INTRODUCTION TO PSYCHOLOGY

INTRODUCTION

TO PSYCHOLOGY

FOURTH EDITION

JAMES W. KALAT

North Carolina State University

Brooks/Cole Publishing Company

I(T)P™ An International Thomson Publishing Company

Pacific Grove • Albany • Bonn • Boston • Cincinnati • Detroit • London • Madrid • Melbourne
Mexico City • New York • Paris • San Francisco • Singapore • Tokyo • Toronto • Washington

Sponsoring Editor: *Jim Brace-Thompson*
Editorial Assistants: *Jodi Hermans and Terry Thomas*
Production Coordinator: *Kirk Bomont*
Project Management, Composition, and Prepress:
  GTS Graphics, Inc.
Marketing Team: *Gay Meixel and Jean Thompson*
Interior Design: *Mel Wanamaker*
Illustrations: *Alexander Teshin Associates, Joel Ito,*
*Mark Stearney, Carlyn Iverson, Graphic Typesetting
Service, John and Judy Waller, Beck Visual Communi-
cations, Jeanne Schreiber, Darwen Hennings*
Cover Design: *Roy R. Neuhaus*
Cover Photograph: *Londie G. Padelsky/Stock
Imagery, Inc.*
Cover and Text Printing and Binding: *Von Hoffman
Press, Inc.*

For more information, contact:

BROOKS/COLE PUBLISHING COMPANY
511 Forest Lodge Road
Pacific Grove, CA 93950
USA

International Thomson Publishing Europe
Berkshire House 168–173
High Holborn
London, WC1V 7AA
England

Thomas Nelson Australia
102 Dodds Street
South Melbourne, 3205
Victoria, Australia

Nelson Canada
1120 Birchmount Road
Scarborough, Ontario
Canada M1K 5G4

International Thomson Editores
Campos Eliseos 385, Piso 7
Col. Polanco
11560 México D.F. México

International Thomson Publishing GmbH
Königswinterer Strasse 418
53227 Bonn
Germany

International Thomson Publishing Asia
221 Henderson Road
#05-10 Henderson Building
Singapore 0315

International Thomson Publishing Japan
Hirakawacho Kyowa Building, 3F
2-2-1 Hirakawacho
Chiyoda-ku, Tokyo 102
Japan

Printed in the United States of America

10 9 8 7 6 5 4 3 2 1

Library of Congress Cataloging-in-Publication Data

Kalat, James W.
  Introduction to psychology / James W. Kalat. —4th ed.
      p.   cm.
  Includes bibliographical references and indexes.
  ISBN 0-534-25014-9
  1. Psychology.   I. Title.
BF121.K26   1996
150—dc20
                                                      95-23816
                                                      CIP

To David and Julie,
Sam,
Robin.

A Note About the Author

Jim Kalat (rhymes with ballot) has been teaching the introductory psychology course at North Carolina State University since 1977. He received a bachelor's degree summa cum laude from Duke University in 1968 and a Ph.D. in psychology from the University of Pennsylvania in 1971. Recipient of Duke's Alumni Outstanding Teacher Award and North Carolina State University's Outstanding Teacher Award, Jim is a Fellow of the American Association for the Advancement of Science, the American Psychological Association, and the American Psychological Society, of which he was the program committee chair in 1991. Besides being the author of the best-selling *Biological Psychology* (the Fifth Edition was published by Brooks/Cole in 1995), Jim has published articles in many psychological journals.

CONTENTS IN BRIEF

CONTENTS

1 WHAT IS PSYCHOLOGY?

2 SCIENTIFIC METHODS IN PSYCHOLOGY

3   BIOLOGICAL PSYCHOLOGY

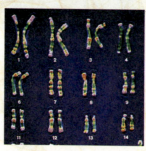

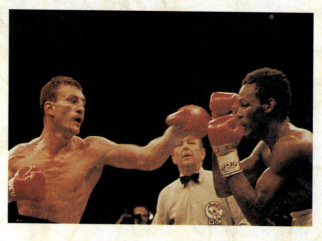

4 SENSATION AND PERCEPTION

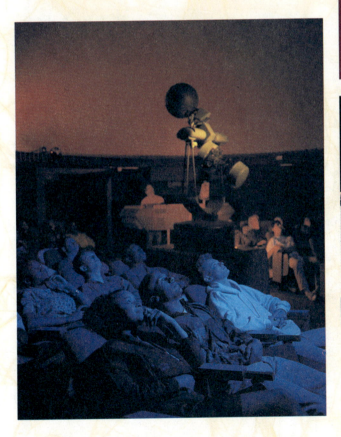

5 ALTERED STATES

6 LEARNING

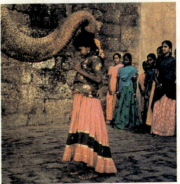

7 MEMORY

8 COGNITION AND LANGUAGE

9 INTELLIGENCE AND ITS MEASUREMENT

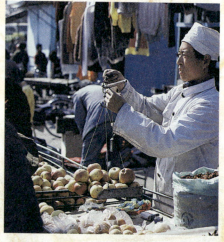

10 DEVELOPMENT

11 MOTIVATION

12 EMOTIONS, HEALTH PSYCHOLOGY, AND COPING WITH STRESS

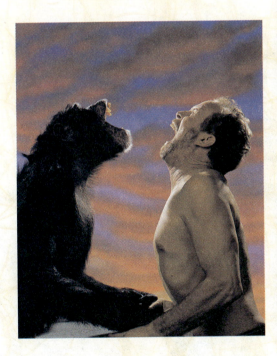

13 PERSONALITY

14 ABNORMAL BEHAVIOR

16 SOCIAL PSYCHOLOGY

APPLIED PSYCHOLOGY

PREFACE TO THE INSTRUCTOR

Teaching psychology means far more than just changing what students know. It means changing how they think. It means ensuring that something worthwhile remains long after they have forgotten the details.

When students leave my Introduction to Psychology classroom, I certainly want them to know the field's important theories and research. But more importantly, I want them to learn the habit of questioning assertions—Freud's assertions, Skinner's, the president's, the newspaper's, their English professor's, their roommate's, mine. I want them to ask for the evidence and to know how to recognize holes in it.

I do not believe that a textbook can instill that habit of questioning assertions merely by means of boxes that are labeled "Critical Thinking." If students are going to form the habit, the author must model it in the normal course of covering the field. I have tried to do so with this book. Consistently, I interweave material that challenges students to examine the evidence (or lack of it) behind some common assertions. "A Guide Through the Book" following the Preface offers specifics on how this textbook can help students question for themselves, look for more than pat answers, and ultimately learn to appreciate the excitement of psychological inquiry.

WHAT'S NEW IN THE FOURTH EDITION

This revision includes more than 400 new references from the 1990s. Every chapter has new material plus reorganization and increased clarification of old material. Many of the figures and photographs have been revised or replaced. Here are a few of the major changes:

- The text includes more cross-cultural examples. These are infused where relevant throughout the text, not set aside as a special section.
- The chapter on development has been moved from Chapter 6 to Chapter 10. Thus the text covers memory, cognition, and language before it covers the development of memory, cognition, and language.
- I have added or enhanced the discussion of some controversial topics in psychology, including extrasensory perception (Chapter 2), the possibility of "recovered memories" (Chapter 7), ethnic differences in IQ performances and *The Bell Curve* (Chapter 9), factors influencing sexual orientation (Chapter 11), lie detection and integrity tests (Chapter 12), why Freud abandoned his seduction theory (Chapter 13), what is "abnormal" (Chapter 14), the effectiveness of psychotherapy (Chapter 15), and the sociobiology of mate choice (Chapter 16).
- New "What's the Evidence?" sections replace the old ones in Chapters 5, 10, 12, and 15.
- Chapter 6 (Learning) now includes a new module on the goals and assumptions of behaviorism.
- Chapter 7 (Memory) has been completely reorganized, with new or much-revised discussion of working memory, how to improve memory, effects of emotional intensity on memory, source amnesia, effects of education on memory strategies, infant amnesia and old-age memory deficits, and story memory.
- Applied Psychology, which was available as a supplementary booklet for the third edition, is now included in the text itself.

TEACHING AND LEARNING AIDS FOR THIS BOOK

A number of important ancillaries accompany the text. For more information about these materials, please contact your local representative.

STUDY GUIDE

Ruth H. Maki of North Dakota State University has prepared a Study Guide that pro-

vides chapter outlines, multiple-choice questions, short-answer essay questions, practice tests, and a new English as a Second Language section contributed by Jack Kirschenbaum of Fullerton College. An interactive electronic Study Guide is available for Mac, DOS, and Windows. For U.S. customers, the text and study guide can be packaged together for a discount (ISBN: 0-534-32951-9).

INSTRUCTOR'S RESOURCE GUIDE

Arthur J. Kohn of Pacific University has prepared a thorough and creative Instructor's Resource Guide. This 1,000-page volume includes suggestions for elaborating on the text, complete lectures, thoughts for promoting discussion, class demonstrations, out-of-class activities, Kalat's answers to the text's "Something to Think About" questions, handouts, and transparency masters.

TEST ITEM FILE

Written by Kalat and Thomas B. Stonebraker of Greenville College, this test bank includes more than 4,000 test items categorized as conceptual, factual, and definition. Most items have been class-tested, and item analysis is provided in the printed form of the test bank. We also offer a computerized testing system for Mac, DOS, and Windows.

TRANSPARENCIES

Two extensive sets of transparencies are available free upon adoption: approximately 140 text-specific, full-color transparencies selected by Kalat, and a set of 95 full-color introductory psychology transparencies.

PSYCH LAB I AND II

Created by Roger Harnish of the Rochester Institute of Technology, these interactive software programs provide psychology demonstrations and simulations, available for DOS and Mac.

CAREER ENCOUNTERS IN PSYCHOLOGY VIDEO

Brooks/Cole has an exclusive agreement to offer this 30-minute video produced by the APA free to adopters of this text.

ANIMATIONS PLUS! VIDEODISC

Produced by Brooks/Cole, this videodisc includes a collection of animations with still frame review and quizzing, diagrams, and video segments. The videodisc comes with an Instructor's Guide including bar codes.

MULTIMEDIA CD/ROM AVAILABLE FALL 1996

Authored by Drs. Arthur and Wendy Kohn and a development team at Pacific University, this CD provides students with dramatic new ways to learn psychology. Exceptionally easy to use, it enables students to independently explore important concepts via interactive experiments, animations, video clips, and images. All materials are directly keyed to the textbook. An instructor's version, available upon adoption of the student version, allows professors to readily assemble and present impressive multimedia lectures.

BROOKS/COLE FILM AND VIDEO LIBRARY FOR PSYCHOLOGY

- *The Pennsylvania State University's PCR: Films and Videos in the Behavioral Sciences*—adopters can choose from the world's largest collection of films and videos on human behavior.
- *The Brain* videotapes—30 video modules and a faculty guide prepared by Frank Vattano of Colorado State University in conjunction with the Annenberg/CPB Project Video Collection.
- *The Mind* videotapes—38 brief video modules offering examples of important concepts in introductory psychology and a faculty guide prepared by Frank Vattano of Colorado State University in cooperation with WNET, New York.
- *Seeing Beyond the Obvious: Understanding Perception in Everyday and Novel Environments*—a videotape that provides an introduction to basic concepts of visual perception, created by NASA Ames Research Center in conjunction with the University of Virginia.
- *Discovering Psychology* videotapes—a series of 26 programs from the Annenberg/CPB Collection.

ACKNOWLEDGMENTS

A potential author needs self-confidence bordering on arrogance just to begin the job of writing a textbook. To complete it, the writer needs the humility to accept criticism of his or her favorite ideas and most carefully written prose. A great many people have provided helpful suggestions that have made this a far better text than it would have been otherwise.

Less than a year before this edition was published, I was frankly doubtful that I would find the time or wherewithal to complete the task on schedule. My wife Ann and my editor, Jim Brace-Thompson, provided consistent encouragement, confidence, support, and patience. To them, my deepest thanks. My special thanks also to Nancy Margolis, whose help made an enormous difference in my completing this edition on time.

John Boykin worked vigorously and creatively to improve the already-outstanding set of figures and illustrations that he orchestrated for the third edition. The fact that I knew I could trust his judgment enabled me to delegate to him much of the work on the illustrations. He has developed illustrations that I consider creative, attractive, and educational; it has been a joy for me to work with him again.

In preparing this edition, I have had the opportunity to work with some very skilled and dedicated people. Kirk Bomont did an excellent job of supervising the production. Eileen Murphy, who managed the art development, and Roy Neuhaus, who designed the cover, had enough patience and artistic judgment to counterbalance their very non-artistic author. Mel Wanamaker, the designer, and Sabu Advani, the copyeditor, were skillful, efficient, and very pleasant colleagues. Faith Stoddard did a marvelous job of coordinating all the supplementary and ancillary materials. May Clark accomplished the nearly impossible task of managing all of the requests for permissions. Gay Meixel planned and executed the marketing strategies. Heather Dutton kept track of all the changes in the illustrations. To each of these, my thanks and congratulations.

My sincere thanks also to the staff of GTS Graphics, the company that produced the book. Richard Lange and Margaret Pinette did a remarkable job of taking a late manuscript and meeting an early publication date. Ann Beurskens, the photo researcher, found wonderful photographs to satisfy my vague descriptions of what the text needed.

Art Kohn has been a source of a number of creative ideas on how to approach certain topics; he has also been a stimulating person to talk to and a good friend. My colleagues at North Carolina State University provided me with encouragement, ideas, and free advice. I thank particularly Lynn Baker-Ward, Rupert Barnes-Nacoste, Don Mershon, and David Martin.

I thank the following people for their helpful reviews on earlier drafts of all or part of the book: Ruth Ault, Davidson College; Susan Baillet, University of Portland; Elaine Baker, Marshall University; Ilene Bernstein, University of Washington; Bob Brown, University of North Carolina at Wilmington; James Calhoun, University of Georgia; Marie Caulfield, Boston VA Medical Center; Tom Collins, Mankato State University; George Domino, University of Arizona; Ralph Erber, DePaul University; Frank Hager, Allegany Community College; Leonard Hamilton, Rutgers University; W. Bruce Haslam, Weber State University; Nils Hovik, Lehigh County Community College; Pam Hufnagel, Pennsylvania State University at Dubois; Craig Jones, Arkansas State University; Ruth Maki, North Dakota State University; Duane McClearn, Elon College; Neil McGrenaghan, Humber College; Bill Moore, Marshall University; Albert Neal, Central Michigan University; Bethany Neal-Beliveau, Indiana University-Purdue University at Indianapolis; Joan Piroch, Coastal Carolina University; Kenneth Rosenberg, SUNY-Oswego; Joan Roy, University of Regina; Susan Schenk, Texas A&M University; Carl Scott, University of St. Thomas; Paul Turner, David Lipscomb University; William F. Vitulli, University of South Alabama; and Amy Wolfson, College of the Holy Cross. I especially thank Mark Leary, Wake Forest University, for his extensive help with Chapter 16.

I also thank the following for their helpful comments and suggestions: Jack Huber of Meredith College, William Moorcroft of Luther College, Craig Jones of Arkansas State University, Richard Pisacreta of Ferris State University, and my good friends Art Kohn and Ken King. I thank Suzanne Corkin and David Amaral for providing research photographs. A great many students who read the previous edition sent me letters with helpful comments and suggestions. I especially thank Janette and Chuck Byers, Amy R. Champion, Kathy Hundley, and Ann Johnson.

James Kalat

PREFACE TO THE STUDENT

Welcome to introductory psychology! I hope you will enjoy reading this text as much as I enjoyed writing it. When you finish, I hope you will write your comments down and mail them to me at: James W. Kalat, Department of Psychology, Box 7801, North Carolina State University, Raleigh, NC 27695-7801. Please include a return address.

The first time I taught introductory psychology, several students complained that the book we were using was interesting to read but impossible to study. What they meant was that they had trouble finding and remembering the main points. I have tried to make this book easy to study in many ways. I have tried to select interesting material and to present it as clearly as possible.

In addition, I have included some special features to aid your study. Each chapter begins with an outline and a brief introduction to the topic. Every chapter except Chapter 1 is divided into two or more major sections, or modules. Each module begins with one or more questions—the fundamental questions that psychologists are trying to answer, the questions that motivate research. In some cases you will be able to answer the question after you read the section; in other cases you will not, because psychologists themselves are not sure about the answers. At the end of each module you will find a summary of some important points, with page references. If you find one of the summary points unfamiliar, you should reread the appropriate section.

Throughout the text you will find certain words highlighted in **boldface** type. These are important terms whose meaning you should understand. All the boldface terms in the text are listed with their definitions at the end of

the chapter. They also appear in the Glossary/Subject Index at the end of the book. You might want to find the Glossary/Subject Index right now and familiarize yourself with it. Note that when you look up a term you find both its definition and page references to help you find it in the text. Note also the Theme Index, which directs you to places in the text that discuss general issues such as gender influences and cultural influences on behavior.

You should learn the meaning of the boldface terms, but don't concentrate your study on them too heavily. I sometimes meet students who think they have mastered the course if they have memorized all the definitions. That's a mistake. You need to understand sentences that use these terms, and you should be able to recognize what is an example of the term and what is not. But don't waste time memorizing definitions word for word.

At various points in the text you will find a question or two under the heading "Concept Check." These questions do not ask you to simply repeat what you have read but rather to use or apply the information in some way. Try to answer each of these questions, and then turn to the indicated page to check your answer. If you cannot answer a Concept Check correctly, you probably have not been reading carefully enough, and you might want to reread the section in which the Concept Check occurs.

You will also find an occasional section marked "Something to Think About." These sections pose questions that require you to go beyond what is discussed in the text. In some cases there is no single right answer; there may be a number of reasonable ways to approach the question. I hope you will think about these questions, perhaps talk about them with fellow students, and maybe ask your instructor what he or she thinks.

I would like to deal with a few of the questions that students sometimes raise about their textbooks:

Do you have any useful suggestions on study habits? Whenever students ask me why they did so badly on the last test, I ask, "When did you read the assignment?" They sometimes answer, "Well, I didn't exactly read *all* of the assignment," or "I read it the night before the test." To do your best, read each assignment *before the lecture*. Within 24 hours after the lecture, read over your lecture notes. Then, before you take the test, reread both the textbook assignment and your lecture notes. If you do not have time to reread everything, at least skim the text and reread the sections on which you need to refresh your memory. As a rule, if you are not satisfied with your test scores, you need to spend more time studying.

Some students, however, spend enough time studying without spending that time effectively. If you are reading the material without remembering it, perhaps you are not thinking about the material while you read it. As you read this book, try to think actively about what you are reading. One way to improve your studying is to read by the SPAR method: *Survey*, *Process* meaningfully, *Ask* questions, *Review*. The steps are as follows:

• *Survey:* When you start a chapter, first look over the chapter outline to get a preview of the chapter's contents. When you start a major section of a chapter, turn to the end of the section and read the summary. Then when you begin to read the chapter you know what to expect and you can focus on the main points.

• *Process meaningfully:* Read the chapter carefully. Stop to think from time to time. Tell your roommate some of the interesting things you learn. Think about how you might apply a certain concept in a real-life situation. Pause when you come to the Concept Checks and try to answer them. Good readers read quickly through unimportant or familiar material, but slowly through difficult and unfamiliar material.

• *Ask questions:* When you finish the chapter, try to anticipate some of the questions you might be asked later. You can take questions from the Study Guide or you can compose your own questions. Write out your questions and think about them, but do not write your answers yet.

• *Review:* Pause for a while—at least several hours, or, better yet, a day or two. If you first read a chapter before class, come back to the chapter the evening after class. Now write out the answers to the questions you wrote earlier. Check your answers against the text or against the answers given in the Study Guide. Reinforcing your memory a day or two after first reading the chapter will help you retain the material longer and with deeper understanding. If you study the same material several times, spaced over lengthy intervals, you increase your chance of remembering it long after the course is over.

Is it worthwhile to buy and use the Study Guide? The Study Guide is designed to help students who have trouble studying, remembering the material, or answering multiple-choice questions. It is most likely to be helpful to freshmen and to students who have had trouble with similar courses in the past. It provides examples of multiple-choice questions, giving not only the correct answers but also explanations of why they are correct.

In the Study Guide for this text, written by Ruth Maki of North Dakota State University, you can work through each chapter in one or two hours. If you are willing to devote that much time to it, I believe the Study Guide will help you.

Does it help to underline or highlight key sentences while reading? Maybe, but don't overdo it. I have seen books in which a student underlined or highlighted more than half the sentences. What good that does, I have no idea.

What do those parentheses mean, as in "(Maki & Serra, 1992)"? Am I supposed to remember the names and dates? Psychologists generally cite references not by footnotes but in parentheses. "(Maki & Serra, 1992)" refers to a publication written by Maki and Serra and published in 1992. All the references cited are listed in alphabetical order according to the author's name in the References section at the back of the book.

You will also notice a few citations that include two dates separated by a slash, such as "(Wundt, 1862/1961)." That citation refers to a publication originally written by Wundt in 1862, republished in 1961. (The original was in German; the republication, in English.)

No one expects you to memorize the names and dates in parentheses. The references are provided in case you want to look up the source of a statement and check for further information. A few names *are* worth remembering, however. For instance, you will read about the research and theories of some famous psychologists, such as B. F. Skinner, Jean Piaget, and Sigmund Freud. You will certainly be expected to remember those names and a few others. But names that are important to remember are emphasized, not buried in parentheses.

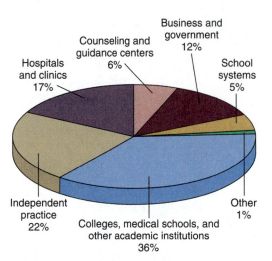

FIGURE 1 *Pie graph*

Can you give me any help on how to read and understand graphs? The graphs in this book are easy to understand. Just take a minute or so to study them carefully. You will find four kinds: pie graphs, bar graphs, line graphs, and scatter plots. Let's look at each kind.

- *Pie graphs* show how a whole is divided into parts. Figure 1 shows that more than one-third of all psychologists take a starting job with a college or some other educational institution. Another one-fifth to one-fourth of psychologists work in independent practice. The total circle represents 100% of all psychologists.

- *Bar graphs* show the frequency of events that fall into one category or another. Figure 2 shows how many adults in the United States suffer from certain psychological disorders. The length of a bar represents the frequency of a particular disorder.

- *Line graphs* show how one variable is related to another variable. In Figure 3 you see that newborn infants spend about 16 hours a day asleep. As they grow older, the amount of time they spend in two types of sleep gradually decreases.

- *Scatter plots* are similar to line graphs, with this difference: A line graph shows averages, whereas a scatter plot shows individual data points. By looking at a scatter plot, we can see how much variation occurs among individuals.

To prepare a scatter plot, we make two observations about each individual. In Figure 4 each student is represented by one point. If you take that point and scan down to the *x*-axis, you find that student's SAT score. If you then scan across to the *y*-axis, you find that student's grade average for the freshman year. A scatter plot shows whether two variables are closely related or only loosely related.

We may have to take multiple-choice tests on this material. How can I do better on those tests?

1. Read all of the choices carefully. Do not choose the first answer that looks correct; first make sure that the other answers are wrong. If two answers seem reasonable, decide which of the two is better.

2. If you don't know the correct answer, make an educated guess. Start by eliminating any answer that you know cannot be right. An answer that includes absolute words such as *always* or *never* is probably wrong. Also eliminate any answer that includes terms that are unfamiliar to you. (Correct choices use only terms that you should know; incorrect choices may include obscure terms or even outright nonsense.)

3. After you finish a test, go back and check your answers and rethink them. You have probably heard the advice, "Don't change your answers; stick with your first impulse." No matter how often you have heard that advice, it is wrong. J. J. Johnston (1975) tested it by looking through the answer sheets of a number of classes that had taken a multiple-choice test. He found that of all

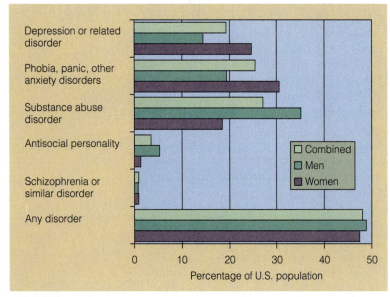

FIGURE 2 *Bar graph*

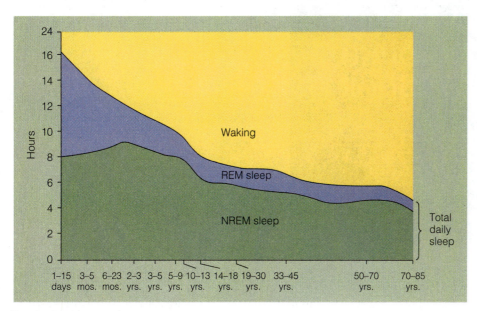

FIGURE 3 *Line graph*

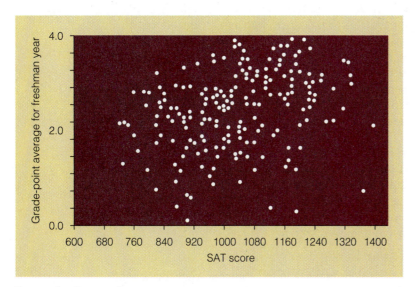

FIGURE 4 *Scatter plot*

the students who changed one or more answers, 71 students improved their scores by doing so and only 31 lowered their scores. Similar results have been reported in a number of other studies. I do not mean that you should make changes just for the sake of making changes. But there are many reasons why your reconsidered answer might be better than your first impulse. For one, sometimes when you read the later questions on a test, one of them may remind you of something that helps you answer an earlier question. Also, you sometimes reread a question and realize that you misunderstood it the first time you read it.

Why, then, do so many students (and professors) believe that it is a mistake to change an answer? Imagine what happens when you take a test and get your paper back. When you look it over, which items do you examine most carefully? The ones you got wrong, of course. You may notice three items that you originally answered correctly and then changed. You never notice the five other items you changed from incorrect to correct.

James Kalat

A Guide Through the Book

A Note from the Publisher

The scientific method is the most powerful tool in the psychologist's—and, indeed, the student's—intellectual armory. In this book, students learn that questioning assertions, challenging evidence, and evaluating results—all components of the scientific method—are second nature to the study of psychology itself. With author Jim Kalat's guidance, students are introduced to psychology in a way that will remain with them long after they may have forgotten specific theories, experiments, and results.

The material that follows demonstrates how Jim Kalat encourages students to experience for themselves the excitement of psychological discovery and how he uses the scientific method as a consistent theme throughout the book. His carefully integrated learning tools clarify psychology's important theories and research.

Kalat's remarkable skill in getting students involved in using the scientific method to question assertions is what distinguishes *Introduction to Psychology, Fourth Edition*. Most books present the research and facts and expect students to memorize what's been discovered. Kalat encourages them to open the doors to further exploration: He helps his readers become more intelligent consumers of psychological research.

A Book Students Truly Love

Throughout the text, Jim Kalat does more than tell students what they ought to know—he engages their desire to learn. He speaks directly to his readers, drawing them into psychological concepts and information in a way that actually changes the way they look at assertions and facts. Kalat's engaging and involving writing style—coupled with humor, personal anecdotes, and exercises students can try themselves—helps make the Fourth Edition an exceptional learning tool, one your students will truly enjoy.

An Introduction to the Power of Questioning Assertions

Chapter 2 is the most important chapter in the book. It not only deals with the procedures for conducting research but also provides a conceptual guide to how psychologists evaluate evidence and theories and, in general, to how they think. For example, it highlights the importance of replicability, the criterion of falsifiability, and the principle of parsimony.

Early in Chapter 2, Kalat presents an overview of the research process. He introduces the *four steps* in gathering and evaluating evidence— ❶ Hypothesis, ❷ Method, ❸ Results, and ❹ Interpretation. This critical material—the heart of the scientific method—is then reinforced throughout the text.

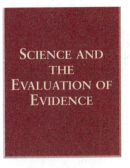

Science and the Evaluation of Evidence

How do scientists evaluate which theories are good and which theories are poor?

Why are most of them so skeptical of new theories and claims that seem to contradict our current understanding?

You will sometimes hear people say that something has been "scientifically proved." Scientists themselves seldom use the word *prove,* except when they are talking about a mathematical proof. As they collect more and better evidence, they may become confident about a given conclusion, but they still hesitate to say they are certain of it.

One distinguishing characteristic of science is that scientists generally agree on how to evaluate competing theories. Even when they disagree on which theory is best, they can still agree on what kinds of evidence they will accept in trying to decide. Most psychologists are quick to concede that our knowledge of psychology is less complete and less systematic than our knowledge of physics, chemistry, and biology. But like physicists, chemists, and biologists, psychologists generally agree on what constitutes good evidence and what does not. They try to rely on the best available evidence, and to draw no conclusion at all if the evidence is weak.

SOMETHING TO THINK ABOUT

If ethicists agreed with each other on how to evaluate theories, could they make progress comparable to that of scientists? Could theologians?

STEPS IN GATHERING AND EVALUATING EVIDENCE

Above all, scientists want to know the evidence behind a given claim. In psychology as in other fields, students should learn to question assertions, to ask what is the evidence behind a given claim and whether that evidence leads to an unambiguous conclusion.

In any scientific field, researchers conduct studies that go through a series of steps described in the following four paragraphs (see also Figure 2.1). Articles in scientific publications generally follow this sequence too. In each of the following chapters, you will find a section titled "What's the Evidence?" Those sections will go through one or more psychological investigations step by step, also in the same order.

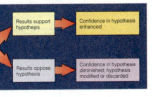

| Results support hypothesis | → | Confidence in hypothesis enhanced |
| Results oppose hypothesis | → | Confidence in hypothesis diminished; hypothesis modified or discarded |

...erimental method tests those pre- ...pports the hypothesis; a disconfir- ...d the hypothesis. Conclusions ...experiment. Most scientists avoid ...sion.

33

Psychologists seek solid evidence to establish that watching televised violence increases the viewer's probability of violent behavior. Good research does more than just establish the connection between the two; it also can tell us how strong the connection is, what kinds of televised violence are most dangerous, and which kinds of viewers are most susceptible.

❶ **Hypothesis** Any study begins with a hypothesis, which is a testable prediction of what will happen under certain conditions. In many cases the hypothesis is the product of someone's casual observations. For example, a psychologist might notice that children who like to watch violent television programs seem to be relatively violent themselves. So it seems, at any rate; we cannot always trust our impressions. The psychologist might then set out to test whether those children who watch the greatest amount of violence on television engage in the greatest amount of aggressive behavior.

❷ **Method** Devising an appropriate method to test a hypothesis can be surprisingly difficult. For example, an investigator wants to measure how much violence each child watches on television. That may sound easy. But what counts as violence? Do we count minutes of violent programming, or do we count violent acts? Do some types of violence count more than others? An experimenter needs to select methods of controlling or measuring all the important events and behaviors in the study. The precision of that control or measurement will determine the usefulness of the research.

❸ **Results** Suppose the investigator somehow measures televised violence and aggressive behavior. Then the task is to determine the relationship between the two measures. Did the children who watched the greatest amount of violence also engage in the most aggressive behavior? If so, how strong was the relationship? Were the results convincing, or might they have arisen by accident? Here the investigator calls upon statistical techniques to evaluate the results.

❹ **Interpretation** Finally, the task is to determine what the results mean. Sometimes the results clearly contradict the hypothesis. For example, an investigator might find that children who watch a great deal of televised violence are no more aggressive than other children in general. In that case we might abandon the hypothesis or we might modify it: Maybe it applies only to certain kinds of children or to certain kinds of violence.

If the results match the prediction, we would look for other possible explanations before we draw a conclusion. Suppose, for example, the investigator finds that the children who watched the most violence on television were also prone to the most aggressive behavior. We should not necessarily conclude that televised violence leads to aggressive behavior, because of an alternative interpretation: Perhaps aggressive children like to watch violent television!

It is almost always possible to suggest more than one interpretation of the results of a given study. At that point the investigator sets up a second study to follow up on the results of the first and tries to decide between the two interpretations. That study too may lead to further studies. Because almost any study has its limitations, the ultimate conclusion comes from a pattern of results from many studies.

REPLICABILITY

Before psychologists trust the results of a study, we like to have other investigators repeat the procedure. If others get consistently similar results, then they have **replicable results**—that is, anyone who follows the same procedure can repeat them. If a result is replicable, we still may not be sure how to interpret it, but at least we think it is worthwhile to try. If the results cannot be replicated, then perhaps there was some hidden flaw in the first study; we base no conclusions on it.

What if a result can be replicated in some studies and not in others? Such a result is not

CHAPTER 2 SCIENTIFIC METHODS IN PSYCHOLOGY

34

plains that a bigger toy just like it is "in the same place" in the bigger room. (For example, if the little toy was behind the sofa in the little room, the big toy would be behind the sofa in the big room.) Most 2½-year-old children look haphazardly for the big toy in the big room without using the little room as a "map." By age 3, most children who see the little toy hidden in the little room go immediately to the correct location in the big room (DeLoache, 1989).

EGOCENTRIC THINKING IN THE PREOPERATIONAL PERIOD

Piaget concluded that children's thought processes are **egocentric**. In using this term, Piaget did *not* mean that children are selfish; instead, he meant that the child sees the world as centered around himself or herself and cannot take the perspective of another person. If you and a preschool child sit on opposite sides of a complicated pile of blocks and you ask the child to draw what the blocks would look like from your side, the child will draw them as they look from his or her own side. When speaking, children often omit to describe the necessary background information, as if assuming that the listener understands everything the speaker understands. (The same can be said for adults, unfortunately. Sometimes someone will start discussing the details of some topic before the listener has any idea what the speaker is talking about.)

2. *Which of the following is the clearest example of egocentric thinking?*
   a. A writer who uses someone else's words without giving credit
   b. A politician who blames others for everything that goes wrong
   c. A professor who gives the same complicated lecture to a freshman class that she gives to a convention of professionals. (Check your answer on page 428.)

To say that a child is egocentric is to say that he or she has trouble understanding other people's point of view, understanding what they know and what they do not know. Psychological researchers have explored this very difficult topic of what children understand about other people's thoughts and knowledge.

Children's Understanding of Other People's Cognitions

How would you feel about walking naked through a room filled with refrigerators, radios, and other machines? You might prefer to have your clothes on, but you probably will feel no great distress. Now, how would you feel about walking naked through a classroom full of other (fully clothed) students? Extremely embarrassed and distressed, I presume, because you regard people as very different from machines. You believe that other students have conscious experiences like your own; you know that people can see you and react to you, whereas electrical appliances cannot.

How and when did we figure that out? At what age do children first understand that other people have minds and knowledge? Experimenters have developed some very clever designs to try to answer that very difficult question.

Hypothesis A child who understands that other people have minds will distinguish between someone who is in a position to know some relevant information and someone who could not know it.

Method A 3- or 4-year-old child sat in front of four cups (figure 10.16). The child watched as one adult hid a candy or toy

Young children's thinking is egocentric: understanding someone else's point of [...] to describe how a complicated pile of [...] to someone else, they describe how it [...] their own position.

WHAT'S THE EVIDENCE?

Appearing in every chapter from Chapter 2 on, each *What's the Evidence?* section presents an interesting problem and then examines one or more experiments in some detail. The format reinforces the steps of the scientific method, until it becomes part of the way students think.

These sections illustrate how scientific research is set into motion by posing a question. Then, using the scientific method of Hypothesis–Method–Results–Interpretation, Kalat walks students through one or two studies that explore the question. Where appropriate, he points out limitations in the research, ethical considerations in the methods, and alternative interpretations of the results so that students have a model of how psychologists evaluate evidence.

FIGURE 10.16
A child sat in front of a screen covering four cups and watched as one adult hid a surprise under one of the cups. Then that adult and another (who had not been present during the hiding) each pointed to one of the cups to signal where the surprise was. Many 4-year-olds consistently followed the advice of the informed adult; 3-year-olds did not.

under one of the cups, although a screen prevented the child from seeing which cup. Then another adult entered the room. The "informed" adult pointed to the cup under which he or she had just hidden the surprise;

the "uninformed" adult pointed to one of the other cups. The child then had an opportunity to look under one cup to try to find the surprise.

This procedure was repeated 10 times for each child in the study. The two adults alternated roles, but on each trial one or the other hid the surprise when the other was absent. That is, one was in a position to know where the surprise was hidden, and the other was not.

Results Of the 4-year-olds, 10 out of 20 chose the correct cup (the one indicated by the informed adult) at least 8 times out of 10 tries. That is, many of the 4-year-olds showed that they understood who had the relevant knowledge and who did not. However, none of 14 3-year-olds chose the correct cup 8 times out of 10; they were as likely to follow the lead of the uninformed adult as that of the informed adult (Povinelli & deBlois, 1992).

Interpretation Evidently, 4-year-olds have a greater understanding of other people's knowledge (or lack of it) than 3-year-olds have.

Other experiments using a somewhat different procedure have yielded similar results. For example, children in one study watched a dramatization in which a girl who had a marble in her basket left the room temporarily, leaving the basket behind. During her absence, a second girl moved the marble from the first girl's basket to her own basket. When the first girl returned to the room, the children were asked, "Where is the marble?" and "Where will the girl look for it?" Most 4-year-olds answered that she would look in her own basket; younger children thought she would look in the other basket (Wimmer & Perner, 1983). As in the previous study, 4-year-olds are better able than younger children are to make inferences about what various people might or might not know.

Although these are important results, we should be careful of drawing too broad a conclusion. Using other methods, we can see evidence that even younger children understand something about the experiences or knowledge of other people. For example, children less than 1 year old act sad and even cry when they see another child get hurt (Hobson, 1993). That is, a child may show

SOMETHING TO THINK ABOUT

Something to Think About questions, found throughout the text, raise provocative issues relevant to the preceding material, and often ask students to use the scientific method as a means of exploring the issues in new and different ways.

These brief segments can be used to trigger class discussion. Many are designed to extend psychology beyond the classroom to real life.

---

the amount of pain at the end, rather than the total sum of pain.

SOMETHING TO THINK ABOUT

Could a dentist make a painful experience seem better by adding a slightly less painful experience at the end?

Would this principle about pain apply to boredom as well? For example, if at the end of a boring lecture someone added a slightly less boring segment, would a listener be inclined to prefer that lecture over a shorter but completely boring lecture?

The Gate Theory of Pain The intensity of a pain depends on the person's other sensory experiences and motivations of the moment. For example, you can make a cut on your leg hurt less if you rub the skin around it or apply cold packs or hot packs (Rollman, 1991). You might not even notice the pain if you are concentrating on other matters. Injured soldiers and athletes sometimes completely ignore a painful injury until the end of the battle or the end of the athletic contest. In other cases, people sometimes complain of severe pain after what appears to be a very minor injury. And some people continue to feel pain long after an injury has healed, almost as if pain had become a learned habit.

Because of observations such as these, Ronald Melzack and P. D. Wall (1965) proposed the **gate theory** of pain, the idea that pain messages have to pass through a gate in the spinal cord on their way to the brain. The brain and receptors in the skin can send messages to the spinal cord to open or close that gate. Although some details of Melzack and Wall's theory are apparently wrong, their basic idea is valid: The activity of the rest of the brain can facilitate or inhibit the transmission of pain messages (Figure 4.25).

Mechanisms of Decreasing Pain Pain alerts us to an injury. A small number of people are completely insensitive to pain. They burn themselves by picking up hot objects; they scald their tongues on hot coffee; they cut themselves without realizing it; they bite their tongues hard, possibly even biting off the tip; they sit in a single position for hours without growing uncomfortable, thereby damaging their bones and tendons. Only with much supervision or considerable luck

Figure 4.25
The Lamaze method of giving birth emphasizes control of pain sensations by changing attitudes, controlling fears and anxieties, and concentrating on breathing. It is one example of how the brain can close "pain gates" and thereby alter pain sensation.

can such a person survive to adulthood (Comings & Amromin, 1974).

Although a pain message serves an essential function of alerting us to danger and damage, a prolonged, intense pain message is unnecessary and sometimes disruptive. One way to reduce the sensation of pain is to provide some distraction. According to the gate theory, the distraction closes the pain gate. For example, surgery patients in a room with a pleasant view complain less about pain, take less painkilling medicine, and recover faster than do patients in a windowless room or a room with a poor view (Ulrich, 1984). Many people relieve their pain by listening to music, by playing games, or by recollecting some pleasant experience (Lavine, Buchsbaum, & Poncy, 1976; McCaul & Malott, 1984).

We also have some biological mechanisms to put the brakes on pain. Pain messages in the nervous system depend on the release of a neurotransmitter called **substance P**. Another set of synapses, which release **endorphins** as their neurotransmitters, inhibit the release of substance P and thereby decrease pain sensations (Reichling, Kwiat, & Basbaum, 1988; Terman, Shavitt, Lewis,

---

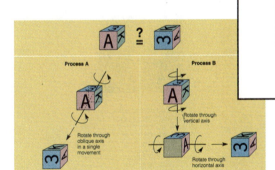

SOMETHING TO THINK ABOUT

Some people report that they have auditory images as well as visual images. They "hear" words or songs "in their head." What kind of evidence would we need to test that claim?

The evidence so far indicates that mental imagery resembles vision in certain ways. Does it confirm that we really do "see little pictures in our heads"? Not necessarily. In several experiments, blind people have heard or felt stimuli and then researchers asked them to "use mental images" to answer various questions. The blind people performed quite similarly to sighted people answering the same questions with the same instructions (Jonides, Kahn, & Rozin, 1975; Kerr, 1983; Loomis et al., 1993). It could be that blind subjects use different kinds of images that simply produce the same results as visual imagery, or the interpretation could be that what we call "imagery" is really a spatial representation, and not exactly a visual representation.

Note an important point about scientific procedure: Even an outstanding, classical experiment does not answer all the relevant questions. Almost always, the results of a pioneering experiment suggest additional questions that require further research.

USING MENTAL IMAGES: COGNITIVE MAPS

You are staying at a hotel in an unfamiliar city. You walk a few blocks to get to a museum; then you turn and walk in another direction to get to a restaurant; after dinner you turn again and walk to a theater. After the performance, how do you get back to the hotel? Do you retrace all of your steps? Can you find a shorter route? Or do you give up and hail a cab?

If you can find your way back, you do so by using a **cognitive map**, a mental image of a spatial arrangement. One way to measure the accuracy of people's cognitive maps is to test how well they can find the route from one place to another. Another way is to ask them to draw a map. As you might expect, people draw a more complete map of the areas they are most familiar with. When students try to draw a map of their college campus, they generally include the central buildings on campus and the buildings they enter most frequently (Saarinen, 1973). The longer students have been on campus, the more detail they include (Cohen & Cohen, 1985).

The errors people make in their cognitive maps follow some interesting patterns. First, they tend to remember street angles as being close to 90°, even when they are not (Moar & Bower, 1983). We can easily understand that error. For practical purposes, all we

accurately.

how many letters or words they can remember and how long they can remember. Given that people differ in this regard, imagine various people reading either of the following sentences:

> Since Ken really liked the boxer, he took a bus to the nearest pet store to buy the animal.

> Since Ken really liked the boxer, he took a bus to the nearest sports arena to see the match.

Then the readers are asked true-false questions such as

T F Ken liked a dog.
T F Ken liked a fighter.

Readers having longer phonological loops answered most such questions correctly; readers having shorter phonological loops had more trouble (Miyake, Just, & Carpenter, 1994). Many words in the English language have several unrelated meanings (for example, boxer, bass, tire, court). When we read such a word, we have to wait until the context of the sentence identifies the correct meaning of the word. In the "Ken" sentences above, the context remained ambiguous about the meaning of "boxer" until eight words later. By that time, readers with a shorter phonological loop had already had to guess which was the correct meaning of *boxer*.

| CONCEPT CHECK |

5. *Would readers who have a shorter phonological loop show greater reading comprehension in English, which has many words with two or more meanings, or in Italian, which has few such words? (Check your answer on page 279.)*

OTHER MEMORY DISTINCTIONS

In addition to distinguishing between long-term memory and either short-term memory or working memory, psychologists also sometimes find it useful to distinguish among long-term memories for different kinds of information. In particular, many psychologists distinguish **semantic memory**, memory for factual information, from **episodic memory**, memory for specific events in a person's life

Episodic memories pertain to particular events, such as the outcome of a recent tennis match. Semantic memories pertain to facts and principles, such as the rules of tennis.

(Tulving, 1989). For example, your memory of the rules of tennis is a semantic memory; your memory of the most recent time you played tennis is an episodic memory. Your memory of the principles of chemistry is a semantic memory; your recollections of what happened during your high-school chemistry course are episodic memories.

Episodic memories are in many cases much more fragile than are semantic memories. For example, people sometimes remember some fact they have heard (a semantic memory) but forget when, where, and from whom they heard it (an episodic memory). That phenomenon is known as **source amnesia**, remembering the content but not where or how one learned the content. Source amnesia is partly responsible for the *sleeper effect,* an interesting phenomenon we shall examine in more detail in Chapter 16: Sometimes someone hears an idea and immediately discards it because it came from an unreliable source. Days or weeks later, the person remembers the idea but forgets the source. "Did I read about this in *Scientific American* or in the *National Enquirer?* Did I hear it from my professor or from Ren and Stimpy? Was it in my textbook or did I imagine it?" Someone who does not remember that the source was unreliable may regard the idea itself as reasonable. In

---

CONCEPT CHECKS

Almost 200 *Concept Checks* are strategically placed at the ends of sections throughout the book. These questions get students to think about, manipulate, and apply the preceding material rather than just repeat what they read. Students go beyond remembering facts to understanding main ideas.

To further enhance continuity and clarity, these checks are presented within the main text, not set off in boxes. Answers are given at the end of each module.

| CONCEPT CHECKS |

7. *Some students who read a chapter slowly get very good grades; others get poor grades. Why?*
8. *Most actors and public speakers who have to memorize lengthy passages spend little time simply repeating the words and more time thinking about them. Why? (Check your answers on page 288.)*

People need to monitor their understanding of a text to decide whether to keep studying or whether they already understand it well enough. Most readers have trouble making that judgment correctly.

SELF-MONITORING OF UNDERSTANDING

Whenever you are studying a text, you periodically have to decide, "Should I keep on studying this section, or do I already understand it well enough?" Most students have trouble monitoring their own understanding. In one study, psychology instructors asked their students before each test to guess whether they would do better or worse on that test than they usually do. Students also guessed after each test whether they had done better or worse than usual. Most students' guesses were no more accurate than chance (Sjostrom & Marks, 1994). Such inaccuracy represents a problem: Students who do not know how well they understand the material will make bad judgments about when to keep on studying and when to quit.

Even when you are reading a single sentence, you have to decide whether you understand the sentence or whether you should stop and reread it. Here is a sentence once published in the student newspaper at North Carolina State University:

> He said Harris told him she and Brothers told French that grades had been changed.

Ordinarily, when good readers come to such a confusing sentence, they notice their own confusion and reread the sentence or, if necessary, the whole paragraph. Poor readers tend to read at their same speed for both easy and difficult materials; they are less likely than good readers to slow down when they come to difficult sentences.

Although monitoring one's own understanding is difficult and often inaccurate, it is not impossible. For example, suppose I tell you that you are to read three chapters dealing with, say, thermodynamics, the history of volleyball, and the Japanese stock market.

Later you will take tests on each chapter. Before you start reading, predict your approximate scores on the three tests. Most people make a guess based on how much they already know about the three topics. If we let them read the three chapters and again make a guess about their test performances, they do in fact make more accurate predictions than they did before reading (Maki & Serra, 1992). That improvement indicates some ability to monitor one's own understanding of a text.

A systematic way to monitor your own understanding of a text is the **SPAR method:** *S*urvey, *P*rocess meaningfully, *A*sk questions, and *R*eview and test yourself. Start with an overview of what a passage is about, read it carefully, and then see whether you can answer questions about the passage or explain it to others. If not, go back and reread.

THE TIMING OF STUDY

Other things being equal, people tend to remember recent experiences better than earlier experiences. For example, suppose someone reads you a list of 20 words and asks you to recall as many of them as possible. The list is far too long for you to recite from your phonological loop; however, you should be able to remember at least a few. Typically, people remember items at the beginning and end of the list better than they remember those in the middle.

That tendency, known as the **serial-order effect,** includes two aspects: The *primacy effect* is the tendency to remember the first items; the *recency effect* refers to the tendency to remember the last items. One explanation for the primacy effect is that the listener gets to rehearse the first few items for a few moments alone with no interference from the others. One explanation for the recency effect is that the last items are still in

HABITUALLY QUESTIONING ASSERTIONS

The theme of questioning assertions is woven throughout the main body of the text. This material permeates the text, sometimes appearing as a sentence or two in the middle of a discussion, sometimes as a paragraph, a full page, or more. This bestselling book is known for the way it encourages students to question the information before them and to ask themselves, *How was a given conclusion reached? Does the evidence really support that conclusion?*

Kalat helps students learn to separate what sounds plausible from what can be substantiated by scientific evidence and how to tell the difference between sound and flawed evidence. The result is a book that challenges students to think carefully about each topic as they read.

Young children forget more rapidly than do adults; they tend to be more suggestible than adults; and they sometimes confuse fantasy with reality. Are they therefore unreliable as witnesses?

Not necessarily. Although researchers do agree that young children yield to suggestion more than adults do, the difference is not enormous (Ceci & Bruck, 1993). Under many circumstances, children remember important personal experiences quite well over surprisingly long periods of time, provided they understood the original experience. For example, children in two studies were asked about events of their medical examinations at delays ranging from 3 days to 6 weeks after the event. Children of ages 3 to 7 reported the events accurately and in detail. Researchers then asked suggestive or leading questions such as "Did the nurse cut your hair?" and "Did the person hit you?" Even at the younger ages, only a few children reported any events that had not happened (Baker-Ward, Gordon, Ornstein, Larus, & Clubb, 1993; Goodman, Aman, & Hirschman, 1987). These results, of course, do not deny that one might induce children to give false testimony by more prolonged and insistent suggestions.

The general recommendations on children's eyewitness testimony are as follows: If a child is simply asked to describe the events in a nonthreatening atmosphere, without suggestions or pressure, reasonably soon after the event, even children as young as 3 are believable (Ceci & Bruck, 1993). Asking a child the same questions repeatedly within a single interview can confuse the child. (Some will change their answers on the assumption that their first answers must have been wrong.) However, asking the child to repeat

the story every few days may help the child to remember—as may be necessary if the child is to testify in a trial many months later (Poole & White, 1995).

THE "FALSE MEMORY" CONTROVERSY

Sigmund Freud, whom we shall consider more fully in Chapter 13, defined **repression** as the process of moving a memory, motivation, or emotion from the conscious mind to the unconscious mind. Earlier, when I was describing explanations of forgetting, I did not include the possibility of repression, simply because the research on memory and forgetting has not supported this concept (Holmes, 1990). However, although most memory researchers doubt this concept, a number of clinical psychologists continue to find it useful and convincing. They are unimpressed with the laboratory research, arguing that repression occurs under circumstances that a laboratory cannot capture.

A significant controversy has arisen over the use of the concept of repression under circumstances of the following type: A client tells a therapist about a variety of distresses and emotional difficulties without any known cause. The therapist, explaining that such symptoms are frequently a result of early sexual abuse, asks whether the client was sexually abused. "No, I don't believe so," the client replies. The therapist, however, persists, explaining that the absence of a memory does not mean that someone was not abused; after all, the person may have repressed the painful memories. The therapist asks the client to try hard to remember, to

Suspect # 3   Suspect # 4   Suspect # 5

...ect" and others chosen to resemble
...t as the probable suspect? (Check

---

fantasize what the abuse might have been if it had occurred. Some therapists employ hypnosis or other techniques to "recover" the repressed memory. Eventually, the client may either claim to remember being sexually abused or may simply agree, "I guess you're right; I must have been sexually abused, even though I don't remember it."

What I have just described is, of course, not representative of all cases and certainly not of all therapists. Sometimes the client clearly recalls being sexually abused and will volunteer that information without any prompting or after the mere question "Were you ever sexually abused?" Instances of that sort are believable and noncontroversial. After all, sexual abuse of children does occur, probably often, and is a serious problem.

The controversy concerns cases in which a psychotherapy client who initially denied remembering any sexual abuse goes through some treatment and eventually reports a recovery of repressed memories. Some patients have reportedly recovered memories that include sexual abuse at a very early age, even less than one year. Others have reported being part of a satanic cult that killed and ate babies and then used their satanic powers to destroy all the evidence. In some cases, people have been tried and convicted of crimes for which the only evidence was the testimony of a person who had not remembered the events until decades later, and regained them through the help of hypnosis or other therapeutic interventions.

Is it possible that people would repress memories of sexual abuse, satanic rituals, and the like, completely forgetting them until the time of therapy? Perhaps, but repression is not common, even after extremely traumatic experiences. One study examined 16 children who were known to have witnessed the murder of one of their parents. All had recurring nightmares, haunting thoughts, and painful flashbacks of the experience; none showed any indication of forgetting or repression (Malmquist, 1986). Another study examined children who at ages of less than 5 years had suffered traumatic experiences ranging from a plane crash to being kidnapped for ransom to being used in pornographic movies. Of those who were at least 3 years old at the time of the trauma, 6 out of 9 had good recall of the events even years later, and the other 3 had partial memories (Terr, 1988). Certainly, such results do

not indicate that repression never occurs; they do indicate, however, that if it occurs it is limited to some other kind of experience, or to certain as yet undefined kinds of people.

People do forget events from before age 3; that forgetting need not be due to repression, however. Also, as discussed in Chapter 5, we have no evidence that hypnosis or any similar treatment can accurately recover such memories.

The alternative to believing that psychotherapy clients recover repressed memories is that the suggestions to remember abusive experiences can "implant" a **false memory**, a report that someone believes to be a memory, but which in fact does not correspond to anything that happened. The advocates of this position point to the evidence showing that suggestions can distort people's memories of what they saw, and that sometimes repeated suggestions can even get people to report experiences that never occurred (Lindsay & Read, 1994; Loftus, 1993).

Critics of this position point out that such evidence shows only that suggestions can implant memories of minor events such as being lost in a shopping mall. Researchers have not demonstrated that suggestions can implant emotionally distressing memories such as those of sexual abuse (Pezdek, 1994).

True, reply those on the other side, but ethics would prohibit us from trying to implant emotionally traumatic memories. Our evidence may seem shaky, but it is better than the evidence that anyone can accurately recover memories, especially infant memories, that have been forgotten for years.

Let us concede a few points which, I believe, ought to be conceded on both sides: First, people do sometimes forget painful memories, and it is at least possible that appropriate reminders might help some of them to remember. Second, people are suggestible; if they are told that something must have happened and that they should try to remember it, at least some people will say they remember events, even though in fact those events never happened.

The real question then is, how common is the accurate recovery of a lost memory and how common is a false memory? If someone says he or she now remembers some long-forgotten event, should we assume it is true or assume it is a false memory? The problem is, psychologists do not know how to distin-

---

Here are some of the assertions students are challenged to reconsider:

- On a multiple-choice test, you should stick with your first impulse.

- We use only 10% of our brains.

- Subliminal messages can control people's behavior in powerful ways.

- Under hypnosis people will not do anything they would refuse to do otherwise.

- Psychotherapists can help people recall long-repressed memories.

- Lie-detector tests can determine accurately who is telling the truth.

- Hypnosis can enable us to remember forgotten materials, including some from early childhood.

- The Rorschach inkblot technique provides information about a person's thoughts and motivations.

- If you want to change people's behavior, you must first change their attitudes.

BEHAVIORISM

How and why did the behaviorist viewpoint arise?

What is its enduring message?

At the beginning of this text, I defined psychology as the study of behavior and experience. Different kinds of psychologists put greater emphasis on one or the other of those two elements. For example, in Chapter 14, we shall encounter *humanistic psychologists*, who are mainly interested in people's personal experiences and values. Here, we discuss **behaviorists**, psychologists who insist that psychologists should study only observable, measurable behaviors, without reference to unobservable mental processes. The discussion of behaviorism will lead into the rest of the chapter's discussion of learning, a field of research that behaviorists have traditionally dominated.

The term *behaviorist* applies to psychologists with quite a range of theoretical views, and we should distinguish between *methodological behaviorists* and *radical behaviorists*. A **methodological behaviorist** maintains that psychologists should study only the events that they can measure and observe—in other words, stimuli and responses. Mental experiences may well exist, and we may even find them interesting, but we cannot include them in our science. Or, if we do include them, we have to make it clear that we are cautiously inferring them from behavioral observations, just as a physicist might talk about unobservable quarks while clearly relating all such discussion to observable events.

In contrast, a **radical behaviorist** argues that the study of behavior is not just an indirect way of studying mental processes or a substitute for studying mental processes. Rather, behavior is the *only* thing for psychologists to study. According to this point of view, any discussion of mental events is just a sloppy use of language. A radical behaviorist accepts references to certain private events, such as headaches, but as a rule resists references to such mental constructs as *hope, intention, imagination,* or *will*. For example, as B. F. Skinner (1990) argued, when you say, "I *intend* to . . . ," what you really mean is "I am about to . . . ," or "In situations like this I usually . . . ," or "This is in the preliminary stages of happening . . ." That is, any statement about intentions or mental experiences can and should be converted into a description of behavior.

THE RISE OF BEHAVIORISM

Behaviorism can be clearly understood only within the historical context in which it arose. During the early 1900s, the *structuralists* were one of the most influential groups within psychology (see Chapter 1). Their method of studying thoughts and ideas was to ask people to describe their own experiences. The early behaviorists were to a large extent a protest group against structuralism. It is useless, the behaviorists insisted, to ask

Behaviorists agree that all psychological investigations should be based on behavioral observations. A methodological behaviorist might use observations of, say, facial expressions to make inferences about such processes as "happiness." A radical behaviorist, however, would be

---

A MODULAR APPROACH

The hallmark of any book by Jim Kalat is the way he organizes the material for students' comprehension. The modular approach, with each chapter divided into two to five freestanding modules, provides logical breaks within chapters, helping students manage the material easily. Each module begins with one or more *key questions* that are important in motivating research. Each module also has its own *introduction, summary, review of terms,* and *answers*. This enables instructors to select or rearrange assigned readings in the order they prefer or to omit sections. Each module ends with a *recommendation of additional readings.*

SUMMARY

• *The origins of behaviorism.* Behaviorism began in part as a protest against structuralists, who were asking people to describe their own mental processes. Behaviorists insisted that the structuralist approach was futile and that psychologists should study observable behaviors. (page 221)

• *Behaviorists' interest in learning.* Prior to the rise of the behaviorist movement, other psychologists had studied animal intelligence. Behaviorists adapted some of the methods used in those studies, but changed the questions, concentrating on the basic mechanisms of learning. (page 222)

• *Behaviorists' assumptions.* Behaviorists assume that all behaviors have causes (determinism), that mental explanations are unhelpful, and that the environment acts to select effective behaviors and suppress ineffective ones. (page 222)

SUGGESTIONS FOR FURTHER READING

Skinner, B. F. (1948). *Walden two.* New York: Macmillan. Skinner's utopian novel, in which he proposes a world based on the principles of behaviorism.

Skinner, B. F. (1974). *About behaviorism.* New York: Knopf. Skinner's elaboration on the behaviorist point of view.

TERMS

behaviorist psychologist who insists that psychologists can study only those behaviors that they can observe and measure, without reference to unobservable mental processes (page 221)

methodological behaviorist psychologist who insists that psychologists should base all their studies on measurements of observable phenomena—in other words, stimuli and responses (page 221)

radical behaviorist psychologist who regards all discussion of mental events as being merely sloppy use of language (page 221)

stimulus-response psychology the attempt to explain behavior in terms of how each stimulus triggers a response (page 222)

MULTICULTURAL AND GENDER-RELATED CONTENT

Where appropriate and relevant, the text includes discussions of how culture, ethnicity, and gender influence behavior. (To make the book more convenient for both instructors and students, a special thematic index helps locate related material.) By studying this diversity, psychologists can investigate the generality of psychological findings more thoroughly.

---

changed. Our biology does not dictate our customs.

Gender roles are not necessarily harmful in all cases, but they sometimes limit the choices children feel will be open to them in later life. Imagine an artistically inclined boy who is told that "real men like sports, not art." Or imagine a girl who wants to become an electrical engineer until someone tells her that "engineering is not a good career for a woman." Ideally, children (and adults) should feel free to develop their own interests and their own talents, whatever they may be.

━━━━━ CONCEPT CHECK ━━━━━

11. *Which of the following (if any) are examples of people following gender roles? (Check your answer on page 457.)*
a. A woman's ability to nurse a baby
b. A boy's interest in playing football
c. A girl's interest in ballet
d. A man's beard growth

ETHNIC AND CULTURAL INFLUENCES

Membership in a minority group molds a child's development in two major ways. First, the customs of the minority group may in fact differ from those of other groups. For example, compared to most other parents, Japanese parents lavish more attention on their infants and teach their children a greater emphasis on educational achievement and on bringing honor to one's family (Yamamoto & Kubota, 1983). Second, members of a minority group are affected by the attitudes of other people, who may treat them differently or expect different behavior from them simply because they are members of that minority group.

Immigrants to the United States or any other country undergo a period of **acculturation**, a transition from feeling part of the culture of their original country to being at ease in the culture of their adopted country. Acculturation is gradual; people sometimes require a generation or more before they or their descendants feel fully comfortable in a new culture.

In many cases, a person may have to

function as a member of two or more cultures or subcultures. For example, people who settle in an Italian-American community may speak Italian and follow Italian customs in their home neighborhood but speak English and follow American customs elsewhere. African Americans and Asian Americans may identify strongly with their ethnic group, live in a neighborhood populated mostly by others of the same group, and rely on the help of an extended family, while also being part of the "melting-pot" American culture at school, on the job, and in other settings. To at least a small extent, all of us learn to function in a variety of subcultures. For example, you enter slightly different subcultures at home, at college, on the job, at a religious ceremony, and so forth. You learn to adjust what you say and do depending on the setting and the people around you. However, while everyone has this experience to some extent, the transitions are more noticeable and more intense for ethnic minority members.

People react to these transitions in different ways. Some minority group members become more or less completely assimilated into the majority or melting-pot culture. However, they may feel a cost in doing so. For example, some high-achieving African-American students worry that their school and occupational success may alienate them from other African Americans, that "if you

Immigrants to a country go through a gradual, sometimes difficult process of acculturation into the customs of the new country. Their children are likely to become much more thoroughly acculturated.

---

succeed, you're betraying your color" (Fordham, 1988).

An alternative to full assimilation is **biculturalism**, an ability to alternate between membership in one culture and in another. Although doing so is difficult, many people succeed. The advantages of biculturalism are similar to those of bilingualism: A bilingual person (one who speaks two languages) can communicate with more people and read a greater variety of literature than can a monolingual person. Also, bilingual people come to understand their primary language from a new perspective, and often become more sensitive to the multiple meanings of a word. Similarly, a bicultural person can speak with and deal with a great variety of other people and may become more aware of both the strengths and the weaknesses of each culture (Harrison, Wilson, Pine, Chan, & Buriel, 1990; LaFromboise, Coleman, & Gerton, 1993).

CLOSING COMMENTS

Each of us can easily fall into the trap of thinking that her or his own way of growing up and of relating to other people is the "right" way, the "normal" way. In fact, people differ substantially in their social development; we have examined some of the major reasons—temperament, family influences, gender, and ethnic and cultural identity. As a society, we are coming both to recognize and to appreciate the resulting diversity of behavior.

SUMMARY

• *Temperament.* Even infants only a few months old show clear differences in temperament, their characteristic way of reacting to new experiences and new people. Temperament is fairly consistent as a person grows older. (page 446)

• *Changes in the U.S. family.* As U.S. society has changed over the decades, the role of women has changed and therefore family life has changed. The research suggests that children who spend much of their early life in a day-care arrangement can develop without difficulties, provided that the day care is of good quality. Most children in nontraditional families develop normally, except for the effects of

the pover[...]
mothers.

• *Effect[...]* families o[...] even befo[...] ally more [...] lies than [...] 448)

• *Male-[...]* ferences b[...] on the av[...] time. Ho[...] associate [...] ciate with females. Males tend to be more competitive, sometimes aggressively. (page 450)

• *Gender roles.* Men and women differ in their behavior partly as a result of gender roles, the behaviors each society specifies for men and for women. (page 452)

• *Ethnic and cultural differences.* People also differ because of ethnic and cultural influences. Acculturation is the process of transition from one culture to another. Many people can function successfully as members of two or more cultures. (page 455)

SUGGESTIONS FOR FURTHER READING

Hetherington, E. M. (1989). Coping with family transitions: Winners, losers, and survivors. *Child Development, 60,* 1–14. Review of the effects of divorce on children.

Maccoby, E. E. (1990). Gender and relationships. *American Psychologist, 45,* 513–520. Review of findings concerning sex differences in social behavior.

Powell, G. J. (Ed.) (1983). *The psychosocial development of minority group children* (pp. 237–247). New York: Brunner/Mazel. Description of research on the psychological effects of minority-group membership.

Tannen, D. (1990). *You just don't understand.* New York: William Morrow. A popular book discussing the ways in which men and women fail to understand one another.

TERMS

temperament people's tendency to be active or inactive, outgoing or reserved (page 446)

gender role the role each person is expected to play because of being male or female (page 452)

acculturation transition from feeling part of the culture of one's original country to the culture of one's adopted country (page 455)

biculturalism alternation between membership in one culture and membership in another (page 456) the sodium gates (van Dyke & Byck, 1982). When your dentist drills a tooth, the receptors in your tooth send out the message "Pain! Pain! Pain!" But that message does not get through to the brain, because a shot of Novocaine has blocked the sodium gates and thereby prevented the sensory axons from sending their message.

CONCEPT CHECK

6. *If you stub your toe, do you feel it immediately or is there a delay before you feel it? Why? (Check your answers on page 98.)*

SYNAPSES: THE JUNCTIONS BETWEEN NEURONS

Ultimately, each neuron must communicate with other neurons. Communication between one neuron and the next follows a different process from the transmission along an axon. At a **synapse** (SIN-aps), the specialized junction between one neuron and another (Figure 3.21), one neuron releases a chemical that either excites or in-

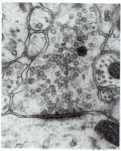

FIGURE 3.21
A synapse, magnified thousands of times in an electron micrograph, includes small round structures in the middle cell called synaptic vesicles, which store neurotransmitter molecules. The thick, dark area at the bottom of the cell is the synapse.

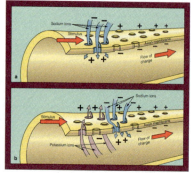

FIGURE 3.20
(a) During an action potential, sodium gates in the neuron membrane open, and sodium ions enter the axon, bringing a positive charge with them. (b) After an action potential occurs at one point along the axon, the sodium gates close at that point and open at the next point along the axon. When the sodium gates close, potassium gates open, and potassium ions flow out of the axon, carrying a positive charge with them. (Modified from Starr & Taggart, 1992.)

hibits the next neuron. The events at the synapses are central to everything your brain does, because the synapses are the source of information for the receiving cell. Drugs that affect behavior—ranging from tranquilizers and antidepressants to illegal drugs such as cocaine and LSD—do so by increasing or decreasing the activity at certain kinds of synapses. The following paragraph summarizes the events at a synapse.

A typical axon has several branches; each branch ends with a little bulge called a *presynaptic ending*, or **terminal button** (Figure 3.22). When an action potential reaches the terminal button, it causes the release of molecules of a **neurotransmitter**, a chemical that has been stored in packets called *synaptic vesicles* and elsewhere in the interior of the terminal button (Figure 3.22). Different neurons use different chemicals as their neurotransmitters, but each neuron uses the same chemical or same combination of [chemicals] at all times and at all branches [of the axon] (Eccles, 1986). The neurotransm[itter mole]cules then diffuse across a narrow [gap called] a *synaptic cleft* to the neuron on [the receiv]ing end of the synapse, the **postsy[naptic neu]ron**. There the neurotransmitter [molecules] attach to receptors, which may be [located on] the neuron's dendrites or cell bo[dy (or for special purposes) on the tip of its a[xon].

AN OPEN, BEAUTIFUL DESIGN AND PEDAGOGICALLY USEFUL ART

This edition contains hundreds of full-color illustrations and photographs, with captions that serve as important learning tools. Rather than simply describing the illustrations and photographs, the captions connect them with textual discussion, often helping to clarify important concepts. Many of the illustrations and photographs have been revised for this edition, and many new ones added. Photojournalism is used whenever possible to show that psychology often means understanding how people function in the real world.

KEY TERMS

Key terms are presented in bold type, making them stand out when they first appear in the text. They are then defined at the end of each module in the order of their appearance in the text. The terms are defined a third time in a combined glossary and subject index at the end of the book.

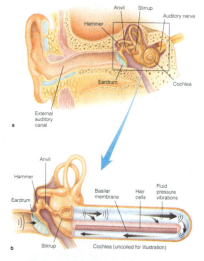

FIGURE 4.19
When sound waves strike the eardrum (a), they cause it to vibrate. The eardrum is connected to three tiny bones—the hammer, anvil, and stirrup—that convert the sound wave into a series of strong vibrations in the fluid-filled cochlea (b). Those vibrations displace the hair cells along the basilar membrane in the cochlea, which is aptly named after the Greek word for snail. Here the dimensions of the cochlea have been changed to make the general principles clear.

than the physical frequency and amplitude of sound waves.

The ear, a complicated organ, converts relatively weak sound waves into more intense waves of pressure in the fluid-filled canals of the snail-shaped **cochlea** (KOCK-lee-uh), which contains the receptors for hearing (Figure 4.19). When sound waves strike the eardrum, they cause it to vibrate. The eardrum is connected to three tiny bones: the hammer, anvil, and stirrup (also known by their Latin names: malleus, incus, and stapes). As the weak vibrations of the large eardrum travel through these bones, they are transformed into stronger vibrations of the much smaller stirrup. The stirrup in turn transmits the vibrations to the fluid-filled cochlea, where the vibrations displace hair cells along the **basilar membrane**, a thin structure within the cochlea. These hair cells, which act much like touch receptors on the skin, are connected to neurons whose axons form the auditory nerve. Impulses are transmitted along this pathway to the areas of the brain responsible for hearing.

A person can lose hearing in two ways. One is **conduction deafness**, which results if the bones connected to the eardrum fail to transmit sound waves properly to the cochlea. Sometimes surgery can correct conduction deafness by removing whatever is obstructing the movement of those bones. A person with conduction deafness can still hear his or her own voice, because it can be conducted through the skull bones to the cochlea, bypassing the eardrum altogether. The other type of hearing loss is **nerve deafness**, which results from damage to the cochlea, the hair cells, or the auditory nerve. Nerve deafness can result from heredity, from multiple sclerosis and other diseases, and from prolonged exposure to loud noises. Nerve deafness is permanent and cannot be corrected by surgery.

Hearing is the sensing of vibrations. Evelyn Glennie, profoundly deaf since childhood, has become a famous percussionist. Although she cannot hear her music, she detects the vibrations through her stocking feet.

INTRODUCTION TO PSYCHOLOGY

1

WHAT IS PSYCHOLOGY?

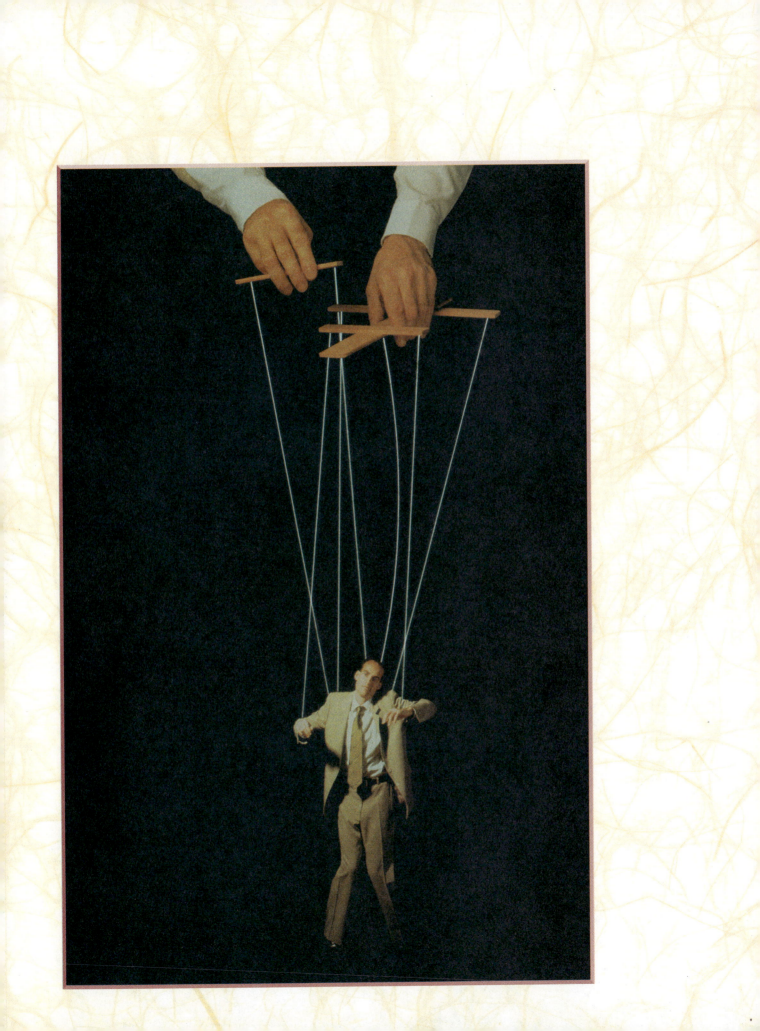

If you are like most students, you start off assuming that just about everything you read in your textbooks and everything your professors tell you must be true. But what if it isn't? Suppose a group of impostors has taken over the faculty of your college. They pretend to know what they are talking about, and they all vouch for one another's competence, but in fact they are all totally unqualified. They have managed to find textbooks that fit their own prejudices, but the information in the textbooks is just as wrong as what the professors themselves are saying. If that happened, how would you know?

As long as we are entertaining such skeptical thoughts, why stop at just your professors? Maybe other people are impostors too. When you read an advice column in the newspaper, or read a book about how to invest money, or listen to a political commentator who "knows" what the country should do, how do you know who has the real answers and who is just an impostor?

The answer is, all of us are impostors—you, me, everybody—at least some of the time. Sometimes we all act a little more confident of our conclusions than we really ought to be. Sometimes we just quote each other, such as, "They say we only use 10% of our brain," or "They say you should always stick with your first impulse on a multiple-choice test," and we don't even pause to find out who "they" are or why they say such things.

The problem is, anybody—even a professor or a textbook writer—has strong reasons for some conclusions, weak ones for others, and absolute certainty for relatively few. I don't mean to imply that you should shift from indiscriminately believing everything you read and hear to indiscriminately disbelieving everything. But what you should insist on is this: Anyone who tells you a conclusion should be able to tell you why he or she drew that conclusion. That is, don't be satisfied if someone suggests, "Take my word for it." Ask what the evidence is. Then perhaps you can draw your own conclusion. You might still not be right, but at least if you make a mistake, it will be your own and not someone else's.

I have just told you the theme of this book: Ask for the evidence. In the past you have heard, and in the future you will continue to hear, all sorts of claims concerning psychology. Some are valid, some are wrong, some are partly valid under certain conditions, and some are so vague or nonsensical that we cannot even evaluate whether or not they are true. By the end of this book, you should be in a better position to evaluate evidence for yourself and to judge on your own which claims are reasonable and which ones are not.

Who has the correct answers? None of us do, at least not always. Even when people we trust seem very confident of their opinions, we should ask what their evidence or reasoning is. Ultimately, we all have to draw our own conclusions.

Handwritten margin notes:
logos – word or study
psyche – soul or mind
roots in philosophy

Psychologists try to understand why people act the way they do + to help understand themselves.

THE GOALS OF PSYCHOLOGISTS

Why do psychological researchers generally assume that every behavior has causes?

How do they deal with the fact that much behavior seems to be unpredictable?

What do psychologists believe about the relationship between mind and brain, and about the roles of nature and nurture in the formation of behavior?

What do psychologists do?

What is the difference between psychologists and psychiatrists?

"Let us, then, make a fresh start and try to determine what soul is and what will be its most comprehensive definition."
ARISTOTLE (384–322 B.C.)

What do you suppose psychologists are really trying to accomplish? If you could ask any one question in psychology and be sure of getting a completely correct answer, what question would that be?

Some years ago, a student in one of my classes asked me, "When will we get to the kind of psychology we can 'use' on people?" Another student asked me whether I, as a psychologist, had any tips for him on how to seduce his girlfriend. (I told him I did not, and that even if I did, I would devote at least equal effort to giving his girlfriend tips on how to resist seduction.) Psychologists do not seek techniques for manipulating or tricking people. They do try to understand

FIGURE 1.1
What controls our behavior? According to advocates of free will, we are not swept along passively like objects in the wind; we control our own destiny. Sure, reply defenders of determinism, but the "we" who do the controlling are, in turn, products of our genetics and our previous experiences. We do not create ourselves.

why people act the way they do, and try to help people to better understand themselves.

THREE MAJOR PHILOSOPHICAL ISSUES IN PSYCHOLOGY

Psychology, broadly defined, is the systematic study of behavior and experience. The term *psychology* derives from the Greek roots *psyche*, meaning "soul" or "mind," and *logos*, meaning "word" or "study." Psychology began as the analysis of the mind or soul. As with most academic disciplines, it had its roots in philosophy. Although it has moved far away from philosophy in its methods, psychology continues to be motivated by some deep philosophical issues. Three of the most profound questions are free will versus determinism, the mind–brain problem, and the nature–nurture issue.

FREE WILL VERSUS DETERMINISM

Beginning with the Renaissance period in Europe, people began looking for scientific explanations for the phenomena they observed. One of the key points of this Scientific Revolution was a shift toward seeking the *immediate* causes of an event (what led to what) instead of the *final* causes (the ultimate purpose of the event in an overall plan).

Scientists analyzed the motion of objects in terms of pushes and pulls and other laws of nature (White, 1990). That is, they made an assumption called **determinism**—the assumption that everything that happens has a cause, or *determinant,* in the observable world.

Is the same true for human behavior? We are, after all, part of the physical world. Your brain and mine are made of chemical compounds subject to the same laws of nature as anything else. According to the *determinist* assumption for human behavior, everything we do has a cause (Figure 1.1).

Clearly, at least some of those causes lie within us. A person walking down a mountainside is not the same as a rock that is rolling or bouncing down the same mountainside. The point of psychological determinism is that even when you make complex decisions about how to get down a mountainside safely, your decision is a product of the combined influence of your genetics, your past experiences, and the current environment (Sappington, 1990). That is, just as an engineer can design a robot to consider information and make appropriate decisions, your genetics and experience have programmed you to make appropriate decisions. (You did not design or program yourself.)

Logically, the opposite of determinism would be *indeterminism*—the idea that events happen randomly with no cause at all. When we are discussing psychology, however, few people argue that important events are truly random or indeterminate. Rather, opponents of determinism defend a position called **free will**, a difficult view to describe. To some extent it is merely a rejection of determinism, claiming that people sometimes make decisions not controlled by their genetics, their past experiences, or their environment. But what is left besides genetics and environment? The answers here are generally vague, but accompanied by an insistence that our decision-making processes are in some way beyond the reach of the natural sciences.

The test of determinism is ultimately empirical: If everything we do has a cause, our behavior should be predictable. To a large extent, it is. For example, suppose a number of students are studying in various rooms of a campus building when they hear an announcement: "A fire has broken out in this building. By the time we bring the fire under control, the smoke and fumes may become hazardous. We therefore request that everyone leave the building." I can predict that almost everyone will promptly leave the building. I can make an even more accurate prediction if I know something about the individual students: I can predict that everyone will leave the building *except* those who are hearing-impaired, those who do not understand English, and those who have been advised by a friend that "every year at about this time someone says to leave the building because of a fire, but it's just a silly exercise to show that psychologists can predict your behavior, so be sure to ignore the warning."

In other situations, however, you might object that no one could possibly predict your behavior, no matter how much he or she knew about you. For example, no one could predict what you will choose to eat for lunch tomorrow or which color of sweater you will buy or how many pages of this book you will read before you quit to do something else.

You are right; certain details of your behavior will probably remain forever unpredictable. However, that unpredictability does not imply a lack of causes. Physicists and mathematicians today talk about *chaos*—the complex effects that result from the influence of many small causes. For example, imagine that I drop a golf ball at the top of a hilly

Your selection of a sweater to buy depends on many factors—your favorite color, the fact that you already have four sweaters in that color, the feel of the fabric, your desire to stay out of the way of another shopper, your eagerness to pick something quickly enough to get home in time for dinner, and so forth. Your final decision may not be predictable until moments before it actually occurs. It is unpredictable because of the large number of influences, not because your choice is independent of influences.

road and measure the exact point at which it eventually comes to rest. Then I take the ball back to the same location at the top of the hill and drop it in the same way as I did the first time. Will it eventually land in the same place as it did the first time? Very unlikely. The first bounce or two will be in nearly the same places as before, but with each succeeding bounce, the ball will veer farther and farther from its original route. The discrepancy does not indicate that the ball has violated the principles of physics; it simply shows the cumulative influence of an enormous number of tiny influences. Similarly, when you are deciding what to eat for lunch or which sweater to buy, your behavior is subject to so many tiny influences that your choice may be no more predictable than the final bounce of that golf ball. The unpredictability stems from the great number of small causes, not from a lack of causes.

Like most scientifically oriented psychologists, I, your author, believe in the concept of determinism. However, let me concede an important point. You will recall that in the introduction to this chapter I said that we all sometimes state something with confidence when it really is only an assumption. Here is such a case. Researchers assume that every behavior has a natural cause, because that assumption seems to work, and because the only way to test the assumption is to see how far we can go with it before we find some limit. Still, to be honest, it is an assumption and not a certainty.

The mind–brain problem includes such questions as, "Does the structure of the brain explain the achievements of a great scientist such as Albert Einstein?" and, "Does the structure of the brain explain why any of us have a mind at all?"

SOMETHING TO THINK ABOUT

What kind of evidence, if any, would support the concept of free will? Demonstrating that a particular theory makes incorrect predictions about behavior under given circumstances would not refute determinism. To support the concept of free will, you need to demonstrate that no conceivable theory would make correct predictions. Should a psychologist who believes in free will conduct the same kind of research that determinists conduct, or a different kind of research, or no research at all?

THE MIND–BRAIN PROBLEM

Every movement we make depends on muscle activity controlled by the nervous system, and every sensory experience depends on the activity of the nervous system. All activities of the nervous system follow the laws of physics and chemistry. What then is the role of the mind? The philosophical question of how experience is related to the brain is the **mind–brain problem** (or mind–body problem). Does the brain produce the mind? If so, how and why? Or does the mind control the brain? If so, how could a nonphysical entity control a physical substance? Or are the mind and the brain just two names for the same thing? If so, what does it mean to say they are the same?

Although the mind–brain problem is a particularly difficult philosophical issue, it does lend itself to examination by research. The research can determine links between brain activity on the one hand and behavior and experience on the other. For example, consider Figure 1.2. A technique called positron-emission tomography, discussed in Chapter 3, enables investigators to measure the amount of activity in different parts of the brain at various times. The nine photos in Figure 1.2 show brain activity while a person is engaged in nine different tasks. Red indicates the highest degree of brain activity, followed by yellow, green, and blue. As you can see, different tasks tend to activate different areas of the brain, although all areas show at least a little activity at all times (Phelps & Mazziotta, 1985).

Data such as these show a very close relationship between brain activity and psychological events. You might well ask, do these results mean that brain activity caused the associated thoughts, or did those thoughts cause that pattern of brain activity?

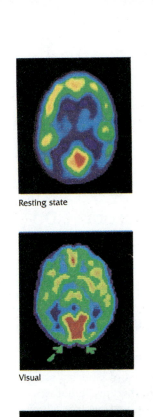

Resting state

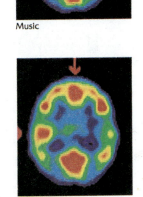

Music

Visual

Language

Auditory

Language and music

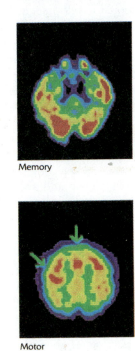

Cognitive

Memory

Motor

FIGURE 1.2

PET scans show brain activity of normal people engaged in different activities. Left column: Brain activity with no special stimulation and while passively watching something or listening to something. Center column: Activity while listening to music, language, or both. Right column: Activity during performance of a cognitive task, an auditory memory task, and a task of moving fingers of the right hand. Red indicates the highest activity, followed by yellow, green, and blue. Arrows indicate the most active areas.

Many brain researchers would be uncomfortable with that question. They would submit that neither brain activity nor mental activity "causes" the other; rather, brain activity and mental activity are different expressions of the same thing. (See Dennett, 1991.)

Even if we accept that position, we are far from understanding the mind–brain relationship fully. Is mental activity associated with all brain activity or just with certain types? Why is there such a thing as conscious experience at all? Couldn't the brain get along without it?

Research studies are not about to resolve the mind–brain problem and put philosophers out of business. But research results do constrain the types of philosophical answers that we can seriously entertain. The hope of learning more about the mind–brain relationship is one of the ultimate motivators for many psychologists, especially the psychologists whose work we shall study in Chapters 3 and 4.

SOMETHING TO THINK ABOUT

One way to think about the mind–brain relationship is to ask whether something other than a brain—a computer, for example—could have a mind. How would we know?

What if we built a computer that could perform all the same intellectual functions that humans perform? Could we then decide that the computer is conscious, as human beings are conscious? If we say the computer is not conscious, must we then conclude that consciousness is unnecessary, that a brain can get along just fine without it?

THE NATURE–NURTURE ISSUE

On the average, little boys spend more time than little girls do playing with toy guns and trucks and less time playing with dolls. Why? Are such behavioral differences mostly the result of genetic differences between boys and girls, or are they mostly the result of differences in the way society treats boys and girls?

In many countries, alcoholism is a serious problem. In other countries—Turkey, for example—alcohol abuse is less prevalent. Why the differences? Are they entirely a matter of social custom, or do certain genes influence how much alcohol people consume?

Certain psychological disorders are more common in large cities than in small towns and in the countryside. Does life in crowded cities somehow cause psychological disorders? Or do people develop such disorders because of some genetic predisposition and then move to a big city because that is the only place they can find jobs, housing, or welfare services?

Each of these questions is related to the **nature–nurture issue** (Figure 1.3). All of behavior depends on both heredity (nature) and environment (nurture), because people could not develop at all unless they had both heredity and environment. But the *differences* between one person and another may depend mostly on differences in heredity or differences in environment.

The relative contributions of hereditary differences and environmental differences vary from one instance to another. For example, how skillfully people play a video game depends mostly on how much time they have spent practicing (nurture). But

how well they can distinguish red from green depends mostly on which people have a particular gene for red-green colorblindness. In other cases, the differences among people depend strongly on both environmental and hereditary differences. The nature–nurture issue shows up from time to time in practically all fields of psychology.

WHAT PSYCHOLOGISTS DO

We have started with some major philosophical issues related to the whole enterprise of psychology. However, few psychologists are so ambitious as to think they can answer these ultimate questions; for the most part, they deal with more specific or more detailed issues.

When most people hear the term *psychologist*, they think first of **clinical psychologists**, who are **psychotherapists**, that is, specialists in helping troubled people. Clinical psychologists are just one of many types of psychologists, but let us distinguish from the start between clinical psychologists and psychiatrists. Psychology is an academic discipline, as are chemistry, history, and economics. If you decide to become a psychologist, you must earn a Ph.D. degree or some other

FIGURE 1.3
To what extent do children resemble their parents, and why? The Burmese reform leader Aung San Suu Kyi and former Soviet President Mikhail S. Gorbachev won Nobel Peace Prizes. Suu Kyi was the daughter of a national hero who led Burma's struggle for independence from Britain; Gorbachev was the son of Russian peasants. The way each person develops depends on both heredity and environment, but not necessarily in ways that are easy to understand or predict.

TABLE 1.1
Clinical Psychologists and Other Psychotherapists

TYPE OF THERAPIST	EDUCATION	APPROXIMATE NUMBER PRACTICING IN U.S.A.*
Clinical psychologist	Ph.D. with clinical emphasis, or Psy.D., plus internship. Total generally 5+ years after undergraduate degree.	60,000
Psychiatrist	M.D. plus psychiatric residency. Total 8 years after undergraduate degree.	55,000
Psychoanalyst	Psychiatry or clinical psychology plus 6–8 years in a psychoanalytic institute. Some others also call themselves psychoanalysts.	9,000
Psychiatric nurse	From 2-year (A.A.) degree to master's degree, plus supervised experience.	60,000
Clinical social worker	Master's degree plus 2 years of supervised experience. Total at least 4 years after undergraduate degree.	80,000

*Based on estimates provided in 1994 by the American Psychological Association, the American Psychiatric Association, the American Psychoanalytic Association, the American Psychiatric Nurses Association, and the National Association of Social Workers

advanced degree in psychology. Some psychology graduate students specialize in clinical psychology; others specialize in other branches of psychology. A few institutions offer the Psy.D. (Doctor of Psychology) degree, which generally requires less research experience than the Ph.D. The education for a Ph.D. or Psy.D. degree requires at least 4 or 5 years of academic work after graduation from college. Clinical psychologists take at least another year of supervised clinical work, called an *internship*.

Psychiatry is the branch of medicine that deals with psychological and emotional disturbances. To become a psychiatrist, you would first earn an M.D. degree and then take an additional 4 years of residency training in psychiatry. Psychiatrists and clinical psychologists provide similar services for most clients: They listen, ask questions, and provide advice. For clients with more serious problems, psychiatrists are authorized to prescribe drugs such as tranquilizers and antidepressants. Because psychologists are not medical doctors, they cannot prescribe drugs. Many clinical psychologists favor a change in the law to enable clinical psychologists with extra training to prescribe drugs. That proposal is highly controversial, and its eventual fate is hard to predict.

(Does psychiatrists' ability to prescribe drugs give them an advantage over psychologists? Not always. Ours is an overmedicated society. Some psychiatrists habitually treat anxiety and depression with drugs, whereas a psychologist would try to treat the problems by changing the person's way of living.)

Several other kinds of professionals also provide help and counsel. Psychiatric nurses and psychiatric social workers have an undergraduate or master's degree in nursing or social work plus additional training in care for emotionally troubled people.

Psychoanalysts are therapists who rely heavily on the theories and methods of the early 20th-century Viennese physician Sigmund Freud. There is some question about who may rightly call themselves psychoanalysts. Some people apply the term to any psychotherapist who relies heavily on Freud's methods. Others apply the term only to graduates of an institute of psychoanalysis. Those institutes admit only people who are already either psychiatrists or clinical psychologists. Training in the institute lasts 6 to 8 years. Thus, if you were to become a psychoanalyst, you would be at least in your late 30s by the time you completed your training.

Table 1.1 shows the differences among various types of psychotherapists.

CONCEPT CHECK

1. Can psychoanalysts prescribe drugs?
(Check your answer on page 19.)

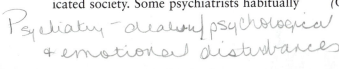

TABLE 1.2
Some Major Specializations in Psychology

SPECIALIZATION	GENERAL INTEREST	EXAMPLE OF SPECIFIC INTEREST OR RESEARCH TOPIC
Clinical psychologist	Emotional difficulties	How can people be helped to overcome severe anxiety?
Community psychologist	Organizations and social structures	Would improved job opportunities decrease certain types of psychological distress?
Counseling psychologist	Helping people to make important decisions and to achieve their potential	Should this person consider changing careers?
Developmental psychologist	Changes in behavior as people grow older	At what age can a child first distinguish between appearance and reality?
Educational psychologist	Improvement of learning in school	What is the best way to test a student's knowledge?
Environmental psychologist	The influence of noise, heat, crowding, and other environmental conditions on human behavior	How can a building be designed to maximize the comfort of the people who use it?
Ergonomist	Communication between person and machine	How can an airplane cockpit be redesigned to increase safety?
Experimental psychologist	Sensation, perception, learning, thinking, memory	Do people have several kinds of learning? Do they have several kinds of memory?
Industrial and organizational psychologist	People at work, production efficiency	Should jobs be made simple and foolproof or interesting and challenging?
Personality researcher	Personality differences	Why are certain people shy and others gregarious?
Biopsychologist	Relationship between brain and behavior	What body signals indicate hunger and satiety?
Psychometrician	Measurement of intelligence, personality, and interests	How fair or unfair are current IQ tests? Can we devise better tests?
School psychologist	Problems that affect schoolchildren	How should the school handle a child who regularly disrupts the classroom?
Social psychologist	Group behavior, social influences	What methods of persuasion are most effective in changing attitudes?

So, a clinical psychologist is one kind of mental-health specialist. However, many psychologists are not clinical psychologists. Nonclinical psychologists conduct research, teach, and provide nonclinical services. The interests of psychologists range from social and cultural influences on human behavior to the effects of brain damage on animal behavior, from helping corporations select among job applicants to helping mentally retarded children walk and talk. Table 1.2 lists some of the major areas of psychological research and practice.

The interests of psychologists range from highly theoretical issues to purely practical concerns. Here are a few examples of theoretical interests:

•   Do we have just one memory store, or do we have several types of memory?

•   What would we have to include in a computer program for it to mimic the performance of an expert chess player?

•   Can chimpanzees or other nonhumans learn to use symbols in a way that resembles the use of language by humans?

Here are a few examples of more practical interests:

•   How can someone help a compulsive gambler stop gambling?

•   Why do certain schoolchildren have academic difficulties, and what can be done to help them?

•   What design of an airplane cockpit would make it easiest for a pilot to find the controls?

Many questions have both theoretical and practical aspects. For example, some

Ergonomics is a field that combines psychology and engineering. Ergonomists, or human factors specialists, try to design machinery controls to make them easier for people to operate.

people claim that patients in psychotherapy can recover long-lost memories of abuse that they experienced during childhood. The question of whether it is possible to lose memories and then regain them has enormous theoretical implications as well as practical consequences. (For example, should juries convict someone of a crime based on memories supposedly recovered 20 or more years after the fact?)

OCCUPATIONAL SETTINGS IN PSYCHOLOGY

Psychologists work in many occupational settings, as shown in Figure 1.4. A little over one-third work in academic institutions—colleges, universities, and medical schools. Almost 40% work in health-provider settings—independent practices, hospitals, and clinics. Others work in business, government, guidance and counseling centers, and public school systems. Those who work in business help companies make decisions about hiring, promotions, training of workers, and job design. Those who work in school systems help teachers deal with discipline problems and underachieving students.

WOMEN AND MINORITIES IN PSYCHOLOGY

For a long time, academic psychology, like most other academic disciplines, was populated mostly by men. Women students were not encouraged to seek a Ph.D. degree; those who did were rarely offered employment at the most prestigious colleges, universities, or research institutions. Today, well over 50% of all graduate students in psychology are women, and the percentage of women among psychologists is high and growing.

Minorities also constitute a growing percentage of psychologists, though the total number is still small. According to a 1988 survey in the United States, African Americans, Hispanics, Asian Americans, and other ethnic minorities combined received 11.4% of the doctorates awarded in clinical psychology. That percentage is low compared to most other academic fields. Many graduate schools are taking active measures to attract more applications from minority students

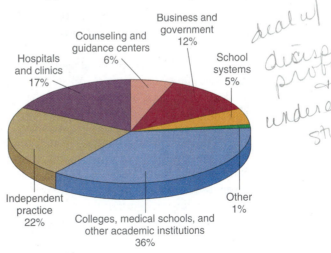

FIGURE 1.4
More than a third of psychologists work in academic institutions, with the remainder finding positions in a variety of settings.

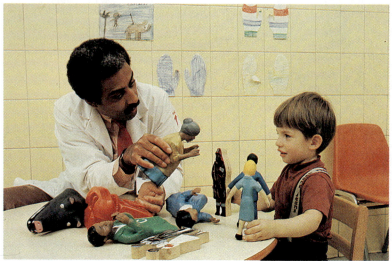

The number of minority individuals starting careers in psychology has been steadily increasing. Diversity among psychologists helps the field in many ways; people from different backgrounds tend to ask different questions and to offer different possible solutions to problems.

who would like to become psychologists (Hammond & Yung, 1993).

SOME APPROACHES TO THE STUDY OF BEHAVIOR AND EXPERIENCE

Consider this question: Why are you reading this book right now? No doubt you could come up with a reason, but it probably would not tell the whole story. We rarely do anything for just one reason. Perhaps you are reading this book because:

- You are curious to learn something about psychology.
- You have found that reading your textbook assignments leads to better grades and other rewards.
- In past years you picked up the habit of completing your school assignments.
- You know you will feel guilty if you spend a lot of money on a college education and then flunk out.
- Your roommate is reading a textbook, so you think you might as well do the same.

Notice that these reasons do not compete with one another. Several influences may combine and lead to a given behavior at a given time. Notice too that these reasons have to do with different things—your thoughts, your past learning, your emotions, and social influences.

Different psychologists explain the same behaviors in different ways and arrive at different answers to the same questions. In other words, they take different approaches

to psychology. Table 1.3 summarizes six examples of psychological approaches. (These are hardly the only approaches in psychology. Sometimes I think there are almost as many approaches as there are psychologists.)

Let us consider a few examples of psychological approaches. To compare them, we shall examine how each approach deals with the question of individual differences: Why does one individual behave differently from another?

THE QUANTITATIVE PSYCHOLOGY APPROACH

Any useful study of natural phenomena must be based on careful measurements. Quantitative psychologists measure individual differences and apply statistical procedures to determine what their measurements indicate. In fact, nearly all psychologists take measurements and apply statistical procedures; quantitative psychologists are those who concentrate more on mathematics and generally give less attention to the theoretical interpretations.

To measure individual differences, psychologists have devised tests of IQ, personality, interests, and attitudes, most of them requiring pencil-and-paper answers. Once they have devised a test, they must determine whether or not it measures what it is supposed to measure.

Tests in psychology only measure; they do not explain. For example, once we determine that a particular child has a low IQ score, we can predict that the child will have trouble in school. The test score does not, however, tell us *why* the child is performing poorly—either on the test or in school. One child may perform poorly because of visual or auditory impairments, another because of a poor educational background, yet another because he or she does not read or speak English. Measuring individual differences is a first step toward explaining them, but it is only a first step.

THE BIOLOGICAL APPROACH

A **biopsychologist** (or behavioral neuroscientist) tries to explain behavior in terms of biological factors such as electrical and chemical activities in the nervous system, the effects of drugs and hormones, genetics, and evolutionary pressures. For example, Huntington's disease is a condition in which the person experiences movement disorders and eventually memory and thought disorders.

TABLE 1.3
Six Examples of Psychological Approaches

APPROACH	DESCRIPTION	HOW PSYCHOLOGISTS MIGHT STUDY, FOR EXAMPLE, ELEMENTARY STUDENTS
Quantitative	Measures individual differences	Administer IQ tests
Biological	Studies nervous system, genetics, hormones, other biological influences	Identify indications of brain damage or disorder
Behavioral	Studies observable behavior	Observe how disruptive students are rewarded with attention
Cognitive	Studies thought and knowledge	Identify the kinds of questions a child can and cannot answer, infer thought processes
Social	Examines behavior in social context	Appraise influence of other people's expectations on child's performance
Clinical	Treats emotional troubles	Let child describe emotional conflicts

Whether or not one gets this disease depends on a single gene (Huntington's Disease Collaborative Research Group, 1993). More frequently, psychologists deal with genes that merely increase the probability of a given behavior or condition, depending on a number of environmental circumstances. For example, one gene has been identified that apparently increases the risk of alcoholism or drug abuse (S. S. Smith et al., 1992). Whether or not the person actually becomes an alcoholic or drug abuser, however, depends on experiences as well as on genes.

Biopsychologists also study the effects of brain damage. Brain damage may result from such things as a sharp blow to the head, a ruptured blood vessel in the brain, an interruption of oxygen supply, prolonged malnutrition, or exposure to toxic chemicals. The effects on behavior vary enormously, depending on the location and extent of the damage.

People have long known that various drugs can alter behavior. For example, opiates generally make people quiet, passive, and insensitive to pain. Amphetamine and cocaine generally stimulate increased activity in most people. Biopsychologists try to understand what drugs do in the brain. They find that most drugs that affect behavior do

Different psychologists ask different questions about the same behavioral observations. For example, does a low-achieving child have a biological disorder? How has the child learned to behave in this way? How is the child influenced by other people's expectations? Is the child reacting to emotional problems at home?

so by altering the chemical communication between one neuron and another at junctions called *synapses.*

So, according to biopsychologists, why do people differ from one another? The reasons are many: People are born with different genes; they develop slightly different brains and different hormonal patterns. Some have suffered brain damage; some are under the influence of drugs or of nutritional deficiencies that affect the brain. Anything that affects the body, especially the brain, will also affect behavior.

THE BEHAVIORAL APPROACH

Another approach to psychology is the behavioral approach. A **behaviorist** is a psychologist who studies observable behaviors instead of trying to analyze thought processes. Behaviorists believe that most behavior depends on the consequences of past behaviors. That is, how often we engage in a particular behavior depends on whether that behavior has usually led to positive, negative, or neutral outcomes in the past. Because many of the principles of learning are similar from one species to another, behaviorists often use animals in their investigations.

Suppose we want to know why most first-grade children follow the teacher's instructions (most of the time) whereas a few constantly chatter, run around, and disrupt class activities. While we could imagine many possible explanations, a behaviorist would look first at the consequences of a child's disruptive behavior: Other children watch and giggle and the teacher stamps and yells. In other words, certain children learn that they can attract more attention by running around noisily than by doing what the teacher asks them to do. How can the teacher get such children to behave better? One way is to praise them when they behave in a quiet, cooperative manner. If that approach fails, the teacher can isolate them from the other children for a few minutes after misbehaviors.

Adult behavior also is governed by its consequences. Whether adults choose to spend their time studying or socializing, running in track meets or running for political office depends in part on the rewards and frustrations that their choices produced in the past. Behaviorists try to relate individual differences to the individual's history of reward and punishment.

THE COGNITIVE APPROACH

Cognition refers to thinking and acquiring knowledge. A **cognitive psychologist** studies those processes. (The root *cogn* also shows up in the word *recognize,* which literally means "to know again.") Cognitive psychologists have learned much from the behaviorists. They do not simply ask people to describe their thought processes; they perform elaborate experiments to measure the consequences of those processes.

A cognitive psychologist who studies individual differences tries to identify the ways in which people think. For example, what do experts know or do that sets them apart from other people? One distinction is simply that the expert knows more facts. Consider a subject on which you are an expert: how to find your way around your college campus. A fellow student asks you, "How do I get from here to the biology building?" To answer, you can draw on the knowledge you share with the other student: "Go over toward the library. Then cut behind the library, between the library and the math building. The biology building will be right in front of you." Now a visitor who has never been on campus before asks you the same question. You say, "Go over toward the library . . ." "Wait, where's the library?" "Well, go out this door, make a right, go to the next street . . ." You will find that someone with little or no previous knowledge needs detailed and extensive instructions (Isaacs & Clark, 1987).

Another distinction between the expert and the nonexpert is that the expert can identify more categories. For example, a nonexpert might look at a group of birds on a beach and say, "Hey, look at all the sea gulls." An expert bird-watcher might reply, "There are three gull species and two tern species."

Moreover, the expert can identify the *right* categories. The inexperienced bird-watcher might say, sheepishly, "Oh, I see. Some of them have darker feathers than others." The expert would reply, "No, the ones with darker feathers are just younger. To tell one species from the other you have to check the color of the beak, the color of the legs, the size of the bird, the color of the eyes . . ." The expert knows what to look for—what is relevant and what is not (Murphy & Medin, 1985).

In short, a cognitive psychologist explains individual differences partly in terms of knowledge: People differ from one another because some of them know more than others do about a particular topic. Cognitive psychologists also study the ways in which people think and remember and how they use their knowledge.

THE SOCIAL PSYCHOLOGY APPROACH

Social psychologists study how an individual's actions, attitudes, emotions, and thought processes are influenced by other people. They also study how people behave in groups. When we are with other people, we tend to take our cues from them on what we should do. You arrive at a party and notice that the other guests are walking around, helping themselves to snacks, and talking. You do the same. When you go to a religious service or an art museum, you notice how other people are acting and again conform your behavior to theirs. Certainly, if you had grown up in a different country, you would have developed vastly different customs from the ones you now have.

Even within a given culture, different people acquire different behaviors because of the people around them. If for some reason you had made friends with a different set of people in high school, you might be a much different person today. According to social psychologists, people are also heavily influenced by other people's expectations. For example, we often intentionally or unintentionally convey expectations that boys will be more competitive and girls will be more cooperative, or that teenagers will be immature and that 25-year-olds will be responsible. At least to some extent, people's behavior tends to live up to—or down to—the expectations of others. Social psychologists study such influences.

THE CLINICAL APPROACH

I want to mention how clinical psychologists deal with individual differences, but I admit there is something wrong with calling clinical psychology an "approach." A clinical psychologist might rely on biological explanations, social explanations, behaviorist explanations, or still others, depending on the situation and the psychologist's own theoretical leanings.

Nevertheless, one point stands out as characteristic of many, though not all clinicians: an emphasis on emotional influences. For example, to explain why a particular child is inattentive in class or why a particular college student has trouble sleeping, a clinician might inquire about conflicts with

According to behaviorists, the probabilities of various behaviors are determined by their consequences in the past. Because this athlete's past efforts have brought him fame and other rewards, he will continue such efforts in the future.

family or friends. Perhaps the child is inattentive in class because his or her parents are constantly fighting at home. Perhaps the college student has conflicts with a boyfriend or girlfriend, or anxieties about living up to parental expectations. Not every problem in life depends on emotional conflicts, but a clinical psychologist is likely to explore that possibility carefully in a given case.

OVERLAP AMONG THE VARIOUS APPROACHES

I have oversimplified the discussion of the approaches of psychology in several ways. First, it is only partly correct to refer to biological psychology, cognitive psychology, social psychology, and other types as approaches. True, each constitutes one way of approaching certain phenomena of interest to all psychologists. But each is also a separate field of study with its own special phenomena. Biological psychologists ask questions about how the brain works; social psychologists ask questions about group behavior. Furthermore, the various approaches overlap significantly. Nearly all psychologists combine insights and information gained from a variety of approaches. To understand why one person differs from another, most psychologists are interested in their biology, their past learning experiences, the social influences that have acted on them, and much more.

As we proceed through later chapters, we shall consider one kind of behavior at a time,

Social psychologists study the ways in which our behavior depends on cultural influences, the expectations of other people, and what we observe of other people's behavior.

and generally one approach at a time. That is simply a necessity; we cannot talk intelligently about all kinds of psychological processes at once. But bear in mind that all these various processes do ultimately fit together; what you do at any moment depends on your biology, your past experiences, your social setting, your emotions, and a great deal more.

SUMMARY*

- *What psychology is.* Psychology is the systematic study of behavior and experience. Psychologists deal with theoretical questions, such as how experience relates to brain activity and how behavior relates to nature and nurture. Psychologists also deal with practical questions, such as selecting among applicants for a job or helping people to overcome bad habits. (page 6)
- *Determinism versus free will.* Determinism is the view that everything that occurs, including human behavior, has a physical cause. That view is difficult to reconcile with the conviction that humans have free will—that we deliberately, consciously decide what to do. (page 6)
- *Mind–brain.* The mind–brain problem is the question of how conscious experience is related to the activity of the brain. (page 8)
- *Nature–nurture.* Behavior depends on

_____

*The page numbers following each item indicate where you can look to review a topic.

both nature (heredity) and nurture (environment). Psychologists try to determine the influence of those two factors on differences in behavior. The relative contributions of nature and nurture vary from one behavior to another. (page 9)

- *Psychology versus psychiatry.* Psychology is an academic field whereas psychiatry is a branch of medicine. Both clinical psychologists and psychiatrists treat people with emotional problems, but only psychiatrists can prescribe medicine and other medical treatments. (page 10)
- *Quantitative approach.* Psychologists pursue different approaches in trying to explain the origin of individual differences. Those following the quantitative approach focus on measuring individual differences through such devices as IQ tests. (page 14)
- *Biological approach.* Psychologists following the biological approach look for explanations of behavior in terms of genetics, brain damage, diet, and other biological factors. (page 14)
- *Behavioral approach.* Psychologists following the behavioral approach study only observable actions and generally emphasize the role of learning. (page 16)
- *Cognitive approach.* Psychologists using the cognitive approach concentrate on people's thought processes and knowledge. They demonstrate, for example, that people's performance on a given task depends largely on their factual knowledge. (page 16)
- *Social approach.* Psychologists using the social approach study how people act in groups and how an individual's behavior is affected by other people. (page 17)

- *Clinical approach.* Clinical psychologists look for influences of emotional conflict on behavior, especially the role of emotional conflicts the person does not consciously recognize. (page 17)
- *Overlap.* The various approaches in psychology overlap partly in their interests, but not entirely. Each approach studies its own particular set of phenomena. (page 17)

SUGGESTIONS FOR FURTHER READING

Dennett, D. C. (1991). *Consciousness explained.* Boston: Little, Brown. A sophisticated, well-informed attempt to grapple with the relationship between brain activity and conscious experience.

Sechenov, I. (1965). *Reflexes of the brain.* Cambridge, MA: MIT Press. (Original work published 1863.) One of the first attempts to deal with behavior scientifically and one of the clearest statements of the argument for determinism in human behavior.

TERMS

psychology the systematic study of behavior and experience (page 6)

determinism the assumption that all behavior has a cause, or *determinant,* in the observable world (page 7)

free will the alleged ability of an individual to make decisions that are not controlled by genetics, past experiences, or environment (page 7)

mind–brain problem the philosophical question of how the conscious mind is related to the physical nervous system, including the brain (page 8)

nature–nurture issue the question of the relative roles played by heredity (nature) and environment (nurture) in determining differences in behavior (page 10)

clinical psychologist specialist in identifying and treating psychological disorders (page 10)

psychotherapist specialist who provides help for troubled people (page 10)

psychiatry the branch of medicine that deals with psychological and emotional disturbances (page 11)

psychoanalyst therapist who relies heavily on the theories of Sigmund Freud (page 11)

quantitative psychologist specialist who measures individual differences in behavior and applies statistical procedures to determine what the measurements indicate (page 14)

biopsychologist (or behavioral neuroscientist) specialist who tries to explain behavior in terms of biological factors such as electrical and chemical activities in the nervous system, the effects of drugs and hormones, genetics, and evolutionary pressures (page 14)

behaviorist psychologist who studies only observable behaviors rather than trying to analyze thought processes (page 16)

cognition thinking and acquiring knowledge (page 16)

cognitive psychologist specialist who studies thought processes and the acquisition of knowledge (page 16)

social psychologist specialist who studies how an individual's actions, attitudes, emotions, and thought processes are influenced by other people and how people behave in groups (page 17)

ANSWER TO CONCEPT CHECK

1. Most psychoanalysts can prescribe drugs, because they are psychiatrists, and psychiatrists are medical doctors. However, those psychoanalysts who are psychologists instead of psychiatrists are not medical doctors and therefore cannot prescribe drugs. (page 11)

PSYCHOLOGY THEN AND NOW

How did psychology get started?
How is it different now from what it was in its earliest era?

Imagine yourself as a young scholar in, say, 1880. Enthusiastic about the new scientific approach in psychology, you have decided to become a psychologist yourself. If you are like the other early psychologists, you have a background in either biology or philosophy. You are determined to apply the scientific methods of biology to the problems of philosophy.

So far, so good. But what questions will you address? A good research question is both important and answerable. You don't want to waste your time on a question that is one but not the other. Back in 1880, how do you decide which questions are important? You cannot get research ideas from the psychological journals, because the first issue won't be published until next year. (And it is going to be all in German!) You cannot follow in the tradition of previous researchers, because there haven't been any previous researchers. You are on your own.

Furthermore, back in the late 1800s and early 1900s, psychologists were not sure which questions were answerable. Sometimes they still are not sure. Should we try to study the nature of human consciousness? Should we skip conscious experience and instead concentrate on describing what people actually do? Many of the changes during the history of psychology have been changes in investigators' decisions about what constitutes a good research question.

In the next several pages we shall explore some of the changes in research questions over the history of psychology, featuring a few projects that dominated psychology for a while and then faded. I shall not mention Sigmund Freud or several other early pioneers whose contributions will appear in later chapters.

PSYCHOLOGY IN THE EARLY ERA (1879 TO ABOUT 1920)

Philosophers at least since Aristotle (384–322 B.C.) have been debating why people act the way they do, why they have the experiences they do, and why one person is different from another. Novelists such as Chaucer, Dostoyevsky, and Goethe have also made profound observations about human behavior.

Without meaning to take anything away from the importance of these great thinkers, a number of 19th-century scholars wondered whether a scientific approach might be fruitful. They were impressed by the great strides made in physics, chemistry, and biology; they wondered whether psychology could make similar progress if it collected and evaluated evidence scientifically.

WILHELM WUNDT AND THE FIRST PSYCHOLOGICAL LABORATORY

The origin of psychology as we now know it is generally dated to 1879, when a medical doctor and sensory researcher named Wilhelm Wundt (pronounced "voont") set up the first psychology laboratory, in Leipzig, Germany. Wundt and others had conducted psychological experiments before then, but this was the first time anyone had established a lab exclusively for psychological research.

Wundt's fundamental question was "What are the components of experience, or mind?" He proposed that psychological experience is composed of compounds, just as chemistry has compounds. Psychology, he maintained, has two kinds of elements—sensations and feelings (Wundt, 1896/1902). So, at a particular moment you might experience the taste of a fine meal, the sound of good music, and a certain degree of pleasure. These would merge together into a single experience, but that experience would still include the separate elements. Furthermore, Wundt maintained, your experience is partly under your control; even when the physical situation stays the same, you can shift your attention from one item to another and get a different experience.

FIGURE 1.5
(Left) In one of Wundt's earliest experiments, the pendulum struck the metal balls (d and b), making a sound each time. However, to an observer the ball appeared to be somewhere else at the time of the sound, generally at a distance it would have traveled in about ⅛ second. Wundt inferred that a person needs about ⅛ second to shift attention from one stimulus to another. (Above) The Walt Disney studios rediscovered Wundt's observation decades later: A character's mouth movements seem to be in synchrony with the sounds if the movements precede the sounds by ⅛ to ⅙ second.

Wundt's question about the components of experience was a philosophical one, and some of his musings about the elements of the mind were not much different from the writings of philosophers before him. But Wundt, unlike the philosophers, tried to test his statements by collecting data. He presented various kinds of lights, touches, and sounds and asked people to report the intensity and quality of their sensations. He measured the changes in people's experiences as he changed the stimulus.

Wundt also demonstrated that it was possible to conduct meaningful experiments in psychology. For example, in one of his earliest studies, Wundt set up a pendulum that struck metal balls and made a sound at two points on its swing (points b and d in the drawing at the left of Figure 1.5). Then he or another subject would watch the pendulum and determine where it appeared to be when they heard the sound. In some cases the pendulum appeared to be slightly in front of the ball and in other cases slightly behind the ball. On the average, the apparent position of the pendulum at the time of the sound differed from its actual position by about ⅛ second (Wundt, 1862/1961). Apparently we can be slightly wrong about the time when we saw or heard something. Wundt's interpretation was that a person needs about ⅛ second to shift attention from one stimulus to another.

Wundt and his students were prolific investigators; the brief treatment here does not do him justice. He contributed a great deal (writing more than 50,000 pages), but his most lasting impact on psychology came from setting the precedent of studying psychological questions by collecting scientific data.

EDWARD TITCHENER AND STRUCTURALISM

For years, most of the world's scientific psychologists received their education from Wundt himself. One of Wundt's students, Edward Titchener, came to the United States in 1892 as a psychology professor at Cornell University. Like Wundt, Titchener thought the main question of psychology was the nature of mental experiences.

Titchener (1910) typically presented a stimulus and asked his subject to analyze it into its separate features—for example, to look at an apple and describe its redness, its brightness, its shape, and so forth. Whereas Wundt believed an experience was composed of these various elements, Titchener thought people could actually *describe* the individual elements of their experience.

He called his approach **structuralism**, because he was trying to describe the structures

Edward Titchener asked subjects to describe their sensations. For example, they might describe their shape sensation, their color sensation, and their texture sensation while looking at a lemon. He had no way to check the accuracy of their reports, however, and later psychologists abandoned his methods.

that compose the mind. He was much less interested in what those elements *do* (their functions).

If you asked some psychologists today whether they thought Titchener had the correct description of the structures of the mind, you would probably get a blank look or shrug of the shoulders. After Titchener died in 1927, psychologists virtually abandoned his research methods and even his questions. Why? Remember that I said a good scientific question is both important and answerable. We may or may not find Titchener's question about the elements of the mind important, but after he had spent his entire adult life working on it, the question seemed less and less answerable. The main reason was that he and his students had to rely on observers to describe their experiences accurately, but they had no convincing way to check that accuracy.

For example, suppose you are the psychologist: I look at a lemon and tell you I have an experience of brightness that is totally separate from my experience of yellowness. How do you know whether I am correct about that? I might be lying to you, telling you what I think you want me to say, or even deceiving myself. You are apparently stuck with taking my word for it, unless you have some other way of seeing into my mind. Psychologists' frustration with this approach eventually turned most of them against the whole idea of studying the mind, leaving them eager to adopt the behaviorist alternative, which we shall discuss later.

WILLIAM JAMES AND FUNCTIONALISM

About simultaneously with the work of Wundt and overlapping the work of Titchener, Harvard's William James articulated

some of the major issues of psychology and won eventual recognition as the founder of American psychology. James's book *The Principles of Psychology* (1890) defined the questions that dominated psychology for years afterward, and still do to some extent today.

James had little patience for Wundt's or Titchener's search for the elements of the mind. He once wrote, "[A] microscopic psychology has arisen in Germany, carried on by experimental methods, asking of course every moment for introspective data, but eliminating their uncertainty by operating on a large scale and taking statistical means. This method taxes patience to the utmost, and hardly could have arisen in a country whose natives could be *bored*. Such Germans as . . . Wundt obviously cannot."

James focused concern on the actions the mind *performs*, rather than the ideas that the mind *has*. That is, he did not care to isolate the elements of consciousness; he preferred to learn how the mind produces useful behaviors. For that reason we call his approach **functionalism**. He suggested the following as examples of good psychological questions (James, 1890):

• How can people strengthen good habits?
• How many objects can a person attend to at once?
• How do people recognize that they have seen something before?
• How does an intention lead to an action?

James himself did little research to answer these questions, although he proposed some reasonable possibilities. His main contribution was to inspire later researchers to address the questions he posed. In focusing on how the mind produces useful behavior, he paved the way for the behaviorists of a later generation, who focused on behavior it-self and ignored "mind" altogether.

STUDIES OF SENSATION

For many early psychologists, the important question was the relationship between physi-cal stimuli and psychological sensations. To a large extent, the study of sensation *was* psychology. The first English-language text-book of the "new," scientifically based psy-chology devoted almost half its pages to the senses and the related topic of attention (Scripture, 1907). By the 1930s, a standard psychology textbook devoted less than 20% of its pages to these topics (Woodworth, 1934); today, the coverage constitutes about 5–10%.

Why were the early psychologists so in-terested in sensation? One reason was philo-sophical: They wanted to understand mental experience, and experience is composed mostly if not entirely of sensations. The other reason was strategic: If they were going to demonstrate the possibility of a scientific psychology, they had to begin with questions that were *answerable,* and many questions about sensation are indeed answerable.

They discovered that what we see, hear, and otherwise sense is not the same as what is really "out there." For example, the *per-ceived* intensity of a stimulus is not directly proportional to the *actual* physical intensity of the stimulus. A light that is twice as in-tense as another light does not *look* twice as bright. Figure 1.6 shows the actual relation-ship between the intensity of light and its perceived brightness. The mathematical de-scription of that relationship is called the **psychophysical function,** because it relates psychology to physics. Such research demon-strated that at least in the study of sensation, scientific methods can provide nonobvious answers to psychological questions.

THE INFLUENCE OF DARWIN AND THE STUDY OF ANIMAL INTELLIGENCE

Charles Darwin's theory of evolution by nat-ural selection (Darwin, 1859, 1871) had an enormous impact not only on biology but also on psychology. Darwin argued that hu-mans and other species share a remote com-mon ancestor. That proposal implied that each species had evolved specializations adapted to different ways of life, but it also implied that all vertebrate species had cer-tain basic features in common. It implied that nonhuman animals should exhibit vary-ing degrees of human characteristics, in-cluding intelligence similar to human intelligence.

Presuming that we accept that implica-tion, what should psychologists do about it? A number of early **comparative psycholo-gists** (psychologists who compare different animal species) did something that seemed reasonable at first, though it later seemed less and less fruitful: They set out to measure an-imal intelligence. They apparently imagined that they would be able to rank-order all an-imals from the smartest to the dullest. To-ward that goal, they put various species into such tasks as the delayed-response problem and the detour problem. In the *delayed-response problem,* an animal was given a sig-nal indicating where it could find food. Then the animal was delayed in its movement to-ward the food (Figure 1.7), to find out how

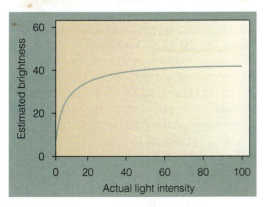

FIGURE 1.6
This graph of a psychophysical event shows the perceived intensity versus its physical intensity. When a light becomes twice as intense physically, it does not seem twice as bright. (Based on Stevens, 1961.)

FIGURE 1.7
One of the tasks used by early comparative psychologists to assess animal intelligence was the delayed-response problem. A stimulus was presented, a delay ensued, and then the animal had to respond to the remembered stimulus. Variations on the delayed-response task are still used today.

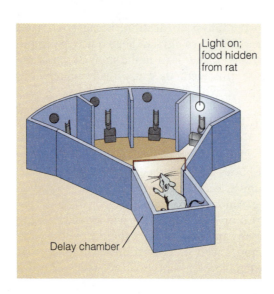

Light on; food hidden from rat

Delay chamber

FIGURE 1.8

Another task popular among early comparative psychologists was the detour problem. An animal had to go away from the food in order to move toward it.

Food

believed that human achievement was hereditary

FIGURE 1.9

In an experiment by Giebel (1958), zebras compared stripe patterns. How "smart" a species is depends in part on what ability or skill is tested.

long each species could remember the signal. In the *detour problem,* an animal was separated from food by a barrier (Figure 1.8), to find out which species would get the idea of taking a detour away from the food at first in order to get to it later.

Comparative psychologists set their animals to other tasks as well (Maier & Schneirla, 1964). But the task of measuring animal intelligence turned out to be much more difficult than it sounded. Too often a species that seemed dull-witted on one task seemed highly capable on a very similar one. For example, zebras are generally slow to learn to approach one pattern instead of another for food, unless the patterns happen to be narrow stripes versus wide stripes, in which case zebras become geniuses (Giebel, 1958). (See Figure 1.9.) Rats perform very poorly when they have to find an object that looks different from the others, but very well when they have to find an object that smells different (Langworthy & Jennings, 1972).

Eventually psychologists realized that the relative intelligence of nonhuman animals would not be an easy question to answer; the question may even be scientifically meaningless. Some researchers today hesitate even to say that monkeys are more intelligent than frogs (Macphail, 1985). They prefer to talk about which particular sensory and learning functions are better developed in one species or another.

THE MEASUREMENT OF HUMAN INTELLIGENCE

While some psychologists had studied animal intelligence, most had an even greater interest in human intelligence. Francis Galton, a first cousin of Charles Darwin, was among the first to try to measure intelligence and to ask whether intellectual variations were based on heredity. Galton was fascinated with measurement of almost anything and pioneered many new methods of measurements (Hergenhahn, 1992). For example, he invented the weather map, measured degrees of boredom during lectures, suggested the use of fingerprints to identify individuals, and—presumably in the name of science—attempted to measure the degree of beauty for women of different countries.

In an effort to determine the role of heredity in human achievement, Galton (1869/1978) examined whether the sons of famous and accomplished men were likely to become equally eminent themselves. (He paid little attention to women, on the grounds that women in 19th-century England had little prospect of attaining eminence.) Galton found that the sons of judges, writers, politicians, and other noted men had a high probability of reaching high levels themselves. He attributed their edge to heredity, although today we would hardly consider his evidence persuasive. (Sons of eminent men clearly had a favorable environment, not just favorable genes.) He furthermore suggested that eminence is partly due to intelligence; thus, he believed a tendency toward high or low intelligence was heritable.

Galton, however, had no test of intelligence. He attempted to measure intelligence by simple tests of sensory capacities and motor coordination, but none of these tests proved satisfactory. The French researcher, Alfred Binet, devised the first useful test in 1905. We shall discuss Binet's contributions and other intelligence tests in Chapter 9. At this point let us just note that the idea of intelligence testing quickly captured a great deal of interest in the United States and other countries. Such tests were widely used during World War I as a means of eliminating "feebleminded" people from military service; soon tests were used by schools and sometimes by employers. Eventually psychologists developed tests of personality, interests, and other psychological characteristics.

THE ROLE OF WOMEN IN THE EARLY DAYS OF PSYCHOLOGY

In the late 1800s and early 1900s, most U.S. colleges provided only very limited opportunities for women, either as students or as faculty. Psychology was not much different from other fields in this regard, but a few women did make major contributions and achieved wide recognition.

One of the first women to make a career in psychology was Mary Calkins (Scarborough & Furomoto, 1987). When Henry Durant founded Wellesley College in 1870, he decided to hire only women to teach the all-female student body. But he could find no woman with an advanced degree in psychology. Finally, in 1890, he hired a bright young woman, Mary Calkins (Figure 1.10), who had a B.A. degree in classics, to teach psychology, promising that he would pay for her graduate education in psychology. Then the

intelligent tests became popular in U.S.

problem was to find a graduate program that would accept a female student. After much debate and stiff resistance, nearby Harvard University finally agreed to let her attend graduate classes. In 1895, when she passed the final examination for the Ph.D. degree, one of her professors remarked that she had performed better on the examination than had any other student in the history of the department.

The Harvard administration, however, was still unwilling to grant a Ph.D. degree to a woman. It suggested a compromise: It would grant her a Ph.D. degree from Radcliffe College, the recently established women's undergraduate college associated with Harvard. Calkins refused, declaring that to accept the compromise would violate the high ideals of education. She never gave in, and neither did Harvard. Although Mary Calkins never received a Ph.D. degree, she became a pioneer in psychological research, inventing a technique of studying memory, known as the paired-associates method, that is still used today. She also became president of the American Psychological Association.

The first woman to receive the Ph.D. degree in psychology was Margaret Washburn, who received it from Cornell University in 1894. She later wrote *The Animal Mind* (1908), the first text on that topic; she too served as president of the American Psychological Association. Christine Ladd-Franklin, another early psychologist, did outstanding research on vision, beginning in 1887.

Studied memory paired-associated method)

THE PERIOD OF BEHAVIORIST DOMINANCE (C. 1920 TO C. 1970)

Earlier in this chapter I casually tossed out a definition of psychology as "the systematic study of behavior and experience." For a substantial period in the history of psychology, most experimental psychologists would have protested violently against those words *and experience*. Some psychologists still object today, but a little less strenuously. From about 1920 to 1970, give or take a little, psychology was the study of behavior, period. Most research psychologists were firmly committed behaviorists. Psychology had little to say about minds, experiences, or anything of the sort. (According to one quip, psychologists had "lost their minds.")

How did psychologists ever reach that conclusion? Recall that Titchener's effort to analyze experience into its components had failed. Most psychologists concluded that questions about the mind were unanswerable. The comparative psychologists also had failed in their efforts to measure animal intelligence, but in the process they had developed techniques for studying animal learning. Behaviorists discarded the question about animal intelligence but kept the research methods.

Behaviorists' primary research question was broad and simple: What do people and other animals do under various conditions? This question is clearly meaningful, although no one knew whether the answer would consist of long lists of details or a short list of general laws.

JOHN B. WATSON AND THE ORIGIN OF BEHAVIORISM

We can regard John B. Watson as the founder of behaviorism. He was not the first behaviorist—actually, it is hard to say who was the first—but Watson systematized behaviorism, stated its goals and assumptions, and popularized the approach. He set forth his views in two major statements, *Psychology from the Standpoint of a Behaviorist* (Watson, 1919) and *Behaviorism* (Watson, 1925). Here are two quotes from Watson:

Psychology as the behaviorist views it is a purely objective experimental branch of natural science. Its theoretical goal is the prediction and control of behavior. (Watson, 1913, p. 158)

The goal of psychological study is the ascertaining of such data and laws that, given the stimulus, psychology can predict what the response will be; or, on the other hand, given the response, it can specify the nature of the effective stimulus. (Watson, 1919, p. 10)

Watson's books and articles set psychology's agenda for many years. The early behaviorists were extremely optimistic, expecting to discover simple, basic laws of behavior comparable to Newton's laws in physics. In the belief that behavioral laws would be more or less the same from one species to another, many experimenters studied animals, especially rats. By 1950, one psychologist found that well over half of all psychological studies on animals dealt with rats (Beach, 1950).

CLARK HULL AND LEARNING THEORY

Inspired by Watson, psychologists set out to study animal behavior, especially animal learning. For a time, the most influential figure in this area was Yale psychologist Clark Hull. Hull was very explicit about what he considered an important psychological question: "One of the most persistently baffling problems which confronts modern psychologists is the finding of an adequate explanation of the phenomena of maze learning" (Hull, 1932). (Today, would you list that topic as one of the most important items you would like to understand in psychology?)

Hull set out to discover laws to account for the behavior of a rat in a maze. He summarized his theory in a mathematical equation showing that a rat increased its "habit strength" rapidly on the first few runs through a maze, and then more slowly on each additional trial (Figure 1.11). As Hull continued his research, he found that he had to make the equation more complicated. First he found that he had to multiply "habit strength" times "drive" to determine the probability that the rat would actually respond. Then he found that rats will run faster for a really tasty tidbit of food than for a barely edible piece. So he added to the equation another term for the amount of incentive. And then he needed another one for

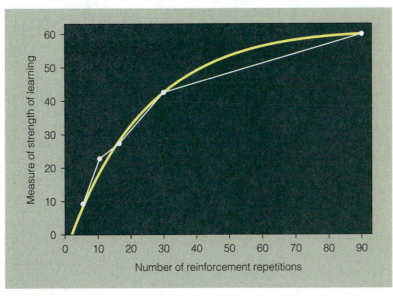

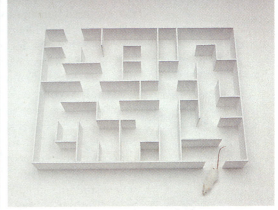

FIGURE 1.11
Clark Hull proposed the formula $sH_R = M - Me^{-iN}$ for the strength of learning (sH_R) by a rat in a maze. As the data points show, a rat improves its running speed rapidly at first and then more slowly as it approaches the maximum level, M. Hull's formula matched these results fairly well. The term i in his formula changed from one experiment to another to match the data. (Based on Hull, 1943.)

the effects of delaying reinforcement. And another to account for the fact that after a rat has been tested many times it starts to slow down. Gradually his equation grew longer and longer.

After the 1943 publication of Hull's major work, *Principles of Behavior,* his ideas dominated experimental psychology for years. His work was mentioned in almost a third of the articles published in the *Journal of Experimental Psychology* between 1950 and 1952. Within a few years after his death in 1952, though, his influence began to decline. Today, few psychologists take Hull's equations seriously.

What happened to Hull's theories? Not much, really. No one ever demonstrated that he was wrong. The problem was that in order to account for the behavior of a rat in a maze, Hull had to make his theory more and more complicated. The theory seemed to be getting more complicated faster than it was getting more accurate. Besides, why were psychologists studying a rat in a maze in the first place? Surely not because of the importance of rats or mazes for their own sake; the hope was to use something simple, like rats in a maze, to discover general principles of behavior. But if the behavior of rats in a maze was not simple and did not lead to general laws of behavior, then psychologists should study something else. Just as psychologists of the 1920s decided that Titchener's structuralist approach was unlikely to answer his questions in a reasonable period of time, psychologists of the late 1950s and 1960s turned away from Hull's approach.

THE CURRENT ERA IN PSYCHOLOGY

The rest of this book deals with the current era in psychology, with occasional flashbacks on the history of a particular subfield. The current era is not a "postbehaviorist" era, but we could call it a "postbehaviorist dominance" era. That is, behaviorism is still alive and well, but it does not dominate psychology as thoroughly as it once did. Some psychologists continue to study animal learning, but other psychologists now study mental images, problem solving, emotions, and other phenomena that behaviorists of the past virtually ignored.

Nevertheless, psychology has definitely *not* returned to prebehaviorist methods. Even the psychologists studying thinking and mental images are careful to do so by measuring behaviors, not by relying on people to describe their own ideas and thought processes. That is, even psychologists who ask nonbehaviorist questions generally rely on behaviorist methods.

Psychologists today also have broadened their scope to include more of human diversity. Psychological researchers of the past were mostly interested in the "general" laws or principles of behavior—the principles of perception or learning or motivation that all people share. In fact, they assumed that those principles were so general that we could probably discover them by studying rats or pigeons or any other convenient species. When they studied some behavior that required human subjects—language, for example—they still assumed that the principles were the same for all people, so the research could focus on any convenient group of people. Most often, the research used students at U.S. colleges. The strategy of simply using any convenient subject is justifiable for certain purposes (such as understanding how the eyes work), but for other purposes the differences among people may be more important than the similarities. For example, when studying child-rearing practices, the growth of self-esteem, or marriage customs, psychologists compare the results from different cultures throughout the world and from various ethnic groups within a given country. They often find at least subtle differences among groups; for example, a word such as *assertive* or *passive* has different meanings for European-American, African-American, and Latina women (Landrine, Klonoff, & Brown-Collins, 1992). Cross-cultural studies that examine such differences have become increasingly influential in psychology. Cross-cultural psychologists have interests that overlap those of cultural anthropologists.

Throughout the discussion of the early history of psychology, I have shown that many psychologists went down some blind alleys, devoting enormous efforts to projects that produced only disappointing results. Not all the efforts of early psychologists were quite so fruitless; in later chapters I shall discuss a variety of early studies that have stood the test of time. Still, if psychologists of the past have spent countless person-years on fashionable projects, only to decide later that those efforts were misguided, how do we know that some psychologists aren't on the wrong track right now?

Well, we don't. Thousands of psychologists are doing various kinds of research, and chances are, some of them are working on projects that will never accomplish much. As you read through later chapters, you are welcome to entertain some doubts. Maybe some of psychologists' questions are not so simple—or their answers not so solid—as they seem; perhaps you can think of a better way to approach certain topics.

In short, psychologists do not have all the answers. But that is not a cause for despair. Much like the rats in the mazes, psychologists make progress by trial and error. They pose a question, try a particular research method, and find out what happens. Sometimes the results turn out to be fascinating and rich in practical consequences. Sometimes they turn out to be puzzling or inconclusive. If one study after another proves to be disappointing, psychologists either look for a new method or change the question. By abandoning enough unsuccessful approaches, they eventually find their way to better questions and better answers.

SUMMARY

- *Choice of research questions.* During its history, psychology has several times changed its opinions of what constitutes an interesting, important, answerable question. (page 20)

- *First experiments.* Wilhelm Wundt established the first laboratory devoted to psychological research in 1879. He demonstrated the possibility of psychological experimentation. (page 20)

- *Limits of self-observation.* Edward Titchener, one of Wundt's students, attempted to analyze the elements of mental experience, relying on people's self-observations. Other psychologists became discouraged with this approach. (page 21)

- *The founding of American psychology.* William James, generally considered the founder of American psychology, focused attention on how the mind guides useful behavior, rather than on the contents of the mind. In doing so he paved the way for the later rise of behaviorism. (page 22)

- *Early sensory research.* In the early days of psychology, many researchers concentrated on studies of the senses, partly because they were more certain to find definite answers on this topic than they were on other topics. (page 23)

- *Darwin's influence.* Charles Darwin's theory of evolution by natural selection influenced psychology in many ways; it prompted some prominent early psychologists to compare the intelligence of different species. That question turned out to be more complicated than anyone had expected. (page 23)

- *Intelligence testing.* The measurement of human intelligence was one concern of early psychologists that has persisted through the years. (page 24)

- *Women in the early days of psychology.* In spite of an environment that discouraged women from pursuing academic careers, several women including Mary Calkins and Margaret Washburn became leaders in the early days of psychology. (page 25)

- *Era of behaviorist dominance.* As psychologists became discouraged with attempts to analyze the mind, they turned to behaviorism. For many years psychological researchers concentrated on behavior, especially animal learning, to the virtual exclusion of mental experience. (page 26)

- *Mathematical models of maze learning.* Clark Hull, who attempted to describe learning with a mathematical formula, exerted great influence for a number of years. Eventually his approach became less popular because rats in mazes did not seem to generate simple or general answers to major questions. (page 26)

- *Psychological research today.* Today, psychologists study a wide variety of topics. We cannot promise that we are not going down some blind alleys, like many psychologists before us. (page 27)

SUGGESTION FOR FURTHER READING

Scarborough, E., & Furomoto, L. (1987). *Untold lives: The first generation of American women psychologists.* New York: Columbia University Press. A rich account of history and biography.

TERMS

structuralism an attempt to describe the structures that compose the mind (page 21)

functionalism an attempt to understand how mental processes produce useful behaviors (page 22)

psychophysical function mathematical description of the relationship between the physical properties of a stimulus and its perceived properties (page 23)

comparative psychologist specialist who compares different species (page 23)

cross-cultural studies research studies that examine differences in behavior among various cultures or ethnic groups (page 28)

2

SCIENTIFIC METHODS IN PSYCHOLOGY

Every year spectacular claims are published about human behavior and related matters, even if little or no evidence supports the claims. Here are some examples:

• *Alien abductions.* Some people claim that they have been abducted by alien invaders, examined aboard a spacecraft, and then returned to Earth. To the question of why other people have not seen or photographed these aliens or their spacecraft, some of the "abductees" reply that the invaders and their craft are invisible, and so are the abductees during the period of their abduction.

• *Age regression.* Some people say that under hypnosis and similar techniques, a person can recall in great detail what it was like to be a young child, a baby, an embryo, or even a sperm cell (Sadger, 1941). (One man said that he and his fellow sperm cells had resented their father because they knew he did not want them to fertilize the egg!)

• *Buried treasures.* According to one group of believers, a vault buried beneath Bruton Parish Church in Williamsburg, Virginia, contains "the missing crown jewels of England," Francis Bacon's birth certificate, the original manuscripts of Shakespeare's plays, and some documents that can establish world peace (Sheaffer, 1992). Leaders of this church have had to get a legal restraining order to make these people stop digging under the church. One point the believers cite as "evidence"

The flag of the state of Virginia. According to one group, the spear in Athena's hand is a coded message that we should dig under the ground beneath a church in Williamsburg, Virginia, to find a buried treasure.

for their belief: Look at the flag of the state of Virginia. It shows the Greek goddess Athena pointing a spear. And where is the spear pointed? *At the ground! Where the vault is buried!*

• *Advanced techniques in channeling.* You have probably heard of "channeling"— the alleged ability of some people to provide a communication link to the soul of some great person of the past, such as Julius Caesar or King Tutankhamen. One woman in California has published a newsletter in which she reports that she channels the spirit of Barbie. That's right, Barbie, as in Barbie doll (Sheaffer, 1993). She claims that she has always had "an intensely personal, growth-oriented relationship" with her Barbie doll.

Most of us quickly dismiss such preposterous claims. Even if we do not dismiss them immediately, we are likely to ask the correct skeptical questions: What is the evidence? How good is that evidence? Can we find some other, more reasonable explanation of the evidence?

The harder step is to discipline ourselves to ask those same questions about more plausible claims. When someone announces a "new scientific finding" that agrees with what we already believe, or want to believe, we may find it very tempting to accept the new finding without subjecting it to careful scrutiny. It is a good habit to check the evidence carefully for every claim, so far as we can; occasionally the evidence forces us to change our opinions. This chapter concerns the kinds of evidence that psychologists use and the ways in which they evaluate theoretical claims.

SCIENCE AND THE EVALUATION OF EVIDENCE

How do scientists evaluate which theories are good and which theories are poor?

Why are most of them so skeptical of new theories and claims that seem to contradict our current understanding?

You will sometimes hear people say that something has been "scientifically proved." Scientists themselves seldom use the word *prove,* except when they are talking about a mathematical proof. As they collect more and better evidence, they may become confident about a given conclusion, but they still hesitate to say they are certain of it.

One distinguishing characteristic of science is that scientists generally agree on how to evaluate competing theories. Even when they disagree on which theory is best, they can still agree on what kinds of evidence they will accept in trying to decide. Most psychologists are quick to concede that our knowledge of psychology is less complete and less systematic than our knowledge of physics, chemistry, and biology. But like physicists, chemists, and biologists, psychologists generally agree on what constitutes good evidence and what does not. They try to rely on the best available evidence, and to draw no conclusion at all if the evidence is weak.

SOMETHING TO THINK ABOUT

If ethicists agreed with each other on how to evaluate theories, could they make progress comparable to that of scientists? Could theologians?

STEPS IN GATHERING AND EVALUATING EVIDENCE

Above all, scientists want to know the evidence behind a given claim. In psychology as in other fields, students should learn to question assertions, to ask what is the evidence behind a given claim and whether that evidence leads to an unambiguous conclusion.

In any scientific field, researchers conduct studies that go through a series of steps described in the following four paragraphs (see also Figure 2.1). Articles in scientific publications generally follow this sequence too. In each of the following chapters, you will find a section titled "What's the Evidence?" Those sections will go through one or more psychological investigations step by step, also in the same order.

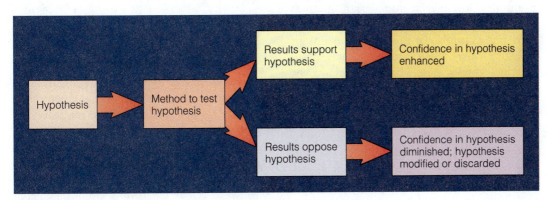

FIGURE 2.1
A hypothesis leads to predictions. An experimental method tests those predictions; a confirmation of a prediction supports the hypothesis; a disconfirmation indicates a need to revise or discard the hypothesis. Conclusions remain tentative, especially after just one experiment. Most scientists avoid saying that their results "prove" a conclusion.

Psychologists seek solid evidence to establish that watching televised violence increases the viewer's probability of violent behavior. Good research does more than just establish the connection between the two; it also can tell us how strong the connection is, what kinds of televised violence are most dangerous, and which kinds of viewers are most susceptible.

Hypothesis Any study begins with a **hypothesis,** which is a testable prediction of what will happen under certain conditions. In many cases the hypothesis is the product of someone's casual observations. For example, a psychologist might notice that children who like to watch violent television programs seem to be relatively violent themselves. So it seems, at any rate; we cannot always trust our impressions. The psychologist might then set out to test whether those children who watch the greatest amount of violence on television engage in the greatest amount of aggressive behavior.

Method Devising an appropriate method to test a hypothesis can be surprisingly difficult. For example, an investigator wants to measure how much violence each child watches on television. That may sound easy. But what counts as violence? Do we count minutes of violent programming, or do we count violent acts? Do some types of violence count more than others? An experimenter needs to select methods of controlling or measuring all the important events and behaviors in the study. The precision of that control or measurement will determine the usefulness of the research.

Results Suppose the investigator somehow measures televised violence and aggressive behavior. Then the task is to determine the relationship between the two measures. Did the children who watched the greatest amount of violence also engage in the most aggressive behavior? If so, how strong was the relationship? Were the results convincing, or might they have arisen by accident? Here the investigator calls upon statistical techniques to evaluate the results.

Interpretation Finally, the task is to determine what the results mean. Sometimes the results clearly contradict the hypothesis. For example, an investigator might find that children who watch a great deal of televised violence are no more aggressive than other children in general. In that case we might abandon the hypothesis or we might modify it: Maybe it applies only to certain kinds of children or to certain kinds of violence.

If the results match the prediction, we would look for other possible explanations before we draw a conclusion. Suppose, for example, the investigator finds that the children who watched the most violence on television were also prone to the most aggressive behavior. We should not necessarily conclude that televised violence leads to aggressive behavior, because of an alternative interpretation: Perhaps aggressive children like to watch violent television!

It is almost always possible to suggest more than one interpretation of the results of a given study. At that point the investigator sets up a second study to follow up on the results of the first and tries to decide between the two interpretations. That study too may lead to further studies. Because almost any study has its limitations, the ultimate conclusion comes from a pattern of results from many studies.

REPLICABILITY

Before psychologists trust the results of a study, we like to have other investigators repeat the procedure. If others get consistently similar results, then they have **replicable results**—that is, anyone who follows the same procedure can repeat them. If a result is replicable, we still may not be sure how to interpret it, but at least we think it is worthwhile to try. If the results cannot be replicated, then perhaps there was some hidden flaw in the first study; we base no conclusions on it.

What if a result can be replicated in some studies and not in others? Such a result is not considered trustworthy. For example, a number of years ago, one group of investigators trained some rats to respond in a certain way, then ground up the rats' brains, injected an extract into other rats, and reported that the new rats remembered what the old rats had learned (Babich, Jacobson, Bubash, & Jacobson, 1965). Many other experimenters tried to replicate this surprising result. A few reported results similar to those of the first experimenters, but most investigators could not (Gaito, 1976; L. T. Smith, 1975).

In a case such as this, psychologists look first for a pattern in the results. Did the procedure produce transfer of training only with certain kinds of rats, or certain kinds of training, or certain methods of taking extracts from the brain? If so, then identifying the key elements of the procedure might lead to a great advance in our understanding. As it turned out in this case, investigators could not identify any conditions under which they could demonstrate the phenomenon consistently, and most laboratories could never demonstrate it at all under any conditions. Eventually, most psychologists decided that the original results must have been an accident. The point is, scientific progress has to be based on replicable data. If results are not consistently replicable, we cannot take them seriously and we should not base any theory upon them.

CRITERIA FOR EVALUATING SCIENTIFIC THEORIES

Up to this point I have alluded to research in psychology without much detail. We shall consider the details of research methods later. Here, let's look at the big picture: After investigators collect mounds of evidence, what do they do with it? As part of the definition of science, I said that investigators agree on how to evaluate competing theories. Exactly how do they decide what is a good theory?

The goal of scientific research is to establish **theories,** comprehensive explanations of natural phenomena that lead to accurate predictions. A good theory predicts many observations in terms of a few assumptions and reduces the amount of information we must keep available for reference. For example, according to the *law of effect* (to be discussed in Chapter 6), if a person or any other

animal makes some response that is consistently followed by a reinforcer (such as food to a hungry person or water to a thirsty one), then the future probability of the response will increase. This law summarizes results for many species, many responses, and many reinforcers.

When we are confronted with several competing theories, we must evaluate them to decide which is the most acceptable. Scientists use several criteria (Figure 2.2). First, *a theory should fit the known facts and predict new observations*. Fitting the known facts (or seeming to fit known facts) is relatively easy; predicting new observations is more difficult and more important. For example, suppose someone says, "I understand why the stock market went down. First the U.S. President did this . . . and then the Japanese Prime Minister said that . . . , and the result was a loss of investor confidence." The correct reply is, "Okay, let's test your theory. Predict the next fall in stock market prices."

Second, *a theory's predictions should be precise, not vague*. For example, "people who are under too much stress will fail to achieve their full potential" is a poor theory; we do not know what constitutes "too much" stress and we have no way to determine someone's "full potential." The theory's prediction is so vague that we can hardly even imagine any evidence that would contradict it. (If someone under great stress made magnificent accomplishments, the possibility remains that the stress was not "too much" or that the person's "full potential" was even greater.) Therefore, scientists insist that a good theory should be **falsifiable.** What they mean is, we should be able to *imagine* some evidence that would, if demonstrated, contradict (falsify) the theory. For example, consider the theory that "vision depends on the stimulation of the eyes by light." This theory is falsifiable: We can *imagine* plenty of evidence that would falsify this prediction. For example, if people could see in a room with absolutely no light, or if they could see after loss of their eyes, such demonstrations would contradict the theory. The fact that no one has ever obtained such evidence is a good sign for the theory. (Note, of course, that *falsifiable* does not mean *falsified*!)

Third, *other things being equal, scientists prefer the theory that explains matters in the simplest possible terms and makes the simplest assumptions*. That is often a difficult criterion to apply, but it is a most important

FIGURE 2.2
Scientists evaluate competing theories by these criteria and rank them as good or perhaps not so good.

one, central to the scientific approach. We shall examine it in detail.

CONCEPT CHECK
---

1. *Identify each of the following theories as falsifiable or not falsifiable:*
    a. An object dropped in a vacuum at a low altitude above Earth will fall with an acceleration of 9.8 m/s².
    b. Some people have supernatural powers that science cannot explain.
    c. Children who suffer any kind of frustration at the oral stage of personality development (in the first year of life) will eventually develop emotional difficulties.
    d. People who use marijuana are more likely than other people to try additional illegal drugs. (Check your answers on page 42).

THE PRINCIPLE OF PARSIMONY

According to the principle of **parsimony** (literally, stinginess), scientists prefer the theory that accounts for the results using the simplest assumptions. In other words, they prefer a new theory that is consistent with other theories that they have already accepted. A theory that makes radically new assumptions

When a light fails, you can imagine many possible explanations: Maybe the power company has gone out of business. Maybe a rodent in your attic has chewed through a wire. Maybe the laws of electricity have temporarily ceased to apply. Before you entertain such unlikely assumptions, you try the more parsimonious explanation that the lightbulb has burned out.

[handwritten margin note: Prefer new theory that is consistent w already accepted theories.]

is acceptable only after we have made every attempt to explain the results in a simpler way.

You will note that parsimony is a very conservative tendency: It tells us to stick as close as possible to what we already believe. You might protest, "Shouldn't we remain open-minded to new possibilities?"

Yes, but with limits; the point is that we resist a change and that we adopt a radically new theory only when the evidence forces us to do so. Open-mindedness should not imply that "anything has as much chance of being true as anything else." The stronger the evidence in favor of a particular theory, the more strongly we should resist any claim that contradicts it. That is, we should have various degrees of open-mindedness. Consider three examples:

Visitors from outer space. I personally do not believe that visitors from other planets have ever landed on Earth, and I regard the prospect of travel between one solar system and another as unlikely. Still, I know that this judgment is based on uncertain assumptions about the technology and the biology of alien life. If I saw some nonhuman pilots step out of an odd-looking spacecraft, I could quickly change my opinion of the possibility of interstellar travel.

Homeopathic medicine. Adherents of homeopathic medicine claim that a good way to cure a disease is to administer a very small amount of a substance that causes similar symptoms. For example, if some disease produces symptoms similar to those of arsenic poisoning, then we can relieve the disease by giving tiny doses of arsenic. By "tiny," I mean really tiny. Homeopathic medicine practitioners sometimes dilute a solution, then pour most of it out, dilute the rest, pour most of it out, and so forth until the final concentration is *extremely* diluted. One study claimed to get biologically meaningful activity from a solution diluted to one part in 10^{120} (Davenas et al., 1988). To put that number in perspective, imagine dissolving one molecule of a substance into the Pacific Ocean. That procedure would yield a concentration of 1 part in 2.4×10^{46}, by my calculation. The authors who claimed biological activity from one part in 10^{120} admitted that their solution probably did not contain even a single molecule of the original substance, but they suggested that the water was somehow influenced by the substance that used to be in it. If you haven't guessed already, I am very skeptical of this claim and of homeopathic medicine in general. Am I open-minded enough that I could change my opinion? Well, maybe, but I am a great deal less open-minded in this case than I am about visitors from outer space.

Perpetual motion machines. A "perpetual motion machine" is one that generates more energy than it uses. For centuries, people have failed in all attempts to develop such a machine. (Figure 2.3 shows one example.) The U.S. Patent Office is officially closed-minded on this issue; it refuses even to consider any patent application for a perpetual motion machine. The reason is that a perpetual motion machine violates the second law of thermodynamics. (According to that law, within a closed system, entropy—disorganization—can never decrease. Any work will increase the entropy, and therefore waste some energy.) The second law of thermodynamics is more than just a summary of careful observations; it is a logical necessity, equivalent to saying that "the more probable state is more probable than the less probable state." Like the U.S. Patent Office, I consider a perpetual motion machine to be an impossibility. What would it take to make me change my mind? I can't even imagine. I am even less open-minded on this issue than I am on homeopathic medicine.

Now, what does all this discussion have to do with psychology? Sometimes people claim spectacular results that would seem to be impossible, according to everything else we know or think we know. While it is only fair to examine the evidence behind such claims, it is also reasonable to maintain a skeptical attitude and to look as hard as possible for a simple, parsimonious explanation of the results. Let us consider two examples.

AN EXAMPLE OF APPLYING PARSIMONY: CLEVER HANS, THE AMAZING HORSE

Early in this century, Mr. von Osten, a German mathematics teacher, set out to prove that his horse, Hans, had great intellectual abilities, particularly in arithmetic (Figure 2.4). To teach Hans arithmetic, he first showed him a single object, said "One," and lifted Hans's foot once. Then he raised Hans's foot twice for two objects, and so on. Eventually, when von Osten presented a group of objects, Hans tapped his foot by himself, and with practice he managed to tap the correct number of times. With more

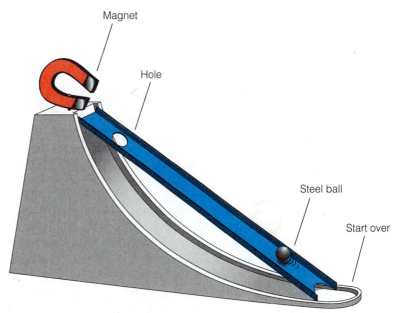

FIGURE 2.3
A proposed "perpetual motion machine": The magnet pulls the metal ball up the inclined plane. When the ball reaches the top, it falls through the hole and returns to its starting point, from which the magnet will again pull it up. Do you see what is wrong with this idea? (Check Answer A on page 42.)

practice, it was no longer necessary for Hans to see the objects. Von Osten would just call out a number, and Hans would tap the appropriate number of times.

Von Osten moved on to addition and then to subtraction, multiplication, and division. Hans seemed to catch on amazingly quickly, soon responding with 90–95% accuracy. Von Osten began touring Germany to exhibit Hans's abilities. He would give Hans a question, either orally or in writing, and Hans would tap out the answer. As time passed, Hans's abilities grew, just from being around humans, without any special training. Soon he was able to add fractions, convert fractions to decimals or vice versa, do simple algebra, tell time to the minute, and give the values of all German coins. Using a letter-to-number code, he could spell out the names of objects and even identify musical notes, such as D or B-flat. (Hans, it seems, had absolute pitch.) He responded correctly

keep skeptical attitude + look for simple explanation

FIGURE 2.4
Clever Hans and his owner, Mr. von Osten, demonstrated that the horse could answer complex mathematical questions with great accuracy. The question was "How?" (After Pfungst, 1911, in Fernald, 1984.)

even when questions were put to him by persons other than von Osten, in unfamiliar places, and with von Osten nowhere in sight.

Given this evidence, many people were ready to assume that Hans had great intellectual prowess. But others were not. Why not? Certainly the evidence was replicable. The problem was parsimony. No previous research had led us to assume that a nonhuman animal could perform complex mathematical calculations. Was there a simpler explanation?

Enter Oskar Pfungst. Pfungst (1911) discovered that Hans could not answer a question correctly if the questioner had not calculated the answer first. Evidently, the horse was not actually doing the calculations by himself but was somehow getting the answers from the questioner. Next Pfungst learned that Hans had to see the experimenter. When the experimenter stood in plain sight, Hans's accuracy was 90% or better; when he could not see the experimenter, he either did not answer or made a wild guess.

Eventually Pfungst observed that any questioner who asked Hans a question would lean forward to watch Hans's foot. Hans had simply learned to start tapping whenever someone stood next to his right forefoot and leaned forward. As soon as Hans had given the correct number of taps, the experimenter would give a slight upward jerk of the head and change facial expression in anticipation that this might be the last tap. (Even skeptical scientists who tested Hans did this involuntarily.) Hans simply continued tapping until he received that cue.

In short, Hans was indeed a clever horse. But what he did could be explained in simple terms that did not involve mathematical calculations or any other advanced cognitive process. We prefer the explanation in terms of facial expressions because it is the more parsimonious.

SOMETHING TO THINK ABOUT

If Clever Hans had died before Pfungst had discovered his secret, we would never have known for sure how the horse was doing it. Would we be obliged to believe forever that this one horse could understand spoken language and could solve complex mathematical problems? How could we have evaluated such a hypothesis years later? (Hint: Would we have had to discover how Hans did answer the questions? Or would it be enough just to determine how he could have answered them?)

ANOTHER EXAMPLE OF APPLYING PARSIMONY: EXTRASENSORY PERCEPTION

A highly controversial claim in psychology is the claim of **extrasensory perception**. Supporters of the idea of extrasensory perception (ESP) claim that certain people can acquire information without using any sense organ and without receiving any form of energy. They claim, for instance, that a person gifted with ESP can identify another person's thoughts (telepathy) even when the two are separated by a thick lead barrier that would block the transmission of almost any form of energy. They also claim that people with telepathic powers can identify thoughts just as accurately from a distance of a thousand kilometers as from an adjacent room, in apparent violation of the inverse-square law of physics.

Some ESP supporters also claim that certain people can perceive inanimate objects that are hidden from sight (clairvoyance), predict the future (precognition), and influence such physical events as the roll of dice by sheer mental concentration (psychokinesis). In other words, they claim it is possible

Magician David Copperfield can make people and animals seem to appear, disappear, float in the air, or do other things we know are impossible. Even if we do not know how he accomplishes these feats, we take it for granted that they are magic tricks, based on methods of misleading the audience. Other performers claim their amazing results depend on psychic powers. A more parsimonious explanation is that their feats, like Copperfield's, depend on misleading the audience.

acquire info without using senses.

1. *The great man will be struck down in the day by a thunderbolt. An evil deed, foretold by the bearer of a petition. According to the prediction another falls at night time. Conflict at Reims, London, and pestilence in Tuscany.*

2. *When the fish that travels over both land and sea is cast up on to the shore by a great wave, its shape foreign, smooth, and frightful. From the sea the enemies soon reach the walls.*

3. *The bird of prey flying to the left, before battle is joined with the French, he makes preparations. Some will regard him as good, others bad or uncertain. The weaker party will regard him as a good omen.*

4. *Shortly afterwards, not a very long interval, a great tumult will be raised by land and sea. The naval battles will be greater than ever. Fires, creatures which will make more tumult.*

FIGURE 2.5
According to the followers of Nostradamus, each of these statements is a specific prophecy of a 20th-century event (Cheetham, 1973). Can you figure out what the prophecies mean? Compare your answers to Answer B on page 42. The prophecies of Nostradamus are so vague that no one knows what they mean until after the "predicted" event. Consequently, they are not really predictions and certainly not falsifiable.

to gain information or to influence physical events without receiving or transmitting any physical energy. A conclusive demonstration of any of these claims would require us not only to overhaul some major concepts in psychology, but also to discard some of the most fundamental tenets of physics.

What evidence is there for ESP?

Anecdotes One kind of evidence consists of anecdotes, which are people's reports of isolated events. Someone has a dream or a hunch that comes true or says something and someone else says, "I was just thinking exactly the same thing!" Such experiences may seem impressive when they occur, but they are meaningless as scientific evidence for several reasons. First, consider the possibility of coincidence. Of all the hunches and dreams that people have, eventually some are bound to come true by chance. Second, people tend to remember and talk about the hunches and dreams that do come true and to forget those that do not. They hardly ever say, "Strangest thing! I had a dream, but then nothing like it actually happened!" Third, people tend to exaggerate the coincidences that occur, both in their own memories and in the retelling. We could evaluate anecdotal evidence only if people recorded their hunches and dreams before the predicted events and then determined how many unlikely predictions came true.

You may have heard of the "prophet Nostradamus," a 16th-century French writer who allegedly predicted many events of later centuries. Figure 2.5 presents four samples of his writings. No one knows what his predictions

mean until after the "predicted" events happen. After something happens, people imaginatively reinterpret his writings to fit the event. (His "predictions" are not falsifiable.)

CONCEPT CHECK

2. *How could someone scientifically evaluate the accuracy of Nostradamus's predictions? (Check your answer on page 42.)*

Professional Psychics A number of stage performers claim to read other people's minds and perform other psychic feats. Two of the most famous are Uri Geller and the Amazing Kreskin. Actually, Kreskin consistently denies doing anything supernatural; he prefers to talk of his "extremely sensitive," rather than "extrasensitive," perception (Kreskin, 1991). Still, part of his success as a performer comes from letting people believe he has mental powers that defy explanation, and his performances are similar to those of people who do call themselves psychics.

After carefully observing Geller, Kreskin, and others, David Marks and Richard Kammann (1980) concluded that the performers exhibited no special powers but only the kinds of deception commonly employed in magic shows. For example, Kreskin (Figure 2.6) sometimes begins his act by asking the audience to read his mind. Let's try to duplicate this trick right now: Try to read my mind. I am thinking of a number between 1 and 50. Both digits are odd numbers, but they are not the same. That is, it could be 15 but it could not be 11. (These are the

FIGURE 2.6

The Amazing Kreskin admits he is using magic tricks and "extremely sensitive" perception. In addition to entertaining people, he also sometimes works to combat superstition and gullibility. Some other performers claim they are using unexplainable powers. Regardless of what a performer claims to be doing, scientists look for the simplest, most parsimonious explanation available.

instructions Kreskin gives.) Have you chosen a number? Please do.

All right, my number was 37. Did you think of 37? If not, how about 35? You see, I started to think 35 and then changed my mind, so you might have got 35.

Probably about half the readers "read my mind." If you were one of them, are you impressed? Don't be. There are not many numbers you could have chosen. The first digit had to be 1 or 3, and the second had to be 1, 3, 5, 7, or 9. You had to eliminate 11 and 33 because both digits are the same, and you probably eliminated 15 because I cited it as a possible example. That leaves only seven possibilities. Most people like to stay far away from the example given and tend to avoid the highest and lowest possible choices. That leaves 37 as the most likely choice and 35 as the second most likely.

Second act: Kreskin asks the audience to write down something they are thinking about while he walks along the aisles talking. Then, back on stage, he "reads people's minds." He might say something like, "Someone is thinking about their mother . . ." In any large crowd, someone is bound to stand up and shout, "Yes, that's me, you read my mind!" On occasion he describes something that someone has written out in great detail. That person generally turns out to be someone sitting along the aisle where Kreskin was walking.

After a variety of other tricks (see Marks & Kammann, 1980), Kreskin goes backstage while the local mayor or some other dignitary hides Kreskin's paycheck somewhere in the audience. Then Kreskin comes back, walks up and down the aisles and across the rows, and eventually shouts, "The check is here!" The rule is that, if he guesses wrong, he does not get paid. (He hardly ever misses.)

How does he do that trick? Think for a moment before reading on. Very simply, it is a Clever Hans trick. Kreskin studies people's faces. Most of the people are silently cheering for him to find the check. Their facial expression changes subtly as he comes close to the check and then moves away. In effect, they are saying, "Now you're getting closer" and "Now you're moving away." At last he closes in on the check. That is, Kreskin has trained himself to use his senses very well; he does not need some extra sense.

We can also explain the performances of many other stage performers in terms of simple tricks and illusions. Of course, someone always objects, "Well, maybe so. But there's this other guy you haven't investigated yet. Maybe he really does possess psychic powers." Until there is solid evidence to the contrary, it is simpler (more parsimonious) to assume that those other performers are also using illusion and deception.

Experiments Because stage performances and anecdotal events always take place under uncontrolled conditions, we cannot determine the probability of coincidence or the possibility of deception. The only evidence worth serious consideration comes from laboratory experiments.

For example, in what is called the *ganzfeld* procedure (from German terms meaning "the entire field"), a "sender" is given a photo or film, selected at random from four possibilities, and a "receiver" in another room is asked to describe his or her thoughts and images. Typically, the receiver wears half Ping-Pong balls over the eyes and listens to static noise over earphones to minimize normal stimuli that might overpower the presumably weaker extrasensory stimuli (Figure 2.7). Later a judge examines a transcript of what the receiver said and compares it to the four photos or films, determining which one it matches most closely. On the average it should match the target about one time in four. If a subject "hits" more often than one in four, we can calculate the probability of accidentally doing that well.

(ESP researchers, or parapsychologists, use a variety of other experimental procedures, but in each case the goal is to determine whether someone can gain information without the senses at a higher-than-chance rate.)

We can summarize the results of ESP experiments as follows: Over the decades we have gone through many cycles. First ESP researchers announce that they have good evidence for a phenomenon. Then critics find flaws in the procedure or report failures to replicate. Then ESP researchers admit that the previous research was inconclusive but claim that they now have a better procedure and better evidence (Hyman, 1994). Currently, ESP researchers seem most enthusiastic about the ganzfeld method described above. According to one review, six of the ten laboratories that have used this method have reported positive results (Bem & Honorton, 1994); perhaps, believers claim, researchers have finally found a replicable experiment.

Perhaps, and certainly the best way to test that claim is for more investigators to conduct more research. However, most psychologists remain skeptical—I would say justifiably skeptical. Why? First, they are aware of the long history of flawed procedures, weak evidence, and nonreplicable results in this field. The ganzfeld procedures appear to be an improvement over those used in the past; still, half of the published research has come from just two laboratories, and one of those laboratories has been strongly criticized for using faulty research methods (Blackmore, 1994). Under the circumstances, it would be premature (at least) to call these results "replicable."

Second, psychologists look in general for the most parsimonious explanation for any phenomenon. If someone claims to have a horse that does mathematics or a person who reads the mind of a person in another room, we should look as hard as possible for a simpler explanation and adopt a radically new explanation only if the evidence absolutely and consistently forces us to do so. (Even then, we cannot accept a new explanation until someone specifies it clearly. Saying that some result demonstrates "an amazing ability that science cannot explain" does not constitute an explanation.)

GENERAL IMPLICATIONS

What have we learned about science in general? Science does not deal with proof or certainty. All scientific conclusions are tentative

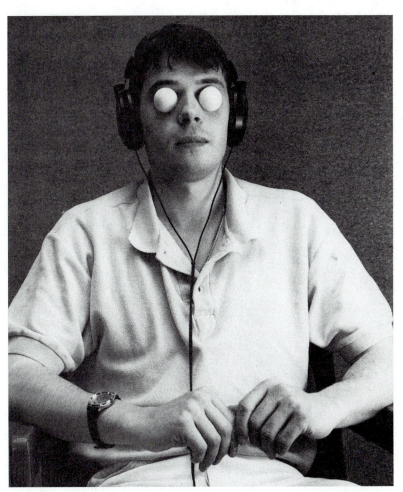

FIGURE 2.7
In the ganzfeld procedure, a "receiver" who is deprived of most normal sensory information tries to describe the photo or film that a "sender" is examining.

and subject to revision. The history of any scientific field contains examples of theories that were once widely accepted and later needed revision. Nevertheless, this tentativeness does not imply a willingness to abandon well-established theories in the face of any apparently contradictory evidence.

Scientists always prefer the most parsimonious theory. They abandon accepted theories and assumptions only when better theories and assumptions become available. Scientists scrutinize any claim that violates the rule of parsimony. Before they will accept any such claim, they insist that it be supported by replicable experiments that rule out simpler explanations.

Scientest prefer for most parsimonious explanation

SUMMARY

- *Scientific approach in psychology.* Although psychology does not have the same wealth of knowledge as other sciences have, it shares with those other fields a commitment to scientific methods, including a set of criteria for evaluating theories. (page 33)

- *Steps in a scientific study.* A scientific study goes through the following sequence of steps: hypothesis, methods, results, interpretation. Because almost any study is subject to more than one possible interpretation, we base conclusions on a pattern of results from many studies. The results of a given study are taken seriously only if other investigators can replicate them. (page 33)

- *Criteria for evaluating theories.* A good theory agrees with known facts and leads to correct predictions of new information. Its predictions are sufficiently precise so that we can imagine possible results that would falsify the theory. Other things being equal, scientists prefer the theory that relies on simpler assumptions. (page 35)

- *Skepticism about extrasensory perception.* Claims of extrasensory perception are scrutinized very cautiously because evidence reported so far has been unreplicable and because the scientific approach includes a search for parsimonious explanations. (page 38)

SUGGESTIONS FOR FURTHER READING

Carey, S. S. (1994). *A beginner's guide to scientific method.* Belmont, CA: Wadsworth. A description of scientific methods, particularly in their application to extraordinary (nonparsimonious) claims.

Kreskin. (1991). *Secrets of the amazing Kreskin.* Buffalo, NY: Prometheus. Kreskin explains some of his stage performances.

Randi, J. (1980). *Flim-flam.* New York: Harper & Row. A master magician exposes a variety of claims of psychic powers and other extraordinary abilities.

TERMS

hypothesis a testable prediction of what will happen under certain conditions (page 34)

replicable result a result that can be repeated (at least approximately) by any competent investigator who follows the same procedure as the original study (page 35)

theory a comprehensive explanation of natural phenomena that leads to accurate predictions (page 35)

falsifiable (with reference to a theory) sufficiently precise that one can imagine some evidence which (if demonstrated) would contradict the theory (page 35)

parsimony literally, stinginess; scientists' preference for the theory that accounts for the results by using the simplest assumptions (page 36)

extrasensory perception (ESP) the alleged ability of certain people to acquire information without using any sense organ and without receiving any form of energy (page 38)

ANSWERS TO CONCEPT CHECKS

1. **a.** Falsifiable. Anyone who found some object that fell with a different acceleration could contradict the theory. No one has ever found such an object. This is a good theory because it is *falsifiable* (in principle) and because it has never been *falsified* (by actual data).

   b. Not falsifiable. Even if researchers could scientifically explain every action of every person they had ever tested, the possibility would remain that some untested people have unexplainable powers. (Can you imagine a way to restate the theory so that it is falsifiable?)

   c. Not falsifiable, unless someone can specify a reliable method to determine whether or not a child has suffered "frustration" at this early stage of development and a reliable way to determine which people have emotional difficulties. As stated, the theory is too vague to be scientifically useful.

   d. Falsifiable. However, note that simply demonstrating that some marijuana users fail to try other drugs would not falsify (disconfirm) the theory. The theory would be falsified if researchers found that marijuana users were equally likely or less likely than other people are to try additional drugs. (page 36)

2. To evaluate Nostradamus's predictions, we would have to ask someone to tell us precisely what his predictions mean before the events they supposedly predict. Then we would ask someone else to estimate the likelihood of those events. Eventually we would compare the accuracy of the predictions to the advance estimates of their probability. That is, we should be impressed with "correct" predictions only if observers had rated them "unlikely" before they occurred. (page 39)

ANSWERS TO OTHER QUESTIONS IN THE TEXT

A. Any magnet strong enough to pull the metal ball up the inclined plane would not release it when it reached the hole at the top. (page 37)

B. The prophecies of Nostradamus (see page 39), as interpreted by Cheetham (1973), refer to the following: (1) the assassinations of John F. Kennedy and Robert F. Kennedy, (2) Polaris ballistic missiles shot from submarines, (3) Hitler's invasion of France, and (4) World War II.

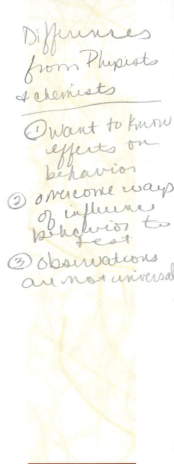

METHODS OF INVESTIGATION IN PSYCHOLOGY

How do psychological researchers try to overcome the problem of vagueness of the terms they use?

What kinds of research designs do they use, and what special problems sometimes arise in interpreting the results?

How do researchers deal with the ethical problems of research with both people and nonhuman animals?

Psychologists try to approach questions scientifically, but they face some special problems that physicists and chemists do not face. A physicist who wondered about the effect of temperature on the length of a steel bar would not pause long to ponder the true meaning of the word *temperature* or the best way to measure the length of a steel bar. However, psychologists who want to know the effect of motivation on a worker's job performance do have to determine what they mean by "motivation" and how they should measure job performance.

Here is a second major difference: When physicists study subatomic particles, they find that they cannot measure events without greatly affecting them. Physicists face that difficulty with subatomic particles; psychologists face it almost all the time. If you saw me watching you and taking notes on everything you did, would you continue acting the way you ordinarily do? Probably not. Psychologists have devised ways of overcoming this problem (Figure 2.8), but they can seldom disregard it.

A third difference is that psychologists study certain phenomena that change from one society to another and from one historical era to another. Physicists' and chemists' measurements of the properties of nitrogen or oxygen are, we believe, universal; they ap-

ply at any point in time at any place in this solar system or any other. In contrast, psychologists' measurements of sexual anxieties or attitudes toward war or child-rearing practices are likely to vary from one time to another or from one place to another.

GENERAL PRINCIPLES OF CONDUCTING PSYCHOLOGICAL RESEARCH

This part of the chapter will trace some of the common methods of doing research in psychology. The goal is not primarily to prepare you to conduct psychological research, although I hope that at least a few readers will eventually do just that. The primary goal is to prepare you to be an intelligent interpreter of psychological research. When you hear about some new study in psychology or related fields, you should be able to ask a few pertinent questions and to decide how good the evidence is and what conclusion (if any) it justifies.

DEFINITIONS OF PSYCHOLOGICAL TERMS

Suppose I want to determine whether hunger affects students' ability to concentrate on their studies. First I have to specify exactly

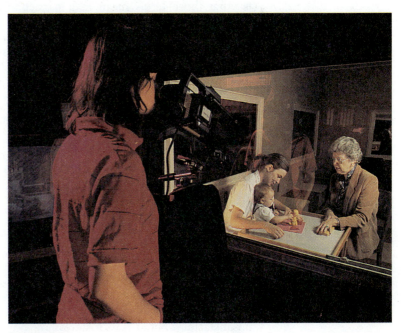

FIGURE 2.8
Observation through a one-way mirror enables psychologists to study subjects without making them self-conscious and influencing their behavior.

43

what I mean by "hunger" and "concentration." You might think that is a trivial question; after all, everyone knows what those words mean, presumably even psychologists. True, but to determine the effect of hunger on concentration, I have to measure the amount of hunger and the degree of concentration. To do so, I shall have to define these terms with greater precision than we do in everyday speech.

Whenever they are trying to measure something, psychologists find it useful to rely on an **operational definition**—a definition that specifies the operations (or procedures) used to measure something, a way to give it a numerical value. An operational definition is not the same as a dictionary definition. A dictionary's definition that *hunger* is a desire for food does not tell us how to measure hunger. Here is a possible operational definition: "Hunger is the duration of time since the most recent meal." That definition tells us a procedure that will produce a measurement (in this case, a measurement of time). Similarly, a psychological researcher might operationally define *concentration* as the length of time that the student continues reading without looking away or doing something else. Note that someone who offers these operational definitions does not insist that they are the best definitions for all purposes; he or she simply explains that this is what those terms mean in a particular piece of research.

Suppose that someone wishes to investigate whether children who watch violence on television are likely to behave aggressively themselves. In that case, the investigator needs operational definitions for *televised violence* and *aggressive behavior*. For example, the investigator might define *televised violence* as "the number of acts shown or described in which one person injures another." According to that definition, a 20-minute stalking scene counts the same as a quick attack, and an on-screen murder counts the same as one that the characters just talk about. An unsuccessful attempt to injure someone would not count as violence at all. It is unclear from this definition whether we should count verbal insults. In many ways this definition might prove to be unsatisfactory, but at least it states how one investigator is measuring violence.

Similarly, the investigator needs an operational definition of *aggressive behavior* (Figure 2.9). To define it as "the number of acts of assault or murder committed within

24 hours after watching a particular television program" would be an operational definition, but not a very useful one. A better operational definition of *aggressive behavior* specifies less extreme, more likely acts. For example, the experimenter might place a large plastic doll in front of a young child and record how often the child punches it.

Let's take one more example: What is love? Never mind what it *really is*. If we are going to measure how it affects some other behavior, or how something else affects it, we need an operational definition. One possibility would be "how many hours someone will spend with another person who asked him or her to stay nearby."

CONCEPT CHECKS

3. *Which of the following is an operational definition of intelligence: (a) the ability to comprehend relationships, (b) a score on an IQ test, (c) the ability to survive in the real world, or (d) the product of the cerebral cortex of the brain?*
4. *What would you propose as an operational definition of friendliness? (Check your answers on page 61.)*

REPRESENTATIVE, RANDOM, AND CROSS-CULTURAL SAMPLES

As a rule, researchers study a small group and derive conclusions that they hope will apply to a larger population, perhaps to everyone. In some cases, broad generalizations are justifiable; for example, the structure of the eye is so similar among all vertebrate species that researchers can study any convenient eye and discover principles that apply to all vertebrate eyes. In other cases, researchers have to be more careful. Someone who wanted to study sexual behavior or political attitudes could not study one small group of people and then assume that the results applied to everyone.

To conduct a meaningful study of a behavior that varies significantly among people, we need either a representative sample or a random sample of the population for which we want to draw conclusions. A **representative sample** closely resembles the entire population in its percentage of males and females, members of various ethnic groups, young and old, Republicans and Democrats, or whatever other characteristics are likely to affect the results. To obtain a representative sample of the people living in a given city, an investigator first would determine what percentage of the city's residents belong to each category and then select people to match those percentages. The disadvantage of this method is that a group may be representative with regard to sex, race, age, and political party and yet be unrepresentative with regard to some factor the investigators ignored, such as religious preference or level of education.

In a **random sample,** every individual in the population has an equal chance of being selected. To get a random sample of city residents, an investigator might select a certain number of households at random from the most recent census listing and then select one person at random from each of those households. If the random sample is large enough, it is likely to be close to the population percentages for sex, race, age, education, and so forth.

Sometimes psychologists are interested only in the members of one particular society. For example, one of my colleagues investigates the psychology of United States jury members. He uses only U.S. citizens in his studies and he draws conclusions that are limited to U.S. citizens and U.S. courts. In other cases, psychologists are interested in humans in general. For example, a psychologist who was studying humor should have no reason for limiting his or her interest to U.S. citizens, and no reason to assume that the conclusions that hold for U.S. humor are the same as those for humor in Pakistan or Venezuela. Consequently, such a researcher would be interested in **cross-cultural studies,** observations comparing the behavior of people in different cultures. Cross-cultural psychologists compare facial expressions in different cultures to determine whether smiles and frowns have the same meaning throughout the world, or whether they vary from one society to another. They also compare the ways in which people in different societies settle their disputes, the ways in which they treat their elderly, their attitudes toward death and dying, and so forth. Such research helps us to determine which aspects of behavior are due to human nature and which aspects are a product of growing up within a particular culture.

Cross-cultural psychology has to deal with some special problems of sampling (Matsumoto, 1994). For example, if you wanted to compare, say, American culture versus Indonesian culture, how would you

FIGURE 2.9

Aggressive behavior is difficult to define and measure. One psychologist might rate these boys' play as aggressive, whereas another might view the play as merely energetic, depending on each psychologist's definition of aggression.

determine what was "typical" of one culture or the other? Even within what we might think of as one culture, we can find major differences in customs and beliefs.

CONCEPT CHECK

5. Suppose I compare the interests and abilities of men and women students at my university. If I find a consistent difference, can I assume that it represents a difference between men in general and women in general? If not, why not? (Check your answers on page 61.)

SINGLE-BLIND AND DOUBLE-BLIND STUDIES

At some point in every psychological study, an investigator measures some aspect of behavior, perhaps by directly observing and recording it. Imagine that you, the investigator, are recording acts of "friendly" behavior by two groups of children. Imagine further that you are testing the hypothesis that Group A will be friendlier than Group B (for whatever reason). You know that, if the results support your hypothesis, you can get your results published and be well on your way to becoming a famous psychologist. Now one child in Group A engages in some mildly friendly act—a borderline case. You are not sure whether to count it or not. You want to be fair. You don't want your hypothesis to influence your decision of whether or not to count this act as friendliness. Just try to ignore that hypothesis.

To overcome the potential source of error in an investigator's bias, psychologists prefer to use a **blind observer**—that is, an observer who does not know which subjects are in which group and what is expected of each. Because blind observers do not know the hypothesis, they can be objective and record observations of behavior as fairly as possible.

Ideally, the experimenter conceals the procedure from the subjects as well. For example, an experimenter who was investigating the effects of some drug on children's friendliness might give that drug to one group and give a **placebo** (a pill with no pharmacological effects) to another group, without telling the children what pill they are taking or what results the experimenter expects. The advantage of this kind of study is that the two groups will not behave differently just because they expected different effects.

A study in which either the observer or the subjects are unaware of which subjects received which treatment is known as a **single-blind study** (Table 2.1). A study in which both the observer and the subjects are unaware is known as a **double-blind study.** (Of course, the experimenter who organized the study would have to keep a record of which subjects received which procedure. A study in which everyone loses track of the procedure is jokingly known as "triple blind.")

VARIETIES OF RESEARCH DESIGN

The general principles I have just discussed apply to a variety of research studies. Psychologists use various methods of investigation, each having its own advantages and disadvantages. Sometimes psychologists simply observe what one person does under certain conditions; on other occasions they perform complicated experiments on large groups. Let us examine some of the major categories of research designs (see Table 2.2).

NATURALISTIC OBSERVATIONS

A good deal of research in psychology is purely descriptive, trying to determine what people know, what they can do, what the special characteristics of certain kinds of people are, and so forth. A **naturalistic observation** is a careful examination of what people or nonhuman animals do under more-or-less natural conditions. For example, Jane Goodall (1971) spent years observing chimpanzees in the wild, recording their food habits, their social interactions, their gestures, their whole way of life (Figure 2.10).

Similarly, psychologists sometimes try to observe human behavior "as an outsider." A psychologist might observe what happens when two unacquainted people get on an elevator together: Do they stand close or far apart? Do they speak? Do they look toward each other or away? Does it matter whether the people are two men, two women, or a man and a woman? A psychologist might also record the behaviors of 6-month-old children, expert chess players, depressed patients, or any other type of people. After all, a first step toward understanding people is to know in detail what they do.

CASE HISTORIES

Psychologists are sometimes interested in conditions that rarely appear. For example, some people can remember what they have seen or heard with amazing accuracy. Others show an amazing inability to remember what they have seen or heard. People with Williams syndrome have normal or above-average language abilities, but in every other regard they are mentally retarded (Bellugi,

TABLE 2.1 Single-Blind and Double-Blind Studies			
Who is aware of which subjects are in which group?			
	OBSERVER	SUBJECTS	EXPERIMENTER WHO ORGANIZED THE STUDY
Single-blind	aware	unaware	aware
Single-blind	unaware	aware	aware
Double-blind	unaware	unaware	aware

TABLE 2.2
Comparison of Five Methods of Research

| | OBSERVATIONAL STUDY | | | | EXPERIMENT |
	Case study	Naturalistic observation	Survey	Correlation	Control of variables
Definition	Detailed description of a single individual	Description of what people or animals do under natural conditions	Description of selected aspects of a population of individuals	Description of the relationship between two variables	Description of the relationship between an independent variable and a dependent variable
Number of individuals studied	Usually one	Usually many	Many	Many	At least a few in each group
Manipulated by investigator	Nothing	Nothing	Questions	Nothing	Independent variable
Advantages	Suitable for studying rare conditions	Unintrusive, natural, source of new information	Determines characteristics of a population	Suitable for studying variables that are impossible or impractical to control	Useful for determining cause-and-effect relationships
Example	Intensive report of the childhood of someone who became a murderer	Report on changes in society's television-watching habits	Survey of how many hours per week most people watch violent TV programs	Correlation between hours of watching violent TV programs and some measure of violent behavior	Two groups randomly assigned; one group watches violent TV and the other watches nonviolent TV; compare probability of violent behavior by members of the two groups

Wang, & Jernigan, 1994). They may not even be able to learn to dress themselves. A psychologist who encounters someone with a rare condition such as this may report a **case history,** a thorough description of the unusual person. In general, a case history is a special kind of naturalistic observation; we distinguish it because it focuses on a single individual.

A case history may include information about the person's medical condition, family background, unusual experiences, current behavior, and details on tasks the person can and cannot perform—in short, anything the investigator thinks might have some bearing on the person's unusual condition. In Chap-

ter 7 you will find an example of a case history of a brain-damaged man who lost his ability to learn facts. Chapter 12 includes a case history of a man who suffered a loss of emotional experiences.

Note that a case history is more than just an anecdote. An anecdote is a report of a single experience, such as "I had a hunch and it came true," or "I think I saw Elvis at the pizza parlor." An anecdote is virtually worthless as evidence because no one can check whether the person misunderstood or misreported the experience. A case history is potentially replicable by anyone who gets a chance to study the same individual or a similar individual again.

replicable by anyone who studies individual.

Case history = anything that has some bearing on unusual condition

FIGURE 2.10
In a naturalistic study, observers record the behavior of people or other species in their natural settings. Here, noted biologist Jane Goodall records her observations on chimpanzees. By patiently staying with the chimpanzees, Goodall gradually won their trust and learned to recognize individual chimps. In this manner she was able to add enormously to our understanding of chimpanzees' natural way of life.

A case history is well suited to exploring an unusual behavioral condition. However, we do not know whether or not the described individual is typical of others with the same condition. Ideally, a series of case histories may reveal a pattern or stimulate investigators to conduct other kinds of research.

SURVEYS

A **survey** is a study of the prevalence of certain beliefs, attitudes, or behaviors based on people's responses to specific questions. A survey is one of the most common methods of investigating people's actions and beliefs, and not just in psychology. Throughout your life you will be reading or hearing about survey results—political surveys, advertising surveys, newspaper public opinion polls, and so forth.

Surveys are deceptively easy to conduct and surprisingly difficult to conduct well. You might imagine that you could simply draw up a list of questions, ask a number of people to answer them, and then report the results. Many people do precisely that, and then discover that they have meaningless results. Here we shall consider a few of the points to watch when conducting a survey. Someday you might conduct a survey yourself. (For example, if you manage a company, you might survey its employees or its customers.) Even if you do not conduct such research, you should be aware of its pitfalls so that you can decide how seriously to take the results of someone else's surveys.

Sampling If I conduct a survey (or any other kind of research) and I want my results to apply to, say, U.S. citizens in general, I should make sure that the people I survey are similar to the population as a whole. Sampling is a serious issue with any kind of research, and particularly with surveys. Consider what happens with a distorted sample: In 1936 the *Literary Digest* mailed 10 million postcards asking people their choice for president of the United States. Of the two million responses, 57% preferred the Republican candidate, Alfred Landon. As it turned out, Landon was soundly defeated by the Democratic candidate, Franklin Roosevelt. The reason for the misleading result was that the *Literary Digest* selected names from the telephone and automobile registration lists. In 1936, at the end of the Great Depression, only fairly well-off people had telephones or cars, and most of them were Republicans. The sample included very few poor people, who voted overwhelmingly Democratic.

The Competence of Those Being Interviewed Suppose a television news commentator reports that "85% of the people surveyed are opposed to increased government spending on kryptonite research." What does that mean? It means that increased spending on kryptonite research is currently an *unpopular* idea, but it does not necessarily mean that such spending would be a *bad* idea. The fact is, a great many people will express an opinion even when they have no idea what they are talking about. For example, one survey in 1994 found that 61% of people in the United States thought that "the information superhighway" was a good or excellent idea. To a follow-up question, however, of what exactly the information superhighway is, 66% admitted that until this moment they had never heard of it, and most of those who said they had heard of it before admitted they did not really know what it meant.

The Wording of the Questions If a survey includes unclear, ambiguous questions, its results will be unclear also. For example, some years ago, just after basketball star Magic Johnson revealed that he was infected with the HIV virus, one survey asked people, "Has the publicity concerning Magic Johnson made you more likely than before to practice safe sex?" To this question, a "yes" answer has a reasonably clear meaning (if we ignore the possibility that the person might

handwritten margin notes:
most common method of invest. peoples action & beliefs.
Pitfalls
Sampling
know what? mean
Ambigious questions
Bia's Questions

be lying). But what does a "no" answer mean? It might mean, "I continue to practice unsafe sex," or "I was already practicing safe sex, and I continue to do so, so I did not become 'more' likely to have safe sex." It might even mean, "I was previously having no sex and I expect to continue having no sex."

Another example: According to a 1993 survey, 92% of high-school boys and 98% of high-school girls said they had been victims of sexual harassment (Shogren, 1993). According to the sponsors of the survey, these results show that sexual harassment has reached "epidemic" proportions. Maybe so, but even if it hasn't, the wording of the survey *defined* sexual harassment into an epidemic. The survey specified that sexual harassment included any of a long list of events, which ranged from very serious offenses (such as having someone rip your clothes off) to a variety of minor annoyances. For example, if someone wrote some sexual graffiti on the rest room wall, and you read it and found it offensive, then you could consider yourself to be sexually harassed. If you tried to make yourself look sexually attractive (as most teenagers do, right?) and then attracted a sexual look from someone you *didn't* want to attract, that look could count as sexual harassment. Sexual harassment is indeed a serious problem, but a survey that lumps together the major offenses with the minor ones fails to tell us the information we need to know.

Surveyor Biases Ideally, a survey question is worded so as not to favor one answer or another. For example, "Which candidate do you plan to support?" or "Do you think that increased parking fees would be a good idea or a bad idea?" If the interviewees know that a certain organization is sponsoring the survey, that knowledge introduces a bias. Many people like to give the answer that they think the interviewer or the sponsoring organization wants to hear.

Someday you may be asked to respond to a mailed survey that explicitly tells you who is conducting and sponsoring the survey. Many such surveys include questions that are intentionally worded in a biased manner, such as "Do you agree that our President is trying to do the right thing in . . ." or "Don't you think it's terrible the way our political enemies are doing the following . . ." If you receive such a biased "survey," you can safely assume that the organization is not ac-

tually interested in recording your opinion. Such mailings are inevitably accompanied by a request for contributions, and they serve only as fund-raisers, not as surveys. (See Figure 2.11.)

CORRELATIONAL STUDIES

Another kind of study is the *correlational study*. A **correlation** is a measure of the relationship between two variables, both of which are outside the investigator's control. Thus, a correlational study is one in which the investigator examines the relationship between two variables, without actually controlling either one of them.

For example, investigators have observed that testosterone levels of male tennis players increase shortly after a successful match and decrease just after a disappointing performance (Booth, Shelley, Mazur, Tharp, & Kittok, 1989). This is a correlational study, because the investigators had no control over the athletes' performances or their testosterone levels. Another example: Students who attend class regularly generally achieve better test scores than do students who frequently miss class (Cavell & Woehr, 1994). Again, investigators exert no control over the attendance or test scores; they merely observe the relationship (or correlation) between them.

A survey can be considered a correlational study if the interviewers compare two or more groups. For example, the interviewers might compare the beliefs of men and women or of young people and old people. The interviewer could thereby measure a relationship between one variable (sex or age) and another variable (beliefs).

THE CORRELATION COEFFICIENT

Some correlations are strong; others are weak. For example, we probably would find a strong positive correlation between hours per week of reading novels and scores on a vocabulary test. We would observe a much lower correlation between hours of reading novels and scores on a chemistry test.

Often it is helpful to have a way of measuring the direction and strength of a correlation. The standard method is known as a **correlation coefficient**, a mathematical estimate of the relationship between two variables, which can range mathematically from $+1$ to -1. A correlation coefficient indicates how accurately we can use measurements of one variable to predict another. A correlation

Survey on Behalf of the Litterers' Society

1. Prior to reading the enclosed letter, were you aware of how little damage litter does to the environment, or how much money the government wastes in an effort to harass innocent citizens who happen to drop a little bit of litter now and then?

_____ yes
_____ no

2. Do you agree that moderate, responsible littering is one of the rights we should expect in a free society?

_____ yes
_____ no
_____ undecided

3. Are you in favor of having the government use your tax dollars to arrest and persecute people whose only "crime" is littering?

_____ yes
_____ no
_____ undecided

4. Do you see a need for an educational campaign to inform the public about the good that littering contributes to _natural_ recycling?

_____ yes
_____ no
_____ undecided

5. Are you outraged that short-sighted do-gooders would pass extremely restrictive, punitive laws against littering, merely to advance their own political careers?

_____ yes
_____ no
_____ undecided

6. Do you support the noble attempts of the Litterers' Society to fight against excessive and unnecessary regulations, and will you support the Society with your generous donation?

_____ Yes! Enclosed is my generous donation!

_____ Sorry, I can't afford a contribution at this time.

FIGURE 2.11

An example of how to bias a survey to get the answers one desires. This is an imaginary survey for an imaginary society, but the style of the questions is similar to those found in many "surveys" sponsored by real political and other organizations. The request for a donation is a reliable clue that the organization is not really seeking your opinion and probably will not even tabulate the results.

coefficient of +1, for example, means that as one variable increases, the other increases also. A correlation coefficient of −1 means that as one variable increases, the other decreases. A correlation of either +1 or −1 enables us to make perfect predictions of either variable whenever we know the other. In real life, psychologists seldom encounter a perfect +1 or −1 correlation coefficient. The closer the correlation coefficient is to +1 or to −1, the stronger the relationship between the two variables and the more accurately we can use one variable to predict the other. Figure 2.12 shows hypothetical (not real) data demonstrating how grades on a final exam in psychology might correlate with five other variables. (This kind of graph is called a scatter plot; each dot represents the measurements of two variables for one person.) Grades on a psychology final exam correlate very strongly with grades on the previous tests in psychology, less strongly with grades on the French final exam, not at all with the person's weight, and negatively with the amount of time spent watching television and the number of times absent from class.

Note that a correlation of +.9 is close to a straight line ascending; a correlation of −.9 is close to a straight line descending.

Here are three examples of the findings of correlational studies:

- The most crowded areas of a city are generally the most impoverished. (Positive correlation between population density and poverty.)
- People's telephone numbers have no relationship to their IQ scores. (Zero correlation between the two.)
- People who trust other people are unlikely to cheat other people. (Negative correlation between trusting and cheating.)

CONCEPT CHECK

6. _Which indicates a stronger relationship between two variables, a +.50 correlation or a −.75 correlation? (Check your answer on page 61.)_

full moon

Illusory Correlations It is difficult to identify a correlation between two variables solely on the basis of casual observation. For example, some years ago, one drug company marketed the drug Bendectin to relieve morning sickness in pregnant women. After a few women who took the drug had babies with birth defects, widespread publicity blamed the drug. From then on, practically every woman who took the drug and had a baby with a birth defect blamed the drug; many sued the company. In fact, only 2–3% of women taking the drug had babies with defects—the same as the percentage among women not taking the drug! When people expect to see a connection between two events (such as Bendectin and birth defects) they remember the cases that support the connection and disregard the exceptions, thus perceiving an **illusory correlation,** an apparent relationship based on casual observations of unrelated or weakly related events. Much of what people believe about differences between women and men, or between members of different ethnic groups, are examples of illusory correlations.

For another example of an illusory correlation, take the widely held belief that a full moon affects human behavior. For hundreds of years, many people have believed that crime and various kinds of mental disturbance are more common under a full moon than at other times. In fact, the term _lunacy_

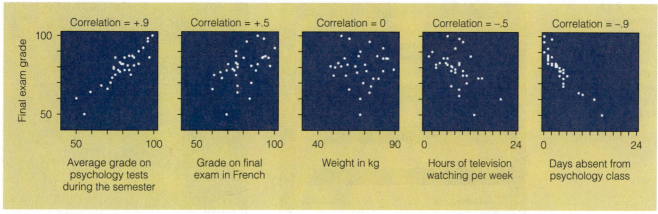

FIGURE 2.12

In a scatter plot, each dot represents data for one person; for example, in the center graph each point tells us the weight of one person and that person's grade on the psychology final exam, in this case using hypothetical data. A positive correlation indicates that as one variable increases, the other generally does also. A negative correlation indicates that as one variable increases, the other generally decreases. The closer a correlation coefficient is to +1 or −1, the stronger the relationship.

(from the Latin word *luna,* meaning "moon") originally meant mental illness caused by the full moon. Some police officers report that they receive more calls on nights of a full moon, and hospital workers report that more emergency cases turn up on such nights. However, those reports are based on what people can recall rather than on carefully analyzed data. James Rotton and I. W. Kelly (1985) examined all available data relating crime, mental illness, and other phenomena to phases of the moon. They concluded that the phase of the moon has either no effect at all on human behavior or so little effect that it is almost impossible to measure.

Why then does the belief persist? We do not know when or how it first arose. (It may have been true many years ago, before the widespread use of artificial lights.) But we can guess why it persists. Suppose, for example, you are working at a hospital and you expect to handle more emergencies on full-moon nights than at other times. Sooner or later, on a full-moon night, you encounter an unusually high number of accidents, assaults, and suicide attempts. You say, "See? There was a full moon and people just went crazy!" You will remember that night for a long time. You disregard all the other full-moon nights when nothing special happened and all the non-full-moon nights when you were swamped with emergency cases.

CORRELATION AND CAUSATION

A correlational study tells us whether two variables are related to each other and, if so, how strongly. It does not tell us *why* they are related. For example, consider the negative correlation between trusting and cheating. That correlation might mean that people who develop a trusting attitude learn not to cheat, or that people who do not cheat develop a trusting attitude, or perhaps that people who grow up in a warm, loving family develop a trusting attitude and (independently) learn not to cheat. *No matter how high the correlation coefficient between two variables A and B, even if it is +1, it does not let us draw a conclusion about which variable controlled the other one.*

Here are some other examples of why we cannot draw cause-and-effect conclusions from correlational data (see also Figure 2.13):

• *Unmarried men are more likely than married men are to wind up in a mental hospital or prison.* So we can say that, for men, marriage is negatively correlated with mental illness and criminal activity. Does the correlation mean that marriage leads to mental health and good social adjustment? Or does it mean that men who are confined to mental hospitals or prisons are unlikely to marry? (Both explanations could, of course, be valid.)

• *People who follow regular exercise habits tend to have high self-esteem and tend not to feel depressed.* This correlation could indicate that exercise helps to raise self-esteem and to decrease the chance of depression. It could also mean that nondepressed people with high self-esteem are more likely than other people are to get some exercise. (Very depressed people seldom do

The common belief that a full moon elicits criminal or mentally ill behavior (if not necessarily werewolfism) is an example of an illusory correlation—a weak or imaginary relationship that is supported only by our tendency to remember the instances that seem to agree with a hypothesis and to forget the instances that contradict it.

FIGURE 2.13

*A strong correlation
between variables A
and B does not tell
us whether A causes
B, B causes A, or
some other variable
C causes both A
and B.*

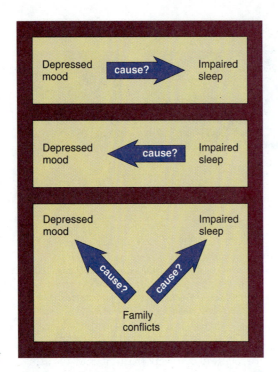

*Doesn't tell us about
causation.*

*experiment - measure
the effect of changes
in one variable on
measurements of
another variable*

*Dependent - what
measures (result)
Independent - change
or control
(influence)*

much of anything.) The correlation could also reflect the fact that being young, healthy, and employed increases the chance that a person will find time to exercise, and that it also (independently) helps to improve self-esteem and guard against depression.

To repeat: A correlation does not tell us about causation. To determine causation, an investigator needs to manipulate one of the variables directly, through a research design known as an *experiment*. When an investigator manipulates one variable and then observes changes in another variable, the causation is clear.

EXPERIMENTAL STUDIES

An **experiment** is a study in which the investigator manipulates at least one variable while measuring at least one other variable. The logic behind the simplest possible experiment is as follows: The investigator assembles a suitable sample of people (or animals), divides them randomly into two groups, and then administers some experimental procedure to one group and not to the other. Someone, preferably a blind observer, records the behavior of the two groups. If the behavior of the two groups differs in some consistent way, then the difference is presumably the result of the experimental procedure.

I shall describe psychological experiments and some of their special difficulties.

For the sake of illustration, let's use the example of experiments to determine whether watching violent television programs leads to an increase in aggressive behavior.

Independent Variables and Dependent Variables   An experiment is an attempt to measure the effect of changes in one variable on measurements of some other variable. A *variable* is anything that can have more than one value, such as age, experience, or performance of a given task. The **independent variable** is the variable that the experimenter changes or controls; for example, the amount of violent television that the subjects are permitted to watch. The **dependent variable** is the variable that the experimenter *measures* to see how it was affected. In our example, the experimenter measures the amount of aggressive behavior the subjects exhibit. You might think of the independent variable as the influence and the dependent variable as the result. (See Figure 2.14)

7. *An instructor wants to find out whether the frequency of tests in introductory psychology has any effect on students' final exam performance. The instructor gives weekly tests in one class, just three tests in a second class, and only a single midterm*

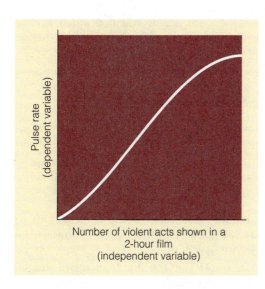

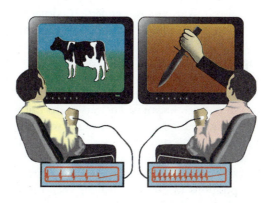

FIGURE 2.14
An experimenter manipulates the independent variable (in this case, the films people watch) so that two or more groups experience different treatments. Then the experimenter measures the dependent variable (in this case, pulse rate) to see how the independent variable affected it. Ordinarily, we plot the independent variable along the x-axis and the dependent variable along the y-axis.

[handwritten margin notes: experiment group – receives treatment. control group – treated same way except for treatment.]

exam in the third class. All three classes take the same final exam, and the instructor compares their performances. Identify the independent variable and the dependent variable. (Check your answers on page 61.)

Experimental Group and Control Group

Here is more terminology you need to understand: The **experimental group** receives the treatment that the experiment is designed to test. In our example, the experimental group would watch televised violence for a specific length of time. The **control group** is treated in the same way as the experimental group except for the treatment the experiment is designed to test. In other words, the control group spends the same amount of time watching television but watches only nonviolent programs (Figure 2.15).

In principle, that procedure sounds easy. In practice, a difficulty arises: We are conducting a study on a group of teenagers who have a history of violent behavior. The experimental group watches a film with lots of action and violence. Exactly what do we ask the control group to watch? Can we find a program without violence that is just as exciting to watch? (It's not easy.)

Random Assignment The preferred way of assigning subjects to groups is **random assignment**: The experimenter uses some chance procedure such as drawing names out of a hat to make sure that every subject has the same probability as any other subject of being assigned to a given group. Imagine what could happen if the experimenter did not assign people at random. Suppose we let the subjects choose whether they want to be

in the experimental group or the control group. The people most prone to aggressive behavior might generally choose to be in the experimental group (the one that watches violent programs). Or suppose we ask people to volunteer for the study, and the first 20 people who volunteer become the experimental group and the next 20 become the control group. Again, we will have trouble analyzing the results, because the people

Pool of subjects	Condition	Independent variable	Dependent variable
Random assignment to groups	Experimental	3 hours per day watching *violent* TV programs	Violent behavior recorded by blind observer
	Control	3 hours per day watching *nonviolent* TV programs	Violent behavior recorded by blind observer

FIGURE 2.15
Once researchers decide on the hypothesis they want to test, they must design the experiment, such as these procedures for testing the effects of watching televised violence. An appropriate, accurate method of measurement is essential.

who are quickest to volunteer may be impulsive in other regards also.

Consider an animal example: We set up a rack of cages and put each rat in a cage by itself. The rack has five rows of six cages each, numbered from 1 in the upper-left corner to 30 in the lower right. Regardless of the procedures we use, we find that the rats with higher cage numbers are more aggressive than those with lower cage numbers. Why?

We might first guess that the difference has to do with location. The rats in the cages with high numbers are farthest from the lights and closest to the floor. They get fed last each day. To test the influence of these factors, we move some of the cages to different positions in the rack, leaving each rat in its own cage. To our surprise, the rats in cages 26–30 are still more aggressive than those in cages 1–5. Why? (How could they possibly know what number is on each cage, and even if they did know, why should they care?)

The answer has to do with how rats get assigned to cages. When an investigator buys a shipment of rats, which one goes into cage 1? The one that is easiest to catch! Which ones go into the last few cages? The vicious, ornery little critters that put up the greatest resistance to being picked up! The rats in the last few cages were already the most aggressive ones before they were put into those cages.

The point is that even with rats, an experimenter must assign individuals to the experimental group and the control group at random. It would not be right to assign the first 15 rats to one group and the second 15 to another group. The same is true, only more so, with humans.

WHAT'S THE EVIDENCE?

Studies of the Effects of Televised Violence on Aggressive Behavior

We have talked in general terms about experiments on the effects of televised violence. Now let us consider some actual examples.

Part of the evidence regarding the effects of televised violence comes from correlational studies. Several such studies have found that people who watch a great deal of televised violence are more likely to engage in aggressive behavior than are people who do not (National Institute of Mental Health, 1982). Those results are suggestive but inconclusive.

They do not tell us whether watching violence leads to aggressive behavior or whether people prone to aggressive behavior like to watch violence on television. To examine a possible cause-and-effect relationship, we must turn to experiments.

Hypothesis Children who watch violent television programs will engage in more acts of aggression than will children who spend the same amount of time watching nonviolent programs.

Method One set of experimenters chose to study male juvenile delinquents in an institution (Parke, Berkowitz, Leyens, West, & Sebastian, 1977). The disadvantage of this selection was that the conclusions of the study might apply only to a limited group. The advantage was that the experimenters could control the choice of television programs (the independent variable) in a detention center much better than they could for youngsters living at home.

The boys were assigned randomly to two cottages. Those in one cottage watched violent films on five consecutive nights, while those in the other cottage watched nonviolent films. Throughout this period, blind observers recorded incidents of aggressive behavior by each boy. On the sixth day, each boy was put into an experimental setting in which he had an opportunity at certain times to press a button that, he thought, would deliver an electric shock to another boy. (In fact, no shocks were given.) The experimenters recorded the frequency and intensity of shocks that each boy chose to deliver (the dependent variable).

Results Compared to the boys who had watched nonviolent films, those who had watched the violent films engaged in more acts of aggression and pressed the button to deliver more frequent and more intense electric shocks.

Interpretation At least in this study, watching violent films led to increased violence. As with most studies, however, this one has its limitations. The boys in the experiment were not representative of boys in general, much less of people in general. Moreover, we cannot assume that we would get similar results with a different choice of violent films or a different method of measuring aggressive behavior.

The only way to get around the limitation of a given experiment is to conduct additional experiments, using different samples of people, different films, and different measures of aggressive behavior. A number of such experiments have been conducted. Although the results vary considerably from one study to another, most psychologists have concluded that watching televised violence does indeed increase aggressive behavior, at least temporarily (Comstock & Strasburger, 1990). However, we have little information about the cumulative effects of years of watching violence on television.

HOW EXPERIMENTS SOMETIMES GO WRONG

Research on behavior poses some thorny problems because it deals with living beings. Sometimes people act strange just because they know they are in an experiment. Sometimes in the middle of a long-term experiment some of the people move out of town or simply announce that they do not want to participate any more. When psychologists cannot avoid such problems, they must at least recognize them and point out the limitations of the research results. Here we consider three examples of the problems that arise in research on human behavior.

DEMAND CHARACTERISTICS

The subjects who take part in a psychological experiment often try to guess what the experimenter wants them to do and say. They believe that "good" results will help the experimenter succeed and will contribute to the advancement of knowledge. As a result, some experiments reveal more about the participants' expectations than about the phenomenon the experimenter is trying to study. Martin Orne (1969) defined **demand characteristics** as cues that tell a subject what is expected of him or her and what the experimenter hopes to find. Experimenters try to minimize the influence of demand characteristics.

One example of the effects of demand characteristics surfaced in an experiment on **sensory deprivation.** In experiments of this sort, subjects are placed in an apparatus that minimizes vision, hearing, touch, and other forms of sensory stimulation. After several hours, many subjects reported hallucinations, anxiety, and difficulty in concentrat-

ing; they exhibited impaired intellectual performance. M. T. Orne and K. E. Scheibe (1964) conducted an experiment to determine whether such effects might be related to the subjects' expectations.

College students participated in the experiment, which was described to them as a study on "meaning deprivation." The experimenter interrogated the students in the experimental group about their medical history and asked them to sign a form that released the hospital in which the experiment took place from legal responsibility for the experiment's consequences. A prominently displayed "emergency tray" contained medicines and various instruments kept on hand "as a precaution." One subject per day entered an "isolation chamber," which was actually an ordinary room that contained two chairs, a desk, a window, a mirror, a sandwich, and a glass of water. The subjects never would have guessed that the room had anything to do with sensory deprivation had they not been told so. Finally, the subjects were shown a microphone they could use to report any hallucinations or other distorted experiences and a "panic button" they could press to escape if the discomfort became unbearable. Students in the control group were led to the same room, but they were not shown the "emergency tray," they were not asked to sign a release form, and they were given no other indication that they were expected to have any unpleasant experiences.

Each subject was left alone in the room for 4 hours. Ordinarily, 4 hours by oneself is not a particularly disturbing experience. But everything the experimenter had said to the experimental group suggested that the experience would be dreadful, and the subjects acted as if it were. One pressed the panic button to demand release. Several others reported that they were hallucinating "multicolored spots on the wall," or that "the walls of the room are starting to waver," or that "the objects on the desk are becoming animated and moving about" (Figure 2.16). Some complained of anxiety, restlessness, difficulty in concentrating, and spatial disorientation. At the end of the 4 hours, most of them showed impaired performance on a series of perceptual and intellectual tasks. The subjects in the control group reported no unusual experiences.

Sensory deprivation may very well have significant effects on behavior. But as this ex-

FIGURE 2.16
*Subjects tend to
report what they
think the experi-
menter wants to hear.
The cues that tell
them what the exper-
imenter hopes to find
are called demand
characteristics.*

peri ment illustrates, we must carefully distinguish between the effects of the independent
variable and the effects of what the subjects
expect of the experiment.

In a sense, demand characteristics set up
self-fulfilling prophecies. In designing the experiment, the experimenter has a certain expectation in mind and then conducts the experiment in a way that may inadvertently
convey that expectation to the subjects,
thereby influencing them to behave as expected. To eliminate demand characteristics,
many experimenters take elaborate steps to
conceal the purpose of the experiment from
the subjects. A double-blind study serves the
purpose: If two groups share the same expectations but behave differently because of the
treatment they receive, then the difference in
behavior is presumably not the result of their
expectations.

EXPERIMENTER BIAS

Experimenters are human beings, not perfectly objective observers. When they record
their data, sometimes they have trouble separating what they really see from what they
had expected to see. Here is a class demonstration to illustrate the point: Students in
one psychology class were told that they
would watch a person engage in a difficult
hand-eye coordination task before and after
drinking alcohol. That person in fact was
drinking only apple juice and performed
equally well before and after drinking. Nevertheless, most of the students observing the
performance described it as sharply deteriorating (Goldstein, Hopkins, & Strube,
1994). They "saw" what they had expected
to see.

Experimenter bias is the tendency of an
experimenter to distort the procedures or results of an experiment, based on the expected outcome of the study. The experimenter does not intend the distortion and
may not even be aware of it. The best way to
guard against such distortions is to use blind
observers, as described earlier (page 45).

SELECTIVE ATTRITION

At Santa Enigma State College, only 50% of
all freshmen have decided on a career,
whereas 90% of all seniors have decided. An
observer concludes that between the freshman year and the senior year, most of the undecided students come to a decision. Sounds
reasonable, right? But wait.

Suppose a creature from outer space is
observing humans for the first time. He/she/it
discovers that about 50% of all human children are males but that only 10–20% of 90-
year-olds are males. The creature concludes
that as human males grow older, most of
them change into females.

You see why that conclusion is wrong.
Males—with a few exceptions—do not
change into females. But they do die earlier,
leaving a greater proportion of older females. So can we really say that a large percentage of undecided freshmen make career
decisions by the time they become seniors?
Not necessarily. Perhaps undecided freshmen
simply drop out of college before reaching
their senior year.

This example represents the problem of
selective attrition, also known as *differential
survival,* which is the tendency for some
kinds of people to be more likely than others
to drop out of a study. If some subjects drop
out of a study (by dying, quitting, or moving
away), then those who remain may be different from those who left. To avoid this problem, psychologists simply report the before-
and-after data only for people who complete
a study; they discard the data for those who
leave.

CONCEPT CHECK

*8. Decide which of the following examples
represent demand characteristics, experimenter bias, or selective attrition:*

*a. Most of the first-year teachers in the
Dismalville public school system complain about the school's policies. Teachers who have been at the school for 15*

When psychologists wish to draw a conclusion that applies to human behavior in general, they need to test a variety of groups to determine in what ways the behaviors differ from one population to another.

Can't generalize in psychology

years or more rarely complain and seem quite satisfied.

b. A political survey reports one set of results when people are told, "This survey is sponsored by the Democratic party," and a different set of results when they are told, "This survey is sponsored by the Republican party."

c. A study of intelligence in one group of older people reports low performance among 70-year-olds, but (surprisingly) improved mean performance for those members of this group who reach age 80.

d. A group of researchers who believe that rats in Group A are especially fast learners spend more time petting and handling the Group A rats. Later they find that the Group A rats learned faster than the Group B rats, even though at the start, rats had been assigned randomly to the two groups. (Check your answers on page 61.)

GENERALIZABILITY OF RESULTS

When chemists find out how two chemicals react in a test tube, they can feel confident that those chemicals will react pretty much the same way anywhere, given similar levels of temperature, pressure, and so forth. Psychologists are not always so certain that they can generalize their results from one set of

people to another or from one set of circumstances to another.

Generalizing the results is especially uncertain if the investigator used a very select or limited sample of people. Imagine that I advertise a study on the effects of marijuana on behavior; what kind of people are most likely to volunteer to participate? Probably not a random sample of the population. What if I advertised a study on hypnosis? I would expect to get mostly volunteers who are curious to experience hypnotism, people who might turn out to be easily hypnotized.

These limitations are not a cause for despair, but only for caution. After studies on a limited sample of people, such as students taking an introductory psychology course at a particular college, a researcher should state conclusions cautiously and tentatively. If the researcher wishes to draw conclusions about humans in general, and not just about a limited population, the researcher will need to compare the results from people of different ages, both sexes, different cultures, different amounts of education, and so forth.

ETHICAL CONSIDERATIONS IN EXPERIMENTATION

In any experiment, psychologists manipulate some variable to see how it affects behavior. Perhaps the idea that someone might try to alter your behavior sounds objectionable. If so, bear in mind that every time you talk to other people, you are trying to alter their be-

According to the results of several experiments, cancer patients who participate in group-therapy sessions with other cancer patients have an improved chance for long-term survival. Generally, research is considered ethical if researchers expect the treatment to produce benefits, as it did here. Research to demonstrate the disadvantages of some procedure is generally prohibited as unethical. Sometimes a new ethical issue arises: If we seriously expect some treatment (such as group therapy for cancer patients) to produce significant benefits, is it ethical to assign anyone to the control group that does not receive the treatment?

havior at least in a slight way. Most experiments in psychology produce effects that are no more disruptive than are the effects of a conversation.

Still, some experiments do raise ethical issues. Psychologists are seriously concerned about ethical issues, both in the experiments they conduct with humans and in those they conduct with animals.

ETHICAL CONCERNS IN EXPERIMENTS ON HUMANS

Earlier in this chapter I discussed experiments on the effects of televised violence. If psychologists believed that watching violent programs on television would really transform viewers into murderers, then it would be unethical for them to conduct any experiment to find out for sure. Moreover, it would be unethical to perform any experimental procedure likely to cause people any significant pain or embarrassment or to exert any long-lasting, undesirable effects on their lives.

The main ethical principle is that experiments should include only procedures that people would agree to experience. No one should leave a study muttering, "If I had known what was going to happen, I never would have agreed to participate." To maintain high ethical standards in the conduct of experiments, psychologists ask prospective participants to give their **informed consent** before proceeding. When experimenters post a sign-up sheet asking for volunteers, or at the start of the experiment itself, they explain what will happen—the participants will receive electrical shocks, or they will be

required to drink concentrated sugar water, or whatever. Any prospective participant who objects to the procedure can simply withdraw.

In addition, experiments conducted at any college or at any other reputable institution must first be approved by a Human Subjects Committee at that institution. Such a committee judges whether or not the proposed experiments are ethical. For example, a committee would not approve an experiment that called for administering large doses of cocaine—even if some of the subjects were eager to give their informed consent. The committee also judges experiments in which the experimenters want to conceal certain procedures from the subjects. For example, suppose the experimenters plan to put subjects through a certain experience and then see whether they are more or less likely than others to obey instructions to pick up a live snake. The experimenters might not want to mention the possible snake handling in their informed-consent instructions. (The whole point of the experiment might depend on an element of surprise.) The Human Subjects Committee would then decide whether or not to permit such an experiment.

Finally, the American Psychological Association, or APA (1982), publishes a booklet detailing the ethical treatment of volunteers in experiments. Any member who disregards the principles may be censured or expelled from membership in the APA.

ETHICAL CONCERNS IN EXPERIMENTS ON ANIMALS

Some types of research require human subjects—for example, research on the effects of televised violence. Animals can be used for research on biological processes, such as mechanisms of sensation, the effects of drugs on behavior, or the effects of brain damage (Figure 2.17). About 7–8% of all published studies in psychology use animals (Gallup & Suarez, 1980). Animal research would be inappropriate for addressing certain issues—such as the effects of televised violence on behavior—but it is extremely helpful for other purposes. Animal research is responsible for much of what we know about the brain, about how drugs affect behavior, and about sensory systems. Research to find treatments for schizophrenia, Huntington's disease, Parkinson's disease, brain damage, and many other conditions begins with animal studies.

Some people nevertheless oppose animal research. Animals, after all, are in no position to give informed consent. Animal rights supporters vary in their views. Some are willing to tolerate experiments that inflict no pain and experiments likely to help solve major human problems. Others believe animals should have all the same rights as humans (Regan, 1986). According to this view, keeping animals (even pets) in cages is slavery and killing an animal is murder. Those who accept this view oppose all animal experiments, even if they appear to be highly useful and even if they cause the animals no apparent discomfort.

Most scientists who conduct animal research strongly support animal *welfare,* including improvements in laboratory care, but they deny that animals have the same *rights* as people (D. Johnson, 1990). They make the following arguments in defense of animal research:

- We certainly agree that animals should not be mistreated, but we also recognize "the right of the incurably ill to hope for cures or relief from suffering through research using animals" (Feeney, 1987). If animal experiments were abolished, certain areas of research, such as how to promote recovery from brain damage, would be almost impossible to pursue.

- Research on animals has produced a wealth of valuable information leading to the development of antianxiety drugs, new methods of treating pain and depression, an understanding of how certain drugs impair the development of the fetus, insight into the effects of old age on memory, and methods of helping people to overcome neuromuscular disorders (N. E. Miller, 1985).

- Extremely painful experiments on animals are rare (Coile & Miller, 1984). Although they undeniably occur, their frequency has been greatly exaggerated.

- Although studies of plants, experiments with tissue cultures, and computer simulations provide useful information on a few issues, they cannot provide much information about animal or human behavior or about brain mechanisms (Gallup & Suarez, 1985).

The debate continues. Meanwhile, professional organizations such as the Neuroscience Society publish guidelines for the proper use of animals in research. Colleges and other research institutions maintain

FIGURE 2.17
A mirror mounted on a young owl's head enables investigators to track the owl's head movements and thereby to discover how it localizes sounds with one ear plugged. The findings may help researchers understand how young children's brains compensate for hearing loss. An experiment such as this subjects the animal to only minor inconvenience. Some experiments, however, inflict pain or discomfort and are more likely to raise ethical objections.

Laboratory Animal Care Committees to ensure that laboratory animals are treated humanely, that their pain and discomfort are kept to a minimum, and that experimenters consider alternatives before they impose potentially painful procedures on animals. Because such committees have to deal with competing values, their decisions are never beyond dispute. How can anyone determine whether the value of the experimental results (which are hard to predict) will outweigh the pain the animals endure (which is hard to measure)? As is often the case with ethical decisions, reasonable arguments can be raised on both sides of the question, and no compromise is fully satisfactory.

SUMMARY

- *Operational definitions.* Psychologists must begin any study by defining their terms. For many purposes they prefer operational definitions, which state how to measure a phenomenon or how to produce it. (page 44)

- *Sampling.* Because psychologists hope to draw conclusions that apply to a large population and not just to the small sample they have studied, they try to select a sample that resembles the total population. They may select either a representative sample or a random sample. (page 44)

- *Blind observers.* To ensure objectivity, investigators use blind observers—observers who do not know how each individual has been treated or what results are expected. In a double-blind study, neither the observer nor the subjects know who has received which treatment. (page 45)

• *Naturalistic observations.* Naturalistic observations provide descriptions of people or other species under natural conditions. (page 46)

• *Case histories.* A case history is a detailed research study of a single individual, generally someone with unusual characteristics. (page 47)

• *Surveys.* A survey is a report of people's answers to a questionnaire. To be valid, a survey should deal with a representative or random sample of the population and should use clear, unambiguous, unbiased questions. We should not assume that everyone who answers a question has a solid basis for an opinion. (page 48)

• *Correlations.* A correlational study is a study of the relationship between variables that are outside the investigator's control. The strength of the relationship is measured by a correlation coefficient, which ranges from 0 (no relationship) to + or − 1 (a perfect relationship). (page 49)

• *Illusory correlations.* Beware of illusory correlations—relationships that people think they observe between variables after casual observation. (page 50)

• *Inferring causation.* A correlational study does not uncover cause-and-effect relationships, but an experiment can. (page 51)

• *Experiments.* Experiments are studies in which the investigator manipulates one variable to determine its effect on another variable. The manipulated variable is the independent variable. Changes in the independent variable may lead to changes in the dependent variable, which is the one the experimenter measures. (page 52)

• *Random assignment.* An experimenter should assign individuals to form the experimental and control groups. That is, all individuals should have an equal probability of being chosen for the experimental group. (page 53)

• *How experiments can go wrong.* Demand characteristics, experimenter bias, and selective attrition sometimes distort the results of an experiment. (page 55)

• *Generalizing conclusions.* If a study is conducted with just one population under one set of circumstances, we should be cautious about generalizing the conclusions to much different populations or different circumstances. (page 57)

• *Ethics of experimentation.* Experimentation on either humans or animals raises ethical questions. Psychologists try to minimize risk to their subjects, but they cannot avoid making difficult ethical decisions. (page 57)

SUGGESTION FOR FURTHER READING

Stanovich, K. E. (1986). *How to think straight about psychology.* Glenview, IL: Scott, Foresman. An excellent treatment of how to evaluate evidence in psychology and how to avoid pitfalls.

TERMS

operational definition a definition that specifies the operations (or procedures) used to measure something, a way to give it a numerical value (page 44)

representative sample a selection of the population chosen to match the entire population with regard to specific variables (page 44)

random sample a group of people picked in such a way that every individual in the population has an equal chance of being selected (page 45)

cross-cultural studies observations on the behavior of people in different cultures (page 45)

blind observer an observer who does not know which subjects are in which group and what is expected of each (page 46)

placebo an inactive pill that has no known pharmacological effect on the subjects in an experiment (page 46)

single-blind study a study in which either the observer or the subjects are unaware of which subjects received which treatment (page 46)

double-blind study a study in which neither the observer nor the subjects know which subjects received which treatment (page 46)

naturalistic observation a careful examination of what many people or nonhuman animals do under natural conditions (page 46)

case history a thorough description of a single individual, including information on both past experiences and current behavior (page 47)

survey a study of the prevalence of certain beliefs, attitudes, or behaviors based on people's responses to specific questions (page 48)

correlation a measure of the relationship between two variables, both of which are outside the investigator's control (page 49)

correlation coefficient a mathematical estimate of the relationship between two variables, ranging from +1 (perfect positive relationship) to 0 (no linear relationship) to −1 (perfect negative relationship) (page 49)

illusory correlation an apparent relationship based on casual observation of unrelated or poorly related events (page 50)

experiment a study in which the investigator manipulates at least one variable while measuring at least one other variable (page 52)

independent variable the variable the experimenter manipulates to see how it affects the dependent variable (page 52)

dependent variable the variable the experimenter measures to see how changes in the independent variable affect it (page 52)

experimental group the group that receives the treatment that an experiment is designed to test (page 53)

control group the group that is treated in the same way as the experimental group except for the treatment the experiment is designed to test (page 53)

random assignment a chance procedure for assigning subjects to groups such that every subject has the same probability as any other of being assigned to a particular group (page 53)

demand characteristics cues that tell a subject what is expected of him or her and what the experimenter hopes to find (page 55)

sensory deprivation temporary reduction of vision, hearing, touch, and other forms of sensory stimulation (page 55)

experimenter bias the tendency of an experimenter to make unintentional distortions in procedures or results, based on the experimenter's expectations of the outcome of the study (page 56)

selective attrition the tendency for some kinds of people to be more likely than others to drop out of a study (page 56)

informed consent a subject's agreement to take part in an experiment after being informed about what will happen (page 58)

ANSWERS TO CONCEPT CHECKS

3. The score on an IQ test is an operational definition of intelligence. (Whether it is a particularly good definition is another question.)
None of the other definitions tells us how to measure or produce intelligence. (page 44)

4. Many operational definitions are possible for "friendliness." One would be "the number of other people that someone speaks to within 24 hours. Perhaps (likely) you can think of a better definition. Remember, it is an operational definition if it specifies a clear method of measurement. (page 44)

5. Clearly not. It is unlikely that the men at a given college are typical of men in general or that the women are typical of women in general. Moreover, a given college may have attracted mostly men who are interested in one major and mostly women who are interested in another. In that case, the men and women are almost certain to differ in ways that have no direct relationship to being male or female. (page 45)

6. The −.75 correlation indicates a stronger relationship—that is, a greater accuracy of predicting one variable based on measurements of the other. A negative correlation is just as useful as a positive one. (page 50)

7. The independent variable is the frequency of tests during the semester. The dependent variable is the students' performance on the final exam. (page 52)

8. **a.** Selective attrition. The least satisfied teachers do not spend 15 years at the school. (page 56)

b. Demand characteristics. Telling people who sponsored the survey suggests they give answers favoring that sponsor.

c. Selective attrition. Perhaps the more intelligent people were more likely to survive to age 80. (page 56)

d. Experimenter bias. Note that the experimenters may not even have been aware of the extra attention they gave the favored rats. (page 56)

MEASURING AND ANALYZING RESULTS

How can one describe the "average" results in a study?

How can one describe the variation among individuals?

How can a researcher determine whether the results reflect some consistent trend, or whether they are likely to have arisen just by chance?

Some time ago, a television program about the alleged dangers of playing the game Dungeons and Dragons reported 28 known cases of D&D players who had committed suicide. Alarming, right?

Not necessarily. At least 3 million young people at the time were playing the game regularly. The reported suicide rate among D&D players—28 per 3 million—was considerably *less* than the suicide rate among teenagers in general.

So do the results mean that playing D&D *prevents* suicide? Hardly. The 28 reported cases probably are not a complete count of all suicides by D&D players. Besides, the correlation between playing D&D and committing suicide, regardless of its direction and magnitude, could not possibly tell us about cause and effect.

Then what conclusion should we draw from these data? *None at all.* Sometimes, as in this case, the data are meaningless because of how they were collected. Even when the data are potentially meaningful, people sometimes present them in a confusing or misleading manner (Figure 2.18). Let's consider some of the proper ways of analyzing and interpreting results.

■ DESCRIPTIVE STATISTICS

To explain the meaning of a study, an investigator must summarize the results in some orderly fashion. When a researcher observes the behavior of 100 people, we have no interest in hearing all the details about every person observed. We want to know what the researcher found in general, on the average. We might also want to know whether most people were similar to the average or whether they varied a great deal. An investigator presents the answers to those questions through **descriptive statistics**, which are mathematical summaries of results, such as measures of the central score and the amount of variation. The correlation coefficient, dis-

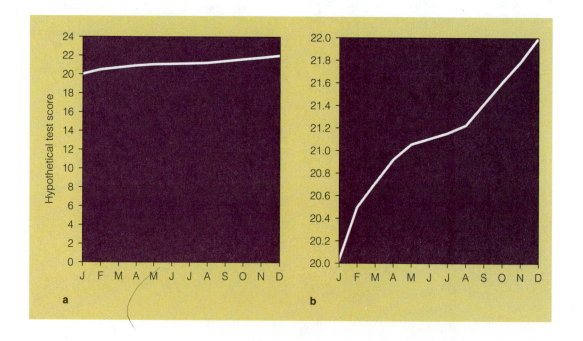

FIGURE 2.18
How statistics can mislead: Both of these graphs present the same data, an increase from 20 to 22 over a year's time. But by ranging only from 20 to 22 (rather than from 0 to 22), graph B makes that increase look much more dramatic. (After Huff, 1954.)

cussed earlier in this chapter, is one kind of descriptive statistic.

MEASUREMENTS OF THE CENTRAL SCORE: MEAN, MEDIAN, AND MODE

There are three ways of representing the central score: mean, median, and mode. The **mean** is the sum of all the scores divided by the number of scores. (Generally, when people say "average," they refer to the mean.) For example, the mean of 2, 10, and 3 is 5 ($\frac{15}{3}$). The mean is a useful term if the scores approximate the **normal distribution** (or normal curve)—a symmetrical frequency of scores clustered around the mean. A normal distribution is sometimes described as a bell-shaped curve. For example, if we measure how long 30 students take to memorize a poem, their times will probably follow a pattern similar to the normal distribution.

In some circumstances, however, the mean can be misleading. Suppose, for example, we want to find out whether some article published in 1995 relied on up-to-date information. We check the dates of the references cited in the article and find the distribution shown in Figure 2.19. Here the scores follow an approximately normal distribution and the mean of 1991 adequately represents the results. However, suppose the author had added three quotes—one from Shakespeare (published in 1610), one from Aristotle (324 B.C.), and one from *Genesis* (4000 B.C.?). The addition of those three references lowers the mean date from 1991 to 1838. The mean is frequently misleading when the distribution is far from normal, as it becomes after adding three items that are very different from the others.

The addition of the three old references has much less effect on the median, however. To determine the **median,** we arrange all the scores in order from the highest score to the lowest score. The middle score is the median. For example, if the scores are 2, 10, and 3, the median is 3. In Figure 2.19 the median date of references is 1991; after adding three very old references, the median is still 1991. If the author added another eight old references, the median would fall to 1990. In short, a few extreme scores have less effect on the median than they do on the mean.

The third way to represent the central score is the **mode,** the score that occurs most frequently. For example, in the distribution of scores 2, 2, 3, 4, and 10, the mode is 2. The mode is not particularly useful for most

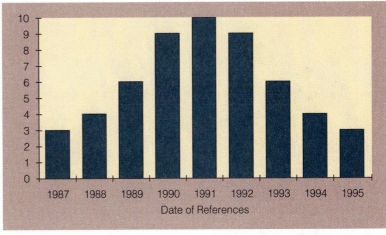

FIGURE 2.19
A distribution of references for a hypothetical publication. Note that the distribution is symmetrical and similar to the normal curve. In this case, the mean, median, and mode are all the same: 1991.

purposes. Here is a case, however, in which we might want to use the mode: The bar graphs in Figure 2.20 illustrate how many times people attend religious services per month in two hypothetical communities. Here the mean and the median are useless for comparison purposes, because for both populations the mean happens to be 2.4 and the median is 2. It might be more interesting to note that the mode (the most common response) is zero times per month in one population and four times per month in the other.

To recap: Roughly speaking, the mean is what most people refer to when they say "average." The median is the middle score;

Occasionally the mode is a useful way of describing results. For example, in a given community, the mode for religious attendance might be once a week or once a month.

mean = average
median = middle
mode = most frequent

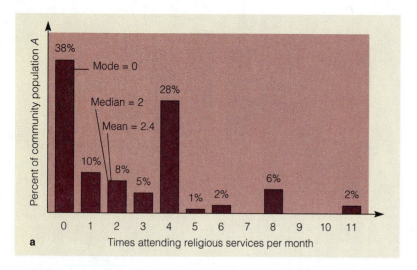

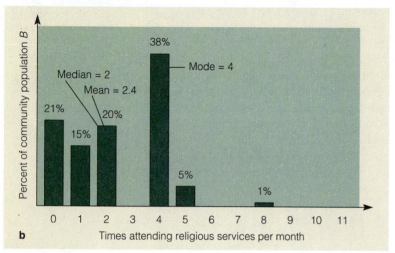

FIGURE 2.20
These two charts, which lack normal distributions, have the same median and mean. Here the difference in modes can be informative. In (a) the mode is 0; in (b) the mode is 4. (In both cases, 38% of people are on the mode, but 38 is not the mode.)

the mode is the most common score (Figure 2.21).

CONCEPT CHECK

9. *a. For the following distribution of scores, determine the mean, the median, and the mode: 5, 2, 2, 2, 8, 3, 1, 6, 7.*
b. Determine the mean, median, and mode for this distribution: 5, 2, 2, 2, 35, 3, 1, 6, 7. (Check your answers on page 67.)

MEASURES OF VARIATION

Figure 2.22 shows two distributions of scores. Suppose they represent scores on two tests of knowledge about introductory psychology. Both tests have the same mean, median, and mode. But if you had a score of 80, then the meaning of that score would be different for the two tests. Such a score on the first test is above average, but nothing un-

usual. The same score on the second test would put you in the top 1% of your class.

To describe the difference between Figure 2.22a and b, we need a measurement of the variation (or spread) around the mean. The simplest such measurement is the **range** of a distribution, a statement of the highest and lowest scores. Thus, the range in Figure 2.22a is 39 to 100 and in Figure 2.22b it is 58 to 92. If we subtract the lower end of the range from the higher number, we see that the range includes more numbers in 2.22a than in 2.22b.

The range is simple but not very useful, because it takes account of only two scores. Statisticians need to know whether nearly all the scores are clustered close to the mean or whether they are more scattered. A good measure should indicate that the scores in 2.22a are much more scattered than those in 2.22b. The most useful measure is the **standard deviation**, a measurement of the amount of variation among scores in a normal distribution. The appendix to this chapter gives a formula for calculating the standard deviation, but for our present purposes you can simply remember that when the scores are closely clustered near the mean, the standard deviation is small; when the scores are more widely scattered, the standard deviation is large.

As Figure 2.23 shows, the Scholastic Assessment Test was designed to produce a mean of 500 and a standard deviation of 100. Of all people taking the test, 68% score within one standard deviation above or below the mean (400–600); 95% score within two standard deviations (300–700). Only 2.5% score above 700; another 2.5% score below 300.

Standard deviations provide a useful way of comparing scores on two tests. For example, if you had a score one standard deviation above the mean on the SAT, you did about as well as someone who scored one standard deviation above the mean on some other test, such as the American College Test. We would say that both of you had a deviation score of +1.

CONCEPT CHECK

10. *On your first psychology test, you get a score of 80. The mean for the class is 70, and the standard deviation is 5. On the second* *test, you get a score of 90. This time the mean for the class is again 70, but the standard deviation is 20. Compared to the other students in your class, did your performance improve, deteriorate, or stay the same? (Check your answer on page 67.)*

EVALUATING RESULTS: INFERENTIAL STATISTICS

Suppose we conduct a study at a local school, comparing second-graders learning arithmetic in the standard way and second-graders in another class who are using a new curriculum. We would probably report the means and standard deviations for each group. But we are interested in not just the performances of these two local groups but also the performances of all the second-graders who might ever use either curriculum. When we talk about the entire population, we use **inferential statistics,** which are statements about large groups based on inferences from small samples.

The most common use of inferential statistics is to decide whether the difference observed between two groups is probably real or probably accidental. Suppose, for example, we find that the second-graders using the new curriculum get a mean score of 85 on a test at the end of the year, while students in the standard curriculum get a mean score of 79. Should we conclude that the new curriculum is better? Or might the apparent difference between the two groups be just an accident?

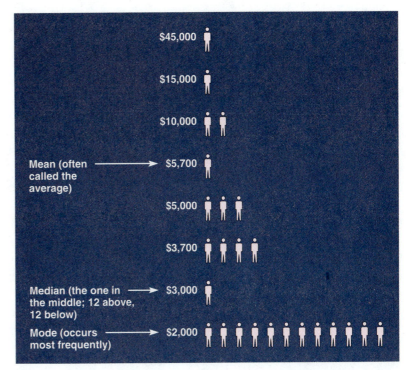

Mean (often called the average) → $5,700

Median (the one in the middle; 12 above, 12 below) → $3,000

Mode (occurs most frequently) → $2,000

FIGURE 2.21
The monthly salaries of the 25 employees of company X, showing the mean, median, and mode. (After Huff, 1954.)

To answer that question, we use statistical techniques. Different formulas are used for different purposes. The appendix at the end of this chapter gives an example of a statistical test. A statistical test determines the probability that a study may produce, *just by accident,* results as impressive as those that were actually obtained. If that probability is low, the results can be taken seriously.

In our example, we want to know how likely it is that two groups we chose at random might differ by accident in their arithmetic scores by at least 85 to 79. That prob-

range = highest + lowest scores.

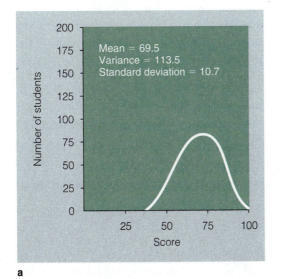

a

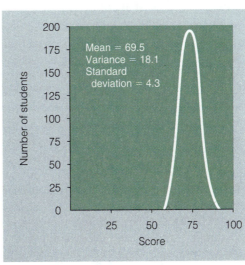

b

FIGURE 2.22
These two distributions of test scores have the same mean but different variances and different standard deviations.

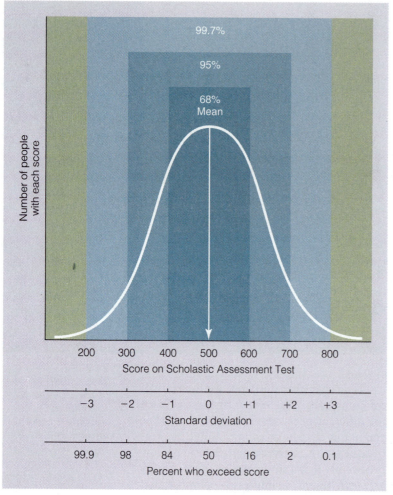

If, however, each group had some children with very high scores and some with very low scores, the difference between the means would be less convincing.

To summarize the results of a statistical test, we use a value known as *p*, which stands for *probability* of accidentally getting results at least as impressive as the reported results. The *lower* the value of *p*, the more convincing the results: If the value of *p* is low, then the probability of accidentally producing similar results is low. That is, *the lower the value of p, the more impressive the results.* Psychologists usually regard a result as significant if the value of *p* is less than 5%, expressed as **p < .05.** This expression means that the probability of getting results similar to those observed is less than 5%. A more cautious experimenter might insist on a stricter standard, such as *p < .01.* In either case, if the *p* value is lower than the standard chosen, then an experiment's results are said to be statistically significant, and the results are sufficiently convincing that we would look for an explanation. If the *p* value is higher than the standard chosen, the results are inconclusive.

11. *You compare the performance of women and men on 20 tasks. On one of the tasks, you find a significant difference (p < .05). How could you check against the possibility that this apparent difference is the result of accident? (Check your answer on page 67.)*

Finding statistically significant results is only the first step toward drawing a conclusion. To say that an experiment has **statistically significant results** means only that the probability is low that the effect arose by chance. The question remains, if not by chance, then what caused the difference? At that point, psychologists call upon all their knowledge to try to determine the most likely interpretation of the results.

FIGURE 2.23
In a normal distribution, the amount of variation of scores from the mean can be measured in standard deviations. In this example, scores between 400 and 600 are said to be within one standard deviation from the mean; scores between 300 and 700 are within two standard deviations.

ability depends on several factors (Figure 2.24):

1. The larger the difference between two groups, the less likely it is that the difference has arisen by accident.

2. Other things being equal, the more subjects each group has, the less likely that the difference observed between the groups is just an accident. If 20 children used the new curriculum and 20 used the old curriculum, the probability is fairly high that one group would accidentally score a few points higher than the other. But if the study included thousands of children, the probability is much lower that the two groups would accidentally differ by as much as six points.

3. The more consistently the members of each group behave, the less likely it is that any difference between the groups has arisen through accident. For example, if almost every child in one curriculum got a score close to 85 and almost every child in the other curriculum got a score close to 79, this difference would be reasonably impressive.

SUMMARY

• *Mean, median, and mode.* One way of presenting the central score of a distribution is the mean, determined by adding all the scores and dividing by the number of individuals. Another way is the median, which is the score in the middle after all the scores have been arranged from highest to lowest. The mode is the score that occurs most frequently. (page 63)

• *Standard deviation.* To indicate whether most scores are clustered close to the mean or whether they are spread out, psychologists report the range of scores or the standard deviation. If we know that a given score is a certain number of standard deviations above or below the mean, then we can determine what percentage of other scores it exceeds. (page 64)

• *Inferential statistics.* Inferential statistics are attempts to deduce the properties of a large population based on the results from a small sample. (page 65)

• *Probability of chance results.* The most common use of inferential statistics is to calculate the probability that a given research result could have arisen by chance. That probability is low if the difference between two groups is large, if the variability within each group is small, and if the number of individuals in each group is large. (page 66)

• *Statistical significance.* When psychologists say "$p < .05$," they mean that the probability that accidental fluctuations could produce the kind of results they obtained is less than 5%. They generally set a standard of 5% or less. If the results meet that standard, then they are said to be statistically significant. (page 66)

SUGGESTION FOR FURTHER READING

Martin, D. (1996). *Doing psychology experiments.* (4th ed.). Pacific Grove, CA: Brooks/Cole. A discussion of all aspects of research, including both methods of conducting research and statistical analysis of results.

TERMS

descriptive statistics mathematical summaries of results, such as measures of the central score and the amount of variation (page 62)

mean the sum of all the scores reported in a study divided by the number of scores (page 63)

normal distribution (or normal curve) a symmetrical frequency of scores, clustered around the mean (page 63)

median the middle score in a list of scores arranged from highest to lowest (page 63)

mode the score that occurs most frequently in a distribution of scores (page 63)

range a statement of the highest and lowest scores in a distribution of scores (page 64)

standard deviation a measurement of the amount of variation among scores in a normal distribution (page 64)

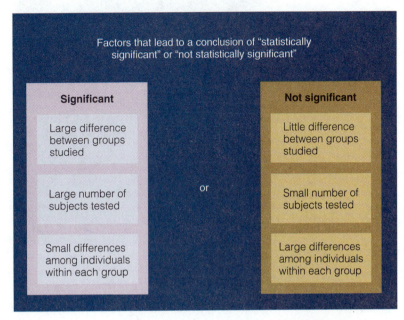

Factors that lead to a conclusion of "statistically significant" or "not statistically significant"

Significant

Large difference between groups studied

Large number of subjects tested

Small differences among individuals within each group

or

Not significant

Little difference between groups studied

Small number of subjects tested

Large differences among individuals within each group

FIGURE 2.24
We cannot draw conclusions from data until they are shown to be "statistically significant," which is why raw data must be subjected to appropriate statistical procedures. The appendix to this chapter describes some of these procedures.

inferential statistics statements about large groups based on inferences from small samples (page 65)

$p < .05$ an expression meaning that the probability of accidentally getting results equal to the reported results is less than 5% (page 66)

statistically significant results effects that have a low probability of having arisen by chance (page 66)

ANSWERS TO CONCEPT CHECKS

9. **a.** Mean = 4; median = 3; mode = 2.
b. Mean = 7; median = 3; mode = 2. Note that changing just one number in the distribution from 8 to 35 greatly altered the mean without affecting the median or the mode. (page 63)

10. Even though your score went up from 80 on the first test to 90 on the second, your performance actually deteriorated in comparison to other students' scores. An 80 on the first test was two standard deviations above the mean, a score better than 98% of all other students. A 90 on the second test was only one standard deviation above the mean, a score that beats only 84% of other students. (page 64)

11. The more comparisons one makes, the greater is the probability that at least one of them will appear to be statistically significant, just by chance. One way to avoid this difficulty would be to set a higher standard of statistical significance, such as $p < .001$, and to discount any difference that does not meet this high standard. Another way would be to repeat the study on a second population to see whether the difference is replicable.) (page 66)

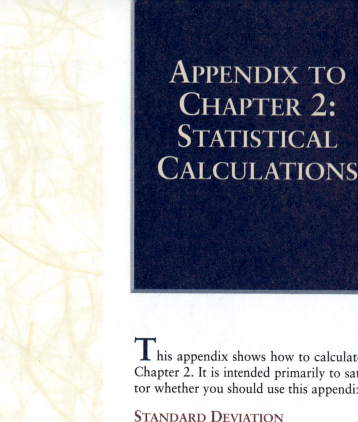

APPENDIX TO CHAPTER 2: STATISTICAL CALCULATIONS

This appendix shows how to calculate a few of the statistics mentioned in Chapter 2. It is intended primarily to satisfy your curiosity. Ask your instructor whether you should use this appendix for any other purpose.

STANDARD DEVIATION

To determine the standard deviation (SD):

1. Determine the mean of the scores.
2. Subtract the mean from each of the individual scores.
3. Square each of those results, add them together, and divide by the total number of scores.

The result is called the *variance*. The standard deviation is the square root of the variance. See Table 2.3 for examples.

STANDARD ERROR OF THE MEAN

One way to infer whether the mean of a sample is close to the true mean of the population is to calculate the *standard error of the mean (SE)*. We calculate the standard error of the mean by dividing the standard deviation of the population by $\sqrt{N-1}$, where N is the number of individuals in the sample:

$$SE = SD/\sqrt{(N-1)}$$

If the sample includes many individuals who vary only slightly from one another, the standard deviation will be small, N will be large, and therefore the standard error of the mean will be small. On the other hand, if the sample includes only a few individuals, and they vary greatly from one another, the standard error will be large.

A TYPICAL STATISTICAL TEST: THE t-TEST

A number of statistical tests are available to suit different kinds of data and different kinds of experiments. For the simple case of comparing two groups, both of which show results that approximate the normal distribution, one of the most popular tests is the *t-test*. Assume that for two populations the means are $\bar{x}_1$ and $\bar{x}_2$, the numbers of individuals measured are n_1 and n_2, and the standard deviations are s_1 and s_2.

We calculate t by using this formula:

$$t = \frac{(\bar{x}_2 - \bar{x}_1)\sqrt{n_1 \cdot n_2 \cdot (n_1 + n_2 - 2)}}{\sqrt{n_1 \cdot s_1^2 + n_2 \cdot s_2^2} \cdot \sqrt{n_1 + n_2}}$$

TABLE 2.3

INDIVIDUAL SCORES	MEAN MINUS THE INDIVIDUAL SCORES	DIFFERENCES SQUARED
12.5	2.5	6.25
17.0	− 2.0	4.00
11.0	4.0	16.00
14.5	0.5	0.25
16.0	− 1.0	1.00
16.5	− 1.5	2.25
17.5	− 2.5	6.25
		36.00

Mean = 15.0
Variance = 36/7 = 5.143
Standard deviation = 2.268

The larger the value of t, the less likely that the difference between the two groups is due to chance. The value of t will be high if the difference between the two means ($\bar{x}_2 - \bar{x}_1$) is large, if the standard deviations (s_1 and s_2) are small relative to the means, and if the number of individuals is large. For example, if a group of 50 people has a mean of 81 and a standard deviation of 7, and a group of 150 people has a mean of 73 and a standard deviation of 9, then

$$t = \frac{(81 - 73)\sqrt{150 \cdot 50 \cdot 198}}{\sqrt{(150 \cdot 81 + 50 \cdot 49)}\sqrt{(200)}} = \frac{9748.8}{120.83 \times 14.14} = 5.71$$

The larger the value of t, the less likely it is that the results have arisen by accident. Statistics books contain tables that show the likelihood of a given t value. In this case, with 200 people in the two groups combined, a t value of 5.71 is significant ($p < .001$).

CORRELATION COEFFICIENTS

To determine the correlation coefficient, we designate one of the variables x and the other one y. We obtain pairs of measures, x_i and y_i. Then we use the following formula:

$$= \frac{[(\Sigma x_i y_i) - n \cdot \bar{x} \cdot \bar{y}]}{n \cdot sx \cdot sy}$$

In this formula, ($\Sigma x_i y_i$) is the sum of the products of x and y. For each pair of observations (x, y), we multiply x times y and then add together all the products. The term $n \cdot \bar{x} \cdot \bar{y}$ means n (the number of pairs) times the mean of x times the mean of y. The denominator, $n \cdot sx \cdot sy$, means n times the standard deviation of x times the standard deviation of y.

3

BIOLOGICAL PSYCHOLOGY

"There is a great deal that we do not know about how the brain works." I have heard that statement many times, sometimes from people who know a great deal about how the brain works, and sometimes from people who know very little. Some of those who know rather little about the brain underestimate how much we do know. While they are right that many questions remain unanswered, our ignorance is not so great as they might suppose.

To illustrate: In 1994, the journal *Brain Research* published 12,500 pages of research articles. The *Journal of Neuroscience* published another 7800; *Journal of Neurophysiology,* 3000; and *Behavioral Neuroscience,* 1200. Those are just four of the dozens of professional journals that publish research in this area. Our knowledge about the brain is growing at an amazing rate. Many of the questions that researchers admit they cannot answer today are questions they did not know enough to ask just a few years ago.

No one can keep up-to-date with all of that literature, of course. Still, psychology has become increasingly tied to biology, and psychologists need to know at least the highlights of the biological research. Discussions of perception, motivation, emotion, and abnormal behavior today rely more and more on information and concepts about genetics and brain functioning. I hope to convince you in this chapter not only that the biology of behavior is essential to any theoretical understanding of psychology, but also that it can be highly interesting. (Try not to get too bogged down in just memorizing the terms.)

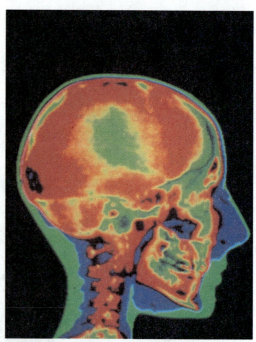

"I think, therefore I am"—René Descartes' declaration points to the mind–body problem facing psychologists: How and why does the brain's activity produce conscious experience?

PSYCHOLOGICAL EXPLANATIONS AT THE LEVEL OF THE GENE

How do heredity and evolution influence behavior?

What makes one person act differently from another? There are two possible explanations: differences in what we were at the start of life (as a single fertilized cell) and what has happened to us since then. In other words, the answers are heredity and environment, nature and nurture. If you wish, you can add a third possibility, the *interaction* between heredity and environment, that is, the possibility that the environment can have different effects on people depending on their heredity. (For example, exposure to a high-fat diet might have a bigger effect on some people than on others, because of differences in their genetics.)

In some cases, a single gene can have an enormous effect on behavior. For example, people with a gene for **Alzheimer's disease** live a normal life until old age, when certain parts of the brain gradually begin to deteriorate (Van Hoesen, Hyman, & Damasio, 1991). In the initial stages, people with Alzheimer's disease become forgetful. As the disease progresses, they grow confused, depressed, and restless, prone to hallucinations and delusions, and unable to eat and sleep normally (Cummings & Victoroff, 1990). All that as the result of a single gene!

And yet the gene alone is not entirely responsible for the condition. Different people with the same gene have different outcomes. Whether they develop Alzheimer's disease at all, and how soon and how severely, apparently depends on many features in the environment. The same is true for many other genes of importance to psychology. Certain

people have genes that increase their likelihood of becoming depressed or of developing an alcohol problem. The actual outcome, however, depends on their environment. For example, someone with a genetic predisposition toward alcohol abuse might grow up in a strict Mormon community that never makes alcohol available.

Often psychologists have trouble determining what behavior is due to the effects of genes and what to the effects of the environment. For example, are boys generally more aggressive than girls—at least in certain circumstances—because of their genes, or because other people somehow encourage them to act that way? And why do identical twins generally resemble each other so closely? How much of that resemblance is due to their shared genes and how much is due to their shared environment?

Such questions illustrate the nature–nurture problem, which shows up in practically all fields of psychology. In this section I shall discuss what genes are, how they exert their effects, and how psychologists try to determine the role of genes in human behavior. I shall also discuss a few points about the evolution of behavior.

PRINCIPLES OF GENETICS

If you have already studied genetics in a biology class, much of this discussion will be a review. I shall, however, add some examples that relate to psychology.

Nearly every cell of every plant and animal contains a nucleus, which in turn contains strands of hereditary material called **chromosomes** (Figure 3.1). Chromosomes provide the chemical basis of heredity. Humans have 23 pairs of chromosomes in each cell of the body, except that an egg or sperm cell has 23 unpaired chromosomes. At fertilization, the 23 chromosomes in the egg cell combine with the 23 in the sperm to form the 23 pairs that will characterize the new person (Figure 3.2).

Sections along each chromosome are known as **genes.** These segments control chemical reactions that ultimately direct the development of the organism. The genes determine whether the individual develops into a tall red-headed woman or a short blond man.

73

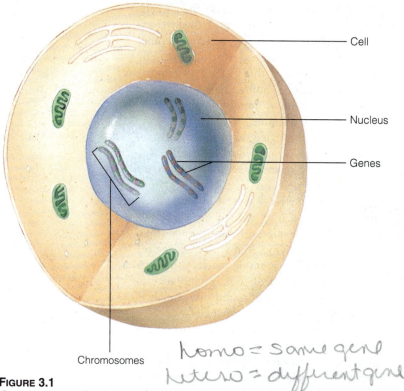

Cell

Nucleus

Genes

Chromosomes

FIGURE 3.1
Genes are sections of chromosomes, which are in the nuclei of cells. Scale is exaggerated for illustration purposes.

[handwritten: homo = same gene; hetero = different gene]

[handwritten: paired genes. except Male has 1 X & 1 Y]

FIGURE 3.2
The nucleus of each human cell contains 46 chromosomes, 23 from the sperm and 23 from the egg cell, united in pairs.

THE TRANSMISSION OF GENES FROM ONE GENERATION TO ANOTHER

All the body cells that contain pairs of chromosomes have pairs of genes, one on each chromosome. You or I have two genes for eye color, two for hair color, two for almost every characteristic. (The exception: Men have one X chromosome and one Y chromo-

some, and therefore unpaired genes on their X and Y chromosomes.)

The two genes of any given pair may be either the same or different. When both genes of a pair are the same, the person is said to be **homozygous** (HO-mo-ZI-gus) for that gene. When the two are different, the person is **heterozygous** (HET-er-o-ZI-gus) for the gene (Figure 3.3). (A *zygote* is a fertilized egg. *Homozygous* means a fertilized egg formed from the same genes; *heterozygous* means a fertilized egg formed from *different* genes.)

Certain genes are considered **dominant genes** because they will exert their effects on development even in a person who is heterozygous for that gene. Very few human behaviors depend on a single gene. One example is the ability to curl the tongue lengthwise (Figure 3.4). Another example is the ability to taste the chemical phenylthiocarbamide (PTC), which tastes bitter to those with the gene. Both of these genes are dominant; you need only one gene to be able to curl your tongue or to taste PTC. The genes for inability to curl the tongue and inability to taste PTC are said to be **recessive genes**. Only people who are homozygous for a recessive gene show its effects. In other words, if you cannot curl your tongue, you must be homozygous for the inability-to-curl gene (not exactly a serious handicap).

A person who is heterozygous for a particular gene will show the effects of the dominant gene but may still pass the recessive gene to a son or a daughter. For example, two parents who are heterozygous for the tongue-curling gene will both be able to curl their tongues, but they could each pass a recessive gene to their child, who would then be a nontongue-curler.

<hr>

CONCEPT CHECKS

1. Suppose you can curl your tongue but cannot taste PTC. Are you homozygous or heterozygous for the tongue-curling gene, or is it impossible to say? Are you homozygous or heterozygous for the inability to taste PTC, or is it impossible to say?
2. If two parents can curl their tongues but cannot taste PTC, what can you predict about their children? (Check your answers on page 86.)

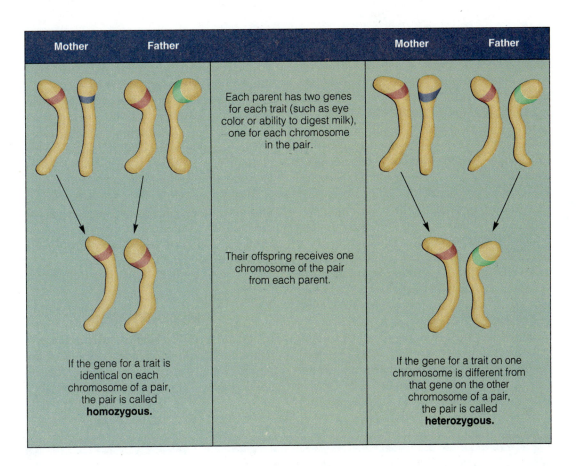

Each parent has two genes for each trait (such as eye color or ability to digest milk), one for each chromosome in the pair.

Their offspring receives one chromosome of the pair from each parent.

If the gene for a trait is identical on each chromosome of a pair, the pair is called **homozygous.**

If the gene for a trait on one chromosome is different from that gene on the other chromosome of a pair, the pair is called **heterozygous.**

SEX-LINKED AND SEX-LIMITED GENES

Some characteristics are more common in men; others are more common in women. Why? There can be many explanations, and a genetic explanation is not always a likely one. Still, genes do account for some of the differences, and it is valuable to know how genes could produce differences between the sexes.

One pair of human chromosomes are known as **sex chromosomes** because they determine whether an individual will develop as a male or as a female. The sex chromosomes are of two types, known as X and Y (Figure 3.5). A female has two **X chromosomes** in each cell; a male has one X chromosome and one **Y chromosome.** The mother contributes one X chromosome to each child, and the father contributes either an X or a Y chromosome.

Genes located on the X chromosome are known as X-linked genes, or as **sex-linked genes.** An X-linked recessive gene shows its effects more often in men than in women. For example, the most common type of color blindness depends on an X-linked recessive

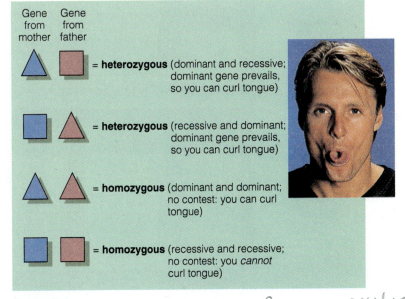

Gene from mother	Gene from father	
△ (blue)	□ (pink)	= **heterozygous** (dominant and recessive; dominant gene prevails, so you can curl tongue)
□ (blue)	△ (pink)	= **heterozygous** (recessive and dominant; dominant gene prevails, so you can curl tongue)
△ (blue)	△ (pink)	= **homozygous** (dominant and dominant; no contest: you can curl tongue)
□ (blue)	□ (pink)	= **homozygous** (recessive and recessive; no contest: you *cannot* curl tongue)

FIGURE 3.4
This figure uses the ability to curl the tongue lengthwise as an example of a behavior that depends on a single gene. The gene that enables you to curl your tongue is a dominant gene, indicated by a triangle here. The square refers to a recessive gene for inability to curl tongue.

[handwritten: female = 2X chromo / male = 1 X + 1 Y chromo]

[handwritten: Sex linked genes = genes located on X chromosomes]

FIGURE 3.5
An electron micrograph of X and Y chromosomes shows the difference in length. (From Ruch, 1984.)

Sex-limited genes: those that affect 1 sex more than the other.

FIGURE 3.6
Why males are more likely than females to be color-blind.

gene. A man with that gene on his X chromosome definitely will be color-blind, because he has no other X chromosome. He has a Y chromosome, but the Y chromosome contains neither the gene for color blindness nor the gene for normal color vision. A woman who has the color blindness gene has a second X chromosome, which probably has a dominant gene for normal color vision. If so, she will not be color-blind. She will, however, be a "carrier" for color blindness; that is, she can transmit the color blindness gene to any of her children (Figure 3.6).

Genetically controlled differences between the sexes do not necessarily depend on sex-linked genes. For example, adult men generally have deeper voices and more facial hair than women do. Those characteristics are controlled by genes not on the X or Y chromosome; the genes are present in both sexes, but activated by hormones that are found mostly in men. Similarly, the genes controlling breast development are present in both sexes, but activated by hormones that are

found mostly in women. **Sex-limited genes** are those that affect one sex only or affect one sex more strongly than the other, even though both sexes have the genes.

Why are men more likely to get into fistfights than women are? We do not have enough evidence to determine whether genes are responsible, but if the difference is because of their genes, the responsible genes are probably *sex-limited* genes rather than sex-linked genes. That is, male hormones may activate certain genes that promote aggressive behavior; we have no evidence indicating an X-linked gene or a Y-linked gene for aggressive behavior.

CONCEPT CHECK

3. Suppose a color-blind man marries a woman who is homozygous for normal color vision. What sort of color vision will their children have? (Check your answer on page 86.)

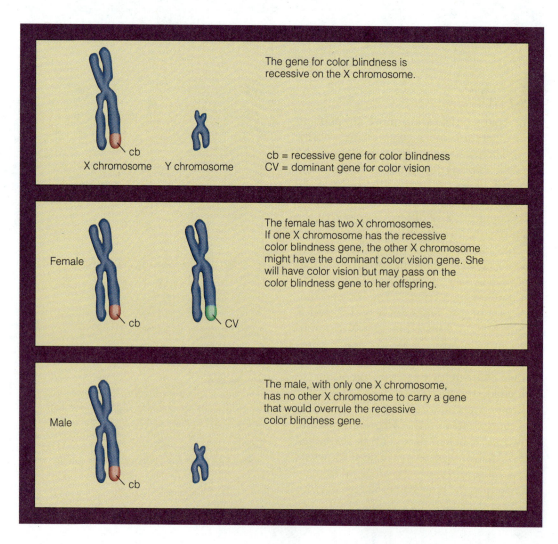

The gene for color blindness is recessive on the X chromosome.

X chromosome   Y chromosome

cb = recessive gene for color blindness
CV = dominant gene for color vision

Female

The female has two X chromosomes. If one X chromosome has the recessive color blindness gene, the other X chromosome might have the dominant color vision gene. She will have color vision but may pass on the color blindness gene to her offspring.

Male

The male, with only one X chromosome, has no other X chromosome to carry a gene that would overrule the recessive color blindness gene.

[handwritten top left: genome - collection of genes / localizing genes + determining effects.]

[handwritten top right: By identifying problem genes can help detect problems and ways of preventing them / - could help undo damage / - prevent further spread of disorder]

IDENTIFYING AND LOCALIZING GENES

In the early days of genetic research, genes were merely inferred. For example, if both parents have blue eyes, then all of their children have blue eyes; we conclude therefore that a gene must exist that causes blue eyes. Today, researchers are trying to identify and localize the genes and then to determine chemically how given genes produce their effects. Ultimately they hope to map the entire human *genome* (collection of genes).

In one early success story, researchers have located the gene that causes **Huntington's disease,** a disease that generally begins in middle-aged people, impairing their voluntary muscle control and causing both mental and physical deterioration, eventually leading to death. The identification of the responsible gene enables physicians to take a tissue sample, look at the chromosomes, examine the appropriate part of chromosome number 4, and thereby determine whether or not a person has the Huntington's gene (Huntington's Disease Collaborative Research Group, 1993). If one of your parents had Huntington's disease, and you knew you therefore had a high probability of having the gene for it yourself, would you want to have your chromosomes examined for this gene? Some people do, because they want to adjust their lives accordingly. (For example, if they found that they had the gene, they might choose not to have children and they might choose to take a job that does not require many years of education.) Other people, however, decide that they would rather live with uncertainty than to run the risk of learning that they have the Huntington's gene. Most people who choose to get tested manage to cope with the outcome, even if the test results are positive (Wiggins et al., 1992).

In the future, researchers may identify other genes with important psychological effects—conceivably, genes that increase the risk of schizophrenia, depression, alcoholism, or other undesirable conditions. If so, such information, like almost any other information, could be used for either helpful or harmful purposes. On the good side, the information might enable therapists to make an early identification of people likely to develop certain problems, and then perhaps to take steps to prevent the problem. Some problems, such as alcohol abuse, are difficult to treat after they have reached a serious level; earlier intervention might be more successful.

Furthermore, identifying responsible genes might help with *genetic counseling.* Suppose researchers found that some serious disorder depends on a recessive, identified gene; physicians might then run tests to tell certain couples, "Each of you carries this recessive gene that predisposes people to such and such disorder. You will not develop the disorder yourselves, but if you choose to have children, about one-fourth will be homozygous for this gene and therefore likely to develop the disorder. You may consider this information when deciding whether to start a family."

One more benefit: After researchers find the gene that causes a particular disorder, it will be possible to trace chemically what the gene does; that information might enable researchers to find a way to undo the damage. In the case of Huntington's disease, finding the responsible gene has not led immediately to a treatment for the disease, but it gives researchers a very encouraging clue of where and how to look for such a treatment.

As I said, however, the information about the genes could be used in more threatening ways. Conceivably, employers or insurance companies could require genetic tests of all applicants and then discriminate against anyone whose test indicated a likelihood of developing some disease or psychological disorder. At this point, no employers or insurance companies seem inclined to start such a policy, but the potential exists for a serious issue that society may have to face in the future.

STUDIES OF HUMAN BEHAVIOR GENETICS

In many regards, understanding the genetics of Huntington's disease is much easier than understanding the genetics of schizophrenia, depression, or alcoholism. With Huntington's disease, everyone who has the gene gets the disease and anyone who lacks the gene definitely will not get the disease. We cannot make the same statement with regard to many important psychological conditions. A condition such as alcoholism is almost certainly influenced by a great many genes as well as by the environment.

In such a case, how can we know that genes have any effect at all? Researchers rely

[handwritten right margin: Alcoholism influenced by many genes + environment]

Identical twins

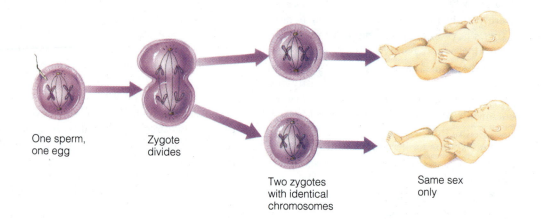

One sperm,
one egg

Zygote
divides

Two zygotes
with identical
chromosomes

Same sex
only

Fraternal twins

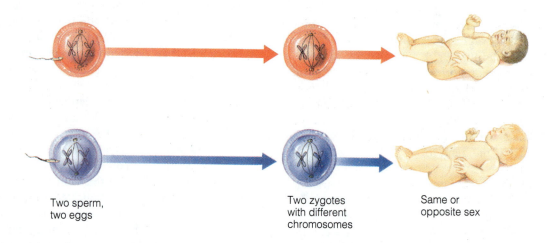

Two sperm,
two eggs

Two zygotes
with different
chromosomes

Same or
opposite sex

[handwritten margin note:] MONOZYGOTIC = identical heredities

dizygotic = resemble only genetically

on the following types of evidence (Segal, 1993):

• Do **monozygotic** (identical; literally, one-egg) **twins** resemble each other more closely than **dizygotic** (fraternal; literally, two-egg) **twins** do (Figure 3.7)? Monozygotic twins have identical heredities; dizygotic twins resemble each other genetically only as much as brother and sister do. A greater resemblance between monozygotic twins is not conclusive evidence for a genetic influence, but a *lack* of such resemblance would argue strongly against a genetic influence.

• Do twins who are adopted by separate families and reared apart resemble each other more closely than we would expect for two unrelated people? If so, genetic similarity is a likely explanation. (It is not the only possibility. A woman who drinks much alcohol while pregnant with twins might impair the brain development of both children, who

would then closely resemble each other for a nongenetic reason.)

• To what extent do adopted children resemble their adoptive parents and their biological parents? If children who are adopted in infancy closely resemble their biological parents in some regard, that resemblance probably reflects a genetic influence.

SOMETHING TO THINK ABOUT

A greater resemblance between a pair of monozygotic twins than between a pair of dizygotic twins is not considered conclusive evidence for a genetic influence. Why not?

Based on evidence of these types, researchers have found at least some genetic influence for a wide variety of behaviors and conditions. Certain people apparently have a genetic predisposition toward schizophrenia, depression, alcohol abuse, or other disorders

(Loehlin, Willerman, & Horn, 1988). Psychologists have also found evidence for genetic tendencies that influence a wide variety of normal and abnormal personality types (Nigg & Goldsmith, 1994) and even people's attitudes (Tesser, 1993). How much time people spend watching television apparently depends in part on genetics; adopted children resemble their birth parents in this regard more than they do their adopting parents (Plomin, Corley, DeFries, & Fulker, 1990). Genetics is apparently a factor even in how deeply people care about religion (Waller, Kojetin, Bouchard, Lykken, & Tellegen, 1990). (Monozygotic twins reared apart resemble each other in their religious devoutness, although their religious affiliation depends on the adoptive family. There is no gene for Presbyterian.) In fact, given the mounting evidence for a genetic contribution to almost everything in behavior, one group of researchers attracted near-headline attention by identifying a behavior that is apparently *not* dependent on genetics: people's attitudes toward romantic love (Waller & Shaver, 1994). That is, psychologists have a growing assumption that hereditary differences influence almost everything we do.

Psychologists who study identical twins often find extremely detailed similarities in behaviors they would never suspect of having a genetic influence if they just looked at nontwin brothers or sisters (Lykken, McGue, Tellegen, & Bouchard, 1992). For example, identical twins reared apart generally resemble each other strongly in their interests (such as hunting, fishing, or arts and crafts), their optimistic or pessimistic outlook on life, and even their hobbies (such as dog training or gun collecting). Why might identical twins resemble each other so closely? One possible answer is that many behavioral traits depend on the combined influences of many genes. For example, genes A, B, C, and D together might produce some effect that we would never suspect from the effects of any one of the genes separately, much as the effects of mixing five ingredients might produce a cake that one could never approximate from only four of the ingredients. Because monozygotic twins share all their genes in common, they will share these combination or configuration results; other people in the same family ordinarily will not.

How Genes Affect Behavior

Does any of this discussion about genetics and behavior strike you as a bit hard to be-

lieve? "How could there be a gene for something like television watching?" you might wonder, for example. "After all, televisions have been around for only a few decades; how could humans have evolved genes to influence a behavior that wasn't even possible until recently?"

Indeed. Let's start by conceding that it is totally implausible that humans would have a gene with effects that are limited to television watching. The explanation is that genes ordinarily have a multitude of effects. A gene that influences people's muscle development, for example, will influence how much time they spend on athletic play and therefore how much time they spend (or don't spend) watching television. A gene that influences attention span will influence how much time people spend watching television, and also how much time they spend reading or holding long conversations, and so forth. With a little imagination you can propose a number of other ways in which genes might indirectly affect television watching, none of which are limited just to television. Presumably, almost every gene has a multitude of indirect effects.

Moreover, a gene might greatly influence behavior through a mechanism completely outside the brain. Here is one example: Most Asian adults, including Americans of Asian ancestry, drink little or no milk and seldom if ever eat dairy products. Within other ethnic groups, some adults enjoy consuming large amounts of dairy products, while others consume only a little. The differences in dairy consumption are known to be largely under genetic control, but those genes affect digestion, not taste or motivation. The relevant genes control the body's ability to digest *lactose*, the sugar in milk (Figure 3.8).

Almost all infants of all ethnic groups can digest lactose. As they grow older, most Asian children and a large number of non-Asian children lose the ability to digest lactose. (They lose that ability even if they drink milk frequently.) They can still consume a little milk, cheese, or ice cream, but if they consume very much, they become nauseated (Flatz, 1987; Rozin & Pelchat, 1988). Figure 3.9 shows how the ability to digest dairy products varies from one part of the world to another. The overall point is that a gene can affect a behavior—in this case, a food preference—by altering chemical reactions outside the brain itself.

genes have a multitude of indirect effects.

genes affect behavior by altering chemical reactions outside the brain ex. milk.

FIGURE 3.8
Genes don't control behavior directly but through many indirect routes. They control chemical reactions in the body, which in turn influence behavior.

4. Why do Asian cooks almost never use cheese or milk? In what other parts of the world would you expect cooks to avoid dairy products? (Check your answers on page 86.)

SOMETHING TO THINK ABOUT

Can you imagine a possible explanation for how some gene might influence religious devoutness? What other behaviors would your proposed gene also influence?

HOW HEREDITY INTERACTS WITH ENVIRONMENT

You will sometimes hear someone say, "I hope researchers never conclude that . . . [fill in the blank: intelligence, depression, alcoholism, etc.] is under genetic control, be-cause if that's the case, we can't do anything about it." That statement is nonsense. In fact, every characteristic that is influenced by genetics is influenced also by the environment, and the fact that genetic differences have a major influence says nothing about how some environmental intervention might change the results. For example, even if you have genes for straight hair, your health condition, your diet, and your grooming habits might give you straight hair, curly hair, or no hair at all.

Here is another example: **Phenylke-tonuria (PKU)** is an inherited condition that, if untreated, leads to mental retardation. (The condition depends on a recessive gene. About 2% of people of European or Asian ancestry are heterozygous carriers for this gene; people of African ancestry do not carry the gene.) People homozygous for PKU lack the chemical reactions that break down a substance called *phenylalanine,* a common

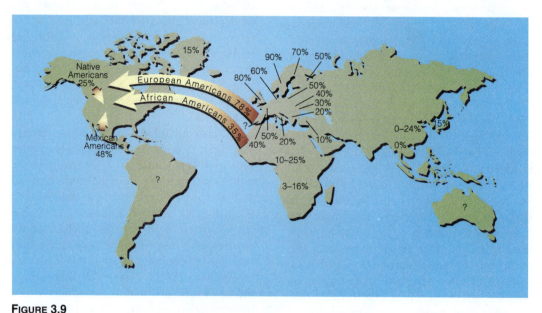

FIGURE 3.9
Adult humans vary in their ability to digest lactose, the main sugar in milk and other dairy products. The numbers in this figure refer to the percentage of each population's adults that can easily digest lactose. In Asian countries and other locations where most adults cannot digest lactose, cooks seldom if ever use dairy products. (Based on Flatz, 1987, and Rozin & Pelchat, 1988.)

environmental intervention can influence condition under genetic control

constituent of the diet, into other chemicals. On an ordinary diet, an affected child accumulates phenylalanine in the brain and becomes mentally retarded. However, an affected child who stays on a diet low in phenylalanine for at least the first 12–15 years of life does not become mentally retarded. That is, an environmental intervention (here, a controlled diet) can greatly influence a condition that is known to be under genetic control.

EVOLUTION

Our genes are a product of evolution. Evolution is more than a well-established theory supported by fossil evidence; it is a logical necessity based on what we know about genetics. The argument goes as follows:

1. The genes an organism inherits from its parents largely control its characteristics. In short, like begets like.

2. On occasion, genetic variations will cause an organism to differ from its parents. Such variations may arise from recombinations of genes (some from one parent and some from the other) or from **mutations** (random changes in the structure of genes). Recombinations and mutations alter the appearance or activity of the organism. Most mutations are disadvantageous, although an occasional mutation will give an individual an advantage in coping with certain situations.

3. If individuals with a certain gene or gene combination reproduce more successfully than others do, the genes that conferred the advantage will spread. Over many generations, the frequency of those genes will increase while the frequency of others will decrease (Weiner, 1994). Such changes in the gene frequencies of a species constitute **evolution**. Because we know that mutations sometimes occur in genes and that an occasional mutation may lead to greater success in reproduction, we can logically deduce that evolution *must* occur.

(Note the conclusion: Evolution must be occurring now and must have been occurring as long as animals and plants have been reproducing the way they do now. This argument does not tell us whether all forms of life evolved from a single common ancestor. To deal with that question, we need other kinds of evidence, such as the fossil record.)

Animal and plant breeders discovered a long time ago that they could develop new strains through **artificial selection,** or selective breeding. By purposefully breeding only those animals with certain traits, breeders developed cocker spaniels, thoroughbred racehorses, and chickens that lay enormous numbers of eggs. Charles Darwin's theory of evolution stated that **natural selection** can accomplish the same thing as selective breeding. If, in nature, individuals with certain genetically controlled characteristics reproduce more successfully than others do, then the species will come to resemble those individuals more and more as time passes.

Some people assume, mistakenly, that evolution means "the survival of the fittest." But what really matters in evolution is not survival but *reproduction* (Figure 3.10). Someone who lives to the age of 100 without having a child has failed to spread his or her genes. By contrast, a person who has five healthy children before dying at age 30 is a big success, evolutionarily speaking.

A gene that increases a person's chance of surviving long enough to reproduce will be favored over a gene that causes death in infancy. But genes that have no influence on the individual's survival may also be favored. For example, a gene that makes an individual more successful at attracting mates would certainly be favored, as would a gene that makes an individual more successful at protecting his or her offspring or other close relatives.

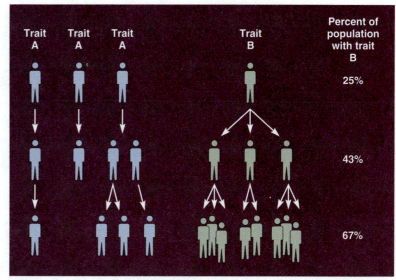

FIGURE 3.10
What's important in evolution is reproduction, not survival. Here, the population starts with three people carrying trait A and one with trait B. The person with B and his or her descendants produce more children, on the average, than people with A do. Consequently, the genes controlling trait B increase in prevalence from one generation to the next.

evolution = reproduction

CONCEPT CHECK

5. *Infertile worker bees are sisters of the queen bee, which lays all the eggs. In comparison with species in which all individuals are fertile, would you expect worker bees to*

FIGURE 3.11

The nesting behavior of kittiwakes is superbly adapted for their survival. For example, the parents build a mud barrier on the edge of the nest, and the young remain motionless until they are able to fly. Ground-nesting gulls, closely related to kittiwakes, do not build mud barriers, and their young walk out of the nest before they are mature enough to fly.

We don't add, change or lose genes because of how we use them.

Evolution doesn't mean long-term improvement

be more likely or less likely to risk their lives to defend their sister? Would you expect a queen bee to be more or less likely than a worker bee to risk her life? (Check your answers on page 86.)

on animal species

Occasionally people say something like "every generation our little toes get smaller and smaller because we don't use them," or "through evolution we will gradually get rid of the human appendix because we don't need it." Such statements reflect a misunderstanding about evolution. We do not add, change, or lose genes because of the way we use some part of the body. A lack of need for an appendix has no effect on the genes controlling the appendix. The only way people could evolve, say, a reduction of the size of the little toe would be if people with genes for "smaller than average little toe" had some reproductive advantage over other people.

One other common misunderstanding: Evolution does not necessarily mean long-term improvement. Genes will spread within a population if they provide some benefit at the moment. The result could be a population that is beautifully adapted to its current environment, but ill-adapted if the environment changes in some way.

THE EVOLUTION OF BEHAVIOR

Various animal species

Psychologists learn about the evolution of behavior largely through studies of animals. The study of animal behavior grew out of

Studies behavior under natural conditions

two separate pursuits: ethology and comparative psychology. **Ethology** is the branch of biology that studies animal behavior under natural or nearly natural conditions. Ethologists emphasize unlearned or **species-specific behaviors**—behaviors that are widespread in one animal species but not others. Species-specific behaviors are sometimes described as *instinctive,* although many investigators shun that term. (Many people use the term *instinct* as if it constituted an explanation. For example, they would say a mother squirrel takes care of her young because of her "maternal instinct." But simply naming what is happening is hardly an explanation.)

Comparative psychology is the branch of psychology that compares the behaviors of various animal species. A comparative psychologist might study which species are best at localizing sounds, how species differ in their means of finding food, or why some species solve a particular problem faster than other species do. Both ethologists and comparative psychologists study how behavioral capacities evolve and how they develop within an individual.

Evolution adapts the behavior of an animal, as well as its anatomy, to its way of life. Consider the mating behavior of the kittiwake, a member of the gull family (Tinbergen, 1958). Kittiwakes, unlike other gulls, nest on narrow ledges of steep cliffs (Figure 3.11). Because there are just so many suitable ledges, kittiwakes fight ferociously to claim a territory. By contrast, herring gulls, which nest on the ground, rarely fight over territory, because for them one nesting site is

Both study how behavior evolve & how develop within individual

about as good as any other. Kittiwakes use mud to build a hard nest with a barrier to prevent their eggs from rolling off the ledge. Herring gulls make no such effort. When kittiwake chicks hatch, they remain virtually motionless until they are old enough to fly. The advantage of this behavioral tendency is clear: A chick that takes even a step or two may fall off the ledge. Herring gull chicks, in contrast, begin to wander out of their nest long before they can fly.

Each of these kittiwake behaviors—fighting over territory, building secure nests, and remaining motionless—is well adapted to life on a narrow ledge. But have these behaviors been built into the animal by evolution, or are they learned anew by each individual? Even in the rare cases when kittiwakes nest on the ground, the chicks remain motionless, even though they are in no danger of falling. If the egg of a herring gull is placed in a kittiwake's nest, the kittiwakes accept the foreign egg and care for the chick after it hatches. But the chick invariably takes a few steps and falls to its death. Evidently some behavioral differences are a product of the evolution of each species rather than anything the individual learns.

■ SOCIOBIOLOGY

Sociobiology is a field that tries to relate the social behaviors of a species to its biology, particularly to its evolutionary history. According to sociobiologists, an animal interacts with others of its species in a particular way because similar behaviors in past generations have increased the probability of survival and mating. That is, individuals with a genetic tendency to engage in these social behaviors passed on their genes; individuals that behaved some other way were less successful at passing on their genes.

ANIMAL EXAMPLES OF SOCIOBIOLOGICAL EXPLANATIONS

Sociobiologists try to understand how various social behaviors may have helped animals to survive and reproduce. Here are two examples:

• Lions generally live in groups made up of one adult male, several adult females, and their young. If a new male succeeds in driving off the old male, he is likely to kill all the young. Why? Female lions are not sexually

FIGURE 3.12
A Tibetan boy gives money to an impoverished monk. Why do humans and some other species sometimes engage in altruistic behaviors? One possibility (kin selection) is that natural selection has favored behaviors that help our relatives, and we sometimes extend those behaviors to nonrelatives. Especially with humans, however, we can also imagine nongenetic explanations.

receptive so long as they are nursing their young. By killing the young, the new male brings the females into sexual receptivity and increases the likelihood of spreading his genes (Wilson, 1975).

• In a species of bird called reed buntings, a male–female pair sticks together fairly closely, although some females will also occasionally mate with neighboring males. Males help with incubating the eggs and taking care of the young; however, some males help more than others do. Researchers have found that females that engage in a large number of "extramarital affairs" with neighboring males elicit the least help from their male partners (Dixon, Ross, O'Malley, & Burke, 1994). That is, apparently a male works hard to help raise the young if the probability is high that he is their father. (We do not assume that he understands all this; evolution has simply prepared him to be more helpful to a faithful mate than to an unfaithful mate.)

SPECULATIONS ON HUMAN SOCIOBIOLOGY

Human social behavior also is partly the product of our evolutionary history. In principle that result is a logical necessity, yet citing precise examples is difficult because we are less certain about which human behaviors are strongly influenced by our genes and which ones are learned from our culture. Consider a couple of speculative, controversial examples:

• People will work very hard to help one another, sometimes even risking their own lives to help other people. Doing something to help others without any direct benefit to

How social behaviors may have helped animals to survive + reproduce

FIGURE 3.13

At different times and places in human history, mating customs have been quite varied, including the familiar one husband–one wife pattern, one wife–many husbands, and one husband–many wives, as illustrated by this Utah polygamist and his spouses. According to sociobiologists, men tend to be more interested in multiple partners than women are because a man with many partners can spread his genes, whereas a woman with many partners does not gain an equal advantage in reproduction.

Human sociobiology is controversial, largely because its adherents sometimes seem to be saying, "This is the way people behave; therefore they must have evolved the tendency to behave this way; and because we have evolved this way, it is natural and necessary that we continue to behave this way." When we observe differences between men and women, or between one culture and another, or between any other groups, we do not always know how much of that difference, if any, is due to genetic differences and how much is due to differences in experiences. If we find, say, that some male–female difference is reasonably consistent across cultures and from one historical era to another, then it probably is a real part of human nature, and sociobiological explanations are as appropriate here as they are for lions or for reed buntings. However, if the behavior is highly variable across cultures, or if we do not know how much it varies across cultures, then we should be skeptical of a sociobiological explanation. Our behavioral tendencies certainly are a product of our evolutionary histories, as the sociobiologists argue, but they also depend on our experiences. Psychologists must keep both kinds of influences in their proper place.

oneself is called **altruistic behavior** (Figure 3.12). Similarly, other species engage in some behaviors that appear to be altruistic; for example, a goose that sees a hawk overhead utters an alarm call that warns other geese. A sociobiological explanation for altruistic behavior is that selection has favored certain genes that somehow promote altruism toward one's relatives (Trivers, 1972). That is, individuals that help their offspring and other relatives tend to spread their genes, simply because those relatives have many of the same genes as the altruistic individual.

• Men are more likely than women to seek multiple sexual partners. A sociobiological interpretation is that a man who impregnates several women is spreading his genes. A woman gains no such advantage in taking multiple sexual partners. Moreover, if she were to do so, she might have trouble getting any one of them to help her rear the children. Therefore, the sociobiologists say, we may have evolved some sex-limited genes that increase males' interest in multiple partners or decrease females' interest (Buss, 1994). (See Figure 3.13.)

SUMMARY

• *Genes.* Genes, which are segments of chromosomes, control heredity. Because chromosomes come in pairs, every person has two of each gene, one received from the father and one from the mother. (page 73)

• *Dominant and recessive genes.* A dominant gene exerts its effects even in people who have only one dominant gene. People must have two of a recessive gene, one on each chromosome, in order to show its effects. (page 74)

• *Sex-linked and sex-limited genes.* Genes on the X chromosome are sex linked. A sex-linked recessive gene will show its effects more frequently in males than in females. A sex-limited gene may be present in both sexes, but it exerts its effects more strongly in one than in the other. (page 75)

• *Identifying and localizing genes.* Researchers have located the gene responsible for Huntington's disease and they are trying to identify and localize as many other human genes as possible. Identifying people's behavioral tendencies and risks by examining their genes offers the potential for significant benefits and also for possible misuse. (page 77)

• *Evidence for genetic influences.* Researchers determine the contribution of genes to human behavior by seeing whether monozygotic twins resemble each other more than dizygotic twins do, by comparing monozygotic twins reared in separate environments, and by examining how adopted children resemble their biological parents and their adoptive parents. (page 78)

• *How genes affect behavior.* Genes apparently affect an amazing variety of behaviors, not just one each; they may affect behavior indirectly, not necessarily even by any influence on brain development. (page 79)

• *Influence of the environment on gene expression.* It is possible for a behavior that reflects a genetic influence to be highly modified by a change in the environment. (page 80)

• *Evolution.* Evolution by natural selection is a logical necessity, given the principles of heredity and the fact that individuals with certain genes leave more offspring than do individuals with other genes. (page 81)

• *Study of animal behavior.* Ethologists and comparative psychologists study animal behavior and try to understand how it evolved. (page 82)

• *Sociobiology.* Sociobiologists try to explain social behaviors in terms of the survival and reproductive advantages of those behaviors. To interpret human behavior in such terms, one must carefully distinguish behaviors that are part of human nature from those that are highly dependent on culture and individual experience. In many cases we simply do not know enough to make that distinction. (page 83)

SUGGESTIONS FOR FURTHER READING

Tinbergen, N. (1958). *Curious naturalists.* New York: Basic Books. One of the best books for stimulating interest in animal behavior.

Weiner, J. (1994). *The beak of the finch.* New York: Knopf. Not really about behavior, but an excellent book for its explanations and illustrations of how evolution works.

TERMS

Alzheimer's disease a disease of old age marked by gradual damage to the brain leading to the gradual loss of memory and other abilities (page 73)

chromosome a strand of hereditary material found in the nucleus of a cell (page 73)

gene a segment of a chromosome that controls chemical reactions that ultimately direct the development of the organism (page 73)

homozygous having the same gene on both members of a pair of chromosomes (page 74)

heterozygous having different genes on a pair of chromosomes (page 74)

dominant gene a gene that will exert its effects on development even in a person who is heterozygous for that gene (page 74)

recessive gene a gene that will affect development only in a person who is homozygous for that gene (page 74)

sex chromosomes the chromosomes that determine whether an individual will develop as a female or as a male (page 75)

X chromosome a sex chromosome of which females have two per cell and males have one (page 75)

Y chromosome a sex chromosome of which males have one per cell and females have none (page 75)

sex-linked gene a gene situated on the X chromosome (page 75)

sex-limited gene a gene that affects one sex only or affects one sex more strongly than the other, even though both sexes have the gene (page 76)

Huntington's disease an inherited condition marked by gradual deterioration of voluntary movement control and other behavioral functions, usually beginning in middle age (page 77)

monozygotic twins (literally, one-egg twins) identical twins who develop from the same fertilized egg (page 78)

dizygotic twins (literally, two-egg twins) fraternal twins who develop from two eggs fertilized by two different sperm. Dizygotic twins are no more closely related than are any other children born to the same parents. (page 78)

phenylketonuria (PKU) an inherited disorder in which a person lacks the chemical reactions that convert a nutrient called phenylalanine into other chemicals; unless the diet is carefully controlled, the affected person becomes mentally retarded (page 80)

mutation a random change in the structure of a gene (page 81)

evolution changes in the gene frequencies of a species (page 81)

artificial selection the purposeful breeding, by humans, of animals with certain traits; also known as selective breeding (page 81)

natural selection the tendency, in nature, of individuals with certain genetically controlled characteristics to reproduce more successfully than others do; eventually the species will come to resemble those individuals more and more (page 81)

ethology the branch of biology that studies animal behavior under natural or nearly natural conditions (page 82)

species-specific behavior a particular behavior that is widespread in one animal species but not in others (page 82)

comparative psychology the branch of psychology that compares the behaviors of various animal species (page 82)

sociobiology a field that tries to relate the social behaviors of a species to its biology, particularly to its evolutionary history (page 83)

altruistic behavior behavior that benefits others without directly benefiting the individual showing the behavior (page 84)

ANSWERS TO CONCEPT CHECKS

1. It is impossible to say whether you are homozygous or heterozygous for the tongue-curling gene. Because that gene is a dominant gene, it produces the same effects in both the homozygous and the heterozygous conditions. If you cannot taste PTC, however, you must be homozygous for the nontasting gene. (page 74)

2. Because both of the parents must be homozygous for the inability to taste PTC, all their children will be unable to taste it also. Because both parents may be heterozygous for the tongue-curling gene, we cannot predict whether or not some of their children will be noncurlers. (page 74)

3. The woman will pass a dominant gene for normal color vision to all the children, so they will all have normal color vision. The man will pass a gene for deficient color vision on his X chromosome; the daughters will be carriers for color blindness. (page 76)

4. Asian cooks almost never use cheese or milk because most Asian adults cannot digest lactose, the primary sugar in dairy products. We also should expect to find little use of dairy products in those parts of Africa and southeastern Europe where few people can digest much lactose. (page 80)

5. Because the infertile worker bees cannot reproduce, the only way they can pass on their genes is by helping the queen bee. Consequently, they will sacrifice their own lives to defend the queen. They will also risk their lives to defend other workers in the hive, because these workers also try to defend the queen. The queen, however, will do little to defend a worker, because doing so would not increase her probability of reproducing. (page 81)

EXPLANATIONS OF BEHAVIOR AT THE LEVEL OF THE NEURON

Can we explain our experiences and our behavior in terms of the actions of single cells in the nervous system?

Your brain, which controls everything you do, is composed of cells. Does this mean that every one of your experiences—every sight, every sound, every thought—represents the activity of cells in your brain?

A highly productive strategy in science is **reductionism**—the attempt to explain complex phenomena by reducing them to combinations of simpler components. Biologists explain breathing, blood circulation, and metabolism in terms of chemical reactions and physical forces. Chemists explain chemical reactions in terms of the properties of the 92 naturally occurring elements. Physicists explain the structure of the atom and the interactions among atoms in terms of a few fundamental forces.

Does reductionism apply to psychology? Can we explain human behavior and experience in terms of chemical and electrical events in the brain? Here we deal with attempts to answer those questions.

THE CELLS OF THE NERVOUS SYSTEM

You experience your "self" as a single entity that senses, thinks, and remembers. And yet neuroscientists find that the nervous system responsible for your experience consists of an enormous number of separate cells. The brain processes information in **neurons** (NOO-rons), or nerve cells. Many of the neurons in the human nervous system are extremely small; the best current estimate is

that the nervous system contains a little less than 100 billion neurons (Williams & Herrup, 1988), as shown in Figure 3.14. The nervous system also contains another kind of cells called **glia** (GLEE-uh), which support the neurons in many ways without actually transmitting information themselves. The glia are about one-tenth the size of neurons but about 10 times more numerous. Until shortly after the year 1900, many researchers thought it likely that all the neurons physically merged, that the tip of each neuron actually joined the next neuron. We now know that it does not; each neuron remains separate. How do so many separate neurons and glia combine forces to produce the single stream of experiences that is "you"?

The secret is communication. Each neuron receives information and transmits it to other cells by conducting electrochemical impulses. Sensory neurons carry information from the sense organs to the central nervous system; neurons of the central nervous system process that sensory information and compare it to past information; motor neurons convey commands to the muscles and glands. Within the central nervous system, each neuron sends information to many others, which send information to still others; eventually some of those neurons may send information back to the first one. Out of all

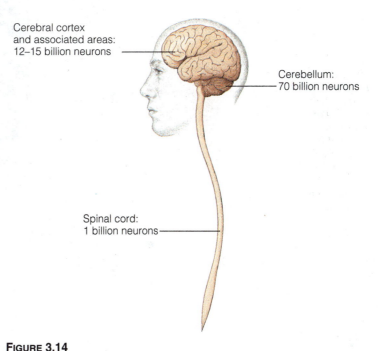

Cerebral cortex and associated areas: 12–15 billion neurons

Cerebellum: 70 billion neurons

Spinal cord: 1 billion neurons

FIGURE 3.14
Distribution of the estimated 83–86 billion neurons in the adult human central nervous system. (Based on data of Williams & Herrup, 1988.)

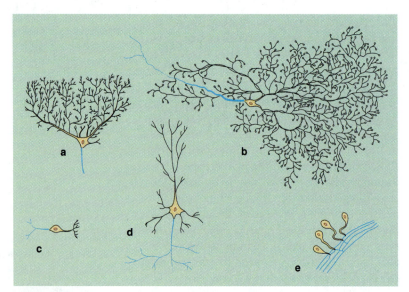

FIGURE 3.15
Neurons vary enormously in their shapes. In each case the neuron consists of its cell body and all the branched attachments, called axons and dendrites. The neurons in (a) and (b) receive input from many sources, the neuron in (c) from only a few sources, and the neuron in (d) from an intermediate number of sources. The neurons in (e) are sensory neurons, which carry messages from sensory receptors to the brain or spinal cord. The axons are coded blue for easy identification. (Part b courtesy of Richard Coss.)

info: excitory or inhibitory
↑ or ↓ the probability that the next
cell will send a message of
its own.

this rapid exchange of information, about 100 billion neurons produce a single functioning system.

To understand the nervous system, we must understand the properties of both the individual neurons and the connections among them. Neurons have a variety of shapes, depending on whether they receive information from a few sources or from many and whether they send impulses over a short distance or over a long distance (Figure 3.15).

A neuron consists of three parts—a cell body, dendrites, and an axon (Figure 3.16). The **cell body** contains the nucleus of the cell. The **dendrites** (from a Greek word meaning "tree") are widely branching structures, usually short; they receive transmissions from other neurons. The **axon** is a single, long, thin, straight fiber with branches near its tip. Some vertebrate axons are covered with *myelin*, an insulating sheath that speeds up the transmission of impulses along an axon. As a rule, an axon transmits information to other cells, and the dendrites or cell body of each other cell receives that information. That information can be either excitatory or inhibitory; that is, it can increase or decrease the probability that the next cell will send a message of its own. Inhibitory messages are important for many purposes. For example,

FIGURE 3.16
The generalized structure of a motor neuron shows the dendrites, the branching structures that receive transmissions from other neurons; and the axon, a single, long, thin, straight fiber with branches near its tip. Axons, which range in length from 1 millimeter to more than 1 meter, carry information toward other cells. (inset) A photomicrograph of a neuron.

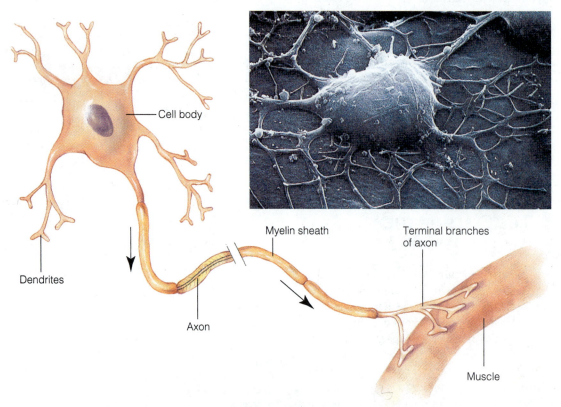

Cell body

Dendrites

Axon

Myelin sheath

Terminal branches of axon

Muscle

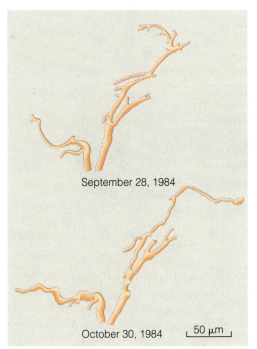

September 28, 1984

October 30, 1984   50 µm

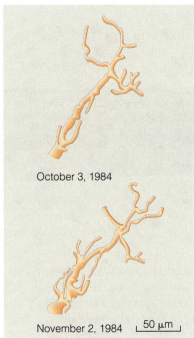

October 3, 1984

November 2, 1984   50 µm

FIGURE 3.17
Dendrites, such as these from rat brains, gradually change their structures. Between one viewing and a second viewing a month later, some branches elongate and others contract. (From Purves & Hadley, 1985.)

Brain does not gain existing neurons but they do grow new branches.

during a period of painful stimulation, your brain has mechanisms to inhibit further sensation of pain.

The structure of the brain, unlike the structure of a computer, is not fixed throughout its life. Although the human brain gains no additional neurons after early infancy, the existing neurons frequently grow new branches of their axons and dendrites and retract other branches (Purves & Hadley, 1985), as shown in Figure 3.17. For example, an enriched social environment leads to increased branching of the dendrites. Rats kept in large cages with other rats and with a variety of objects to explore develop a wider pattern of dendritic branching than do rats kept in individual cages (Camel, Withers, & Greenough, 1986; Greenough, 1975). The increased branching enables each dendrite to integrate information from a greater number of sources.

THE ACTION POTENTIAL

Imagine what would happen if axons conveyed information the same way a wire conducts electricity: Because axons are made of biological materials and not copper wire, the electrical impulses decrease in intensity as they travel along the axon. A pinch on your nose would reach the brain at nearly its full intensity; a pinch on your stomach would feel much weaker and a pinch on your toe

would feel weaker yet. Short people would be able to feel a pinch on the toe more intensely than tall people would.

Instead of transmitting electrical impulses, axons convey information by a special process called an *action potential*, which maintains the impulse at a constant strength, no matter how far it has to travel. The advantage over electrical conduction is that action potentials from distant places like your toes reach the brain at full strength. The disadvantage is that impulses reach your brain more slowly than they would by electrical conduction. Your brain's processing lags almost a tenth of a second behind what is happening to your toes. Fortunately, that delay does not inconvenience you very often.

To explain how the action potential works we start with the resting condition of the axon: Ordinarily, there is an electrical polarization across the membrane (or covering) of an axon, with a negative charge on the inside of the axon. This electrical polarization, called the **resting potential** of the membrane, amounts to about 70 millivolts in a typical cell. It is maintained by the different distributions of sodium and potassium ions across the membrane. A mechanism called the sodium-potassium pump slowly and steadily pulls potassium ions into the cell and simultaneously ejects sodium ions; thus, sodium ions become much more concentrated outside the axon and potassium ions are much more concentrated inside. Now, as

action potential full force all at once.

resting potential — 70 millivolts polarized — covered

negative inside positive outside

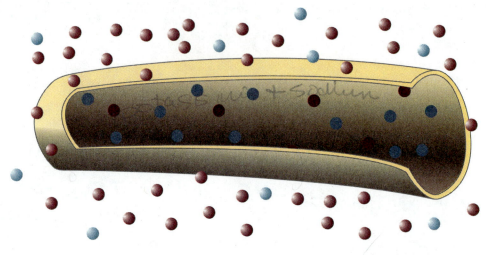

Sodium (handwritten)

Potassium + Sodium (handwritten, on axon)

FIGURE 3.18
When not conveying an action potential, the axon membrane has a resting potential, with the outside being relatively positive and the inside being relatively negative. This difference in electrical potential depends on the distribution of positive ions. The more numerous sodium ions (Na+) are located mostly outside the axon, whereas the less numerous potassium ions (K+) are located mostly inside. Here, red spheres represent sodium; blue spheres represent potassium.

Action potential: (handwritten)
Allow sodium to enter the axon eliminating regions.
potassium gate opens allow to release potassium returning to resting potential

I hope you remember from your chemistry class, both sodium ions and potassium ions have a +1 charge, so you might imagine that the sodium and potassium effects would cancel each other out. However, the body has a great deal more sodium than it has potassium, so the distribution of sodium makes more difference than the distribution of potassium. The net result is that the outside of the axon (where sodium is mostly located) is relatively positive; the inside is relatively negative. (See Figure 3.18.) (Naturally, sodium and potassium are not the only ions present; there are also positively charged calcium, negatively charged chloride, and other types as well. Sodium and potassium are the critical ions for understanding the action potential, however.)

Certain kinds of stimulation can disrupt this stable resting potential and evoke an **action potential,** an event in which sodium gates in the membrane open for just a moment and allow many sodium ions to enter the axon (Figure 3.19). As those sodium ions cross the membrane, they eliminate the negative potential that is usually present inside the cell; in fact, the inside develops an extremely brief positive potential. At that point the sodium gates close; meanwhile potassium gates open to allow enough potassium ions to leave the axon, returning the axon to its original resting potential (Figure 3.20b). Eventually but much more slowly, the sodium-potassium pump brings the potassium ions back in while ejecting the invading sodium ions.

You will recall that I said the axon does not conduct electrical current like a wire. Indeed it does not. The action potential at each point along the axon provides a stimulus to excite the next point along the axon to have its own action potential. You could imagine the process a bit like a fire burning along a string: The fire at each point along the string ignites the next point, which ignites the next point. That is, after sodium ions cross at one point along an axon, the electrical excitation opens channels at the next point along the axon, enabling sodium ions to cross there, as shown in Figure 3.20, and so forth. In this manner, the action potential remains equally strong all the way to the end of the axon.

Now, all of this information is clearly important to investigators of the nervous system, but why is it important to you as a general psychology student? First, it explains why sensations from points on your fingers and toes do not fade away by the time they reach your brain. Second, an understanding of action potentials helps to explain the communication between one neuron and the next. Third, an understanding of action potentials helps to explain the effects of certain drugs. For example, anesthetic drugs (such as Novocaine) silence neurons by clogging

FIGURE 3.19
Ion movements conduct an action potential along an axon. At each point along the membrane, sodium ions enter the axon and alter the distribution of positive and negative charges. As one point along the membrane returns to its original state, the action potential flows to the next point.

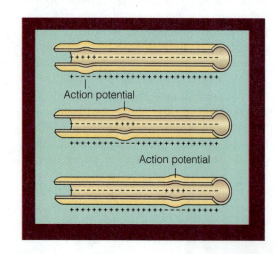

Action potential

Action potential

the sodium gates (van Dyke & Byck, 1982). When your dentist drills a tooth, the receptors in your tooth send out the message "Pain! Pain! Pain!" But that message does not get through to the brain, because a shot of Novocaine has blocked the sodium gates and thereby prevented the sensory axons from sending their message.

CONCEPT CHECK

6. If you stub your toe, do you feel it immediately or is there a delay before you feel it? Why? (Check your answers on page 98.)

SYNAPSES: THE JUNCTIONS BETWEEN NEURONS

Ultimately, each neuron must communicate with other neurons. Communication between one neuron and the next follows a different process from the transmission along an axon. At a **synapse** (SIN-aps), the specialized junction between one neuron and another (Figure 3.21), one neuron releases a chemical that either excites or in-

Communicate through Synapses.

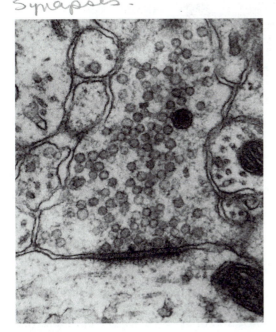

FIGURE 3.21

A synapse, magnified thousands of times in an electron micrograph, includes small round structures in the middle cell called synaptic vesicles, which store neurotransmitter molecules. The thick, dark area at the bottom of the cell is the synapse.

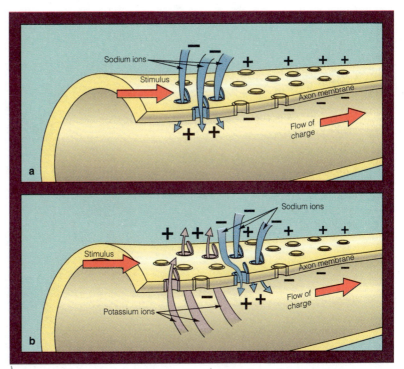

drugs increas or decreas certain kinds of synapses

hibits the next neuron. The events at the synapses are central to everything your brain does, because the synapses are the source of information for the receiving cell. Drugs that affect behavior—ranging from tranquilizers and antidepressants to illegal drugs such as cocaine and LSD—do so by increasing or decreasing the activity at certain kinds of synapses. The following paragraph summarizes the events at a synapse.

A typical axon has several branches; each branch ends with a little bulge called a *presynaptic ending*, or **terminal button** (Figure 3.22). When an action potential reaches the terminal button, it causes the release of molecules of a **neurotransmitter**, a chemical that has been stored in packets called *synaptic vesicles* and elsewhere in the interior of the terminal button (Figure 3.22). Different neurons use different chemicals as their neurotransmitters, but each neuron uses the same chemical or same combination of chemicals at all times and at all branches of its axon (Eccles, 1986). The neurotransmitter molecules then diffuse across a narrow gap called a *synaptic cleft* to the neuron on the receiving end of the synapse, the **postsynaptic neuron**. There the neurotransmitter molecules attach to receptors, which may be located on the neuron's dendrites or cell body or (for special purposes) on the tip of its axon. The

FIGURE 3.20

(a) During an action potential, sodium gates in the neuron membrane open, and sodium ions enter the axon, bringing a positive charge with them. (b) After an action potential occurs at one point along the axon, the sodium gates close at that point and open at the next point along the axon. When the sodium gates close, potassium gates open, and potassium ions flow out of the axon, carrying a positive charge with them. (Modified from Starr & Taggart, 1992.)

Synaptic Vesicles contain neurotransmitters (a chemical)

FIGURE 3.22

The synapse is the junction of the pre-synaptic (message-sending) neuron and the postsynaptic (message-receiving) neuron. At the end of the presynaptic axon is the terminal button, which contains many molecules of the neurotransmitter, ready for release.

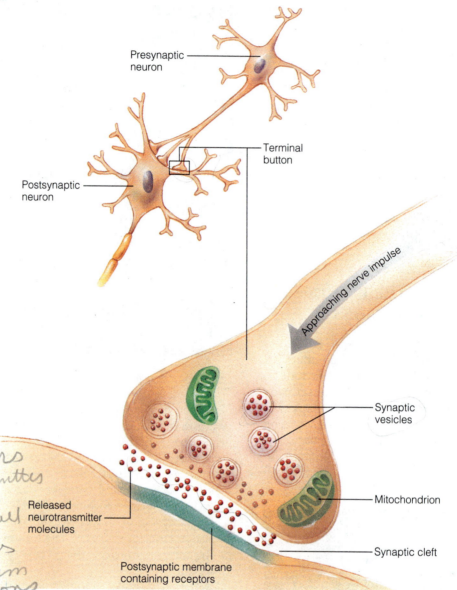

Presynaptic neuron

Terminal button

Postsynaptic neuron

Approaching nerve impulse

Synaptic vesicles

Mitochondrion

Released neurotransmitter molecules

Synaptic cleft

Postsynaptic membrane containing receptors

[Handwritten margin notes:]

Excitation occurs if the neurotransmitter open gates & lets Sodium into the cell

Inhibition occurs if it lets potassium out or lets neg ions in (chloride)

INHibitioN:
① Absence of Excitat
② Active braking process

neural communication process is summarized in Figure 3.23.

Depending on the chemical used as a neurotransmitter and on the type of receptor, the result may be either excitation or inhibition of the neuron. Excitation occurs if the neurotransmitter opens gates to let sodium into the cell; inhibition occurs if it lets potassium out or lets negatively charged chloride in. The postsynaptic neuron may be receiving nearly simultaneous excitation and inhibition from a great many other neurons. It produces an action potential of its own if the total amount of excitation outweighs the total amount of inhibition. That is, positively charged ions may be flowing into the cell at some locations in the cell and out at others, while negatively charged ions are

also flowing one direction or the other. The net effect of all these flows may be to produce action potentials, to decrease the probability of action potentials, or to leave the axon unchanged. This process resembles a decision: When you are trying to decide whether to do something, you weigh all the pros and cons and act if the pros outweigh the cons.

Note that inhibition is not just the absence of excitation; it is an active braking process. For example, when a pinch on your foot causes you to raise it by contracting one set of muscles, inhibitory synapses in your spinal cord block activity in the opposing set of muscles, those that would move your leg the opposite direction. Those inhibitory synapses prevent your spinal cord from

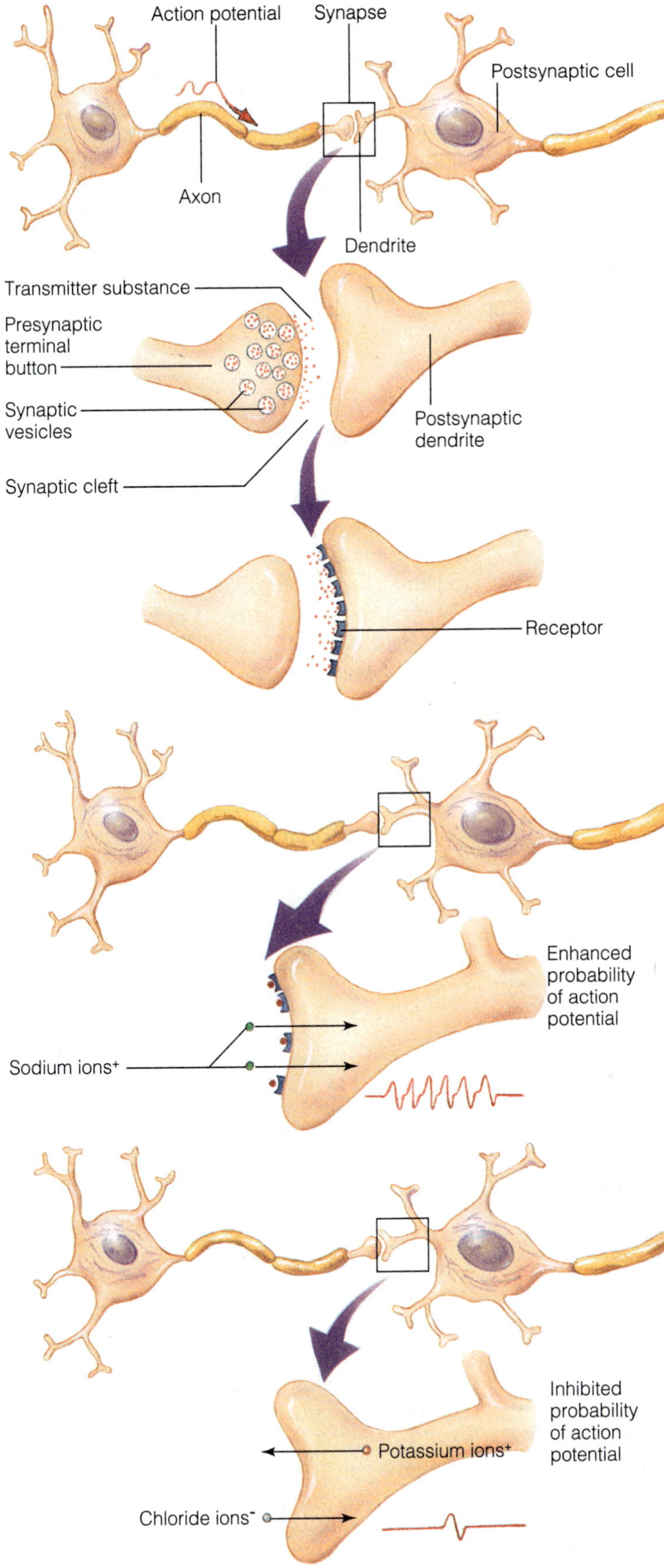

Action potential
Synapse
Postsynaptic cell
Axon
Axon
Dendrite

Action potential travels down the axon toward the synapse.

Transmitter substance
Presynaptic terminal button
Synaptic vesicles
Synaptic cleft
Postsynaptic dendrite

At the synapse, the transmitter substance is released.

Receptor

The transmitter crosses the synaptic cleft, where it binds to the receptors on the surface of the postsynaptic cell, usually on its dendrites, though not necessarily.

Enhanced probability of action potential

Sodium ions+

If binding of the transmitter to the receptor cell causes positively charged sodium ions to enter the cell, that cell will produce more action potentials. This is an *excitatory synapse*.

Inhibited probability of action potential

Potassium ions+

Chloride ions−

If binding of the transmitter to the receptor cell causes positively charged potassium ions to leave the cell or negatively charged chloride ions to enter the cell, that cell will produce fewer action potentials. This is an *inhibitory synapse*.

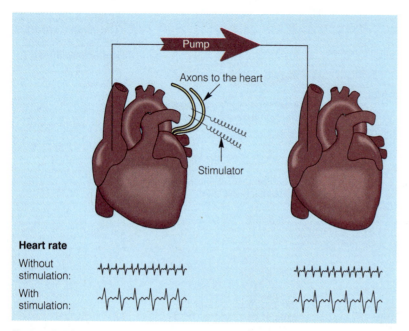

Heart rate

Without
stimulation:

With
stimulation:

FIGURE 3.24
Otto Loewi demonstrated that axons release chemicals that can affect other cells. Using a frog, he electrically stimulated a set of axons known to decrease the heart rate. Then he collected some fluid from around that heart and transferred it to the surface of another frog's heart. When that heart slowed its beat, Loewi concluded that the axons of the first heart must have released a chemical that slows the heart rate.

sending messages to raise your leg and extend it at the same time.

CONCEPT CHECKS

7. *As mentioned earlier, under some conditions the axons and dendrites of a neuron increase their branching. How will that affect the number of synapses?*
8. *Norepinephrine is a neurotransmitter that inhibits postsynaptic neurons. If a drug were injected that prevents norepinephrine from attaching to its receptors, what would happen to the postsynaptic neuron? (Check your answers on page 98.)*

WHAT'S THE EVIDENCE?

Neurons Communicate by Releasing Chemicals

I have just finished telling you that neurons communicate by releasing chemicals at synapses. Perhaps you are perfectly content to take my word for it and go on with something else. Still, it is good to pause and contemplate the evidence responsible for an important conclusion.

Today, neuroscientists have a wealth of evidence that neurons release chemicals at synapses. They can work with radioactively labeled chemicals that enable investigators to

trace where chemicals go and what happens when they get there; they also can inject purified chemicals at a synapse and use extremely fine electrodes to measure the response of the postsynaptic neuron. But scientists have known since the 1920s that neurons communicate by releasing chemicals; at that time they had none of the fancy equipment they have today. Otto Loewi found evidence of chemical transmission by a very simple, clever experiment, as he later described in his autobiography (Loewi, 1960).

Hypothesis If a neuron releases chemicals, an investigator should be able to collect some of those chemicals and transfer them from one animal to another and thereby get the second animal to do what the first animal had been doing. Loewi had no way to collect chemicals released within the brain itself, so he worked with axons communicating with the heart muscle. (Much later research confirmed, as Loewi suspected, that the communication between a neuron and a muscle is similar to that between two neurons.)

Method Loewi began by electrically stimulating some axons connected to a frog's heart. These particular axons slowed down the heart rate. As he continued stimulating those axons, he collected some of the fluid on and around that heart and transferred it to the heart of a second frog.

Results When Loewi transferred the fluid from the first frog's heart, the second frog's heart rate slowed down also (Figure 3.24).

Interpretation Evidently the stimulated axons had released some chemical that slows heart rate. At least in this case, neurons send messages by releasing chemicals.

This experiment was remarkably clever; indeed, Loewi eventually won a Nobel Prize in physiology for this and related experiments. Even outstanding experiments have limitations, however. In this case, the main limitation was the uncertainty about whether the conclusion applied only to frog hearts or whether it applied to all communication by neurons. Answering *that* question required enormous efforts and much more elaborate equipment. (The answer is that *almost* all communication by neurons depends on the release of chemicals. A few exceptional neurons communicate electrically.)

TABLE 3.1
Important Neurotransmitters and Some of Their Functions

NEUROTRANSMITTER	BEHAVIORAL CONSEQUENCES OF NEUROTRANSMITTER EXCESS	BEHAVIORAL CONSEQUENCES OF NEUROTRANSMITTER DEFICIT	COMMENTS
Acetylcholine	Muscle paralysis or convulsions, sometimes death	Memory impairment	Acetylcholine is also released at the junction between motor neuron and muscle.
Dopamine	Involuntary movements; schizophrenia?	Impaired movement (Parkinson's disease); memory impairment; depression?	The brain has several dopamine paths. Some are important for movement; others for thought and emotion.
Norepinephrine	Autonomic arousal; anxiety; symptoms resembling schizophrenia	Memory impairment; depression?	Several transmitters contribute to depression in complex ways not yet understood.
Serotonin	?	Increased aggressive behavior; sleeplessness; depression?	Serotonin synapses are disrupted or damaged by LSD, ecstasy, and several other abused drugs.
GABA (gamma-amino-butyric acid)	?	Anxiety	Tranquilizers facilitate GABA synapses and thereby reduce anxiety.
Glutamate; glycine; other amino acids	Various, including cell death	Various	The most abundant transmitters in the central nervous system; their functions are diverse.
Endorphins	Inhibition of pain	Increased pain	The effects of endorphins are partly mimicked by morphine, heroin, and other opiates.
Neuropeptides	Various	Various	These are small chains of amino acids. The brain uses many neuropeptides; their functions vary and remain mostly unknown.

Sources: Kalat, 1995; Spring, Chiodo, & Bowen, 1987.

THE ROLE OF DIFFERENT NEUROTRANSMITTERS IN BEHAVIOR

Different neurons release different chemicals as their neurotransmitters; dozens of chemicals serve as neurotransmitters at one location or another, each playing a distinct role in the control of behavior (Snyder, 1984). Table 3.1 summarizes a few of the major transmitters and some of their known functions; however, this table barely hints at the diversity of effects. The major transmitters affect several different types of receptor, and each type of receptor has different effects on behavior. For example, certain serotonin receptors affect mood and movement. Others affect nausea; a drug such as Zofran® that blocks just the latter type of receptors can reduce nausea without otherwise impairing experience or behavior.

Because different transmitters control different aspects of behavior, an excess or a deficit of a particular transmitter or of its receptor can produce a specific impairment of some aspect of behavior. Such imbalances may be caused by genetic factors, by brain damage, by drugs, and even by changes in the amount of some ingredient in a person's diet.

One example of a behavioral disorder related to a particular neurotransmitter is **Parkinson's disease,** a condition that affects many elderly people. Its main symptoms are difficulty in initiating voluntary movement, slowness of movement, tremors, and depressed mood. Without medical treatment, Parkinson's disease generally grows worse and worse as time passes, until the person dies.

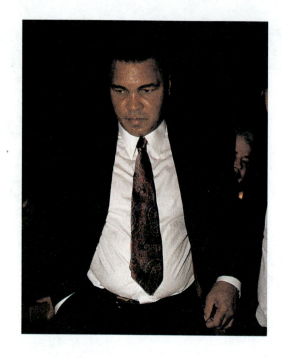

Former heavyweight boxing champion Muhammad Ali suffers from symptoms similar to those of Parkinson's disease. The disease itself is caused by the loss of a set of axons that release dopamine as their neurotransmitter.

In Parkinson's disease one set of neurons gradually die (Figure 3.25). Those neurons give rise to a path of axons that all use the same neurotransmitter, a chemical known as **dopamine** (DOPE-uh-meen), which promotes activity levels and facilitates movement. One way to treat Parkinson's disease is the drug *deprenyl,* which slows the loss of neurons (Tetrud & Langston, 1989). Another treatment is to furnish the damaged brain area with extra dopamine. Dopamine, like many other chemicals, cannot cross directly from the blood into the brain. But another chemical, L-dopa, taken in the form of pills, can enter the blood and cross into the brain, where it is converted into dopamine. Although the L-dopa does not prevent the continuing loss of neurons, it reduces the symptoms of the disease and gives the victim additional years of normal, active life.

Some additional treatments currently in the experimental stage may become useful in the future. One approach is to implant dopamine-containing neurons from the brain of a human fetus. However, that approach faces not only the ethical difficulties of dealing with aborted fetuses, but also serious practical and scientific problems (Freed et al., 1992; Spencer et al., 1992). Another experimental approach is to inject certain chemicals that promote the survival and growth of the remaining neurons in the damaged brain area (Tomac et al., 1995). That approach appears promising, but needs much additional research.

Although the cause of Parkinson's disease probably differs from one case to another, one possible cause is exposure to toxic substances. In 1982 several young adults (ages 22–42) developed Parkinson's disease after using illegal drugs that they had all bought from the same dealer. Investigators eventually identified the drug as a mixture of two chemicals known as MPPP and MPTP. L-dopa reduced the symptoms for these people, as it does for more typical Parkinson's patients. Experiments with animals disclosed that MPTP causes damage to the *substantia nigra,* the same part of the brain known to be damaged in Parkinson's disease (Chiueh, 1988).

FIGURE 3.25
In Parkinson's disease, one path of axons from the substantia nigra *gradually dies. Patients can gain years of active life by taking a chemical called L-dopa, which is converted to the neurotransmitter dopamine in the brain.*

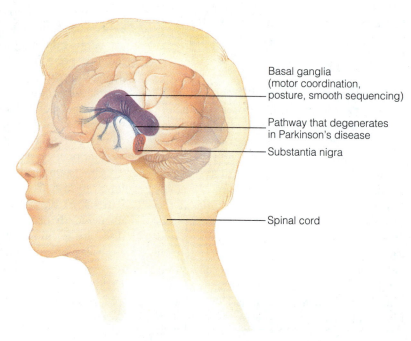

Basal ganglia (motor coordination, posture, smooth sequencing)

Pathway that degenerates in Parkinson's disease

Substantia nigra

Spinal cord

9. People suffering from certain disorders are given haloperidol, a drug that blocks activity at dopamine synapses. How would haloperidol affect a person suffering from Parkinson's disease? (Check your answer on page 98.)

CHEMICAL INTERFERENCE WITH THE FUNCTIONING OF NEURONS

Many factors can interfere with the healthy functioning of neurons. One is a lack of adequate vitamin B_1 (thiamine), a substance abundant in yeast, grain, beans, peas, liver, and pork. Although most other organs of the body can use a variety of fuels, most cells in the brain use only **glucose** (GLOO-kose), a sugar. However, for the brain to use glucose, it must have an adequate supply of vitamin B_1. If a person's diet is deficient in that vitamin over a period of weeks, parts of the brain deteriorate or die, and other parts function below their normal capacity. Vitamin B_1 deficiency is common among severe alcoholics and causes some of them gradually to develop *Korsakoff's syndrome*, a kind of brain damage that produces severe memory loss.

A number of drugs can interfere with the activity of a particular type of synapse. Common-cold remedies, for example, decrease the flow of sinus fluids by blocking acetylcholine synapses and stimulating norepinephrine synapses. Because the same neurotransmitters are used at other synapses as well, cold remedies have the side effects of increasing heart rate, decreasing salivation, and impeding sexual arousal.

Lysergic acid diethylamide (LSD) and most other hallucinogenic drugs (drugs that cause hallucinations) also are believed to act on the synapses. LSD is chemically similar to the neurotransmitter **serotonin,** which plays an important role in mood changes. LSD stimulates one of several kind of serotonin synapses (Jacobs, 1987). Mescaline (the active substance in peyote), "angel dust," "ecstasy," and other hallucinogenic drugs also stimulate or block serotonin synapses and other kinds of synapses. Heroin and morphine stimulate the synapses that normally respond to **endorphins** (en-DOR-fins), neurotransmitters that inhibit the sensation of pain. The active chemicals in marijuana stimulate synapses responsive to the neurotransmitter *anandamide,* which was first discovered in the 1990s; the behavioral functions of that transmitter are still unknown (Devane et al., 1992). We shall consider drugs and their effects in more detail in Chapter 5.

10. One way in which society could prevent Korsakoff's syndrome would be to prevent alcoholism. What would be another way? (Check your answer on page 98.)

SUMMARY

- *Neuron structure.* A neuron, or nerve cell, consists of a cell body, dendrites, and an axon. The axon conveys information to other neurons, where it is received by the dendrites or cell body or occasionally by another axon. (page 88)

- *Changes in neuron structure.* The branching of a neuron's axon and dendrites changes over time as a result of experience. (page 89)

- *The action potential.* Information is conveyed along an axon by an action potential, which is regenerated without loss of strength at each point along the axon. (page 89)

- *Mechanism of the action potential.* An action potential depends on the entry of sodium into the axon. Anything blocking that flow will block the action potential. (page 89)

- *How neurons communicate.* A neuron communicates with another neuron by releasing a chemical called a neurotransmitter at a specialized junction called a synapse. A neurotransmitter can either excite or inhibit the next neuron. (page 91)

- *Neurotransmitters and behavioral disorders.* An excess or a deficit of a particular neurotransmitter may lead to abnormal behavior, such as Parkinson's disease. (page 95)

- *Chemical impairment of neuronal activity.* The functioning of neurons may be impaired by a deficit of vitamin B_1 or by certain chemicals that resemble neurotransmitters. (page 97)

SUGGESTIONS FOR FURTHER READING

Kalat, J. W. (1995). *Biological psychology* (5th ed.). Pacific Grove, CA: Brooks/Cole. Chapters 1 through 5 deal with the material discussed in this chapter, but in more detail.

Levitan, I. B., & Kaczmarek, L. K. (1991). *The neuron.* New York: Oxford University Press. For those who want a lot more information about neurons and synapses.

TERMS

reductionism the attempt to explain complex phenomena by reducing them to combinations of simpler components (page 87)

neuron a cell of the nervous system that receives information and transmits it to other cells by conducting electrochemical impulses (page 87)

glia a cell of the nervous system that insulates neurons, removes waste materials (such as dead cells), and performs other supportive functions (page 87)

cell body the part of the neuron that contains the nucleus of the cell (page 88)

dendrite one of the widely branching structures of a neuron that receive transmissions from other neurons (page 88)

axon a single long, thin, straight fiber that transmits information from a neuron to other neurons or to muscle cells (page 88)

resting potential electrical polarization that ordinarily occurs across the membrane of an axon that is not undergoing an action potential (page 89)

action potential a sudden decrease or reversal in electrical charge across the membrane (or covering) of an axon (page 90)

synapse the specialized junction between one neuron and another at which one neuron releases a neurotransmitter, which either excites or inhibits the next neuron (page 91)

terminal button a bulge at the end of an axon from which the axon releases a chemical called a neurotransmitter (page 91)

neurotransmitter a chemical that is stored in the terminal of an axon and periodically released at a synapse (page 91)

postsynaptic neuron a neuron on the receiving end of a synapse (page 91)

Parkinson's disease a behavioral disorder caused by the deterioration of a path of axons, characterized by difficulty in initiating voluntary movement (page 95)

dopamine a neurotransmitter that promotes activity levels and facilitates movement (page 96)

glucose a sugar, the main source of nutrition for the brain (page 97)

lysergic acid diethylamide (LSD) a chemical that can affect the brain, sometimes producing hallucinations (page 97)

serotonin a neurotransmitter that plays an important role in sleep and mood changes (page 97)

endorphin a neurotransmitter that inhibits the sensation of pain (page 97)

ANSWERS TO CONCEPT CHECKS

6. You will not feel the pain immediately because the action potential must travel from your foot to your brain. (If the action potential travels at, say, 10 meters per second and your toe is about 2 meters from your brain, you will feel the pain about 0.2 seconds after you stub your toe.) (page 91)

7. Increased branching of the axons and dendrites will increase the number of synapses. (page 94)

8. Under the influence of a drug that prevents norepinephrine from attaching to its receptors, the postsynaptic neuron will receive less inhibition than usual. If we presume that the neuron continues to receive a certain amount of excitation, it will produce action potentials more frequently than usual. (page 94)

9. Haloperidol would increase the severity of Parkinson's disease. In fact, large doses of haloperidol can induce symptoms of Parkinson's disease in anyone. (page 97)

10. Another way to prevent Korsakoff's syndrome would be to require all alcoholic beverages to be fortified with vitamin B_1. (page 97)

EXPLANATIONS OF BEHAVIOR AT THE LEVEL OF THE NERVOUS SYSTEM

Does a person who loses part of the brain also lose part of the mind?

Why should psychologists care about the organization of the brain and the effects of brain damage? They have at least two reasons, one practical and one theoretical.

The practical reason is that they need to distinguish between people who act strangely because they have had bad experiences and people who act strangely because they have a brain disorder. To do so, one has to know how brain damage affects behavior.

The theoretical reason is simply that the study of brain damage helps to explain the organization of behavior. In some manner or another, behavior must be made up of component parts. But what are those parts? Is behavior composed of ideas? Sensations? Movements? Personality characteristics? And how do the various components combine to produce the overall behavior and experience? One way to answer such questions is to examine the effects of brain damage.

A SURVEY OF THE NERVOUS SYSTEM

Psychologists and biologists distinguish between the central nervous system and the peripheral nervous system. The **central nervous**

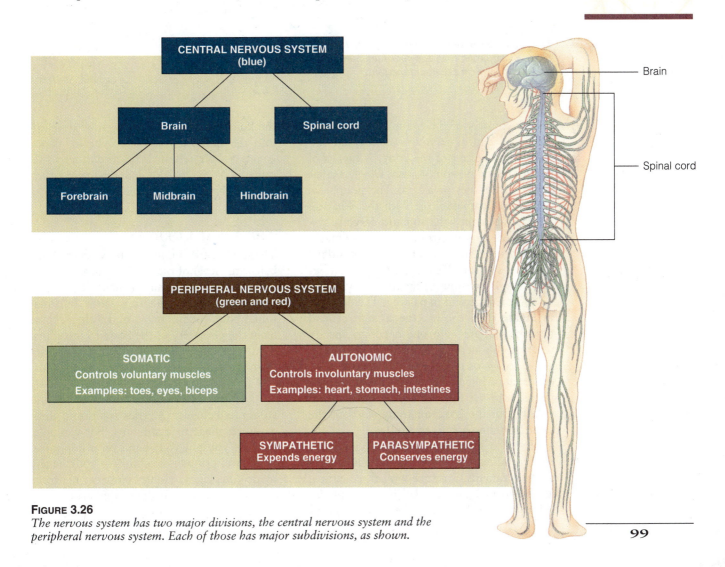

FIGURE 3.26
The nervous system has two major divisions, the central nervous system and the peripheral nervous system. Each of those has major subdivisions, as shown.

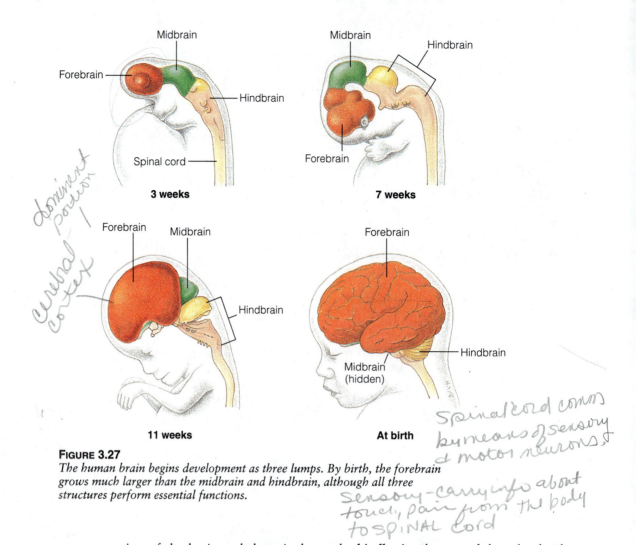

FIGURE 3.27

The human brain begins development as three lumps. By birth, the forebrain grows much larger than the midbrain and hindbrain, although all three structures perform essential functions.

system consists of the brain and the spinal cord. The central nervous system communicates with the rest of the body by means of the **peripheral nervous system,** which is composed of bundles of axons. The peripheral nerves that communicate with the skin and muscles are called the **somatic nervous system.** Those that control the heart, stomach, and other organs are called the **autonomic nervous system.** Figure 3.26 summarizes these major divisions of the nervous system.

(Just a comment in passing: The drawing in Figure 3.26 shows "the human central nervous system." No one needs to specify whether this nervous system is male or female, young or old, Asian or African, well-educated or ill-educated. How different people learn to use their nervous systems varies greatly, but the gross anatomy is about the same from one person to another.)

Early in its embryological development, the central nervous system of vertebrates, including humans, is a tube with three lumps, as shown in Figure 3.27. Those lumps develop into the **forebrain,** the **midbrain,** and

the **hindbrain;** the rest of the tube develops into the spinal cord. The forebrain, which contains the cerebral cortex and other structures, is by far the dominant portion of the brain in mammals, especially humans.

THE SPINAL CORD

The **spinal cord** communicates with the body below the level of the head by means of sensory neurons and motor neurons (Figure 3.28). The **sensory neurons** carry information about touch, pain, and other senses from the periphery of the body to the spinal cord. The **motor neurons** transmit impulses from the central nervous system to the muscles and glands.

The spinal cord serves both reflexive and voluntary behavior. A **reflex** is a rapid, automatic response to a stimulus. For example, suppose you put your hand on a hot stove. Stimulation of pain receptors in your fingers sends messages along sensory neurons; within the spinal cord these neurons send messages via interneurons to motor neurons,

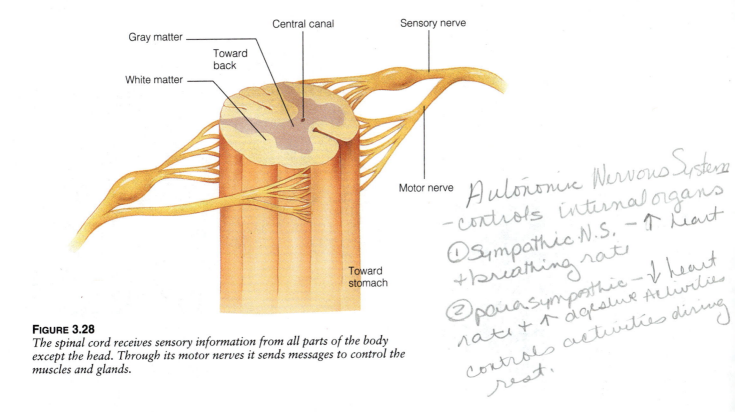

Gray matter
Central canal
Sensory nerve
Toward back
White matter
Motor nerve
Toward stomach

FIGURE 3.28
The spinal cord receives sensory information from all parts of the body except the head. Through its motor nerves it sends messages to control the muscles and glands.

which send impulses to the muscles that jerk your hand away from the hot stove.

The spinal cord is also necessary for voluntary behaviors. Every command to walk, talk, or make any other movement requires a message from the brain to the spinal cord, and from the spinal cord to the muscles. People who have suffered damage to the spinal cord lose some part of their muscle control. For example, after damage in the lower part of the spinal cord, a person cannot get messages from the brain to the bottom of the spinal cord, which controls leg movements as well as bowel and bladder functions. After damage to a higher part of the spinal cord, the person would also lose control of the arm muscles.

THE AUTONOMIC NERVOUS SYSTEM

The autonomic nervous system, closely associated with the spinal cord, controls the internal organs such as the heart. The term *autonomic* means involuntary or automatic. The autonomic nervous system is partly, though not entirely, automatic. We are generally not aware of its activity, although it does receive information from, and send information to, the brain and spinal cord.

The autonomic nervous system consists of two parts: (1) The *sympathetic nervous*

system, controlled by a chain of neurons lying just outside the spinal cord, increases heart rate and breathing rate and readies the body for vigorous "fight or flight" activities. (2) The *parasympathetic nervous system,* controlled by neurons in the very top and very bottom levels of the spinal cord, decreases heart rate, increases digestive activities, and in general promotes the body's activities that take place during rest (Figure 3.29). We shall return to this topic in more detail in the chapter about emotions (Chapter 12).

THE ENDOCRINE SYSTEM

Although the endocrine system is not part of the nervous system, it is closely related to it, especially to the autonomic nervous system. The **endocrine system** is a set of glands that produce hormones and release them into the blood. Figure 3.30 shows some of the major endocrine glands.

Hormones are chemicals released by certain glands and conveyed by the blood to other parts of the body, where they alter activity. They are similar to neurotransmitters in that both affect the nervous system. The same chemical may be used both as a hormone and as a neurotransmitter. The difference is that when a chemical is used as a

Sympathetic system	Parasympathetic system
uses much energy	conserves energy
Pupils open	Pupils constrict
Saliva decreases	Saliva flows
Pulse quickens	Pulse slows
Sweat increases	
Stomach less active	Stomach churns
Epinephrine (adrenaline) secreted	

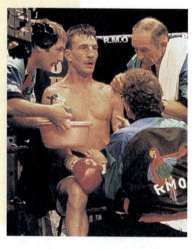

FIGURE 3.29

The sympathetic nervous system prepares the body for brief bouts of vigorous activity; the parasympathetic nervous system promotes digestion and other nonemergency functions. Although both systems are active at all times, the balance may shift from predominance of one to predominance of the other.

neurotransmitter, it is released immediately adjacent to the cell that it is to excite or inhibit. When it is used as a hormone, it is released into the blood, which diffuses it throughout the body.

Hormones can control effects that last from minutes (such as changes in blood pressure) to months (such as preparation for migration in birds). Some hormonal effects are nearly permanent. For example, the amount of the male sex hormone testosterone present during prenatal development determines whether one develops a penis and scrotum or a clitoris and labia.

CONCEPT CHECK

11. Just after a meal, the pancreas produces increased amounts of the hormone insulin, which increases the conversion of the digested food into fats in many cells throughout the body. In what way is a hormone more effective for this purpose than a neurotransmitter would be? (Check your answer on page 119.)

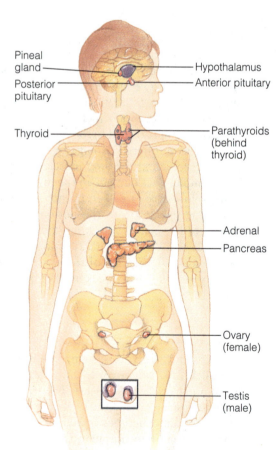

FIGURE 3.30

Glands in the endocrine system produce hormones and release them into the blood.

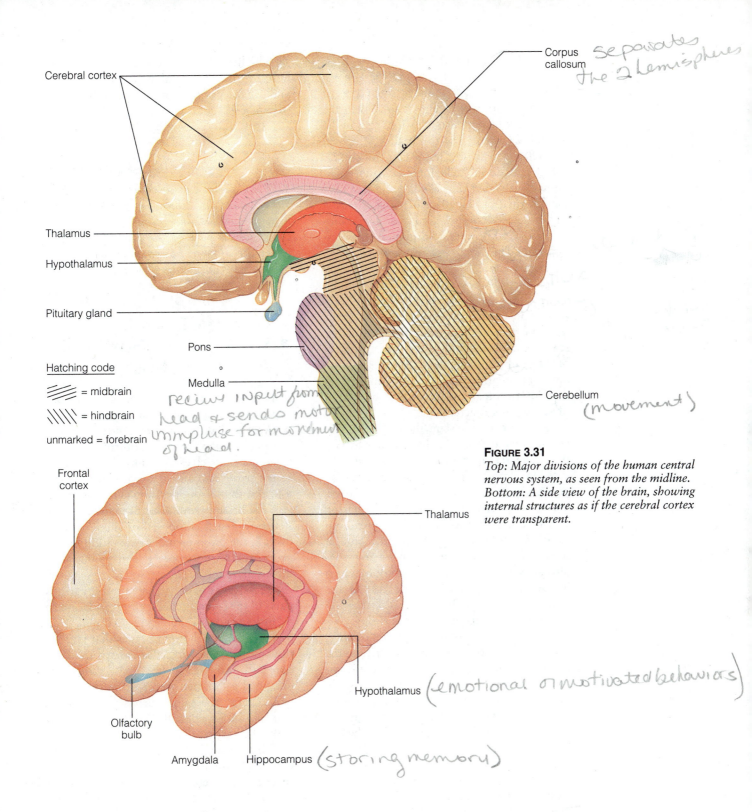

Cerebral cortex

Thalamus

Hypothalamus

Pituitary gland

Pons

Hatching code

⬚ = midbrain

⬚ = hindbrain

unmarked = forebrain

Medulla

Corpus callosum *separates the 2 hemispheres*

Cerebellum *(movement)*

recieves input from head & sends motor impulse for movement of head.

FIGURE 3.31
Top: Major divisions of the human central nervous system, as seen from the midline. Bottom: A side view of the brain, showing internal structures as if the cerebral cortex were transparent.

Frontal cortex

Thalamus

Hypothalamus *(emotional or motivated behaviors)*

Olfactory bulb

Amygdala

Hippocampus *(storing memory)*

BETWEEN THE SPINAL CORD AND THE CEREBRAL CORTEX

Beyond the spinal cord, we find the hindbrain, the midbrain, the subcortical areas of the forebrain, and finally the cerebral cortex. (See Figure 3.31.) Information passing between the spinal cord and the cerebral cortex (in either direction) travels through other structures on the way. In some cases that route is simple. For example, the primary motor area of the cerebral cortex sends axons that simply pass through other structures until they reach the spinal cord, where they form synapses with cells that control the muscles. In other cases, the route is complex. For example, when you feel something with your fingers, the axons from your touch receptors send information to the spinal cord, which relays it to cells in the medulla (part of the hindbrain), which relay it to cells in the midbrain, which in turn relay it to cells in the thalamus (part of the forebrain), which in turn relay it to an area in the cerebral cortex. When I mention "relaying" information, I do not mean that the cells literally just take the information and pass it along. At each stage, the cells combine and contrast this information with other information, processing it and changing it in various ways.

Furthermore, structures along the way have functions of their own. The **medulla** and **pons,** structures located in the hindbrain (Figure 3.31), receive sensory input from the head (taste, hearing, touch sensations on the scalp) and send impulses for motor control of the head (for example, chewing, swallowing, and breathing). They also send axons that control breathing, heart rate, and other life-preserving functions.

activated by any sensory stimulus

An important system that originates in the medulla and pons is the **reticular formation.** The reticular formation can be activated by almost any sensory stimulus; it also generates spontaneous activity of its own. When activated, the reticular formation sends messages via its axons that spread out to areas throughout the forebrain. Thus it serves a function of arousal; almost any stimulus activates the reticular formation, which in turn activates much of the rest of the brain. Damage to the reticular formation leaves an individual inactive and sleepy.

The **cerebellum** (Latin for "little brain"), another part of the hindbrain, is active in the control of movement, especially for complex, rapid motor skills, such as playing the piano or dribbling a basketball. A person who suffers damage to the cerebellum can still make muscular movements, but has to plan each series of movements slowly, one at a time, instead of executing them in a smooth sequence. Such a person has difficulty walking a straight line and speaks haltingly, slurring the words. (Words have to be planned as units; you cannot speak a word clearly by pronouncing one sound at a time.)

In later chapters we shall return to some of the subcortical areas of the forebrain shown in Figure 3.31. The hippocampus is important for storing memories; people with damage to the hippocampus can remember most of what happened before the damage but little of what happened after it (Chapter 7). The hypothalamus makes critical contributions to eating, drinking, sexual behavior, and other emotional or motivated behaviors (Chapter 11).

CONCEPT CHECK

12. People who have become intoxicated by alcohol have slow, slurred speech and cannot walk a straight line. From these observations, which part of the brain would you guess the alcohol has impaired the most? (Check your answer on page 119.)

HOW THE BRAIN DOESN'T WORK . . . AND HOW IT APPARENTLY DOES

Somehow, the brain is responsible for all our experiences and all our actions. When we try to explain how this process happens, we immediately come upon a problem: We each experience ourselves as a unity. That is, there seems to be just one "I" who sees, hears, touches, thinks, decides, and acts. Nevertheless, the brain is composed of many separate structures, each composed of substructures; overall, the brain includes tens of billions of neurons. How does one "I" emerge out of all these separate voices?

A naive answer is that all the various parts of the brain funnel their information to a "little person in the head" who puts it all together. Although no one takes that idea seriously, the underlying idea is hard to abandon and brain researchers have sometimes imagined a "master area" of the brain that would serve the same purpose as the little person—integrating all the information and making decisions.

That master area, if there is such a thing, would presumably be part of the cerebral cortex. The **cerebral cortex** is the outer surface of the forebrain, in humans constituting about 90% of the total brain. The cerebral cortex consists of two **hemispheres,** the left and the right (Figure 3.32). Each hemisphere is responsible for sensation and motor control on the opposite side of the body. (Why the reversal? Why does each hemisphere control the opposite side instead of its own side? Frankly, no one knows.) You have probably heard people talk about "having a lot of gray matter." The cerebral cortex in the forebrain

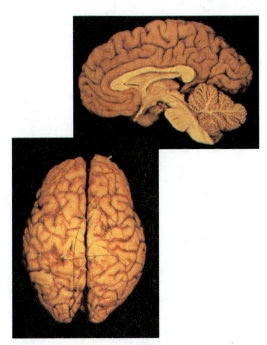

FIGURE 3.32

The human cerebral cortex: (bottom) left and right hemispheres; (top) inside view of a complete hemisphere. The folds greatly extend its surface area.

is that *gray matter*; it contains a great many cell bodies, which are grayer than the axons. The interior of the forebrain beneath the cerebral cortex contains large numbers of axons, many of them covered with *myelin,* a white insulation. You can see areas of gray matter and white matter in Figure 3.33.

How does the cerebral cortex work, and does some part of it function as a "master area" or "central processor"? Here is one idea of how the brain works, an idea that was popular in the early 20th century (with indications of which parts were based on fact and which parts were just guesswork):

- *(Fact):* Sensory information enters the nervous system through well-defined pathways, such as the optic nerves and the auditory nerves. (See Figure 3.34a.)
- *(Fact):* The sensory nerves send their information to subcortical areas of the nervous system, which relay the information to the cerebral cortex. Different areas of the cerebral cortex receive different kinds of sensory information. (See Figure 3.34b.)
- *(Guess):* The various sensory areas of the cortex feed their information into one or more "association areas" that compare different kinds of sensory information, combine

it with memories and motivations, and decide what to do. (See Figure 3.34c.)
- *(Fact):* The sensory or association areas somehow pass on their information to the motor areas of the brain, which send messages to the medulla and spinal cord, which in turn send messages to control the activity of the muscles and glands. (See Figure 3.34d.)

That guess about combining all the information in association areas certainly sounds reasonable; it corresponds to our common-sense notion that we perceive something, think about it, and then act. However, the research over the last half of the 20th century has failed to find any "think-about-it" area. Brain researchers have sometimes designated certain cortical areas as "association cortex," but those association areas are really additional sensory areas (Diamond, 1983; Van Hoesen, 1993). That is, the visual-association areas elaborate visual information, auditory-association areas elaborate auditory information, and so forth. Researchers find few neurons that receive a combination of visual and auditory information or visual and touch information. Apparently the sensory information does *not* all funnel into one central processor in the cerebral cortex.

The fact that the information fails to funnel into one area raises some puzzling questions. You will recall that I said in the introduction to this chapter that many of the questions brain researchers find unanswerable today are questions they would not have known to ask a few years ago. One of those questions is how we detect a similarity between what we see and what we hear, or between what we see and what we touch. Even newborn infants can do so (Kaye & Bower,

Sensory info doesn't funnel into 1 central processor

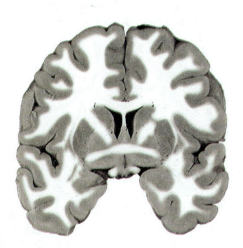

FIGURE 3.33

This cross section through a human brain shows the distinction between gray matter (composed mostly of cell bodies and dendrites) and white matter (composed almost entirely of axons). Myelin, a fatty sheath that surrounds many axons, provides the whiteness of the white matter.

FIGURE 3.34

According to a once popular but now obsolete idea of how the brain works, (a) sensory information coming from sensory receptors enters into the central nervous system, (b) subcortical areas relay this information to the primary sensory areas of the cerebral cortex, (c) the primary sensory areas funnel their information into association areas that think about it, and (d) the association areas send information to the motor areas of the cortex, which prompt appropriate muscle movements. The error in this scheme pertains to part (c): The primary sensory areas do not, in fact, funnel their information into any one location. Different sensory systems operate independently and in parallel.

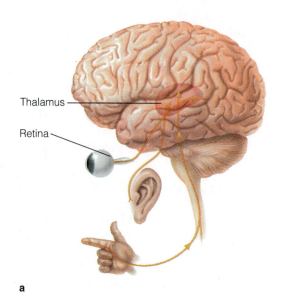

a

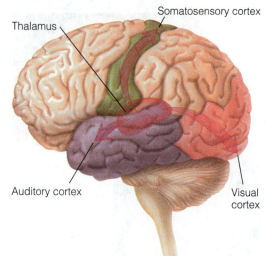

b

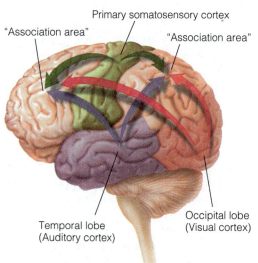

c

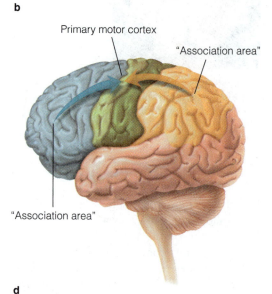

d

1994). That ability may depend on cells in subcortical areas of the brain; it would be hard to explain from what we know about the cerebral cortex.

If the brain does not work by funneling all of its information into one area, how then does it work? A famous psychologist named Karl Lashley (1929, 1950) suggested that the cerebral cortex operates as a whole. Lashley was not interested in explaining consciousness or why we experience ourselves as a unity instead of many separate voices. Still, his proposal must have appealed to those who were interested in such issues; if the brain operates as a whole, then information does not have to funnel into one spot within the brain. Lashley proposed that every important behavioral function depends on all brain areas more or less equally.

Lashley, alas, was wrong. He concluded that all parts of the brain contribute about equally to behavior only because he examined some very complicated behaviors, such as rats' maze learning. (Learning the way through a maze might sound to you like a fairly simple behavior. It did to Lashley, too. In fact, it requires a complicated combination of visual information, touch, smell, detection of body position, and so forth.)

Today, brain researchers find that the brain does not operate as an undifferentiated whole; tiny areas within the brain make very specific contributions to behavior. If you lose a small part of your brain, you will lose a part of your capacity for behavior and experience. We shall examine some examples of brain damage and the specialized deficits that result. The overall picture that emerges of brain functioning is that the brain consists of a great many separate pathways or modules, each acting in parallel with the others. Overall behavior emerges from these parallel

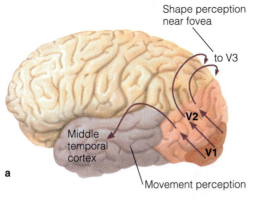

Shape perception near fovea

to V3

V2

V1

Middle temporal cortex

Movement perception

a

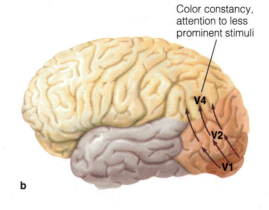

Color constancy, attention to less prominent stimuli

V4

V2

V1

b

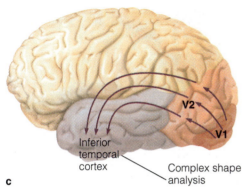

V2

V1

Inferior temporal cortex

Complex shape analysis

c

FIGURE 3.35

Three major visual pathways in the cerebral cortex: One path is responsible for movement perception (a); a second path deals with color and brightness (b); the third path provides analysis of complex shapes (c). Because the three paths are largely independent of one another, brain damage can impair one aspect of visual perception without blocking the others.

paths much as the behavior of a society emerges from the independent actions of many separate members.

EFFECTS OF LOCALIZED BRAIN DAMAGE: VISUAL SYSTEM

I have told you the mysterious fact that the visual, auditory, and other systems of the brain operate almost independently of one another. The mystery deepens: Even within a given system, such as vision, the brain processes different aspects of the stimulus separately and in parallel. Figure 3.35 illustrates three major pathways in the visual areas of the human cerebral cortex. All three pathways begin in the *primary visual cortex,* designated here as "V1" (meaning visual area 1), although they begin with different neurons within that area. They send their information to different neurons in the *sec-*

ondary visual area, V2, and from there the information branches out to areas V3, V4, V5, and others. One pathway is responsible mostly for analysis of shape details; another for color; another for motion.[1]

A person who suffers damage to the entire primary visual cortex (V1) becomes completely blind. In contrast, consider what happens to someone with damage to part of a single pathway. After damage to parts of the inferior temporal cortex, which is part of the shape pathway, some people suffer a specific **face blindness,** also known by the fancier name *prosopagnosia.* Such a person may still be able to read, and can see faces well enough to say, "That person is almost bald and has a somewhat thin face, and dark eyes," but lacks the ability to say, "Aha, that's my cousin Ross." The affected person may also fail to identify specific plants, animals, cars, and so forth (Farah, 1990, 1992).

Now consider damage to area V4 in the cortex. People with damage in this area lose an ability called **color constancy,** which is the ability to continue recognizing colors even after a change in the lighting. For example, suppose you put on blue-tinted glasses. You would not suddenly see everything as blue; you could still identify which

---

[1] Relax; you do not need to memorize the different locations of areas V1 through V5 or which pathway controls which function. The point of this discussion is that different pathways in the visual area of the brain handle different aspects of visual perception. I can make that point most easily if I show you some examples of what I mean by a pathway. Not every detail in a text is there for you to memorize.

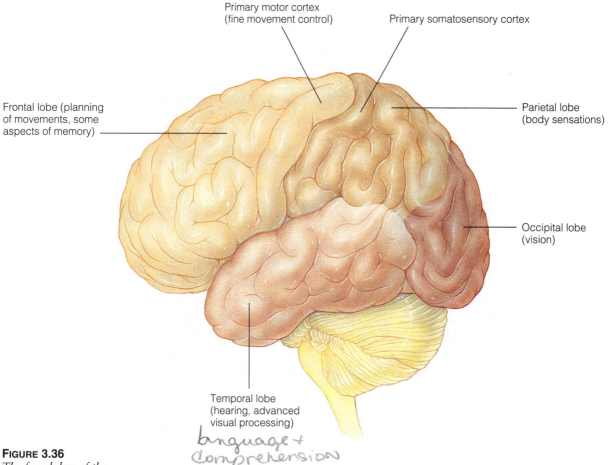

Primary motor cortex
(fine movement control)

Primary somatosensory cortex

Frontal lobe (planning
of movements, some
aspects of memory)

Parietal lobe
(body sensations)

Occipital lobe
(vision)

Temporal lobe
(hearing, advanced
visual processing)

*language +
comprehension*

FIGURE 3.36
*The four lobes of the
human cerebral
cortex, with indica-
tions of some of their
major functions.*

FIGURE 3.37
*A person with dam-
age to the right pari-
etal lobe will draw
only the right side of
an object, as this
attempt to copy a
picture of a flower
shows. (From Heil-
man & Valenstein,
1993.)*

objects are red, yellow, and so forth. People
with damage to area V4 have trouble with
color constancy; for them, everything in the
room would indeed look blue (Zeki, 1980,
1983).

Damage to area V5 produces a very surprising deficit: **motion blindness.** People with
such damage have trouble detecting the
movement of objects (Zihl, von Cramon, &
Mai, 1983). One such patient found that she
could not safely cross a road, because she
could not see which cars were moving, or
how fast. She had trouble pouring coffee into
a cup, because she could not see the liquid
level gradually rising in the cup. (Eventually
she would stop when she saw coffee all over
the table.)

In short, different parts of the visual system of your cerebral cortex process different
aspects of each visual stimulus—one part at-
tends to shape, another to color, another to
motion. How do you put it all together?
Again, we have reached the limitations of
current knowledge; although the brain must
somehow be able to combine different kinds
of information, we do not currently understand how.

EFFECTS OF LOCALIZED BRAIN DAMAGE: UNILATERAL NEGLECT

Let's now consider a kind of brain damage
that affects attention rather than sensation.
Damage in the parietal lobe (see Figure
3.36), especially if it is in the right parietal
lobe, leads to **neglect** of the opposite side of
the body and the opposite side of the world.
Such people may put clothing on only the
right side of the body, insisting that the left
half is someone else. They read only the right
side of a page and draw only the right side of
an object, using only the right side of the paper (Heilman, 1979; see Figure 3.37).

If you were to tickle such a person simultaneously on the left and right sides of the
wrist (of either hand, left or right), he or she
would report the sensation on the right side
of that wrist, ignoring the sensation on the
left side. Now suppose you turn the person's
hand upside down and repeat the experiment. He or she now reports the sensation on
what has *now* become the right side of the
hand, as illustrated in Figure 3.38 (Moscovitch & Behrmann, 1994). That is, the person
does not simply neglect a certain area of skin,
but detects what part of the arm is on the left,

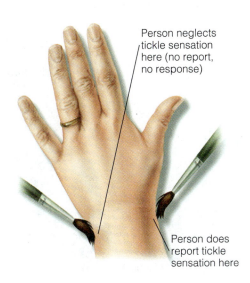

Person neglects tickle sensation here (no report, no response)

Person does report tickle sensation here

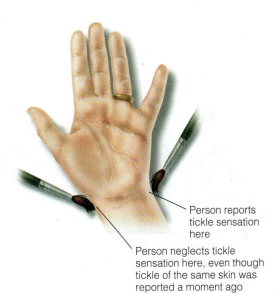

Person reports tickle sensation here

Person neglects tickle sensation here, even though tickle of the same skin was reported a moment ago

FIGURE 3.38
Patients who have had damage in the parietal lobe of the right hemisphere of the brain neglect (ignore) stimuli on the left side of either wrist. After the hand is rotated to a new position, the patient ignores what is now on the left, even though they attended to that same skin in the previous position. That is, their problem is one of attention, not of simple sensation.

and then neglects it. The impairment is not a loss of sensation; it is a loss of attention.

EFFECTS OF LOCALIZED BRAIN DAMAGE: SPECIFIC MEMORY LOSS

Brain-damaged people sometimes show remarkably specialized kinds of memory loss, which we shall discuss Chapter 7. Here, I wish to describe an even more specific kind of memory loss, which so far has been demonstrated only in monkeys.

The brain damage is localized in a tiny portion of the frontal cortex, and the behavior to be measured is a kind of delayed response. **Delayed response** is any task in which an individual gets a signal and then has to wait before making the necessary response. In one set of studies, monkeys were trained to stare at a dot on a screen, as shown in Figure 3.39. A signal light flashed briefly at some spot away from the fixation point. The monkey had to continue looking at the fixation point until it went off several seconds later, and then move its eyes to the location where the signal light had been. Monkeys with extensive damage to one area in the frontal lobes of the cerebral cortex show severe deficits on the task, apparently forgetting where the signal was. With very tiny damage within this area, monkeys lose their spatial memory *for just one spot.* For example, a monkey might be unable to remember a spot directly at the top of the circle or a spot at the left (Goldman-Rakic, 1994). We know the monkey can still see

these spots, because it can respond to them on a task requiring no delay. But as soon as we introduce a short delay, the monkey's performance deteriorates. Evidently it has lost its memory for just one location.

CONCLUSIONS ABOUT BRAIN ORGANIZATION

We have considered examples of damage to the visual system, neglect of half of the body, and loss of a tiny area of spatial memory. I hope you find the examples interesting for their own sake, but beyond that, the main point is that the brain is full of separate systems operating in parallel. The various systems do not funnel their information into one central processor; each part of the brain does its own task. Moreover, a small area of brain damage can lead to a significant loss of a narrowly defined behavioral function, with little loss of other, seemingly related functions.

Another way of stating the same conclusion, with greater emphasis on the philosophical implications: *If part of the brain is lost, part of behavior and experience is lost as well. So far as we can tell, brain activity and "mind" are inseparable; we cannot have one without the other.*

DIVISION OF LABOR: THE FOUR LOBES OF THE CEREBRAL CORTEX

In the process of telling you about certain kinds of brain damage, I have already told you the functions of certain parts of the

[handwritten margin note: Damage to Frontal cortex result in memory loss.]

[handwritten margin note: brain is full of separate systems operating in parallel.]

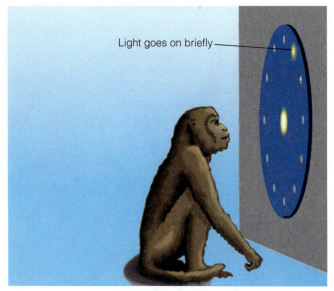

FIGURE 3.39

In one version of the delayed-response task, a monkey is trained to stare at a central fixation point. A light appears briefly at some point along the circle surrounding the fixation point. The monkey keeps its eyes focused on the fixation point during a delay, then must look at the point where the light appeared. That is, the monkey must remember the location of the light during the delay.

cerebral cortex. Let us now survey the major areas of the cortex more systematically.

For the sake of convenience, we describe the cerebral cortex in terms of four *lobes*— occipital, parietal, temporal, and frontal, as shown in Figure 3.36. The functions of the **occipital lobe** are easy to describe: This area is specialized for vision. As already discussed, different areas within (and outside) the occipital lobe contribute to different aspects of vision, such as shape, color, and motion. However, apparently all of the occipital lobe contributes to vision in one way or another.

The **parietal lobe** is specialized for the body senses, including touch, pain, temperature, and awareness of the location of body parts. A strip in the anterior (forward) part of the parietal lobe, known as the **primary somatosensory** (body-sensory) **cortex**, has neurons sensitive to touch in different body areas, as shown in Figure 3.40. Note in Figure 3.40 that larger areas are devoted to touch from the more sensitive parts of the body, such as the lips and hands, than to less sensitive areas, such as the abdomen and the back. Damage to any part of the somatosensory cortex impairs sensation from the corresponding part of the body.

The **temporal lobe** of each hemisphere, located toward the temples, is the main processing area for hearing, as well as contributing to some of the more complex aspects of vision. One area in the temporal lobe in the left hemisphere is important for language comprehension. Damage centered here impairs people's ability to understand what other people are saying; they also have trouble remembering the names of objects when they are speaking themselves.

The temporal lobe also apparently plays an important role in emotional behavior. Tumors, epilepsy, or other abnormalities affecting the temporal lobe sometimes cause severe emotional outbursts. Some people, for example, exhibit unprovoked violent behavior (Mark & Ervin, 1970), periods of uncontrollable laughter (Swash, 1972), or periods of ecstatic pleasure (Cirignotta, Todesco, & Lugaresi, 1980).

The **frontal lobe** includes the **primary motor cortex** (Figure 3.40), which is important for the control of fine movements, such as moving one finger at a time. As with the primary somatosensory cortex, each area of the primary motor cortex controls a different part of the body, and larger areas are devoted to precise movements of the tongue and fingers than to, say, the shoulder and elbow muscles. The anterior sections of the frontal lobe, called the **prefrontal cortex**, contribute to the organization and planning of movements, as well as to certain aspects of mem-

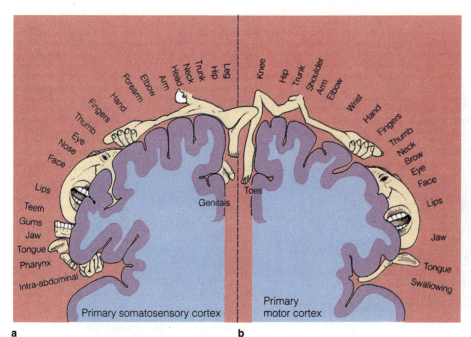

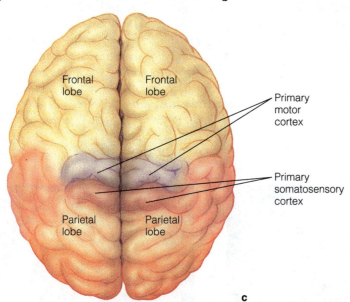

FIGURE 3.40
(a) The primary somatosensory cortex and (b) the primary motor cortex, illustrating which part of the body each brain area controls. Larger areas of the cortex are devoted to body parts that need to be controlled with great precision, such as the face and hands. The figure shows the left primary somatosensory cortex, which receives information from the right side of the body, and the right primary motor cortex, which controls the muscles on the left side of the body. (c) Locations of the primary somatosensory cortex and the primary motor cortex. [(a) and (b) from Geschwind, 1979.]

ory. Indeed, planning a movement depends on memory. Recall, for example, the delayed response task (page 109): The individual has to remember a signal during a delay, and then make the appropriate movement. In Chapter 15 we shall discuss the effects of *prefrontal lobotomies,* which damage the prefrontal cortex.

Certain areas in the left frontal lobe are important for human language production. People with extensive damage in the left frontal lobe have trouble speaking, writing, or gesturing in sign language (Bellugi, Poizner, & Klima, 1983; Geschwind, 1970). What they say makes sense, although they generally omit prepositions, conjunctions, and word endings.

How do we know that these brain areas have the functions that I have described? For many years, nearly all the evidence came from observations on brain damage. Researchers can now supplement such evidence with modern techniques that measure activity in an unanesthetized brain. For example, the **regional cerebral blood flow technique (rCBF)** measures the blood flow to various brain areas. Generally, blood flow increases to the most active areas, so an increase in blood flow indicates increased brain activity.

↑blood flow
↑brain activity

FIGURE 3.41
This apparatus records regional cerebral blood flow (rCBF) in the brain, allowing investigators to measure activity in different parts of the brain.

To measure rCBF, investigators inject into the person's blood a small amount of radioactively labeled xenon, an inert gas. The more active a certain area of the brain is, the greater the amount of xenon-carrying blood that will enter that area. Figure 3.41 shows the apparatus used in measuring rCBF. Figure 3.42 shows the results of one study comparing rCBF during rest and during speech (Wallesch, Henriksen, Kornhuber, & Paulson, 1985). Reds indicate areas of highest activity; yellows, greens, blues, and purples indicate progressively lower activity. This figure demonstrates that while a person is speaking, blood flow increases to much of the left hemisphere, including the left frontal cortex but other areas as well. Similar research has identified the brain areas active during a variety of other behaviors.

13. *The following five people are known to have suffered damage to the cerebral cortex. From their behavioral symptoms, determine the probable location of the damage for each person: (a) impaired perception of the left half of the body and a tendency to ignore the left half of the body and the left half of the world, (b) impaired hearing and some changes in emotional experience, (c) inability to make fine movements with the right hand, (d) loss of vision in the left visual field, and (e) poor performance on a delayed response task, indicating difficulty remembering what has just happened. (Check your answers on page 119.)*

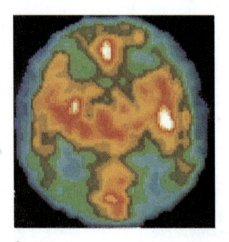

a

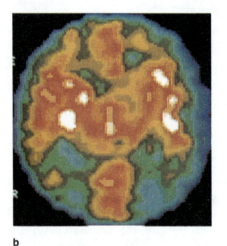

b

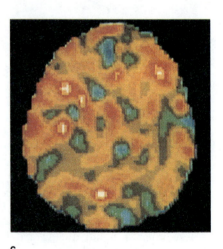

c

FIGURE 3.42
These rCBF records indicate the relative amounts of blood flow to various brain areas of a normal human brain under differing conditions. Red indicates the greatest amount of blood flow, and therefore brain activity; yellow indicates the next-greatest amount, followed by green, blue, and purple. (a) Blood flow to the brain at rest. (b) Blood flow while the person describes a magazine story. (c) Difference between (b) and (a). The record in (c) indicates the areas that increased their activity during speech. Note the widespread areas of activity, especially in the left hemisphere. (From Wallesch, Henriksen, Kornhuber, & Paulson, 1985.)

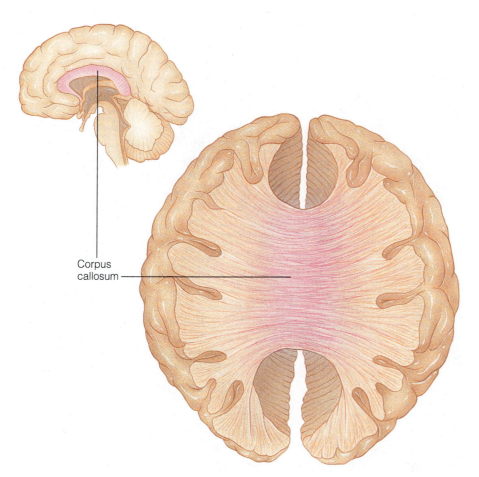

FIGURE 3.43
The corpus callosum is a large set of axons that convey information between the two hemispheres of the cerebral cortex. (left) A midline view showing the location of the corpus callosum. (right) A horizontal section, showing how each axon of the corpus callosum links a spot in the left hemisphere to a corresponding spot in the right hemisphere.

Corpus callosum

THE CORPUS CALLOSUM AND THE SPLIT-BRAIN PHENOMENON

What would happen if the sensory input from one half of your body, represented in one hemisphere, could not get to the motor cortex in the opposite hemisphere? Such a situation arises after damage to the **corpus callosum,** a set of axons connecting the two hemispheres (Figure 3.43). Corpus callosum damage also prevents someone from comparing sights seen on one side of the world against sights seen on the other side of the world, and from comparing something felt with one hand to something felt with the other hand. Information that reaches one hemisphere must stay in that hemisphere; the person no longer has a single cerebral cortex, but rather has two half-cortexes operating side by side. Research on some unusual surgical patients suggests that the result is two separate spheres of consciousness.

Several teams of brain surgeons have cut the corpus callosum in an effort to relieve a condition called **epilepsy,** in which neurons somewhere in the brain begin to emit abnormal rhythmic, spontaneous impulses. Such impulses originate in different locations for different people. They quickly spread to other areas of the brain, including neurons in the opposite hemisphere. The effects on behavior can vary widely, depending on where the epilepsy originates in the brain and where it spreads. Most people with epilepsy respond well to antiepileptic drugs and live normal lives. A few people, however, do not respond to any of the known drugs and continue to have major seizures so frequently that they cannot work, go to school, or travel far from medical help. Such people are willing to try almost anything to get relief. In certain cases, surgeons recommended cutting the corpus callosum. The reasoning was that epileptic seizures would be prevented from spreading across the corpus callosum to the other hemisphere and so would be less severe.

The operation was more successful than expected. Not only were the seizures limited to one side of the body, but they also became far less frequent. A possible explanation is that the operation interrupted the feedback loop between the two hemispheres that

FIGURE 3.44

A mythical beast, the cyclops, sees each side of the world in the opposite side of its one retina. Humans have two eyes like that of the cyclops: For each eye, the left half of the retina sees the right half of the world and the right half of the retina sees the left half of the world.

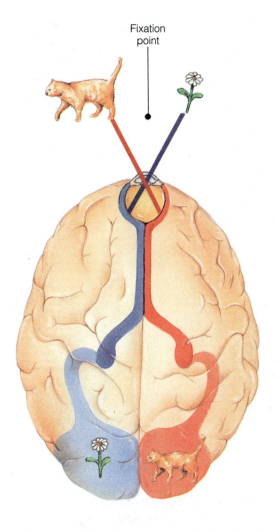

Fixation point

most the same view with both eyes. You see the left half of the world with part of your left eye and part of your right eye.

To illustrate, consider Figure 3.44, which shows the visual system of the mythical one-eyed beast, the cyclops. In this view, you are looking at the head of the cyclops from above. Light from either half of the world crosses through the pupil to strike the opposite side of the **retina** (the visual receptors lining the back of the eyeball). That is, light from the left strikes the right half of the retina and light from the right strikes the left half of the retina. Then axons from each half of the retina go to their own side of the brain.

The human visual system is organized just like that of the cyclops, except that humans have two "cyclopean" eyes. Figure 3.45, which shows the human system, warrants careful study. In us as in the cyclops, light from each half of the world strikes receptors on the opposite side of the retina, but we (unlike the cyclops) have two such retinas. Information from the left half of *each* retina travels via the **optic nerves** to the left hemisphere of the cerebral cortex; information from the right half of each retina travels via the optic nerves to the right hemisphere.

Here is one way to remember this material: *Light from each side of the world strikes the opposite side of the retina. The brain is connected to the eyes in such a way that each hemisphere sees the opposite side of the world.* If you remember those two statements, you should be able to sketch the connections shown in Figure 3.45.

What about the very center of the retina? Cells in a thin strip down the center of each retina send axons to both sides of the brain.

allows an epileptic seizure to echo back and forth. These split-brain patients were able to return to work and to resume other normal activities. There were, however, some interesting behavioral side effects. But before I can discuss them, we need to consider the links between the eyes and the brain.

CONNECTIONS BETWEEN THE EYES AND THE BRAIN

Note: This section presents a simple concept that is contrary to most people's expectations. Even when students are warned that this material will appear on a test and are practically told what the question will be, many of them still miss it. So pay attention!

Because each hemisphere of the brain controls the muscles on the opposite side of the body, it needs to see the opposite side of the world. This does not mean that your left hemisphere sees with the right eye or that your right hemisphere sees with the left eye. Convince yourself: Close one eye, then open it and close the other. Note that you see al-

BEHAVIORAL EFFECTS OF SEVERING THE CORPUS CALLOSUM

For almost all right-handed people and for about 60% of left-handed people, the brain area that controls speech is located in the left hemisphere of the brain. When visual or other information comes into your right hemisphere, you have no difficulty talking about it, because the corpus callosum readily transfers information between the hemispheres.

But what happens when the corpus callosum is severed? When a woman with a severed corpus callosum touches something with her right hand without looking at it, she can say what it is, because the touch information reaches her left hemisphere (Nebes,

1974; Sperry, 1967). However, if she touches something with her left hand, then she cannot say what it is, because the information reaches only her right hemisphere. If she is given several choices and is asked to point to what her left hand has felt, she can point to it correctly—but only with her left hand. In fact, she will sometimes point to the correct object with her left hand while saying, "I have no idea what it was. I didn't feel anything." Evidently the right hemisphere can understand the instructions and answer with the hand it controls, but it cannot talk. Roger Sperry won a Nobel Prize in physiology and medicine in 1981 for these pioneering discoveries.

Now consider what happens when this split-brain woman looks at something (Figure 3.46b). Under ordinary conditions, when her eyes are free to move about, she sees almost the same thing in both hemispheres. In the laboratory, however, it is possible to restrict information to one side or the other by presenting it faster than the eyes can move. The woman in Figure 3.46b focuses her eyes on a point in the middle of the screen. The investigator flashes a word such as *hatband* on the screen for a split second so that the woman does not have enough time to move her eyes. If she is asked what she saw, she replies "band," which is what the left hemisphere saw. Information from the right side of the screen, you will recall, goes to the left side of each retina and from there to the left hemisphere. If she is asked what *kind* of band it might be, she is puzzled: "I don't know. Jazz band? Rubber band?"

What the right hemisphere saw cannot get to the left hemisphere, which does the talking. However, if the investigator displays a set of objects and asks the woman to *point* to what she just saw, using her *left* hand, she points to a hat, which is what the right hemisphere saw! The left hemisphere and right hemisphere answer questions independently, as if they were separate people.

Split-brain people get along reasonably well in everyday life. Walking, for example, is no problem; it is controlled largely by subcortical areas of the brain that exchange information through connections below the corpus callosum.

In special circumstances, the two hemispheres find clever ways to cooperate. In one experiment, a split-brain person was looking at pictures flashed on a screen, as in Figure 3.46a. He could not name the objects flashed

in the left visual field, but after some delay, he could name such simple shapes as round, square, or triangular. Here is how he did it: After seeing the object (with the right hemisphere), he let his eyes move around the room. (Both hemispheres have control of the eye muscles.) When the right hemisphere saw something with the same shape as the object it had seen on the screen, it would stop moving the eyes. The left hemisphere just waited for the eyes to stop moving and then called out the shape of the object it saw.

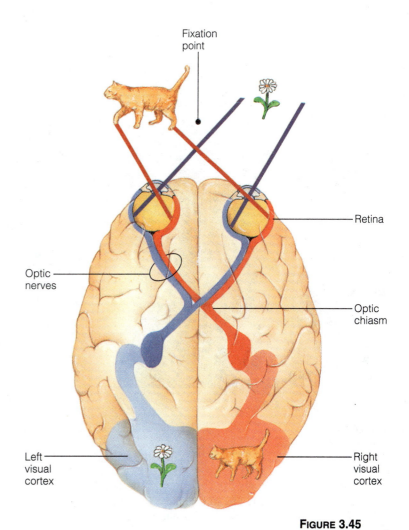

FIGURE 3.45
In the human visual system (viewed here from above), light from either half of the world crosses through the pupils to strike the opposite side of each retina. Axons from the left half of each retina travel to the left hemisphere of the brain; axons from the right half of each retina travel to the right hemisphere of the brain.

CONCEPT CHECK

14. *After damage to the corpus callosum, a person can describe some of what he or she sees, but not all. Where does the person have to see something in order to describe it in words? One eye or the other? One half of the retina? One visual field or the other? (Check your answers on page 119.)*

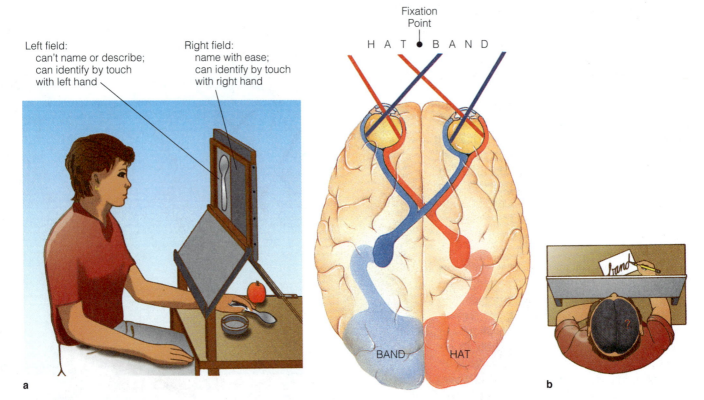

Left field:
  can't name or describe;
  can identify by touch
  with left hand

Right field:
  name with ease;
  can identify by touch
  with right hand

Fixation
Point

H A T ● B A N D

BAND   HAT

a   b

FIGURE 3.46

(a) A woman with a severed corpus callosum can name something she sees in her right visual field, but not something she sees in her left visual field. Information from the left goes to the right hemisphere, which cannot talk. (b) When the word hatband *is flashed on a screen, a woman with a split brain can report only what her left hemisphere saw,* band. *However, with her left hand she can point to a hat, which is what the right hemisphere saw.*

Split-brain surgery is extremely rare. We study such patients not because you are likely to encounter one but because they teach us something about the organization of the brain: Although we cannot fully explain our experience of a unified consciousness, we do see that it depends on communication across brain areas. If communication between the two hemispheres is lost, then each hemisphere begins to act and experience independently of the other.

COMMON MISUNDERSTANDINGS ABOUT THE BRAIN

Before closing this chapter, I want to caution you about some widespread misstatements and misunderstandings concerning the brain. One has to do with the left hemisphere and the right hemisphere. Research on split-brain patients and on people who have suffered widespread damage to one hemisphere has demonstrated that the two hemispheres have different specializations. The left hemisphere is specialized for language in nearly all right-handers and even in most left-handers. The right hemisphere is important for some complex visual-spatial tasks, such as drawing a

picture or imagining what something might look like from a different angle. So far, so good. However, some writers have gone beyond this generalization to claim that the left hemisphere is logical and the right hemisphere is creative, so some people are logical because they are left-brain people and others are creative because they are right-brain people. Some writers have even suggested that we could all become more creative if we could find some way to stimulate the right hemisphere or to suppress the competing left hemisphere.

In fact, every task, even the most logical or the most creative, uses both sides of the brain. Certain tasks activate one hemisphere a bit more than the other, but no task relies on just one hemisphere. As for the idea that some people are left-brained or that others are right-brained, we simply have no evidence to support that claim. It is merely a guess that a person who seems better at creative tasks than at logical reasoning must be relying mostly on the right hemisphere, a guess based on the person's behavior, and not on any measurement of brain activity. This is an example of *neuromythology*—making up a guess about the brain to account for an observation about behavior.

A second misunderstanding: You probably have heard the expression "They say we use only 10% of our brain." Stop and think about that for a moment. Who are "they"? No brain researcher says anything of the sort. What does the statement really mean? Does it mean that someone could lose 90% of the brain and still function normally? If so, the statement is false. Does it mean that only 10% of the neurons in the brain are active at any given time? If so, false again. Perhaps it means simply that we could all know more and do more than we know and do now. That is undeniably true, though it has nothing to do with the estimated 10% (or any other numerical estimate). I am not much of an athlete, but that does not mean that I am using only 10% of my muscles. We all use all of our brain (even those who do not seem to be using their brains very well).

The claim that we use only some small percentage of our brain has been popular at least since the 1920s; it is evidently something that people like to believe. Where and how did the belief begin? One possibility is that it began when researchers could not find a clear function for the "association areas" of the brain and therefore some observers imagined that those areas might be doing nothing. Another possibility is that early researchers noticed that the brain includes many very small neurons; some researchers supposed that the tiny neurons were immature, perhaps capable of later developing and adding to the power of the brain. The message of the story is clear: Beware when anyone says "They say that . . ." and then cannot tell you who "they" are or what evidence they have for the conclusion.

A number of advertisements and articles in the popular media rely on unsubstantiated claims about the brain.

trols the body's organs, preparing them for emergency activities or for vegetative activities. The endocrine system consists of organs that release hormones into the blood. (page 101)

- *Early conceptions of brain organization.* One early idea of brain organization was that various brain areas funnel all kinds of sensory information into a single "master area." Another idea was that the cerebral cortex operates as a single, undifferentiated whole. Later research has disconfirmed both of these views. (page 104)

- *Parallel paths and specialized functions of brain areas.* Contemporary research indicates that different brain areas have specialized functions and that localized brain damage can produce specialized defects. Various brain functions occur in parallel, largely independently. Loss of part of the brain leads to loss of part of behavior and experience. (page 106)

- *Lobes of the cerebral cortex.* The four lobes of the cerebral cortex and their primary functions are: occipital lobe, vision; temporal lobe, hearing and some aspects of vision; parietal lobe, body sensations; frontal lobe, movement and preparation for movement. (page 110)

- *Imaging brain activity.* Modern technology enables researchers to develop images

SUMMARY

- *Central and peripheral nervous systems.* The central nervous system consists of the brain (forebrain, midbrain, and hindbrain) and the spinal cord. The peripheral nervous system consists of nerves that communicate between the central nervous system and the rest of the body. (page 99)

- *Structures of the central nervous system.* Information passing between the cerebral cortex and the spinal cord goes through several intervening structures such as the midbrain and medulla. All the intervening structures have important functions of their own. (page 100)

- *Autonomic nervous system and endocrine system.* The autonomic nervous system con-

showing the structure and activity of various brain areas in living, unanesthetized people. (page 111)

- *Corpus callosum.* The corpus callosum is a set of axons through which the left and right hemispheres of the cortex communicate. After it is damaged, information that reaches one hemisphere cannot be shared with the other. (page 113)

- *Connections from eyes to brain.* In humans, information from the left visual field strikes the right half of both retinas, from which it is sent to the right hemisphere of the brain. Information from the right visual field strikes the left half of both retinas, from which it is sent to the left hemisphere. (page 114)

- *Split-brain patients.* The left hemisphere is specialized for language in most people. Split-brain patients can describe information only if it enters the left hemisphere. Because of the lack of direct communication between left and right hemispheres in split-brain patients, such people show signs of having separate fields of awareness. (page 114)

- *Common misunderstandings.* Many people try to explain logical thinking or creative thinking by attributing it to extra activity in the left or right hemisphere. That guess is at best a half-truth, unsupported by direct evidence. Another common misunderstanding is the assertion that we use only some small percentage of the brain. In fact, people are using all of their brain, even when they are not using it very well. (page 116)

SUGGESTIONS FOR FURTHER READING

Klawans, H. L. (1988). *Toscanini's fumble and other tales of clinical neurology.* Chicago: Contemporary Books. Interesting and informative examples of the effects of human brain damage.

Zeki, S. (1993). *A vision of the brain,* Oxford, England: Blackwell Scientific Publishers. Provides more information about the effects of localized damage in the visual areas of the brain.

TERMS

central nervous system the brain and the spinal cord (page 99)

peripheral nervous system the nerves that convey messages from the sense organs to the central nervous system and from the central nervous system to the muscles and glands (page 100)

somatic nervous system the nerves that control the muscles (page 100)

autonomic nervous system a set of neurons lying in and alongside the spinal cord that receive information from and send information to the organs, such as the heart (page 100)

forebrain the most anterior (forward) part of the brain, including the cerebral cortex and other structures (page 100)

midbrain the middle part of the brain, more prominent in fish, reptiles, and birds than in mammals (page 100)

hindbrain the most posterior (hind) part of the brain, including the medulla, pons, and cerebellum (page 100)

spinal cord the part of the central nervous system that communicates with sensory neurons and motor neurons below the level of the head (page 100)

sensory neuron a neuron that carries information about touch, pain, and other senses from the periphery of the body to the spinal cord (page 100)

motor neuron a neuron that transmits impulses from the central nervous system to the muscles or glands (page 100)

reflex a rapid, automatic response to a stimulus (page 100)

endocrine system a set of glands that produce hormones and release them into the blood (page 101)

hormone a chemical released by a gland and conveyed by the blood to other parts of the body, where it alters activity (page 101)

medulla a structure located in the hindbrain that is an elaboration of the spinal cord; controls many muscles in the head and several life-preserving functions, such as breathing (page 104)

pons a structure adjacent to the medulla that receives sensory input from the head and controls many muscles in the head (page 104)

reticular formation set of neurons in the medulla and pons that receive information from sensory systems and respond by sending arousal messages to many areas of the forebrain (page 104)

cerebellum (Latin for "little brain") a hindbrain structure that is active in the control of movement, especially for complex, rapid motor skills (page 104)

cerebral cortex the outer surface of the forebrain (page 104)

hemisphere the left or the right half of the brain; each hemisphere is responsible for sensation and motor control on the opposite side of the body (page 104)

face blindness impairment of the ability to recognize faces, despite otherwise satisfactory vision (page 107)

color constancy ability to continue recognizing colors even after a change in the lighting (page 107)

motion blindness impaired ability to detect motion in visual perception, despite otherwise satisfactory vision (page 108)

neglect tendency to ignore stimuli on one side of the body or one side of the world (page 108)

delayed response task in which an individual has to wait during a delay after a signal before being given the opportunity to make the necessary response (page 109)

occipital lobe the rear portion of each cerebral hemisphere, critical for vision (page 110)

parietal lobe a portion of each cerebral hemisphere, the main receiving area for the sense of touch and for perception of one's own body (page 110)

primary somatosensory cortex a strip in the anterior (forward) part of the parietal lobe that receives most touch sensation and other information about the body (page 110)

temporal lobe a portion of each cerebral hemisphere, the main processing area for hearing, complex aspects of vision, and certain aspects of emotional behavior (page 110)

frontal lobe portion of each cerebral hemisphere, critical for precise control of movement, preparation for movement, and certain aspects of memory (page 110)

primary motor cortex strip in the posterior (rear) part of the frontal cortex that controls fine movements, such as hand and finger movements (page 110)

prefrontal cortex area in the anterior portion of the frontal lobes, critical for planning movements and for certain aspects of memory (page 110)

regional cerebral blood flow technique (rCBF) a technique for estimating the level of activity in an area of the brain by dissolving radioactive xenon in the blood and measuring the radioactivity emitted in that area (page 111)

corpus callosum a large set of axons connecting the left and right hemispheres of the cerebral cortex and enabling the two hemispheres to communicate with each other (page 113)

epilepsy a condition characterized by abnormal rhythmic activity of brain neurons (page 113)

retina the visual receptors lining the back of the eyeball (page 114)

optic nerve bundle of axons from the retina to the brain (page 114)

ANSWERS TO CONCEPT CHECKS

11. The storage of fats takes place at many sites throughout the body. A hormone diffuses throughout the body; a neurotransmitter exerts its effects only on the neurons immediately adjacent to where it was released. (page 102)

12. Although alcohol impairs activity throughout the brain, one of the first areas to show a substantial effect is the cerebellum. The typical symptoms of alcohol intoxication are also symptoms of impairment to the cerebellum. (page 104)

13. (a) right parietal lobe; (b) temporal lobe; (c) primary motor cortex of the left frontal lobe; (d) right occipital lobe; (e) prefrontal cortex. (page 112)

14. To describe something, the person must see it with the left half of the retina of either eye. The left half of the retina sees the right visual field. (page 115)

4

SENSATION AND PERCEPTION

When my son Sam was 8 years old, he asked me, "If we went to some other planet, would we see different colors?" He did not mean just a new shade or a new mixture of familiar colors. He meant colors that were truly new, as different from the colors we are familiar with as yellow is from red or blue. I told him no, that would be impossible, and I tried to explain why.

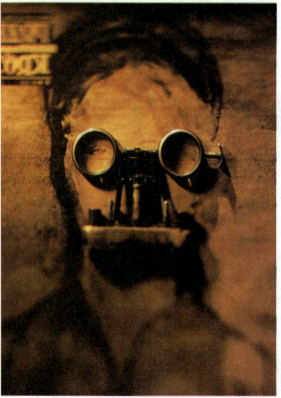

No matter where we might go in outer space, no matter what unfamiliar objects or atmospheres we might encounter, we could never experience a color, or a sound, or any other sensation that would be fundamentally different from what we experience on Earth. Different combinations, perhaps. But fundamentally different sensory experiences, no.

Three years later, Sam told me he was wondering whether people who look at the same thing are all having the same experience. When different people look at something and call it "green," how can we know whether they are all seeing the same "green"? I agreed that there was no sure way of knowing.

Why am I certain that colors on a different planet would look the same as they do on Earth and yet uncertain that colors look the same to different people here? You may find the answer obvious. If not, I hope it will be after you have read this chapter.

Sensation is the conversion of energy from the environment into a pattern of response by the nervous system. It is the registration of information. **Perception** is interpreting that information. For example, light rays striking your eyes give rise to sensation. When you conclude from that sensation, "I see my roommate," you are expressing your perception. (In practice, the distinction between sensation and perception is often difficult to draw. Let us not waste time arguing about what is a sensation and what is a perception.)

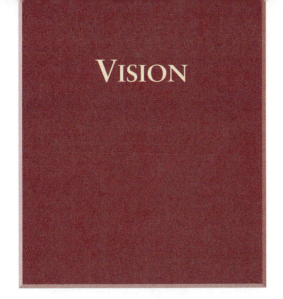

VISION

How do our eyes convert light energy into something we can experience?

How do we perceive colors?

We live in a world full of **stimuli**—energies that affect what we do. Our eyes, ears, and other sensory organs are packed with **receptors**—specialized cells that convert environmental energies into signals for the nervous system. Somehow the nervous system builds a representation of the useful information in the outside world. But how?

When we think about vision, we easily fall into the trap of imagining that the brain simply builds a little copy of what the eyes see, perhaps projecting an image of the outside world onto a screen of some sort inside the head. Today, neuroscientists have rejected any idea of a "little person in the head" who examines a projected image. Still, many people find it hard to shake that idea. To get away from such confusions, let us

consider for a moment the way your brain represents odors. Although no one yet knows the details of this process, we are not even tempted to assume that the brain builds little copies of what we smell. Are the neurons that smell a rose arranged in the shape of a rose? Of course not. The way the brain represents the smell of a rose need not physically resemble anything about the rose.

The same goes for vision. The representation of a visual stimulus in the brain need not physically resemble what we see, any more than the representation of a smell resembles the flower. Furthermore, what we experience is not the same as what is "out there." As a light grows more intense, we describe it as "brighter," but brightness is not the same thing as intensity. If the wavelength of a light changes, we see it as a different color, but color is not the same thing as wavelength. Our experiences do not *copy* the outside world; they *translate* it into a very different representation.

THE DETECTION OF LIGHT

What we refer to as *light* is just one part of the electromagnetic spectrum. As Figure 4.1 shows, the **electromagnetic spectrum** is the continuum of all the frequencies of radiated energy, from gamma rays and X rays, which have very short wavelengths, through ultraviolet, visible light, and infrared to radio and TV transmissions, which have very long wavelengths.

What exactly makes "visible light" visible? The answer is "our receptors," which are equipped to respond to wavelengths

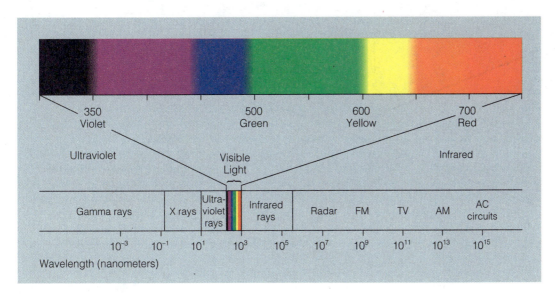

FIGURE 4.1
Visible light, what human eyes can see, is a small part of the electromagnetic spectrum. Experimenting with prisms, Isaac Newton discovered that white light is a mixture of all colors, and color is a property of light. A carrot looks orange because it reflects orange and absorbs all the other colors.

The red you see in some snapshots is the color of the retina, reflecting light from a flash that is mounted on the camera so that light bounces straight back.

from 400 nm to 700 nm. With different receptors, we might see a different range of wavelengths. Some species—bees, for example—see some wavelengths shorter than 350 nm, which are invisible to humans. However, bees fail to see some of the longer wavelengths, those that appear red to most humans.

STRUCTURE OF THE EYE

When we see an object, light reflected from that object passes through the **pupil,** an adjustable opening in the eye through which light enters. The **iris** is the colored structure on the surface of the eye, surrounding the pupil. It is the structure we describe when we say someone has brown eyes, blue eyes, or whatever. When the light is dim, muscles open the pupil to let in more light. When the light is bright, muscles narrow the pupil.

After light passes through the pupil, it travels through the *vitreous humor* (a clear, jellylike substance) and strikes the retina at the back of the eyeball. The **retina** is a layer of visual receptors that covers the back surface of the eyeball (Figure 4.2). As light passes through the eye, the cornea and the lens focus the light on the retina as shown in Figure 4.2.

The **cornea,** a rigid, transparent structure on the outer surface of the eyeball, focuses light in the same way at all times. The

lens, however, is a flexible structure that can vary in thickness, enabling the eye to **accommodate**—that is, to adjust its focus for objects at different distances. When we look at a distant object, for example, our eye muscles relax and let the lens become thinner and flatter, as shown in Figure 4.3a. When we look at a close object, our eye muscles tighten and make the lens thicker and rounder (Figure 4.3b).

SOME COMMON DISORDERS OF VISION

Our vision is best when our eyeballs are nearly spherical. A person whose eyeballs are elongated, as shown in Figure 4.4a, can focus well on nearby objects but has difficulty focusing on distant objects. Such a person is said to be *nearsighted,* or to have **myopia** (mi-O-pee-ah). About half of all 20-year-olds are nearsighted and must wear glasses or contact lenses in order to see well at a distance. A person whose eyeballs are flattened, as shown in Figure 4.4b, has **presbyopia,** or *farsightedness.* Such a person can focus well on distant objects but has difficulty focusing on close objects. Presbyopia occurs uncommonly in young people as a result of a flattened eyeball. It occurs very commonly in old age because the aging lens becomes less flexible and therefore less capable of focusing on nearby objects. (The Greek root

FIGURE 4.2
The lens gets its name from Latin for lentil, *referring to its shape—an appropriate choice, as this cross section of the eye shows. The names of other parts of the eye also refer to their appearance.*

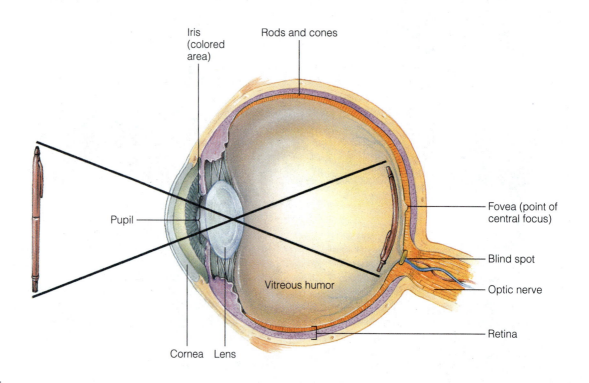

Iris (colored area)

Rods and cones

Pupil

Cornea   Lens

Vitreous humor

Fovea (point of central focus)

Blind spot

Optic nerve

Retina

presby- means old. It also shows up in the word *presbyterian*, which means *governed by the elders.*) Many older people have both myopia (because of an elongated eyeball) and presbyopia (because of a stiff lens). Such people need bifocal glasses to help with both near focus and distant focus.

Two other common visual disorders are glaucoma and cataracts. **Glaucoma** is a condition characterized by increased pressure within the eyeball; the result can be damage to the optic nerve and therefore a loss of peripheral vision ("tunnel vision") and eventually blindness, unless the disorder is successfully treated. A **cataract** is a disorder in which the lens becomes cloudy. People with severe cataracts may have a lens surgically removed and replaced with a contact lens. Because the normal lens filters out more blue and ultraviolet light than other light, people with artificial lenses sometimes report seeing

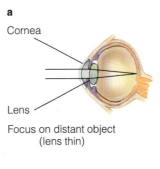

a

Cornea

Lens

Focus on distant object
(lens thin)

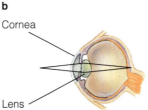

b

Cornea

Lens

Focus on close object
(lens thick)

FIGURE 4.3
Changing shape so that objects (a) far and (b) near can come into focus, the flexible, transparent lens bends entering light rays so that they fall on the retina. In old age, the lens becomes rigid and people find it harder to focus on nearby objects.

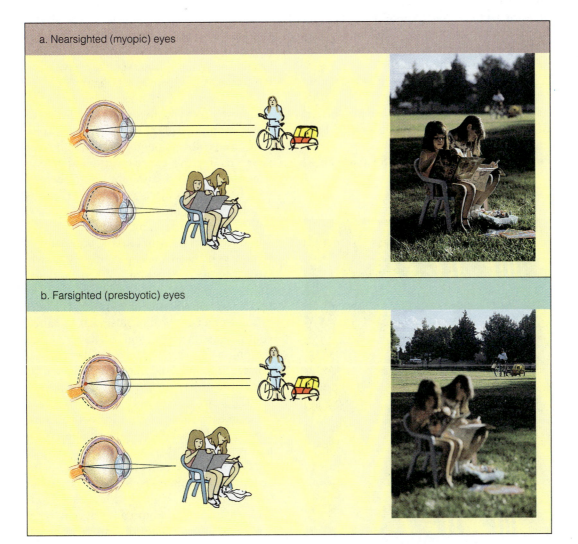

a. Nearsighted (myopic) eyes

b. Farsighted (presbyotic) eyes

FIGURE 4.4
The structure of (a) nearsighted and (b) farsighted eyes distort vision. Because the nearsighted eye is elongated, light from a distant object focuses in front of the retina. Because the farsighted eye is flattened, light from a nearby object focuses behind the retina. The photographs simulate (a) nearsightedness and (b) farsightedness.

blue more clearly and distinctly than they ever had before (Davenport & Foley, 1979). They do, however, suffer increased risk of damage to the retina from ultraviolet light.

CONCEPT CHECK

1. Suppose you have normal vision and you try on a pair of glasses made for a person with myopia. How will the glasses affect your vision? (Check your answer on page 137.)

THE VISUAL RECEPTORS

The visual receptors of the eye are specialized neurons in the retina, at the back of the eyeball. They are so sensitive to light that they are capable of responding to a single photon, the smallest possible quantity of light.

These visual receptors are of two types: cones and rods. The two differ in appearance, as Figure 4.5 shows, and in function. The **cones** are adapted for color vision, daytime vision, and detailed vision. The **rods** are adapted for vision in dim light.

About 5–10% of all the visual receptors in the human retina are cones. Most birds have about the same or a higher proportion of cones than humans have; they also have good color vision. Species with very few cones in their retina—rats, for example—

make little use of color vision. Nearly all vertebrates have at least some cones (Dowling, 1987), although many species fail to show any clear evidence of color perception.

The proportion of cones is highest toward the center of the retina. The **fovea** (FOE-vee-uh), the central area of the human retina, is adapted for highly detailed vision (Figure 4.2). The fovea has a greater density of receptors than any other part of the retina; also, receptors in the fovea send their information to a great number of cells at later stages in the nervous system. If you want to see something in detail, you focus it on the fovea; for example, you can read letters of the alphabet only if you see them in or near the fovea.

Other animal species have eyes that are organized somewhat differently from human eyes. For example, hawks, owls, and other predatory birds have a greater density of receptors on the top of the retina (looking down) than on the bottom of the retina (looking up). When these birds are flying, this arrangement enables them to see the ground beneath them in detail. When they are on the ground, however, they have trouble seeing above themselves (Figure 4.6).

The fovea consists solely of cones (Figure 4.2). Away from the fovea, the proportion of cones drops sharply. That is why you have little or no color vision in the far periphery of your eye. Try this experiment: Hold several pens or pencils of different colors behind your back. (Any objects will work so long as they have about the same size and shape and approximately the same brightness.) Pick one at random without looking at it. Hold it behind your head and bring it very slowly into your field of vision. When you just barely begin to see it, you will probably not be able to tell what color it is. (If glaucoma or some other medical problem has impaired your peripheral vision, you will have to bring the object closer to your fovea before you can see it at all, and then you will see its color at once.)

The rods are more effective than the cones in detecting dim light for two reasons: First, a rod is slightly more responsive to faint stimulation than a cone is. Second, the rods pool their resources. More than a hundred rods send messages to the next cell in the visual system, but only a few cones converge their messages onto a given cell. Table 4.1 summarizes some key differences between rods and cones.

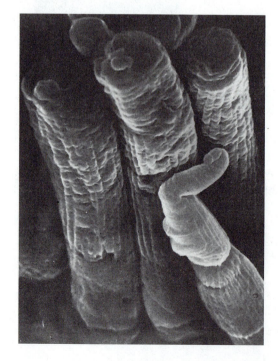

FIGURE 4.5
Rods and cones seen through a scanning electron microscope. The rods, which number more than 120 million, help us see in dim light. The 6 million cones in the retina can distinguish gradations of color in bright light.

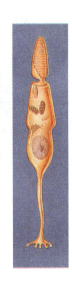

RODS	Shape	CONES
Nearly cylindrical	Shape	Tapered at one end
90–95%	Prevalence in human retina	5–10%
In species that are active at night	Greatest incidence by species	In birds, primates, and other species that are active during the day
Toward the periphery	Area of the retina	Toward the fovea
No direct contribution	Contribution to color vision	Critical for color vision
Strong	Response to dim light	Weak
Little	Contribution to perception of detail	Much

TABLE 4.1
Differences Between Rods and Cones

CONCEPT CHECK

2. Why is it easier to see a faint star in the sky if you look slightly to the side of the star instead of straight at it? (Check your answer on page 137.)

DARK ADAPTATION

You go into a basement at night trying to find your flashlight. The only light bulb in the basement is burned out. A little moonlight comes through the basement windows, but not much. At first you can hardly see anything. A couple of minutes later, you are beginning to see well enough to find your way around. After 10 minutes, you can see well enough to find the flashlight. This gradual improvement in the ability to see under dim light is called **dark adaptation.**

Dark adaptation occurs because the visual receptors gradually become more sensitive as they "rest" in dim light. The cones and rods adapt to the dark at different rates. Ordinarily, during the day our vision relies overwhelmingly on cones, and even as we begin adapting to the dark, we are seeing mostly with cones. However, if we stay long enough in a very dim location, the rods continue adapting longer than the cones do, until eventually the rods become significantly more sensitive than the cones. At that point we are seeing mostly with rods.

Here is how a psychologist can demonstrate this process of dark adaptation (Goldstein, 1989): You are taken into a room that is completely dark except for one tiny flashing light. You have a knob that controls the intensity of the light; you are told to make the light so dim that you can barely see it.

Over the course of 3 or 4 minutes you will gradually decrease the intensity of the light, as shown in Figure 4.7a. Note that a decrease in the intensity of the light indicates an increase in the sensitivity of your eyes.

If you stared straight at the point of light, your results demonstrate the adaptation of your cones to the dim light. (You have been focusing the light on your fovea, which has no rods.) Now the psychologist repeats the study, with one change in procedure:

You are told to stare at a very faint light while another light flashes in the periphery of your vision, where it stimulates rods as well

FIGURE 4.6
Birds of prey, such as these owlets, can see down much more clearly than they can see up. In flight, that arrangement is helpful. On the ground, they have to turn their heads almost upside down in order to see above them.

FIGURE 4.7

These graphs show dark adaptation to (a) a light you stare at directly, using only cones, and (b) a light in your peripheral vision, which you see with both cones and rods. (Based on Goldstein, 1989.)

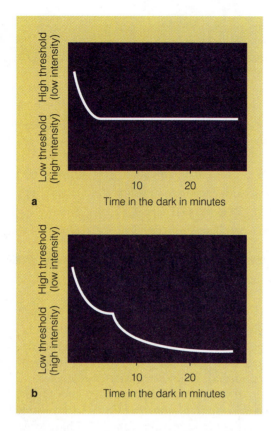

a

Time in the dark in minutes

b

Time in the dark in minutes

In a coal mine or a dark movie theater, we see little at first. As our eyes adapt from bright to dim light, we see more and more.

gin to see even fainter lights. Your rods continue to adapt to the dark over the next 20 minutes or so.

If you would like to demonstrate dark adaptation for yourself without any apparatus, try this: On a dark night, with only slight amounts of light coming through your windows, turn on a light in your room. Close one eye and cover it tightly with your hand for 10–20 minutes. By the end of that time, your covered eye will be adapted to the dark and your open eye will be adapted to the light. Next, turn off your light and then open both eyes. You will see well with your dark-adapted eye and poorly with your light-adapted eye.

CONCEPT CHECKS

3. You may have heard people say that cats can see in the dark. Is that possible?
4. After you have thoroughly adapted to extremely dim light, will you see more objects in your fovea or in the periphery of your eye? (Check your answers on page 137.)

THE VISUAL PATHWAY

If you were designing an eye, you would probably run the axons of the cones and rods straight to the brain. Nature chose a different method. The visual receptors send their impulses *away from* the brain, toward the center of the eye, where they make synaptic contacts with other neurons called bipolar cells. The *bipolar cells* in turn make contact with still other neurons, the **ganglion cells,** which are located still closer to the center of the eye. The axons from the ganglion cells join to form the **optic nerve,** which turns around and exits the eye, as Figure 4.2 and Figure 4.8 show. Half of each optic nerve crosses to the opposite side of the brain at the optic chiasm (KI-az-m). Axons from the optic nerve separate and go to several locations in the brain. In humans the largest number go to the thalamus, which then sends information to the occipital lobe, the primary area of the cortex for visual processing.

The area at which the optic nerve exits the retina is called the **blind spot.** There is no room for receptors here because the exiting axons take up all the space. You can find

as cones. You turn a control knob until the flashing light in the periphery is just barely visible. Figure 4.7b shows the results. During the first 7–10 minutes, the results are the same as before. But then your rods become more sensitive than your cones, and you be-

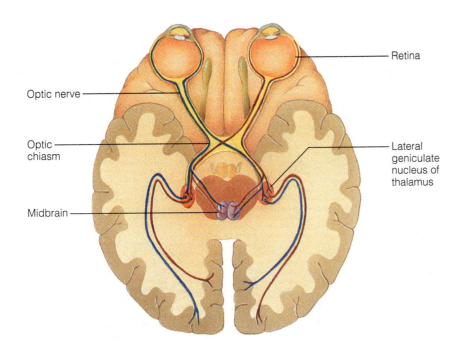

Retina

Optic nerve

Optic chiasm

Lateral geniculate nucleus of thalamus

Midbrain

your own blind spot by covering your left eye and staring at the x below or by covering your right eye and staring at the o. Then slowly move the page forward and backward. When your eye is about 15–20 cm away from the page, the letter you are not staring at will disappear, because you are focusing that letter onto the blind spot of your eye.

x   o

Ordinarily, we are unaware of our blind spot. You do not see blackness in the blind spot, any more than you see black behind your head. Rather, you have a gap in your experience. Ordinarily, your brain makes an inference about what is in that gap. To illustrate, cover your left eye and stare at the center of Figure 4.9, then slowly move the page forward and backward, as you did with the first demonstration. Notice what happens when the lion disappears: You see a complete circle! If you attend carefully, however, you will discover that the part of the circle running through your blind spot is not at all clear. You do not see it in quite the same way that you see the rest of the circle; your experience here is an inference rather than a normal perception. Furthermore, the inferences we make are fairly simple; we infer the extension of a line as in Figure 4.9; we do not infer corners or other more complicated features (Ramachandran, 1992).

COLOR VISION

As Figure 4.1 shows, different colors of light correspond to different wavelengths of electromagnetic energy. (White light consists of an equal mixture of all visible wavelengths.) How does the visual system convert those wavelengths into our perception of color? The process begins with three kinds of cones, which respond to different wavelengths of light. Later cells in the visual path code this wavelength information in terms of pairs of opposites—roughly, red versus green, yellow versus blue, and white versus black. Finally, cells in the cerebral cortex compare the input from various parts of the visual field to synthesize a color experience for each object. We shall examine these three stages in order.

THE TRICHROMATIC THEORY

Thomas Young was an English physician of the 1700s who, among many other accomplishments, helped to decode the Rosetta stone (making it possible to understand Egyptian hieroglyphics), introduced the modern concept of energy, revived and popularized the wave theory of light, and offered the first theory of how people perceive color. His theory, elaborated and modified by Hermann von Helmholtz in the 1800s, came to be known as the **trichromatic theory** or the **Young-Helmholtz theory.** It is called *trichromatic* because it claims that our receptors respond to three primary col-

FIGURE 4.9

Close your left eye and focus your right eye on the animal trainer. Move the page toward your eyes and away from them until you find a point at which the lion on the right disappears. At that point the lion is focused on the blind spot of your retina, where you have no receptors. Note what you see in its place— not a blank spot, but a continuation of the circle.

ors. In modern terms, we say that color vision depends on the relative rate of response by three types of cones. Each type of cone is most sensitive to a particular range of light wavelengths (Figure 4.10). One type is most sensitive to short wavelengths (which we generally see as blue), another to medium wavelengths (seen as green), and another to long wavelengths (red). Each wavelength prompts varying levels of activity in the three types of cones. For example, green light excites mostly the medium-wavelength cones, red light excites mostly the long-wavelength cones, and yellow light excites the medium-wavelength and long-wavelength cones about equally. Every wavelength of light produces its own distinct ratio of responses by the three kinds of cones. White light excites all three kinds of cones equally.

Young and Helmholtz proposed their theory long before experiments confirmed the existence of three types of cones (Wald, 1968). They relied entirely on a behavioral observation: Observers can take three different colors of light and then, by mixing them in various proportions, match all other colors of light. (Note that mixing light of different colors is not the same as mixing paints of different colors. Mixing yellow and blue *paints* produces green; mixing yellow and blue *lights* produces white.)

The short-wavelength cones, which respond most strongly to blue, are less numerous than the other two types, especially in the fovea. Consequently, a tiny blue point may look black. In order for the retina to detect blueness, the blue must extend over a moderately large area. Figure 4.11 illustrates this effect. Count the red spots and then the blue spots. Then stand farther away and count the spots again. You will probably see as many red spots as before but fewer blue spots.

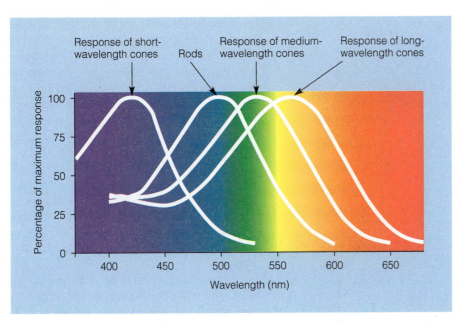

FIGURE 4.10
Sensitivity of the rods and three types of cones to different wavelengths of light. (Based on data of Bowmaker & Dartnall, 1980.)

CONCEPT CHECK

5. According to the trichromatic theory, how does our nervous system tell the difference between bright yellow-green and dim yellow-green light? (Check your answer on page 137.)

THE OPPONENT-PROCESS THEORY

Young and Helmholtz were right about how many cones we have, but our perception of color has some complicated features that the trichromatic theory fails to explain. Another 19th-century scientist, Ewald Hering, having noticed that color perceptions seem to occur in pairs, proposed the **opponent-process theory** of color vision, which accounts for much of what happens to visual information after it leaves the cones in the retina. According to this theory, we perceive color not in terms of independent colors but in terms of a system of paired opposites: red versus green, yellow versus blue, and white versus black. Any light stimulus leads to a perception somewhere along each of the three dimensions. Although Hering did not know it, the dimen-

sions correspond to excitation and inhibition of many cells in the visual system (DeValois, 1965; Michael, 1978). For example, some bipolar cells in the eye are excited when green light strikes the cones that connect to them and are inhibited when red light strikes.* Other bipolar cells are excited by red and inhibited by green. Still other cells are excited by yellow and inhibited by blue or excited by blue and inhibited by yellow. The white-black system is more complicated: If a cell is excited by white light, we cannot meaningfully say that it is inhibited by black. Rather, the cell is inhibited when the light on neighboring areas of the retina is brighter than the light in its own area.

For example, in Figure 4.12, bipolar cell 1 receives an excitatory synaptic message from the long-wavelength cone and an inhibitory synaptic message from the medium-wavelength cone. The cell increases its

---

*Technically, it is wrong to talk about red, green, or blue light. I should say "long-wavelength," "medium-wavelength," or "short-wavelength" light. The light itself is not red, green, or any other color; the color perception takes place within us. Furthermore, light that is predominantly medium wavelength can, under certain circumstances, be seen as a color other than green.

FIGURE 4.11
Blue spots look black unless they cover a sizable area. Count the red dots, then count the blue dots. Try again while standing farther away from the page.

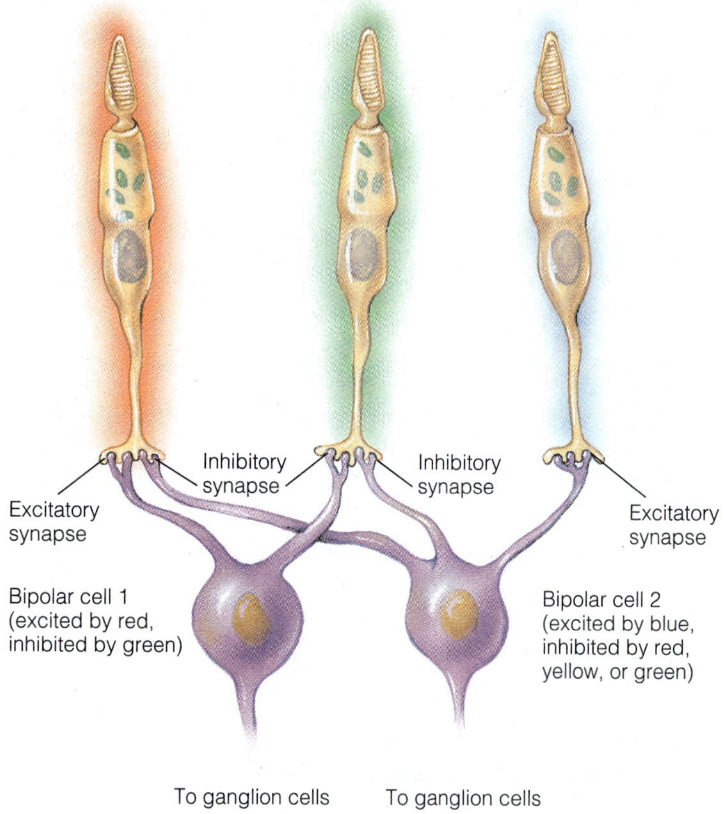

Long-wavelength cone (responds well to red or yellow)

Medium-wavelength cone (responds best to green, less to yellow)

Short-wavelength cone (responds best to blue)

Inhibitory synapse

Inhibitory synapse

Excitatory synapse

Excitatory synapse

Bipolar cell 1 (excited by red, inhibited by green)

Bipolar cell 2 (excited by blue, inhibited by red, yellow, or green)

To ganglion cells

To ganglion cells

FIGURE 4.12

According to the opponent-process theory of color vision, the responses of three kinds of cones excite and inhibit bipolar cells, which relay their responses to later cells in the visual system. For example, red light excites the long-wavelength cone and thereby excites bipolar cell 1; green light excites the medium-wavelength cone and thereby inhibits bipolar cell 1. Therefore, bipolar cell 1 increases its response in the presence of red light and decreases its response in the presence of green light. After prolonged exposure to red light, the cell will "rebound" to an inhibition of response, and therefore report a message of "green."

response in the presence of red light and decreases its response in the presence of green light. Bipolar cell 2 receives excitatory synaptic messages from the short-wavelength cone; it is therefore excited by blue light. Cell 2 receives inhibitory messages from both the long-wavelength cone and the medium-wavelength cone; it will be inhibited by red, yellow, or green light.

Figure 4.13 lends support to the opponent-process theory. Stare at the white dot near the center of the figure for a minute or so, preferably under a bright light, without moving your eyes or your head. Then look at a plain white or gray background. *Do this now.*

If you have normal or near-normal vision, you saw the red, white, and blue U.S. flag when you looked away. After the cells in your visual system have been activated in one direction long enough, removal of the stimulus makes them rebound in the opposite direction. Thus, if you stare at something bright green and then look away, you will see red; if you stare at something yellow and then look away, you will see blue. The rebound colors are called **negative afterimages.**

6. *How would bipolar cell 1 in Figure 4.12 respond to yellow light? Why?*

FIGURE 4.13
Use this figure to see the negative afterimages of opposite colors, which rebound after sufficient stimulation.

7. *The negative afterimage that you created by staring at Figure 4.13 may seem to move against the background. Why doesn't it stay in one place? (Check your answers on page 137.)*

THE RETINEX THEORY

The opponent-process theory, though it accounts for many phenomena of color vision, overlooks a very important one. Suppose you look at a large white screen illuminated entirely with green light, in an otherwise dark room. How would you know whether this is a white screen illuminated with green light or a green screen illuminated with white light? (Or a blue screen illuminated with yellow light? Actually the possibilities go on and on.) The answer is that you would not know. But now someone wearing a brown shirt and blue jeans stands in front of the screen. By comparing what you see of this person to what you see on the screen, you immediately see the shirt as brown, the jeans as blue, and the screen as white, even though all these objects are reflecting more green light than anything else. The point is, we do not ordinarily perceive the color of an object in isolation. We perceive the color of an object by comparing the light it reflects to the light that other objects in the scene reflect. As a result, we can perceive blue jeans as blue and bananas as yellow regardless of whether we are in dim light or bright light, outdoors or indoors, wearing red-tinted glasses or green-tinted glasses, and so forth. This tendency of an object to appear nearly the same color under a variety of lighting conditions is called **color constancy**. (See Figure 4.14.)

In response to such observations, Edwin Land (the inventor of the Polaroid Land camera) proposed the **retinex theory**. According to this theory, we perceive color through the cerebral cortex's comparison of various retinal patterns (Figure 4.15). (*Retinex* is a combination of *retina* and *cortex*.) The cerebral cortex compares the patterns of light coming from different areas of the retina and synthesizes a color perception for each area (Land, Hubel, Livingstone, Perry, & Burns, 1983; Land & McCann, 1971).

The strongest evidence for this theory comes from brain-damaged patients. Damage to one region in the occipital cortex destroys color constancy (Wild, Butler, Carden, & Kulikowski, 1985; Zeki, 1993). To a per-

FIGURE 4.14
Despite the green and red filters used in producing the lower two photographs, you can still identify the colors of the objects in the photos. The effect would be much more convincing if you were actually on location, looking at this scene through tinted glasses. Here, each photo is surrounded by the white page, which sets an effective standard. Your ability to identify the color of an object despite changes in the light striking the environment is called color constancy.

son with such brain damage, an object that looks orange under one light looks red under another. The same object looks yellow, greenish, or even white under still other lights. As the retinex theory predicts, the phenomenon of color constancy depends on the activity of the cerebral cortex.

Note that each of the three theories of color vision deals with different aspects of color vision and that they are not directly in competition with one another. That is, the retinex theory does not deny that we see colors in terms of three pairs of opposites, and

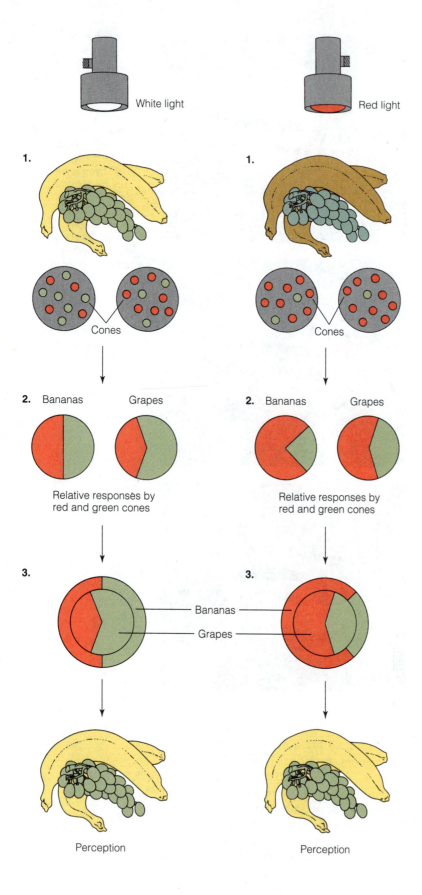

White light

1.

Cones

2. Bananas   Grapes

Relative responses by
red and green cones

3.

Bananas

Grapes

Perception

Red light

1.

Cones

2. Bananas   Grapes

Relative responses by
red and green cones

3.

Perception

FIGURE 4.15
When bananas and grapes reflect red light, they excite a higher percentage of long-wavelength (red) cones than usual. According to the retinex theory, brain cells determine the red-green percentage for each fruit. Then cells in the visual cortex divide the "red-greenness" of the bananas by the "red-greenness" of the grapes to produce color sensations. In red and white light, the ratios between the fruits are nearly constant.

all theories agree that color vision begins with the stimulation of three kinds of cones.

SOMETHING TO THINK ABOUT

If you stare for a minute at a small green object on a white background and then look away, you see a red afterimage. But if you stare at a green wall near you so that you see nothing but green in all directions, then when you look away you do not see a red afterimage. Why not?

COLOR BLINDNESS

For a long time, people apparently assumed that anyone with normal vision could see and recognize colors (Fletcher & Voke, 1985). Then, during the 1600s, the phenomenon of color blindness was unambiguously recognized. Here was the first clue that color vision is a function of our eyes and brains, and not just of the light itself.

The total inability to distinguish one color from another is extremely rare, except as the result of certain kinds of brain damage. However, about 4% of all people are partially color blind. Investigators believe that most cases of color blindness result from either the absence of one of the three types of cones or a decreased responsiveness by one of those types (Fletcher & Voke, 1985). People with a deficiency of the medium-wavelength cones are relatively insensitive to medium-wavelength (green) light. I do not mean that they are unable to see such light; I mean rather that they have trouble discriminating green from other colors. Such people perceive a green patch as almost gray, although they might see very large green patches as green (Boynton, 1988).

The most common type of color blindness is sometimes known as **red-green color blindness.** People with red-green color blindness have difficulty distinguishing red from green and either red or green from yellow.

Actually, red-green color blindness has two forms: *protanopia* and *deuteranopia*. People with protanopia lack long-wavelength cones; people with deuteranopia lack medium-wavelength cones. People with the rare *yellow-blue color blindness* (also known as *tritanopia*) have trouble distinguishing yellows and blues. They are believed to lack short-wavelength cones.

Figure 4.16 gives a crude but usually satisfactory test for red-green color blindness. What do you see in each part of the figure? (To interpret your answers, refer to answer A on page 137.)

How does the world look to color-blind people? Their descriptions use all the usual color words: Roses are red, violets are blue, bananas are yellow, grass is green. But that does not mean that they perceive colors the same way as does a person with normal color vision. Can they tell us what that "red" rose actually looks like to them? In most cases, no. Certain rare individuals, however, are red-green color blind in one eye but have normal vision in the other eye. Because they know what the color words really mean (from experience with their normal eye), they can tell us what their color-blind eye sees. They say that objects that look red or green to the normal eye look yellow or yellow-gray to the color-blind eye (Marriott, 1976).

If you have normal color vision, Figure 4.17 will show you what it is like to be red-green color blind. First cover part b, a typical item from a color-blindness test, and stare at part a, a red field, under a bright light for about a minute. (The brighter the light and the longer you stare, the greater the effect will be.) Then look at part b. Staring at the red field has fatigued your red cones, and you now have only a weak sensation of red.

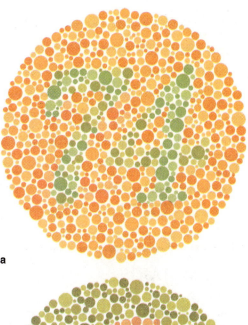

FIGURE 4.16
These items provide an informal test for red-green color blindness, an inherited condition that affects mostly men. What do you see? Compare your answers to answer A, page 137.

a

b

As the red cones recover, you will see part b normally.

Now stare at part c, a green field, for about a minute and look at part b again. Because you have fatigued your green cones, the figure in b will stand out even more strongly than usual. In fact, certain red-green

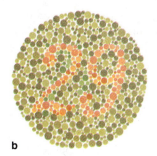

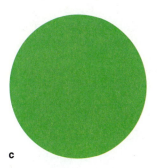

a

b

c

FIGURE 4.17
These stimuli induce temporary red-green color blindness and temporarily enhance color vision. First stare at pattern a under a bright light for about a minute, then look at b. What do you see? Next stare at c for a minute and look at b again. Now what do you see? Compare your answer to answer B, page 137.

color-blind people may be able to see the number in b only after staring at c. (Refer to answer B on page 137.)

(Refer to answer B on page 137.)

SOMETHING TO THINK ABOUT

The introduction to this chapter suggested that we would see no new colors on another planet and that we cannot be certain that different people on Earth really have the same color experiences. Try now to explain the reasons behind those statements.

SUMMARY

- *The coding of sensory information.* The brain does not build little copies of the stimuli it senses. It converts or translates sensory stimuli into an arbitrary code that represents the information. (page 123)

- *Focus.* The cornea and lens focus the light that enters through the pupil of the eye. If the eye is not spherical or if the lens is not flexible, corrective lenses may be needed. (page 124)

- *Cones and rods.* The retina contains two kinds of receptors: cones and rods. Cones are specialized for detailed vision and color perception. Rods detect dim light. (page 126)

- *Blind spot.* The blind spot is the area of the retina through which the optic nerve exits; this area has no receptors and is therefore blind. (page 128)

- *Three types of cones.* Color vision depends on three types of cones, each most sensitive to a particular range of light wavelengths. The cones transmit messages so that the bipolar and ganglion cells in the visual system are excited by light of one color and inhibited by light of the opposite color. Then the cerebral cortex compares the responses from different parts of the retina to determine the color of light coming from each area of the visual field. (page 129)

- *Color blindness.* Complete color blindness is rare. Certain people have difficulty distinguishing reds from greens; in rare cases, some have difficulty distinguishing yellows from blues. (page 134)

SUGGESTIONS FOR FURTHER READING

Goldstein, E. B. (1989). *Sensation and perception* (3rd ed.). Belmont, CA: Wadsworth. An excellent textbook covering sensory processes.

Hubel, D. H. (1988). *Eye, brain, and vision.* New York: Scientific American Library. A treatment by an investigator who shared the Nobel Prize in physiology and medicine for his research on the physiology of vision.

TERMS

sensation the conversion of energy from the environment into a pattern of response by the nervous system (page 122)

perception the interpretation of sensory information (page 122)

stimulus an energy in the environment that affects what we do (page 123)

receptor a specialized cell that converts environmental energies into signals for the nervous system (page 123)

electromagnetic spectrum the continuum of all the frequencies of radiated energy (page 123)

pupil the adjustable opening in the eye through which light enters (page 124)

iris the colored structure on the surface of the eye, surrounding the pupil (page 124)

retina a layer of visual receptors covering the back surface of the eyeball (page 124)

cornea a rigid, transparent structure on the surface of the eyeball (page 124)

lens a flexible structure that can vary its thickness to enable the eye to focus on objects at different distances (page 124)

accommodation of the lens adjustment of the thickness of the lens in order to focus on objects at different distances (page 124)

myopia nearsightedness, the inability to focus on distant objects (page 124)

presbyopia farsightedness, the inability to focus on nearby objects (page 124)

glaucoma condition characterized by increased pressure within the eyeball, resulting in damage to the optic nerve and therefore a loss of vision (page 125)

cataract disorder in which the lens of the eye becomes cloudy (page 125)

cone the type of visual receptor that is adapted for color vision, daytime vision, and detailed vision (page 126)

rod the type of visual receptor that is adapted for vision in dim light (page 126)

fovea the central part of the retina that has a greater density of receptors, especially cones, than any other part of the retina (page 126)

dark adaptation a gradual improvement in the ability to see under dim light (page 127)

ganglion cells neurons in the eye that receive input from the visual receptors and send impulses via the optic nerve to the brain (page 128)

optic nerve a set of axons that extends from the ganglion cells of the eye to the thalamus and

blind spot the area of the retina through which the optic nerve exits (page 128)

trichromatic theory or **Young-Helmholtz theory** the theory that color vision depends on the relative rate of response by three types of cones (page 129)

opponent-process theory (of color vision) the theory that we perceive color in terms of a system of paired opposites: red versus green, yellow versus blue, and white versus black (page 131)

negative afterimage a color that a person sees after staring at the opposite color for a while (page 132)

color constancy the tendency of an object to appear nearly the same color under a variety of lighting conditions (page 133)

retinex theory the theory that color perception results from the cerebral cortex's comparison of various retinal patterns (page 133)

red-green color blindness the inability to distinguish red from green and either red or green from yellow (page 134)

ANSWERS TO CONCEPT CHECKS

1. If your vision is normal, wearing glasses intended for a myopic person will make your vision blurry. Such glasses alter the light as if they were bringing the object closer to the viewer. Unless the glasses are very strong, you may not notice much difference when you are looking at distant objects, because you can adjust the lens of your eyes to compensate for what the glasses do. However, nearby objects will appear blurry in spite of the best compensations you can make with the lenses of your eyes. (page 126)
2. The center of the retina consists entirely of cones. If you look slightly to the side, the light falls on an area of the retina that consists partly of rods, which are more sensitive to faint light. (page 127)
3. As with people, cats can adapt well to dim light. No animal, however, can see in complete darkness. Vision is the detection of light that strikes the eye. (Similarly, the X-ray vision attributed to the comic book character Superman is impossible. Even if he could send out X rays, he would not see anything unless those X rays bounced off some object and back into his eyes.) (page 128)
4. You will see more objects in the periphery of your eye. The fovea contains only cones, which cannot become as sensitive as the rods do in the periphery. (page 128)
5. Although bright yellow-green and dim yellow-green light would evoke the same ratio of activity by the three cone types, the total amount of activity would be greater for the bright yellow-green light. (page 131)
6. Bipolar cell 1 would be almost unaffected by yellow light. Yellow light would stimulate the long-wavelength cone, which excites bipolar cell 1, but it would stimulate the medium-wavelength cone, which inhibits bipolar cell 1, about equally. (page 132)
7. The afterimage is on your eye, not on the background. When you try to focus on a different part of the afterimage, you move your eyes and the afterimage moves with them. (page 133)

ANSWERS TO OTHER QUESTIONS IN THE TEXT

A. In Figure 4.16a, a person with normal color vision sees the numeral 74; in Figure 4.16b, the numeral 8.
B. In Figure 4.17b, you should see the numeral 29.

THE NONVISUAL SENSES

How do hearing, the vestibular sense, skin senses, pain, taste, and olfaction work?

Consider these common expressions:

I *see* what you mean.

I *feel* sympathetic toward your plight.

I am deeply *touched* by everyone's support and concern.

The Senate will *hold* hearings on the budget proposal.

She is a person of great *taste*.

He was *dizzy* with success.

The policies of this company *stink*.

That *sounds* like a good job offer.

Each sentence expresses an idea in terms of sensation, though we know that the terms are not meant to be taken literally. When we say, "He has great taste," we are not talking about his tongue. Rather, we use such terms to describe a wide variety of concepts.

That usage is not accidental. Our thinking and brain activity deal mostly, if not entirely, with sensory stimuli. Perhaps you doubt that assertion: "What about abstract concepts?" you might object. "Sometimes I think about numbers, time, love, justice, and all sorts of other nonsensory concepts." Yes, but how did you learn those concepts? Didn't you learn numbers by counting objects you could see or touch? Didn't you learn about time by observing changes in sensory stimuli? Didn't you learn about love and justice from specific events that you saw, heard, and felt? Could you explain any abstract concept without referring to examples that we detect through our senses?

Sensations bring us in contact with the energies of the outside world. We have al-ready considered how we detect light. Now let us deal with the the ways in which we detect sounds, head tilt, skin stimulation, and chemicals.

◾ HEARING

Fish detect vibrations in the water by means of a long row of touch receptors along their sides, called the *lateral line system*. The mammalian ear, which probably evolved as a modification of the lateral line system, converts sound waves into mechanical displacements of a membrane that a row of receptor cells can detect.

Sound waves are vibrations of the air or of some other medium. They vary in both frequency and amplitude (Figure 4.18). The *frequency* of a sound wave is the number of cycles (vibrations) it goes through per second. **Pitch** is a perception closely related to frequency. We perceive a high-frequency sound wave as high pitched and a low-frequency sound as low pitched. **Loudness** is our perception that depends on the amplitude of a sound wave—the vertical range of its cycles. Other things being equal, the greater the *amplitude* of a sound, the louder it sounds to us. Because pitch and loudness are psychological concepts, however, they can sometimes be influenced by factors other

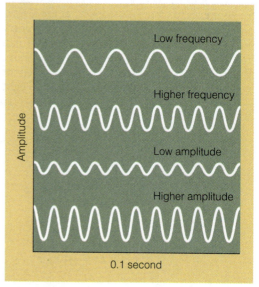

FIGURE 4.18
The period (time) between the peaks of a sound wave determines the frequency of the sound; we experience frequencies as different pitches. The vertical range, or amplitude, of a wave determines the sound's intensity and loudness.

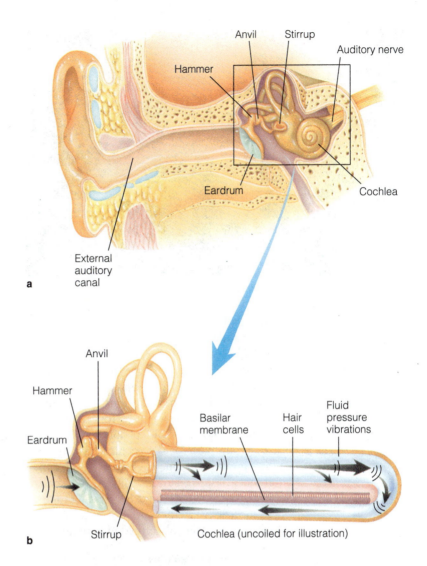

than the physical frequency and amplitude of sound waves.

The ear, a complicated organ, converts relatively weak sound waves into more intense waves of pressure in the fluid-filled canals of the snail-shaped **cochlea** (KOCK-lee-uh), which contains the receptors for hearing (Figure 4.19). When sound waves strike the eardrum, they cause it to vibrate. The eardrum is connected to three tiny bones: the hammer, anvil, and stirrup (also known by their Latin names: malleus, incus, and stapes). As the weak vibrations of the large eardrum travel through these bones, they are transformed into stronger vibrations of the much smaller stirrup. The stirrup in turn transmits the vibrations to the fluid-filled cochlea, where the vibrations displace hair cells along the **basilar membrane,** a thin structure within the cochlea. These hair cells, which act much like touch receptors on the skin, are connected to neurons whose axons form the auditory nerve. Impulses are transmitted along this pathway to the areas of the brain responsible for hearing.

A person can lose hearing in two ways. One is **conduction deafness,** which results if the bones connected to the eardrum fail to transmit sound waves properly to the cochlea. Sometimes surgery can correct conduction deafness by removing whatever is obstructing the movement of those bones. A person with conduction deafness can still hear his or her own voice, because it can be conducted through the skull bones to the cochlea, bypassing the eardrum altogether. The other type of hearing loss is **nerve deafness,** which results from damage to the cochlea, the hair cells, or the auditory nerve. Nerve deafness can result from heredity, from multiple sclerosis and other diseases, and from prolonged exposure to loud noises. Nerve deafness is permanent and cannot be corrected by surgery.

Hearing is the sensing of vibrations. Evelyn Glennie, profoundly deaf since childhood, has become a famous percussionist. Although she cannot hear her music, she detects the vibrations through her stocking feet.

Most older people experience some loss of hearing, which may be restored by a hearing aid. Younger people may also experience a hearing loss, especially after frequent or prolonged exposure to loud sounds. Both rock performers and their audiences risk a hearing loss.

Hearing aids can compensate for the hearing loss in most people with either conduction deafness or nerve deafness (Moore, 1989). Hearing aids merely increase the intensity of the sound, so they are of little help to people with severe damage to the cochlea or the auditory nerve. Many people have hearing impairments only for certain frequencies. For example, people with damage to certain parts of the cochlea have trouble hearing high frequencies or medium-range frequencies. Modern hearing aids can be adjusted to intensify only a certain range of sounds so that they do not intensify the sounds that were already loud enough.

PITCH PERCEPTION

The adult human ear responds to sound waves from about 15–20 hertz to about 15,000–20,000 hertz (Hz). (A **hertz,** named for German physicist Heinrich Hertz, is a unit of frequency equaling one cycle per second.) The low frequencies are perceived as deep tones of low pitch; the high frequencies are perceived as tones of high pitch. The upper limit of hearing declines suddenly after exposure to loud noises and declines steadily as a person grows older. Thus, children sometimes hear high-frequency sounds that adults do not.

The ability to perceive pitch depends on the *frequency* of vibrations along the basilar membrane, *volleys* of such vibrations, and the *place* along the membrane where the vibrations are greatest. At low frequencies (up to about 100 Hz), the basilar membrane in the cochlea vibrates in synchrony with the sound waves; that is, it produces action potentials at the same frequency as the sound. This is the **frequency principle.** A sound with a frequency of 50 Hz excites each hair cell along the membrane 50 times per second, sending 50 impulses per second to the brain.

At intermediate frequencies (about 100–5000 Hz), the basilar membrane continues to vibrate in synchrony with the sound waves. However, the individual hair cells are unable to send an impulse to the brain every time the membrane vibrates. (A neuron cannot fire more than about 1000 action potentials per second, and it cannot maintain that pace for long.) Even so, each vibration of the membrane excites at least a few hair cells, and groups of them (volleys) respond to each vibration by producing an action potential (Rose, Brugge, Anderson, & Hind, 1967). This is the **volley principle.** Thus, a tone at 2000 Hz might send impulses to the brain 2000 times per second, even though no neuron by itself could produce all those impulses.

At high frequencies, sound waves of different frequencies cause vibrations at different locations along the basilar membrane. The membrane is thin and stiff near the stirrup and wide and floppy at the other end. Consequently, high-frequency sounds cause maximum vibration near the stirrup end, and lower-frequency sounds cause maximum vibration at points farther along the membrane. During a high-frequency sound, hair cells near the stirrup become active; during a low-frequency sound, hair cells at the opposite end become active. This is the **place principle.** The brain can identify the frequency by noting which cells are most active.

The reason we can discriminate among pitches is that different pitches excite different hair cells along the basilar membrane (Zwislocki, 1981). Figure 4.20 shows how we perceive pitches of low, medium, and high frequency.

CONCEPT CHECKS

8. Suppose a mouse emits a soft, high-frequency squeak in a room full of people. Which kinds of people are least likely to hear the squeak?

9. When hair cells at one point along the basilar membrane produce 50 impulses per second, we hear a tone at 5000 Hz. What do we hear when those same hair cells produce 100 impulses per second? (Check your answers on pages 151–152.)

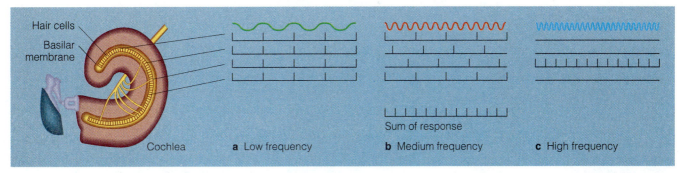

Hair cells
Basilar membrane

Cochlea
a Low frequency
Sum of response
b Medium frequency
c High frequency

ABSOLUTE PITCH PERCEPTION

Suppose a violinist plays a note and then invites the listeners to guess what that note was. Most of the listeners look at one another blankly as if to say, "How should I know?" One of the listeners, however, announces confidently, "That was an F-sharp above middle C." People who can identify a note correctly are said to have **absolute pitch**. When they make an error, they are usually close, such as saying F-sharp when the actual note was F-natural. If such a person consistently misses by half a note (either too sharp or too flat), the explanation generally turns out to be that the violin or piano used for the test was tuned a bit differently from the one the person most often uses.

Fewer than 1 person in 10,000 possesses absolute pitch (Takeuchi & Hulse, 1993). Is this a special talent that some people inherit? No, the research indicates that the ability is acquired through years of musical training. "Ah," you ask, "then I could learn this ability?" Sorry, you asked too late, unless you happen to be a remarkably young reader of this book. As in many other cases of perceptual development, early experience has more powerful effects than later experience. Absolute pitch develops only in those who begin intensive musical training well before age six and then continue it on a consistent basis into adulthood (Takeuchi & Hulse, 1993). Unless people have already refined the ability to identify a note (absolute pitch) by the age of six, they will from then on attend almost entirely to the relationships among notes (the melodies).

Curiously, researchers have found some consistent differences between the brains of adult musicians with absolute pitch and those without it (Scheibel, 1984; Schlaug, Jäncke, Huang, & Steinmetz, 1995). Because of the evidence linking absolute pitch to early practice, we infer that the early practice led to the differences in brain structure. If so, this example is one of the most striking cases of how experience can influence brain development.

LOCALIZATION OF SOUNDS

When you hear something, the stimulus is actually on the basilar membrane of your ear, but you do not experience it as such. You experience it as "out there," and you can generally estimate approximately where it came from. How do you do that?

The auditory system determines the direction of a source of sound by comparing the messages coming from the two ears. If a sound is coming from a source directly in front, the messages will arrive at the two ears at the same time and will be equal in loudness. If the sound is coming from a source on the left, however, it will arrive at the left ear slightly before it arrives at the right ear, and it will be louder in the left ear (Figure 4.21). Yet you do not hear two sounds; you have an experience of a single sound coming from the left. A difference between the messages in the two ears indicates how far the sound source is to the left or right of center. (Someone who wears a hearing aid in just one ear may experience inaccuracy in localizing sounds.)

The auditory system also can detect the approximate distance of a sound source. If a sound grows louder, you interpret it as coming closer. If one sound includes more high-frequency tones than another does, you assume the one with the high-frequency tones is closer. (Low-frequency tones carry better over a long distance than high-frequency tones do.) However, loudness and frequency tell you only the *relative* distances of sound sources; neither one provides information about the *absolute* distance. The only cue for absolute distance is the amount of reverberation (Mershon & King, 1975). In a closed room, you first hear the sound waves that

FIGURE 4.20
The auditory system responds differently to low-, medium-, and high-frequency tones. (a) At low frequencies, hair cells at many points along the basilar membrane produce impulses in synchrony with the sound waves. (b) At medium frequencies, different cells produce impulses in synchrony with different waves, but the group as a whole still produces one or more impulses for each wave. (c) At high frequencies, only one point along the basilar membrane vibrates; hair cells at other locations are silent.

FIGURE 4.21

The stereophonic hearing of our ears enables us to determine where a sound is coming from. The ear located closest to the sound will receive the sound waves first. A change of less than one ten-thousandth of a second can alter our perception of the location of a sound source.

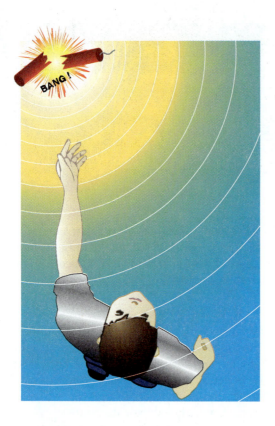

THE VESTIBULAR SENSE

In the inner ear, on each side of the head, adjacent to the structures responsible for hearing, is a structure called the *vestibule*. The **vestibular sense** that it controls tells us the direction of tilt and amount of acceleration of our head, and the position of our head with respect to gravity. It plays a key role in posture and balance and is responsible for the sensations we experience when we are riding on a roller coaster or sitting in an airplane during takeoff.

The vestibular sense also enables us to keep our eyes focused even when our head is moving. When you walk down the street, you can keep your eyes focused on a distant street sign even though your head is bobbing up and down. The vestibular sense detects each head movement and controls the movement of your eyes to compensate for it.

Do this experiment: Try to read this page while you are jiggling the book up and down and from side to side, keeping your head steady. Now hold the book steady and move your head up and down and from side to side, keeping the book steady. If you are like most people, you will find it much easier to read when you are moving your head than when you are jiggling the book. That is because your vestibular sense keeps your eyes focused on the print during head movements. People who have suffered injury to their vestibular sense report that they have to hold their head perfectly steady in order to read street signs or clocks. If they move their head even a bit, their vision becomes blurred.

The vestibular system is composed of three semicircular canals, oriented in three separate directions, and two otolith organs (Figure 4.22b). The *semicircular canals* are lined with hair cells and filled with a jellylike substance. When the body accelerates in any direction, the jellylike substance in the corresponding semicircular canal pushes against the hair cells, which send messages to the brain. The two *otolith organs* shown in Figure 4.22b also contain hair cells (Figure 4.22c), which lie next to the *otoliths* (calcium carbonate particles). Depending on which way the head tilts, the particles move about in the direction of the gravitational pull and excite different sets of hair cells. The otolith organs report the direction from which gravity is pulling and tell us which way is "up."

What happens if the otoliths fail to pro-

come directly from the source and then, after a delay, the waves that are reflected off the walls, floor, ceiling, and objects in the room. The more distant the source, the greater the percentage of reflected and delayed sound you hear. When you hear many reflected sounds (echoes), you judge the source of the sound to be far away. In a noisy room, the noise interferes mostly with the weakest sounds, the echoes. In such a room, people have trouble estimating the distances of sounds; because they hear few echoes, they interpret all sounds as coming from short distances (McMurtry & Mershon, 1985).

CONCEPT CHECKS

10. Why is it difficult to tell whether a sound is originating directly in front of or directly behind you?

11. Suppose you are listening to a radio with just one speaker (not stereo). Can the station play sounds that you will localize as coming from different directions, such as left, center, and right? Can it play sounds that you will localize as coming from different distances? Why or why not? (Check your answers on page 152.)

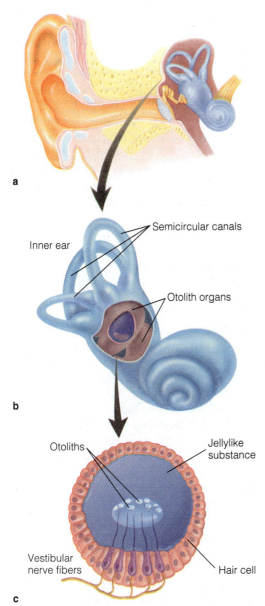

FIGURE 4.22
(a) Location of and (b) structures of the vestibule. (c) Moving your head or body displaces hair cells that report the tilt of your head and the direction and acceleration of movement.

a

Inner ear

Semicircular canals

b

Otolith organs

c

Otoliths

Jellylike substance

Vestibular nerve fibers

Hair cell

These Turkish whirling dervishes subject their heads to enormous vestibular sensation. Nevertheless, through long practice, they have learned to maintain their direction and balance without showing overt signs of dizziness.

■ THE CUTANEOUS SENSES

What we commonly think of as the sense of touch actually consists of several partly independent senses: pressure on the skin, warmth, cold, pain, vibration, movement across the skin, and stretch of the skin. These sensations depend on several kinds of receptors in the skin, as Figure 4.23 shows (Iggo & Andres, 1982). A pinch on the skin feels different from a tickle, and both feel different from a cut or a burn, because each of these stimuli excites different receptors. Collectively, these sensations are known as the **cutaneous senses,** meaning the skin senses. Although they are most prominent in the skin, we have some of the same receptors in

vide reliable information? Astronauts in the zero-gravity environment of outer space, for whom the otoliths provide no useful information about up or down, have to rely entirely on visual signals instead. They have to inhibit lifelong habits such as placing an object on a table. (Unless the object is tied down, it will float away.) Because they store each object in a consistent place, the places for different objects help to define the axes of their environment—up and down, front and back (Lackner, 1993).

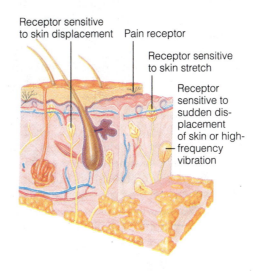

Receptor sensitive to skin displacement

Pain receptor

Receptor sensitive to skin stretch

Receptor sensitive to sudden displacement of skin or high-frequency vibration

FIGURE 4.23
Cutaneous sensation is the product of many kinds of receptors, each sensitive to a particular kind of information.

FIGURE 4.24
Sighted and blind subjects felt these raised-line drawings and tried to identify what they represented. Most sighted subjects and subjects blind since birth found the task very difficult and seldom answered correctly. Subjects who had become blind later in life performed much better. (From Heller, 1989.)

our internal organs as well, enabling us to feel internal pain, pressure, or temperature changes. Therefore, the cutaneous senses are sometimes known by the broader term *somatosensory system,* meaning *body-sensory system.*

On the fingertips, the lips, and other highly sensitive areas of skin, the receptors are densely packed, and each receptor detects stimulation in only a small area of the skin. On the back and other less sensitive areas, the receptors are scattered more widely, and each one is responsible for detecting stimulation over a large surface. Similarly, much more of the parietal lobe is devoted to sensation from the lips and fingers than from the less sensitive areas.

If you ask someone to place some everyday object (such as a pencil or a spoon) in your hand without showing it to you or telling you what it is, you will find that you can probably identify the object just by feeling it. With a more complicated or less familiar object, such as a scale model of the Statue of Liberty, you will probably fail to identify it, even though you would identify it easily by sight. With extensive practice, you could improve on your ability to identify objects by touch. Subjects in one study felt raised-line drawings, like those in Figure 4.24, without

seeing them. Some of the subjects were sighted; some were blind since birth; and some had become blind later in life. Most sighted people found it very difficult to identify what the drawings represented, presumably because they had little practice at paying close attention to touch. People blind since birth also had little success on this task, but for a different reason: A raised-line drawing of an umbrella or similar object makes little sense to someone who has never seen the object. In contrast, people who had lost their vision later in life were able to identify many of the objects (Heller, 1989). They had the advantage of previous experience with visual drawings, plus years of practice in paying close attention to touch.

PAIN

We experience pain in many ways: when we cut a finger, spill an irritating chemical on our skin, or suffer exposure to extreme heat or cold. Pain receptors are simple, bare nerve endings that send messages to the spinal cord. However, the experience of pain is a complicated mixture of sensation (the information about tissue damage) and emotion (the unpleasant reaction). The intensity of the emotional response is not closely related to the sensory response; in fact, the sensory and emotional qualities are probably handled by different parts of the brain (Craig, Bushnell, Zhang, & Blomqvist, 1994; Fernandez & Turk, 1992).

Here is one peculiarity of pain: One's memory of a painful experience relates more closely to the average intensity of the pain than to the duration of the pain. In one experiment, college students were given two painful experiences and then asked to choose which of the two they would prefer to repeat. One (not always the first) was to immerse a hand in water kept at 14.1 °C (painfully cold) for 60 seconds. The other was to immerse the other hand in water that was kept at 14.1 °C for 60 seconds and then gradually increased to 15.2 °C (still unpleasantly cold) for the next 30 seconds. Of 32 subjects in this experiment, 22 preferred the longer of the two painful experiences (Kahneman, Fredrickson, Schreiber, & Redelmeier, 1993). Note that the first 60 seconds produced the same pain in both experiences; the "advantage" of the second experience was the addition of 30 seconds of slightly less intense pain. That is, our memory of pain depends on the average intensity of the pain or the amount of pain at the end, rather than the total sum of pain.

SOMETHING TO THINK ABOUT

Could a dentist make a painful experience seem better by adding a slightly less painful experience at the end?

Would this principle about pain apply to boredom as well? For example, if at the end of a boring lecture someone added a slightly less boring segment, would a listener be inclined to prefer that lecture over a shorter but completely boring lecture?

The Gate Theory of Pain The intensity of a pain depends on the person's other sensory experiences and motivations of the moment. For example, you can make a cut on your leg hurt less if you rub the skin around it or apply cold packs or hot packs (Rollman, 1991). You might not even notice the pain if you are concentrating on other matters. Injured soldiers and athletes sometimes completely ignore a painful injury until the end of the battle or the end of the athletic contest. In other cases, people sometimes complain of severe pain after what appears to be a very minor injury. And some people continue to feel pain long after an injury has healed, almost as if pain had become a learned habit.

Because of observations such as these, Ronald Melzack and P. D. Wall (1965) proposed the **gate theory** of pain, the idea that pain messages have to pass through a gate in the spinal cord on their way to the brain. The brain and receptors in the skin can send messages to the spinal cord to open or close that gate. Although some details of Melzack and Wall's theory are apparently wrong, their basic idea is valid: The activity of the rest of the brain can facilitate or inhibit the transmission of pain messages (Figure 4.25).

Mechanisms of Decreasing Pain Pain alerts us to an injury. A small number of people are completely insensitive to pain. They burn themselves by picking up hot objects; they scald their tongues on hot coffee; they cut themselves without realizing it; they bite their tongues hard, possibly even biting off the tip; they sit in a single position for hours without growing uncomfortable, thereby damaging their bones and tendons. Only with much supervision or considerable luck

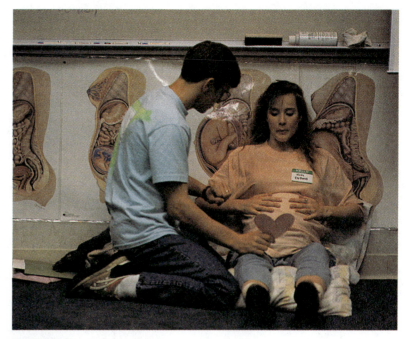

FIGURE 4.25
The Lamaze method of giving birth emphasizes control of pain sensations by changing attitudes, controlling fears and anxieties, and concentrating on breathing. It is one example of how the brain can close "pain gates" and thereby alter pain sensation.

can such a person survive to adulthood (Comings & Amromin, 1974).

Although a pain message serves an essential function of alerting us to danger and damage, a prolonged, intense pain message is unnecessary and sometimes disruptive. One way to reduce the sensation of pain is to provide some distraction. According to the gate theory, the distraction closes the pain gate. For example, surgery patients in a room with a pleasant view complain less about pain, take less painkilling medicine, and recover faster than do patients in a windowless room or a room with a poor view (Ulrich, 1984). Many people relieve their pain by listening to music, by playing games, or by recollecting some pleasant experience (Lavine, Buchsbaum, & Poncy, 1976; McCaul & Malott, 1984).

We also have some biological mechanisms to put the brakes on pain. Pain messages in the nervous system depend on the release of a neurotransmitter called **substance P.** Another set of synapses, which release **endorphins** as their neurotransmitters, inhibit the release of substance P and thereby decrease pain sensations (Reichling, Kwiat, & Basbaum, 1988; Terman, Shavitt, Lewis,

FIGURE 4.26
Substance P is the neurotransmitter most responsible for pain sensations. Endorphins are neurotransmitters that block the release of substance P, thereby decreasing pain sensations. Opiates decrease pain by mimicking the effects of endorphins.

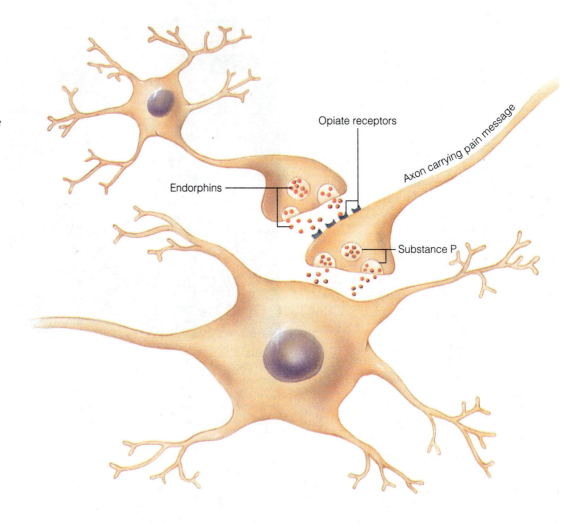

Opiate receptors

Axon carrying pain message

Endorphins

Substance P

Cannon, & Liebeskind, 1984). (See Figure 4.26.) The term *endorphin* is a combination of the terms *endogenous* (self-produced) and *morphine*. The drug morphine has long been known for its ability to inhibit pain; it does so by stimulating the endorphin synapses in the brain. A variety of nondrug stimuli can also release endorphins. Under some circumstances, a painful stimulus itself releases endorphins so that exposure to one painful stimulus decreases sensitivity to the next painful stimulus (Terman & Liebeskind, 1986). Pleasant stimuli may also release endorphins. (That effect may help explain why a pleasant view helps to ease postsurgical pain.) In short, endorphins are a powerful method, perhaps the main method, of closing pain "gates."

Paradoxically, another method of decreasing pain begins by inducing it. The chemical **capsaicin** causes the release of substance P. Injecting capsaicin or rubbing it on the skin produces a temporary burning or stinging sensation (Karrer & Bartoshuk, 1991; Yarsh, Farb, Leeman, & Jessell, 1979).

However, because capsaicin releases substance P faster than the neurons can resynthesize it, the result is a fairly long-lasting decrease in pain sensitivity after the burning sensation subsides. A number of skin creams intended for the relief of aching muscles contain capsaicin. (Don't rub them on right before you go to bed. They produce a burning sensation before they relieve the muscle pain.)

Jalapeños and other hot peppers contain capsaicin. The reason they taste hot is that their capsaicin releases enough substance P from the tongue to cause a stinging, hot sensation.

CONCEPT CHECKS

12. *Naloxone, a drug used as an antidote for an overdose of morphine, is known to block the endorphin synapses. How could we use naloxone to determine whether a pleasant stimulus releases endorphins?*

13. *Psychologist Linda Bartoshuk recommends candies containing moderate amounts of jalapeño peppers as a treatment for people*

CHAPTER 4
SENSATION AND
PERCEPTION

146

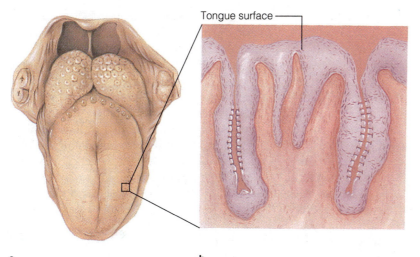

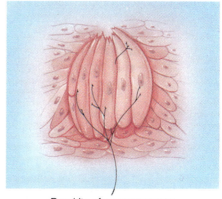

Tongue surface

Dendrite of sensory neuron

a   b   c

FIGURE 4.27
(a) The tongue, a powerful muscle used in speaking and eating. Taste buds, which react to chemicals dissolved in saliva, are located along the edge of the tongue in adult humans, but are more widely distributed in children. (b) A cross section through part of the surface of the tongue, showing taste buds. (c) A cross section of one taste bud. Each taste bud has about 50 receptor cells within it.

with pain in the mouth. Why? (Check your answers on page 152.)

THE CHEMICAL SENSES: TASTE AND SMELL

The **chemical receptors** responsible for taste and smell are evolutionarily ancient and found throughout the animal kingdom. Most textbooks on sensation concentrate on vision and hearing; some ignore taste and smell or include them in a chapter titled "The Other Senses" or even "The Minor Senses." For most of the animal kingdom, however, these senses are not so minor. If rats or raccoons wrote sensation textbooks, they would probably devote as much coverage to taste and smell as they would to hearing; vision would be one of the "minor senses." A number of invertebrates have no vision or hearing at all, getting by with only chemical senses and touch.

TASTE

Vision and hearing enable us to do many different things: to find food and water, to avoid danger, to keep our balance, and to find suitable mates. The sense of **taste,** which detects chemicals on the tongue, serves just one function: It tells us what is safe to eat and drink.

The taste receptors are located in **taste buds,** located almost exclusively along the outside edge of the tongue in adults (Figure 4.27). (Children's taste buds are more widely scattered.) Try this demonstration (based on Bartoshuk, 1991): Soak something small (the tip of a paper napkin will do) in sugar water, salt water, or vinegar. Then dab it onto the center of your tongue. You will taste nothing. Then slowly move the substance toward the side of the tongue. Suddenly you taste it.

If you go the other direction (first touching the side of the tongue and then moving toward the center), you will continue to taste the substance even when it reaches the center of your tongue. The explanation is not that you suddenly grew new taste buds. Rather, your taste buds provide no information about location. Once you have stimulated the taste buds near the edge of the tongue, you will continue tasting the substance, but the taste receptors do not tell you *where* you are tasting it. If you now stimulate *touch* receptors elsewhere on your tongue, your brain interprets the taste perception as coming from the spot you are touching, even though in fact the taste sensation is coming from a different location (the side of your tongue).

Different Types of Taste Receptors Researchers now have a reasonably clear understanding of the structures of the taste receptors and how they work (Margolskee, 1993). Actually, long before neuroscientists began characterizing taste receptors, behavioral researchers had solid evidence that different tastes depend on different kinds of receptors, representing sweet, sour, salty, and bitter. That conclusion rested partly on the demonstrations that people can match almost any taste by mixing sweet, sour, salty, and bitter substances (Schiffman & Erickson, 1971). The conclusion was also supported by evidence that certain procedures can affect one taste without affecting others, presumably by acting on only one type of receptor. Here are two examples:

• Cooling the tongue decreases one's sensitivity to the taste of sucrose and other sweet substances with little or no effect on other tastes (Frankmann & Green, 1988). This finding suggests that the receptors for sweet tastes have different properties from the receptors for other tastes. (It also implies that hot apple pie should taste sweeter than cold apple pie.)

• Have you ever drunk a glass of orange juice just after brushing your teeth? How can something that ordinarily tastes so good suddenly taste so bad? The reason is that most toothpastes contain sodium lauryl sulfate, a chemical that weakens our response to sweet tastes and intensifies our response to sour and bitter tastes (Schiffman, 1983). Again, the implication is that different taste receptors have different properties.

People in different parts of the world have different taste preferences. Contrast, for example, Greek cuisine, Mexican cuisine, and Chinese cuisine. Do cultures' different food preferences relate in any way to differences in people's sense of taste? Evidently not. People throughout the world are very much alike in their ability to taste various substances (e.g., Laing et al., 1993). Their food preferences depend mainly on what is familiar to them.

OLFACTION

Olfaction is the sense of smell. The olfactory receptors, located on the mucous membrane in the rear air passages of the nose (Figure 4.28b), detect the presence of certain airborne molecules. Chemically, these receptors are much like synaptic receptors, except that they are stimulated by chemicals from the environment instead of chemicals released by other neurons. The axons of the olfactory receptors form the olfactory tract, which extends to the olfactory bulbs at the base of the brain.

How many kinds of olfactory receptors do we have? Investigators have long known that color vision depends on three kinds of receptors; they have also long known at least approximately how many receptor types we have for hearing, touch, and taste. In olfaction, however, until 1991 researchers had virtually no idea how many types of receptors might exist.

In principle, researchers can determine the number of receptor types through behavioral data, without chemically isolating the receptors. In color vision, for example, researchers of the 1800s established that people can mix three colors of light in various amounts to match any other color. Therefore, even before they had the technology to examine the cones in the retina, they had reason to believe that the retina has three kinds of cones. In taste, the fact that we can mix sweet, sour, salty, and bitter substances to match almost any other taste implies that the tongue has perhaps only four kinds of taste receptors. When we come to olfaction, no one knew how many kinds of receptors to expect. Can people match all possible odors by mixing appropriate amounts of three, four, seven, or ten "primary" odors? Or do they need fifty, a hundred, or what? No researcher had ever demonstrated that it was possible to match all the possible odors by mixing some number of primaries.

Perhaps it is just as well that no one spent a lifetime trying. In 1991, Linda Buck and Richard Axel used the latest biochemical technology to demonstrate that the nose has at least a hundred types of olfactory receptors, and probably several hundred (Buck & Axel, 1991). In most cases, a given receptor responds well to only a limited family of odorant molecules (Ressler, Sullivan, & Buck, 1994). Exactly how the brain makes sense of hundreds of channels of olfactory information, we do not know (Figure 4.29). What we can say is that our olfactory system is set up to detect and discriminate among an enormous number of possible molecules. When perfume chemists synthesize some brand-new molecule, people do not need to evolve a new receptor to detect it; we can detect the chemical with some combination of the receptors we already have.

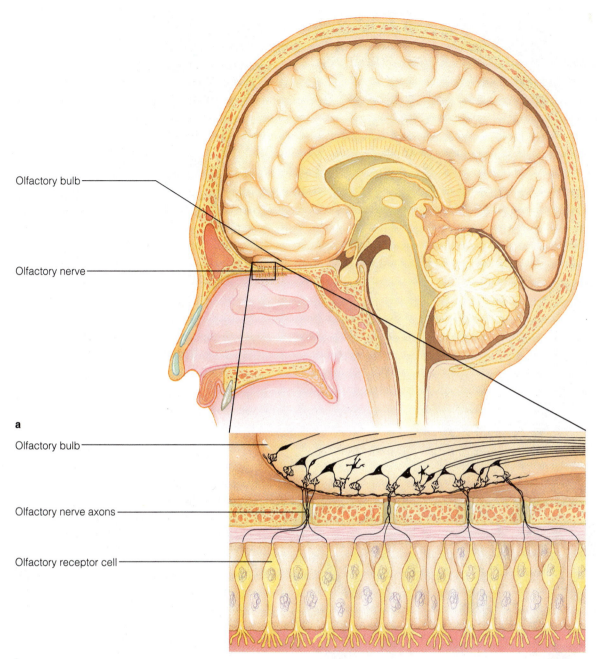

Olfactory bulb

Olfactory nerve

a

Olfactory bulb

Olfactory nerve axons

Olfactory receptor cell

b

FIGURE 4.28
The olfactory receptor cells lining the nasal cavity send information to the olfactory bulb in the brain. There are at least a hundred types of receptors with specialized responses to airborne chemicals.

Humans' olfactory abilities are unimpressive compared to most other mammals. A single olfactory receptor is probably about as sensitive in humans as it is in any other species, but other species have a greater number of receptors. For example, trained dogs can track a person's olfactory trail across fields and through woods. It is difficult (though humorous) to imagine any human even attempting such a task.

Many mammals identify one another by means of **pheromones,** odorous chemicals they release into the environment. In nearly all nonhuman mammals, the males rely on pheromones to distinguish sexually receptive females from unreceptive females.

Humans prefer *not* to recognize one another by smell. The deodorant and perfume industries exist for the sole purpose of removing and covering up human odors. But perhaps we respond to pheromones anyway, at least under certain conditions. For exam-

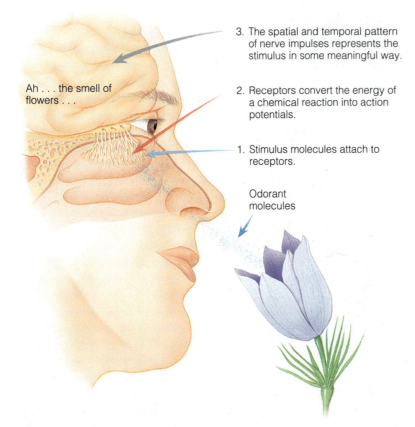

3. The spatial and temporal pattern of nerve impulses represents the stimulus in some meaningful way.

2. Receptors convert the energy of a chemical reaction into action potentials.

1. Stimulus molecules attach to receptors.

Ah . . . the smell of flowers . . .

Odorant molecules

FIGURE 4.29
Olfaction, like any other sensory system, converts a physical energy into a complex pattern of brain activity.

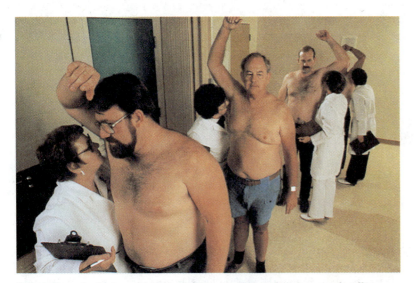

Secret, Ban, Arrid—as these names suggest, U.S. industries spend millions developing and promoting deodorants and antiperspirants so we can secretly banish sweat and have arid armpits. In the past, people used strong perfume to mask odors.

ple, young women who are in frequent contact with one another, such as roommates in a college dormitory, tend to synchronize their menstrual cycles, probably as a result of pheromones they secrete (McClintock, 1971). (If the women are taking birth-control pills, the synchronization does not occur.)

In addition to its role in responding to pheromones, olfaction plays a key role in food selection. What we call the flavor of a food is produced by both its taste and its smell. When a meat or other food is spoiled, olfaction alerts us to that fact before we even try to taste it.

SUMMARY

• *Pitch.* At low frequencies of sound, we identify pitch by the frequency of vibrations on the basilar membrane. At intermediate frequencies, we identify pitch by volleys of responses from a number of neurons. At high frequencies, we identify pitch by the area of the basilar membrane that vibrates most strongly. (page 140)

• *Localizing sounds.* We localize the source of a sound by detecting differences in the time and loudness of sounds our two ears receive. We localize the distance of a sound source mostly by the amount of reverberation, or echoes, following the main sound. (page 141)

• *Vestibular system.* The vestibular system detects movement of the head and its position with respect to gravity. The vestibular system enables us to keep our eyes focused on an object while the rest of our body is in motion. (page 142)

• *Cutaneous receptors.* We experience many types of sensation on the skin, each dependent on different receptors. The fingertips, lips, and face have especially rich supplies of such receptors. (page 143)

• *Pain.* The sense of pain can be alleviated by a variety of events that release endorphins in the central nervous system. (page 145)

• *Taste receptors.* Even before researchers identified the taste receptors, they knew there had to be at least four kinds, because certain procedures affect one taste quality (such as sweetness) without affecting the others. An adult human has taste receptors only along the edges of the tongue. (page 147)

• *Olfactory receptors.* The olfactory system—the sense of smell—depends on at least a hundred types of receptors, each with its own special sensitivity. (page 148)

- *Pheromones.* Mammals, probably including humans, use odorous chemicals called pheromones for certain types of communication. (page 149)

SUGGESTIONS FOR FURTHER READING

Heller, M. A., & Schiff, W. (1991). *The psychology of touch*. Hillsdale, NJ: Erlbaum. Describes research on touch and how people learn to use it for braille reading and other functions.

McLaughlin, S., & Margolskee, R. F. (1994). The sense of taste. *American Scientist, 82,* 538–545. Highly informative discussion of the physiology and psychology of taste.

Melzack, R., & Wall, P. D. (1983). *The challenge of pain.* New York: Basic Books. Discussion of factors that evoke and inhibit pain.

Zwislocki, J. J. (1981). Sound analysis in the ear: A history of discoveries. *American Scientist, 69,* 184–192. Review of research on the mechanisms of hearing.

TERMS

sound waves vibrations of the air or of some other medium (page 138)

pitch a perception closely related to the frequency of sound waves (page 138)

loudness a perception that depends on the amplitude of sound waves (page 138)

cochlea the snail-shaped, fluid-filled structure that contains the receptors for hearing (page 139)

basilar membrane a thin structure in the cochlea that vibrates after sound waves strike the eardrum (page 139)

conduction deafness hearing loss that results if the bones connected to the eardrum fail to transmit sound waves properly to the cochlea (page 139)

nerve deafness hearing loss that results from damage to the cochlea, the hair cells, or the auditory nerve (page 139)

hertz a unit of frequency representing one cycle per second (page 140)

frequency principle identification of pitch by the frequency of action potentials in neurons along the basilar membrane of the cochlea, synchronized with the frequency of sound waves (page 140)

volley principle identification of pitch by the fact that groups of hair cells respond to each vibration by producing an action potential (page 140)

place principle identification of pitch by which auditory neurons are most active (page 140)

absolute pitch the ability to identify a given isolated note after hearing it (page 141)

vestibular sense a specialized sense that detects the direction of tilt and amount of acceleration of the head and the position of the head with respect to gravity (page 142)

cutaneous senses the skin senses, including pressure on the skin, warmth, cold, pain, vibration, movement across the skin, and stretch of the skin (page 143)

gate theory a theory that pain messages have to pass through a gate in the spinal cord on their way to the brain, and that the brain and receptors in the skin can send messages to the spinal cord to open or close that gate (page 145)

substance P neurotransmitter responsible for much of the transmission of pain information in the nervous system (page 145)

endorphin any of the neurotransmitters that decrease the perception of pain and induce pleasant feelings (page 145)

capsaicin chemical that stimulates the release of substance P (page 146)

chemical receptors the receptors that respond to the chemicals that come into contact with the nose and mouth (page 147)

taste the sensory system that responds to chemicals on the tongue (page 147)

taste buds the site of the taste receptors, located in the folds on the surface of the tongue (page 147)

olfaction the sense of smell, the detection of chemicals in contact with the membranes inside the nose (page 148)

pheromone an odorous chemical released by an animal that changes the way other members of its species respond to it socially (page 149)

ANSWERS TO CONCEPT CHECKS

8. Obviously, the people farthest from the mouse are least likely to hear it. In addition, older people would be less likely than young people to hear the squeak, because the ability to hear high frequencies declines in old age. Another group unlikely to hear the squeak are those who have had repeated exposure to loud noises. For that reason, you should beware of attending loud rock music concerts, and of listening to recorded music played at a loud volume, especially when you listen on a Walkman or similar device. In the long run, you could damage your hearing, even if you do not realize it now. (page 140)

9. We still hear a tone at 5000 Hz, but it is louder than before. For high-frequency tones, the pitch we hear depends on which hair cells are most active, not on how many impulses per second they fire. (page 140)

10. We localize sounds by comparing the input into the left ear with the input into the right ear. If a sound comes from straight ahead or from straight behind (or from straight above or below), the input into the left ear is identical with the input into the right ear. (page 142)

11. Various sounds from the radio cannot seem to come from different directions, because your localization of the direction of a sound depends on a comparison between the responses of the two ears. However, the radio can play sounds that seem to come from different distances, because distance localization does not depend on a difference between the ears. It depends on the amount of reverberation, loudness, and high-frequency tones, all of which can be varied with a single speaker. Consequently, the radio can easily give an impression of people walking toward you or away from you, but not of people walking left to right or right to left. (page 142)

12. First determine how much the pleasant stimulus decreases the experience of pain for several people. Then give half of them naloxone and half of them a placebo. Again measure how much the pleasant stimulus decreases the pain. If the pleasant stimulus decreases pain by releasing endorphins, then naloxone should impair its painkilling effects. (page 146)

13. The capsaicin in the jalapeños will release substance P faster than it can be resynthesized, thus decreasing sensitivity to pain in the mouth. (page 146)

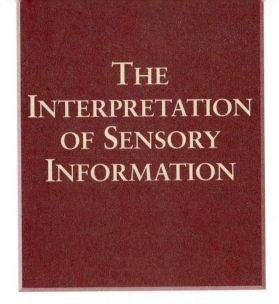

THE INTERPRETATION OF SENSORY INFORMATION

What is the relationship between the real world and the way we perceive it?

Why are we sometimes wrong about what we think we see?

No doubt you have heard people say that "a picture is worth a thousand words." If so, what is one one-thousandth of a picture worth? One word? Ordinarily, one one-thousandth of a picture is worth nothing. (Of course, I grant, "nothing" is *one word!*)

Printed photographs, such as the one on page 150, consist of a great many dots. Ordinarily, you are aware of only the overall patterns and objects, but if you magnify a photo, as in Figure 4.30, you can see the individual dots. Although one dot by itself tells us almost nothing, the pattern of dots as a whole constitutes a meaningful picture.

Actually, our vision is like this all the time. Your retina is composed of about 126 million rods and cones, each of which sees one dot of the visual field. What you perceive is not dots, however, but lines, curves, and complex objects. In a variety of ways your nervous system starts with an enormous array of details and extracts the meaningful information.

PERCEPTION OF MINIMAL STIMULI

Right now your receptors are no doubt bombarded by a large number of sensory stimuli. You are (I hope) focusing much of your attention on what you see in this book. You ignore a great many other stimuli, although you could easily shift your attention to them if you had a reason to do so. For example, you probably have not been aware of the feeling of your clothes against your skin, but now that I have called your attention to it, you do notice it.

Can you detect extremely weak stimuli, if you try? Also, do stimuli that you do not consciously notice have any effect on your behavior?

SENSORY THRESHOLDS

Under ideal circumstances, your sensory receptors can respond to extremely weak stimuli. For example, once your eyes have become adapted to darkness, the rods will respond to as little as a single photon of light (Baylor, Lamb, & Yau, 1979). How intense does a stimulus have to be for you to detect it under ordinary conditions? In a typical experiment to determine the threshold of hearing—that is, the minimum intensity at which

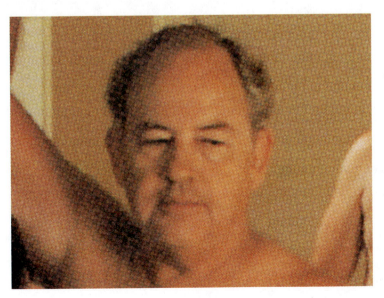

FIGURE 4.30
Printed photographs are composed of tiny dots. Ordinarily you see the photo on page 150 as a group of people. If you magnify a part of that or any other photo, you can see the dots. If you magnify still more or look closely enough, you see only dots and no people. In fact, because your retina is composed of separate cells, all your visual perceptions begin as an array of millions of dots, from which your brain derives the shapes and objects.

FIGURE 4.31

Typical results of an experiment to measure a sensory threshold. There is no sharp boundary between stimuli that you can perceive and stimuli that you cannot perceive.

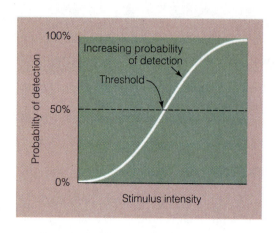

we can detect sound—subjects are presented with tones of varying intensity in random order, including some trials with no tone at all. On each trial the subjects are asked to say whether or not they heard a tone. Figure 4.31 presents typical results. Notice that as loudness increases, the probability of detection also increases, with no sharp dividing line between detectable and nondetectable stimuli. A similar pattern of results applies to other sensory systems.

Because perception researchers find no sharp dividing line between detectable and nondetectable, they define a **sensory threshold** as the intensity at which a given individual can detect a stimulus 50% of the time. Note, however, that an individual will frequently detect stimuli that are weaker than the threshold and sometimes fail to detect stimuli above the threshold.

An individual's sensory threshold may change as a result of **sensory adaptation,** the tendency of a sensory threshold to rise or fall after a period of strong or weak stimulation. For example, if you have been outdoors on a bright, sunny day and you walk into a darkened movie theater, you have trouble seeing the seats at first. After a few minutes your threshold drops (that is, your sensitivity increases) and you see the seats well. If you stayed in the dark theater after the movie ended, your ability to detect dim light would increase still further. The sensory threshold at the time of maximum sensory adaptation is called the **absolute threshold.**

When people try to detect weak stimuli, they can make two kinds of errors: They can fail to detect a stimulus (a "miss"), or they can say they detected a stimulus when none was present (a "false alarm"). **Signal-detection theory** is the study of people's tendencies to make correct judgments, misses, and false alarms (Green & Swets, 1966). (Psycholo-

gists borrowed signal-detection theory from engineering, where this system is applied to such matters as detecting radio signals in the presence of interfering noise.) According to signal-detection theory, people's responses depend both on the ability of their senses to detect a stimulus and on their willingness to risk a miss or a false alarm. (When in doubt, they have to risk one or the other.)

Suppose you are the subject and I tell you that you will receive a 10-cent reward every time you correctly report that a light is present, but you will be fined 1 cent for saying "yes" when a light is not present. Whenever you are unsure, you probably will say yes, taking the risk of making a false alarm. The results will resemble those in Figure 4.32a. Then I change the rules: You will receive a 1-cent reward for correctly reporting the presence of a light, but you will suffer a 10-

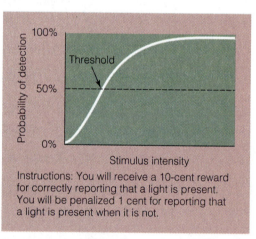

Instructions: You will receive a 10-cent reward for correctly reporting that a light is present. You will be penalized 1 cent for reporting that a light is present when it is not.

a

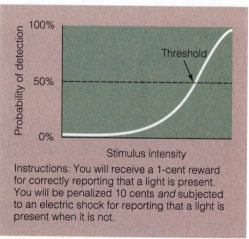

Instructions: You will receive a 1-cent reward for correctly reporting that a light is present. You will be penalized 10 cents *and* subjected to an electric shock for reporting that a light is present when it is not.

b

FIGURE 4.32

Results of experiments to measure a sensory threshold using two different sets of instructions.

This ad pokes fun at the idea of subliminal perception, because it's so obvious. Yet the technique effectively conveys two messages simultaneously.

cent penalty *and* an electric shock for reporting a light when none is present. Now you will say yes only if you are certain you saw a light, and the results will look like those in Figure 4.32b. *Clearly, if we want to determine which subjects are more sensitive to light, we have to take into account their misses and false alarms as well as their correct judgments.* Subjects whose measured thresholds are high may simply be exercising great caution in making their responses.

This same tendency toward caution shows up when subjects are tested to determine their threshold for recognizing words. For example, in one experiment the subjects were asked to try to read words that were flashed on a screen for just a split second. They performed well when ordinary words like *river* or *peach* were shown. For emotionally loaded words like *penis* or *bitch,* however, they generally said they were not sure what they saw. Psychologists have suggested a number of possible explanations for such results (e.g., Blum & Barbour, 1979); one possibility is that subjects hesitate to blurt out an emotionally charged word unless they are certain they are right.

SUBLIMINAL PERCEPTION

You probably have heard of **subliminal perception,** the idea that a brief, faint stimulus can influence our behavior even if we do not perceive it consciously. (*Limen* is Latin for "threshold"; thus, *subliminal* means *below the threshold.*) Some people claim that subliminal perception can have a powerful, even manipulative, effect on human behavior.

Are such claims plausible or outright nonsense? Problem number one is to define *subliminal.* I just finished telling you that *subliminal* means *below the threshold.* Fine, except that I already told you there is no sharp division between perceptible stimuli and imperceptible stimuli. If we define *subliminal* stimuli as stimuli that people detect on fewer than 50% of occasions, then subliminal perception is hardly surprising. In practical terms, when psychologists refer to a "subliminal stimulus," they generally mean "a stimulus that a person *did not* consciously detect on a given occasion," regardless of whether the person *could have* detected it under other circumstances.

That definition does not end the problem, however. How do we know whether or not someone *did* detect a given stimulus? We ask, of course. But how do we know what the person's answers really mean? Suppose someone insists that he or she "did not see" some word an experimenter flashed instantaneously on a screen. That reply could mean "I never saw anything," "I'm unsure of what I saw," or "I forgot what I saw." You can see why this kind of research is often difficult to interpret.

WHAT SUBLIMINAL PERCEPTION CANNOT DO

Although subliminal perception may have some effects on behavior, they tend to be very modest effects. Unfortunately, many of the claims regarding subliminal effects have been so wild, and so lacking in evidence, that many scientists became very skeptical that subliminal perception could have any effect at all.

Many years ago, claims were made that subliminal messages could control people's

PEOPLE HAVE BEEN TRYING TO FIND THE BREASTS IN THESE ICE CUBES SINCE 1957.

The advertising industry is sometimes charged with sneaking seductive little pictures into ads.

Supposedly, these pictures can get you to buy a product without your even seeing them.

Consider the photograph above. According to some people, there's a pair of female breasts

hidden in the patterns of light refracted by the ice cubes.

Well, if you really searched you probably *could* see the breasts. For that matter, you could also see Millard Fillmore, a stuffed pork chop and a 1946 Dodge.

The point is that so-called "subliminal advertising" simply

doesn't exist. Overactive imaginations, however, most certainly do.

So if anyone claims to see breasts in that drink up there, they aren't in the ice cubes.

They're in the eye of the beholder.

ADVERTISING
ANOTHER WORD FOR FREEDOM OF CHOICE.
American Association of Advertising Agencies

buying habits. For example, an unscrupulous theater owner might insert a single frame reading "EAT POPCORN" in the middle of a film. Customers not consciously aware of the message would not be able to resist it, so they would flock to the concession stand to buy popcorn. Despite many tests of that claim, no one has found any evidence for it (Bornstein, 1989).

Another claim is that certain rock records contain satanic messages that have been recorded backward and superimposed on the songs. Some people allege that listeners unconsciously perceive these messages and turn to drugs or devil worship. So far as psychology is concerned, the issue is whether people who heard a backward message could understand it and whether it would influence their behavior. Psychologists have recorded various messages (fairly tame, nothing "satanic") and asked people to listen to them played backward. So far, no one listening to the backward messages has been able to discern what they would sound like forward. And listening to those messages has not influenced anyone's behavior in any detectable way (Vokey & Read, 1985). In other words, even if certain records do contain backward messages, we have no reason to believe that listeners will be influenced by them.

A third unsupported claim: Many book stores and music stores sell "subliminal audiotapes" that claim they can help you improve your memory, quit smoking, lose weight, raise your self-esteem, and so forth. In one study, psychologists asked more than 200 volunteers to listen to a popular brand of audiotape. But they intentionally mislabeled some of the tapes. That is, some tapes with "self-esteem" messages were labeled "memory tapes" and some tapes with "memory" messages were labeled "self-esteem tapes." After a month of listening, most who *thought* they were listening to self-esteem tapes said they had greatly improved their self-esteem; those who *thought* they were listening to memory tapes said their memory had greatly improved. What they were *actually* hearing had no bearing on the results. In other words, if people improved their memory—and some of them did improve, although not nearly as much as they thought they did—the improvement depended on their expectations, and not on the tapes themselves (Greenwald, Spangenberg, Pratkanis, & Eskanazi, 1991).

WHAT SUBLIMINAL PERCEPTION CAN DO

We have just considered what subliminal messages *cannot* do. Now let's consider examples of what they apparently *can* do.

If people are subliminally exposed to a simple picture and then asked to choose between that picture and another one (both now plainly visible), about 60–65% choose the picture they had seen subliminally. Although this is not a very strong effect, it does last a week or more (Bornstein, 1989).

If people see a word subliminally, it influences their later perception of an easily visible stimulus (Dixon, 1981). For example, people watch a screen where the word PENCIL is flashed briefly in the midst of a cluttered background. Then they see a set of letters such as TERIW or WRITE and they are supposed to say, as quickly as possible, whether it is a word. People who have just seen the subliminal stimulus PENCIL respond a little quicker than usual that WRITE is a word. This is a dependable effect, although it apparently wears off quickly after the subliminal stimulus.

A number of researchers have made claims that brief, subliminal exposure to an

High-school photos

a b c d e

25 years later

1 2 3 4 5

6 7 8 9 10

FIGURE 4.33
High-school photos and the same people 25 years later, along with five other people. Can you match the photos in the two sets? (Check answer C on page 179.) (From Bruck, Cavanagh, & Ceci, 1991.)

emotional message produces an emotional response. In one study, undergraduate students showed mild signs of nervousness or discomfort after viewing a very brief presentation of the message NO ONE LOVES ME, but not after viewing the unemotional message NO ONE LIFTS IT (Masling, Bornstein, Poynton, Reid, & Katkin, 1991). This study was not set up to measure how long the effect might last. Other studies have reported fairly long-lasting emotional effects of subliminal stimuli (Hardaway, 1990), but such results remain highly controversial.

With various refinements in technique, could subliminal perception become an effective means of influencing people, for either worthwhile or dangerous purposes? Maybe, say some psychologists (e.g., Bornstein, 1989); very unlikely, say others (e.g., McConnell, 1989). So far, the best-documented effects are either weak or short-lived, and in some cases the subliminal message actually influences behavior in the opposite direction from the predicted effect (Underwood, 1994).

PERCEPTION AND THE RECOGNITION OF PATTERNS

Now let us consider how we perceive strong, well-above-threshold stimuli. Human perception of complex scenes, especially faces, can be quite amazing. When you go back to your 25th high-school reunion, you probably will recognize many people whom you haven't seen since graduation, despite major changes in their appearance. Can you match the high-school photos in Figure 4.33 with the photos of the same people as they looked 25 years later? Probably not, but other people who had gone to that same high school succeeded with a respectable 49% accuracy (Bruck, Cavanagh, & Ceci, 1991).

THE FEATURE-DETECTOR APPROACH

To explain how we identify faces is quite challenging. In fact, explaining how we recognize even a letter of the alphabet is difficult

CAT HAT

a

12
ABC
14

b

FIGURE 4.34
We perceive elements differently depending on their context. In (a), the A in CAT is the same as the H in HAT, but we perceive them differently. In (b), the central character can appear to be a B or the number 13, depending on whether we read horizontally or vertically. (Part b from Kim, 1989.)

enough. According to one explanation, we begin recognition by breaking a complex stimulus into its component parts. For example, when we look at the letter *A*, specialized neurons called **feature detectors**, located in the visual cortex, identify the three lines and then some other more advanced feature detector reacts to the activity of the first set of feature detectors to identify the letter *A*.

Feature detectors certainly cannot provide the whole explanation for how we perceive letters, much less faces. For example, we perceive the words in Figure 4.34a as CAT and HAT, even though the A in CAT is identical to the H in HAT. Likewise, the character in the center of 4.34b can be read as either the letter *B* or the number *13*. Feature detectors are essential in the early stages of visual perception, but the perception of a complex pattern requires more than just feature detectors.

WHAT'S THE EVIDENCE?

Feature Detectors in the Human Visual System

We can easily imagine feature detectors in the human brain and we can imagine all kinds of properties for them. What evidence do we have for their existence? We have two kinds of evidence, one from laboratory animals and one from humans.

EXPERIMENT 1

Hypothesis Neurons in the visual cortex of cats and monkeys will respond specifically when light strikes the retina in a particular pattern, such as a line.

Method Two pioneers in the study of the visual cortex, David Hubel and Torsten Wiesel (1981 Nobel Prize winners in physiology and medicine), inserted thin electrodes into cells of the occipital cortex of cats and

monkeys and then recorded the activity of those cells when various light patterns struck the animals' retinas (Figure 4.35).

Results They found that each cell responds to a preferred stimulus (Hubel & Wiesel, 1968). Some cells become active only when a vertical bar of light strikes a given portion of the retina. Others become active only when a horizontal bar strikes the retina. In other words, such cells act as feature detectors.

In later experiments, Hubel and Wiesel and other investigators found a variety of other feature detectors, including some that respond to objects of a particular color or lines moving in a particular direction.

Interpretation Hubel and Wiesel found feature-detector cells in both cats and monkeys. If the organization of the occipital cortex is similar in species as distantly related as cats and monkeys, it is likely (though not certain) to be similar in humans as well.

A second line of evidence is based on the following reasoning: If the human cortex does contain feature-detector cells, one type of cell should become fatigued after we stare for a time at the features that excite it. When we look away, we should see an aftereffect created by the inactivity of that type of cell. (Recall the negative afterimage in color vision, as shown by Figure 4.13.)

One example of this phenomenon is the **waterfall illusion:** If you stare at a waterfall for a minute or more and then turn your eyes to nearby cliffs, the cliffs will appear to flow *upward*. In staring at the waterfall, you fatigue neurons that respond to downward motion. When you look away, those neurons become inactive, but others that respond to upward motion continue their normal activity. Even though the motionless cliffs stimulate those neurons only weakly, the stimulation is enough to produce an illusion of upward motion.

For another example, here is a demonstration you can perform yourself.

EXPERIMENT 2

Hypothesis After you stare at one set of vertical lines, you will fatigue the feature detectors that respond to lines of a particular width. If you then look at lines slightly wider or narrower than the original ones, they will appear to be even wider or narrower than they really are.

Method Cover the right half of Figure 4.36 and stare at the little rectangle in the middle

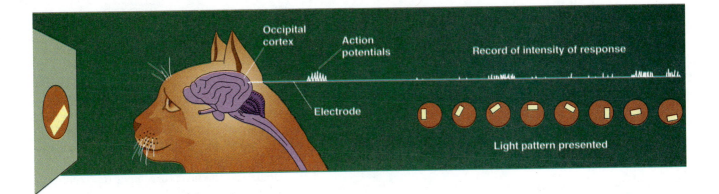

FIGURE 4.35
Hubel and Wiesel implanted electrodes to record the activity of neurons in the occipital cortex of a cat. Then they compared the responses evoked by various patterns of light and darkness on the retina. In most cases, a neuron responded vigorously when a portion of the retina saw a bar of light oriented at a particular angle. When the angle of the bar changed, that cell became silent but some other cell responded.

of the left half for at least 1 minute. (The effect will grow stronger the longer you stare.) Do not stare at just one point; move your focus around within the rectangle. Then look at the square in the center of the right part of the figure, and compare the spacing between the lines of the top and bottom gratings (Blakemore & Sutton, 1969).

Results What did you perceive in the right half of the figure? People generally report that the top set of lines looks narrower than it really is and that the bottom set of lines looks wider.

Interpretation Staring at the left part of the figure fatigues one set of cells sensitive to wide lines in the top part of the figure and another set sensitive to narrow lines in the bottom part. When you then look at intermediate lines, the fatigued cells become inactive. Therefore, your perception is dominated by cells sensitive to narrower lines in the top part and to wider lines in the bottom part.

To summarize, we have two types of evidence for the existence of visual feature detectors: (1) The brains of other species contain cells with the properties of feature detectors, and (2) after staring at certain patterns, we see aftereffects that can be explained as fatigue of feature-detector cells in the brain.

Note one important point here about scientific evidence: A single line of evidence—even excellent, Nobel Prize–winning evidence—is seldom enough to establish a conclusion to our complete satisfaction.

Whenever possible, we look for independent lines of evidence that confirm the same conclusion.

DO FEATURE DETECTORS EXPLAIN PERCEPTION?

The feature detectors I have been describing are active during the early stages of visual processing. They detect lines of a certain width and angle and objects moving in a certain direction, for example. How do you perceive something more complicated, such as your grandmother's face, the Eiffel Tower, or even the letter *A*?

One possibility requires increasingly complex feature detectors. One set of neurons responds to single lines; another set receives input from the first set and responds

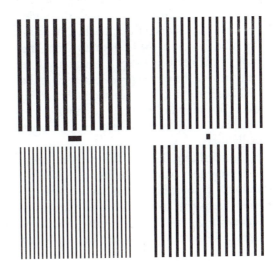

FIGURE 4.36
Use this display to fatigue your feature detectors and create an afterimage. Follow the directions in Experiment 2 in the What's the Evidence? section. (From Blakemore & Sutton, 1969.)

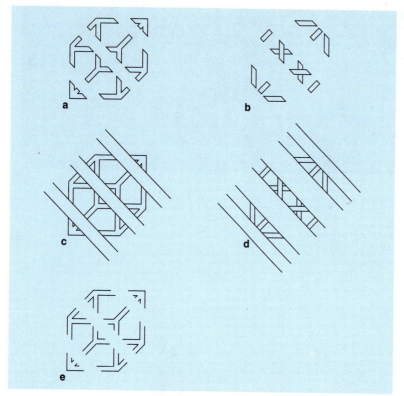

FIGURE 4.37
This picture is a puzzle until a context is introduced. Then a cube "emerges" from meaningless lines. (From Kanizsa, 1979.)

by imposing an active interpretation on the pattern.

When you are trying to identify some visual stimulus, additional visual stimuli at other times or locations may either help or hurt. For example, suppose you are told to focus at a fixation point on a computer screen, and at various times a set of stimuli are briefly flashed on the screen. In the display below, the arrow represents the fixation point and the next three lines represent possible arrays of stimuli.

```
                ↓
ΘΘΘΘΘΘΘΘΘΘΘΘΘΘΘΘF
ΘΘΘΘΘΘΘWΘΘΘΘΘΘΘΘF
ΘΘΘΘΘΘΘFΘΘΘΘΘΘΘΘF
```

The first array, with just an F at the end, is difficult. Adding a different letter at the fixation point (the W) makes the task even more difficult, by interference. But if an F appears at the fixation point, the task becomes much easier (Geiger & Lettvin, 1986). Your identification of the F in the center of your vision "primes" you to identify another F at another location.

A related example: Suppose you look at a computer screen. A simple, small figure such as a white circle or rectangle appears on the screen for 50 ms or so and then disappears. Despite the short duration of the stimulus, you have no trouble reporting and describing the stimulus. Now we repeat the procedure, except that 50 ms after the stimulus, two additional stimuli appear in positions flanking the first stimulus:

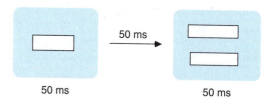

The second pair of stimuli blots out the first stimulus altogether. That is, you will report seeing the second pair of stimuli, but not the first stimulus (e.g., Ramachandran & Cobb, 1995). The ability of a second visual stimulus to erase a first stimulus is called **backward masking**. The fact that it occurs indicates that we do not see stimuli one at a time, as they occur. Instead, we integrate information over a period of at least a fraction of a second, just as we integrate

only to certain combinations of lines—such as the lines that make up the letter *A* or the lines that compose a face.

If we try to explain all of vision by means of feature detectors, however, we soon encounter problems. We do not perceive a scene simply by adding up points, lines, or other simple features. The way we perceive part of a scene depends on the context provided by the rest of the scene. In Figure 4.37 (based on Kanizsa, 1979) parts a and b are composed of small geometric forms. Although we might guess that part a is made up of segments of a three-dimensional cube, we cannot "see" the cube. Part b does not even suggest a cube. In parts c and d, the added lines provide a context that enables us to see the cube. In part e, the deletion of short lines from a enables us to "see" imaginary lines that provide the same context. In c, d, and e, we have perceptually organized the meaningless forms of a and b into a meaningful pattern; we are perceiving something that is not really there.

Similarly, in Figure 4.38a we see a series of meaningless patches. In Figure 4.38b, the addition of some black glop immediately enables us to perceive those same patches to represent the word *psychology* (Bregman, 1981). We perceive the letters in part b only

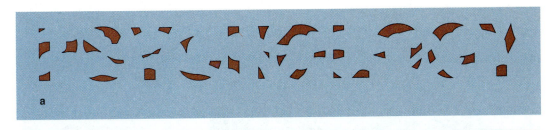

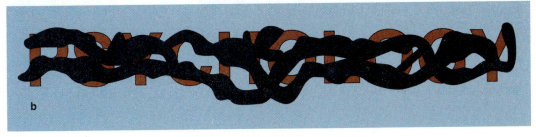

information from different locations in the visual field.

THE GESTALT PSYCHOLOGY APPROACH

Figure 4.39 is a photo of several hundred people. Yet you probably see the overall shape of an airplane. Out of context, one person is no more a piece of an airplane than a piece of anything else. The plane is not the sum of the people; it is the overall pattern. Recall also Figure 4.30 from earlier in this chapter: The photograph is composed entirely of dots, but you perceive a face, not just a collection of dots.

Such observations derive from **Gestalt psychology.** *Gestalt* (geh-SHTALT) is a German word for which there is no exact English equivalent; *configuration* and *overall pattern* come close. The founders of Gestalt psychology rejected the idea that a perception can be broken down into its component parts. If a melody is broken up into individual notes, the melody is lost. Their slogan was "The whole is different from the sum of its parts."

According to Gestalt psychologists, visual perception is an active production, not just the passive adding up of lines and dots. We considered examples of this principle in Figures 4.37 and 4.38. Here are some further examples:

Figure 4.40 shows two animals. When you first look at these pictures, you will probably see nothing but meaningless black and white patches. As you continue to look at them, you may suddenly see the animals. (If you give up, check answer D, page 179.) Once you have seen them, you will see them again whenever you look at the pictures.

To perceive the animals, you must separate **figure and ground**—that is, you must distinguish the object from the background. Ordinarily that process takes place almost instantaneously; only in special cases like this one do you become aware of the process.

Figure 4.41 contains five **reversible figures,** stimuli that may be perceived in more than one way. In effect, we test hypotheses: "Is this the front of the object or is that the front? Is this object facing left or facing

FIGURE 4.39
According to Gestalt psychology, the whole is more than the sum of its parts. Here we perceive an assembly of several hundred people as an airplane.

THE INTERPRETATION
OF SENSORY INFORMATION

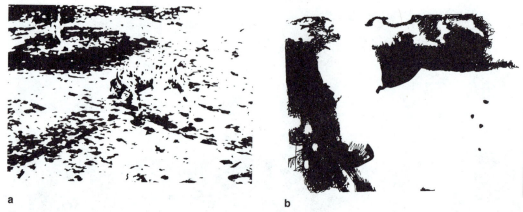

FIGURE 4.40

Do you see an animal in each picture? If not, check answer D, page 179. (Part b from Dallenbach, 1951.)

right? Is this section the foreground or the background?" Depending on what we are looking for, we may organize the scene in different ways. In Figure 4.41, part a is called the *Necker cube,* after the psychologist who first called attention to it. Which is the front face of the cube? If you look long enough, you will see it two ways. In fact, you can choose to see it one way or the other. You can see part b either as a vase or as two profiles. In part c (from Shepard, 1990) you have to use some imagination to see anything meaningful. You might see a woman's face or a man blowing a horn. (If you need help, check answer E on page 179.) Part d (from Boring, 1930) shows both an old woman and a young woman. Almost everyone sees one or the other immediately, but many people lock into one perception so tightly that they cannot see the other one. Part e was drawn by an 8-year-old girl who intended it as the picture of a face. Some people claim it looks like an apple. Can you find a third possibility? (If you have trouble with parts d or e, check answers F and G, page 179.) Note that when you change from one perception

to another on any of these reversible figures, you suddenly reinterpret each piece of the figure. For example, in part c, when you see the man's face and nose, that context almost forces you to see another part of the figure as a horn.

It is difficult to explain *how* we perceive organized wholes, though the Gestalt psychologists offered a few principles of how we organize perceptions. Figure 4.42 gives examples of each principle. **Proximity** is the tendency to perceive objects that are close together as belonging to a group. The objects in part a form two groups because of proximity. The tendency to perceive objects that resemble each other as forming a group is called **similarity.** The objects in b group into Xs and Os because of similarity. When lines are interrupted, as in c, we may perceive a **continuation** of the lines. We can perceive this illustration as a green rectangle covering the front of one horse and the rear of another, but we can also perceive it as a rectangle covering the center of one very elongated horse.

When a familiar figure is interrupted, as in d, we perceive a **closure** of the figure—

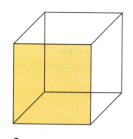

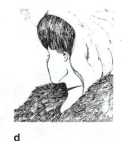

a   b   c   d   e

FIGURE 4.41

Reversible figures. (a) The Necker cube. Which is the front face? (b) Faces or a vase. (c) Sax player and woman's face ("Sara Nader"). (d) An old woman and a young woman. (e) A face or what? (Part c from Shepard, 1990; d from Boring, 1930.)

FIGURE 4.42
Gestalt principles of (a) proximity, (b) similarity, (c) continuation, (d) closure, and (e) good figure.

that is, we imagine the rest of the figure. (Because of closure you perceive the head, two arms, and two legs as belonging to the same woman. How might magicians use this principle?) Closure depends on. the entire pattern, not just on a small part of the stimulus (Finkel & Sajda, 1994; Sekuler, Palmer, & Flynn, 1994). For example, note the

books overlapping pencils in Figure 4.43. In part a of that figure, we perceive a book overlapping three long pencils. By adding additional elements in parts b and c, we can greatly alter the perception of the pencils. In other words, closure depends on our concept of the objects in the display, and that concept in turn depends on everything in the picture

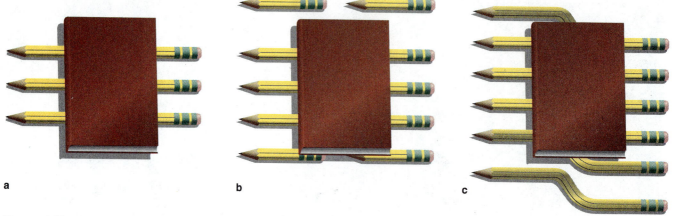

a   b   c

FIGURE 4.43

Closure depends on the whole pattern, not just the part that gets interrupted by another object. In part a, we perceive a book overlapping three long pencils. In part b, because of the added pencil stubs, we see the original three long pencils as six pencil stubs. In part c, the additions make us see the original pencils as parts of novelty twisted pencils. The overall point is that our perception of the closure of an object depends on what we identify as an object. Such an apparently simple process as closure taps into all of our experiences about objects in the world.

as well as our previous experiences with objects in the world.

Finally, we tend to perceive a **good figure**—a simple, symmetrical figure—even when the pattern can be perceived in some other way. In Figure 4.42e, even after we see that the right-hand drawing is a green backward L overlapping part of an irregular object, we continue to perceive it as a red square overlapping a green square. In general, a good figure is a symmetrical figure or a figure composed of continuous lines.

CONCEPT CHECK

14. *Which of the Gestalt principles were operating in your perception of Figures 4.37 and 4.38? (Check your answer on page 179.)*

GESTALT PRINCIPLES IN HEARING

The perceptual organization principles of Gestalt psychology apply to hearing as well as to vision. There are reversible figures in sound, just as there are in vision. For instance, you can hear the sound of a clock as "tick, tock, tick, tock" or as "tock, tick, tock, tick." You can hear your windshield wipers going "dunga, dunga" or "gadung, gadung."

As with visual reversible figures, people occasionally get so locked into one interpretation of something they hear that they have

This assemblage, Celia, Los Angeles, is by the English artist David Hockney. According to Gestalt psychologists, the whole picture is more than its 32 parts combined.

People who are looking for an image or a message in some random pattern sometimes convince themselves that they have found what they were seeking. Crowds in one town believed they saw the image of a recently murdered girl (inset) on a blank billboard. Perception results from a combination of sensory stimulation and our expectations.

trouble hearing it any other way. For example, read this sentence to a friend: "The matadors fish on Friday." Pause long enough to make sure your friend has understood the sentence. Then say: "The cat on the mat adores fish on Friday." If you read the second sentence normally, without pausing between mat and adores, your friend is likely to be puzzled. "Huh? The cat on the matadors . . .?" Had you not read the first sentence, your friend would not have had trouble understanding the second sentence.

FEATURE DETECTORS AND GESTALT PSYCHOLOGY: BOTTOM-UP VERSUS TOP-DOWN PROCESSING

The Gestalt approach to perception does not conflict with the feature-detector approach as much as it might seem. The feature-detector approach describes how perception, especially vision, develops from the bottom up. It takes the individual points of light identified by the receptors and connects them into lines and then connects lines into more complex features. According to the feature-detector approach, the brain says, "I see these points here, here, and here, so there must be a line. I see a line here and another

line connecting with it here, so there must be a letter L."

The Gestalt approach describes how perception develops from the top down. It starts with an overall expectation and then fits in the pieces. According to the Gestalt interpretation, the brain says, "I see what looks like a circle, so the missing piece must be part of a circle too."

Which view is correct? Both, of course. Our perception has to assemble the individual points of light or bits of sound, but once it forms a tentative interpretation of the pattern, it uses that interpretation to organize or reorganize the information.

PREATTENTIVE AND ATTENTIVE PROCESSES IN VISION

When you look at a scene made up of many shapes and relationships among objects, you automatically notice certain details even if you are not trying to find them. Consider Figures 4.44a and b. In each figure, find the circle that is intersected by a vertical line. Most people spot the vertical line in b about as quickly as the vertical line in a, even though b has far more distractors (circles without lines) (Treisman & Souther, 1985). Apparently people examine all the

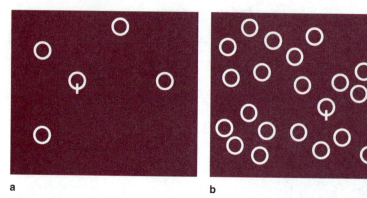

FIGURE 4.44
Demonstration of the preattentive processes. Find the vertical line in parts a and b. Most people find it about equally fast in both.

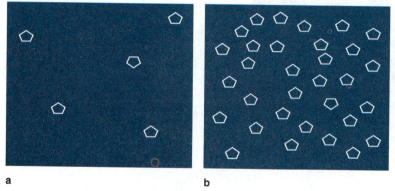

FIGURE 4.45
Demonstration of attentive processes. Find the pentagon pointing down in parts a and b. Most people take longer to find it in b.

FIGURE 4.46
A photograph of a photo taken from the side appears distorted. Yet when you view a movie screen from an angle, you are seldom aware of the distortion.

circles *in parallel,* rather than attending to them one at a time. That is, they can look at all the circles at once; finding the vertical line does not require one-circle-at-a-time attention. Finding the line relies on a **preattentive process**—one that takes place automatically and simultaneously across a large portion of the visual field. Our preattentive processes probably use feature detectors to identify simple elements (Enns & Rensink, 1990).

Now look at Figures 4.45a and b. Each part contains several pentagons, most of them pointing upward. Find the one pentagon in each part that points downward.

Most people take longer to find the pentagon pointing down in part b than in part a, because part b contains more distractors. The greater the number of distractors, the longer it takes to find the pentagon that is different. People must turn their attention to one pentagon at a time until they come to the correct one. In contrast to the preceding example, this task requires an **attentive process**—that is, a procedure that considers only one part of the visual field at a time. An attentive process is a *serial* process because a person must pay attention to each part in the series.

PERCEPTION OF MOVEMENT AND DEPTH

As an automobile drives away from us, its image on the retina grows smaller, yet we perceive it as moving, not as shrinking. That perception illustrates **visual constancy**—our tendency to perceive objects as keeping their shape, size, and color, even though what actually strikes our retina may be changing from time to time. When we sit off to the side in a movie theater, for example, the images that strike our retina may be badly distorted (see Figure 4.46). Yet we perceive a normal scene, not a slanted one (Cutting, 1987). Figure 4.47 shows examples of two visual constancies: shape constancy and size constancy. Constancies depend on our familiarity with objects and on our ability to estimate distances and angles of view. For example, we know that a door is still rectangular even when we view it from an odd angle. But to recognize that an object has kept its shape and size, we have to perceive movement or changes in distance or angle. How do we do so?

PERCEPTION OF MOVEMENT

It is common sense to assume that anyone who can see a rabbit should be able to see its size, shape, color, and direction and speed of movement. In this case, common sense is wrong. You already know that some people are color blind. You may not have known that some people are motion blind. Motion blindness results from damage to a small area in the temporal lobe of the cortex (Zihl, von Cramon, & Mai, 1983). This rare condition illustrates a major point: The visual system of the brain has separate pathways that analyze different aspects of what we see. One pathway analyzes shape; another analyzes color; another analyzes movement (Zeki, 1993).

The detection of motion in the visual world raises some interesting issues, including how we distinguish between our own movement and the movement of objects. Try this simple demonstration: Hold an object in front of your eyes and then move it to the right. Now hold the object in front of your eyes and move your eyes to the left. The image of the object moves across your retina in the same way, regardless of whether you move the object or move your eyes. Yet you perceive the object as moving in one case and not in the other. Why is that?

FIGURE 4.47

(a) Shape constancy. We perceive all three doors as rectangles. (b) Size constancy. We perceive all three hands as equal in size.

There are two reasons why the object does not appear to move when you move your eyes. One reason is that the vestibular system constantly informs the visual areas of the brain about movements of your head. When your brain knows that your eyes have moved to the left, it interprets a change in what you see as being a result of that movement.

The second reason is that we perceive motion when an object moves *relative to the background* (Gibson, 1968). For example, when you walk forward, stationary objects in your environment move across your retina. If something fails to move across your retina, you perceive it as moving in the same direction that you are.

What do we perceive when an object is stationary and the background is moving? That hardly ever happens, but when it does, we incorrectly perceive the object as moving and the background as stationary. For example, when you watch clouds moving slowly across the moon from left to right, you generally perceive the clouds as a stationary background and the moon as an object

FIGURE 4.48

Motion pictures: When you watch a movie, you are unaware of its thousands of still photographs flickering by at a rate of 86,400 an hour. The sequence of photographs printed here conveys a sense of motion in another way.

moving from right to left. This perception, known as **induced movement,** is a form of *apparent movement,* as opposed to *real movement.*

I have already mentioned the waterfall illusion (page 158) as an example of apparent movement. Another example is **stroboscopic movement,** an illusion of movement created by a rapid succession of stationary images. When a scene is flashed on a screen and is followed a split second later by a second scene slightly different from the first, you perceive the objects as having moved smoothly from their location in the first scene to their location in the second scene (Figure 4.48). Motion pictures are actually a series of still photos flashed on the screen at a rate of 24 per second. Thus, the perceived movement is an illusion produced by the rapid succession of photos.

We also experience an illusion of movement when two or more stationary lights separated by a short distance blink on and off at regular intervals. Your brain creates the sense of motion in what is called the **phi effect.** You may have noticed signs in front of restaurants or motels that make use of this effect. As the lights blink on and off, an arrow seems to be moving and inviting you to come in.

Our ability to detect visual movement played an interesting role in the history of astronomy. In 1930, Clyde Tombaugh was searching the skies for a possible unknown planet beyond Neptune. He photographed each region of the sky twice, several days apart. A planet, unlike a star, would move from one photo to the next. However, how would he find one tiny dot that moved, among all the countless unmoving dots in the sky? He put each pair of photos on a machine that would flip back and forth between showing one photo and showing the other. When he came to the correct pair of photos, the machine flipped back and forth between them and he immediately—preattentively—noticed the one moving dot (Tombaugh, 1980). We now know that little dot as the planet Pluto (Figure 4.49).

DEPTH PERCEPTION

Depth perception is our perception of distance; it enables us to experience the world in three dimensions. Depth perception depends on several factors.

We use **retinal disparity**—the difference in the apparent position of an object as seen by the left and right retinas—to compare the views the two eyes see (Figure 4.50). Try this: Hold one finger at arm's length. Focus on it with one eye and then with the other. Note that the apparent position of your finger shifts with respect to the background. Now hold your finger closer to your face and repeat the experiment. Notice that the apparent position of your finger shifts by a greater amount. *The discrepancy between the slightly different views the two eyes see be-*

FIGURE 4.49
Clyde Tombaugh used preattentive detection of movement to discover the planet Pluto. He photographed each area of the sky twice, several days apart. Then he had a machine flip back and forth between the two photos of each pair. When he came to one part of the sky, he immediately (preattentively) noticed one dot that had moved between the two photos. That dot was the planet Pluto.

comes greater as the object comes closer. We use the amount of discrepancy to gauge distance.

A second cue for depth perception is the **convergence** of our eyes—that is, the degree to which they turn in to focus on a close object (Figure 4.51). When you focus on a distant object, your eyes are looking in almost parallel directions. When you focus on some-

thing close, your eyes turn inward; you can sense the tension of your eye muscles. The more the muscles pull, the closer the object must be.

Retinal disparity and convergence are called **binocular cues,** because they depend on the action of both eyes. **Monocular cues** enable a person to judge depth and distance effectively with just one eye, or if both eyes

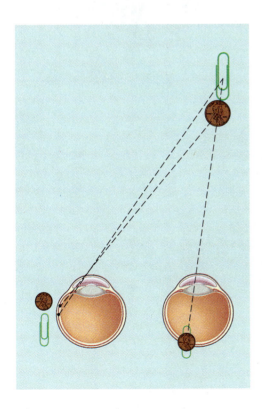

FIGURE 4.50
Retinal disparity is one cue to distance. The left and right eyes see slightly different versions of any scene; the difference between the image on the left retina and the image on the right retina indicates the distance to each object.

FIGURE 4.51
Convergence of the eyes as a cue to distance. The more the viewer on the right has to converge her eyes toward each other in order to focus on an object, the closer the object must be.

see the same image, as they do when you look at a picture. Several monocular cues help us judge the approximate distance of the objects in Figure 4.52:

• *Object size.* Other things being equal, an object close to us produces a larger image than does one farther away. This cue is useful only if we already knew the approximate actual size of the objects. For example, the roller skater in the photo produces a larger image than does the parked van, which we know is actually larger. So we see the skater as closer. The rocks in the sea, however, are not equally large in reality, so the relative sizes of their images are not a cue to their distance.

• *Linear perspective.* As parallel lines stretch out toward the horizon, they come closer and closer together. Examine the road in Figure 4.52. At the bottom of the photo (close to the viewer), the edges of the road are far apart; at greater distances, the edges of the road come closer together. The closer the lines come, the more distant we perceive them to be.

• *Detail.* We see nearby objects, such as the roller skater, in much detail. More distant objects are increasingly hazy and less detailed.

• *Interposition.* A nearby object interrupts our view of a more distant object. Interposition is our surest way of seeing which rocks are closer than others.

FIGURE 4.52
We can judge depth and distance in a photograph, using certain cues that are useful even if we use only one eye. (1) Closer objects occupy more space on the retina (or on the photograph) than do distant objects of the same type. (2) Nearer objects show more detail. (3) Closer objects overlap certain distant objects. (4) Objects in the foreground look sharper than do objects on the horizon. These are known as monocular cues.

- *Texture gradient*. Notice the posts on the safety rail on the right side of the road. At greater distances, the posts come closer and closer together. The "packed together" appearance of objects gives us another cue to their approximate distance.

- *Shadows*. Shadows are hardly prominent in Figure 4.52, but when present they can provide another cue to help us interpret the sizes and positions of objects in a picture.

The ability to use these monocular cues to interpret an illustration depends partly on our experience with photographs and drawings. For example, in the two drawings of Figure 4.53, it appears to me that the hunter is aiming his spear at the antelope. When these drawings were shown to people in certain African cultures that do much sculpture but very little drawing, many people said the hunter was aiming at a baby elephant (Hudson, 1960). That is, people do not automatically use monocular cues to depth in interpreting simple drawings like these; we have to learn how to use such cues.

Motion parallax, another monocular cue, helps us to perceive depth when we are looking at a three-dimensional scene, though it is of no help when we are looking at a photograph. When we are moving—riding along in a car or train, for example—close objects seem to pass by swiftly while distant objects seem to pass by very slowly. The faster an object passes by, the closer it must be. That principle is motion parallax.

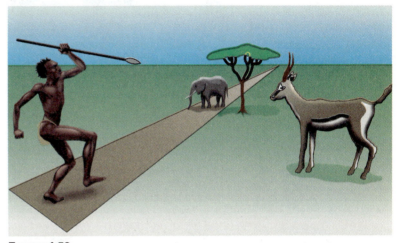

FIGURE 4.53
Which animal is the hunter attacking in each of these pictures? Most readers of this text, using monocular cues to distance, will reply that he is attacking the antelope. However, Hudson (1960) found that many African subjects thought he was attacking a baby elephant. Evidently the tendency to use monocular cues to distance depends on experience with photographs and drawings; the African subjects were from cultures that had little such experience. (Based on Hudson, 1960.)

This photo of people from Monterrey, Mexico, includes several monocular cues to distance, especially size. We interpret the people shown larger to be closer. Linear perspective and detail also contribute to our perception of distance.

If you were a passenger on this train, the ground beside the tracks would appear to pass by more quickly than the more distant elements in the landscape. The photo's version of motion parallax is that the ground is blurred, the more distant objects crisp.

15. Which monocular cues to depth are available in Figure 4.53?
16. In three-dimensional photography, cameras take two views of the same scene from different locations through lenses with different color filters or with different polarized-light filters. The two views are then superimposed. The viewer looks at the composite view through special glasses so that one eye sees the view taken with one camera and the other eye sees the view taken with the other camera. Which depth cue is at work here? (Check your answers on page 179.)

OPTICAL ILLUSIONS

Many people claim to have seen ghosts, flying saucers, the Loch Ness monster, Bigfoot, Santa's elves, or people floating in the air. Maybe they are lying; maybe they did see something extraordinary. Another possibility is that they saw something ordinary but misinterpreted it. An **optical illusion** is a misinterpretation of a visual stimulus. Figure 4.54 shows a few examples. Psychologists would like to develop a single explanation for all

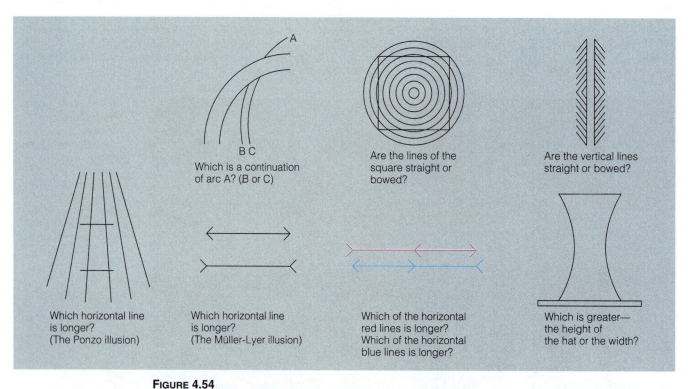

Which is a continuation of arc A? (B or C)

Are the lines of the square straight or bowed?

Are the vertical lines straight or bowed?

Which horizontal line is longer? (The Ponzo illusion)

Which horizontal line is longer? (The Müller-Lyer illusion)

Which of the horizontal red lines is longer? Which of the horizontal blue lines is longer?

Which is greater— the height of the hat or the width?

FIGURE 4.54
Many paintings rely on some optical illusion, but we are more aware of it in geometric figures. (Check your answers with a ruler and a compass.)

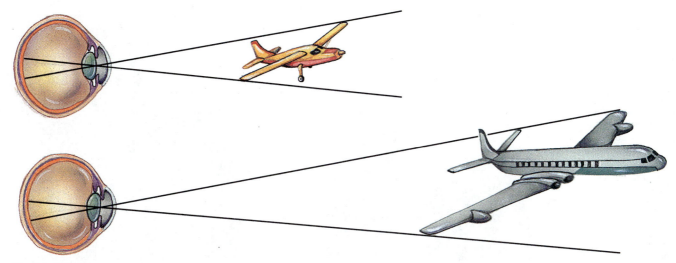

FIGURE 4.55
The trade-off between size and distance. A given image on the retina may indicate either a small, close object or a large, distant object.

optical illusions. (Remember the principle of parsimony from Chapter 2.) Although they have not fully succeeded, they can explain a fair number of optical illusions based on the relationship between size perception and depth perception.

THE RELATIONSHIP BETWEEN DEPTH PERCEPTION AND SIZE PERCEPTION

If you can estimate the size of an object, you can deduce its distance. If you can estimate its distance, you can deduce its size. Figure 4.55 shows that a given image on the retina may represent either a small, close object or a large, distant object. Watch what happens when you take a single image and change its apparent distance: Stare at Figure 4.13 again to form a negative afterimage. First examine the afterimage while you are looking at the wall across the room. Your afterimage looks like a fairly large flag. Then look at the afterimage against the palm of your hand. Suddenly the image becomes very small. Move your hand backward and forward; you can make the apparent size of the flag grow and then shrink.

In the real world, we seldom have trouble estimating the size and distance of objects. When you walk along the street, for instance, you never wonder whether the people you see are giants a kilometer away or miniature people a few centimeters away. However, when you have fewer cues about the size or distance of an object, you may become confused (Figure 4.56). I once saw an airplane overhead and for a minute or two

was unsure whether it was a small, remote-controlled toy airplane or a distant, full-size airplane. Airplanes come in many sizes and the sky has few cues as to distance.

A similar issue arises in reported sightings of UFOs. When people see an unfamiliar object in the sky, they may easily misjudge its distance. If they overestimate its distance, they also will overestimate its size and speed.

What does all this have to do with optical illusions? Whenever we misjudge distance, we are likely to misjudge size as well.

FIGURE 4.56
Because fish come in all sizes, we can estimate the size of a fish only if we know how far away it is or if we can compare its size to other nearby objects. See what happens when you cover the man and then cover the hand.

Figure 4.57

A study in deceptive perception, the Ames room is designed to be viewed through a peephole with one eye. (a) Both of these people are actually the same height. We are so accustomed to rooms with right angles that we can't imagine how this apparently ordinary room creates this optical illusion. (b) This diagram shows the positions of the people in the Ames room and demonstrates how the illusion of distance is created. (Part b from Wilson et al., 1964.)

a

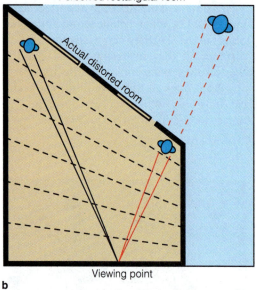

Perceived rectangular room

Actual distorted room

Viewing point

b

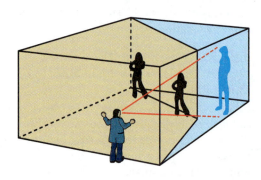

For example, Figure 4.57a shows people in the Ames room (named for its designer, Adelbert Ames). The room is designed to look like a normal rectangular room, though its true dimensions are as shown in Figure 4.57b. The right corner is much closer than the left corner. The two young women are actually the same height. If we eliminated all the background cues, then we would correctly perceive the women as being the same size but at different distances. However, the apparently rectangular room provides such powerful (though misleading) cues to distance that the women appear to differ greatly in height.

Even a two-dimensional drawing on a flat surface may offer cues that lead to erroneous depth perception. People who have had much experience with photos and drawings tend to interpret two-dimensional drawings as if they were three-dimensional. Figure 4.58 shows a bewildering two-prong/three-prong device and a round staircase that seems to run uphill all the way clockwise or downhill all the way counterclockwise. Both drawings puzzle us because we try to interpret them as three-dimensional objects.

In Figure 4.59a, we interpret the railroad track as heading into the distance. Similarly, because the background cues in part b suggest that the upper line is farther away than the lower line, we perceive the upper line as being larger. The same is true of the right-hand cylinder in part c. Recall from Figure 4.55 that when two objects produce the same-size image on the retina, we perceive the more distant one as being larger. In short, by perceiving two-dimensional representations as if they were three-dimensional, we misjudge distance and consequently misjudge size. When we are somehow misled by the cues that ordinarily ensure constancy in size and shape, we end up experiencing an optical illusion (Day, 1972).

We can also experience an *auditory illusion* by a similar principle: If we misestimate the distance to a sound source, we will misestimate the intensity of the sound. In one study, experimenters misled students about the distance of a sound by using the **visual capture effect,** the tendency of people to hear a sound as coming from a visually prominent source. (You experience this effect when you "hear" a voice coming from a ventriloquist's dummy or from a movie or television screen.) The experimenters had an unchanging sound source that the students never saw, plus a silent "dummy loudspeaker" that moved. The students always thought they heard the sound coming from the dummy loudspeaker, regardless of where the experimenters put it. When the loudspeaker was far away, most students said the sound was *louder* than when the speaker was close (Mershon, Desaulniers, Kiefer, Amerson, & Mills, 1981). Remember, the actual sound was the same in all cases. When people thought they heard such a sound from a great distance, they interpreted it as being very intense.

CROSS-CULTURAL DIFFERENCES IN SEEING OPTICAL ILLUSIONS

For most of us, the Müller-Lyer illusion is one of the most convincing. (See Figure 4.60.) According to one attempt at explaining it, the lines with outward-facing arrowheads (on the left in Figure 4.60) appear

FIGURE 4.58
Expectations shape perceptions. These two-dimensional drawings puzzle us because we try to interpret them as three-dimensional objects.

FIGURE 4.59
Some optical illusions depend on misjudgment of distances. In b, the top line looks longer because the perspective (resembling the railroad tracks in a) suggests a difference in distance. In c, the jar on the right seems larger because the context makes it appear farther away.

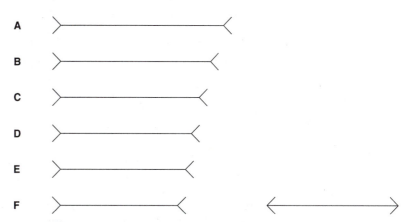

FIGURE 4.60
The Müller-Lyer illusion: Ignoring (or trying to ignore) the arrowheads, which of the horizontal lines on the left is the same length as the horizontal line at the right? (Check answer H on page 179.) For most people in the United States, Canada, and Europe, this is a strong and convincing illusion. The illusion is present but apparently weaker in many people from less technological societies.

a   b

FIGURE 4.61

According to one interpretation of the Müller-Lyer illusion, inward-facing arrowheads make a line appear shorter because they make the line resemble the front of a building (as in a), while outward-facing arrowheads make the line resemble the back of a building (as in b). If we interpret the line with inward-facing arrowheads as closer, we will also interpret the line as shorter.

larger because they resemble the edge and corners of the back of a room; the lines with inward-facing arrowheads resemble the front of a room. (See Figure 4.61.) If we perceive one line (a) as being closer than the other line (b), we are likely to interpret the closer one as shorter.

For a number of reasons, this explanation is not altogether convincing, but it does lead to one interesting prediction: The Müller-Lyer illusion might be stronger in cultures that have much experience with rooms and buildings and other cubical objects, and weaker in cultures that build circular huts or live in rain forests or other un-citylike environments. The illusion might also depend on people's experience with drawings of objects.

To test this hypothesis, researchers showed subjects stimuli similar to those in Figure 4.60 and determined which of the horizontal lines with outward arrows appeared the same length as the line with inward arrows. They found that the illusion was strongest for people who lived in U.S. or South African cities, and weaker for people from rural, nontechnological cultures such as African bushmen (Segall, Campbell, & Herskovits, 1966). A similar study found the illusion stronger for city dwellers in Zambia than for farm dwellers in the same country (Stewart, 1973).

The apparent conclusion is that people's experience with objects in their environment modifies the strength of certain optical illusions. However, people in all cultures experienced the illusion; the difference was merely one of how large the illusion was. Furthermore, in most cultures, children experienced a larger illusion than adults did; although the illusions may depend on visual experience, they apparently do not require many years of experience.

THE MOON ILLUSION

To most people, the moon close to the horizon appears about 30% larger than it appears when higher in the sky. This **moon illusion** is so convincing that some people have tried to explain it by referring to the bending of light rays by the atmosphere or to some other physical phenomenon. The explanation, however, must depend on the observer, not the light rays. If you actually measure the moon image with navigational or photographic equipment, you will find that its size is the same at the horizon as it is higher in the sky. For example, Figure 4.62 shows the moon at two positions in the sky; you can measure the two images to demonstrate that they really are the same size. (The atmosphere's bending of light rays makes the moon look orange near the horizon, but it does not increase the size of the image.) However, photographs do not capture the full strength of the moon illusion as we see it in real life. In Figure 4.62 (or any similar pair of photos), the moon looks almost the same at each position; in the actual night sky the moon at the horizon looks enormous.

One possible explanation is that the vast terrain between the viewer and the horizon provides a basis for size comparison. When you see the moon at the horizon, you can compare it to the other objects you see at the horizon, all of which look tiny. By contrast, the moon looks large. When you see the moon high in the sky, however, it is surrounded only by the vast, featureless sky, and in contrast the moon appears relatively small (Baird, 1982; Restle, 1970).

A second possible explanation is that the terrain between the viewer and the horizon gives an impression of great distance. When the moon is high in the sky, we have no basis to judge distance, and perhaps we unconsciously see the overhead moon as closer than the moon is at the horizon. If we see the horizon moon as more distant, we will perceive it as larger (Kaufman & Rock, 1989;

Rock & Kaufman, 1962). This explanation is appealing, because it relates the moon illusion to our misperceptions of distance, a factor already accepted as important for many other illusions.

Many psychologists are not satisfied, however, mostly because they are not convinced that the horizon moon looks farther away than the overhead moon. If we ask people which looks farther away, many hesitate or say they are not sure. If we prevail upon them to answer, most say the horizon moon looks *closer,* in direct contradiction to the theory. Some psychologists reply that the situation is complicated: Unconsciously we perceive the horizon as farther away; consequently we perceive the horizon moon as very large; then, because of the perceived large size of the horizon moon, we secondarily and consciously perceive it as closer (as people report), while we continue to unconsciously perceive it as farther away (Rock & Kaufman, 1962).

That theory is worth taking seriously, even if it sounds a bit far-fetched. But many psychologists continue to search for other explanations that do not require such awkward assumptions (Hershenson, 1989). In spite of extensive research, the moon illusion remains surprisingly difficult to explain.

One major message arises from work on optical illusions, and indeed from all the research on visual perception: What we perceive is not the same as what is "out there." The visual system does an amazing job of providing us with useful information about the world around us, but under unusual circumstances we can be very wrong about what we think we saw.

SUMMARY

- *Perception of minimal stimuli.* There is no sharp dividing line between sensory stimuli that can be perceived and sensory stimuli that cannot be perceived. A threshold stimulus is one that is intense enough to be perceived 50% of the time. (page 153)

- *Subliminal perception.* Under some circumstances, a weak stimulus that we do not consciously identify may influence our behavior, at least weakly or briefly. However, the claims of powerful or irresistible effects of subliminal perception are unfounded. (page 155)

FIGURE 4.62
Ordinarily, the moon at the horizon looks much larger than the moon overhead. In photographs this illusion disappears completely or almost completely, but the photographs do serve to demonstrate that the physical image of the moon is the same in both cases. The moon illusion requires a psychological explanation, not a physical explanation.

- *Detection of simple visual features.* In the first stages of the process of perception, feature-detector cells identify lines, points, and simple movement. Feature detectors cannot account for many of the active, interpretive aspects of perception, however. (page 157)

- *Perception of organized wholes.* According to Gestalt psychologists, we perceive an organized whole by identifying similarities and continuous patterns across a large area of the visual field. (page 161)

- *Attentive and preattentive processes.* We can identify some features of the visual field immediately even without paying attention to them. We identify others only by attending to one part of the visual field at a time. (page 165)

- *Visual constancies.* We ordinarily perceive the shape, size, and color of objects as constant even though the pattern of light striking the retina varies from time to time. (page 167)

- *Motion perception.* We perceive an object as moving if it moves relative to its background. We can generally distinguish between an object that is actually moving and a similar pattern of retinal stimulation that results from our own movement. (page 167)

- *Depth perception.* To perceive depth, we use retinal discrepancy between the views our two eyes see. We also use other cues that are just as effective with one eye as with two. People need some experience with photos or drawings before they can use depth cues to interpret sizes and distances in the drawings. (page 168)

- *The size-distance relationship.* Our estimate of an object's size depends on our estimate of its distance from us. If we overestimate its distance, we will also overestimate its size. (page 170)

- *Optical illusions.* Many, but not all, optical illusions result from interpreting a two-dimensional display as three-dimensional or from other faulty estimates of depth. The strength of an optical illusion may depend on a person's experiences. One of the strongest illusions, the moon illusion, has still not been convincingly explained. (page 172)

SUGGESTIONS FOR FURTHER READING

Kanizsa, G. (1979). *Organization in vision.* New York: Praeger. Emphasizes the Gestalt approach to vision.

Livingstone, M. S. (1988, January). Art, illusion, and the visual system. *Scientific American, 258* (1), 78–85. Discusses implications of the finding that different parts of the brain deal with different aspects of visual information, such as shape, color, and movement.

Rock, I. (1984). *Perception.* New York: Scientific American Books. Includes discussions of visual constancies, illusions, motion perception, and the relationship between perception and art.

TERMS

sensory threshold the minimum intensity at which a given individual can detect a sensory stimulus 50% of the time; a low threshold indicates ability to detect faint stimuli (page 154)

sensory adaptation the tendency of a sensory threshold to fall after a period when the sensory receptors have not been stimulated and to rise after exposure to intense stimuli (page 154)

absolute threshold the sensory threshold at a time of maximum sensory adaptation (page 154)

signal-detection theory the study of people's tendencies to make correct judgments, misses, and false alarms (page 154)

subliminal perception the ability of a stimulus to influence our behavior even when it is presented so faintly or briefly or along with such strong distractors that we do not perceive it consciously (page 155)

feature detector a neuron in the visual system of the brain that responds to particular lines or other features of a visual stimulus (page 158)

waterfall illusion phenomenon in which prolonged staring at a waterfall and then looking at nearby cliffs causes those cliffs to appear to flow upward (page 158)

backward masking the ability of a visual stimulus to erase the perceptual record of an immediately preceding different visual stimulus (page 160)

Gestalt psychology an approach to psychology that seeks explanations of how we perceive overall patterns (page 161)

figure and ground an object and its background (page 161)

reversible figure a stimulus that you can perceive in more than one way (page 161)

proximity in Gestalt psychology, the tendency to perceive objects that are close together as belonging to a group (page 162)

similarity in Gestalt psychology, the tendency to perceive objects that resemble each other as belonging to a group (page 162)

continuation in Gestalt psychology, the tendency to fill in the gaps in an interrupted line (page 162)

closure in Gestalt psychology, the tendency to imagine the rest of an incomplete familiar figure (page 162)

good figure in Gestalt psychology, the tendency to perceive simple, symmetrical figures (page 164)

preattentive process a perceptual activity that occurs automatically and simultaneously across a large portion of the visual field (page 166)

attentive process a perceptual activity that considers only one part of a visual field at a time (page 166)

visual constancy the tendency to perceive objects as being unchanging in shape, size, and color, despite variations in what actually reaches the retina (page 167)

induced movement a perception that an object is moving and the background is stationary when in fact the object is stationary and the background is moving (page 168)

stroboscopic movement an illusion of movement created by a rapid succession of stationary images (page 168)

phi effect the illusion of movement created when two or more stationary lights separated by a short distance flash on and off at regular intervals (page 168)

depth perception the perception of distance, which enables us to experience the world in three dimensions (page 168)

retinal disparity the difference in the apparent position of an object as seen by the left and right retinas (page 168)

convergence the degree to which the eyes turn in to focus on a close object (page 169)

binocular cues visual cues that depend on the action of both eyes (page 169)

monocular cues visual cues that are just as effective with one eye as with both (page 169)

motion parallax the apparently swift motion of objects close to a moving observer and the apparently slow motion of objects farther away (page 171)

optical illusion a misinterpretation of a visual stimulus as being larger or smaller or straighter or more curved than it really is (page 172)

visual capture effect tendency to localize a sound as coming from a prominent visual feature (such as a loudspeaker or a ventriloquist's dummy) (page 175)

moon illusion the apparent difference between the size of the moon at the horizon and its size higher in the sky (page 176)

ANSWERS TO CONCEPT CHECKS

14. In Figure 4.37, continuation, closure, and perhaps good figure; in Figure 4.38, closure. (page 164)
15. Object size is a cue that the elephant (usually larger than an antelope) must be far away. Interposition is a cue in part a; the antelope overlaps a hill that overlaps the hill with the elephant. Linear perspective is a cue in part b. (page 172)
16. Retinal disparity. (page 172)

ANSWERS TO OTHER QUESTIONS IN THE TEXT

C. a. (7); b. (1); c. (5); d. (9); e. (4)

D.

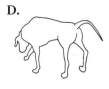

E.

F.

Eye
Ear
Cheek
Jaw
Necklace

Young woman

Eye
Nose
Mouth
Chin

Old woman

G.

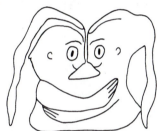

H. Line D is the same length as the one on the right. (Check it with a ruler.)

5 ALTERED STATES

My colleague Art Kohn tells a story of an old man who displayed what he said had been Abraham Lincoln's hand ax. Of course, the man explained, the blade had worn out some years after Lincoln died, so it had to be replaced. And some years later the handle broke and had to be replaced. But this was still Lincoln's ax.

Was it? In a sense, no: Not one scrap of material remained from the ax Lincoln had used. In another sense, yes: We see an unbroken continuity between the ax Lincoln used and this ax.

Now, what about *you*: Are you still the same person as that little 5-year-old who toddled off to kindergarten so many years ago? Since childhood, your body has grown many new cells and has repeatedly replaced

many old cells. Daily, each cell replaces many of its molecules with new ones. The material in your body has been replaced far more times than Lincoln's ax ever was. It is the same *you* only in the same sense that "Lincoln's ax" is still the same ax as the one Lincoln used long ago.

And yet, you may reply, the exchange of chemicals in your body is irrelevant to your sense of identity. What really constitutes *you* is not the particular molecules in your body at any given instant; the real *you* is your continuing experience, your unbroken "stream of consciousness," in the phrase of William James (1899/1962).

What is consciousness? Given that this is a chapter about altered states of consciousness, you might assume that I have something intelligent to say about the nature of consciousness. I wish I did. On the one hand, consciousness is undeniable. The philosopher René Descartes said that "I think, therefore I am" was the one statement he could not doubt. On the other hand, consciousness is impossible to observe directly and is therefore a difficult topic for scientific study. Psychologists of today are more willing to discuss consciousness than they were in, say, the 1950s; today's psychologists are even willing to consider the topic of nonhuman consciousness (Ristau, 1991). Still, anything we say about consciousness, even the simple statement "I believe that other people are conscious," is an inference, not an observation.

Oddly, although it is difficult to say much about consciousness itself, it is not difficult to discuss certain factors that alter, limit, or impair consciousness: sleep, hypnosis, and drugs. This chapter focuses on those three factors.

Since the time of your birth, you have repeatedly replaced the material in your body and added new material. Only a minuscule fraction of the molecules in your body today are the same as the molecules that were present in infancy. What makes you the same person from one year to the next is your continuous stream of conscious experience.

SLEEP AND DREAMS

Why do we sleep?
What accounts for the content of our dreams?

Ground squirrels hibernate during the winter, a time when they would have trouble finding enough food. The females awaken in spring at almost exactly the time when food becomes available. The males also need to awaken in time to eat, but they have another concern as well: The females are ready to mate as soon as they come out of their winter burrows, and each female mates only once a year. If some of the males woke up before the females and some woke up afterward, the late risers would pay for their extra sleep by missing out on their mating opportunity for a *whole year*. So the males don't take any chances; they all awaken from hibernation a full week before the females are due. And then they sit around waiting for a week . . . with no females, nothing to eat, and little to do except to fight with one another (French, 1988).

The point is that animals have evolved timing mechanisms to prepare their behavior for the situations they are likely to encounter. Male ground squirrels have some mechanism that awakens them from hibernation while the air is still cold and well before food is available. They awaken not in response to their current situation but in preparation for their future situation. Similarly, most migrating birds start south in the fall well before their northern homes become inhospitable.

Humans also have built-in timing mechanisms. We do not have any annual mechanism to prepare us to migrate or hibernate, but we do have mechanisms to prepare us for activity during the day and sleep during the night.

OUR CIRCADIAN RHYTHMS

Humans and other animals that rely on vision for survival are active during the day and inactive at night (Figure 5.1). Rats, mice, and other less visual animals are active at night and inactive during the day. Each species generates a rhythm of activity and inactivity lasting about one day. We call these rhythms **circadian rhythms.** (The term *circadian* comes from the Latin roots *circa* and *dies,* meaning "about a day.") The rising and setting of the sun provide a cue to reset our rhythm each day and keep it at exactly 24 hours; in an environment with no cues to time, most people generate a waking-sleeping rhythm lasting 24½ to 25 hours (Moore-Ede, Czeisler, & Richardson, 1983).

One of the earliest demonstrations of humans' circadian rhythms was a study of two people who spent a few weeks in a remote part of Mammoth Caves in Kentucky, isolated from the outside world (Kleitman, 1963). For 24 hours a day, the temperature was a constant 12° Celsius, and the relative humidity was a steady 100%. They saw no light except the light from lamps that they could control, and they heard no noises except the ones they made themselves. Any decision about when to sleep and when to awaken had to come from within themselves, not from the environment. Yet, they

FIGURE 5.1
The rising and setting of the sun does not directly produce our daily rhythm of wakefulness and sleepiness, but it synchronizes that rhythm. We adjust our internally generated cycles so that we feel alert during the day and sleepy at night.

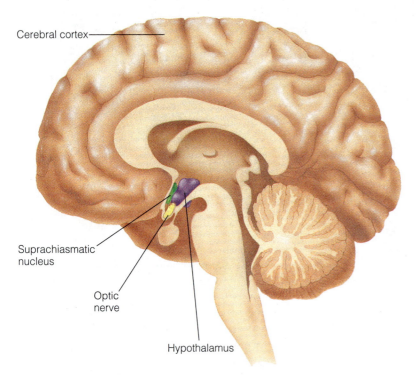

Cerebral cortex

Suprachiasmatic
nucleus

Optic
nerve

Hypothalamus

FIGURE 5.2
The suprachiasmatic nucleus, a small area at the base of the brain, produces the circadian rhythm. Ordinarily, information about light intensity reaches this area by way of the optic nerves from the eyes; such information resets the circadian rhythm but is not necessary for its generation. Cells in the suprachiasmatic nucleus can generate a 24- to 25-hour rhythm of activity on their own, even if they are separated from the rest of the brain.

ally rise later in the day. They also reach their intellectual and physical peaks at about 5–10 P.M. Self-described "morning people" reach their peak for body temperature as well as intellectual and physical work in the mornings (Horne, Brass, & Pettitt, 1980). Not everyone is a pure morning person or evening person; many are intermediates. Furthermore, these classifications are not permanent. You might be an evening person while in your 20s and become a morning person in your 40s or 50s.

SHIFTING SLEEP SCHEDULES

In ordinary life, the light of early morning serves to reset the body's clock each day to prevent it from gradually slipping out of synchrony with the outside world. If you travel across time zones, the light in your new location will eventually reset your clock to the new time, but until it does so, your internal rhythms are out of phase with the light and dark cycles of your environment. For example, if you travel from the west coast of North America to western Europe, it will be 7:00 A.M. (time to get up and go) when your body says it is 10:00 P.M. (almost bedtime). The resulting **jet lag** will make it difficult for you to fall asleep at night, to awaken in the morning, and to function during the day. Over a few days you will gradually adjust to your new schedule, but you will experience jet lag again when you return home. Back on the west coast, your body will scream, "Bedtime! Bedtime!" before anyone else thinks it is time for dinner.

Most people find it easier to adjust to flying west, where they go to bed later, than to flying east, where they go to bed earlier (Désir et al., 1981). East-coast people tend to adjust to west-coast time more easily than west-coast people adjust to east-coast time (Figure 5.3).

It is possible to have an experience akin to jet lag without even leaving town. Suppose you stay up late on Friday night and wake up late on Saturday morning. (Many readers will not find it difficult to "suppose" that assumption.) Then you stay up late again on Saturday and wake up late on Sunday. By Monday morning, when you are supposed to awaken early to go to school or work, you have reset your circadian rhythm, and even though the clock on your table may say 7:00 A.M., your internal clock thinks you are about two thousand miles west and the time is 5:00 A.M.

went to sleep and awoke at about the same time every day.

Later research has established that one tiny structure at the base of the brain, known as the *suprachiasmatic nucleus,* generates the body's circadian rhythm. If that area of the brain is damaged, the body's activity cycles become erratic (Rusak, 1977); if cells from that area are kept alive outside the body, they generate a circadian rhythm on their own (Green & Gillette, 1982; Inouye & Kawamura, 1979). In short, this area serves as the body's built-in clock. (See Figure 5.2.)

Our circadian rhythms do not affect us all in exactly the same way. You have probably heard some people describe themselves as "morning people," who awaken early and full of energy, doing their best work before noon; other people, who call themselves "evening people," take longer to warm up in the morning, and feel their best and do their best work in the late afternoon or evening. Those reported differences are real. One study found that people who call themselves "evening people" are quite literally slow to warm up in the mornings; their body temperatures are low in the morning and gradu-

Companies that want to keep their factories going nonstop run three work shifts, generally midnight–8:00 A.M., 8:00 A.M.–4:00 P.M., and 4:00 P.M.–midnight. Because it is difficult to find people to work regularly on the "graveyard shift" (midnight–8:00 A.M.), many companies ask their workers to rotate among the three shifts. People working the night shift, especially those who have just switched to the night shift, are responsible for a disproportionate number of industrial accidents and medical complaints. Even people who work the night shift month after month may not fully adjust; they continue feeling groggy on the job and sleeping fitfully during the day.

Employers can ease the burden on their workers in two ways: First, when they transfer workers from one shift to another, they should transfer workers to a *later* shift, not an earlier shift (Czeisler, Moore-Ede, & Coleman, 1982) (Figure 5.4). That is, someone working the 8:00 A.M–4:00 P.M. shift should switch to the 4:00 P.M.–midnight shift (equivalent to traveling west), instead of the midnight–8:00 A.M. shift (equivalent to traveling east).

Second, employers can help workers adjust to the night shift by providing bright lights to mimic sunlight. In one study, young men exposed to very bright lights at night adjusted well to working at night and sleeping during the day. Within 6 days, their circadian rhythms had shifted to the new schedule. Another group of men who worked on the same schedule but under less bright lights showed no indications of altering their circadian rhythms (Czeisler et al., 1990).

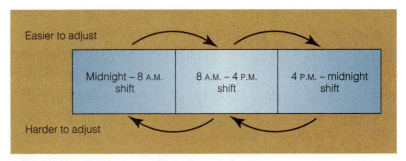

FIGURE 5.4
The graveyard shift is aptly named—serious industrial accidents, including those at nuclear power plants, usually occur at night, when workers are least alert. Night-shift jobs providing emergency services are essential. But since few people want to work at night permanently, workers rotate among three shifts. As in jet lag, the direction of change is critical. Moving forward—clockwise—is easier than going backward.

CONCEPT CHECK

1. Suppose you are the president of Consolidated Generic Products in the U.S.A., and you are negotiating a difficult business deal with someone from the opposite side of the world. Should you prefer a meeting place in Europe or on an island in the Pacific Ocean? (Check your answer on page 200.)

SOMETHING TO THINK ABOUT

What advice would you give someone who suffered severe, lasting insomnia because that person's body was not ready for sleep until 3:00 A.M.? (Assume this person has repeatedly tried going to bed earlier, but has failed.) Remember, the internal clock can shift more easily to a later time than to an earlier time. How could such a person reset his or her internal clock to the correct time?

WHY WE SLEEP

We would not have been born with a mechanism that forces us to sleep for 8 hours or so out of every 24 unless sleep did us some good. But what good does it do? Scientists have proposed two theories.

THE REPAIR AND RESTORATION THEORY OF WHY WE SLEEP

According to the **repair and restoration theory**, the purpose of sleep is to enable the body to recover from the exertions of the day. During sleep the body increases its rate of cell division and the rate at which it

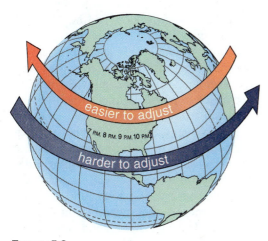

FIGURE 5.3
Jet lag: time zones and sleeping times.

SLEEP AND DREAMS

FIGURE 5.5
Even near the end of his 264 consecutive hours without sleep, Randy Gardner was able to perform tasks requiring strength and skill. Here, observers dutifully record his every move.

produces new proteins (Adam, 1980). It also digests food. There is no doubt that these and perhaps other restorative processes do occur during sleep. However, nearly all of the same processes also take place when we are awake but sitting quietly. Evidently we do not need sleep in order to rest the muscles or any other tissues, other than perhaps the brain (Horne, 1988). We have several other reasons to doubt that sleeping is like resting to catch your breath after extensive exercise.

First, if sleep were simply a means of recovering from the exertions of the day, it would resemble the rest periods we have after bouts of activity. But people need only a little more sleep after a day of extreme physical or mental activity than after a day of inactivity (Horne & Minard, 1985).

Second, some people get by with much less than the "normal" 7½ to 8 hours of sleep a day. An extreme case was a 70-year-old woman who claimed that she slept only about 1 hour a night. Researchers who observed her over a number of days confirmed her claim; some nights she did not sleep at all (Meddis, Pearson, & Langford, 1973). Nevertheless, she remained healthy.

Third, some people have intentionally gone without sleep for a week or more, suffering less severely than we might have expected (Figure 5.5). In 1965 a San Diego high-school student, Randy Gardner, stayed awake for 264 hours and 12 minutes—11

days—in a project for a high-school science fair. Gardner suffered no serious psychological consequences (Dement, 1972). On the last night of his ordeal he played about a hundred arcade games against sleep researcher William Dement and won every game. Just before the end of the 264 hours he held a television press conference and handled himself well. After sleeping 14 hours and 40 minutes, he awoke refreshed and apparently fully recovered.

You may have heard that unscrupulous people have used sleep deprivation as a means of brainwashing or torturing prisoners. Why would sleep deprivation produce so many more drastic effects on prisoners than it did on, say, Randy Gardner? Two reasons: First, Gardner may have been better able to tolerate sleep deprivation than most other people. Quite likely, many other people have tried to deprive themselves of sleep, but we never heard about them because they gave up after two or three days. Second, Gardner knew he was in control of the situation. If he became unbearably miserable, he could simply quit and go to sleep. Tortured prisoners do not have that option; if they stay awake night after night, they do so because of constant prodding, not because of their own decision. For the same reason, rats that have been forced to go without sleep for several days suffer severe health problems that human volunteers seldom experience after similar periods of sleep deprivation (Rechtschaffen, Gilliland, Bergmann, & Winter, 1983).

If you go without sleep some night—as most college students do at one time or another—you probably will grow very sleepy by about 4:00 or 5:00 A.M. But if you are still awake at 7:00 or 8:00 A.M., you will feel less sleepy than you did before. For the rest of the day you may feel a little peculiar, but you probably will stay awake and keep reasonably alert. That night, however, you will feel very sleepy indeed. Apparently, the need to sleep is tied to particular time periods.

In one study, volunteers went without sleep for 3 nights; an experimenter periodically took their temperature and measured their performance on logical reasoning tasks. Both temperature and logical reasoning declined during the first night and then increased almost to their normal level the next morning. During the second and third nights, temperature and logical reasoning decreased more than they had the first night,

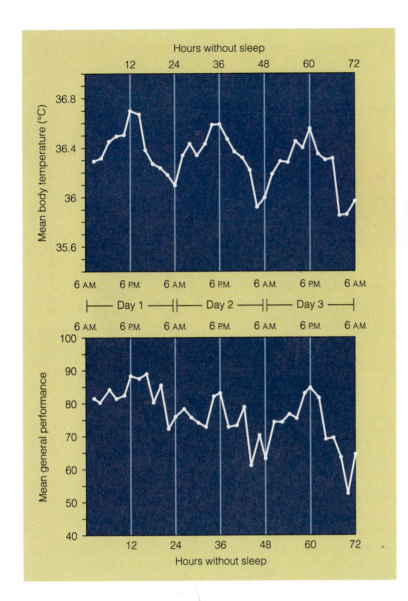

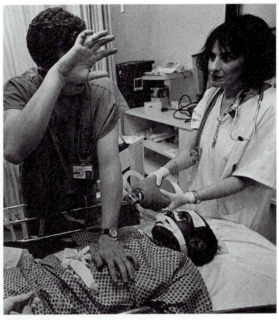

FIGURE 5.6
Cumulative effects of 3 nights without sleep. Both body temperature and logical reasoning decrease each night and increase the next morning. They also deteriorate from one day to the next. Medical interns have to fight this loss of efficiency when they stay on duty for extended periods. (From Babkoff, Caspy, Mikulincer, & Sing, 1991.)

but again they improved the following morning (Figure 5.6). Thus, sleep deprivation produces a pattern of progressive deterioration that is superimposed on the normal circadian cycle of rising and falling body temperature and reasoning ability (Babkoff, Caspy, Mikulincer, & Sing, 1991).

In short, sleepiness apparently depends partly on how long one has gone without sleep and partly on the time of day (that is, where one is within the circadian rhythm). Evidently, sleep contributes to repair and restoration of the body, even if that is not its only reason for existence.

THE EVOLUTIONARY THEORY OF WHY WE SLEEP

Sleep may be a way of conserving energy. If we built a solar-powered robot to explore the planet Mars, we probably would pro-

gram it to shut down almost all its activities at night in order to conserve fuel and in order to avoid walking into rocks that it could not see.

According to the **evolutionary theory of sleep,** evolution equipped us with a regular pattern of sleeping and waking for the same reason (Kleitman, 1963; Webb, 1979). The theory does not deny that sleep provides some important restorative functions. It merely says that evolution has programmed us to perform those functions at a time when activity would be inefficient and possibly dangerous.

Note, however, that sleep protects us only from the sort of trouble we might walk into; it does not protect us from trouble that comes looking for us! So we sleep well when we are in a familiar, safe place; but we sleep lightly, if at all, when we fear that burglars

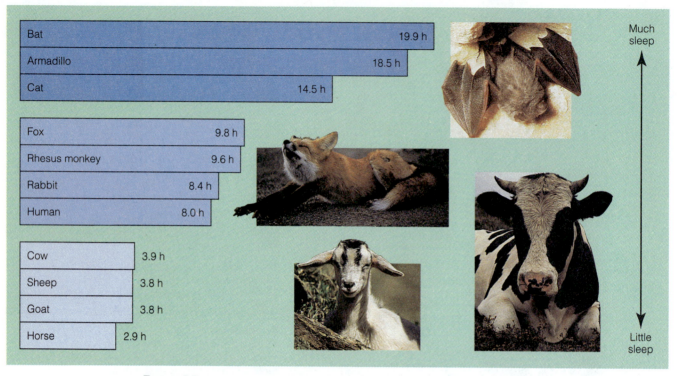

Bat	19.9 h	
Armadillo	18.5 h	
Cat	14.5 h	
Fox	9.8 h	
Rhesus monkey	9.6 h	
Rabbit	8.4 h	
Human	8.0 h	
Cow	3.9 h	
Sheep	3.8 h	
Goat	3.8 h	
Horse	2.9 h	

Much sleep ↑

Little sleep ↓

FIGURE 5.7
*Sleep time for mammals varies widely. Animals that are rarely attacked sleep
a lot; those in danger of attack sleep only a few hours. Diet also relates to
sleep. (Based on data from Zepelin & Rechtschaffen, 1974.)*

will break into the room or that bears will nose into the tent.

The evolutionary theory accounts well for differences in sleep among species (Campbell & Tobler, 1984). Why do cats, for instance, sleep so much, whereas horses and sheep sleep so little? Surely cats do not need five times as much repair and restoration as horses do. But cats can afford to have long periods of inactivity because they spend little time eating and are unlikely to be attacked while they sleep. Horses and sheep must spend almost all their waking hours eating, because their diet is very low in calories (Figure 5.7). Moreover, they cannot afford to sleep too long or too soundly, because their survival depends on their ability to run away from attackers. (Woody Allen once said, "The lion and the calf shall lie down together, but the calf won't get much sleep.")

Which of the two theories of sleep is correct? Both are, to a large degree. Supporters of the repair and restoration theory concede that the timing and even amount of sleep depend on when the animal is least efficient at finding food and defending itself. Supporters of the evolutionary theory concede that during a time that evolution has set aside for an animal to conserve energy, the animal takes that opportunity to perform repair and restoration functions.

STAGES OF SLEEP

In the mid-1950s, Michel Jouvet, a French scientist, discovered that brain activity and body activity vary from time to time during sleep. While trying to record the very small head movements that a severely brain-damaged cat made while asleep, he found periods in which its brain was relatively active even though its muscles were completely relaxed. Further research indicated that such periods occur not only in brain-damaged cats but also in normal cats (Jouvet, Michel, & Courjon, 1959). Jouvet referred to these periods as *paradoxical sleep*. (A paradox is an apparent self-contradiction.) The paradox is that such sleep is very light in some respects but very deep in other ways. The brain is active, and the body's heart rate, breathing rate, and temperature fluctuate substantially (Parmeggiani, 1982). In these respects paradoxical sleep is very light. And yet most of the muscles, especially the large muscles involved in posture and locomotion, are very relaxed. In these respects paradoxical sleep is deep.

At about the same time that Jouvet discovered paradoxical sleep, American researchers William Dement and Nathaniel Kleitman (1957a, 1957b) observed that in one recurrent stage of human sleep, the sleeper's eyes move rapidly back and forth under the closed lids. They referred to this stage as **rapid eye movement (REM) sleep.** (All other stages of sleep are known as **non-REM, or NREM, sleep.**) Almost at once investigators realized that REM sleep is the same as paradoxical sleep. When Dement and Kleitman awakened people during REM sleep, the sleepers usually reported that they had been dreaming. Apparently, the rapid eye movements were external indications of an internal event; for the first time, it became possible to undertake scientific studies of dreaming.

SLEEP CYCLES DURING THE NIGHT

Sleep researchers have identified four stages of sleep: After we fall asleep, we progress from stage 1 sleep, in which the brain remains fairly active, through stages 2, 3, and 4. Researchers can detect the stages by recording brain waves with electrodes attached to the scalp (Figure 5.8). A device called an **electroencephalograph,** abbreviated **EEG,** measures and amplifies slight electrical changes on the scalp that reflect patterns of activity in the brain. An awake, alert brain produces an EEG record with many short, choppy waves like the one shown in Figure 5.9a. In sleep stages 1 through 4, the brain produces an increasing number of long, slow waves, as shown in Figure 5.9b through e. These large waves indicate *decreased* brain activity. They grow larger from one stage to the next because a larger proportion of the active neurons are active at the same time. During wakefulness, by contrast, the neurons are out of synchrony and their activities nearly cancel each other out, rather like a crowd of people talking at the same time.

After we have reached stage 4 of sleep, we gradually move back through stages 3 and 2 to stage 1 again. A normal young adult cycles from stage 1 to stage 4 and back to stage 1 again in about 90 to 100 minutes. Then he or she repeats the sequence, again and again, all through the night (Figure 5.10).

During the first part of the night, stages 3

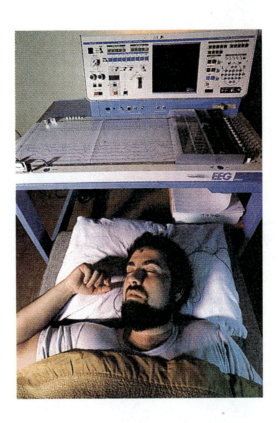

FIGURE 5.8
These electrodes monitor the activity in a sleeper's brain, and an EEG then records and displays brain-wave patterns.

and 4 predominate. Later in the night, the duration of stages 1 and 2 increases. Except for the first occurrence of stage 1 (when the person is just entering sleep), REM periods replace most of the stage 1 periods. Figure 5.9f shows a period of REM sleep. Note both the active EEG recordings and the eye movements.

CONCEPT CHECK

2. *Would REM sleep and dreaming be more common toward the end of the night's sleep or toward the beginning? (Check your answer on page 198.)*

SLEEP STAGES AND DREAMING

Dement's early research indicated that people who were awakened during REM sleep usually reported they had been dreaming but that people who were awakened during any other period seldom reported dreaming. So, for a time, REM sleep was thought to be almost synonymous with dreaming. However, later studies found a fair amount of dreaming during non-REM sleep as well. Non-REM dreams, however, are less vivid, less visual, less bizarre, and less likely to be experienced as something really happening. We can describe these experiences as dreams

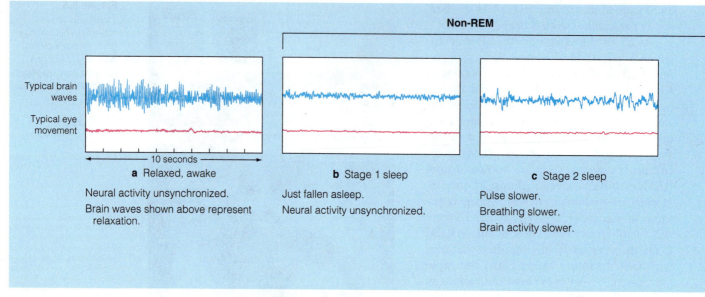

Non-REM

Typical brain waves
Typical eye movement

← 10 seconds →

a Relaxed, awake

Neural activity unsynchronized.
Brain waves shown above represent relaxation.

b Stage 1 sleep

Just fallen asleep.
Neural activity unsynchronized.

c Stage 2 sleep

Pulse slower.
Breathing slower.
Brain activity slower.

FIGURE 5.9
During sleep, people progress through stages that vary in brain activity. The blue line indicates brain waves, as shown by an EEG. The red line shows eye movements. Note that REM sleep resembles stage 1 sleep except for the addition of rapid eye movements. (Courtesy of Le Vere.)

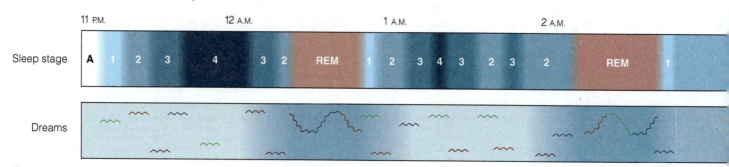

11 P.M.   12 A.M.   1 A.M.   2 A.M.

Sleep stage A 1 2 3 4 3 2 REM 1 2 3 4 3 2 3 2 REM 1

Dreams

FIGURE 5.10
Condensing hundreds of pages of EEG recordings over a night, this graph shows that a person had five cycles of REM and non-REM sleep and woke up briefly three times (A = Awake). The large amount of stage 3 and 4 sleep early in the night is typical of most people. During such non-REM sleep, the body uses little energy. Brain activity, respiration, and temperature decrease. (Based on Dement, 1972.)

if we wish, or we can simply classify them as thoughts.

The link between REM sleep and highly vivid dreams enabled sleep investigators to determine with fair accuracy whether or not someone was dreaming. Scientific progress frequently depends on an improved way of measuring something; in this case, a method of measuring dreaming enabled researchers to answer some basic questions.

For example, does everyone dream? People who claim they do not dream have been taken into the laboratory so that researchers could examine brain waves and eye movements. The people who claimed not to dream had normal periods of REM sleep. If awakened during one of these periods, they reported dreams (to their own surprise). Apparently, these people dream as much as anyone else; they simply forget their dreams faster.

Another question: How long do dreams last? Before the discovery of REM sleep, this was an unanswerable question; now, sud-

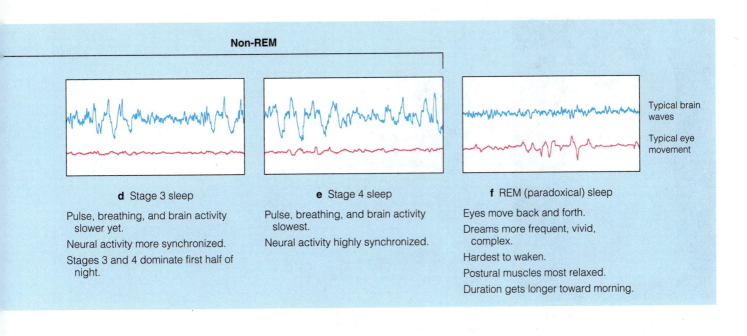

Non-REM

Typical brain waves

Typical eye movement

d Stage 3 sleep

Pulse, breathing, and brain activity slower yet.

Neural activity more synchronized.

Stages 3 and 4 dominate first half of night.

e Stage 4 sleep

Pulse, breathing, and brain activity slowest.

Neural activity highly synchronized.

f REM (paradoxical) sleep

Eyes move back and forth.

Dreams more frequent, vivid, complex.

Hardest to waken.

Postural muscles most relaxed.

Duration gets longer toward morning.

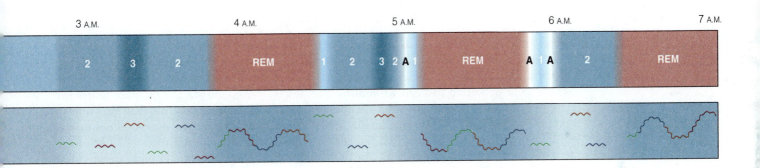

3 A.M.   4 A.M.   5 A.M.   6 A.M.   7 A.M.

2   3   2   REM   1   2   3 2 A 1   REM   A 1 A   2   REM

denly, researchers had a method to answer it. William Dement and Edward Wolpert (1958) awakened people after REM periods of various durations and asked them to describe their dreams, if any. A person awakened after 1 minute of REM sleep usually would tell a brief story; a person awakened after 5 minutes of REM sleep usually would tell a story about 5 times as long, and so on. Evidently, dreams take place in "real time." That is, a dream is not over in a split second; if it seemed to last several minutes, it probably did.

THE FUNCTIONS OF REM SLEEP

Given that people spend about 20–25% of an average night in the specialized state of REM sleep, presumably REM sleep serves some important function. But what is that function? The most direct way to approach this question is to deprive people of REM sleep and see how the deprivation affects their health or behavior.

In one study, William Dement (1960) monitored the sleep of eight young men for seven consecutive nights and awakened them for a few minutes whenever their EEG and eye movements indicated the onset of REM sleep. He awakened the members of a control group equally often but at random times, so that he did not necessarily interrupt their REM sleep. Over the course of a week, Dement found it harder and harder to prevent REM sleep in the experimental group. On the first night, the average subject had to be awakened 12 times. By the seventh night, the average was 26 times, and the awakening process had become more difficult.

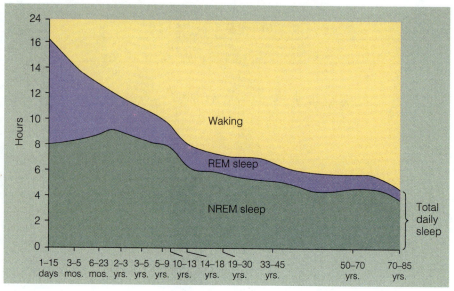

FIGURE 5.11

The percentage of time in REM and non-REM sleep varies with age. As the total amount of sleep declines over age, the percentage of REM sleep also declines. Thus it is uncertain whether REM is particularly important for infants, or just particularly prevalent in those who spend many hours asleep. (From Roffwarg, Muzio, & Dement, 1966.)

During the day, REM-deprived subjects experienced anxiety, irritability, and impaired concentration. On the eighth night, all the subjects were permitted to sleep without interruption. Most of them showed a "REM rebound," spending 29% of the night in REM sleep as compared with 19% before the experiment started. The subjects in the control group, who had not been deprived of REM sleep, showed no such REM rebound.

So, evidently REM sleep satisfies some need and the body works to catch up on at least some of the REM sleep that it has been forced to miss. However, in this and related studies, the effects of REM deprivation have not been catastrophic, and the question remained as to exactly why we need REM sleep.

A second approach to the question is to determine which people get more REM sleep than others. One clear pattern is that infants get more REM sleep than children do and that children get more than adults do (Figure 5.11). From that observation, a number of people have inferred that REM sleep serves some function that is more acute in younger people. Maybe so, but we should be cautious about interpreting this evidence. Infants not only get more REM sleep but also get more total sleep. If we compare species, we find

that the species that get the most total sleep (such as cats) also generally have the greatest percentage of REM sleep. Among adult humans, those who sleep 9 or more hours per night spend a large percentage of that time in REM sleep; those who sleep 6 hours or less spend a smaller percentage in REM sleep. In short, the individuals with the greatest amount of total sleep time spend the greatest percentage of that time in REM. It is as if a certain amount of non-REM sleep is necessary each night, and additional amounts of REM sleep can be added if sleep continues long enough (Horne, 1988).

A growing body of research suggests that one function of REM sleep, though not necessarily the only or main function, is to improve memory storage. After days when animals are given new learning experiences, they generally get more than the usual amount of REM sleep, and animals prevented from getting REM sleep learn slowly (Hobson, 1992). As a rule, the animals that learn fastest are also the ones that show the greatest increase in REM sleep (Smith & Wong, 1991). In humans, certain kinds of skilled performances learned on a given day generally improve the next morning, following a normal night's sleep. However, that improvement does not occur in people who are deprived of REM sleep during the night (Karni, Tanne, Rubenstein, Askenasy, & Sagi, 1994). Exactly how REM sleep facilitates learning, or how learning prompts extra REM sleep, remains unknown.

THE CONTENT OF OUR DREAMS

"Even a saint is not responsible for what happens in his dreams."

ST. THOMAS AQUINAS

What do we dream about and why? At one time, people believed that dreams foretold the future. Occasionally, of course, they do, either by coincidence or because the dreamer had some reason to expect a certain event to happen. Sigmund Freud maintained that dreams reveal a person's unconscious thoughts and motivations (Chapter 15). To some extent they do; the content of most dreams comes from events the person experienced or thought about in the previous day or two (Arkin & Antrobus, 1978). (See Figure 5.12.) For example, people deprived of fluids frequently dream about drinking; people who have been kept in isolation dream about talking in groups. People who have watched violent movies tend to have unusually clear, vivid, and emotional dreams, though not necessarily violent ones. After watching movies with a great deal of explicit sexual content, people who are asked about their dreams frequently say, "I, uhh . . . forget what I was dreaming about."

Furthermore, a frequently repeated dream may suggest that something is worrying the person. People who have the same dream over and over tend to report more anxiety, depression, and stress in their waking lives than do other people (Brown & Donderi, 1986).

Occasionally a person's dream about some personal problem suggests a solution. Here is one example (Barrett, 1993): A college senior majoring in psychology had applied to two university programs in clinical psychology and two in industrial psychology, and was trying to decide which of the two fields to enter. The dream:

A map of the United States. I am in a plane flying over this map. The pilot says we are having engine trouble and need to land and

FIGURE 5.12
The content of most dreams comes from what we think about or do in the day or two prior to the dream.

we look for a safe place on the map indicated by a light. I ask about Massachusetts which we seem to be over right then and he says all of Massachusetts is very dangerous. The lights seem to be further west. I wake up and realize that my two clinical schools are both in Massachusetts, where I have spent my whole life and where my parents live. Both industrial programs are far away, Texas and California. That was because originally I was looking to stay close to home and there were no good industrial programs nearby. I realize that there is a lot wrong with staying at home and that, funny as it sounds, getting away is probably more important than which kind of program I go to.

Dreams are a product of brain activity, and even a sleeping brain experiences a fair amount of sensory information. While you sleep, you hear, feel, and smell the world

For 50,000 years, Australia's aborigines have been interpreting their dreams through music, dance, and art about their Dreamtime, a mythical period when spirit ancestors created everything on the earth. The paintings, which were once done on the sandy soil of the desert, are now created on canvas, with dots of acrylic paint to reproduce the stones or clumps of plant matter that made up the traditional designs. Here a father is explaining his dreaming to his children.

around you, and your vestibular system detects the position of your head. Meanwhile, especially during REM sleep periods, many parts of your brain, especially the visual areas, have substantial amounts of spontaneous activity. According to the **activation-synthesis theory of dreams,** the brain experiences this spontaneous activity as sensations, links the sensations together, and tries to synthesize them into a coherent pattern (Hobson, 1988). A dream is your brain's best effort to make sense of the limited information it is receiving.

This theory suffers the flaws of being vague and not easily testable. Still, as the theory assumes, people who are experiencing various stimuli often incorporate them into their dreams (Arkin & Antrobus, 1978; Dement, 1972). For example, if you happened to feel a spray of water on your face, you might dream about standing in the rain or going swimming. A sudden loud noise might become a dream about an earthquake or a plane crash. A bright light might become a dream about flashes of lightning or a fire.

We can relate certain common dreams to sensory stimuli, although the explanations are admittedly based more on speculation than on evidence. For example, most people have occasional dreams of flying or falling. Perhaps those dreams relate to the fact that you are lying down when you sleep; your

vestibular system detects your prone position and your brain interprets the sensation as if you were flying (Hobson & McCarley, 1977). Most people also have occasional dreams in which they are trying to run away from something but find that they cannot move. A possible reason is that the major postural muscles really are paralyzed during REM sleep. Thus, your brain could send messages telling your muscles to move but then receive sensory feedback indicating that they have not moved at all.

As I said, these explanations are speculative. One objection is that most people almost always sleep in a prone position but only occasionally dream of flying, and that our muscles are always paralyzed during REM sleep but we only occasionally dream of being unable to move. The activation-synthesis theory makes only vague predictions about who will dream what and when, so it can be criticized for being not falsifiable (see Chapter 2).

Most people experience visual imagery during their dreams. Blind people may or may not, depending on when and how they became blind. A person who has had vision and then lost it because of damage to the eyes continues to see during dreams. (The visual cortex is still intact and becomes spontaneously active during REM sleep.) But a person who has never had vision or who has lost it because of damage to the visual cortex has no visual imagery during dreams. People with any degree of visual impairment are more likely than sighted people to dream about touching something (Sabo & Kirtley, 1982).

Many questions about dreams are more easily asked than answered. For example, many people ask, "Do we dream in color?" That sounds like a simple question, perhaps one that should be simple to answer. However, the very fact that people ask this question reveals why it is difficult to answer. People ask because they do not remember whether or not their dreams were in color. But how can an investigator determine whether people dream in color except by asking them? The best answer we have is that when people are awakened during REM sleep, when their recall should be as sharp as possible, they report color at least half the time (Herman, Roffwarg, & Tauber, 1968; Padgham, 1975). This result does not mean that their other dreams are necessarily in black and white; it may mean only that the colors in those dreams are not memorable.

ABNORMALITIES OF SLEEP

Comedian Steven Wright says that someone asked him, "Did you sleep well last night?" He replied, "No, I made a few mistakes."

We laugh because sleep isn't the kind of activity on which a person makes mistakes; sleep just happens. Sometimes, however, sleep doesn't happen, or it happens at the wrong time, or it does not seem restful, or we have bad dreams. We probably do not wish to call these unpleasant experiences "mistakes," but in one way or another, our sleep is not what we wanted it to be.

INSOMNIA

The term **insomnia** literally means "lack of sleep." However, we cannot usefully define insomnia in terms of the number of hours of sleep. Some people feel well rested after 5 or 6 hours of sleep per night; others feel poorly rested after 8 or 9. Furthermore, many people who seek help for their insomnia greatly underestimate how much they sleep. Some of the insomniacs who have been studied in sleep laboratories get to sleep almost as fast as other people and accumulate almost a normal amount of sleep per night. However, when they are awakened, even from stage 4 sleep, they claim that they were not asleep! Evidently they are getting many hours of sleep without feeling rested. Many of these same people report feeling "much better rested" after a night when they took sleeping pills, even though the sleeping pills increased their total sleep time by only about half an hour (Mendelson, 1990). In short, insomnia is a subjective condition. *A complaint of insomnia indicates that the person feels poorly rested at the end of the night.* By this definition, about one third of all adults have occasional insomnia and about one tenth have serious or chronic insomnia (Lilie & Rosenberg, 1990).

It is convenient to distinguish three main types of insomnia: People with **onset insomnia** have trouble falling asleep. Those with **termination insomnia** awaken early and cannot get back to sleep. Those with **maintenance insomnia** awaken frequently during the night, though they get back to sleep each time. In many cases, onset insomnia and termination insomnia are related to a circadian rhythm that is out of synchrony with the outside world. At 11:00 P.M. a person with onset insomnia may feel as if it were still only 6:00 P.M. At 2:00 A.M. a person with termi-

Insomnia is identified not by how many hours one sleeps at night, but by how sleepy the person is the following day.

nation insomnia may already feel as if it were 7:00 A.M. In such cases, therapy is a matter of trying to readjust the circadian rhythms so that the person can feel sleepy and wakeful at the normal times.

In addition to an out-of-synch circadian rhythm, we can identify many other causes of insomnia (Kales & Kales, 1984). People sometimes have trouble sleeping because of noise, worries, uncomfortable temperatures, use of various drugs including alcohol, indigestion, and miscellaneous other problems. Overuse of tranquilizers can also become a cause of insomnia. That statement may be surprising, because people often take tranquilizers as a way of *relieving* insomnia. Tranquilizers do induce sleep and help people get a restful sleep. The problem is, no pill exerts its effects for exactly the period of time that someone wanted to sleep. Some tranquilizers produce brief effects that wear off before morning, so the person awakens early (Kales, Soldatos, Bixler, & Kales, 1983). Others have effects that last too long, so the person remains sleepy for part of the next day.

An additional problem with tranquilizers is that a consistent user may come to depend on them to get to sleep (Kales, Scharf, & Kales, 1978). When such a person tries to sleep without taking a pill, he or she may experience more severe insomnia than the original insomnia the pill was supposed to relieve.

Sleep Apnea

One cause of extremely poor sleep is known as **sleep apnea** (AP-nee-uh). *Apnea* means "no breathing." Many people have irregular breathing or occasional periods of 10 seconds or so without breathing during their sleep. People with sleep apnea, however, may fail to breathe for a minute or more and then wake up gasping for breath (Weitzman, 1981). When they do manage to breathe during their sleep, they generally snore. They may lie in bed for 8 to 10 hours a night but actually sleep less than half that time. During the following day they are likely to feel sleepy and may have headaches.

Many people with sleep apnea are obese, especially obese middle-aged or older men, and are unable to find a sleeping position that lets them breathe easily. Others with sleep apnea have brain abnormalities, especially in the medulla, that interfere with breathing during sleep. Sleep apnea can be a serious problem, especially in older people. In many cases in which old people die in their sleep, physicians suspect that the actual cause of death was sleep apnea (Bliwise, Bliwise, Partinen, Pursley, & Dement, 1988).

Narcolepsy

People who have sudden attacks of extreme, even irresistible, sleepiness in the middle of the day are said to have **narcolepsy** (Aldrich, 1993). Such people may also experience sudden attacks of muscle weakness, especially after a period of strong emotions. Sometimes they have dreamlike experiences that they have trouble distinguishing from reality. Each of these symptoms could be interpreted as a sudden intrusion of sleep, especially REM sleep, into the waking period of the day.

Narcolepsy is a rare condition, affecting about one person in a thousand. Its causes are unknown, except that it often runs in families. Physicians prescribe stimulant drugs and anti-depressant drugs, both of which are somewhat helpful, but are also capable of producing unwanted side effects (Kryger, 1993).

Sleep Talking, Sleepwalking, Nightmares, and Night Terrors

Many people who may or may not suffer insomnia have certain unusual experiences during their sleep. Sleep talking is probably the most common and least troublesome. Most people talk in their sleep far more often

than they realize, because people do not remember sleep talking themselves and usually no one else is awake to hear them. Sleep talking occurs with about equal probability in REM sleep and non-REM sleep. It may range from a single, indistinct word or grunt to a clearly articulated paragraph. Sleep talkers sometimes pause between utterances, as if they were carrying on a conversation. In fact, you can engage some sleep talkers in a dialogue. Sleep talking is nothing to worry about. It is not related to any mental or emotional disorder, and sleep talkers rarely say anything they would be embarrassed to say when awake.

Sleepwalking tends to run (walk?) in families. A person who appears to be sleepwalking may really be awake but confused. True sleepwalking occurs mostly in children during stage 4 sleep and lasts less than 15 minutes. Few children hurt themselves when sleepwalking, and most children outgrow it (Dement, 1972). You have no doubt heard people say, "You should never awaken a sleepwalker." This is another of those statements like "We only use 10% of our brain" in which people are quoting each other, each person confident that the others know what they are talking about. In fact, sleep researchers report that waking a sleepwalker is neither dangerous nor harmful, although the person may be disoriented and confused (Moorcroft, 1993).

Finally, what about nightmares? Psychologists distinguish between nightmares and night terrors. A *nightmare* is an unpleasant dream, but a dream nevertheless. A *night terror*, however, creates a sudden arousal from sleep accompanied by extreme panic, including a heart rate three times the normal rate. Night terrors occur during stage 3 or stage 4, never during REM sleep. They are fairly common in young children, but their frequency declines with age (Salzarulo & Chevalier, 1983).

Leg Movements While Trying to Sleep

Have you ever lain in bed, trying to fall asleep, when suddenly one of your legs kicked? Don't worry; an occasional leg jerk while trying to fall asleep is a common experience and not a sign of some disorder. Apparently some neurons in the brain or spinal cord become spontaneously active in synchrony with one another, causing a leg movement. Beyond this meager effort at explanation, psychologists have little to say.

In contrast to the minor inconvenience of an occasional kick, some people have prolonged "creepy-crawly" sensations in their legs, accompanied by many repetitive leg movements strong enough to awaken the person, especially during the first half of the night (Moorcroft, 1993). Sufferers can stop the kicks by standing and walking, but in doing so they of course interrupt their sleep. This condition, known as **periodic limb movement disorder,** or more informally as restless leg syndrome, is a common cause of poor sleep in people over age 50. At present neither causes nor any good treatment is known, except for the advice to avoid factors that aggravate the condition—such as caffeine, stress, or fatigue.

CONCEPT CHECK

3. Why would it be unlikely, if not impossible, for sleepwalking to occur during REM sleep? (Check your answer on page 198.)

IF YOU HAVE TROUBLE SLEEPING . . .

Insomnia can be a brief, minor annoyance or a sign of some potentially serious disorder. If you suffer prolonged insomnia, you should consult a physician, but for occasional or minor insomnia there are some steps you can try yourself (Hauri, 1982; Lilie & Rosenberg, 1990):

• Try to wake up at the same time each day. (It is hard to get to sleep at a regular time if you don't also wake up at a regular time.)

• Avoid caffeine and nicotine, especially in the evenings.

• Avoid habitual use of alcohol or sleeping pills. (Either may help you get to sleep occasionally, but they become counterproductive after repeated use.)

• Avoid trying to sleep in a room that is too warm or too noisy.

• Get a steady amount of exercise daily. (Irregular exercise does little good.)

• If you find that you just can't get to sleep, don't lie in bed worrying about it. Get up, do something else, and try again later.

One recommended strategy if you have trouble sleeping: If you cannot get to sleep, don't just lie in bed worrying about your lack of sleep. Get up, do something else, and try going to sleep later.

SUMMARY

• *Circadian rhythms.* Sleepiness depends on the time of day. Even in an unchanging environment, people become sleepy in cycles of approximately 24 hours. (page 183)

• *Theories of the need for sleep.* A number of repair and restoration functions take place during sleep. Sleep also serves to conserve energy at times of relative inefficiency. (page 185)

• *Sleep stages.* During sleep, people cycle through sleep stages 1 through 4 and back through stages 3 and 2 to 1 again. The complete cycle, beginning and ending with stage 1, lasts about 90 to 100 minutes. (page 188)

• *REM sleep and dreams.* A special stage known as REM sleep replaces many of the stage 1 periods. REM sleep is characterized by rapid eye movements, a high level of brain activity, and relaxed muscles. People usually dream during this stage. (page 189)

• *Insomnia.* Insomnia—subjectively unsatisfactory sleep—may result from many influences, including a biological rhythm that is out of phase with the outside world, sleep apnea, narcolepsy, overuse of sleeping pills, and periodic limb movement disorder. (page 195)

Suggestions for Further Reading

Dement, W. C. (1992). *The sleepwatchers.* Stanford, CA: Stanford Alumni Association. Account by one of the founders of sleep research.

Moorcroft, W. (1993). *Sleep, dreaming, and sleep disorders: An introduction* (2nd ed.). Lanham, MD: University Press of America. An excellent review of research on many aspects of sleep and dreams.

Terms

circadian rhythm rhythm of increase and decrease in some process lasting approximately one day (page 183)

jet lag the discomfort that travelers feel in a new time zone because their internal clocks are out of phase with the light–dark cycle of the new environment (page 184)

repair and restoration theory the theory that the purpose of sleep is to enable the body to recover from the exertions of the day (page 185)

evolutionary theory of sleep the theory that sleep evolved primarily as a means of forcing animals to conserve their energy when they are relatively inefficient (page 187)

rapid eye movement (REM) sleep a stage of sleep characterized by rapid eye movements, a high level of brain activity, and deep relaxation of the postural muscles; also known as paradoxical sleep (page 189)

non-REM (NREM) sleep all stages of sleep other than REM sleep (page 189)

electroencephalograph (EEG) a device that measures and amplifies slight electrical changes on the scalp that reflect brain activity (page 189)

activation-synthesis theory of dreams the theory that parts of the brain are spontaneously activated during REM sleep and that a dream is the brain's attempt to synthesize that activation into a coherent pattern (page 194)

insomnia failure to get enough sleep at night in order to feel well rested the next day (page 195)

onset insomnia trouble falling asleep (page 195)

termination insomnia a tendency to awaken early and to be unable to get back to sleep (page 195)

maintenance insomnia trouble staying asleep, with a tendency to awaken briefly but frequently (page 195)

sleep apnea a condition in which a person has trouble breathing while asleep (page 196)

narcolepsy a condition characterized by suddenly falling asleep, or at least feeling very sleepy, during the day (page 196)

periodic limb movement disorder condition occuring during sleep, marked by unpleasant sensations in the legs and many repetitive leg movements strong enough to interrupt sleep (page 197)

Answers to Concept Checks

1. You should prefer to schedule the meeting on a Pacific island so that you will travel west and the other person will travel east. (page 185)

2. REM sleep and dreaming are more common toward the end of the night's sleep. (page 189)

3. During REM sleep the major postural muscles of the body are completely relaxed. (page 197)

HYPNOSIS

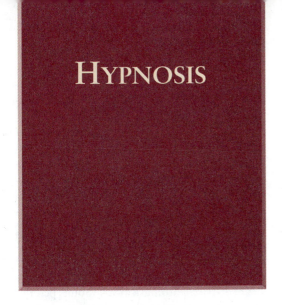

What can hypnosis do?
What are its limitations?

"Truth is nothing but a path traced between errors." *

FRANZ ANTON MESMER

If a hypnotist told you that you were 4 years old, and you suddenly starting acting like a 4-year-old, we would say that you were a good hypnotic subject. If the hypnotist said that you see your cousin sitting in the empty chair in front of you, and you said yes, you see her, then again we would remark on the fact that you are deeply hypnotized.

But what if you had *not* been hypnotized and you started acting like a 4-year-old? Or insisted that you see someone in that empty chair? In that case, psychologists would suspect that you were suffering from some serious psychological disorder. Hypnosis induces a temporary state that is sometimes bizarre. No wonder we find it so fascinating.

Psychologists define **hypnosis** as a condition of increased suggestibility that occurs in the context of a special hypnotist–subject relationship. The term *hypnosis* comes from Hypnos, the Greek god of sleep. Although it has long been assumed that hypnosis is somehow related to sleep, the connection is rather superficial. It is true that in both states the eyes are usually closed and the person is without initiative. Moreover, in both hypnosis and dreams, a person accepts contradictory information without protest. A hypno-

*Does this sound profound? Or is it nonsense? Mesmer said a lot of things that sound profound at first, but the more we think about them, the less sense they make.

tized person resembles a waking person, however, in his or her ability to move about and to respond to stimuli. Also, the EEG of a hypnotized person is like that of a waking person with closed eyes, not like that of a sleeping person.

Hypnosis was first practiced by an Austrian philosopher and physician, Franz Anton Mesmer (1734–1815). In treating certain medical problems, Mesmer would pass a magnet back and forth across the patient's body to redirect the flow of blood, nerve activity, and certain undefined "fluids." His novel form of therapy seemed to help some patients dramatically.

Later, Mesmer discovered that he could dispense with the magnet; a piece of wood, or even his own hand, would work just as well. From this observation, you or I would conclude that magnetism had nothing to do with the phenomenon. Mesmer, however, drew the quirky conclusion that he did not need a magnet because *he himself* was a magnet. With that claim, he gave us the term "animal magnetism."

In his later years Mesmer grew stranger yet. After his death, his followers carried out serious studies of "animal magnetism" or "Mesmerism," eventually giving it the name "hypnotism." But by that time, many physicians and scientists associated hypnosis with eccentrics, charlatans, and other practitioners of hocus-pocus. Legitimate users

Although Mesmer is often depicted as irresistibly controlling people, psychologists now recognize that hypnosis reflects a willingness by the hypnotized person, not a special power by the hypnotist.

of hypnosis have had to fight against that reputation ever since.

WAYS OF INDUCING HYPNOSIS

Mesmer thought that hypnosis was a power emanating from his own body, like the power a magnet exerts on metals. If so, only certain people would have the power to hypnotize others. Today we believe that becoming a successful hypnotist requires a fair amount of practice but no unusual powers or personality traits.

Some people still use hypnosis as part of a stage act. We should carefully distinguish stage hypnotists from psychologists and psychiatrists who are licensed to practice hypnosis. Hypnosis can be useful for many therapeutic purposes, including pain reduction and breaking bad habits.

There are several ways of inducing hypnosis. The first step toward being hypnotized is simply agreeing to give it a try. Contrary to what you may have seen in movies or on television, no one can hypnotize an uncooperative person.

A hypnotist might then ask the subject to concentrate while the hypnotist monotonously repeats such suggestions as, "You are starting to fall asleep. Your eyelids are getting heavy. Your eyelids are getting very heavy. They are starting to close. You are falling into a deep, deep sleep" (Figure 5.13).

In another popular technique, described by R. Udolf (1981), the hypnotist suggests, "After you go under hypnosis, your arm will begin to rise automatically." (Some people, eager for the hypnosis to succeed, shoot their arm up immediately and have to be told, "No, not yet. Just relax; that will happen later.") Then the hypnotist encourages the subject to relax and suggests that the arm is starting to feel lighter, as if it were tied to a helium balloon. Later the hypnotist suggests that the arm is beginning to feel a little strange and is beginning to twitch. The timing of this suggestion is important, because after people stand or sit in one position long enough, their limbs really do begin to feel strange and twitch a bit. If the hypnotist's suggestion comes at just the right moment, the subject thinks, "Wow, that's right, my arm does feel a little strange. This is really starting to work!" Wanting to be hypnotized or believing that you are being hypnotized is a big step toward actually being hypnotized.

A little later the hypnotist may suggest that the subject's arm is starting to rise. If that fails, the suggestion may be revised a bit: "Your arm is so light that when I push it upward a little, it will keep rising by itself." If the arm rises and then begins to waver and drop, a skilled hypnotist may say, "Now you can lower your arm." At some point along the way, the subject's eyelids will close, even if the hypnotist has not suggested closing them.

Gradually, the hypnotist brings the subject into a condition of heightened suggestibility. When people talk about the "depth" of hypnosis, they are making an estimate of how likely the subject is to do what the hypnotist suggests. A "deeply" hypnotized person will do what the hypnotist says to do and will experience (or at least will *report* experiencing) what the hypnotist says to experience.

A hypnotic experience is not much different from many other experiences. When you

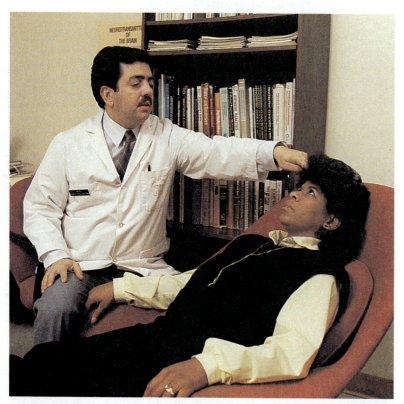

FIGURE 5.13
A hypnotist induces hypnosis by repeating suggestions, relying on the hypnotized person's cooperation and willingness to accept suggestions. No one can enforce hypnosis on an unwilling person.

watch a good movie or play or read a good novel, you may become captivated by its "suggestions" (Figure 5.14). You may focus your attention on the story and experience the emotions just as strongly as if you were one of the characters. Hypnosis has much the same effect (Barber, 1979).

Hypnosis, nevertheless, produces some paradoxical effects. A hypnotist says, "Your hand is rising; you can do nothing to stop it," and the person's hand does indeed rise. When asked about it later, people who have been through this experience often insist that they had "lost control" over their own behavior. Still, the behavior is neither reflexive nor involuntary in any usual sense of the word *involuntary;* the hypnotized people are certainly producing the behavior themselves. Psychologists have wrestled with this problem of how a behavior can be both voluntary and involuntary. One resolution is that the hypnotized people have voluntarily *decided* to be open to this new experience of hypnosis. Having done so, these people regard the hypnotist's words as the cause of their behavior. They experience the behavior as "just happening," and they do not have the usual feeling of deciding whether or not to do something (Lynn, Rhue, & Weekes, 1990).

THE USES AND LIMITATIONS OF HYPNOSIS

Hypnosis can produce relaxation, concentration, temporary changes in behavior, and sometimes changes that persist beyond the end of the hypnotic state. There is no evidence, however, that it enables you to do anything you could not do ordinarily, given sufficient motivation.

WHAT HYPNOSIS CAN DO

One well-established effect of hypnosis is to inhibit pain. For some people, a hypnotic suggestion to feel no pain can be so effective that they can undergo medical or dental surgery without anesthesia (Figure 5.15). The use of hypnosis to block pain is particularly helpful for people who have developed a great tolerance to painkilling opiates or who have allergic or otherwise unfavorable reactions to anesthetic drugs. Apparently, hypnosis has only a slight effect on the actual

FIGURE 5.14
Hypnosis, which gets its name from hypnos, *the Greek word for sleep, resembles the suspended consciousness of sleep. When a novel or video game draws you deeply into its world, you are "mesmerized" or "hypnotized" by it.*

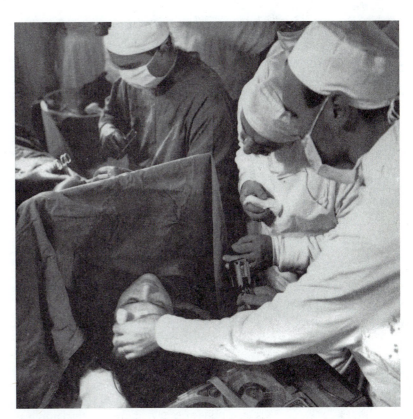

FIGURE 5.15
This woman is undergoing an appendectomy using only hypnotic suggestions as pain reducers. In patients sufficiently responsive to hypnotic suggestions, this procedure reduces the risks associated with anesthesia.

FIGURE 5.16
The U.S. Supreme Court ruled in 1987 that criminal defendants may testify about details they recalled under hypnosis. Its decision sparked this protest by the magician known as "the Amazing Kreskin," who borrowed a stunt usually used to demonstrate the power of hypnosis—standing on a person suspended between two chairs.

sensation of pain but a significant effect on the emotional distress that accompanies pain (Hilgard, 1979). You may recall from Chapter 4 that pain has separate sensory and emotional components. A painful stimulus produces as much change in heart rate and blood pressure in hypnotized people as it does in nonhypnotized people (Hilgard, 1973). However, in many cases the hypnotized people are simply not bothered by the pain.

Another constructive use of hypnosis is a **posthypnotic suggestion,** a suggestion that the person will do or experience something particular after coming out of hypnosis. The posthypnotic suggestion could be to do something trivial, such as to smile at the end of the hypnotic session or to scratch one's left ear at exactly 9 o'clock. Posthypnotic suggestions also have more practical applications, such as helping people give up tobacco or alcohol, lose weight, stop nail biting, break other bad habits, become more sexually responsive, or stop having night terrors

(Kihlstrom, 1979; Udolf, 1981). The suggestions do not force any change in behavior; the people who agree to be hypnotized have already decided to try to quit smoking or to break some other habit. The hypnosis underscores that resolve.

Posthypnotic suggestions seem to be quite effective in helping people change their habits, although the effect of a single session wears off in a few days or weeks. In one study, people were taught to use repeated self-hypnosis to quit cigarette smoking. Almost one-fourth of those who learned this technique managed to quit smoking for at least the next 2 years (Spiegel, Frischholz, Fleiss, & Spiegel, 1993).

WHAT HYPNOSIS CANNOT DO

Some spectacular claims have been made for the power of hypnotic suggestion, but on closer scrutiny most of them turn out to be less impressive. For instance, people under hypnosis can become as stiff as a board, so stiff that they can balance their head and neck on one chair and their feet on another chair and allow someone to stand on their body (Figure 5.16)! Amazing? Not really. You probably can make yourself stiff enough to balance in this way without being hypnotized. It is easier than it looks. (But I do not recommend that you invite anyone to stand on you. Someone who does not balance just right could injure you.)

Often it would be helpful to find some way to improve someone's memory. For example, a distressed person tells a psychotherapist, "I don't know why I have such troubles. Maybe I had some extemely upsetting experience when I was much younger, but I just can't remember." Or a witness to a crime says, "I saw the culprit for a second or two, but now my memory is vague and I can't give you a good description. And I tried to memorize the license plate of the getaway car, but now I forget it." Faced with such situations, therapists and police alike have sometimes turned to hypnotism in hopes of uncovering a hidden memory. The problem is that people under hypnosis are highly suggestible. If they are given a description of a possible suspect and asked whether the description is right, most hypnotized people agree with the suggested description, whatever it was. Even if given such an innocent suggestion as "you will remember more than you told us before," hypnotized people generally comply by providing new information, most of it wrong. One hypnotized witness confidently reported eating a pizza at a restaurant that does not serve pizza. Another person, who reported being stabbed repeatedly with a knife, had none of the scars that would result from such an injury. A third person reported seeing tattoos on a person who had none (Orne, Whitehouse, Dinges, & Orne, 1988).

To gain better control of the situation and to gain better measurement of how hypnosis affects memory, many psychologists have turned to laboratory experiments. In one typical study (Dwyman & Bowers, 1983), researchers showed subjects photos and then asked them to recall as many as they could. After the subjects had done their best, they were hypnotized and asked to try again. Under hypnosis, the subjects recalled more items than before, but most of the additional items were wrong. Even so, they were just as sure about the additional wrong items as they were about the additional correct ones.

In response to such findings, a panel appointed by the American Medical Association (1986) concluded that testimony elicited under hypnosis should not be used in courts of law. The panel did not insist that the police should never use hypnosis. If an investigation has reached a dead end, hypnotizing a witness may yield information that leads the police to solid evidence (Figure 5.17). For example, if a hypnotized witness reports a license plate, and the police track down the car with that license plate and find blood on it, the blood is certainly admissible evidence. However, success stories of that type are extremely rare. If a hypnotized witness says nothing that leads to independent confirmation, the police investigators should simply ignore the witness's report.

An even more doubtful claim is that hypnosis can help people recall their early childhoods. A hypnotist might say, "You are getting younger. It is now the year _____; now it is _____; now you are only 6 years old." Under hypnosis a person may give a convincing performance of being a 10-year-old, a 6-year-old, or a 3-year-old, even playing with teddy bears and blankets as a 3-year-old would (Nash, Johnson, & Tipton, 1979).

But is the subject reliving early childhood experiences? Evidently not. First, the childhood "memories" that the hypnotized subject so confidently recalls, such as the names

FIGURE 5.17
Los Angeles has used special "hypnocops" who hypnotize witnesses to a crime to get additional (or more confident) testimony. It also sends some witnesses to psychotherapists who practice hypnosis. Critics of this procedure point to research showing that hypnosis often leads to confident but inaccurate recall.

of friends and teachers and the details of birthday parties, are generally inaccurate (Nash, 1987). Second, a person who has presumably regressed under hypnosis to early childhood retains spelling and other skills learned later in life. When asked to draw a picture, the subject does not draw as children draw but as adults imagine that children draw (Orne, 1951). (See Figure 5.18.) Third, hypnotized subjects respond to suggestions that they are growing older as well as to suggestions that they are growing younger. They give just as convincing a performance of being an older person and "remembering" events in the future (!) as of being a younger person (Rubenstein & Newman, 1954). Because they must be acting out an imagined future, we should assume they are doing the same for the past.

Finally, an even more astounding claim is that hypnosis can help someone to recall memories from a previous life. Hypnotized people who claim to be recollecting a previous life generally describe the life of a person similar to themselves and married to someone who bears an uncanny resemblance to their current boyfriend or girlfriend. If subjects are asked whether their country (in their past life) is at war or what kind of money is in use, their guesses are seldom correct (Spanos, 1987–88).

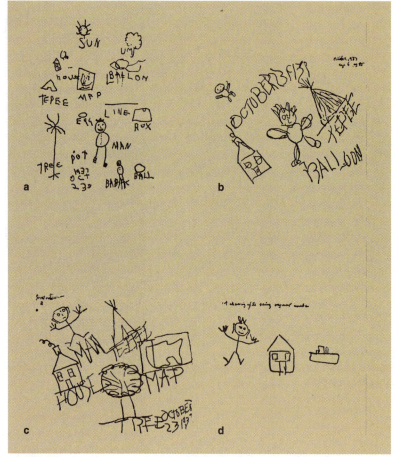

FIGURE 5.18
Regression or role playing? One person made drawing (a) at age 6 and the other three drawings (b, c, d) as a college student under hypnosis. While under hypnosis, the person was asked to regress to age 6. The drawings under hypnosis are not like drawings done in childhood. Orne (1951) concluded that the hypnotized students played the role of a 6-year-old and drew as they thought a child would.

WHAT'S THE EVIDENCE?

The Limits of Hypnosis

Most hypnotists seem to agree about one limit of hypnosis: "You don't have to worry," a hypnotist will reassure you. "People never do anything under hypnosis that they would ordinarily refuse to do." That reassurance is an important strategy in getting you to agree to be hypnotized. But is it true? And how does anyone know whether or not it is true? Do you suppose that hypnotists have frequently asked clients to perform criminal or immoral acts, so that they know that clients consistently refuse? No, they have not; the statement that hypnotized people will refuse to do criminal or immoral acts is more a statement of faith than

it is a statement of fact. Furthermore, when a few investigators have tried to test this statement, they have found results that are difficult to interpret. The following is one example.

Hypothesis Hypnotized people will sometimes perform acts that nonhypnotized people would refuse to do.

Method Eighteen college students were randomly assigned to three groups. The investigator hypnotized those in one group, instructed those in the second group to pretend they had been hypnotized, and merely asked those in the third group to participate in the study (making no mention of hypnosis). All students were then asked to perform three acts. First, they were told to go to a box in a corner of the room and pick up a poisonous snake. The box actually did contain a poisonous snake. If a subject got too close to the snake, he or she was restrained at the last moment. Second, the hypnotist poured some highly concentrated, fuming nitric acid into a large container and said distinctly that it was nitric acid. To dispel any doubts, he threw a coin into the acid and let the subjects watch it as it started to dissolve. The hypnotist then told a subject to reach into the acid with bare hands and remove the coin. Here there was no last-second restraint. Anyone who followed the instructions was told to wash his or her hands in warm soapy water immediately afterward. (This experiment took place before the adoption of ethical procedures to protect subjects in psychological experiments.) Third, the hypnotist told a subject to throw the nitric acid into the face of the hypnotist's assistant. Unnoticed, the hypnotist had swapped the container of nitric acid for a container of water, but the hypnotized subject had no way of knowing that.

Results Five of the six hypnotized students followed all three directions (Orne & Evans, 1965). Moreover, the six control-group students who were pretending to be hypnotized also followed all three commands! So did two of the six students who were just told to take these actions as part of an experiment, with no mention of hypnosis. (Nonhypnotized subjects did, however, hesitate much longer than the hypnotized subjects.)

Why would people do such extraordinary things? They explained that they simply trusted the experimenter: "If he tells me to do something, it can't really be dangerous."

Will hypnotized people do anything that they would otherwise refuse to do? The problem in answering that question is that nonhypnotized people will sometimes perform some strange and dangerous acts, either because an experimenter asked them to or on their own.

Interpretation Hypnotized people will do some strange things that we assume they would not ordinarily do. However, nonhypnotized people will do the same strange things, at least if they know they are in an experiment conducted by someone they regard as reputable.

In short, we simply do not have adequate evidence to decide whether people under hypnosis will do anything that they would utterly refuse to do otherwise, because it is difficult to find any act that nonhypnotized people consistently refuse to do!

The message here about conducting psychological research: If the control groups do not behave in the way the experimenter expects them to behave, it becomes very difficult to interpret the behavior of the experimental groups.

DISTORTIONS OF PERCEPTION UNDER HYPNOSIS

A few people report visual or auditory **hallucinations** (sensory experiences not corresponding to reality) under hypnosis; a larger number report touch hallucinations (Udolf, 1981). A hypnotist can bring about a touch hallucination by such suggestions as "Your nose itches" or "Your left hand feels numb."

When hypnotized people say that they see or hear something, or that they fail to see or hear something, are they telling the truth or are they just saying what the hypnotist wants them to say? Or do they perhaps believe they see or hear something, when in fact they do not?

In one experiment to test this question, people who were highly susceptible to hypnosis looked at the Ponzo illusion, shown in Figure 5.19a. Like other people, they reported that the top horizontal line looked longer than the bottom horizontal line. Then they were hypnotized and told not to see the radiating lines, but to see just the two horizontal ones. Those who said that they no longer saw the radiating lines still perceived the top line as longer than the bottom one (Miller, Hennessy, & Leibowitz, 1973). If the radiating lines had truly disappeared, then the subjects would have seen something like Figure 5.19b, in which the horizontal lines look equal.

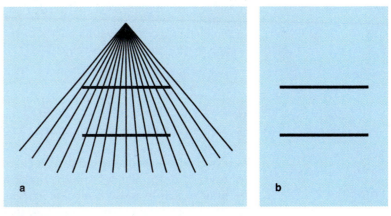

FIGURE 5.19
Horizontal lines of equal length in (a) the Ponzo illusion and (b) without the optical illusion. Researchers employ such visual stimuli to determine how hypnosis may alter sensory perception.

In another experiment, hypnotized subjects were told that they would hear nothing. From that point on, they appeared to be deaf, ignoring even shouts. Then the experimenter spoke a series of words such as *dream,* and after each word showed the subjects four written words. They had been instructed that, upon seeing a group of four words, they should choose any one of the words that they wished. In each case, one of the words rhymed with the original word (such as *cream*) and one had a related meaning (such as *sleep*). The other two words were unrelated to the original word. A person who really did not hear the word *dream* would have a 50% chance of choosing one of the related words. The hypnotized subjects chose a related word 40% of the time—significantly less than they would have by random choice (Nash, Lynn, Stanley, & Carlson, 1987). Evidently the hypnotized subjects did hear the word but in some manner avoided it to make themselves appear to be deaf. (We cannot say whether they did so deliberately.) Therefore we conclude that they were not really hypnotically deafened, even though they claimed to be.

So, does hypnosis alter perception? It does not alter the information that the sensory receptors send to the nervous system. It merely alters the way people react to that information, what they do about it.

CONCEPT CHECK

4. In the experiment in which hypnotized people were told that they were deaf, what conclusion would we draw if they chose one of the related words more than 50% of the time? (Check your answer on page 208.)

IS HYPNOSIS AN ALTERED STATE OF CONSCIOUSNESS?

Because I have included hypnosis in a chapter titled "Altered States," you may take it for granted that hypnosis is an altered state, whatever that means. Not all psychologists concede that point. Some claim that hypnosis does not really alter a person's state of awareness in anything like the manner of sleep or drugs. Rather, they suggest, a hypnotized person is in a normal, waking state but playing a role, much like a performer in a play. Just as actors and actresses do what the author and play director tell them to do, hypnotized people do what the hypnotist tells them to do. But in both cases, people are fully awake and acting voluntarily.

One way to determine whether hypnosis is a special state of consciousness is to see whether nonhypnotized people can do everything that hypnotized people do. That is, if you agreed to pretend you were hypnotized, could you fake it well enough to convince an experienced hypnotist?

HOW WELL CAN A NONHYPNOTIZED PERSON PRETEND TO BE HYPNOTIZED?

In several experiments, one group of college students was hypnotized while another group was told to pretend they were hypnotized. An experienced hypnotist then examined all the people and tried to determine which ones were really hypnotized.

Fooling the hypnotist turned out to be easier than expected. The pretenders were able to tolerate sharp pain without flinching and could recall or pretend to recall old memories. They could make their bodies as stiff as a board and lie rigid between two chairs. When standing people were told to sit down, they did so immediately (as hypnotized people do) without first checking to make sure there was a chair behind them (Orne, 1959, 1979). When told to experience anger or some other emotion, they exhibited physiological changes such as increased heart rate and sweating, just like hypnotized people (Damaser, Shor, & Orne, 1963). Not even highly experienced hypnotists could identify the pretenders accurately.

However, a few differences between hypnotized people and pretenders did emerge (Orne, 1979). The pretenders did certain things differently from the way the hypnotized subjects did them—not because they were unable to do them but because they did not know how a hypnotized subject would act. For instance, when the hypnotist suggested, "You see Professor Schmaltz sitting in that chair," people in both groups reported seeing the professor. Some of the hypnotized subjects, however, said they were puzzled. "How is it that I see the professor there, but I can also see the entire chair?" Pretenders never reported seeing this "double reality."

At that point in the experiment, Professor Schmaltz actually walked into the room.

"Who is that entering the room?" asked the hypnotist. The pretenders either would say they saw no one or would identify Schmaltz as someone else. The hypnotized subjects would say, "That's Professor Schmaltz." Some of them said that they were confused by seeing the same person in two places at the same time. For some of them, the hallucinated professor faded at that moment, whereas others continued to accept the double image.

So . . . what is the conclusion? Is hypnosis an altered state, or are hypnotized people just playing a role? This is not an easy question. Apparently, nonhypnotized people playing the role of "hypnotized subjects" can mimic most of the effects of hypnosis, and they probably could have mimicked the other effects if they had just known what those effects were. However, the fact that nonhypnotized role players resemble hypnotized people does not necessarily mean that hypnosis is "nothing but" role playing (Hilgard, 1971). The induction of hypnosis produces a variety of effects that other people have to learn to imitate; those effects happen spontaneously for the hypnotized subjects.

FAKED HYPNOSIS BY A CRIMINAL DEFENDANT

In 1979 Kenneth Bianchi was arrested for raping and strangling two women. He was suspected of raping and strangling many others in similar fashion—of being the "Hillside Strangler" who had been terrifying the Los Angeles area. While he was awaiting trial, a psychiatrist hypnotized him and claimed to uncover a second personality, "Steve Walker," who had first appeared when Bianchi was 9 years old and who had, Bianchi said, actually committed the crimes. Bianchi pleaded not guilty by reason of insanity.

But was Bianchi really insane, or was he faking the second personality and, indeed, only pretending to be hypnotized (Figure 5.20)? Six psychiatrists were asked to examine Bianchi and try to answer these questions. One of them was Martin Orne, the psychiatrist who had conducted the research on whether college students could effectively pretend to be hypnotized. He knew how hard it was to detect the pretenders, but he had also picked up a few tricks in the course of the research. And, more important, he had cultivated a healthy skepticism. At first, the six psychiatrists were divided on whether

FIGURE 5.20
Kenneth Bianchi, accused of being the Hillside Strangler, pleaded not guilty on the grounds that he had a "multiple personality" and that his evil second personality was responsible for the crimes. Psychiatrist Martin Orne, however, persuaded the court that Bianchi was faking his second personality, and indeed that he was only pretending to be hypnotized.

Bianchi was insane or faking. Eventually, Orne convinced them that Bianchi was faking, for a variety of reasons including the following (Orne, Dinges, & Orne, 1984):

- Bianchi behaved under hypnosis in ways that Orne had never seen in other hypnotized people. When Orne suggested that someone was sitting in the empty chair opposite Bianchi, Bianchi not only claimed to see that person but also reached out to shake hands with the imaginary person! He also tried to get Orne to talk to the imaginary person. Orne concluded that Bianchi was trying too hard to prove that he was hypnotized.

- In one hypnosis session, Bianchi's "Steve" personality tore the filter tip off a cigarette. After the hypnosis was over, the "Ken" personality expressed amazement at the filter tip and said he couldn't imagine who might have torn it off. This episode might suggest that Bianchi had completely forgotten the experience under hypnosis. However, Orne observed that Bianchi did exactly the same thing with three other hypnotists. Again, the natural conclusion was that Bianchi was trying to convince everyone that he had been deeply hypnotized.

- At one point Orne told Bianchi that he doubted Bianchi was a true case of multiple personality because "real" multiple personalities have three personalities, not just two. (This statement is not true; Orne just wanted to see what would happen.) Later that day, Bianchi developed a third personality.

By uncovering these facts, Orne exposed Bianchi's pretense. Bianchi agreed to plead guilty in return for the state's dropping its request for the death penalty. He also stopped claiming to have multiple personalities.

In short, it is sometimes possible to distinguish between hypnotized people and those who are only pretending. But it is not easy.

SUMMARY

*   *Nature of hypnosis.* Hypnosis is a condition of increased suggestibility that occurs in the context of a special hypnotist–subject relationship. Psychologists try to distinguish the genuine phenomenon, which deserves serious study, from exaggerated claims. (page 199)

*   *Hypnosis induction.* To induce hypnosis, a hypnotist asks a person to concentrate and then makes repetitive suggestions. The first steps toward being hypnotized are to be willing to be hypnotized and to believe that one is becoming hypnotized. (page 200)

*   *Uses.* Hypnosis can alleviate pain, and through posthypnotic suggestions it can help someone overcome bad habits, at least temporarily. (page 201)

*   *Non-uses.* Hypnosis does not give people special strength or unusual powers. Most of the new "memories" evoked under hypnosis are incorrect. (page 202)

*   *Uncertain limits.* Although many hypnotists insist that hypnotized people will not do anything that they would refuse to do when not hypnotized, little solid evidence backs this claim. In experiments, it is difficult to find anything that either hypnotized person or nonhypnotized people will consistently refuse to do. (page 204)

*   *Sensory distortions.* People under hypnosis can be induced to ignore certain stimuli as if

they were blind or deaf. However, they are not really blind or deaf; the visual or auditory information still influences behavior in subtle or indirect ways. (page 205)

*   *Hypnosis as an altered state.* Controversy continues about whether hypnosis is a special state of consciousness or whether it is the product of role playing. (page 206)

SUGGESTIONS FOR FURTHER READING

Hilgard, E. R. (1971). Hypnotic phenomena: The struggle for scientific acceptance. *American Scientist, 59,* 567–577. A brief history of hypnosis and an introduction to the research controversies.

Pettinati, H. M. (Ed.). (1988). *Hypnosis and memory.* New York: Guilford Press. A collection of articles covering research on how hypnosis does and does not alter memory.

TERMS

hypnosis a condition of increased suggestibility that occurs in the context of a special hypnotist–subject relationship (page 199)

posthypnotic suggestion a suggestion made to hypnotized subjects that they will do or experience something particular after coming out of hypnosis (page 202)

hallucination a sensory experience not corresponding to reality, such as seeing or hearing something that is not present or failing to see or hear something that is present (page 205)

ANSWER TO CONCEPT CHECK

4. We would conclude that they really had heard the words. Note that this is the same conclusion that we drew when people chose the related words less than 50% of the time. If they really did not hear anything, then they would choose a related word 50% of the time; any other result indicates the words were heard. (page 206)

DRUGS AND THEIR EFFECTS

What experiences do drugs of abuse produce?
Why do people experiment with such drugs?

Many people assume (incorrectly) that any drug they get from a physician or a pharmacy must be safe. In fact, almost any drug is dangerous in large doses, and many legal drugs can become habit-forming after repeated use. Furthermore, many abused drugs (including amphetamine, morphine, and even cocaine) have legitimate medical uses. The dividing line between "good drugs" and "bad drugs" is a blurry one; it depends more on the quantities used and reasons for use than it does on the chemistry of the drugs themselves.

The abuse of alcohol and other drugs is one of the most widespread problems of our society. In Chapter 14 I shall take up the question of addictions and what can be done about them. Here I briefly survey some common drugs of abuse, what experiences they produce, and how the effects change after repeated use. I have tried to present only the information that is backed by solid evidence, but in the study of drug effects it is more difficult than usual to separate fact from fiction. Many people who are trying to discourage drug use have made exaggerated claims about the harm that comes from using various drugs. The risk in presenting exaggerated claims is that people stop believing the warnings, even the legitimate, nonexaggerated ones. On the opposite extreme, many people who defend their own use of drugs have minimized the dangers; again, many of their claims go beyond the facts. As with other topics, we should be skeptical of exaggerated claims.

A SURVEY OF ABUSED DRUGS AND THEIR EFFECTS

Some abused drugs, such as alcohol and opiates, have predominantly calming effects. Others, such as amphetamines and cocaine,

Even legal drugs, such as sedatives, can leave a person dazed and unresponsive.

TABLE 5.1
Commonly Abused Drugs and Their Effects

DRUG CATEGORY	EFFECTS ON BEHAVIOR	EFFECTS ON CENTRAL NERVOUS SYSTEM AND ORGANS
Depressants		
Alcohol	Relaxant; relieves inhibitions; impairs memory and judgment	Widespread effects on membranes of neurons; facilitates activity at GABA synapses
Tranquilizers: barbiturates; benzodiazepines (Valium, Xanax)	Relieve anxiety; relax muscles; induce sleep	Facilitate activity at GABA synapses
Opiates: morphine, heroin	Decrease pain; decrease attention to real world; unpleasant withdrawal effects as drug leaves synapses	Stimulate endorphin synapses
Stimulants		
Caffeine	Increases energy, alertness	Increases heart rate; indirectly increases activity at glutamate synapses
Amphetamines; cocaine	Increase energy, alertness	Increase or prolong activity at dopamine synapses
Mixed Stimulant-Depressant		
Nicotine	Stimulates brain activity, but most smokers say cigarettes relax them	Stimulates activity at some (not all) acetylcholine synapses; increases heart rate
Distortion of Experience		
Marijuana (THC)	Intensifies sensory experiences; distorts perception of time; can relieve glaucoma, nausea; sometimes impairs learning, memory	Attaches to receptors sensitive to the neurotransmitter anandamide
Hallucinogens		
LSD; mescaline	Cause hallucinations, sensory distortions, and occasionally panic	Alter pattern of release and binding of serotonin

have predominantly stimulating effects. Still others, such as LSD, produce unusual sensory experiences. Table 5.1 lists some commonly abused drugs and their most prominent effects. Do they have anything in common that would account for their abuse tendency? Apparently yes. All or nearly all of the commonly abused drugs stimulate type D_2 dopamine receptors in the brain, thus mimicking certain effects of the neurotransmitter dopamine (Uhl, Blum, Noble, & Smith, 1993). Those receptors contribute to pleasurable feelings.

ALCOHOL

Alcohol is a class of molecules that includes methanol, ethanol, propyl alcohol (rubbing alcohol), and others. Ethanol is the one that

people drink; the others are highly dangerous if consumed. Alcohol acts primarily as a relaxant (Sudzak et al., 1986), although it has certain stimulating effects as well. It leads to heightened aggressive, sexual, or playful behaviors, mainly by depressing the brain areas that ordinarily inhibit such behaviors. Moderate use of alcohol serves as a tension reducer and a social lubricant. It helps people forget their problems, at least for the moment.

Excessive use can damage the liver and other organs, aggravate or prolong many medical conditions, and impair memory and motor control. After years of use, alcohol may lead to a long-lasting impairment of memory and judgment that persists even during periods of abstinence (Forsberg &

Goldman, 1987). Alcohol abuse is particularly harmful to memory in older people (Nelson, McSpadden, Fromme, & Marlatt, 1986). A woman who uses alcohol during pregnancy risks impairment to her baby's brain development.

Alcohol abuse occurs throughout the world, although it is more common in some populations than in others. Within the United States, alcohol abuse is more common among Native Americans than among other ethnic groups, more widespread among people of African ancestry than those of European ancestry, and more common among people of European ancestry than those of Asian ancestry. The explanation for these ethnic differences remains speculative. Whatever the explanation, the differences are worth taking seriously; many observers believe that differences in alcohol use are a major reason for the shorter average life spans of Native Americans and African Americans, as compared with other groups (Rivers, 1994).

TRANQUILIZERS

Tranquilizers help people relax and fall asleep; they have miscellaneous other effects including decrease of muscle tension and suppression of epileptic seizures. Tranquilizers are widely prescribed for medical reasons; sometimes people continue using them long after they have satisfied the medical need.

Barbiturates were once the most commonly used tranquilizing drug. When it turned out that they were highly habit-forming, however, and that an overdose could easily be fatal, investigators looked for a substitute. Today the most commonly used tranquilizers are a class of chemicals called *benzodiazepines,* which include the drugs Valium and Xanax. Thousands of tons of benzodiazepines are taken in pill form every year in the United States. Benzodiazepines can be habit-forming, although less so than barbiturates.

Barbiturates exert their calming effects by facilitating transmission at synapses that use the neurotransmitter GABA. Alcohol facilitates transmission at those same synapses, though by a different mechanism (Sudzak et al., 1986). Taking alcohol and tranquilizers together can be dangerous, because together they increase GABA transmission more effectively than either alcohol or tranquilizers could alone.

The addictive potential of a drug depends on who takes the drug and how and why, not just on the drug itself. Although surgical patients frequently receive morphine as a painkiller, almost none of them develop a morphine addiction.

OPIATES

Opiates are either natural drugs derived from the opium poppy or synthetic drugs with a chemical structure similar to that of the natural opiates. Shortly after taking an opiate drug, in most cases the user feels happy, is nearly insensitive to pain, and tends to ignore real-world stimuli; he or she feels warmth, contentment, a loss of anxiety, and (on the unpleasant side) nausea. Once these drugs have left the brain, the affected synapses become understimulated and the user enters withdrawal. Elation gives way to anxiety, heightened sensitivity to pain, and acute sensitivity to external stimuli.

Morphine (named after Morpheus, the Greek god of dreams) has medical uses as a painkiller. When given in controlled doses, generally just enough to block the pain, morphine is almost never habit-forming. Note here an important point: No drug is automatically habit-forming. The probability of abuse or habit-formation depends partly on the drug but largely on the person taking it and the reasons for taking it.

The most common opiate drugs, morphine and heroin, bind to a specific set of neurotransmitter receptors in the brain (Pert & Snyder, 1973). The discovery of neurotransmitter receptors prompted neuroscientists to look for naturally occurring brain chemicals that bind to those receptors, as it hardly seemed likely that evolution would equip us with receptors just to respond to extracts of the opium poppy. Researchers found that the brain produces several chemicals, called **endorphins,** that bind to the opiate receptors (Hughes et al., 1975), as noted in Chapter 3. Endorphins serve to inhibit the sensation of prolonged or repetitive pain.

MARIJUANA

Marijuana produces a variety of effects, including drowsiness, an intensification of sensory experiences, and an illusion that time is passing very slowly (Weil, Zinberg, & Nelson, 1968). It also has certain medical uses. By reducing pressure in the eyes, it helps relieve glaucoma, a common cause of blindness. It reduces nausea and acts as a weak painkiller. Marijuana suppresses tremors and other involuntary movements that are a problem for people with certain kinds of brain damage.

Although people are aware of marijuana's effects for no more than 2 or 3 hours after using it, more subtle effects may persist much longer. Marijuana dissolves in the fats of the body, and traces of it persist for weeks after it has been used (Dackis, Pottash, Annitto, & Gold, 1982).

A number of early reports claimed that marijuana use leads to crime, mental illness, sexual debauchery, and a loss of motivation and ambition. It now appears, however, that those reports confused correlation with causation (see Chapter 2.) Although marijuana use tends to be prevalent among people with a history of such behaviors, it does not cause them. Marijuana may, however, aggravate those behaviors in people who are already predisposed toward them (Hollister, 1986). By interfering with the ability to concentrate, it may also impair learning and memory (Miller & Branconnier, 1983), especially among people using marijuana for the first time. Some marijuana users experience a general loss of motivation.

The active ingredient in marijuana *(Cannabis)* is THC, or tetrahydrocannabinol. For many years, researchers were unable to find any brain receptor to which THC attached and believed it operated by altering neuronal membranes in general. Apparently they failed to find THC receptors because of some limitations in the chemical procedures they were using. THC does indeed attach to some specialized receptors, which are found mostly in the hippocampus (an important brain area for memory) and several areas that are important for the control of movement (Herkenham et al., 1990). Additional THC receptors are found scattered in much of the forebrain. In fact, THC receptors appear to be among the most numerous receptor types in the brain (Herkenham, Lynn, deCosta, & Richfield, 1991).

Obviously, evolution did not give us an abundance of THC receptors in order for us to abuse marijuana, any more than it gave us opiate receptors to abuse opiates. The brain produces a neurotransmitter called *anandamide* that binds to the same receptors as THC (Devane et al., 1992). Now, why are your brain and mine producing a chemical similar to marijuana? At present we do not know; researchers have not yet determined the normal functions of anandamide.

Although marijuana use is certainly not good for one's health, it does not produce sudden or immediate harmful consequences. Many people die of an overdose of opiates; hardly anyone dies of an overdose of marijuana. We now understand why: Opiate receptors are densely located in the medulla and other brain areas that control heart rate and breathing, whereas those same areas have very few THC receptors (Herkenham et al., 1990). So even rather large dosages of marijuana are unlikely to stop the heart or to interfere with breathing. Smoking marijuana cigarettes has some of the same risks as smoking unfiltered tobacco cigarettes, including exposure to tars that increase the risk of lung cancer. According to studies with rats and monkeys, exposure to marijuana smoke can shrink the dendrites of neurons in the hippocampus. (The animals were exposed to piped-in marijuana smoke; don't picture them sitting around with tiny cigarettes in their mouths.) However, these effects are apparently temporary; the brains eventually returned to normal (Westlake et al., 1991).

CONCEPT CHECK

5. Some employers conduct urine tests at random times to determine whether their employees have been taking drugs on the job. What special problem is likely to arise when they test for marijuana? (Check your answer on page 217.)

Stimulants: Caffeine, Nicotine, Amphetamine, and Cocaine

Stimulants are drugs that boost energy, heighten alertness, increase activity, and produce a pleasant feeling. Coffee, tea, and many soft drinks contain caffeine, a stimulant. People who drink much coffee become dependent on caffeine; if someone replaces their regular coffee with decaffeinated coffee, they experience headaches and drowsiness (Hughes et al., 1991). Sometimes surgical patients report various kinds of distress that can be mistaken for effects of the operation, when in fact the patients are suffering results of caffeine withdrawal.

Tobacco cigarettes deliver nicotine, a chemical which is generally classed as a stimulant although it has complex effects on the body (Stolerman, 1991). Although it increases heart rate and blood pressure, for many people it decreases breathing rate (Jones, 1987). Perhaps because of the decreased breathing rate, many smokers say that they find cigarettes relaxing.

Amphetamine and cocaine are powerful stimulants with wide-ranging effects. Both drugs prevent neurons from reabsorbing the dopamine they have released; they thereby prolong the effects of the dopamine (Ritz, Lamb, Goldberg, & Kuhar, 1987). Because both drugs also increase the activity at norepinephrine and serotonin synapses, their effects on behavior are complex. Both drugs increase heart rate, blood pressure, and body temperature. Cocaine has additional anesthetic (sensation-blocking) effects, similar to the effects of Novocaine and Lidocaine.

We regard cocaine as a stimulant, because it increases the heart rate, makes people excited and alert, and interferes with their sleep. However, cocaine actually *decreases* the overall activity within the brain (London et al., 1990). That effect may seem to contradict the statement that cocaine prolongs activity of a couple of neurotransmitters; however, those transmitters are predominantly inhibitory transmitters. Thus, by increasing dopamine and norepinephrine activity, cocaine decreases the activity of many brain neurons (Figure 5.21).

If cocaine is decreasing the activity of neurons, you might ask, how does it act as a stimulant for behavior? The brain is a complicated organ that often acts on the principle of double negatives: Cocaine decreases the activity of neurons, which in turn were acting to inhibit still other neurons. By in-

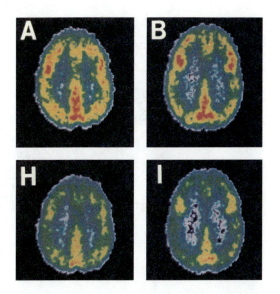

Figure 5.21
"Your brain on drugs." Parts A and B show the activity of a normal brain in horizontal section, as measured by PET scans. Parts H and I show activity of the same brain under the influence of cocaine. Red indicates the highest amount of activity, followed by yellow, green, and blue. Note that cocaine has decreased the total amount of activity in the brain.

hibiting an inhibitor, cocaine has the net effect of stimulating the final behavioral outcome.

Cocaine has long been available in the powdery form of cocaine hydrochloride, a chemical that can be sniffed or injected. When sniffed, it produces mostly enjoyable effects that increase gradually over a few minutes and then decline gradually over about half an hour. It also anesthetizes the nostrils and in some cases damages the lungs. Sniffed cocaine hydrochloride is only occasionally habit-forming.

Before 1985, the only way to get a more intense effect from cocaine hydrochloride was to treat it with ether to convert it into *freebase cocaine*—cocaine with the hydrochloride removed. Smoking freebase cocaine enables a high percentage of it to enter the body rapidly and thereby to enter the brain rapidly. The faster a drug enters the brain, the more intense the resulting experience.

The drug known as *crack* first became available in 1985. Crack is cocaine that has already been converted into freebase rocks, ready to be smoked (Brower & Anglin, 1987; Kozel & Adams, 1986). (See Figure 5.22.) It is called "crack" because it makes popping noises when smoked. Crack produces a rush of potent effects within a few seconds, much faster than sniffed cocaine hydrochloride. The effects are generally described as pleasant, although some people report intense anxiety instead, and some people suffer heart attacks or other severe medical complications. Long-term use can lead to sore throat, mental confusion, lung diseases, loss of teeth, and other problems.

FIGURE 5.22
*Because crack is
smoked, this form of
cocaine reaches the
brain in 8 seconds;
much faster—and in
more potent form—
than most other
drugs, which is why
crack is so addictive.*

Crack cocaine is powerfully habit-forming, unlike sniffed cocaine, although the habit forms so gradually over 2–4 years that frequent users may lull themselves into a false sense of security that "I can take it or leave it" (Gawin, 1991). During periods of using the drug, the drug experience itself becomes the focus of so much attention that the person neglects usual activities such as eating, sleeping, going to work, or taking care of family members.

Because selling crack is so lucrative, rival gangs in large cities compete with one another to control the sales. The resulting violence has created a problem for society that goes beyond the direct harm done by the drug itself.

HALLUCINOGENS

Drugs that induce sensory distortions are **hallucinogens** (Jacobs, 1987). Most of them are derived from certain mushrooms or other plants (Figure 5.23); some are manufactured in chemistry laboratories. The hallucinogenic drugs LSD, PCP, and mescaline intensify sensations and sometimes produce a dreamlike state or an intense mystical experience. Peyote, a hallucinogenic mushroom, has a long history of use in Native American religious ceremonies.

LSD attaches mainly to one kind of brain receptor sensitive to the neurotransmitter serotonin (Jacobs, 1987). It stimulates those receptors at irregular times and prevents the brain's neurotransmitter from stimulating the receptors at the normal times. We have an interesting gap in our knowledge at this point. We know that LSD's disruption of certain kinds of serotonin receptors leads to hallucinogenic experiences, but we do not understand the relationship between those receptors and the experiences. That is, we know where the hallucinogenic event happens, but not how it happens.

OTHER DRUGS

Imagine being a drug dealer. (I don't want you to imagine this for long; just for a moment while I make a point.) If you sell heroin, cocaine, or any other well-known illegal drug, you have to be constantly careful to avoid detection by the police. An alternative strategy is to synthesize some new chemical that will satisfy the users' craving for a high. Now, even if you get caught, you are probably safe from prosecution. The government passes laws against selling heroin, cocaine, and all the other dangerous drugs it knows about. It has no law about some new drug. So, even if you just modified some old drug in a small way, such as adding a chloride or methyl group to the molecule, you are safe until the government finds out about this drug and passes a new law against it. New modifications of illegal drugs are sometimes called "designer drugs." In some cases,

FIGURE 5.23
Tablas, or yarn paintings, created by members of the Huichol tribe (Mexico), evoke the beautiful lights, vivid colors, and "peculiar creatures" experienced after the people eat the hallucinogenic peyote cactus in highly ritualized ceremonies.

they are designed to try to enhance or prolong some psychological effect. In all cases, they are dangerous. In fact, some new drugs or designer drugs produce medical side effects that are more dangerous than those of the original illegal drugs.

CHRONIC DRUG EFFECTS

The intended effects of any drug are temporary. Initially they produce some effect, such as excitement, relaxation, or a distortion of experience. As the drug leaves the brain and the effects wear off, the person experiences **withdrawal effects,** which are generally about the opposite of the initial effects. After someone has taken a given drug repeatedly, its effects grow weaker and weaker, unless the person increases the dosage. This decrease in effect is called **tolerance.** Drug users often seek the drug as a way of fighting the withdrawal effects; they increase their dosage to compensate for the tolerance. That is, withdrawal effects and tolerance tend to promote increased use of a drug.

DRUG WITHDRAWAL

When habitual users suddenly stop using alcohol or opiate drugs (such as morphine or heroin), they gradually enter a state of withdrawal (Gawin & Kleber, 1986). With alcohol, the typical withdrawal symptoms are sweating, nausea, sleeplessness, and, in severe cases, hallucinations and seizures (Mello & Mendelson, 1978). With opiate drugs, the typical withdrawal symptoms are anxiety, restlessness, loss of appetite, vomiting, diarrhea, sweating, and gagging (Mansky, 1978). Users who quit tranquilizers may experience sleeplessness and nervousness. Users who quit cocaine or other stimulant drugs experience a state of depression.

Quitting an abused drug is much like removing some event that elicited an emotion (Solomon & Corbit, 1974). For example, if you lose something that made you happy, you become sad. Take away something that frightened you and you become relieved. Similarly, withdraw from a drug that gave you a "high" and you will experience a "low."

Earlier I mentioned that abused drugs all seem to stimulate D_2-type receptors for the neurotransmitter dopamine. The use of an abused drug, such as morphine or amphetamine, stimulates those receptors. During a period of abstention from the drug, the decreased stimulation of those receptors is the main reason for withdrawal symptoms. Any procedure that activates those D_2 receptors prevents withdrawal symptoms during a period without drug use. Conversely, a drug that blocks activity of D_2 receptors produces withdrawal symptoms, in spite of current drug use (Harris & Aston-Jones, 1994).

After someone has used a drug for months or years, the withdrawal state during periods of abstinence grows more intense and more unpleasant. Eventually, the driving motive of a drug user is no longer primarily one of reaching a "high," but merely one of escaping from the miseries of withdrawal. A user who reaches that point is said to have a **physical dependence** on the drug.

Many psychologists distinguish between physical dependence and **psychological dependence,** which is a strong repetitive desire without any physical symptoms of withdrawal. For example, habitual gamblers have a psychological dependence on placing bets, even though they can abstain from gambling without undergoing anything like the "cold turkey" withdrawal effects of a heroin user. A psychological dependence can

People who are addicted to heroin, morphine, or similar drugs experience anxiety, restlessness, nausea, diarrhea, and loss of appetite when they withdraw from the drug. For a chronic user, the avoidance of such withdrawal effects becomes a major reason to continue using the drug.

be extremely insistent, and in many cases we find it difficult and probably pointless to try to decide whether someone's dependence is physical or psychological. (For example, the withdrawal effects for someone who quits cocaine include mostly "psychological" effects such as a lack of pleasure, with only fairly brief physiological effects. So is the dependence physiological or psychological?)

DRUG TOLERANCE

People who take a drug repeatedly develop a tolerance to its effects. To achieve the desired high, drug users have to increase the dose. Some longtime users inject three or four times more heroin or morphine into their veins than it would take to kill a nonuser.

What brings about drug tolerance? It may result in part from automatic chemical changes that occur in cells throughout the body to counteract the drug's effects (Baker & Tiffany, 1985). It may also result in part from psychological causes. For example, alcohol impairs the coordination of rats as well as that of humans. If rats are simply injected with alcohol every day for 24 days and then tested, the results show that their coordination has been seriously impaired. Apparently such rats develop no tolerance to the alcohol. However, if their coordination is tested after each of the 24 injections, each test session offers the rats an opportunity to practice their coordination, and their performance steadily improves (Wenger, Tiffany, Bombardier, Nicholls, & Woods, 1981). In other words, by practicing coordination while under the influence of the alcohol, the rats develop a tolerance to alcohol. Similarly, although amphetamine suppresses appetite, rats or people that eat a little food after each amphetamine dose gradually develop tolerance to the drug's effects (Streather & Hinson, 1985; Wolgin & Salisbury, 1985). For this reason, "diet pills" based on amphetamine or related compounds become less and less effective over time. We shall discuss the learning of drug tolerance in more detail in the next chapter.

CONCEPT CHECK

6. *People who use amphetamines or related drugs as appetite suppressants generally find that the effect wears off after a week or two. How could they prolong the effect? (Check your answer on page 217.)*

SUMMARY

• *Alcohol.* Alcohol, the most widely abused drug in our society, relaxes people and relieves their inhibitions. It can also impair judgment and reasoning. (page 210)

• *Tranquilizers.* Benzodiazepine tranquilizers are widely used to relieve anxiety; they are also sometimes used to relax muscles or to promote sleep. (page 211)

• *Opiates.* Opiate drugs bind to endorphin receptors in the nervous system. The immediate effect of opiates is pleasure and relief from pain. (page 211)

• *Marijuana.* Marijuana's active compound, THC, acts on abundant receptors, found mostly in the hippocampus and certain brain areas important for control of movement. Because it dissolves in the body's fats, it can exert subtle effects over a period of days or weeks after use. Because the medulla has few THC receptors, a large dose of marijuana is seldom fatal. (page 212)

• *Stimulants.* Stimulant drugs such as amphetamine and cocaine increase activity levels and pleasure. Compared to other forms of cocaine, crack produces more rapid effects on behavior, greater risk of addiction, and greater risk of damage to the heart and other organs. (page 213)

• *Hallucinogens.* Hallucinogens induce sensory distortions. LSD acts at one type of serotonin synapse; we do not know why activity at that type of synapse should produce these effects. (page 214)

• *Withdrawal.* After using a drug, the user enters a rebound state known as withdrawal. Drug users often crave drugs as a way of decreasing the withdrawal symptoms. (page 215)

• *Tolerance.* People who use certain drugs repeatedly become less and less sensitive to them. (page 216)

SUGGESTIONS FOR FURTHER READING

Hamilton, L. W., & Timmons, C. R. (1990). *Principles of behavioral pharmacology.* Englewood Cliffs, NJ: Prentice-Hall. Clear, interesting descriptions of the effects of both medical drugs and abused drugs.

Rivers, P. C. (1994). *Alcohol and human behavior.* Englewood Cliffs, NJ: Prentice-Hall. Covers all aspects of alcohol use from its effects on physiology to its role in society and culture.

TERMS

alcohol a class of molecules that includes ethanol, methanol, propyl alcohol (rubbing alcohol), and others (page 210)

tranquilizers drugs that help people to relax (page 211)

opiates drugs derived from the opium poppy or drugs that produce effects similar to those of opium derivatives (page 211)

endorphins chemicals produced by the brain that have effects resembling those of opiates (page 212)

hallucinogens drugs that induce sensory distortions (page 214)

withdrawal effects experiences that occur as a result of the removal of a drug from the brain (page 215)

tolerance the weakened effect of a drug after repeated use (page 215)

physical dependence condition in which a habitual drug user is driven to seek the drug in order to escape or avoid the unpleasant withdrawal effects that occur during abstention from the drug (page 215)

psychological dependence strong repetitive desire for something without any physical symptoms of withdrawal (page 215)

ANSWERS TO CONCEPT CHECKS

5. Because marijuana dissolves in the fats and leaves the body very slowly, people may still test positive for the drug weeks after the last time they used it. (page 212)

6. Instead of taking a pill just before a meal, they should take it between meals, when they are not planning to eat right away or when they plan to skip a meal altogether. If they eat right after taking a pill, they soon develop a tolerance to its appetite-suppressing effects. However, even if they follow the advice to take the pills when planning to eat nothing, people are not likely to lose weight in the long run. After their appetite is suppressed for a while, they are likely to experience increased appetite later. (page 216)

6

LEARNING

Suppose we set up a simple experiment on animal learning. We put a monkey midway between a green wall and a red wall. If it approaches the green wall, we give it a few raisins; if it approaches the red wall, it gets nothing. After a few trials, the monkey always approaches the green wall. After it has made the correct choice, say, 15 times in a row, we are satisfied that the monkey has learned.

Now let's suppose we conduct the same experiment on an alligator. We use the same procedure as with the monkey, but we get different results. The alligator strains our patience, sitting for hours at a time without approaching either wall. When it finally moves, it is as likely to approach one wall as the other. After hundreds of trials, *we* have learned something: not to go into the alligator-training business. But we see little evidence that the alligator has learned anything.

Does this mean that alligators are slow learners? Not necessarily. Maybe they are just not motivated to seek food. Maybe they cannot see the difference between red and green. Maybe they learn but also forget fast, so that

they can never put together a long streak of consecutive correct turns. To decide whether or not alligators can learn, we would have to test them under a wide variety of circumstances. (I don't know whether you care, but yes, alligators can learn. They're not much good at learning to find food, but they can learn how to get away from unpleasant stimuli, according to Davidson, 1966.)

Some similar problems arise in evaluating human learning. Suppose little Joey is having great academic troubles. Should we consider him a "slow learner"? Not necessarily. Like the alligator, Joey may not be properly motivated, or he may have trouble seeing or hearing, or he may have a tendency to forget. Maybe he has trouble in school because he is distracted by his emotional troubles at home. (That's a possibility we probably wouldn't consider for the alligator.) We can imagine all sorts of other reasons why he might be having trouble.

Psychologists have spent an enormous amount of time studying learning. One of the main things they have discovered is how important it is to consider all sorts of confounding influences that might interfere with learned performance. Psychologists developed and polished many of their skills through experiments on learning.

This chapter is about learning *behaviors:* why you lick your lips at the sight of tasty food, why you turn away from a food that once made you sick, why you get nervous if a police car starts to follow you, and why you shudder at the sight of a ferocious person with a chain saw. It is also about why you work harder at some tasks than at others and why you sometimes take so long before you give up. Chapter 7 deals with the memorizing of factual information.

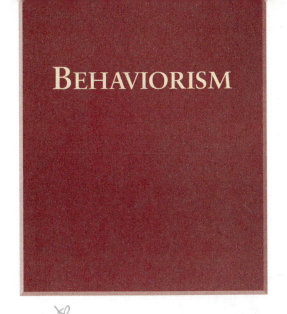

BEHAVIORISM

How and why did the behaviorist viewpoint arise?

What is its enduring message?
Observable, measurable behaviors

At the beginning of this text, I defined psychology as the study of behavior and experience. Different kinds of psychologists put greater emphasis on one or the other of those two elements. For example, in Chapter 14, we shall encounter *humanistic psychologists,* who are mainly interested in people's personal experiences and values. Here, we discuss **behaviorists,** psychologists who insist that psychologists should study only observable, measurable behaviors, without reference to unobservable mental processes. The discussion of behaviorism will lead into the rest of the chapter's discussion of learning, a field of research that behaviorists have traditionally dominated.

The term *behaviorist* applies to psychologists with quite a range of theoretical views, and we should distinguish between *methodological behaviorists* and *radical behaviorists.* A **methodological behaviorist** maintains that psychologists should study only the events that they can measure and observe—in other words, stimuli and responses. Mental experiences may well exist, and we may even find them interesting, but we cannot include them in our science. Or, if we do include them, we have to make it clear that we are cautiously inferring them from behavioral observations, just as a physicist might talk about unobservable quarks while clearly relating all such discussion to observable events.

In contrast, a **radical behaviorist** argues that the study of behavior is not just an indirect way of studying mental processes or a substitute for studying mental processes. Rather, behavior is the *only* thing for psychologists to study. According to this point of view, any discussion of mental events is just a sloppy use of language. A radical behaviorist accepts references to certain private events, such as headaches, but as a rule resists references to such mental constructs as *hope, intention, imagination,* or *will.* For example, as B. F. Skinner (1990) argued, when you say, "I *intend* to . . . ," what you really mean is "I am about to . . . ," or "In situations like this I usually . . . ," or "This is in the preliminary stages of happening . . ." That is, any statement about intentions or mental experiences can and should be converted into a description of behavior.

THE RISE OF BEHAVIORISM

Behaviorism can be clearly understood only within the historical context in which it arose. During the early 1900s, the *structuralists* were one of the most influential groups within psychology (see Chapter 1). Their method of studying thoughts and ideas was to ask people to describe their own experiences. The early behaviorists were to a large extent a protest group against structuralism. It is useless, the behaviorists insisted, to ask

Behaviorists agree that all psychological investigations should be based on behavioral observations. A methodological behaviorist might use observations of, say, facial expressions to make inferences about such processes as "happiness." A radical behaviorist, however, would be interested in the facial expressions themselves, as behaviors, not as a means of inferring something else.

[Handwritten margin notes: methodolgial B – study only events that can be measured & observed. Radical B – Behavior is the only thing for Psych to study. Structuralist- most influential groups within psyc. early Behav. were against Structuralism]

people for self-reports on their private experiences. For example, if someone says, "My idea of roundness is stronger than my idea of color," we have no way to check the accuracy of the statement. We are not even certain what it means. *If psychology is to be a scientific enterprise, behaviorists insisted, it must deal only with observable, measurable events—that is, behaviors.*

In order to avoid any mention of minds, thoughts, or knowledge, some behaviorists went to the opposite extreme. One of the early forerunners of behaviorism, Jacques Loeb (1918/1973), argued that much of animal behavior, and perhaps human behavior as well, could be described as simple responses to simple stimuli—for example, approaching light, turning away from strong smells, clinging to hard surfaces, moving toward or away from moisture, and so forth. (See Figure 6.1.) Complex behavior, he surmised, was just the result of adding together many changes of speed and direction elicited by various stimuli. Loeb's view of behavior

was an example of **stimulus-response psychology,** the attempt to explain behavior in terms of how each stimulus triggers a response.

Although the term *stimulus-response psychology* may have been an appropriate term for Loeb and certain others of his era, it is an inaccurate and badly misleading description for the behaviorists of today. Behaviorists do not believe that an organism is simply a bundle of reflexes or that we can point to a simple stimulus, or change in stimulus, to explain every action an individual takes. Behavior is a product of the individual's past history of stimuli and responses, not simply a product of the current stimuli.

If the behaviorist approach is to deal successfully with complex behaviors, it must be able to explain changes in behavior—and most changes depend on learning. The behaviorist movement, which was developing during the early 1900s, became the heir to a tradition of animal learning research which had begun for quite different reasons. Charles Darwin's theory of evolution by natural selection inspired many early psychologists to study animal learning and intelligence (Kalat, 1983). At first those psychologists were interested in comparing the intelligence of different species. By about 1920 to 1930, however, most psychologists lost interest in that topic, because differences among species in their learning performances proved to be small and inconsistent. Nevertheless, the early researchers had begun a tradition of studying animal learning in an objective manner; behaviorists carried forth with this tradition, although they asked different questions. If nonhumans learn in more or less the same way as humans, behaviorists reasoned, then it should be possible to discover the basic laws of learning by studying the behavior of a convenient laboratory animal, such as a pigeon or a rat. Most of the rest of this chapter will deal with those attempts to outline the basic laws of learning.

THE ASSUMPTIONS OF BEHAVIORISM

Behaviorists make several assumptions, including determinism, the ineffectiveness of mental explanations, and the power of the environment to select behaviors (Delprato & Midgley, 1992). Let us consider each of these points.

FIGURE 6.1
Jacques Loeb, an early student of animal behavior, argued that much or all of invertebrate behavior could be described as responses to simple stimuli, such as approaching light, turning away from light, or moving opposite to the direction of gravity.

① DETERMINISM

Behaviorists assume that every behavior has causes—presumably, causes that can be understood through scientific methods. (Recall the discussion of free will and determinism in Chapter 1.) In other words, all behavior obeys certain laws. One example of such a law is that an individual will increase or decrease the rate of producing some behavior depending on the consequences of that behavior. Behaviorists seek to increase their understanding of the laws of behavior; they test their understanding by trying to predict or control behavior. However, as you will remember from Chapter 1, in many situations no one can expect completely accurate predictions. *Every behavior has causes.*

② THE INEFFECTIVENESS OF MENTAL EXPLANATIONS

In everyday life, we commonly "explain" people's behavior in terms of their motivations, or emotions, or mental state. However, behaviorists insist that such explanations explain nothing:

Q. Why did she yell at that man?

A. She yelled because she was angry.

Q. How do you know she was angry?

A. We can tell she was angry because she was yelling.

Clearly, reference to mental states runs the risk of luring us into circular reasoning that explains nothing and leads us away from more fruitful explanations. To understand the causes of behavior, we should look to the environment, or the individual's history of experiences.

Many behaviorists today do discuss the influence of certain internal states, and they explore ways of probing those states, even in nonhumans (e.g., Lubinski & Thompson, 1993). Still, when they do so, they insist on precise operational definitions to specify how to measure internal states.

④ THE POWER OF THE ENVIRONMENT TO MOLD BEHAVIOR

Every organism emits a great variety of responses, based on its genetics, its past experiences, and the current stimuli. Some of those behaviors lead to favorable outcomes and others lead to neutral or unfavorable outcomes. Those that lead to favorable outcomes persist and grow more likely; the others become less likely. In effect, the environment selects the successful behaviors, much as evolution selects successful animals.

Behaviorists have sometimes been accused of believing that the environment controls practically all aspects of behavior. The most extreme statement of environmental determinism came from John B. Watson, one of the founders of behaviorism, who said, "Give me a dozen healthy infants, well-formed, and my own specified world to bring them up in and I'll guarantee to take any one at random and train him to become any type of specialist I might select—doctor, lawyer, artist, merchant-chief, and yes, even beggar-man thief, regardless of his talents, penchants, tendencies, abilities, vocations, and race of his ancestors" (1925, p. 82).

To be fair, however, Watson himself admitted that his statement was an exaggeration. He defended it by saying that many other people had similarly exaggerated the role of heredity in molding behavior. Today, neither behaviorists nor any other kind of psychologist would claim that all variations in behavior depend on the environment (or that they all depend on heredity, for that matter). However, although behaviorists do not deny the importance of heredity, they also do not emphasize it. Behaviorists concentrate most of their research on environmental factors and on the role of learning in behavior.

Behaviorists emphasize the power of experience to mold behavior. This boy living in Sarajevo has learned to rely on violence; in another time or place, he would have learned different ways of behaving.

SUMMARY

• *The origins of behaviorism.* Behaviorism began in part as a protest against structuralists, who were asking people to describe their own mental processes. Behaviorists insisted that the structuralist approach was futile and that psychologists should study observable behaviors. (page 221)

• *Behaviorists' interest in learning.* Prior to the rise of the behaviorist movement, other psychologists had studied animal intelligence. Behaviorists adapted some of the methods used in those studies, but changed the questions, concentrating on the basic mechanisms of learning. (page 222)

• *Behaviorists' assumptions.* Behaviorists assume that all behaviors have causes (determinism), that mental explanations are unhelpful, and that the environment acts to select effective behaviors and suppress ineffective ones. (page 222)

SUGGESTIONS FOR FURTHER READING

Skinner, B. F. (1948). *Walden two.* New York: Macmillan. Skinner's utopian novel, in which he proposes a world based on the principles of behaviorism.

Skinner, B. F. (1974). *About behaviorism.* New York: Knopf. Skinner's elaboration on the behaviorist point of view.

TERMS

behaviorist psychologist who insists that psychologists can study only those behaviors that they can observe and measure, without reference to unobservable mental processes (page 221)

methodological behaviorist psychologist who insists that psychologists should base all their studies on measurements of observable phenomena—in other words, stimuli and responses (page 221)

radical behaviorist psychologist who regards all discussion of mental events as being merely sloppy use of language (page 221)

stimulus-response psychology the attempt to explain behavior in terms of how each stimulus triggers a response (page 222)

CLASSICAL CONDITIONING

When we learn a relationship between two stimuli, what happens?

Do we start responding to one stimulus as if it were the other?

Or do we learn how to use information from one stimulus to predict something about the other?

You are sitting in your room when your roommate flicks a switch on the stereo. You flinch because you know the stereo is set to a deafening noise level. In a case like this, you are not just responding to a stimulus itself; you are responding to what it predicts.

Certain aspects of our behavior consist of learned responses to signals. However, even those apparently simple responses to simple stimuli no longer seem as simple as they once did. To explain even the simplest learned responses, we have to give the individual credit for having processed a great deal of information.

In their efforts to discover what takes place during learning, psychologists have conducted thousands of experiments, many of them on nonhuman animals. The underlying idea is that the behavior of a rat or a pigeon is likely to be easier to understand than that of a human. Furthermore, if we discover that the learned behavior of, say, a rat is highly complex, then it is safe to assume that the learned behavior of a human is at least equally complex.

PAVLOV AND CLASSICAL CONDITIONING

Suppose you always feed your cat at 4:00 P.M. with food you keep in the refrigerator. As 4:00 P.M. approaches, your cat goes to the kitchen, claws at the refrigerator, meows, and salivates. You might explain the cat's behavior by saying that it "expects" food, that it "knows" there is food in the refrigerator, or that it is "trying to get someone to feed it." Behaviorists reject such mental explanations in favor of a more descriptive approach. When Ivan P. Pavlov proposed a simple, highly mechanical theory of learning, other researchers accepted it quickly. The mood of the time was ready for his message.

Pavlov, a Russian physiologist, won a Nobel Prize in physiology in 1904 for his research on digestion. He continued his research by measuring the secretion of digestive juices in a dog's stomach. One day he noticed that a dog would salivate or secrete

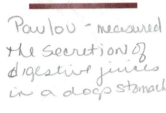

[handwritten note: Pavlov - measured the secretion of digestive juices in a dogs stomach]

Ivan P. Pavlov (with the white beard) with students and an experimental dog. Pavlov focused on limited aspects of the dog's behavior—mostly salivation—and found some apparently simple principles to describe that behavior.

digestive juices as soon as it saw the lab worker who ordinarily brought the dogs their food. Because this secretion presumably depended on the dog's previous experiences, Pavlov called it a "psychological" secretion.

PAVLOV'S PROCEDURES

Pavlov guessed that animals are born with certain automatic connections—he called them **unconditioned reflexes**—between a stimulus such as food and a response such as secreting digestive juices. He conjectured that animals also acquire certain reflexes as a result of experience. If so, he reasoned, it might be possible to transfer a reflex from one stimulus to another. For example, if a neutral stimulus—say, a flashing light or a buzzer—always preceded food, an animal might begin to respond to the light the same way it responds to food. Thus, the flashing light or buzzer would also prompt digestive secretions. The process by which an organism learns a new association between two paired stimuli—a neutral one and one that already evokes a reflexive response—has come to be known as **classical conditioning** or **Pavlovian conditioning.** (It is called classical simply because it has been known and studied for a long time.)

Pavlov used an experimental setup like the one Figure 6.2 shows (Goodwin, 1991). First he carefully selected dogs with a mod-

erate degree of arousal. (Highly excitable dogs would not hold still long enough; docile dogs would fall asleep during the study.) Then he attached a tube to one of the salivary ducts in the dog's mouth to measure salivation. He could have measured stomach secretions, but it was easier to measure salivation.

Pavlov found that whenever he gave the dog food, saliva flowed in the dog's mouth. The food→ salivation connection was automatic; it required no training. Pavlov called the food the **unconditioned stimulus (UCS)** and the salivation the **unconditioned response (UCR).** In other words, before Pavlov started to train the dog, the unconditioned stimulus (UCS) elicited the unconditioned response (UCR) consistently, automatically, reflexively. Throughout any classical conditioning procedure, the unconditioned stimulus continues to elicit the unconditioned response.

Next, Pavlov introduced a new stimulus, a buzzer. On hearing the buzzer, the dog made certain orienting responses: It got up, lifted its ears, and looked around. It did not salivate, however, so we can consider the buzzer at the start of the experiment a neutral stimulus with regard to salivation. Pavlov sounded the buzzer a few seconds before giving food to the dog and repeated this pairing over and over again; eventually, the dog would salivate as soon as it heard the buzzer (Pavlov, 1927/1960).

Pavlov called the buzzer the **conditioned stimulus (CS),** because the dog's response to it depended on the preceding conditions. He called the salivation that followed the buzzer the **conditioned response (CR).** The conditioned response is simply whatever response the conditioned stimulus begins to elicit *as a result* of the conditioning (training) procedure. At the start of the conditioning procedure, the conditioned stimulus does *not* elicit a conditioned response.

In Pavlov's experiments, the unconditioned response was salivation and so was the conditioned response; the only difference was whether the dog salivated because of the conditioned stimulus or because of the unconditioned stimulus. In other experiments, however, the conditioned response may differ from the unconditioned response. The conditioned response is whatever response the conditioned stimulus starts to elicit as a result of training.

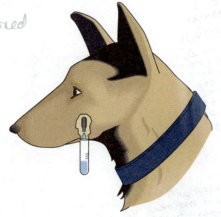

FIGURE 6.2
Pavlov used dogs for his experiments on classical conditioning of salivation. The experimenter can ring a bell (CS), present food (UCS), and measure the response (CR and UCR). Pavlov himself collected saliva with a simple measuring pouch attached to the dog's cheek; later, his colleagues used a more complex device.

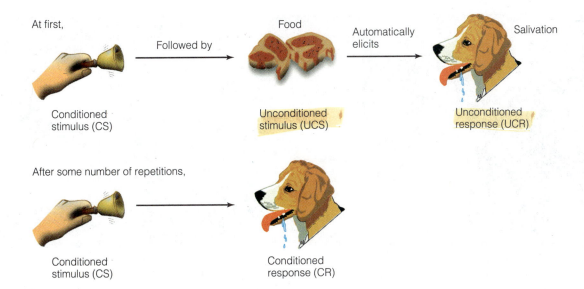

At first,

Conditioned
stimulus (CS)

Followed by

Food

Unconditioned
stimulus (UCS)

Automatically
elicits

Salivation

Unconditioned
response (UCR)

After some number of repetitions,

Conditioned
stimulus (CS)

Conditioned
response (CR)

FIGURE 6.3

In classical conditioning, a conditioned stimulus is followed by an unconditioned stimulus. At first the conditioned stimulus elicits no response, while the unconditioned stimulus elicits the unconditioned response. After sufficient pairings, the conditioned stimulus begins to elicit the conditioned response, which may resemble the unconditioned response.

To summarize: The *unconditioned stimulus* (UCS), such as food or shock, automatically elicits the *unconditioned response* (UCR) at all times. A neutral stimulus, such as a tone or buzzer, that is paired with the UCS becomes a *conditioned stimulus* (CS). At first it elicits either no response at all or an irrelevant response, such as just looking around. After some number of pairings of the CS with the UCS, the conditioned stimulus elicits the *conditioned response* (CR). Figure 6.3 diagrams these relationships.

Here are some other examples of classical conditioning:

• Your alarm clock makes a faint clicking sound a couple of seconds before the alarm goes off. At first, the click by itself does not awaken you, but the alarm does. After a week or so, however, you awaken as soon as you hear the click.

| Unconditioned stimulus (alarm) | → | Unconditioned response (awakening) |
| Conditioned stimulus (clicking) | → | Conditioned response (awakening) |

• You hear the sound of a dentist's drill shortly before the painful and frightening experience of feeling that drill on your teeth. From then on, the sound of a dentist's drill arouses anxiety.

| Unconditioned stimulus (drill on your teeth) | → | Unconditioned response (anxiety) |
| Conditioned stimulus (drill sound) | → | Conditioned response (anxiety) |

• You take a romantic walk along the beach with your new love. Later, when you watch a movie in which a couple takes a walk along the beach, you feel pleasant emotional excitement.

| Unconditioned stimulus (romantic walk) | → | Unconditioned response (pleasant excitement) |
| Conditioned stimulus (beach movie) | → | Conditioned response (pleasant excitement) |

The unconditioned stimulus may be almost any stimulus that evokes an automatic response. The conditioned stimulus may be almost any detectable stimulus—a light, a sound, the interruption of a constant light or sound, a smell. . . . Other things being equal, conditioning occurs more rapidly when the conditioned stimulus is unfamiliar than when it is familiar. For example, if someone hears a tone a thousand times and then the tone is paired with a puff of air in the person's eyes, the person will take a long time to show any signs of conditioning. Similarly, imagine two people who are bitten by a snake. The one who has never been close to a snake before may develop an intense fear of snakes; the one who has spent the past 5 years tending snakes at the zoo will develop much less fear. In both cases, the snake is a conditioned stimulus and the bite is an unconditioned stimulus, but the familiarity of the snake determines the strength of the conditioning.

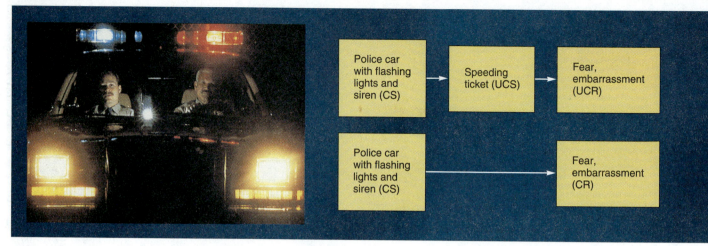

Classical conditioning is not just for dogs. A stimulus that signals some other event can develop the ability to evoke strong conditioned responses.

Acquisition - the process that establishes or strengthens a conditioned response.

extinction - dying out of the conditioned response.

acquisition - learning to do something

extinction - learning to stop doing it

We shall start with mostly laboratory studies, but eventually come to an application of classical conditioning to the human phenomenon of drug tolerance. Later in this book we shall consider the role of classical conditioning in the development of phobias (Chapter 14).

CONCEPT CHECK

1. A nursing mother consistently responds to her baby's crying by putting the baby to her breast. The baby's sucking causes the release of milk. Within a few days, as soon as the mother hears the baby crying, the milk starts to flow, even before she puts the baby to her breast. What is the conditioned stimulus? The conditioned response? The unconditioned stimulus? The unconditioned response? (Check your answers on page 238.)

THE PHENOMENA OF CLASSICAL CONDITIONING

The process that establishes or strengthens a conditioned response is known as **acquisition.** Figure 6.4 shows how the strength of a conditioned response increases as the conditioned and unconditioned stimuli are repeatedly presented together. However, acquisition is not the end of the story, because any response that can be learned can also be unlearned or changed.

Once Pavlov had demonstrated the manner in which classical conditioning occurs, inquisitive psychologists wondered what would happen after various changes in the procedures. Their investigations, prompted by practical concerns, theoretical concerns, or mere curiosity, have revealed many phenomena that are related to classical conditioning. Here are a few of the main ones:

Extinction Suppose I sound a buzzer and then blow a puff of air into your eyes. After a few repetitions, you start closing your eyes as soon as you hear the buzzer (Figure 6.5). Now I sound the buzzer repeatedly without puffing any air. What do you do?

If you are like most people, you will blink your eyes the first time and perhaps the second and third times, but before long you will stop blinking. This dying out of the conditioned response is called **extinction** (Figure 6.4). *To extinguish a classically conditioned response, repeatedly present the conditioned stimulus (CS) without the unconditioned stimulus (UCS).*

Be careful to distinguish between extinction and forgetting. Both serve to weaken a learned response, but they arise in different ways. Forgetting occurs when we have no opportunity to practice a certain behavior over a long time. Extinction occurs as the result of a specific experience—namely, the presentation of the conditioned stimulus without the unconditioned stimulus.

Extinction does not erase the original connection between CS and UCS. You might think of acquisition as learning to do something and extinction as learning to stop do-

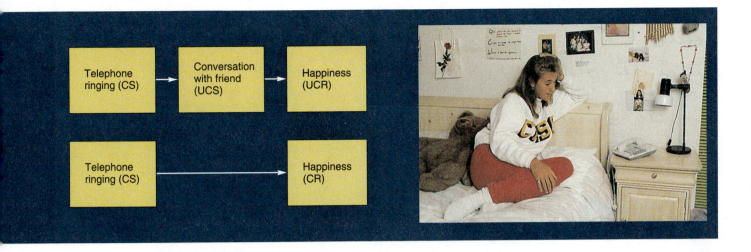

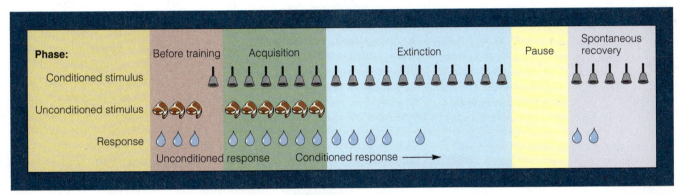

FIGURE 6.4
Phases of classical conditioning. Classical conditioning proceeds through several phases, depending on the time of presentation of the two stimuli. If the conditioned stimulus regularly precedes the unconditioned stimulus, acquisition occurs. If the conditioned stimulus is presented by itself, extinction occurs. A pause after extinction yields a brief spontaneous recovery.

ing it. You could learn to stop without losing or forgetting the original response. For example, suppose you have gone through original learning in which a tone regularly preceded a puff of air to your eyes. You learned to blink your eyes to the tone. Then you went through an extinction process in which you heard the tone many times but received no air puffs. You extinguished, so that the tone no longer elicited a blink. Now, with no warning you get another puff of air to your eyes. As a result, the next time you hear the tone, you will blink your eyes! Extinction inhibited your response to the CS (here, the tone), but a sudden air puff can disinhibit that response (Bouton, 1994).

Spontaneous Recovery Suppose we classically condition a response and then extinguish it. Several hours or days later, we present the conditioned stimulus again. In many cases, the conditioned response will reappear. But this return is temporary, lasting

FIGURE 6.5
The procedure for classical conditioning of the eyeblink response.

only one or a few trials, unless CS-UCS pairings are resumed. **Spontaneous recovery** refers to this temporary return of an extinguished response after a delay (Figure 6.4). For example, the sound of a buzzer (CS) is followed by a puff of air blown into the eyes (UCS) many times until the person learns to blink at the sound of the buzzer. Then the buzzer is presented repeatedly by itself until the person learns to stop blinking. Neither the buzzer nor the puff of air is presented for the next few hours. Then the buzzer is sounded again and the person blinks—not strongly, perhaps, but more than at the end of the extinction training.

Why does spontaneous recovery take place? Think of it this way: At first, the buzzer predicted a puff of air blown into the eyes. Then it predicted nothing. The two sets of experiences conflict with each other, but the more recent one predominates and the person stops blinking. Hours later, neither experience is significantly more recent than the other and the effects of the original acquisition are almost as strong as the effects of the extinction.

CONCEPT CHECK

2. *In Pavlov's experiment on conditioned salivation in response to a buzzer, what procedure could you use to produce extinction? What procedure could you use to produce spontaneous recovery? (Check your answers on page 238.)*

STIMULUS GENERALIZATION

Suppose I play a tone—say, middle C—and then blow a puff of air into your eyes. After a few repetitions you start to blink your eyes as soon as you hear middle C. What happens if I play some other note?

You probably will blink your eyes in response to the new tone as well. The closer the new tone is to the training note (middle C), the more likely you are to blink (Figure 6.6). **Stimulus generalization** is the extension of a conditioned response from the training stimulus to similar stimuli.

That definition may sound pretty straightforward, but in fact psychologists find it difficult to specify exactly what "similar" means. For example, if you learn to respond to middle C in a room with yellow walls and an experimenter standing behind you, you will respond slightly less vigorously if the experimenter changes the tone to B-flat, or turns off the lights, or moves you to a room with green walls, or even if the experimenter starts pacing back and forth. Your response at any moment depends on how similar the total configuration of stimuli is to the set on which you were trained, and that similarity will be hard to measure. At this point, I do not expect you to worry much about how to measure similarity; I merely cite that as an example of the kind of issue that concerns researchers in the field of learning (Pearce, 1994).

Discrimination Now suppose I always follow middle C with a puff of air but never follow F-sharp with a puff of air. Eventually you will **discriminate** between the two tones: You will respond differently to the two stimuli because different outcomes followed them. You will blink your eyes when you hear middle C but not when you hear F-sharp. In everyday life we rely constantly on discrimination: We learn that one bell signals the beginning of class and a different bell signals a fire.

SOMETHING TO THINK ABOUT

We can easily determine how well human subjects discriminate between two stimuli. We can simply ask, "Which note has the higher pitch?" or "Which light is brighter?"

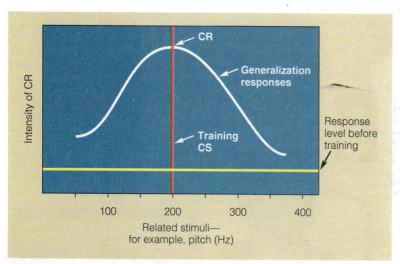

FIGURE 6.6
Stimulus generalization is the process of extending a learned response to new stimuli that resemble the one used in training. As a rule, a stimulus similar to the training stimulus elicits a strong response; a less similar stimulus elicits a weaker response.

drug tolerance is learned ←

① *drug tolerance — users of certain drugs experience progressively weaker effects after taking those drugs repeatedly.*

How could we determine how well an animal can discriminate between stimuli?

DRUG TOLERANCE AS AN EXAMPLE OF CLASSICAL CONDITIONING

Classical conditioning occurs in many laboratory settings; it also occurs in the outside world, sometimes in settings where we might not have expected it. One such setting is **drug tolerance,** the fact that users of certain drugs experience progressively weaker effects after taking those drugs repeatedly.

Drug tolerance occurs for a variety of reasons, which vary from one case to another (Poulos & Cappell, 1991). In many cases, however, drug tolerance is learned. When drug users inject themselves with morphine or heroin, the injection procedure is a stimulus that reliably predicts a second stimulus: the drug's entry into the brain. The drug alters experience but it also triggers a variety of body defenses and countermeasures against the drug's effects—for example, changes in hormone secretions, heart rate, and breathing rate.

Whenever one stimulus predicts a second stimulus that produces a response, we have the conditions necessary for classical conditioning. Shepard Siegel (1977, 1983) has demonstrated that classical conditioning does indeed take place during drug injection episodes. Initially, the injection ritual is a neutral stimulus that gives rise to no relevant response. After many pairings of that stimulus with the entry of the drug into the brain, however, the injection procedure by itself is able to evoke the body's antidrug defenses (Figure 6.7).

How might classical conditioning contribute to drug tolerance? The first time someone takes a drug, a delay intervenes between the time the drug enters the brain and the time the brain mobilizes its defenses. After classical conditioning has taken place, the injection procedure, acting as a conditioned stimulus, may itself trigger the defense reactions, even before the drug has entered the brain. As the defense reactions are aroused earlier and earlier, the effects of the drug grow weaker and the user can tolerate heavier and heavier dosages.

Here is an example of the evidence supporting the classical-conditioning interpretation of drug tolerance. If we assume that the injection procedure serves as a conditioned stimulus, then the body's defense reactions should be strongest when the drug is given with the usual injection procedure (the conditioned stimulus). The evidence strongly supports this prediction (Eikelboom & Stewart, 1982; Lê, Poulos, & Cappell, 1979; Poulos, Wilkinson, & Cappell, 1981; Siegel, 1983; Tiffany & Baker, 1981). *To show strong tolerance in a particular environment, the individual must have previously received the drug in that environment.*

Why do some people die of a drug overdose that is no greater than the dose they normally tolerated? According to the classical-conditioning interpretation, they probably took the fatal overdose in an unfamiliar setting. For example, someone who is accustomed to taking a drug at home in the evening may suffer a fatal reaction from taking it at a friend's house in the morning. Because that setting did not serve as a CS, it failed to trigger the usual tolerance.

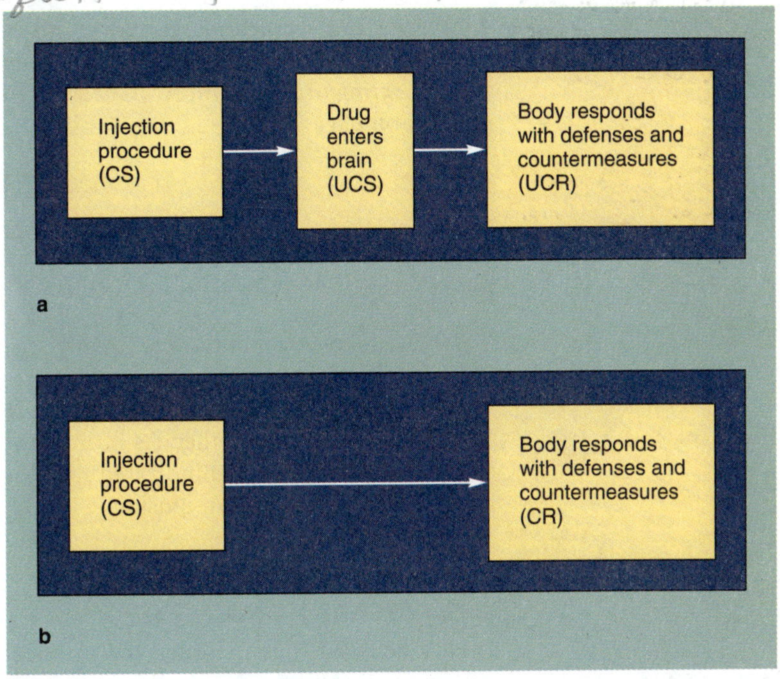

a

b

FIGURE 6.7

If a particular injection procedure consistently predicts the entry of a drug, an individual can develop a conditioned response to defend him- or herself against the drug. This conditioned response is an important part of drug tolerance.

the injection itself triggers the body's antidrug defenses.

CONCEPT CHECKS

3. When an individual develops tolerance to the effects of a drug injection, what are the conditioned stimulus, the unconditioned stimulus, the conditioned response, and the unconditioned response?

temporal contiguity –
CS & the UCS must
be close together in
time.
– caused Conditioning

4. *Within the classical-conditioning interpretation of drug tolerance, what procedure should extinguish tolerance? (Check your answers on page 238.)*

EXPLANATIONS OF CLASSICAL CONDITIONING

What is classical conditioning, really? At first, psychologists thought it was a fairly simple process of transferring a response from one stimulus to another. As is often the case, further investigation indicated that the apparent simplicity was an illusion.

PAVLOV'S THEORY OF THE CAUSES OF CLASSICAL CONDITIONING

Pavlov believed that in order for classical conditioning to occur, the conditioned stimulus and the unconditioned stimulus must be close together in time. Nearness in time is called temporal contiguity. With rare exceptions, the conditioned stimulus must be presented first, followed quickly by the unconditioned stimulus. In some cases, the conditioned stimulus (such as a tone) continues until the presentation of the unconditioned stimulus; in other cases, the conditioned stimulus stops before the unconditioned stimulus. In either case, however, the delay is short between the start of one stimulus and the start of the other. All other things being equal, the longer the delay between CS and UCS, the weaker the conditioning will be.

Pavlov believed not only that temporal contiguity facilitated conditioning but also that temporal contiguity actually *caused* it. According to his theory, every stimulus excites a specific area of the brain. A buzzer excites a "buzzer center," and meat excites a "meat center." Exciting both centers at the same time establishes and strengthens a connection between them. From then on, any excitation of the buzzer center (CS) also excites the meat center (UCS) and evokes salivation (Figure 6.8).

Pavlov's theory appealed to behaviorists at the time because it offered a simple, mechanical explanation of learning. However, most psychologists now believe that classical conditioning requires a more complex explanation.

CONDITIONING: MORE THAN A TRANSFER OF RESPONSES

According to Pavlov's view of classical conditioning, an animal comes to respond to the conditioned stimulus as if it were the unconditioned stimulus. For his results, that interpretation was reasonable; the conditioned response was virtually the same as the unconditioned response.

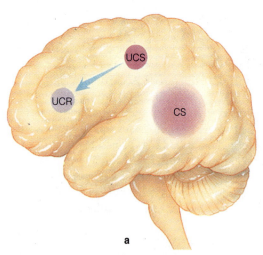
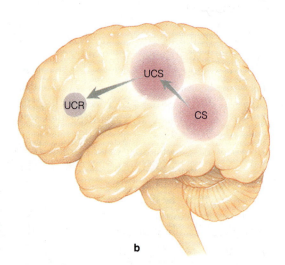

a   b

FIGURE 6.8
Pavlov believed that conditioning depended on temporal contiguity. (a) At the start of conditioning, activity in the UCS center automatically causes activation of the UCR center. At this time activity of the CS center does not affect the UCS center. (b) After sufficient pairings of the CS and UCS, their simultaneous activity causes the growth of a connection between the CS and UCS centers. Afterward, activity in the CS center will flow to the UCS center and therefore excite the UCR center.

However, in some situations the conditioned response can be quite different from the unconditioned response. For example, if a buzzer (CS) signals a forthcoming shock (UCS), animals respond to the buzzer by freezing in position. They do not react to it as if it were a shock; they react to it as they would to signals of possible danger in the real world. In short, the conditioned response serves to prepare the individual for the unconditioned stimulus.

WHAT'S THE EVIDENCE?

Temporal Contiguity Is Not Enough

Contrary to what Pavlov believed, repeatedly pairing a conditioned stimulus with an unconditioned stimulus may, under certain conditions, establish very little connection between the two stimuli. We shall consider two experiments, both of which have been quite influential in the study of animal learning:

EXPERIMENT 1

Hypothesis   For this study we compare two hypotheses. One is that pairing a new stimulus repeatedly with shock will produce a conditioned response to that stimulus. The other hypothesis is that conditioning to this stimulus will fail if some other stimulus had already predicted the shock.

Method   For some rats, a light (CS) was repeatedly followed by a shock (UCS) until the rats showed a clear, consistent response to the light. For other rats, a tone (CS) was followed by the shock until the rats consistently responded to the tone. Then the experimenter presented a light and a tone simultaneously, followed by the same shock. Later the experimenter tested the rats' reactions to the light and the tone, each presented separately (Kamin, 1969). (See Figure 6.9.)

Results   After pairing of the combined light-plus-tone with shock, rats continued to respond as before to whichever stimulus they had originally associated with shock (light for some rats, tone for others). However, they responded very weakly to the new, added stimulus. That is, even though the new

Group 1

Frozen in fear position   Calm

Group 2

Calm   Frozen in fear position

FIGURE 6.9
In Kamin's experiment, each rat learned first to associate either light or sound with shock. Then it received a combination of both light and sound followed by shock. Even after many pairings, each rat continued showing fear of its old stimulus (the one that predicted shock). The rat showed little response to the new stimulus.

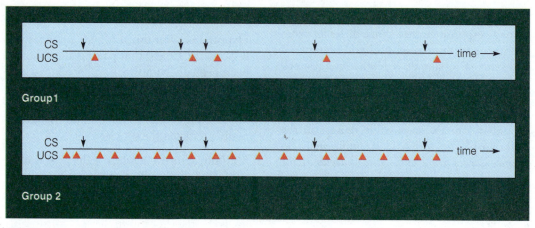

FIGURE 6.10
In Rescorla's experiment, the CS was always followed by the UCS in both groups. However, Group 2 received the UCS so frequently at other times that the CS was not a useful predictor. Group 1 developed a strong conditioned response to the CS; Group 2 did not.

stimulus was always followed by the shock, animals developed little response to it. These results demonstrate the **blocking effect:** The previously established association to one stimulus blocks the formation of an association to the added stimulus.

Interpretation If temporal contiguity were the only factor responsible for learning, the rats should have learned a strong response to both the light and the tone, because both were presented just before the shock. The failure of rats to learn a response to the new stimulus indicates that conditioning depends on something more than just presenting two stimuli together in time. The first stimulus has to be informative or predictive of the second stimulus.

EXPERIMENT 2

Hypothesis Again we compare two hypotheses. The first is that a certain number of CS-UCS pairings will necessarily produce conditioning. The second hypothesis is that the CS-UCS pairings will produce no conditioning if the UCS frequently occurs in the absence of the CS.

Method For some rats, conditioned stimulus and unconditioned stimulus were presented in the sequence shown in Figure 6.10 (top). The horizontal line represents time; the vertical arrows represent times of stimuli presentation. For other rats, the two stimuli were presented in the sequence shown for Group 2 (bottom). In both cases, every pre-

sentation of the conditioned stimulus immediately preceded a presentation of the unconditioned stimulus. But in the second case the unconditioned stimulus also occurred frequently in the *absence* of the conditioned stimulus; therefore, the CS was a poor predictor of the UCS (Rescorla, 1968, 1988).

Results Rats given the first sequence of stimuli formed a strong association between conditioned stimulus and unconditioned stimulus. Those given the second sequence of stimuli formed little or no association between the two stimuli and thus failed to respond to the conditioned stimulus (Rescorla, 1968, 1988).

Interpretation Although both groups of rats received the same number of CS-UCS pairings, one group learned a response to the CS and the other group did not. Evidently *animals (including humans) associate a conditioned stimulus with an unconditioned stimulus only when the CS predicts the occurrence of the UCS.* If the conditioned stimulus comes immediately before the unconditioned stimulus but provides no new information, the animal will not associate the CS with the UCS.

CONCEPT CHECKS

5. If temporal contiguity were the only factor responsible for classical conditioning, what result should the experimenters have obtained in Experiment 2?

6. Suppose you have already learned to flinch when you hear the sound of a dentist's drill, because of the association between that sound and pain. Now your dentist begins turning on some soothing background music at the same time as the drill. That is, the background music is paired with pain just as much as the drill sound is. Will you learn to flinch at the sound of the background music, if it is presented by itself? (Check your answers on page 238.)

CONDITIONING, CONTIGUITY, AND CONTINGENCY

The results just discussed indicate that classical conditioning depends on more than just contiguity. For an animal to form a strong association between two stimuli, the first stimulus must be a good predictor of the second. Therefore, one possible explanation of conditioning is that it depends not on contiguity (being close together in time) but on **contingency** (predictability).

However, we should not imagine that the rat literally calculates the probability of a shock after a tone versus the probability of a shock during a period without a tone (Papini & Bitterman, 1990). Furthermore, contiguity is certainly an important contributor to conditioning, even if it is not the only contributor. Psychologists have been searching for an explanation of classical conditioning that accounts for the importance of both contiguity and contingency.

One possibility goes as follows: *We tend to associate unusual or unexpected stimuli with one another, especially if those stimuli come close together in time* (Holyoak, Koh, & Nisbett, 1989). For example, if you hear an unusual sound and then quickly receive an unexpected shock, you are likely to associate the sound with the shock. However, if you have already heard that sound many times before, you have already associated it with "nothing particular happening afterward," and you are not strongly disposed to associate it with shock. Similarly, if the shock was already predictable for any reason, you will be unlikely to associate it with the sound.

SPECIALIZED LEARNING: CONDITIONED TASTE AVERSIONS

At one time, psychologists believed that all learning follows the same laws; if they could describe what happens in any one convenient situation, they would understand learning in all situations. That was a reasonable starting assumption, but only an assumption. Eventually psychologists discovered that associating a food with illness is a special situation that calls forth a specialized type of learning.

We see that specialization most clearly when we examine associations over long delays. For many kinds of conditioned responses, such as salivating and blinking, learning is greatest with a short delay between the conditioned stimulus and the unconditioned stimulus—on the order of 1 or 2 seconds—and learning is hard to demonstrate with delays greater than 20 seconds (Kimble, 1961).

However, animals (including humans) have no trouble learning which foods are safe to eat and which are harmful, even though they may not feel the consequences of a spoiled food until long after eating it. John Garcia and his colleagues (Garcia, Ervin, & Koelling, 1966) demonstrated that rats can associate food with illness over delays lasting minutes, even hours. They gave rats a saccharin solution that the rats had never tasted before. Ordinarily, rats readily drink saccharin and show a strong preference for it. However, 15 minutes or more after the rats had stopped drinking, the experimenters injected mild doses of poisons to make them slightly ill. When the rats had recovered, the experimenters again offered them a saccharin solution. The rats avoided it, even though they readily drank plain water. Evidently the rats had learned a connection between taste and illness, in spite of the long delay and having experienced the pairing only once. **Conditioned taste aversion** is the phenomenon of avoiding eating something that has in the past been followed by illness.

An animal that learns a conditioned taste aversion to a food treats that food as if it were foul-tasting (Garcia, 1990). Some ranchers in the western United States occasionally use this type of learning to deter coyotes from eating sheep. They offer the coyotes sheep meat containing low levels of lithium salts or similar poisons. Afterward,

[handwritten margin notes: conditioning depends not on contiguity but on contingency (predictability)]

[handwritten margin notes: learning is greatest w/ a short delay between the CS & the UCS.]

[handwritten margin notes: conditioned taste aversion — avoiding eating something that has in the past been followed by illness]

Garcia & Koelling
Animals associate
poison mostly w/
foods + to associate
shocks mostly w/
lights + sounds

Classical Conditioning
alters our motivational
or emotional reactions
to stimuli.

as shown in Figure 6.11, the coyotes no longer attack sheep, acting as if sheep meat tasted bad. This technique has the advantage of protecting the ranchers' sheep without killing the coyotes, which are a threatened species.

John Garcia and R. A. Koelling (1966) demonstrated another specialization of learning: Animals are predisposed to associate poison mostly with foods, and to associate shocks mostly with lights and sounds (not with foods). In Garcia and Koelling's experiment, rats were allowed to drink saccharin-flavored water from tubes that were set up so that whenever the rats licked the water, a bright light flashed and a loud noise sounded. Some of the rats were exposed to X rays (which can induce nausea) while they drank. Others were given electric shocks to their feet 2 seconds after they began to drink. After the training was complete, each rat was tested separately with a tube of saccharin-flavored water and with a tube of unflavored water that produced lights and noises. Figure 6.12 illustrates the experiment.

The rats that had been exposed to X rays avoided only the flavored water. The rats that had received shocks while drinking avoided only the tube that produced lights and noises. Evidently, rats (and other species)

have a built-in predisposition to associate illness mostly with what they have eaten or drunk and to associate skin pain mostly with what they have seen or heard. Such predispositions are presumably beneficial because foods are more likely to cause internal events, and lights and sounds are more likely to signal external events.

CLASSICAL CONDITIONING AS INFORMATION PROCESSING

Classical conditioning is important for some aspects of our behavior, less important for others. It alters our motivational or emotional reactions to stimuli, our "gut feelings"—including responses related to fear, preparations for eating, preparations for a drug injection, and so forth. But it does not control our body movements toward or away from various stimuli. That is, classical conditioning might tell us to be afraid, but it does not tell us how to get away from whatever is frightening us. It might tell us to salivate in preparation for eating, but it does not tell us where to look for food. We have other types of learning to

FIGURE 6.11
This coyote previously got ill by eating sheep meat containing a mild dose of lithium salts. Now it reacts toward both live and dead sheep as it would toward bad-tasting food.

answer these other questions, as we shall see later in this chapter.

According to the current view of classical conditioning, the learner is an active processor of information. Psychologists no longer view conditioning as the passive connection of two stimuli that happened to come close together in time. Each individual enters the world with certain predispositions—such as the predisposition to associate illness with what it eats instead of what it sees or hears. When it experiences a series of stimuli, it determines what each predicts. In a sense, an individual undergoing classical conditioning resembles a scientist who is trying to figure out what causes what (Rescorla, 1985).

SUMMARY

- *Classical conditioning.* Ivan Pavlov discovered classical conditioning, the process by which an organism learns a new association between two stimuli that have been paired with each other—a neutral stimulus (the conditioned stimulus) and one that already evokes a reflexive response (the unconditioned stimulus). The organism displays this association by responding in a new way (the conditioned response) to the conditioned stimulus. (page 225)

- *Extinction.* After classical conditioning has established a conditioned response to a stimulus, the response can be extinguished by presenting that stimulus repeatedly by itself. (page 228)

- *Spontaneous recovery.* If the conditioned stimulus is not presented at all for some time after extinction and then is presented again, the conditioned response may return to some degree. That return is called spontaneous recovery. (page 229)

- *Stimulus generalization.* An individual who learns to respond to one stimulus will respond similarly to similar stimuli. However, it is difficult to specify the dimensions along which we should measure similarity. (page 230)

- *Discrimination.* If one stimulus is followed by an unconditioned stimulus, and another similar stimulus is not, the individual will come to discriminate between them. (page 230)

- *Drug tolerance.* Drug tolerance is partly a form of classical conditioning in which the drug administration procedure becomes associated with the effects of the drug. (page 231)

- *Temporal contiguity versus contingency.* Pavlov believed that temporal contiguity between two stimuli caused classical conditioning. We now believe that conditioning depends

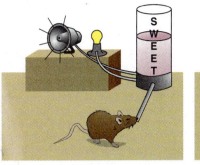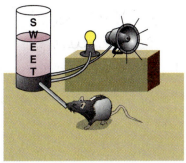

Rats drink saccharin-flavored water. Whenever they make contact with the tube, they turn on a bright light and a noisy buzzer.

Then

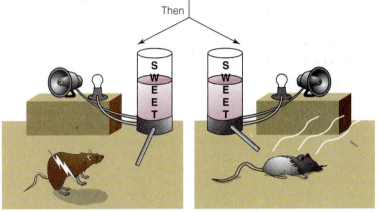

Some rats get electric shock.

Some rats are made nauseated by X rays.

Next day: Rats are given a choice between a tube of saccharin-flavored water and a tube of unflavored water hooked up to the light and the buzzer.

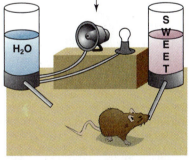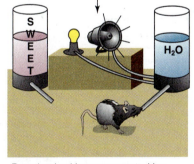

Rats that had been shocked avoided the tube with the lights and noises but drank the saccharin-flavored water.

Rats that had been nauseated by X rays avoided the saccharin-flavored water but drank the water with the lights and the buzzer.

FIGURE 6.12
The experiment by Garcia and Koelling (1966). Rats "blame" tastes for their illness, lights and sounds for their pain.

also on contingency, or the extent to which the occurrence of the first stimulus predicts the occurrence of the second. (page 232)

- *Predispositions.* Conditioning is based on certain predispositions, such as the predisposition to associate illness with foods rather than with other events. (page 236)

SUGGESTION FOR FURTHER READING

Rescorla, R. A. (1988). Pavlovian conditioning: It's not what you think it is. *American Psychologist, 43,* 151–160. A theoretical review by an investigator who has contributed significantly to changing views of classical conditioning.

TERMS

unconditioned reflex an automatic connection between a stimulus and a response (page 226)

classical conditioning or **Pavlovian conditioning** the process by which an organism learns a new association between two paired stimuli—a neutral stimulus and one that already evokes a reflexive response (page 226)

unconditioned stimulus (UCS) a stimulus that automatically elicits an unconditioned response (page 226)

unconditioned response (UCR) an automatic response to an unconditioned stimulus (page 226)

conditioned stimulus (CS) a stimulus that comes to evoke a particular response after being paired with the unconditioned stimulus (page 226)

conditioned response (CR) a response that the conditioned stimulus elicits only because it has previously been paired with the unconditioned stimulus (page 226)

acquisition the process by which a conditioned response is established or strengthened (page 228)

extinction in classical conditioning, the dying out of the conditioned response after repeated presentations of the conditioned stimulus unaccompanied by the unconditioned stimulus (page 228)

spontaneous recovery the temporary return of an extinguished response after a delay (page 230)

stimulus generalization the extension of a conditioned response from the training stimulus to similar stimuli (page 230)

discrimination in classical conditioning, making different responses to different stimuli that have been followed by different outcomes (page 230)

drug tolerance the weakened effect of a drug after repeated use (page 231)

temporal contiguity nearness in time (page 232)

blocking effect tendency for a previously established association to one stimulus to block the formation of an association to an added stimulus (page 234)

contingency the degree to which the occurrence of one stimulus predicts the occurrence of a second stimulus (page 235)

conditioned taste aversion the tendency to avoid eating a substance that has been followed by illness when eaten in the past (page 235)

ANSWERS TO CONCEPT CHECKS

1. The conditioned stimulus is the baby's crying. The unconditioned stimulus is the baby's sucking at the breast. Both the conditioned response and the unconditioned response are the release of milk. Many nursing mothers experience this classically conditioned reflex. (page 228)

2. To bring about extinction, present the buzzer repeatedly without presenting any food. To bring about spontaneous recovery, first bring about extinction and then wait hours or days and present the buzzer again. (page 230)

3. The conditioned stimulus is the injection procedure. The unconditioned stimulus is the entry of the drug into the brain. Both the conditioned response and the unconditioned response are the body's defenses against the drug. (page 231)

4. To extinguish tolerance, present the injection procedure (conditioned stimulus) without injecting the drug (unconditioned stimulus). Instead, inject just water or salt water. Shepard Siegel (1977) demonstrated that repeated injections of salt water do reduce tolerance to morphine in rats. (page 232)

5. If temporal contiguity were the only factor responsible for classical conditioning, rats exposed to the first sequence of stimuli should have responded the same as those exposed to the second sequence of stimuli. (page 234)

6. No, you will not learn to flinch at the sound of the background music. Because the drill sound already predicted the pain, the new stimulus is uninformative and will not be strongly associated with the pain. (page 235)

Operant Conditioning

How do the consequences of our behaviors affect future behaviors?

Sometimes a very simple idea can be amazingly powerful. Take democracy, for example: What could be simpler than the idea that every person gets one vote? Yet that simple idea has played an enormous role in human history. Or consider the idea of natural selection, an extremely simple idea that brings order to an enormous array of biological facts that would otherwise seem unrelated.

In this module we shall consider the idea that behaviors become more likely or less likely because of their consequences. In other words, we repeat a behavior or cease doing it, depending on its outcomes. This simple, even obvious, idea turns out to be extremely powerful.

Thorndike and Operant Conditioning

Shortly before Pavlov performed his innovative experiments, Edward L. Thorndike (1911/1970), a Harvard graduate student, had begun to train and test cats in his basement. Saying that earlier experiments had dealt only with animal intelligence, never with animal stupidity, he devised a simple, behavioristic explanation of learning.

Thorndike put the cats into puzzle boxes (Figure 6.13) from which they could escape by pressing a lever, pulling a string, or tilting a pole. Sometimes he placed food outside the box. (Usually, though, just escaping from a small box was reward enough.) The cats learned to make whatever response was required to open the box. Thorndike discov-

ered that they learned faster if the response opened the box immediately; any delay would impair learning.

When the cat had to tilt a pole in order to escape, it would first paw or gnaw at the door, scratch the walls, or pace back and forth. Eventually, by accident, it would bump against the pole and open the door. The next time, the cat would go through the same repertoire of behaviors but might bump against the pole a little sooner. Over many trials, the time it took the cat to escape grew shorter in a gradual and irregular fashion. Figure 6.14 shows a learning curve to represent this behavior. A *learning curve* is a graph of the changes in behavior that occur over successive trials in a learning experiment.

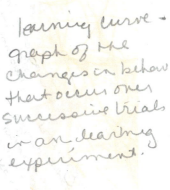
learning curve – graph of the changes in behav that occur over successive trials in an learning experiment.

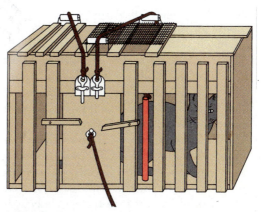

Figure 6.13
Each of Thorndike's puzzle boxes had a device that could open it. Here, tilting the red pole will open the door. (Based on Thorndike, 1911/1970.)

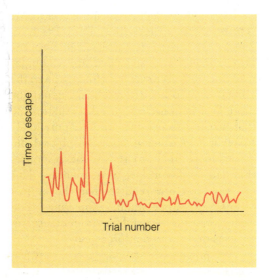

Figure 6.14
Trial and error or insight? As data from one of Thorndike's experiments show, the time a cat needs to escape from a puzzle box gradually grows shorter, but in an irregular manner. Thorndike concluded that the cat did not at some point "suddenly get the idea." Instead, reinforcement gradually increased the probability of the most successful behavior.

Had the cat "figured out" how to escape? Had it come to "understand" the connection between bumping against the pole and opening the door? No, said Thorndike, a true behaviorist. If the cat had gained some new insight at some point along the way, he explained, its speed of escaping would have increased suddenly and would have remained constant for all later trials. Actually, the cat's performance improved only slowly and gradually. Clearly, something other than understanding must have been at work.

Thorndike eventually concluded that learning occurs only as certain behaviors are strengthened at the expense of others. An animal enters a given situation with a certain repertoire of responses—pawing the door, scratching the walls, pacing, and so forth (labeled R_1, R_2, R_3, . . . in Figure 6.15a). First, the animal engages in its most probable response for this situation (response R_1 in the figure). If nothing special happens, it proceeds to other responses. Eventually, it gets to a lower-probability response—for example, bumping against the pole that opens the door (response R_7 in the figure). The opening of the door serves as a reinforcement.

A **reinforcement** is an event that increases the future probability of the most recent response. In other words, it "stamps in," or strengthens, the response. The next time Thorndike's cat is in the puzzle box, it may have a .04 probability of bumping the lever instead of .03; after another reinforcement, the probability may go up to .05. Eventually, the pole-bumping response will occur with greater probability than any other response, and the cat escapes quickly (Figure 6.15c).

Thorndike summarized his views in the **law of effect** (Thorndike, 1911/1970, p. 244): "Of several responses made to the same situation, those which are accompanied or closely followed by satisfaction to the animal will, other things being equal, be more firmly connected with the situation, so that, when it recurs, they will be more likely to recur." In other words, the animal becomes more likely to repeat the responses that led to favorable consequences. This process does not require that the animal "think" or "understand." Someone could easily program a machine to increase responses that led to reinforcement.

The process of changing behavior by following a response with reinforcement is known as **operant conditioning** (because the subject operates on the environment to produce an outcome) or **instrumental conditioning** (because the subject's behavior is *instrumental* in producing the outcome). The defining difference between operant conditioning and classical conditioning is one of procedure: *In operant conditioning, the subject's behavior determines an outcome and is affected by that outcome. In classical conditioning, the subject's behavior has no effect on the outcome (the presentation of either the CS or the UCS).*

In general, the two kinds of conditioning also differ in the behaviors they affect. That is, classical conditioning applies primarily to **visceral** responses (responses of the internal organs), such as salivation and digestion, whereas operant conditioning applies primarily to **skeletal** responses—that is, movements of leg muscles, arm muscles, and so forth. However, this distinction between visceral effects and skeletal effects sometimes breaks down. For example, if a tone is followed by an electric shock (a classical-conditioning procedure), the tone will make the animal freeze in position (a skeletal response) as well as increase its heart rate (a visceral response).

CONCEPT CHECK

7. *When I ring a bell, an animal sits up on its hind legs and drools; then I give it some food. Is the animal's behavior an example of classical conditioning or of operant conditioning? Actually I have just asked you a trick question; you do not have enough information to answer it. What else would you have to know before you could answer? (Check your answer on page 255.)*

EXTINCTION, GENERALIZATION, DISCRIMINATION, AND DISCRIMINATIVE STIMULI

No doubt you are familiar with the saying "If at first you don't succeed, try, try again." That is good advice in some situations but not in others. For example, the first time you tried to ride a bicycle you probably fell, but you kept trying until eventually you could ride with ease. However, what if you tried riding your bicycle on icy or snowy roads and found that you kept slipping and sliding? Should you try, try again? No. Sometimes you should try something else.

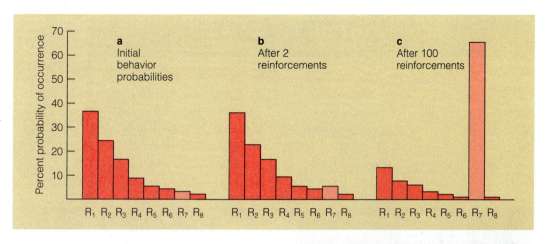

FIGURE 6.15

According to Thorndike, an animal enters any situation with a repertoire of responses (R_1 through R_8 here, with R_1 representing its most likely response). If reinforcement always follows R_7, the probability steadily increases that the animal will make that response in that situation. Note that learning occurs by increasing the probability of one response, not by insight or understanding.

- extinction - response stops producing reinforcement

In other words, you should extinguish your unsuccessful responses. In operant conditioning, **extinction** occurs if responses stop producing reinforcements. For example, you were once in the habit of asking your roommate to join you for supper. The last five times you asked, your roommate said no, so now you stop asking. In classical conditioning, you will recall, extinction is achieved by presenting the CS without the UCS. Table 6.1 compares operant conditioning and classical conditioning.

You will recall the phenomena of stimulus generalization and discrimination in classical conditioning. Similar phenomena occur in operant conditioning, although the procedures are different. If a subject receives reinforcement for making a particular response in the presence of a certain stimulus, the subject will make the same response in the presence of a similar stimulus. The greater the difference between the original stimulus and the new stimulus, however, the less vigorously the subject is likely to respond. This phenomenon is known as **stimulus generalization.** For example, you might smile at a stranger who reminds you of an old friend. Or you might reach for the turn signal in a rented car in the place where you would find it in your own car.

If an individual is reinforced for responding to one stimulus and is reinforced less strongly (or not at all) for responding to another stimulus, then he or she will learn to **discriminate** between them and will respond more vigorously to one than to the other. For example, you walk toward a parked car you think is yours and then you realize it is not. After several such experiences you learn to identify your own car from a distance.

A stimulus that indicates which response is appropriate or inappropriate is called a **discriminative stimulus**. A great deal of our behavior is governed by discriminative stimuli. For example, your professor standing at the front of the class is a discriminative stimulus to cease conversations and get ready to take notes. When class is about over, a

Stimulus generalization
↑ difference between the original stimulus & the new stimulus the less vigorously the subject will respond

discriminate - will respond more vigorously to one stimulus than to another because of reinforcement.

Discriminative Stimulus
Stimulus that indicates which response is appropriate or inappropriate

TABLE 6.1
Comparison of Classical Conditioning and Operant Conditioning

CLASSICAL CONDITIONING		OPERANT CONDITIONING
CS, UCS, CR, UCR	*Terminology*	Response, reinforcement
Does not control UCS	*Subject's behavior . . .*	Controls reinforcement
Two stimuli (CS and UCS)	*Paired during acquisition*	Response and reinforcement (in the presence of certain stimuli)
Mostly visceral (internal organs)	*Responses studied*	Mostly skeletal (movements)
CS without UCS	*Extinction procedure*	Response without reinforcement

display on the clock is a discriminative stimulus to get ready to leave class. A scowl on your roommate's face is a discriminative stimulus for you to keep quiet. Road signs provide discriminative stimuli to tell you when to speed up, slow down, or change lanes. Throughout your day, one stimulus after another signals which behaviors are likely to be reinforced and which ones are not.

WHY ARE CERTAIN RESPONSES LEARNED MORE EASILY THAN OTHERS?

Thorndike's cats quickly learned to push and pull various devices in their efforts to escape from his puzzle boxes. But when Thorndike tried to teach them to scratch themselves or lick themselves to receive the same reinforcement, they learned slowly and performed inconsistently. Why?

One possible reason is **belongingness**, the concept that certain stimuli "belong" together, or that a given response might be more readily associated with certain outcomes than with others. Belongingness is an idea Thorndike himself suggested, although psychologists neglected it for decades, preferring to believe that animals could associate almost any stimulus with any response equally easily. Eventually, psychologists revived the concept of belongingness, also sometimes known as "preparedness" (Seligman, 1970). I mentioned one example of this principle in the discussion of classical condi-

tioning: Rats are predisposed to associate illness with something they ate rather than with something they saw or heard. Another example: Dogs can readily learn that a sound coming from one location means "raise your left leg," while a sound coming from another location means "raise your right leg." But it takes them virtually forever to learn that a ticking metronome means raise the left leg while a buzzer means raise the right leg (Dobrzecka, Szwejkowska, & Konorski, 1966). (See Figure 6.16.) Somehow the location of a sound and a location on the body "belong" together; a type of sound does not belong with a location on the body.

Presumably, Thorndike's cats were slow to associate scratching themselves with escaping from a box because the two activities do not "belong" together. (Cats evolved the ability to learn "what leads to what" in the real world, and scratching oneself is very unlikely to open doors in the real world.) But there is another possible explanation why cats have trouble learning to scratch themselves for reinforcement: Perhaps a cat can scratch itself only when it itches (Charlton, 1983). Consider what would happen if you knew that you would be handsomely reinforced for swallowing rapidly and repeatedly. You quickly swallow a few times, but after those first few swallows, you find additional swallows more and more difficult. (If you doubt me, go ahead and try.) Some behaviors are just not easy to produce in large quantity.

Dog easily learns to raise the leg closer to the sound source.

Dog does not easily learn to raise one leg when it hears a metronome and a different leg when it hears a buzzer.

[handwritten margin notes: Skinner — parsimony simple explanations. Skinner Box — rat presses a lever or pigeon pecks an illuminated dish to receive food.]

B. F. SKINNER AND THE SHAPING OF RESPONSES

The most influential behaviorist, B. F. Skinner (1904/1990), demonstrated many uses of operant conditioning. Skinner was an ardent practitioner of parsimony, always seeking simple explanations in terms of reinforcement histories rather than explanations in terms of mental states.

Although we ordinarily expect scientific progress to emerge from a logical sequence of experiments designed to test certain hypotheses, it sometimes results from simple accident. For example, in one of Skinner's early experiments, he arranged for rats to run down an 8-foot-long alley to get food. After he grew tired of picking the rats up every time and returning them to the starting position, he built a circular runway. Now the rats, after getting the food, could run around the circle and back to the start box on their own. But Skinner still had to replenish the food in the goal box each time. He rigged it so the rats could do that too. Eventually he decided there was no need for the alley to be 8 feet long. In fact, he dispensed with the alley altogether. What was left was a simple box, now called the *Skinner box* (Figure 6.17), in which a rat presses a lever or a pigeon pecks an illuminated disk (or "key") to receive food (Skinner, 1956).

FIGURE 6.17
B. F. Skinner examines one of his laboratory animals in an operant-conditioning chamber, or "Skinner box." When the light above the bar is on, pressing the bar is reinforced. A food pellet rolls out of the storage device (left) and down the tube into the cage.

SHAPING BEHAVIOR

Suppose we want to train a rat to press a lever. If we simply put the rat in the box and wait, the rat might never press the lever. To avoid interminable waits, Skinner devised a powerful technique, called shaping, for establishing a new response by reinforcing successive approximations to it.

To shape a rat to press a lever, we might begin by reinforcing the rat for standing up, a common behavior in rats. Before long the rat has received several reinforcements and is beginning to stand up more frequently. Now we change the rules, giving food only when the rat stands up while facing in the general direction of the lever. Soon the rat spends much of its time standing up and facing the lever. (It extinguishes its behavior of standing and facing any other direction, because those responses are not reinforced.) Now we provide reinforcement only when the rat stands in the part of the cage nearest the lever. Gradually the rat moves closer and closer to the wall on which the lever is mounted. Then the rat must touch the lever and finally apply weight to it. Through a series of short, easy steps, the rat might progress from mere standing to actual lever-pressing in a matter of minutes.

CHAINING BEHAVIOR

To produce more complex sequences of behavior, psychologists use a procedure called chaining. Assume that you want to train an animal to go through a sequence of actions in a particular order. For example, you might be training a Seeing Eye dog or a show horse. You want the animal to go through a whole sequence of actions and not to wait for a reinforcement after each one. You could chain the behaviors, reinforcing each one by the opportunity to make the next behavior. That is, first the animal learns the final behavior for some reinforcement; then it learns the next-to-last behavior, which is reinforced by the opportunity to perform the final behavior. And so on.

For example, a rat might first be placed on the top platform in Figure 6.18, where it eats food. Then it is placed on the intermediate platform with a ladder in place to the top platform. It learns to climb the ladder. After it has done so repeatedly, it is placed on the intermediate platform but the ladder is not present. The rat has to learn to pull a string to raise the ladder so that it can climb to the top platform. Finally the rat is put on the bottom platform. It has to learn to climb the ladder to the intermediate platform, pull a string to raise the ladder, and then climb the ladder again. For each response in the chain, the reinforcement is the opportunity to engage in the next behavior, until the final response in the chain leads to food.

Humans learn to make chains of responses, too. As an infant you learned to eat with a fork and a spoon. Later you learned to put your own food on the plate before eating. Eventually you learned to plan a menu, go to the store, buy the ingredients, cook the meal, put it on the plate, and then eat it. Each behavior is reinforced by the opportunity to engage in the next behavior.

To show how effective shaping and chaining can be, Skinner sometimes per-

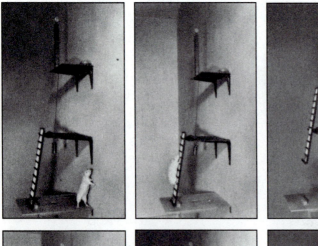

FIGURE 6.18
Chaining is a procedure in which the reinforcement for one behavior is the opportunity to engage in the next behavior. To reach food on the top platform, this rat must climb a ladder and pull a string to raise the ladder so that it can climb up again. Behavior chains longer than this can be sustained by one reinforcement at the end.

TABLE 6.2
Four Categories of Operant Conditioning

	AN EVENT THAT INCREASES BEHAVIOR		AN EVENT THAT DECREASES BEHAVIOR	
Behavior produces the event	**Positive Reinforcement** (Behavior increased in frequency) Example: You write a short stroy and *receive a prize* for it. (You learn to write more stories and submit them in contests.)		**Punishment** also called **Passive Avoidance** (Behavior decreases in frequency) Example: You insult someone who then *slaps* your face. (You learn not to insult people.)	
Behavior prevents or removes the event	**Omission Training** also called **Punishment** or **Negative Punishment** (Behavior decreases in frequency) Example: You put too much salt on your food and therefore find you *cannot eat it.* (You learn to omit the extra salt.)		**Escape** or **Avoidance Learning** also called **Negative Reinforcement** (Behavior increased in frequency) Example: you carry an umbrella with you all day and as a result you *avoid getting wet* when the rains come. (You learn to carry your umbrella when you hear a forecast of rain.)	

formed this demonstration: First, he trained a rat to go to the center of a cage. Then he trained it to do so only when he was playing a certain record. Then he trained it to wait for the record to start, go to the center of the cage, and sit up on its hind legs. Step by step Skinner eventually trained the rat to wait for the record to start (which happened to be the "Star-Spangled Banner"), move to the center of the cage, sit up on its hind legs, put its claws on a string next to a pole, pull the string to hoist a flag, and then salute the flag until the record had finished. Only then did it get its reinforcement. Needless to say, shows of patriotism are not part of a rat's natural repertoire of behaviors; it learns to go through the motions only by successive approximations.

INCREASING AND DECREASING THE FREQUENCY OF RESPONSES

Nearly all of our behavior is governed by its consequences. We engage in acts that in-

crease the number of good things and decrease the bad things that happen to us. Investigators of operant conditioning try to determine in detail how those good things and bad things change our behavior.

REINFORCEMENT AND PUNISHMENT

A few pages back, I defined *reinforcement* as an event that increases the probability that a response will be repeated. A **punishment** is an event that decreases the probability that a response will be repeated. A reinforcement can be either the presentation of an event (such as food) or the *removal or avoidance* of an event (such as the removal of pain). A punishment can be either the presentation of an event (such as pain) or the removal of an event (such as the removal of food). Table 6.2 outlines the four possibilities for reinforcement and punishment and provides some terms, including a couple of terms that are potentially confusing. Let us go through these terms and procedures carefully.

Positive reinforcement, the term in the upper left of the table, is the presentation of an event that increases behavior. Examples

punishment — an event that ↓ the probability that a response will be repeated presentation or removal of an event

Being ejected from a game for using foul language is an example of effective punishment: It is quick and consistent, and the player has other behaviors available that can achieve good results without punishment.

are food, water, or access to a sexual partner. You might well imagine that if positive reinforcement strengthens a behavior, negative reinforcement should weaken it. It does not, at least not by the traditional use of that term. **Negative reinforcement** *strengthens* a behavior *by the negation* of some unpleasant event that would have occurred. For example, a behavior that turns off an electric shock is strengthened by negative reinforcement (escape from the shock). Coming indoors when a storm is brewing is also strengthened by negative reinforcement (avoidance of getting wet). Negative reinforcement is also known as **escape learning** or **avoidance learning,** because the responses lead to escape from or avoidance of some unpleasant event. The terms *escape learning* and *avoidance learning* are probably used more widely than the term *negative reinforcement,* and are in many ways preferable terms (see Kimble, 1993). However, you should be prepared to understand any of these terms.

Punishment occurs when a response is followed by some aversive (unpleasant) event. For example, you put your hand on a hot stove and burn yourself; you insult someone and that person slaps you. Punishment is also called **passive avoidance learning** because the individual learns to avoid some unpleasant event by being passive (for example,

by *not* putting one's hand on the stove or by *not* insulting people).

Finally, consider the element in the lower left of the chart in Table 6.2: Suppose that if you do nothing (that is, you *omit* the response in question) you will receive a reinforcement. For example, "If you make one more snotty remark, you will get no dessert!" Such a situation is called **omission training,** because the omission of the response produces reinforcement. Making the response leads to loss of reinforcement. We may regard the loss of reinforcement as a kind of punishment; thus, the individual is reinforced for omitting the response, punished for making the response. (This kind of punishment is occasionally called *negative punishment* to emphasize that the punishment here is the negation of an event.)

To recap, note that reinforcement increases a behavior; punishment decreases it. "Positive" means that a response leads to some event; "negative" means that a response prevents the event. Practice these distinctions in Concept Check 8.

8. *Identify each of the following examples using the terms shown in Table 6.2:*
    a. *Your employer gives you bonus pay for working overtime.*
    b. *You learn to stop playing your accordion at 5:00 A.M. because your roommate threatens to kill you if you do it again.*
    c. *You turn off a dripping faucet, ending the "drip-drip-drip" sound.*
    d. *You drink less beer than you once did, because you feel sick after drinking more than one glass.*
    e. *Your swimming coach says you cannot go to the next swim meet (which you were looking forward to), because you broke a training rule.*
    f. *Because you drive recklessly, you temporarily lose the privilege of driving the family car.*
    g. *You stay away from some fellow students who are coughing and sneezing, because you do not want to catch whatever illness they have. (Check your answers on page 255.)*

How effective is punishment? Is a harsh punishment more effective than a mild punishment? Psychologists are not in full agreement on these matters.

If an individual has a strong motivation to engage in a certain behavior and has no other way to satisfy that motivation, punishment is generally ineffective. In one experiment, B. F. Skinner (1938) first trained some rats to press a bar to get food and then switched procedures so that pressing the bar no longer produced food. For some of the rats, Skinner arranged the apparatus so that the bar slapped their paws every time they pressed it during the first 10 minutes of the extinction period. The other rats received no punishment. For the first 10 minutes, the punished rats lowered their response rate. In the long run, however, they made as many total responses as the unpunished rats did.

(1) Skinner concluded that punishment suppresses a behavior but does not cause anything similar to forgetting or extinction. That is, the animal still has its learned tendency to make the response, even though punishment causes the animal to suppress or resist the behavior.

(2) The fact that punishment does not produce forgetting or extinction does not stop it from being effective. Punishment suppresses a behavior if it occurs quickly and consistently after the punished response, and if the behaving individual has an alternative way of getting reinforcement (Walters & Grusec, 1977). For example, if you received a painful shock every time you tried to open the refrigerator door, you would quickly stop touching that door if you had other ways of getting food. But if you were locked in the room for three days with no other source of food, you would go on trying to open the refrigerator, despite the punishment.

The effectiveness of punishment depends on other factors as well. For example, children respond more readily to mild punishment accompanied by a parent's explanation of why they were punished than they do to more intense punishment without an explanation. Punishment is ineffective if children learn that they can get more attention for "bad" behavior than for "good" behavior. (Attention is, for most people, a powerful reinforcer.) Punishment may even stimulate the very behaviors it is meant to discourage. For example, a parent who spanks a child for nervous fidgeting may find that the spanking makes the child even more nervous and fidgety.

In practical situations, the question is not whether punishment will work but whether it is the best way to achieve the desired results. If you want to teach your young son or daughter not to touch the top of the stove, you may get good results from a swift but gentle slap on the wrist or even a sharp NO! A few years later, if you want to teach the same child to speak politely to others, an occasional reinforcement for politeness is likely to work much better than punishment for rudeness.

<hr/>

CONCEPT CHECK

9. *The U.S. government imposes strict punishments for selling illegal drugs. Based on what you have just read, why are those punishments ineffective for many people? (Check your answer on page 255.)*

SOMETHING TO THINK ABOUT

Your local school board proposes to improve class attendance by lowering the grades of any student who misses a certain number of classes. How might it achieve the same goal through positive reinforcement?

WHAT CONSTITUTES REINFORCEMENT?

In operant conditioning, the probability of some response increases because a reinforcer follows it. But what is a reinforcer? It is "something that increases the probability of the preceding response." So far we are just going around in circles, unless we can find some way to specify what will reinforce a behavior and what will not. We want to specify the basis of reinforcement for a practical reason as well: When we want to reinforce a child for doing well in school or a worker for doing well on the job (or anyone for doing well at anything), we have to know what will be an effective reinforcer.

Thorndike suggested a trial-and-error approach to finding reinforcers: We could simply try a number of likely reinforcers and see what works. If some event serves as a reinforcer for one behavior, it will also serve as a reinforcer for other behaviors. That approach is, however, theoretically

Different items can serve as reinforcements for different people. This man has devoted enormous time, effort, and money to collecting buttons. Some people pay thousands of dollars for old comic books, stamps, coins, or baseball cards.

ance at some other time. True, we could say that a given drive increases and decreases, but we need some way to predict when it will increase or decrease.

The Premack Principle David Premack (1965) proposed that the world's events are not divided into reinforcers and nonreinforcers. Rather, the opportunity to engage in some behavior (such as eating) will be a reinforcer for any lower-probability behavior. This relationship is known as the **Premack principle.** Thus, for example, if you spend more time reading novels than watching television, then someone could increase your television watching by reinforcing you with novels. For someone else, it might be possible to reinforce novel-reading by means of opportunities to watch television. In short, a given opportunity may or may not be a reinforcer, depending on the individual and the response to be reinforced.

unsatisfactory. *Why* is food, for example, reinforcing?

A simple, though not entirely correct, answer is that reinforcing events satisfy biological needs. Certainly many reinforcers satisfy biological needs (hunger, thirst, sex, temperature regulation, and so forth). However, for many people, alcohol and tobacco (which are biologically harmful) act as stronger reinforcers than exercise and a healthy diet. Furthermore, we are also reinforced by events with no biological value, such as the taste of saccharin, a sweet but undigestible chemical. A modified version of this need-reduction theory is the **drive-reduction theory,** which holds that reinforcers satisfy our drives, such as the drive to consume sweet substances, even if they do not satisfy needs. The drive-reduction theory can handle a great variety of data if we assume that people have drives not only to eat, drink, and copulate, but also drives to socialize with others, to experience art and music, and so forth. The risk, of course, is that we infer many new drives to explain why various reinforcers work.

A further limitation of drive-reduction theory is that a given reinforcer may be more effective at one time than at others. For example, the opportunity to talk to a long-lost friend might be a great reinforcer at one time, a weak reinforcer or even an annoy-

10. *Anorexia nervosa is a condition in which an otherwise healthy person refuses to eat enough to survive and is obsessed with weight loss. Suppose you are a psychologist trying to encourage such a person to eat and you wish to use positive reinforcement. According to the Premack principle, how should you begin? (Check your answer on page 255.)*

The Disequilibrium Principle The limitation of the Premack principle is that we are sometimes reinforced by the opportunity to engage in some uncommon behavior. For example, I do not ordinarily spend much time clipping my toenails, but if I am badly overdue for clipping them, the opportunity to do so will be a strong reinforcer.

According to the **disequilibrium principle** of reinforcement, each of us has a normal, or "equilibrium," state in which we divide our time among various activities in some preferred way. If you or I have recently spent less time than usual clipping toenails, playing video games, or talking with friends, then the opportunity to do so will be a reinforcer. However, if we have already completed our usual amount of some activity, then the opportunity to do it again will be an ineffective reinforcer (Timberlake & Farmer-Dougan, 1991).

Unconditioned and Conditioned Reinforcement

We can easily see why food and water are reinforcers; we all need to eat and drink in order to survive. But we will also work for a dollar bill or a college diploma. We distinguish between **unconditioned reinforcers** such as food and water, which satisfy biological needs, and **conditioned reinforcers** such as dollar bills, which became reinforcing because of their association with an unconditioned reinforcer in the past. Dollar bills have no value to us at first, but become reinforcing once we learn that we can exchange them for food or other unconditioned reinforcers. A student learns that good grades will win the approval of parents and teachers; an employee learns that increased sales will win the approval of the employer. We spend most of our time working for conditioned reinforcers.

Reinforcement as Learning What Leads to What

Thorndike, you will recall, held that reinforcement strengthens the response that preceded it. According to that view, reinforcement is a mechanical process; the person who experiences reinforcement simply engages in the response more frequently, without understanding *why*.

According to another view, individuals learn what leads to what (Tolman, 1932). A rat may learn that running down an alley leads to food. Having learned that, the rat does not automatically go running down the alley all the time. It runs down the alley only when it needs food.

For example, suppose an animal has managed to find its way through a maze. We present it with something it does not need at the moment, such as food just after it has eaten a meal. If we test the rat again after its next meal, it shows no increased speed at getting through the maze. However, if tested several hours after its most recent meal, the rat scurries through the maze, indicating that it had learned more than it had previously shown (Tolman & Honzik, 1930).

Another example: A rat is reinforced with sugar water for making response A and is reinforced with food pellets for making response B. After both responses have become well established, the rat is made ill after consuming, say, the sugar water. Now, when given the opportunity to make either response, the rat makes mostly response B. Evidently the original training did not just increase two responses; the rat learned which

According to the disequilibrium principle, an opportunity to engage in some previously forbidden or deprived behavior will be reinforcing.

response produced which outcome (Colwill, 1993).

In other words, we must distinguish between learning and performance. A subject's behavior depends upon what outcome is associated with that behavior and upon how strongly motivated the subject is to achieve that outcome.

Many conditioned reinforcers are surprisingly powerful. Consider, for example, how hard some first-graders work for a little gold star that the teacher pastes on an assignment.

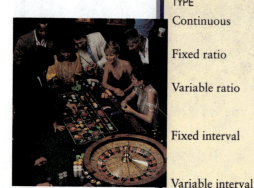
Variable ratio

TABLE 6.3	
Some Schedules of Reinforcement	
TYPE	DESCRIPTION
Continuous	Reinforcement for every response of the correct type
Fixed ratio	Reinforcement for a certain number of responses, regardless of their timing
Variable ratio	Reinforcement for an unpredictable number of responses that varies around some mean value
Fixed interval	Reinforcement for the first response that follows a given delay since the previous reinforcement
Variable interval	Reinforcement for the first response that follows an unpredictable delay since the previous reinforcement

Fixed ratio

SCHEDULES OF REINFORCEMENT

The simplest procedure in operant conditioning is to provide reinforcement every time the correct response occurs. **Continuous reinforcement** refers to reinforcement for every correct response. As you know, not every response in the real world leads to reinforcement. Generally, we need fairly steady reinforcement when we are first learning a new skill, but after a while we can continue with only occasional reinforcement.

Reinforcement for some responses and not others is known as **intermittent reinforcement.** We behave differently when we know that only some of our responses will be reinforced. Psychologists have investigated the effects of many **schedules of reinforcement,** which are rules for the delivery of reinforcement. Continuous reinforcement is the simplest schedule of reinforcement. Four schedules for intermittent reinforcement are fixed ratio, variable ratio, fixed interval, and variable interval. (See Table 6.3.) A ratio schedule provides reinforcements depending on the number of responses. An interval schedule provides reinforcements depending on the timing of responses.

Fixed-Ratio Schedule   A **fixed-ratio schedule** provides reinforcement only after a certain (fixed) number of correct responses have been made—after every fifth response, for example. Even with a fixed-ratio schedule that reinforces every one-hundredth or every two-hundredth response, some animals will

continue to respond until they get reinforcement. We see similar behavior among pieceworkers in a factory, whose pay depends on how many pieces they turn out, or among fruit pickers who get paid by the bushel.

The response rate on a fixed-ratio schedule tends to be rapid and steady. However, if the schedule requires a large number of responses for a reinforcement, there may be a temporary interruption. For example, a student who has just completed 10 calculus problems may pause briefly before starting her French assignment; after completing 100 problems, she will pause even longer.

Variable-Ratio Schedule   A **variable-ratio schedule** is similar to a fixed-ratio schedule except that reinforcement is provided after a variable number of correct responses. For example, reinforcement may come after 10 responses, then after 17 more responses, then after another 9. Variable-ratio schedules generate steady response rates. Gambling is reinforced on a variable-ratio schedule, because the gambler receives payment for some responses and not others on an irregular basis.

In everyday life we sometimes perform some behavior in which every response has an equal, fairly low probability of yielding a reinforcement. When that is true, we are reinforced on a variable-ratio schedule. For example, a radio station announces it will give free concert tickets to the next 40 people who call. When you call, you find that the line is busy. Each time you call you may have, say, 1 chance in 20 of getting a free line. So if you call repeatedly, you are reinforced for an average of 1/20 of your calls. (In this case, of course, you would be reinforced only once.)

Fixed-Interval Schedule A **fixed-interval schedule** provides reinforcement for the first response made after a specific time interval. For instance, an animal might get food only for the first response it makes after each 2-minute interval. Then it would have to wait another 2 minutes before another response would count. Animals (including humans) on such a schedule usually learn to pause after each reinforcement and begin to respond again only as the end of the time interval approaches.

Checking your mailbox is an example of behavior on a fixed-interval schedule. If your mail is delivered at about 3:00 P.M., you will get no reinforcement for checking your mailbox at 2:00 P.M. If you are eagerly awaiting an important letter, you will begin to check around 2:30 and continue checking every few minutes until it arrives.

Variable-Interval Schedule In a **variable-interval schedule**, reinforcement is available after a variable amount of time has elapsed. For example, reinforcement may come for the first response after 2 minutes, then for the first response after 7 seconds, then for the first response after 3 minutes 20 seconds, and so forth. There is no way for the learner to know how long it will be before the next response is reinforced. Consequently, animals usually respond to a variable-interval schedule at a slow but steady rate. In an office where employees are rewarded if they are at work when the boss appears, they will work steadily but not necessarily vigorously so long as the boss's appearances are irregular and unpredictable.

Stargazing is another example of a response reinforced on a variable-interval schedule. The reinforcement for stargazing—seeing a new comet, for example—appears at irregular, unpredictable intervals. Consequently, both professional and amateur astronomers scan the skies regularly.

Extinction of Responses Maintained by Ratio or Interval Reinforcement After a schedule of intermittent reinforcement (either a ratio schedule or an interval schedule), the extinction of responses tends to be slower than it is after a schedule of continuous reinforcement (reinforcement for every response). If you have been reinforced for every time you did something, and now the reinforcements cease, you will notice the change at once and extinguish your response quickly. However, if you have been reinforced on a ratio or interval schedule, you have become accustomed to responding without reinforcement, and the cessation of reinforcement will not produce any quick effect.

CONCEPT CHECKS

11. *Identify which schedule of reinforcement applies to each of the following examples:*
    a. You attend every new movie that appears at your local theater; you find most of them dull (not reinforcing) but really enjoy about one-fourth of them.
    b. You occasionally check your e-mail to find out whether you have any new messages.
    c. You tune your television set to an all-news cable channel, and you look up from your studies to check the sports scores every 30 minutes.
12. *A novice gambler and a longtime gambler both lose 20 bets in a row. Which is more likely to continue betting? Why? (Check your answers on page 255.)*

Some Practical Applications of Operant Conditioning

Although operant conditioning arose from purely theoretical concerns, it has had a long history of practical applications. Here are four examples.

Animal Training

Most animal acts today are based on training methods similar to Skinner's. To get an animal to perform a trick, the trainer first trains it to perform some simple act that is similar to its natural behavior. Then the trainer shapes the animal, step by step, to perform progressively more complex behaviors. Most animal trainers rely on

The high-tech hope of robots handling housekeeping chores has yet to materialize, but in the meantime, simian aides—trained monkeys—are helping the disabled. Monkeys are proving useful for doing indoor tasks for people with limited mobility. The monkey at right is being trained to retrieve objects identified with a laser beam. Such training relies on shaping behavior Skinner-style—building a new response by reinforcing sequential approximations to it.

Skinner

pigeon pecking at target

Chinese POW' essay contest

reinforce behaviors then shape for complex behaviors

positive reinforcement rather than on punishment.

During the Second World War, Skinner proposed a military application of his training methods (Skinner, 1960). The military was having trouble designing a guidance system for its air-to-ground missiles. It needed an apparatus that could recognize a target and guide a missile toward it but would be compact enough to leave room for explosives. Skinner said that he could teach pigeons to recognize a target and peck in its direction. If pigeons were placed in the nose cone of a missile, the direction of their pecking would guide the missile to the target. Skinner demonstrated that pigeons would do the job more cheaply and more accurately than the apparatus then in use and would take up less space. But the military laughed off the whole idea.

PERSUASION

How could you get someone to do something he or she did not want to do? To take an extreme example, how could you convince a prisoner of war to cooperate with the enemy?

The best way is to start by reinforcing a very small degree of cooperation and then working up from there. This principle has been applied by people who had probably never heard of B. F. Skinner, positive reinforcement, or shaping. During the Korean War, for example, the Chinese Communists forwarded some of the letters written home by prisoners of war but intercepted others. (The prisoners could tell from the replies which letters had been forwarded.) The prisoners began to suspect they would have better luck getting their letters through if they said something mildly favorable about their captors. So from time to time they would include a brief remark that the Communists were not really so bad, or that certain aspects of the Chinese system seemed to work pretty well, or that they hoped the war would end soon. After a while the Chinese captors ran essay contests in which the soldier who wrote the best essay (in the captors' opinion) would win a little extra food or some other privilege. Most of the winning essays contained a statement or two that complimented the Communists on some minor matter or that admitted "the United States is not perfect." Gradually, more and more soldiers started to include such statements in their essays. Occasionally, the Chinese might ask one of them, "You said the United States is not perfect. We wonder whether you could tell us some of the ways in which it is not perfect, so that we can better understand your system." Then they would ask the soldiers who cooperated to read aloud their lists of what was wrong with the United States. And so on. Gradually, without torture or coercion, and with only modest reinforcements, the Chinese induced many prisoners to make public statements denouncing the United States, to make false confessions, to inform on fellow prisoners, and even to reveal military secrets (Cialdini, 1985).

The point is clear: Whether we want to get rats to salute the flag or soldiers to denounce it, the most effective training technique is to start with easy behaviors, to reinforce those behaviors, and then gradually to shape more complex behaviors.

APPLIED BEHAVIOR ANALYSIS

Say what you will about ethics, we often try to change people's behavior—in prisons, for example, and mental hospitals and schools. The principles of operant conditioning have proved very useful in efforts to modify behavior.

In **applied behavior analysis,** a psychologist first determines the reinforcers that are sustaining some unwanted behavior, and then tries to alter that behavior by setting specific behavior goals and providing suitable reinforcers for approximating those goals. For example, consider the use of safety belts in cars. Many adults do not habitually wear safety belts, even though the use of such belts would prevent an estimated 50% of the fatalities and serious injuries in automobile accidents. Many states impose fines for failing to wear seat belts, but such laws are only moderately effective.

An alternative is to reinforce people for wearing safety belts. One university, Virginia Polytechnic Institute, invited people parking on campus to sign cards pledging to wear safety belts. All those signing the pledge were entered in a raffle. Drivers were also invited to display a sticker on their car windows indicating that they wear seat belts. Campus police randomly distributed prize coupons to cars that were so identified. This procedure increased the percentage of drivers wearing safety belts from 53% to 72% (Thyer & Geller, 1990).

Similarly, applied behavior analysis is used in therapy for psychologically disturbed people, in techniques of effective parenting, in encouraging medical patients to follow the doctor's instructions, and in business and industry. In each case, the idea is to provide clear and immediate reinforcements for the desired behaviors.

CONCEPT CHECK

13. Of the procedures characterized in Table 6.2, which one applies to laws that penalize people for not wearing seat belts? Which one applies to giving prizes to people who do wear seat belts? (Check your answers on page 255.)

BREAKING BAD HABITS

Some people learn to conquer their own bad habits by means of reinforcements, with a little outside help. Nathan Azrin and Robert Nunn (1973) recommend this three-step method:

1. Become more aware of your bad habit. Interrupt the behavior and isolate it from the chain of normal activities. As an extension of this step, Brian Yates (1985) suggests you imagine an association between the behavior and something repulsive. For example, to break a fingernail-biting habit, imagine your fingernails covered with sewage.

2. If no one else will reinforce you for making progress, provide your own reinforcements. For example, buy yourself a special treat for abandoning your bad habit for a certain period of time.

3. Do something incompatible with the offending habit. For example, if you have a nervous habit of hunching up your shoulders, practice depressing your shoulders.

Figure 6.19 shows an example in which a college student set up a list of reinforcements and punishments to support his goal of decreased smoking. If he successfully limited his smoking, he would treat himself to a movie. If he exceeded the limit he had set for himself, he would have to clean the room by himself on the weekend, and he would not go to a movie. Many people set up similar patterns of reinforcement and punishment for themselves, generally without a written contract.

You might try drawing up for yourself a plan to break your bad habits or establish new good habits. Choose some realistic reinforcers, and keep track of your successes and failures over time.

SUMMARY

- *Reinforcement.* Edward Thorndike introduced the concept of reinforcement. A reinforcement increases the probability that the preceding response will be repeated. (page 239)

- *Operant conditioning.* Operant conditioning is the process of controlling the rate of a behavior through reinforcement. (page 240)

- *Extinction.* In operant conditioning, a response becomes extinguished if it is no longer followed by reinforcement. (page 241)

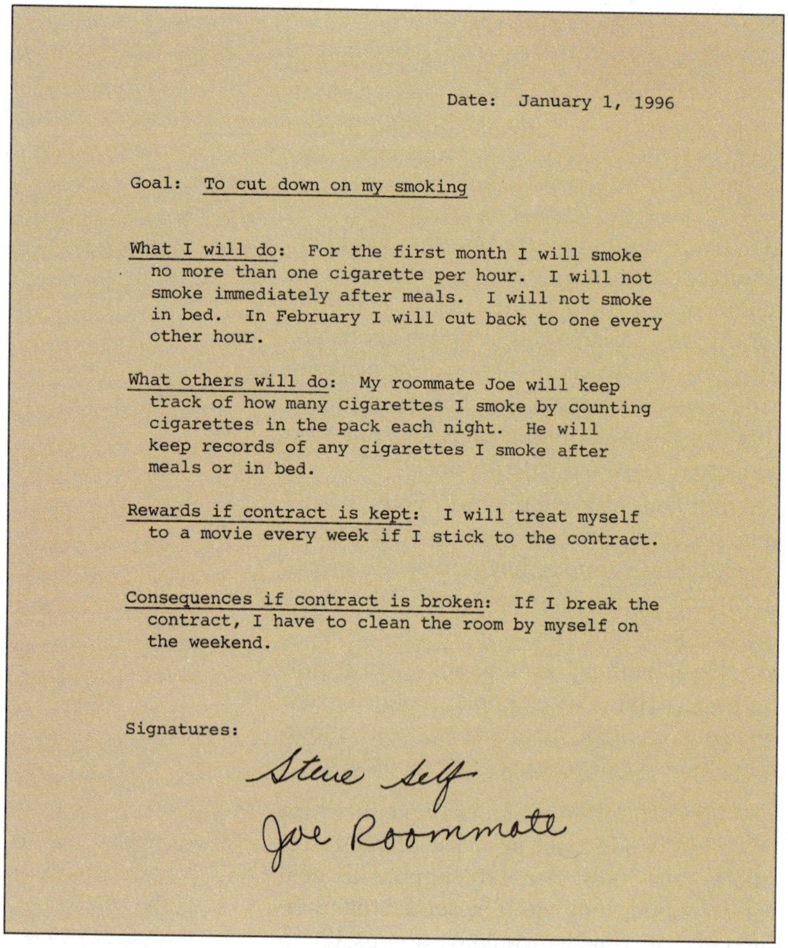

Date: January 1, 1996

Goal: <u>To cut down on my smoking</u>

<u>What I will do:</u> For the first month I will smoke no more than one cigarette per hour. I will not smoke immediately after meals. I will not smoke in bed. In February I will cut back to one every other hour.

<u>What others will do:</u> My roommate Joe will keep track of how many cigarettes I smoke by counting cigarettes in the pack each night. He will keep records of any cigarettes I smoke after meals or in bed.

<u>Rewards if contract is kept:</u> I will treat myself to a movie every week if I stick to the contract.

<u>Consequences if contract is broken:</u> If I break the contract, I have to clean the room by myself on the weekend.

Signatures:

Steve Self

Joe Roommate

FIGURE 6.19
Sometimes people try to change their own behavior by setting up a system of reinforcements and punishments.

- *Shaping.* Shaping is a technique for training subjects to perform difficult acts by reinforcing them for successive approximations to the desired behavior. (page 243)
- *Reinforcement and punishment.* Behaviors can be reinforced (strengthened) by presenting favorable events or by omitting unfavorable events. Behaviors can be punished (suppressed) by presenting unfavorable events or by omitting favorable events. (page 245)
- *The nature of reinforcement.* The opportunity to engage in a more probable behavior will reinforce a less probable behavior. Something that an individual can exchange for a reinforcer becomes a reinforcer itself. (page 247)
- *Learning what leads to what.* Animals (including humans) learn which reinforcement is associated with which behavior. The frequency with which they repeat a given behavior depends on the strength of their motivation to receive the reinforcement at the moment. (page 249)
- *Schedules of reinforcement.* The timing of a response depends on the schedule of reinforcement. In a ratio schedule of reinforce-

ment, an individual is given reinforcement after a fixed or variable number of responses. In an interval schedule of reinforcement, an individual is given reinforcement after a fixed or variable period of time. (page 250)

- *Applications.* People have applied operant conditioning to animal training, persuasion, applied behavior analysis, and habit breaking. (page 251)

SUGGESTION FOR FURTHER READING

Glaser, R. (1990). The reemergence of learning theory within instructional research. *American Psychologist, 45,* 29–39. Discussion of applications of operant conditioning to education.

TERMS

reinforcement an event that increases the future probability of the most recent response (page 240)

law of effect Thorndike's theory that a response which is followed by favorable consequences becomes more probable and a response which is followed by unfavorable consequences becomes less probable (page 240)

operant conditioning or **instrumental conditioning** the process of changing behavior by following a response with reinforcement (page 240)

visceral pertaining to the internal organs (page 240)

skeletal pertaining to the muscles that move the limbs, trunk, and head (page 240)

extinction in operant conditioning, the weakening of a response after a period of no reinforcement (page 241)

stimulus generalization in operant conditioning, the tendency to make a similar response to a stimulus that resembles one that has been associated with reinforcement (page 241)

discrimination in operant conditioning, the learning of different behaviors in response to stimuli associated with different levels of reinforcement (page 241)

discriminative stimulus stimulus that indicates which response is appropriate or inappropriate (page 241)

belongingness the concept that certain stimuli are readily associated with each other and that certain responses are readily associated with certain outcomes (page 242)

shaping a technique for establishing a new response by reinforcing successive approximations to it (page 244)

chaining a procedure for developing a sequence of behaviors in which the reinforcement for one response is the opportunity to engage in the next response (page 244)

punishment an event that decreases the probability that a response will be repeated (page 245)

positive reinforcement strengthening a behavior through the presentation of a favorable event (page 245)

negative reinforcement strengthening a behavior by the negation (avoidance or escape) of some unpleasant event that would have occurred (page 246)

escape learning learning to escape from some unpleasant event (page 246)

avoidance learning learning to avoid some unpleasant event (page 246)

passive avoidance learning learning to avoid some unpleasant event by being passive, that is, by inhibiting a response that would lead to the unpleasant event (page 246)

omission training learning to suppress a behavior that would lead to the omission of some favorable experience (page 246)

drive-reduction theory theory which holds that reinforcers satisfy our drives, even if they do not satisfy biological needs (page 248)

Premack principle the principle that the opportunity to engage in a frequent behavior will reinforce a less frequent behavior (page 248)

disequilibrium principle principle that an opportunity to engage in any deprived activity will be a reinforcer because it restores equilibrium (page 248)

unconditioned reinforcer an event that satisfies a biological need (page 249)

conditioned reinforcer an event that becomes reinforcing when it is associated with a primary reinforcer (page 249)

continuous reinforcement reinforcement for every correct response (page 250)

intermittent reinforcement reinforcement for some responses and not others (page 250)

schedule of reinforcement a rule for the delivery of reinforcement following various patterns of responding (page 250)

fixed-ratio schedule a rule for delivering reinforcement only after the subject has made a certain number of responses (page 250)

variable-ratio schedule a rule for delivering reinforcement after varying numbers of responses (page 250)

fixed-interval schedule a rule for delivering reinforcement for the first response the subject makes after a specified period of time has passed (page 251)

variable-interval schedule a rule for delivering reinforcement after varying amounts of time (page 251)

applied behavior analysis a procedure for determining the reinforcers that sustain some un-

wanted behavior and then altering the behavior by setting specific behavior goals and providing suitable reinforcers for approximating those goals (page 253)

ANSWERS TO CONCEPT CHECKS

7. You would have to know whether the bell was always followed by food (classical conditioning) or whether food was presented only if the animal sat up on its hind legs (operant conditioning). (page 240)

8. a. positive reinforcement **b.** punishment or passive avoidance **c.** escape learning or negative reinforcement **d.** punishment or passive avoidance **e.** omission training or negative punishment **f.** omission training or negative punishment **g.** avoidance learning or negative reinforcement. (page 246)

9. To be effective, punishments have to be quick and consistent. Punishments for drug dealing are neither quick nor consistent. Furthermore, punishment can most effectively suppress a response if the individual has alternative responses that can gain reinforcements. Many people who gain enormous profits by selling drugs would have no alternative legal way to gain similar profits. (page 247)

10. Begin by determining how this person spends his or her time—for example, exercising, reading, watching television, visiting with friends. Offer those opportunities as reinforcers for gaining weight. (We shall discuss this approach more fully in Chapter 15.) (page 248)

11. a. variable ratio. (You will be reinforced for about one-fourth of your movie attendances, but on an irregular basis.) **b.** variable interval. (The messages appear at unpredictable times, and so your responses are reinforced at unpredictable intervals.) **c.** fixed interval. (page 251)

12. The habitual gambler will continue longer, because he or she has a history of being reinforced for gambling on a variable-ratio schedule, which retards extinction. (For the same reason, an alcoholic who has had both good and bad experiences while drunk is likely to keep on drinking even after several consecutive bad experiences.) (page 251)

13. If you think of "not wearing seat belts" as a behavior, then penalizing people for that behavior is a punishment. If (more reasonably) you think of wearing seat belts as the behavior to be acquired, wearing seat belts is a way of avoiding punishment, and therefore the example is one of avoidance behavior or negative reinforcement. Giving prizes to people who agree to wear seat belts is an example of positive reinforcement. (page 253)

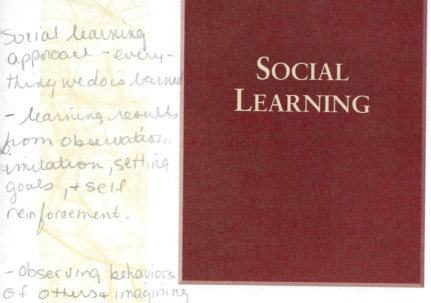

SOCIAL LEARNING

How do we learn from the successes and failures of others without trying every response ourselves?

How do you learn how fast you should drive your car? Classical conditioning plays a role: You notice that your speedometer has hit 70 mph and a few seconds later you hear a police siren. The next time you notice your speedometer hitting 70, you experience a conditioned response: nervousness.

Reinforcement too plays a role in your

According to the social-learning approach, we learn many behaviors by observing what others do, imitating behaviors that are reinforced, and avoiding behaviors that are punished. This girl is being blessed by the temple elephant for making an offering. Others who watch may later imitate her example.

behavior: When you drive at a steady 55 mph, the fact that you reach your destination sooner than if you had driven at 45 provides positive reinforcement. When you drive at 70, reaching your destination even sooner will provide further reinforcement. But it may also bring punishment, causing you to reach your destination both later and poorer.

You also learn from observing the behavior of others. You read that the police plan to enforce the speed laws more rigorously than usual during a holiday weekend, so you stay within the limit. But you notice that everyone is passing you, so you speed up. Then you pass a three-car wreck and recognize some of the cars that had passed you a minute before, so you slow down again. Note that you speed up and slow down even though you are experiencing no direct reinforcement or punishment. You learn about the reinforcements and punishments that your own behavior is likely to provoke by observing what happens to others.

THE SOCIAL-LEARNING APPROACH

According to the **social-learning approach** (Bandura, 1977, 1986), just about everything we do has been learned, even what we call "personality." But not all of it is learned by trial and error with reinforcement; we learn about many behaviors before we try them the first time. Much learning, especially in humans, results from observing the behavior of others and from imagining the consequences of our own behavior. That is, we can learn what leads to what, long before we actually perform any of the actions.

Although psychologists frequently speak of "social-learning theory," it is not a theory in the sense described in Chapter 2. The social-learning approach is more a point of view or a field of emphasis. It focuses on the effects of observation, imitation, setting goals, and self-reinforcement. In this sense, much of human behavior depends on social learning; after all, most school learning is an attempt to learn from the experiences of other people.

MODELING AND IMITATION

When you join a religious organization, a fraternity, or a sorority, or when you start a new job, you discover that the people already there observe certain customs. They will explain some of those customs to you, but the only way you will learn about other customs is by watching. Those who already know them serve as models (or examples) for you; when you copy their example, we say that you are **modeling your behavior after theirs**, or that you are **imitating**.

We are selective in choosing whom to imitate. We imitate people we regard as successful, people with whom we identify, people we would like to resemble. Advertisers, keenly aware of this tendency, try to feature endorsements from people whom consumers are likely to admire and imitate. Cereal and candy advertisements feature happy, healthy children; soft-drink ads feature attractive young adults; ads for luxury cars feature wealthy executives and their impeccably groomed spouses.

This tendency to identify with role models is especially powerful in children. Parents sometimes tell their children, "Do as I say and not as I do." But children are more likely to copy what the parents do (Young-Ok & Stevens, 1987). They also learn how to be a parent by watching their own parents. If and when you become a parent, you probably will treat your own children in much the same way your own parents treated you—even if you *disliked* the way your parents treated you. For example, many people who were yelled at, spanked, slapped, and paddled as children tend to yell at, spank, slap, and paddle their own children (Simons, Whitbeck, Conger, & Wu, 1991). It is, of course, *possible* for you to treat your children differently from the way your parents treated you, but the natural tendency is to imitate what you have observed.

Children also take behavioral cues from other adults and from television characters. They tend to imitate adults of their own sex more than adults of the opposite sex, even when the behaviors are fairly trivial. In one experiment, children watched adults choose between an apple and a banana. If all the men chose, say, the apple and all the women chose the banana, the boys who were watching wanted an apple and the girls wanted a banana (Perry & Bussey, 1979). In other words, children learn about gender roles and sex stereotypes by observation.

Albert Bandura, Dorothea Ross, and

Learning a new skill, such as how to hunt with bow and arrow, may require a combination of verbal instruction, imitating a model, and trial-and-error learning. That is, social learning combines with classical or operant conditioning.

Sheila Ross (1963) studied the role of imitation in learning aggressive behavior. They had two groups of children watch films in which an adult or a cartoon character violently attacked an inflated "Bobo" doll. They had another group watch a film in which the characters did not attack the doll. Then they left the children in a room with a Bobo doll. The children who had watched films showing attacks on the doll (and only those children) attacked the doll vigorously, using many of the same movements they had just seen (Figure 6.20). The clear implication is that children copy the aggressive behavior they have seen in others.

Is the same true for adolescents and adults? This issue is cause for much concern, because so many popular movies include so much violence. As we saw in Chapter 2, the available evidence does not demonstrate that watching violence on television or in movies necessarily causes violent behavior. However, some individuals are more highly influenced than others; some viewers (especially adolescents with a history of violent behavior) may identify strongly with a

FIGURE 6.20
A child will mimic an adult's behavior even when neither one is reinforced for the behavior. This girl attacks a doll after seeing a film of a woman hitting it. People who witness violent behavior, including violence at home, may be more prone than others to turn to violent behavior themselves.

highly violent character in a film. Others may be highly influenced by a film because it resembles some event they have witnessed in their own lives. Many cases have been reported in which people have reenacted scenes they had just seen in a film (Snyder, 1991).

CONCEPT CHECK
---

14. Many people complain that they cannot tell much difference between the two major political parties in the United States, because so many American politicians campaign in similar styles and take similar stands on the issues. Explain this observation in terms of social learning. (Check your answer on page 261.)

VICARIOUS REINFORCEMENT AND PUNISHMENT

Six months ago your best friend quit a job with Consolidated Generic Products in order to open a restaurant. Now you are considering whether you should quit your job with Consolidated Generic and open your own restaurant. How do you decide whether or not to take this step?

Perhaps the first thing you do is to find out how successful your friend has been. You do not automatically imitate the behavior of someone else, even someone you admire. Rather, you imitate behavior that has proved reinforcing for that person. In other words,

you learn by **vicarious reinforcement** or **vicarious punishment**—that is, by substituting someone else's experience for your own.

When a new business venture succeeds, other companies try to figure out the reasons for that success and try to follow the same course. When a venture fails, other companies try to learn the reasons for that failure and try to avoid making the same mistakes. When a football team wins consistently, other teams copy its style of play. And when a television program wins high ratings, other producers are sure to present look-alikes the following year.

SOMETHING TO THINK ABOUT

Might vicarious learning lead to a certain monotony of behavior? Might it contribute to the lack of variety in the television programs and movies that are offered to the public? How can we learn vicariously without becoming like everyone else?

As a rule, vicarious punishment seems to affect behavior less than vicarious reinforcement does. We are bombarded by reminders that failure to wear seat belts will lead to injury or death, and yet many of us fail to buckle up. Despite widespread publicity about the consequences of driving drunk, using addictive drugs, or engaging in "unsafe sex," many people ignore the dangers. Even the death penalty, an extreme example of vicarious punishment, has little demonstrable effect on the murder rate.

Why does vicarious punishment so frequently produce such weak effects? One explanation is that to be influenced, we must identify with the person who is receiving a vicarious reinforcement or punishment. Most of us think of ourselves as successful people; we see someone who is getting punished as a "loser" and "not like us." We can therefore continue to ignore the dangers.

THE ROLE OF SELF-EFFICACY IN SOCIAL LEARNING

You watch an Olympic diver win a gold medal for a superb display of physical control. Presumably you would like to earn an Olympic medal too; so because of this vicarious reinforcement you should go out and try to make some spectacular dives into a pool.

Do you? Probably not. Why not? Why does that vicarious reinforcement fail to motivate you to engage in imitative behavior?

If you are like most people, the reason is that you doubt that you are capable of duplicating the diver's performance. People imitate someone else's behavior only if they have a sense of **self-efficacy**—the perception that they themselves could perform the task successfully.

We achieve or fail to achieve a sense of self-efficacy in two ways. One way is by observing ourselves. Someone who has already succeeded in diving competitions will have a strong sense of self-efficacy concerning the possibility of learning new diving skills. Someone else, who has consistently failed to master even simple athletic skills, will have no sense of self-efficacy.

We also learn about self-efficacy from role models. If your older cousin has studied hard and has gained admission to medical school, you may believe that you can do the same. Psychologists sometimes help students overcome test anxiety by having them watch students similar to themselves displaying good test-taking skills (Dykeman, 1989).

People's sense of self-efficacy generally correlates well with their persistence at a task. For example, people who believe they can succeed at losing weight, or quitting smoking, or quitting alcohol have a much better chance of prolonged success than do people who doubt their own ability to succeed (Curry, Marlatt, & Gordon, 1987). Of course, as with other correlations, we cannot draw conclusions about cause and effect. Perhaps their sense of self-efficacy helps people to break bad habits; just as likely, people may develop that sense of self-efficacy because they know they have the ability to break their bad habits.

Not only do individuals vary in their tendency to imitate successful behaviors; cultures vary too. For example, the Japanese copied and then improved on many of the products and technological methods of the United States and Western Europe. In contrast, the people in a number of Third World countries, though exposed to those products and technology, did not imitate them (Sowell, 1994). Similarly, new advances in farming and medicine spread to some cultures, while other cultures cling to older, traditional methods. We do not know much about why new customs spread more easily

Robert Sandifer, age 11, was killed by his own gang three days after he accidentally killed a 14-year-old girl while attempting to kill someone else. A speaker at his funeral said, "Cry if you will, but make up your mind that you will never let your life end like this." Such a message, if effective, would be an example of vicarious punishment. Unfortunately, people often fail to learn from vicarious punishment.

to some cultures than they do to others, but the answer may have to do with self-efficacy: Cultures that (for whatever reason) believe they can imitate a successful product or procedure are likely to do so; others may be unreceptive even to trying.

SELF-REINFORCEMENT AND SELF-PUNISHMENT IN SOCIAL LEARNING

We learn by observing others who are doing what we would like to do. If our sense of self-efficacy is strong enough, we try to imitate their behavior. But actually succeeding is another matter, which often requires prolonged efforts. People typically set a goal for themselves and monitor their progress toward it. They even provide reinforcement or punishment for themselves just as if they were training someone else. They say to themselves, "If I finish this math assignment on time, I'll treat myself to a movie and a new magazine. If I don't finish on time, I'll make myself clean the stove and the sink." (Self-punishments are usually pretty mild, and seldom actually imposed.)

People who have never learned to use self-reinforcement can be taught to do so.

We acquire a sense of self-efficacy mostly through our own successes, but also partly by watching and identifying with role models.

Donald Meichenbaum and Joseph Goodman (1971) worked with a group of elementary-school children who acted impulsively, blurting out answers and failing to consider the consequences of their actions. To encourage them to set appropriate goals for themselves and to practice self-reinforcement in achieving them, Meichenbaum and Goodman taught the children to talk to themselves while working on a task. For example, a child might say, "Okay, what do I have to do? You want me to copy the picture. . . . Okay, draw the line down, down, good; then to the right, that's it; now down some more and to the left. Good, I'm doing fine so far. Remember, go slowly. Now back up again. No, I was supposed to go down. That's okay. Just erase the line carefully. . . ." After only four training sessions, the children had learned to pause before answering questions and were answering more questions correctly.

Unfortunately, self-reinforcement and self-punishment do not always succeed. One psychologist, Ron Ash (1986), tried to teach himself to stop smoking by means of punishment. He decided to smoke only while he was reading *Psychological Bulletin* and other highly respected but tedious publications. By associating smoking with boredom, he hoped to eliminate his desire to smoke. Two months later he was smoking as much as ever, but he was starting to *enjoy* reading *Psychological Bulletin*!

IN CLOSING: WHY WE DO WHAT WE DO

Almost everything you have done today was a learned behavior—from getting dressed and combing your hair this morning through reading this chapter right now. In fact, you probably would have trouble listing many things you have done today that were not learned. Even your bad habits are examples of learning, or mislearning.

One point that I hope has emerged in this chapter is that learning takes many forms. Classically conditioned salivation, conditioned taste aversions, operantly conditioned movements, and socially learned behaviors occur under diverse circumstances. The underlying mechanisms in the brain may overlap, but at a descriptive level these types of learning differ in some important ways. In short, your behavior is subject to a wide variety of learned influences.

SUMMARY

• *Learning by observation.* We learn much by observing what other people do and what consequences they experience. (page 256)

• *Whom we imitate.* We are more likely to imitate the actions of people we admire and people with whom we identify. (page 257)

• *What we imitate.* We tend to imitate behaviors that have led to reinforcement for other people. We are less consistent in avoiding behaviors that have led to punishment. (page 258)

• *Self-efficacy.* Whether or not we decide to imitate a behavior that has led to reinforcement for others depends on whether we believe we are capable of duplicating that behavior. (page 258)

• *Self-reinforcement and self-punishment.* Once people have decided to try to imitate a certain behavior, they set goals for themselves and may even provide their own reinforcements and punishments. (page 259)

Suggestion for Further Reading

Bandura, A. (1986). *Social foundations of thought and action*. Englewood Cliffs, NJ: Prentice-Hall. A review of social learning by its most influential investigator.

Terms

social-learning approach the view that people learn by observing and imitating the behavior of others and by imagining the consequences of their own behavior (page 256)

modeling or **imitating** copying a behavior or custom (page 257)

vicarious reinforcement or **vicarious punishment** reinforcement or punishment observed to have been experienced by someone else (page 258)

self-efficacy the perception of one's own ability to perform a task successfully (page 259)

Answer to Concept Check

14. One reason why most American politicians run similar campaigns and take similar stands is that they all tend to copy the same models— candidates who have won elections in the past. Another reason is that they all pay attention to the same public-opinion polls. (page 258)

7

MEMORY

Suppose I offer you—for a price—an opportunity to do absolutely anything you want to do for one day. You will not be limited by any of the usual constraints on what is possible. You can travel in a flash from one place to another, visiting as many places as you care to crowd into that single day. You can even travel into outer space, searching for possible life on other planets. You can travel forward and backward through time, finding out what the future holds in store and witnessing the great events of history, or even of prehistoric times. (But you will not be able to alter history.) Anything you want to do—just name it and it is yours. Furthermore, I guarantee your safety: No matter where you choose to go or what you choose to do, you will not get hurt.

Now, how much would you be willing to pay for this once-in-a-lifetime opportunity? Oh, yes, I should mention . . . there is one catch. When the day is over, you will forget everything that happened. You will never be able to recover any memory of that day. Any notes or photos you might have made will vanish. And anyone else who takes part in your special day will forget it, too.

Now how much would you be willing to pay? Much less, I am sure; perhaps nothing. Living without remembering is hardly living at all. Our memories are almost the same thing as our "selves."

Kutbidin Atamkulov travels from one Central Asian village to another, singing from memory the tale of the Kirghiz hero, Manas. The song, which lasts 3 hours, has been passed from master to student for centuries. Human memory can hold an amazing amount of information.

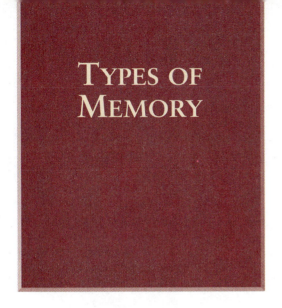

TYPES OF MEMORY

Do we have different types of memory?

Why do we remember some types of material better than others?

People will compete with one another at just about anything, and memory is no exception. In the annual World Memory Championship, contestants compete in such events as speed of memorizing a shuffled pack of 52 playing cards (the record is 58.79 seconds); repeating a long number after hearing it spoken once (the record is a 142-digit number); and memorizing an imaginary 80-day trip around the world, including details about cities, hotels, flight numbers, and car rentals. Dominic O'Brien, the 1993 champion and 1994 runner-up, admits that

his "championship-level" memory sometimes fails him in practical situations. Once he was so busy trying to memorize a shuffled stack of 312 playing cards that he forgot to pick up a friend whom he had promised to meet at the airport. When the angry friend called to remind him, O'Brien apologized and then drove to London's Gatwick airport, busily practicing his card-stack memorization along the way. When he got there and could not find his friend, he finally remembered that the friend was at Heathrow, London's other major airport (Johnstone, 1994).

Examples such as this one illustrate a point that psychologists took decades to learn: People have several kinds of memory. It is possible to have an excellent memory for some kinds of material but only an average or poor memory for other kinds of material.

WHY NO ONE EXPERIMENT CHARACTERIZES ALL THE FEATURES OF MEMORY

If you have an important test on Wednesday morning, how much do you study on Tuesday night? Some professors advise their students that last-minute "cramming" is useless, and occasionally students misinterpret that advice to mean that last-minute *reviewing* is useless. (I met one student who proudly told me that he did no studying at all

Jonathan Hancock defeated Dominic O'Brien in the 1994 World Memory Championship, based on such events as memorizing decks of shuffled cards in order.

the entire day before a test. I'll let you guess what kind of grades he was getting.) What the professors mean—or what they *should* mean—is that waiting until the night before the test to start reading the assignment is a foolish strategy. You should study as you go, and then refresh your memory with a good review the night before the test. That last-minute refresher is, however, very useful.

A few years ago I read a manuscript by someone whose advice went to the opposite extreme. A manuscript for a proposed book on "How to Study in College" recommended that students postpone their study until the last possible moment, because studying any earlier was an almost complete waste of time. If you have ever waited until the night before a test to start your study, you *know* this manuscript was offering bad advice. So how could its author, a college professor who had read at least a little of the research on memory, have come to such an incorrect conclusion? And what evidence do we have to refute it?

EBBINGHAUS'S PIONEERING STUDIES OF MEMORY

The German psychologist Hermann Ebbinghaus (1850–1909) founded the experimental study of memory. Previous researchers had asked people to describe their memories, but they had no way to measure the accuracy of people's recollections. Ebbinghaus did his research by teaching new material and then measuring memory for that material after various delays. To make sure that the material to be memorized would be unfamiliar, Ebbinghaus invented **nonsense syllables**, meaningless three-letter combinations such as GAK or VUB. He wrote out 2300 such syllables and arranged them in random lists (Figure 7.1), and then set out to determine how rapidly people could memorize such lists and how long they could remember them. He had no cooperative introductory psychology students to draw on for his study, nor any friends who were interested in memorizing lists of nonsense syllables, so he ran all the tests on himself. Over the course of about 6 years he memorized thousands of lists of nonsense syllables. (He must have been unusually dedicated to his science or uncommonly tolerant of boredom.)

In one experiment, Ebbinghaus memorized several lists of 13 nonsense syllables each and then tested his memory after various delays. The results appear in Figure 7.2. He forgot a mean of more than 50% of each

FIGURE 7.1
Hermann Ebbinghaus pioneered the scientific study of memory by observing his own capacity for memorizing lists of nonsense syllables.

list after an hour and still more after 24 hours. If we take this result seriously, we would come to the same conclusion as the author of that manuscript I told you about: If you are going to forget everything you learn as fast as Ebbinghaus did, then you should do your studying as close as possible to the time of the test. Any earlier study is likely to be forgotten.

Of course, we should then also conclude that education itself is pointless. If you are going to forget most of what you learn within 24 hours, how much will you still remember by the time of graduation, much less a few years after graduation? Unless the whole idea of education is fundamentally flawed, Ebbinghaus's results must not apply to all memory.

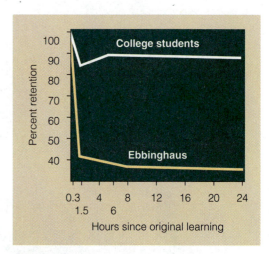

FIGURE 7.2
Yellow line: Recall of lists of syllables by Ebbinghaus (1913) after delays of various lengths. White line: Recall of lists of words by college students after delays of various lengths. (Based on Koppenaal, 1963.) Ebbinghaus learned as fast as other people but forgot faster.

DIFFERENCES AMONG INDIVIDUALS BECAUSE OF INTERFERENCE

Suppose we repeat Ebbinghaus's experiment, but instead of doing all the studies on one person, we persuade a large number of college students to learn a list of words or nonsense syllables, testing some of them after short delays and some after long delays. The top line of Figure 7.2 shows the results of one such study: Even after 24 hours, most students remember most of the items on the list (Koppenaal, 1963).

Why do you suppose most college students remember a list so much better than Ebbinghaus did? You may be tempted to say college students did so well because they are so intelligent. True, no doubt, but Ebbinghaus was no dummy either. Or you might suggest that college students have had "so much practice at memorizing nonsense." (Sorry if you think that's true.) But Ebbinghaus had memorized a lot of nonsense himself. In fact, the problem was that poor Hermann Ebbinghaus had memorized *too much* nonsense—literally thousands of lists of syllables (Figure 7.3). When people memorize many lists of similar material, the similar memories start to interfere with one another. Such people can still memorize new lists just as fast as before (maybe faster), but they tend to confuse the various lists with one another and therefore forget them rapidly. The old materials promote forgetting of the new materials through **proactive interference** (acting *forward* in time); the new materials promote forgetting of the old materials through **retroactive interference** (acting *backward* in time). Figure 7.4 shows the difference between the two kinds of interference.

The application to Ebbinghaus is simple: Because he had memorized so many lists of syllables, he had massive proactive interference and he forgot new lists much faster than other people would. Therefore the results he collected on himself are very misleading if applied to anyone else.

One moral of the story is this: When you want to memorize something, beware of studying anything else too similar to it. (Studying unrelated material poses no problem, though.)

CONCEPT CHECKS

1. *Professor Tryhard learns the names of his students every semester. After a number of years, he finds that he learns them as*

FIGURE 7.3
Ebbinghaus could learn new lists of nonsense syllables, but he forgot them quickly because of interference from all the previous lists he had learned. People who memorize many similar lists start to confuse them with one another.

quickly as ever but forgets them faster. Does he forget because of retroactive interference or proactive interference?
2. *Remember spontaneous recovery from Chapter 6, page 230? Can you explain it in terms of proactive interference? (What is learned first? What is learned second? What would happen if the first interfered with the second?) (Check your answers on page 279.)*

THE IMPORTANCE OF MEANINGFULNESS

Ebbinghaus, you will recall, was memorizing nonsense syllables. As you might guess, people tend to remember meaningful material better than they remember nonsense.

J. D. Bransford and M. K. Johnson (1972) described one clever experiment illus-

Proactive interference:
Old memory impairs recall of newer memory.

Retroactive interference:
New memory impairs recall of older memory.

FIGURE 7.4
Suppose you have two memories. Call the first one O and the second one X. If they are similar but not identical, each will interfere with the other. The interference of the first (O) on the second (X) is proactive interference. Interference of the second (X) on the first (O) is retroactive interference.

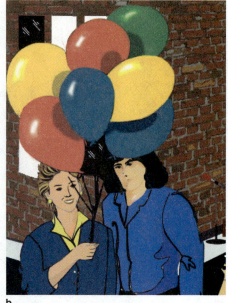

If the balloons popped, the sound would not be able to carry since everything would be too far away from the correct floor. A closed window would also prevent the sound from carrying since most buildings tend to be well insulated. Since the whole operation depends on a steady flow of electricity, a break in the middle of the wire would also cause problems. Of course, the fellow could shout, but the human voice is not loud enough to carry that far. An additional problem is that a string could break on the instrument. Then there could be no accompaniment to the message. It is clear that the best situation would involve less distance. Then there would be fewer potential problems. With face to face contact, the least number of things could go wrong.

a   b   c

FIGURE 7.5

In an experiment by Bransford and Johnson (1972), one group of people looked at a picture similar to a and another group looked at a picture similar to b. Then both groups heard the paragraph in part c. The paragraph is meaningful only if you have seen picture a.

trating the influence of meaningfulness. After looking at either picture a or picture b in Figure 7.5, two groups of people listened to the paragraph in part c (Bransford & Johnson, 1972, p. 131). Note that the paragraph makes sense if you have seen picture b but is nearly incomprehensible if you have seen only picture b. As you might expect, the people who had seen picture a remembered about twice as much of the paragraph as those who had seen only picture b.

How well do you suppose you remember the meaningful, important events of your life? Marigold Linton (1982) wrote notes about at least two important personal events

each day for 6 years and recorded the date on the back of each note. At various times she drew notes at random from the pile and tested her ability to recall the approximate date of each event. She found that she remembered the dates of about 95% of events a year old and a slightly lower percentage of older events. Similarly, Willem Wagenaar (1986) recorded on cards 2400 personal events over 6 years. At the end of the 6 years, he tested himself by reading part of each card (for example, "what happened") and trying to recall the rest (for example, who, where, and when). He was able to recall at least a little information about almost every event. In short, we generally remember meaningful events well, even years later.

IMPORTANCE OF DISTINCTIVENESS

Not only do we tend to remember meaningful material; we also tend to remember distinctive or unusual material (Figure 7.6). Read the following list and then recall immediately, in any order, as many items as you can:

> potato, asparagus, cauliflower, turnip, broccoli, Egypt, beans, corn, peas, rutabaga, squash, cabbage

One of the items you are most likely to recall is *Egypt,* because it is different from the others: It is the only word beginning with a capital letter and the only word that refers to anything other than a vegetable.

Similarly, we tend to remember unusual people or people with unusual names. If you meet several men with rather ordinary ap-

FIGURE 7.6

Which of these four men are you most likely to remember? Other things being equal, we remember the most unusual individuals.

TABLE 7.1
Illustration of the Difference Between Recall and Cued Recall

Instructions: First try to identify each person in the left column while covering the right column (recall method). Then expose the right column, which gives each person's initials, and try again (cued recall).

Author of *Moby Dick*	H. M.
Only woman with face on a U.S. coin ($1)	S. B. A.
Author of Hercule Poirot stories	A. C.
President of the Soviet Union when it collapsed	M. G.
Discoverer of classical conditioning	I. P.
First elected leader of South Africa after end of apartheid	N. M.
Author of Sherlock Holmes stories	A. C. D.
First U.S. woman astronaut	S. R.
Author of this book	J. K.
Author of *Gone with the Wind*	M. M.
First names of the Wright brothers (airplane inventors)	W. & O.

For answers, see page 279, Answer A.

---

pearances and similar names, like John Stevens, Steve Johnson, and Joe Stevenson, it may take you a long time to get their names straight. You would have much less trouble remembering a 7-foot-tall redheaded man named Stinky Rockefeller. The tendency to remember unusual items better than the more common items is known as the **von Restorff effect,** after the psychologist who first demonstrated it (von Restorff, 1933).

DEPENDENCE OF MEMORY ON THE METHOD OF TESTING

Ebbinghaus tested his memory by requiring himself to say the correct syllables in the correct order. Might his method have underestimated his memory? For example, most of us occasionally find ourselves unable to remember someone's name, or the formula for the volume of a sphere, or some other fact that we once knew. Still, we know we haven't forgotten it altogether; later on, some reminder may bring back the memory.

Psychologists find that how well someone appears to remember something depends on how a psychologist tests the memory. The simplest way is to ask for recall. To recall something is to produce it, as you do on essay tests or short-answer tests. For instance, I might ask you, "Please name all the children in your fourth-grade class." You will probably have trouble, partly because you confuse the names of the children in your fourth-grade class with those you knew in other grades. (Remember the influence of proactive and retroactive interference.)

Your memory probably will seem to improve if we use **cued recall,** a method in which you get significant hints about the material. For example, I might show you a photograph of all the children in your fourth-grade class or I might give you a list of their initials (Figure 7.7). Try this: Cover the right side of Table 7.1 with a piece of paper and try to identify each of the people described. (This is the recall method.) Then uncover the right side, revealing each person's initials, and try again. (This is cued recall.)

In **recognition,** a third method of testing memory, a person is asked to identify the correct item from several choices. People can usually recognize more items than they can recall. For example, I might give you a list of 60 names and ask you to check off the correct names of children in your fourth-grade class. Multiple-choice tests use the recognition method to test memory.

A fourth method, the **savings,** or **relearning, method,** will sometimes detect weaker memories than the other methods will. Suppose you cannot name some of the children in your fourth-grade class (recall method) and cannot pick out their names from a list of choices (recognition method). If I presented you with the correct list of names, you might learn it faster than you would learn an unfamiliar list of names. The fact that you *relearn* something more quickly than you learn something new is evidence that some memory has persisted (MacLeod, 1988). In other words, you *save time* when you relearn material that you learned in the past. The

FIGURE 7.7

Could you recall the names of the students in your fourth-grade class? Trying to remember without any hints is recall. Using a photo or a list of initials is cued recall. If you tried to choose the correct names from a list, you would be engaged in recognition. If you compared how fast you relearned the correct names and how fast you learned another list, you would be using the savings (or relearning) method.

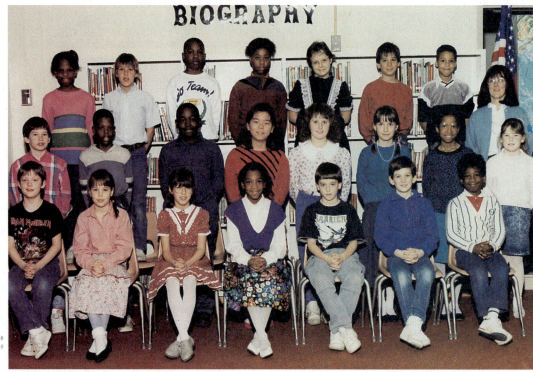

INFO process model:

1st enters temp storage

2nd enters permanent
stores
(INFO processed)

Person Then recovers info.

3 types of memory
① sensory store
② Short-term memory
③ long-Term memory

amount of time saved (time needed for original learning minus the time for relearning) is a measure of memory.

An overall conclusion: We revere Ebbinghaus as the pioneer who started scientific memory research. However, many memories are remembered far longer and better than Ebbinghaus's results implied. His memory was impaired by proactive interference and by the fact that he dealt with meaningless and nondistinctive information. Also, other methods of testing memory, such as recognition, sometimes reveal persisting memories that could not be recalled.

CONCEPT CHECK

3. *Each of the following is an example of one method of testing memory. Identify each method. (Check your answers on page 279.)*
a. Although you thought you had completely forgotten your high-school French, you do much better in your college French course than does your roommate, who never took French in high school.
b. You don't have a telephone directory and are trying to remember the phone number of the local pizza parlor.
c. After witnessing a robbery, you have trouble describing the thief. The police show you several photographs and ask whether any of them is the robber.
d. Your friend asks, "What's the name of our chemistry lab instructor? I think it's Julie or Judy something."

THE INFORMATION-PROCESSING VIEW OF MEMORY

Ebbinghaus apparently thought of memory as a haphazard collection of associations, with no one memory being much different from another. One overall theme of memory research since about 1950 has been the search for distinctions among types of memory.

According to one view, the **information-processing model** of memory, human memory is analogous to the memory system of a computer: Information enters the system, is processed and coded in various ways, and is then stored (Figure 7.8). According to one version of this model that was for a long time considered the standard, memory first enters temporary storage (as when information is typed into a computer) and later enters permanent storage (as when information is entered onto a disk). Still later, in response to a retrieval cue, a person can recover the information (Atkinson & Shiffrin, 1968). According to this model, we should distinguish among three types of memory: a very brief sensory store, short-term memory, and long-term memory. We shall examine this model and its strengths and weaknesses, and then consider some modifications and modern alternatives to this theory.

THE SENSORY STORE

Every memory begins as an exposure to a sensory stimulus. After you see or hear something for even a split second, you can report minor details about it before the memory vanishes. This recall is possible because it has been temporarily entered into the sensory store, a very brief storage of sensory information. However, unless you immediately and actively attend to this sensory information, it will fade in less than a second as new information replaces it in the sensory store.

George Sperling (1960) tested how much information people can retain in the sensory store. He flashed an array like the one shown in Figure 7.9 onto a screen for 50 milliseconds (50 × .001 second). When he asked viewers to report as much of the whole array as they could, he found that they could recall a mean of only about four items. If he had stopped at that point, he might have concluded that viewers could store only a small fraction of an array.

But Sperling knew that it takes several seconds for a person to report even a few items, and he knew it was likely that memories in the sensory store would fade over those seconds. In other words, much of the array that entered the sensory store may have faded while people were reporting the first few items. To test that possibility, he told viewers he would ask them to report only one row of the array, but he did not tell them which row. After flashing the array on the screen, he immediately used a tone to signal which row the viewers were to recall. Most people could name all the items in whichever row he indicated. Evidently, nearly all of the information in the array was available to them for a split second. When he waited for even a second before signaling which row to recall, viewers could recall few, if any, of the items in that row. "Use it or lose it" is certainly true for information in the sensory store—and you had better use it fast or it will fade rapidly.

Is this phenomenon really memory, or is it perception? It is really on the border between the two, and we need not try to make a distinction. We might even regard memory as a long-persisting or restorable perception.

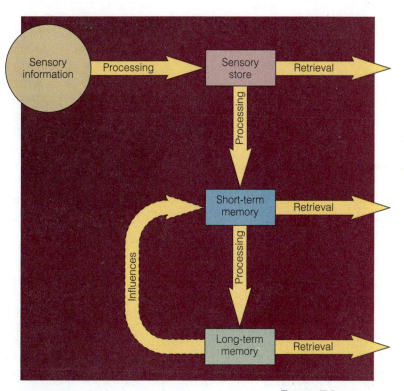

FIGURE 7.8
The information-processing model of memory resembles a computer's memory system, including temporary and permanent memory.

SOMETHING TO THINK ABOUT

Sperling demonstrated the capacity of the sensory store for visual information. How could you demonstrate the capacity of the sensory store for *auditory* information?

SHORT-TERM MEMORY VERSUS LONG-TERM MEMORY

According to the traditional version of information-processing theory, we should distinguish between long-term memory, a relatively permanent store of mostly meaningful information, and short-term memory, the particular information that a person has just experienced. Figure 7.10 compares the rates

FIGURE 7.9
George Sperling flashed arrays like this on a screen for 50 milliseconds. After the display went off, a signal told the viewer which row to recite.

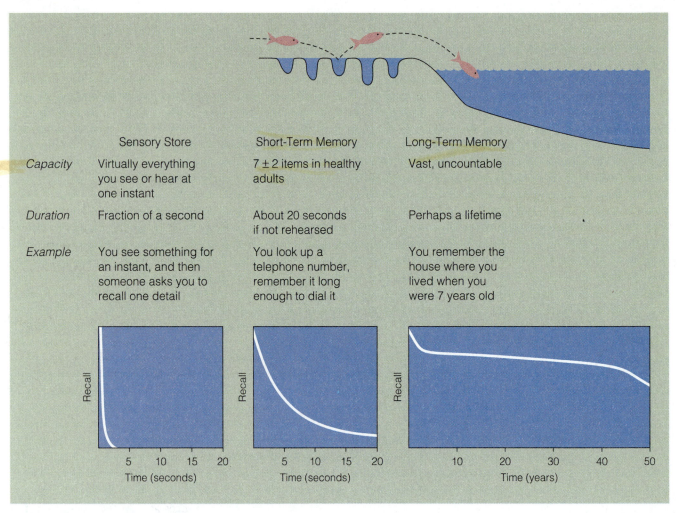

	Sensory Store	Short-Term Memory	Long-Term Memory
Capacity	Virtually everything you see or hear at one instant	7 ± 2 items in healthy adults	Vast, uncountable
Duration	Fraction of a second	About 20 seconds if not rehearsed	Perhaps a lifetime
Example	You see something for an instant, and then someone asks you to recall one detail	You look up a telephone number, remember it long enough to dial it	You remember the house where you lived when you were 7 years old

FIGURE 7.10

After about 1 second, you cannot recall information from the sensory store. Short-term memories can be recalled up to about 20 seconds without rehearsal—much longer if you keep rehearsing them. Long-term memories decline somewhat, especially at first, but you may be able to retrieve them for a lifetime. Your address from years ago is probably in your long-term memory and will continue to be there for the rest of your life.

of decay of the sensory store and short- and long-term memory.

Information in short-term memory is available only temporarily. After attention is distracted, the information fades rapidly though perhaps is not lost altogether. Someone comes up to you at a party and says, "Hello, I'm Sally Davis." "I'm pleased to meet you, Sally," you reply. Two minutes later you want to introduce her to someone else, but you have already forgotten her name. (Curiously, you seem to remember what her name was *not*. For example, if someone asks whether her name might have been "Beulah Budweiser," you say you are sure it was not, even though you have no idea what her name really was.)

In contrast, the information stored in long-term memory can be available at any time. To get information from long-term memory, a person needs a *retrieval cue*, an association that retrieves the memory. Some retrieval cues work better than others. For example, the retrieval cue "the city you were born in" should enable you to retrieve the name of one city from your long-term memory. The retrieval cue "U.S. city whose name is also the name of a type of animal" probably does not enable you to retrieve anything quickly. You laboriously go through all the cities (or animals) you can think of until eventually you come upon an answer, most likely Buffalo, New York. (Conceivably, you might think of Caribou, Maine; Turkey, North Carolina; Anaconda, Montana; or Deadhorse, Alaska.) Retrieving long-term memories is sometimes a difficult, effortful task.

CHARACTERISTICS OF SHORT-TERM MEMORY

If short-term memory is qualitatively different from long-term memory, it should have some special properties. Let us consider the reported characteristics of short-term memory.

The Limited Capacity of Short-Term Memory People can store a vast amount of information in their long-term memory. The musical conductor Arturo Toscanini knew every note for every instrument for 250 symphonies, 100 operas, and many other compositions (Marek, 1975).

In contrast, short-term memory can apparently store only a limited amount of information. Read each of the following sequences of letters and then look away and try to repeat them from memory. Or read each aloud and ask a friend to repeat it.

EHGPH
JROZNQ
SRBWRCN
MPDIWFBS
ZYBPIAFMO
BOJFKFLTRC
XUGJDPFSVCL

Most normal adults can repeat a list of approximately seven items (letters in this case). Some people can remember eight or nine; others, only five or six. George Miller (1956) referred to the short-term memory capacity as "the magical number seven, plus or minus two." When people try to repeat a longer list, however, they may fail to remember even the first seven items. It is somewhat like trying to hold several eggs in one hand: You can hold a certain number, depending on their size, but if you try to hold too many you drop them all (Figure 7.11).

Short-Term Memory and Chunking In some cases, a person can repeat a list of much more than seven items after hearing it only once. For illustration, examine each of these sequences of numbers and then try to repeat them:

106614921776

3141627182814141732

Could you do it? You might have recognized the first sequence as three historical dates (the Norman invasion of England in 1066, Columbus's arrival in America in 1492, and the Declaration of Independence in 1776). If you have a strong background in mathematics, you may have recognized the second sequence as the approximate values of four mathematical constants (pi, 3.1416 . . . ; *e*, 2.71828 . . . ; the square root of two, 1.414 . . . ; and the square root of three, 1.732). If you recognized neither sequence, you had to try to remember 12 digits in the first sequence, 19 in the second—an impossible task in a short time. However, if you organized the sequences as three dates or four mathematical constants, you had just a small number of meaningful units, or **chunks,** to remember. (See Figure 7.12.)

FIGURE 7.11
Short-term memory is like a hand full of eggs; it can hold only a limited number of items at a time.

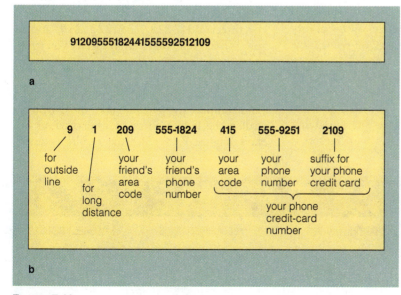

FIGURE 7.12
We overcome the limits of short-term memory through chunking. You probably could not remember the 26-digit number (a), but by breaking it up into a series of chunks (b), you remember it and dial the number correctly.

FIGURE 7.13

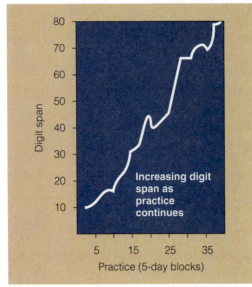

*Most people can
repeat a list of about
7 numbers. Over 18
months of practice
one college student
gradually increased
his ability to repeat a
list of numbers.
(From Ericsson,
Chase, & Falcon,
1980.)*

[Handwritten margin notes: people can learn to recognize larger & larger chunks

If people don't rehearse info in ST memory - it fades. - simple decay

Forgetting of LT memory depends on proactive + retroactive interference]

With practice, people can learn to recognize larger and larger chunks. One student from Carnegie-Mellon University (Ericsson, Chase, & Falcon, 1980) volunteered for an experiment on the memorization of digits. At the beginning, he could repeat only about 7 digits at a time. Over the course of a year and a half, working 3 to 5 hours a week, he gradually improved until he could repeat a sequence of up to 80 digits, as shown in Figure 7.13. He had developed some extraordinary strategies for chunking. He was a competitive runner, so he might store the sequence "3492 . . ." as "3 minutes, 49.2 seconds, a near world-record time for running a mile." He might store the next set of numbers as a good time for running a kilometer, a mediocre marathon time, or a date in history. These strategies, however, applied only to numbers. When he was tested on his ability to remember a list of letters or words, his performance was only average.

A comment: As a rule, a psychologist who reads a list of numbers and asks someone to repeat them assumes that the results measure short-term memory. The possibility of chunking, however, shows that the test is not a pure measure of short-term memory. Someone who recognizes 1492 and 1776 as meaningful units is clearly bringing long-term memories into this short-term memory test. In the case of the Carnegie-Mellon student, it is not even clear whether he was using short-term memory at all, or whether he had developed ways to organize large amounts of information rapidly into long-term memory.

Decay of Short-Term Memories Over Time
Short-term memory may also differ from long-term memory in the mechanism of forgetting. Forgetting of long-term memories depends largely on proactive and retroactive interference. In contrast, certain researchers have suggested that short-term memories are forgotten through simple decay. That is, unless people continually rehearse the material in short-term memory, it gradually fades away.

Lloyd Peterson and Margaret Peterson (1959) demonstrated the decay of short-term memory with an experiment that you can easily repeat if you can trick some friend into volunteering. First read aloud a meaningless sequence of letters, such as HOZDF. Then wait for a bit and ask your friend to repeat it. He or she will have no difficulty doing so. The reason is that your friend suspected you would ask for a recall of the letters and spent the delay rehearsing, "H-O-Z-D-F, H-O-Z-D-F, . . ."

If you prevent rehearsal during the delay period, however, your friend will forget quickly. Say "I am going to read you a list of letters, such as HOZDF. Then I'm going to tell you a number, such as 231. When you hear the number, begin counting backward by threes: 231, 228, 225, 222, 219, and so on. When I tell you to stop, I'll ask you to repeat the sequence of letters." You can record your data as in Table 7.2.

Try this experiment with several friends, and compute the percentage of those who recalled the letters correctly after various delays. Figure 7.14 gives the results Peterson

	TABLE 7.2		
LETTER SEQUENCE	STARTING NUMBER	DELAY IN SECONDS	CORRECT RECALL?
BKLRE	712	5	
ZIWOJ	380	10	
CNVIU	416	5	
DSJGT	289	20	
NFMXS	601	25	

and Peterson obtained. Note that fewer than 10% of their subjects could recall the letters correctly after a delay of 18 seconds. In other words, if we fail to rehearse something that has entered short-term memory, it will generally fade away within 20 seconds or less.

This demonstration works well, however, only when the person is trying to memorize something fairly meaningless, like HOZDF. If you ask your friend to memorize "There is a poisonous snake under your chair," he or she is likely to remember it well even after counting backward by threes from 231. Highly meaningful material does not rapidly decay.

Furthermore, Peterson and Peterson's experiment does not demonstrate such a complete difference between short-term and long-term memory as we once thought it did. Let's reconsider the demonstration: You read off, say, "BKLRE," asked someone to count backward by threes for 5 seconds, and then probably found that the person could recall the letters. After two more trials you came to "DSJGT" and a 20-second delay. At that point the person probably did not give the correct answer. But DSJGT was the fourth trial, potentially subject to a fair amount of proactive interference. Suppose you try this

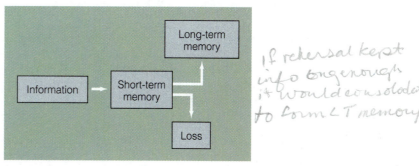

FIGURE 7.15
According to the original conception of the relationship between short-term and long-term memory, a short-term memory becomes a long-term memory if it is rehearsed long enough. Without consolidation, it is lost. This view is now considered oversimplified.

with another volunteer, but now you *start* with DSJGT and a 20-second delay. Under these conditions, most participants remember DSJGT without difficulty (Keppel & Underwood, 1962; Wickens, 1970). Evidently the forgetting that occurs in this situation depends partly on interference, as it does in long-term memory.

CONCEPT CHECK

4. Name one way in which short-term memory and long-term memory are evidently different, and one way in which they are similar. (Check your answers on page 279.)

The Transfer from Short-Term Memory to Long-Term Memory For many years, psychologists thought of short-term memory and long-term memory as separate stages: Information first enters short-term memory and stays there a while. If rehearsal kept it there long enough, it would **consolidate** to form a long-term memory (Figure 7.15).

However, the data contradict this simple view. Simply rehearsing something in short-term memory is no guarantee that it will become a long-term memory, and how long it stays in short-term memory is a poor predictor of whether it will become a long-term memory. For illustration, try the following experiment (based on Craik & Watkins, 1973): Read the list of words below to yourself, or read them to your roommate. Some of the words start with *g*. The instruction for part 1 of the experiment is to keep track of what is the most recent *g*-word. At the end of the list,

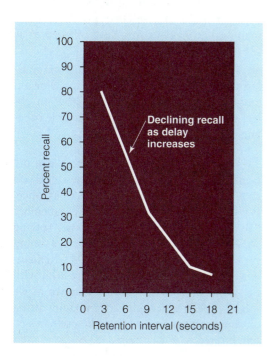

FIGURE 7.14
In the study by Peterson and Peterson (1959), people remembered a set of letters well after a short delay, but their memory faded greatly over 20 seconds.

you (or your roommate) should say what was the *last* word on the list that began with *g*:

> table, giraffe, frog, goose, key, window, banana, pencil, spoon, grass, road, garden, house, tree, lake, paper, chicken, glove, paint, garlic, stone.

The correct answer is *garlic,* and I assume you or your roommate had no trouble getting this answer. So far, so good. Note that what you had to do was to store each *g*-word in short-term memory until you dumped it to replace it with the next *g*-word. You had to hold some of the words briefly and others for longer times. Okay, now that I have distracted you for a while, let's move on to part 2 of the experiment: I didn't warn you about this, but I now want you (or your roommate) to write a list of *all* the *g*-words on that list. (Try this before you continue reading.)

The correct answers are giraffe, goose, grass, garden, glove, and garlic. Considering the delay between when you read the words and when you recalled them, we have to assume you recalled them from long-term memory. The question is, which terms made it into your long-term memory? In general, researchers find that people are about equally likely to remember giraffe, grass, and glove (which stayed in short-term memory only briefly) as to remember goose or garden (which had to stay longer in short-term memory before being replaced). Evidently, how long a word stays in short-term memory has little to do with whether it moves into long-term memory.

A further problem with the traditional concept of short-term memory as a holding station on the way to long-term memory: Such a concept implies that any defect in short-term memory would greatly impair the formation of long-term memories. However, a few brain-damaged patients have been observed to form and retrieve new long-term memories without any apparent difficulty, in spite of having a serious weakness in short-term memory. One such patient had a short-term memory capacity of only *two*. For example, he might be able to repeat "7, 4," but would fail at repeating "7, 4, 8." Even with only two letters, his memory usually failed after delays of just a couple of seconds (Shallice & Warrington, 1970). Evidently it is possible to have a very poor short-term memory and still store a great deal into long-term memory. That conclusion implies that short-term memory has some function other than

just holding onto something long enough to form a long-term memory.

A MODIFIED VERSION OF INFORMATION-PROCESSING THEORY: WORKING MEMORY

Short-term memory has a status similar to that of many other psychological concepts: Although it captures certain elements of the truth, the traditional version of the concept is incomplete or misleading. Instead of trying to redefine short-term memory, a number of leading memory researchers have substituted a different term, *working memory.* Working memory is seen not just as a system that temporarily stores information, but as a system for processing or working with current information. That is, the concept is almost synonymous with one's current sphere of attention. Working memory includes three major components (Baddeley & Hitch, 1994):

- A *central executive* that governs shifts of attention.
- A *phonological loop* that stores and rehearses speech information. The phonological loop enables us to repeat about seven numbers or letters immediately after hearing them; it more or less corresponds to what many other investigators have referred to as short-term memory.
- A *visuospatial sketchpad* that manipulates visual and spatial information. For example, it enables us to imagine how an object would appear if viewed from some other angle.

The evidence for making these distinctions is that people can sometimes work on two unrelated "short-term" tasks at once. For example, you could probably remember "B 7 Q 8 J 4" while simultaneously solving some difficult visual, spatial, or reasoning problem (Baddeley & Hitch, 1974). Remembering those items would interfere a bit with the problem-solving, but not as much as we might expect, especially if we imagined that all short-term tasks had to make use of a system limited to 7 ± 2 items.

The concept of a phonological loop helps to explain why some people have better reading comprehension than other people do. First, psychologists have determined that certain people have a larger phonological loop than others do; that is, people differ in how many letters or words they can remember and how long they can remember. Given that people differ in this regard, imagine various people reading either of the following sentences:

Since Ken really liked the boxer, he took a bus to the nearest pet store to buy the animal.

Since Ken really liked the boxer, he took a bus to the nearest sports arena to see the match.

Then the readers are asked true-false questions such as

T F   Ken liked a dog.
T F   Ken liked a fighter.

Readers having longer phonological loops answered most such questions correctly; readers having shorter phonological loops had more trouble (Miyake, Just, & Carpenter, 1994). Many words in the English language have several unrelated meanings (for example, boxer, bass, tire, court). When we read such a word, we have to wait until the context of the sentence identifies the correct meaning of the word. In the "Ken" sentences above, the context remained ambiguous about the meaning of "boxer" until eight words later. By that time, readers with a shorter phonological loop had already had to guess which was the correct meaning of *boxer*.

CONCEPT CHECK

5. Would readers who have a shorter phonological loop show greater reading comprehension in English, which has many words with two or more meanings, or in Italian, which has few such words? (Check your answer on page 279.)

OTHER MEMORY DISTINCTIONS

In addition to distinguishing between long-term memory and either short-term memory or working memory, psychologists also sometimes find it useful to distinguish among long-term memories for different kinds of information. In particular, many psychologists distinguish **semantic memory,** memory for factual information, from **episodic memory,** memory for specific events in a person's life

Episodic memories pertain to particular events, such as the outcome of a recent tennis match. Semantic memories pertain to facts and principles, such as the rules of tennis.

(Tulving, 1989). For example, your memory of the rules of tennis is a semantic memory; your memory of the most recent time you played tennis is an episodic memory. Your memory of the principles of chemistry is a semantic memory; your recollections of what happened during your high-school chemistry course are episodic memories.

Episodic memories are in many cases much more fragile than are semantic memories. For example, people sometimes remember some fact they have heard (a semantic memory) but forget when, where, and from whom they heard it (an episodic memory). That phenomenon is known as **source amnesia,** remembering the content but not where or how one learned the content. Source amnesia is partly responsible for the *sleeper effect,* an interesting phenomenon we shall examine in more detail in Chapter 16: Sometimes someone hears an idea and immediately discards it because it came from an unreliable source. Days or weeks later, the person remembers the idea but forgets the source. "Did I read about this in *Scientific American* or in the *National Enquirer*? Did I hear it from my professor or from *Ren and Stimpy*? Was it in my textbook or did I just imagine it?" Someone who does not remember that the source was unreliable may regard the idea itself as reasonable. In this manner, a suggestion that seemed to be ineffective at first may become more persuasive over time (Johnson, Hashtroudi, & Lindsay, 1993; Riccio, 1994).

a suggestion that seemed to be ineffective at first may become more persuasive over time because you can't remember that the source was unreliable

CONCEPT CHECK

6. *Is your memory of your current mailing address a semantic memory or an episodic memory? What about your memory of the events of moving to your current address? (Check your answers on page 279.)*

RETROSPECT

Although researchers still disagree with one another on many points concerning memory, they agree on what memory is *not*: Memory is not a single store into which we simply dump things and later take them out. When Ebbinghaus conducted his studies of memory in the late 1800s, he thought he was measuring the properties of memory, period. We now know that the properties of memory depend on the type of material being memorized, the individual's experience with similar materials, and the method of testing. We know also that short-term or working memory is quite different from long-term memory. Memory is not one process, but many.

memory is not a single store into which we dump things + later take them out

Properties of memory
type of material memorized
individuals experience w/ similar material
method of testing

SUMMARY

• *Ebbinghaus's approach.* Hermann Ebbinghaus pioneered the experimental study of memory by testing his own ability to memorize and retain lists of nonsense syllables. Although the general principles he reported were valid, his measurements of the speed of learning and forgetting do not apply to all memory. (page 266)

• *Variations in memory strength.* People remember material best if they have minimal interference from similar materials, if the material is meaningful and distinctive, and if the method of testing is one that is capable of detecting a weak memory. (page 267)

• *The information-processing model.* Psychologists distinguish among various types of memory. According to the information-processing model of memory, information is stored first as short-term memories and later processed to become long-term memories. (page 270)

• *Memory capacity.* Short-term memory has a capacity of only about seven items in nor-mal adults, although chunking enables us to store much information in each item. Long-term memory has a very large, not easily measured capacity. (page 273)

• *Weaknesses of the traditional information-processing model.* Contrary to what psychologists once believed, how long an item remains in short-term memory is a poor predictor of whether it will enter long-term memory. Furthermore, some people with a defective short-term memory have a normal long-term memory. Evidently short-term memory is not simply a holding station on the way to long-term memory. (page 275)

• *Working memory.* As an alternative to the traditional description of short-term memory, some researchers identify working memory as a system for storing and processing several kinds of current information. (page 276)

• *Semantic and episodic memories.* An additional distinction is drawn between semantic memories (memories of facts and knowledge) and episodic memories (memories of personal experiences). (page 277)

SUGGESTION FOR FURTHER READING

Baddeley, A. (1990). *Human memory: Theory and practice.* Boston: Allyn and Bacon. Careful development of the concept of working memory and a review of research on the properties of memory.

TERMS

nonsense syllable a meaningless three-letter combination (page 266)

proactive interference the hindrance an older memory produces on a newer one (page 267)

retroactive interference the impairment a newer memory produces on an older one (page 267)

von Restorff effect tendency to remember the distinctive or unusual items on a list better than other items (page 269)

recall method of testing memory by asking someone to produce a certain item (such as a word) (page 269)

cued recall method of testing memory by asking someone to remember a certain item after being given a hint (page 269)

recognition method of testing memory by asking someone to choose the correct item from a set of alternatives (page 269)

savings method or **relearning method** method of testing memory by measuring how much faster someone can relearn something learned in the past than something being learned for the first time (page 269)

information-processing model view that information is processed, coded, and stored in various ways in human memory as it is in a computer (page 270)

sensory store a very brief storage of sensory information (page 271)

long-term memory a relatively permanent store of information (page 271)

short-term memory a temporary storage of a limited amount of information (page 271)

chunking process of grouping digits or letters into meaningful sequences (page 273)

consolidation the formation and strengthening of long-term memories (page 275)

working memory a system that processes and works with current information, including three components—a central executive, a phonological loop, and a visuospatial sketchpad (page 276)

semantic memory memory for factual information (page 277)

episodic memory memory for specific events in a person's life (page 277)

source amnesia remembering content but forgetting the manner of learning that content (page 277)

ANSWERS TO CONCEPT CHECKS

1. It is due to proactive interference—interference from memories learned earlier. Much of the difficulty in retrieving long-term memories is due to proactive interference. (page 267)

2. First, the subject learns the response; second, the subject learns the extinction of the response. If the first learning proactively interferes with the later learning, spontaneous recovery will result. (page 267)

3. (a) savings; (b) recall; (c) recognition; (d) cued recall. (page 270)

4. Short-term memory has a capacity limited to about seven items in normal adults, whereas long-term memory has an extremely large capacity (difficult to estimate). Both short-term memory and long-term memory are more rapidly forgotten in the presence of interference. (page 275)

5. Readers with a shorter phonological loop should show greater comprehension of Italian, which will seldom require them to remember a word for a long time before deciding on its meaning. (page 277)

6. Your memory of your current address is a semantic memory. Your memory of the events of moving is an episodic memory. (page 278)

ANSWER TO OTHER QUESTION IN THE TEXT

A. Herman Melville, Susan B. Anthony, Agatha Christie, Mikhail Gorbachev, Ivan Pavlov, Nelson Mandela, Arthur Conan Doyle, Sally Ride, James Kalat, Margaret Mitchell, Wilbur and Orville (page 269)

MEMORY IMPROVEMENT

How can we improve our memory?

Once in a while I cross paths with someone who was a student in one of my classes 10 or more years ago. Sometimes the former student says, "Oh, yeah. I remember you. I remember that time in class when . . . " and then, all too often, he or she describes some trivial event or some stupid joke or funny example I told. I have mixed feelings about all this. I suppose I should be glad that my students remember anything about my class. Still, it would be nice if someday someone said, "Oh, yeah. I remember you. I remember that brilliant lecture you gave about classical conditioning."

The unfortunate fact is, all of us vividly remember a great deal of useless information and sometimes forget more important material. How can we improve our memory?

The short answer is, to improve your memory, improve the way you store the material in the first place. The rest of this module elaborates on that point.

THE INFLUENCE OF EMOTIONAL AROUSAL

Generally, people are likely to remember events that were personally arousing to them. Chances are, you can vividly remember your first day of college, your first kiss, the time your team won the big game, various times when you were extremely frightened or extremely excited. Psychologists have found that many people report very detailed memories of where they were, what they were doing, and even what the weather was when they first heard the news of an assassination, the start of a war, or some major disaster (Brown & Kulik, 1977). (See Figure 7.16.)

People have apparently known for centuries about this influence of arousal on memory. In England in the early 1600s, people did not have the custom of recording the sale of land on paper. (Paper was expensive and most people were illiterate anyway.) In-

FIGURE 7.16
People experience "flashbulb memories" for the details surrounding intense emotional events, such as an earthquake or other natural disaster, a personal tragedy, or hearing of the assassination of a political leader. However, although such memories are intense, they are not always accurate.

stead, residents of the city or village would gather together in a ceremony in which someone announced the sale and instructed everyone to remember it. The children's memory was especially important, because they would live the longest. To increase the chance that the children would remember, the adults would kick the children while telling them of the business deal. (Avoiding such abuse is just another of the benefits of literacy.)

Unfortunately, although emotional intensity increases the vividness and intensity of a memory, it does not guarantee the memory's accuracy. One investigator asked people in England to remember the moment they first heard about the Hillsborough soccer disaster, in which a stampede of fans trying to enter the stadium crushed 95 people to death. Large numbers of people claimed to remember clearly the moment when they first heard about the disaster, but as time passed after the disaster, their "vivid" memories changed (Wright, 1993). So, emotionally charged memories are subject to change and distortion, just as other memories are.

Why are emotionally arousing events so memorable (even if the memories are not always accurate)? First, emotionally exciting events stimulate certain kinds of norepinephrine synapses in the brain, known as β-adrenergic synapses, which enhance memory storage. Drugs that block those synapses decrease the storage of emotionally exciting events (Cahill, Prins, Weber, & McGaugh, 1994). Second, exciting experiences arouse your sympathetic nervous system, increasing the conversion of stored glycogen into glucose (a sugar) and therefore raising the level of blood glucose (McGaugh, 1990). Recall from Chapter 3 that glucose is the brain's primary fuel; elevating the glucose level facilitates brain functioning.

Is it possible to enhance your memory by taking drugs that stimulate β-adrenergic synapses? In principle, maybe; however, such drugs produce unwanted side effects. Could you enhance your memory by increasing your blood glucose levels? Yes, and in fact such benefits have been demonstrated in laboratory animals (Gold, 1987; Hall & Gold, 1990; Lee, Graham, & Gold, 1988). However, it is not easy to raise blood glucose levels for long without causing medical problems. Simply eating carbohydrates has only brief effects; the body compensates for in-

creased sugar intake by mobilizing hormones that convert the excess carbohydrates into fats.

MEANINGFUL STORAGE AND LEVELS OF PROCESSING

Long-term memories are not all alike. For example, I assume you can always remember your own name without hesitation; you can probably remember the name of your tenth-grade math teacher with a little more effort; and you may need still greater effort and a few good hints in order to recall the name of the current U.S. Secretary of Agriculture.

According to the levels-of-processing principle (Craik & Lockhart, 1972), we store some memories in a way that makes them easy to retrieve and others in a way that makes them harder to retrieve, depending on the number and types of associations we form. When you read something—this chapter, for example—you might simply read over the words, giving them no more thought than necessary to complete your reading assignment. In that case, you have engaged in shallow processing and whatever memories you store will be hard to retrieve if you try to remember the chapter later. Alternatively, you might stop and think about various points that you read, relate them to your own experiences, and think of your own examples of the principles discussed. The more ways you think about the material, the deeper your processing and the more easily you will remember the material later. Table 7.3 summarizes this model.

Here is one example of the effects of shallow processing: Figure 7.17 shows a real U.S. penny and 14 fakes. Chances are, you

TABLE 7.3
Levels-of-Processing Model of Memory

Superficial processing	Simply repeat the material to be remembered: "Hawk, Oriole, Tiger, Timberwolf, Blue Jay, Bull."
Deeper processing	Think about each item. Note that two start with T and two with B.
Still deeper processing	Note that three are birds and three are mammals. Also, three are major-league baseball teams, and three are NBA basketball teams.

Handwritten margin notes:
① Emotionally charged memories are subject to change + distortion

why arousing events memorable:
① Drugs that block those synapses decrease the storage of emotionally excited events
② Exciting experiences arouse your sympathetic Nervous system, ↑ the conversion of stored glycogen into glucose ↑ the level of blood glucose

Not easy to ↑ blood glucose w/out side effects

levels of processing principle:
we store some memories in a way thats easy to retrieve + others that are harder to retrieve depend of # classes we form.

Read Chapter + understanding

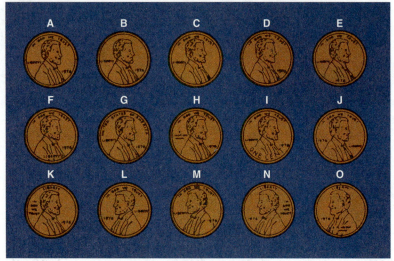

A   B   C   D   E
F   G   H   I   J
K   L   M   N   O

FIGURE 7.17

Can you spot the genuine penny among 14 fakes? (Based on Nickerson & Adams, 1979.) If you're not sure (and you don't have a penny with you), check answer B on page 288.

relationships among the items. You might notice, for example, that the list consists of five animals, six foods, four methods of transportation, and five objects made of wood.

In the United States and in Europe, few young children organize their list-learning this way, whereas most teenagers and adults do. Does that difference reflect some sort of overall intellectual maturation, or does it reflect the influence of schooling? To answer that question, we have to look at a culture in which not all children go to school. According to one study of Kpelle children in West Africa, teenage children who had gone to school organized a list of words into categories, such as foods, types of clothing, and hunting materials. Unschooled children did not sort the list into categories, and generally did not remember words on the list very well (Scribner, 1974).

have examined countless pennies countless times without giving their structure much thought. Can you now identify the real penny? In one study (Nickerson & Adams, 1979), only 15 of 36 U.S. citizens chose the correct coin. (If you do not have a penny in your pocket, check answer B on page 288.) In short, shallow processing of a stimulus does not produce a strong memory.

For an example of contrasting shallow versus deeper levels of processing, imagine several groups of students who study a list of 20 words in several ways. One group simply reads the list over and over, producing a very shallow level of processing (Greene, 1987a). A second group counts the letters in each word. This is also a superficial level of processing, because it does not focus on the meaning of the words. A third group tries to think of a synonym for each word or tries to use each word in a sentence. As they think about the words, they store them at a deeper level of processing. Even though all the students spent the same amount of time studying the list, the third group remembers the words far better than the other two. That is, the deeper the level of processing, the easier it is to recall the material.

If you are trying to memorize, say, a list of words, you can improve your level of processing in either of two ways (Einstein & Hunt, 1980; McDaniel, Einstein, & Lollis, 1988). First, you can think about each individual item. Second, you can look for

When Mozart was a boy he visited the Vatican, where he heard a performance of a piece of music. The next day he had a handwritten score of the piece. The pope was furious, because he had decreed that no one could copy the score of that music. Mozart had written down the entire piece from memory—eight voice parts—after one hearing. The pope was so impressed, he awarded him a medal.

[Handwritten margin notes:]
Shallow processing doesn't produce a strong memory.

The deeper the level of processing the easier to recall.

2 ways of remembering a list:
1.) Think of ea. individual item
2.) Look for relationship among words.

7. Some students who read a chapter slowly get very good grades; others get poor grades. Why?

8. Most actors and public speakers who have to memorize lengthy passages spend little time simply repeating the words and more time thinking about them. Why? (Check your answers on page 288.)

People need to monitor their understanding of a text to decide whether to keep studying or whether they already understand it well enough. Most readers have trouble making that judgment correctly.

SELF-MONITORING OF UNDERSTANDING

Whenever you are studying a text, you periodically have to decide, "Should I keep on studying this section, or do I already understand it well enough?" Most students have trouble monitoring their own understanding. In one study, psychology instructors asked their students before each test to guess whether they would do better or worse on that test than they usually do. Students also guessed after each test whether they had done better or worse than usual. Most students' guesses were no more accurate than chance (Sjostrom & Marks, 1994). Such inaccuracy represents a problem: Students who do not know how well they understand the material will make bad judgments about when to keep on studying and when to quit.

Even when you are reading a single sentence, you have to decide whether you understand the sentence or whether you should stop and reread it. Here is a sentence once published in the student newspaper at North Carolina State University:

He said Harris told him she and Brothers told French that grades had been changed.

Ordinarily, when good readers come to such a confusing sentence, they notice their own confusion and reread the sentence or, if necessary, the whole paragraph. Poor readers tend to read at their same speed for both easy and difficult materials; they are less likely than good readers to slow down when they come to difficult sentences.

Although monitoring one's own understanding is difficult and often inaccurate, it is not impossible. For example, suppose I tell you that you are to read three chapters dealing with, say, thermodynamics, the history of volleyball, and the Japanese stock market.

Later you will take tests on each chapter. Before you start reading, predict your approximate scores on the three tests. Most people make a guess based on how much they already know about the three topics. If we let them read the three chapters and again make a guess about their test performances, they do in fact make more accurate predictions than they did before reading (Maki & Serra, 1992). That improvement indicates some ability to monitor one's own understanding of a text.

A systematic way to monitor your own understanding of a text is the SPAR method: Survey, Process meaningfully, Ask questions, and Review and test yourself. Start with an overview of what a passage is about, read it carefully, and then see whether you can answer questions about the passage or explain it to others. If not, go back and reread.

THE TIMING OF STUDY

Other things being equal, people tend to remember recent experiences better than earlier experiences. For example, suppose someone reads you a list of 20 words and asks you to recall as many of them as possible. The list is far too long for you to recite from your phonological loop; however, you should be able to remember at least a few. Typically, people remember items at the beginning and end of the list better than they remember those in the middle.

That tendency, known as the serial-order effect, includes two aspects: The *primacy effect* is the tendency to remember the first items; the *recency effect* refers to the tendency to remember the last items. One explanation for the primacy effect is that the listener gets to rehearse the first few items for a few moments alone with no interference from the others. One explanation for the recency effect is that the last items are still in

[handwritten margin notes:]
Students have trouble monitoring their own understanding

A way to monitor understanding:
SPAR method
Survey, Process, Ask, & Review

People remember recent experiences better than earlier experience

Serial-order effect:
① Primacy effect: remember 1st items
② recency effect - remember last items

the listener's phonological loop at the time of the test.

The phonological loop cannot be the whole explanation for the recency effect, however. In one study, British rugby players were asked to name the teams they had played against in the current season. Players were most likely to remember the last couple of teams they had played against, thus showing a clear recency effect even though they were recalling events that occurred weeks apart (Baddeley & Hitch, 1977). (The phonological loop holds information only for a matter of seconds.)

So, studying material—or, rather, *reviewing* material—shortly before a test is likely to improve recall. Now let's consider the opposite: Suppose you studied something years ago and have not reviewed it since then. For example, suppose you studied a foreign language in high school several years ago. Now you are considering taking a college course in the language, but you are hesitant because you are sure you have forgotten it all. Have you?

Harry Bahrick (1984) tested people who had studied Spanish in school 1 to 50 years previously. Nearly all agreed that they had rarely used Spanish and had not refreshed their memories at all since their school days. (That is a disturbing comment, but beside the point.) Their retention of Spanish dropped noticeably in the first 3 to 6 years, but remained fairly stable from then on (Fig-

ure 7.18). In other words, we do not completely forget even very old memories that we seldom use.

In a later study, Bahrick and members of his family studied foreign-language vocabulary either on a moderately frequent basis (practicing once every 2 weeks) or on a less frequent basis (as seldom as once every 8 weeks), and tested their knowledge years later. The result: More frequent study led to faster learning; however, less frequent study led to better long-term retention, measured years later (Bahrick, Bahrick, Bahrick, & Bahrick, 1993).

The principle here is far more general than just the study of foreign languages. *If you want to remember something well for a test,* your best strategy is to study it as close as possible to the time of the test, in order to take advantage of the recency effect and decrease the effects of retroactive interference. Obviously, I do not mean that you should wait until the night before the test to start studying, but you might rely on an extensive review at that time. You should also, ideally, study under conditions similar to the conditions of the test. For example, you might study in the same room where the test will be given, or at the same time of day.

However, *if you want to remember something long after the test is over,* then the advice I have just given you is all wrong. To be able to remember something when-

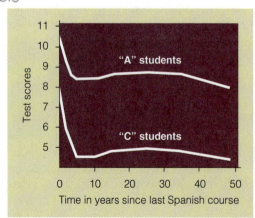

FIGURE 7.18
(Left) Spanish vocabulary as measured by a recognition test shows a rapid decline in the first few years but then long-term stability. (From Bahrick, 1984.) (Right) Within a few years after taking your last foreign-language course, you may think you have forgotten it all. You have not, and even the part you have forgotten will come back (through relearning) if you visit a country where you can practice the language.

ever you want, wherever you are, and whatever you are doing, you should study it under as varied circumstances as possible. Study and review at various times and places with long, irregular intervals between study sessions. Studying under such inconsistent conditions will slow down your original learning, but it will improve your ability to recall it long afterwards (Schmidt & Bjork, 1992).

CONCEPT CHECKS

9. The results shown in Figure 7.18 demonstrate how well people recall the Spanish they studied years ago. Might they actually remember more than this figure indicates? If so, how might you determine how much more they remember?

10. If you want to do well on the final exam in this course, which should you do now, review this chapter or review the first three chapters in the book? (Check your answers on page 288.)

THE USE OF SPECIAL CODING STRATEGIES

A librarian who places a new book on the shelf also enters some information into the retrieval system, so that library users can find the book if they know the title, author, or topic of the book. Similarly, when you store a memory, you store it in terms of **retrieval cues**, associated information that might help you regain the memory later. We shall examine two illustrations of retrieval cues, the encoding specificity effect and the use of mnemonic devices.

ENCODING SPECIFICITY

At the time you learn something, the associations you form with the learned material become retrieval cues that could remind you of the material later. According to the **encoding specificity principle** (Tulving & Thomson, 1973), the associations you form at the time of learning will be effective retrieval cues; other associations will be less effective or ineffective (Figure 7.19).

Here is an example of encoding specificity (modified from Thieman, 1984). First, read the pairs of words (in psychological jargon, *paired associates*) in Table 7.4a. Then turn to Table 7.4b on page 286. For each of

TABLE 7.4a		
Clergyman	—	Cardinal
Trinket	—	Charm
Social event	—	Ball
Shrubbery	—	Bush
Inches	—	Feet
Take a test	—	Pass
Weather	—	Fair
Geometry	—	Plane
Tennis	—	Racket
Stone	—	Rock
Magic	—	Spell
Envelope	—	Seal
Cashiers	—	Checkers

the words on the list there, try to recall a related word from the second column of Table 7.4a. *Do this now.*

The answers are on page 288, answer C. Most people find this task difficult and make only a few of the correct pairings. Because they initially coded the word *cardinal* as a type of clergyman, for example, the retrieval cue *bird* does not remind them of the word *cardinal*. The cue *bird* is most effective for people who think of *cardinal* as a bird at the time of storage. In short, you can improve

FIGURE 7.19
According to the principle of encoding specificity, the way we code a word during original learning determines which cues will remind us of that word later. For example, when you hear the word queen, *you may think of that word in any of several ways. If you think of* queen bee, *then the cue* playing card *will not remind you of it later. If you think of the* Queen of England, *then* chess piece *will not be a good reminder.*

MEMORY IMPROVEMENT

285

① mnemonic device!
any memory aid that
is based on encoding
ea. item in some
special way.

- literary story
- method of loci
 (method of places)

- peg method
 form mental images
 to link the names
 w/ peg words

TABLE 7.4b

Instructions: For each of these words, write a related word that you remember from the second column of the list in Table 7.4a.

Exhibition	_____
Animal	_____
Part of body	_____
Transportation	_____
Football	_____
Crime	_____
Former U.S. president	_____
Music	_____
Personality	_____
Write	_____
Bird	_____
Board game	_____
Sports	_____

Nobel Peace Prize Winners

1901	H. Dunant and F. Passy
1902	E. Ducommun and A. Gobat
1903	Sir W. R. Cremer
1904	Institute of International Law
1905	Baroness von Suttner
1906	T. Roosevelt
1907	E. T. Moneta and L. Renault
1908	K. P. Arnoldson and F. Bajer
1909	A. M. F. Beernaert and Baron d'Estournelles de Constant
1910	International Peace Bureau
1911	T. M. C. Asser and A. H. Fried

1957	L. B. Pearson
1958	G. Pire
1959	P. J. Noel-Baker
1960	A. Luthuli
1961	D. Hammarskjöld (posthumously)
1962	L. Pauling (awarded 1963)

1990	M. Gorbachev
1991	A. S. Suu Kyi
1992	Rigoberta Menchu
1993	Yasir Arafat, Yitzhak Rabin, and Shimon Peres
1994	Nelson Mandela and Frederik W. de Klerk

FIGURE 7.20
A list of Nobel Peace Prize winners. Mnemonic devices can be useful when people try to memorize long lists like this one.

your memory by storing information in terms of retrieval cues and by using the same retrieval cues when you try to recall the information.

MNEMONIC DEVICES

If you had to memorize something lengthy and not altogether meaningful—for example, a list of all the bones in the body—what would you do? One effective strategy is to attach systematic retrieval cues to each term, so that you can remind yourself of the terms when you need them.

A **mnemonic device** is any memory aid that is based on encoding each item in some special way. The word *mnemonic* ("nee-MAHN-ik") comes from a Greek root meaning "memory." (The same root appears in the word *amnesia,* "lack of memory.")

Mnemonic devices come in many varieties. Some are simple, as in thinking up a little story that reminds you of each item to be remembered (such as "Every Good Boy Does Fine" to remember the notes E G B D F on the musical staff). Suppose you had to memorize the list of Nobel Peace Prize winners (Figure 7.20). You might try making up a little story: "Dun (Dunant) passed (Passy) the Duke (Ducommun) of Gob (Gobat) some cream (Cremer). That made him internally ILL (Institute of International Law). He suited (von Suttner) up with some roses (Roosevelt) and spent some money (Moneta) on a Renault (Renault). . . ." You still have to study the names, but your story might help you to remember them all in order.

Another effective **mnemonic device is the method of loci** (method of places). First you memorize a series of places and then you use some vivid image to associate each of these locations with something you want to remember. For example, you might start by memorizing every location along the route from your dormitory room to, say, your psychology classroom. Then you link the locations, in order, to the names.

For example, suppose the first three locations you pass are the desk in your room, the door to your room, and the corridor. You should first form a mental image linking the first pair of Nobel Peace Prize winners, Dunant and Passy, to the first location, your desk. You might imagine a Monopoly game board on your desk, with a big sign "DO NOT (Dunant) PASS (Passy) GO." Then you link the second pair of names to the second location, your door: A DUKE (as in Ducommun) is standing at the door, giving confusing signals. He says "DO COME IN (Ducommun)" and "GO BACK (Gobat)." Then you link the corridor to Cremer, perhaps by imagining someone has spilled CREAM (Cremer) all over the floor (Figure 7.21). You continue in this manner until you have linked every name to a location. Now, if you can remember all those locations in order and if you have imagined good images for each one, you can recite the list of Nobel Peace Prize winners.

A similar mnemonic device is called the **peg method.** You start by memorizing a list of objects, such as "One is a bun, two is a shoe, three is a tree, . . ." Then you form mental images to link the names with these peg words, just as you would with the method of loci. For example, for number one, "I ate a BUN at the DUNE PASS (Dunant, Passy)," imagining *dune pass* as a passageway between sand dunes. Later you use all your peg words to help remember the list of names. One trouble with the method of loci and the peg method is the difficulty of thinking of good images for all the items. (What image can you devise for Nobel Peace Prize winner Gorbachev?)

How useful are elaborate mnemonic devices, such as the method of loci or the peg method? That depends. Such devices can be very helpful for memorizing long lists of unrelated words in order, or for competing in the World Memory Championship. Some people find such devices useful for remembering people's names. (For example, you might remember someone named Harry Moore by picturing him as "more hairy" than everyone else.) However, few people find mnemonics helpful for everyday tasks such as remembering your school assignments or remembering to meet your friend at Heathrow airport.

FIGURE 7.21
The method of loci is one of the oldest mnemonic devices. First learn a list of places, such as "my desk, the door of my room, the corridor, . . ." Then link each of these places to the items on a list of words or names, such as a list of the names of Nobel Peace Prize winners.

understand. Self-monitoring is difficult but not impossible, and people can learn techniques to improve their self-monitoring. (page 283)

- *Timing of study.* Studying under consistent conditions as close as possible to the time of the test will increase memory on the test. However, reviewing under varied conditions at long, irregular intervals is better for establishing memories that will be available at varied times and places. (page 283)

- *Encoding specificity.* When we form a memory, we store it with links to the way we thought about it at that time. When we try to recall the memory, a cue is most effective if it is similar to the links we formed at the time of storage. (page 285)

- *Mnemonics.* Specialized techniques for establishing systematic retrieval cues can help people remember ordered lists of names or terms. (page 286)

SUGGESTION FOR FURTHER READING

Cermak, L. S. (1975). *Improving your memory.* New York: McGraw-Hill. A lively book about mnemonic devices and other ways to improve memory.

TERMS

levels-of-processing **principle** concept that the number and types of associations established

SUMMARY

- *Emotional arousal.* Emotionally exciting events tend to be remembered vividly, if not always accurately. Such events stimulate β-adrenergic synapses in the brain and act to increase blood glucose levels. (page 280)

- *Levels-of-processing principle.* According to the levels-of-processing principle, a memory becomes stronger (and easier to recall) if we think about the meaning of the material and relate it to other material. (page 281)

- *Self-monitoring of understanding.* Good readers check their own understanding of a text and slow down or reread when they do not during learning determines the ease of later retrieval of a memory (page 281)

SPAR method a systematic way to monitor and improve understanding of a text by surveying, processing meaningfully, asking questions, and reviewing (page 283)

serial-order effect tendency to remember the first and last items on a list better than those in the middle (page 283)

retrieval cue information associated with remembered material, which can be useful in helping to recall that material (page 285)

encoding specificity principle tendency for the associations formed at the time of learning to be more effective retrieval cues than are other associations (page 285)

mnemonic device any memory aid that is based on encoding each item in some special way (page 286)

method of loci mnemonic device that calls for linking the items on a list with a memorized list of places (page 286)

peg method mnemonic device in which a person first memorizes a list of objects and then forms mental images linking those objects to a list of names to be memorized (page 287)

ANSWERS TO CONCEPT CHECKS

7. The results depend on why the students are slow readers. Students who read slowly because they have trouble understanding the material are likely to get poor grades. Students who read slowly because they frequently pause to think about the meaning of the material are engaging in deep processing and are likely to remember the material well, probably better than those who read through the material quickly. (page 283)

8. Simply repeating the words would produce a shallow level of processing and poor retention. A more efficient means of memorizing is to spend most of one's time thinking about the meaning of the speech and only a little time actually memorizing the words. (page 283)

9. People would remember even more if they were tested by the recognition method, as Bahrick (1984) demonstrated. (page 285)

10. To prepare well for the final exam, you should review all the material at irregular intervals. Thus, you might profit by skimming over chapters 2 and 3 right now. Of course, if you have a test on Chapter 7 a day or two from now, your goal is different and your strategy should be different. (page 285)

ANSWERS TO OTHER QUESTIONS IN THE TEXT

B. The correct coin is A. (page 282)

C. (page 285)

Exhibition	Fair
Animal	Seal
Part of body	Feet
Transportation	Plane
Football	Pass
Crime	Racket
Former U.S. president	Bush
Music	Rock
Personality	Charm
Write	Spell
Bird	Cardinal
Board game	Checkers
Sports	Ball

MEMORY LOSS

What are some causes of memory loss?
What do various types of memory loss teach us about memory?

Computer operators are advised to protect their computers from strong magnetic fields. Suppose you defied that advice and passed your computer through the strongest magnetic field you could find. Chances are, you would thereby erase all the memory in your computer. But suppose you didn't; what if it erased all of the text files but none of the graphics files? Or what if it left all the old memories intact but made it impossible to store new ones? You would in the process learn something about how your computer's memory works.

The same is true of human memory. Passing your head through a magnet would not erase your memories. (At least not with ordinary magnets; I can't promise what would happen at extreme levels.) Other kinds of damage, however, do impair memory and produce different effects on different kinds of memories. The study of severe memory losses contributes much to our understanding of memory.

"NORMAL" FORGETTING

Already in this chapter we have encountered several of the possible reasons why all of us forget from time to time. Let us review.

One explanation of forgetting is interference. For example, sports fans ordinarily forget the details of a game they saw a month ago or a year ago, largely because of interference from memories of all the games they saw before it (proactive interference) and af-

ter it (retroactive interference). You probably remember well many of your most unusual or highly distinctive experiences; the details would blur if you now had a number of similar experiences.

An alternative explanation of forgetting is the idea that memory traces gradually decay, like old photographs that fade in the sunlight. The effects of decay and interference are difficult to disentangle experimentally. That is, any delay necessarily includes some experiences that could produce interference. Nevertheless, researchers have considered decay as a reasonable possibility to explain forgetting from working memory, because some information in the phonological loop disappears within seconds if it is not rehearsed. Decay is a less popular explanation of forgetting from long-term memory, because some long-term memories remain available after years without use. That is, not all long-term memories fade.

A third possible explanation is that memories seem to be forgotten because we no longer have the appropriate retrieval cues. For example, if you learned certain facts in an eighth-grade geography class, the retrieval cues included not only the content (discussions of rivers, mountains, and continents), but also the context of when and where you learned it (the classroom, the city,

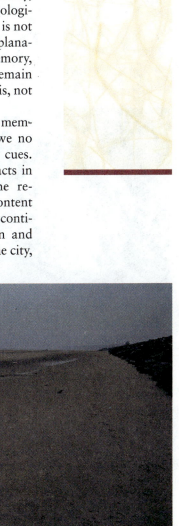

Bob Williams was one of 40 aging former paratroopers who reenacted his parachute jump on the 50th anniversary of D-Day. Ordinarily we forget most events from 50 years ago. However, this was a distinctive, emotionally arousing event, followed by very few other experiences that were similar enough to produce interference. Returning to the scene of the original jump provides contextual cues that would help to retrieve the memory.

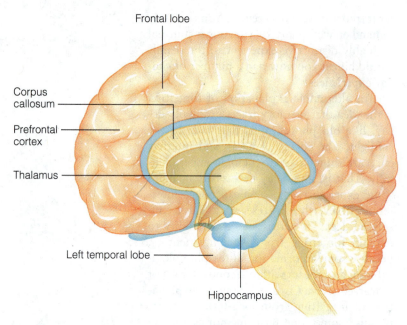

Frontal lobe

Corpus callosum

Prefrontal cortex

Thalamus

Left temporal lobe

Hippocampus

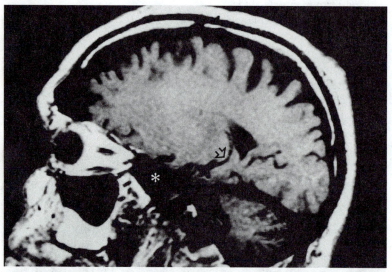

FIGURE 7.22

The hippocampus is a large subcortical structure of the brain. After damage to the hippocampus and related structures, patient H. M. had great trouble storing new long-term memories. The photo shows a scan of the brain of H. M. formed by magnetic resonance imaging. The * indicates the area from which the hippocampus is missing. The arrow indicates a portion of the hippocampus that is preserved. (Photo courtesy of Suzanne Corkin and David Amaral.)

the other students around you). Years later, if you try to remember those facts, you do not have the contextual cues to help remind you. Sometimes if people return to the place where they learned something (at least in their imagination), they remember information that they thought they had forgotten.

AMNESIA AFTER BRAIN DAMAGE

In contrast to normal forgetting, **amnesia** is a severe loss or deterioration of memory. Even in the most severe cases of amnesia, people do not forget everything they have ever learned. They may lose one kind of memory while performing normally on another kind. The specific deficits of amnesic patients tell us much about the types of memory that people have. We shall consider amnesia based on several types of brain damage, plus amnesia of infancy and old age.

THE CASE OF H. M., A MAN WITH HIPPOCAMPAL DAMAGE

In 1953 a man with the initials H. M. was subjected to unusual brain surgery in an attempt to control his extreme epilepsy. H. M., who had failed to respond to antiepileptic drugs, had suffered such frequent and severe seizures that he was unable to keep a job or live a normal life. As a last resort, surgeons removed from his brain the **hippocampus** and several neighboring structures (Figure 7.22), where they believed his epileptic seizures were originating. Although the surgeons did not know what to expect from the operation, they acted in the belief that desperate cases call for desperate measures.

The results of the surgery were favorable in some regards. H. M.'s epileptic seizures decreased in frequency and severity. His personality and intellect remained the same; in fact, his IQ score increased slightly after the operation, presumably because of the decreased epileptic interference.

However, he suffered severe memory problems (Corkin, 1984; Milner, 1959), particularly a massive **anterograde** (ANT-eh-ro-grade) **amnesia** (inability to store new long-term memories). For years after the operation, he gave the year as 1953 and his own age as 27. Later, he took wild guesses (Corkin, 1984). He would read the same issue of a magazine repeatedly without realizing that he had read it before. He could not even remember where he had lived for the last few years. He also suffered a moderate **retrograde amnesia** for long-term factual memories (loss of memory for events that occurred shortly prior to the brain damage; see Figure 7.23). That is, he had some trouble recalling events that happened within the last 1

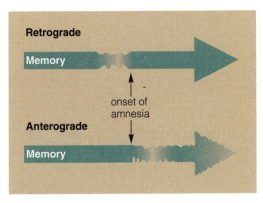

FIGURE 7.23
Retrograde amnesia is loss of memory for events in a certain period before brain damage or some other trauma. Anterograde amnesia is a difficulty forming new memories after some trauma.

to 3 years before the operation, although he could recall still older events. He could form normal short-term memories, such as repeating a brief list of items, and if he was permitted to rehearse them without distraction, he could even retain the list of items for several minutes. He could also learn new skills, as we shall see in a moment. Researchers have reported deficits similar to those of H. M. in other people with hippocampal damage and (temporarily) in normal people who have taken large doses of certain drugs, including tranquilizers (Polster, 1993).

H. M. is a modern Rip van Winkle who becomes more and more out of date with each passing year (Gabrieli, Cohen, & Corkin, 1988; M. L. Smith, 1988). He does not recognize the names or faces of people who became famous after the mid-1950s. He could not name the president of the United States even when Ronald Reagan was president, though he remembered Reagan as an actor from before 1953. He does not understand the meaning of words that entered the English language after the time of his surgery. For example, he guessed that *biodegradable* means "two grades," that *soul food* means "forgiveness," and that a *closet queen* is a "moth." For H. M., watching the evening news is like visiting another planet.

In spite of H. M.'s massive memory difficulties, he can acquire new skills and retain them later. We refer to skill retention as **procedural memory,** in contrast to **declarative memory,** the ability to recall factual information. For example, H. M. has learned to read

material written in mirror fashion (Cohen & Squire, 1980):

with the words reversed like this

Although he has learned to read mirror writing, he does not remember having learned it. He has also learned a simple finger maze, and he has learned the correct solution to the Tower of Hanoi puzzle shown in Figure 7.24 (Cohen, Eichenbaum, Deacedo, & Corkin, 1985). He does not *remember* learning these skills, however. He claims he has never seen any of these tasks before, and he is always a bit surprised by his success.

FRONTAL-LOBE AMNESIA

Amnesia can also arise after damage to the frontal lobes, especially the prefrontal cortex (Figure 7.22). Because the frontal lobes receive a great deal of input from the hippocampus, the symptoms of frontal-lobe damage overlap those of hippocampal damage. However, frontal-lobe damage produces some special memory impairments of its own.

Frontal-lobe damage can be the result of a stroke or of trauma to the head. Frontal-lobe deterioration is also commonly associated with **Korsakoff's syndrome,** also known as the *alcohol amnestic disorder,* a condition caused by a prolonged deficiency of vitamin B_1, usually as a result of chronic alcoholism. The vitamin deficiency leads to a loss or shrinkage of neurons in many parts of the brain, especially the prefrontal cortex and parts of the thalamus. Patients suffer

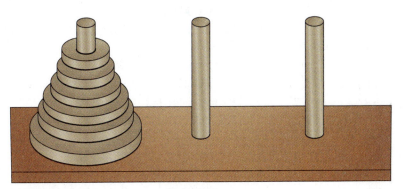

FIGURE 7.24
In the Tower of Hanoi puzzle, the task is to transfer all the disks to another peg, moving only one at a time and never placing a larger disk onto a smaller disk. Patient H. M. learned the correct strategy and retained it from one test period to another, although he did not remember ever seeing the task before. That is, he showed procedural memory but not declarative memory.

Suffer from retrograde + anterograde amnesia

Can't remember when & where various events took place.

Confabulations - attempts to fill in the gaps in their memory.

-answer ? s/w info. from past.

frontal lobes are necessary for working w/memory

Alzheimer's disease cerebral cortex, hippocampus & other areas lose cells

multiple impairments of memory, apathy, and confusion (Oscar-Berman, 1980; Squire, Amaral, & Press, 1990). Patients with Korsakoff's syndrome suffer severe retrograde amnesia, generally covering most events beginning about 15 years before the onset of their illness (Squire, Haist, & Shimamura, 1989). They also suffer from anterograde amnesia. If given a list of words to remember, they temporarily remember the words at the end of the list, but they forget the beginning of the list (Stuss et al., 1994). A few minutes later, they forget even the words at the end.

Such patients have particular trouble remembering when and where various events took place (Shimamura, Janowsky, & Squire, 1990). For example, if asked what they ate this morning or what they did last night, they describe something they did sometime in the past. In spite of their severe loss of declarative memories, they acquire new procedural memories reasonably well.

Patients with frontal-lobe damage, whatever the cause, have a characteristic pattern of answering questions with a bewildering mixture of correct information, out-of-date information, and wild guesses. Their guesses, or **confabulations,** are apparent attempts to fill in the gaps in their memory. The result is sometimes self-contradictory or preposterous, as the following example illustrates (Moscovitch, 1989, pp. 135–136):

Psychologist: How old are you?
Patient: I'm 40, 42, pardon me, 62.
Psychologist: Are you married or single?
Patient: Married.
Psychologist: How long have you been married?
Patient: About 4 months.
Psychologist: What's your wife's name?
Patient: Martha.
Psychologist: How many children do you have?
Patient: Four. (He laughs.) Not bad for 4 months.
Psychologist: How old are your children?
Patient: The eldest is 32; his name is Bob. And the youngest is 22; his name is Joe.
Psychologist: How did you get these children in 4 months?
Patient: They're adopted.
Psychologist: Who adopted them?
Patient: Martha and I.

Psychologist: Immediately after you got married you wanted to adopt these older children?
Patient: Before we were married we adopted one of them, two of them. The eldest girl Brenda and Bob, and Joe and Dina since we were married.
Psychologist: Does it all sound a little strange to you, what you are saying?
Patient: I think it is a little strange.
Psychologist: I think when I looked at your record it said that you've been married for over 30 years. Does that sound more reasonable to you if I told you that?
Patient: No.
Psychologist: Do you really believe that you have been married for 4 months?
Patient: Yes.

What accounts for this tendency to confabulation? According to Morris Moscovitch (1992), the frontal lobes are necessary for *working with memory,* the strategies we use to reconstruct memories that we cannot immediately recall. For example, if you are asked who Romeo's girlfriend was, or whether you have ever been to Puerto Rico, you can probably answer at once without any apparent effort. But if you are asked what you did Tuesday evening last week, or if a 62-year-old man is asked how long he has been married, the answer requires some effort and a process of inferring what *must* be true. People with frontal-lobe damage have trouble inferring what must have happened in their past and so they make guesses that other people recognize to be wrong.

ALZHEIMER'S DISEASE

A third example of amnesia caused by brain damage is **Alzheimer's disease,** a degenerative condition that generally occurs in old age. The cerebral cortex, hippocampus, and other areas lose cells, as Figure 7.25 shows (Hyman, van Hoesen, Damasio, & Barnes, 1984). According to one estimate, almost 50% of all people over age 85 develop Alzheimer's (Evans et al., 1989). The symptoms start with minor forgetfulness and progress (sometimes rapidly) to more serious memory loss, confusion, depression, restlessness, hallucinations, delusions, and disturbances of eating, sleeping, and other daily activities (Cummings & Victoroff, 1990). Many Alzheimer's patients are not fully

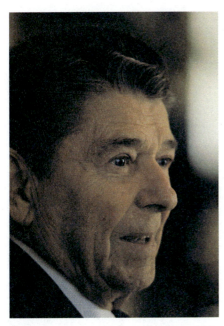

In 1994, former U.S. President Ronald Reagan disclosed that he had Alzheimer's disease. Alzheimer's disease, which severely damages memory, becomes increasingly common as people age.

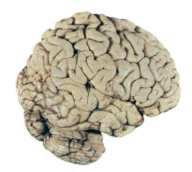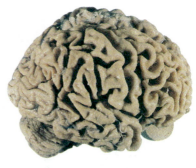

FIGURE 7.25

Compared with a normal brain, the brain of an Alzheimer's patient (right) has significant shrinkage in the cerebral cortex and other areas. As the brain shrinks, patients also show deficits of memory and reasoning.

[handwritten: has both genetic & nongenetic causes]

aware of their own memory loss (McGlynn & Kaszniak, 1991).

Alzheimer's disease has both genetic and nongenetic causes. Researchers have identified at least two genes that increase one's risk of early-onset Alzheimer's disease, with onset before age 60 to 65 (Goate et al., 1991; Murrell, Farlow, Ghetti, & Benson, 1991; Schellenberg et al., 1992), and another gene that increases the risk of late-onset Alzheimer's disease (Corder et al., 1993; Pericak-Vance et al., 1991). However, Alzheimer's disease, especially the late-onset type, often occurs in people with no family history of the disease, and some people who have an identical twin with Alzheimer's fail to get the disease themselves (Nee et al., 1987).

People in an early stage of Alzheimer's disease can recall events from long ago, but they have trouble remembering new information. When one investigator played a round of golf with an Alzheimer's patient (Schacter, 1983), the patient could remember the rules and terminology of golf perfectly well but could not remember how many strokes he had taken on a hole. He often forgot whether he had already teed off or was still waiting his turn. Unless he went directly to his ball after hitting it, he could not remember where it was. He could not say what label was on his ball, although when he

picked up a ball he could recognize whether it was his.

As with other psychological deficits and disorders, researchers would like to find ways to identify Alzheimer's disease in its early stages, before the symptoms become severe. Investigators in one study repeatedly studied a group of people who had close relatives with Alzheimer's disease; many of the studied people also developed the disease. Such people showed a number of mild deficits in memory experiments about a year or two before they started showing symptoms that were troublesome in everyday life. For example, a year or two before they had recognizable Alzheimer's disease, these people learned word lists slowly and failed to show the usual primacy effect—the tendency

People with Alzheimer's disease lose their use of factual memory. Procedural memory is less impaired; those with the disease forget to do things more than they forget how to do them. Posting reminders to turn off appliances is often useful.

TABLE 7.5
Five Ways to Test Memory

	DESCRIPTION	EXAMPLE
Explicit (direct) tests		
Recall	You are asked to say what you remember.	Name the Seven Dwarfs.
Cued recall	You are given significant hints to help you remember.	Name the Seven Dwarfs. Hint: One was always smiling, one was smart, one never talked, one seemed always to have a cold. . . .
Recognition	You are asked to choose the correct item from among several items.	Which of the following were among the Seven Dwarfs: Sneezy, Sleazy, Dopey, Dippy, Hippy, Happy?
Savings (relearning)	You are asked to relearn something: If it takes you less time than when you first learned that material, some memory has persisted.	Try memorizing this list: Sleepy, Sneezy, Doc, Dopey, Grumpy, Happy, Bashful. Can you memorize it faster than this list: Sleazy, Snoopy, Duke, Dippy, Gripey, Hippy, Blushy?
Implicit (indirect) tests		
Priming	You are asked to generate words, without necessarily recognizing them as memories.	You hear the story "Snow White and the Seven Dwarfs." Some time later you are asked to fill in these blanks to make words: __ L __ __ P __ __ __ N __ __ Z __ __ __ C __ O __ E __ __ R __ __ P __ __ __ P P __ __ A __ H __ U __

to remember words at the beginning of the list better than those in the middle (Bondi et al., 1994).

IMPLICIT MEMORY AND ITS PERSISTENCE IN AMNESIC PATIENTS

Although H. M., frontal-lobe patients, and Alzheimer's patients all have severe memory deficits, certain aspects of their memory re-

main almost intact. For example, they acquire new procedural memories. Moreover, although amnesic patients perform poorly on explicit tests of memory (such as recall, cued recall, or recognition), H. M. and frontal-lobe patients perform about normally on *implicit* tests of memory (Shimamura, Salmon, Squire, & Butters, 1987).

The kinds of memory tests we have considered so far—recall, recognition, and so forth—have been tests of **explicit memory**; a person who states the correct answer generally recognizes that it *is* the correct answer. For example, as a reply to the question "Who is your psychology instructor?" you would have to state the name or choose it from a list of choices. In contrast to such explicit or direct tests of memory, a test of implicit or *indirect* memory does not require any conscious recognition of a memory. In fact, the subjects may not even realize that they are taking part in a memory test.

For example, you might read a list of words, including CHAIRMAN, LECTURES, PENDULUM, and DONATION. You read them just once, perhaps not even realizing that you will be tested on them, and when you are asked to repeat the list a few minutes later, you cannot. Then you are asked to fill in the missing letters to make words from the following:

        __HA__R___N
        M___N_T_C
        _E_D_L_M
        _EC__ _R_S
        A___A___IN

You probably will find it easy to fill in the letters for the words you had read (CHAIRMAN, PENDULUM, and LECTURES) but more difficult for the other words (MAGNETIC and ASSASSIN). Reading a word temporarily *primes* the word and increases the chance that you will recognize it in a word fragment (Graf & Mandler, 1984; Schacter, 1987a). Table 7.5 contrasts a test of implicit memory with several ways of testing explicit memory.

Brain-damaged amnesic patients show good evidence of implicit, but not explicit, memory. For example, if they are asked to read a list of words, such as DEFEND, TINSEL, and BATHED, they are later unable to remember any of the words on the list. Then they are given three-letter combinations and asked to complete each stem to make a complete word, any word:

        DEF___   TIN___   BAT___

Instead of coming up with other words that could be built on the stems, frontal-lobe patients and other amnesic patients generally fill in the letters that will form the words on the original list (Schacter, 1985). Somehow these words are "activated" in the patients' brains, even though they insist they do not remember seeing them on the original list. (Some people do not even remember that there *was* a list.)

Figure 7.26 summarizes the relationships among some of the types of memory: Explicit memories can be either declarative or procedural; so can implicit memories. Declarative memories can be either episodic or

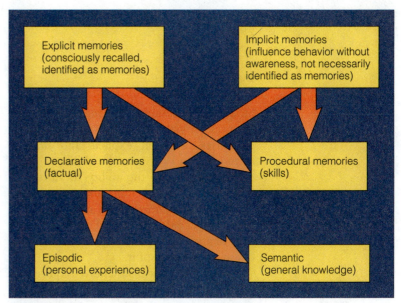

FIGURE 7.26

Psychologists draw several distinctions among types of memories. Explicit memories can be either declarative or procedural; so can implicit memories. Declarative memories can be either episodic or semantic; procedural memories are not divided in that way.

semantic; procedural memories deal with skills and are not described as either episodic or semantic.

CONCEPT CHECKS

11. (a) Is remembering how to tie your shoes a procedural memory or a declarative memory? (b) You remember an event that happened to you the first day of high school. Is that a procedural or a declarative memory?

12. Which of the following is an example of implicit memory?

   a. You read a chapter about Central America and then try to answer some practice questions about it. Although you cannot answer questions in the format, "Name the capital of Honduras," you do answer most of the multiple-choice items correctly.

   b. Two people near you are talking about Central America, and you are paying no attention. After they leave, someone asks you what they had been talking about and you reply that you have no idea. A few minutes later you spontaneously comment, "I wonder what's going on in Central America these days."

13. Which kinds of memory are most impaired in H. M., frontal-lobe patients, and Alzheimer's patients? Which kinds are least impaired? (Check your answers on page 298.)

IMPLICATIONS OF BRAIN-DAMAGE AMNESIA

Studies of amnesic patients highlight the differences between declarative and procedural memories, between explicit and implicit memories, and between the ability to recall old memories and the ability to store new memories. The phenomenon of implicit memory demonstrates that a memory can be active and capable of influencing behavior, at least temporarily, even in a person who is not consciously aware of it.

These memory distinctions require further research, however. Many researchers are not at all sure that they can usefully distinguish between explicit and implicit memories on the basis of whether they require "conscious awareness" (Rudy & Sutherland, 1992). In the future, psychologists may clarify the current distinctions or introduce different ones. The growing consensus, however, is that some sort of distinction is necessary; we have different kinds of memory and not just one.

INFANT AMNESIA

Most adults can remember nothing from before age 3½ years, and only a little from between 3½ and 5. Some can remember earlier events, occasionally even from as early as age 2, but such events are isolated and fragmentary. The relative lack of early memories, known as **infant amnesia** or **childhood amnesia,** is difficult to explain (Howe & Courage, 1993). Infants do form some reasonably long-lasting memories. For example, many 4-year-olds can clearly remember what happened last Christmas and maybe even the Christmas before that, as well as a variety of events from age 3 or earlier. However, those memories are forgotten by the time the child reaches about age 10 or so. By contrast, many memories formed at ages 5 and 6 remain available for a lifetime.

Psychologists have proposed a number of theories to explain infant amnesia, none of them fully convincing. Sigmund Freud's theory was that infant memories are hidden or repressed because of the emotional traumas of infancy. Nevertheless, he claimed, therapists might be able to access those memories

through special techniques. That theory, although historically influential, has little evidence to support it. Patients in therapy do sometimes tell their therapists about events they claim happened in infancy, but it is almost always impossible to demonstrate that those reports represent accurate infant memories, as opposed to guesses, fantasies, or statements of what someone else has told the patients about their infancy.

Another possibility is that early memories are nonverbal and later memories are verbal. One fault with that hypothesis is that 4- and 5-year-olds (who clearly rely on language) do remember events from ages 2 and 3; it is only older children who do not. Besides, even nonhuman animals (which never develop language) forget most of what they learned as infants (Bachevalier & Mishkin, 1984).

Another possibility is that infant amnesia may be related to the slow maturation of the hippocampus (Moscovitch, 1985). Although we recall few early factual memories, we retain an enormous number of procedural memories gained in infancy—how to walk, talk, put on clothing, and conduct other daily activities. That pattern of retaining procedural memories while losing factual memories is characteristic of impaired functioning of the hippocampus. Again, however, the problem with this theory is that infants do form factual memories that last at least a

People retain many procedural memories from early childhood, such as how to eat with chopsticks or a fork and spoon, but they forget nearly all the events from that time of their life.

year or two. What we need to explain, and the hippocampal theory fails to explain, is why the infant memories last for a year or two and then fade.

Still another possibility is that a permanent memory of a personal experience requires a "sense of self" that develops between ages 3 and 4 (Howe & Courage, 1993). That theory, though certainly worth considering, is vague and difficult to test. It also leaves us wondering whether the long-term memories of adult rats and pigeons imply that they have a "sense of self." In summary, the phenomenon of infant amnesia remains open for further hypotheses and further evidence.

SOMETHING TO THINK ABOUT

Does the encoding specificity principle (page 285) suggest another possible explanation for infant amnesia? (Hint: Your physiological condition always differs somewhat at the time of attempted recall from what it was at the time of original learning.)

AMNESIA OF OLD AGE

Most elderly people also experience a certain amount of memory loss, ranging from a slight increase in forgetfulness to the severe losses associated with Alzheimer's disease. Memory skills vary from one person to another and from one time to another. On the average, older adults show only mild deficits on the simplest memory tasks, such as short-term retention of a list of words; they show greater deficits on more complex memory tasks (Babcock & Salthouse, 1990; Salthouse, Mitchell, Skovronek, & Babcock, 1989). If given a short narrative to remember, older adults remember the central points of the narrative almost as well as younger adults but they show a substantial deficit in memory of the odd and irrelevant details (Hess, Donley, & Vandermaas, 1989).

One aspect likely to suffer especially is memory for context and time. Older people may wonder, "Did I already tell this story to my daughter, or was it someone else?" "Where did I park my car today?" "Is my appointment for today or for tomorrow?" In one study, young people (20–30 years) and old people (65–87 years) tried to memorize a long list of words. When recalling the words,

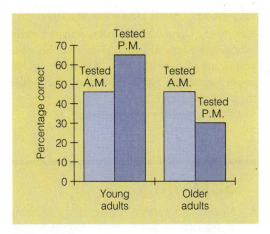

FIGURE 7.27
Older people (ages 66–78) reach their peak of alertness early in the morning, while younger people (ages 18–22) are more variable but generally reach their peak in late afternoon or evening. If both groups are tested early in the morning, older people perform about as well as younger people. Late in the afternoon, younger people greatly outperform older people. (Based on data of May, Hasher, & Stoltzfus, 1993.)

memory for context + time.
- all older are morning people

the older people were more likely to say the same word two or three times, forgetting that they had already said it (Koriat, Ben-Zur, & Sheffer, 1988).

Although increased forgetfulness is undeniably common in old age, many studies have exaggerated this phenomenon because of an overlooked detail in the design of the experiments: As you might remember from Chapter 5, some people are "morning people" and some are "evening people." Most young people are either neutral (about equally alert at all times) or "evening people" (most alert in late afternoon and evening). In contrast, nearly all older people (over age 65) are "morning people"; they reach their peak early in the day and decline sharply from then on. Who does most research on memory? Graduate students. How old are graduate students? Most often, they are in their 20s. So what time do graduate students choose for their studies? Late afternoon, a fine time for a 25-year-old, but a poor time for a 65-year-old. Researchers in one study compared the memories of young adults (18–22 years old) and older adults (66–78 years old) at different times of day. Late in the afternoon, the younger adults greatly outperformed the older adults, as they had in most previous memory studies. However, when the research took place early in the morning, the older adults did just as well as the younger adults (May, Hasher, & Stoltzfus, 1993). Figure 7.27 shows the results.

Are most college classes offered in the early morning or late afternoon? Is that because you want to take them at that time, or because your aging professors want to schedule them at that time?

SUMMARY

- *Normal forgetting.* Forgetting depends partly on interference from related memories. At least for memories in the phonological loop, passive decay also contributes to forgetting. We also have trouble remembering if we do not have adequate retrieval cues. (page 289)

- *Amnesia after damage to the hippocampus.* H. M. and other patients with damage to the hippocampus have great trouble storing new declarative memories, although they form normal procedural and implicit memories. (page 290)

- *Korsakoff's syndrome and other damage to the frontal lobes.* After damage to the frontal lobes, people make illogical inferences about their past and therefore make odd confabulations. (page 291)

- *Alzheimer's disease.* Alzheimer's disease, common in old age, produces a progressive loss of memory and reasoning. (page 292)

- *Lessons from amnesia.* Studies of brain-damaged people demonstrate the value of distinguishing among different types of memory, such as declarative and procedural, or explicit and implicit. (page 296)

- *Infant amnesia.* Most people remember little or nothing from before about age 3½. Psychologists have proposed several theories to explain this loss of early memories, but no convincing evidence backs any of the theories so far. (page 296)

- *Loss of memory in old age.* Most older people suffer some loss of memory, especially for details and for the contexts of events. As a rule, older people show much better memory early in the morning than late in the afternoon. (page 297)

SUGGESTION FOR FURTHER READING

Squire, L. R., & Butters, N. (Eds.) (1992). *Neuropsychology of memory* (2nd ed.). New York: Guilford Press. Collection of chapters by a number of leading investigators of memory and amnesia.

TERMS

amnesia severe loss or deterioration of memory (page 290)

hippocampus forebrain structure believed to be important for certain aspects of memory (page 290)

anterograde amnesia inability to store new long-term memories (page 290)

retrograde amnesia loss of memory for events that occurred prior to brain damage or other trauma (page 290)

procedural memory retention of learned skills (page 291)

declarative memory recall of factual information (page 291)

Korsakoff's syndrome condition caused by prolonged deficiency of vitamin B_1, which results in both retrograde amnesia and anterograde amnesia (page 291)

confabulation guesses made by an amnesic patient to fill in memory gaps (page 292)

Alzheimer's disease degenerative condition that generally occurs in old age, characterized by progressive loss of memory (page 292)

explicit memory memory that a person can state, generally recognizing that it is the correct answer (page 294)

implicit memory memory that influences behavior without requiring conscious recognition that one is using a memory (page 295)

infant amnesia or **childhood amnesia** relative lack of declarative memories from early in one's life, especially before age 3½ (page 296)

ANSWERS TO CONCEPT CHECKS

11. Remembering how to tie your shoes (a) is a procedural memory. Remembering the first day of school (b) is a declarative memory. (page 295)

12. Item b is an example of implicit memory. Both recall and recognition are examples of explicit memory. (page 295)

13. In H. M. and other amnesic patients, declarative memories are most impaired and procedural memories are least impaired. (page 295)

THE RECONSTRUCTION OF MEMORY

Why do we sometimes report memories that turn out to be incorrect?

How do later events sometimes change people's recollections?

At one point, while I was doing the research for this book, I tried to find an article that I remembered reading. I was pretty sure I remembered the author, the name of the journal, and the date of the article within a year, and I expected to find the article quickly.

About 4 hours later I finally located it. I was right about the author, but I was wrong about the journal and the year. Worst of all, I discovered that the results the article reported were quite different from what I remembered. (The way I remembered the results made a lot more sense than the actual results!)

Why do we sometimes forget things? And why do we sometimes remember something all wrong and think we are right?

RECONSTRUCTION OF PAST EXPERIENCES

Certain tasks in everyday life require us to remember information exactly. If you want to call someone on the phone, you won't gain much from remembering the "approximate" telephone number. If you try to recite a famous poem, or the Pledge of Allegiance, or the Twenty-third Psalm, no one will be impressed if you can "explain the main idea." Either you say it exactly right, or you don't know it.

In other circumstances, however, your goal is just to remember the main events.

When you try to describe an event from your life, you start with the details that you remember clearly and you reconstruct the rest to fill in the gaps. (During an original experience we *construct* a memory. When we try to retrieve that memory, we *reconstruct* it from what survives.) For example, suppose you try to recall your experience of studying in the library last night. You may remember where you sat, what you were reading, who sat down next to you, and where you went for a snack afterward. As time passes, you probably will forget most or all of that information. However, if you happen to fall in love with the person who sat down next to you and went with you for a snack, you may remember the experience forever. In that case, however, you will remember meeting that person and perhaps where you went for a snack, but probably not which book you were reading. If you wanted to recall which book it was, you might reconstruct the memory this way: "Let's see, that semester I was taking a chemistry course that took a lot of study, so maybe I was reading a chemistry book. No, wait, I remember that when we went out for a snack we talked about politics. So maybe I was reading a political science text."

We also reconstruct the times when various experiences occurred. If you are asked when you last ate a pizza, or saw your cousin, you can with a little effort generate an approximate date (Friedman, 1993). You do not have a time-tag on every memory, but you can logically surmise, for example, that you saw your cousin the last time the two families got together during a holiday get-together, or perhaps at someone's wedding. Then you figure out when that event took place.

RECONSTRUCTION IN STORY MEMORIES

When we reconstruct a memory of an experience, we generally fit it into a series of expectations, which F. C. Bartlett called a schema. For example, if you try to recall your last trip to the dentist, you probably will fill in the gaps with a schema of what usually happens at the dentist's office.

Bartlett demonstrated this tendency in a study of British participants who read stories and then tried to retell them after various delays (Bartlett, 1932). One of the stories, "The War of the Ghosts," was a Native American tale about two young men who

A witness at a trial is asked to recall an event that happened months or years ago. It is neither likely nor necessary that this witness will recall every detail or every word of a conversation. Rather, the report will be a mixture of clear memories and reconstructions.

In another study, U.S. and Mexican adults were asked to listen to three stories and try to recall them. Some were given U.S. versions of the stories; others were given Mexican versions that differed in certain details. (For example, in the "going on a date" story, the Mexican version had the man's sister go along as a chaperone.) On the average, U.S. participants remembered the U.S. versions better, whereas the Mexicans remembered the Mexican versions better (Harris, Schoen, & Hensley, 1992).

Suppose you were asked to remember a story that was mostly logical but which included a few incongruous elements—for example, you are told that a teenager, clutching a teddy bear, parked a bicycle in the kitchen. How well would you expect someone to remember such an odd event? On the one hand, you might expect poor memory because the event violates the schema for a teenager's day. On the other hand, you might predict that the odd events will stand out as distinctive, unusual, and therefore memorable. The answer is, the results vary, depending on the exact procedure used (Maki, 1990). People who remember the story well frequently mention the odd, surprising information, and people who are tested by the recognition method are very likely to agree, "Yes, I remember the teenager with the teddy bear who parked a bicycle in the kitchen." People who are asked to recall the story, as opposed to just answering recognition questions, rely more on their schemas, especially if they do not remember the story well. As they reconstruct the story, they are likely to omit the unexpected events, and may even include some events that "should have happened" even though the story did not mention them (such as "the teenager went to school in the morning"). In short, people combine their memories with their expectations; the less certain the memory, the more they rely on their expectations (Heit, 1993).

HINDSIGHT BIAS

To illustrate another way in which we reconstruct memories, let's try a little demonstration. First read the following paragraph, then answer the question following it:

For some years after the arrival of Hastings as governor-general of India, the consolidation of British power involved serious war. The first of these wars took place on the northern frontier of Bengal where the

met five other men who later turned out to be ghosts; one of the young men went home, while the other went with the ghosts to a battle in which he sustained an injury that later killed him. Most of Bartlett's subjects found the story confusing, even incoherent. It contained the unfamiliar place names "Egulac" and "Kalama," an unfamiliar sequence of events, and an assortment of seemingly unimportant details. In short, it did not fit neatly into any of the subjects' schemas.

If subjects are asked to learn such a story and then retell it on frequent occasions, they maintain a consistent, fairly accurate version of the story (Wheeler & Roediger, 1992). However, if they are asked to tell it weeks or months apart, as they were in Bartlett's study, they omit many details and change others. With long delays, they have serious gaps in their memories and fill them with inferences of what must have been true, or what would have made sense. As a result the later versions are less and less accurate, but make more sense than the original—at least to the people retelling the story, if perhaps not to those who told it originally. In other words, we distort memories to make them more logical, to make them fit our expectations and inferences.

[handwritten margin notes:] w/long delays they have serious gaps in their memory & fill them w/ inferences of what must have been true or what would have made sense.

people combine memories w/ expectations ; the less certain the mem the more they rely on their expectations

British were faced by the plundering raids of the Gurkas of Nepal. Attempts had been made to stop the raids by an exchange of lands, but the Gurkas would not give up their claims to country under British control, and Hastings decided to deal with them once and for all. The campaign began in November, 1814. It was not glorious. The Gurkas were only some 12,000 strong; but they were brave fighters, fighting in territory well-suited to their raiding tactics. The older British commanders were used to war in the plains where the enemy ran away from a resolute attack. In the mountains of Nepal it was not easy even to find the enemy. The troops and transport animals suffered from the extremes of heat and cold, and the officers learned caution only after sharp reverses. Major-General Sir D. Octerlony was the one commander to escape from these minor defeats. (Woodward, 1938, pp. 383–384)

Question: In the light of the information appearing in the passage, what was the probability of occurrence of each of the four possible outcomes listed below? (The probabilities should sum to 100%.)

a. a British victory   ____ %
b. a Gurka victory   ____ %
c. stalemate with no peace settlement ____ %
d. stalemate with a peace settlement ____ %

Note that some of the facts pointed in one direction and some pointed in another direction; each of the possible outcomes had some probability of occurring. Now that you have made your estimates of the probabilities, I can tell you what really happened: The two sides had a military stalemate without any settlement. The British had the advantages of superior numbers and superior equipment, but the Gurkas knew the territory and refused to give up. Battles continued sporadically and indecisively for years.

Now that you know the outcome, would you like to revise your estimates of the probabilities? Perhaps if you reread the paragraph you will decide that you had overestimated the probabilities of some outcomes and underestimated others.

Subjects in one experiment read the preceding passage about the British and the Gurkas. Some were told the correct outcome, and others were told one of the other outcomes; all were then told to estimate the probabilities of the four possible outcomes.

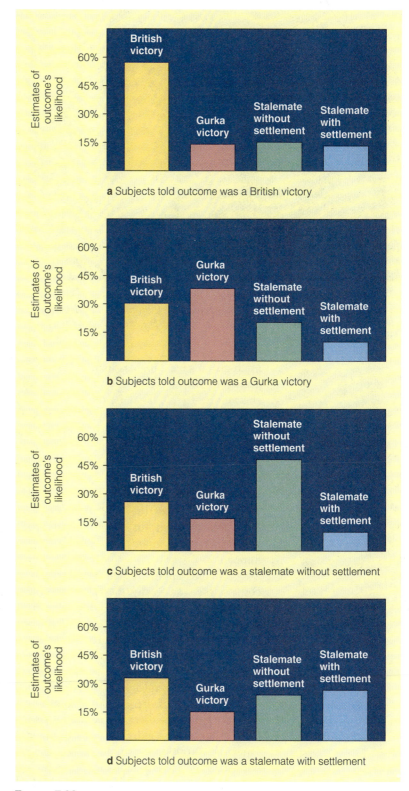

FIGURE 7.28
Mean estimates of the likelihood of four outcomes varied, depending on what each group was told about the "actual" outcome. Those who thought the British had won said that under the circumstances, the British had a very high probability of victory. Those who thought the Gurkas had won said that was the most likely outcome under the circumstances. And so forth. (Based on data of Fischhoff, 1975.)

Nicholas Leeson, whose early investments earned large profits for the Barings firm, made later investments that cost a $1 billion loss. Hindsight was clearer than any original perception; his associates suddenly said they had known they should not have trusted him.

hindsight bias – the tendency to mold our recollection of the past to fit the way later events turned out.

Each group gave a high estimate to the probability of the outcome they had been told (Fischhoff, 1975). That is, once they knew what "really" happened (or incorrectly *thought* they knew), they reinterpreted the previous interpretation to make that outcome seem likely, or perhaps even inevitable (Figure 7.28). The subjects' behavior illustrates **hindsight bias,** the tendency to mold our recollection of the past to fit the way later events turned out. Something happens and we say, "I *knew* that was going to happen!"

(Oh, incidentally, I lied about the outcome of the war. Really, the British won. Because of their poor leadership, the war dragged on for 2 years, but eventually their superior power and resources prevailed. Now would you like to reevaluate your estimates *again?*)

Examples of hindsight bias are abundant in many phases of life. A couple announces they are getting a divorce and their friends say, "I *knew* that marriage was doomed." Later the couple cancels their plans for a divorce and the same friends say, "I knew they would get back together." Historians look at events over a period of time and perceive a "trend" in those events that "had to" turn out the way they did. The government makes a controversial decision that turns out well; later, people forget their doubts and agree that "of course" it had been a good idea.

We can explain hindsight bias in several

ways (Hawkins & Hastie, 1990). To some extent, people may misrepresent their previous beliefs to make themselves look smart. ("See how smart I am? I knew this was going to happen.") Also, people frequently cannot quite remember what they had expected before the event occurred. After the event, they remember best the previous facts that fit with the eventual outcome. From the facts that stand out in their memory, they reconstruct an expectation of what was likely to occur— an expectation that fits the events that actually did occur, and not the expectation they really had before they knew the outcome.

SOMETHING TO THINK ABOUT

Can you interpret people's beliefs that they had a "psychic hunch" in terms of hindsight bias?

WHAT'S THE EVIDENCE?

The Suggestibility of Memory

When people in a psychologist's laboratory distort a story or alter their recollections of previous beliefs in hindsight, no harm is done. But sometimes a great deal is riding on the accuracy of someone's memory.

You have just watched a robbery being committed by a man you had never seen before. When the police ask you to describe the thief, you do your best, but you saw him for only a few seconds and cannot recall many details. The police ask, "Did he have a mustache? Did he have a tattoo on his right hand? Two other robberies were pulled off around here in the last few days by a man with a mustache and a tattoo on his right hand." Suddenly it comes back to you: "Yes, he definitely had a mustache. And I'm almost sure he had a tattoo." Did the suggestion help you to recall those details? Or did it prompt you to reconstruct details that you never actually saw?

EXPERIMENT 1

Hypothesis If people are asked questions that suggest or presuppose a certain fact, many people will later report remembering that "fact," even if it never happened.

Method Elizabeth Loftus (1975) asked two groups of students to watch a videotape of an automobile accident. Then she asked one group, and not the other, "Did you see the children getting on the school bus?" In fact, the videotape did not show a school bus. A week later, she asked both groups 20 new questions about the accident, including this one: "Did you see a school bus in the film?"

Results Of the first group (those who were asked about seeing children get on a school bus), 26% reported they had seen a school bus; of the second group, only 6% said they had seen a school bus.

Interpretation The question "Did you see the children getting on the school bus?" presupposes that there was a school bus. Some of the people who heard that question reconstructed what happened by combining what they actually saw with what they believed might reasonably have happened and with what someone suggested to them afterward.

What do results of this type mean? They might mean that the first question added a school bus to the listeners' memory. But they might also mean that the listeners thought, "Hmm . . . I don't remember a school bus, but the experimenters asked about one before, and I suppose they should know. So I'll say I remember a school bus." Does the experimenters' suggestion actually change people's memory or does it just change their answers?

EXPERIMENT 2

Hypothesis When people are given a misleading suggestion and then asked about what they saw, they may give answers that follow the suggestion. But if they are asked questions that eliminate the suggested information as a possible answer, they will return to the original information.

Method College students saw a series of slides about a man who entered a room, stole some money and a calculator, and left (Figure 7.29). One of the slides showed a coffee jar on a file cabinet. After the last slide, the students were asked a series of questions, and some were asked the misleading question of whether they saw a jar of sugar on the file cabinet. Others were just asked about a jar. Later, some of the misled students and some of the other students were asked what kind of jar they saw on the file cabinet, a jar of coffee or a jar of sugar. The remaining

FIGURE 7.29
Subjects in one experiment saw this slide (among others) and later answered a series of questions. Some subjects answered a question about whether they remembered seeing a jar of sugar on the file cabinet. Many said they did. However, when they were asked whether the jar contained coffee or cookies, they remembered the coffee. The misleading question had not destroyed the original memory.

students were asked whether they saw a jar of coffee or a jar of cookies (Zaragoza, McCloskey, & Jamis, 1987).

Results Of those who were asked whether they saw a jar of sugar or a jar of coffee, 39% of those who had heard the misleading question about a jar of sugar said they remembered a jar of sugar. Of those who had not heard the misleading question, only 18% said they remembered a jar of sugar.

However, of students who were asked whether they saw a jar of coffee or a jar of cookies, about the same percentage remembered the jar of coffee, regardless of whether they had heard the misleading question about a jar of sugar.

Interpretation A misleading suggestion does sometimes lead people to answer a question incorrectly, but it does not necessarily impair the original memory. Perhaps people are saying "sugar" even though they still remember "coffee."

That conclusion may not always hold either, however. Consider one more study.

EXPERIMENT 3

Hypothesis People who view something and get misleading information about it afterward will forget which information came from the original experience and which came later.

Method College students viewed a set of slides and then read a description that, as they were warned, contained many inaccuracies. Then they were asked to list various items, such as magazine titles or soft-drink brands, but to be sure to *omit* any titles that they saw in the slides.

Results Subjects not only omitted titles they saw in the slides, but they also omitted many titles they read in the narrative. When asked why, they replied that they thought they had seen those titles in the slides (Weingardt, Loftus, & Lindsay, 1995).

Interpretation Remember the concept of *source amnesia:* People often have trouble remembering when and where they learned something. As a result, in an experiment like this one, people fully confuse the original experience with a later description of it, even if they are warned that the later description is wrong.

Overall Conclusion Sometimes misleading information just alters how people report their memories, and sometimes it actually impairs or distorts the original memory (Loftus, 1992).

There is a message in all this about how psychologists do research: What seems like the obvious interpretation for a given set of results may not apply in all circumstances. We need to examine a phenomenon in many ways before drawing a conclusion.

SUGGESTIBILITY AND EYEWITNESS TESTIMONY

Regardless of whether suggestions actually alter people's memories or just alter what they report, the implications are equally ominous for the legal profession. That is, if a police officer or other interviewer can ask questions that alter a witness's reports of the event, we may end up with faulty information and perhaps the conviction of an innocent person. What do we know about eyewitness testimony?

The news is neither all good nor all bad. Eyewitnesses sometimes report accurately and sometimes inaccurately; a series of misleading or suggestive questions can bias people to report what the interrogator wants them to report, but not everyone yields to such pressure. Perhaps the broadest generalization we can make is that most people, from police to juries, put too much faith in eyewitness reports (Wells, 1993).

EYEWITNESS IDENTIFICATION FROM LINEUPS

Some special memory problems arise with a *lineup,* a procedure in which a crime witness or victim is asked to examine a set of people and identify which of them, if any, committed the crime. People who saw the culprit only once, perhaps just briefly, have trouble remembering the exact appearance, and yet they feel an obligation to try to identify someone. Too often, if the actual culprit is not in the lineup, witnesses identify someone who looks similar to the culprit, and then declare with confidence, "Yes, that's the one."

If the police suspect one person of the crime, who should be the *foils* (nonsuspects included in the lineup)? Obviously, they should look reasonably similar to the suspect. For example, if the lineup includes one short person and all the others are tall, or one young person and all the others are middle-aged, the one that is different will stand out. The police could, of course, intentionally bias the lineup in this way in order to get an identification of the person they suspect, but let's assume they are trying to play fair.

The obvious alternative is to start with the suspect and then add other people who resemble the suspect as much as possible. That procedure turns out to be troublesome also, for a subtler reason (Wogalter, Marwitz, & Leonard, 1992): If all the others are selected because they resemble the suspect, the suspect stands out as the one who is *most similar* to the others in the group! For instance, examine the lineup in Figure 7.30. If you had to pick out one of them, without even having seen the crime, would one of these people stand out? (Check answer D, page 307.) The point is not that lineups are always unfair, but that making them fair is difficult (Wells, 1993; Wogalter et al., 1992).

CHILDREN AS EYEWITNESSES

Another special problem arises when children are witnesses to or victims of a crime.

Young children forget more rapidly than do adults; they tend to be more suggestible than adults; and they sometimes confuse fantasy with reality. Are they therefore unreliable as witnesses?

Not necessarily. Although researchers do agree that young children yield to suggestion more than adults do, the difference is not enormous (Ceci & Bruck, 1993). Under many circumstances, children remember important personal experiences quite well over surprisingly long periods of time, provided they understood the original experience. For example, children in two studies were asked about events of their medical examinations at delays ranging from 3 days to 6 weeks after the event. Children of ages 3 to 7 reported the events accurately and in detail. Researchers then asked suggestive or leading questions such as "Did the nurse cut your hair?" and "Did the person hit you?" Even at the younger ages, only a few children reported any events that had not happened (Baker-Ward, Gordon, Ornstein, Larus, & Clubb, 1993; Goodman, Aman, & Hirschman, 1987). These results, of course, do not deny that one might induce children to give false testimony by more prolonged and insistent suggestions.

The general recommendations on children's eyewitness testimony are as follows: If a child is simply asked to describe the events in a nonthreatening atmosphere, without suggestions or pressure, reasonably soon after the event, even children as young as 3 are believable (Ceci & Bruck, 1993). Asking a child the same questions repeatedly within a single interview can confuse the child. (Some will change their answers on the assumption that their first answers must have been wrong.) However, asking the child to repeat the story every few days may help the child to remember—as may be necessary if the child is to testify in a trial many months later (Poole & White, 1995).

THE "FALSE MEMORY" CONTROVERSY

Sigmund Freud, whom we shall consider more fully in Chapter 13, defined **repression** as the process of moving a memory, motivation, or emotion from the conscious mind to the unconscious mind. Earlier, when I was describing explanations of forgetting, I did not include the possibility of repression, simply because the research on memory and forgetting has not supported this concept (Holmes, 1990). However, although most memory researchers doubt this concept, a number of clinical psychologists continue to find it useful and convincing. They are unimpressed with the laboratory research, arguing that repression occurs under circumstances that a laboratory cannot capture.

A significant controversy has arisen over the use of the concept of repression under circumstances of the following type: A client tells a therapist about a variety of distresses and emotional difficulties without any known cause. The therapist, explaining that such symptoms are frequently a result of early sexual abuse, asks whether the client was sexually abused. "No, I don't believe so," the client replies. The therapist, however, persists, explaining that the absence of a memory does not mean that someone was not abused; after all, the person may have repressed the painful memories. The therapist asks the client to try hard to remember, to

| Suspect # 1 | Suspect # 2 | Suspect # 3 | Suspect # 4 | Suspect # 5 |

FIGURE 7.30
Here a lineup is composed of one "suspect" and others chosen to resemble the suspect. Does one of these stand out as the probable suspect? (Check answer D, page 307.)

fantasize what the abuse might have been if it had occurred. Some therapists employ hypnosis or other techniques to "recover" the repressed memory. Eventually, the client may either claim to remember being sexually abused or may simply agree, "I guess you're right; I must have been sexually abused, even though I don't remember it."

What I have just described is, of course, not representative of all cases and certainly not of all therapists. Sometimes the client clearly recalls being sexually abused and will volunteer that information without any prompting or after the mere question "Were you ever sexually abused?" Instances of that sort are believable and noncontroversial. After all, sexual abuse of children does occur, probably often, and is a serious problem.

The controversy concerns cases in which a psychotherapy client who initially denied remembering any sexual abuse goes through some treatment and eventually reports a recovery of repressed memories. Some patients have reportedly recovered memories that include sexual abuse at a very early age, even less than one year. Others have reported being part of a satanic cult that killed and ate babies and then used their satanic powers to destroy all the evidence. In some cases, people have been tried and convicted of crimes for which the only evidence was the testimony of a person who had not remembered the events until decades later, and regained them through the help of hypnosis or other therapeutic interventions.

Is it possible that people would repress memories of sexual abuse, satanic rituals, and the like, completely forgetting them until the time of therapy? Perhaps, but repression is not common, even after extremely traumatic experiences. One study examined 16 children who were known to have witnessed the murder of one of their parents. All had recurring nightmares, haunting thoughts, and painful flashbacks of the experience; none showed any indication of forgetting or repression (Malmquist, 1986). Another study examined children who at ages of less than 5 years had suffered traumatic experiences ranging from a plane crash to being kidnapped for ransom to being used in pornographic movies. Of those who were at least 3 years old at the time of the trauma, 6 out of 9 had good recall of the events even years later, and the other 3 had partial memories (Terr, 1988). Certainly, such results do not indicate that repression never occurs; they do indicate, however, that if it occurs it is limited to some other kind of experience, or to certain as yet undefined kinds of people.

People do forget events from before age 3; that forgetting need not be due to repression, however. Also, as discussed in Chapter 5, we have no evidence that hypnosis or any similar treatment can accurately recover such memories.

The alternative to believing that psychotherapy clients recover repressed memories is that the suggestions to remember abusive experiences can "implant" a **false memory**, a report that someone believes to be a memory, but which in fact does not correspond to anything that happened. The advocates of this position point to the evidence showing that suggestions can distort people's memories of what they saw, and that sometimes repeated suggestions can even get people to report experiences that never occurred (Lindsay & Read, 1994; Loftus, 1993).

Critics of this position point out that such evidence shows only that suggestions can implant memories of minor events such as being lost in a shopping mall. Researchers have not demonstrated that suggestions can implant emotionally distressing memories such as those of sexual abuse (Pezdek, 1994).

True, reply those on the other side, but ethics would prohibit us from trying to implant emotionally traumatic memories. Our evidence may seem shaky, but it is better than the evidence that anyone can accurately recover memories, especially infant memories, that have been forgotten for years.

Let us concede a few points which, I believe, ought to be conceded on both sides: First, people do sometimes forget painful memories, and it is at least possible that appropriate reminders might help some of them to remember. Second, people are suggestible; if they are told that something must have happened and that they should try to remember it, at least some people will say they remember events, even though in fact those events never happened.

The real question then is, how common is the accurate recovery of a lost memory and how common is a false memory? If someone says he or she now remembers some long-forgotten event, should we assume it is true or assume it is a false memory? The problem is, psychologists do not know how to distinguish true memories from false memories, or even between people having amnesia and people just pretending to have amnesia (Schacter, 1986a, 1986b). Especially when much is at stake, as in a court trial, a good policy might be this: First, use a little common sense. If someone reports extreme or unlikely events, insist on some independent evidence and don't just take the person's word for it. Second, consider the circumstances: Did the person report the events spontaneously or after repeated suggestions and prompts? For how long were the events forgotten? Did they occur recently, or far in the past, or in infancy? We may not be able to distinguish fantasy from memory in every case, but surely we should make an effort.

SOMETHING TO THINK ABOUT

Do you see any parallels between some of the undocumented reports of abuse and the Salem witchcraft trials?

Should anyone believe reports that therapists can help people recover memories of infantile sexual abuse? Some of those who have been accused of such acts have successfully struck back, such as this man, who sued the therapist for implanting "false memories."

SUMMARY

• *Reconstruction.* In remembering stories or events from their own lives, people recall some of the facts and fill in the gaps based on logical inferences of what must have happened. They rely particularly heavily on schemas and inferences when they are uncertain about their memory of the events. (page 299)

• *Hindsight bias.* People often revise their memories of what they previously expected, saying that the way that events turned out was what they had expected all along. (page 300)

• *The suggestibility of memory.* Misleading questions can bias individuals to report events differently from what they saw. In some cases, people confuse what they saw and what was suggested to them later. (page 302)

• *Eyewitness testimony.* Eyewitness testimony is sometimes accurate, sometimes not. Lineups can bias a witness toward identifying a particular suspect. Children can be reliable witnesses if they are interviewed properly. (page 304)

• *False memory debate.* Some therapists have used hypnosis or very suggestive lines of questioning to try to help people remember painful experiences. Some of the reported memories include extreme or bizarre events and some allegedly occurred in infancy. It is im-

portant to try to distinguish actual cases of abuse from false memories that depend on suggestion. (page 305)

TERMS

reconstruction putting together an account of past events, based partly on memories and partly on expectations of what must have happened (page 299)

schema in memory, a series of expectations used to guide one's reconstruction of events (page 299)

hindsight bias tendency to mold our recollection of the past to fit the way later events turned out (page 302)

repression according to Freudian theory, the process of moving a memory, motivation, or emotion from the conscious mind to the unconscious mind (page 305)

false memory report that someone believes to be a memory, but which in fact does not correspond to anything that happened (page 306)

ANSWER TO OTHER QUESTION IN THE TEXT

D. Face 5 is the suspect. All the others have been chosen to resemble him, but each has one unusual feature—a different unusual feature in each case. (page 304)

8 COGNITION AND LANGUAGE

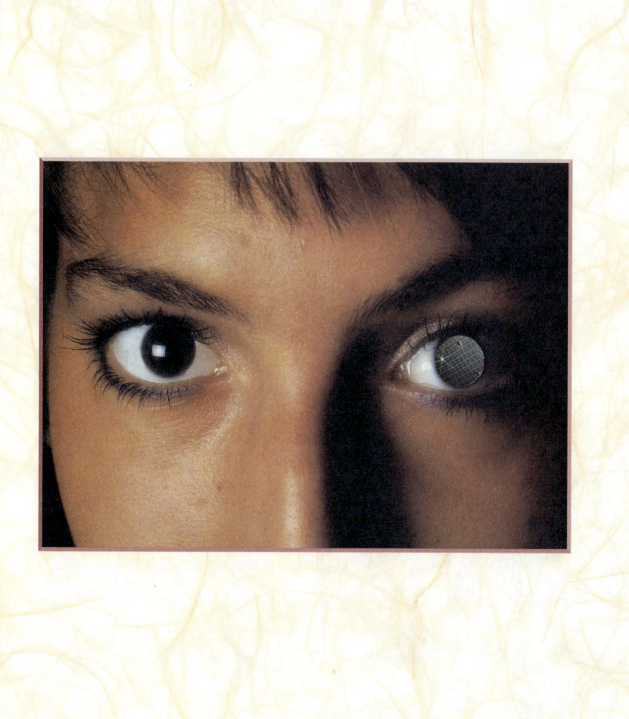

How does a television set work? We can answer that question in two ways: One way is to describe the internal wiring and what each electronic device does. The other way is to describe how the set as a whole operates. (For example, if I flip a certain switch, the set comes on. If I turn a dial, the channel changes.)

How does a human work—that is, behave? We can also answer that question in two ways: One way is to describe what each neuron does and how the various neurons communicate with one another. The other way is to describe the behavior of the person as a whole. (For example, when the weather turns cold or rainy, I go indoors. At noon I walk across the street to get lunch.)

Do we need a third way of describing behavior? Might we describe behavior as something caused by thoughts, knowledge, expectations, and desires?

As we saw in Chapter 6, behaviorists do not think so. We do not need such terms to describe human behavior any more than we need them to explain how televisions work. Moreover, neurons and behavior are easily observed and measured. Thoughts and knowledge are not. A scientific study, say the behaviorists, should deal only with what can be observed and measured.

And yet we all are directly aware of our own thoughts. Even if we cannot observe or measure other people's thoughts directly, we are sure of the reality of our own. In fact, my own conscious mind is the thing I am most sure of. (After all, the external world might be just an illusion.)

Granting that thoughts and knowledge exist, we ask, "What are they?" Even if we cannot observe them directly, can we measure them indirectly through their effects on behavior? This chapter deals with the attempts of psychologists to grapple with such questions.

Cognition is knowledge and the use of knowledge.

THINKING AND MENTAL PROCESSES

How is it possible to measure thought processes?

Are mental images similar to visual images?

How do people categorize items?

Cognition is the psychologists' word for thinking, gaining knowledge, and dealing with knowledge. Cognitive psychologists study how people think, how they acquire knowledge, what they know, how they imagine, how they plan, and how they solve problems. It also deals with how people organize their thoughts into language and communicate their thoughts to others.

Perhaps it seems to you that cognitive psychology should be trivially easy. "If you want to find out what people think or what they know, why not just ask them?" Sometimes we can and do; however, in many cases people are not fully aware of their own thought processes (Kihlstrom, Barnhardt, & Tataryn, 1992). Recall, for example, implicit memory as discussed in Chapter 7: Sometimes you see or hear something that will influence your behavior in the next minute or so, without your noticing that influence. Similarly, some people who are influenced by a posthypnotic suggestion will say or do something and not understand why. We often solve a problem so fast that we do not know how we did it. And when we come to a wrong conclusion, we can be very puzzled as to why it was wrong.

Cognitive psychology began to become popular in the 1970s, not coincidentally at about the time that people began widely using computers. Although a brain and a computer do not work the same way, computers provide a valuable way of modeling theories of cognitive processes. A researcher may say, "Imagine that cognitive processes work as follows. . . . Now let's program a computer to go through those same steps in the same order. If we then give the computer the same information a human has, will it draw the same conclusions and make the same errors humans do?" In short, computer modeling provides a good method to test theories of cognition. Cognitive psychology today uses a variety of methods to measure mental processes and test theories of what we know and how we know it.

SOMETHING TO THINK ABOUT

The Turing Test, suggested by computer pioneer Alan Turing, proposes the following operational definition of artificial intelligence: A person poses questions to a human source and to a computer, both in another room. The human and the computer send back typewritten replies, which are identified only as coming from "source A" or "source B." If the questioner cannot determine which replies are coming from the computer, then the computer has passed a significant test of understanding.

Suppose a computer did pass the Turing Test. Would we then say that the computer "understands," just as a human does? Or would we say that it is merely mimicking human understanding?

CATEGORIZATION

An ancient Greek philosopher wrote that we can never step into the same river twice. In a sense, of course, he was right; everything is constantly changing. However, we generally find it useful to think of the Nile as "the same" river from one minute to the next, even one century to the next. It also suits our purposes to use "river" as a general concept, lumping together the Nile, the Amazon, the Mississippi, and thousands of other rivers, despite their differences from one another.

Forming useful categories enables us to make educated guesses about features we have never seen for ourselves (Anderson, 1991). For example, your concept of river enables you to infer that a river that you have never previously seen probably has many of the features of familiar rivers, such as a flow of water, navigability by boats, a certain degree of curviness, and the presence of certain kinds of wildlife.

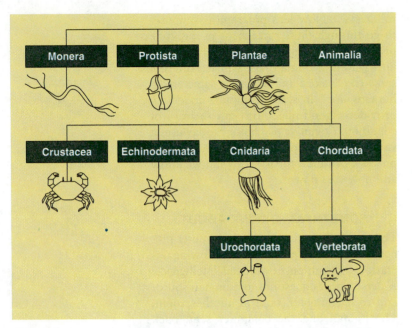

Animals that belong to the emperor

Embalmed ones

Trained ones

Suckling pigs

Mermaids

Fabulous ones

Stray dogs

Those that are included in this classification

Those that tremble as if they were mad

Innumerable ones

Those drawn with a very fine camel's hair brush

Others

Those that have just broken a flower vase

Those that resemble flies from a distance

FIGURE 8.1
Left: A much-abridged chart of the current scientific classification of the animal kingdom. Right: an alleged listing from an ancient Chinese encyclopedia—actually the creation of someone's imagination (Rosch, 1978). The point is, there are many ways to categorize animals or anything else, and some methods of categorizing are better than others.

What makes something a table? Many of our categories have no simple definition.

We often take our categories for granted, as if our own way of categorizing objects were the only possible way (Figure 8.1). But people in other cultures sometimes use categories that seem strange to us (Lakoff, 1987). The Japanese word *hon* refers to long, thin things, including sticks, pencils, trees, and hair. It also includes items that do not strike English-speaking people as obvious examples of long, thin things: hits in baseball, shots in basketball, telephone calls, television programs, a mental contest between a Zen master and a student, and medical injections. Clearly, people from different cultures categorize objects in different ways.

How do people decide how to categorize objects? That question is part of the more basic question of how we think.

CATEGORIZATION BY PROTOTYPES

If you look up a word such as "river" in a dictionary, you will find a definition. Do we also look up our concepts in a mental dictionary to determine their meaning? In some cases, probably yes. For example, the term *bachelor* denotes *an unmarried male*. Because we would not ordinarily apply the term *bachelor* to a 3-year-old boy or to a Catholic priest, we might want to modify the definition to *a man who has not married so far but who could get married*. Such a description pretty well explains the concept *bachelor*.

Very few of our concepts can be so clearly defined, however. Frequently we also deal with such loosely defined categories as *interesting novels* or *embarrassing experiences* that have no clear defining features. Even for such a simple, everyday concept as *table*, we have trouble describing necessary and sufficient features. (Most tables are made of wood, but they need not be. Most have four legs, but they may have more or fewer. The top surface must be reasonably flat, but not everything with a flat surface is a table.)

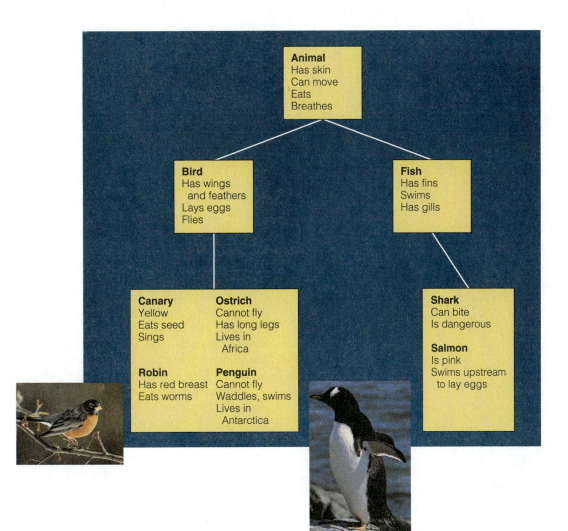

Animal
Has skin
Can move
Eats
Breathes

Bird
Has wings
  and feathers
Lays eggs
Flies

Fish
Has fins
Swims
Has gills

Canary
Yellow
Eats seed
Sings

Ostrich
Cannot fly
Has long legs
Lives in
  Africa

Robin
Has red breast
Eats worms

Penguin
Cannot fly
Waddles, swims
Lives in
  Antarctica

Shark
Can bite
Is dangerous

Salmon
Is pink
Swims upstream
  to lay eggs

According to Eleanor Rosch (1978; Rosch & Mervis, 1975), many categories are defined by some familiar or typical examples, called **prototypes.** According to the **categorization by prototypes** approach, we decide whether an object belongs to a category by determining how well it resembles the protypical members of the category.

For example, we define the category *vehicle* by giving examples: car, bus, train, airplane, boat. To decide whether some other object is a vehicle, we compare it to these examples. If we ask people whether *truck* is a vehicle, they respond "yes" after a short reaction time. They have longer reaction times to the atypical example *blimp* and still longer reaction times to *elevator* or *wheelchair.*

The main point of Rosch's prototype approach is that category membership is sometimes a matter of degree. When we are asked whether a penguin is a bird, there is a correct answer ("yes"), but when we are asked whether an elevator is a vehicle or whether our next-door neighbor is an intelligent person, we may have to answer "sort of" or "not exactly."

Do we always define categories by prototypes? No. We can deal with odd categories such as *repentant turtles* or *sarcastic toddlers,* even though we probably cannot think of a clear example of either category (Smith, Osherson, Rips, & Keane, 1988).

THINKING ABOUT CATEGORIES

One key point about human thought is that we relate different categories to one another. For example, *river* is related to *water* and to *boat; boat* is related to *sailing* and to *anchor.* According to one description, the **categorization by levels** approach (Collins & Quillian, 1969, 1970), we categorize items in terms of a hierarchy. For example, the concepts *bird* and *fish* are both subordinate to *animal,* a variety of specific birds are subordinate to *bird,* and so forth, as shown in Figure 8.2. This kind of hierarchy simplifies our thinking. For example, I tell you that a crested caracara is a bird. Although you had probably never heard of

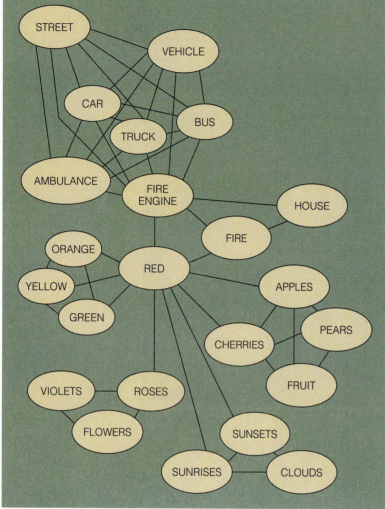

FIGURE 8.3
We link each concept to a number of others that relate to it in various ways. Any stimulus that activates one of these concepts will also partly activate (or "prime") the ones that are linked to it. (From Collins & Loftus, 1975.)

that bird before and still have not seen one, you can correctly answer questions about whether the crested caracara has wings, whether it has feathers, whether it lays eggs, and whether it can fly. You answer those questions by relating *crested caracara* to the next higher level, *bird,* and noting the features of *bird.* You also, of course, have to learn some exceptions, such as the fact that penguins and ostriches are birds that do not fly.

The ways in which we relate one level of categories to another influences our reaction times to certain questions. Suppose you are asked true-false questions about canaries. To the statement "A canary is yellow," you respond rapidly, because *yellow* is a distinctive feature of *canary.* To the statement "A ca-

nary lays eggs," you respond more slowly, because *laying eggs* is not a particularly distinctive feature of *canaries.* You have to relate canaries to the next higher level: "Canaries are birds, and birds lay eggs. So canaries lay eggs." Finally, to the statement "Canaries have skin," your reaction is slower yet. *Skin* is not a distinctive feature of either *canaries* or *birds.* So you have to go from the *canary* level to the *bird* level to the *animal* level before you find the distinctive feature *skin.*

Your responses are not quite so simple as Figure 8.2 implies. For example, you will probably respond faster to whether robins can fly than to whether crested caracaras can fly, and you respond faster to whether robins have feathers than to whether penguins have feathers. The reasons are twofold: First, because you are familiar with robins, you have seen them fly and you have seen their feathers. Therefore, you probably store *flight* and *feathers* as features of robins themselves, and you may not have to refer to the superordinate category *bird.* Second, even if you do have to refer to the category *bird,* a robin is a familiar example of a bird whereas a crested caracara is an unfamiliar example and a penguin is such a weird bird that we have to carefully memorize the fact that it is a bird at all. Thus, our thinking slides easily from *robin* to *bird,* but less easily for the other examples (Rips, Shoben, & Smith, 1973; Smith, Shoben, & Rips, 1974).

CONCEPT CHECK

1. Which would take longer to decide: "Do Eskimos wear parkas?" or "Do Eskimos wear clothes?" Why? (Check your answers on page 320.)

NETWORKS OF RELATED CONCEPTS

When we think about a concept, we relate it not only to those that are linked in a hierarchy (such as *robin—bird—animal*), but also to other concepts that relate to it in a variety of ways. Figure 8.3 shows a possible network of conceptual links for one person (Collins & Loftus, 1975). The links will, of course, vary from one person to another or even from one time to another for a given individual. For example, if you have been talking about hair, *gray* will be closer to *white* than it is to *black,* but if you have been talking about clouds, *gray* will be closer to *black* (Medin & Shoben, 1988).

Suppose this network describes your own concepts. When you hear about or think about one of the concepts shown in this figure, the excitation of that concept will activate, or prime, the concepts linked to it (Collins & Loftus, 1975). The process of doing so is called **spreading activation.** As a result of spreading activation, thinking of one concept makes it easier to think of its related concepts. For example, if you hear the word *roses,* you are temporarily more likely than usual to think of the word *flowers.* If you hear *roses* and then see the word *flowers* flashed briefly on a screen or hear it spoken very softly, you will have a greater-than-usual probability of identifying *flowers* correctly. Spreading activation can combine from more than one source. For example, if you hear the words *clouds* and *red,* you have a high probability of thinking of the word *sunset.*

As this theory would predict, a concept that is linked to many other concepts will activate each of them only slightly, whereas a concept that is linked to only a few will activate them more strongly. For example, *fruit* is linked with a relatively small number of items—more than shown in Figure 8.3, but still not an enormous number. The concept *red* is linked to a much larger number of other items. Suppose we ask various people the following questions and measure their speed of response:

What is something red that is a fruit?

What is something that is a fruit and is red?

People generally respond faster to the second question, and the spreading-activation theory explains why (Collins & Loftus, 1975). In the first question, *red* produces only a small spreading activation for *apple* (the most likely correct answer). So the person answering the question does not get much of a start on this question until hearing the word *fruit.* In the second question, the word *fruit* provides a good start and has significantly activated *apple* before the person hears *red.*

CONCEPT CHECK

2. Would people respond faster to naming a "black-and-white thing that stinks" or to

"a stinky thing that is black-and-white"? (Check your answer on page 321.)

THINKING IN SERIES VERSUS THINKING IN PARALLEL

Suppose I give you a name and you try to decide whether it is the name of a famous person. To answer correctly, you have to look for a match between that name and the name of any famous person you have ever heard of. How do you do something like that? Do you go through all the famous names one by one, or do you somehow compare them all at once? And what if I made it a little more difficult: I am interested only in people who became famous by being a classical music composer, or a poet, or a baseball player. (If the person became famous in some other way, you say "no.") Would you have to go through any different mental processes with this task than with the simpler "famous or not famous" task?

As before, we cannot rely on you to describe your mental processes. But we can learn something about those processes by measuring how long it takes you to answer various questions.

The subjects in one classic experiment watched a number flashed on a screen (Sternberg, 1967). They were told to pull one lever if the number was, say, either 3 or 7, and a different lever if it was any other number. To make the correct response, the subjects had to go through three steps: First, they had to perceive what number was being flashed on the screen. Second, they had to compare that number to the numbers they had memorized (3 and 7) to determine whether it was one of them. Third, they had to pull a lever.

To perform that second step of determining whether the number was either a 3 or a 7, did subjects ask first "Was it a 3?" and then "Was it a 7?" Or did they somehow compare it to both the 3 and the 7 simultaneously?

Saul Sternberg (1967) measured their reaction times under various conditions. Sometimes the subjects had to decide whether the number on the screen was a single number, such as 3. Sometimes they had to decide whether it was either of two numbers, such as 3 or 7. Sometimes they had to decide whether it was one of four numbers, such as 3, 4, 6, or 7. Figure 8.4 gives the results.

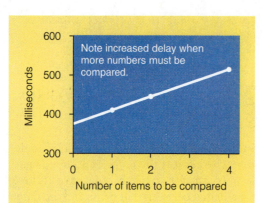

FIGURE 8.4

When people were asked to compare a number on the screen to one, two, or four memorized numbers, they took longer when they had to compare it to more numbers. The line is extrapolated to zero to show how much time is taken for other elements of the response besides the comparison process. These results suggest that people compare the number on the screen to those in memory one at a time (in series), not all at once (in parallel). (Based on Sternberg, 1967.)

When the subjects had memorized two numbers to compare to the displayed number, they took 35 milliseconds (ms) longer per response than when they had one number. When they had four numbers, they took 71 ms longer than when they had two. Apparently, they took about 35 ms to compare the displayed number to each of the memorized numbers. Because the relationship was so regular, Sternberg concluded that the subjects were comparing the number on the screen to each of the numbers they had memorized, one at a time. That is, they conducted their comparisons *in series,* not *in parallel.*

That one study did not settle the matter, though. Other research has shown that people sometimes *do* conduct a parallel search. If the task is to decide whether the number on the screen was 2, 4, 6, 8, or 0—that is, an even number—they answer very rapidly, implying a parallel search. The same is true if the task is to decide whether the number was 1, 2, 3, 4, or 5. That is, depending on the difficulty of the task, people may search through a mental list of items either in series or in parallel. And sometimes the results are difficult to interpret (Townsend, 1990). But in any case, psychologists try to understand people's cognitive processes not by asking them to describe their own thought processes but by timing their responses.

3. In studies similar to Sternberg's, experimenters made it harder to perceive the numbers on the screen by making them blurry. The results were slightly different from those shown in Figure 8.4: The slope of the graph line was the same, but the line started higher. Which step in a subject's response was affected by the blurred numbers: perceiving the number, comparing it to the numbers in memory, or pulling the lever?

4. Figure 8.4 shows the results for subjects who are making a serial comparison of an item they just saw to one or more items held in memory. What would the results look like if they conducted their comparisons in parallel? (Check your answers on page 321.)

ATTENTION

In the case of a parallel search, people have no trouble attending to several stimuli at the same time. Perception is different from action, however. If people have to perform different activities at the same time, they discover certain limits to their attention.

Sometimes doing two things at the same time poses no apparent problem—such as riding an exercise bicycle and listening to the radio. We can create a problem, however, by making the two tasks a bit more difficult: You must try to pedal your exercise bicycle at a steady, high rate. And instead of just listening to the radio, you must count the grammatical errors on a radio talk show. Under such demanding conditions, either you will miss some of the grammatical errors or you will have occasional decelerations in your pedaling. You can do two things at once if one of them is so routine that it requires no effort or attention; however, if both tasks require some cognitive effort, they will interfere with each other (Pashler, 1994).

If you try to do two nonroutine tasks at once, you will shift your attention back and forth between the two. However, that shift requires at least a certain delay. For example, consider the display shown in Figure 8.5. Participants watched a screen that briefly displayed a green character and a red character. A nonsense pattern followed both stimuli to make the identification more difficult. If the two stimuli appeared on the screen simultaneously, participants could identify both of them with reasonable accuracy.

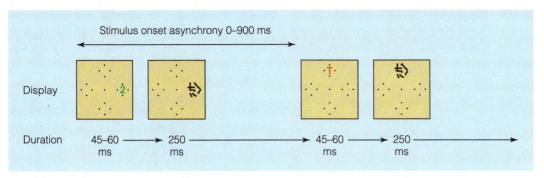

FIGURE 8.5
Participants watched a screen that showed a green character (2 or 5) and a red character (L or T). Sometimes they appeared simultaneously, sometimes with a delay of up to 900 ms between them. Immediately after each stimulus disappeared, an interfering nonsense pattern took its place. The results demonstrated interference from the first stimulus upon the second stimulus. (Modified from Duncan, Ward, & Shapiro, 1994).

However, if one stimulus preceded the other, participants named the first one correctly but had more trouble with the second one. The interference was especially severe with a delay of 200 ms, but still noticeable at a delay of 600 ms (Duncan, Ward, & Shapiro, 1994).

A second experiment was similar, except that it required participants to make only one response. The screen displayed two stimuli, a combination of L or Γ or ⌐. Participants had to answer whether at least one of the stimuli was an L. If the first stimulus was an L, participants had no problem. However, if the first was one of the other stimuli and the second was an L, a delay of 100–200 ms reduced participants to 50% guessing on the identity of the second stimulus. Even a delay of 600 ms produced substantial interference (Duncan et al., 1994).

In other words, attending to a stimulus occupies an attentional process, a "bottleneck" at some point along the way (Pashler, 1994). After one stimulus has engaged our attention, we need more than half a second to shift attention to another stimulus.

MENTAL IMAGERY

When people think about three-dimensional objects or about places where they have been, they generally report that they "see" images in their head. Do those mental images resemble actual vision?

"Well, of course they do," you might reply. "I see mental images all the time." Your self-reports are not solid evidence, however. After all, people sometimes insist that they have a clear mental image of some object and then find that they cannot correctly answer simple questions about it.

To illustrate: Imagine a simple cube balanced with one point (corner) on the table and the opposite point straight up. Imagine that you hold the highest point with one finger. Now, with a finger of the opposite hand, point to all the remaining corners of the cube. How many corners do you touch?

You probably will say that you answered this question by "picturing" a cube in your mind as if you were actually seeing it. However, most people answer the question incorrectly, and few people get the right answer quickly (Hinton, 1979). (Check answer A, page 321.)

So our mental images are sometimes incomplete or vague. Further, it is not obvious that we need mental images to answer visual or spatial questions. Computers can answer such questions quite accurately without drawing little pictures inside themselves. Can we demonstrate that mental images are at least sometimes useful and that they have some of the properties we ordinarily associate with vision? Answering this question was one of the early triumphs of the experimental method in cognitive psychology.

WHAT'S THE EVIDENCE?

Mental Imagery

Roger Shepard and Jacqueline Metzler (1971) conducted a classic study of how humans solve visual problems. They reasoned that if people actually visualize mental images, then the time it takes them to rotate a mental image should be similar to the time it takes to rotate a real object.

Hypothesis When people have to rotate a mental image to answer a question, the farther they have to rotate it, the longer it will take them to answer the question.

Method The experimenters showed subjects pairs of two-dimensional drawings of three-dimensional objects, as in Figure 8.6, and asked whether the drawings in each pair represented the same object rotated in different directions or whether they represented different objects. (Try to answer this question yourself before reading further. Then check answer B, page 321.)

The subjects could answer by pulling one lever to indicate *same* and another lever to indicate *different*. When the correct answer

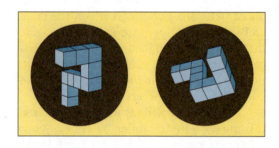

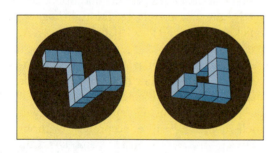

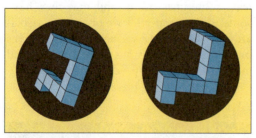

FIGURE 8.6
Examples of pairs of drawings used in an experiment by Shepard and Metzler (1971). Do the drawings for each pair represent the same object being rotated, or are they different objects? (See answer B on page 321.)

was *same,* a subject might determine that answer by rotating a mental image of the first picture until it matched the second. If so, the delay should depend on how far the image had to be rotated.

The delays before answering *different* were generally longer and less consistent than those for answering same—as is generally the case. Subjects could answer *same* as soon as they found a way to rotate the first object to match the second. However, to be sure that the objects were *different,* subjects might have to double-check several times and imagine more than one way of rotating the object.

Results Subjects were almost 97% accurate in determining both *same* and *different.* As predicted, their reaction time for responding *same* depended on the angular difference in orientation between the two views. For example, if the first image of a pair had to be rotated 30° to match the second image, the subject took a certain amount of time to pull the *same* lever. If the two images looked the same after the first one had been rotated 60°, the subject took twice as long to pull the lever. In other words, the subjects reacted as if they were actually watching a little model of the object rotate in their head; the more the object needed to be rotated, the longer they took to determine the answer.

Interpretation Viewing a mental image is at least partly like real vision.

In a related experiment, subjects were shown pairs of cubes. Each face of a particular cube was labeled with a different letter or number. For each pair, subjects were asked whether it was possible that the two cubes were identical. To answer, they had to imagine the rotation of one of the cubes. The rotation could be completed either by one turn through an oblique angle, as process A in Figure 8.7 shows, or by two 90° turns, as process B in Figure 8.7 shows. Those who reported that they could imagine turns through oblique angles answered the questions more accurately even though they answered faster than other subjects did (Just & Carpenter, 1985). An experiment such as this helps us understand why certain people answer a problem faster or more accurately than others do: They go through different identifiable mental processes.

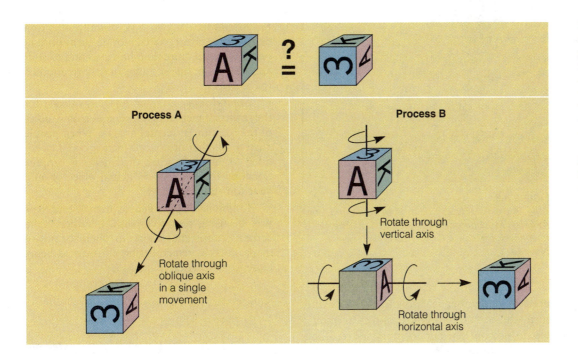

Process A

Rotate through oblique axis in a single movement

Process B

Rotate through vertical axis

Rotate through horizontal axis

SOMETHING TO THINK ABOUT

Some people report that they have auditory images as well as visual images. They "hear" words or songs "in their head." What kind of evidence would we need to test that claim?

The evidence so far indicates that mental imagery resembles vision in certain ways. Does it confirm that we really do "see little pictures in our heads"? Not necessarily. In several experiments, blind people have heard or felt stimuli and then researchers asked them to "use mental images" to answer various questions. The blind people performed quite similarly to sighted people answering the same questions with the same instructions (Jonides, Kahn, & Rozin, 1975; Kerr, 1983; Loomis et al., 1993). It could be that blind subjects use different kinds of images that simply produce the same results as visual imagery, or the interpretation could be that what we call "imagery" is really a spatial representation, and not exactly a visual representation.

Note an important point about scientific procedure: Even an outstanding, classical experiment does not answer all the relevant questions. Almost always, the results of a pioneering experiment suggest additional questions that require further research.

USING MENTAL IMAGES: COGNITIVE MAPS

You are staying at a hotel in an unfamiliar city. You walk a few blocks to get to a museum; then you turn and walk in another direction to get to a restaurant; after dinner you turn again and walk to a theater. After the performance, how do you get back to the hotel? Do you retrace all of your steps? Can you find a shorter route? Or do you give up and hail a cab?

If you can find your way back, you do so by using a **cognitive map**, a mental image of a spatial arrangement. One way to measure the accuracy of people's cognitive maps is to test how well they can find the route from one place to another. Another way is to ask them to draw a map. As you might expect, people draw a more complete map of the areas they are most familiar with. When students try to draw a map of their college campus, they generally include the central buildings on campus and the buildings they enter most frequently (Saarinen, 1973). The longer students have been on campus, the more detail they include (Cohen & Cohen, 1985).

The errors people make in their cognitive maps follow some interesting patterns. First, they tend to remember street angles as being close to 90°, even when they are not (Moar & Bower, 1983). We can easily understand that error. For practical purposes, all we

FIGURE 8.8
Logical versus actual: Location of Reno and Los Angeles. Most people imagine that Los Angeles is farther west because California is west of Nevada.

need to remember is "go three blocks and turn left" or "go two blocks and turn right"; we do not burden our memory by recalling "turn 72° to the right."

Second, people generally image geographic areas as being aligned neatly along a north-to-south axis and an east-to-west axis (Stevens & Coupe, 1978; B. Tversky, 1981). Try these questions, for example: Which city is farther west—Reno, Nevada or Los Angeles, California? And which is farther north—Philadelphia, Pennsylvania or Rome, Italy? Most people reason that, because California is west of Nevada, Los Angeles is "obviously" west of Reno. (Figure 8.8 shows the true position of the cities.) Rome is in southern Europe, and Philadelphia is in the northern part of the United States; therefore, Philadelphia should be north of Rome. In fact, Rome is north of Philadelphia.

You see now the differences between a cognitive map and a real map: Cognitive maps, like other mental images, highlight some details, distort some, and omit some. Nevertheless, they are accurate enough for most practical purposes.

SUMMARY

*   *Categorizing.* People can form categories of objects either by lists of common features or by examples or prototypes that represent a category. (page 311)
*   *Mental searches.* When people search through a mental list, they can search the items either in series or in parallel, depending on the difficulty of the task. (page 315)

*   *Attention.* If two tasks require attention or cognitive effort, we cannot do them both at once. We need more than half a second to shift attention from one stimulus or task to another. (page 316)
*   *Mental images.* One line of evidence for the reality of mental images comes from studies of the rotation of mental images. When people answer whether or not one picture could be rotated to match another, their delay is proportional to the distance an actual object would have to rotate. (page 317)
*   *Cognitive maps.* People learn to find their way by using cognitive maps, but they make certain consistent errors in their cognitive maps, such as remembering all turns as being close to 90° angles. (page 319)

SUGGESTIONS FOR FURTHER READING

Johnson-Laird, P. N. (1988). *The computer and the mind.* Cambridge, MA: Harvard University Press. Description of cognitive psychology and its relationship to computer science, written in nontechnical language.

Lakoff, G. (1987). *Women, fire, and dangerous things.* Chicago: University of Chicago Press. A discussion of how we conceptualize categories.

TERMS

cognition the processes that enable us to imagine, to gain knowledge, to reason about knowledge, and to judge its meaning (page 311)

prototype a highly typical member of a category (page 313)

categorization by prototypes theory that we decide whether an object belongs to a category by determining how well it resembles the prototypes of the category (page 313)

categorization by levels theory that we categorize each item at a level with similar items; each item has distinctive features of its own plus all the features of higher-level categories that include it (page 313)

spreading activation process by which the activation of one concept activates or primes the other concepts that are linked to it in a network (page 315)

cognitive map a mental representation of a spatial arrangement (page 319)

ANSWERS TO CONCEPT CHECKS

1. It should take longer to respond that Eskimos wear clothes. Wearing parkas is a distinctive feature of Eskimos, along with living in igloos. To answer whether Eskimos wear clothes we have to go a level up, either to "Eskimos are human; humans wear clothes" or to "parkas are clothes." (page 314)

2. You will respond faster to the second question. The concept *stinky* is presumably linked to fewer concepts and will activate all of them, including *skunk*, fairly strongly. Thus it provides a good start on answering the question. The concept *black-and-white* is more weakly linked to a great many concepts. (page 315)

3. Making the letters blurry slowed the perception of the number. If it had slowed the process of comparing a number to the numbers in memory, the slope of the line would have become steeper. (page 316)

4. The line in Figure 8.4 would be horizontal instead of increasing. (page 316)

ANSWERS TO OTHER QUESTIONS IN THE TEXT

A. The cube has six (not four) remaining corners. (page 317)

B. The objects in pair *a* are the same; in *b* they are the same; and in *c* they are different. (page 318)

PROBLEM SOLVING, EXPERTISE, AND ERROR

What do experts know or do that sets them apart from other people?

How can we improve our ability to solve problems?

Why do people sometimes reason illogically?

On a college physics exam, a student was once asked how to use a barometer to determine the height of a building. He answered that he would tie a long string to the barometer, go to the top of the building, and carefully lower the barometer until it reached the ground. Then he would cut the string and measure its length.

How would you carry 98 water bottles—all at one time, with no wheelbarrow or truck? When faced with a new problem, sometimes people find a novel and effective solution, and sometimes they do not.

When the professor marked this answer incorrect, the student asked why. "Well," said the professor, "your method would work, but it's not the method I wanted you to use." The student objected. The professor then offered, as a compromise, to let the student try again.

"All right," the student said. "Take the barometer to the top of the building, drop it, and measure the time that it takes to hit the ground. Then from the formula for the speed of a falling object, using the gravitational constant, calculate the height of the building."

"Hmmm," replied the professor. "That too would work. And it does make use of physical principles. But it still isn't the answer I had in mind. Can you think of another way to use the barometer to determine the height of the building?"

"Another way? Sure," replied the student. "Place the barometer next to the building on a sunny day. Measure the height of the barometer and the length of its shadow. Also measure the length of the building's shadow. Then use the formula

$$\frac{\text{height of barometer}}{\text{length of barometer's shadow}} = \frac{\text{height of building}}{\text{length of building's shadow}}$$

The professor was becoming more and more impressed with the student, but he was still reluctant to give credit for the answer. He asked for yet another way.

The student suggested, "Measure the barometer's height. Then walk up the stairs of the building, marking it off in units of the barometer's height. At the top, take the number of barometer units and multiply by the height of the barometer to get the height of the building."

The professor sighed. "Just give me one more way—any other way—and I'll give you credit, even if it's not the answer I wanted."

"Really?" asked the student with a smile. "Any other way?"

"Yes, any other way."

"All right," said the student. "Go to the man who owns the building and say, 'Hey, buddy, if you tell me how tall this building is, I'll give you this neat barometer!'"

We sometimes face a logical or practical problem that we have never tried to solve before. We have to devise a new solution; we cannot rely on a memorized or practiced solution. Sometimes people develop creative, imaginative solutions, like the ones the physics student proposed. Sometimes they offer less imaginative, but still reasonable, solutions. Sometimes they suggest something quite illogical, or no solution at all. Psychologists study problem-solving behavior partly to understand the thought processes behind it and partly to look for ways to help people reason more effectively.

■ EXPERTISE

People vary in their performance on problem-solving and decision-making tasks. In the barometer story just described we probably would talk about the student's creativity; in other cases we talk of someone's expertise. In either case, some people seem more able than other people to understand a problem or to find feasible solutions.

HOW DOES ONE BECOME AN EXPERT?

What does it take to become an expert in any field—say, competing in a sport, solving crossword puzzles, or writing songs? Most of us are so impressed with expert performances that we assume the experts were born with a special talent.

Psychologists who have studied expert performances doubt that assumption (Ericsson & Charness, 1994; Ericsson, Krampe, & Tesch-Römer, 1993). Granted, a person with genes for being short and slow is not likely to become an expert basketball player, and a person born blind is not likely to become an expert photographer. However, in any field, most of the difference between the great expert and the merely average-to-good performer reflects the expert's greater effort and practice.

As a general rule, becoming an expert in a field depends on about 10 years of concentrated effort. Obviously, the amount of needed practice will vary a little depending on the field, but the 10-year rule applies pretty well to many fields that have clearly defined standards of expertise, including musical composition, playing a musical instrument, and playing chess.

Hungarian author Laszlo Polgar set out to demonstrate his conviction that almost anyone can become an expert at something, with sufficient effort. He allowed his three young daughters to explore several fields;

when they showed an interest in chess, he devoted enormous efforts to nurturing their chess skills. Today, all three daughters are outstanding chess players. One of them, Judit Polgar, reached grand master status about 10 years after she started studying the game; today she is rated among the 20 best chess players in the world. (See Figure 8.9.)

Similarly, most of the world's best violinists began learning the violin in early childhood and continue practicing 3–4 hours a day throughout their lives. Those hours of "practice" do not include the hours of performance. While performing, one does not have an opportunity to work on perfecting one's skills or correcting one's mistakes. Thus, an expert violinist devotes practice time to working on especially difficult passages. A tennis player may spend hours working on just the backhand, and a golfer may spend hours practicing a chip shot. The practice is even more effective if a coach is present to provide extra feedback.

So, does all this mean that you could become an expert at something? If you have waited until college age to start on a skill as competitive as chess or violin, you are very late; still, the answer is yes, if you choose an appropriate field and devote enough effort, you can become an expert at something. However, do not underestimate the effort and sacrifice that will be necessary. For Judit

FIGURE 8.9
Judit Polgar confirmed her father's confidence that prolonged effort could make her an expert in her chosen field, chess. She became the fourth woman ever to achieve grand master status in chess. By reaching that status at age 15 years and 5 months, she beat Bobby Fischer's previous record for being the youngest grand master.

a

b

FIGURE 8.10
Pieces arranged on a chessboard in a way that might actually occur in a game (a) and in a random manner (b). Master chess players can memorize the realistic pattern much better than average players can, but they are no better than average at memorizing the random pattern.

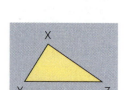

FIGURE 8.11
A question to test mathematical problem-solving skills: What line drawn parallel to the base of the triangle will divide the area in half?

Polgar to become a grand master at chess, she devoted about 8 hours a day to chess, beginning at age 5. She did not go to school and she spent little time on the usual childhood activities. Whatever your chosen field, if you want to be really outstanding in it, you have to commit yourself to an enormous amount of work.

EXPERT PATTERN RECOGNITION

Once someone has become an expert, what exactly does that person do that other people do not? In other words, what makes someone an expert? One important characteristic of experts is that they can look at a pattern and recognize its important features quickly. In a typical experiment (de Groot, 1966), people were shown pieces on a chessboard, as in Figure 8.10, for 5 seconds. Then they were asked to recall the position of all the pieces. When the pieces were arranged as they might occur in an actual game, expert players could recall the position of 91% of them, while novices could recall only 41%. When the pieces were arranged randomly, however, the expert players did no better than the nonexperts. That is, expert chess players do not have a superior overall memory; they have simply learned to recognize and remember a great many of the most common chessboard patterns.

Similarly, expert figure skaters can memorize a sequence of skating moves better than an average skater can. In one study, six members of the Canadian women's ice-skating team and four other, moderately skilled skaters were asked to memorize a sequence of eight skating elements and then either to describe or to perform them. If the elements were arranged in a haphazard order, the two

groups of skaters remembered about equally well. But when the elements were choreographed in a logical order, the expert skaters remembered much better (Deakin & Allard, 1991). In this and other situations, an expert excels at recognizing and memorizing meaningful patterns of information.

EXPERT PROBLEM SOLVING

Some people manage to solve unfamiliar problems, while other people fail to do so. For example, try this difficult problem: Given a triangle, as shown in Figure 8.11, find the line parallel to the base that will divide the area of the triangle in half.

Alan Schoenfeld (1985) observed the steps people went through as they tried to solve this problem. One pair of college students who had just completed a calculus course began by guessing that the line should be drawn halfway between the base and the vertex of the triangle. After carefully drawing that line, they realized it was wrong. Then they drew a line from the vertex to the midpoint of the base, forgetting that the line had to be parallel to the base. One of them suggested that they go back to the problem and "underline the important parts." When the allotted 30 minutes expired, they were no closer to a solution than when they began.

By contrast, one professional mathematician noticed that any line drawn parallel to the base will create a small triangle *Xyz* similar to the large triangle *XYZ*, as shown in Figure 8.12. Because the angles of the two triangles are the same, the height-to-base ratio of the small triangle (*h*/*b*) must be the same as the height-to-base ratio of the large triangle (*H*/*B*). Because the problem specified that the area of the small triangle is half the area of the large triangle, he calculated that the ratio of *h* to *H* must be the ratio of 1 to the square root of 2 (Figure 8.12).

The two students knew how to do everything the professional mathematician did. Why, then, could they not solve the problem? The expert almost immediately picked out the relevant information, rejected some fruitless approaches, and plotted a direct route to the solution. The nonexperts wasted much time on wild-goose chases without realizing that they were doing something irrelevant. Evidently, expertise is a matter not just of having the right tools but also of knowing which tools to use and when.

PROBLEM SOLVING

Can people learn general skills of problem solving that they could apply to new and unfamiliar questions? To some extent, yes (Bransford & Stein, 1984).

Generally we go through four phases when we set about solving a problem (Polya, 1957): (1) understanding the problem, (2) generating one or more hypotheses, (3) testing the hypotheses, and (4) checking the results (Figure 8.13). A scientist goes through those four phases in approaching a new, complex phenomenon, and you probably would go through them in trying to assemble a bicycle that came with garbled instructions. We shall go through the four phases of problem solving, with advice on each phase.

UNDERSTANDING AND SIMPLIFYING A DIFFICULT PROBLEM

You are facing a question or a problem, and you have no idea how to begin. You may even think the problem is unsolvable. Then someone shows you how to solve it and you realize, "I could have done that, if I had only thought of trying it that way."

When you do not see how to solve a problem, try starting with a simpler version of it. For example, here is what may appear to be a difficult, even impossible, problem:

A professor hands back students' test papers at random. On the average, how many students will accidentally receive their own paper?

Note that the problem fails to specify how many students are in the class. At first you may not see any way to approach the problem, but see what happens if we start with simpler cases: How many students will get their own paper back if there is only one student in the class? One, of course. What if there are two students? There is a 50% chance that both will get their own paper back and a 50% chance that neither will. On the average, one student will get the correct paper. What if there are three students? Each student has one chance in three of getting his or her own paper. One-third chance times three students means that, on the average, one student will get the correct paper. Having worked through a few simple examples, we suddenly see the pattern: The number of students in the class does not matter; on the

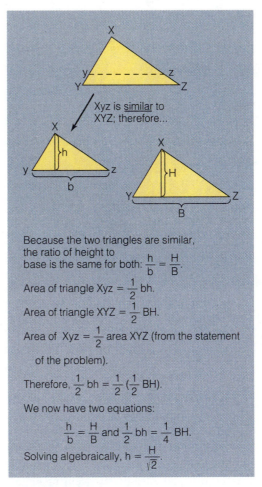

Xyz is <u>similar</u> to XYZ; therefore...

Because the two triangles are similar, the ratio of height to base is the same for both: $\frac{h}{b} = \frac{H}{B}$.

Area of triangle Xyz $= \frac{1}{2}$ bh.

Area of triangle XYZ $= \frac{1}{2}$ BH.

Area of Xyz $= \frac{1}{2}$ area XYZ (from the statement of the problem).

Therefore, $\frac{1}{2}$ bh $= \frac{1}{2}$ ($\frac{1}{2}$ BH).

We now have two equations:

$\frac{h}{b} = \frac{H}{B}$ and $\frac{1}{2}$ bh $= \frac{1}{4}$ BH.

Solving algebraically, $h = \frac{H}{\sqrt{2}}$.

FIGURE 8.12
An expert solution for how to divide the area of a triangle in half by a line drawn parallel to the base. The impossible may seem easy once you see the answer.

average, one student will get his or her own paper back.

Often you can also find ways to simplify a factual question and to generate a decent estimate of the correct answer (von Baeyer, 1988). For example, what is the circumference of Earth? Even if you do not know the answer, you might know the distance from New York to Los Angeles—about 3,000 miles (4,800 km). The distance from New York to Los Angeles is also a change of three time zones. How many times zones would a traveler cross in going completely around the planet? Twenty-four (one for each hour in the day). So the distance from New York is ³⁄₂₄ (or one eighth) of the distance around Earth. Eight times the distance from New York to Los Angeles is 8 × 3,000 miles (4,800 km) = 24,000 miles (38,400 km). That is a decent approximation of the actual circumference of Earth, 24,902.4 miles (40,068 km).

GENERATING HYPOTHESES

Suppose that after simplifying a problem as well as possible, you realize that many

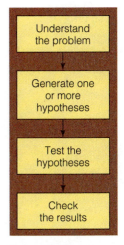

FIGURE 8.13
The four steps in solving problems.

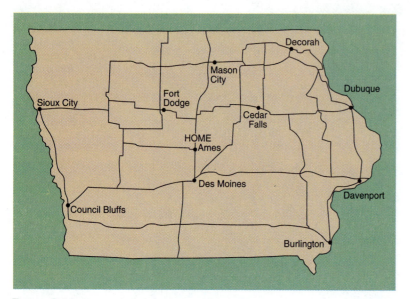

FIGURE 8.14
In the "traveling-salesperson problem," the task is to find the shortest route from home through all the other destinations. If the number of destinations is large, the number of possible routes can be extremely large. Therefore, we look for some heuristic to simplify the problem.

answers are possible. At that point you need to generate hypotheses—preliminary interpretations that you can evaluate or test.

In some cases, you can generate more hypotheses than you can test. Consider the traveling-salesperson problem in Figure 8.14. Starting and finishing at Ames, how could you travel through each of the marked cities while keeping your total travel distance to a minimum? You could set up an algorithm to solve the problem. An **algorithm** is a mechanical, repetitive mathematical procedure for solving a problem such as "Calculate the distance from Ames to a first city, then to a second city, and so on through all cities and back to Ames again. Repeat the same procedure for all possible orders of the cities. Compare the distances of all the possible routes."

That algorithm tests all the possible hypotheses (routes) and is sure to lead to the best answer . . . eventually. But even with just 10 cities to visit, there are nearly 2 million possible routes (10 factorial divided by 2). As the number of cities increases, the task becomes unmanageable even for computers. To make the problem manageable, we must narrow the number of hypotheses. We do so by resorting to **heuristics**, strategies for simplifying a problem or for guiding an investigation. A heuristic is a rule for checking the most likely possibilities. For instance, we might decide to test only those routes in

which each move takes us to one of the four closest cities, rejecting all routes in which the salesperson has to go from one end of the state to the other. Or we might limit the search to routes in which the salesperson finishes one part of the state before starting a new one.

Heuristics are important for many kinds of problem solving. Suppose you and a friend you haven't seen for years find you are both visiting the same state at the same time and decide to meet halfway between where you are and where your friend is. But this turns out to be a city where neither of you has ever been before, so neither of you can suggest a landmark where you can meet. You might think of some heuristic to simplify the problem. For example, "Go to the city limits on the western side and look for the nearest fast-food place." Once you arrived, you might have to look for your friend in several nearby fast-food places, but at least you would have narrowed the search. (Perhaps you could think of a better heuristic for solving this problem.)

CONCEPT CHECK

5. The government wants to know how much the average citizen pays for groceries each week. So it finds a city with only one grocery store, asks the store manager how much money he or she receives for sales in a given week, and divides that amount by the number of people who live in the city. Is that approach to the problem an example of an algorithm or an example of heuristics? (Check your answer on page 344.)

TESTING HYPOTHESES AND CHECKING THE RESULTS

If you think you have solved a problem, test your idea to see whether it will work. Many people who think they have a great idea never bother to try it out, even on a small scale. One inventor applied for a patent on the "perpetual motion machine" shown in Figure 8.15. Rubber balls, being lighter than water, rise in a column of water and overflow at the top. Being heavier than air, they fall, moving a belt and thereby generating energy. At the bottom, they reenter the water column. Do you see why this system could never work? You would if you tried to build it. (Check answer C on page 344.)

The final step in solving a problem is to check and recheck the results, or at least to check whether the results are plausible. For example, one article in the journal *Science* reported that fields in California's Imperial Valley produce 750,000 melons per acre. One reader, who had grown up on a farm, wrote to the journal to point out that 750,000 melons per acre equates to about 17 melons per square foot. With tongue in cheek, he asked whether the weight of all those melons might be causing California's earthquakes (Hoffman, 1992).

GENERALIZING SOLUTIONS TO SIMILAR PROBLEMS

After laboriously solving one problem, can people then solve a related problem more easily? Can they at least recognize that the new problem is related to the old problem, so they know where to start?

Sometimes yes, but all too frequently no. Many people who understand the laws of probability fail to see how those laws might apply to real-life situations (Nisbett, Fong, Lehman, & Cheng, 1987). For example, most people who flipped a coin 10 times and got 10 consecutive heads would not expect more than 5 heads out of the next 10 flips. But the same people might expect a basket-

FIGURE 8.16
(a) Draw the trajectory of water as it flows out of a coiled garden hose.
(b) Draw the trajectory of a bullet as it leaves a coiled gun barrel.

a

b

ball team that won 10 consecutive games to win the next 10 games as well. The basketball situation is not exactly the same as coin flipping, but it does have some similarity: A long winning streak depends partly on chance.

In other situations as well, people who have solved one problem correctly fail to solve a second problem that is basically similar, unless someone gives them a hint explaining that the problems are similar (Gick & Holyoak, 1980). For example, Figure 8.16 shows a coiled garden hose. When the water spurts out, what path will it take? (Draw it.) Figure 8.16 shows a curved gun barrel. When the bullet comes out, what path will it take? (Draw it.)

Almost everyone draws the water coming out of the garden hose in a straight path. Even after doing so, however, many people draw a bullet coming out of a gun in a curved path, as if the bullet remembered the curved path it had just taken (Kaiser, Jonides, & Alexander, 1986). The physics is the same in both situations: Both the water and the bullet will follow a straight path (except for the effects of gravity).

Sometimes we recognize similar problems and use our solution to an old problem as a guide to solving a new one (Figure 8.17); sometimes we do not. What accounts for the difference? One reason is that it is easier to generalize a solution after we have seen several examples of it; if we have seen only a single example, we may think of the solution in only that one context (Gick &

FIGURE 8.17
The computer mouse was invented by a computer scientist who was familiar with an engineering device called a planimeter and decided that it could be modified for use with computers. Such insights are unusual; most people do not generalize a solution from one task to another.

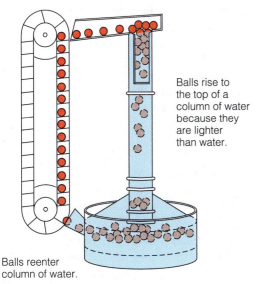

Balls overflow onto conveyor belt and pull it down because they are heavier than air.

Balls rise to the top of a column of water because they are lighter than water.

Balls reenter column of water.

FIGURE 8.15
What is wrong with this perpetual motion machine?

Holyoak, 1983). For example, one group of high-school students had learned to solve arithmetic-progression problems in algebra, practicing on a variety of problems. When they were given a fundamentally similar problem in physics, they recognized the similarity and solved it (Figure 8.18). A different group of students had been taught to solve the physics problem; when they were given the related problem in algebra, most of them failed to recognize the similarity (Bassok & Holyoak, 1989). Apparently the physics students associated the solution entirely with physics, and they failed to see it as a general principle that could be applied more widely.

Although people often fail to transfer a solution from one problem to an analogous problem, most people transfer general approaches to problems. For example, people might learn to represent certain kinds of problems graphically or to break up a problem into subproblems. Once they have learned these skills, they readily apply them to other problems (Novick, 1990).

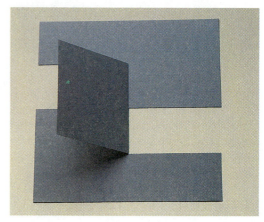

FIGURE 8.19
An object made by cutting and folding an ordinary piece of cardboard with nothing left over. How was it done?

SPECIAL FEATURES OF INSIGHT PROBLEMS

Some of the problems we have been discussing are "insight" problems or "Aha!" problems—the kind in which you think of the correct answer suddenly, if you think of it at all. Here is a clear example of an insight problem (Gardner, 1978): Figure 8.19 shows an object that was made by just cutting and bending an ordinary piece of cardboard. How was it made? If you think you know, take a piece of paper and try to make it yourself.

People react to this problem in different ways. Some see the solution almost at once; others take a long time before insight suddenly strikes them; still others never figure it out. Some people have looked at this illustration and told me that it was impossible, that I must have pasted two pieces together or bought a custom-made piece of "trick cardboard." (The correct answer is on page 344, answer D.)

INSIGHTFUL PROBLEM SOLVING: SUDDEN OR GRADUAL?

Solving insight problems differs from solving, say, algebra problems. Most people can look at an algebra problem and rather accurately predict whether or not they will be able to solve it, and if so, how quickly. As they work on it, they can estimate how close they are to reaching a solution. On insight problems, however, they give poor estimates of whether they are about to solve the prob-

---

a An arithmetic-progression problem in algebra:

Q: A boy was given an allowance of 50 cents a week beginning on his 6th birthday. On each birthday following this, the weekly allowance was increased 25 cents. What is the weekly allowance beginning on his 15th birthday?

Solution: Let a_n = allowance beginning on nth birthday
d = difference added on each birthday

$a_{15} = a_6 + (9)d$

Number of birthdays from age 6 to 15

$= \$.50 + (9) \times .25 = \$2.75$

b A constant-acceleration problem in physics:

Q: An express train, traveling at 30 meters per second at the start of the 3rd second of its travel, uniformly accelerates increasing in speed 5 meters per second each succeeding second. What is its final speed at the end of the 9th second?

Solution: Let s_n = speed at beginning of nth second
d = difference added each second

$s_{10} = s_3 + (7)d$

Speed at beginning of 10th second (end of 9th)

Number of seconds from the start of 3rd second to end of the 9th

$= 30 + (7) \times 5 = 65$ m/s

FIGURE 8.18
An arithmetic-progression problem in algebra (a) is similar to a constant-acceleration problem in physics (b). Students who had learned to solve the algebra problem recognized the physics problem as similar and solved it successfully. Most students who had learned to solve the physics problem, however, failed to recognize the algebra problem as similar and failed to solve it. (From Bassok and Holyoak, 1989.)

lem or not (Metcalfe & Wiebe, 1987). Frequently someone will say, "I have no idea whether I will ever solve this problem," and then suddenly announce the correct answer the next minute.

So it appears that the answer comes suddenly, all or none. But does it really? If you were groping your way around in a dark room, you would have no idea how soon you were going to find the door, but that does not mean that you have made no progress. You would have learned much about the room, including many places where the door was *not*.

So maybe people are making progress without realizing it when they struggle with insight problems. To test this possibility, psychologists gave students problems of the following form:

> The three words below are all associated with one other word. What is that word?
>
> color   numbers   oil

In this case, the correct answer is *paint*. Like other insight questions, subjects reported that they got the answer suddenly or not at all and that they could not tell whether they were about to think of the answer or not. Then the experimenters gave the subjects paired sets of three words each to examine for 12 seconds. In each pair, one set had a correct answer (like *paint* in the example just given). For the other set, no one word was associated with all three items. Subjects were to try to generate a correct answer if they could; if not, they were to guess *which* set had a correct answer and say how confident they were of their guess. Examples:

First pair of sets:
playing credit report OR still pages music

Second pair of sets:
town root car OR ticket shop broker

(You can check your answers on page 344, answer E.)

The main result was that when subjects could not find the correct answer, they still guessed with greater than 50% accuracy which was the set that had a correct answer (Bowers, Regehr, Balthazard, & Parker, 1990). Even on pairs for which subjects said they had "no confidence" at all in their guesses, they were still right more often than not. In short, insight solutions are not altogether sudden; people may be "getting warm" even without realizing it.

CHARACTERISTICS OF CREATIVE PROBLEM SOLVING

Solving a problem or developing a new product is always to some extent a creative activity, but some solutions and products seem more creative than others. Psychologists frequently define **creativity** as the development of novel, socially valued products (Mumford & Gustafson, 1988). In principle that is a reasonable definition, although in practice it can be hard to apply. Many unusual works of art and literature were not held in high esteem in their own time but later hailed as classics. By the usual definition of *creative*, these works became creative many decades after they were produced!

One of the important characteristics of a creative contribution is choosing an appropriate task or problem. For example, we admire the works of Darwin, Newton, or Einstein not just because they found the answers to their questions, but also because they identified important unanswered but answerable questions. Similarly, the mark of great political leaders is not just that they propose good solutions to problems, but that they focus attention on the right problems.

Could you or I develop a great scientific theory, if we addressed the right question and had all the necessary information? If you want to try this challenge, examine the data

DD Dolby®

Dolby sound is one example of an insight solution to a problem. Engineer Ray Dolby was trying to find ways to reduce hissing noises on tapes when he suddenly got the idea to treat high-level signals differently from low-level signals. (Noise is a problem when the music is soft; we do not notice it when the music is loud.)

Creative problem solving, such as making a bridge out of whatever supplies are available, has two elements: novelty and social value.

in the table below. Five pairs of numbers, arbitrarily labeled s and q, are measurements of two physical variables. I won't tell you what the variables are, because you might be familiar with the theory in question. Examine each of the pairs of variables and see whether you can find a single mathematical equation relating s to q.

In one study, 4 of 14 university students managed to find the correct equation within 1 hour, thus reproducing a great scientific discovery (Qin & Simon, 1990). You may use a calculator. Recommendation: Either copy these data onto another sheet of paper or cover the text to the right so that you do not accidentally read the correct formula.

s	q
36	88
67.25	224.7
93	365.3
141	687
483.8	4332.1

An example of creative problem solving: United Nations field worker Peter Dalglish, wanting to help homeless orphans in Khartoum, Sudan, decided to put their knowledge of the streets to good use as bicycle couriers in a city where telephones are unreliable. On another occasion, Dalglish caught a boy breaking into his car. Instead of calling the police, he thought, "This kid would make a great mechanic," and set up a technical training school for Khartoum's homeless children.

The data represent measurements on the first five planets of our solar system. Column s gives the distance from the sun in millions of miles; column q gives the time (in Earth days) required for rotation around the sun. The German astronomer Johannes Kepler (1571–1630) is regarded as a great genius and the founder of modern astronomy for

discerning the relationship between these two sets of data.

The correct formula can be expressed in any of the following ways:

$$s^3/q^2 = 6.025$$
$$s^3/6.025 = q^2$$
$$q^{2/3} = 0.55\, s$$
$$s^{1.5} = 2.45\, q$$

That is, the cube of the distance from the sun is related to the square of the period of rotation. The fact that 4 university students solved this problem, and in fact solved it in less time than Kepler needed, indicates that the actual problem solving requires only good mathematical skill and a fair degree of persistence, not some special talent available to only one person in a million. Kepler's true genius emerged in the fact that he guessed that there *was* a relationship between the two sets of numbers; that is, he guessed that it was a solvable problem.

SOMETHING TO THINK ABOUT

Are people of normal ability also capable of great creative achievements in art and literature? How could we test that ability?

THE CHARACTERISTICS OF CREATIVE PEOPLE

Are some people naturally more creative than other people are? The Torrance Tests of Creative Thinking use items similar to the one shown in Figure 8.20 to measure creativity (Torrance, 1980, 1981, 1982). We know that such tests are measuring *something*; certain individuals consistently score high when they

FIGURE 8.20
A "what-is-it?" picture similar to those in one part of the Torrance Tests of Creative Thinking.

take any of these tests, and other individuals consistently score low. However, the tests do not seem to be measuring a general ability to perform creatively regardless of the situation. That is, the people who score high on such tests tend to perform well, even creatively, on the kinds of tasks the tests are measuring, but not necessarily on other tasks.

We should not fault the tests for this shortcoming; they fail to measure "general creative ability" only because such a thing does not exist. Highly creative people are creative only within the domains that they know well (Gardner, 1993). That is, a creative scientist who tries writing a poem is not likely to produce a fine, creative poem. A creative poet may not be a creative sculptor, and a creative sculptor may not devise creative solutions to problems in automobile repair.

Howard Gardner (1993) studied creativity by examining in detail the lives of seven individuals of the 20th century who are widely regarded as creative and who made their contributions to very different fields: Sigmund Freud (psychology), Albert Einstein (physics), Pablo Picasso (painting), Igor Stravinsky (musical composition), T. S. Eliot (poetry), Martha Graham (dance), and Mahatma Gandhi (political resistance, religion, and spirituality). Gardner inquired what, if anything, these highly creative people had in common. He found a few patterns, which may perhaps be accidents that depend on his particular choice of "creative people," but which deserve at least serious consideration. Among those patterns were the following:

- Creativity thrives in an atmosphere of moderate tension, in which the person senses that the old ways of doing things are not quite adequate.

- The highly creative person has to have enough familiarity with the topic to feel self-confident, but not so much experience that he or she has become trapped in the traditional habits of procedure. Just as people need about 10 years to become an expert in a field, people generally need about 10 years in a field before they are ready to make their first major creative contribution.

- During a period early in life when a creative genius is working on new ideas, he or she is likely to rely heavily on one or a few close, trusted friends for advice and encouragement. The advice is necessary for polishing the ideas and the encouragement is nec-

Howard Gardner compared seven highly creative people, including dance pioneer Martha Graham, to find the features that promote creativity.

essary to build persistence in the face of criticism.

- A creative genius throws himself or herself wholeheartedly into the work, sacrificing any possibility of a "well-rounded" life. Each of the creative people that Gardner studied had a very limited family life and very strained relationships with other people. Even Gandhi, famous as an advocate of love and justice, loved people only in the abstract and had trouble developing close relationships with actual individuals.

COMMON ERRORS IN HUMAN COGNITION

Although we humans pride ourselves on our intelligence and on our ability to solve problems, we sometimes err on fairly simple problems. After someone points out the correct answer, we are surprised at our own mistake. Sometimes we err because we relied on inappropriate heuristics. Recall that heuristics are methods for simplifying a problem and facilitating an investigation. Ordinarily, relying on heuristics enables us to find a reasonable, if not perfect, answer. Occasionally,

According to Philip Tetlock's research, most news analysts who confidently predict national and world events are no more accurate than you or I would be—just more confident. Analysts who consistently favored a particular political viewpoint were less accurate than those who tried to see both sides of an issue.

however, certain heuristics can lead us astray. Let's now consider several reasons why people sometimes arrive at illogical conclusions.

OVERCONFIDENCE

Let's try a little demonstration. Answer each of the questions in the box at the bottom of the page and then estimate the probability that your answer is correct. For example, you might feel 99% sure, 50% sure, or 10% sure that you are correct.

Most people are overconfident of their answers to such questions as 1–4 and underconfident of their affirmative answer to question 5. (You did say "yes," didn't you?) For statistical reasons, it is almost a sure thing that the average person will be underconfident of his or her answer to question 5: Be-

cause the actual probability is virtually 100%, no one will overstate the probability, and if anyone understates it, the average will be an understatement (Erev, Wallsten, & Budescu, 1994).

However, in cases in which people try to predict events that are actually quite uncertain, most people tend to be overconfident of their predictions (Kahneman, Slovic, & Tversky, 1982). People are especially likely to be overconfident when predicting their own accomplishments. For example, at the beginning of each semester, most students (even poor students) estimate that they will get mostly A's and B's (Prohaska, 1994). (See Figure 8.21.) Similarly, most athletes and athletic teams predict that they will have better seasons this year than they had last year, and most people entering a contest think they have a better-than-average chance of winning. A certain amount of optimism and self-confidence is probably good for our mental health, but objectively speaking, people are overestimating their probable success. (Most students will not get all A's and B's, and it is impossible for every team in the league to win more games this year than they won last year.)

Philip Tetlock (1994) conducted a study of government officials and consultants, foreign policy professors, newspaper columnists, and others who make their living by analyzing and predicting world events. He asked them to predict a number of events in U.S. and world politics over the next several years—such as what would happen in Korea, the Middle East, Eastern Europe, and Cuba—and to state, in percent, their confidence in the predictions. Five years later he checked their accuracy. He found that most of the experts' predictions were no more accurate than the guesses you or I might have

	Your answer	% confidence
1. What grade will you get in psychology this semester?		
2. Who will be elected president of the United States in the next election?		
3. Over the next three months, will the stock market go up, down, or stay steady?		
4. What will happen in the next two years in Cuba?		
5. Will there be at least one hurricane and at least one earthquake somewhere in the world next year?		

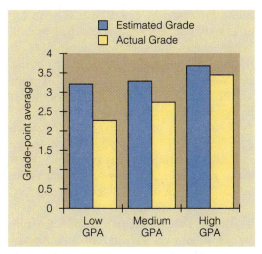

FIGURE 8.21
At the beginning of a semester, undergraduates in an advanced psychology course estimated their probable semester grade. Students with low, medium, or high grade-point averages generally predicted that they would get an A or a B. The best students were slightly overpredicting their success; the worst students were greatly overpredicting. (Based on data of Prohaska, 1994.)

made, although they had expressed great confidence in their predictions. That is, they were overconfident. Curiously, the few experts whose predictions showed more than random accuracy shared the following features:

- They showed no strong political leaning. (Experts who consistently favored one political party or a conservative or liberal viewpoint were wrong as often as they were right.)
- They relied on complex information, instead of arguing from analogy to a single historical pattern.
- They were not too sure of themselves. That is, the ones most likely to be right were the ones who admitted they might be wrong.

Of all the people who make their livings by predicting the future, weather forecasters are among the most accurate. Although we tend to remember the spectacular errors, of all the times when meteorologists forecast a "70% chance of rain," it actually does rain close to 70% of the time. One advantage of weather forecasting over predicting political events is that meteorologists get day-by-day feedback on their predictions; when they are wrong, they cannot avoid admitting they were wrong.

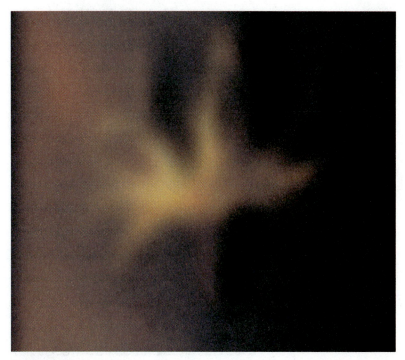

FIGURE 8.22a
People who form a hypothesis based on the first photo look at succeeding photos trying to find evidence that they are right. Because their first guess is generally wrong, they do less well than do people who look at the later photos before making any preliminary guesses. Try to guess what this shows. Then examine parts b and c on the following pages.

PREMATURE COMMITMENT TO A HYPOTHESIS

Sometimes we make mistakes because we commit ourselves prematurely to a particular hypothesis and fail to consider other possibilities. Suppose a psychologist asks subjects to look at a photo way out of focus, as in Figure 8.22a, and asks them what they think the photo shows. Then the psychologist shows them a series of photos, each one in slightly sharper focus, until they correctly identify what is shown in the photos. Most people try to simplify the task by forming a hypothesis such as, "Maybe it's a picture of a military emblem." That is a heuristic of sorts; it guides further exploration of the photos. However, if the initial hypothesis is wrong, it can mislead. Subjects who first see an extremely blurry photo are generally *less* accurate at identifying a slightly blurry photo than are subjects who looked first at the slightly blurry photo (Bruner & Potter, 1964). Those who see the extremely blurry photo are impaired even if they check their initial hypothesis and find out that it is wrong (Snodgrass & Hirshman, 1991). Somehow, their initial

If something looks, waddles, and quacks like a duck, it's probably a duck. However, sometimes this "representativeness heuristic" leads us astray, especially if something resembles a rare type of item.

interpretation continues to interfere with any new interpretation.

Peter Wason (1960) asked students to discover a certain rule he had in mind for generating sequences of numbers. One example of the numbers the rule might generate, he explained, was "2, 4, 6." He told the students that they could ask about other sequences, and he would tell them whether or not those sequences fit the rule. As soon as they thought they had enough evidence, they could guess what the rule was.

Most students started by asking, "8, 10, 12?" When told "yes," they proceeded with, "14, 16, 18?" Each time, they were told, "yes, that sequence fits the rule." Soon most of them guessed, "The rule is three consecutive even numbers."

"No," came the reply. "That is not the rule." Many students persisted, trying "20, 22, 24?" "26, 28, 30?" "250, 252, 254?" And so forth. Eventually they would say, "Three even numbers in which the second is two more than the first and the third is two more than the second." Again, they were told that the guess was wrong. "But how can it be wrong?" they complained. "It always works!"

The rule Wason had in mind was, "Any three positive numbers of increasing magni-tude." For instance, 1, 2, 3, would be acceptable; so would 4, 19, 22, or 3, 76, 9 million. Where many students went wrong was in testing only the cases that their hypothesis said would fit the rule. One must also examine the cases that the hypothesis says will not fit the rule (Klayman & Ha, 1987).

A follow-up study used the same procedure but added one complication: Investigators told the students that when they asked about a sequence, the answers they received might be wrong on 0–20% of all occasions. Under these conditions, students were even less likely than usual to discover the rule. Whenever they got a result that did not match their hypothesis, they "explained it away" by assuming this was one of those occasions on which they received an incorrect answer (Gorman, 1989). In short, we all tend to look for evidence that supports our beliefs and to overlook or disregard evidence that conflicts with our beliefs. This is a hard tendency to overcome; we should at least be aware of it.

THE REPRESENTATIVENESS HEURISTIC AND BASE-RATE INFORMATION

Perhaps you have heard the saying: "If some-thing looks like a duck, waddles like a duck, and quacks like a duck, chances are it's a duck." This saying is an example of the **representativeness heuristic,** the tendency to assume that if an item is similar to members of a particular category, it is probably a member of that category itself. This assumption is reasonable in most cases.

It can lead us astray, however, if we are dealing with something unusual. For example, suppose you see a bird that looks like an Eskimo curlew, walks like an Eskimo curlew, and whistles like an Eskimo curlew. Does that mean you have found an Eskimo curlew?

Not likely. Eskimo curlews are extremely rare, almost extinct; chances are, you have sighted some more common bird that resembles an Eskimo curlew.

When we have to decide whether some-thing belongs in category A or category B, such as Eskimo curlew versus other bird, we should consider three questions: (1) How closely does it resemble the items in category A? (2) How closely does it resemble the items in category B? (3) Which is more common, category A or category B? The answer to the third question is known as **base-rate infor-mation**—that is, data about the frequency or probability of a given item, how rare or how common it is.

People frequently overlook the base-rate information and follow only the representativeness heuristic. As a result, they identify something as a member of some uncommon category, disregarding the more likely category. For example, consider the following question (modified from Kahneman & Tversky, 1973):

Psychologists have interviewed 30 engineers and 70 lawyers. One of them is Jack, a 45-year-old married man with four children. He is generally conservative, careful, and ambitious. He shows no interest in political and social issues and spends most of his free time on home carpentry, sailing, and mathematical puzzles. What is the probability that Jack is one of the 30 engineers in the sample of 100?

Most people think that the description is more representative of engineers than it is of lawyers. Based on representativeness, they estimate that Jack is probably an engineer. But what about the fact that the sample includes more than twice as many lawyers as engineers? That base-rate information should influence their estimates. In fact, however, most people pay little attention to the base-rate information. They make about the same estimates of how likely Jack is to be an engineer, regardless of whether the sample includes 30% engineers or 70% engineers (Kahneman & Tversky, 1973).

Here is another example of overreliance on the representativeness heuristic. Read the following description, and then answer the questions following it:

Linda was a philosophy major. She is 31, bright, outspoken, and concerned with issues of discrimination and social justice.

Now, what would you estimate the probability to be that Linda is a bank teller? What is the probability that she is a *feminist* bank teller? (Answer before you read on.)

It is hard to know what the true probabilities are, but that is not the point. The interesting result is that most people estimate a higher probability that Linda is a feminist bank teller than the probability that she is a bank teller (Tversky & Kahneman, 1983). That estimate is self-contradictory, as she clearly could not be a feminist bank teller without being a bank teller. The reason is that people regard the description as fairly typical for a feminist, and therefore also for a feminist bank teller (or feminist *anything*). But it is not an especially typical description for bank tellers in general (Shafir, Smith, & Osherson,

FIGURE 8.22b

1990). Because of the representativeness heuristic, most people overestimate the probability that Linda is a feminist bank teller.

CONCEPT CHECK

6. *Suppose an improved lie-detector test can determine with 90% accuracy whether people are telling the truth. An employer proposes to administer the test to all employees, asking them whether they have ever stolen from the company and firing everyone who fails the test. Is that policy reasonable? Assume that the company has 1,000 employees, of whom only 20 have ever stolen anything. Hint: Think about the base-rate probability of finding a dishonest employee. (Check your answer on page 344.)*

THE AVAILABILITY HEURISTIC

When asked how common something is, or how often something happens, we generally start by trying to think of examples. Try this question: In the English language, are there more words that start with *k* or more words that have *k* as the third letter? If you are like most people, you guessed that there are more words that start with *k*. How did you decide that? You tried to think of words that start with *k*: "king, kitchen, kangaroo, key, knowledge, . . ." Then you tried to think of

If you worked at a U.S. federal building and you saw a truck parked outside the building, how would you react? During the weeks just after a truck bomb destroyed a federal building in Oklahoma City, the ready availability of that memory made a parked truck seem dangerous. Here, a driver left his truck just long enough to get coffee and returned to find the police suspiciously inspecting it. The availability heuristic is often useful, but it can also mislead us.

words that have *k* as the third letter: "ask, ink, bake, . . . uh . . ." You were relying on the **availability heuristic,** the strategy of assuming that how many memories of an event are available indicates how common the event actually is (Table 8.1). Because it was easier to think of words that start with *k* than words with *k* as the third letter, you assumed that there really are more words that start with *k*. In fact, however, words with *k* as the third letter are considerably more common.

The availability heuristic leads to illusory correlations, as we saw in Chapter 2. Someone asks, "Do people act strange on nights of a full moon?" If you have always expected people to act strange on such nights, you may be able to remember more examples when they did act strange than examples when they did not.

Here is another example of the availability heuristic: Suppose I ask you to fill out a survey of your beliefs on a variety of controversial political, social, and religious issues. Then I ask you for each of those questions to estimate what percentage of other people agree with your position. You will probably overestimate that percentage, for two reasons. One is that, as mentioned before, most people are overconfident of their own opinions. The other reason is that you probably associate with friends who share most of your opinions. You can think of many people who share your opinions; you consequently overestimate how many other people share those views.

Still another example: Do you consider yourself a better than average driver, an average driver, or a worse than average driver? A great many people consider themselves better than average; the rest consider themselves average. One reason why people tend to overestimate their driving skills is this: When you think about other drivers, the ones you remember most vividly are the unusually bad drivers. Because the worst drivers are the easiest to remember, we overestimate their numbers.

	IS A TENDENCY TO ASSUME THAT . . .	LEADS US ASTRAY WHEN . . .	EXAMPLE
TABLE 8.1 **The Representativeness Heuristic and the Availability Heuristic**			
Representativeness heuristic	any item that resembles members of some category is probably itself a member of that category.	an item resembles members of a rare category.	You see something that looks the way you think a UFO would look, so you decide it is a UFO.
Availability heuristic	how easily we can think of examples of some category indicates how many examples really occur.	one kind of example is easier to think of than another is.	You remember more newspaper reports of airline crashes than of car crashes, so you assume that air crashes are more common than car crashes.

You can guard against overuse of the availability heuristic. When you try to estimate whether one type of event is more common than another, look for systematic data. Don't just trust your memory of how often various events occur. (See Table 8.2.)

THE FRAMING OF QUESTIONS

If we were truly logical beings, we would give the same answer to a question no matter how it was worded. In fact, we do not. Most people give one answer to a question that is phrased in terms of gain and give a different answer to the same question when it is phrased in terms of loss.

For example: You have recently been appointed head of the Public Health Service. A new contagious disease has been detected, and you have to choose between two plans for combating it. If you do nothing, 600 people will die. If you adopt plan A, you will save the lives of 200 people. If you adopt plan B, there is a 33% chance that you will save all 600 and a 67% chance that you will save no one. (Choose one of the plans before reading further.)

Now another contagious disease breaks out; you must again choose between two plans. If you adopt plan C, 400 people will die. If you adopt plan D, there is a 33% chance that no one will die and a 67% chance that 600 will die. (Choose one now, then compare your choices with the results in Figure 8.23.)

Consider another example, this one dealing with money instead of lives. Which would you rather have?

  W. A gain of $240

or X. A 25% chance to win $1,000

Now you have to make another decision. You have just received an outright gift of $1,000, but you must choose between two unpleasant alternatives:

  Y. A loss of $750

or Z. A 75% chance of losing the whole $1,000 (a 25% chance of losing nothing)

Tversky and Kahneman found that 84% of all people chose W over X (avoiding risk), whereas 87% chose Z over Y (taking a risk). Note that W is actually $10 less than choice Y and that X is the same as Z. Again, people generally avoid taking a risk when considering gains but accept the risk when consider-

FIGURE 8.22c

ing losses. Put another way, people try to avoid losses.

This tendency sometimes leads people to decisions that economists would consider irrational. For example, 2 months ago you bought an expensive ticket to a football game. Today, the day of the game, the weather is cold and rainy. The team you were cheering for is having a dismal season, and several key players are out with injuries. You do not look forward to attending. In fact, if you did not have tickets and someone offered you a free one, you would refuse. And yet, you may decide to go to the game anyway, because you already paid for the tickets

TABLE 8.2
Your Odds of Dying

How much do you think each of the following activities increases your chance of dying? Rank them from most dangerous (7) to least dangerous (1). Compare your ranking with answer F on page 344.

_____Traveling 50 miles in a motor vehicle (cause of death: accident)
_____Traveling 400 miles in a school bus (cause: accident)
_____Flying 4 minutes, general aviation (cause: accident)
_____Flying 4 hours, scheduled airline (cause: accident)
_____Getting a chest X ray in a good hospital (cause: cancer from radiation)
_____Working for 3 hours as a miner (cause: accident)
_____Drinking 2 glasses of wine (cause: alcohol-related cirrhosis and automobile accident)

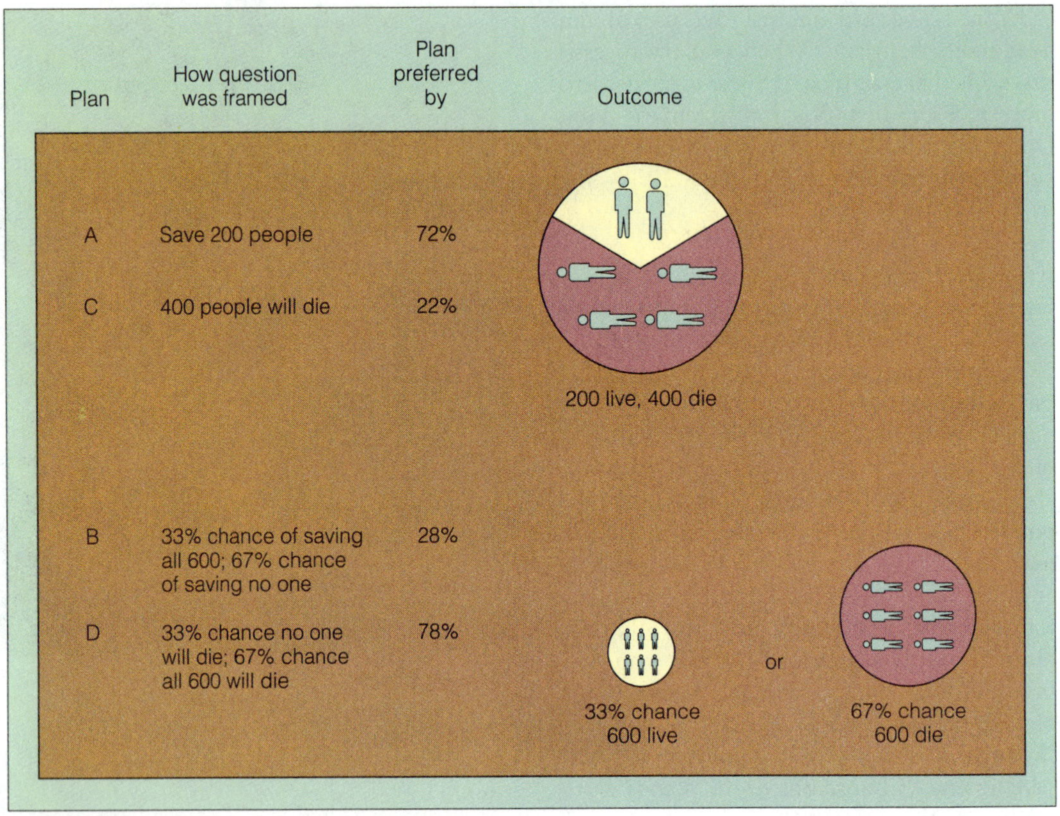

Plan	How question was framed	Plan preferred by	Outcome
A	Save 200 people	72%	
C	400 people will die	22%	

200 live, 400 die

| B | 33% chance of saving all 600; 67% chance of saving no one | 28% | |
| D | 33% chance no one will die; 67% chance all 600 will die | 78% | |

33% chance 600 live   or   67% chance 600 die

FIGURE 8.23

When Amos Tversky and Daniel Kahneman (1981) offered these choices to more than 150 people, 72% chose A over B and 78% chose D over C. However, plan A is exactly the same as plan C (200 live, 400 die), and plan B is exactly the same as plan D. Why then did so many people choose both A and D? The reason, according to Tversky and Kahneman, is that most people avoid taking a risk when a question is phrased in terms of gain, but they are willing to take a risk when a question is phrased in terms of loss.

and you "don't want to take a loss." (In fact, you lose twice—first by buying the ticket and second by attending an uninteresting game in the rain.) People can, however, learn to make more rational decisions in situations like this (Larrick, Morgan, & Nisbett, 1990).

CONCEPT CHECK

7. **a.** Someone says, *"More than 90% of all college students like to watch late-late night television, whereas only 20% of older adults do. Therefore, most watchers of late-late night television are college students."* What error in thinking has this person made?

b. Someone tells me that if I say "abracadabra" every morning I will stay healthy. I say it daily, and, sure enough, I stay healthy. I conclude that saying this magic word really does ensure health. What error of thinking have I made? (Check your answers on page 344.)

LEARNING, MEMORY, COGNITION, AND THE PSYCHOLOGY OF GAMBLING

Suppose your professor asks everyone in class to hand in 10 dollars. The professor collects all the money, keeps half of it, and hands the other half to one of the students, chosen at random. Presuming you were not the winner of the money, would you enjoy this little exercise? Would you encourage your professor to do it again every week from now on?

Casino gambling and state lotteries operate much like this example. Table 8.3 illustrates the odds for one state lottery game. Actually, casinos offer much better odds than a state lottery; a casino keeps less than 5% of the gambled money whereas a state government keeps about 50%. In either case, the great majority of the bettors are going to lose money, although they continue gambling anyway. For illustration, the Hilton Hotel company, which owns 230 hotels plus a

State and national lotteries have been called a "tax on stupidity." Both psychologists and economists try to understand why some people repeatedly bet large amounts of money despite knowing that they have only an extremely small chance of winning.

TABLE 8.3					
Expected Winnings on a $1 Decco Ticket (a California Lottery Game)					
	PROBABILITY	×	PAYOFF	=	EXPECTED VALUE
	.9573084	×	$0	=	$0.000
	.040404	×	$5	=	$0.202
	.0022409	×	$50	=	$0.112
	.0000467	×	$5,000	=	$0.233
Total	1.0				$0.547

Note: Someone who purchases a $1 ticket has more than a 95% chance of winning nothing, slightly more than a 4% chance of winning $5, and so forth. Overall, the person should expect to receive about 55 cents back for the $1. No one actually receives the 55 cents for a single ticket, but that should be the average payoff after someone has bought many Decco tickets.

gambling riverboat and a handful of hotel-casinos, reported that 62% of its 1993 income came from gambling (Dorfman, 1994).

Gambling has been a common part of human behavior throughout history and throughout the world. Why people gamble at all is an interesting question, but here we shall focus on why people make apparently illogical bets, in which they are likely to lose more than they win. We shall use this issue as a way of illustrating and reviewing some of the principles of learning, memory, and thinking that we have encountered in the last three chapters.

OVERESTIMATION OF CONTROL

Rationally, you should not spend $1 on a 1-in-21-thousand chance at winning $5,000 in a lottery. But what if you thought that *your* chances (unlike everyone else's) were significantly better than that? Perhaps you believe that you have some special skill or luck that will enable you to pick winning numbers. If so, then gambling might make sense for you. Most gamblers do believe that some people can win consistently at games of chance. Even most people who play the slot machines (Figure 8.24) believe that their skill in pulling the arm can influence their winnings (Griffiths, 1990).

In fact, this is part of a more general principle: Most people are overconfident about the accuracy of their own judgments. For example, we ask people questions of the form "What is *absinthe*—a precious stone, a liqueur, or a Caribbean island?" After each question we ask people to estimate their

probability of being correct. Most people overestimate (Lichtenstein, Fischhoff, & Phillips, 1982). That is, on questions where they estimate 60% accuracy, they are correct less than 60% of the time; when they estimate 70% accuracy, they are correct less than 70% of the time. So, when confronted with a roulette wheel or some other game of chance, it is not surprising that people overestimate their chances of winning.

Here is a quote from one habitual lottery gambler who makes clear his beliefs about the possibility of skillfully picking winning numbers: "Working the lottery is a lot of work, and you need the time between games to work on your systems and number combinations. You need to get books with systems

FIGURE 8.24
Most chronic gamblers believe that some people can win consistently at games of chance. Even with slot machines, many people believe their skill in pulling the handle can influence their results.

and work out possible repeat combinations and go over your charts to check the highs and lows [numbers with many hits and numbers with few hits] and the number of times since a number hit last, if a number is hot, and combinations of pairs that are hot, etc., etc." (in Lorenz, 1990, p. 385). (This man's gambling losses eventually led him to criminal offenses that landed him in prison.)

In one study, people were given a chance to buy $1 lottery tickets for a $50 prize (Langer, 1975). Some of them were simply handed a ticket, while others were permitted to choose their own ticket. Those who chose their own ticket thought they had a better chance of winning. Days later, all the ticket holders were asked whether they were willing to sell their ticket to someone else. Those who had been handed a ticket were generally willing to sell, asking for a price only slightly higher than what they had paid for their ticket. Those who had chosen their own ticket asked a mean of more than $8 per ticket, and some refused to sell for less than the full $50 they expected to win!

PEOPLE'S AFFINITY FOR LONG-SHOT BETS

Which would you rather have, $100,000 for sure, or a 10% chance of winning a million dollars? If you are like most college students who have been offered this choice, you will choose the $100,000 for sure. What about a choice between $10,000 for sure and a 1% chance at a million dollars? Again, you will probably choose the sure gain of $10,000.

The choices continue: Would you prefer $1,000 for sure or a 0.1% chance at a million? A sure profit of $100 or a 0.01% chance at a million? A $10 profit or a 0.001% chance at a million? A $1 profit or a 0.0001% chance at a million? At some point in this progression, most college students switch from the sure profit to the gamble. For most students, if the sure profit is $10 or less, they prefer a chance at winning a million. In fact, almost half of the students would forego $10 to have even one chance in a million of winning a million (Rachlin, Siegel, & Cross, 1994).

Why? First, for most students, $10 does not sound like very much. Oh, sure, you would rather have the $10 than not have it, but unless you happen to need the money to pay a bill right now, $10 is not going to raise your standard of living enough to notice.

A million dollars would. Furthermore, although it is easy to understand the difference between a 10% chance and a 1% chance, most of us are not very sensitive to the difference between a 0.001% chance and a 0.0001% or even a 0.000001% chance. Beyond a certain point, they all blur together as just "unlikely," and as long as the chance is even slightly above 0, we think, "Someone is going to win, and it might be me."

SCHEDULES OF REINFORCEMENT

Most gamblers make a long series of bets, not just one bet. They win some; they lose some. They get reinforced on a variable-ratio schedule; that is, the more bets they place, the more times they win, but the order of wins and losses is random. As we discussed in Chapter 6, such a schedule induces a steady rate of responding, even during a long period without reinforcement.

Still, some people who have never won a lottery persist in buying tickets, whereas other people quit buying tickets immediately after winning a million-dollar jackpot (Kaplan, 1988). That is, a win does not always reinforce gambling and a loss may not particularly weaken it. Howard Rachlin (1990) suggests that a gambler evaluates his or her success at the end of a string of bets that ends in a win. For example, suppose you lose bets on six horse races and then bet on a winner. If your bet on the winner pays more than the amount you lost on the first six bets, then you don't count your progress as "six losses, one win," but as "a net gain on the day, one overall win." (Horse-race gamblers who have lost money on the first few races of the day generally make large bets on the final race. Do you see why?)

Similarly, if you bet on a single number at roulette (at a payoff of 35 to 1), you would count yourself a winner if you picked a winning number before losing $35. The situation is a little like that of a pigeon pecking at a disk, receiving rare but large reinforcements.

Now, imagine a man who buys tickets in a state lottery. Every year he spends hundreds of dollars, maybe thousands, without winning anything. Does he give up? If so, he admits that all he invested is a loss. If he continues buying tickets, he maintains the hope of eventually hitting the jackpot, winning more than enough to make up for all the money he lost. A single payoff could make the whole string of bets a net win.

VICARIOUS REINFORCEMENT AND PUNISHMENT

Recall from the discussion of social-learning theory that people learn what to do and what to avoid by observing what happens to others. Recall also that vicarious reinforcement tends to be more effective than vicarious punishment.

State governments want to encourage people to buy lottery tickets (because they provide revenue for the government), so what do you suppose they do? They encourage massive publicity for everyone who wins a big jackpot (Figure 8.25). You will often see news reports showing some instant millionaire, delirious with excitement. (The state hopes this vicarious reinforcement will induce you to buy lottery tickets.) You seldom see reports about the millions of people who bought tickets and won nothing.

THE INFLUENCE OF HEURISTICS

Using the availability heuristic, people assume that if they can recall many examples of an event, the event must be common. You can see how this combines forces with vicarious reinforcement. Someone who sees a big lottery winner on television almost every week remembers many such examples and therefore overestimates the likelihood of winning a lottery.

The representativeness heuristic also plays a role in gambling. Suppose you are flipping a coin, recording the order of heads (H) and tails (T). Which of these sequences do you think is the least likely:

1. H H H H H H H H
2. H H H H T T T T
3. H H H H H H H T

Although in fact all three sequences are equally likely, most people who have no training in probability theory think sequence 1 is the least likely (Kahneman & Tversky, 1973). A sequence of all heads seems *unrepresentative* of the usual experiences. However, representativeness does not alter the odds: After a run of four heads or even seven heads, another head is as likely as a tail on the next flip.

The gambler's fallacy is an example of the representativeness heuristic. The **gambler's fallacy** is the belief that if a particular random outcome has not occurred for a while, its "turn" has come. For example, if the last seven spins on the roulette wheel landed on black numbers, the next spin probably will land on a red number. If your

FIGURE 8.25
States that sponsor lotteries provide publicity and an exciting atmosphere for each big payoff. They hope this publicity will provide vicarious reinforcement to encourage other people to buy lottery tickets. They do not publicize all the people who lost money on the lottery.

last 20 bets have lost, you are due to win on the next bet. However, because each random event is really independent of all the preceding events, the gambler's fallacy leads to misplaced confidence.

SELF-ESTEEM

Many gamblers have an additional reason for gambling, which we cannot explain in terms of learning, memory, or errors in reasoning: They want to beat their opponent. For many habitual gamblers, an important part of their self-esteem is tied to proving themselves to be "winners," and they like to make that point by winning someone else's money (Peck, 1986). Their self-esteem becomes more of an issue when gambling among friends and acquaintances than it does when gambling in a casino. Consequently, a habitual gambler who has been losing at a game of craps or poker will sometimes bet wildly and foolishly in an effort to catch up.

In summary, we have the following explanations for why some people continue to gamble despite consistent losses:

- They believe that by skillfully choosing the right numbers they can increase their probability of winning a game of chance.

- If the potential prize is large, people act as if they do not understand the difference between a small chance of winning and an extremely small chance of winning.

- They can continue through a long losing streak if the (imagined) eventual payoff is big enough to repay all the losses.

- They remember seeing or hearing about many people who have won big jackpots.

Thus they receive vicarious reinforcement for gambling and they overestimate the probability of winning.

- They may believe that after a long series of losses, the probability of winning increases.
- They are so eager to beat an opponent that they will take risks they know to be foolish.

Similar explanations apply to the gambles people take in everyday life. If you drink and drive, or go out on a date with someone who mistreated you in the past, you are taking a gamble—perhaps a foolish gamble. People take such risks for some of the same reasons just described.

One general point from all this is that people usually have multiple reasons for their behavior. People do not gamble for just one reason any more than you went to college for just one reason. A second general point is that the principles of learning, memory, and cognition do not apply to separate domains; we can apply all of those principles to a single behavior, such as gambling.

SOMETHING TO THINK ABOUT

Recall the discussion on page 337 of how the phrasing of a question may influence someone's decision. For example, most people

Most of our decisions in everyday life are gambles. Your choice of a college is a gamble; your choice of a career is a gamble; riding a motorcycle without a helmet is a gamble. Although we cannot avoid taking gambles, we can try to make intelligent gambles instead of foolish gambles.

will take more risks to avoid a loss than they will to increase a gain. Can you use this principle to explain why many gamblers on a losing streak will continue betting, sometimes increasing their bets? Is there a different way for a gambler to think about the situation so as to decrease the temptation to continue gambling?

SUMMARY

- *Becoming an expert.* Experts are made, not born. Becoming an expert requires about 10 years of full-time effort; the difference between experts and ordinary performers is mostly a matter of practice and effort. (page 323)
- *Expert pattern recognition.* Experts recognize and memorize familiar and meaningful patterns more rapidly than less experienced people do. (page 324)
- *Expert problem solving.* Experts solve problems in their field rapidly because they recognize the appropriate method and avoid wasting time on ineffective methods. (page 324)
- *Steps in solving a problem.* People go through four steps in solving a problem: understanding the problem, generating hypotheses, testing the hypotheses, and checking the results. (page 325)
- *Algorithms and heuristics.* People can solve problems through algorithms (repetitive means of checking every possibility) or heuristics (ways of simplifying the problem to get a reasonable solution). (page 326)
- *Generalizing.* Many people who have learned how to solve a problem fail to apply that solution to a similar problem. (page 327)
- *Insight.* With insight problems, people have trouble estimating how close they are to a solution. However, they may be making progress even if they do not realize they are. (page 328)
- *Creativity.* Creative people do their creating in a field in which they have knowledge and self-confidence; creativity does not translate well from one field of endeavor to another. Many highly creative people go through a life period in which they rely on a small group of friends, perhaps just one, for support and encouragement. They dedicate their lives to their work, often to the exclusion of all else. (page 329)
- *Reasons for errors.* People tend to be overconfident about their own judgments. Other

common mistakes in human reasoning include premature commitment to a hypothesis and overreliance on the representativeness heuristic and the availability heuristic. (page 332)

- *Reasons for gambling.* Gambling illustrates the combined influences of learning, memory, and cognition. Many people gamble despite consistent losses because they overestimate their control, because they are insensitive to the difference between a small chance and an extremely small chance of winning, because they experience vicarious reinforcement, and because they believe a series of losses makes an eventual win more likely. Some people gamble as a way of competing with others and of establishing their own self-esteem. (page 338)

SUGGESTIONS FOR FURTHER READING

Bransford, J. B., & Stein, B. S. (1984). *The ideal problem solver.* New York: Freeman. Advice on how to approach and solve both "mind-bender" problems and practical problems.

Dostoevsky, F. (1972). *The gambler.* Chicago: University of Chicago Press. (Original work written 1866.) A classic novel that captures the enticement of gambling.

Kahneman, D., Slovic, P., & Tversky, A. (Eds.) (1982). *Judgment under uncertainty.* Cambridge, England: Cambridge University Press. Describes research on the representativeness heuristic, the availability heuristic, and other heuristics that can lead to systematic errors in decision making.

TERMS

algorithm a mechanical, repetitive mathematical procedure for solving a problem (page 326)

heuristics strategies for simplifying a problem or for guiding an investigation (page 326)

creativity the development of novel, socially valued products (page 329)

representativeness heuristic the tendency to assume that if an item is similar to members of a particular category, it is probably a member of that category itself (page 334)

base-rate information data about the frequency or probability of a given item (page 334)

availability heuristic the strategy of assuming that the number of available memories of an event indicates how common the event actually is (page 336)

gambler's fallacy the belief that if a particular random outcome has not occurred recently, its probability of occurrence will increase (page 341)

ANSWERS TO CONCEPT CHECKS

5. It is an example of heuristics; someone has devised a simple way to obtain an approximate answer. (page 326)

6. The employer would fire 18 dishonest employees (90% of the 20 who had stolen). The employer would also fire 98 honest employees (10% of the 980 who had not stolen). Because the base rate of dishonesty is low, a clear majority of those identified as dishonest are actually honest. (page 335)

7. a. Failure to consider the base rate: 20% of all older adults is a larger number than 90% of all college students.
b. Premature commitment to one hypothesis without considering other hypotheses (such as that one could stay healthy without any magic words). (page 338)

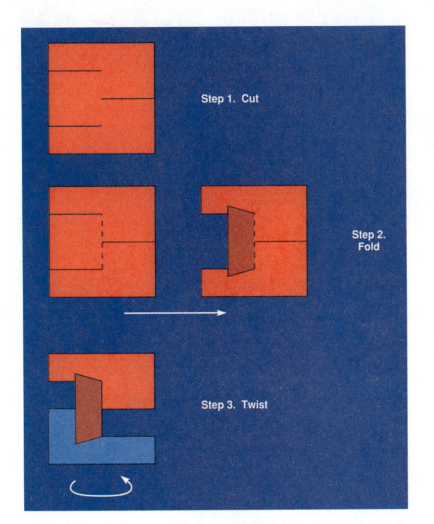

Step 1. Cut

Step 2. Fold

Step 3. Twist

C. The water in the tube would leak out of the hole in the bottom. Any membrane heavy enough to keep the water in would also keep the rubber balls out. (page 327)

D. The illustration at left shows how to cut and fold an ordinary piece of paper or cardboard to match the figure with nothing left over. (page 328)

E. Set 1: The words *playing, credit,* and *report* are all associated with *card.* Set 2: The words *ticket, shop,* and *broker* are all associated with *pawn.* (page 329)

F. All of the activities listed increase your odds of dying equally, by one in a million (Source: Failure Analysis Associates). Some of these activities may seem more dangerous than others, because some kinds of accidents and risks receive more publicity than others. That is, our overestimation of certain risks is another example of the availability heuristic. (page 337)

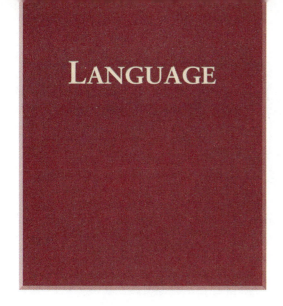

LANGUAGE

How do we learn to understand language, to speak, and to read?

Does language have special properties that set it apart from other intelligent behaviors?

Rats can learn mazes about as fast as humans can. Given enough practice, a chimpanzee or an elephant can learn to perform some rather complicated tasks. Apparently, other species have many intellectual abilities similar to those of humans.

And yet the achievements of humans far surpass those of other species. We build bridges, discover cures for diseases, cultivate crops, write and read psychology textbooks, and put other species into zoos. What enables us to do so much more than other animals?

One answer to that question is language, a complex system that enables us to convert our thoughts into words and to convert other people's words into thoughts. By age 3, almost all children have learned language well enough to put it to some very important uses: They use it to acquire knowledge. ("Don't touch the stove!" "Stay away from the poison ivy.") They use it to inform others. ("Swing me around more, Daddy!" "Not so fast, Daddy!") A few years later they are using language to learn history, science, and the accumulated knowledge and wisdom of humanity.

NONHUMAN PRECURSORS TO LANGUAGE

Language is an immensely useful ability. Without it, each of us would have only the benefit of our own experiences. With it, we can profit from the experiences of people on the other side of the world and people who lived thousands of years ago.

So, if language is such a useful ability, why have no other species evolved it? One hypothesis is that humans' large brains and great intelligence enable us to develop language; other species simply have too small brains and too little intelligence. That hypothesis fails for two reasons. First, several other species, including dolphins and whales, have larger brains than humans have. Although those species do communicate, their communication lacks the flexibility and complexity that characterize human languages. (See Figure 8.26.) Second, if we compare human brains with those of our nearest relatives, including chimpanzees and gorillas, we find that the human brain is not merely larger, but also organized in ways that seem especially suited to promoting language. For example, the prefrontal cortex, which contains areas necessary for language production, forms twice as large a percentage of the human brain as it does of chimpanzee, gorilla, or monkey brains (Deacon, 1990). Connections among cortical areas and connections from the cortex to the speech muscles are much more extensive in humans than they are in any related species (Deacon, 1992). Evolution has given our brains a major overhaul to make language not only possible but easy. (*Why* evolution favored language for us and not for other species remains a puzzle.)

FIGURE 8.26
Nonhuman species certainly communicate with each other, and with training many species can learn to communicate with people. However, so far as we can determine, no nonhumans develop a language comparable to human languages.

345

a

b

c

d

e

FIGURE 8.27
Speaking is physically impossible for chimpanzees, but some psychologists have tried to teach them to communicate by gesture or symbols. (a) One of the Premacks' chimps arranges plastic chips to make a "sentence" request for food. (b) Viki in her human home, helping with the housework. After years with the Hayeses, she could make only a few sounds similar to English words. (c) Kanzi, a bonobo, presses symbols to indicate words. Bonobos have shown the most promising ability to acquire language among the higher primates. (d) A chimp signing toothbrush. *(e) Roger Fouts with Alley the chimp, who is signing* lizard.

Still, even if language is a highly evolved human adaptation, we might expect to find some limited, similar capacities in other species. After all, evolution seldom makes something entirely new; more often, it modifies old structures for new functions, such as modifying hairs to become porcupine quills or modifying arms to become bat wings.

ATTEMPTS TO TEACH LANGUAGE TO CHIMPANZEES

Beginning in the 1920s, several psychologists reared chimpanzees in their homes and tried to teach them to talk. The chimpanzees

learned a number of human habits (Figure 8.27), but showed only very limited understanding of language and only brief, unsuccessful attempts to speak. In the 1960s and 1970s, Allen Gardner and Beatrice Gardner (1969) taught a chimpanzee, Washoe, to use the sign language that American deaf people use (Ameslan). Sign language is closer to the hand gestures that chimpanzees use naturally, and it does not require them to imitate human voice sounds, for which their vocal tracts are poorly adapted. Washoe eventually learned the symbols for about a hundred words, which she occasionally linked into meaningful combinations, such as "cry hurt food" for a radish and "baby in my drink" when someone put a doll into her cup.

Other chimpanzees also learned to use such symbols, but a controversy arose about whether their use of symbols and gestures really resembles human language. In many cases, chimpanzees' gestures were an imitation of symbols their human trainers had used recently (Terrace, Petitto, Sanders, & Bever, 1979). Moreover, they used their symbols almost exclusively to make requests, rarely if ever to describe things, and they seldom linked gestures together in anything like a sentence (Pate & Rumbaugh, 1983; Terrace et al., 1979; Thompson & Church, 1980). By contrast, a child with a vocabulary of a hundred words or so starts linking them together to make many original combinations and short sentences. In short, the chimps' use of symbols showed little of the flexibility of human language.

That, at any rate, was the conclusion from studies of the common chimpanzee, *Pan troglodytes.* Closely related to the common chimp is a rare and endangered species, *Pan paniscus,* sometimes known as the pygmy chimpanzee (a misleading term because these animals are almost as large as common chimpanzees) and sometimes known as the bonobo. The social behavior of *Pan paniscus* resembles that of humans in several regards: Males and females form strong, long-lasting attachments; females are sexually responsive throughout the month, not just during their fertile period; males contribute much more to infant care than other nonhuman primate males do; and adults often share food with one another.

Several bonobos studied by Sue Savage-Rumbaugh and Duane Rumbaugh have used symbols in ways that go beyond the productions of common chimpanzees. First, they occasionally use the symbols to name and describe objects even when they are not requesting them. Second, they sometimes use the symbols to relate events of the past. (One explained a cut on his hand by using gestures to indicate that his mother had bit him.) Third, they frequently make original, creative requests, such as asking one person to chase another person while the bonobo watched. The bonobos' symbol production is, nevertheless, limited. They often produce two- or three-symbol combinations, but not full sentences. Their comprehension is better than their production; a couple of bonobos seem to comprehend symbols about as well

FIGURE 8.28

Kanzi, a bonobo, points to answers on a board in response to questions he hears through earphones. Experimenter Rose Sevcik sits with him but does not hear the questions and cannot intentionally or accidentally signal the correct answer.

as a 2- to 2½-year-old child understands language (Savage-Rumbaugh et al., 1993).

A couple of bonobos have also shown considerable understanding of spoken English, responding correctly to unfamiliar spoken commands such as "throw your ball into the river" and "go to the refrigerator and get out a tomato" (Savage-Rumbaugh, 1990; Savage-Rumbaugh, Sevcik, Brakke, & Rumbaugh, 1992). They even pass the test of responding to commands over earphones, used to eliminate the possibility of unintentional "Clever Hans"-type signals, as discussed in Chapter 2 (Figure 8.28).

Part of the explanation for this impressive success probably pertains to species differences: Perhaps bonobos have greater language capacities than common chimpanzees. Another part of the explanation may pertain to the method of training: The bonobos learned by observation and imitation, probably a better way of learning language than the formal training methods used in previous studies (Savage-Rumbaugh, Sevcik, Brakke, & Rumbaugh, 1992). Finally, the bonobos began their language experience early in life.

CONCEPT CHECK

8. *Based on the studies of bonobos, what would be good advice on how to teach*

language to children born with some disability that impairs language learning? (Check your answer on page 360).

LANGUAGE AND THOUGHT

How is language related to thought? Many years ago certain psychologists maintained that they are identical; thought was just "subvocal" speech, and we could in principle figure out what someone is thinking by recording muscle movements in the throat. Among other problems with that theory, it seems to imply that preverbal children, brain-damaged adults, and nonhuman animals cannot think at all. Today we look for more subtle and complex ways in which language and thought influence each other.

THE PRODUCTIVITY OF LANGUAGE

Language is productive—that is, we can use language to express a never-ending variety of new ideas. Every day we say and hear a few stock sentences, such as "Nice weather we're having," or "I can't find my shoes," but we also say and hear sentences that probably no one has ever said before.

You might ask, "How can you *know* that no one has ever said a particular sentence before?!" Well, of course, we *cannot* know that a *particular* sentence is new, but we can be confident that *some* sentences are new (not specifying which ones). Try this exercise (Slobin, 1979): Pick any sentence of 10 to 20 words from any book you choose. How long would you have to keep reading, in that book or any other, until you found exactly the same sentence again?

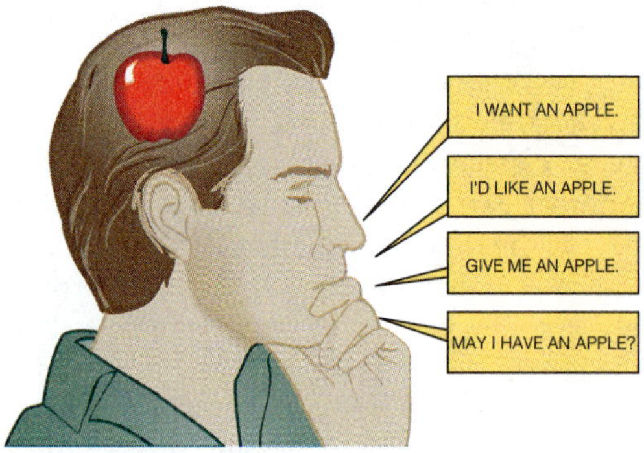

In short, we do not memorize all the sentences we will ever use; instead, we learn rules for making sentences and for interpreting other people's sentences. Noam Chomsky (1980) has described those rules as a transformational grammar, which is a system for converting a deep structure into a surface structure. The deep structure is the underlying logic of the language. The surface structure is the sequence of words as they are actually spoken or written (Figure 8.29). According to this theory, whenever we speak we transform the deep structure of the language into a surface structure. Two surface structures may resemble each other without representing the same deep structure, or they may represent the same deep structure without resembling each other.

For example, "John is easy to please" has the same deep structure as "Pleasing John is easy" and "It is easy to please John." They all represent the same underlying idea: When people try to please John, they find it easy to do.

In contrast, consider the sentence "Never threaten someone with a chain saw." The surface structure of that one sentence maps into two quite different deep structures:

1. It is not nice to swing a chain saw around and threaten someone with it.

2. If you meet someone carrying a chain saw, don't make any threatening gestures.

Transformational grammar consists of a set of rules for converting one surface structure into another. For example, it specifies that we can transform "John is easy to please" into "Pleasing John is easy." But we cannot transform "John is eager to please" into "Pleasing John is eager."

Ordinarily, when we listen to language, we attend only briefly to the surface structure, quickly extracting and remembering the deep structure—that is, the meaning (Sachs, 1967). To illustrate: Several paragraphs ago you read one of the following sentences. Without peeking, can you remember which one it was?

1. Two surface structures may represent the same deep structure without resembling each other, or they may resemble each other without representing the same deep structure.

FIGURE 8.29
According to transformational grammar, we can transform a sentence with a given surface structure into any of several other sentences with different surface structures. All of them represent the same deep structure, which is the underlying logic of the sentence.

I WANT AN APPLE.

I'D LIKE AN APPLE.

GIVE ME AN APPLE.

MAY I HAVE AN APPLE?

2. Two surface structures may resemble each other without representing the same deep structure, or they may represent the same deep structure without resembling each other.

3. Two deep structures may resemble each other, but two surface structures cannot.

If you are like most people, you had trouble remembering whether it was 1 or 2. (If you thought it was 3, you haven't been reading very carefully.) Generally, once people understand a sentence, they remember its meaning, not its word-for-word sequence.

Understanding a sentence is a complex matter that requires knowledge about the world. For example, consider the following sentences (from Just & Carpenter, 1987):

That store sells horse shoes.
That store sells alligator shoes.

We would not interpret the second sentence as referring to "shoes for alligators to wear," because alligators do not wear shoes. But that is a fact you had to know; the sentences themselves do not tell you that horses wear horse shoes but people wear alligator shoes. Here is another example:

I'm going to buy a pet hamster at the store, if it's open.
I'm going to buy a pet hamster at the store, if it's healthy.

You understand at once that *it* in the first sentence refers to the store and in the second sentence to the hamster. Nothing about the sentence structure tells you that, however. (If you were communicating with a computer or a being from another planet, you would have to specify what each *it* meant.) You understood because you know that stores (but not hamsters) can be open, whereas hamsters (but not stores) can be healthy. In short, language comprehension depends on assumptions that the speaker and the listener—or writer and reader—share.

THE WHORF HYPOTHESIS

Language enables us to think about topics that would be hard to consider in nonlinguistic terms. For example, it is doubtful that anyone could discover the Pythagorean theorem without having words for *right triangle* and *hypotenuse*. Certainly, language facilitates thought.

What is less certain is whether different languages facilitate different thoughts. Any-

thing that people say in one language can be translated into any other language, although sometimes a translation is long and awkward, or has a slightly different meaning from the original (Rudmin, 1994). If people have trouble saying something in certain languages, do they also have trouble thinking it in those languages?

According to one view, the **Whorf hypothesis** (or *Sapir-Whorf hypothesis*), our language determines the way we think (Whorf, 1941), and people who speak different languages think differently. This vague hypothesis does not specify *how* language affects thought, just *that* it affects thought in some way. Therefore, testing the hypothesis is a matter of trying to find a good example, any example, of some such effect. For the most part, that search has produced such weak, unconvincing examples that many psychologists say we should not even waste our time discussing the Whorf hypothesis. In spite of the weak evidence, however, many people *act* as if they believe the hypothesis is correct. For example, certain anthropologists are trying to get members of various Native American societies to preserve their native languages, apparently on the theory that they have to speak their traditional languages in order to maintain their traditional cultures (Bilger, 1994). Also, consider all the

Years ago, the favorite example to illustrate the Whorf hypothesis was the alleged fact that Eskimos have countless words for snow. Laura Martin (1986) demonstrated that this claim was enormously exaggerated. Even if true, it would be a poor example of the Whorf hypothesis.

concern about what we should call certain people. For example, should we call people "mentally retarded" or "intellectually challenged" or "differently abled"? Is it ever acceptable to call certain people "schizophrenics" or should it always be "people with schizophrenia"? People care strongly about such issues because they believe that what we call people influences what we think about them. That belief assumes, as Whorf did, that language influences thought.

For many years one of the examples cited most frequently in support of the Whorf hypothesis was the alleged fact that Eskimos had dozens of words for snow, enabling them to describe some of the fine points of snow that speakers of other languages overlook. Even if true, this would hardly be powerful evidence. Ornithologists know hundreds of words for birds; astronomers have a great vocabulary for stars and galaxies; every expert knows many specialized words. But having a large vocabulary on a topic is not the same as thinking *differently* about it.

Furthermore, most of the claims about Eskimo snow words came from people who never met an Eskimo in their lives, much less talked with one. A 1911 publication identified four Eskimo snow words, roughly corresponding to snowflake, snow on the ground, drifting snow, and snowdrift. Later authors who had read this publication (or heard about it) exaggerated its findings; still later authors exaggerated still further. Eventually, people were quoting each other without any idea of the original source of the information. By the 1970s, magazines and encyclopedias variously announced that Eskimos had 50, 100, or 200 words for snow (Martin, 1986; Pullum, 1991).

(You may wonder how many snow words the Eskimos really have. Actually, "Eskimo" is a family of languages, and the vocabulary varies from one language to another. According to Laura Martin [1986], West Greenlandic has two roots, meaning snowflake and snow on the ground. It can add suffixes to these roots to make many additional words, just as English can: *snowed, snowing, snowy, snowfall,* and so forth. And, like English, it has words that can apply to snow as well as to other objects, depending on context: *drift, powder, avalanche, . . .* If we count all of these as "snow" words, then West Greenlandic has a large number of snow words. But then so does English.)

Can we find a better example to support the Whorf hypothesis? I read once that the Quechua people of the Andes have trouble thinking about the concept of *flatness* because their language has no word for *flat* (Hunt & Agnoli, 1991). Several years later I happened to meet a woman who spoke English and Quechuan. When I asked her about this claim, she looked puzzled and responded that of course Quechuan has a word for *flat*. According to Benjamin Whorf (1941), the Hopi language has no way of saying "10 days," although one can say "after the 10th day." According to Whorf, the consequence is that Hopi speakers cannot easily think about lengths of time or about time as an abstract concept. However, later scholars who were more familiar with the Hopi language than Whorf was have assured us that Hopi does indeed have words for time and that the Hopi people have no trouble thinking about time.

If the Whorf hypothesis is both valid and important, we should be able to support it by comparing speakers of widely spoken languages. For example, many languages have gender endings on nouns. The German word for pigeon (*Taube*) is female; the Italian word (*piccione*) is masculine. So Germans call a pigeon "she" and Italians call it "he." Conversely, Germans call a buzzard "he," while Italians call it "she." Do Germans and Italians think about pigeons and buzzards differently from each other, and from English speakers, who call both kinds of bird "it"? Unfortunately, research on this question is surprisingly sparse (Hunt & Agnoli, 1991).

We do have evidence to support the Whorf hypothesis in one case: The effects of gender-related words in various situations. In English it used to be customary to use the pronoun *he* to refer to a person of unknown gender—such as "a doctor should do what he thinks is best," or "a professor should know his topic well." Many people objected that this custom implied that doctors, professors, and so forth were necessarily *men*. And indeed the language does have this effect. In one study, students read sentences such as:

The average American believes that he watches too much TV.

or

The average American believes that he or she watches too much TV.

or

Average Americans believe that they watch too much TV.

After each sentence, students described the image it suggested. Students who read the *he* sentence almost always described a man. When they read a sentence with *he* or *she*, men described an image with a man; women described an image with a woman. When they heard a *they* sentence, most described a group composed of both men and women (Gastil, 1990). In short, the way we speak does influence the way we think, at least in this situation. For that reason, speakers and writers today are encouraged to use gender-neutral expressions, such as "a doctor should do what *he* or *she* thinks is best," or "professors should know *their* topics well."

SEARCHING FOR THE RIGHT WORD

"The . . . uh . . . Whorf hypothesis is . . . uh . . . not widely accepted . . . um . . . because most of the . . . er . . . evidence has . . . uh . . . failed to show . . . " We have all sat through lectures punctuated by excessive numbers of um's, uh's and er's, and, to be honest, most of us say a few uh's and er's ourselves. Why? The answer is simply that we are searching for the right word; we say "uh" or "er" during the pause while we find the word we want.

Stanley Schachter and his colleagues sat through an assortment of undergraduate lec-

FIGURE 8.30
College lecturers in scientific fields tend to say few "uh's" and "er's" per minute; lecturers in art history and English literature use such fillers much more frequently.

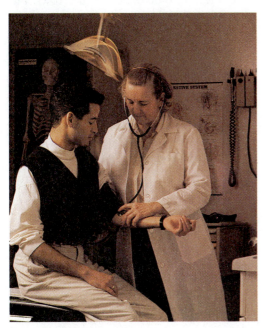

When people use the pronoun he *to refer to a person of unknown sex, such as "the doctor does what he thinks best," people tend to think of the unknown person as a man. Using a gender-neutral expression (such as "he or she") does influence people's thinking—as the Whorf hypothesis suggests.*

tures in various departments at Columbia University, counting all the um's, uh's, and er's. Which departments would you guess had the most, and which had the least?

The results are shown in Figure 8.30 (Schachter, Christenfeld, Ravina, & Bilous, 1991). On the average, lecturers in the humanities, such as art history and English literature, uttered more than 6 uh's and er's per minute—that is, more than 1 every 10 seconds. Lecturers in scientific fields and mathematics uttered only 1–2 per minute. The explanation has to do with their fields, not with the kinds of people who enter them. When these lecturers held conversations outside class on "neutral" topics such as graduate school policies, they all had about the same number of uh's and er's per minute. The differences among fields occurred only when the instructors were talking about their own fields. People say "uh" and "er" when they are trying to think of the right word. Lecturers in science and math have little trouble finding the right word. For example, a biologist giving a lecture on mitochondria is going to say "mitochondria" over and over; a chemist talking about electrons and protons will say "electrons" and "protons" many times. Biology has no synonyms for *mitochondria* and chemistry has no other ways of saying *electrons* and *protons*. In English literature, however, professors have many possible ways of expressing a given idea. Someone who says "plot" early in the lecture may want to say "story line" later in the lecture, either to express a slightly different shade of meaning or just for the sake of variety. Similarly, in published articles, professors of history and literature use a large and varied vocabulary; mathematicians and natural scientists tend to use the same words repeatedly within an article (Schachter, Rauscher, Christenfeld, & Crone, 1994).

UNDERSTANDING LANGUAGE

Making sense of what we see and hear is a complex process. A single letter, such as *a*, sounds different in different words, sounds different for different speakers, and looks different in different handwritings. Yet we learn to treat all of these expressions as the same. A single word can have different meanings in different contexts; for example, *net* can refer to something on a basketball or tennis court, something to catch fish or butterflies, or the profit of a corporation. Even a phrase or sentence has different meanings in different contexts (Just & Carpenter, 1987). (See Figure 8.31.) For example, we generally interpret the proverb "Time flies like an arrow" to mean that time passes quickly. But consider the same sentence in two other (far-fetched) contexts:

> **Q:** You taught me how to use this device to time the motion of cars, and a different way to time the flight of arrows. But how should I time the flight of house-flies?
> **A:** *Time flies like an arrow.*

> There were all sorts of weird insects in this place—space flies, gravity flies, and time flies. They all eat wood, but each fly likes a different kind. Space flies like to eat a desk. Most gravity flies like chairs. *Time flies like an arrow.*

Language comprehension is immensely complicated, as people discover when they try to program a computer to understand language (Just & Carpenter, 1987). And yet most of the time we understand what we hear and read without any noticeable effort. Although many questions remain to be answered, researchers have also made some discoveries about how all this takes place.

HEARING A WORD AS A WHOLE

We customarily describe the word *cat* as being composed of three sounds, *Kuh, Ah,* and *Tuh.* In a sense that is misleading: The first

Great wall of china.

Our new china patterns underscore Gorham's commitment to dinnerware that can proudly stand next to our highly popular crystal stemware and our inveterately successful sterling flatware. To see it all, talk to your Gorham representative or write Gorham, P.O. Box 6150, Providence, RI 02940.

GORHAM THE PERFECT SETTING.

GORHAM

FIGURE 8.31
Many clever ads take advantage of the fact that a given word can have several meanings and that people will figure out the intended meaning based on context.

sound in *cat* is not quite the same as the consonant sound in *Kuh;* the *a* and *t* sounds are changed also. Each letter changes its sound depending on the other sounds that precede it and follow it. We cannot hear the separate letters of a word; we must hear the word as a whole.

One of the clearest demonstrations was an experiment in which students listened to a tape recording of a sentence with one sound missing (Warren, 1970). The sentence was "The state governors met with their respective legislatures convening in the capital city." However, the sound of the first *s* in the word *legislatures,* along with part of the adjacent *i* and *l,* had been replaced by a cough or a tone. The students were asked to listen to the recording and try to identify the location of the cough or tone. None of the 20 students identified the location correctly, and half thought the cough or tone interrupted one of the other words on the tape. They all claimed to have heard the *s* plainly. In fact, even those who had been told that the *s* sound was missing insisted that they had heard the sound. Apparently the brain had used the context to fill in the missing sound.

UNDERSTANDING WORDS IN CONTEXT

Many words have different meanings in different contexts. Some words have meanings that seem almost completely unrelated to one another. *Rose* can refer to a flower, or it can be the past tense of the verb to *rise.* Consider the word *mean* in this sentence: "What did that mean old statistician mean by asking us to find the mean and mode of this distribution?"

Just as we hear the word *legislatures* as a whole, not as a string of separate letters, we interpret a sequence of words as a whole, not one at a time. For example, suppose you hear a tape-recorded sound that is carefully engineered to sound like something halfway between *dent* and *tent.* If you simply hear it and have to say what you heard, you might reply "dent," "tent," or "something sort of intermediate between dent and tent." But now suppose you hear that same sound in context:

1. When the **ent* in the fender was well camouflaged, we sold the car.
2. When the **ent* in the forest was well camouflaged, we began our hike.

People who hear sentence 1 tend to report the word *dent.* People who hear sentence 2 tend to report *tent.* Now consider two more sentences:

3. When the **ent* was noticed in the fender, we sold the car.
4. When the **ent* was noticed in the forest, we stopped to rest.

For sentences 3 and 4, the context does not matter. People are as likely to report hearing *dent* in one sentence as they are in the other (Connine, Blasko, & Hall, 1991). Think for a moment what this means: In the first two sentences, the fender or forest showed up three syllables after **ent.* In the second pair, the fender or forest showed up six syllables later. Evidently, when you hear an ambiguous sound you can hold it in some temporary "undecided" state for about three syllables to find out whether the context helps you to understand it. Beyond that point it is too late for the context to help; you hear it one way or the other and stick with it even if the later context contradicts your decision.

Although a delayed context cannot help you hear an ambiguous word correctly, it can help you understand what it means. Consider the following sentence from Karl Lashley (1951):

> Rapid righting with his uninjured hand saved from loss the contents of the capsized canoe.

If you hear this sentence spoken aloud, so that spelling is not a clue, you are likely to interpret the second word as "writing." That is a perfectly reasonable interpretation until we come to the final two words of the sentence. Suddenly the phrase *capsized canoe* changes the whole scenario; now we understand that "righting" meant pushing with a paddle. In summary, the immediate context can influence what you think you heard, but even a much delayed context can influence what you think the sentence means.

UNDERSTANDING NEGATIVES

"I am angry." "I am not angry." Seemingly, the second sentence is not much more complicated than the first, and yet people often have more trouble understanding negative sentences than affirmatives. In one study,

FIGURE 8.32
Most students preferred Kool-Aid made with sugar labeled "sugar" instead of sugar labeled "not cyanide," even though they had placed the labels themselves. Evidently, people do not fully believe the word "not." (Based on results of Rozin, Markwith, & Ross, 1990.)

college students looked at displays showing either ⧈ or ⧈. Then they were asked true-false questions such as "The star is above the plus" or "The plus isn't below the star." On the average, students took 685 ms longer to answer questions containing the negative word *isn't* (Clark & Chase, 1972).

In many cases, people also fail to fully understand or fully remember the *not*. When they hear "I am not angry," they may remember only that they heard something about angry. If they hear or read that "Bob Talbert is not linked with the Mafia," they tend to remember the hint that he *might* have been linked with the Mafia (Wegner, Wenzlaff, Kerker, & Beattie, 1981).

Another example: Students in one study watched as an experimenter poured sugar into two jars. Then they were told to place two labels on the jars, putting whichever label they wanted on each jar. One label said "sucrose, table sugar." The other said "not sodium cyanide, not poison." Then the experimenter made two cups of Kool-Aid, one with sugar from one jar and one with sugar from the other jar, and asked the students to choose one cup of Kool-Aid (Figure 8.32). Almost half the students said they had no preference, but of those who did have a preference, 35 of 44 wanted the Kool-Aid made from the jar marked "sucrose," not from the one that denied having cyanide and poison (Rozin, Markwith, & Ross, 1990). The students acted as if the label "not cyanide" meant something was wrong with the sugar in that jar.

People have particular trouble understanding double negatives, such as "She is

not unfriendly." The state of Illinois gives the following instructions to jurors in a murder case; note the four (!) negatives in this one sentence (emphasis added):

If you do not unanimously find from your consideration of all the evidence that there are no mitigating factors sufficient to preclude the imposition of a death sentence, then you should sign the verdict requiring the court to impose a sentence other than death.

Does that sound clear to you? Do you think the author of these instructions was trying to make the point clear to a jury?

READING

Before the abolition of slavery in the United States, it was illegal in certain places to teach a slave how to read. Slaves who could read might be dangerous, the reasoning went. They might get new ideas; they might learn things their masters did not want them to know.

Since then, many totalitarian governments probably wished they could prevent people from reading, but because that was impossible, they tried to control *what* people read. Anything opposing the government in power was banned; so were nonpolitical works that might stimulate new thoughts.

Reading can be a powerful force against a repressive government; it can also be a powerful force to strengthen a modern, progressive society. In a highly technological society, an illiterate person is unqualified for most jobs and seriously disadvantaged in many aspects of everyday life.

To figure out how best to teach reading, we need to understand what people do when they read. As they move their eyes over a page, do they read one letter at a time, a word at a time, or more? Do they have to finish reading one item before they start on the next, or can they work on several items at once? If we knew more about reading, we might be able to help people to read faster and with better comprehension.

READING AND EYE MOVEMENTS

In an alphabetic language such as English, the printed page consists of letters, which often form familiar clusters, which in turn form words, which form sentences. One kind of cluster is a **phoneme**, a unit of sound. A phoneme can be a single letter (such as *f*) or a short combination of letters (such as *sh*). Another kind of cluster is a **morpheme**, a unit of meaning. For example, *thrills* has two morphemes (*thrill* and *s*). The final *s* is a unit of meaning because it indicates that the word is plural. (See Figure 8.33.)

FIGURE 8.33
The word shamelessness *has nine phonemes (units of sound) and three morphemes (units of meaning).*

CONCEPT CHECK

9. *How many phonemes are there in the word* thoughtfully? *How many morphemes? (Check your answers on page 361.)*

When we read, do we ordinarily read one letter, one phoneme, one morpheme, or one word at a time, or do we read several words at once? And do we move our eyes steadily or in a jerky fashion? These movements are so fast that we are unable to answer these questions by self-inspection. Psychologists have arranged devices to monitor people's eye movements during reading. Their first discovery was that a reader's eyes move in a jerky fashion, not steadily. You can move your eyes steadily when they are following a moving object, but when you are scanning a stationary object such as a page of print, your eyes move from one fixation point to another in quick jumps called **saccades.** You read during your fixations; you are virtually blind during the saccades. To illustrate that point, try the following demonstration: Look at yourself in the mirror and focus on the image of your left eye. Then move your focus to the right eye. Can you see your eyes moving in the mirror? No; you see no movement. (Go ahead; try it.) The reason is that while your eyes were making that brief saccadic movement, your visual processing became inactive; you cannot see while making the saccade (Burr, Morrone, & Ross, 1994).

"Oh, but wait," you say. "That slight movement of my eyes in the mirror was simply too quick and too small a movement to be seen." Wrong. Try this: Get your roommate to look at your left eye and then shift his or her focus to your right eye. Now you do see the eye movement, so the movement itself is not too fast or too small to be seen. Go back and try your own eyes in the mirror again and observe the difference. You can see someone else's eyes moving their focus, but you cannot see your own eyes moving in the mirror. The reason is, I emphasize, that your brain virtually ignores visual input during your saccades.

An average person reading an average page of text focuses on each point for about 200 ms on the average. The fixation varies from a duration of less than 100 ms on short, familiar words like *girl* or *cake* to a second or more on difficult words like *ghoul* or *khaki*. Good readers generally have shorter fixations than poor readers do (Just & Carpenter, 1987). After each fixation, the saccade lasts about 25–50 ms. Thus, a typical person has about four fixations per second while reading; better readers can average five or six.

How much can a person read during one fixation? Many people have the impression that they see quite a bit of the page at each instant. Like many informal impressions, this one is wrong. The research says that we

Reading is a complex skill that includes stages from eye movements through understanding and using the material. Investigators find that they cannot separate these stages; how well a reader understands the material influences the speed of the eye movements.

generally read only one or two words at a time, while "previewing" the next word (Pollatsek & Rayner, 1989). Recall from Chapter 4 that human vision has its greatest acuity in the fovea, an area in the center of the retina. You can read letters when you fixate them in the fovea, but your ability to read drops sharply in the surrounding area. To demonstrate this phenomenon, focus on the point marked by an arrow (↓) in the sentences below.

↓

1. This is a sentence with no misspelled words.

↓

2. Xboc lx zji rxunce with no mijvgab zucn.

↓

3. Xboc lx zji rxuhnj with zw cjvvgab zucn.

If you permit your eyes to wander back and forth, you quickly notice that sentences 2 and 3 are mostly gibberish. But as long as you dutifully keep your eyes on the fixation point in sentence 2, it may look all right. You can read the letter on which you fixated plus about 3 or 4 characters (including spaces) to the left and about 7 to the right. This is enough for you to see —*ce with no m*—, or possibly —*nce with no mi*—. You cannot see the more distant letters well enough to be sure whether or not they spell out real words.

In sentence 3, however, you do notice something wrong. Even while keeping your eyes carefully fixated on the *i* in *with,* you can see that the next word is the nonsense combination *zw* and that the previous word ends with *j*, unlike any English word you can think of. Evidently you can read about 11 characters in one fixation.

In a study documenting this phenomenon, college students read text on a computer screen while a machine monitored their eye positions and fed that information to the computer. The computer correctly displayed whatever word a student was fixating on, plus a certain number of letters on each side of it. Beyond those letters, the computer displayed only gibberish. Students almost never noticed that anything was unusual, unless the computer started displaying gibberish letters closer than 3 characters to the left or 7 characters to the right of the fixation point (Underwood & McConkie, 1985). Evidently we read in a "window" of about 11 letters—the fixated letter, about 3 characters to its left, and about 7 to its right.

10. Why can we sometimes read two or three short words at a time, whereas we need a saccade or two to read the same number of longer words?
11. If a word is longer than 11 letters, will a reader need more than one fixation to read it? (Check your answers on page 361.)

In many cases, that window includes one word plus a fragment of the next word. For example, suppose you have fixated on the point shown by an arrow in the sentence below:

↓

The government made serious mistakes.

Because of the research just described, we know that readers can see the word *serious* plus about the first three letters of *mistakes.* That does not provide enough information to read the word *mistakes;* from what the reader knows, the next word could be *misspellings, misbehavior, missiles, mishmash,* or any of a number of other *mis*-things that a government might make. Does that little "preview" of the next word facilitate reading? Yes. In one study, college students again read passages on a computer screen while a machine monitored their eye movements. The computer correctly displayed the word the student fixated on plus the next zero, three, or four letters. So the display might look like this:

↓

The government made xxxxxxx xxxxxxxx.

↓

The government made serious xxxxxxxx.

↓

The government made serious mistakes.

or like this:

↓

The government made serxxxx xxxxxxxx.

↓

The government made serious misxxxxx.

↓

The government made serious mistakes.

Students who could preview the first three or four letters of the next word read significantly faster than those who could not (Inhoff, 1989). Evidently we do not read just one word at a time. While we are reading one word, we are previewing the next.

Would it be possible to learn to read more letters in each fixation? Perhaps, but

FIGURE 8.34
Do you C a J? A student watches either a word or a single letter flashed on a screen. An interfering pattern is then flashed on the screen and the student is asked, "Which was presented, C or J?" or "Was the first letter C or J?" More students were able to identify the letter correctly when it was part of a word.

doing so would probably not be helpful. Actually, some people do read more letters per fixation, especially to the right of the fixation point. They can read letters far to the right almost as well as they read letters at the fixation point itself. Far from gaining an advantage, such people suffer from **dyslexia**, a specific impairment of reading (Geiger, Lettvin, & Zegarra-Moran, 1992). Evidently, the letters they see to the right interfere with their perception of letters at the fixation point; they see too many words at once and consequently have trouble identifying any of them.

Some people read much faster than others, and you might wonder, for example, what "speed readers" do differently from normal readers. Some people who have learned to speed-read can cover a page in less than one-fifth the time a normal reader takes. Clearly, they do not do so by reading more letters in each eye fixation. Speed readers save time partly by keeping each fixation short and partly by skipping over many words altogether. Compared to most other readers, speed readers generally understand the basic points of their reading quite well; however, they do miss a fair amount of detail (Just & Carpenter, 1987).

THE WORD-SUPERIORITY EFFECT

When we read a word, do we identify the letters one at a time, or do we process several letters simultaneously, in parallel? Beginning readers have to sound out a word one letter at a time—for example, "Kuh . . . Ah . . . Tuh . . . CAT." When experienced readers come to an unfamiliar word, like *eleemosynary* or *metrorrhagia,* they sound it out one syllable at a time. But with short, familiar words we apparently attend to all letters simultaneously.

In one experiment, the investigator flashed a single letter on a screen for less than a quarter of a second and then flashed an interfering pattern on the screen and asked, "What was the letter, C or J?" Then the experimenter flashed a whole word on the screen for the same length of time and asked, "What was the first letter of the word, C or J?" (Figure 8.34). Which question do you think the subjects answered correctly more often? Most of them identified the letter more accurately when it was part of a whole word than when it was presented by itself (Reicher, 1969; Wheeler, 1970). This is known as the **word-superiority effect.**

In a follow-up experiment, James Johnston and James McClelland (1974) briefly flashed words on the screen and asked students to identify one letter (whose position was marked) in each word (Figure 8.35). On some trials they told the students to focus on the center of the area where the word would appear and to try to see the whole word. On other trials they showed the students exactly where the critical letter would appear on the screen and told them to focus on that spot and ignore the rest of the screen. Most students did better at identifying the critical letter when they were told to look at the whole word than when they focused on just the letter itself!

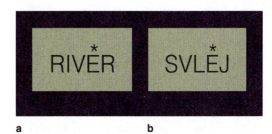

a   b

FIGURE 8.35
Students were better at identifying an indicated letter when they focused on an entire word (a) than when they were asked to remember a single letter in a designated spot among random letters (b).

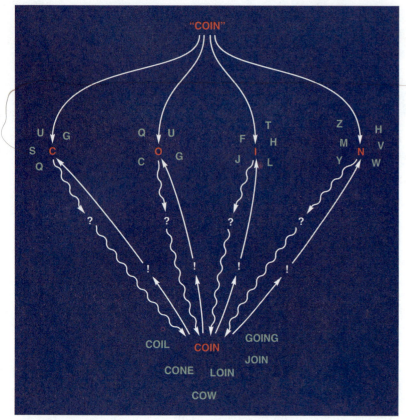

FIGURE 8.36

According to one version of the connectionist model, a visual stimulus activates certain letter units, some more strongly than others. Those letter units then activate a word unit, which in turn strengthens the letter units that compose it. For this reason, we recognize a whole word more easily than we recognize a single letter.

The context of other letters aids recognition only if the combination is a word or something resembling a word. For example, it is easier to recognize the difference between *COIN* and *JOIN* than the difference between *C* and *J*. But it is easier to recognize the difference between *C* and *J* than the difference between *XQCF* and *XQJF* (Rumelhart & McClelland, 1982).

You may have experienced the word-superiority effect yourself. A common game on long car trips is to try to find every letter of the alphabet on the billboards along the way. Many people find it easier to spot a particular letter by reading whole words than by checking each word letter by letter.

THE CONNECTIONIST MODEL

What accounts for the word-superiority effect? One possibility is the **connectionist model.** Actually, psychologists have proposed several connectionist models. According to one version (McClelland, 1988; Rumelhart, McClelland, & the PDP Research Group,

1986), our perceptions and memories are represented by vast numbers of connections among "units," presumably corresponding to neurons or sets of neurons. Each unit is connected to other units (Figure 8.36).

Each unit, when activated, excites some of its neighbors and inhibits others to varying degrees. Suppose that at a given moment units corresponding to the letters *C, O, I,* and *N* are moderately active—not quite active enough for a firm identification of each letter. These units excite a higher-order unit corresponding to the word *COIN.* Although none of the four-letter units sends a strong message by itself, the collective impact is strong (McClelland & Rumelhart, 1981). This higher-level perception *COIN* then feeds excitation back to the letter-identifying units and confirms their tentative decisions because they make sense in the context.

Figure 8.37 is an example of the kind of phenomenon this model attempts to explain. Why do you see the top word in that figure as RED instead of *PFB*? After all, in the other three words of that figure, you do see those letters as *P, F,* and *B*. But in the top word, one ambiguous figure activates some *P* units and some *R* units; the next figure activates *E* and *F* units, and the third figure activates *D* and *B* units. All of those units in turn activate other, more complex units corresponding to *RFB, PFB, PFD,* and *RED*. Because *RED* is the only English word in the group, the units that correspond to *RED* are easier to activate than those for *PFB* and the others. Consequently, you perceive the word as *RED*. As the *RED* unit becomes active, it in turn provides feedback to strengthen the activity of the *R, E,* and *D* units.

READING AS AN AUTOMATIC HABIT: THE STROOP EFFECT

Experienced readers identify familiar words almost without effort. It is difficult for us to avoid reading them as words, even if we try. For example, read the following instructions and then examine Figure 8.38 on the next page and follow them:

Notice the blocks of color at the top of the figure. Scanning from left to right, give the name of each color as fast as you can. Then notice the nonsense syllables printed in different colors in the center of the figure. Don't try to pronounce them; just say the color of each one as fast as possible. Then turn to the real words at the bottom. Don't read them; quickly say the color in which each one is printed.

If you are like most people, you found it very difficult not to read the words at the bottom of the figure. After all the practice you have had reading English, you can hardly bring yourself to look at the word *RED*, written in green letters, and say "green." This is known as the **Stroop effect**, after the psychologist who discovered it. Because you can read familiar words faster than you can name colors, the tendency to say "red" seriously interferes with your saying "green" (Cohen, Dunbar, & McClelland, 1990). (One way to read the colors instead of the words, reported by bilingual students, is to name the colors in a language other than English. Another way is to blur your vision intentionally so that you cannot make out the letters.)

READING AND UNDERSTANDING IN CONTEXT

Good reading requires understanding word meanings. Some English words, such as *bachelor* and *uranium,* have only one common meaning and understanding them poses no special problems. Other English words, however, have multiple meanings and we have to discern the correct one in context. For example, consider this sentence: *A pelican dove into the water and scared away the*

dove. The word *dove* is potentially ambiguous, but the context enables you to infer—so fast that you were unaware of what you were doing—that the first *dove* rhymes with *stove* and means *plunged,* and the second *dove* rhymes with *love* and means a pigeonlike *bird.* Now consider another sentence: *A flying fish jumped out of the water and scared the pigeon and dove away.* In this case, the word *dove* is hopelessly ambiguous. The sentence might mean that the flying fish scared two birds (a pigeon and a dove), or that the fish scared the pigeon and then dove (plunged) away.

Good writers try to avoid severe ambiguities of this type; however, the context of a sentence is usually sufficient to clarify the meaning of each word. In some cases, a word appears early in a sentence and the context that explains it occurs later. Consider the italicized words in each of the following sentences:

The *table* that was full of errors was an embarrassment to the owners of the furniture store.

The *table* that was full of errors was an embarrassment to the publishers of the mathematics text.

When they chose the *lead,* they were very careful, because they wanted the new play to be a success.

FIGURE 8.37
A pattern across letters enables us to identify a word; word recognition in turn helps to confirm the letter identifications. Although each of the letters in the top word is ambiguous, a whole word— RED—is perceived. (From Rumelhart, McClelland, & the PDP Research Group, 1986.)

ZYK	TUV	MRK	VLB	YIU	ZNG	GAK	NYL	WVB
ACJ	BDC	DSR	VNW	CAJ	KFI	NOZ	RFL	HIY
XNE	PZQ	PDN	RBY	SOV	ALA	GNT	URF	PNR

RED	BROWN	RED	BLUE	BLUE	GREEN	RED	BROWN	RED
GREEN	RED	RED	BROWN	BLUE	BROWN	GREEN	GREEN	BLUE
BROWN	RED	RED	GREEN	RED	GREEN	BROWN	RED	BLUE

FIGURE 8.38
Read (left to right) the color of the ink in each part. Try to ignore the words themselves. Your difficulties on the lowest part illustrate the Stroop effect.

When they chose the *lead,* they were very careful, because they wanted to produce high-quality pencils.

In cases such as these, most readers have a fairly long fixation time when they read the ambiguous word *table* or *lead.* If the previous context made it clear which meaning is correct, a good reader almost immediately selects the correct meaning and discards the other possibilities. If the previous context provided no help, good readers keep in mind several possible meanings of the ambiguous word until later in the sentence. They show long fixation times on later words (such as *furniture* or *mathematics, play* or *pencils*) that clarify the meaning of the ambiguous word (MacDonald, Pearlmutter, & Seidenberg, 1994; Sereno, Pacht, & Rayner, 1992).

Poor readers are less efficient at selecting the correct meaning. When people read a sentence such as "He dug with the spade" or "A spade was used for digging," the word *spade* initially activates several possible meanings, but a good reader quickly activates the relevant meaning (shovel) and suppresses all the others. Poor readers, however, are less efficient at suppressing the irrelevant meanings (Gernsbacher, 1993; Gernsbacher & Faust, 1991). For example, if an experimenter asks whether the sentence included anything related to the word "ace," good readers promptly say no, but poor readers hesitate and sometimes say yes. Evidently, the poor readers failed completely to suppress the irrelevant meaning of *spade* as a playing card.

SUMMARY

- *Language in animals.* The ability to acquire language evolved from precursors present in our ancestors and still detectable in other species. Certain species, such as the bonobo, have made striking progress in language use, although their exact potential is still uncertain. (page 345)

- *Thought and language.* People are capable of expressing an enormous number of ideas in words, linking them in creative ways. Understanding what others say requires a great deal of factual knowledge as well as an understanding of the language. (page 348)

- *Whorf hypothesis.* According to the Whorf hypothesis, our language influences how we think. Good evidence to support this theory is hard to find, although the effects of

gender-related words may be one example. (page 349)

- *Hesitations.* Speakers tend to say *uh, um,* and *er* to fill the pauses while they search for the right word. (page 351)

- *Ambiguity.* We hear a word as a whole, not as a sequence of parts. We can change how we hear an ambiguous word, depending on approximately the next three syllables. (page 352)

- *Reading.* When we read, we have fixation periods separated by eye movements called saccades. Even good readers can read only about 11 letters per fixation. (page 354)

- *Word-superiority effect.* Good readers can identify a letter faster and more accurately when they see it as part of a word than when they see it by itself. (page 357)

- *Good readers.* Good readers suppress the irrelevant meanings of ambiguous words. (page 359)

SUGGESTIONS FOR FURTHER READING

Adams, M. J. (1990). *Beginning to read.* Cambridge, MA: MIT Press. Excellent review of research on how people read.

Pinker, S. (1994). *The language instinct.* New York: William Morrow and Company. Clear, often entertaining discussion of the psychology of language.

TERMS

Whorf hypothesis hypothesis that our language determines the way we think (page 349)

phoneme a unit of sound (page 354)

morpheme a unit of meaning (page 355)

saccade a quick jump in the focus of the eyes from one point to another (page 355)

dyslexia specific impairment of reading (page 357)

word-superiority effect greater ease of identifying a letter when it is part of a whole word than when it is presented by itself (page 357)

connectionist model theory that our perceptions and memories are represented by vast numbers of connections among "units," each of them connected to other units (page 358)

Stroop effect the difficulty of naming the colors in which words are written instead of reading the words themselves (page 359)

ANSWERS TO CONCEPT CHECKS

8. Start language learning when a child is young. Rely on imitation as much as possible instead of providing direct reinforcements for correct responses. (page 347)

9. *Thoughtfully* has seven phonemes: *th-ough-t-f-u-ll-y*. (A phoneme is a unit of sound, not necessarily a letter of the alphabet.) It has three morphemes: *thought-ful-ly*. (Each morpheme has a distinct meaning.) (page 355)

10. Two or three short words can fall within the "window" of about 11 letters that we can fixate on the fovea at one time. If the words are longer, it may be impossible to get them all onto the fovea at once. (page 356)

11. Probably, but not always. Suppose your eyes fixate on the fourth letter of *memorization*. You should be able to see the three letters to its left and the seven to its right—in other words, all except the final letter. Because there is only one English word of the form *memorizatio-*, you have enough information to recognize the word. (page 356)

9 INTELLIGENCE AND ITS MEASUREMENT

The famous mathematician Alan Turing bicycled to and from work each day. Occasionally the chain fell off his bicycle and he had to put it back on. Eventually, Turing began keeping records and noticed that the chain fell off at regular intervals. In fact, it repeatedly fell off after a certain number of revolutions of the front wheel. Turing then calculated that this number was an even multiple of the number of spokes in the front wheel, the number of links in the chain, and the number of cogs in the sprocket. From these data he deduced that the chain came

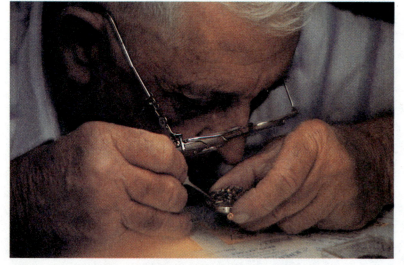

The term intelligence *refers both to generalized problem solving and to highly practiced skills.*

loose whenever a particular link in the chain came in contact with a particular bent spoke on the wheel. He identified that spoke, repaired it, and never again had trouble with the chain (Stewart, 1987).

Turing's solution to his problem qualifies as highly intelligent, according to what we usually mean by *intelligent*. But hold your applause. Your local bicycle mechanic could have solved the problem in just a few minutes, without using any mathematics at all.

So, you might ask, what's my point? Was Turing unintelligent? Not at all. He was highly intelligent, and if you have some new, complicated, unfamiliar problem to solve, you probably should take it to someone like Turing, not to your favorite bicycle mechanic.

My point is that intelligence is a combination of general abilities and practiced skills. The term *intelligence* can refer to the highly practiced skills shown by a good bicycle mechanic, a Micronesian sailor, a hunter-gatherer of the Serengeti plains, or any other person with extensive experience and special expertise in a particular area. *Intelligence* can also refer to the generalized problem-solving ability that Turing displayed—the kind of ability that one can apply in an unfamiliar situation. But even that ability develops gradually, reflecting contributions of many kinds of experience.

INTELLIGENCE AND INTELLIGENCE TESTS

What is intelligence?
What is the purpose of IQ tests?
What do the scores on IQ tests mean?

Intelligence testing has a long history of controversy, partly because of misconceptions about its purpose. Consider the following analogy:

You and I have just been put in charge of choosing members of the next U.S. Olympic team. To choose the best-qualified people, we decide to hold tryouts in basketball, gymnastics, high jump, and all the other events. Suddenly the Olympic rules are changed: Each country can send only 30 men and 30 women, and each athlete must compete in every event. Furthermore, the competitive events will be new ones, not exactly like any of the familiar events, and the Olympic Committee will not publish the rules for any of the new events until all of our athletes have arrived at the Olympic site. Clearly, we cannot hold regular tryouts. How shall we choose the team?

Our best bet would be to devise a test of "general athletic ability." We would measure the abilities of all the applicants to run, jump, change direction, maintain balance, throw and catch, kick, lift weights, respond rapidly to signals, and perform other athletic feats. Then we would choose the applicants who had the best scores.

No doubt our test would be imperfect, and we would make some mistakes in our selection of athletes. But if we must choose 60 athletes, and if we want to maximize their chances of winning, we certainly have to use some sort of test. So we go ahead with our Test of General Athletic Ability.

As time passes, other people begin to use our test. It becomes well accepted and widely used. Does its acceptance imply that athletic ability is a single quantity, like speed or weight? Not necessarily. When we devised the test, it merely suited our purposes to ignore the differences between one sport and another.

WHAT IS INTELLIGENCE?

Intelligence tests resemble our imaginary test of athletic ability. If we have to choose from among applicants to a school or college, we want to select those who will profit most from the experience. Because students may be studying subjects that they have never studied before, we want to measure their general ability to profit from education rather than any specific knowledge or specialized ability. By the same token, if we want to identify children who belong in a special education program for slow-learning children, we need to measure their general likelihood of academic success.

Intelligence tests were developed for the practical function of selecting students for special classes. They were not based on any theory of intelligence, and those who administer them are often content to define *intelligence* as the ability to do well in school. Given that definition, IQ tests do measure intelligence.

I. tests were used for selecting students for special classes.

IQ tests measure intelligence

IQ tests serve the practical function of helping schools identify which applicants are most likely to succeed in their schoolwork. Problems and controversies arise when people assume that IQ tests can, or should, serve much wider functions.

For theoretical purposes, however, that definition is hardly satisfactory. What would be a better definition? Here are some of the ways psychologists have defined *intelligence* (Wolman, 1989):

- The ability to cope with the environment through learning.
- The ability to judge, comprehend, and reason.
- The ability to understand and deal with people, objects, and symbols.
- The ability to act purposefully, think rationally, and deal effectively with the environment.

Note that these definitions use such terms as *judge, comprehend, understand,* and *think rationally*—terms that are themselves only vaguely defined. Psychologists would like to organize this list of intelligent abilities more intelligently. Intelligence should not consist of a haphazard set of unrelated abilities; the list should have some structure or organization. Just as all the objects in the world are composed of compounds of 92 elements, most psychologists expect to find that all the kinds of intelligence are compounds of a few basic abilities. They have proposed several models of how intelligence is organized.

SPEARMAN'S PSYCHOMETRIC APPROACH AND THE *g* FACTOR

Charles Spearman (1904) took a **psychometric** approach to intelligence. Psychometric means the measurement *(metric)* of individual differences in behaviors and abilities. Spearman began by measuring how well a variety of people performed a variety of

tasks, such as following complex directions, judging musical pitch, matching colors, and performing arithmetic calculations. He then found that their performance on any single task correlated positively with their performance on all the other tasks. He deduced that all the tasks must have something in common. To perform well on any test of mental ability, Spearman argued, people need a certain "general" ability, which he called *g*. Psychologists generally describe the *g* factor as the ability to perceive and manipulate relationships, or to deal with abstract concepts.

To account for the fact that performance on various tasks does not correlate perfectly, Spearman suggested that each task requires the use of a "specific" ability, *s*, in addition to the general ability, *g*, that all tasks require (Figure 9.1). Thus, intelligence consists of a general ability plus an unknown number of specific abilities, such as mechanical, musical, arithmetical, logical, and spatial. Later research has found that many of these specific abilities develop somewhat independently and may rely on partly separate genetic influences (Loehlin, Horn, & Willerman, 1994; Pedersen, Plomin, & McClearn, 1994). Spearman called his theory a "monarchic" theory of intelligence because it includes a dominant ability, or monarch (*g*), that rules over the lesser abilities.

Psychologists have not entirely agreed on what *g* represents. That is, the ability to do well on one task correlates with the ability to do well on another task, but why? Consider two possibilities:

First, consider the high correlation among the tasks shown in Figure 9.2: People who excel at running a 100-meter race also generally do well at the high jump and the long jump. A particular athlete might be a little better at one of these events than at others, but we can hardly imagine, say, an Olympic-class high jumper who could not manage a decent long jump. The reason for the high correlation is that all three events depend on the same leg muscles. An injury that impaired performance on one event would impair performance on all three events.

Second, consider the lengths of three body parts—left leg, right arm, and left index finger—as illustrated in Figure 9.3: Within a normal population of people, these three measurements will correlate strongly with one another. That is, people with a long left leg tend also to have a long right arm and

FIGURE 9.1
According to Spearman, all intelligent abilities have an area of overlap, which he called g (for "general"). Each ability also depends partly on an s (for "specific") factor.

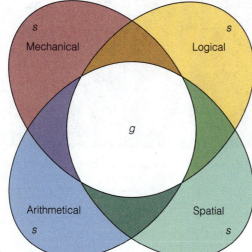

(handwritten margin notes:) Intelligence should have organization—structure

Psychometric—measure of indiv. diff. in behaviors + abilities a long left index finger. Why? In the athletic example, we found a high correlation because different events measured the same thing (leg muscles), but here the measurements of leg, arm, and finger definitely do not measure the same thing. (Amputation of one of them would not affect the others at all.) Lengths of leg, arm, and finger correlate because the *causes* of growth are the same for all three. That is, growth of your leg depends on nutrition, health, age, and certain genes; growth of your arm and finger depend on those same factors.

Now, which of these cases is more like intelligence? Do we find a positive correlation among performances of various intellectual skills because they all measure some single underlying ability, or because they all grow together, dependent on the same factors of health, nutrition, education, and so forth?

The evidence suggests that both explanations are partly correct. For example, certain kinds of brain damage impair performance on a wide variety of intellectual tasks, because the damage impairs a function such as attention that is necessary for almost any task. Thus, various intellectual abilities will correlate with one another partly because they depend on some of the same underlying processes. However, as we have seen in previous chapters, it is also true that some people lose a specific kind of memory or perceptual ability without much loss in other abilities. That is, different intellectual abilities do not share *all* of their underlying processes. To a considerable degree, various intellectual skills correlate with one another because the health, nutrition, education, and other factors that promote the development of any one skill also promote the development of others.

FLUID INTELLIGENCE AND CRYSTALLIZED INTELLIGENCE

Raymond Cattell followed Spearman's psychometric approach but proposed an important modification. According to Cattell (1987), the *g* factor has two components: fluid intelligence and crystallized intelligence. The analogy is to water: Water in its liquid state (fluid) can take any shape, whereas ice crystals are rigid. **Fluid intelligence** is the power of reasoning and using information. It includes the ability to perceive relationships, deal with unfamiliar problems, and gain new types of knowledge. **Crystallized intelligence** consists of acquired skills and knowledge and the application of that

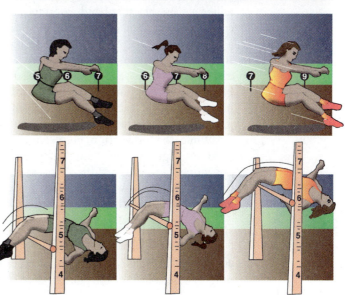

FIGURE 9.2

Measurements of sprinting, high jumping, and long jumping correlate with one another because they all depend on the same leg muscles. Similarly, the g *factor that emerges in IQ testing could reflect a single ability that all tests tap.*

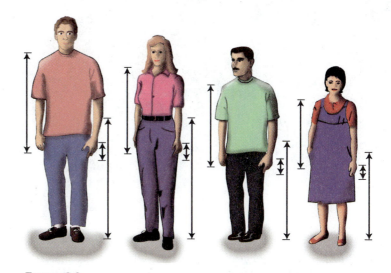

FIGURE 9.3

Measurements of leg, arm, and finger length correlate with one another only because the nutritional and health factors that promote the growth of any one of these also promote growth of the others. Similarly, the g *factor that emerges in IQ testing could reflect the fact that different intellectual abilities depend on the same nutritional, health, and educational influences.*

knowledge to specific content in a person's experience. For example, fluid intelligence is the ability to learn new skills in a new job. Crystallized intelligence includes the skills already learned by a good auto mechanic, salesperson, or accountant.

Fluid intelligence, according to Cattell and his colleagues, reaches its peak before age 20; beyond that age it may either remain constant or begin to decline. Crystallized intelligence, on the other hand, continues to increase as long as a person remains healthy and active (Cattell, 1987; Horn & Donaldson, 1976). A 20-year-old may be more successful than a 65-year-old at solving some problem that is unfamiliar to both of them, but the 65-year-old will excel at solving problems in his or her area of specialization.

While the distinction between crystallized intelligence and fluid intelligence is appealing, it is often difficult to apply in practice. Almost any task requires a combination of fluid and crystallized intelligence.

CONCEPT CHECK

1. *Was Alan Turing's solution to the slipping bicycle chain (at the start of this chapter) an example of fluid or crystallized intelligence? Was the solution provided by a bicycle mechanic an example of fluid or crystallized intelligence? (Check your answers on page 380.)*

GARDNER'S THEORY OF MULTIPLE INTELLIGENCES

The traditional defense of a single kind of intelligence has rested on the concept of *g*: Scores on all kinds of intellectual tests—mathematical, verbal, and other—correlate with one another and therefore with *g*, representing a single ability. However, critics reply, the statistical emergence of *g* merely indicates that mathematics, language use, and the other skills we have chosen to test happen to be related. If we expand the concept of *intelligence* to include other skills that society values, *g* may fade away or even disappear.

In particular, Howard Gardner (1985) has claimed that people have **multiple intelligences**—numerous unrelated forms of intelligence. Gardner distinguishes language abilities, musical abilities, logical and mathematical reasoning, spatial reasoning, body movement skills, self-control and self-understanding, and sensitivity to other people's social signals. He points out that people may be outstanding in one type of intelligence but not in others. For example, a *savant* (literally, "learned one") is a person who has an outstanding ability in one limited skill but no more than ordinary abilities in other areas. (An *idiot savant* is outstanding at one skill and very poor in other areas.) More generally, an athlete may excel at body movement skills but lack musical abilities, an outstanding musician may be poor at sensitivity to other people, and a politician may be outstanding at understanding other people's needs but quite inept at controlling body movements. Because of the differences among multiple kinds of intelligence, someone who seems very intelligent in certain regards may surprise us by doing something foolish in a different setting.

Gardner certainly makes an important point: People do have a variety of socially valued abilities, and almost no one is strong in all abilities or weak in all abilities. Gardner encourages us to seek better ways of teaching and encouraging a full range of abilities, including self-control, social responsiveness, and other intelligent skills that educators have not traditionally emphasized.

In Garrison Keillor's fictional Lake Wobegon, "all the children are above average." Although that description sounds impossible, in one sense it is true: Virtually everyone is above average at something. A given individual may excel at mathematics, dancing, piano playing, juggling, poetry, cooking, or whatever. A single measurement of "intelligence" necessarily overlooks people's specialized skills.

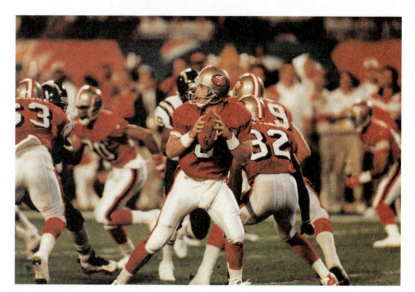

According to Howard Gardner, we have not one intelligence but many intelligences, including mathematics, artistic skills, muscle skills, and musical abilities.

cognitive ability- math, logical, and verbal skills

Do we want to use one word, *intelligence*, to refer to every valued skill from writing a novel to dribbling a basketball? If we do, then Gardner is right that people have many unrelated kinds of intelligence. However, in that case we shall need a new term (perhaps *cognitive ability*) to refer more narrowly to mathematical, logical, and verbal skills.

STERNBERG'S TRIARCHIC THEORY OF INTELLIGENCE

Spearman concluded that intelligence depends on one overall ability; Cattell suggested

FIGURE 9.4
In these two photos, which person is the supervisor and which is the worker? Robert Sternberg has used these photos to evaluate people's "practical intelligence"—their ability to understand non-verbal cues.

two kinds of ability, and Gardner suggested many. Still, the concept of "ability" tells us nothing about *how* a person processes information or engages in "intelligent" behavior (Das, 1992).

Robert Sternberg (1985) has offered one of the most influential attempts to specify in more detail what happens during intelligent behavior. Sternberg's description is called a **triarchic theory** (in contrast to Spearman's monarchic theory) because Sternberg deals with three aspects of intelligence: (1) the cognitive processes that occur within the individual, (2) the situations that require intelligence, and (3) how intelligence relates to the external world.

According to Sternberg, the first part of the triarchy—the cognitive processes within the individual—includes three components: learning the necessary information, planning an approach to a problem, and combining the knowledge with the plan so as actually to solve a problem.

Standard IQ tests do not try to measure the learning or planning components; they concentrate on the third component, how well someone actually solves a problem. For example, a test might ask you to complete an analogy, such as

Washington is to 1 as Lincoln is to:
(a) 5, (b) 10, (c) 20, (d) 50.

To solve this problem you must have already learned a fair amount of relevant information and you must develop a strategy for applying it to this question. Ultimately, if you are successful, you decide that the question must be about George Washington and the $1 bill and that the answer is (a), because Abraham Lincoln's picture is on the $5 bill. This question is reasonable, so far as it goes,

although we need to recognize that it is measuring only the final outcome, not the steps that led to it. An improved measure of intelligence might separate the learning and planning components from the performance component.

The second part of Sternberg's triarchy is the identification of situations that require intelligence. It is important to distinguish novel situations from repeated situations, because they require different responses from us. In a novel situation, we have to examine a problem in various ways until we find a successful approach. (Recall, for example, the insight problems of Chapter 8.) In a repeated situation, we profit from developing automatic habits so that we make a successful response quickly.

The third part of the triarchy is the relationship between intelligence and the outside world. An intelligent person either adapts to the environment, or tries to improve the environment, or, if all else fails, escapes to a better environment. Sternberg and others (Sternberg, 1985; Weinberg, 1989) have tried to develop special tests of people's practical intelligence—for example, the ability of a young person to identify the steps most likely to lead to career advancement. (See Figure 9.4.) Sternberg explicitly recognizes that because intelligent behavior has to be practical, the term *intelligence* is meaningful only in a sociocultural context. For example, we cannot meaningfully compare the intelligence of a European city dweller with that of someone living in the Amazon rain forests or the Serengeti plains. What is important and practical for one may not be for the other.

Table 9.1 summarizes four theories of intelligence.

TABLE 9.1
Four Theories of Intelligence

THEORY	PRINCIPAL THEORIST	KEY IDEAS AND TERMS	EXAMPLES
Psychometric approach	Charles Spearman	*g* factor: general abstract reasoning ability common to various tasks	Perceiving and manipulating relationships
		s factor: specific ability required for a given task	Mechanical, verbal, spatial abilities
Fluid and crystallized intelligence	Raymond Cattell	Fluid intelligence: reasoning and using information; peaks in young adulthood	Finding a solution to an unfamiliar problem
		Crystallized intelligence: acquired skills and knowledge; continues growing throughout life	Knowing how to play a piano, build a cabinet, write a novel, calculate sales tax
Multiple intelligences	Howard Gardner	Intelligence includes all the abilities that one's society values	Music, social attentiveness, dancing, language skills, mathematics, etc.
Triarchic theory	Robert Sternberg	Cognitive mechanisms	Gaining knowledge, planning a strategy, actually solving a problem
		Situations that require intelligence	Novel situations, repeated situations
		Relationship to the environment	Adapt to one's environment, improve it, or escape from it

CONCEPT CHECK

2. In Sternberg's theory, novel situations call for problem solving, whereas repeated situations call for automatic habits. Using Cattell's terminology, which kind of situation calls for fluid intelligence and which calls for crystallized intelligence? (Check your answer on page 380.)

THEORIES OF INTELLIGENCE AND TESTS OF INTELLIGENCE

The standard IQ tests, which we shall consider momentarily, were devised decades ago, before most of the discoveries about memory and cognition discussed in the last two chapters were made. Today we have several theories about intelligence and a variety of intelligence tests, but the theories have little relationship to the tests.

Can we measure something—in this case intelligence—without fundamentally understanding what it is? Possibly so; physicists measured gravity and magnetism long before they had any sophisticated understanding of these forces. Maybe psychologists can do the same with intelligence.

But then again, maybe not. Physicists of the past measured not only gravity and magnetism, but also "phlogiston," a substance that, as they later discovered, does not exist. Measurements of a poorly understood phenomenon are risky. Many psychologists are dissatisfied with the currently available intelligence tests, and some are working on efforts to produce a fundamentally better test.

[handwritten margin note: Measure of a poorly understood phenomenon is risky]

In the meantime, the currently available tests have both strengths and weaknesses. Let us examine some of those tests.

■ IQ TESTS

If you have been in school long enough to go on to college, chances are you have spent a significant portion of your life getting tested in one way or another. Our society probably overdoes the testing; still, the need for testing is often clear. More students want to attend medical school than the schools could possibly accommodate; more people would like to be actors than the movie studios can hire; and more people would like to play on their college basketball teams than the teams can include. Choosing future doctors or actors at random would be as foolhardy as choosing members of a basketball team at random; in some way or another, someone has to determine which applicants are most likely to perform the task well.

Schools and colleges try to base their admissions decisions on accurate information. They look at the students' grades and the recommendations of their teachers, but they know that such information has its limita-

Special classes have long been provided for children believed to be unready for ordinary classes. IQ tests are a way of determining who belongs in these special classes, and—perhaps more importantly—who does not.

tions. (Some schools are better than others; some teachers grade harder than others.) To compare students from different schools, they also look at students' scores on standardized tests.

Intelligence quotient (IQ) tests attempt to measure an individual's probable performance in school and similar settings. (The term *quotient* dates from the time when IQ was determined by dividing *mental age* by *chronological age*. That method is now obsolete, but the term remains.) The first IQ tests were devised for a practical purpose by two French psychologists, Alfred Binet and Theophile Simon (1905). The French Ministry of Public Instruction wanted a fair way to identify children who had such serious intellectual deficiencies that they could not succeed in the public school system of Paris. Those children were to be put into special classes. Formerly, the task of identifying retarded children had been left to medical doctors. However, different doctors had different standards for judging retardation. A fair, impartial test of some sort was needed. Binet and Simon produced a test to measure the skills that children need for success in school, such as understanding and using language, computational skills, memory, and the ability to follow instructions.

Such a test can make useful predictions. For example, it can tell us that Susie is likely to do better in school than Nancy will. Now, suppose Susie does well and Nancy does poorly. Can we say that Susie does better in school *because* she has a higher IQ score?

No. Consider this analogy: Suppose we ask why a certain baseball player strikes out so often. Someone answers, "Because he has a low batting average." Clearly, that explains nothing. (The reason for the low batting average is that he strikes out so often.) Similarly, saying that a student does poorly in school because he or she does poorly on an IQ test isn't much of an explanation; after all, the IQ test was designed to measure the very skills schoolwork requires. _An IQ score is like any other score: It measures current performance. It does not explain differences in performance._

THE STANFORD-BINET TEST

The test Binet and Simon designed was later modified for English speakers by Lewis Terman and other Stanford psychologists and published as the **Stanford-Binet IQ test.** This test is administered to individual students by someone who has been carefully trained in how to present the items and how to score the answers. It contains items that range in difficulty, as designated by age. (See Table 9.2.) An item designated as "age 8," for example, will be answered correctly by 60–90% of all 8-year-olds. (A higher percentage of older children will answer it correctly, as will a lower percentage of younger children.) Those who take the test are asked to answer only those items that are pegged at about their level of functioning. For example, the psychologist testing an 8-year-old might start with the items designated for 7-year-olds. If the child missed many of them, the psychologist would go back to the items for 6-year-olds. But if the child answered all or nearly all of the 7-year-old items correctly, the psychologist would proceed to the items for 8-year-olds, 9-year-olds, and so forth, until the child began to miss item after item. At that point, the test is over.

Ordinarily, the entire test lasts no more than 60 to 90 minutes. However, unlike most other IQ tests, the current edition of the Stanford-Binet imposes no time limit; people are allowed to think about each item as long as they wish (McCall, Yates, Hendricks, Turner, & McNabb, 1989).

Stanford-Binet IQ scores are computed from tables set up to ensure that a given IQ score will mean the same thing at different ages. A 6-year-old with an IQ score of, say, 116 has performed better on the test than 84% of other 6-year-olds. Similarly, an adult with an IQ score of 116 has performed better than 84% of other adults. The mean IQ at each age is 100. In addition to the overall IQ, the Stanford-Binet provides subscores reflecting verbal reasoning, quantitative reasoning, and abstract visual reasoning (McCall et al., 1989).

In Table 9.2 notice that the Stanford-Binet test includes questions designated for ages as low as 2 years. For children younger than 4 or 5 years old, scores are likely to fluctuate widely between one test and the next (Honzik, 1974; Morrow & Morrow, 1974). Tests of very young children have low accuracy and few uses.

THE WECHSLER TESTS

Two IQ tests devised by David Wechsler are now more commonly used than the Stanford-Binet. Known as the **Wechsler Adult Intelligence Scale–Revised (WAIS-R)** and the **Wechsler Intelligence Scale for Children–**

TABLE 9.2
Examples of the Types of Items on the Stanford-Binet Test

AGE	SAMPLE TEST ITEM
2	Test administrator points at pictures of everyday objects and asks, "What is this?" "Here are some pegs of different sizes and shapes. See whether you can put each one into the correct hole."
4	"Why do people live in houses?" "Birds fly in the air; fish swim in the _____."
6	"Here is a picture of a horse. Do you see what part of the horse is missing?" "Here are some candies. Can you count how many there are?"
8	"What should you do if you find a lost puppy?" "Stephanie can't write today because she twisted her ankle. What is wrong with that?"
10	"Why should people be quiet in a library?" "Repeat after me: 4 8 3 7 1 4."
12	"What does regret mean?" "Here is a picture. Can you tell me what is wrong with it?"
14	"What is the similarity between high and low?" "Watch me fold this paper and cut it. Now, when I unfold it, how many holes will there be?"
Adult	"Make up a sentence using the words *celebrate, reverse,* and *appointment.*" "What do people mean when they say, 'People who live in glass houses should not throw stones'?"

Source: Modified from Nietzel and Bernstein, 1987.

Third Edition (WISC-III), these tests produce the same average, 100, and almost the same distribution of scores as the Stanford-Binet produces. As with the Stanford-Binet, the Wechsler tests are administered to one individual at a time. The main advantage of a Wechsler test is its multiple scores; in addition to an overall score, it provides scores in two major categories (verbal and performance), each of which is divided into component abilities. (Table 9.3 shows examples of test items, and Figure 9.5 shows one individual's test profile.) Thus, a Wechsler test may indicate the individual's pattern of strengths and weaknesses. For example, a Navajo child whose family speaks Navajo as well as English is likely to get a higher score on the performance scales than on the verbal scales (Naglieri, 1984).

Each of the 12 parts of the WISC-III and the WAIS-R begins with very simple questions that almost everyone answers correctly and then progresses to increasingly difficult items. Six of the 12 parts constitute the Verbal Scale of the test; these parts require the use of spoken or written language. The other

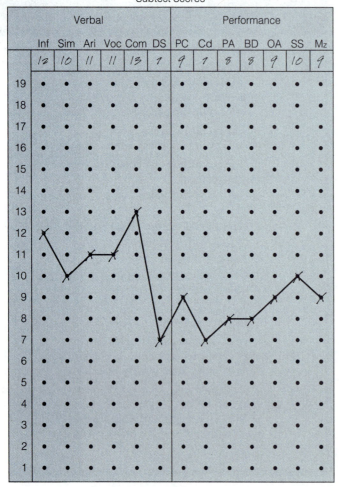

Subtest Scores

Verbal						Performance						
Inf	Sim	Ari	Voc	Com	DS	PC	Cd	PA	BD	OA	SS	Mz
12	10	11	11	13	7	9	7	8	8	9	10	9

FIGURE 9.5
A score profile for one child on the WISC-III IQ test. Each subtest score represents this child's performance on one type of task compared with other children of the same age. In addition to providing an overall IQ score, a profile such as this highlights an individual's strengths and weaknesses. Note this child's better performance on verbal tasks than on performance tasks. (Data courtesy of Patricia Collins.)

6 parts constitute the Performance Scale. Although a person must know English well enough to understand the instructions, the answers are nonverbal (Figure 9.6).

The inclusion of questions that ask for factual information (such as "From what animal do we get milk?") has caused much controversy. Critics complain that such items measure knowledge, not ability. Defenders reply as follows:

• "Intelligent" people tend to learn more facts than others do, even if they have had no more exposure to the information.

• As researchers in artificial intelligence have discovered, most of what we call intelligence requires a vast store of factual knowledge (Schank & Birnbaum, 1994). That is, factual knowledge is not *sufficient* to demonstrate intelligence, but it is *necessary*.

• The purpose of an IQ test is to predict performance in school, and in that respect it works. Students who already know a great many facts tend to do well in school.

We shall consider further criticisms of intelligence tests in the second module of this chapter.

RAVEN'S PROGRESSIVE MATRICES

The Stanford-Binet and Wechsler tests, though useful for many purposes, have certain limitations. First, they call for specific information that may be much more familiar to some people than to others. Second, because they require comprehension and use of the English language, they are unfair to people who do not speak English well, including immigrants and hearing-impaired people. "Why not simply translate the tests into other languages?" you might ask. Sometimes psychologists do, but it is very difficult to equate the translation with the original. For example, one part of the Stanford-Binet gives

FIGURE 9.6
Much of the WAIS-R involves nonverbal tests in which a person is asked to perform certain tasks. Here, to evaluate visual-spatial organization, a woman arranges colored blocks according to a specified pattern while a psychologist times her.

TABLE 9.3
Items from the Wechsler Intelligence Scale for Children (WISC)

TEST	EXAMPLE

Verbal Scale

Information
From what animal do we get milk?
(Either "cow" or "goat" is an acceptable answer.)

Similarities
How are a plum and a peach similar?
(Correct answer: "They are both fruits." Half credit is given for "Both are food."
or "Both are round.")

Arithmetic
Count these blocks: ■ ■ ■ ■ ■ ■ ■ ■

Vocabulary
Define the word *letter*.

Comprehension
What should you do if you see a train approaching a broken track?
(A correct answer is "Stand safely out of the way and wave something to warn
the train." Half credit is given for "Tell someone at the railroad station."
No credit is given for "I would try to fix the track."

Digit Span
Repeat these numbers after I say them: 3 6 2.

Performance Scale

Picture completion
What part is missing from this picture?

Picture arrangement
Here are some cards with a gardener on them.
Can you put them in order?

Block design
See how I have arranged these four blocks? Here are four more blocks.
Can you arrange your blocks like mine?

Object assembly
Can you put these five puzzle pieces together to make a dog?

Coding
Here is a page full of shapes. Put a slash (/) through all the circles and
an × through all the squares.

Mazes
Here is a maze. Start with your pencil here and trace a path
to the other end of the maze without crossing any lines.

Source: Based on Wechsler, 1949.

people certain words and asks for words that rhyme with them. Generating rhymes is moderately easy in English, extremely easy in Italian, and, I am told, virtually impossible in Zulu (Smith, 1974).

To overcome such problems, psychologists have tried to devise a culture-fair, or culture-reduced, test that would make minimal use of language and would not ask for any specific facts. One example of a culture-reduced test is the **Progressive Matrices** test devised by John C. Raven. Figure 9.7 presents matrices of the type this test uses. These matrices, which "progress" gradually from easy items to difficult items, attempt to measure abstract reasoning; to answer them, a person must generate hypotheses, test them, and infer rules (Carpenter, Just, & Shell, 1990).

The Progressive Matrices test calls for no verbal responses and no specific information.

The instructions are easy to translate into any language. How "culture-fair" is the Progressive Matrices test? Certainly, it gives a non-English-speaking immigrant or a deaf person a much better opportunity than most other IQ tests do (Powers, Barkan, & Jones, 1986; Vernon, 1967). However, the Progressive Matrices test does assume that the test-taker is at least familiar with pencil-and-paper tests and with the idea of looking for visual patterns. It is not so culture-fair that it would be appropriate for an unschooled person from a nontechnological society.

For disadvantaged subcultures within the United States, the Progressive Matrices test offers no clear advantage. On the average, African Americans and European Americans differ about as much on the Progressive Matrices as they do on the Wechsler and Stanford-Binet tests. In fact, the Progressive Matrices test has one possible disadvantage

(Sternberg, 1991): By reporting only a single overall score, the test fails to show an individual's areas of strength and weakness, as the other IQ tests do.

THE SCHOLASTIC ASSESSMENT TEST

The test once known as the Scholastic Aptitude Test is now titled the **Scholastic Assessment Test (SAT)**. Because the term *assessment* means *test*, the title really means *school-based test test*. Many people call it the "SAT test," adding yet another layer of redundancy.

The Scholastic Assessment Test serves the same function as an IQ test: It predicts performance in college. (Figure 9.8 shows the relationship between SAT scores and grade-point average during the freshman year in college at one university.) Administered to large groups of students at one time, the SAT consists of multiple-choice items divided into two sets, verbal and quantitative. Each set is scored on a scale from 200 to 800. The mean was originally set at 500. Over the years, the mean gradually drifted downward, partly because a wider range of students was taking the test, instead of only the best. In 1995 the scoring system was readjusted to return the mean to 500. (Thus, scores reported before the readjustment do not mean the same thing as scores reported after the readjustment.)

Figure 9.9 presents examples of the types of items found on the SAT. If you are a college student in the United States, you are probably familiar with the SAT or with the similar American College Test (ACT). Recent changes in the SAT have included the addition of a test of writing and the possibility of taking the test on a computer.

The SAT was designed to help colleges select among applicants for admission. Although the best predictor of college success is success in high school, high-school grades by themselves are not entirely satisfactory. A student who earned a B- average while taking challenging courses at a very competitive high school may in fact be a better student than someone who earned a straight-A average while taking easy courses at some other high school. The SAT offers a way to compare students from different high-school backgrounds. As a predictor of college success, the SAT by itself is less satisfactory than high-school grades by themselves. However, a combination of high-school grades and SAT scores significantly improves the prediction of college success (Weitzman, 1982).

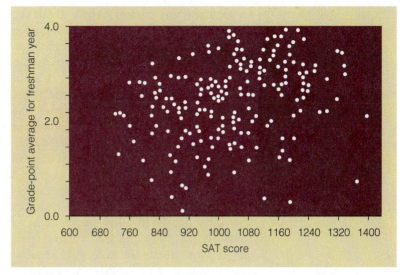

FIGURE 9.8
In this scatter plot, each point represents one freshman student at a particular state university. That student's SAT score is given on the x-axis; his or her grade-point average on the y-axis. Note that SAT scores predict college grades moderately well, with a correlation of .3 for this sample. Note also a number of exceptions—students with high SAT scores but poor grades and students with low SAT scores but good grades.

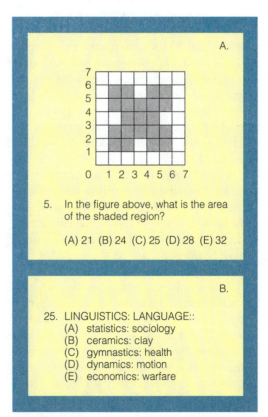

FIGURE 9.9
These two sample items from the Scholastic Assessment Test reflect its two parts, which measure mathematical and verbal skills. (From the College Entrance Examination Board and the Educational Testing Service.)

Because many students worry about doing well on the SAT, a coaching industry has developed. Students can pay to attend sessions after school or on weekends. If you attended such sessions, did you get your money's worth? If you did not attend them, did you miss a chance for a much higher SAT score? Several studies have compared the SAT scores of students who attended coaching sessions to the scores of students of similar ability who did not. The results have been consistent: On the average, participation in SAT coaching sessions raises a student's score by about 10 to 20 points (on a scale from 200 to 800). Students who attend longer, more intensive coaching sessions score only slightly higher than those who attend briefer sessions. To improve scores by more than about 30 points, a student has to spend almost as much time in the coaching sessions as in school (Kulik, Bangert-Drowns, & Kulik, 1984; Messick & Jungeblut, 1981).

TESTING APTITUDE VERSUS TESTING ACHIEVEMENT

The SAT and IQ tests are considered aptitude or ability tests. Psychologists and educators distinguish aptitude tests from *achievement* tests, which are intended to measure the skills or knowledge someone has gained in a particular area of study. For example, the tests you take in your college courses are considered achievement tests.

In fact, however, both kinds of tests measure a combination of aptitude and achievement. People with good reasoning ability have an advantage on any achievement test, and those people who have acquired a great deal of knowledge can use it on tests of supposed reasoning ability.

Here is a demonstration of the difficulty of measuring aptitude separately from knowledge: The SAT includes many reading passages, each followed by a set of questions concerning the reading. Supposedly, these items measure the students' ability to draw conclusions from what they just read. However, one study found that college students could answer almost half the questions correctly even *without* reading the passages (Katz, Lautenschlager, Blackburn, & Harris, 1990). That is, they could call upon their knowledge of related material to choose the most likely answers. These items were supposed to measure how well students could learn from their readings, but they in fact measured (in part) how much the students already knew.

The point to remember is this: *No test measures pure ability, and perhaps no test ever will. Every test necessarily measures some complex mixture of abilities and knowledge.*

TESTS OF THE FUTURE

Standard IQ tests and related tests have been used for decades, despite persistent criticism. They have their advantages as well as their disadvantages. An IQ score is useful for certain practical purposes, such as selecting students for special programs. It also serves as a rough gauge of certain crude biological variables. For example, studies using modern methods such as MRI scans have found a moderate, positive correlation between students' IQ scores and their brain volumes (Willerman, Schultz, Rutledge, & Bigler, 1991). IQ scores also correlate positively with speed of information processing (Hale & Jansen, 1994; Jensen, 1993).

In a way, the overall intelligence of an individual is like the gross national product of a country; both figures provides a summary that may be useful for certain purposes. However, if we want to understand what is happening in any detail, we have to go beyond those summaries and explore the detailed components and processes.

Many psychologists hope to develop new IQ tests that differ significantly from the current tests—perhaps tests that focus less on knowledge and more on ability to learn or tests that cover a wider range of abilities (Sternberg, 1991). Unfortunately, producing a significantly improved IQ test is not as easy as it may sound. The present tests, even with their shortcomings, are the product of decades of research and effort; devising an accurate measure of more complex and varied abilities will not be easy.

In the next module of this chapter we shall consider the ways in which psychologists evaluate tests, including the currently available IQ tests and any new tests that might be proposed to take their place. Psychologists have worked out clear criteria for evaluating tests and deciding which tests are better than others.

A ski mask can be used to protect a skier from harsh weather or to hide the face of a thief during a robbery. Similarly, IQ tests can be used for their originally intended purposes or for other, more doubtful purposes.

At this point let us simply stress that the value of an IQ test, like that of any tool, depends on how it is used. A hammer can be used to build a door or to break one down; similarly, a test score can be used to open the doors of opportunity or to close them. A test score, if cautiously interpreted, can aid schools in making placement decisions. If it is treated as an infallible guide, it can be seriously misleading.

SUMMARY

- *Defining intelligence.* The designers of the standard IQ tests defined intelligence simply as the ability to do well in school. Psychologists with a more theoretical interest have defined intelligence by listing the abilities it includes. (page 365)
- *g factor.* A number of "intelligent" abilities apparently share a common element, known as the *g* factor, which is closely related to abstract reasoning. The *g* factor may arise either because various tests tap the same ability, or because the health and educational factors that promote growth of one intellectual ability also promote the development of other intellectual abilities. (page 366)
- *Fluid and crystallized intelligence.* Psychologists distinguish between fluid intelligence (a basic reasoning ability that a person can apply to any problem, including unfamiliar types) and crystallized intelligence (acquired abilities to solve familiar types of problems). (page 367)

- *Abilities that make up intelligence.* Different psychologists have drawn up different lists of the abilities that make up intelligence. Some define intelligence fairly narrowly; others include such abilities as social attentiveness, musical abilities, and motor skills. According to the multiple intelligences view, people possess many independent types of intelligence. (page 368)
- *Triarchic theory.* According to Sternberg's triarchic theory of intelligence, intelligence consists of three aspects—the cognitive mechanisms within the individual, the situations that require intelligence, and the ways in which intelligent behavior relates to the environment. (page 369)
- *IQ tests.* The Stanford-Binet and other IQ tests were devised to predict the level of performance in school. (page 372)
- *Wechsler IQ tests.* The Wechsler IQ tests measure separate abilities, grouped into a Verbal Scale of six parts and a Performance Scale of six parts. (page 373)
- *Culture-reduced tests.* Culture-reduced tests such as Raven's Progressive Matrices can be used with people who are unfamiliar with English. (page 376)
- *SAT.* The Scholastic Assessment Test is similar to IQ tests because it predicts performance in school, specifically in college. (page 377)

SUGGESTION FOR FURTHER READING

Ceci, S. J. (1990). *On intelligence . . . more or less.* Englewood Cliffs, NJ: Prentice-Hall. Perceptive critique of traditional assumptions about intelligence.

TERMS

psychometric the measurement of individual differences in abilities and behaviors (page 366)

g Spearman's "general" factor that all IQ tests and all parts of an IQ test are believed to have in common (page 366)

s a "specific" factor that is more important for performance on some scales of an intelligence test than it is on others (page 366)

fluid intelligence the basic power of reasoning and using information, including the ability to perceive relationships, deal with unfamiliar problems, and gain new types of knowledge (page 367)

crystallized intelligence acquired skills and knowledge and the application of that knowledge to specific content in a person's experience (page 367)

multiple intelligences Gardner's theory that intelligence is composed of numerous unrelated forms of intelligent behavior (page 368)

triarchic theory Sternberg's theory that deals with three aspects of intelligence: The cognitive processes that occur, the situations that require intelligence, and how intelligence relates to the external world (page 370)

intelligence quotient (IQ) a measure of an individual's probable performance in school and in similar settings (page 372)

Stanford-Binet IQ test a test of intelligence, the first important IQ test in the English language (page 372)

Wechsler Adult Intelligence Scale–Revised (WAIS-R) an IQ test originally devised by David Wechsler, commonly used with adults (page 373)

Wechsler Intelligence Scale for Children–Third Edition (WISC-III) an IQ test originally devised by David Wechsler, commonly used with children (page 373)

Progressive Matrices an IQ test that attempts to measure abstract reasoning without use of language or recall of facts (page 376)

Scholastic Assessment Test (SAT) a test of students' likelihood of performing well in college (page 377)

ANSWERS TO CONCEPT CHECKS

1. Turing's solution reflected fluid intelligence, a generalized ability that he could apply to any topic. The solution provided by a bicycle mechanic reflects crystallized intelligence, an ability developed in a particular area of experience. (page 368)

2. In Cattell's terminology, a novel situation calls for fluid intelligence, whereas a repeated situation calls for crystallized intelligence. (page 371)

ANSWERS TO OTHER QUESTIONS IN THE TEXT

A. 1. 8 2. 6 3. 3 4. 4 5. 6 6. 2 (page 376)

EVALUATION OF INTELLIGENCE TESTS

What do the scores on IQ tests mean?

Are variations in intelligence between groups of people the result of differences in genes?

Edward Thorndike, a pioneer in the study of both animal and human learning, is often quoted as saying, "If something exists, it exists in some amount. If it exists in some amount, it can be measured." Douglas Detterman (1979) countered, "Anything which exists can be measured incorrectly."

We can apply both of these quotes to intelligence: If intelligence exists at all, it must be measurable, but it can be measured incorrectly. One of the major tasks for researchers in this field is to test the tests—to determine whether the tests measure what their designers claim they measure, how accurately they measure it, and whether they apply fairly to all groups. This is an area of heated arguments, an area in which it is often difficult to separate science from politics and social beliefs.

THE STANDARDIZATION OF IQ TESTS

In order to specify what various scores mean, those who devise a test must *standardize* it. **Standardization** is the process of establishing rules for administering a test and for interpreting its scores. One of the main steps in standardization is to find the **norms,** which are descriptions of the frequencies at which particular scores occur.

Psychologists try to standardize a test on a large, representative population. For example, if a test is to be used with children throughout the United States and Canada, psychologists need to measure the norms for a large random or representative sample of U.S. and Canadian children, not just for children of one ethnic group or one geographic region.

THE DISTRIBUTION OF IQ SCORES

Binet, Wechsler, and the other pioneers who devised the first IQ tests chose items and arranged the scoring method to establish the mean score at 100, with a standard deviation of 15 for the Wechsler test (as Figure 9.10

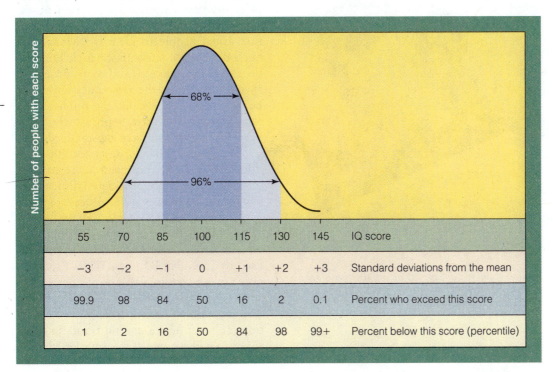

IQ score	55	70	85	100	115	130	145	IQ score
Standard deviations	−3	−2	−1	0	+1	+2	+3	Standard deviations from the mean
Percent exceed	99.9	98	84	50	16	2	0.1	Percent who exceed this score
Percent below	1	2	16	50	84	98	99+	Percent below this score (percentile)

FIGURE 9.10
The scores on an IQ test form an approximately bell-shaped curve. The curve shown here represents scores on the Wechsler IQ test, with a standard deviation of 15 (15 points above and below the mean, 100). The results on the Stanford-Binet test are very similar, except that the standard deviation is 16, so the spread is slightly wider.

Periodically merchants should check their scales to make sure they are measuring accurately. Similarly, psychologists carefully check IQ tests and other psychological tests to find out the reliability and validity of their results.

shows) and 16 for the Stanford-Binet. (The standard deviation, you may recall from Chapter 2, is a measure of the degree of variability of performance. If most scores are close to the mean, the standard deviation is small; if scores vary widely, the standard deviation is larger.)

In any normal distribution, 68% of all people are within one standard deviation above or below the mean; 96% are within two standard deviations. Someone with a

People with IQ scores at least two standard deviations below the mean are classified as "retarded." Many can be "mainstreamed" in regular classes; severely retarded children are taught in special classes.

score of 115 on the Wechsler test exceeds the scores of those people within one standard deviation from the mean, plus all of those more than one standard deviation below the mean—a total of 84% of all people, as shown in Figure 9.10. We say that such a person is "in the 84th percentile." Someone with an IQ score of 130 is in the 98th percentile, which means that his or her score is higher than the scores of 98% of others of the same age.

Psychologists sometimes refer to people more than two standard deviations above the mean as "gifted." That designation is arbitrary. There is not much difference between an allegedly "gifted" child with an IQ of 130 and an allegedly "nongifted" child with an IQ of 129.

Psychologists also classify people more than two standard deviations below the mean as "retarded." Many retarded children, especially those who are severely retarded, suffer from biological disorders, including chromosomal abnormalities and fetal alcohol syndrome (Zigler & Hodapp, 1991). Since 1975, U.S. law has required schools to provide "free, appropriate" education to all retarded children. Those with severe retardation are placed in separate classes; those with milder problems are "mainstreamed" (placed in regular classes with some extra attention).

RESTANDARDIZATION OF IQ TESTS

Over the years, the standardization of any IQ test becomes obsolete. In 1920 a question that asked people to identify "Mars" was fairly difficult, because most people knew little about the planets. Today, in an era of space exploration, the same question would be very easy. Periodically, the publishers of each IQ test update it, rephrase the questions, and change the scoring standards.

The result is that IQ tests become more difficult. To keep the mean score at 100, items that were once considered difficult but have since become easy have been replaced with more difficult items (Flynn, 1984, 1987). In other words, people are doing better and better at answering the questions that used to appear in IQ tests. Why? Psychologists are not certain. Evolution is not a plausible explanation for such a rapid change. The explanation may lie in improved education, in better health and nutrition, in exposure to a wider range of information via television, in greater test-taking skills, or in other environmental changes.

EVALUATION OF TESTS

At some point in your academic career, you probably complained that a test was unfair. You were sure you knew the important material, but the test concentrated on minor details or penalized you for not saying something in quite the right way. Your instructor may or may not have agreed with your criticism.

Similarly, many people complain about intelligence tests. Much is at stake in this dispute; intelligence tests substantially influence the future of millions of people. Psychologists try to avoid simply arguing about whether or not a test appears to be reasonable; they look at specific kinds of evidence to determine whether the test achieves what it is intended to achieve. The two basic ways of evaluating any test are to check its reliability and its validity.

RELIABILITY

The **reliability** of a test is defined as the repeatability of its scores (Rogers, 1995). A reliable test measures something consistently. To determine the reliability of a test, psychologists use a correlation coefficient. They may test the same people twice, either with the same test or with equivalent versions of it, and compare the two sets of scores. Or they may compare the scores on the first and second halves of the test or the scores on the test's odd- and even-numbered items. If all the items measure approximately the same abilities, the scores on one set of items should be highly correlated with the scores on the other set of items. As with any other correlation coefficient, the reliability of a test can (theoretically) range from +1 to −1. In the real world, however, reliabilities are always positive. (A negative reliability would mean that people who do better than average the first time they take a test will do worse than average the next time. That pattern simply never happens.) Figure 9.11 illustrates **test-retest reliability.**

If a test's reliability is perfect (+1), the person who scores the highest on the first test will also score highest on the retest, and the person who receives the 127th-best score will again make the 127th-best score. If the

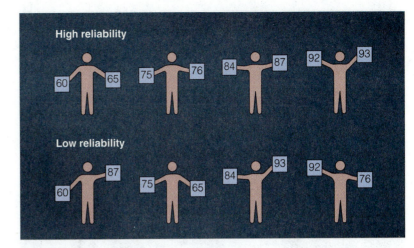

FIGURE 9.11
On a test with high reliability, people who score high one time will score high again when they take the test a second time. On a test with low reliability, scores fluctuate randomly.

reliability is 0, a person's scores will vary randomly from one test to another. The reliability of the WISC-III has been measured at about .95; the reliabilities of the Stanford-Binet, Progressive Matrices, and SAT are also in the range of about .90 to .95 (Anastasi, 1988; Burke, 1985; Siegler & Richards, 1982). These figures indicate that the IQ tests are measuring *something* in a consistent, repeatable manner. (They do not tell us what that something is.)

CONCEPT CHECKS

3. I have just devised a new "intelligence test." I measure your intelligence by dividing the length of your head by its width and then multiplying by 100. Would that be a reliable test?
4. Most students find that if they retake the SAT, their scores increase the second time. Does that improvement indicate that the test is unreliable? (Check your answers on page 397.)

VALIDITY

A test's **validity** is a determination of how well it measures what it claims to measure. One type of validity is **content validity.** We say that a test has high content validity if its items accurately represent the information the test is meant to measure. For example, a licensing examination for psychologists would have high content validity if it tested

In some countries test scores can determine a student's future almost irrevocably. Students who perform well are almost assured of future success; those who perform poorly may have very limited opportunities.

information that a practicing psychologist is expected to know. A test for a driver's license has content validity if it includes important laws and regulations that pertain to driving.

A second type of validity is **construct validity**. A test has construct validity if what it measures corresponds to a theoretical construct. For example, intelligence is a theoretical construct. Psychologists expect it to have certain properties, such as increasing as a child grows older. They also expect it to include several component abilities, such as mathematics, memorization, and verbal reasoning. For an IQ test to have construct validity, it must reflect those properties. For example, older children should, as a rule, answer more questions correctly than younger children do.

Predictive validity, a third type of validity, is the ability of a test's scores to predict real-world performance. For example, an interest test that accurately predicts what courses a student will enjoy has predictive validity. Similarly, an IQ test that accurately predicts how well a student will perform in school has predictive validity.

As with reliability, psychologists measure predictive validity by means of a correlation coefficient. For example, to determine the predictive validity of an IQ test or of the SAT, psychologists determine how well those scores predict students' grades. A validity of +1 would mean that the scores perfectly pre-

dicted performance; a validity of 0 would mean that the scores were worthless as predictors. The predictive validity of such tests as the WISC-III, Stanford-Binet, Progressive Matrices, and SAT generally ranges from about .3 to .6, varying from one school to another (Anastasi, 1988; Siegler & Richards, 1982). As these figures suggest, success in school depends on many factors, not just on the skills the tests measure.

IQ tests also have some validity for predicting success in a variety of jobs, especially for performance in entry-level jobs (Barrett & Depinet, 1991). One reason for that tendency is that people with high IQ scores generally receive the advantage of extensive education. How well IQ predicts job success *independently of education* is more controversial (McClelland, 1993). In the long run, job performance depends on both how fast people learn (intelligence) and how much time they have spent learning the job (experience). The relative importance of these two factors no doubt varies from one job to another (Schmidt & Hunter, 1993).

Sometimes the reported predictive validity of a test such as the SAT can be misleading. Consider some data for the Graduate Record Examination (GRE), a test similar to the SAT. For predicting grades in the first year of graduate school, the verbal and quantitative parts of the GRE have the following predictive validities (Educational Testing Service, 1994):

Graduate students in	GRE verbal score	GRE quantitative score
physics	.19	.13
English	.23	.29

Note that for physics students, the verbal score is the better predictor of grades, whereas for English students, the quantitative score is a better predictor! How can we explain these surprising results? Simply, almost all graduate students in physics have about the same (very high) score on the quantitative test, and almost all English graduate students have nearly the same (very high) score on the verbal test. When almost all the students in a department have practically the same score, that score cannot predict which students will be more successful than others. *A test can have a high predictive validity only for a population whose scores vary over a substantial range.*

TABLE 9.4
Evaluating Intelligence Tests

RELIABILITY	VALIDITY	UTILITY	BIAS
How consistent are the same person's scores?	How well does the test measure what it claims to measure?	How useful is the test for some practical purpose?	Do test scores make equally accurate predictions for all groups?
	Content—Do the test items represent the pertinent information?		
	Construct—Do the results match theoretical expectations?		
	Prediction—Do the test scores predict real-world performance?		

CONCEPT CHECKS

5. Can a test have high reliability and low validity? Can a test have low reliability and high validity?

6. If physics graduate departments tried admitting some students with low GRE quantitative scores and English departments tried admitting some students with low GRE verbal scores, what would happen to the predictive validity of those tests?

7. Would you expect the SAT scores to show higher predictive validity at a university with extremely competitive admissions standards, such as MIT, or at a university that admits almost anyone who applies? (Check your answers on page 397.)

UTILITY

In addition to reliability and validity, a good test should have utility. **Utility** is defined as usefulness for a practical purpose. Not every test that is reliable and valid is also useful.

For example, one study found that first-year grades at the University of Pennsylvania correlated positively with both SAT aptitude test scores and SAT achievement test scores. That is, both aptitude scores and achievement scores were valid. However, the investigators found that they could predict first-year grades just as well from achievement scores alone as they could from a combination of aptitude and achievement scores (Baron & Norman, 1992). That is, if the university already had students' SAT achievement scores, the SAT aptitude test had little or no utility. Those results may not apply to

other colleges, and they are of course irrelevant to colleges that do not require the achievement tests. The point is that any institution should check whether a given test has utility for its purposes.

Table 9.4 summarizes criteria for evaluating intelligence tests.

INTERPRETING FLUCTUATIONS IN SCORES

Suppose you have a score of 94% correct on the first test in your psychology course. On the second test (which was equally difficult), you make a score of 88%. Does that score indicate that you studied harder for the first test than for the second test? Not necessarily. Whenever you take tests that are not perfectly reliable, your scores are likely to fluctuate. The lower the reliability, the greater the fluctuation.

When people lose sight of that fact, they sometimes offer complex explanations for random fluctuations in results. In one well-known study, Harold M. Skeels (1966) tested infants in an orphanage and identified those who had the lowest IQ scores. He then placed those infants in an institution that provided more personal attention. Several years later, most of those infants showed major increases in their IQ scores. Should we conclude, as many psychologists did, that the extra attention improved the children's IQ performances? Not necessarily (Longstreth, 1981). IQ tests for infants have low reliabilities—in other words, the scores fluctuate widely from one time to another. If someone selects a group of infants with low IQ scores

Most first-generation immigrants to the United States do not score high on English-language IQ tests. As a rule, their children get higher scores.

and retests them later, the mean IQ score is almost certain to improve, simply because the early scores were poor estimates of the children's abilities. Or, to put it another way, the scores had nowhere to go but up.

SOMETHING TO THINK ABOUT

What would be the proper control group for the study by Skeels?

GROUP DIFFERENCES IN IQ SCORES

Binet and the other pioneers in IQ testing discovered that girls tend to do better than boys on language tasks, whereas boys tend to do better than girls on some visual-spatial and mathematical tasks. By loading the test with one type of item, they could have "demonstrated" that girls are smarter than boys or that boys are smarter than girls. Instead, they carefully balanced the two types of items to ensure that the mean score of both girls and boys would be 100.

Mean differences between males and females are small on most tests of language and mathematics (Feingold, 1988; Hyde, Fennema, & Lamon, 1990). However, males tend to show greater individual variability. Thus, the data on a variety of intellectual measures show a higher percentage of males than females at the very top of the range and at the very bottom of the range (Lubinski &

Benbow, 1992). (*Why* that is true, we do not know.)

Ethnic groups in the United States also differ in their mean performance on IQ tests (Herrnstein & Murray, 1994). The mean score of European Americans as a whole is about 100, with the Jewish subpopulation averaging a few points above that. The mean for African Americans has generally been stated as 85, although several studies indicate an increase to about 88 for the current younger generation. The available data indicate that East Asians (those of Japanese, Chinese, or Korean descent) have a mean score above 100; it is hard to specify the mean more precisely because much of our information comes from small and possibly unrepresentative samples. Data on Latinos indicate a mean score several points below 100; however, many of the individuals tested were first-generation immigrants to the United States, and their results are undoubtedly impaired by language difficulties. Figure 9.12 shows mean test scores on the SAT from 1975 to 1991; SAT scores show a pattern similar to the results reported for IQ scores (Carson, Huelskamp, & Woodall, 1993).

Please bear in mind: These data reflect the means for whole populations. Each ethnic group includes individuals with extremely high scores and others with very low scores. The data do not justify prejudices or assumptions about any individual.

What accounts for the observed differences among ethnic groups? In a famous and controversial book, *The Bell Curve*, Richard

Herrnstein and Charles Murray (1994) argued as follows:

- IQ tests, imperfect as they are, reliably measure something, regardless of whether we call it intelligence.
- Whatever it is that IQ tests measure, it correlates with school performance, likelihood of getting certain jobs, and many other behavioral measures. It is not an all-important characteristic of a person, but it is not trivial, either.
- Measured differences among groups are not illusions that we can attribute to faulty tests.
- IQ differences within the European-American population reflect a combination of environmental and genetic differences.
- IQ differences among ethnic groups may also reflect a combination of environmental and genetic differences.

The first and second of those points say, in effect, that IQ tests are reliable and valid for certain purposes. As already mentioned earlier in this chapter, the data clearly support those two points. Let us now consider the controversies and evidence for the remaining points. To preview the eventual conclusions, according to a consensus of 52 leading researchers in the field (Arvey et al., 1994): Herrnstein and Murray's third and fourth points also fit the data. The apparent group differences are not due to faulty testing, and differences among European Americans are probably due to both genetic and environmental influences. On the fifth point, the evidence is too weak to justify any conclusion. The available evidence does not demonstrate a genetic basis for ethnic differences, but it also fails to eliminate the possibility. With that preview in mind, let us proceed.

SHOULD WE EVEN CONSIDER SUCH MATTERS?

As mentioned, the conclusions of *The Bell Curve* are highly controversial. A number of critics have heatedly attacked the book's authors for even raising issues about ethnic differences. According to such critics, a public airing of the book's conclusions can only increase interethnic hostility and provide excuses for racists bent on unfair treatment of minority groups.

We should take that point seriously. However, consider two arguments in favor of discussing these difficult issues:

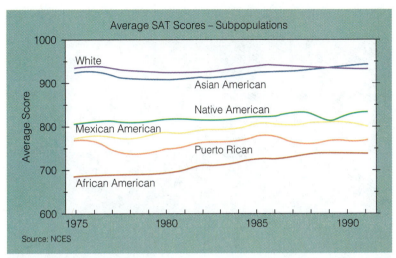

FIGURE 9.12
Various U.S. ethnic groups differ on their SAT (and IQ test) scores. Note the gradual increase in scores among African Americans during this period. (From Carson, Huelskamp, & Woodall, 1993.)

First, in spite of the taboo on discussing ethnic differences in public, a great many people do in fact form private opinions, many of them not based on any evidence, and some of them far more extreme than anything in *The Bell Curve*. Presumably, many people would like to know what the evidence is.

Second, attempts to silence an unwanted viewpoint tend to backfire. For example, for

People form opinions, sometimes heated opinions, about the causes of race differences, even if they know nothing about the scientific evidence. Discussing the scientific evidence poses definite risks, but keeping people ignorant of the evidence poses risks, too.

A test is biased if its scores underpredict the performance of a particular group. But if its scores make equally accurate predictions for all groups, then it is not biased; group differences in scores evidently report an actual difference among groups. Note that calling a test "unbiased" does not mean its scores measure fixed or innate potential. It just means that whatever is responsible for group differences in school performance or some other performance shows up in test scores as well.

many years the Communist governments of the Soviet Union and Eastern Europe forbade any public criticism of Communism. As a result, citizens who heard pro-Communist speeches immediately discounted them as "only what the speaker was required to say." When they occasionally heard someone express contrary views, listeners assumed the speaker must have a very strong basis for such punishable opinions. Analogously, in the U.S. and Canada, some proponents of a genetic basis for group IQ differences have been subjected to personal harassment, vandalism, lawsuits, and death threats just for presenting those views (e.g., Rushton, 1994). That kind of persecution can easily promote a fascination with "those views that are too dangerous for us to hear." In short, an open discussion may do more good than would a timid avoidance of the issues.

◼ ARE IQ TESTS BIASED?

One frequently proposed explanation for group differences in IQ scores is that the tests are biased against certain groups. That is, ethnic groups do not actually differ in mean IQ; they merely appear to differ because of unfair or inappropriate tests. Presumably, according to this viewpoint, a better test would indicate no group differences.

The first point to emphasize is that the existence of measurable group differences does not, by itself, demonstrate bias in the tests. An apparent difference can arise either because the tests measure certain groups inaccurately, or because the groups really do differ. This is an *empirical question;* that is, a question to be decided by the evidence.

To determine whether or not a test is **biased** against a group, psychologists determine whether the test *systematically underestimates* that group's performance. To understand what it means for a test to be biased, consider two examples of demonstrable test bias: First, the Stanford-Binet and Wechsler IQ tests are biased against non-English-speaking immigrants to the United States. In the long run (after they have learned the language), such immigrants succeed beyond what their initial test scores would indicate. That is, the test scores underestimate the immigrants' likely performance. Psychologists of an earlier era, unaware of this bias or insensitive to it, drew some conclusions concerning the "feeblemindedness" of immigrants that now seem ludicrous (Gelb, 1986).

Second example: Women who enter or return to college in their 30s, 40s, or 50s generally get better grades than their scores on the SAT, ACT, or any other test would predict. They also do better than their high-school grades would predict. When we say, therefore, that the tests are biased against such women, we are not saying that the test authors rigged the test against them. We are merely saying that a given test score means something different for a 40-year-old woman than it does for a 19-year-old. (Colleges that are aware of this tendency often take a chance on some middle-aged applicants with disappointing test scores.)

To determine whether a test is biased—against middle-aged women, ethnic minorities, or whatever—psychologists find out whether such individuals do better in school or college than the test scores predict. Psychologists try to identify bias both in individual test items and in the test as a whole.

EVALUATING POSSIBLE BIAS IN SINGLE TEST ITEMS

To determine whether a particular item on a test is biased, psychologists have to go beyond an "armchair analysis" that says "this item looks unfair." They look for evidence that an item that is one of the easiest on the test for one

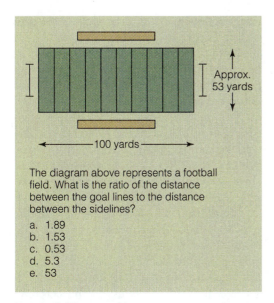

FIGURE 9.13

This item was once included on the SAT until psychologists determined that it was biased against women. Many women did not know which were the goal lines and which were the sidelines.

group might be one of the more difficult items for another group (Schmitt & Dorans, 1990).

Figure 9.13, an item that once appeared on the SAT, shows a diagram of a football field and asks for the ratio of the distance between the goal lines to the distance between the sidelines. For men, this was one of the easiest items on the test. The few men who missed it generally did poorly on the rest of the test as well. However, a higher percentage of women missed this item, including some women who did very well on the rest of the test. The reason was that a number of very bright women did not know which were the goal lines and which were the sidelines. This pattern of evidence indicated that the item was biased against women, and the publishers of the SAT therefore removed the item from the test. As a rule, standardized tests such as the SAT are purged of any items with demonstrable bias against any group.

EVALUATING POSSIBLE BIAS IN A TEST AS A WHOLE

By definition, a biased test is one that systematically underestimates (underpredicts) the performance of a group. If an IQ test is indeed biased against African Americans, for example, then African Americans who score, say, 100 really have greater abilities than European Americans with the same score.

The evidence, however, indicates that minority-group students with a given IQ score generally do about as well in school and at school-related tasks as do European Americans with the same IQ score (Barrett & Depinet, 1991; Cole, 1981; Lambert, 1981; Svanum & Bringle, 1982). Likewise, minority-group students with a given SAT score generally do about as well in college as do European Americans with the same scores (McCornack, 1983). The unpleasant fact is that on the average, European-American students get better grades in school than do African Americans in the United States. The IQ tests accurately report that fact. In short, the tests show no evidence of ethnic-group bias, and continued claims of test bias could be described as "blaming the messenger" (the IQ tests) for the bad news.

Some critics have tried to document a charge of bias against the standard tests by developing tests with a "reverse bias," favoring African Americans over European Americans. Figure 9.14 shows examples from one such test, the Black Intelligence Test of

Circle the letter that indicates the correct meaning of the word or phrase.

1. *running a game*
   a. writing a bad check
   b. looking at something
   c. directing a contest
   d. getting what one wants from another person or thing

2. *to get down*
   a. to dominate
   b. to travel
   c. to lower a position
   d. to have sexual intercourse

3. *cop an attitude*
   a. leave
   b. become angry
   c. sit down
   d. protect a neighborhood

4. *alley apple*
   a. brick
   b. piece of fruit
   c. dog
   d. horse

5. *boogie jugie*
   a. tired
   b. worthless
   c. old
   d. well put together

FIGURE 9.14

Some items from the Black Intelligence Test of Cultural Homogeneity (BITCH). Check your answers against answer B, page 397.

Cultural Homogeneity (BITCH). Tests such as this one certainly underscore the point that some information is more familiar to members of one group than it is to members of another. However, we cannot reasonably regard the BITCH as an intelligence test; even for African Americans, high scores on this test do not predict good performance in school or on the job (Matarazzo & Wiens, 1977).

Charges of test bias sometimes take another form: Some critics have argued that African-American students perform less well on various tests because they are intimidated by a European-American tester or confused by the language of the test. However, research studies have found no consistent increase in minority children's test scores when the test is administered by an African-American examiner, using an African-American dialect (Sattler & Gwynne, 1982).

Note that when I say the IQ tests show no demonstrable bias against minority groups, I am *not* saying that the differences in scores are due to differences in innate ability. I am merely saying that whatever causes children to differ in school performance also causes them to differ in test performance. Whether the difference reflects hereditary or environmental influences is an entirely separate question.

Note that I am also not saying that the tests are perfect. They measure just one kind of intelligence, the kind of intelligence that helps people to do well in school. They do not measure the multiple kinds of intelligence that Gardner discusses, and certainly not all the kinds of skills that any human culture might value.

"Students will rise to your level of expectation," says Jaime Escalante, the high-school teacher portrayed by Edward James Olmos in Stand and Deliver. *The movie chronicles his talent for inspiring average students to excel in calculus. School counselors warned that he was asking too much of his students; parents said their kids didn't need calculus. And when his students first passed the advance placement test in calculus, they were accused of cheating, a charge that seemed to reflect bias against the students, who were not European-American, middle-class, college-prep types. What does this success suggest about intelligence?*

CONCEPT CHECKS

8. *A test of driving skills includes items requiring people to describe what they see. People with visual impairments score lower than do people with good vision. Is the test therefore biased against people with visual impairments?*

9. *Suppose someone devises a new IQ test and we discover that tall people generally get higher scores on this test than short people do. How could we determine whether or not this test is biased against short people? (Check your answers on page 397.)*

HOW DO HEREDITY AND ENVIRONMENT AFFECT IQ SCORES?

The British scholar Francis Galton (1869/1978) was the first to offer evidence that a tendency toward high intelligence is hereditary. As evidence he simply pointed out that eminent and distinguished men—politicians, judges, and the like—generally had a number of distinguished relatives. We no longer consider that evidence convincing, because distinguished people share environment as well as genes with their relatives. Besides, becoming distinguished is only partly a matter of intelligence.

The question of how heredity affects intelligence has persisted to this day and has turned out to be difficult to answer to everyone's satisfaction. Here are descriptions of the available kinds of evidence, with their strengths and limitations:

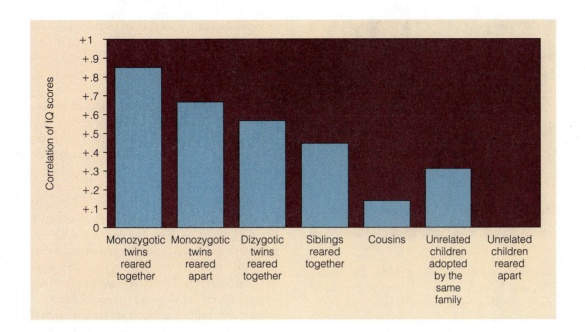

FIGURE 9.15

Mean correlations for the IQs of children with various degrees of genetic and environmental similarity. (Siblings are nontwin children in the same family, such as two brothers, two sisters, or brother and sister.) (Adapted from Bouchard & McGue, 1981.)

FAMILY RESEMBLANCES

Figure 9.15, based on a review of the literature by Thomas Bouchard and Matthew McGue (1981), shows the correlations of IQ scores for people with various degrees of genetic relationship. These data are based almost entirely on European-American families; we do not know how well the results apply to other ethnic groups.

Because no IQ test has perfect reliability, a single individual taking the test on two occasions will get slightly different scores and a correlation between the two test scores near .9. The scores of monozygotic (identical) twins correlate with each other to a similarly high degree (Plomin & DeFries, 1980). Fraternal twins differ by a larger amount and nontwin siblings by a still larger amount. Remoter relatives, such as cousins, have IQ scores that correlate positively, but not strongly. A resemblance among relatives is consistent with the possibility of a genetic influence, but it is also consistent with the possibility of an environmental influence. (Closer relatives generally share more of their environment as well as more of their heredity.)

Note also in Figure 9.15 the correlation between unrelated children adopted in the same family. That correlation indicates a significant contribution of the environment. However, the fact that this correlation is lower than the correlation between siblings (brothers or sisters) suggests that family environment does not account for all variations in IQ. (Alternatives include genetics, prenatal environment, and "nonshared" factors in

the environment that differ from one family member to another.)

Note also the comparison between monozygotic (identical) and dizygotic (fraternal) twins. The greater correlation between monozygotic twins than between dizygotic twins presumably reflects a genetic contribution, unless we can attribute these results to a tendency for monozygotic twins to spend more time together and to be treated more alike. However, researchers have found that identical twins who always *thought* they were fraternal twins resemble each other as much as other identical twins do; fraternal twins who always *thought* they were identical twins resemble each other only as much as other fraternal twins do (Scarr, 1968; Scarr & Carter-Saltzman, 1979). That is, the main determinant of similarity in IQ is whether twins are actually identical, not whether they think they are identical.

IDENTICAL TWINS REARED APART

In Figure 9.15, note the high correlation between monozygotic twins reared apart. That is, identical twins who have been adopted by different parents and reared in separate environments strongly resemble each other in IQ scores (Bouchard & McGue, 1981; Farber, 1981). That resemblance implies a genetic contribution to IQ. Skeptics point out that the "separate" environments have often been very similar (Farber, 1981; Kamin, 1974). In some cases, the biological parents raised one twin and close relatives or next-door

In most cases, identical twins resemble each other in IQ score more closely than do fraternal twins, even in cases in which the identical twins did not know they were identical.

neighbors raised the other twin. Nevertheless, it is hard to escape the suggestion of at least a small genetic contribution, unless the monozygotic twins reared apart have *more* similar environments than do dizygotic twins who grow up in the same household.

ADOPTED CHILDREN

Another line of evidence comes from studies of adopted children. Children who are reared by their biological parents generally have IQ scores similar to those of their parents (Figure 9.16). Adopted children generally have IQ scores more similar to those of

their biological parents than to those of their adoptive parents, and the similarity to the biological parents actually *increases* as the children grow older (Loehlin, Horn, & Willerman, 1989). Furthermore, the IQ scores of unrelated children adopted by the same family resemble each other less closely than do the IQs of related children who are adopted by separate families (Teasdale & Owen, 1984).

The interpretation of these results is confounded to some extent by the policies of adoption agencies. Many adoption agencies place children of high-IQ parents with the brightest available adoptive parents. Thus, adopted children with high-IQ parents may develop high IQs themselves not just because of their heredity but also because of their environment. Still, the fact that adopted children resemble their biological parents *more* than they resemble their adoptive parents implies a significant role of heredity in IQ scores.

Most (though not all) researchers now agree that hereditary and environmental factors both contribute to the observed variations in IQ scores, at least within the European-American population (Thompson, Detterman, & Plomin, 1991; Turkheimer, 1991). The important question is no longer *do* heredity and environment contribute, but *how* they contribute.

The fact that heredity contributes to variations in IQ scores does not mean that people are somehow stuck with the potential they had at birth. "Hereditary" does not mean "unmodifiable"; heredity controls how the individual reacts to the environment. It is possible that the "best" environment for one group of children may not be the best for some other group. We need more research to address this issue.

HEREDITY, ENVIRONMENT, AND ETHNIC DIFFERENCES

Is it likely that hereditary differences contribute to some part of the observed differences in IQ scores among ethnic groups? Some psychologists have answered "yes" and others "no." However, many on either side of the argument state their case with more confidence than their data would seem to support.

Those who believe that heredity is a likely contributor to ethnic differences offer the following simple proposition: Hereditary differences do appear to contribute to IQ differences within at least one ethnic group (European Americans), and therefore they prob-

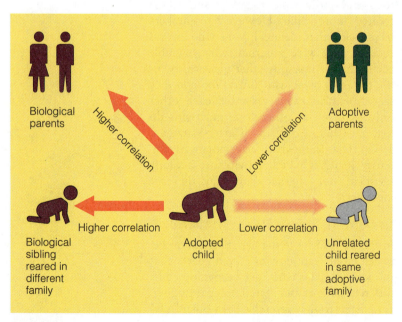

Biological parents

Adoptive parents

Higher correlation

Lower correlation

Higher correlation

Lower correlation

Biological sibling reared in different family

Adopted child

Unrelated child reared in same adoptive family

FIGURE 9.16
The IQ scores of adopted children correlate more highly with the IQ scores of their biological relatives than they do with the IQ scores of their adoptive relatives. Such data point to a hereditary influence on IQ scores.

ably also contribute to the differences among ethnic groups. To see the flaw in this reasoning, consider the analogy in Figure 9.17: One population of wheat is growing on top of a hill, exposed to the sun; another population is growing in a shaded valley. The variations among plants within the sunlit population are due largely to heredity, because they all live in the same advantageous environment. Similarly, variation among plants within the shaded population are probably due largely to heredity. Nevertheless, the difference *between* the two populations is attributable to differences in sunlight.

Those who say that heredity is not a likely contributor to ethnic differences argue as follows: The various human ethnic groups have diverged for only a brief period of evolutionary history. The great majority of human genes either show no variation at all among individuals, or differ widely *within* each ethnic group. Only a few genes (such as the genes controlling hair and skin color) have a greater difference between ethnic groups than they have within each group.

Granting all of that, the implication for the genetics of intelligence is unfortunately not clear. Different ethnic groups do share most of their genes in common, but within a given country, such as the United States, different ethnic groups also share a good deal of their environment in common and their children mature through the same developmental processes (Rowe, Vazsonyi, & Flannery, 1994). Furthermore, researchers do not know which genes, or even how many genes, make significant contributions to intelligence, or how such genes exert their influence. Do such genes differ more within each human population than they differ between populations? Or are they among those few genes that differ significantly between one population and another? We really do not know, and arguing about probabilities and likelihoods is no substitute for collecting evidence.

WHAT'S THE EVIDENCE?

Environmental Contributors to Ethnic Differences

Many studies attempting to evaluate the role of environmental factors have followed the design of providing improved early education, improved nutrition, or a change in

FIGURE 9.17
Even if the size variation within *each population of wheat is due mostly to hereditary differences, the difference between one population and the other may be due entirely to environmental factors. Similarly, the demonstration that hereditary factors contribute to IQ variation within the European-American population does not necessarily indicate a hereditary basis for the differences among ethnic groups.*

some other environmental factor for an experimental group of extremely low-income children, and then examining the effect on the children's eventual IQ scores and school performances. Most such studies have found genuine but fairly small benefits (e.g., Darlington, Royce, Snipper, Murray, & Lazar, 1980).

A more drastic approach is to examine African-American children who have been adopted by upper-middle-class European-American families. The idea behind this approach is that such families are likely to provide a variety of environmental supports helpful for performance on IQ tests, including nutrition, education, and general familiarity with "the culture of the test."

Hypothesis If the IQ difference between the races is due partly to early experiences, then African-American children reared by European-American families will perform better on IQ tests than most other African-American children will.

Method Sandra Scarr and Richard Weinberg (1976) studied European-American families in Minnesota that had adopted African-American children (with two African-American parents) or ethnically mixed children (one African-American and one European-American parent). Many of them also had biological children of their own; many also had adopted European-

FIGURE 9.18

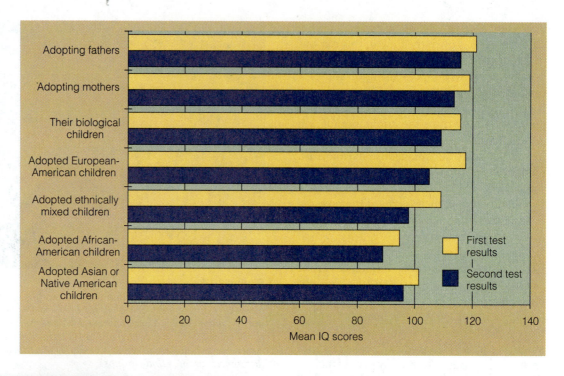

African-American children adopted by upper-middle-class European-American families showed IQ scores well above the national average for African Americans in childhood, but showed only small benefits 10 years later. (Data from Weinberg, Scarr, & Waldman, 1992.)

If ethnic differences in IQ relate largely to environmental differences, then African-American children adopted by upper-middle-class European-American families should score higher than similar children reared in African-American homes. The results have been unimpressive, but also hard to interpret because many of those children were adopted fairly late.

American or Asian or Native American children. The investigators tested the IQs of the children and the adopting parents, and tested them again 10 years later (Scarr & Weinberg, 1976; Weinberg, Scarr, & Waldman, 1992).

Results Figure 9.18 shows the mean scores only for those individuals who were tested both times. All the means were lower at the second test because of changes in the IQ test itself. (As mentioned earlier, psychologists restandardize the test every few years, generally making it more difficult.)

Interpretation The data of interest are the means for the adopted children. The adopted European-American children scored higher than adopted children with one African-American parent ("ethnically mixed"), who in turn scored higher than adopted children with two African-American parents. However, the ethnically mixed adopted children scored near 100 (above it on the first test, slightly below it on the second). Adopted children with two African-American parents scored a mean of 95 on the first test, 89 on the second test 10 years later.

Psychologists are frankly divided and uncertain about how to interpret these results (e.g., Levin, 1994; Waldman, Weinberg, & Scarr, 1994). African-American children adopted by upper-middle-class European-American families did perform better on IQ tests than the national average for African Americans (85), but not by much. Furthermore, the mean for African Americans in Minnesota is not 85, but 88.

If these data suggest a disappointingly small environmental influence, one possible reason is that the presumed benefits of an "advantaged" family began well after birth. For whatever reason, the African-American mothers of the adopted children in this study gave their babies up for adoption significantly later than did the European-American mothers. Many of those adopted African-American and ethnically mixed children lived in several foster homes of uncertain quality before being adopted. These children may be showing the effects of their very early environment, as well as perhaps their prenatal environment. (Many African-American mothers who give their babies up for adoption are teenagers who had poor health care and nutrition during their pregnancy.) In short, this study—potentially a strong one for showing environmental influences—produced small and equivocal effects.

WHAT'S THE EVIDENCE?

Hereditary Contributors to Ethnic Differences

In comparison, let us now examine a well-designed study with the potential to show a strong hereditary contribution.

Hypothesis If heredity is responsible for even part of the difference in IQ performance between the races, then African Americans with a high percentage of European ancestry should obtain higher IQ scores than African Americans with a lower percentage. (Few African Americans have 100% African ancestry. The mean for the African-American population is about 75–80% African ancestry and 20–25% European ancestry.)

Method Determining the ethnic ancestry of an African-American child is difficult. Most of the family trees do not go back enough generations, and skin color is an inaccurate indicator. (Even in Africa, skin darkness varies greatly from one subpopulation to another.) Blood-typing, however, provides a moderately accurate estimator.

The investigators (Scarr, Pakstis, Katz, & Barker, 1977) examined 362 African-American children in Philadelphia, testing 14 different blood factors—the familiar ABO blood types, the Rh factor, the Duffy factor, and 11 others. Certain blood factors are more common in Europe than in Africa and vice versa. For example, type B blood is present in only 9% of Europeans but in 21% of Africans. No Europeans have Duffy type A− B− blood, whereas 94% of Africans do. By comparing each child's blood factors to the frequency of those blood factors in both

Europe and Africa, the investigators estimated the degree of European ancestry for each child. They were under no illusion that their estimates were highly precise, but great precision was unnecessary. All that mattered was that, in general, children with higher estimated European ancestry had more actual European ancestry. Then the investigators correlated their estimates of European ancestry with performance on Raven's Progressive Matrices and four other tests of intellectual performance.

Results The investigators tried several methods of weighting the importance of various blood factors to estimate European and African ancestry. Regardless of which method they used, they found virtually zero correlation between the estimates of European ancestry and measures of performance.

Interpretation If hereditary factors were a major contributor to ethnic differences in IQ scores, we would expect to find a positive correlation between degree of European ancestry and IQ scores. The absence of such a correlation indicates either that heredity contributes nothing to the ethnic difference, or that it contributes so little that this research method could not detect it.

CLOSING COMMENTS

Where does all this leave us? The best-designed studies attempting to demonstrate an environmental contributor to ethnic differences found only weak and uncertain effects. The best study capable of demonstrating a hereditary contributor failed to find even a weak or debatable effect; it found none at all. Sometimes even good research fails to answer the question, and here we have such a case. Presumably, future research will help resolve the issues; in the meantime, the best recommendation is to draw no conclusion at all, and to be suspicious of anyone who seems too sure of what the answer must be. It is also important to bear in mind that regardless of the answers concerning heredity and environment, an IQ score is merely a measure of current performance on one kind of task, not a measure of overall worth.

What kind of research should psychologists do in the future? Actually, I would not encourage a young psychologist to begin research on the roles of heredity and environment in IQ differences. Never mind the political explosiveness of the issue; the topic is scientifically difficult, and it is not clear what (if anything) we would do with the results. There is, however, a related topic that definitely does deserve more and improved research: Given that environmental factors do contribute to differences in intelligence (as everyone agrees, even if not everyone agrees how much they contribute), which are the important environmental factors? Simply growing up in an upper-middle-class home is apparently not enough to boost IQ or school performance enormously. But what is? Prenatal health and nutrition, perhaps? Other factors in the infant's environment? If we could identify those factors, we might be able to accomplish benefits for everyone.

SUMMARY

• *Standardization.* To determine the meaning of a test's scores, the authors of a test determine the mean and the distribution of scores for a random or representative sample of the population. IQ tests are revised periodically. To keep the same mean, test authors have made the tests more difficult from time to time. (page 381)

• *Distribution of IQ scores.* IQ tests have a mean of 100 and a standard deviation of about 15 or 16, depending on the test. Items are carefully selected so that performance on each item correlates positively with performance on the test as a whole. (page 381)

• *Reliability and validity.* Tests are evaluated in terms of reliability and validity. Reliability is a measure of a test's consistency, or the repeatability of its scores. Validity is a determination of how well a test measures what it claims to measure. (page 383)

• *Test bias.* Psychologists try to remove from a test any item that is easy for one group of people but difficult for another. They also try to evaluate the possible bias of a test as a whole. Bias is defined as a systematically incorrect estimation of how well some group will perform. By that definition, IQ tests are biased against immigrants but apparently not against ethnic minorities; they predict school performance of African Americans about as accurately as that of European Americans. (page 388)

• *Hereditary and environmental influences.* To determine the contribution of heredity to the variation in scores on IQ tests, investigators compare identical twins and fraternal twins,

study identical twins reared apart, and compare adopted children with their biological and adoptive parents. For European-American families (on whom we have the most information), both hereditary and environmental factors appear to contribute to observed differences in performance. (page 390)

• *The controversy concerning racial differences in IQ.* Ethnic groups differ, on the average, in IQ performance, although the group means cannot tell us what to expect from each individual. Research designed to show environmental contributors to the ethnic differences has generally produced disappointingly small effects that are difficult to interpret. The best-designed study capable of demonstrating a hereditary contribution failed to show even marginal effects. At present, the research evidence does not justify a confident conclusion about the origin of ethnic differences. (page 392)

SUGGESTIONS FOR FURTHER READING

Mackenzie, B. (1984). Explaining race differences in IQ: The logic, the methodology, and the evidence. *American Psychologist, 39,* 1214–1233. A few years old, but still an excellent source describing the strengths and weaknesses of various kinds of data concerning ethnic differences in IQ.

Rogers, T. B. (1995). *The psychological testing enterprise: An introduction.* Pacific Grove, CA: Brooks/Cole. A textbook covering both intelligence testing and personality testing.

TERMS

standardization the process of establishing rules for administering a test and for interpreting its scores (page 381)

norms descriptions of the frequencies at which particular scores occur (page 381)

reliability repeatability of a test's scores (page 383)

test–retest reliability repeatability of a test's scores between a test and a retest (page 383)

validity determination of how well a test measures what it claims to measure (page 383)

content validity similarity between the items in a test and the information the test is meant to measure (page 383)

construct validity correspondence of a test's measurements to a theoretical construct (page 384)

predictive validity ability of a test's scores to predict real-world performance (page 384)

utility usefulness of a test for a practical purpose (page 385)

bias tendency for test scores to exaggerate a difference between groups or to report a difference that does not exist at all (page 388)

ANSWERS TO CONCEPT CHECKS

3. Yes! To say that a test is "reliable" is simply to say that its scores are repeatable—that and only that. My test would give perfectly reliable (repeatable) measurements. True, they would be utterly useless, but that is beside the point. Reliability is not a measure of usefulness. (page 383)

4. No. An individual's score may be higher on the retest, either because of the practice at taking the test or because of the additional months of education. But the rank order of scores does not change much. That is, if a number of people retake the test, all of them are likely to improve their scores, but those who had the highest scores the first time probably will have the highest scores the second time. (page 383)

5. Yes, a test can have high reliability and low validity. A measure of intelligence determined by dividing head length by head width has high reliability (repeatability) but presumably no validity. A test with low reliability cannot have high validity, however. Low reliability means that the scores fluctuate randomly. If the test scores cannot even predict a later score on the same test, then they can hardly predict anything else. (page 385)

6. The predictive validity of the tests would increase. Predictive validity tends to be low when almost all students have practically the same score; it is higher when students' scores are highly variable. (page 385)

7. The predictive validity of SAT scores will be higher at the university that admits almost anyone. At the university with extremely competitive admissions standards, almost all students have nearly the same SAT scores, and the slight variation in scores cannot predict which students will get the best grades. (page 385)

8. No, this test is not biased against people with visual impairments. It correctly determines that they are likely to be poor drivers. (page 390)

9. We would have to determine whether the test accurately predicts the school performances of both short and tall people. If short people with an IQ score of 100 perform better in school than tall people with an IQ score of 100, then the test is underpredicting the performances of short people and we can conclude the test is biased against them. (The mere fact that the test reports a difference between short and tall people is not in itself evidence of test bias.) (page 390)

ANSWERS TO OTHER QUESTIONS IN THE TEXT

B. 1. d 2. d 3. b 4. a 5. b (page 389)

10 DEVELOPMENT

Suppose you buy a robot. When you get it home, you discover that it does nothing useful. It cannot even maintain its balance. It makes irritating, high-pitched noises, moves its limbs about haphazardly, and leaks. The store you bought it from refuses to take it back. And you discover that, for some reason, it is illegal to turn it off. So you are stuck with this useless machine.

A few years later, your robot can walk and talk, read and write, draw pictures, and do arithmetic. It will follow your directions (most of the time), and sometimes it will even find useful things to do without being told. It beats you consistently at chess and destroys you at memory games.

How did all this happen? After all, you knew nothing about how to program a robot. Did your robot have some sort of built-in programming that simply took a long time to phase in? Or was it programmed to learn all these skills by imitating what it saw?

Children are a great deal like that robot. Nearly every parent wonders, "How did my children get to be the way they are?" The goal of developmental psychology is to understand everything that influences human behavior "from womb to tomb."

As we grow older, we change in many ways—we gain in some ways and lose in others. Developmental psychologists seek to understand the changes in our behavior and the reasons behind them.

THE STUDY OF EARLY DEVELOPMENT

What are the capacities of the newborn and the young infant?

How can psychologists determine those capacities?

The art works of young children can be amazingly inventive and can reveal a great deal of what the children are thinking. One toddler, 1½ years old, showed off a drawing that consisted only of dots on a sheet of paper. Puzzled adults did not understand the drawing. It was a rabbit, the child explained, while making more dots: "Look: Hop, hop, hop . . ." (Winner, 1986).

When my daughter, Robin, was 6 years old, she drew a picture of a boy and a girl drawing pictures (Figure 10.1). The overall picture has a number of miscellaneous features that may not be clear, such as the fact that both children are wearing Halloween costumes. For the little girl's drawing, Robin pasted on some wildlife photos. This array, she maintained, was what the little girl had drawn. Now look at the little boy's drawing: It's just a scribble. When I asked why the little girl's drawing was so much better than the little boy's, Robin replied, "Don't make fun of him, Daddy. He's doing the best he can."

Sometimes, as in this case, a child's drawing shows not just what the child sees, but what the child thinks. As children grow older, their art changes. Robin Kalat, now a high-school student, produces drawings that are technically much more skilled than what she could draw a few years ago. Still, sometimes I miss the highly expressive drawings of her early childhood.

The point is this: As we grow older, we develop; we gain many new abilities and skills. But we lose something too.

Studying the abilities of children, especially very young children and infants, is extremely challenging. The very young are often capable of far more than we realize, simply because they misunderstand our questions or because we misunderstand their answers. Sometimes the same is true for the very old. Developmental psychologists have made much of their progress by devising increasingly careful and sensitive ways to measure what people can and cannot do.

FIGURE 10.1
A drawing of two children drawing pictures, courtesy of 6-year-old Robin Kalat.

THE FETUS AND THE NEWBORN

Early one morning while a human mother is giving birth, a horse is also giving birth. By mid-afternoon, the newborn horse is following its mother around the field; within a few days it is starting to run (Figure 10.2). By age 2 or 3 years it approaches its potential as a race horse or a work horse.

In contrast, that human baby needs several months of development before it can crawl, much less run. When we look at a helpless newborn baby, we are tempted to underestimate its capacities. Actually, it can do quite a lot; it can see, hear, learn . . . but I am getting ahead of the story. The point is that a substantial degree of development takes place even before birth.

PRENATAL DEVELOPMENT

During **prenatal** (before-birth) development, everyone starts life as a fertilized egg cell. That fertilized egg quickly becomes an **embryo,** dividing into many cells and starting to grow. A human embryo does not look much different from a chicken embryo or any other vertebrate embryo (Figure 10.3).

From about 8 weeks after conception until birth, we call the developing human a **fetus.** The fetus looks more human than the embryo did, but it still has a long way to go. All of its organs, including the brain, must mature a great deal before birth. Different structures and substructures mature at dif-

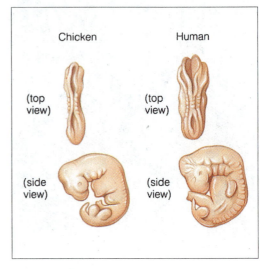

FIGURE 10.3
During the earliest stages, a human embryo looks much the same as the embryo of any other vertebrate species. The differences emerge later.

ferent times; consequently, traumas and poisons produce different kinds of impairments at different ages.

The growing body receives its nutrition from the mother. If she eats little, the baby receives little nourishment. If she takes drugs, the baby gets them too. Undernourished mothers generally give birth to small babies (Figure 10.4), and investigators have long known that newborns weighing less than about 1,750–2,000 grams (4 pounds) have a high risk of dying in infancy (Kopp, 1990). If such babies survive, they have an increased risk of eventual mental retarda-

FIGURE 10.2
A newborn horse. Horses and their relatives are born much more mature than human infants. Many other species, however, are born far less mature than humans.

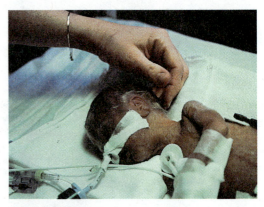

FIGURE 10.4
Advances in medicine enable us to keep babies alive even if they are born premature or very small. Low-birth-weight babies are prone to a number of physical and behavioral difficulties later in life; however, we cannot be sure that low birth weight causes these problems. Many of these babies are born to mothers who are very young or impoverished, taking drugs, or failing to provide good nutrition and care.

tion, low academic achievement, and various behavior problems (Morgan & Winick, 1989). Those facts are beyond dispute, but consider how difficult it is to interpret what they mean.

The apparently obvious interpretation is that a low birth weight leads to impaired brain development, and thus to later academic and behavior problems. But the apparently obvious interpretation is not the only possibility. Most low-birth-weight babies are born to unmarried teenage mothers or to mothers who are poor, uneducated, living under difficult circumstances, eating a low-vitamin or low-mineral diet, possibly smoking or drinking during pregnancy, and not visiting a doctor for care and advice during pregnancy (Garcia Coll, 1990; McCormick, 1985). Mothers who did not have good nutrition or medical care before giving birth may not provide their babies a very good environment afterward. In short, these mothers' babies may have some problems independent of their low birth weight (Brooks-Gunn & Furstenberg, 1986).

How, then, could we determine the effect of low birth weight on later development? Answering this question might seem impossible, because birth weight is so hopelessly entangled with the mother's age, health, financial situation, education, and so forth. But one clever research strategy minimizes these problems: Psychologists have examined pairs of twins in which one twin was born much heavier than the other. In such cases we have a low-birth-weight child *and* a second child with a higher birth weight but the same parents, similar prenatal exposure to alcohol or other substances, and the same environment. Investigators find that if the low-birth-weight infant gets adequate care, it generally develops about as well as the heavier twin (Wilson, 1987). In short, low birth weight *by itself* is not an insurmountable problem for a child's long-term development; it correlates with developmental difficulties largely because many low-birth-weight babies encounter other disadvantages.

A more severe risk arises if the fetus is exposed to alcohol or other substances. If the mother drinks alcohol during pregnancy, the infant may show signs of the **fetal alcohol syndrome,** a condition marked by stunted growth of the head and body; malformations of the face, heart, and ears; and nervous system damage, including seizures, hyperactivity, learning disabilities, and sometimes mental retardation (Streissguth, Barr, & Martin, 1983). The more alcohol the mother drinks and the longer she drinks during pregnancy, the greater the risk to the fetus (see Figure 10.5); researchers are not sure what, if anything, is a "safe" level of alcohol during pregnancy. Cocaine, opiates, and tobacco are also dangerous to the fetus; so are certain prescription drugs (Kerns, 1986). Many drugs simply have not been in use long enough for investigators to determine the long-term effects of exposing fetuses to them. To be safe, pregnant women should

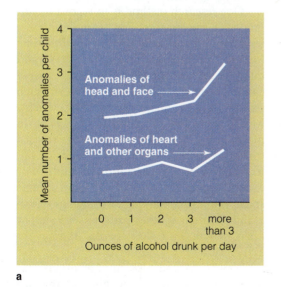

a

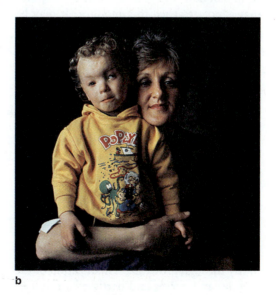

b

FIGURE 10.5

(a) The more alcohol a woman drinks during pregnancy, the more likely her baby is to have anomalies of the head, face, and organs. (Based on data of Ernhart et al., 1987.) (b) A child with fetal alcohol syndrome. Notice especially the wide separation between the eyes, a common feature of this syndrome.

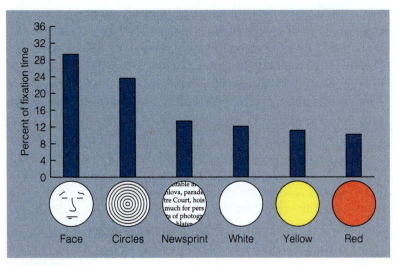

FIGURE 10.6
Infants pay more attention to faces than to other patterns. (Based on Fantz, 1963.) These results suggest that infants are born with certain visual preferences that do not depend on learned associations. The preference for faces facilitates the development of social attachments.

avoid alcohol and tobacco and should get a physician's advice before taking even routine, over-the-counter drugs.

Still, it is remarkable that an occasional "high risk" child—small at birth, perhaps exposed to alcohol or other drugs before birth, perhaps from an impoverished or very turbulent family—overcomes all odds and becomes a healthy, productive, even outstanding person (Werner, 1989). What makes some children so "resilient" to such severe stress, we do not know.

BEHAVIORAL CAPACITIES OF THE NEWBORN

A human newborn is a little like a computer that is not attached to a monitor: It may be processing a great deal of information, but it cannot tell us about it. The challenge in studying the newborn is to figure out how to attach some sort of "monitor" to find out what is going on inside the head.

Newborns have very little control of their muscles. At first they cannot keep their head from flopping over, and their arms and legs flail about aimlessly. The lack of movement control may actually be adaptive for the infant; completely inexperienced infants could only get into trouble if they were capable of crawling or walking briskly around the room (Bjorklund & Green, 1992). Infants gradually gain more muscle control, partly through growth and maturation of the muscles and nerves and partly as a result of practice. For example, babies are much more persistent at waving their arms if they can see their arms than if they have to wave without

watching (van der Meer, van der Weel, & Lee, 1995). Also, babies who are too young to support their weight flail their arms and legs in varied and haphazard ways; as soon as they are capable of supporting their weight, they quickly abandon most of their varied movement patterns and settle on the standard patterns and rhythms of human crawling (Freedland & Bertenthal, 1994).

About the only useful movements newborns can make are mouth movements and eye movements. As the months pass, and as their control spreads from the head muscles downward, they are able to make progressively finer movements, eventually culminating in the ability to move a single finger at a time.

If we want to test the infant's sensory and learning abilities, we have to test them by means of responses the infant can control. For example, if we want to test what an infant can see, we should examine eye movements or head movements; we should not try to train the infant to reach out and grab something. Researchers insensitive to this problem have frequently underestimated the sensory and learning capacities of infants.

THE VISION OF NEWBORNS

William James, a pioneer in American psychology, once said that so far as an infant can tell, the world is a "buzzing confusion," full of meaningless sights and sounds. Since the time of James, psychologists have slowly but substantially increased their estimate of what an infant can see.

One research method is to record the infant's eye movements. For example, infants less than 3 months old spend very little time looking at narrow diagonal stripes, and many investigators believe infants simply cannot see any difference between such stripes and a plain gray field (Leehy, Moskowitz-Cook, Brill, & Held, 1975). In many cases, infants direct their eyes toward (or pay attention to) the same kinds of objects that attract the attention of adults. For example, even at the age of 2 days infants spend more time looking at drawings of human faces than at other patterns with similar areas of light and dark (Fantz, 1963). (See Figure 10.6.)

Newborns can also imitate mouth expressions—pursing or opening of the lips (Figure 10.7). Similar results have been described for newborns in both the United States and Nepal (Meltzoff & Moore, 1977;

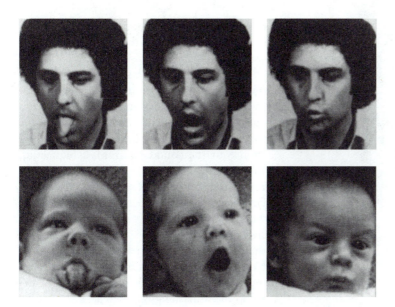

FIGURE 10.7
Infants 2 to 3 weeks old sometimes imitate adults' mouth expressions without knowing what they express. (Photos at left from Meltzoff & Moore, 1977.)

Reissland, 1988). How and why they imitate, we do not know, but the fact that they do indicates reasonably adept perception.

Although infants tend to look mostly at the same kinds of objects that adults look at—colorful objects, faces, rotating objects, and so forth—they do not control their visual attention in the same way that adults do. Infants less than 3 or 4 months old have trouble shifting their attention *away* from an attractive display (Johnson, Posner, & Rothbart, 1991). For example, once they begin looking at a set of moving dots on a computer screen, they seem unable to turn their eyes away from it, even to look at an equally interesting display nearby. Sometimes, 1-month-old infants continue staring at something until they literally begin crying in distress!

As infants become slightly older (about 3 to 6 months old), they can shift their eyes from one object to another, but then they are likely to shift their gaze *back* to the first object. Adults who look at a complicated scene generally look at one object, then another, then another, and may check most of the objects in the display before returning to the first object; infants seem unable to inhibit their eyes from turning back to an object they have already examined (Clohessy, Posner, Rothbart, & Veccra, 1991).

This peculiarity is apparently due to the immaturity of a path in the brain from the cerebral cortex to an area in the midbrain that controls eye movements. In effect, the cortex cannot tell the midbrain that it has seen enough of one object and that it is ready to move on to something else.

THE DEVELOPMENT OF VISUAL-MOTOR COORDINATION

By age 5 months or so, infants have had extensive visual experience but almost no experience at crawling or reaching for objects. Suddenly, as they start to gain control of their arm and leg movements, they have to reach out to pick up toys, crawl around objects, avoid crawling off ledges, and in other ways coordinate what they see with what they do.

Apparently infants have to have some experience of controlling their movements before they show a fear of heights. Infants begin to show a fear of heights shortly after they begin to crawl—presumably also the age when they have their first experiences of slipping and falling. Infants who crawl early develop fear of heights early; infants who are late to crawl are also late to develop fear of heights (Campos, Bertenthal, & Kermoian, 1992).

Although visual-motor coordination develops quickly, infants need practice to maintain and improve that coordination. Several studies have been made of kittens, which are ideal for such studies because kittens can move about quite well by the time they first open their eyes. In one experiment, kittens were permitted to walk around in a dark room for 21 hours a day (Held & Hein, 1963). For the other 3 hours, half the kittens (the "active" group) were permitted to walk around in a well-lit cylindrical room, as Figure 10.8 shows. The other kittens (the "passive" group) were confined to boxes that were propelled around the room by the active kittens.

FIGURE 10.8
As the kitten carousel experiment demonstrates, experience influences development. These two kittens see the same thing, but only one can correlate what it sees with its own movements. Only the active kitten develops normal paw-eye coordination. (Modified from Held & Hein, 1963.)

The active kittens gradually developed good paw-eye coordination, but the passive kittens lagged far behind. In fact, the passive kittens' coordination actually grew worse instead of better as the experiment continued. Evidently, kittens need to see and move at the same time in order to maintain and improve their visually guided behavior. The same is almost certainly true for humans as well.

THE HEARING OF NEWBORNS

At first it might seem difficult to measure newborns' responses to sounds; after all, we cannot observe anything similar to eye movements. However, we can record the effects of sounds on the infant's sucking. Infants suck more vigorously when they are aroused, and certain sounds arouse them more than others do.

In one study, the experimenters played a brief sound and noted how it affected the infant's sucking rate (Figure 10.9). On the first few occasions, the sound increased the sucking rate. After the sound had been played repeatedly, it produced less and less effect. We say that the infant **habituated** to the sound (that is, the infant showed less response after the sound had been repeated). But when the experimenters substituted a new sound, it produced a sharp increase in the sucking

rate. Evidently, the infant was aroused because he or she heard a new, unfamiliar sound.

Psychologists use this technique to determine whether an infant hears a difference between two sounds (Jusczyk, 1985). For example, an infant who has habituated to the sound *ba* will increase the sucking rate in response to the sound *pa* (Eimas, Siqueland, Jusczyk, & Vigorito, 1971). Apparently, even month-old infants can tell the difference between *ba* and *pa*. That ability is surprising when we consider that children show little sign of language use or comprehension until they are nearly 1 year old. Evidently they have some of the preliminary skills of attending to language sounds long before they develop the other language skills.

THE LEARNING AND MEMORY OF NEWBORNS

Infants certainly cannot describe their memories to us. But if they respond differently to some stimulus because of previous experience with it, we can infer that they remember it.

Several studies have begun with the fact that infants learn to suck harder on a nipple if their sucking turns on some sound. Investigators then tried to determine whether the infants will work harder to turn on certain sounds than they will for others. In one

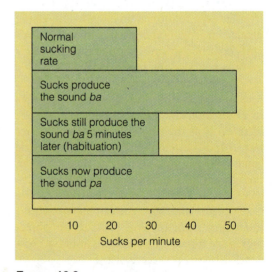

FIGURE 10.9
After 5 minutes of hearing the same sound, the infant's sucking habituates. When a new sound, pa, follows, the sucking rate increases, indicating that infants hear a difference between the sounds ba and pa. (Based on results of Eimas, Siqueland, Jusczyk, & Vigorito, 1971.)

study, 26 babies less than 3 days old could turn on a tape recording of their mother's voice by sucking on a nipple at certain times and at certain rates. By sucking at different times or at different rates, they could turn on a tape recording of some other woman's voice. When their manner of sucking produced their own mother's voice, their rate of sucking increased significantly (DeCasper & Fifer, 1980); it increased less when it produced a different voice. Apparently, even very young infants recognized their own mother's voice and preferred it to an unfamiliar voice. Because they showed this preference so early—in some cases, on the day of birth—developmental psychologists believe the infants are displaying a memory of what they heard *before* birth (Figure 10.10).

FIGURE 10.10
Inspired by research showing that a fetus learns to recognize its mother's voice, some women have made special efforts to talk to their fetuses—and some enterprising capitalists have sold them "pregaphones," manuals, tapes, and lessons. (Don't count on the fetus to be the one getting the greatest benefit from all of this.)

CONCEPT CHECK

1. Suppose a newborn sucks to turn on a tape recording of its father's voice. Eventually the baby habituates and the sucking rate decreases. Now the experimenters substitute the recording of a different man's voice for the father's. What would you conclude if the sucking rate increased? What would you conclude if it remained the same? What would you conclude if it decreased? (Check your answers on page 409.)

Investigators have also demonstrated infant learning and memory by studying head movements—another of the few types of movements an infant can control. For example, in certain studies an experimenter tickled an infant's cheek while sounding either a tone or a buzzer. A movement of the infant's head after one sound (tone for half the infants, buzzer for the other half) brought a reward of sugar water; a movement after the other sound brought no reward. Newborns learned to turn their head more often in response to whichever sound was paired with reward (Clifton, Siqueland, & Lipsitt, 1972; Siqueland & Lipsitt, 1966).

Using somewhat older infants, Carolyn Rovee-Collier (1984) demonstrated an ability to learn a response and remember it for days afterward. She attached a ribbon to one ankle so that an infant could activate a mobile by kicking with one leg (Figure 10.11). Two-month-old infants quickly learned this response and generally kept the mobile going

nonstop for a full 45-minute session. (I know I said infants cannot control their leg muscles, but they don't need much control to keep the mobile going.) Once they have learned, they quickly remember what to do when the ribbon is reattached several days later—to the infants' evident delight.

FIGURE 10.11
By the age of 8 weeks, infants can rapidly learn to kick one of their legs to activate a mobile attached to their ankle with a ribbon. After just a little practice, they can keep the mobile going for a full 45 minutes. In addition, these infants remember how to activate the mobile from one session to the next. (From Rovee-Collier, 1984.)

THE DIFFICULTIES OF INFERRING THE INFANT'S THOUGHTS AND KNOWLEDGE

When we watch the behavior of an infant, we are tempted to speculate on what the infant is thinking. Sometimes we can make a reasonable inference, but we should always use great caution.

Consider an example: You place a toy in front of a 6-month-old, who reaches out and grabs it. Later you place a toy in the same place, but before the infant has a chance to grab it you cover it with a clear glass. No problem; the infant removes the glass and takes the toy. Now you repeat that procedure, but this time you cover the toy with an opaque (nonclear) glass. The infant, who watched you place the glass over the toy, makes no effort to remove the glass and obtain the toy. Or you put the toy down and then put a thin barrier between the infant and the toy. If the toy is partially visible, the infant will reach for it; otherwise, he or she makes no effort to reach for the toy (Piaget, 1937/1954). (See Figure 10.12.)

Why not? And what can we infer about the baby's thought processes? According to Jean Piaget, whose theories we shall consider later in this chapter, the baby's failure to reach out for the toy means that the baby *does not know* the toy is there. "How could that be?" you might ask. "If the baby watched me hide the toy, of course the baby knows where the toy is." Not necessarily; perhaps babies have not yet attained the concept of **object permanence,** the idea that objects continue to exist even when we do not see or hear them.

Still, instead of unquestioningly accepting Piaget's interpretation, we should test babies under other conditions, to find out whether they will ever reach for something they do not see. Here are two other observations to consider before drawing a conclusion:

First observation: If we show an infant a toy and then turn off the lights before the infant can grab it, the infant will still reach out to grab it in the dark (Bower & Wishart, 1972).

Possible interpretation: Evidently, infants can reach out for something they do not see, provided that they see nothing else. In other words, it's wrong to assume that the infant believes the unseen toy has ceased to exist. Maybe the infant concentrates so completely on the seen objects that he or she simply ignores the unseen objects.

Second observation: From about 9 to 11 months, an infant who watches you hide a toy will reach out to retrieve it. But if you hide the toy several times on the right side and then hide it on the left side, the infant will continue to reach out to the right side.

Interpretation: One possibility is that the infant even at this age does not understand that a hidden object remains in place. Another possibility is that infants quickly forget where the object was hidden. Still another possibility is that the infant simply gets into a motor habit of reaching in one direction, regardless of what he or she sees (or thinks).

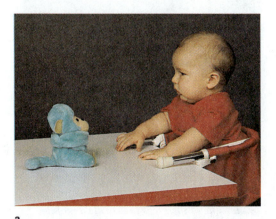
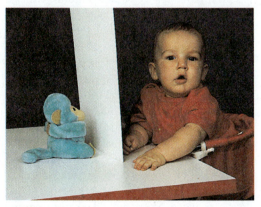

a   b

FIGURE 10.12
During the sensorimotor period, a child will reach for a visible toy (a) but not one that is hidden behind a barrier (b)—even if he or she sees someone hide the toy. According to Piaget, this observation indicates the child lacks the concept of object permanence.

Which interpretation is correct? What is the *real* reason why 6-month-old infants will not reach out to grab a toy they just saw you hide? We don't really know, and I apologize if our uncertainty frustrates you. (If it does, you might want to choose a career outside psychology. Psychologists have to get used to uncertainty.)

The main point is that we should not jump to conclusions, particularly when we are dealing with infants or anyone else whose thought processes are likely to be very different from our own. When we study an infant, we get very different results depending on exactly how we conduct the study. We may believe we understand the infant's vision, hearing, memory, or thinking, but we should always be prepared to modify our conclusions if someone finds a better way to measure the infant's capacities.

SUMMARY

• *Prenatal development.* Behavioral development begins before birth. During prenatal development, an individual is especially vulnerable to the damaging effects of alcohol and other drugs. Babies who are very small at birth have a high risk of later problems, but mostly because many such babies do not get good care or stimulation later in life. (page 402)

• *Inferring infant capacities.* It is easy to underestimate the capacities of newborn human infants because they have so little control over their muscles. With careful testing procedures, we can demonstrate that newborns can see, hear, and remember more than we might have supposed. Unlike adults, however, they have great trouble shifting their visual attention from one stimulus to another. (page 404)

• *Inferring infant thought processes.* Infants behave differently from older children in many ways. For example, infants fail to reach for a toy after watching someone hide it within their reach. We can try to draw inferences about infants' thinking, but we have to be cautious about those inferences. An infant might fail to reach for a toy because she does not know the toy still exists, because she is distracted by other things she sees, because she has forgotten the hiding place, or because she is following a motor habit inconsistent with reaching in the correct direction. (page 408)

SUGGESTION FOR FURTHER READING

Mandler, J. M. (1990). A new perspective on cognitive development in infancy. *American Scientist, 78,* 236–243. An interesting article describing the often surprising capabilities of infants less than half a year old.

TERMS

prenatal before birth (page 402)

embryo an organism at a very early stage of development (from about 3 to 8 weeks in humans) (page 402)

fetus an organism more developed than an embryo but not yet born (from about 8 weeks until birth in humans) (page 402)

fetal alcohol syndrome a condition marked by decreased alertness and other signs of impaired development, caused by exposure to alcohol prior to birth (page 403)

habituate to decrease a person's response to a stimulus when it is presented repeatedly (page 406)

object permanence the concept that an object continues to exist even when one does not see, hear, or otherwise sense it (page 408)

ANSWER TO CONCEPT CHECK

1. If the rate increased, we would conclude that the infant recognizes the difference between the father's voice and the other voice. If it remained the same, we would conclude that the infant did not notice a difference. If it decreased, we would assume that the infant for some reason preferred the sound of the father's voice to that of the other man. (That would be a puzzler, because it is difficult to imagine how a newborn would recognize his or her father's voice.) (page 407)

THE DEVELOPMENT OF THINKING AND REASONING

What goes on in the mind of a small child?

How does the thinking of children differ from that of adults?

How do language abilities and moral reasoning develop?

Preschool children ask some profound questions: "Why is the sky blue? What makes ice cubes cold? If it's dangerous to look at the sun, why is it safe to look at a picture of the sun? Where does the sun go at night?" They are relentlessly curious about how things work. (Moreover, when you answer their questions, they never interrupt to ask, "Is this going to be on the test?")

These same budding little scientists also believe in Santa Claus, the Easter Bunny, and the Tooth Fairy. Adults find it difficult to recapture what it was like to be a child. It is clear that children think differently from adults in a number of ways, although it is not easy to specify those ways. Nevertheless, we try.

THE DEVELOPMENT OF THOUGHT AND KNOWLEDGE: PIAGET'S CONTRIBUTIONS

Attending a rousing political rally may have a profound effect on a young adult, less effect on a preteen, and no effect at all on an infant. However, playing with a pile of blocks will be a more stimulating experience for a young child than for someone older. *The effect of a certain experience on a person's thinking processes and knowledge depends on that person's maturity and previous experiences.* The theorist who made this point most strongly and most influentially

was Jean Piaget (peah-ZHAY) (1896–1980). (See Figure 10.13.)

Early in his career, Piaget administered IQ tests to French-speaking children in Switzerland. He grew bored with the IQ tests because he felt he was not learning anything about intelligence, but he was fascinated by the incorrect answers that children consistently gave to certain questions. For example, when asked, "If you mix some water at a temperature of 50 degrees with an equal amount of water at 70 degrees, what temperature will the mixture be?" most 9-year-olds answer, "120 degrees" (Jensen, 1980).

Unless someone was going around mischievously misinforming all the children in Switzerland, the children must be coming to some incorrect conclusions on their own. In other words—and this is one of Piaget's central insights—*children's thought processes are different from those of adults.* Children are not merely inexperienced adults, and they are not just less skillfully going through the same thought processes adults use. The difference between children's thought processes and those of adults is *qualitative* as

FIGURE 10.13
Jean Piaget (1896–1980), the most influential theorist on intellectual development in children, demonstrated that an experience's influence on a person's way of thinking depends on that person's age and previous experience.

well as *quantitative*—that is, it is a difference in kind and a difference in degree. Piaget supported this conclusion with extensive longitudinal studies of children, especially his own.

HOW THOUGHT PROCESSES AND KNOWLEDGE GROW: SOME PIAGETIAN TERMINOLOGY

According to Piaget, a child's intellectual development is not merely an accumulation of experience or a maturational unfolding. Rather, the child constructs new mental processes as he or she interacts with the environment.

In Piaget's terminology, behavior is based on schemata (plural of *schema*). A schema is an organized way of interacting with objects in the world. For instance, infants have a grasping schema and a sucking schema. Older infants gradually add new schemata to their repertoire and adapt their old ones. This adaptation takes place through the processes of assimilation and accommodation.

In **assimilation** a person applies an old schema to new objects—for example, an infant may suck an unfamiliar object or use the grasp response in trying to manipulate it. In **accommodation** a person modifies an old schema to fit a new object—for example, an infant may suck a breast, a bottle, and a pacifier in different ways or may modify the grasp response to accommodate the size or shape of a new toy (Figure 10.14).

Infants shift back and forth from assimilation to accommodation. For example, an infant who tries to suck on a rubber ball (assimilating it to her sucking schema) may find that she cannot fit it into her mouth. First she may try to accommodate her sucking schema to fit the ball; if that fails, she may try to shake the ball. She is assimilating the new object to her grasping schema, but at the same time, she is accommodating that schema—changing it—to fit the ball.

Adults do much the same thing. You are given a new mathematical problem to solve. You try several of the methods you have already learned until you hit on the one schema that works. In other words, you assimilate the new problem to your old schema. If, however, the new problem is quite different from any problem you have ever solved before, you will modify (accommodate) your schema until you work out a solution. It is through processes like these, said Piaget, that intellectual growth occurs.

PIAGET'S STAGES OF INTELLECTUAL DEVELOPMENT

Piaget contended that children progress through four major stages of intellectual development:

1. *The sensorimotor stage* (from birth to about 1½ years)

2. *The preoperational stage* (from about 1½ to 7 years)

3. *The concrete-operations stage* (from about 7 to 11 years)

4. *The formal-operations stage* (from about 11 years onward)

FIGURE 10.14

According to Piaget, assimilation and accommodation occur whenever we deal with an object. Here, the infant assimilates new objects to the grasp schema, applying an established behavior to them. However, the infant also accommodates the grasp schema, adjusting it to fit objects of different shapes and sizes.

The ages given here are approximate. Many people do not reach the stage of formal operations until well beyond age 11, if they reach it at all. Piaget recognized that some children develop at a faster rate than others, but he insisted that all children go through these four stages in the same order. Let us consider the capacities of children at each of these stages.

THE SENSORIMOTOR STAGE: INFANCY

Piaget called the first stage of intellectual development the **sensorimotor stage** because at this early age (birth to 1½ years) behavior consists mostly of simple motor responses to sensory stimuli—for example, the grasp reflex and the sucking reflex. The fact that infants do not look for objects that they cannot see indicated to Piaget that infants respond only to what they see and hear, rather than to what they might remember or imagine.

Infants do, nevertheless, notice relationships among their experiences (Mandler, 1990). For example, even infants as young as 4 months old pay more attention to a film in which the sound track matches the action than one in which the sound track is unrelated to the action. Also, an infant who has been sucking on a pacifier will look more at a pacifier of the same shape than at a pacifier of a different shape.

As children progress through the sensorimotor stage of development, they appear to gain some concept of self. The data are as follows: A mother puts a spot of unscented rouge on an infant's nose and then places the infant in front of a mirror. Infants less than 1½ years old either ignore the red spot they see on the baby in the mirror or reach out to touch the red spot on the mirror. At some point after age 1½ years, infants in the same situation touch themselves on the nose, indicating that they recognize themselves in the mirror (Figure 10.15). Different infants show this sign of self-recognition at somewhat different ages; the age at which they start to show self-recognition is also the age at which they begin sometimes to act embarrassed (Lewis, Sullivan, Stanger, & Weiss, 1991). That is, they show a sense of self either in both situations or in neither.

THE PREOPERATIONAL STAGE: EARLY CHILDHOOD

By about age 1½, most children are learning to speak; within a few years they have nearly mastered their language. Neverthe-less, they do not understand everything the same way adults do. For example, they have difficulty understanding that a mother can be someone else's daughter. A boy with one brother will assert that his brother has no brother. Piaget refers to this period as the **preoperational stage.** The child is said to lack **operations,** which are reversible mental processes. For example, for a boy to understand that his brother has a brother, he must be able to reverse the concept "having a brother."

Distinguishing Appearance from Reality in the Preoperational Stage Children in the early preoperational stage do not distinguish clearly between appearance and reality. A child who sees you put a white ball behind a blue filter will say that the ball is blue. When you ask, "Yes, I know the ball *looks* blue, but what color is it *really*?" the child grows confused. So far as the child is concerned, any ball that *looks* blue *is* blue (Flavell, 1986).

Children in the early part of the preoperational stage also have trouble using one object as a symbol or representation for another. For example, a psychologist shows a child a playhouse room that is a scale model of a full-size room. Then the psychologist hides a tiny toy in the small room and ex-

FIGURE 10.15
If someone places a bit of unscented rouge on a child's nose, a child older than about 2 years shows self-recognition by touching his or her own nose. A younger child ignores the red spot or points at the mirror.

plains that a bigger toy just like it is "in the same place" in the bigger room. (For example, if the little toy was behind the sofa in the little room, the big toy would be behind the sofa in the big room.) Most 2½-year-old children look haphazardly for the big toy in the big room without using the little room as a "map." By age 3, most children who see the little toy hidden in the little room go immediately to the correct location in the big room (DeLoache, 1989).

EGOCENTRIC THINKING IN THE PREOPERATIONAL PERIOD

Piaget concluded that children's thought processes are egocentric. In using this term, Piaget did *not* mean that children are selfish; instead, he meant that the child sees the world as centered around himself or herself and cannot take the perspective of another person. If you and a preschool child sit on opposite sides of a complicated pile of blocks and you ask the child to draw what the blocks would look like from your side, the child will draw them as they look from his or her own side. When speaking, children often omit to describe the necessary background information, as if assuming that the listener understands everything the speaker understands. (The same can be said for adults, unfortunately. Sometimes someone will start discussing the details of some topic before the listener has any idea what the speaker is talking about.)

CONCEPT CHECK

2. Which of the following is the clearest example of egocentric thinking?
a. A writer who uses someone else's words without giving credit
b. A politician who blames others for everything that goes wrong
c. A professor who gives the same complicated lecture to a freshman class that she gives to a convention of professionals. (Check your answer on page 428.)

To say that a child is egocentric is to say that he or she has trouble understanding other people's point of view, understanding what they know and what they do not know. Psychological researchers have explored this very difficult topic of what children understand about other people's thoughts and knowledge.

WHAT'S THE EVIDENCE?

Children's Understanding of Other People's Cognitions

How would you feel about walking naked through a room filled with refrigerators, radios, and other machines? You might prefer to have your clothes on, but you probably will feel no great distress. Now, how would you feel about walking naked through a classroom full of other (fully clothed) students? Extremely embarrassed and distressed, I presume, because you regard people as very different from machines. You believe that other students have conscious experiences like your own; you know that people can see you and react to you, whereas electrical appliances cannot.

How and when did we figure that out? At what age do children first understand that other people have minds and knowledge? Experimenters have developed some very clever designs to try to answer that very difficult question.

Hypothesis   A child who understands that other people have minds will distinguish between someone who is in a position to know some relevant information and someone who could not know it.

Method   A 3- or 4-year-old child sat in front of four cups (figure 10.16). The child watched as one adult hid a candy or toy

Young children's thinking is egocentric: They have trouble understanding someone else's point of view. If asked to describe how a complicated pile of blocks appears to someone else, they describe how it appears from their own position.

FIGURE 10.16

A child sat in front of a screen covering four cups and watched as one adult hid a surprise under one of the cups. Then that adult and another (who had not been present during the hiding) each pointed to one of the cups to signal where the surprise was. Many 4-year-olds consistently followed the advice of the informed adult; 3-year-olds did not.

under one of the cups, although a screen prevented the child from seeing which cup. Then another adult entered the room. The "informed" adult pointed to the cup under which he or she had just hidden the surprise;

the "uninformed" adult pointed to one of the other cups. The child then had an opportunity to look under one cup to try to find the surprise.

This procedure was repeated 10 times for each child in the study. The two adults alternated roles, but on each trial one or the other hid the surprise when the other was absent. That is, one was in a position to know where the surprise was hidden, and the other was not.

Results Of the 4-year-olds, 10 out of 20 chose the correct cup (the one indicated by the informed adult) at least 8 times out of 10 tries. That is, many of the 4-year-olds showed that they understood who had the relevant knowledge and who did not. However, none of 14 3-year-olds chose the correct cup 8 times out of 10; they were as likely to follow the lead of the uninformed adult as that of the informed adult (Povinelli & deBlois, 1992).

Interpretation Evidently, 4-year-olds have a greater understanding of other people's knowledge (or lack of it) than 3-year-olds have.

Other experiments using a somewhat different procedure have yielded similar results. For example, children in one study watched a dramatization in which a girl who had a marble in her basket left the room temporarily, leaving the basket behind. During her absence, a second girl moved the marble from the first girl's basket to her own basket. When the first girl returned to the room, the children were asked, "Where is the marble?" and "Where will the girl look for it?" Most 4-year-olds answered that she would look in her own basket; younger children thought she would look in the other basket (Wimmer & Perner, 1983). As in the previous study, 4-year-olds are better able than younger children are to make inferences about what various people might or might not know.

Although these are important results, we should be careful of drawing too broad a conclusion. Using other methods, we can see evidence that even younger children understand something about the experiences or knowledge of other people. For example, children less than 1 year old act sad and even cry when they see another child get hurt (Hobson, 1993). That is, a child may show

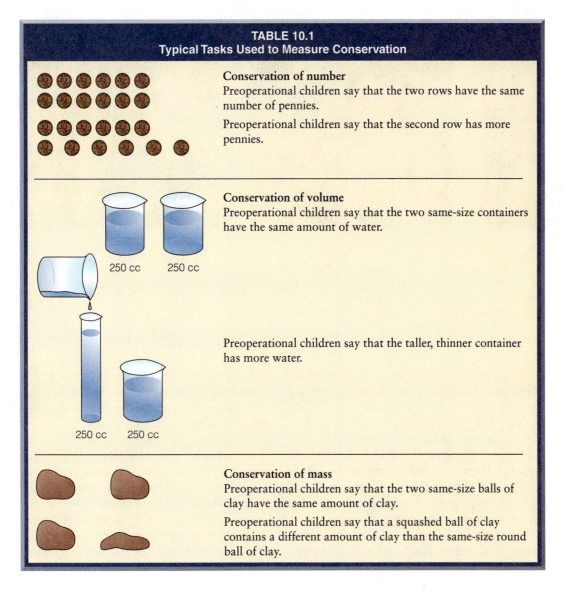

TABLE 10.1
Typical Tasks Used to Measure Conservation

Conservation of number
Preoperational children say that the two rows have the same number of pennies.

Preoperational children say that the second row has more pennies.

Conservation of volume
Preoperational children say that the two same-size containers have the same amount of water.

250 cc   250 cc

Preoperational children say that the taller, thinner container has more water.

250 cc   250 cc

Conservation of mass
Preoperational children say that the two same-size balls of clay have the same amount of clay.

Preoperational children say that a squashed ball of clay contains a different amount of clay than the same-size round ball of clay.

an understanding of other people's thoughts and feelings in some ways and not in others.

LACK OF THE CONCEPT OF CONSERVATION IN THE PREOPERATIONAL PERIOD

According to Piaget, preoperational children lack the concept of **conservation.** Just as they fail to understand that something can still be white even though it looks blue, they fail to understand that objects conserve such properties as number, length, volume, area, and mass after the shape or arrangement of the objects has changed. They cannot perform the mental operations necessary to understand such transformations. (Table 10.1 shows some typical conservation tasks.)

For example, if we set up two glasses of the same size containing the same amount of water and then pour the contents of one glass into a taller, thinner glass, preopera-

tional children will say that the second glass contains more water (Figure 10.17).

I once doubted whether children really believed what they were saying in such a situation. Perhaps, I thought, the way the questions are phrased somehow tricks them into saying something they do not believe. Then something happened to convince me that preoperational children really believe their answers. One year, when I was discussing Piaget in my introductory psychology class, I invited my son Sam, then 5½ years old, to take part in a class demonstration. I started with two glasses of water, which he agreed contained equal amounts of water. Then I poured the water from one glass into a wider glass, lowering the water level. When I asked Sam which glass contained more water, he confidently pointed to the tall, thin one. After class he complained, "Daddy, why did you ask me such an easy question? Everyone

FIGURE 10.17

Looks can be deceptive: The conservation concept shows one way children think less logically than adults do. Preoperational children, up to about age 7 years, don't understand that some property of a substance—such as the volume of water—remains constant despite changes in its appearance. At around age 7, during the transition from preoperational thinking to concrete operations, the conservation tasks seem difficult and confusing.

could see that there was more water in that glass! You should have asked me something harder to show how smart I am!"

The following year I brought Sam to class again for the same demonstration. He was now 6½ years old, about the age at which children make the transition from preoperational thinking to the next stage. I again poured the water from one of the tall glasses into a wider one and asked him which glass contained more water. He looked and paused. His face got red. Finally he whispered, "Daddy, I don't know!" After class he complained, "Why did you ask me such a hard question? I'm never coming back to any of your classes again!" The question that was embarrassingly easy a year ago had become embarrassingly difficult.

The next year, when he was 7½, I tried again (at home). This time he answered confidently, "Both glasses have the same amount of water, of course. Why? Is this some sort of trick question?"

THE CONCRETE-OPERATIONS STAGE: LATER CHILDHOOD

At about age 7, children enter the stage of concrete operations and begin to understand the conservation of physical properties. The transition is not sharp, however. The ability to understand the conservation of various properties emerges sequentially, at different ages. For instance, a 6-year-old child may understand that squashing a ball of clay will

not change its weight, but may not realize until years later that squashing the ball will not change the volume of water it displaces when it is dropped into a glass.

The **stage of concrete operations** is Piaget's term for the stage when children can perform mental operations on concrete objects. But they still have trouble with abstract or hypothetical ideas. For example, ask this question: "How could you move a 4-mile-high mountain of whipped cream from one side of the city to the other?" Older children find the question amusing and try to think of an imaginative answer. But children in the concrete-operations stage (or younger) are likely to complain that the question is silly.

Or ask, "If you could have a third eye anywhere on your body, where would you put it?" Children in this stage generally respond immediately that they would put it right between the other two, on their forehead. They seem to regard the question as not very interesting. Older children come up with more imaginative possibilities, such as on the back of their head or at the tip of a finger (so they could peek around corners).

THE FORMAL-OPERATIONS STAGE: ADOLESCENCE AND ADULTHOOD

The **stage of formal operations** is Piaget's term referring to the mental processes used in dealing with abstract, hypothetical situations. Those processes demand logical, deductive reasoning and systematic planning.

TABLE 10.2
Summary of Piaget's Stages of Cognitive Development

STAGE AND APPROXIMATE AGE	ACHIEVEMENTS AND ACTIVITIES	LIMITATIONS
Sensorimotor (birth to 1½ years)	Reacts to sensory stimuli through reflexes and other responses	Little use of language; seems not to understand object permanence; does not distinguish appearance from reality
Preoperational (1½ to 7 years)	Develops language; can represent objects mentally by words and other symbols; can respond to objects that are remembered but not present at the moment	Lacks operations (reversible mental processes); lacks concept of conservation; focuses on one property at a time (such as length or width), not on both at once; still has some trouble distinguishing appearance from reality
Concrete operations (7 to 11 years)	Understands conservation of mass, number, and volume; can reason logically with regard to concrete objects that can be seen or touched	Has trouble reasoning about abstract concepts and hypothetical situations
Formal operations (11 years onward)	Can reason logically about abstract and hypothetical concepts; develops strategies; plans actions in advance	None beyond the occasional irrationalities of all human thought

Piaget set the beginning of the formal-operations stage at about age 11. He attributed some fairly sophisticated abilities to children in this stage, although later research indicates that many children take much longer to reach it, if they ever do.

Suppose we ask three children, ages 6, 10, and 14, to arrange a set of 12 sticks in order from longest to shortest. The 6-year-old (preoperational) child fails to order the sticks correctly. The 10-year-old (concrete operations) eventually gets them in the right order, but only after a great deal of trial and error. The 14-year-old (formal operations) holds the sticks upright with their bottom ends on the table and then removes the longest one, the second-longest one, and so on.

A second example: We set up five bottles of clear liquid and explain that it is possible, by mixing the liquids together in a certain combination, to produce a yellow liquid. The task is to find the right combination. Children in the concrete-operations stage plunge right in with an unsystematic trial-and-error search. They try combining bottles A and B, then C and D, then perhaps A, C, and E, and so on. By the time they work through five or six combinations they forget which ones they have already tried. They may try one combination several times and others not at all; if and when they do stumble onto the correct combination, it is mostly by luck.

Children in the formal-operations stage approach the problem more systematically. They may first try all the two-bottle combinations: AB, AC, AD, AE, BC, and so forth. If all those fail, they turn to three-bottle combinations: ABC, ABD, ABE, ACD, and so on. By adopting a strategy for trying every possible combination one time and one time only, they are bound to succeed.

Children do not reach the stage of formal operations any more suddenly than they reach the concrete-operations stage. Before they can reason logically about a particular problem, they must first have had a fair amount of experience in dealing with that problem. A 9-year-old who has spent a great deal of time playing chess reasons logically about chess problems and plans several moves ahead. The same child reverts to concrete reasoning when faced with an unfamiliar problem.

Table 10.2 summarizes Piaget's four stages.

3. You are given the following information about four children. Assign each of them to one of Piaget's stages of intellectual development. (Check your answers on page 428.)

a. Child has mastered the concept of conservation; still has trouble with abstract and hypothetical questions.

b. Child performs well on tests of object permanence; still has trouble with conservation.

c. Child has schemata; does not speak in complete sentences; fails tests of object permanence.

d. Child performs well on tests of object permanence, conservation, and hypothetical questions.

ARE PIAGET'S STAGES DISTINCT?

According to Piaget, the four stages of intellectual development are distinct, and each transition from one stage to the next requires a major reorganization of the child's way of thinking. He contended that children in the sensorimotor stage fail certain tasks because they lack the concept of object permanence and that children in the preoperational stage fail conservation tasks because they lack the necessary mental processes. In other words, intellectual growth is marked by periods of revolutionary reorganization as a child advances from one stage of thinking to another.

Later research has thrown much doubt upon that conclusion. If it were true, then a child in a given stage of development, say the preoperational stage, should perform consistently at that level, neither advancing to a higher level nor sinking to a lower level. In fact, a child's performance fluctuates, and one can increase that fluctuation by altering the difficulty of a task. For example, preschool children ordinarily fail conservation-of-number tasks, in which an investigator presents two rows of coins or candies with seven or more objects in each row, then spreads out one row and asks which row "has more." Preoperational children reply that the spread-out row has more. However, when Rochel Gelman (1982) presented two rows of just three objects each (Figure 10.18) and then spread out one of the rows, even 3- and 4-year-old children answered that the rows had the same number of items. (Most of the 3-year-olds counted first, to make sure.) After much practice with these short rows, most of the 3- and 4-year-olds also answered correctly that a spread-out row of eight items had the same number as the tightly packed row of eight.

In general, the progression from one stage of thinking to another appears to be gradual and not sudden (Siegler, 1994). That is, the difference between older children and younger children is not so much a matter of "having" an ability or of "lacking" it; the difference is one of readily using the ability and using it only in simple tasks.

IMPLICATIONS FOR EDUCATION: PIAGET AND LEV VYGOTSKY

One implication of Piaget's findings is that children have to discover certain concepts, such as the concept of conservation, mainly on their own. Teaching such concepts is mostly a matter of directing children's attention to the key aspects and then letting them discover the concepts for themselves.

Another implication frequently drawn from Piaget's work is that teachers should determine a child's level of functioning and then teach material that is appropriate to that level. For example, teachers should not try to introduce abstract concepts to children who are at the concrete-operations stage of development.

In contrast to this view, the Russian psychologist Lev Vygotsky (1978) argued that

FIGURE 10.18
(a) With the standard conservation-of-number task, preoperational children answer that the lower row has more. (b) With a simplified task, the same children say that both rows have the same number.

Lev Vygotsky called attention to a child's zone of proximal development: the gap between what a child can do alone and what the child can do with help. Education within the zone of proximal development can advance a child's reasoning abilities.

education cannot simply wait for children to reach the next stage of development on their own; children have to learn in order to develop. According to Vygotsky, children have a **zone of proximal development,** which he defined as the distance between what a child can do on his or her own and what the child can do with the help of adults or other children. For example, children improve their recall of a story if adults provide appropriate hints and reminders; children can solve more complicated math problems with an adult's help than they can alone; and some children can solve Piaget's conservation tasks with just a bit of adult help and encouragement. After an adult has provided help for a while, the child will begin to solve the same kind of problems without help.

Good advice for an educator, therefore, is to try to be sensitive to a child's zone of proximal development, to try to detect how much further the educator can successfully push the child's development. In some cases, the child may provide clues to how far that might be. For example, several preoperational children who are asked which beaker has more water may all point to the tall, thin one; however, the children who could most easily learn conservation of volume describe the various beakers while using hand gestures that indicate both height and width (Goldin-Meadow, Alibali, & Church, 1993).

An educator sensitive to those gestures could infer which children have the largest zone of proximal development, and therefore which children are ready for particular kinds of instruction.

LANGUAGE DEVELOPMENT

Susan Carey (1978) has estimated that children between the ages of 1½ and 6 learn an average of nine new words per day—almost one new word per hour—thereby increasing their ability to tell us what they know and think (see Table 10.3). Imagine what it is like for a young child to learn a language. Deciphering the meanings of words would be extraordinarily difficult unless the infant in effect made some assumptions to simplify the task (Markman, 1990). When an adult points at an object and says "bed," the infant refers the sound to the type of object the adult is pointing at. That assumption seems so natural that we may not even recognize it as an assumption. But so far as the infant knows, the sound *could* have referred to "thing that is important at bedtime," in which case it would refer also to pajamas, darkened rooms, and goodnight kisses.

Infants do not confuse beds with goodnight kisses because they assume that most words refer to a type of object or a type of action. Ellen Markman and Jean Hutchinson (1984) showed 2-year-old and 3-year-old children pictures of common objects, gave the objects nonsense names, and then found out what other objects the children would apply those names to. For example, the experimenters called a birthday cake a *zig.* Then they showed pictures of a chocolate

TABLE 10.3
Conversations with Some Children at the Preoperational Stage

Q:	Are you an American?
A:	No, my father is an American. I'm a girl.
Q:	Do you have to go to the bathroom?
A:	No. Don't have to go. Mine peanut not working. Don't have any juice in it.
Q:	Do you understand what's happening in this movie (a nature film)?
A:	Yes. When the baby skunks grow up, they turn into raccoons.

TABLE 10.4	
Stages of Language Development in Children	
AVERAGE AGE	LANGUAGE ABILITIES
3 months	Random vocalizations and cooing
6 months	Babbling
1 year	More babbling; some language comprehension; probably a few words, including "Mama"
1½ years	Some individual words, mostly nouns, but no phrases
2 years	Large vocabulary (more than 50 words); many 2-word phrases; no sentences
2½ years	Good language comprehension; longer phrases and short sentences; still many errors
3 years	Vocabulary around a thousand words; fewer errors; longer sentences
4 years	Close to basic adult speech competence

cake and a birthday present and asked which of them was another *zig*. Eighty-three percent of the children chose the chocolate cake. Evidently, even 2- and 3-year-old children know that a particular word applies to various objects in the same category, not to objects that are part of the same "theme."

STAGES OF LANGUAGE DEVELOPMENT

Language development in children follows a distinct sequence. Table 10.4 lists the average ages at which children reach various stages of language ability (Lenneberg, 1969; Moskowitz, 1978). Although there is great variation from one child to another, the rate of language development is not closely related to intelligence. A child who advances through these stages faster or slower than the average is not necessarily more intelligent or less intelligent than the average child. (Retarded children do, however, progress very slowly, and some never develop good language skills.)

Infants begin by babbling. For the first 6 months or so, their babbling has no apparent relationship to what they hear; deaf infants babble as much as hearing infants do. Beyond about age 6 months, hearing infants

babble more and deaf infants babble less. As a rule, the infants who babble the most learn language the fastest. At first, babbling produces only haphazard sounds, but soon the infant starts repeating the sounds that are common in the language that he or she has been hearing, while discarding sounds that the baby has not been hearing. Thus, as infants approach the age of 1 year, French babies' babbling sounds French, Chinese babies' babbling sounds Chinese, and so forth (Locke, 1994).

By the time they are 1 year old, infants begin to understand language and most of them can say at least a word or two. For most infants throughout the world, one of the first sounds is *muh*. Parents in most parts of the world have defined *muh-muh* (or something similar to it) as meaning "mother." Infants also typically make the sounds *duh, puh,* and *buh;* they almost never make the sound *s*. In many languages, the word for father is similar to *daddy* or *papa*. *Baba* is the word for grandmother in several languages. In effect, infants tell their parents what words to use for certain concepts.

By age 1½, most toddlers can say a few words. Their vocabulary may be small or large—the average is about 50 words—but

TABLE 10.5	
Sample Two-Word Phrases Spoken by a 2-Year-Old Child	
PHRASE	MEANING
Mommy bath.	Mommy is taking a bath.
Throw Daddy.	Throw it to Daddy.
More page.	Don't stop reading.
More high.	More food is up there on top.
Allgone sticky.	My hands have been washed.
Allgone outside.	Someone closed the door.
No hug!	I'm angry at you!

they almost never link words together. Thus, a toddler who can say "Daddy" and "bye-bye" may be unable to say "Bye-bye, Daddy." These single-word utterances generally convey a great deal of information, however, and parents can usually make out their meaning from the context. *Mama* might mean "That's a picture of Mama," "Take me to Mama," "Mama went away and left me here," or "Mama, get me something to eat."

Some toddlers follow a pattern of language development different from the usual one (Nelson, 1981). Instead of speaking one word at a time and learning the names of objects, they speak poorly articulated, compressed phrases, such as "Do-it-again" or "I-like-read-Goodnight-Moon." At first these expressions are so poorly pronounced that adults, unless they listen carefully, may not realize that the child is doing anything but babbling. Children who start off by generating complex requests and phrases tend to do so consistently over much of the period of language development (Nelson, Baker, Denninger, Bonvillian, & Kaplan, 1985).

At about age 2, children start to produce many two-word phrases and occasional longer phrases (see examples in Table 10.5). Even at this early stage, much of what children say is creative rather than just imitative. It is unlikely that they have ever heard their parents say, "More page," "Allgone sticky," or "Allgone outside." Such statements are contrary to adult speech habits and adult thought. A child who says "Allgone outside" seems to be saying that the outside is not there any more. (As Piaget said, young chil-

dren do seem to think differently from adults.)

By age 2½ to 3 years, most children are generating full sentences, though each child maintains a few peculiarities. For example, many children have their own rules for making negative sentences. One of the most common is to add *no* or *not* to the beginning or end of a sentence, such as "No I want to go to bed!" One little girl made her negatives just by saying something louder and at a higher pitch; for instance, if she shrieked, "I want to share my toys," she meant, "I do not want to share my toys." Presumably she had learned this "rule" by remembering that people screamed at her when they told her not to do something. My son Sam made negatives at this stage by adding the word *either* to the end of a sentence: "I want to eat lima beans either." Apparently he had heard people say, "I don't want to do that either," and had decided that an *either* at the end of the sentence made it an emphatic negative.

At this same age, children act as if they were applying grammatical rules. (I say "as if" because they cannot state the rules. By the same token, baseball players who anticipate exactly where a fly ball will come down act "as if" they understood complex physics and calculus.) For example, a child may learn the word *feet* at an early age and then, after learning other plurals, abandon it in favor of *foots*.

Later, he or she begins to compromise by saying "feets," "footses," or "feetses" before eventually returning to "feet." Children at this stage say many things they have never heard anyone else say, such as "The mans comed" or "The womans goed and doed something." Clearly, they are applying rules of how to form plurals and past tenses, although they overregularize those rules. My

FIGURE 10.19

Some overeager parents try to coach their children on language usage at a very early age. The attention may be enjoyable, but it is not likely to accelerate progress through the stages of language development.

son David invented the word *shis* to mean "belonging to a female." He had apparently generalized the rule "He—his, she—shis." Note that all these inventions imply that children are doing something more than just imitating, and more than just producing responses that win them reinforcements. They are trying their best to learn rules.

CONCEPT CHECK

4. At what age do children begin to string words into novel combinations that they have never heard anyone say before? Why do psychologists believe that even very young children learn some of the rules of grammar? (Check your answers on page 428.)

People at a low stage of moral reasoning equate "wrong" with "being punished." At a higher stage of reasoning, people's moral judgments depend on whether the person intended to help or to harm other people.

LANGUAGE DEVELOPMENT AS MATURATION

Language development depends largely on maturation rather than on the mere accumulation of experience (Lenneberg, 1967, 1969). Part of the evidence for this conclusion is that the sequence of stages outlined in Table 10.4 is about the same in all known cultures. The average ages differ a bit from one culture to another, but the various stages are easily recognizable worldwide, in all languages, at approximately the same ages.

Furthermore, parents who expose their children to as much language as possible find that they hardly speed up the children's language development at all (Figure 10.19). The children may acquire a slightly larger vocabulary than usual, but they still go through each stage at about the normal age. At the opposite end in terms of exposure to language, hearing children of deaf parents are exposed to very little spoken language, but if they have periodic contact with speaking people, they progress through the various stages almost on schedule.

If children weren't exposed to any language at all, would they make up one of their own? Some parents of deaf children have unintentionally conducted such an experiment on their own children. A child who cannot hear well enough to learn speech and who never sees anyone using sign language is effectively isolated from all language. The results are consistent: The children make up their own sign language (Goldin-Meadow, 1985). As they grow older, they make the system more complex, linking signs together into sentences with some consistency of word order. Most of the children manage to teach their system, or at least part of it, to one or both parents. Children who spend much time together adopt each other's signs and eventually develop a unified system.

DEVELOPMENT OF MORAL REASONING

As children develop their reasoning powers, they apply their new reasoning abilities to moral issues. Just as 11-year-olds reason differently from 5-year-olds about what happens when water is poured from one beaker to another, they also reason differently about issues of right and wrong.

KOHLBERG'S METHOD OF EVALUATING LEVELS OF MORAL REASONING

Psychologists once regarded morality as a set of arbitrary, learned rules with no logical basis. Lawrence Kohlberg (1969; Kohlberg & Hersh, 1977) rejected that view, arguing instead that moral reasoning is the result of a reasoning process that resembles Piaget's stages of intellectual development. Young children mostly equate "wrong" with "punished." Adults understand that certain acts are wrong even though they may never lead to punishment and that other acts are right even if they do lead to punishment. Children younger than about 6 years old think that accidentally breaking something valuable is worse than intentionally breaking something of less value; older children and adults give more regard to people's intentions.

Kohlberg proposed that people pass through distinct stages as they develop moral reasoning. Although those stages are analogous to Piaget's stages, they do not follow the same time sequence. For example, an individual may progress rapidly through Piaget's stages while moving more slowly through Kohlberg's stages.

Kohlberg suggested that moral reasoning should not be evaluated according to the decisions a person makes but according to the reasoning behind them. For example, do you think that designing nuclear bombs is a moral way to make a living? According to Kohlberg, it might or might not show good moral reasoning, depending on one's reasons for taking the job. Hugh Gusterson (1992) interviewed a number of nuclear bomb designers at the Lawrence Livermore National Laboratory. When he asked them about the morality of their actions, nearly everyone said something like, "You're lucky you chose me to interview, because I, unlike all the others, think deeply about these matters." (Clearly, all of them were thinking about the morality of their actions but they were not talking with one another about it.) The vast majority said they were confident that the weapons would never be used, and that the only function of the bombs was to threaten, and thereby to deter other countries from starting a war. If you disagree with these bomb designers' assumptions, you might disagree with the morality of their *actions*, but according to Kohlberg's system, you should concede that

they are operating at a high level of moral *reasoning*, because they justified their actions in terms of the expected benefits to humanity.

Kohlberg believed that we all start with a low level of moral reasoning and mature through higher stages. To measure the maturity of a person's moral judgments, Kohlberg devised a series of **moral dilemmas**—problems that pit one moral value against another. Each dilemma is accompanied by a question, such as "What should this person do?" or "Did this person do the right thing?" Kohlberg was not concerned about the choice a person makes, because the dilemmas pit one value against another and well-meaning people do disagree on the best answer. More revealing than the answer is the explanation and justification the respondent gives. The respondent's explanations are then matched to one of Kohlberg's six stages, which are grouped into three levels (see Table 10.6). Because very few people operate consistently at stage 6, many authorities combine stages 5 and 6. Note that, in Kohlberg's scheme, what counts is not the decision you make but the reasons behind it. There are no moral or immoral decisions, just moral and immoral reasons for a decision (Darley & Shultz, 1990). (See Figure 10.20.)

FIGURE 10.20

Here is a real-life moral dilemma: Michigan physician Jack Kevorkian developed a device to help terminally ill patients kill themselves painlessly. Is it morally right or wrong to aid in someone's suicide? According to Kohlberg's viewpoint, the morality of an act does not depend on the act itself, but on the reasoning behind the act.

TABLE 10.6
Responses to One of Kohlberg's Moral Dilemmas by People at Six Levels of Moral Reasoning

The dilemma: Heinz's wife was near death from a type of cancer. A druggist had recently discovered a drug that might be able to save her. The druggist was charging $2,000 for the drug, which cost him $200 to make. Heinz could not afford to pay for it, and he could borrow only $1,000 from friends. He offered to pay the rest later. The druggist refused to sell the drug for less than the full price paid in advance. "I discovered the drug and I'm going to make money from it." Late that night Heinz broke into the store to steal the drug for his wife. Did Heinz do the right thing?

LEVEL/STAGE	TYPICAL ANSWER	BASIS FOR JUDGING RIGHT FROM WRONG	DESCRIPTION OF STAGE
The Level of Preconventional Morality			
1. Punishment and obedience orientation	"No. If he steals the drug he might go to jail." "Yes. If he can't afford the drug, he can't afford a funeral, either."	Wrong is equated with punishment. What is good is whatever is in the man's immediate self-interest.	Decisions are based on their immediate consequences. Whatever is rewarded is "good" and whatever is punished is "bad." If you break something and are punished, then what you did was bad.
2. Instrumental relativist orientation	"He can steal the drug and save his wife, and he'll be with her when he gets out of jail."	Again, what is good is whatever is in the man's own best interests, but his interests include delayed benefits.	It is good to help other people, but only because they may one day return the favor: "You scratch my back and I'll scratch yours."
The Level of Conventional Morality			
3. Interpersonal concordance, or "good boy/nice girl" orientation	"People will understand if you steal the drug to save your wife, but they'll think you're cruel and a coward if you don't."	Public opinion is the main basis for judging what is good.	The "right" thing to do is whatever pleases others, especially those in authority. Be a good person so others will think you are good. Conformity to the dictates of public opinion is important.
4. "Law and order" orientation	"No, because stealing is illegal." "It is the husband's duty to save his wife even if he feels guilty afterward for stealing the drug."	Right and wrong can be determined by duty, or by one's role in society.	You should respect the law—simply because it *is* the law—and should work to strengthen the social order that enforces it.
The Level of Postconventional or Principled Morality			
5. Social-contract legalistic orientation	"The husband has a right to the drug even if he can't pay now. If the druggist won't charge it, the government should look after it."	Laws are made for people's benefit. They should be flexible. If necessary, we may have to change certain laws or allow for exceptions to them.	The "right" thing to do is whatever people have agreed is best for society. As in stage 4, you respect the law, but in addition recognize that a majority of the people can agree to change the rules. Anyone who makes a promise is obligated to keep the promise.
6. Universal ethical principle orientation	"Although it is legally wrong to steal, the husband would be morally wrong not to steal to save his wife. A life is more precious than financial gain."	Right and wrong are based on absolute values such as human life. Sometimes these values take precedence over human laws.	In special cases it may be right to violate a law that conflicts with higher ethical principles, such as justice and respect for human life. Among those who have obeyed a "higher law" are Jesus, Mahatma Gandhi, and Martin Luther King, Jr.

Source: Kohlberg, 1981.

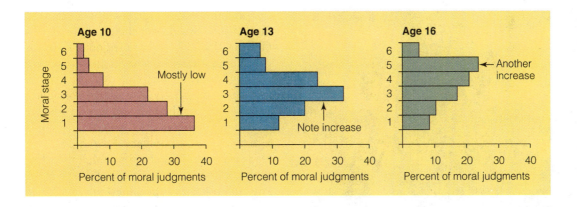

SOMETHING TO THINK ABOUT

Suppose a military junta overthrows a democratic government and sets up a dictatorship. In which of Kohlberg's stages of moral reasoning would you classify the members of the junta? Would your answer depend on the reasons they gave for setting up the dictatorship?

The responses people make to Kohlberg's moral dilemmas suggest the level of moral reasoning at which they *usually* operate. Few people are absolutely consistent in their moral reasoning, any more than they are consistent in any other kind of reasoning.

The consistent pattern is that people begin at the first stage and progress through the others in the order Kohlberg suggests, although they may not all reach the highest stages. (The order of progression is an important point. If people were as likely to progress in the order 3-5-4 as in the order 3-4-5, then we would have no justification for regarding stage 5 as higher than stage 4.) Apparently, people do not skip a stage, and few revert to an earlier stage after reaching a higher one. The progression of moral reasoning is similar in cultures throughout the world, with a few variations. For example, people in India, as compared to those in the United States, tend to put a higher emphasis on an obligation to help one's friends and less emphasis on property rights (Miller & Bersoff, 1992).

Figure 10.21 shows that most 10-year-olds' judgments are at Kohlberg's first or second stage, but that the mode of 16-year-olds' judgments is at stage 5. What accounts for this rather swift development of moral reasoning? Kohlberg suggests that it results from cognitive growth: Sixteen-year-olds are capable of more mature reasoning than are 10-year-olds. Rachael Henry (1983) proposes a different possibility: Adolescents reject parental authority. In stages 1 and 2, parents are the source of moral judgments, and what they say determines what is right and what is wrong. In stage 3, other people become the source of moral judgments. In stage 4, the source is the law; in stages 5 and 6, society as a whole or some abstract truth is the source of moral judgments. As adolescents continue to mature, they move farther and farther away from regarding their parents as the ultimate authority on questions of morality.

CONCEPT CHECK

5. For the moral dilemma described at the top of Table 10.6, suppose someone says that Heinz was wrong to steal the drug to save his wife. Which level of moral reasoning is characteristic of this judgment? (Check your answer on page 428.)

LIMITATIONS OF KOHLBERG'S VIEWS OF MORAL DEVELOPMENT

Although Kohlberg's theories have had an enormous impact on psychology, they do have certain limitations. Some critics point out that moral reasoning is just one part of moral behavior. James Rest (1983) divides moral behavior into four components:

1. Interpreting the situation
2. Deciding on the morally correct thing to do
3. Deciding what you actually will do, which may not be the same as the morally correct thing to do
4. Actually doing what you have decided to do

FIGURE 10.22
Critics of Kohlberg's approach to moral reasoning point out that moral reasoning is not the same thing as moral action. This cadet at a Russian military academy probably could explain why cheating is immoral, but he cheats nevertheless.

Kohlberg's stages relate only to the first and second of these components. Many juvenile delinquents and adult criminals make mature responses to Kohlberg's moral dilemmas but then engage in destructive behavior (Jurkovic, 1980; Link, Sherer, & Byrne, 1977). Apparently a person can distinguish between right and wrong in the abstract and then behave in a way that ignores the reasoning (Figure 10.22).

Another criticism is that Kohlberg's theories imply that moral reasoning is entirely a logical process. For example, we decide that it is wrong to hurt another person because human life and welfare are fundamentally valuable. But moral reasoning is an emotional process, too. We do not want to hurt other people because we feel bad when we see other people suffering (Kagan, 1984).

Still another criticism is that Kohlberg concentrated entirely on one type of moral

reasoning, which we might call the "justice" orientation, based on people's rights. Carol Gilligan (1977, 1979) pointed out a different way of approaching moral decisions, the "caring" orientation (what would help or hurt other people). For example, consider a situation during the Vietnam War, in which a group of soldiers were ordered to kill a group of unarmed civilians. One soldier, who regarded the order as immoral, refused to shoot. However, his actions did not make any difference, as the other soldiers killed all the civilians. In terms of "justice," this soldier acted at a high moral level, following a "higher law" that required him not to kill. But in terms of "caring," his actions were not especially moral. A better action would have been to find a way to hide a few of the Vietnamese civilians (Linn & Gilligan, 1990).

Initially, Gilligan (1977, 1979) proposed that the "justice" and "caring" orientations represented a sex difference. Men, she said, focus mostly on rights and duties; women focus more on caring and relationships. For example, when asked about the ethics of abortion, men might say that abortion is wrong because it takes a life, or they might say it is acceptable because a woman has the right to make decisions about her own body. Either answer could get a high evaluation in Kohlberg's system, if explained clearly. But a woman might answer the same question by saying the ethics of abortion depends on many of the details of the situation. An "it depends" answer does not get high marks in Kohlberg's system, because it does not rely on abstract principles of right and wrong. Nevertheless, it may reflect a sympathetic, caring approach to solving people's problems.

Gilligan therefore proposed an alternative set of stages of moral development, outlined in Table 10.7. The postconventional stage is the most mature; the preconventional stage is the least mature. Like Kohlberg, Gilligan concentrates on the reasons behind someone's moral decisions, not on the decisions themselves. But unlike Kohlberg, Gilligan emphasizes the "caring" aspect of the reasons: Will this action help or hurt the people it affects?

Later researchers have agreed with Gilligan that people have two ways of reasoning about moral issues, one based on justice and the other based on caring. However, they have not found that these ways are consis-

TABLE 10.7
Carol Gilligan's Stages of Moral Development

STAGE	BASIS FOR DECIDING RIGHT FROM WRONG
Preconventional	What is helpful or harmful to myself?
Conventional	What is helpful or harmful to other people?
Postconventional	What is helpful or harmful to myself as well as to others?

Figure 10.23

Sometimes the two "voices" of moral reasoning—justice and caring—are in conflict with each other. From a caring standpoint, you want to help a person in distress. From a justice standpoint, you may think it wrong to encourage begging. In many situations, ranging from abortion to the death penalty to animal protection, well-meaning people disagree about what action is moral.

tently related to whether one is male or female (Shweder & Haidt, 1993). The probability of a justice or a caring orientation may vary a bit between men and women, or from one culture to another, but the differences are small. Nearly everyone shows concern with both kinds of moral reasoning.

Gilligan has therefore modified her position: Each of us has within ourselves two "voices" of morality—a voice of justice and rights, and a voice of caring and relationships. One voice may speak a little louder in some people and the other voice in other people, but both voices are valid (Gilligan & Attanucci, 1988). Sometimes the two voices are in conflict; that is, one may feel an obligation to help some person and yet find that the only way to help requires breaking some general principle of justice (Linn & Gilligan, 1990). In short, sometimes situations are complicated and moral reasoning difficult. (See Figure 10.23.)

SUMMARY

• *Piaget's view of children's thinking.* According to Jean Piaget, children's thought processes are more intuitive, less logical, and more egocentric than adults' thought processes are. (page 410)

• *Piaget's stages of development.* Piaget described four stages of development of thought processes and knowledge. Children progress through those stages in order. (page 411)

• *Egocentric thinking.* Young children sometimes have trouble understanding other people's point of view. Before about age 4, children have trouble inferring what someone else is likely or unlikely to know. (page 413)

• *Restricted uses of abilities.* Young children do not always use all the abilities they have. Although children in the preoperational stage ordinarily fail to demonstrate conservation of number, it is clear from other tasks that they do understand the concept of number. (page 418)

• *Implications for education.* Teaching must be at a level appropriate to the developmental stage of a child. However, as Lev Vygotsky argued, children can advance with an adult's help to do more than they could on their own. Therefore, education should try to push a child somewhat beyond his or her current level of performance. (page 418)

• *Language development.* Children begin rapidly learning language at about age 1½. From the start, their speech is creative and not just imitative. (page 419)

• *Kohlberg's view of moral reasoning.* Lawrence Kohlberg contended that moral reasoning also can be described in terms of stages. According to Kohlberg, a person's moral reasoning should be evaluated on the basis of the reasons the person gives for a decision, rather than on the basis of the decision itself. (page 423)

• *Gilligan's view of moral reasoning.* Carol Gilligan demonstrated that not all people decide moral dilemmas primarily on the basis of principles of justice. Some decide primarily on the basis of a caring orientation. (page 426)

SUGGESTIONS FOR FURTHER READING

Hobson, R. P. (1993). *Autism and the development of mind.* Hove, East Sussex, UK: Lawrence Erlbaum Associates. In spite of the title, this book is only partly about autism; it is about how children come to understand other people and to communicate with them.

Locke, J. L. (1994). Phases in the child's development of language. *American Scientist, 82,* 436–445. Fine description of how children learn language.

TERMS

schema (plural: schemata) an organized way of interacting with objects in the world (page 411)

assimilation Piaget's term for the application of an established schema to new objects (page 411)

accommodation Piaget's term for the modification of an established schema to fit new objects (page 411)

sensorimotor stage according to Piaget, the first stage of intellectual development, in which an infant's behavior is limited to making simple motor responses to sensory stimuli (page 412)

preoperational stage according to Piaget, the second stage of intellectual development, in which children lack operations (page 412)

operation according to Piaget, a mental process that can be reversed (page 412)

egocentric an inability to take the perspective of another person, a tendency to view the world as centered around oneself (page 413)

conservation the concept that objects retain their weight, volume, and certain other properties in spite of changes in their shape or arrangement (page 415)

stage of concrete operations according to Piaget, the third stage of intellectual development, in which children can deal with the properties of concrete objects but cannot readily deal with hypothetical or abstract questions (page 416)

stage of formal operations according to Piaget, the fourth and final stage of intellectual development, in which people deal with abstract, hypothetical situations, which demand logical, deductive reasoning and systematic planning (page 416)

zone of proximal development the distance between what a child can do on his or her own and what the child can do with the help of adults or other children (page 419)

moral dilemma a problem that pits one moral value against another (page 423)

ANSWERS TO CONCEPT CHECKS

2. (c) is the clearest case of egocentric thought, a failure to recognize another person's point of view. Egocentric thought is not the same thing as selfishness. (page 413)

3. (a) Stage of concrete operations; (b) preoperational stage; (c) sensorimotor stage; (d) stage of formal operations. (page 418)

4. Children begin to string words into novel combinations as soon as they begin to speak two words at a time. We believe that they learn rules of grammar because they overgeneralize those rules, saying such "words" as *womans* and *goed*. (page 422)

5. Not enough information is provided to answer this question. In Kohlberg's system, any judgment can represent either a high or a low level of moral reasoning. We evaluate a person's moral reasoning entirely by the explanation for the judgment, not by the judgment itself. (page 425)

SOCIAL AND EMOTIONAL DEVELOPMENT

What are the special social and emotional problems that people face at different ages of life?

What determines how we develop socially and emotionally?

You are a contestant on a new TV game show called "What's My Worry?" Behind the curtain is someone with an overriding concern. You are to identify that concern by questioning a psychologist who knows what it is. (You can neither see nor hear the person.) You must ask questions that can be answered with a single word or a short phrase. If you identify the concern correctly, you can win up to $50,000.

But there is one catch: The more questions you ask, the smaller your prize. If you guess correctly after one question, you win $50,000. After two questions, you win $25,000. And so on. It would be poor strategy to go on asking questions until you were sure of the answer; instead, you should ask one or two questions and then guess.

What would your first question be? Mine would be: "How old is this person?" The principal worries of teenagers are different from those of most 20-year-olds, which in turn differ from those of most 40-year-olds and 70-year-olds. Each age has its own characteristic concerns and decisions, opportunities and pleasures.

RESEARCH DESIGNS FOR STUDYING DEVELOPMENT

Comparing the psychology of people of different ages sounds easy: We study a group of, say, 10-year-olds and a group of 20-year-olds and see how they differ. But how do we know whether those differences are due to age or to some other difference between the groups? We may get different results depending on exactly how we conduct the study. Depending on circumstances, psychologists can use either cross-sectional studies or longitudinal studies. A **cross-sectional study** compares groups of individuals of different ages all at the same time. For example, we could compare the drawing abilities of 6-year-olds, 8-year-olds, and 10-year-olds.

A **longitudinal study** follows a single group of individuals as they develop. For example, we could study a group of 6-year-olds, and then restudy the same children when they reach ages 9 and 12. Table 10.8 contrasts the two kinds of studies.

Longitudinal studies face certain obvious practical difficulties. A longitudinal study of children from age 6 to 12 necessarily requires 6 years to complete; some longitudinal studies last decades. To make matters worse, many of the children who begin in a study at, say, age 6 may move out of town by age 9 or 12. A longitudinal study of the elderly faces the problem that many people will die or become seriously ill before the end of the study. (This is the problem of "selective attrition" mentioned in Chapter 2.) By

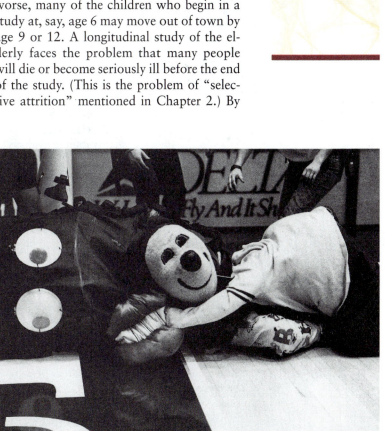

As people grow older, they mature in their social and emotional development. However, in a situation where people think that childish behavior is acceptable, they can revert to some amazingly immature actions. At one college basketball game, the two college mascots (college students in costumes) had to be arrested after a disorderly brawl.

TABLE 10.8
Cross-sectional and Longitudinal Studies

	DESCRIPTION	ADVANTAGES	DISADVANTAGES	EXAMPLE
Cross-sectional	Several groups of subjects of various ages studied at one time	1. Quick 2. No risk of confusing age effects with effects of changes in society	1. Risk of sampling error by getting different kinds of people at different ages 2. Risk of cohort effects	Compare memory abilities of 3-, 5-, and 7-year-olds.
Longitudinal	One group of subjects studied repeatedly as they grow older	1. No risk of sampling differences 2. Can study effects of one experience on later development 3. Can study consistency within individuals over time	1. Takes long time 2. Some subjects quit 3. Sometimes hard to separate effects of age from changes in society	Study social and emotional behavior of children at time of parents' divorce and at various times afterward.

choosing a cross-sectional study, we avoid such problems.

A longitudinal study also faces the difficulty of separating the effects of age from the effects of changes in society. For example, suppose we found that a group of people who were 20 years old in 1970 became politically more conservative by age 40. We would not know whether these people became more conservative because of age or because of changes in the political situation between 1970 and 1990.

Why, then, would investigators ever conduct a longitudinal study? One reason is that certain questions logically require a longitudinal study. For example, to study the effects of divorce on children, we learn much by comparing how each child reacts at first with how that same child reacts several years later. To study whether happy children are likely to become happy adults, we would

have to follow a single group of people for a substantial period of time.

What happens if a cross-sectional study gives one result and a longitudinal study gives another? Psychologists do not just throw up their hands in despair; they look for reasons behind the different results. For example, suppose someone conducting a study in 1955 finds that the mean IQ score of the 20-year-olds is much higher than that of the 60-year-olds. However, on a retest in 1995, the former 20-year-olds (now 60 years old) score as high as they did in 1955. Thus, the longitudinal part of the study indicates that IQ scores are fairly stable from age 20 to age 60. Why, then, did the 20-year-olds score so much higher than the 60-year-olds in 1955? Two possible reasons: First, perhaps the investigators in 1955 selected a particularly bright group of 20-year-olds or a dull group of 60-year-olds. Second, maybe the

FIGURE 10.24
One reason why the young people of today differ from their elders is that they grew up in a different historical era, with different education, nutrition, and health care. Differences among age groups based on such influences are called cohort effects.

generation of people who were 20 years old in 1955 were healthier and better educated than the older generation had ever been. That is, the 20-year-olds of 1955 may have performed better than the 20-year-olds of 1915 would have. Psychologists call this a *cohort effect* (Figure 10.24). A **cohort** is a group of people born at a particular time or a group of people who entered some organization at a particular time. Psychologists try to distinguish whether a difference among people of different ages is really due to age or whether it is a difference among cohorts.

CONCEPT CHECKS
---

6. *Suppose you want to study the effect of age on artistic abilities, and you want to be sure that any apparent differences are due to age and not to a cohort effect. Which should you use, a longitudinal study or a cross-sectional study?*
7. *Suppose you want to study the effect of age on choice of clothing, but you are worried because clothing fashions change from one year to the next. (It would not be fair to compare the people of today with people of previous years.) Which should you use, a longitudinal study or a cross-sectional study? (Check your answers on page 445.)*

Using a combination of cross-sectional and longitudinal studies, psychologists study changes in people's abilities, but also changes in their life situations. The decisions and so-

cial environment young adults face are very different from the experiences of children on one hand or old people on the other.

ERIKSON'S AGES OF HUMAN DEVELOPMENT

How people spend their time is largely determined by their current role in life—preschool child, student, worker, or retired person. Moreover, a person's role in life is determined largely, though not entirely, by his or her age. To understand why people behave as they do, we need to know the decisions they are facing at their current stage of life.

Erik Erikson (Figure 10.25), a pioneer in child psychoanalysis, divided the human life span into eight ages, each with its own social and emotional conflicts. First is the age of the newborn infant, whose main conflict is **basic trust versus mistrust.** The infant asks, in effect, "Is my social world predictable and supportive?" An infant whose early environment is supportive, nurturing, and loving will form an attachment to the parents that will also influence future relationships with other people (Erikson, 1963).

Erikson's second age is the age of the toddler, 1–3 years old, whose main conflict is **autonomy versus shame and doubt.** The toddler faces the issue "Can I do things by myself or must I always rely on others?" Experiencing independence for the first time, the

FIGURE 10.25
Erik Erikson, a highly influential theorist, argued that each age has its own special social and emotional conflicts.

TABLE 10.9
Erikson's Ages of Human Development

AGE	MAIN CONFLICT	TYPICAL QUESTION
Infant	Basic trust versus mistrust	Is my social world predictable and supportive?
Toddler (ages 1–3)	Autonomy versus shame and doubt	Can I do things by myself or must I always rely on others?
Preschool child (ages 3–6)	Initiative versus guilt	Am I good or bad?
Preadolescent (ages 6–12)	Industry versus inferiority	Am I successful or worthless?
Adolescent (early teens)	Identity versus role confusion	Who am I?
Young adult (late teens and early 20s)	Intimacy versus isolation	Shall I share my life with another person or shall I live alone?
Middle adult (late 20s to retirement)	Generativity versus stagnation	Will I succeed in my life, both as a parent and as a worker?
Older adult (after retirement)	Ego integrity versus despair	Have I lived a full life or have I failed?

toddler begins to walk and talk, to be toilet trained, to obey some instructions and defy others. Depending on how the parents react, children may develop a healthy feeling of autonomy (independence) or a self-critical sense of shame and doubt that they can accomplish things on their own.

Erikson's third age is the age of the preschool child, whose main conflict is **initiative versus guilt.** At ages 3–6, as children begin to broaden their horizons, their boundless energy comes into conflict with parental restrictions. Sooner or later the child breaks something or makes a big mess. The child faces the question "Am I good or bad?" In contrast to the previous stage, where the child was concerned about what he or she is *capable* of doing, at this stage the child is concerned about the morality or acceptability of his or her actions.

In the fourth age, preadolescence (about ages 6–12), **industry versus inferiority** is the main conflict. The question is "Am I successful or worthless?" Children widen their focus from the immediate family to society at large and begin to prepare for adult roles. They fantasize about the great successes ahead, and they begin to compete with their peers in an effort to excel in the activities of their age. Children who feel that they are failing may be plagued with long-lasting feelings of inferiority. Children who take pride in their accomplishments gain a long-lasting feeling of competence.

Erikson's fifth age is adolescence (the early teens), in which the main conflict is **identity versus role confusion.** Adolescents begin to seek independence from their parents and try to answer the question "Who am I?" or "Who will I be?" They may eventually settle on a satisfactory answer—an identity—or they may continue to experiment with goals and lifestyles—a state of role confusion.

Erikson's sixth age is young adulthood (the late teens and early 20s), in which **inti-**

macy versus isolation is the main conflict. Shall I share my life with another person or shall I live alone? Young adults who marry or who live with a friend find that they have to adjust their habits in order to make the relationship succeed. Those who choose to live alone may experience loneliness and pressure from their parents and friends to find a suitable partner.

Erikson's seventh age is middle adulthood (from the late 20s through retirement), in which the major conflict is **generativity versus stagnation.** Will I produce something of real value? Will I succeed in my life, both as a parent and as a worker? Or will the quality of my life simply dwindle with the years?

Erikson's eighth age is old age (the years after retirement), in which the main conflict is **ego integrity versus despair.** Have I lived a full life or have I failed? Integrity is a state of contentment about one's life, past, present, and future. Despair is a state of disappointment about the past and the present, coupled with fear of the future. Table 10.9 summarizes Erikson's ages.

Is Erikson's view of development correct? That is almost an unanswerable question. Some psychologists find Erikson's description of development a useful way to organize our thinking about human life; others find it less useful; almost no one finds it easy to test scientifically. Erikson described development; he did not explain it. For example, he hardly addressed the question of how or why a person progresses from one stage to the next. Still, Erikson called attention to the fact that the social and emotional concerns of one age differ from those of another, and his writings inspired interest in development across the entire life span.

Now let's take a closer look at some of the major issues that confront people in their social and emotional development at different ages. Beyond the primary conflicts that Erikson highlighted, development is marked by a succession of other significant problems.

SOMETHING TO THINK ABOUT

Suppose you disagreed with Erikson's analysis; for example, suppose you believed that the main concern of young adults was not "intimacy versus isolation" but "earning money versus not earning money" or "finding meaning in life versus meaninglessness." How might you determine whether your theory or Erikson's is more correct?

FIGURE 10.26
In Harlow's studies, monkeys who got milk from the wire mother still clung to the cloth mother as much as they could.

INFANCY: FORMING THE FIRST ATTACHMENTS

Before the late 1950s, if someone had asked, "What causes an infant to develop an attachment to its mother?" almost all psychologists would have replied, "Mother's milk." They were wrong.

STUDIES OF ATTACHMENT AMONG MONKEYS

Attachment—a long-term feeling of closeness between a child and a care giver—depends on more than just being fed. Attachment is part of trust, in Erikson's sense of "trust versus mistrust." That attachment or trust comes only partly from the satisfaction of biological needs. It also depends on the emotional responses provoked by such acts as hugging.

Some highly influential evidence comes from an experiment that Harry Harlow conducted with monkeys. Harlow (1958) separated eight newborn rhesus monkeys from their mothers and isolated each of them in a room containing two artificial mothers. Four of the infant monkeys had a mother made out of wire and equipped with a milk bottle in the breast position and a mother made out of cloth with no bottle (Figure 10.26); the other four had a cloth mother with a bottle

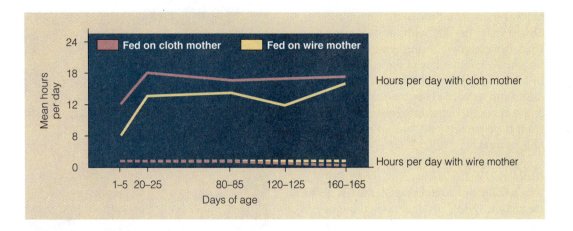

Hours per day with cloth mother

Hours per day with wire mother

and a wire mother with no bottle. Harlow wanted to find out how much time the baby monkeys would spend with the artificial mother that fed them.

Figure 10.27 shows the mean number of hours per day that the monkeys spent with the two kinds of mothers. Regardless of whether they got their milk from the cloth mother or from the wire mother, they all spent more than half their time clinging to the cloth mother and very little time with the wire mother. Evidently their attachment depended more on *contact comfort*—comfortable skin sensations—than on the satisfaction of their hunger or sucking needs.

At first Harlow thought that the cloth mothers were serving the infants' emotional needs adequately. He discovered, however, that the monkeys failed to develop normal social and sexual behavior (Harlow, Harlow, & Suomi, 1971). (See Figure 10.28.) When some of the females finally became pregnant, they proved to be woefully inadequate mothers, rejecting every attempt their babies made to cling to them or to be nursed. Clearly, the monkeys that had been reared by artificial

mothers did not know how to react to other monkeys. In monkeys, as in humans, a good parent interacts with the infant, giving social signals as well as responding to the infant's signals. Merely being warm and cuddly is a good start, but hardly enough.

What are the messages of this study for humans? The data do *not* mean that an infant needs a mother's constant attention. They do mean that an infant needs social attention from *someone*. In later studies, Harry Harlow and Margaret Harlow (1965) found that infant monkeys reared by artificial mothers could develop fairly normally if they had frequent opportunities to play with other infant monkeys.

EARLY ATTACHMENT IN HUMANS

Early social experience is, we would assume, at least as important for human social development as it is for monkeys. Although we cannot conduct deliberate experiments to test this point, all indications support it. In the early 1900s, many foundling homes and orphanages raised infants under conditions that were little better than those of the Harlows' monkeys. The supervisors, trained to believe that unnecessary stimulation should be avoided, ruled that each infant be kept in a crib in a narrow cubicle. The nurses seldom cuddled the infants or played with them, and the infants rarely had an opportunity even to see other babies.

In various institutions, 30–100% of the babies died within 1 year (Spitz, 1945, 1946). Those who survived were retarded in physical growth and in language and intellectual development; they were socially inept and unresponsive to their environment (Bowlby, 1952). We cannot ascribe these results solely to early social isolation because many of the children were ill to begin with, and a number of those who survived continued to be reared under poor conditions (Clarke & Clarke, 1976). Still, severe deprivation of human contact early in life clearly can be extremely harmful.

CONCEPT CHECK

8. *In what way were the unstimulating institutions similar to the Harlows' artificial monkeys? (Check your answer on page 445.)*

EFFECTS OF DIFFERENT PARENTING STYLES

What is the best way to rear children? The answer depends on how one hopes the children will develop; different parents and different cultures have different ideas of what constitutes a favorable outcome.

Diana Baumrind (1971) conducted extensive studies of the behaviors of parents and children. She tentatively identified the several styles of parenting, of which the following are the most common or most basic:

Authoritative parents: These parents are demanding and impose firm controls, but they are also warm and responsive to the child's communications. They encourage their children to set appropriate independent goals. Their children show self-reliance and self-control, cooperating with others and generally doing well in school.

Authoritarian parents: Like the *authoritative* parents, *authoritarian* parents set firm controls. However, they tend to be less warm and less close to the child; they set rules without explaining why they are good rules. Their children tend to be socially responsible, law-abiding citizens, but they tend also to be discontent, distrustful, and not very independent.

Permissive parents: Permissive parents are warm and loving but not demanding. Their children generally lack self-control and lack a sense of social responsibility.

We should be careful not to assume that the parents' behavior caused the children's behavior. These are correlational studies, and as with nearly all correlational studies, we can imagine other possible explanations for the results. For example, the children's behavior can affect the parents as much as the parents affect the children. (Perhaps chil-

Physical contact and cuddling are essential for the attachment that develops between parent and child. The early parent-child relationship serves as a prototype for later social attachments.

dren who act in self-reliant, self-controlled ways elicit authoritative parenting styles.) Another possibility is that parents and children show certain patterns of behavior because they share certain genes. (Perhaps the genes that promote permissive behavior in parents increase the probability of irresponsible behavior in children.)

Baumrind's research focused mainly on European-American children; later research has found that the effects of different parenting styles may vary somewhat among different ethnic groups (Darling & Steinberg, 1993). For example, the authoritative parenting style is associated with strong academic success and social cooperativeness for European-American children; the effects are less consistent for Asian-American and African-American families. Also, authoritarian European-American parents tend to have somewhat withdrawn children; authoritarian African-American parents have rather assertive children. At present, the reasons for these apparent differences are uncertain. They remind us not to assume that the results found in one group will apply to all groups; they also emphasize the need for further research.

FIGURE 10.29
Children learn their social skills by interacting with brothers, sisters, and friends close to their own age.

SOCIAL DEVELOPMENT IN CHILDHOOD

Infants less than 1 year old seldom play with one another. They show interest in one another, but they do not have enough social skills to continue any meaningful social interactions. From age 1 to 2, we can see the beginnings of social play, but still it is mostly **parallel play:** Two or more infants play at the same time, in the same place, but almost independently. After about age 2, children start playing with one another more and more.

The social and emotional development of children depends in part on how successful they are in forming friendships with other children (Figure 10.29). Some children are "popular," having many friends and admirers. Others are "rejected," with most other children avoiding their company. Still others are "controversial," liked by some and rejected by others. Controversial children are generally those with some social skills but an aggressive streak. A child's status as popular, rejected, or controversial tends to be fairly consistent from year to year (Coie & Dodge, 1983). Children with few friends tend to suffer low self-esteem and to do poorly in both schoolwork and athletics. (But does the lack of friends lead to poor performance or does poor performance lead to the lack of friends?)

Many studies have been made of the effects of being a firstborn child or being born later. A number of those birth-order studies report that firstborn children do better in school, are more ambitious, are more honest, and have a greater need to affiliate with others. Children born later tend to be more popular, more independent, less conforming, better adjusted emotionally, and possibly more creative. These tendencies are slight and inconsistent, however, and some of the evidence is based on poorly conducted studies (Ernst & Angst, 1983; Schooler, 1972). Be skeptical of recommendations that parents should space their children many years apart in order to give each of them the alleged benefits of the firstborn.

SOMETHING TO THINK ABOUT

Psychologists have offered two explanations for the effects of birth order on behavior: (1) Depending on whether there are older, younger, or no other children in the family, each child is subjected to different social influences. (2) Because the mother undergoes physical changes, such as changes in her hormones after giving birth, younger children experience different prenatal influences from those experienced by the firstborn child. What kind of evidence would you need to decide whether one of these explanations was more satisfactory than the other?

ADOLESCENCE

Adolescence begins when the body shows signs of sexual maturation. In North America, the mean ages are around 12 to 13 in girls and about a year or two later in boys. The end of adolescence is harder to identify. Adolescence merges into adulthood, and adulthood is more a state of mind than a condition of the body. Some 12-year-olds act like adults, and some 30-year-olds act like adolescents.

Adolescence is a time of transition from childhood to adulthood. Children think of themselves as part of their parents' family; young adults are ready to become parents. Adolescents are somewhere in between, still closely tied to their parents but also spending more and more time with their peer group. Their relationship with their parents changes, often in turbulent ways. From the parents' standpoint, adolescents are no longer acting like dutiful, obedient children, but they are also not acting like responsible adults. The adolescents are asserting their independence, but they are sometimes making big mistakes, at least in the parents' judgment. The relationship between the parents and teenagers may include episodes of serious conflict (Paikoff & Brooks-Gunn, 1991).

Adolescence is also, for many young people in western cultures, a time of disruptive behavior, ranging from mere mischief or mild vandalism to serious delinquency. The probability of delinquent misconduct is higher at age 16 than at any other age (Wolfgang, Figlio, & Selin, 1972; see Figure 10.30). Some of those who engage in delinquent behavior in their teenage years continue with antisocial and criminal behavior later in life, but a large number of others cease their misbehavior (Moffitt, 1993). Few who are well-behaved at 16 and 17 begin a pattern of antisocial behavior later. Note that the adolescent outburst of vandalism and delinquency is culture-dependent; it is absent in many traditional cultures with strong family units.

A number of programs have attempted to prevent juvenile delinquency; most have had only limited success. So far, the most impressive results have come from programs that attempt to improve young people's educational performance, rather than those attempting to discourage delinquent behavior itself (Zigler, Taussig, & Black, 1992).

Adolescence is a time of "finding yourself," of determining "Who am I?" or "Who will I be?" As Erikson said, identity is a major issue at this age.

IDENTITY CRISIS

In some societies, children are expected eventually to enter the same occupation as their parents and to live in the same town. The parents may even choose marriage partners for their children. In such societies, adolescents have few major choices to make.

Western society offers young people a great many choices. They can decide how much education to get, what job to seek, and where to live. They can decide whether to marry and whom and when. They can choose their own political and religious affiliation. They can choose their own standards of behavior for sex, alcohol, and drugs. In making each of these choices, they may face conflicting pressures from peers, parents, and teachers.

Adolescents, realizing that they must make such decisions within a few years, face an **identity crisis**. The search for identity or

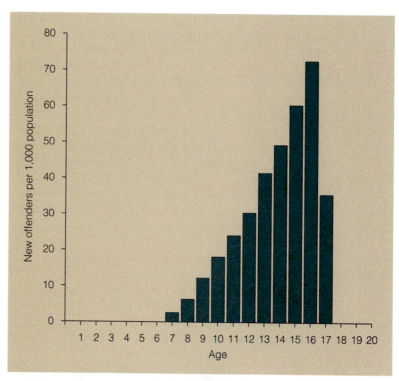

FIGURE 10.30
The probability of a first delinquent act increases until age 16; few people commit a first delinquent act after age 17. That is, someone who has not committed such an act by age 17 is unlikely to do so later. (From Wolfgang, Figlio, & Selin, 1972.)

self-understanding may lead an adolescent in several directions (Marcia, 1980). **Identity foreclosure,** for example, is the passive acceptance of a role defined by one's parents. An adolescent's father may declare, for example, "When you graduate from high school, you will go on to college and study electrical engineering, just as I did when I was your age. Then you will go into the family business with me." Adolescents who accept such parental prescriptions enjoy at least one advantage: They avoid the uncertainty and anxiety that other adolescents endure while trying to "find themselves."

Until fairly recently, identity foreclosure was the norm for most young women. Parents and society both decreed, "You will be a full-time wife and mother." Today, young women have greater freedom to choose what to do with their life, and consequently a greater probability of experiencing an identity crisis during adolescence.

The search for identity may also lead to **role diffusion.** The uncertain sense of identity and the low self-esteem that many adolescents experience may prompt them to experiment with a variety of roles, alternately playing the "party goer," the "rebel," the "serious student," the "loner," and the "class clown." Role diffusion is not necessarily a bad thing, at least as a temporary measure. It is natural to experiment with several roles before a person finds the one that seems most suitable.

Another possible outcome is a **moratorium**—a delay in resolving an identity crisis. The adolescent simply postpones making any lasting decision.

Finally, the search for identity may lead to **identity achievement.** Some adolescents deliberately decide what their values, goals, and place in society will be. That identity may or may not be permanent; we all continue to change in various ways throughout life, and from time to time we need to rethink our values and goals.

THE "PERSONAL FABLE" OF TEENAGERS

Respond to the following statements. Are they true or false?

- Other people will fail to realize their life ambitions, but I will realize mine.
- I understand love and sex in a way my parents never did.
- Tragedy may strike other people, but it will probably never strike me.

- Almost everyone notices how I look and how I dress.

You know perfectly well that all these statements are false, and yet you may nurture a secret belief in them. According to David Elkind (1984), teenagers are particularly likely to harbor such beliefs. Taken together, he calls them the "personal fable," the conviction that "I am special; what is true for everyone else is not true for me." Up to a point, that fable may help us to maintain a cheerful, optimistic outlook on life. It becomes dangerous when it leads people to take foolish chances. (See Figure 10.31.)

For example, one study found that high-school girls who were having sexual intercourse without contraception estimated that they had only a low chance of becoming pregnant through unprotected sex. Girls who were either having no sex or having sex only with contraception estimated a much higher probability that unprotected sex would lead to pregnancy (Arnett, 1990). Because this was a correlational study, we do not know which came first—the girls' under-

FIGURE 10.31
Some teenagers seriously risk their health and safety. According to David Elkind, one reason for such risky behavior is the "personal fable," the secret belief that "nothing bad will happen to me."

estimation of the risk of pregnancy, or their willingness to have unprotected sex. Nevertheless, in either case, these results illustrate the "it can't happen to me" attitude common to many teenagers.

That attitude is hardly unique to teenagers, however. Middle-aged adults also overestimate their own chances of winning a lottery, regard themselves as more likely than other people are to succeed on the job, and regard themselves as less likely than average to have an injury or a serious illness (Quadrel, Fischhoff, & Davis, 1993). That is, the "personal fable" is characteristic of all people, not just teenagers.

YOUNG ADULTHOOD

In young adulthood, marriage and career no longer lie in the future. Ready or not, the future has arrived. According to Erikson, the main concern at this age is "Shall I live by myself or share my life with another person?"

DATING AND LEARNING ABOUT EACH OTHER

Dating couples gradually share a great deal of information about themselves, including their political and religious beliefs, their feelings toward their parents, and their deepest hopes and fears (Rubin, Hill, Peplau, & Dunkel-Schetter, 1980). Still, most people are generally reluctant at first to reveal themselves fully to a dating partner and to enter into intimate communication. What causes that reluctance?

As a rule, people exchange information about their private lives only after a long, gradual, give-and-take process (Figure 10.32). If an old friend opens up to you about his failure at work or tells you about his brother in jail, you may feel privileged. If the man who just moved in next door shares the same sort of information, you probably wonder what strange sort of person he is.

When people feel they have nothing to lose, they are more likely to reveal themselves. For instance, couples who are facing serious difficulties in their marriage speak more candidly to each other than happily married couples do (Tolstedt & Stokes, 1984). Zick Rubin (1974) found that strangers who meet by accident on a train or a plane on their way to different destinations often reveal intimate information they would never reveal to their closest friends.

FIGURE 10.32
Dating is marked by cautious self-disclosure. Both partners want to get to know each other, but each also wants to avoid saying anything that could make the wrong impression.

Dating couples who have many acquaintances in common feel that they have a great deal to lose if they open up too freely or too quickly. Many couples are therefore very slow to explore certain matters that are likely to cause friction if they decide to marry.

Table 10.10 provides some questions that are important in a long-term relationship that couples seldom discuss early in a relationship. Answer the questions in Table 10.10 *as you think your dating partner* would answer them. (Several of these questions assume a heterosexual relationship; please disregard any items that do not apply to you.)

Were you uncertain about how your dating partner would answer any of the questions? If so, you are in the majority. And yet disagreements on such questions are among the most common reasons for conflict in marriage or other long-term relationships.

BALANCING FAMILY AND CAREER

In early adulthood, most people start both a family and a career. Sometimes the two come into conflict, most frequently for women. Traditionally in Europe and the United States, mothers have devoted much more time to care for small children than fathers have. The amount of time mothers devoted has been variable; wealthy European mothers might leave their children with "nannies" during most of the day or send them to a boarding school at an early age. Still, most

TABLE 10.10
Premarital Questionnaire

1. After marriage, how often would you want to visit your parents? Your in-laws?

2. How many children do you want to have? How soon?

3. How do you want to raise your children? Should the mother stay home with the children full-time while they are young? Or should the father and mother share the responsibility for child care? Or should the children be put in a day-care center?

4. Suppose the husband is offered a good job in one city and the wife is offered a good job in a city a hundred miles away. Neither spouse can find a satisfactory job in the other's city. How would you decide where to live?

5. Suppose a sudden financial crisis strikes. Where would you cut expenses to balance the budget? Clothes? Food? Housing? Entertainment?

6. How often do you plan to attend religious services?

7. Where and how do you like to spend your vacations?

8. How often would you expect to spend an evening with friends, apart from your spouse?

Today it is common for a woman to have a career and to be the primary caretaker for one or more children. Balancing the demands of career and family can be taxing.

mothers stayed at home while their children were young.

Did that interrupt their careers? Well, staying at home does not interrupt your career if you do not have a career. Before the late 1960s and early 1970s, career opportunities for women were distinctly limited. Job discrimination against women still exists today, but it is much less severe than in times past. Many young women are in the midst of promising careers when they contemplate having a baby. Suddenly they have a difficult decision to face: After delivering the baby, do they return to work at least part-time? And if so, how soon? Most families need the income from the mother's job; even if they don't, the mother may enjoy working outside the home. But getting affordable, high-quality day care is difficult in most areas (Scarr, Phillips, & McCartney, 1989).

Different families make different decisions. The mother may interrupt her career to stay with the baby; less frequently the father may stay with the baby full-time; in some cases, the mother and father arrange their work schedules so that they can take turns being with the baby. In still other families, both parents work full-time and try to find decent day-care facilities.

In any of these cases, but especially if both parents work full-time, the parents discover that they do not have enough hours in the day. One survey found many families in which each parent worked a full-time job and spent an average of 3 to 5 hours per day on housework and child care (Burley, 1991). Under those circumstances, the parents have little time left for recreation or romance.

In many such families, the father and mother find very little time to spend with each other, and their relationship may encounter some tensions. One study reported an interesting but hard-to-interpret correlation: In two-income families, the *more* time the father spent with the child, the *less* the father reported loving the mother (Crouter, Perry-Jenkins, Huston, & McHale, 1987). What does that correlation mean: The less time he spends with the child, the more time he has for the mother? Or the less he loves the mother, the more he prefers to spend his time with the child instead? Or what? In any event, balancing career needs and family needs is a serious, widespread problem.

Later in this chapter we will discuss two-paycheck families from the child's point of view.

MIDDLE ADULTHOOD

From the 20s until retirement, the main concern of most adults is "What and how much will I produce? Will I make a valuable contribution and achieve significant success?"

These are generally highly productive years in which people take pride and satisfaction in their accomplishments. Middle adulthood lacks some of the excitement of young adulthood but brings a greater sense of security and accomplishment. Middle-aged adults generally have a good sense of how successful they are going to be in their marriage and career.

JOB SATISFACTION

Adults who are satisfied with their job are generally satisfied with their life, and people who like their life generally like their job (Keon & McDonald, 1982). Some adults manage to be happy even though they work at an unrewarding job, but the daily work routine is bound to influence their satisfaction with life.

How satisfied *are* most workers with their job? The answer depends on how we word the question. When pollsters ask simply, "Are you satisfied with your job?" about 85–90% say "yes" (Weaver, 1980). But when pollsters ask, "If you could start over, would you seek the same job you have now?" less than half of white-collar workers and only one-fourth of blue-collar workers say "yes." Although most workers say they are "satisfied" with their job, they could easily imagine being *more* satisfied.

The level of satisfaction is lower, on the average, among young workers than among long-term workers (Bass & Ryterband, 1979). (See Figure 10.33.) One explanation is that older workers have better, higher-

Possible reasons why older workers report greater job satisfaction than younger workers

Better pay

Greater responsibility

Greater challenges

Comfort of status quo

Lower expectations

Previous experience in less suitable jobs

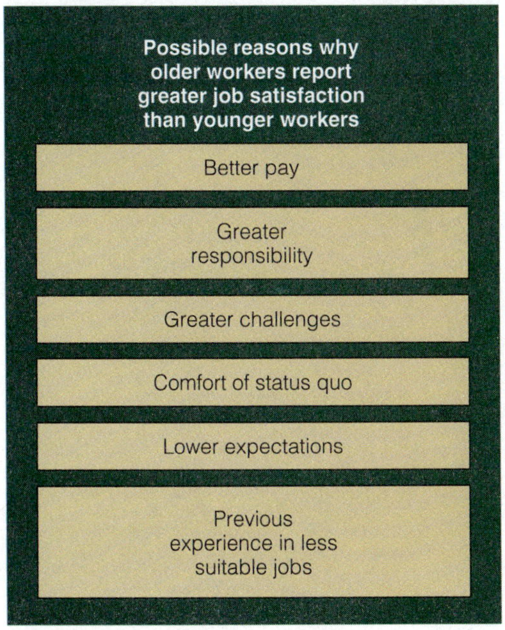

FIGURE 10.33
Most older workers report higher job satisfaction than younger workers do. Psychologists propose several reasons.

paying jobs that offer greater responsibility and challenge. Another is that today's young people are harder to satisfy. But neither of those explanations accounts for all the results (Janson & Martin, 1982). Another possibility is that many young workers start in the wrong job and find a more suitable one later on. Yet another is that many young people are still considering the possibility of changing jobs; by age 40, people reconcile themselves to whatever job they have.

Your choice of career has a profound effect on the quality of your life. A student once told me that he found the courses in his major boring, but at least they were preparing him for a job. I cautioned him that he probably would find that job just as boring. Between the ages of 20 and 70 you will probably spend about half your waking hours on the job—a long time to live with work you find unsatisfying.

THE MIDLIFE TRANSITION

People enter adulthood with a great many hopes and goals. Then as they settle into the daily round of activities, they tend to postpone their ambitions. Around age 40, some adults experience a **midlife transition**, a reassessment of their personal goals. Up to this point, they had clung to the personal fable that their life would be a success in every way. There was always plenty of time to get that better job, start that family, write that great novel, take that trip up the Amazon, or get an advanced degree. But at some point they begin to realize that the opportunity to make major life changes is rapidly fading.

The Russian novelist Leo Tolstoy wrote at age 47:

I have lived through the period of childhood, adolescence and youth when I climbed higher and higher up the mysterious hill of life, hoping to find at its summit a result worthy of the effort put in; I have also lived through the period of maturity during which, having reached the summit, I went on calmly and contentedly . . . searching all round me for the fruits of life which I had attained . . . and I have lived through the conviction that nothing of what I expected on this summit was there and that now, only one thing remained to me— to descend to the other side to the place where I came from. And I have begun that descent. . . . I call such a condition old age, and at the present moment I have reached

"Adults hope that life begins at 40— but the great anxiety is that it ends there."
DANIEL LEVINSON
(1978)

that condition. (Tolstoy, 1875/1978, pp. 288–289.)

Daniel Levinson (1977, 1978) reports that about 80% of all adults experience such a midlife transition. Other psychologists deny that the prevalence of the experience is anywhere near that figure. The disagreement may be a matter of definition. Most middle-aged adults do not experience a painful midlife transition like the one Tolstoy described, but many go through a minor, non-traumatic readjustment. They review their successes and failures, examine the direction their life is taking, and set new, more realistic goals.

Some adults who go through a midlife transition accept their life as it is. Others refuse to abandon their early goals. Declaring "It's now or never," they train for a new job or take some other positive step—sometimes over the protests of family members who would prefer to play it safe. Still others become depressed and may turn to alcohol or other means of escape.

CONCEPT CHECK

9. *In what way does a midlife transition resemble an adolescent identity crisis? (Check your answer on page 445.)*

OLD AGE

The percentage of people who live into their 70s and 80s has grown steadily throughout the 20th century. So has their health, their activity, and their intellectual performance (Schaie, 1994). Different people age in different ways. Some people, especially those with Alzheimer's disease or other serious ailments, deteriorate both intellectually and physically, in some cases rapidly. Other older people remain almost as active and alert as ever, well into their 80s or even 90s.

One common concern of old age is to maintain a sense of dignity and self-esteem. How well older people maintain their dignity depends in large part on how they are treated by their family, their community, and their society (Figure 10.34). Some cultures, including the people of Korea, observe a special ceremony to celebrate a person's retirement or 70th birthday (Damron-Rodriguez, 1991). African-American and Native Ameri-

can families traditionally honor their elders, giving them a position of status and calling upon them for advice. Japanese families follow a similar tradition, at least publicly, although many admit in private that they have a less positive attitude toward the elderly (Koyano, 1991).

Many of the changes that people experience as they grow older are determined by society rather than by biology (Schlossberg, 1984). One of those changes is enforced (or encouraged) retirement. Figure 10.35 shows the percentage of people in the United States who are employed at various ages (U.S. Department of Labor, 1989). For about 40 to 50 years of their life, people spend much of their time at work, taking pride in their accomplishments and enjoying their status. Then sometime between 60 and 70 they face voluntary or mandatory retirement. Many continue to be active, doing volunteer work, taking a part-time job, or even serving as a U.S. senator.

People adjust to retirement in different ways (Atchley, 1980). Those who had a variety of interests and engaged in different activities before retirement usually find the ad-

FIGURE 10.34
In Tibet and many other cultures, children treat old people with respect and honor. Most old people say that maintaining a sense of dignity is very important to them.

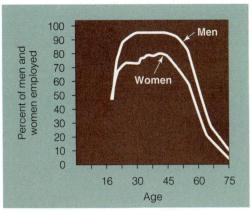

FIGURE 10.35
The percentage of people employed rises and falls as a function of age. These figures include students, patients in hospitals, and others who are not looking for a job. (Based on data from U.S. Department of Labor, 1989.)

justment easiest. Most retirees go through a "honeymoon" period at first, doing all the things they never had time to do before. However, their reborn hopes for great achievement soon fade. Just as many 20-year-olds start out with goals they can never achieve, many 65-year-olds enter retirement with unrealistic expectations. Within a few months or a few years, they experience something similar to the midlife transition, review their prospects, and revise their goals.

It is helpful for old people to maintain some sense of control over their lives even when their health begins to fail. Consider a person who has spent half a century managing a household or running a business. Now he or she may be living in a nursing home where staff members make all the decisions, from scheduling meals to choosing television programs. The loss of control can be frustrating and degrading. If the staff lets the residents make certain choices on their own and perform some tasks by themselves, their health, alertness, and memory tend to improve (Rodin, 1986; Rowe & Kahn, 1987).

THE PSYCHOLOGY OF FACING DEATH

We commonly associate death with old people, although a person can die at any age. Not only do we have trouble dealing with the prospect of our own death, but we also find it difficult to deal with the death of others. Each society provides standards and guidance for how people should deal with

the death of a loved one, and western society has changed its standards over the last hundred years. In the 1800s, the expectation was that the death of a spouse would lead to a "broken heart" and long-lasting grief. Today, society encourages people to recover from the emotional distress and to try to return to normal functioning (Stroebe, Gergen, Gergen, & Stroebe, 1992). As you can imagine, some people find it difficult to follow that advice.

Most people deal with anxiety about their own death by telling themselves that death is far in the future. When they learn they have a fatal disease, they react in special ways. In her book *On Death and Dying*, Elisabeth Kübler-Ross (1969) suggests that dying people go through five stages of adjustment (see Table 10.11).

Kübler-Ross suggests that all dying people progress through these five stages in the same order. Other observers, however, report that dying people may move from stage to stage in any order and may skip some stages altogether. In any case, these stages represent five common ways of coping with the imminent prospect of death.

SOMETHING TO THINK ABOUT

Do Kübler-Ross's stages apply only to people who are dying? Or do people react in similar fashion to lesser losses, such as a poor grade

In the "acceptance" stage of facing death, people take a realistic approach to their impending death. AIDS activist Elizabeth Glaser reached this stage relatively early after learning of her disease; she used the final part of her life productively to inform people of the dangers of AIDS and of the need for better methods of prevention and treatment.

"A man who has not found something he is willing to die for is not fit to live."
MARTIN LUTHER KING, JR.

"This is perhaps the greatest lesson we learned from our patients: LIVE, so you do not have to look back and say, 'God, how I have wasted my life!'"
ELISABETH KÜBLER-ROSS (1975)

"The worst thing about death is the fact that when a man is dead it's impossible any longer to undo the harm you have done him, or to do the good you haven't done him. They say: live in such a way as to be always ready to die. I would say: live in such a way that anyone can die without you having anything to regret."
LEO TOLSTOY (1865/1978, P. 192)

TABLE 10.11
Kübler-Ross's Five Stages of Adjustment to Death

STAGE	BEHAVIOR OR EXPERIENCE OF PEOPLE WHO ARE DYING	CHARACTERISTIC EXPRESSION
Denial	Refuse to acknowledge their condition; may visit several physicians or faith healers in search of someone to restore their health	"No, not me; it cannot be true"
Anger	Criticize and rage at doctors, nurses, and relatives	"Why me?"
Bargaining	Promise good behavior in exchange for the granting of a wish, usually the extension of life; those who do not believe in God may try to strike a bargain with the doctor	"Get me through this, God, and I'll give half my money to the church" or "Doc, give me some medicine that will make me well again, and here's what I'll do for you"
Depression	Sadness at losing what is past and sadness because of impending losses	"All I can do is wait for the bitter end"
Acceptance	Show little emotion of any sort; do not wish to be stirred up by news of the outside world, even by a potential new treatment to prolong life; psychologically ready to die	"The final rest before the long journey"

Source: Based on Kübler-Ross, 1969.

or the loss of a job? Have you ever had a personal experience in which you went through some of these same stages?

SUMMARY

• *Cross-sectional and longitudinal studies.* Psychologists study development by means of cross-sectional studies, which examine people of different ages at the same time, and by means of longitudinal studies, which look at a single group of people at different times as they grow older. Each method has its advantages and disadvantages. (page 429)

• *Cohort effects.* In some cases a difference between young people and old people is not due to age itself but to a cohort effect: The people born in one era differ from those born in a different era. (page 431)

• *Erikson's ages of development.* Erik Erikson described the human life span as a series of eight ages, each with its own social and emotional conflicts. (page 431)

• *Infant attachment.* The attachment of an infant to his or her mother depends on the comfort of physical contact rather than on be-

ing fed. Both infant monkeys and infant humans need social contact and attention if they are to develop normal social behaviors. Different parenting styles are associated with different behavior patterns in the children; the nature of that association appears to vary across ethnic groups. (page 433)

• *Social development of children.* The social development of a child depends on the influences of other children, including brothers and sisters. (page 436)

• *Adolescent identity crisis.* Adolescents have to deal with an identity crisis, the question "Who am I?" Many experiment with several identities before deciding which one seems right. (page 437)

• *Young adults' concerns.* One of the main concerns of young adults is the decision to marry or to establish some other lasting relationship. Many also have to deal with the competing demands of family and career. (page 439)

• *Middle adulthood.* For most adults, satisfaction with life is closely linked with satisfaction on the job. Some adults experience a midlife transition in which they reevaluate their goals. (page 440)

• *Old age.* In old age, people make new adjustments, including the adjustment to retirement. Maintaining dignity and independence is a key concern. (page 442)

- *Facing death*. People at all ages have to face the anxieties associated with the fact that we eventually die. People go through some characteristic reactions when they know that they are likely to die soon. (page 443)

SUGGESTION FOR FURTHER READING

Elkind, D. (1984). *All grown up and no place to go*. Reading, MA: Addison-Wesley. An account of the problems teenagers and young adults face.

TERMS

cross-sectional study a study of groups of individuals of different ages all at the same time (page 429)

longitudinal study a study of a single group of individuals over time (page 429)

cohort a group of people born at a particular time (as compared to people born at different times) (page 431)

basic trust versus mistrust the conflict between trusting and mistrusting that one's parents and other key figures will meet one's basic needs; first conflict in Erikson's eight ages of human development (page 431)

autonomy versus shame and doubt the conflict between independence and doubt about one's abilities (page 431)

initiative versus guilt the conflict between independent behavior and behavior inhibited by guilt (page 432)

industry versus inferiority the conflict between feelings of accomplishment and feelings of worthlessness (page 432)

identity versus role confusion the conflict between the sense of self and the confusion over one's identity (page 432)

intimacy versus isolation the conflict between establishing a long-term relationship with another person and remaining alone (page 432)

generativity versus stagnation the conflict between a productive life and an unproductive life (page 433)

ego integrity versus despair the conflict between satisfaction and dissatisfaction with one's life; final conflict in Erikson's eight ages of human development (page 433)

attachment a long-term feeling of closeness between people, such as a child and a care giver (page 433)

authoritative parents parents who are demanding and impose firm controls, but who are also warm and responsive to the child's communications (page 435)

authoritarian parents parents who set firm controls on their children, generally without explaining the reasons for the rules and without providing much warmth (page 435)

permissive parents parents who are warm and loving but not demanding (page 435)

parallel play simultaneous but independent play, common in young children (page 436)

identity crisis the search for self-understanding (page 437)

identity foreclosure the acceptance of a role that a person's parents prescribe (page 438)

role diffusion experimentation with various roles or identities (page 438)

moratorium a delay in resolving an identity crisis (page 438)

identity achievement the deliberate choice of a role or identity (page 438)

midlife transition a time of reassessment of one's goals (page 441)

ANSWERS TO CONCEPT CHECKS

6. Use a longitudinal study. A longitudinal study studies the same people repeatedly instead of comparing one cohort with another. (page 431)

7. Use a cross-sectional study, comparing people of different ages all in the same year. (page 431)

8. Both the institutions and the Harlows' monkeys failed to provide the social contact necessary for infants to learn how to relate to others. (page 435)

9. In both a midlife transition and an adolescent identity crisis, people reexamine their goals, plan for the future, and decide who they are or who they want to be. (page 442)

GROWING UP THE SAME AND DIFFERENT: TEMPERAMENT, FAMILY, GENDER, AND CULTURAL INFLUENCES

Are people's temperamental differences consistent as they grow older?

How does family life guide children's social and emotional development?

In what ways do boys and girls differ, and why?

How does ethnic identity influence development?

If you had to describe yourself in 200 words or less, what would you say? You would probably mention your age, whether you are male or female, where you live, your main interests and activities, and something about your family. You might mention your political or religious affiliation, if they are important to you. Would you also mention your ethnic identity? Some would; some would not.

The point is this: You are a unique individual, and you are also a member of various identifiable groups. Your group memberships mold what you think of yourself and how other people treat you. You are a complex product of both what you bring to a situation (your personality and temperament) and what a situation does to you. Let us begin with temperament.

TEMPERAMENT AND LIFELONG DEVELOPMENT

People differ markedly in their **temperament**—their tendency to be active or inactive, outgoing or reserved. Would you rather go to a party where you will meet new people, or would you prefer to spend a quiet evening with a few old friends? Do you like to try a new, somewhat risky adventure, or would you prefer to watch while someone else tries it first? In general, are you more impulsive or more reserved than most of the people you know?

Now, the way you just described yourself: Is that the way you have always been, more or less? Or have you changed considerably? Were you at one time a great deal more outgoing and adventurous, or more shy and reserved, than you are now?

According to the research, most people are fairly consistent in their temperament over long periods of time, at least in certain regards. We can begin to measure temperament even before birth. During the last two months before birth, infants differ substantially in their degree of kicking and other movements, and the infants that are most active before birth tend to remain the most active after birth (Eaton & Saudino, 1992).

Jerome Kagan and Nancy Snidman (1991) measured how often 4-month-old infants kicked, how often they cried, and how tense their hands were. A few months later they examined the same infants' responses to mildly frightening situations. (For example, the experimenter might uncover a rotating toy, frown, and scream a nonsense phrase.) Infants who showed the most kicking, crying, and tension at age 4 months tended to show the most fears at ages 9 and 14 months. That is, their temperament was consistent from one test to the next.

As a child grows older, his or her interests change, but an underlying temperament stays fairly constant in most cases.

10. *Was Kagan and Snidman's study longitudinal or cross-sectional? (Check your answer on page 457.)*

Infants who seldom kick, cry, or show fears are called "easy" or "uninhibited" (Thomas & Chess, 1980; Thomas, Chess, & Birch, 1968). Easy infants develop regular sleeping and eating habits, show interest in new people and new objects, and are easily comforted. The kicking, crying, highly fearful infants are, as you might guess, termed "difficult" or "inhibited." Their eating and sleeping habits are irregular, they show frequent signs of tension, and they are hard to comfort (Kagan, 1989). They are also more likely to contract various contagious diseases (Lewis, Thomas, & Worobey, 1990). Evidently, temperament is connected to all aspects of how the body functions. Not all infants fit into either the "inhibited" or "uninhibited" categories; many are intermediate. Some fit the special category "slow to warm up": They withdraw at first from unfamiliar people and new experiences, but after repeated exposures they begin to react positively.

How long do temperaments last? The answer varies. A fair number of infants identified as highly inhibited at the age of 21 months end up as shy, quiet, nervous, and fearful 7½-year-olds (Kagan, Reznick, & Snidman, 1988). Similarly, many uninhibited infants develop into socially interactive, highly talkative 7½-year-olds. However, major changes occur, too; about 10% of uninhibited infants develop into shy 7½-year-olds (Kagan, 1989).

What causes differences in temperament? Genetic differences make some contribution. Monozygotic (identical) twins resemble each other in temperament more than dizygotic (fraternal) twins do (Matheny, 1989). Even monozygotic twins reared in separate and apparently rather different environments generally end up with similar temperaments (Bouchard, Lykken, McGue, Segal, & Tellegen, 1990). Environmental factors obviously play a major role also; otherwise, monozygotic twins would always match each other exactly in temperament.

Heredity and environment can interact in some complex ways to influence temperament. Furthermore, a child's developing temperament can alter the environment, which in turn influences the further development of temperament (Bouchard et al., 1990; Collins & Gunnar, 1990). For example, a child with an uninhibited temperament will meet more people and try more new experiences than an inhibited child will; in doing so, the child learns new skills and develops new behaviors that alter later reactions to new situations.

Most people's temperaments are fairly consistent over time. A reserved, inhibited child will probably continue to be reserved and inhibited for years, perhaps even into adulthood.

THE FAMILY

One of the most powerful influences in the human environment is the family. Children in a loving family gain a sense of security and learn, "I am a lovable person." By playing with brothers, sisters, or other children, they begin to learn social skills. They also learn social skills by observation, especially by watching how their parents relate to each other. How do variations in early family environments affect a child's social and emotional development?

PARENTAL EMPLOYMENT AND CHILD CARE

Styles of infant and child care vary across cultures and across historical eras. For many years, the usual pattern in the United States, Canada, and Europe was for the mother to provide for almost all of an infant's care and companionship, although she might leave the infant alone for a long time while she was in another part of the house. By contrast, in the Efe culture of Africa, a mother is with her infant only about half the day, but the infant is seldom alone. Within the first few months, the infant will establish strong, long-lasting bonds with several adults and children who have shared in providing the infant care (Tronick, Morelli, & Ivey, 1992).

In western society today, most mothers have at least a part-time job; although the pattern is not quite the same as that of the Efe, young children today do develop attachments to several adult care givers. In 1960, only one-fifth of American mothers of preschool children had jobs outside the home. By the 1980s, half or more had jobs (Rubenstein, 1985). When both the father and the mother spend most of the day at work and have only a limited amount of time to spend with their children, what happens to the child?

The results vary. Some mothers of young children work at unsatisfying jobs because they need the money. If they are unhappy about working, they return from work in an unpleasant mood that interferes with their effectiveness as mothers (Lamb, 1982). Other mothers work because they enjoy their careers. They return from work with high self-esteem and make good use of the time they have available with their children. They become role models for their children, who are likely to develop attitudes about the roles of men and women that are less sex-stereotyped than the typical attitudes of children whose mothers have no job outside the home (Hoffman, 1989).

Preschool children in two-paycheck families are left in various day-care arrangements while the parents are at work (Figure 10.36). The effects on the children depend on the quality of the day care and the age of the child. When children less than a year old are entrusted to day-care centers where the staff is indifferent and unstable, the children are likely to feel insecure. If the day care is reasonably good, however, and if the parents provide good attention at night and on weekends, the children seem to develop about as well as children who spend all day with a parent (Scarr, Phillips, & McCartney, 1990). Children who spend much of their first year of life in day care tend to be a bit "bossy" and disobedient, but they also develop self-confidence and social skills in dealing with other children (Clarke-Stewart, 1989).

"NONTRADITIONAL" FAMILIES

The "traditional" family consisted of a mother, a father, and their children. Many people who grew up in a reasonably happy traditional family have thought of such an arrangement as so "right" that anything else must be wrong.

Nevertheless, a large number of children grow up in families significantly different from the traditional model. For example, psychologists have studied the children of unmarried mothers (Weissman, Leaf, & Bruce, 1987), children reared by a gay or lesbian couple (Patterson, 1994), and children of families in which the mother works full-time and the father stays home with the children (Lamb, Frodi, Hwang, & Frodi, 1982; Radin, 1982). In each case, the usual finding is that the children develop normally; one finds no major or consistent personality difference between these children and the children of the more traditional families. To the extent that differences emerge at all, the causes are mostly due to economics: Most unmarried mothers have very limited finances and cannot provide their children with the same opportunities that middle-class children have.

FIGURE 10.36
As you might guess, the effects of day care on children's development depend on the quality of that care; the quality varies enormously within the United States.

PARENTAL CONFLICT AND DIVORCE

At an earlier time in the United States, divorce was unusual and frowned upon. When Adlai Stevenson was defeated in the presidential campaign of 1952, one explanation was that "American voters will never elect a divorced candidate as President." By 1980, when Ronald Reagan was elected president, hardly anyone considered his divorce and remarriage to be an issue at all. Divorce was simply a fact of life.

An estimated 75% of African-American and 38% of European-American children will experience the divorce of their parents before the children reach age 16. Most of those children show a variety of academic, social, and emotional problems, compared to children in two-parent households. One reason is that children in divorced families receive less attention and suffer greater economic hardships. The main reason, however, is that children in divorced families have to endure prolonged conflict and hostility between their parents (Amato & Keith, 1991). If the divorce is completed while the children are still too young to realize what is happening, the effects on the children are milder (Tschann, Johnston, Kline, & Wallerstein, 1990).

Mavis Hetherington and her associates have conducted longitudinal studies of middle-class elementary-school children and their families following divorce (Hetherington, 1989; Hetherington, Cox, & Cox, 1982). In each case, the mother had custody of the children. Hetherington found that most of the children and many of the parents suffered considerable upheaval after the divorce, especially during the first year.

During this first year the children resorted to pouting and seeking attention. They were generally angry about their parents' divorce, and they let the parents know about it. Many of the mothers had very difficult relationships with their sons; one exasperated divorced mother described the relationship as "like getting bitten to death by ducks." Boys in particular became very aggressive toward other children, and much of their aggressive behavior was unprovoked and ineffective (Figure 10.37). After 2 years they became better adjusted, but by then they had been rejected by their peers. Boys who changed schools after the first year managed to escape their reputation and make a fresh start.

The degree of distress varied from one child to another. Generally, a child's distress was greater if the mother had not worked before the divorce and had taken a job immedi-

FIGURE 10.37
Sons of divorced parents often go through a period in which they act out their frustrations by starting fights.

ately afterward—often an economic necessity. The children in such families felt they had lost both their parents. In the studies by Hetherington and her associates, boys showed more distress and more negative behavior than girls did, partly because the mothers retained custody of the children. When the father had custody, the boys reacted better than the girls did (Santrock, Warshak, & Elliott, 1982). (However, because many other factors are at work, we cannot conclude that a father should always be granted custody of sons or that a mother should always be granted custody of daughters.)

In families in which the mother remarried, girls generally had more trouble accepting the stepfather than boys did. Hetherington (1989) found that many of the girls rejected every attempt their stepfathers made to establish a positive relationship; eventually the stepfather simply gave up. When stepfathers were asked to name all the "members of your family," most did not even mention their stepdaughters.

Hetherington's studies concentrated on European-American middle-class children, and the results are somewhat different for other cultures. Divorce is more common in African-American families, and in most cases less stressful (Fine & Schwebel, 1987). Apparently, most African-American families accept the idea of single parenthood better than most European-American families do. In addition, many African-American families ease the burden of single parenthood by having a grandmother or other relative share in the child care. As in European-American families, the more upset the mother is by the divorce, the more upset the children are likely to be (Phillips & Alcebo, 1986).

To almost any generalization about the effects of divorce on children, exceptions can be found (Hetherington, Stanley-Hagan, & Anderson, 1989). Some children show emotional distress for a year or two and then gradually feel better. Others continue to act depressed 5 or 10 years after the divorce. A few seem to do well for a while and then show signs of distress years later, especially during adolescence. Some children are amazingly resilient throughout their parents' divorce and afterward. They keep their friends; they do all right in school; they maintain good relationships with both parents. Generally these are children who were well adjusted before the divorce and whose parents displayed a minimum of conflict toward each other (Hetherington, 1989; Kline, Tschann, Johnston, & Wallerstein, 1989).

Given the emotional trauma commonly associated with divorce, should parents stick together? Staying together is not always a workable solution. Children who grow up in households in which the parents are constantly in conflict develop emotional problems similar to those of children in divorced families (Emery, 1982). Indeed, most children (especially boys) in divorced families begin to show signs of distress years *before* the divorce itself, perhaps in response to the parental conflict they already see (Cherlin et al., 1991).

■ THE INFLUENCE OF GENDER

In what ways would you be different if you had been born female instead of male, or male instead of female? We all have certain impressions of how boys act differently from girls, and men from women. But how many of those impressions are correct, how many are exaggerations, and how many are simply false? Remember the phenomenon of *illusory correlations* from Chapter 2: We tend to remember most clearly the examples that fit some pattern we expect to find; we therefore convince ourselves that our expectations were correct. Sex differences do oc-

cur, but we have to base our conclusions on systematic data, not casual impressions.

SEX DIFFERENCES IN BEHAVIOR

In 1974, Eleanor Maccoby and Carol Jacklin published an extensive review of the literature on sex differences in behavior. They concluded that the evidence supported a few generalizations. For example, females tend to perform better on certain aspects of language use, whereas males tend to perform better on certain mathematical and visual-spatial tasks. Those differences are marked in adolescents and adults, but doubtful in children. In addition, males tend to fight more. Sex differences in other aspects of behavior were possible, but not clear from the evidence (Maccoby & Jacklin, 1974).

Maccoby and Jacklin's review drew two kinds of criticisms. First, some argued that they had ignored or understated many behavioral differences between the sexes: On the average, men swear more than women. Women tend to know more than men do about flowers. Men and women generally carry books and packages in different ways (Figure 10.38). A list of miscellaneous differences could go on.

FIGURE 10.38
One of many poorly understood differences between the sexes: Beyond the age of puberty, most males carry packages at their side, whereas females carry them in an elevated position.

FIGURE 10.39

One girl tested alone behaves about the same as one boy tested alone. But when boys play together, they "show off" to one another and to other observers.

Second, others argued that Maccoby and Jacklin had overstated the differences, and that in fact males and females hardly differ at all. According to this point of view, boys and girls—and men and women—act differently only because our society tells them to. (Actually, even if true, this is not a fair criticism of Maccoby and Jacklin, who were trying to *describe* the differences, not to *explain* them.)

Much time has passed since Maccoby and Jacklin's 1974 review. Most of the same conclusions still hold, although we must modify them somewhat (Maccoby, 1990). For example, the advantage of females on verbal tasks seems to have faded (for reasons unknown). New evidence has indicated that women are, on the average, more easily influenced by other people's opinions. (Depending on your point of view, you could say that women are more "conformist" or that men are more "stubborn.") New evidence also indicates sex differences in helping behavior. It is not a simple case of one sex being more helpful than the other; men and women tend to help in different ways. For example, men are generally more likely to help a stranger change a flat tire; women are more likely to help people who need long-term nurturing support (Eagly & Crowley, 1986).

Sex Differences in Social Situations It is now clear that certain important differences between males and females emerge only in a social context (Maccoby, 1990). Psychologists ordinarily test people in isolation. When tested one at a time, boys and girls tend to behave about the same in most regards. However, in a group setting, boys usually get together with other boys while girls get together with other girls; suddenly the two groups act very differently (Figure 10.39).

Girls sometimes play competitive games, but they are more likely than boys to spend long times at quiet, cooperative play. They take turns; they present their desires as "suggestions" instead of demands; they exchange compliments; and they generally try to avoid hurting each other's feelings.

Meanwhile, boys are almost always competing with each other. They compete even when they are just talking: They shout orders, they interrupt, they make threats and boasts, and they exchange insults. Their play is often rough and aggressive and almost always competitive. When elementary-school boys play baseball, sooner or later they have some dispute about the rules; invariably they work out some compromise and continue playing, but they may continue screaming "you cheater" or "you liar" while they continue playing. Still, when the game is over, they almost always part as friends.

When they grow up, do boys change their way of interacting with one another? Not entirely. Deborah Tannen (1990) reports one episode at a college basketball game: At the University of Michigan, student tickets have seat numbers on them, but students generally ignore those assignments and take seats on a first-come, first-served basis. One night several men from the visiting team, Michigan State, tried to go to the seats listed on their tickets, only to find some University of Michigan students already seated there, including both men and women. The Michigan State students asked the others to get out of their seats; the men in those seats then replied rudely, and the dispute quickly grew loud, heated, and insulting. The women with these men were mortified.

Within a few minutes, however, the Michigan State men settled into seats next to the University of Michigan students, and before long the two sets of men were happily discussing basketball strategies. The women didn't understand why the men had screamed insults at each other in the first place, much less why they had made friends so quickly afterwards.

MALE-FEMALE RELATIONSHIPS IN CHILDHOOD AND ADULTHOOD

What do you suppose happens when boys and girls play together? If they are working on a task that requires cooperation, few sex differences are evident (Powlishta & Maccoby, 1990). However, in an unsupervised situation with no need to cooperate, the boys often dominate and intimidate the girls. In some cases, the boys take control and the girls simply watch (Maccoby, 1990).

When boys and girls become young men and women, romantic interests may draw them together. Both are ill prepared to deal with the other sex. Men are used to demanding their way; women are used to a cooperative give-and-take. Men worry about their status in relation to other men; women often do not understand these status contests. When women discuss their problems, they expect their listeners to express sympathy; men often do not understand this need. Here are some examples of the resultant misunderstanding (Tannen, 1990):

• A man invites an out-of-town friend to spend the night in a guest bedroom. The man's wife is upset that her husband did not check with her before inviting his friend. He replies that he would feel embarrassed to say "I have to ask my wife first."

• A woman asks her husband to get their VCR to record television movies. The husband says this particular kind of VCR plays tapes but cannot record. The woman then asks their next-door neighbor to check the VCR. He too tells her the VCR cannot record tapes. The husband remains angry about this episode for years, because his wife implied he was incompetent to understand their VCR.

• A woman who has breast surgery tells her husband she is unhappy about the scar left by the surgery. Instead of expressing sympathy, he replies, "You can have plastic surgery. . . ." She is upset with the implication that he doesn't like the way she looks. He replies that he doesn't care about the scar; he was trying to help because *she* said she was unhappy.

Are male-female relationships always like this? Of course not. Men are not all the same, and neither are women. The point is that the sexes differ on the average, and that men and women need to work at understanding one another's point of view.

GENDER ROLES

Given that men and women differ on the average in many social behaviors, the question is: Why? Chances are, there are several reasons. Biology is probably one factor. Competition among males for status is extremely widespread in the animal kingdom; it is probably part of our basic nature. People are also molded by culture. Even if males are biologically predisposed to be more aggressive or females to be more cooperative, their culture channels the ways they express those tendencies.

In one way or another, each society prepares boys for the tasks expected of men and prepares women for the tasks expected of women. That is, it teaches them their *gender role*. A gender role is the psychological aspect of being male or female, as opposed to sex, which is the biological aspect. **Gender role** is the role each person is expected to play because of being male or female.

When we say that "society" teaches children their gender role, we do not necessarily mean that *parents* teach children their gender role, or that *anyone* teaches gender roles deliberately or intentionally. Parents do dress boys differently from girls, give them different toys, and offer them different kinds of

Children learn their gender roles partly from their parents. But parents who try to treat their sons and daughters alike discover that children also learn roles from other children.

experiences (Figure 10.40). The choice of toys in turn determines how much the parents talk with the children while they are playing. When parents and their children play with dolls, they talk a great deal; when they play with cars and trucks, they talk less (O'Brien & Nagle, 1987). Adults also teach gender roles by example. Boys tend to imitate their father, and girls tend to imitate their mother. Television presents certain images of what men and women do. Children also pay attention to role models outside the home. For instance, a girl who goes to a female pediatrician may think of becoming a doctor herself.

However, in our society, most adults do *not* teach boys that they are supposed to fight with one another. In fact, they usually try to curb the fighting. Little boys tend to be bossy and aggressive toward little girls if they think no adults are watching; with an adult present, they become more cooperative (Powlishta & Maccoby, 1990).

And yet, clearly, little boys do learn to compete and fight with one another, even if adults are trying to teach them to stop. From whom are boys learning this part of their gender role? Quite simply, they learn it from other children. Children have a "playground culture" of their own; each cohort of children teaches the slightly younger set

what is expected of them. Even parents who try to raise their sons and daughters without gender roles find that their children come back from the playground with strong prejudices about what boys do and what girls do.

Gender roles interact with biology. For example, consider boys' tendency to fight more than girls do. Assuming that boys have, on the average, at least a slight biological predisposition to be aggressive and competitive, boys learn by observation on the playground that other boys tend to be aggressive. To get along in that environment, they have to learn to compete, and what they learn in turn augments their biological predisposition.

In many cases, of course, gender roles have no close relationship with biology. In western society, tradition tells us that women should wear their hair longer than men, that women will do more of the cooking, and that men will try to repair cars and other machinery. Such arbitrary gender distinctions vary drastically from one society to another (Figure 10.41) and from one time to another in a given society. In the United States of the early 20th century, women could not vote, few attended college, and employment opportunities for women were very limited. In a period of decades all those customs and more have

FIGURE 10.41
Gender roles vary greatly from one culture to another. In the United States, gender roles are more flexible now than they once were. Many women hold jobs previously reserved for men.

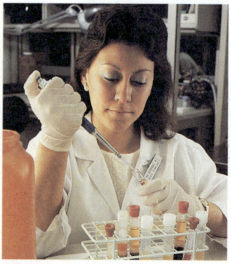

changed. Our biology does not dictate our customs.

Gender roles are not necessarily harmful in all cases, but they sometimes limit the choices children feel will be open to them in later life. Imagine an artistically inclined boy who is told that "real men like sports, not art." Or imagine a girl who wants to become an electrical engineer until someone tells her that "engineering is not a good career for a woman." Ideally, children (and adults) should feel free to develop their own interests and their own talents, whatever they may be.

CONCEPT CHECK

11. *Which of the following (if any) are examples of people following gender roles? (Check your answer on page 457.)*
   a. *A woman's ability to nurse a baby*
   b. *A boy's interest in playing football*
   c. *A girl's interest in ballet*
   d. *A man's beard growth*

ETHNIC AND CULTURAL INFLUENCES

Membership in a minority group molds a child's development in two major ways. First, the customs of the minority group may in fact differ from those of other groups. For example, compared to most other parents, Japanese parents lavish more attention on their infants and teach their children a greater emphasis on educational achievement and on bringing honor to one's family (Yamamoto & Kubota, 1983). Second, members of a minority group are affected by the attitudes of other people, who may treat them differently or expect different behavior from them simply because they are members of that minority group.

Immigrants to the United States or any other country undergo a period of **acculturation,** a transition from feeling part of the culture of their original country to being at ease in the culture of their adopted country. Acculturation is gradual; people sometimes require a generation or more before they or their descendants feel fully comfortable in a new culture.

In many cases, a person may have to function as a member of two or more cultures or subcultures. For example, people who settle in an Italian-American community may speak Italian and follow Italian customs in their home neighborhood but speak English and follow American customs elsewhere. African Americans and Asian Americans may identify strongly with their ethnic group, live in a neighborhood populated mostly by others of the same group, and rely on the help of an extended family, while also being part of the "melting-pot" American culture at school, on the job, and in other settings. To at least a small extent, all of us learn to function in a variety of subcultures. For example, you enter slightly different subcultures at home, at college, on the job, at a religious ceremony, and so forth. You learn to adjust what you say and do depending on the setting and the people around you. However, while everyone has this experience to some extent, the transitions are more noticeable and more intense for ethnic minority members.

People react to these transitions in different ways. Some minority group members become more or less completely assimilated into the majority or melting-pot culture. However, they may feel a cost in doing so. For example, some high-achieving African-American students worry that their school and occupational success may alienate them from other African Americans, that "if you

Immigrants to a country go through a gradual, sometimes difficult process of acculturation into the customs of the new country. Their children are likely to become much more thoroughly acculturated.

succeed, you're betraying your color" (Fordham, 1988).

An alternative to full assimilation is **biculturalism,** an ability to alternate between membership in one culture and in another. Although doing so is difficult, many people succeed. The advantages of biculturalism are similar to those of bilingualism: A bilingual person (one who speaks two languages) can communicate with more people and read a greater variety of literature than can a monolingual person. Also, bilingual people come to understand their primary language from a new perspective, and often become more sensitive to the multiple meanings of a word. Similarly, a bicultural person can speak with and deal with a great variety of other people and may become more aware of both the strengths and the weaknesses of each culture (Harrison, Wilson, Pine, Chan, & Buriel, 1990; LaFromboise, Coleman, & Gerton, 1993).

▌ CLOSING COMMENTS

Each of us can easily fall into the trap of thinking that her or his own way of growing up and of relating to other people is the "right" way, the "normal" way. In fact, people differ substantially in their social development; we have examined some of the major reasons—temperament, family influences, gender, and ethnic and cultural identity. As a society, we are coming both to recognize and to appreciate the resulting diversity of behavior.

SUMMARY

- *Temperament.* Even infants only a few months old show clear differences in temperament, their characteristic way of reacting to new experiences and new people. Temperament is fairly consistent as a person grows older. (page 446)
- *Changes in the U.S. family.* As U.S. society has changed over the decades, the role of women has changed and therefore family life has changed. The research suggests that children who spend much of their early life in a day-care arrangement can develop without difficulties, provided that the day care is of good quality. Most children in nontraditional families develop normally, except for the effects of

the poverty that is common among unmarried mothers. (page 447)
- *Effects of divorce.* Children of divorcing families often show signs of distress, sometimes even before the divorce. The distress is generally more marked in European-American families than in African-American families. (page 448)
- *Male-female differences.* Behavioral differences between males and females are small, on the average, when people are tested one at a time. However, in social settings males tend to associate with other males while females associate with females. Males tend to be more competitive, sometimes aggressively. (page 450)
- *Gender roles.* Men and women differ in their behavior partly as a result of gender roles, the behaviors each society specifies for men and for women. (page 452)
- *Ethnic and cultural differences.* People also differ because of ethnic and cultural influences. Acculturation is the process of transition from one culture to another. Many people can function successfully as members of two or more cultures. (page 455)

SUGGESTIONS FOR FURTHER READING

Hetherington, E. M. (1989). Coping with family transitions: Winners, losers, and survivors. *Child Development, 60,* 1–14. Review of the effects of divorce on children.

Maccoby, E. E. (1990). Gender and relationships. *American Psychologist, 45,* 513–520. Review of findings concerning sex differences in social behavior.

Powell, G. J. (Ed.) (1983). *The psychosocial development of minority group children* (pp. 237–247). New York: Brunner/Mazel. Description of research on the psychological effects of minority-group membership.

Tannen, D. (1990). *You just don't understand.* New York: William Morrow. A popular book discussing the ways in which men and women fail to understand one another.

TERMS

temperament people's tendency to be active or inactive, outgoing or reserved (page 446)

gender role the role each person is expected to play because of being male or female (page 452)

acculturation transition from feeling part of the culture of one's original country to the culture of one's adopted country (page 455)

biculturalism alternation between membership in one culture and membership in another (page 456)

Answers to Concept Checks

10. Kagan and Snidman's study was longitudinal; they studied the same children at more than one age. (page 447)

11. A boy who becomes interested in football and a girl who becomes interested in ballet are examples of people following gender roles. The other two are not. (Gender roles are psychological, not physical.) (page 455)

11

MOTIVATION

NASA is searching for a volunteer to make a solo trip to Mars. If you volunteer, you will journey for two or three years in a small, uncomfortable spacecraft, eating synthetic food and having no human companionship. You will have about a 20% chance of coming back to Earth alive. What you are offered in return is a chance to be the first human being to set foot on Mars. How would you respond to this opportunity? When I pose this question to large groups of students, most decline, but at least a few say they are ready to volunteer.

If we assume that humans are rational beings who try to maximize their probability

How motivated would you be to get into The Guinness Book of World Records *as the person covered with the largest number of bees?*

of surviving and passing on their genes, then volunteering for that trip to Mars does not make a whole lot of sense. Neither does it make sense to risk one's life for a political or religious cause. And yet many people do. For many people, various abstract goals take priority over all of their practical goals, such as surviving and reproducing. Why? How do these abstract goals become so strong, and why are they so much stronger for some people than for others?

A great deal about human motivation is puzzling. Unfortunately, it will still be puzzling by the end of this chapter. This chapter deals with some of the better-understood aspects of motivation. We begin with an overview of some general principles of motivation. Then we shall explore three examples of motivated behaviors: hunger, sexual activity, and striving for achievement.

I have selected these examples for emphasis, largely because they are an important part of human life but also because they illustrate how our biology interacts with the social setting. Hunger is based on a biological need, but what, when, and how much we eat also depends on what we learn from other people. Sexual motivation also serves a biological need, but the search for a suitable partner is fundamentally a social behavior. Striving for achievement is learned as a method of pleasing and impressing others. Although it is primarily a social motivation, it is an outgrowth of the competition for dominance that we can observe throughout the animal kingdom.

GENERAL PRINCIPLES OF MOTIVATION

What is motivation?

How could a psychologist determine whether or not an act is motivated?

You are sitting quietly, reading a book, when suddenly you hear a loud noise. You jump a little and gasp. Was that action motivated? "No," you say. "I jumped involuntarily." Now I tell you that I want to do a little experiment. I shall tap my pencil; as soon as you hear it, you should try to jump and gasp just as you did the first time. I tap my pencil and, sure enough, you jump and gasp—not exactly as you did the first time, but approximately so. Was that action motivated? "Yes," you reply.

In both cases, I accept your answer. If I had not asked you whether or not your behavior was motivated, or if I did not trust your answer, could I have figured it out any other way? Remember, your motivated behavior and your unmotivated behavior looked about the same. We cannot always trust people's self-reports. Someone accused of murder says, "I didn't mean to kill. It was an accident." Your friend, who promised to drive you somewhere and then left without you, says, "I didn't do it on purpose. I just forgot." Maybe so and maybe not. How do we decide whether or not a behavior is motivated? We need a clear understanding of how motivated behaviors differ from unmotivated behaviors.

▮ VIEWS OF MOTIVATION

What is motivation? Let's try some definitions: "Motivation is what activates and directs behavior." Will that do? That descrip-

tion fits motivation fairly well, but it also fits some other, nonmotivational phenomena. For example, light activates and directs the growth of plants, but we would hardly say that light "motivates" plants.

"Motivation is what makes our behavior more vigorous and energetic." That definition ignores some important motivational phenomena. For example, some people are strongly motivated to lie motionless for hours on end.

How about this: "Motivation is what changes one's preferences or choices"? That might do, except that we would first have to define preference and choice.

To be honest, it is hard to state precisely what we mean by motivation. Psychologists have repeatedly altered their views of motivation. By considering one theory after another, they have seen the shortcomings of each and have developed some idea of what is and is not motivation.

MOTIVATION AS AN ENERGY

Motivation, which comes from the same root as *motion,* is literally something that "moves" a person. So we might think of it as a type of energy. Sigmund Freud, the founder of psychoanalysis, proposed that the human nervous system is a reservoir of **libido,** a kind of sexual energy. As libido builds up, it demands an outlet, like air in an overinflated balloon or hot water trapped under a geyser. If its normal outlet is blocked, it will discharge itself through some other channel. Freud used this concept to explain why people who are unable to release their libido in a normal way sometimes engage in irrational, self-defeating behaviors. If, for example, you had an impulse or an energy for engaging in some forbidden sex act, it might manifest itself in the form of nervous twitches (Freud, 1908/1963).

Konrad Lorenz, a pioneer in the field of ethology (the study of animal behavior under natural conditions), proposed a similar theory. According to Lorenz (1950), animals engage in instinctive acts when specific energies reach a critical level. For example, a male stickleback fish outside the breeding season has no specific energy for mating, and it will not respond sexually. At the start of the breeding season, it has a small amount of mating energy and it will court female stickleback fish, as well as attack male stickleback fish. At the height of the breeding season, it has a great amount of mating energy and it

will court females vigorously; it may even respond sexually to a piece of wood painted to resemble a female of its species.

Figure 11.1 illustrates Lorenz's model. A specific kind of energy builds up in the reservoir and flows into the tray below. The outlets in that tray represent ways of releasing the energy. If conditions are right, the energy is released through the lowest outlet—for example, mating with a normal partner. If that outlet is blocked and energy continues to build up, the energy will spill through one of the higher, less preferred outlets.

Both Freud and Lorenz based their theories on a conception of the nervous system that is now obsolete. They believed that every impulse to action had to be carried out in one way or another. We now know that an individual can simply inhibit the impulses for a disadvantageous behavior.

DRIVE THEORIES

Closely related to the instinctive energy theories, such as those of Freud and Lorenz, are theories that describe motivation as a **drive,** an internal state of unrest or irritation that energizes one behavior after another until one of them removes the irritation (Hull, 1943). For example, when you get a splinter in your finger, the discomfort motivates you to engage in various actions until you get rid of the splinter.

According to *drive-reduction theory,* popular among psychologists of an earlier

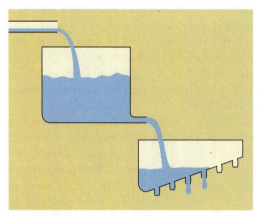

FIGURE 11.1
According to Konrad Lorenz, energy (represented as a fluid) builds up in a "reservoir" in the brain; it needs to be discharged. Ordinarily, an instinct is released through natural or preferred outlets. If those are blocked, however, energy spills into another outlet, and the animal engages in an irrelevant behavior. (After Lorenz, 1950.)

era, animals including humans strive to reduce their needs and drives as much as possible. That is, they eat to reduce their hunger, drink to reduce their thirst, have sexual relations to reduce their sex drive, and so forth. This view implies that one's ideal condition is to have no unmet needs or drives; an individual in this state would become completely inactive.

The primary shortcoming of drive theory is that it implies that people (and other animals) always try to reduce their drives and thereby their level of stimulation. In fact, we all seek variety and activity in our lives; the ideal state is one with a moderate amount of stimulation, not one with as little as possible.

Another flaw in drive theory is that it ignores the role of external stimulation. For example, a person's interest in food depends not only on hunger (an internal drive) but also on what foods are available. Similarly, interest in sex depends partly on an internal drive and partly on the presence or absence of a suitable partner.

HOMEOSTASIS

An important advance from the idea of drive reduction is the concept of **homeostasis,** the maintenance of an optimum level of biological conditions within an organism (Cannon, 1929). The idea of homeostasis recognizes that we are motivated to seek a state of equilibrium, not to reduce all drives and stimuli to zero. For example, people maintain a body temperature of about 37 °C (98.6 °F) through a combination of physiological and behavioral means. We fight against both increases and decreases in body temperature. Each of us also works to maintain a fairly steady body weight, a nearly constant amount of water in the body, a reasonably stable level of sensory stimulation, and so on.

Unlike a rock, which remains static only because nothing is acting on it, the homeostasis of the body is more like a spinning top; someone has to apply additional energy from time to time to keep it spinning. For example, we maintain constant body temperature partly by shivering, sweating, and other involuntary physiological responses and partly by putting on extra clothing, taking off excess clothing, or finding a more comfortable location.

Motivated behaviors of humans differ from the actions of a home thermostat control in one important regard: Human behav-

We eat because of both intrinsic and extrinsic motivations. Even when the hunger (an intrinsic motivation) is satisfied, we eat because of the taste and the desire to socialize (extrinsic motivations).

ior often acts in anticipation of future needs. For example, you might eat a large breakfast some morning, even though you are not hungry, just because you know that you are going to be too busy to stop for lunch. If you are angry or frightened, you begin to sweat even before you begin the vigorous actions that might heat your body. (We call this phenomenon a "cold sweat.") Thus, one promising description of motivation is to say that it maintains current homeostasis and anticipates future needs to maintain future homeostasis (Appley, 1991).

Still, even that conception of motivation overlooks the power of new stimuli to arouse motivated behaviors. For example, nonhungry people may eat or drink just to be sociable or because someone has offered them something especially tasty.

INCENTIVE THEORIES

Why do people ride roller coasters? It is doubtful that they have any special need to go thundering down a steep decline. Or suppose you have just finished a big meal and someone offers you a slice of a very special cake. If you are like most people, you eat it—but hardly because you need it. Evidently, motivation includes more than the internal forces that push us toward certain behaviors; it also includes incentives—external stimuli that *pull* us toward certain actions.

The distinction between a drive and an incentive is not clear-cut. Jumping into a swimming pool on a hot summer day may satisfy your biological drive to maintain normal body temperature, but the prospect of

splashing around in the water may serve as a strong incentive as well.

Most motivated behaviors are controlled by a combination of drives and incentives. You eat because you are hungry (a drive) and because you see appealing food in front of you (an incentive). How much you eat depends on both the strength of the drive and the appeal of the incentive.

INTRINSIC AND EXTRINSIC MOTIVATIONS

Similar to the distinction between drives and incentives is the differentiation psychologists make between intrinsic motivations and extrinsic motivations. An intrinsic motivation is a motivation to engage in an act for its own sake; an extrinsic motivation is based on the rewards and punishments the act may bring. For example, if you eat because you are hungry, you are following an intrinsic motivation; if you eat something you don't like in order to please the cook, you are following an extrinsic motivation. Most of our behavior is motivated by a combination of intrinsic and extrinsic motivations. An artist paints partly for the joy of creation (intrinsic) and partly for the eventual profit (extrinsic). You read this book partly because you enjoy reading it (I hope) and partly because you want to get a good grade in the course.

Does a combination of intrinsic and extrinsic motivations lead to more persistent and effective performance than an intrinsic motivation alone? Not always. In a classic

Why would someone devote enormous time and energy to building up muscles, as Arnold Schwarzenegger has? We assume such people have both intrinsic and extrinsic motivations. An intrinsic motivation is the enjoyment of exercising and bodybuilding for their own sake. An extrinsic motivation is to obtain the attention and admiration of other people.

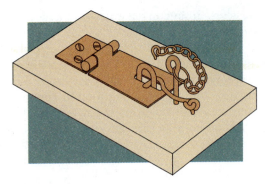

FIGURE 11.2
Monkeys learned to open this device by removing the pin, the hook, and the hasp, in that order. At first they received no reward, opening the device just for the fun of it. When a raisin was placed (as an extrinsic motivation) in the device, their performance deteriorated. Evidently in some cases an individual performs better with just intrinsic motivation (here, the joy of the task itself) than with a combination of intrinsic and extrinsic motivations.

study, researchers gave four monkeys a device like the one in Figure 11.2 to play with. To open it, a monkey had to remove the pin, lift the hook, and lift the hasp, in that order. The monkeys played with the device from time to time over a period of 10 days. They received no reinforcements; they played with it apparently just for the fun of it (an intrinsic motivation). By the end of the 10 days, each monkey was able to open the device quickly, almost never getting the steps out of order. Then the device was placed over a food well in a place where the monkeys were accustomed to finding a raisin (an extrinsic motivation). If they opened the device they could get it. Suddenly their ability to open the device deteriorated. Instead of patiently removing the pin, the hook, and the hasp as they had done before, they attacked the hasp forcefully. They took longer to open the device for food than they had for play. Later, when they were given the device by itself with no food available, they opened it less frequently than before and made more errors in their attempts (Harlow, Harlow, & Meyer, 1950). Evidently, opening the device for food had become work, and the monkeys no longer saw it as play.

The same principle applies to human behavior: If people are given extrinsic reinforcements just for participating in an interesting activity, they lose interest in that activity, at least temporarily. For example, college students in one experiment were asked to try to arrange seven plastic pieces

with complex shapes to match figures in a drawing. At one point halfway through the experiment, students in the experimental group were paid $1 for each correct match. (Students in the control group did not know that the experimental group was being paid.) Then the experiment continued without pay for anyone. So long as the students in the experimental group were being paid, they worked harder than the students in the control group. After pay was suspended, the experimental group worked less than the control group did (Deci, 1971). Results such as these illustrate the **overjustification effect**: When people are given more extrinsic motivation than necessary to perform a task, their intrinsic motivation declines. According to one interpretation, people ask themselves, "Why am I doing this task?" They answer, "It's not because I enjoy the task. It's because I'm being paid." Once the extrinsic motivation is removed, the task seems uninteresting. The overjustification effect has been reported in a variety of settings, among both children and adults (Kassin & Lepper, 1984).

The overjustification effect has its limits, however (Deci & Ryan, 1991). Paying people to do something they enjoy does not always undermine their enjoyment of it or their intrinsic motivation to improve their performance. In many cases parents have to offer children some sort of inducement to get them to finish their homework, clean their room, or do some other task, and nevertheless the children may eventually "internalize" the motivation and enjoy performing the task without further inducement. Similarly, many adult workers enjoy their work, strive for excellence at it, and try to help their organization even in ways that earn them no bonuses. The overall message is not that extrinsic motivation for a task always damages intrinsic motivation. (Sometimes it does; sometimes it does not, depending on a variety of conditions.) Rather, the more dependable message is that if someone is already performing a task for an intrinsic motivation, adding an extrinsic motivation is not likely to improve performance.

Table 11.1 summarizes four views of motivation.

CONCEPT CHECK

1. Given the overjustification effect, would you expect retired professional players to enjoy playing tennis more or less than other

TABLE 11.1
Four Views of Motivation

VIEW	BASIC POSITION	MAJOR WEAKNESSES
Instinct theories  *According to instinct theories, motivation is a kind of energy that builds up until it finds a release.*	Motivations are energies that accumulate; each energy specifies a preferred action, although it might spill over into a less preferred outlet.	Based on obsolete view of the nervous system.
Drive theories  *According to drive theories, motivation is an irritation that continues until we find some way to reduce it.*	Motivations are based on needs or irritations that we try to reduce; they do not specify particular actions.	Implies that we always try to reduce stimulation, never to increase it. Also overlooks importance of external stimuli.
Homeostasis (plus anticipation)  *Homeostasis is the process of maintaining some variable, such as body temperature, within a set range.*	Motivations tend to maintain body states near some optimum, intermediate level. They may anticipate future needs as well as react to current needs.	Overlooks importance of external stimuli.
Incentive theories  *Incentives are external stimuli that attract us, even if we have no biological need for them.*	Motivations are responses to attractive stimuli.	Incomplete unless combined with drive or homeostasis.

people do? *(Check your answer on page 469.)*

TYPES OF MOTIVATIONS

How many motivations do people have? They are motivated to obtain food, water, shelter, clothing, companionship, sexual activity. . . . The list could go on. Can we group these into a few coherent categories?

PRIMARY AND SECONDARY MOTIVATIONS

One way to categorize motivations is to distinguish primary motivations from secondary motivations. Primary motivations—such as the desire for food and water—serve obvious biological needs. Secondary motivations develop as a result of specific learning experiences; they do not serve any biological need directly, although they may lead indirectly to the satisfaction of primary motiva-

TABLE 11.2
Four Lists of Primary Motivations

W. McDOUGALL (1932)	P. T. YOUNG (1936)	H. A. MURRAY (1938)	K. B. MADSEN (1959)
Food seeking	Hunger	Inspiration	Hunger
Disgust	Nausea	Water	Thirst
Sex	Thirst	Food	Sex
Fear	Sex	Sentience	Nursing
Curiosity	Nursing	Sex	Temperature
Protective/parental	Urinating	Lactation	Pain avoidance
Gregarious	Defecating	Expiration	Excretion
Self-assertive	Avoiding heat	Urination	Oxygen
Submissive	Avoiding cold	Defecation	Rest/sleep
Anger	Avoiding pain	Pain avoidance	Activity
Appeal	Air	Heat avoidance	Security
Constructive	Fear/anger	Cold avoidance	Aggression
Acquisitive	Fatigue	Harm avoidance	
Laughter	Sleep		
Comfort	Curiosity		
Rest/sleep	Social instinct		
Migratory	Tickle		
Coughing/breathing			

Note: I have rephrased some of the words in more familiar language—for example, *pain avoidance* instead of *noxavoidance*.

tions. Primary motivations and secondary motivations are analogous to *unconditioned reinforcers* and *conditioned reinforcers,* discussed in Chapter 7.

Presumably, we learn secondary motivations because they help us to satisfy primary motivations. For example, we learn a desire for money (a secondary motivation) because it helps us to obtain food, water, and shelter (primary motivations). In some cases, however, a secondary motivation seems to develop a momentum of its own, becoming apparently independent of the original primary motivations associated with it. For example, someone may start collecting coins or stamps (a secondary motivation) in hopes of making a profit or because the collection leads to praise from other coin or stamp enthusiasts. Eventually some collectors devote enormous money and effort to their collections, demonstrating that they have become interested in the stamps for their own sake and not just as a means to make money or impress friends.

People may have an unlimited number of secondary motivations. Because the biological needs of the body are limited, psychologists expect to find only a limited number of primary motivations. Table 11.2 presents four examples of psychologists' attempts to list all the primary motivations.

CONCEPT CHECK

2. *Is your interest in graduating from college a primary motivation or a secondary motivation? (Check your answer on page 469.)*

MASLOW'S HIERARCHY OF NEEDS

If you study the lists in Table 11.2 closely, you may see the complexity of the task. Each list includes one or more debatable entries, and none of them seems complete. Moreover, none of these lists has any structure or organization. Wouldn't it make sense to group certain motivations together, such as the different kinds of avoidance? And shouldn't some motivations be distinguished as more important, or at least more urgent, than others?

Abraham Maslow (1970) attempted to bring some organization to the listing of human motivations, including both primary and secondary motivations. According to Maslow, our behavior is governed by a **hierarchy of needs**. The most basic are the physiological needs for food, drink, oxygen, and temperature, as shown at the bottom level of Figure 11.3. Maslow holds that these basic needs ordinarily take priority over all others (Figure 11.4). For example, people who are gasping for breath will not take time out to do something else until they have satisfied their need for oxygen. Once people have satisfied all of their physiological needs, they seek to satisfy their safety needs, such as security from attack and avoidance of pain. When those needs are satisfied, they proceed to the needs for love and belonging—making friends and socializing with them. Next come the needs for esteem, such as gaining prestige and a feeling of accomplishment. At the apex of Maslow's hierarchy is the need for **self-actualization, the need to achieve one's full potential.**

Maslow's theory is appealing because it recognizes a wide range of human motivations—from satisfying our biological needs to savoring the joy of accomplishment. Moreover, it suggests that the various motivations are not equal. When they conflict, the basic physiological needs take priority over safety needs, which take priority over the need for love, and so on.

Maslow's hierarchy has been widely accepted, although it has inspired little research, and what research has been done has often failed to support the theory (Wahba & Bridwell, 1976). No evidence supports the idea that motivations fall into five distinct categories. That is, the differences between the need for oxygen and the need for food (both basic physiological needs) are as great as the differences between the need for love and the need for self-esteem. More important, people sometimes work to satisfy higher-level needs before they satisfy lower-level needs. Even when you are ravenously hungry, you might skip a meal to be with someone you love, or to study for a test, or to accept an award. Martyrs have willingly sacrificed their lives to advance some political or religious cause. Depending on the circumstances, almost any motivation may take priority over the others, at least temporarily.

GENERAL PROPERTIES OF MOTIVATED BEHAVIOR

What, if anything, do various types of motivated behavior have in common? The foremost characteristic of motivated behaviors is that they are goal directed (Pervin, 1983). They have a quality of "persistence until." A person or an animal engages in one behavior after another until reaching the goal. When you feel cold, you do not always do one par-

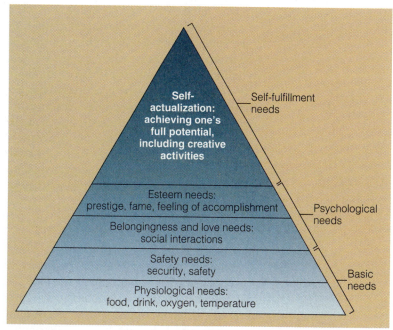

FIGURE 11.3

Maslow's hierarchy of needs suggests a hierarchical order of human motivations. If you are thirsty, you will want to drink something to meet that basic need. If your primary physical needs are met, you can focus on meeting psychological needs for companionship and achievement. Your final efforts will be devoted to reaching your full potential. But do all people follow this principle? Some people, such as Olympic performers, sacrifice eating, drinking, and companionship to strive toward athletic accomplishment and prestige. Artists might also give up some physical comforts and social pleasures to focus on an inner vision and to realize their creative potential.

FIGURE 11.4

According to Maslow's hierarchy of needs, we concentrate first on the lowest level of needs—such as the needs for food, oxygen, and temperature—until we meet them. Then we move on to higher and higher needs. Thus, an impoverished and homeless person would be unlikely to devote much effort to creative endeavors. (Some exceptions to that rule do occur, however.)

ticular thing. You may go inside, put on a sweater, huddle with others, run around, or just stand and shiver, depending on the circumstances. Similarly, when you are hungry, you may act in a number of ways to obtain food. To determine whether a particular behavior is motivated, as opposed to automatic or reflexive, an observer needs to watch the individual over a period of time in a variety of circumstances. If the individual varies the behavior at different times and persists until reaching a goal, then the behavior is motivated, or intentional.

SOMETHING TO THINK ABOUT

A frog flicks its tongue at a passing insect, captures it, and swallows it. The behavior serves to satisfy the frog's need for food, so we might guess that it is motivated. However, the behavior appears to be as constant as a reflex. How might you determine whether or not the behavior is motivated?

A second characteristic of motivated behaviors is that they vary from time to time, under the influence of both internal (biological) and external (social) controls (Pervin, 1983). For example, you wear clothes to keep warm, to look attractive, to display your exquisite taste, and to avoid arrest for indecent exposure. Exactly what clothing and how much clothing you wear depends on what you feel like doing, today's weather, and the people you expect to see. We have more than one motivation for almost everything we do.

Motivated behaviors vary from person to person as well as from situation to situation. People do not differ much in their drive for oxygen, but they differ significantly in their search for food, still more in their motivation for sexual activity, self-esteem, and self-fulfillment—the needs near the top of Maslow's hierarchy. In the rest of this chapter, we shall return periodically to the ways in which people differ in their motivations.

SUMMARY

- *Motivation as an energy.* Sigmund Freud and Konrad Lorenz viewed motivated behaviors as outlets for instinctive energies. They be-

lieved that specific energies accumulated in the nervous system and had to be released in one way or another. Their theories were based on a now obsolete concept of the nervous system. (page 461)

- *Motivation as drive reduction.* Some psychologists have described motivation as a drive that energizes behaviors which persist until they reduce the drive. This view implies that we strive to achieve a state of minimal drive and minimal stimulation. (page 462)

- *Motivation as a way of maintaining homeostasis.* To a large degree, motivated behaviors tend to maintain body conditions and stimulation at a near-constant, or homeostatic, level. This view of motivation can account for much behavior if we also assume that behaviors anticipate future needs instead of just responding to current needs. However, the homeostatic view of motivation overlooks the role of external stimuli in arousing behavior. (page 462)

- *Motivation as incentive.* Motivations are partly under the control of incentives—external stimuli that pull us toward certain actions. Both drives and incentives control most motivated behaviors. (page 463)

- *Intrinsic and extrinsic motivations.* People and animals engage in some actions because the actions themselves are interesting or pleasing (intrinsic motivation). Providing an external reinforcement (extrinsic motivation) for the actions may actually reduce the interest or pleasure they provide. (page 463)

- *Types of motivations.* Psychologists have made several attempts to list or categorize various motivations. One prominent attempt, offered by Abraham Maslow, arranged needs in a hierarchy ranging from basic physiological needs at the bottom to the need for self-actualization at the top. His claim that people satisfy their lower needs before their higher needs does not, however, apply in all cases. (page 465)

- *Characteristics of motivated behaviors.* Motivated behaviors persist until the individual reaches a goal. They are controlled by internal and external forces and by biological and social forces. Motivated behaviors vary from time to time, from situation to situation, and from person to person. (page 467)

SUGGESTION FOR FURTHER READING

Mook, D. G. (1987). *Motivation: The organization of action.* New York: Norton. A theoretical treatment of the basic principles of motivation.

TERMS

libido according to Sigmund Freud, a kind of sexual energy (page 461)

drive an internal state of unrest or irritation that energizes one behavior after another until one of them removes the irritation (page 462)

homeostasis the maintenance of an optimum level of biological conditions within an organism (page 462)

incentive an external stimulus that prompts an action to obtain the stimulus (page 463)

intrinsic motivation motivation to engage in an act for its own sake (page 463)

extrinsic motivation motivation based on the rewards and punishments an act may bring (page 463)

overjustification effect tendency for people who are given more extrinsic motivation than necessary to perform a task to experience a decline in their intrinsic motivation (page 464)

primary motivation motivation that serves biological needs (page 465)

secondary motivation motivation that serves no biological need directly but develops as a result of specific learning experiences (page 465)

hierarchy of needs Maslow's categorization of human motivations, ranging from basic physiological needs at the bottom to the need for self-actualization at the top (page 466)

self-actualization the need to achieve one's full potential (page 467)

ANSWERS TO CONCEPT CHECKS

1. According to the overjustification effect, you should expect a retired professional tennis player to enjoy playing tennis less than other people do—at least less than other players of high ability. (page 464)

2. Your interest in graduating from college is a secondary motivation, because it is something you had to learn to value. Such secondary motivations can become very strong. (page 466)

MOTIVATION AND BIOLOGICAL STATES: THE CASE OF HUNGER

What causes us to feel hungry?

How do we choose which foods to eat?

Why do some people gain excessive weight and others deliberately lose weight to a dangerous level?

In the 1970s, the United States suffered a gasoline shortage. Sometimes, drivers found that every service station in their area was out of gas. After a few such experiences, they stopped taking chances. Whenever they saw a station that still sold gas, they would stop and fill their tank, even if it wasn't empty yet.

If you expect to have trouble finding food from time to time, a good strategy is to fill up your "tank" whenever you can. Throughout most of human existence, people have had to contend with periodic food shortages and famines. To many of our ancestors, the idea of going on a diet to lose weight would have made no sense at all. The

Eating is a complex behavior that depends on more than just hunger. Sometimes people refuse to eat for symbolic reasons, such as when Cesar Chavez went on a hunger strike to protest against the unfair treatment of migrant workers.

same is true for many impoverished people today. However, for people who have almost constant access to a variety of high-calorie foods, the strategy of filling the tank as often as possible is no longer useful.

Social pressures can make matters even worse. When you visit friends or relatives, they may offer you food as a gesture of affection, and they may act hurt if you refuse their hospitality. Say you visit the family of your boyfriend or girlfriend, and you want to make a good impression. "Dinner's ready!" someone calls. You go into the dining room and find a huge meal, which your hosts clearly expect you to enjoy. Do you explain that you are not hungry because you already made a pig of yourself at lunch? Probably not.

Eating is controlled by many motives, both physiological and social. We eat to get needed nutrition but also to experience tastes and to socialize (Figure 11.5).

PHYSIOLOGICAL MECHANISMS OF HUNGER

Hunger is a (partly) homeostatic drive that serves to keep fuel available for the body to use. Specialized mechanisms in the brain monitor how much fuel is available; when supplies begin to drop, the brain triggers behaviors that lead to eating. But how does the brain know how much fuel is available and therefore how much a person should eat and how often?

The problem is far more complex than keeping enough fuel in a car's gas tank. When the fuel gauge shows that the tank is running low, you fill it with gas. By contrast, keeping track of how much fuel is in your stomach does not tell you how much more you need. Right now, in addition to the fuel in your stomach and intestines, a fair amount of fuel is present in every cell of your body, ready to be used. Additional fuel is circulating in your blood, ready to enter cells that need it. Still more fuel is stored in fat cells, available to be converted into a form that can enter the blood. If necessary, your body can break down muscle tissues to provide additional fuel. Whereas your car's engine will stop running within seconds after it uses all the fuel in the gas tank, your body can keep going for days, even weeks, after your stomach is empty.

Unlike your car, which uses only gas, your body needs a complex mixture of proteins, fats, and carbohydrates, plus assorted vitamins and minerals. How much you should eat at a given meal depends both on how much nutrition you need and on exactly what combination of nutrients is present in the foods you are eating. How can your brain possibly get it right?

Fortunately, it doesn't need to. The brain monitors how much fuel you need, based on the fuel available in your cells and circulating in your blood. When the need for more fuel is great enough, you feel hungry. How much you eat in your next meal corresponds only loosely to how much you need. If you eat too little, you will feel hungry again soon. If you eat too much, part of the excess will be temporarily stored as fat and later converted from fat to sugars that can enter your bloodstream. As a result, you won't feel hungry again as soon as usual. You do not have to eat exactly the correct amount in a given meal; you can correct your errors over the next few meals.

GLUCOSE, INSULIN, AND THE SHORT-TERM REGULATION OF HUNGER

To determine how much fuel your body needs at a given moment, your brain keeps track of many factors (Friedman & Stricker, 1976). One of the most important factors is glucose, the most abundant sugar in your blood. Many of the foods you eat can be converted into glucose; so can your body's fats. An important source of energy for all parts of the body, glucose is the main source of energy for the brain.

A decreased supply of glucose and other cell nutrients leads to a sensation of hunger (Figure 11.6). Ordinarily, the amount of nutrients present in the blood does not vary widely over time; what varies is the amount leaving the blood and entering the cells. The flow of nutrients into the cells depends largely on insulin, a hormone which the pancreas releases. Insulin is the body's way of preventing enormous fluctuations in blood glucose and other nutrients (Woods, 1991).

At the beginning of a meal, long before the nutrients have started entering the blood, the brain sends messages to the pancreas to increase its secretion of insulin. Insulin promotes movement of nutrients out of the blood and into the cells—both the cells that

FIGURE 11.5
Mealtime is more than just an opportunity to satisfy hunger: It is an occasion to bring the family and sometimes friends together, to share a pleasant experience, to discuss the events of the day, and even to pass on a culture from one generation to the next. We expect people to participate in the family's meals, even if they are not hungry.

need fuel and the cells that store the nutrients as fats and other supplies for later use. As the meal continues, the digested food enters the blood, but almost as fast as it enters, insulin helps to move excess nutrients out of the blood and into the liver or fat cells. In that manner the insulin holds down the surge of glucose and other nutrients in the blood. Later, long after the meal, when the nutrient supply in the blood starts to drop, the pancreas secretes the hormone **glucagon** instead of insulin. Glucagon helps to convert stored energy supplies back into blood glucose; it continues to do so until the next meal.

At least that is what happens in healthy people. Consider what happens if insulin levels stay too high or too low for long times: When insulin levels are consistently low, as in the medical condition diabetes, nutrients enter the cells very slowly and hunger increases (Figure 11.7 on page 473). Animal studies have demonstrated that low insulin levels prevent digested food from entering the cells—even the fat cells. Consequently, most of each meal is excreted.

At the opposite extreme, if insulin levels are consistently high, nutrients enter the cells easily, but a high percentage of every meal is converted to fats and stored in fat cells. Because the insulin level remains high, the food stored in fat cells simply stays there; glucagon cannot mobilize it back into blood

[handwritten margin note:] low insulin prevents digested food from entering the cells meal is excreted

[handwritten margin note:] high insulin - nutrients enter cells easily but high % of meal is converted to fat & stored in fat cells.

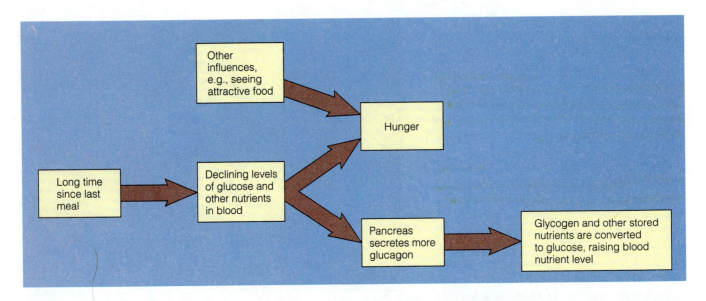

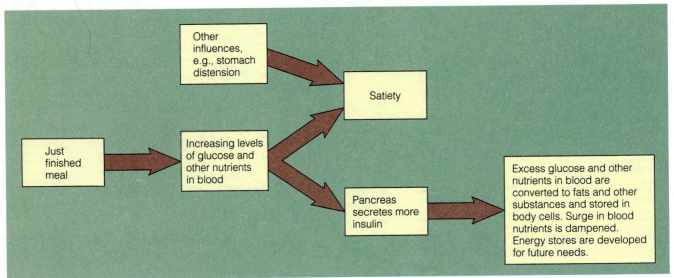

FIGURE 11.6
The short-term regulation of eating depends on the levels of glucose and other nutrients in the blood; it also depends on the appearance and flavor of the food, social influences, and so forth. Varying secretions of the hormones insulin and glucagon help to keep the blood nutrient levels reasonably constant. During and shortly after a meal, insulin moves blood nutrients into storage in the liver and fat cells; during a period without food, glucagon converts stored nutrients into blood glucose.

increased high
or low insulin
results in increased
appetite

glucose a couple of hours later. Consequently, soon after a person with high insulin levels finishes digesting a meal, he or she has a low level of blood glucose *(hypoglycemia)* and increased appetite. (Figure 11.8 shows the relationship between glucose level and food intake.) Note that if the insulin level is either consistently low or consistently high, the result will be an increased appetite; however, very low insulin leads to weight loss and very high insulin leads to weight gain.

CONCEPT CHECK

3. Insulin levels fluctuate cyclically over the course of a day. Would you guess that they are higher in the middle of the day, when hunger is high, or late at night, when hunger is generally low? (Check your answer on page 484.)

SATIETY

The brain monitors the levels of glucose and other nutrients in the cells to determine when the body needs more fuel. How does your brain know when you should stop?

Satiety (sah-TI-uht-ee) is the experience of being full, of feeling no more hunger. Ordinarily, satiety depends mostly on stomach distention. When the stomach is full, satiety increases (Deutsch, Young, & Kalogeris, 1978). Food entering the small intestine may also contribute to the feeling of satiety, possibly by causing the intestine to release a certain hormone (Smith & Gibbs, 1987). Moreover, if you are eating a familiar, calorie-rich diet, you may stop eating long before your stomach is full because you have learned how much energy to expect from the food (Deutsch, 1983).

We also have ways of becoming satiated on a specific food, to prevent an imbalance among different kinds of nutrients (Mook, 1990). For example, after eating a meal high in protein, you might be interested in eating some sweets, but not more proteins. If you had just finished eating sweets, you might be willing to eat a high-protein food, but not more sweets.

THE LONG-TERM REGULATION OF HUNGER

During your next meal, you will almost certainly eat either a bit more or a bit less than your body needs. Your misjudgment will create no difficulties unless you misjudge in the same direction on every meal. If you consistently ate just 5% more than you needed, you would gain 15 pounds (7 kilograms) per year (Jéquier, 1987). If you consistently ate 5% less than you needed, you would eventually starve to death.

The brain corrects for the error of a given meal by monitoring body weight over time. If you undereat for several meals, you lose weight and then get hungry earlier than usual. Conversely, if you overeat for several meals (at Thanksgiving, for example), you gain weight but then you feel less hungry. All of this happens automatically; you do not need to check the scales each day. Over the course of months, most people maintain a nearly constant body weight. That weight is referred to as a set point—a level that the body attempts to maintain (Figure 11.9).

Note that the physiological regulators maintain a constant weight, but not necessarily a normal or healthy weight. Some people fluctuate around a low weight; others fluctuate around a much higher weight. Most adults maintain almost the same weight year after year, unless they become ill,

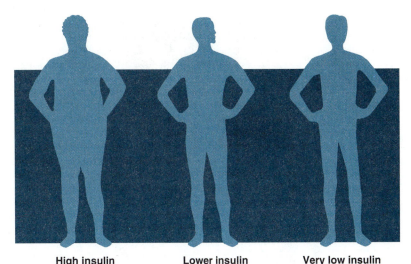

High insulin
Food is stored as fat. Little glucose in blood. Appetite increases. Weight increases.

Lower insulin
Fat supplies are converted to glucose. Appetite is lower.

Very low insulin
Glucose cannot enter cells. Appetite is high, but much of nutrition is excreted. Weight decreases.

FIGURE 11.7
How insulin affects glucose, appetite, and weight.

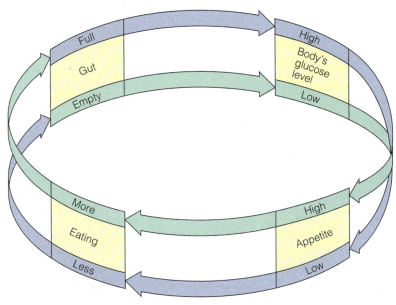

FIGURE 11.8
To maintain equilibrium, homeostatic regulating systems, such as the one for food intake shown here, provide a feedback mechanism. Low levels of glucose—the brain's primary energy source—stimulate the hypothalamus, which prompts the pancreas to release insulin and raise the levels of glucose. Once the glucose reaches a certain level, control mechanisms act to lower it.

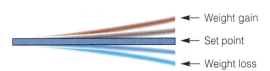

← Weight gain
← Set point
← Weight loss

FIGURE 11.9
For most people most of the time, weight fluctuates around a set point, somewhat like a diving board that bounces up and down from a central position.

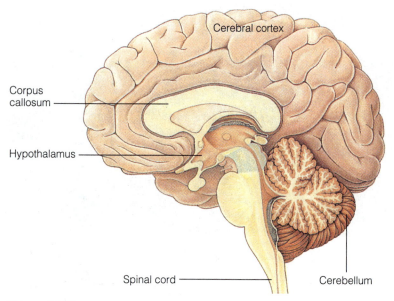

Cerebral cortex

Corpus callosum

Hypothalamus

Spinal cord

Cerebellum

FIGURE 11.10

The hypothalamus, a small area on the underside of the brain, contains a number of subareas that contribute in various ways to eating, drinking, sexual behavior, and other motivated activities. Damage to the lateral hypothalamus inhibits eating; damage to other hypothalamic areas can provoke overeating.

change their way of life, or make a deliberate effort to lose weight.

BRAIN MECHANISMS OF HUNGER AND SATIETY

Somehow the brain has to monitor information from the blood, cells, and digestive system to determine when to eat and when to stop. Several brain areas, especially in the hypothalamus (Figure 11.10) are especially important in this process.

The **lateral hypothalamus** appears to be a critical area for starting meals. An individual with damage to the lateral hypothalamus has trouble salivating, swallowing, and digesting foods (Hernandez, Murzi, Schwartz, & Hoebel, 1992). Also, such an individual secretes higher levels of glucagon than of insulin; consequently, the fat supplies are constantly converted into blood glucose and the individual has little immediate need for further nutrition.

Two areas of the hypothalamus are important for ending meals. One is the **ventromedial hypothalamus.** After damage that includes the ventromedial hypothalamus and the axons that pass nearby, an individual digests food more rapidly than usual and secretes more insulin. The high insulin level

causes a disproportionate amount of each meal to be stored as fat. Because the food passes quickly through the digestive system and quickly into the fat cells, where it stays, the individual becomes hungry again shortly after each meal (Hoebel & Hernandez, 1993). Figure 11.11 shows a very obese rat with this kind of brain damage. One woman with a tumor in this area gained an average of more than 10 kg (15 pounds) per month (Reeves & Plum, 1969).

Another area of the hypothalamus contributes to ending meals in a different way. After damage to or chemical inhibition of the **paraventricular hypothalamus,** meals are of normal frequency but each individual meal is enormous (Leibowitz & Alexander, 1991; Leibowitz, Hammer, & Chang, 1981). An individual with such damage may continue eating until the stomach and intestines are about to burst, as if he or she did not feel the usual sensation of distention.

CONCEPT CHECK

4. After damage to the ventromedial hypothalamus, an animal's weight eventually reaches a higher-than-usual level and then fluctuates around that amount. What has happened to the set point? (Check your answer on page 484.)

MOTIVES IN FOOD SELECTIONS

So far I have discussed how you determine when and how much to eat. A separate issue, just as important, is how you determine which foods to eat.

FIGURE 11.11

An obese rat with a damaged ventromedial hypothalamus (left) can eat less than an ordinary rat (right) and still gain weight. This rat's excess fat prevents it from grooming its fur.

We learn our food choices mainly by learning what *not* to eat. Toddlers around the age of 1½ will try to eat almost anything they can fit into their mouth (Figure 11.12). Up to age 7 or 8, almost the only reason children give for refusing to eat something is that they think it would taste bad (Rozin, Fallon, & Augustoni-Ziskind, 1986). As they grow older, they give a wider variety of reasons for accepting certain foods and rejecting others. Food selection is a complex matter; as with other motivations, it depends on a combination of physiological, social, and cognitive factors. Let's consider some of the most important factors.

ACCEPTANCE OR REJECTION OF FOODS BASED ON TASTE

Some taste preferences are present at birth. Infants readily consume sweet liquids; when they taste something bitter or sour, they turn their head and spit it out.

At least one taste preference can be triggered by an abnormal condition within the body. One boy showed a strong craving for salt. As an infant, he licked the salt off crackers and bacon but refused to eat the food itself. One of the first words he learned was *salt*. He put a thick layer of salt on everything he ate, and sometimes he ate salt by itself. When deprived of salt, he ate almost nothing and began to waste away. At the age of 3½, he was taken to the hospital and fed the usual hospital fare. He soon died of salt deficiency (Wilkins & Richter, 1940).

It turned out that the boy's adrenal glands were defective. These glands secrete hormones that enable the body to retain salt. The boy craved great amounts of salt because salt was being excreted so rapidly from his body. (We are often told to limit our salt intake for health reasons, but too little salt can also be dangerous.)

Research on animals confirms that a deficiency of salt in the body triggers an immediate craving for salty foods. As soon as animals, including humans, become salt-deficient, they show a heightened preference for salty tastes (Rozin & Kalat, 1971). Those who have lost large quantities of salt as a result of bleeding or heavy sweating often express a craving for salt. Apparently, salt actually tastes better to salt-deficient rats and people than it does to others (Jacobs, Mark, & Scott, 1988). In short, changes in body chemistry can alter a person's motivation to choose a particular food.

FIGURE 11.12
Infants and young children will try eating almost anything and refuse a food only if it tastes bad. As they grow older they learn to avoid foods for other reasons. People avoid eating some substances to avoid getting sick; they avoid other substances because the very idea of eating them is disgusting.

PREFERENCE FOR FAMILIAR FOODS

Although people eat a wide variety of foods, they are cautious about eating foods they have never eaten before. Think about the first time you tried artichokes, jalapeño peppers, or coffee, for example. Although you probably enjoy new combinations of familiar ingredients, you tend to be wary of anything with a flavor that is new to you. If you ever become ill after eating something, you are likely to be even more cautious about eating something new (Rozin, 1968).

Members of every culture and every ethnic group become familiar with its preferred ways of preparing and seasoning foods. Children who grow up in Italian families come to prefer foods flavored with tomato, garlic, and olive oil. Mexican children at first dislike hot peppers, but within a few years, many insist on having them with almost every meal. Cuisine is one of the most stable features of human cultures. In the United States, for example, the children and grandchildren of immigrants tend to follow the food choices of

FIGURE 11.13
People associate the foods they eat, especially unfamiliar foods, with the way they feel afterward. If you ate corn dogs and cotton candy just before getting on a wild roller coaster ride and then got sick from the ride, you would find that something in your brain had "blamed" the food for your feeling ill, even though you consciously believe that the food had nothing to do with your illness. Ordinarily, however, this kind of learning enables us to learn to avoid harmful substances.

their forebears long after they have discarded other old-country customs.

LEARNED ASSOCIATIONS WITH FOOD

As mentioned in Chapter 6, animals associate foods with the gastrointestinal consequences of eating them. The same is true of humans. When you eat something and later get sick, you may form a strong aversion to that food, especially if it was unfamiliar. Ordinarily, that aversion occurs because something in the food made you ill, but the same learning takes place even if something else caused the illness. A person who eats a greasy corn dog at an amusement park and then goes on a wild ride and gets sick may find corn dogs repulsive from then on (Figure 11.13). The person may "know" the ride was at fault, but somehow an area deep in the brain associates the food with the sickness.

Moreover, people sometimes reject safe, nutritious foods because they have learned to associate them with something that evokes repulsive associations (Rozin & Fallon, 1987; Rozin, Millman, & Nemeroff, 1986). In our society, most people refuse to eat dog meat, cat meat, or horse meat. How would you like to try the tasty morsels described in Figure 11.14? Most people find the idea of eating insects repulsive, even if the insects were sterilized to kill all germs (Rozin & Fallon, 1987). They also say they would refuse to drink a

glass of apple juice after a dead, sterilized cockroach had been dipped into it. After seeing a cockroach dipped into a glass of apple juice, some people even refuse to drink other apple juice poured into a different glass (Rozin, Millman, & Nemeroff, 1986).

▌ EATING DISORDERS

The mechanisms I have discussed so far enable most people to select a reasonable, well-balanced diet and to maintain their weight within normal limits. In some individuals, the motivational mechanisms go awry. They feel hungry all the time and eat too much, or they alternate between stuffing themselves and starving themselves, or they feel hungry but refuse to eat. Some of these disorders result from physiological abnormalities; others result from social and cognitive influences that compete with the normal physiological mechanisms.

OBESITY

Obesity is the excessive accumulation of body fat. A body weight 20–40% above the standard for a person's height is considered mild obesity. Weight 41–100% above the standard is considered moderate obesity. Weight more than 100% above the standard is considered severe obesity (Berkow, 1987). Why do some people become seriously overweight? Obviously because they take in more calories than they use up. But *why* do they do that? One reason, as we have seen, is that some people have high levels of insulin, which causes much of the food they eat to be stored as fats. Let's consider some other possible explanations.

THE LIMITED ROLE OF EMOTIONAL DISTURBANCES

Are overweight people more likely than others are to have psychological problems? One prevalent idea is that anxiety, depression, or other emotional problems lead to overeating and weight gain. Another is that extreme weight gain leads to anxiety or depression. The research, however, fails to support either hypothesis. Anxiety, depression, and other psychological concerns are not unusually common among obese people (Wadden & Stunkard, 1987). There may, nevertheless, be a subpopulation of obese people who react strongly to the unfavorable way in which they are treated. Because prejudices against

Crispy Cajun Crickets

(Adapted from a recipe in the *Food Insects Newsletter,* March 1990)

Tired of the same old snack food? Perk up your next party with Crispy Cajun Crickets ("pampered" house crickets, *Acheta domesticus,* available from Flucker's Cricket Farm, P.O. Box 378, Baton Rouge, LA 70821, 800-735-8537).

   1 cup crickets
   1 pinch oatmeal
   4 ounces butter, melted
    Salt
    Garlic
    Cayenne

1. Put crickets in a clean, airy container with oatmeal for food. After one day, discard sick crickets and freeze the rest.
2. Wash frozen crickets in warm water and spread on a cookie sheet. Roast in a 250-degree oven until crunchy.
3. Meanwhile, heat butter with remaining ingredients and sprinkle this sauce on crickets before serving.

Yield: 1 serving

FIGURE 11.14
People avoid eating some potential foods because they are disgusted by the very idea of eating them. For example, most people would refuse to eat insects, regardless of any assurances that the insects were nutritious and harmless.

Different cultures have different taboos. Here is an assortment of insect and reptile dishes. (Yum, yum?)

the obese are so common, many obese people have a restricted social life and have trouble getting a good job. Dealing with such prejudices and barriers leads to psychological distress and low self-esteem in a minority of obese people (Friedman & Brownell, 1995).

Although emotional distress is not the cause of obesity, it can produce temporary fluctuations in eating and body weight for almost anyone. In one survey of 100 adults (Edelman, 1981), 40 said that they overeat three or more times a month when they feel nervous, tired, lonely, or sorry for themselves. The eating binge enables them to focus their attention on eating and away from their other concerns (Heatherton & Baumeister, 1991). Such eating binges are most frequent and most extreme in people who have been dieting to lose weight (Greeno & Wing, 1994). Evidently, dieters actively inhibit their desire to eat, until a stressful experience breaks the inhibitions and releases the pent-up desire to eat.

GENETICS

Obesity tends to run in families, and the weight of adopted children correlates more closely with that of their birth parents than with that of their adopting parents (Stunkard et al., 1986). Researchers studying mice have located a particular gene that leads to obesity. (See Figure 11.15.) That is, by examining chromosomes they can identify which mice are likely to become obese and which ones are not (Zhang et al., 1994). The "obese" gene causes a mouse to secrete

Although obesity is not significantly linked with anxiety or depression, some obese people feel distress and low self-esteem because of the way other people react to them.

FIGURE 11.15
The mouse on the right has a gene called obese *(for an obvious reason). That gene has been located on the chromosomes of mice. Some humans are believed to have a similar gene. (From Zhang et al., 1994.)*

[handwritten margin note: Obese genes causes secretion of excessive amts of a particular protein. function: unknown]

excessive amounts of a particular protein. The function of that protein is not known; it may have direct effects on the brain or it may alter activities of the digestive system and other organs. In any case, humans have a very similar protein, and it is likely that genetic variations in the production of that protein contribute to people's probabilities of becoming obese. Future research on that protein may enable researchers to plan logical biomedical treatments to help people avoid obesity.

DECREASED ENERGY OUTPUT

Some overweight people think they are eating normal or even small meals when in fact they are overeating. Many others, however, really do eat consistently normal to small meals without losing weight (DeLuise, Blackburn, & Flier, 1980). Their overweight condition is not due to high energy intake, but to low energy output. I refer here not just to their lack of exercise but also to their failure to burn off enough calories in their overall metabolism. Presumably, one way in which the genes for obesity act is by decreasing the use of energy.

One group of investigators compared the infants of 12 overweight mothers and 6 normal-weight mothers over their first year of life. All the babies weighed about the same at birth, but 6 of the babies of the overweight mothers had become overweight by the end

of the year. Those babies also had been relatively inactive since birth. During the first 3 months they had expended about 20% less energy per day than had the babies who maintained normal weight (Roberts, Savage, Coward, Chew, & Lucas, 1988).

Low energy expenditure is a good predictor of weight gain in adults as well. Eric Ravussin and his associates (1988) found that the adults with the lowest energy expenditure over a 24-hour period were the most likely to gain weight over the next 2 to 4 years. Figure 11.16 summarizes factors involved in being overweight.

LOSING WEIGHT

The best way to lose weight is to eat less—no surprise in that conclusion. Most dieters do in fact succeed in losing weight, and some keep it off permanently (Schachter, 1982). Others, however, despite good intentions, consistently fail to lose weight or alternate between losing it and gaining it back. Some become so desperate they will try almost anything—including surgery to remove fat, implanting a balloon in the stomach (to reduce its capacity), taking drugs that suppress appetite, and having their jaws wired shut (Munro, Stewart, Seidelin, Mackenzie, & Dewhurst, 1987). Even these desperate solutions are often ineffective, and they introduce serious health risks of their own.

Besides decreasing their eating, dieters are also advised to get regular exercise, as a way of both burning off extra calories and improving overall health. The difficulty is that most overweight people have trouble sticking to a regular exercise program, and even if they do stick to it, they do not lose much weight unless they also eat less (Segal & Pi-Sunyer, 1989). In one study, 13 overweight women exercised fairly vigorously for 90 minutes a day, 4 or 5 times a week, for 14 months. By the end of that time, their mean weight had dropped from 90 kilograms (198 pounds) to 86.3 kilograms (190 pounds). Even that mild weight loss is beneficial, but the point is that exercise by itself is unlikely to turn a fat person into a thin person (Després et al., 1991).

THE EFFECT OF INTENTIONAL WEIGHT LOSS ON APPETITE

Many people in our society, especially women, believe they should lose weight even though their weight is already well within normal limits. The motivation to lose weight

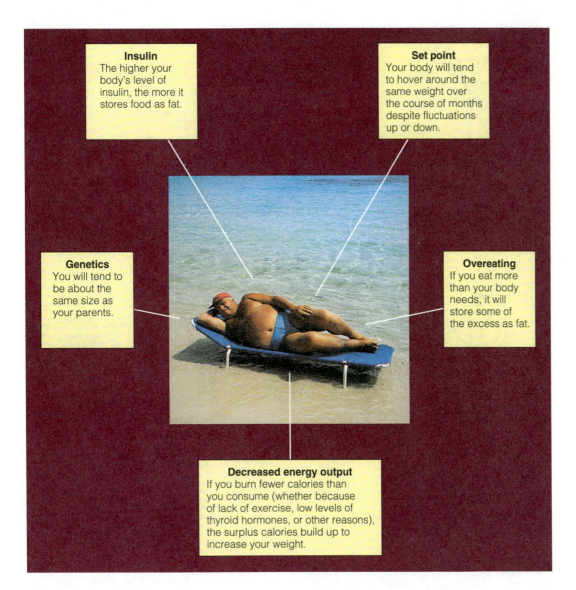

Insulin
The higher your body's level of insulin, the more it stores food as fat.

Set point
Your body will tend to hover around the same weight over the course of months despite fluctuations up or down.

Genetics
You will tend to be about the same size as your parents.

Overeating
If you eat more than your body needs, it will store some of the excess as fat.

Decreased energy output
If you burn fewer calories than you consume (whether because of lack of exercise, low levels of thyroid hormones, or other reasons), the surplus calories build up to increase your weight.

is a product of cultural standards that depict thin women as especially attractive. April Fallon and Paul Rozin (1985) asked women to indicate on a diagram which body figure they thought men considered most attractive. The investigators also asked men which female figure *they* considered most attractive. As Figure 11.17 shows, women thought that men preferred thinner women than most men actually do. (The same study also found that men thought women preferred heavier men than most women actually do.)

Given the social pressure to be thin, many normal-weight people deprive themselves of food they would like to eat, keeping themselves thinner than they would have been by eating naturally (Polivy & Herman, 1987). They continue to have a strong drive to eat, however, and many factors can weaken their inhibition against eating. In one experiment, participants were told that they were taking part in market research on the flavors of ice creams. Some of them were first asked to drink a milkshake, while others were not. Then they were all asked to taste three flavors of ice cream. (The dependent variable was how much ice cream they ate.) When this experiment was conducted with people who were not dieting, the ones who had first drunk a milkshake ate *less* ice cream than those who had not (Figure 11.18). No surprise here; drinking a milkshake made people less hungry. But when the experiment was conducted with people who were dieting, those who had first drunk a milkshake ate just as much ice cream and sometimes even *more* than those who had not drunk a milkshake (Ruderman, 1986; Ruderman & Christensen, 1983). Apparently the dieters said to themselves, "What the heck. As long as I've already broken my diet, I may as well eat all I want." Not all

FIGURE 11.17
In a study by Fallon and Rozin (1985), women and men were asked which figure they considered most attractive in the opposite sex and which figure they thought the opposite sex considered most attractive. Each sex had systematic misestimates of the other's preferences.

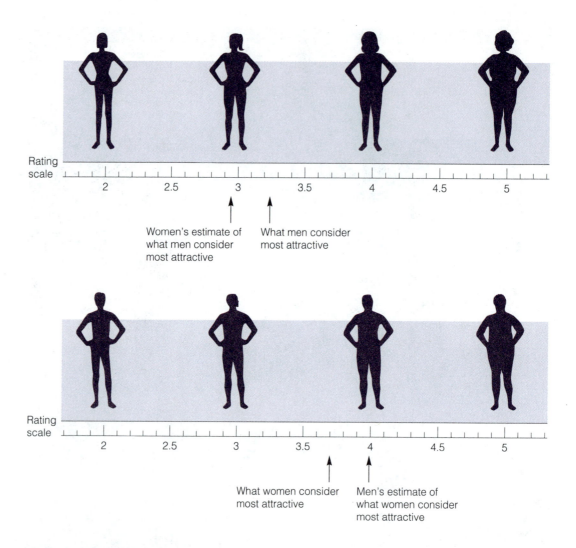

Rating scale

Women's estimate of what men consider most attractive

What men consider most attractive

What women consider most attractive

Men's estimate of what women consider most attractive

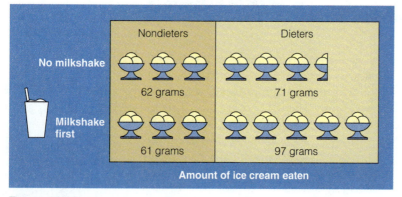

Nondieters | Dieters

No milkshake — 62 grams | 71 grams

Milkshake first — 61 grams | 97 grams

Amount of ice cream eaten

FIGURE 11.18
Dieters who drank a milkshake before tasting ice cream ate more ice cream than did dieters who had not drunk a milkshake. Apparently those who drank a milkshake thought, "I've broken my diet anyway, so I may as well eat all I want." (Data from Ruderman & Christensen, 1983.)

dieters react this way when they have consumed a calorie-rich snack; as is generally the case in psychology, we can find many individual differences (Lowe, 1993). The point is that many dieting people can be easily shaken off their diet.

Some become "yo-yo dieters," alternating periods of weight loss with periods of weight gain. The resulting fluctuations in body weight may be harmful to health, although we have little research to measure the degree of that risk. Consequently, authorities are not certain what advice to give to people of near-normal weight who consider trying to lose weight. Certainly, if someone is extremely obese, losing weight is medically important. When less obese people succeed at keeping their weight down it is clear that dieting is beneficial. However, when people who are already close to a normal weight find themselves repeatedly losing and regaining weight by "yo-yo dieting," no one is sure whether the benefits outweigh the risks (Brownell & Rodin, 1994).

ANOREXIA NERVOSA

Some people go beyond reasonable limits in their passion to lose weight. The Duchess of Windsor once said, "You can't be too rich or too thin." She may have been right about being too rich, but she was definitely wrong about being too thin. Some people are so strongly motivated to be thin (for social and cognitive reasons) that they manage to overrule their physiological drives almost completely.

Here is a case history: A somewhat chubby 11-year-old girl, who weighed 118 pounds (53 kilograms), was told to watch her weight (Bachrach, Erwin, & Mohr, 1965). She did so all through her teens. Along the way she suffered certain hormonal difficulties, including menstrual irregularity, heavy menstrual bleeding, and deficient activity of her thyroid gland. At age 18 she still weighed 118 pounds (53 kilograms), but with her taller frame that weight was normal for her.

After she was married, she moved from her home in Virginia to her husband's place of employment in California. She immediately became homesick. Because the couple could afford only a small apartment with no cooking facilities, they ate most of their meals at a very cheap restaurant. Soon she began to lose weight and stopped menstruating. Sexual relations were painful and unpleasant for her. Her physician warned her that she was losing far too much weight and said that if she did not start regaining some of it he would be forced to send her home to her parents. He intended this as a threat, but she took it as a promise. By the time she visited the physician again, she had lost even more weight. She went back to Virginia.

Even after returning to familiar surroundings and home cooking, however, she continued to lose weight. The weight loss seemed to have developed a momentum of its own, and she continued to get thinner, eventually reaching a weight of only 47 pounds (21 kilograms).

This is a case of **anorexia nervosa,** a condition in which a person refuses to eat adequate food and steadily loses weight. (*Anorexia* means "loss of appetite." *Nervosa* means "for nervous reasons," as opposed to organic reasons.) At the outset, the person may have decided to lose weight for health reasons, or to become a dancer, or for some other reason. But the person continues losing weight well beyond the original goal. Surprisingly, even when they are on the verge of starvation, anorexic women have unusually high energy levels (Falk, Halmi, & Tryon, 1985). They run long distances, engage in sports, work diligently on their school as-

signments, and sleep very little. As with other psychological conditions, anorexia nervosa comes in all degrees. Of those who are so seriously afflicted that they consult a physician, about 5–10% die of starvation or other complications due to severe weight loss.

Anorexia nervosa usually begins during the teenage years. Earlier onset is almost unheard of. Onset in the 20s is possible but uncommon, although anorexia that begins in the teenage years may continue into the 20s or beyond. Women with anorexia outnumber men with anorexia by about 10 to 1. Relatively little is known about men with anorexia, except that anorexia seems to have something to do with their sexuality. One study found that about one-fourth of anorexic men had a homosexual orientation, most of the rest had almost no sexual activity, and a large percentage felt conflicts and doubts about their sexuality (Herzog, Norman, Gordon, & Pepose, 1984).

Reports from before the 1980s described anorexia as almost culture-specific, being found almost solely in western cultures, and overwhelmingly in women of European ancestry. We have to modify that description somewhat today. The prevalence of anorexia is still very low in India, Singapore, Malaysia, and most of Africa, but it has been increasing in Japan and among African Americans (Pate, Pumariega, Hester, & Garner, 1992). The best guess is that one of the major contributors to anorexia is societal pressure, especially on women, to be very thin. Anorexia is less likely to occur in cultures that tolerate or cherish a somewhat plumper look, such as Jamaica (Smith & Cogswell, 1994) or even Europe in an earlier era (Figure 11.19).

Some psychologists have tried to explain anorexia nervosa in terms of a misfunction of the lateral hypothalamus, the brain area that seems to be so central for hunger. That explanation is unlikely, however. Many people with anorexia enjoy preparing food and seem quite interested in food, and yet they avoid eating it in far more extreme ways than do people who are merely not hungry. For example, some people with anorexia refuse even to lick postage stamps, for fear that the glue might contain some tiny fraction of a calorie. A mere lack of hunger could not explain such an extreme and misguided behavior.

A better description of anorexia nervosa is that it reflects a "pathological fear of

FIGURE 11.19
Beauty is in the eye of the beholder. Many cultures, including Europe in earlier centuries, have had a standard of female beauty that is noticeably plumper than that of western society today. Presumably, a society with no pressure for extreme thinness is also a culture with little likelihood of anorexia nervosa.

fatness." Even when anorexic women grow painfully thin, they often describe themselves as "looking fat" and "needing to lose weight" (Figure 11.20). Anorexia might be described as a special case of Maslow's hierarchy of needs: An anorexic woman manages to suppress her lower-level hunger needs in order to pursue higher-level goals of self-control and self-esteem. But her biology does not give up; even while she refuses to eat, her thoughts may be preoccupied with food.

BULIMIA

Other people, again mostly young women, starve themselves at times but occasionally throw themselves into an eating binge. They may consume up to 20,000 calories at a time (Schlesier-Stropp, 1984)—the equivalent of about 30 Big Macs, 10 helpings of french fries, and 10 chocolate milkshakes. Some, but not all, force themselves to vomit or use laxatives after gorging on these enormous meals. People who alternate between self-starvation and excessive eating are said to suffer from bulimia (literally, "ox hunger"). Like anorexic women, they are preoccupied with food and show an exaggerated fear of growing fat (Striegel-Moore, Silberstein, & Rodin, 1986). Unlike anorexic women, they do not necessarily remain thin.

We might imagine that people who go on eating binges might starve themselves for a while to make up for it. According to Janet Polivy and Peter Herman (1985), however, the causation goes in the other direction: It is the dieting that causes the binges. Bulimic people starve themselves far below their normal weight; they then fight their persistent feelings of hunger for a while and then go on an eating binge.

IMPLICATIONS

The research on anorexia and bulimia underscores an important point about motivation in general: Our motivations are controlled by a complex mixture of physiological, social, and cognitive forces. People become overweight (or perceive themselves as overweight) for a variety of reasons, and then try to lose weight mostly for social reasons, such as trying to look attractive. Sometimes the physiological factors and the social factors collide, as when normal-weight people try to make themselves thinner and thinner.

What motivates someone to become anorexic? First, many women who become anorexic have always prized self-control. Their extreme weight loss demonstrates extreme self-control and thereby raises their self-esteem. Also, maintaining a dangerously low weight is a way of rebelling quietly and of attracting attention. Before the onset of the disorder, most anorexic girls are described as having been obedient, conforming, and highly intelligent perfectionists—girls who never gave their parents or teachers any trouble (Bruch, 1980; Goldstein, 1981; Rowland, 1970). Their severe weight loss attracts attention and even prestige. The anorexic girl who comes to enjoy the attention may be reluctant to lose it by gaining weight.

The overall point is this: All motivations interact and combine. How much we eat depends on the need for food, but also on social and self-esteem needs.

FIGURE 11.20
A fun house mirror causes a temporary distortion of anyone's body appearance. People with anorexia nervosa experience a similar distortion of body image at all times, seeing themselves as much fatter than they really are.

foods, we can learn how much to eat, based on the number of calories in the food. (page 472)

- *Long-term regulation of intake.* An individual meal may be larger or smaller than necessary to provide the energy the body needs. In the long run, a person compensates for such fluctuations by regulating body weight. When weight increases, hunger decreases; when weight decreases, hunger increases. (page 473)

- *Food selection.* Food preferences can be altered by changes in body chemistry, such as a deficiency of salt. Other things being equal, we tend to prefer familiar foods. We avoid foods that have been followed by illness and foods that we associate with something repulsive, even if the food itself is harmless. (page 474)

- *Causes of being overweight.* Several factors contribute to a person becoming overweight. High levels of insulin increase weight by causing blood glucose to be stored as fats. Genetic factors predispose certain people to become obese, through increased levels of a particular protein that is currently not well understood. Inactive people are more likely to gain weight than active people. (page 476)

SUMMARY

- *Hunger.* Mechanisms that monitor the amount of glucose and other fuels in the cells regulate hunger. The availability of glucose depends on the hormone insulin, which facilitates the entry of glucose into the cells. (page 470)

- *Satiety.* We stop eating when food distends the stomach, if not before. With familiar

- *Weight-loss techniques.* People in our society resort to a variety of strategies to lose weight, with varying degrees of success. (page 478)
- *Effects of unnecessary weight loss.* Normal-weight people who follow a strict diet have a strong desire to eat more than they do. On occasion, they abandon their diet and indulge in eating binges. (page 478)
- *Anorexia nervosa.* People suffering from anorexia nervosa deprive themselves of food, sometimes to the point of starvation. They suppress their physiological drives to satisfy other motivations, such as self-esteem. People suffering from bulimia alternate between periods of strict dieting and brief but spectacular eating binges. (page 480)

SUGGESTIONS FOR FURTHER READING

Logue, A. W. (1991). *The psychology of eating and drinking* (2nd ed.). New York: Freeman. Discusses normal and abnormal eating, including anorexia and bulimia.

Rozin, P., & Vollmecke, T. A. (1986). Food likes and dislikes. *Annual Review of Nutrition, 6,* 433–456. A review of the factors that influence our choice of foods.

TERMS

glucose the most abundant sugar in the blood (page 471)

insulin a hormone which the pancreas releases to increase the entry of glucose and other nutrients into the cells (page 471)

glucagon a hormone which the pancreas releases to convert stored energy supplies into blood glucose (page 471)

satiety the experience of being full, of feeling no more hunger (page 473)

set point a level of some variable (such as weight) that the body attempts to maintain (page 473)

lateral hypothalamus an area of the brain that contributes to the control of hunger (page 474)

ventromedial hypothalamus an area of the brain in which damage leads to weight gain via an increase in the frequency of meals (page 474)

paraventricular hypothalamus an area of the brain in which damage leads to weight gain via an increase in the size of meals (page 474)

obesity the excessive accumulation of body fat (page 476)

anorexia nervosa a condition in which a person refuses to eat adequate food and steadily loses weight (page 481)

bulimia a condition in which a person alternates between self-starvation and excessive eating (page 482)

ANSWERS TO CONCEPT CHECKS

3. Insulin levels are higher in the middle of the day (LeMagnen, 1981). As a result, much of the food you eat is stored as fats and you become hungry again soon. Late at night, when insulin levels are lower, some of your fat supplies are converted to glucose, which enters the blood. (page 472)

4. The set point has increased. (page 474)

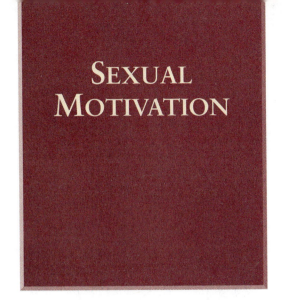

SEXUAL MOTIVATION

What causes sexual arousal?

What sexual customs are prevalent in our society?

What accounts for some of the variations in sexual practices?

For most of us, sexual activity does not occupy a major fraction of the average day—but thinking about sex does. If you have any doubts about people's interest in sex, consult the television listings, popular books and magazines, and films. In fact, one way that people can tell they are getting old is that they only think about sex most of the time, instead of all the time.

Humans, unlike most other mammalian species, are interested in sex even at those times of the month when a woman is unlikely to get pregnant; in fact, we often take measures to prevent pregnancy. Most couples stay together not only long enough to rear children but also long after the children are grown up. Sexual motivation is a force that binds people together in powerful and intimate relationships, and also sometimes drives them apart.

Like hunger, sexual motivation depends on both a physiological drive and available incentives. Again as with hunger, the sex drive increases during a time of deprivation, at least up to a point, and it can be inhibited for social and symbolic reasons, including religious vows.

However, the sex drive differs from hunger in important ways. We do not need to be around food in order to feel hungry; many people do need the presence of an attractive partner to feel sexual arousal. We eat in public; having sex in public is not recommended. Moreover, many people have sexual preferences that other people find hard to understand.

WHAT DO PEOPLE DO AND HOW OFTEN DO THEY DO IT?

Researchers have many reasons for inquiring about the frequency of various sexual behaviors. For example, if we want to predict how fast and how far the AIDS virus is likely to spread in the population, it is important to know how many people are having unsafe sex with a variety of partners.

In addition to the important scientific and medical reasons for investigating sexual behavior, let's admit it: Most of us are curious about what other people do. We would like to know, "Am I normal? Am I doing something wrong or shameful? Am I missing out on pleasures that everyone else is having?"

The answers depend on what we mean by "normal." If that term means "common within the population," then almost anything you are doing or not doing is normal.

Sexual customs vary sharply from one society to another. These people play "kiss-a-girl" in traditional Ukrainian costumes while riding galloping horses. The point of the game is ostensibly to develop horse-riding skills, but clearly that is not the only motivation.

People vary enormously in their sexual behavior and interests.

THE KINSEY SURVEY

The first important survey of human sexual behavior was conducted by Alfred C. Kinsey (Figure 11.21), a shy and studious insect biologist who once agreed to teach the biological portion of Indiana University's course on marriage. When he found that the library included very little information about human sexuality, he decided to conduct a survey. What he intended as a small-scale project eventually grew into a survey of 18,000 people.

Although Kinsey had a large sample, it was neither random nor representative. He obtained most of his interviews by going to organizations, ranging from fraternities to nunneries, and trying to get everyone in the organization to talk to him. As a result, he interviewed mostly midwesterners, mostly European Americans, who belonged to organizations that agreed to cooperate. Because of Kinsey's unrepresentative sample, his data do not provide a trustworthy estimate of the frequencies of various behaviors in the U.S. population.

Nevertheless, he did document the great variation that occurs in human sexual behavior (Kinsey, Pomeroy, & Martin, 1948; Kinsey, Pomeroy, Martin, & Gebhard, 1953). For example, he found some men and women who had rarely or never experienced orgasm. At the other extreme, he found one man who reported an average of four to five orgasms a day over the preceding 30 years, and several women who sometimes had 50 or more orgasms within 20 minutes.

Kinsey found that most people were unaware of the great variation in sexual behavior in the population at large. For example, when he asked people whether they believed that "excessive masturbation" causes physical and mental illness, most said they did. (We now know it does not.) He then asked what would constitute "excessive." For each person, "excessive" meant a little more than what he or she did. One young man who masturbated about once a month said he thought three times a month would be excessive and would cause mental illness. Another man, who masturbated three times a day, said he thought five times a day would be excessive. (In reaction to these findings, Kinsey once defined *nymphomaniac* as "someone who wants sex more than you do.")

MODERN SURVEYS

Kinsey did not even try to interview a random sample of the population, because he assumed that most people would refuse to cooperate and perhaps even take offense at being asked. He may have been right about people in the 1940s; however, his assumptions clearly do not hold today. In the 1980s and 1990s, researchers identified random samples of the U.S. population and managed to get cooperation from most of the people they approached (Fay, Turner, Klassen, & Gagnon, 1989; Laumann, Gagnon, Michael, & Michaels, 1994).

(Some advice if anyone asks you to participate in a sex survey: Do not cooperate until you know who the questioner is. Legitimate researchers are careful to present their credentials to show their affiliation with a research institute. They also take elaborate precautions to guarantee the confidentiality of people's responses. If "researchers" who want to ask you sex questions fail to present their credentials or seem unconcerned about your confidentiality, do not trust them. Be especially wary of sex surveys by telephone. Although a few sex researchers do conduct research by telephone, most prefer a face-to-face interview. If in doubt, assume the alleged "survey" is an obscene phone call in disguise.)

FIGURE 11.21

Alfred C. Kinsey pioneered survey studies of sexual behavior. As an interviewer he was peerless—he always put people at ease so that they could speak freely, but he was also alert to detect probable lies. His results should be interpreted cautiously, because he did not obtain a random or representative sample of the population.

A modern survey of a random sample of almost 3,500 U.S. adults (Laumann, Gagnon, Michael, & Michaels, 1994) has added greatly to our knowledge of U.S. sexual practices and customs. First, what would people *like* to be doing? Figure 11.22 shows the percentage of men and women who describe various sexual activities as "very appealing." Clearly, the most popular sexual activity is vaginal intercourse. Watching one's partner undress is "very appealing" to a large minority of people; so is oral sex. Other possible options lag well behind. Note an ambiguity in people's responses: A response of "very appealing" might mean, "I have enjoyed doing that activity," "I would like to try that activity," or "I greatly enjoy fantasizing about that activity, although I might decline to do it in real life." (One wonders, for example, about the 13% of men who find group sex very appealing.)

Note that a higher percentage of men than women report an interest in every activity on the list. Other studies have reported similar results. In addition to the differences shown in Figure 11.22, men are much more likely than women to masturbate frequently and to look forward to opportunities for casual sex (Oliver & Hyde, 1993). However, in spite of men's desire for more frequent and more varied sexual activities, men and women are about equally likely to express satisfaction with their current sex lives.

Figure 11.23 shows the number of sex partners in the last year for people of various ages. At all ages, most report either one partner or none. The percentage of people having multiple partners is greatest in young adulthood and declines steadily at older ages.

The results in Figure 11.23 are cross-sectional, not longitudinal. That is, the 20-year-olds and 50-year-olds grew up in different eras. Figure 11.24 emphasizes these differences among cohorts. People were asked how many sex partners they had had in their lifetime. As Figure 11.24 shows, people in their forties were more likely to report a large number of partners than were people in their fifties. The reason is that people who were in their 50s at the time of the survey (1992) grew up before the so-called "sexual revolution." A "reverse sexual revolution" may be happening today, as many young people, fearful of AIDS, become more cautious about having multiple sex partners.

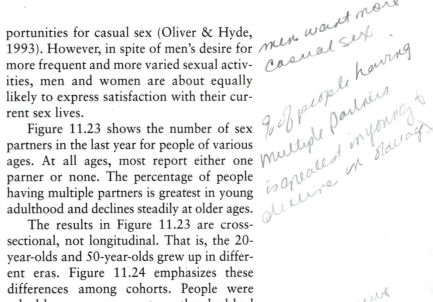

men want more casual sex

% of people having multiple partners is greatest in young adulthood or decline in stds age

Today experience reverse sexual revolution because of aids

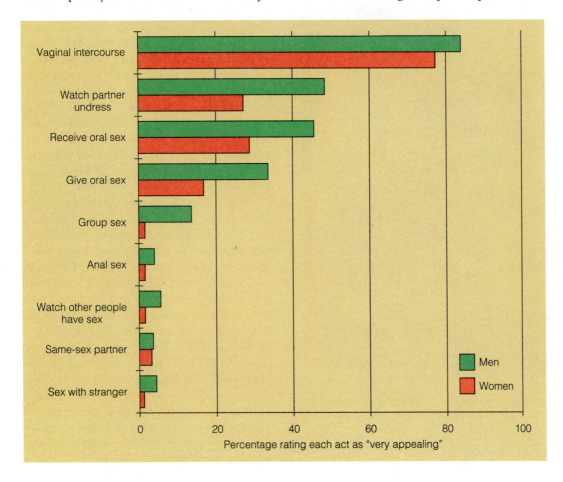

FIGURE 11.22
Percentage of U.S. adults who rate various sexual activities as very appealing, *as opposed to* somewhat, not, *or* not at all. *(Based on data of Laumann, Gagnon, Michael, & Michaels, 1994.)*

Vaginal intercourse

Watch partner undress

Receive oral sex

Give oral sex

Group sex

Anal sex

Watch other people have sex

Same-sex partner

Sex with stranger

Men
Women

0   20   40   60   80   100

Percentage rating each act as "very appealing"

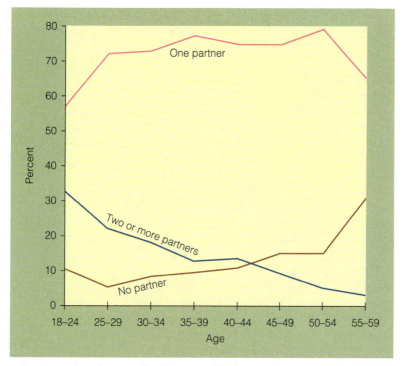

FIGURE 11.23
Number of sex partners in the last 12 months, by U.S. adults of various ages, both sexes combined. (Based on data of Laumann, Gagnon, Michael, & Michaels, 1994.)

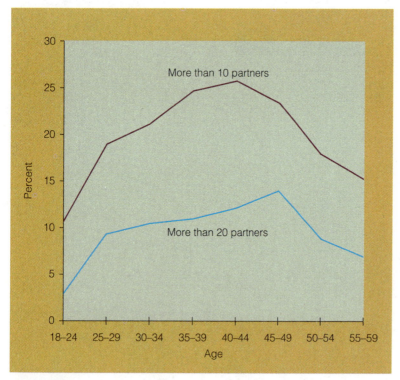

FIGURE 11.24
Percentage of U.S. adults (both sexes combined) reporting more than 10 or 20 sex partners over their lifetime. (Based on data of Laumann, Gagnon, Michael, & Michaels, 1994.)

In Figure 11.25 you can see differences in sexual activity by people of different ages. Note that the older respondents are less likely than the young to report having sex more than twice a week. That trend is probably a real effect of age, not a cohort effect. That is, most 50- to 60-year-olds agree that they are having sexual relations less often than they did when they were younger.

Finally, how many people have a homosexual orientation? You have probably heard many people announce the figure "10 percent" as if it were an established fact. That number derives from Kinsey's survey from the 1940s and 1950s. Kinsey reported that about 13% of the men and 7% of the women he interviewed reported a predominantly homosexual orientation. The often quoted figure of 10% is simply the mean of Kinsey's results for men and women. However, Kinsey's data were based on a very nonrandom sample of the population.

According to a survey of a random sample of 3,500 U.S. adults, 2.8% of men and 1.4% of women describe themselves as having a homosexual (gay or lesbian) orientation (Laumann et al., 1994). As Figure 11.26 illustrates, heterosexuality versus homosexuality is a continuum. Just as many left-handed people perform some tasks with their right hand, and most right-handed people have at least tried various tasks with their left hand, similarly a number of people have at least experimented with both homosexual and heterosexual activities. Over 4% of both men and women report at least one adult homosexual experience. If we expand the scope to "lifetime" (including early puberty), 9% of men report at least one homosexual experience.

If you have frequently heard the prevalence of homosexual orientations estimated at "10%," you may be skeptical of the report that only 1–3% of people regard themselves as mostly gay or lesbian. However, three other large surveys of U.S. men reported that 1–2%, 3%, or 6% of U.S. men were gay or bisexual (Billy, Tanfer, Grady, & Klepinger, 1993; Cameron, Proctor, Coburn, & Forde, 1985; Fay, Turner, Klassen, & Gagnon, 1989). The study reporting the 6% figure had the least satisfactory sampling technique. Surveys in Britain and France have reported a slightly lower prevalence of homosexual orientations, as shown in Figure 11.27 (Spira, et al. 1993; Wellings, Field, Johnson, & Wadsworth, 1994).

The frequencies of various sexual practices vary, of course, among cultures and historical eras. Certainly a sex survey of the United States in 1992 does not apply to other locations or other times. A number of studies have reported on the exotic sexual customs of people in certain nonwestern cultures (Davenport, 1977). When we consider how difficult it has been to get reasonably accurate data about U.S. sexual practices, we should be a bit skeptical about studies in which anthropologists have interviewed a few people about the sexual customs of their culture. Nevertheless, observable practices (such as dating, marriage, and public display of the human body) vary so strikingly that we can clearly say that much of sexual behavior is the product of learned customs, not just of biological necessity.

SEXUAL BEHAVIOR IN THE AIDS ERA

During the 1980s, a new factor entered into people's sexual motivations: The fear of **acquired immune deficiency syndrome (AIDS)**, a new and deadly sexually transmitted disease that gradually destroys the body's immune system.

For the AIDS virus to spread from one person to another, it must enter the second person's blood. (Outside the blood or the body's cells, the virus cannot survive.) There are three common routes of transmission: transfusions of contaminated blood, sharing needles used for intravenous injections, and sexual contact. Casual contact between people, even kissing, does not spread the virus (unless perhaps both people had a cut on the mouth that was actively bleeding at the time of the kiss).

An infected male has about a 3% chance of transmitting the virus to a female during vaginal intercourse; an infected woman has no more than a 2% chance, probably much less, of transmitting it to a male (Kaplan, 1988). The likelihood of transmission increases if either partner has an open wound on the genitals or if the woman is menstruating. The probability of transmission during anal intercourse is much higher, about 7–10%, because the lining of the rectum is likely to be torn (Kaplan, 1988). None of these estimates can be completely accurate, of course.

For generations, people have known how to avoid contracting syphilis, gonorrhea, and other sexually transmitted diseases: Don't have sex with someone who might be infected, or when in doubt, use a condom. (To be completely safe, don't have

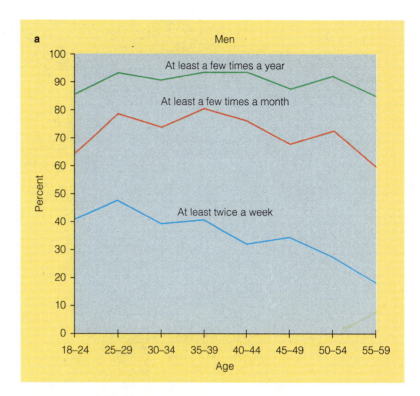

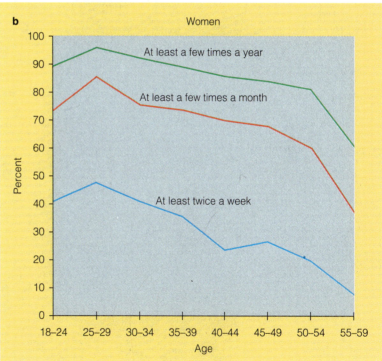

FIGURE 11.25
Percentage of U.S. adults who have had sexual relations with a partner at various frequencies in the last year. (a) Results for men. (b) Results for women. (Based on data of Laumann, Gagnon, Michael, & Michaels, 1994.)

sex at all.) Because AIDS is life-threatening and (so far) incurable, it has had a greater impact on sexual customs than other sexually transmitted diseases have had. Since the advent of AIDS, many people, especially homosexual men, have grown more cautious,

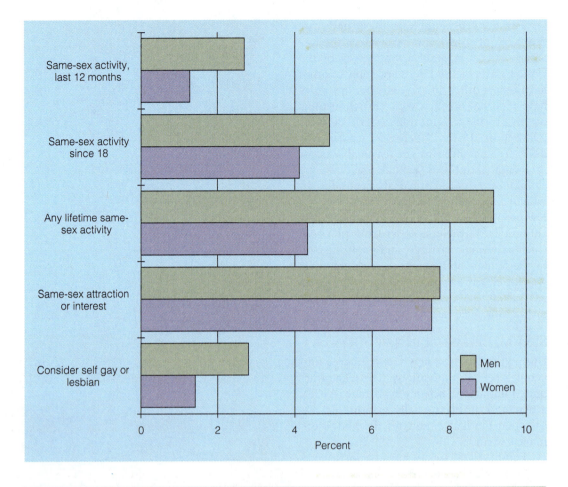

FIGURE 11.26
Percentage of U.S. adults who report sexual activity or interest in sexual activity with members of their own sex. (Based on data of Laumann, Gagnon, Michael, & Michaels, 1994.)

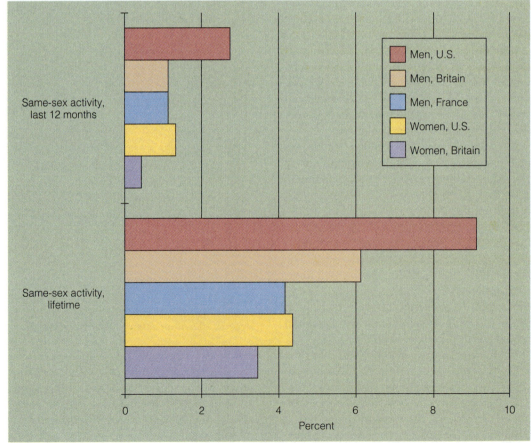

FIGURE 11.27
Comparisons of results of surveys in three countries asking people whether they have engaged in homosexual activity. (Based on data of Laumann, Gagnon, Michael, & Michaels, 1994; Spira et al., 1993; Wellings, Field, Johnson, & Wadsworth, 1994.)

Human cultures set very different standards about public display of the human body, as well as about dating, marriage, and premarital sex.

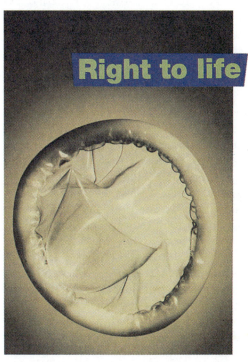

Right to life

AIDS is a preventable disease. By using condoms during sex and by not sharing injection needles with other people, one can greatly decrease the probability of transmitting or receiving the AIDS virus. Advertisements such as this one have prompted many people to change their behaviors.

choosing long-term sexual partners and using condoms to reduce the likelihood of transmitting the virus. One study of men leaving a homosexual bathhouse found that only 10% were engaging in anal sex without a condom—a far lower percentage than was common prior to the AIDS crisis (Richwald et al., 1988).

Some heterosexual couples also have become more cautious, although that increase is not impressive overall. According to one national survey in 1990, only 17% of heterosexuals with multiple sexual partners and 12.6% of heterosexuals with "risky" sexual partners used condoms consistently (Catania et al., 1992). Choosing whether or not to have sex, or how or with whom, is a special kind of decision-making. The continuing spread of the AIDS virus and the continuing number of unwanted pregnancies indicate that a large number of people continue to make unwise decisions about sex (Wyatt, 1994).

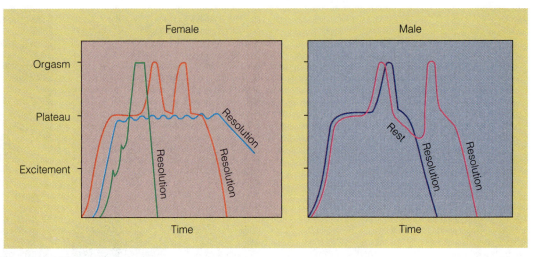

FIGURE 11.28

Sexual arousal usually proceeds through four stages—excitement, plateau, orgasm, and resolution. Each line represents the response of a different individual. (After Masters & Johnson, 1966.)

SEXUAL AROUSAL

Sexual motivation depends on both physiological and cognitive influences. William Masters and Virginia Johnson (1966), who pioneered the study of human sexual response, discovered that physiological arousal during the sex act is about the same in men and women. They observed hundreds of people engaging in masturbation and sexual intercourse in a laboratory and monitored their physiological responses, including heart rate, breathing, muscle tension, blood engorgement of the genitals and breasts, and nipple erection. Masters and Johnson identified four physiological stages in sexual arousal (Figure 11.28). During the first stage, *excitement,* a man's penis becomes erect and a woman's vagina becomes lubricated. Breathing grows rapid and deep. Heart rate and blood pressure increase. Many people experience a flush of the skin, which sometimes resembles a measles rash. Women's nipples become erect, and, if they have never nursed a baby, their breasts swell slightly. Although this stage is referred to as excitement, it actually requires some degree of relaxation. Nervousness interferes with sexual excitement; so do stimulant drugs (even coffee).

During the second stage, called the *plateau,* excitement remains fairly constant. This stage lasts for varying lengths of time, depending on the person's age and the intensity of the stimulation. During the third stage, excitement becomes intense and is followed by a sudden relief of tension known as *climax* or *orgasm,* which is felt throughout the entire body. During the fourth and final stage, *resolution,* the person returns to an unaroused state.

As Figure 11.28 shows, the pattern of excitation varies from one person to another. During a given episode, a woman may experience no orgasm at all, a single orgasm, or many. Men do not experience multiple consecutive orgasms, although they may achieve orgasm again following a rest (or refractory) period. In both sexes, the intensity of orgasm ranges from something like a sigh to an extremely intense experience.

At any rate, that is the usual pattern. Some people are unable to complete the four stages of arousal. Some men cannot get or maintain an erection. Others have premature ejaculations; they advance from excitement to orgasm sooner than they or their partners wish. A substantial number of women, perhaps as many as 10%, and a few men stay at the plateau stage without experiencing orgasm. The reasons for such sexual dysfunctions include both physiological disorders and competing motivations. For example, some people are inhibited in their sexual arousal because they have been taught that sex is shameful. When the problems are motivational rather than physiological, a therapist can work with people to reduce their anxieties or to help them learn new patterns of sexual activity more satisfactory to both themselves and their partners (Andersen, 1983).

SEXUAL IDENTITY AND ORIENTATION

Just as hunger includes two major aspects—how much food to eat and which foods to choose—sexual motivation includes two aspects: how frequently to have sex and with whom. People vary in their sexual preferences, just as they do in their food preferences or any other aspect of life. Why do some people prefer partners of the opposite sex and others prefer partners of their own sex?

Psychologists distinguish two aspects of being male or female: sexual identity and sexual orientation. Sexual identity is the sex the person regards himself or herself as being. With rare exceptions, people who look male call themselves male and people who look female call themselves female. Sexual orientation is the person's preference for male or female sex partners (or both). People who prefer partners of their own sex have a homosexual (gay or lesbian) orientation. Sexual identity is based partly on anatomical and physiological factors, partly on social influences. Psychologists do not yet fully understand the causes of sexual orientation.

INFLUENCES ON SEXUAL ANATOMY

In the earliest stages of development, the human fetus has a "unisex" appearance (Figure 11.29). One structure subsequently develops into either a penis or a clitoris; another structure develops into either a scrotum or labia. The direction this development takes depends on hormonal influences during prenatal development. For humans, the most important period for development of sexual anatomy is the third and fourth month of pregnancy. At that time, genetic male fetuses generally secrete relatively high levels of the hormone testosterone, and the testosterone causes the tiny fetal structures to grow into a penis and a scrotum. Genetic female fetuses ordinarily secrete lower levels of testosterone; because of the low testosterone, their structures develop into a clitoris and labia. High levels of the hormone estrogen are also present at this time, especially in females but also in males. However,

because sexual development depends mostly on the testosterone levels, the estrogen levels in the blood have little effect on sexual development.

Remember: In humans and other mammals, high testosterone levels produce a male anatomy; low testosterone levels produce a female anatomy. Within normal limits, the amount of circulating estrogen is not an important influence on the development of sexual anatomy.

In rare cases, a female fetus may be subject to a somewhat elevated testosterone level. For example, the mother might have a tumor that produces testosterone, or the mother might be taking medications with effects similar to testosterone. Under the influence of elevated testosterone, the genetic female may then develop a sexual anatomy that looks intermediate between male and female (Money & Ehrhardt, 1972).

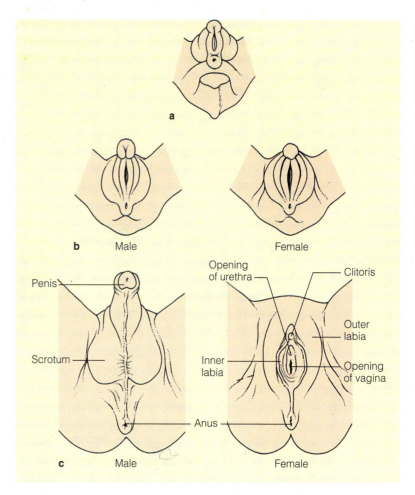

FIGURE 11.29
The human genitals look the same for male and female for about the first 6 weeks after conception (a). Differences begin to emerge in the second trimester (b) and are clearly developed at birth (c).

Sexual orientation probably depends on the combined influences of many factors, some biological and some experiential, but the full explanation is far from certain at this point.

[handwritten margin note:] lesbian because sexually abuse by men or genetics

Some psychologists believe that the psychological makeup of adults reflects the early unisex nature of the fetus. According to this view, we go through life with the potential to adopt either the male or the female role in our relationships with others and to respond sexually to either male or female partners. For most people, only half of that potential expresses itself. What activates one half or the other—or both? It may be that hormonal levels in the fetus influence subsequent sexual behavior, as they influence sexual anatomy. However, the evidence is not conclusive (Hines, 1982). I shall discuss some of it later in this section.

CONCEPT CHECK

5. If a human fetus were exposed to very low levels of both testosterone and estrogen throughout prenatal development, how would the sexual anatomy appear? (Check your answer on page 499.)

INFLUENCES ON SEXUAL ORIENTATION

The origins and determinants of sexual orientation are not yet well understood. Adult homosexuals often report that their sexual preference was apparent to them from as early an age as they can remember. They did not choose it voluntarily, and they could not change it any more easily than a left-hander could become a right-hander. (A left-hander could learn to use the right hand for certain tasks, but doing so would not make the person right-handed.) What causes some

people to develop a heterosexual preference and others to develop a homosexual preference? There probably are several contributing factors.

The research I shall discuss deals almost entirely with gay men. Lesbians (women with a homosexual orientation) are less likely than gay men to frequent gay bars, join gay organizations, or subscribe to gay publications. Many are sufficiently private about their orientation that they become "invisible" to researchers. The research we do have suggests that some women become lesbians after being sexually abused by men, especially in childhood (Gundlach, 1977). Others are predisposed toward lesbianism for other reasons, possibly including genetics (Bailey, Pillard, Neale, & Agyei, 1993).

Society's attitudes toward homosexuality have changed repeatedly over time. So far as we can tell, the ancient Greeks and Romans considered it fairly typical for men to engage in occasional sexual activities with each other as well as with women (Boswell, 1990). (The Greek and Roman writers had little to say about women's sexual interests.) In a later era, Europeans regarded male homosexuality as sinful or criminal. By the early 20th century, the "enlightened" view was that homosexuality was not sinful, but merely a sign of disease or mental illness. The evidence, however, was based on a badly distorted sample: Psychiatrists and psychologists were acquainted with homosexual men who had sought help for psychological troubles. But homosexual men without psychological problems never consulted therapists, and therefore the therapists did not know that such men existed. Studies of homosexual men who have never gone to a therapist revealed that many homosexual men are content and well adjusted (Siegelman, 1974). Consequently, psychologists and psychiatrists today consider a homosexual orientation to be a natural variation in sexual motivation.

Many factors influence sexual orientation, differing from one person to another. Genetics is one possible contributing factor. Figure 11.30 shows the results of one study concerning homosexuality in twins and other relatives of adult gays and lesbians (Bailey & Pillard, 1991; Bailey, Pillard, Neale, & Agyei, 1993). Note that homosexuality is more prevalent in the monozygotic (identical) twins than in the dizygotic (fraternal) twins. That trend suggests a possible

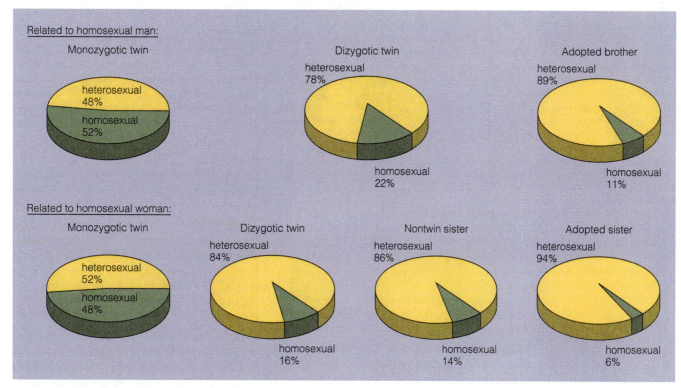

FIGURE 11.30

The probability of a homosexual orientation is higher among monozygotic twins of adult homosexuals than among their dizygotic twins. The probability is higher among dizygotic twins than among adopted brothers or sisters who grew up in the same family. These data suggest a possible role of genes in the development of sexual orientation. (Based on results of Bailey & Pillard, 1991; Bailey, Pillard, Neale, & Agyei, 1993.)

genetic influence toward homosexuality, although a gene could hardly be the only factor. (If it were, then 100% of the monozygotic twins would have homosexual orientations.) Note also that homosexuality is more common among the dizygotic twins than among adopted brothers. That trend also suggests a genetic factor, although it could also indicate the influence of some factor in the prenatal environment, shared by twins but not by boys who simply grow up in the same family. If genetic influences contribute to homosexuality, the genes influencing males are different from those influencing females. That is, gay men have a high percentage of gay relatives but not of lesbian relatives; lesbian women have a high percentage of lesbian relatives but not of gay relatives.

If genes affect sexual orientation, they must do so by altering the development of some part of the body, possibly the brain. Other possible influences on sexual orientation, such as prenatal hormones, may also alter brain anatomy. Regardless of the roles of genetics, hormones, and other factors, the evidence suggests a measurable difference in brain anatomy between homosexual and heterosexual men. Let us examine that evidence.

WHAT'S THE EVIDENCE?

Relationship Between Sexual Orientation and Brain Anatomy

Animal studies have demonstrated that one section of the anterior hypothalamus, known to neuroanatomists as INAH3, is generally larger in males than it is in females and that it is necessary for the display of male-typical sexual activity. Its growth is known to depend on prenatal hormones. This, then, is an interesting area to compare in the brains of homosexual and heterosexual men.

Hypothesis INAH3, a particular cluster of neurons in the anterior hypothalamus, will be larger, on average, in the brains of heterosexual men than in the brains of homosexual men or heterosexual women.

Method Simon LeVay (1991) examined the brains of 41 young or middle-aged adults

neurons in hypothalamus is larger in heterosexual men than homosexual men.

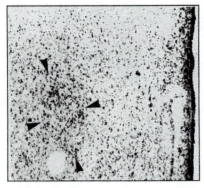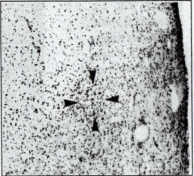

FIGURE 11.31
One section of the anterior hypothalamus (marked by arrows) is larger, on the average, in the brains of heterosexual men (left) than in the brains of homosexual men (right) or heterosexual women (LeVay, 1991). Review Figure 11.10 for the location of the hypothalamus.

(ages 26–59) who had died of AIDS or other causes. AIDS was the cause of death for all 19 of the homosexual men in the study, 6 of the 16 heterosexual men, and 1 of the 6 heterosexual women. No brains of homosexual women were available for study. LeVay measured the sizes of four clusters of neurons in the anterior hypothalamus, including two clusters for which sex differences are common and two which do not differ between the sexes.

Results LeVay found that three of the four neuron clusters did not consistently vary in size among the groups he studied. However, area INAH3 was, on the average, about twice as large in heterosexual men as it was in homosexual men, and about the same size in homosexual men as it was in heterosexual women. Figure 11.31 shows results for two representative individuals. The results probably do not simply reflect the cause of death; among heterosexual men, the size of this brain area did not depend on whether the men died of AIDS or of other causes.

Interpretation These results suggest that the size of the INAH3 area of the anterior hypothalamus may be related to heterosexual versus homosexual orientation, at least for some individuals. These results are consistent with the idea that genes or prenatal hormones guide brain development, thus altering the probabilities of developing various sexual orientations. However, they are not entirely conclusive. Conceivably, a homosexual or heterosexual lifestyle might alter brain anatomy instead of the other way around. Also, we do not know whether the people LeVay studied were representative of other

people; certainly we must await replications on other samples. Finally, the variations in brain structure from one person to another indicate that brain anatomy does not completely control sexual orientation. (The INAH3 nucleus was fairly large in some homosexual men and fairly small in some heterosexual men.)

So, where do all these studies leave us? At this point, the evidence links certain biological factors, including genes and brain anatomy, to male homosexuality, at least for some individuals. We know little, however, about how those biological predispositions combine with experience to produce sexual orientation. Indeed, researchers do not know which kinds of experiences are most crucial. We shall need to await additional studies before we can draw any confident conclusion.

Uncertainty and tentative conclusions are not unusual in psychology. If you decide to become a psychologist, you will have to get used to the words *maybe* and *probably*. As I pointed out in Chapter 2, psychologists rarely talk about "proving" a conclusion; they merely increase or decrease their confidence in a conclusion.

CONCEPT CHECK

6. *Most studies find that adult homosexual men have approximately the same levels of testosterone in their blood as heterosexual men of the same age. Do such results conflict with the suggestion that prenatal hormonal conditions predispose certain men to homosexuality? (Check your answer on page 499.)*

MOTIVATION AND RAPE

Up to this point we have been considering sexual behavior among consenting adults. Not all behavior meets that description. Rape is sexual contact obtained through violence, threats, or intimidation. The perpetrator may be guided by various combinations of sexual and violent motivations. Although, theoretically, both men and women can commit rape, virtually all rapes are, in fact, attacks by men.

In principle, rape is easy to define; in practice, we find a continuum from forcible rape through cases of mild, ambiguous resistance. For example, 9% of the women surveyed at 32 colleges reported that they had been forced into unwanted sexual intercourse, and 25% said they had participated in unwanted intercourse in response to verbal coaxing or while under the influence of alcohol (Koss, Gidycz, & Wisniewski, 1987; see Figure 11.32). At the same colleges, only 4.4% of the men said they had forced a woman to have sex (Koss & Dinero, 1988). Although it is possible that a small percentage of the men forced themselves sexually on a large percentage of the women, a more likely interpretation is that men and women interpreted the same events differently. Most of the unwanted sex was in the context of dates, not assaults by a stranger. In many cases the couple had kissed and petted voluntarily; when the man progressed to intercourse, evidently the woman declined and the man either disbelieved or disregarded her refusal.

What motivates men to rape? That is a hard question to answer, because most of our data are based on men who have been actually *convicted* of rape. The men most likely to be convicted are those who commit repeated, violent attacks. Such men may not be representative of other rapists; indeed, it is hard to imagine how researchers could obtain a representative sample. Still, the best available evidence indicates that most men who sexually attack women have a history of hostility and violence against men as well as women (Malamuth, Sockloskie, Koss, & Tanaka, 1991). Many rapists were abused children; many feel anger toward women and a need to dominate or control them. Although much less is known about date rapists, one survey of admitted date rapists found that they also reported anger toward women and a drive to dominate them (Lisak & Roth, 1988).

Some psychologists distinguish between rapists who intended to humiliate and injure their victims and those who used only enough force to subdue their victims. However, it is difficult to determine whether a rapist is using force just to obtain compliance or is indulging in violence for its own sake (Prentky, Knight, & Rosenberg, 1988).

Some rapists have a weak sex drive or are almost impotent; they hope to find sexual satisfaction by being "completely in charge," something they cannot manage with a willing partner. Most rapists are sexually

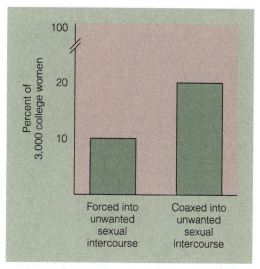

FIGURE 11.32
Date rape is prevalent among college students. Knowing the assailant doesn't mean it isn't rape.

aroused by photos and audiotapes of rape, whereas most other men are either unaroused or repulsed (Earls, 1988). To judge whether a convicted rapist is still dangerous, measurements of his sexual arousal are sometimes made while he listens to tapes. Men who develop erections while listening to descriptions of rape are considered to be still dangerous.

Rape is a complex matter, and, like other motivated behaviors, it has a variety of causes. While a rapist may have been an abused child or may feel anger toward women, these circumstances do not explain why he commits an attack at a particular moment. In many cases, he is so intoxicated from alcohol or other drugs that he sheds the inhibitions that would ordinarily prevent such an attack (Lisak & Roth, 1988). Psychologists have much to learn before they can understand rape and contribute to its prevention.

What should a woman do if a man is trying to rape her? Some psychologists recommend fighting back; others recommend trying to appeal to the would-be rapist's better nature; others recommend doing something to upset or offend the rapist, such as vomiting. However, for each of these recommendations, one can find other psychologists who say it is a bad idea, likely to backfire (Fischhoff, 1992). The problem is that no one approach is sure to succeed or sure to fail; the results depend on the woman, the man, and the setting.

Unless people call attention to the phenomenon of date rape, it is easily ignored. Women raped on a date seldom report it to the police; the men who force a woman to have sex on a date seldom perceive their act as rape.

SOMETHING TO THINK ABOUT

Rapists and child molesters sometimes pore over sexually explicit magazines and videotapes just before committing an offense (Malamuth & Donnerstein, 1982; Marshall, 1988). Can we conclude that such materials lead to the offenses? (Remember, correlation does not mean causation.) What kind of evidence would we need to determine whether sexually explicit materials lead to sex offenses?

SUMMARY

• *Variability in human sexual behavior.* Alfred Kinsey, who conducted the first extensive survey of human sexual behavior, found that sexual activity varies more widely than most people realize. (page 486)

• *Prevalence of sexual behaviors.* Modern surveys indicate that most U.S. adults have either one sex partner or none during a given year. Men express a greater interest than women do in varied sexual practices with varied partners. Nevertheless, sexual satisfaction is about equal for men and women. (page 486)

• *Prevalence of homosexuality.* According to several surveys, about 1–3% of U.S. and Western European adults regard themselves as gay or lesbian. A larger number of people, especially men, who regard themselves as heterosexual have experimented with homosexual activities, especially during adolescence. (page 488)

• *Sexual arousal.* Sexual arousal proceeds through four stages: excitement, plateau, orgasm, and resolution. For a combination of physiological and motivational reasons, some people fail to pass through all four stages or pass through them more quickly than they wish. (page 492)

• *Development of genitals.* In the early stages of development, the human fetus possesses anatomical structures that may develop into either male genitalia (if testosterone levels are high enough) or female genitalia (if testosterone levels are lower). (page 493)

• *Homosexuality.* The reasons are not clear as to why some people develop a heterosexual orientation and others develop a homosexual orientation. Genetic influences can apparently alter the probability of a homosexual orientation, although genetic influences alone cannot account for all variations in sexual orientation. On the average, heterosexual and homosexual men differ in the size of one structure in the hypothalamus that contributes to certain aspects of sexual behavior. (page 494)

• *Rape and related offenses.* Unwanted sex ranges from violent attacks to mild force against mild resistance. Instances of date rape are often perceived differently by the man and the woman. Most rapists have a history of violence and antisocial behavior against men as well as women. (page 496)

SUGGESTION FOR FURTHER READING

Laumann, E. O., Gagnon, J. H., Michael, R. T., & Michaels, S. (1994). *The social organization of sexuality in the United States.* Chicago, IL: University of Chicago Press. Provides not only survey data, but also a discussion of the role of sexuality in human life.

TERMS

acquired immune deficiency syndrome (AIDS) a disease often transmitted sexually that gradually destroys the body's immune system (page 489)

sexual identity the sex a person regards himself or herself as being (page 493)

sexual orientation a person's preference for male or female sex partners (page 493)

testosterone a hormone present in higher quantities in males than in females (page 493)

estrogen a hormone present in higher quantities in females than in males (page 493)

rape sexual contact obtained through violence, threats, or intimidation (page 496)

Answers to Concept Checks

5. A fetus exposed to very low levels of both testosterone and estrogen throughout prenatal development would develop a normal female appearance. High levels of testosterone lead to male anatomy; low levels lead to female anatomy. The level of estrogen does not play a decisive role. (page 494)

6. Not necessarily. It would be possible for some process to block the prenatal effects of testosterone without decreasing adult testosterone levels. (page 496)

ACHIEVEMENT MOTIVATION

What motivates some people to work harder than others?

How do we learn an achievement motivation?

How do people with a strong achievement motivation differ from others?

Your 2-year-old nephew is building a stack of blocks. You say, "Here, let me help you," and you finish stacking the blocks. Will he smile and thank you? Hardly. He is more likely to cry, "I wanted to do it myself!" His goal was not to *have* a tall stack, but to *build* a tall stack.

Now you are doing something creative yourself—painting a picture, writing a story,

Dave Thomas, a high-school dropout, set out to disprove his father's prediction that he would never earn enough money to support himself. By age 30 Thomas had made a million dollars by improving Kentucky Fried Chicken franchises; then he founded the Wendy's chain. Most high-school dropouts do not develop success stories like this. Psychologists try to understand why some people strive for achievement so much more vigorously than others do.

playing chess perhaps—something you do moderately well. Someone more expert than you says, "Here, let me help you. I see you're having a little trouble, and I think I can fix it." How do you react? You might not burst into tears, but you probably resent the help. You are more interested in completing the task yourself than in having a perfect final product.

Most of us strive for the joy of accomplishment, some more than others. What occupation do you hope to enter after graduation? Have you chosen it because it is your surest way to earn a lot of money? Or have you chosen it because it will enable you to take pride in your achievements? Many people forgo a better-paying job to take one that gives them a greater feeling of achievement. (I bet your psychology professor is one such person.)

THE MEASUREMENT OF NEED FOR ACHIEVEMENT

The **need for achievement** is a striving for accomplishment and excellence. That sounds like a rather straightforward definition, but it confuses two quite distinct types of motivation (McClelland, Koestner, & Weinberger, 1989). As a rule, when people describe themselves as possessing a strong achievement motivation, they refer to an extrinsic motivation. That is, they are drawn by the rewards they have been receiving or expect to receive for various accomplishments. But, as we saw in the first module of this chapter, there is a second kind of need for achievement, a more intrinsic motivation. People with this intrinsic kind of need for achievement may or may not describe themselves as striving for achievement, but they take pleasure in accomplishing goals for their own sake. They are likely to persist at a task for a long time and probably develop great skills in the long run. For example, people who spend every spare moment playing and studying chess may be driven by an intrinsic motivation to excel at chess, even if they do not think of themselves as "highly motivated" for achievement. (They may even think of themselves as wasting their time.) We shall concentrate here on the intrinsic need for achievement.

The intrinsic need for achievement was first inferred from the performance of schoolchildren. Some children are much

Need for achievement includes both extrinsic and intrinsic motivation. The artist who created this wooden cow probably hoped for recognition and money (an extrinsic motivation), but also must have enjoyed the creative process itself (an intrinsic motivation). The inside of the back of the cow folds out to form a desk.

more successful in school than others who, so far as we can tell, are equal in ability and equally interested in the rewards that good grades might eventually bring. The same is true in athletics, business, and other aspects of life. Apparently, some people simply try harder than others. If that is true, then we should be able to measure and study this tendency as a personality variable.

But how? If you wanted to determine which workers or schoolchildren were most highly motivated to achieve, what would you measure and how? You could not simply measure how much people achieve because you are trying to explain *why* some people achieve more than others. You would need some measure of the need for achievement that is separate from the achievements themselves.

Another way *not* to measure the need for achievement is to ask people whether they are strongly motivated for success. Many people say yes because they believe it is socially desirable to do so. Psychologists measure achievement motivation indirectly, without even telling people what they are measuring.

One of the most popular methods of measuring need for achievement makes use of the *Thematic Apperception Test,* which we shall examine again in Chapter 13. Investigators show people pictures like the one in Figure 11.33 and ask them to tell a story about each picture, including what is going on, what led up to this scene, and what will happen next (McClelland, Atkinson, Clark, & Lowell, 1953). The investigators then count the number of times each person men-

tions striving for goals and achievements. For example, this story would score high:

This girl is taking an important test. First she went through the test and answered all the items she knew well. Now she is trying to remember the answer to one of the more difficult questions. She gazes off into the

FIGURE 11.33
In the Thematic Apperception Test, each person looks at a series of pictures similar to this one and tells a story about each one. Psychologists count the number of achievement themes to measure the person's need for achievement. They can also measure other motivations by counting other kinds of themes.

distance, trying to remember everything she has read about this topic. She finally remembers, writes down the correct answer, and gets a perfect score. Later she goes on to college, becomes a Rhodes scholar, and eventually becomes a famous inventor.

Contrast that story with this one:

This girl is sitting through a very boring class. She is gazing off into the distance, thinking about the party she went to last weekend. As soon as class is over, she goes out and has a good time with her friends.

Such a story would rate a zero on need for achievement. (It might rate high on other motives, of course.)

How well does the Thematic Apperception Test measure need for achievement? The data suggest that it provides a moderately useful measure. Children who score high on need for achievement generally work harder and get higher grades in school than do children of equal IQ who score low on need for achievement (Khalid, 1991). Need for achievement also correlates reasonably well with various measures of career success (Spangler, 1992). It does not correlate highly with people's self-reports of their "strength of motivation." In other words, the test does seem to tap something about intrinsic motivation.

NEED FOR ACHIEVEMENT AND SETTING GOALS

Suppose you have a choice of three video games to play. One game is easy; you know you can get a high score on it, but so could anyone else. The second game is more difficult; you are not sure how well you would do. The third is so difficult that you are sure you would lose quickly, as most people do. Which do you choose? Most people prefer the difficult but not impossible game, especially people with a strong need for achievement (Atkinson & Birch, 1978).

People sometimes prefer especially easy or especially difficult tasks if they are dominated by a **fear of failure**. When they try very easy tasks, they avoid failure, although they never achieve any remarkable success. When they try very difficult tasks, they provide themselves an excuse for failure. Apparently, they would rather fail at an impossible task than run the risk of failing at a realistic task.

People with a strong fear of failure make a normal effort, or even an extraordinary ef-

fort, on an easy task or in a relaxed, low-pressure situation. But if they are told, "This is an important test; you are going to be evaluated, so do your best," they lower their effort. By contrast, people with a strong need for achievement make little effort on an easy task or when the situation puts little pressure on them. When they are told that they are going to be evaluated, they try harder (Nygard, 1982).

When people receive feedback on their performance, such as "You got 82% correct on the first test," those with a strong need for achievement usually increase their efforts, no matter what the results were. Apparently, they interpret almost any feedback as meaning that they are behind schedule and need to try harder. People with a low need for achievement or a high fear of failure react to feedback by decreasing their efforts. The feedback either tells them that they are achieving their low goals, or that they are failing and may as well quit (Matsui, Okada, & Kakuyama, 1982).

SOMETHING TO THINK ABOUT

Some people have suggested that our society has become less ambitious and less motivated by achievement than it once was. How could we test that hypothesis?

CONCEPT CHECK

7. *The new football coach at Generic Tech has set up a schedule for next year. The team will play only opponents that had a won-lost record of 5-6 or 6-5 last year. Does this coach have a high need for achievement or a high fear of failure? (Check your answer on page 507.)*

EFFECTIVE AND INEFFECTIVE GOALS

High goals are especially effective in motivating people with a strong need for achievement, and they tend to be somewhat effective with most people. (See Figure 11.34.) At the start of the college semester, four young women are asked to state their goals. One is aiming for a straight-A average. Another hopes to get at least a C average. A third plans to "do as well as I can." A fourth has no set goals. Which student will work hardest and get the best grades?

FIGURE 11.34
People with a high need for achievement prefer high goals. Research findings indicate that people work hardest when they set high goals for themselves, provided they think they have a realistic chance of success.

The student aiming for a straight-A average will do the best, under certain circumstances (Locke & Latham, 1991):

- She must have enough ability for the goal to be realistic. If she has previously struggled just to get passing grades, she will quickly become discouraged.

- She must take her goal seriously. If she casually says she is aiming for straight A's and then never thinks about it again, it will make no difference to her. She can increase her commitment to the goal by stating it publicly. The more people who know about her goal, the harder it will be for her to ignore it.

- She must get some feedback from periodic test scores and grades on assignments to tell her what she needs to study harder (Figure 11.35).

- She will be most likely to pursue her goal diligently if she is *not* being paid to achieve it. If she must get all A's in order to earn a financial reward, she may become discouraged and quit trying if it appears that she might get even one B.

The same conditions hold for workers (Locke, Shaw, Saari, & Latham, 1981). A very high goal leads to the best performance, provided the goal seems realistic. A vague "do your best" goal is no better than no goal at all. For a goal to be effective, workers must be committed to achieving it and must receive periodic feedback on their progress.

CONCEPT CHECK

8. *Under what conditions would people be most likely to keep their New Year's resolutions? (Check your answer on page 507.)*

AGE AND SEX DIFFERENCES AND THE NEED FOR ACHIEVEMENT

Some people have such a strong need for achievement that they will devote every available moment to an ambitious task they have set for themselves. How does the need for achievement develop, and why does it become stronger in some people than in others?

THE DEVELOPMENT OF NEED FOR ACHIEVEMENT IN CHILDHOOD

Achievement and success mean different things to different people (Phalet & Claeys, 1993). In some cultures, and for some people within a given culture, the emphasis is on individual accomplishments, such as gaining wealth, fame, and influence. For others, the emphasis is on identification with the group, such as serving one's country or helping one's family. The Japanese culture in particular stresses bringing honor to one's family. In nontechnological societies, success is defined in terms other than jobs and money.

Achievement also has different meanings for people of different ages. For older people, jobs and earnings become less important goals (Maehr & Kleiber, 1981); hobbies become more important, and even mere competence in taking care of one's own needs may be a source of feelings of accomplishment. Still, even within a sometimes restricted range, people strive for some kind of achievement.

In early childhood also, achievement means something more like competence than it does something like prestige. Even children 18 months old clearly show pride in their

Setting goals leads to vigorous activity if:

| The goal is realistic. |
| A serious commitment is made, especially if it is made publicly. |
| Feedback is received. |

FIGURE 11.35
Conditions for high activity toward achieving goals.

Preschool children show delight in their successes, but show no clear sign of discouragement after their failures. Perhaps they are ever-confident of their eventual success, or perhaps they simply do not understand the concept of failure.

accomplishments, such as building a tall stack of blocks. By age 2½, they understand the idea of competition; they show pleasure at beating someone else, disappointment at losing (Heckhausen, 1984).

Although preschool children show great pleasure at completing a task, they seldom appear distressed by their inability to complete it. Heinz Heckhausen (1984) tried to find out how children less than 4 years old would react to failure. He rigged up various contraptions so that a child's stack of blocks would topple or fall through a trap door. He often managed to arouse the children's curiosity, never their discouragement. He could not find a way to make young children feel that they had failed.

Preschool children are highly optimistic about their own abilities. Even if they have failed a task repeatedly, they announce confidently that they will succeed the next time. An adult asks, "Who is going to win this game the next time we play?" Most preschool children shout "Me!" even if they have lost time after time in the past (Stipek, 1984).

Perhaps optimism comes naturally to humans. We quickly learn how it feels to succeed; we learn more slowly what it means to fail. When children enter school, their teachers force them to compare themselves to one another. Within a few years, some children approach tasks with a fear of failure instead of a joyful striving for success (Stipek, 1984).

Psychologists have not yet determined when and why children change their attitudes toward success and failure, but they suspect teachers unintentionally convey the message, "You probably aren't going to like this or do it very well, but you have to do it anyway." Jere Brophy (1987, p. 190) reports the following quotes from junior-high teachers:

- "If you get done by 10 o'clock, you can go outside."

- "This penmanship assignment means that sometimes in life you just can't do what you want to do. The next time you have to do something you don't want to do, just think: 'Well, that's part of life.'"

- "You'll have to work real quietly, otherwise you'll have to do more assignments."

- "This test is to see who the really smart ones are."

SEX DIFFERENCES AND THE NEED FOR ACHIEVEMENT

According to some reports, women score lower than men do on need for achievement as measured by the Thematic Apperception Test. The difference is subject to both biological and environmental interpretations. Male hormones may encourage aggressiveness and competition in humans, as they clearly do in other species. Aggressiveness and competition are not the same as striving for achievement, but they may facilitate it.

In addition, our society tends to encourage boys to set higher personal goals than it encourages for girls (McCormick & Wolf, 1993). Although high-school girls set goals about as high as those of high-school boys (Farmer, 1983), many women lower their goals within a few years after finishing high school. Why?

One explanation is that women are influenced more by criticism than men are (Roberts, 1991). A woman who is told that she is doing poorly or that she is unlikely to succeed often takes the advice seriously. Many men tend to ignore such criticisms and proceed as before. Ignoring criticism is not necessarily a good idea, but the net result is that women may become discouraged faster than men.

Furthermore, women have historically faced serious discrimination against them in most jobs; consequently, many have chosen to enter certain fields where women predominate. In one study, a group of adult women filled out a job-interest questionnaire. The interests they checked most frequently included secretary, elementary teacher, home economics teacher, and dietician. Two weeks later they filled out the questionnaire again, but this time they were given these instructions:

I want you to pretend with me that men have come of age and that: (1) Men like intelligent women; (2) Men and women are promoted equally in business and the professions; and (3) Raising a family well is very possible for a career woman. (Farmer & Bohn, 1970, p. 229).

After hearing these instructions, the women expressed a significantly increased interest in becoming an author, psychologist, lawyer, insurance salesperson, or physician. They largely lost interest in becoming a secretary, teacher, or dietician (Farmer & Bohn, 1970). Evidently, women lower their career aspirations because they fear that high ambitions will scare men away, or because they believe businesses will not promote them fairly, or because they fear that a full-time career will interfere with raising a family (Farmer, 1987).

Women have often been led to believe, perhaps correctly, that men resent and dislike highly successful women. Matina Horner (1972) proposed that women have low motivation for achievement because they have a *fear of success*. She did not mean that women try to fail, but merely that they might try to avoid high, conspicuous levels of success. Horner asked 90 college women to complete a story beginning, "After the first-term finals, Anne finds herself at the top of her medical school class." She asked 88 men to do the same, except that she substituted "John" for "Anne." Almost two thirds of the women told stories in which Anne quit medical school or suffered social rejection or other misfortunes. Less than one tenth of the men said that anything unpleasant happened to John. Horner concluded that women have been taught that high levels of achievement are unfeminine; once they approach those levels, they begin to fear the consequences.

However, these results have been difficult to replicate. They have a "now you see it, now you don't" quality. In most later studies, about an equal percentage of men and women raised concerns about fear of success (Zuckerman & Wheeler, 1975). Was Horner therefore wrong? Not necessarily. The results could have differed because of changes in procedure, including slight changes in instructions. The results probably also vary from one historical era to another and from one culture to another (Llaneza-Ramos, 1991). Perhaps women today have less reason

Although women tend to avoid activities in which men discriminate heavily against them, some women do manage to succeed at such activities. Sex differences in need for achievement vary depending on the historical era and the method of measuring motivations.

to fear success than women did in the 1960s, when Horner collected her first results.

Are women right in believing that businesses will not promote them fairly? It is difficult to say. On the one hand, many businesses make a deliberate effort to recruit and promote women. On the other hand, as one observer has pointed out, "Two facts matter to business: Only women have babies and only men make rules" (Schwartz, 1989, p. 65). Although many women want to take an extended leave from a job after they give birth, many employers prefer that they quit altogether. The result is that everyone loses: The woman leaves a promising career and later returns to the workforce with much lower aspirations. The company loses a talented worker permanently. And observers conclude that it is a mistake to hire women for top jobs, because they are likely to quit (Schwartz, 1989). Perhaps our society will find better ways to enable women (and men) to combine career ambitions with family commitments.

WHAT NEED FOR ACHIEVEMENT TELLS US ABOUT MOTIVATION

Although we sometimes regard hunger as a "typical" motivation, it differs in some striking ways from need for achievement. For example, people can satisfy their

People who have reached the highest levels of achievement seldom relax; they set goals for new achievements. Andrew Lloyd Webber, composer of Phantom of the Opera, Cats, *and other extremely successful shows, continues composing new shows, such as* Sunset Boulevard.

hunger, but seldom their need for achievement. At the end of a big meal, you are quite uninterested in any more food. In contrast, no matter how marvelous people's achievements are, very few people lose interest in further achievements. Almost no one "reaches" his or her life goal and then stops; after reaching a previous life goal, people set new goals (Cantor & Fleeson, 1994). We would be distressed if we had no further goals. We constantly strive to build a perfect world, but we might not enjoy living in one.

In the words of the Russian novelist Fyodor Dostoevsky (1864/1960, pp. 29, 30), "Man likes to create and build roads; that is beyond dispute. But why does he also have such a passionate love for destruction and chaos? . . . May it not be that he loves chaos and destruction . . . because he is instinctively afraid of attaining his goal and completing the edifice he is constructing? . . . [P]erhaps the only goal on earth to which mankind is striving lies in this incessant process of attaining, or in other words, in life itself, and not particularly in the goal. . . . He feels that as soon as he has found it there will be nothing for him to look for. . . . He

likes the process of attaining, but does not quite like to have attained."

SUMMARY

• *Measurement of need for achievement.* Some people work harder than others because of their strong need for achievement. Need for achievement can be measured by the stories a person tells when looking at a picture in the Thematic Apperception Test. (page 500)

• *Goal setting.* People with a strong need for achievement prefer to set goals that are high but realistic. Given such a goal, they will work as hard as possible. In contrast, people with a low need for achievement or a strong fear of failure prefer goals that are either easy to achieve or so difficult that they provide a ready excuse for failure. (page 502)

• *Effectiveness of goal setting.* Almost everyone is motivated to achieve a goal if the goal is realistic, if the person makes a serious commitment to achieving it, and if the person gets feedback on his or her efforts to reach the goal. (page 502)

• *Achievement motivation in children.* Children begin showing delight in their accomplishments by age 1½. Preschool children are highly optimistic about their own abilities. After they enter school, they learn the meaning of failure and start to show discouragement. (page 503)

• *Sex differences in need for achievement.* According to some reports, men have, on the average, a stronger need for achievement than women have, although some of the results are difficult to replicate. To some extent, women lower their aspirations because they fear that their high success may displease men or because they believe that employers will not promote them fairly. Studies in the 1960s indicated that women were inhibited by a fear of success, but that fear is no longer evident. (page 504)

SUGGESTION FOR FURTHER READING

McClelland, D. C. (1985). *Human motivation.* Glenview, IL: Scott, Foresman. A text by one of the pioneers in the study of achievement motivation.

TERMS

need for achievement a striving for accomplishment and excellence (page 500)

fear of failure a preoccupation with avoiding failure, rather than taking risks in order to succeed (page 502)

Answers to Concept Checks

7. The answer depends on how good the Generic Tech team is. If they won most of their games last year and return most of their top players, then the coach has set a very low goal for them, and we can assume that the coach has more fear of failure than need for achievement. If, however, Generic Tech has a mediocre team, then the coach may have set a high yet realistic challenge. We would then assume the coach has a high need for achievement. (page 502)

8. A New Year's resolution is like any other goal: People are more likely to keep it if it is realistic, if they state the resolution publicly, and if they receive feedback on how well they are achieving it. (page 503)

12

EMOTIONS, HEALTH PSYCHOLOGY, AND COPING WITH STRESS

The *Star Trek* character Mr. Spock is reputed to feel very little emotion because he is half Vulcan—and people from the planet Vulcan feel little or no emotion. Suppose you are the first astronaut to land on Vulcan. The Vulcans gather around and ask you, their first visitor from Earth, what *emotion* is. What do you tell them?

"Well," you might say, "emotion is how you feel when something surprisingly good or surprisingly bad happens to you."

"Wait a minute," they reply. "We don't understand these words *feel* and *surprisingly*."

"All right, how about this: Emotions are experiences like anger, fear, happiness, sadness. . . ."

"Anger, fear. . . . what do those terms mean?" the Vulcans ask.

Defining such terms would be more diffi-

cult than trying to explain *color* to a blind person. Even though blind people cannot experience color, they can determine whether someone else has color vision by showing the appropriate stimuli. Could you set up a similar test that would let the Vulcans determine whether someone was experiencing an emotion? If so, what sort of test could you use? The problem is that *color vision* has a well-established meaning, whereas *emotion* has an imprecise meaning that is defined mostly by example.

In this chapter we shall consider what psychologists have learned so far about emotions, while leaving some major questions unanswered. We begin with general theories and principles. Later we turn to the role of emotions in health and the ways in which people cope with the emotions associated with stress.

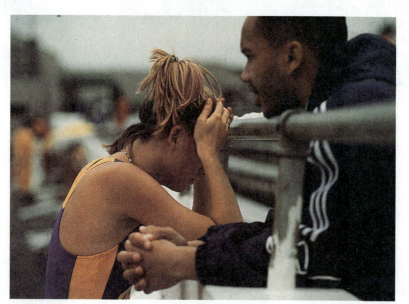

When we experience emotions, we are in some way moved. (Movement is the root of emotion.) Our feeling of disturbance is a positive or negative excitement; sometimes we cry for joy, sometimes for grief.

EMOTIONAL BEHAVIORS

What causes us to feel one emotion or another?
How many kinds of emotion do people have?

Let me start with this confession: Psychologists' progress toward understanding emotion has left some major gaps. Scientific progress depends on accurate measurement, and emotions are difficult to measure. Psychologists can measure learning, memory, hunger, and vision without difficulty, even in nonhuman species. They can even discuss memory and problem-solving in machines. But when they come to emotions, psychologists are reduced largely to asking people for self-reports—a method of uncertain accuracy even with adult humans, and totally inapplicable to infants, many brain-damaged people, and nonhuman species.

Perhaps some day psychologists will find better ways to measure emotions. In the meantime, our answers to certain questions will remain incomplete and tentative. In this chapter we shall concentrate on the observable aspects of emotion—its physiology, expressions, and effects on behavior.

EMOTION AND PHYSIOLOGICAL AROUSAL

Originally, the word *emotion* was a general term for any sort of turbulent movement. People used to talk about thunder as an "emotion of the atmosphere." Eventually, the word came to refer only to feelings associated with vigorous motion of the body, such as fear, anger, and joy.

We experience emotional arousal when we have a strong tendency either to approach or to avoid something, generally in an energetic way. For example, love includes a strong drive to come close to another person. Anger includes a tendency to charge toward someone and to attack through either speech or action. Fear and disgust are associated with a tendency to escape. All emotions share certain features related to physiological arousal. So although anger, fear, and happiness are very different emotional states, we may express any one of them by screaming or by engaging in frenzied activity.

"But wait," you say. "Sometimes when I feel highly emotional I can hardly do anything at all. Like the time I borrowed a friend's car and then wrecked it. When I had to explain what had happened to the car, I could hardly speak." True, but even then your emotion was associated with a tendency to take vigorous action. While you were reporting the wreck to your friend, you undoubtedly felt a strong urge to run away. Although you suppressed that urge, it made itself apparent in your trembling voice and shaking hands.

THE USEFULNESS OF EMOTIONS

When drawing conclusions, you are generally advised to look at the evidence "calmly, rationally, unemotionally." The *Star Trek* character Spock is the personification of this advice: extremely logical, almost never emotional. If emotions just get in the way of intelligent decision-making, why do we have them at all?

[handwritten note: Tendency to avoid or approach something]

Ordinarily an emotional state elicits a tendency toward vigorous action, even if we suppress that tendency. Here, a soldier disarms a mine during the war in the former Yugoslavia. No doubt he feels an emotional desire to run away, and no doubt his heart is racing, but he manages to restrain his actions.

FIGURE 12.1

Researchers in the 1990s used modern technology to reconstruct the path that an iron bar must have taken through the brain of Phineas Gage, who survived this injury in 1848. The damage impaired Gage's judgment and decision-making. (From Damasio, Grabowski, Frank, Galaburda, & Damasio, 1994.)

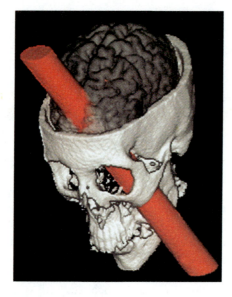

emotions designated in prefrontal cortex

The answer is they don't get in the way, at least within a moderate range of emotional strength. In fact, the capacity to feel emotions is helpful, perhaps even necessary, to decision-making. Antonio Damasio (1994) reported on some patients who suffered a great impoverishment of emotions following damage to parts of the prefrontal cortex. One was the famous patient Phineas Gage, who in 1848 survived a freak accident in which an iron bar shot through his head, damaging his prefrontal cortex. Nearly one-and-a-half centuries later, researchers examined his skull (which is still on display in a Boston museum) and reconstructed the route that the bar must have taken through Gage's brain (Damasio, Grabowski, Frank, Galaburda, & Damasio, 1994). As you can see in Figure 12.1, the accident damaged a portion of his prefrontal cortex. The result, according to medical reports of the time, was that Gage showed little emotion and also seemed to lose his former values. Formerly a conscientious worker, he became unreliable in both his work and his personal habits. He followed each whim of the moment, unable to follow any long-term plans.

A parallel case in more recent times is known to us as "Elliot" (Damasio, 1994). Elliot too suffered damage to his prefrontal cortex, the outcome of surgery to remove a brain tumor. As a result, he has extremely limited emotions. He shows no impatience, no frustration; he experiences no joy from music or art; he rarely expresses anger; he describes his brain surgery and the resulting deterioration of his life with calm detachment, as if he were describing events that happened to a stranger. In addition to his loss of emo-

lack of decision making

tions, he has great trouble making or following any reasonable plans. If given an array of information, he can discuss the probable outcome of each decision he might make, but after describing those outcomes, he seems to have no idea which decision to make. Or if he does announce a decision, he abandons it soon after. As a result, Elliot cannot keep a job, cannot invest his money intelligently, cannot maintain normal relationships with his friends or acquaintances.

According to Damasio (1994), Elliot's difficulty with decision-making is closely related to his lack of emotions. Ordinarily, when you or I consider possible decisions, we contemplate the possible outcomes and feel a brief "as if" emotion with each. For example, you consider a job offer from a company that pollutes the environment, and you get a feeling of revulsion. So you decide at once to reject the offer. You consider another offer from a company that recently fired your best friend. You imagine facing that friend, imagine the unpleasant scene, and again decide to reject the offer. You continue until you come to a job offer that you feel good about, and you take it. Now, imagine eliminating all those emotions, and you can see how the capacity for emotion is helpful, even necessary, for certain kinds of decision-making.

THE ROLE OF THE AUTONOMIC NERVOUS SYSTEM

Any stimulus that arouses an emotion—such as a hug, a fire alarm, or a slap on the face—alters the activity of the autonomic nervous system, the section of the nervous system that controls the functioning of the internal organs. The word *autonomic* means independent; biologists once believed that the autonomic nervous system operated independently of the brain and the spinal cord. We now know that the brain and the spinal cord send messages to alter the activity of the autonomic nervous system, but we continue to use the term *autonomic*.

The autonomic nervous system consists of the sympathetic nervous system and the parasympathetic nervous system (Figure 12.2). Two chains of neuron clusters just to the left and right of the spinal cord make up the **sympathetic nervous system**. The **parasympathetic nervous system** consists of neurons whose axons extend from the medulla (Figure 3.32) and the lower part of the spinal cord to neuron clusters near the internal organs. Both the sympathetic and parasympathetic systems

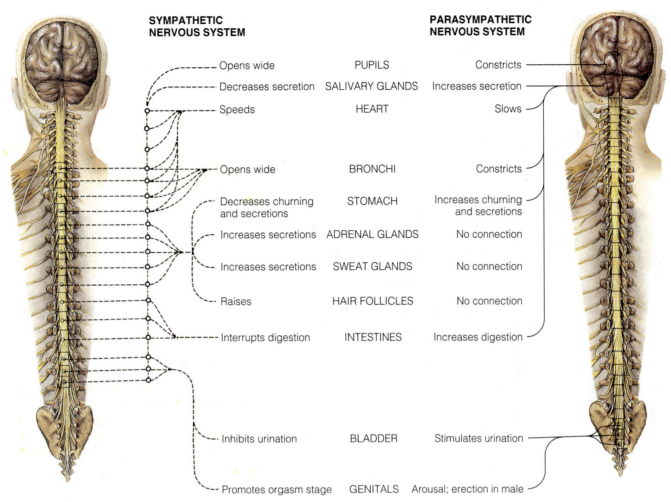

SYMPATHETIC NERVOUS SYSTEM		PARASYMPATHETIC NERVOUS SYSTEM
Opens wide	PUPILS	Constricts
Decreases secretion	SALIVARY GLANDS	Increases secretion
Speeds	HEART	Slows
Opens wide	BRONCHI	Constricts
Decreases churning and secretions	STOMACH	Increases churning and secretions
Increases secretions	ADRENAL GLANDS	No connection
Increases secretions	SWEAT GLANDS	No connection
Raises	HAIR FOLLICLES	No connection
Interrupts digestion	INTESTINES	Increases digestion
Inhibits urination	BLADDER	Stimulates urination
Promotes orgasm stage	GENITALS	Arousal; erection in male

FIGURE 12.2

The autonomic nervous system consists of the sympathetic and parasympathetic nervous systems, which act sometimes in opposing ways and sometimes in cooperative ways. The sympathetic nervous system readies the body for emergency actions; the parasympathetic nervous system supports digestive and other nonemergency actions.

send axons to various organs of the body, such as the heart and digestive organs. A few organs, such as the adrenal glands, receive input from the sympathetic system only.

The sympathetic nervous system arouses the body for "fight or flight" (Figure 12.3). For example, if someone charges at you, you may have to choose between fighting and running away; in either case, your sympathetic nervous system prepares you for a burst of vigorous activity. It does so by increasing your heart rate, breathing rate, production of sweat, and flow of epinephrine (EP-i-NEF-rin; also known as adrenaline). The parasympathetic nervous system decreases the heart rate, promotes digestion, and in general supports nonemergency functions.

Both systems are constantly active, though one may be more active than the other at any given time. An emergency that demands a vigorous response will predominantly activate the sympathetic system; a restful situation predominantly activates the parasympathetic system. Some situations activate parts of both systems at once (Berntson, Cacioppo, & Quigley, 1993). For example, a frightening situation may increase your heart rate and sweating (sympathetic responses) and promote bowel and bladder emptying (parasympathetic responses). Remember the last time you were seriously frightened—perhaps your professor asked you to explain why your term paper was so similar to one that another student turned in last semester, or perhaps your boss asked whether you knew why $500 was missing from the cash register. Chances are, your heart was beating wildly, you found

FIGURE 12.3
The sympathetic nervous system prepares the body for a vigorous burst of activity.

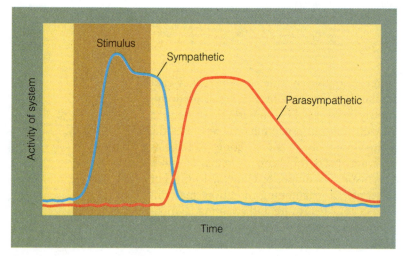

FIGURE 12.4
After removal of the stimulus eliciting the sympathetic response, the sympathetic response is reduced, while the opposing parasympathetic response is enhanced. This is why people feel almost faint at the end of an exciting experience.

yourself gasping for breath, and you were afraid you were going to lose your bladder control. Both your sympathetic and parasympathetic systems were responsible for those responses.

THE OPPONENT-PROCESS PRINCIPLE OF EMOTIONS

After a stimulus that has excited sympathetic activity ceases, there is sometimes a "rebound" of increased parasympathetic activity (Gellhorn, 1970). (See Figure 12.4.) For example, while you are running away from an attacker, your sympathetic nervous system increases your heart rate and your breathing rate. If the police suddenly intercept your attacker, your sympathetic arousal ceases, and your parasympathetic system becomes highly activated as a rebound. If the rebound is great enough, a person who has just escaped from danger may faint because of the sudden decrease in heart rate.

This tendency is related to a larger, general principle, the opponent-process principle of emotions (Solomon, 1980; Solomon & Corbit, 1974). According to this principle, the removal of a stimulus that excites one emotion causes a swing to an opposite emotion (Figure 12.5). This principle is similar to the opponent-process principle of color vision (discussed in Chapter 4). Recall that when you stare for a long time at one color and then look away, you see its opposite. (After staring at yellow, you see blue.) Solomon and Corbit suggest that the same principle holds for emotional states.

For example, suppose you make a parachute jump for the first time. As you start to fall, you probably experience a state akin to terror. As you continue to fall and your parachute opens, your terror begins to subside. When you land safely, your emotional state does not simply return to normal; it rebounds to relief. As time passes, your relief gradually fades until at last you return to a normal state. Figure 12.6 shows these changes in emotional response over time. Solomon and Corbit refer to the initial emotion as the A state and the opposite, rebound emotion as the B state.

Here is another example: You hear on the radio that you have just won a million dollars in a lottery; you become excited and elated. Later you discover that the winner was not you, but someone else with a similar name. Now you feel sad, even though you "lost" something you never had.

FIGURE 12.5
According to the opponent-process principle of emotions, removing the stimulus for one emotion elicits a rebound to the opposite emotion. A hiker who sees a snake may feel terrified; when the threat passes, the terror gives way to relief and elation.

Solomon and Corbit further propose that repetition of an experience strengthens the B state but not the A state. For example, after you have made several parachute jumps, your rebound pleasure becomes greater and starts to occur earlier and earlier. Over time, you may not be aware of any initial terror at all; the entire experience becomes pleasant.

Figure 12.6 illustrates the changes in emotional response that occur when the experience-and-rebound cycle is repeated many times. Note that the A state has become weaker and the B state has become stronger and more prolonged.

CONCEPT CHECKS

1. When you ride a roller coaster, does your heart rate increase or decrease? What happens after you get off?
2. If we apply the opponent-process principle to the experiences drugs produce, we can describe the initial "high" as the A state and the subsequent unpleasant withdrawal experience as the B state. If someone takes a drug repeatedly, how will the A state and the B state change? (Check your answers on page 532.)

THE SYMPATHETIC NERVOUS SYSTEM AND LIE DETECTION

Frequently the police interview a suspect who denies any participation in a crime, or an employer interviews a prospective employee who claims to be skillful, honest, and trustworthy. In such cases, the interviewer would like to know whether the person is

telling the truth. Unfortunately, most of us are not very good at detecting lies. In one study, a well-known British political commentator gave two consecutive interviews about his favorite films. One time he told the truth; the other time he lied on every question. Both interviews were broadcast on radio and television and printed in a newspaper. Members of the public were invited to guess which of the interviews was the honest one and which one was full of lies. Of the more than 41,000 people who responded,

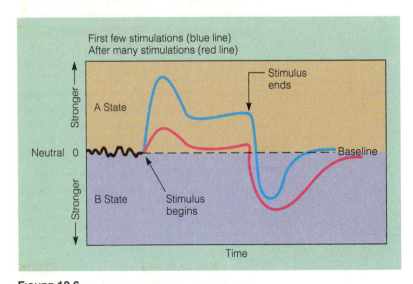

FIGURE 12.6
According to the opponent-process theory of emotions, removal of the stimulus for one emotion (A state) induces the opposite emotion (B state). The blue line shows emotional responses to a stimulus that is introduced and then withdrawn. The red line shows emotional responses to a stimulus that has been introduced and withdrawn repeatedly. Note how the intensity of the responses changes over time. (Based on Solomon & Corbit, 1974.)

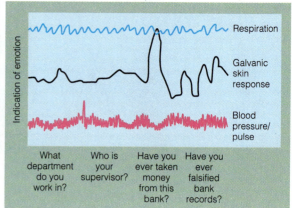

Respiration

Galvanic
skin
response

Blood
pressure/
pulse

| What department do you work in? | Who is your supervisor? | Have you ever taken money from this bank? | Have you ever falsified bank records? |

FIGURE 12.7

The polygraph, a method for detecting nervous arousal, is the basis for the so-called lie detector test. The polygraph operator asks a series of nonthreatening questions to establish baseline readings of the subject's autonomic responses, then asks questions relevant to some investigation. The underlying assumption is that an increase in arousal indicates nervousness, which in turn indicates lying. Unfortunately, a large percentage of innocent people also become nervous.

only 53% got the right answer (Wiseman, 1995). Curiously, the television viewers were less accurate than the radio listeners or newspaper readers.

For centuries people have tried to find some simple test to determine who is lying. One of the best-known attempts is the **polygraph,** a special instrument that simultaneously records several indications of sympathetic nervous system arousal, generally including blood pressure, heart rate, breathing rate, and electrical conduction of the skin (Figure 12.7). (Slight sweating, a sympathetic nervous system response, increases electrical conduction of the skin.) The assumption is that people feel nervous when they lie, and consequently their sympathetic nervous system will show more arousal when they lie than when they tell the truth.

The polygraph often succeeds in a practical sense, simply because a person hooked up to a polygraph sometimes says, "Oh, what's the use? You're going to figure it out now anyway, so I may as well confess. . . ." Similarly, for research purposes, psychologists have sometimes attached people to a device called a **bogus pipeline.** Although the device itself actually does nothing, psychologists *convince* people that it detects lies. They ask a few questions to which the psychologists already know the correct answers, and then say, "Ah, the machine says you told the truth on number 1. You lied on number 2. . . ." When people believe the machine can detect lying, they start telling the truth on additional questions (Roese & Jamieson, 1993).

To some degree, a polygraph works the same way.

For people who do not break down and confess, how effectively does a polygraph detect lying? Let us examine the evidence.

WHAT'S THE EVIDENCE?

The Effectiveness of a Polygraph in Detecting Lies

Hypothesis Polygraph administrators should call guilty suspects liars more often than they call innocent suspects liars.

Method To test this hypothesis, the investigators need a sample of people who are known to be guilty, and another sample who are known to be innocent but who are otherwise similar to the guilty people. In one study, the investigators selected 50 criminal cases in which two suspects had taken a polygraph test, and one suspect had later confessed to the crime (Kleinmuntz & Szucko, 1984). Thus, the investigators knew which 50 suspects were guilty, and they knew that the 50 innocent people were similar enough to have been plausible suspects. It is important to note that all suspects were denying their guilt at the time of the polygraph test.

During the polygraph administration, suspects were asked two kinds of questions. *Relevant* questions pertained to the crime itself; for example, "Did you steal $125 from

[Handwritten margin note: people feel nervous when we lie, SNS will show more arousal when they lie.]

the convenience store last Tuesday?" *Control* questions were of the form, "Have you ever taken anything of value that was not yours?" Theoretically, someone who robbed the convenience store should be more nervous about the first question; other people should be, if anything, more nervous about the second.

Six professional polygraph administrators examined all the polygraph results and judged which suspects were lying and which were telling the truth.

Results   Figure 12.8 shows the results. The polygraph administrators did manage to identify 76% of the guilty suspects as lying; however, they also classified 37% of the innocent suspects as lying.

Interpretation   The polygraph test identifies lying a bit more accurately than most people do. However, it makes too many mistakes, especially in falsely identifying innocent people as lying.

These results are typical of similar research; in fact, this study may have underestimated the tendency of polygraph administrators to call innocent people liars. In some studies, the polygraph administrators have called 50% or more of the innocent people liars (Forman & McCauley, 1986; Horvath, 1977; Patrick & Iacono, 1989).

Imagine the consequences. Suppose we give polygraph tests to 10 suspects, one of whom is guilty. The test would have about a 76% chance of identifying the guilty person as lying, but it would also identify several of the innocent people. Or imagine giving a polygraph test to all the employees of a company, asking whether they have stolen from the company. Even if every employee is loyal and innocent, the test may identify close to half of them as liars. Because of the low accuracy of polygraph tests, the U.S. Congress passed a law in 1988 prohibiting private employers from giving polygraph tests to employees or job applicants, except under special circumstances (Camara, 1988).

AN ALTERNATIVE: THE GUILTY-KNOWLEDGE TEST

The **guilty-knowledge test**, a modified version of the polygraph test, produces more accurate results by asking a different type of question (Lykken, 1979). Instead of asking, "Did you rob the gas station?" the interrogator asks, "Was the gas station robbed at 8:00 P.M.? At 10:30? At midnight? At 1:30 in the

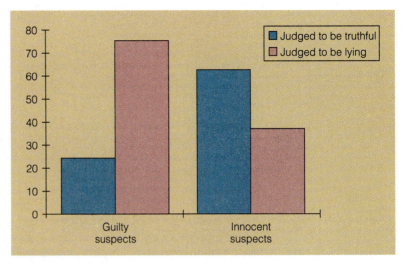

FIGURE 12.8
Polygraph examiners correctly identified 76% of guilty suspects as lying. However, they also identified 37% of innocent suspects as lying. (Based on data of Kleinmuntz & Szucko, 1984.)

morning? Did the robber carry a gun? A knife? A club?" So long as the questions deal with facts that have not yet been publicized, innocent people should be no more nervous about one question than about another. A person who shows greater arousal when asked about the correct details of the crime than when asked other questions must have "guilty knowledge"—knowledge that only someone who had committed the crime or had talked to the person who committed it could possess. The guilty-knowledge test, when properly administered, identifies a large percentage of the guilty people and only rarely makes the mistake of classifying an innocent person as guilty (Balloun & Holmes, 1979; Bashore & Rapp, 1993; Elaad, 1990).

The guilty-knowledge test, however, is not suitable to all situations. Suppose you are an employer and you want to know whether someone who is applying for a job at your company is likely to steal from the cash register. Giving a polygraph test is illegal, and would not be very accurate anyway, so what do you do?

One approach is to administer pencil-and-paper "integrity tests" that ask such questions as:

- Have you ever stolen money or property from a previous employer?

- Do you think that most employees occasionally steal from their employers?

- On previous jobs, have you ever left work early while claiming to have worked a full day?

- Have you sometimes come to work while under the influence of illegal drugs?
- If you were sure you wouldn't get caught, would you ever make personal long-distance telephone calls and charge them to your employer?

You might assume that anyone who has a history of dishonest dealings with previous employers would lie about it. Strangely, a number of people fill out the questionnaire honestly, admitting a long history of past dishonesty. (Perhaps they assume the new employer will find out about this history anyway by checking with previous employers.) Research on such tests, though limited, suggests that they manage to identify a good percentage of dishonest people (Camara & Schneider, 1994). However, they also misidentify an unknown percentage of highly honest and conscientious people. For example, someone may read the question "Have you ever stolen property from a previous employer?" and think, "Well, there was that one time when I used a business envelope to mail a personal letter." That is, some people "confess" to dishonest acts even though their actual transgressions were trivial (Lilienfeld,

1993). At this point, the overall accuracy of "integrity" tests is difficult to assess, and their future role is hard to predict.

SOMETHING TO THINK ABOUT

How might results of a guilty-knowledge test be biased by a questioner who knows the correct details of the crime? How should the test be administered to minimize bias?

THREE GENERAL THEORIES OF EMOTION

Psychologists generally agree that emotions are related to the activity of the autonomic nervous system and the activity of the body in general. What is less clear is the nature of that relationship. Let us consider three theories that have offered different descriptions of that relationship.

THE JAMES-LANGE THEORY OF EMOTIONS

In 1884, William James and Carl Lange independently proposed a theory that immediately became highly influential and remains so to this day, in spite of the fact that psychologists have often misunderstood it. Indeed, even today people often confuse what James and Lange actually said, what they meant to say, and what casual readers thought they said (Ellsworth, 1994).

Common sense suggests that an outside stimulus causes an emotion and that the emotion in turn causes autonomic changes and body movements: We feel sad and therefore we cry; we become afraid and therefore we tremble; we feel angry and therefore we attack. James and Lange turned this concept around. According to the **James-Lange theory** (Figure 12.9), our interpretation of a stimulus evokes the autonomic changes and body movements first and directly; what we call an emotion is our perception of those changes and movements. We decide we are sad *because* we cry, we feel afraid *because* we tremble, we feel angry *because* we attack. Similarly, the act of smiling makes us happy and frowning makes us unhappy. The body responses, James and Lange would agree, are not sufficient for emotions, but they are necessary. For example, trembling itself would not make you afraid. (You might be trembling because you are cold.) Nevertheless, if

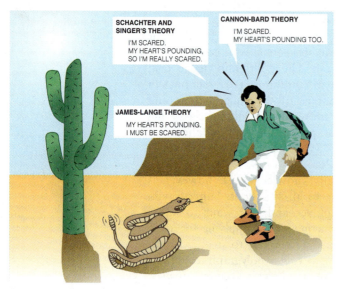

FIGURE 12.9
Three traditional theories of emotion differ concerning the relationship between physiological arousal and the cognitive experience of emotion. According to the James-Lange theory, the physiological arousal determines the nature of the emotion. According to the Cannon-Bard theory, the physiological arousal is independent of the cognitive experience. According to Schachter and Singer's theory, the physiological arousal determines the intensity of the emotion, but it does not determine which emotion one experiences.

feel sad cause me cry.

you did not tremble, you could not feel the full experience of fear.

According to this theory, how would you know which emotion you are feeling? Actually, William James was skeptical of separating emotion into different categories such as fear, anger, and disgust. He regarded emotions as endlessly varying, with no firm border between one and the next. Still, so far as it makes sense to label emotions as one state or another, the James-Lange theory suggests that we distinguish among our emotions by observing our bodily responses, especially our autonomic responses. We feel one pattern of autonomic responses when angry, another pattern when happy, still another when frightened or sad. (Remember, according to this theory, an emotion is the *perception* of change in the body, not the *cause* of that change.) But is the autonomic state associated with anger noticeably different from the state associated with anxiety or any other emotion?

Heart rate and respiration increase during almost any emotion. Beyond that basic similarity, each emotional state has certain distinguishing physiological features (Levenson, 1992). With its "butterflies in the stomach" sensation, anxiety is probably the most distinctive emotional experience (Neiss, 1988). Your heart rate increases a little more when you are angry or frightened than when you are happy; the temperature of your hands increases more when you are angry than when you feel any other emotion. Your facial muscles respond in different ways when you experience different emotions, even though you are not actually smiling or frowning (Tassinary & Cacioppo, 1992).

Granted that emotional states produce different physiological states, can those differences account for the differences in emotions, as James and Lange suggested? If you begin to breathe rapidly and your heart begins to race, do you decide whether you are angry or frightened by checking the temperature of your hands—or any other physiological indicator? Probably not. The physiological differences among emotions are small, probably too small to identify an emotional state accurately (Lang, 1994). In fact, most people are rather inaccurate even at reporting the intensity of their autonomic arousal.

A somewhat more promising explanation is that we judge our emotions by monitoring our facial expressions, or at least that having a certain facial expression increases the prob-

ability of feeling the associated emotion. James Laird (1974) molded people's faces into a smile or a frown by telling them to contract first this muscle, then that one, without ever using the words *smile* or *frown*. He found that an induced smile made people more likely to feel happy and that an induced frown made them more likely to feel sad or angry.

But remember the problem of *demand characteristics:* Subjects in an experiment often report what they think the experimenter expects them to report. Even though Laird never used the words *smile* or *frown,* the subjects may have identified their expressions and guessed that they were supposed to be related to their mood.

In another study, the experimenters found a clever way to conceal their purpose. They told subjects that the experiment had to do with how people with disabilities learn to write after losing control of their arms. The subjects were told to hold a pen either with their teeth or with their protruded lips, as Figure 12.10 shows. Then they were to use the pen in various ways, such as drawing lines between dots and making checkmarks to rate the funniness of cartoons. When they held the pen with their teeth, their face was forced into a near-smile and they rated the cartoons as very funny. When they held the pen with protruded lips, they rated the cartoons as significantly less funny (Strack,

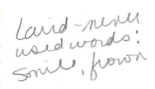

a   b

FIGURE 12.10

Facial expression can influence mood. When people hold a pen with their teeth (a), they rate cartoons as funnier than when they hold a pen with their protruded lips (b).

Martin, & Stepper, 1988). (You might try holding a pen in one way and then the other while reading newspaper cartoons. Do you notice any difference?)

THE CANNON-BARD THEORY OF EMOTIONS

Walter Cannon (1927), a prominent American physiologist, argued against the idea that autonomic responses were essential to emotion. Instead, he said, emotions produce autonomic changes and the cognitive experience of emotion independently. This view, as modified by Philip Bard (1934), is known as the **Cannon-Bard theory of emotions** (Figure 12.9). According to this theory, certain areas of the brain evaluate sensory information and, when appropriate, send one set of impulses to the autonomic nervous system and another set to the forebrain, which is responsible for the subjective and cognitive aspects of emotion.

The key assumption here is that the cognitive aspect of emotions is independent of the autonomic aspect. That assumption is only partly true. After spinal cord damage, people experience little sensation from their heartbeat, stomach fluttering, and other autonomic responses, and yet they continue to experience fear, anger, and other emotions. They may, however, report that their emotions feel less intense than they did before. For example, one man with spinal cord damage reported that he occasionally *acted* angry without actually feeling angry, just because he knew that if he did not respond to some situation with anger, other people would take advantage of him (Hohmann, 1966).

Similarly, after people with an intact nervous system take tranquilizing drugs, they generally report that their emotions, especially anxiety, seem less intense than before. That is, the cognitive aspect of emotions may be partly independent of the autonomic changes, but it is not as independent as Cannon and Bard suggested.

SCHACHTER AND SINGER'S THEORY OF EMOTIONS

Suppose we wire you to another person in such a way that you share the other person's heart rate, breathing rate, skin temperature, and muscle tension. When the other person feels a particular emotion, will you feel it too?

We cannot perform that experiment, but we can do the next best thing: We can use a drug to induce nearly the same physiological state in two people and then see whether they both report the same emotion. To make things a little more interesting, we can put them in different situations. If emotion depends only on a person's physiological state, then both people will report the same emotion, even if they happen to be in different situations. Stanley Schachter and Jerome Singer (1962) put these ideas to the test in a now famous experiment.

Schachter and Singer gave injections of the hormone epinephrine (adrenaline) to a group of college students who agreed to participate in the experiment. (Epinephrine mimics the effects of arousal of the sympathetic nervous system for about 20 to 30 minutes.) The experimenters told some of the subjects that the injections were vitamins; they did not warn them about the likely autonomic effects. Others were told to expect increased heart rate, butterflies in the stomach, and so forth. (Therefore, when they did have such experiences, they would attribute the effects to the injection, not to the situation.)

Subjects were then placed in different situations. Some were placed, one at a time, in a situation designed to arouse euphoria, or excited happiness. The others were placed in a situation designed to arouse anger.

Each student in the euphoria situation was asked to wait in a room with a very playful confederate, or accomplice, of the experimenter. The confederate flipped wads of paper into a trash can, sailed paper airplanes, built a tower with manila folders, shot paper wads at the tower with a rubber band, and played with a hula hoop. He encouraged the subject to join him in play.

Each subject in the anger situation was put in a waiting room with an angry confederate and asked to fill out an insulting questionnaire that included items such as these:

Which member of your immediate family does not bathe or wash regularly?

With how many men (other than your father) has your mother had extramarital relationships?

4 or fewer   5–9   10 or more

Most students in the euphoria situation showed strong emotional responses. Some joined the confederate in his play (Figure 12.11), and some of them initiated play of their own. (One jumped up and down on the desk, and another opened a window and threw paper wads at passersby.) The students in the anger situation responded in various ways; some muttered angry comments, and a few refused to complete the questionnaire.

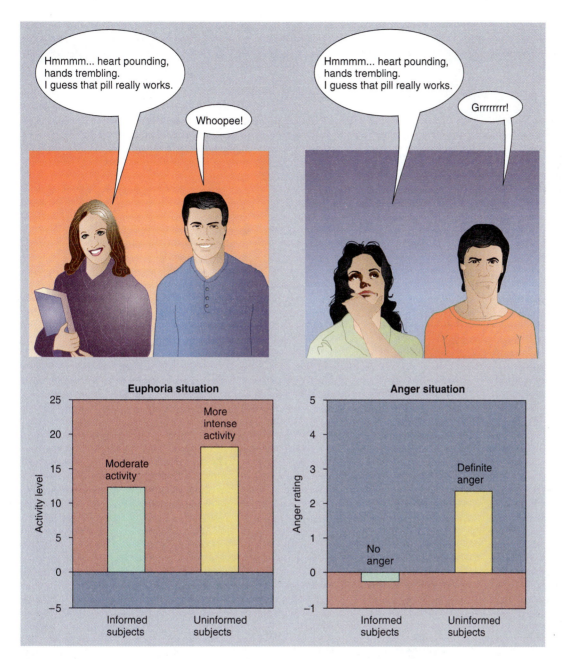

FIGURE 12.11
In Schachter and Singer's experiment, people who were uninformed about the effects of epinephrine reported strong emotions appropriate to their situation. According to Schachter and Singer, the autonomic arousal controls the strength of the emotion, but cognitive factors tell us which emotion we are experiencing.

But another factor was important in this experiment. Some of the subjects had been informed beforehand that the injections would produce certain autonomic effects, including hand tremor and increased heart rate. No matter which situation they were in, those subjects showed only slight emotional responses. When they felt themselves sweating and their hands trembling, they said to themselves, "Aha! I'm getting the side effects, just as they said I would."

What can we conclude from this experiment? According to **Schachter and Singer's theory of emotions,** a given physiological state is not the same thing as an emotion (see Figure 12.9). The intensity of the physiological state—that is, the degree of sympathetic nervous system arousal—determines the *in-*

tensity of the emotion, but not the type of emotion. Depending on all the information people have about themselves and the situation, they could interpret a particular type of arousal as anger, euphoria, or just an interesting side effect of taking a pill. That is, arousal intensifies an emotion, but cognitive appraisal of the situation tells us *which* emotion we are feeling. Table 12.1 contrasts Schachter and Singer's theory with the James-Lange and Cannon-Bard theories.

Unfortunately, these conclusions neglect another group of subjects—subjects whose results raise problems for Schachter and Singer's theory. These subjects, who were given placebo injections instead of epinephrine, showed about as much euphoria in the euphoria situation and as much anger in the

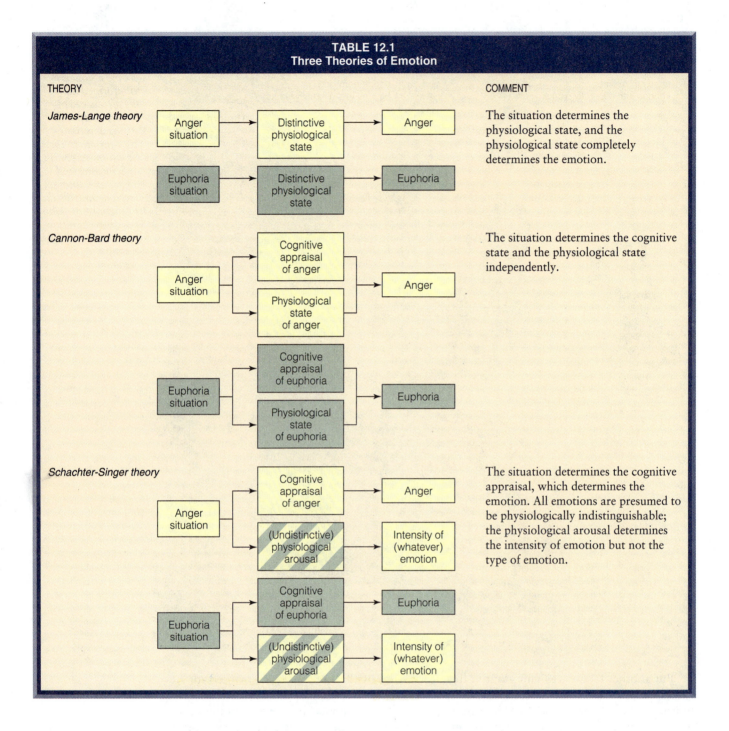

TABLE 12.1
Three Theories of Emotion

THEORY				COMMENT
James-Lange theory	Anger situation → Distinctive physiological state → Anger			The situation determines the physiological state, and the physiological state completely determines the emotion.
	Euphoria situation → Distinctive physiological state → Euphoria			
Cannon-Bard theory	Anger situation → Cognitive appraisal of anger / Physiological state of anger → Anger			The situation determines the cognitive state and the physiological state independently.
	Euphoria situation → Cognitive appraisal of euphoria / Physiological state of euphoria → Euphoria			
Schachter-Singer theory	Anger situation → Cognitive appraisal of anger → Anger / (Undistinctive) physiological arousal → Intensity of (whatever) emotion			The situation determines the cognitive appraisal, which determines the emotion. All emotions are presumed to be physiologically indistinguishable; the physiological arousal determines the intensity of emotion but not the type of emotion.
	Euphoria situation → Cognitive appraisal of euphoria → Euphoria / (Undistinctive) physiological arousal → Intensity of (whatever) emotion			

anger situation as did the subjects injected with epinephrine. Therefore, critics argue, the epinephrine injections may have had nothing to do with the results. If we accept that possibility, we are left with this summary of Schachter and Singer's experiment: People in a euphoria situation act happy; people in an anger situation act angry. That result is not very interesting (Plutchik & Ax, 1967).

Schachter and Singer were right in calling attention to the importance of cognition, but they may have gone too far. In emphasizing how cognition determines our emotions, they downplayed the contributions of physiological states. To some extent, fear, anger, and happiness really do feel different physiologically, and those physiological differences contribute to emotions.

The overall questions related to the James-Lange, Cannon-Bard, and Schachter-Singer theories are complex and difficult to investigate. Most investigators today believe that a more fruitful strategy is to explore the nature of specific emotions and their causes and expressions. Perhaps some day after we know enough about specific emotions we can come back to the issue of emotions in general.

CONCEPT CHECK

3. *You are in a small boat far from shore, and you see a storm approaching. You feel frightened and start to tremble. According to the James-Lange theory, which came first, the fright or the trembling? According to Schachter and Singer's theory, which came first? (Check your answers on page 532.)*

THE RANGE OF EMOTIONS

How many different emotions do humans experience? Do we perhaps have a few "basic" emotions that combine to form our other emotional experiences, just as three basic colors combine to produce all the other colors we see?

If so, how could we identify those basic emotions? Psychologists have generally accepted the following criteria:

- Basic emotions should emerge early in life, without requiring much experience. For example, *fear* and *anger* are reasonable candidates to be considered basic emotions, because we see them even in infants. *Nostalgia* and *pride,* which emerge later in life, are less likely to be considered basic emotions (Lewis, 1995).

- Basic emotions should have distinct biological bases. That is, each emotion probably depends on its own system of brain activity and triggers its own pattern of body activity, including perhaps a facial expression.

- The basic emotions should be about the same for people in different cultures. For example, if happiness and sadness are basic emotions, then people in different cultures should experience them similarly and express them similarly. The expected similarity in emotions does not, however, conflict with the fact that different cultures impose different rules for the expression of emotions. For example, cultures vary in their rules for when and where people should laugh and cry, what events should provoke jealousy, how much fear is appropriate for a normal person on a normal day, and how often people should get angry at others instead of taking the blame themselves (Mesquita &

FIGURE 12.12
For years psychologists have sought a list of "basic" emotions but have so far found no consensus. An alternative approach is to discard the concept of basic emotions. Perhaps even anger is a compound of "basic" components that have separate causes and meanings even though they often occur together.

Frijda, 1992; Roseman, Dhawan, Rettek, Naidu, & Thapa, 1995).

Given such criteria, psychologists have, unfortunately, not yet agreed on a single list of basic emotions. Some psychologists have proposed a very short list, such as "pain and pleasure" or "happiness, sadness, and anger." A number of psychologists list six emotions: happiness, sadness, anger, fear, disgust, and surprise. Others have added more to this list, such as distress, contempt, shame, guilt, courage, wonder, and hope. Still others have raised doubts about the whole concept of basic emotions (e.g., Ortony & Turner, 1990). For example, anger, which is ordinarily considered a basic emotion, may be formed from several components, as shown in Figure 12.12. Those behavioral components would then be the "elements" and what we have been calling basic emotions are really compounds.

THE PRODUCTION OF FACIAL EXPRESSIONS

Does each emotion have its own special expression? And why do we have facial expressions of emotions, anyway?

Quite simply, the function of facial expressions is communication. All primates (humans, apes, and monkeys) communicate their emotional states through gestures and

fear + anger are basic emotions

FIGURE 12.13
The facial expressions of chimpanzees are similar to those of humans.

facial expressions (Redican, 1982). (See Figure 12.13.) We humans can use spoken language as well, but we ordinarily prefer to use nonverbal expressions. You wink, nod, or smile to show a possible romantic interest; you withhold such expressions to indicate a lack of interest. (You *could* actually tell a stranger "I find you sexually attractive" or "Please don't approach me." If you try this direct verbal approach, you will probably discover why most people prefer to rely on facial expressions.)

Facial expressions provide a kind of "truth in advertising." That is, your expression reflects your internal state—such as happy, sad, or angry—and therefore tells other people whether you are likely to interact with them in a friendly or an uncooperative manner (Buck, 1994). Having other people around tends to exaggerate emotional expressions. For example, one study found that people bowling with friends often smiled after making a strike or a spare; people bowling alone seldom smiled (Kraut & Johnston, 1979). Even 10-month-old infants at play smile more when their mothers are watching than when their mothers are sitting nearby but reading a magazine (Jones, Collins, & Hong, 1991).

People can also smile, frown, or produce other facial expressions voluntarily. However, voluntary expressions do not exactly match the full, spontaneous expressions (except in the case of skilled actors). For example, the smile of a happy person includes movements of the mouth muscles and the muscles around the eyes (Figure 12.14a). Voluntary smiles (Figure 12.14b) include the mouth movements but generally do not include the muscles around the eyes (Ekman &

a   b

FIGURE 12.14
A spontaneous, happy smile (a) includes movements of both the mouth muscles and the muscles surrounding the eyes. This expression is sometimes called the "Duchenne smile." A voluntary smile (b) ordinarily includes only the mouth muscles. Most people cannot voluntarily control the eye muscles associated with the Duchenne smile.

Voluntary expression doent mater the fall

Davidson, 1993). The full expression including the muscles around the eyes is called the **Duchenne smile,** named after Duchenne de Boulogne, the first person to describe it.

CROSS-CULTURAL COMPARISONS OF FACIAL EXPRESSIONS

Do we learn how to make appropriate facial expressions, or are they part of our biological heritage? One way to approach this question is through naturalistic observations. Charles Darwin (1872/1965) asked missionaries and other people stationed in remote parts of the world to describe the facial expressions of the people who lived there. He found that people everywhere had similar facial expressions, including expressions of grief, determination, anger, surprise, terror, and disgust.

A century later, Irenäus Eibl-Eibesfeldt (1973, 1974) photographed people in different cultures, documenting the similarities in their facial expressions. He found smiling, frowning, laughing, and crying throughout the world, even in children who are born deaf and blind (Figures 12.15 and 12.16). Evidently, at least some of our facial expressions develop spontaneously, without any

FIGURE 12.15
This laughing girl was born deaf and blind. (From Eibl-Eibesfeldt, 1973.)

need for imitation. Eibl-Eibesfeldt also found that people everywhere expressed a friendly greeting by briefly raising their eyebrows (Figure 12.17). The mean duration of that expression is the same in all cultures: 1/3 second from start to finish, including 1/6 second in the fully elevated position.

raising of eyebrow.

FIGURE 12.16
A boy, blind since birth, covers his face in embarrassment. He prevents others from seeing his face, even though he himself has never experienced sight. (From Eibl-Eibesfeldt, 1973.)

FIGURE 12.17
People throughout the world, such as this man from New Guinea, raise their eyebrows as a greeting. Traveling around the world, you could communicate anywhere by using such universal facial expressions of emotion as smiling and frowning. But you might give the wrong message if you didn't know that nodding your head in some cultures means "no" or which hand and foot gestures are insulting. (From Eibl-Eibesfeldt, 1973.)

FIGURE 12.18

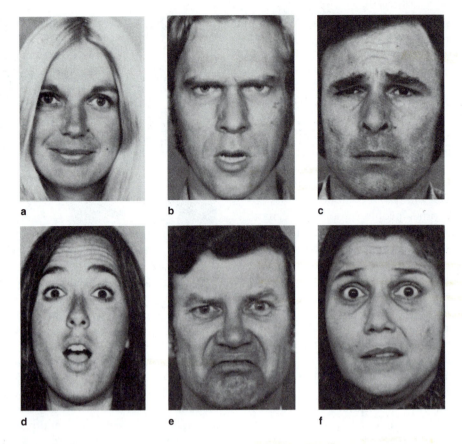

To move beyond naturalistic observations, researchers typically use photos of people showing the presumed "basic" facial expressions, as shown in Figure 12.18. Researchers show these photos to people in various cultures and ask them to identify which face shows anger, disgust, fear, happiness, sadness, and surprise. Naturally, terms such as *happiness* and *disgust* have to be translated into the various languages. However, researchers use the same photos with all cultures; the intention is to demonstrate that all people can recognize the same facial expressions. (In other experiments, the procedure is reversed and European Americans are asked to identify the facial expressions of people from other parts of the world.) The results: People in all cultures label the expressions with high, although not perfect, accuracy (Ekman, 1992).

What can we conclude from such data? We can conclude that people throughout the world use similar facial expressions, much as they see the same colors (Ekman, 1994). However, we cannot conclude that the facial expressions are clearly distinct for exactly six basic emotions (Russell, 1994). For example, you probably had little trouble matching the six expressions of Figure 12.18 to the six labels. However, if you had examined just one expression, you might have been less certain.

(Might you have identified photo d as fear or photo e as anger if you had seen each one by itself?)

Furthermore, the fact that people of all cultures can recognize facial expressions for six emotions does not necessarily mean that those are basic emotions, much less that they are the *only* basic emotions. For example, we could add to the photo set a new photo representing, say, *slight happiness*. If people of all cultures could correctly label this photo, we should conclude only that people of all cultures show degrees of happiness in the same way. We should not conclude that slight happiness is a seventh "basic emotion." Similarly, the fact that people can correctly label six photos does not necessarily identify each of those six emotions as basic.

A BIOLOGICAL APPROACH TO IDENTIFYING BASIC EMOTIONS

If people do have basic emotions, one way to identify them would be to find procedures that would eliminate just one emotion or another. For example, if we found six kinds of brain damage, each of which eliminated one kind of emotion, we could justifiably classify those emotions as basic.

As one step toward that goal, researchers have identified the brain circuits responsible for fears and learned fears. Figure 12.19 pre-

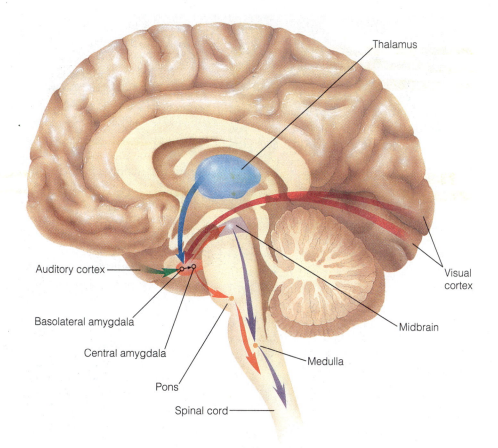

Thalamus

Auditory cortex

Basolateral amygdala

Central amygdala

Pons

Spinal cord

Visual cortex

Midbrain

Medulla

FIGURE 12.19

Certain small structures in the pons and medulla control unlearned fear reactions, such as a startle response to an unexpected loud sound. Damage to those areas can eliminate fear responses. Another structure, the amygdala, sends information to the pons and medulla. Damage to the amygdala eliminates learned fears, but does not affect the unlearned startle response to a loud sound. This diagram shows the human brain, although the relevant experiments were conducted with rats.

sents a diagram of certain structures in the human brain. Damage to the tiny areas shown in the pons and medulla can impair or eliminate all fears, including the unlearned startle response that all hearing people, even babies, display after an unexpected loud noise. In rat experiments, damage to the areas shown in the amygdala has no effect on the startle response, but can eliminate learned fears, such as the response learned to some signal that predicts an electric shock (Phillips & LeDoux, 1992).

That is, the damage that destroys unlearned fears destroys learned fears as well. Damage that destroys learned fears does not impair unlearned fears. It is fair, therefore, to say that unlearned fears are more basic than learned fears.

Extensions of this research approach might answer some additional questions about emotions. For example, after brain damage that eliminates fear, does an individual show any impairment of disgust, anger,

surprise, or other emotions? If so, then the other emotions are related to fear, and not really basic. But if a loss of fear entails no significant change in the other emotions, then we draw a different conclusion. If we found, for example, that one kind of brain damage eliminates fear without affecting other emotions, another kind of damage eliminates anger, still another eliminates disgust, and so forth, then we would at last have a solid basis for describing each of those emotions as basic.

■ EXAMPLES OF EMOTIONS

I shall not try to discuss each type of emotion, partly because no one is sure how many types there are. Instead, I shall focus on two important types of emotional experience, anger and happiness. What makes us angry and what do we do about it? And what makes us happy?

ANGER AND AGGRESSIVE BEHAVIOR

An experience of anger requires two elements: (1) something goes wrong, and (2) we attribute that event to someone else's actions. For example, if you get injured in an earthquake, you probably do not become angry, because you do not blame anyone else. If you get injured because someone tripped you, your reaction is much different.

Most people become angry far more often than they become physically aggressive. In one study, some people were asked to describe their most recent experience of anger; others kept an "anger diary" for a week (Averill, 1983). They reported that most experiences of anger were directed against family or friends. People usually dealt with their anger by saying something to the person who had aroused it or by talking about the experience to someone else. Very rarely did they physically attack the person who had provoked their anger.

FACTORS THAT ELICIT ANGER AND AGGRESSION

A great many instances of anger fall under the heading "times when I felt mistreated." According to the frustration-aggression hypothesis, much or all of anger and aggressive behavior is caused by "frustration" (Dollard, Miller, Doob, Mowrer, & Sears, 1939). You experience frustration when an obstacle prevents you from reaching some expected goal, such as when a barking dog prevents you from sleeping or a traffic jam prevents you from reaching an important appointment on time. Frustration leads to anger and hostile aggression; it is not a factor in the calm ag-

The facial expression of anger represents a threat of possible attack, but for most of us that threat seldom develops into a reality. We deal with our anger by discussing the problem or by walking away from the situation; rarely if ever do we strike someone.

gressive behaviors that people learn as strategies for getting what they want (Berkowitz, 1989).

However, unpleasant events that do not cause frustration sometimes also lead to aggressive behavior. Leonard Berkowitz (1983) has proposed a more comprehensive theory: All unpleasant events—including frustration, pain, foul odors, a hot environment, and frightening information—give rise to both the impulse to fight and the impulse to flee. Which impulse dominates depends on the circumstances, such as the availability of avoidance responses, the targets available for attack, and the individual's previous experiences with fighting and fleeing. For example, if someone bumps into you and spills hot coffee all over you, do you scream angrily? Perhaps. But if that person is your boss, or the loan and scholarship officer at your college, or the biggest and meanest-looking person you have ever seen, you may smile and apologize for being in the way.

The probability of attacking also depends on one's biological state at the moment. A variety of drugs, notably alcohol and tranquilizers, increase the probability of violent behavior (Bushman, 1993; Bushman & Cooper, 1990). Tranquilizers presumably increase violent behavior by decreasing one's fear of the possible retaliation by the person attacked. High levels of the hormone testosterone also increase the probability of aggressive behavior, although this tendency is not a strong one (Dabbs & Morris, 1990; Moyer, 1974). High temperatures also increase the probability of violence (Anderson, 1989).

PREDICTION AND CONTROL OF VIOLENT BEHAVIOR

People who cannot control their anger sometimes commit acts of violence, even criminal acts. Anger is hardly the only cause of violence, but because it is one important cause, let's now consider how psychologists try to predict violent behavior.

A parole board is trying to decide whether or not to release a prisoner who is eligible for parole. The staff of a mental hospital is debating whether or not to discharge a patient with a history of violent behavior. A judge is trying to decide whether or not to send a first-time offender to jail. In each case, the authorities ask a psychologist or a psychiatrist for a professional opinion on whether the person is dangerous.

How accurate are such opinions? If they are based mainly on interviews, they are accurate only a little more often than random guesses would be (Monahan, 1984). Some dangerous people manage to convince others that they are harmless.

The most accurate predictions are those based on biographical information. People who were physically abused as children and who witnessed violence between their parents are more likely than others are to commit repeated acts of violence, including murder (Malinosky-Rummell & Hansen, 1993). The physical pain of being beaten may provoke future violence, and a violent parent provides a model for the child eventually to imitate. (Recall the principles of social learning from Chapter 6.) Even this predictor is far from foolproof, however; only about one-third of abused children become abusive parents (Widom, 1989).

Several other factors are associated with a tendency toward violent behavior (Eron, 1987; Lewis et al., 1985; Raine, Venables, & Williams, 1990):

- A history of acting violently during childhood
- Not feeling guilty after hurting someone
- Symptoms of brain damage or of major psychological disorders
- Weaker-than-normal physiological responses to arousal
- Being closely related to someone who has been committed to a psychiatric hospital
- A history of suicide attempts
- Watching a great deal of violence on television

How can anyone help people control their violent behavior? Punishment is sometimes effective and may be necessary in extreme cases, but it is often counterproductive. Excessively painful punishment actually triggers aggressive behavior.

Sometimes cognitive approaches are effective. People can be taught to stop making unrealistic, perfectionistic demands on themselves and others. They can be taught to tolerate frustration.

Encouraging people to learn new behaviors is another way to control violent behavior (Fehrenbach & Thelen, 1982). Eliminating reinforcement may extinguish or reduce the offensive behavior. If a child has learned to win attention by throwing temper tantrums, for example, then parents and teach-

When a convicted criminal, such as kidnapper John Esposito, is eligible for parole, courts sometimes call on psychologists or psychiatrists to estimate how dangerous the person is. That judgment is difficult to make and is frequently inaccurate. Generally, the best predictor of future violence is a person's previous history of violent behavior.

ers should ignore the tantrums. Or they can impose "time-out" periods after an episode of violent behavior, perhaps by temporarily isolating a child who regularly attacks other children. Finally, they can reinforce acceptable behavior, perhaps by giving points toward a reward for every hour spent in calm interaction with others.

HAPPINESS

What makes you happy? What makes you unhappy? The answers are more elusive than you might expect. The following quote is from Leo Tolstoy, the author of *War and Peace*, *Anna Karenina*, and other famous novels. At the time of this writing, Tolstoy was rich and famous, but desperately unhappy:

I wandered about in the forest of human knowledge. . . . From one branch of human knowledge I received an endless number of precise answers to questions I had not asked, answers concerning the chemical composition of the stars, the movement of the sun toward the constellation Hercules, the origin of the species and of man, the forms of infinitely small atoms. . . . But the answer given by this branch of knowledge to my question about the meaning of my life was only this: You . . . are a temporary, random conglomeration of particles. The thing that you have been led to refer to as your life is simply the mutual interaction and alteration of these particles. This conglomeration will continue for a certain period of time; then the interaction of these particles will come to a halt, and the thing you call your life will come to an end and with it all your questions. You are a little

lump of something randomly stuck together. The lump decomposes. . . . There is no more to be said.

My life came to a stop. . . . There was no life in me because I had no desires whose satisfaction I would have found reasonable. . . . If a fairy had come and offered to fulfill my every wish, I would not have known what to wish for. . . . I did not even want to discover truth anymore because I had guessed what it was. The truth was that life is meaningless. (Tolstoy, 1882/1983, pp. 40–41, 27–28)

What would it take to make Tolstoy happy? Fame, wealth, family, and friends had failed to bring him happiness. If he were alive today, no doubt someone would recommend giving him antidepressant drugs. But I wouldn't count on drugs to do him much good either. What Tolstoy needed was a belief—a belief that the universe made sense and that life had meaning.

Eventually he found contentment, if not exactly happiness, by changing his life, seeking spiritual (though not church-oriented) values, and giving away much of his wealth—over the protests of his wife and children.

Many things can make people happy, but mere *things* don't keep people happy for long. Within a given country, at a given time, wealthy people tend to be happier than poor people are, but we find many exceptions to this rule. Furthermore, as a given country— say, the United States—becomes wealthier and wealthier, the average person in that country does not become happier and happier (Diener, 1984).

Then what does make people happy? We can list many possibilities—family activities, enjoyment of nature, having a belief in the value of life, having goals to work toward, and so on. But it is difficult to conduct research on the contribution of each factor. Good scientific research requires good measurement, and measuring happiness is difficult.

Most frequently psychologists measure happiness simply by asking people how happy they are. Based on people's self-reports, psychologists find that religious people and people with many friends tend to be happier than nonreligious people and people with few social contacts. Also, people who are healthy and who are achieving their goals tend to be happy (Diener, 1984). However, these trends represent correlational data and therefore tell

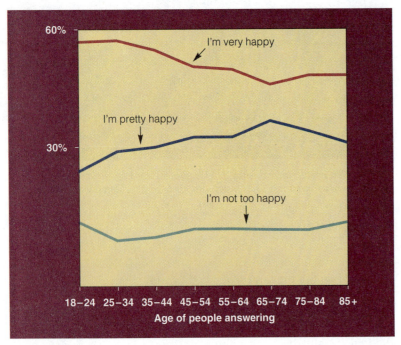

FIGURE 12.20

Between 1972 and 1986, more than 20,000 people in the United States were asked how happy they were—very happy, pretty happy, or not too happy. Results varied only slightly from one age group to another or from one year to another. (Based on data of Russell & Megaard, 1988.)

On self-report questionnaires, old people describe themselves as about as happy as 20-year-olds describe themselves. These data are difficult to interpret, because we do not know whether all people mean the same thing by the expression "I'm happy."

us nothing about cause and effect. (For example, we do not know whether having friends makes a person happy or whether being happy helps someone attract friends.)

Moreover, people's self-reports of happiness may not be entirely accurate. For example, consider Figure 12.20, which shows that *reported* happiness is nearly constant from young adulthood through old age (Russell & Megaard, 1988). Are people in their 70s really just as happy as young adults? Maybe. But it is also possible that "I feel very happy" means something different to an older person than it does to a younger person.

SUMMARY

- *The usefulness of emotions.* We make many decisions by imagining the emotional consequences of the possible outcomes. Brain-damaged people who suffer a loss of emotions also have trouble making and keeping long-term plans. (page 511)

- *Emotions and autonomic arousal.* Emotions are generally associated with arousal of the sympathetic or parasympathetic branch of the autonomic nervous system. The sympathetic nervous system readies the body for emergency action. The parasympathetic nervous system promotes digestion and other less vigorous activities. (page 512)

- *Opponent-process principle.* As stated by the opponent-process principle of emotions, the removal of the impetus for a given emotion brings about a sudden swing to the opposite emotion. (page 514)

- *Polygraph.* The polygraph measures the activity of the sympathetic nervous system through such variables as heart rate, breathing rate, blood pressure, and electrical conductance of the skin. The polygraph is sometimes used as a "lie detector," although its accuracy for that purpose is low. (page 516)

- *James-Lange theory.* According to the James-Lange theory of emotions, an emotion is the perception of a change in the body's physiological state. (page 518)

- *Cannon-Bard theory.* According to the Cannon-Bard theory, the cognitive experience of an emotion is independent of physiological arousal. (page 520)

- *Schachter and Singer's theory.* According to Schachter and Singer's theory, autonomic arousal determines the intensity of an emotion but does not determine what that emotion will be. We identify an emotion on the basis of how we perceive the situation. (page 520)

- *Limitations of these theories.* None of these three theories of emotion is fully satisfactory. Physiological and cognitive influences interact in complex ways to produce emotional experiences. (page 522)

- *Facial expressions.* Facial expressions are closely tied to emotions. When people move their facial muscles into something that resembles a smile, they are more likely to be happy than if they maintain other expressions. (page 523)

- *Cultural similarities.* Many human facial expressions are largely the same for cultures throughout the world. (page 525)

- *Anger.* People report frequently experiencing anger, although it seldom leads to violent acts. Aggressive behavior often occurs in defense of territory or in competition for a mate. Frustration or other unpleasant experiences often prompt aggressive behavior. (page 528)

- *Predicting violence.* Psychologists and psychiatrists find it difficult to predict whether a particular prisoner would be dangerous if released. Currently, the best way to make such predictions is to review the prisoner's biographical information, especially the history of violent behavior. (page 528)

- *Measuring happiness.* Happiness is difficult to measure, and most of what we know about it is based on correlational data. Possessions alone cannot guarantee happiness. (page 529)

SUGGESTION FOR FURTHER READING

Damasio, A. R. (1994). *Descartes' error.* New York: G. P. Putnam's sons. Argues that emotion is not just something that interferes with rational behavior; it is a necessary contributor to intelligent decision-making.

TERMS

autonomic nervous system a section of the nervous system that controls the functioning of the internal organs (page 512)

sympathetic nervous system a system composed of two chains of neuron clusters lying just to the left and right of the spinal cord; the neurons send messages to the internal organs to prepare them for a burst of vigorous activity (page 512)

parasympathetic nervous system a system of neurons located at the top and bottom of the spinal cord; the neurons send messages to the internal organs that prepare the body for digestion and related processes (page 512)

opponent-process principle of emotions principle that the removal of a stimulus that excites one emotion causes a swing to an opposite emotion (page 514)

polygraph a machine that simultaneously measures heart rate, breathing rate, blood pressure, and galvanic skin response (page 516)

bogus pipeline device that in fact measures nothing, but which psychologists attach to people in an attempt to convince them that it measures honesty or lying (page 516)

guilty-knowledge test a test that uses the polygraph to measure whether a person has information that only someone guilty of a certain crime could know (page 517)

James-Lange theory the theory that emotion is merely our perception of autonomic changes and movements evoked directly by various stimuli (page 518)

Cannon-Bard theory of emotions theory that certain areas of the brain evaluate sensory information and, when appropriate, send one set of impulses to the autonomic nervous system and another set to the forebrain, which is responsible for the subjective and cognitive aspects of emotion (page 520)

Schachter and Singer's theory of emotions theory that emotions are our interpretation of autonomic arousal in light of all the information we have about ourselves and the situation (page 521)

Duchenne smile expression that includes movement of both the mouth muscles and certain muscles near the eyes (page 525)

frustration-aggression hypothesis the theory that frustration leads to aggressive behavior (page 528)

ANSWERS TO CONCEPT CHECKS

1. When you ride a roller coaster, your heart rate increases (sympathetic activity). After you get off, your heart rate falls to lower than usual (rebound increase in parasympathetic activity). (page 515)

2. After someone takes a drug repeatedly, the A state becomes weaker. (That is known as tolerance, as discussed in Chapter 6.) The B state (withdrawal) becomes stronger. (page 515)

3. According to the James-Lange theory, the trembling and shaking came first. Schachter and Singer's theory agrees. However, according to the James-Lange theory, your perception of the trembling and shaking leads immediately and automatically to the experience of fear. According to Schachter and Singer's theory, you first interpret your trembling on the basis of circumstances before you experience fear: "Am I shaking because of that pill I took? Because someone made me angry? Because I'm excited? Because I'm frightened?" (page 523)

ANSWER TO OTHER QUESTION IN THE TEXT

A. (a) happiness (b) anger (c) sadness (d) surprise (e) disgust and (f) fear. (page 526)

HEALTH PSYCHOLOGY

How do our emotions affect our health?

Imagine you meet a man who is suffering from, say, multiple sclerosis. Would you say, "It's his own fault he's sick; he's being punished for his sins"? I presume you would neither say nor believe anything so cruel. However, in the Middle Ages and in ancient times, many people believed just that. We congratulate ourselves today on having advanced beyond that way of thinking; we know it is wrong to "blame the victim."

Or do we? We may think cigarette smokers are at least partly at fault if they develop lung cancer. We note that AIDS usually occurs in people with a history of intravenous drug use or unsafe sex. If women drink alcohol during pregnancy, we hold them partly responsible for the deformities or mental retardation of their infants. As we learn more and more about the causes of various illnesses, we expect people to accept more responsibility for their own health, even if we do not exactly use the word *blame* when people become ill.

People's behavior does, in fact, influence their health. Unfortunately, we can easily overstate the amount of that influence. Some people are always as careful as possible about their diet, exercise regularly, and have healthy habits but develop serious illnesses anyway. Psychological factors influence our health, but they are not the only influence.

Health psychology deals with the ways in which people's behavior can enhance health and prevent illness and how behavior contributes to recovery from illness (Brannon & Feist, 1992). It deals with such issues as why people smoke, why they may ignore their physician's advice, and how to reduce pain.

In this section, we shall focus mainly on how stress and other emotional conditions affect health.

▌ STRESS

Have you ever gone without sleep several nights in a row trying to finish an assignment before a deadline? Or waited what seemed like forever for someone who was supposed to pick you up? Or had a close friend suddenly not want to see you anymore? Or tried to explain why you no longer want to date someone? Each of these experiences provokes an emotional response and causes stress.

SELYE'S CONCEPT OF STRESS

According to Hans Selye (1979), an Austrian-born physician who worked at McGill University in Montreal, stress is *the nonspecific response of the body to any demand made upon it.* Every demand on the body evokes certain specific responses as well. The body responds in one way to the loss of blood, in another way to the lack of sleep. But all demands on the body evoke generalized, nonspecific responses. For example,

Health psychology deals with all the ways in which people's behavior affects their health, ranging from why some people neglect to take their prescribed medication to why some people persist in smoking, drinking, and other risky behaviors.

they all activate the sympathetic nervous system, increase the release of the hormone epinephrine, and interfere with your ability to concentrate.

When people say, "I've been under a lot of stress lately," they are generally referring to a string of unpleasant experiences. Selye's concept of stress is broader than that: He includes any experience that brings about change in a person's life. For example, getting married or being promoted is presumably a pleasant experience, but it also demands that you make a number of changes in the way you live, and so, in Selye's sense, it produces stress. It is unclear, however, that a favorable stressor makes the same demands on the body as does an unfavorable stressor. Note also that, according to Selye, dealing with the effects of poverty, racism, sexism, or a lifelong disability would *not* count as stress; only *changes* in your life count as stress.

According to Selye, the body goes through three stages in its response to a stressor: The first is **alarm,** a brief period of high arousal of the sympathetic nervous system, readying the body for vigorous activity. However, some stressors last longer than the body can maintain this high state of arousal. Perhaps you live down the street from a nuclear power plant, or you have a high-stress job. If so, you cannot overcome your problem with a brief burst of intense activity. You enter **resistance,** a stage of prolonged but moderate arousal. Your epinephrine levels remain high day after day, week after week (Figure 12.21). Your adrenal cortex secretes **cortisol** and several other hormones that elevate blood sugar and enhance metabolism. The increased fuel supply to the cells enables them to sustain a high, steady level of activity to endure prolonged stress. However, you no longer feel ready for vigorous activity; you feel withdrawn and inactive much of the time, your performance deteriorates, and you complain of emotional distress (Baum, Gatchel, & Schaeffer, 1983; Frankenhaeuser, 1980).

If the stress is even more intense and long-lasting, the body enters the third stage, **exhaustion.** As cortisol and other hormones shift energy toward increasing blood sugar and metabolism, they shift it away from the synthesis of proteins, including the proteins necessary for the immune system. In the short term that shift may not be a problem; however, severe stress over many months may weaken the immune system and leave the individual vulnerable to a variety of illnesses (O'Leary, 1990). The end result is what Selye calls the **general adaptation syndrome,** which is characterized by weakness, fatigue, loss of appetite, and a general lack of interest.

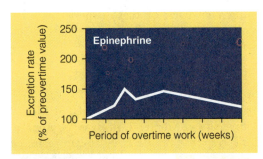

FIGURE 12.21
Epinephrine levels rose for a group of women before, during, and after a long period of working overtime. To establish a baseline, each woman's epinephrine level prior to the overtime period was taken as 100%; thus any number above 100% represents an increase. (Based on Frankenhaeuser, 1980.)

Dealing with a child who has a chronic illness creates a long-term stress for parents, possibly leading to the resistance or exhaustion stage.

POSTTRAUMATIC STRESS DISORDER

Perhaps the most powerful demonstration of the effects of severe stress is **posttraumatic stress disorder (PTSD),** a condition in which people who have endured extreme stress feel prolonged anxiety and depression (Pitman, Orr, Forgue, deJong, & Claiborn, 1987). This condition has been recognized after wars throughout history, under such names as "battle fatigue" or "shell shock." One nationwide survey reported posttraumatic stress disorder in 20% of the American veterans who were wounded in Vietnam (Helzer, Robins, & McEnvoy, 1987). It also occurs in rape or assault victims, torture victims, survivors of an airplane crash or a severe automobile crash, and witnesses to a murder.

Anyone who suffers through a traumatic event experiences severe stress at the time and shortly afterward. People differ greatly, however, in their long-term reactions. For example, in 1980 a man kidnapped three college cheerleaders and raped and murdered one of them. The other two escaped and eventually testified against their assailant. One of the two quickly put the events behind her; she completed her education, married, got a job, had children, and only occasionally thought about her gruesome ordeal. The other woman suffered a clear case of PTSD, including long bouts of depression and intense flashbacks. She found herself unable to focus on her studies and very uneasy in her relationships with men. At one point she got a room with a view of the prison so she could keep an eye on it, to make sure her assailant was not escaping (Krueger & Neff, 1995). Why PTSD strikes some people and not others, following the same experience, psychologists do not yet know.

People with posttraumatic stress disorder may suffer from frequent nightmares, outbursts of anger, constant unhappiness, and guilt. The guilt is a special kind of experience, often called *survivor's guilt,* common in people who survive a catastrophe in which many other people died. People with PTSD may have difficulty concentrating or relating emotionally to other people (Keane, Wolfe, & Taylor, 1987). A brief reminder of the tragic experience can trigger a flashback that borders on panic. Many day-to-day events become stressful, even years after the original event (Solomon, Mikulincer, & Flum, 1988). In one study, eight Vietnam veterans with PTSD watched a 15-minute videotape of dramatized combat. Watching the film elevated their endorphin levels in the same way in which people generally react to an actual injury (Pitman, van der Kolk, Orr, & Greenberg, 1990).

This group of Vietnam vets met regularly for a year to work on problems related to posttraumatic stress. Since the group disbanded, one member has had a show of his hand-colored photographs. (This group portrait is a sample of his work.) Another member has started his own company. Some members have created new careers; some have been in and out of substance-abuse programs. Most continue to experience vivid dreams full of war images.

MEASURING STRESS AND ITS EFFECT ON HEALTH

Most investigators agree that severe stress can endanger a person's health. For example, prolonged job stress is significantly correlated with anxiety and depression (deWolff, 1985). People who experience severe stress on the job report frequent illnesses as well. (At least they often call in sick and stay home from work!)

How much stress is injurious to one's health? Is it true that the more stress a person experiences, the more that person's health suffers?

To answer such questions, we need to measure both stress and health. Measuring health is tough enough; measuring stress is even more difficult. One approach is to give people a checklist of stressful experiences. For example, Thomas Holmes and Richard Rahe (1967) devised a Social Readjustment Rating Scale (Table 12.2) that assigns points for both desirable and undesirable events, in accordance with Selye's idea that any change in a person's life is stressful. Note, for example, that you could get 35 points for "change in number of arguments with spouse"—the same number of stress points for an increase or a decrease in arguments! To measure your amount of stress, you are supposed to check off all the experiences you have had within a given period of time, such as the last 6 months, and total up the points assigned to each.

TABLE 12.2
Social Readjustment Rating Scale

RANK	LIFE EVENT	POINT VALUE	RANK	LIFE EVENT	POINT VALUE
1	Death of spouse	100	22	Change in responsibilities at work	29
2	Divorce	73	23	Son or daughter leaving home	29
3	Marital separation	65	24	Trouble with in-laws	29
4	Jail term	63	25	Outstanding personal achievement	28
5	Death of close family member	63	26	Wife begin or stop work	26
6	Personal injury or illness	53	27	Begin or end school	26
7	Marriage	50	28	Change in living conditions	25
8	Fired at work	47	29	Revision of personal habits	24
9	Marital reconciliation	45	30	Trouble with boss	23
10	Retirement	45	31	Change in work hours or conditions	20
11	Change in health of family member	44	32	Change in residence	20
12	Pregnancy	40	33	Change in schools	20
13	Sex difficulties	39	34	Change in recreation	19
14	Gain of new family member	39	35	Change in church activities	19
15	Business readjustment	39	36	Change in social activities	18
16	Change in financial state	38	37	Mortgage or loan less than $10,000	17
17	Death of close friend	37	38	Change in sleeping habits	16
18	Change to different line of work	36	39	Change in number of family get-togethers	15
19	Change in number of arguments with spouse	35	40	Change in eating habits	15
			41	Vacation	13
20	Mortgage over $10,000	31	42	Christmas	12
21	Foreclosure of mortgage or loan	30	43	Minor violations of the law	11

Source: Homes & Rahe, 1967.

The Social Readjustment Rating Scale is based on Selye's theory that stress results from any change in one's life, good or bad—marriage, divorce, birth of a child, death of a relative, entering or leaving school, getting a job or losing one. However, according to this view, long-term miserable experiences do not count as stressful if they are unchanging.

Although this scale has been widely used, it is subject to many criticisms: First, the assumption that we can add stress points from various events is probably wrong (Birnbaum & Sotoodeh, 1991). For example, suppose you graduate from college (26 points), treat yourself to a vacation (13), and then start a new job (36). That adds up to 75 points—more than you would get for a divorce (73) or the death of a close family member (63).

Second problem: The scale includes 53 points for suffering the stress associated with "personal injury or illness." It also ascribes points for sex difficulties, change in sleeping habits, and change in eating habits—all of which are symptoms of illness. So it is not very impressive to find that people with high stress scores have an increased probability of being ill.

Third, the scale fails to measure some important stressors. Selye defined stress as a response to changes in one's life; accordingly, this scale ignores the stress of coping with unchanging problems, such as racism or poverty. It also ignores the stress we experience from events that *almost* happened. For example, all year long you expect to be laid off from your job. You keep waiting, but the

The amount of stress an individual feels depends on the meaning of an event for that person. An event that is very stressful for one person may be only mildly stressful for another. Pregnancy means one thing to a 27-year-old married woman and something different to an unwed 16-year-old—one reason stress rating scales are of dubious value.

rumored plant closing never happens. Or you have been counting on a promotion at work, and you have told all your friends that you are expecting it, but then you do not get promoted. You get no points on the rating scale for "not getting fired" or "not being promoted." And yet anyone who has lived through such an experience can tell you that it was very stressful.

SOMETHING TO THINK ABOUT

Can you think of a better way to measure stress? Some psychologists have given people a list of events and have asked them both to check off events they have experienced and to assign a value to each event on the basis of how stressful they found it. Is that an improvement, or does it introduce problems of its own?

LAZARUS'S APPROACH TO STRESS

Aside from the problems with the Social Readjustment Rating Scale, however, many psychologists challenge the basic assumption that a particular life change produces a specific amount of stress and that a given event will be equally stressful for all people. As Richard Lazarus (1977) pointed out, the stress evoked by an event depends on how people interpret the event and what they can do about it. Pregnancy may be much more

stressful for a 16-year-old unmarried woman than it is for a 27-year-old married woman. Being fired may be a disaster for a 50-year-old who expects to have trouble finding another job; it may be only a minor annoyance to a 19-year-old.

According to Lazarus, *stress is a situation that someone regards as threatening and as possibly exceeding his or her resources* (Lazarus, 1977). (See Figure 12.22.) Note that this view allows for much greater

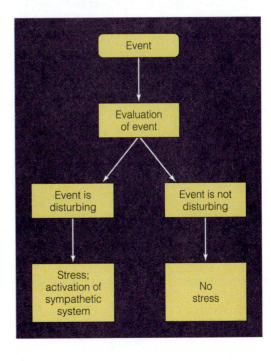

FIGURE 12.22
Lazarus believes that evaluation of some kind, conscious or unconscious, always precedes emotion. Thus a given event may be highly stressful for one person, only slightly stressful or not at all for a second person.

emphasis on people's knowledge, experience, and cognitions: Two women are bitten by a snake. The first woman panics; the second woman remains calm, because she recognizes the snake as a harmless variety. Two men are criticized by their boss. One is deeply hurt; the other (who has seen the boss act this way before) shrugs and says, "I guess the boss is in a bad mood again today."

To the extent that stress is related to our interpretation of an event, not simply to the event itself, people can learn to cope with potentially stressful events, as we shall see later in this chapter. They can learn to deal with events actively instead of feeling threatened by them. Given this view, the proper measure of stress would have to include not only the unpleasant events ("hassles") that we have to deal with but also the pleasant events ("uplifts") that brighten our day and help to cancel out the unpleasant events (Kanner, Coyne, Schaefer, & Lazarus, 1981). Table 12.3 presents one example of this approach.

We can conclude this section by emphasizing that stress is difficult to measure accurately. Nevertheless, we can identify particular kinds of stressful experiences that endanger many people's health. Studying the effects of experience on health and illness can offer us insights into the relationship among stressful experiences, interpretation of those experiences, and body functioning.

STRESS AND PSYCHOSOMATIC ILLNESS

A **psychosomatic illness** is *not* an imagined or a pretended illness. Rather, it is an illness that is influenced by a person's experiences—particularly stressful experiences—or by his or her reactions to those experiences. That is, something about the person's behavior or way of life influenced what disease he or she got and how long it lasted. Most illnesses are partly psychosomatic in this sense.

For many years, physicians looking for the sources of illness concentrated on physical agents such as germs or injuries, giving no thought to the possibility of a psychosomatic influence. Then, in the early 1800s, they found soldiers who were suffering from what we would now call posttraumatic stress disorder. Some of the soldiers showed serious (though temporary) physical ailments, including blindness or paralysis, even though they had never been injured. A few even died on the battlefield when a cannonball landed nearby without striking them. Physicians of the time suggested that the soldiers were injured by the wind of the cannonball passing by, or by atmospheric electricity stirred up by the wind, or by the heat or the temporary vacuum left in its wake. Today those hypotheses sound extremely far-fetched; at the time they seemed more reasonable than the "ridiculous" idea that mere fear or other psychological states could influence someone's health (McMahon, 1975).

Physicians and psychologists still have trouble explaining how emotional states affect the body. They do not assume that emotions lead directly to illness. They know, however, that people who have certain emotional experiences are more likely than others to overeat, to smoke, or to engage in other habits that increase the risk of illness. Certain behaviors and experiences can damage the immune system and increase a person's susceptibility to a variety of disorders ranging from minor infections to cancer (Shavit et al., 1985).

One young woman died of fear in a most peculiar way: When she was born, on Friday the 13th, the midwife who delivered her and two other babies that day announced that all three were hexed and would die before their 23rd birthday. The other two did die young. As the third woman approached her 23rd birthday, she checked into a hospital and in-

---

TABLE 12.3 Ten Most Frequent Hassles and Uplifts	
HASSLES	**UPLIFTS**
1. Concerns about weight	1. Relating well with your spouse or lover
2. Health of a family member	2. Relating well with friends
3. Rising prices of common goods	3. Completing a task
4. Home maintenance	4. Feeling healthy
5. Too many things to do	5. Getting enough sleep
6. Misplacing or losing things	6. Eating out
7. Yard work or outside home maintenance	7. Meeting your responsibilities
8. Property, investment, or taxes	8. Visiting, phoning, or writing someone
9. Crime	9. Spending time with family
10. Physical appearance	10. Home (inside) pleasing to you

Source: Kanner, Coyne, Schaefer, & Lazarus, 1981.

formed the staff of her fears. The staff noted that she dealt with her anxiety by extreme hyperventilation (deep breathing). Shortly before her birthday, she hyperventilated to death.

How did that happen? Ordinarily, when people do not breathe voluntarily they breathe reflexively; the reflex is triggered by carbon dioxide in the blood. By extreme hyperventilation, this woman had exhaled so much carbon dioxide that she did not have enough left to trigger reflexive breathing. When she stopped breathing voluntarily, she stopped breathing altogether ("Clinicopathologic conference," 1967). This is a clear example of a self-fulfilling prophecy: The fact that the woman believed in the hex caused its fulfillment. It is also a clear example of an indirect influence of emotions on health.

We shall examine heart disease and cancer as examples of diseases that may be linked to particular emotional experiences or personality types. In both cases, the evidence has its strengths and weaknesses.

HEART DISEASE

An upholsterer repairing the chairs in a physician's waiting room once noticed that the fronts of the chairs wore out before the backs. To figure out why, the physician began watching patients in the waiting room.

He noticed that his heart patients habitually sat on the front edges of their seats, waiting impatiently to be called in for their appointments. This observation led the physician to hypothesize a link between heart disease and an impatient, success-driven personality, now known as the Type A personality (Friedman & Rosenman, 1974).

People with a Type A personality are highly competitive; they must always win. They are impatient, always in a hurry, and often angry and hostile. By contrast, people with a Type B personality are relatively easygoing, less hurried, and less hostile. For example, Gary Schwartz (1987) describes observations of two men fishing: One (a Type B) slowly baited his hook, dropped his line into the water, and sat back watching the gulls and waiting for a bite. Another man (a Type A), fishing with two poles, spent much of his time rushing back and forth between the two poles, cursing when the two lines got tangled with each other. When another fisher caught a large fish, this man pulled up his anchor in frustration and raced his boat off to another part of the bay. (Are you a Type A or a Type B? Check yourself by answering the questions in Figure 12.23.)

Statistically, a link does exist between Type A personality and susceptibility to

Measuring the Type A Personality

_____ 1. Do you find it difficult to restrain yourself from hurrying others' speech (finishing their sentences for them)?

_____ 2. Do you often try to do more than one thing at a time (such as eat and read simultaneously)?

_____ 3. Do you often feel guilty if you use extra time to relax?

_____ 4. Do you tend to get involved in a great number of projects at once?

_____ 5. Do you find yourself racing through yellow lights when you drive?

_____ 6. Do you need to win in order to derive enjoyment from games and sports?

_____ 7. Do you generally move, walk, and eat rapidly?

_____ 8. Do you agree to take on too many responsibilities?

_____ 9. Do you detest waiting in lines?

_____ 10. Do you have an intense desire to better your position in life and impress others?

FIGURE 12.23
If you answer yes to a majority of the questions from the quiz on the left, Friedman and Rosenman (1974) would say you probably have a Type A personality. But they would also consider your explanation of your answers, so this questionnaire gives only a rough estimate of your personality. Friedman and Rosenman classified everyone as either Type A or Type B, but most psychologists believe people can have any degree of Type A traits from low to high.

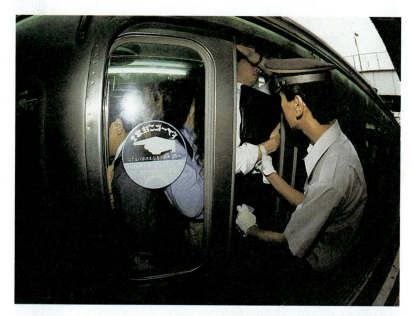

FIGURE 12.24
People in some cultures have a frantic pace of life: Everyone seems to be in a rush; people walk fast, talk fast, and push one another around. In other cultures, no one is sure what time it is and no one cares. The risk of heart disease is greatest in cultures or subcultures with a frantic pace of life.

heart disease. People with a Type A personality tend to have a higher heart rate and higher blood pressure than most other people. The difference grows larger in competitive situations, in which people with a Type A personality show great increases in heart rate and blood pressure (Lyness, 1993).

Additional evidence for a linkage comes from studies comparing heart disease in various cultures (Levine, 1990). Some cultures have a hurried pace of life; people walk fast; they talk fast; almost everyone wears a watch; storekeepers pay prompt attention to their customers. Other cultures have a more relaxed pace of life; people are seldom in a

rush; few people wear watches; buses and trains seldom arrive on schedule, but no one seems to care (Figure 12.24). As you might guess, the rate of heart disease is higher in countries with a hurried pace of life than it is in countries with a more relaxed pace. In the United States, the risk of heart attacks and the pace of life are generally at their highest in large northeastern cities; they are at their lowest in small towns of the West and the South. Note, of course, that these are correlational data; they do not demonstrate conclusively that a frantic pace of life causes heart problems. (For example, something about cultural differences in diet or climate might simultaneously influence people's activity levels and their heart muscles.)

At first, researchers focused mostly on the role of impatience and competitiveness as the main links between Type A behavior and heart disease. When Type A people perform competitive tasks, their muscle tension increases and their sympathetic nervous system is aroused (Williams et al., 1982). Because they seek competitive tasks, their hearts are working hard much of the time.

However, later evidence has indicated that heart disease correlates more strongly with unpleasant emotions, especially depression and hostility (Booth-Kewley & Friedman, 1987). Perhaps a highly responsive sympathetic nervous system predisposes people to feel tense, while it also overstimulates the heart. Future research will tell us more about how depression and anger contribute to heart disease.

CONCEPT CHECK

4. People with a Type A personality are likely to develop stress-related heart disease. Yet when they fill out the Social Readjustment Rating Scale mentioned earlier, their scores are often low. Why might that scale understate the stress levels of Type A people? (Check your answer on page 542.)

CANCER

Among the causes of cancer are genetics and exposure to toxic substances. Behavior also can influence the onset and spread of cancer, at least indirectly. For example, people who smoke cigarettes increase their risk of cancer. Women who examine their breasts regularly can detect breast cancer at an early stage, when treatment is more likely to be successful. Do emotions contribute directly to cancer? Because the brain influences the immune system, which fights cancer, an emotional experience might lead to an impairment of the immune system and therefore to a greater risk of certain kinds of cancer.

The two emotional states most likely to lead to cancer are depression and stress. Many cancer patients are depressed (Weinstock, 1984), and many of them report that they were depressed, often following the death of a loved one, long before they knew they had cancer. Severe depression suppresses the activity of the immune system and leaves a person more vulnerable than usual to all sorts of infection and disease, including the spread of certain types of tumors (Anisman & Zacharko, 1983; Baker, 1987).

In research on the effects of stress in animals, investigators have found that stress increases the spread of cancer and shortens the animal's survival. But it is difficult to generalize those results to humans. First, the results vary from one study to another, depending on the duration and type of stress and the genetic makeup of the animals. Second, nearly all the animal studies deal with cancers caused by viruses, and viruses cause fewer than 5% of human cancers (Fox, 1983).

Depression, stress, and severe emotional problems probably do increase the risk of cancer in humans. Still, the influence is minor; emotional factors are far less important in causing cancer than are genes and toxic substances (Anisman & Zacharko, 1983; Derogatis, 1986; Fox, 1983). Keeping a positive outlook on life may help to prevent cancer; still, many people suffering from serious, long-lasting depression manage to survive to old age (Stein, Miller, & Trestman, 1991).

Psychological factors may exert a stronger influence on what happens after the onset of cancer. For many people, the stress of dealing with cancer decreases the pleasures of life, impairs eating and sleeping, and directly or indirectly weakens the ability of the immune system to attack the cancer cells (Andersen, Kiecolt-Glaser, & Glaser, 1994). People who receive steady support from their family and friends, or from a psychotherapist or a cancer patients self-help group, have a better chance of recovery and a better quality of life while fighting the disease (Fawzy, Fawzy, Arndt, & Pasnau, 1995).

SUMMARY

• *Selye's concept of stress.* According to Hans Selye, stress is "the nonspecific response of the body to any demand made upon it." Any event, pleasant or unpleasant, that brings about some change in a person's life produces some measure of stress. This theory, though influential, has some problems and limitations. (page 533)

• *Stages of response to stress.* The body goes through three stages in response to a stressful experience: alarm, resistance, and exhaustion. In resistance and exhaustion, prolonged channeling of energy toward resisting stress may weaken the immune system. (page 534)

• *Influence of past experiences.* The degree of stress an event evokes depends not only on the event itself but also on the person's interpretation of the event. People with posttraumatic stress disorder react strongly to daily events because of their previous experiences with war, rape, or other deeply upsetting events. (page 534)

• *Difficulties of measuring stress.* The stress an individual experiences is difficult to measure. Two people who have gone through similar experiences may show different levels of stress. (page 535)

• *Psychosomatic illness.* Stress, hostility, and other emotional experiences may increase the probability of certain illnesses. A psychosomatic illness is somehow related to a person's experiences or to his or her reactions to those experiences. (page 538)

• *Heart disease.* People with a Type A personality are competitive, impatient, and hostile. They are more likely than others to suffer heart disease, although the strength of that relationship and the reasons behind it are still in dispute. The emotional states of depression and hostility pose a greater risk than do competitiveness and impatience. (page 539)

• *Cancer.* Depression and stress may increase the risk of cancer, at least slightly. Social support improves people's chance of recovery from cancer and improves the quality of life while fighting the disease. (page 540)

SUGGESTION FOR FURTHER READING

Brannon, L., & Feist, J. (1992). *Health psychology* (2nd ed.). Belmont, CA: Wadsworth. A textbook that surveys the relationship between behavior and health.

TERMS

health psychology field of psychology that deals with the ways in which people's behavior can enhance health and prevent illness and how behavior contributes to recovery from illness (page 533)

stress according to Hans Selye, the nonspecific response of the body to any demand made upon it; according to Lazarus, a situation that someone regards as threatening and as possibly exceeding his or her resources (page 533)

alarm first stage of response to stress, a brief period of high arousal of the sympathetic nervous system, readying the body for vigorous activity (page 534)

resistance second stage of response to stress, a stage of prolonged but moderate arousal (page 534)

cortisol hormone that elevates blood sugar and enhances metabolism (page 534)

exhaustion third stage of response to stress, when the body's prolonged response to stress decreases the synthesis of proteins, including the proteins necessary for the immune system (page 534)

general adaptation syndrome condition characterized by weakness, fatigue, loss of appetite, and a general lack of interest (page 534)

posttraumatic stress disorder (PTSD) condition in which people who have endured extreme stress feel prolonged anxiety and depression (page 534)

psychosomatic illness an illness that is influenced by a person's experiences—particularly stressful experiences—or by the reactions to those experiences (page 538)

Type A personality personality characterized by constant competitiveness, impatience, anger, and hostility (page 539)

Type B personality personality characterized by easygoingness, lack of hurry, and lack of hostility (page 539)

ANSWER TO CONCEPT CHECK

4. The Social Readjustment Rating Scale measures events that change a person's life; it does not measure constant sources of stress such as the pressures of work. It also fails to measure people's reactions to events, responses such as impatience, competitiveness, and hostility. (page 540)

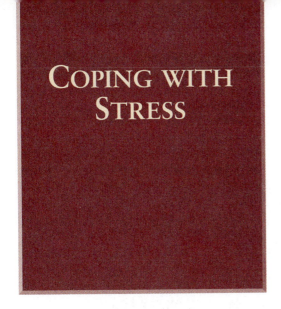

COPING WITH STRESS

How can we reduce the harmful effects of stress on the body?

How can we learn to cope with stress?

An eccentric millionaire whom you have never met before hands you a $10 bill for no apparent reason, no strings attached. How do you feel? Happy, I presume.

Now let's change the circumstances a bit: That generous person had been handing out $100 bills until it was your turn. Then the millionaire said, "Sorry, I just ran out of $100 bills. So I'll have to give you a $10 bill instead." Now how do you feel? Disappointed, sad, angry? You may even feel *cheated,* even though you have just received something for nothing.

Just as your reaction to a free $10 bill depends on the circumstances, so does your reaction to bad news. How would you feel if you had studied hard for a test and then got a C-? Unhappy, I presume. But if you then discovered that everyone around you had failed the test, you would begin to feel much better about your C-.

How you feel about an event depends not just on the event itself but also on how you interpret it (Frijda, 1988; Lazarus, Averill, & Opton, 1970). Was the event better or worse than you had expected? Better or worse than what happened to someone else? Was it a one-time event, or did it carry some hint of what might happen in the future? How you feel about an event also depends on your personality. Some people manage to keep their spirits high even in the face of tragedy while others are devastated by lesser setbacks.

Coping with stress is the process of developing ways to decrease its effects, to get through difficult tasks despite the stress.

How do people cope with disappointments, anxieties, and stress? And can we learn to cope more successfully?

COPING WITH STRESS BY ATTACKING THE PROBLEM

The best advice on coping with stress is also the most obvious: If some problem is causing you stress, don't just deal with the stress; try to solve the problem itself. For example, if you have a great deal of anxiety about test-taking, you could spend an hour or two on relaxation procedures before each test, but you might get better results if you spent that time studying for the test. Similarly, if you have trouble in your marriage or in your job, don't just learn ways to live with the stress; find some way to fix the situation and reduce the stress.

Uncontrollable and unpredictable events tend to be very stressful; people feel better if they gain some sense of control. For example, in the winter of 1988, an unusually severe snowstorm hit my hometown of Raleigh, North Carolina. Because the city had little snow-removal equipment, and because most residents had scant experience driving through snow, the schools and many businesses closed down for 5 days. It didn't take long until many people started

The stressfulness of an event depends on how we interpret it, not just on the event itself. For example, most people would be delighted to finish second or third in an Olympic event, but a person who was expecting to finish first may consider any lower result to be a defeat and a disappointment.

complaining of "cabin fever": "I can't stand being cooped up in this house another day! I've got to get out!" Staying at home, in itself, was not the problem. After all, what is wrong with spending 5 days at home? The problem was the unpredictability; people had no way of knowing whether they would be staying home the next day or going to school or work.

In several experiments, people were asked to perform difficult tasks while listening to loud bursts of noise that might impair their performance. Some participants had no power to control the noise; others were shown a switch that could cut off the noise, although the experimenters preferred that the subjects not use that switch unless necessary. Even though none of the subjects flipped the switch, simply knowing that they *could* turn off the noise made it less disturbing to them. They performed better on a proofreading task than did the subjects with no sense of control (Glass, Singer, & Pennebaker, 1977; Sherrod, Hage, Halpern, & Moore, 1977).

As a rule, people who consistently blame someone else for their misfortunes tend to have a poor psychological adjustment (Tennen & Affleck, 1990). Apparently the reason is their lost sense of control. If you think your misfortunes are your own fault, you may feel somewhat depressed about your failure, but at least you have some control. You can say, "I won't make that mistake

again" or "Next time I'll try harder." But if you think other people are maliciously thwarting your plans, you no longer feel control.

CONCEPT CHECK

5. Which would disrupt your studying more, your own radio or your roommate's radio? Why? (Check your answers on page 549.)

HOW DO PREDICTABILITY AND CONTROLLABILITY HELP?

Why does a predictable or controllable event produce less stress than an unpredictable or uncontrollable event does? One explanation is that we fear an unpredictable, uncontrollable event may grow so intense that it will eventually become unbearable (Thompson, 1981). So long as we know what is likely to happen next, we assume that things won't get any worse. And so long as we have some measure of control over an event, we tell ourselves that we can take some action if the situation becomes unbearable.

A second explanation is that when an event is predictable we have a chance to prepare for it at just the correct time. Suppose you dread being called on in class to answer questions. If your professor calls upon students in alphabetic order, you can relax until just before your turn comes, and then get ready. However, if your professor calls on students at random, you have to remain tense and ready at all times.

IS PREDICTABILITY ALWAYS HELPFUL?

As a general rule, knowing what to expect reduces the stressfulness of an experience. But if you are not likely to face the experience for some time, and if there is nothing you can do about it anyway, then just knowing about it may not be helpful. If someone could tell you when and how you were going to die—and you knew you could do nothing to avoid it—would you want to know? Maybe you would, on the grounds that you could make better decisions about how to live whatever life is left to you. But you might prefer not to know.

People with a family history of Huntington's disease are faced with precisely that decision. Huntington's disease is an uncommon, inherited disorder that typically strikes

A soldier on patrol in a war zone is under high stress because of the unpredictability of danger. Because danger could erupt at any moment, the soldier has no opportunities to relax.

at about age 40. People with the disease undergo a gradual deterioration in their muscle control and mental functioning until they die about 15 years later. If your father or mother had the disease, you would have a 50% chance of getting it too.

Before the 1980s, people with a family history of Huntington's disease had to live with prolonged uncertainty about whether they would ever get the disease. Today, they can find the answer through an examination of their chromosomes. Such information helps people make decisions about their future, particularly about whether or not to have children. However, they have no way of preventing or delaying the onset of the disease. Some people who know they are at risk decide to take the chromosome test. Others choose to remain uncertain. In short, people are not always sure they want to know what to expect if they can do nothing about it.

RELAXATION

Sometimes even after we have exerted as much control over a situation as we can, we still have a problem. And some people get nervous even when they have no real problem (Manuck, Cohen, Rabin, Muldoon, & Bachen, 1991). In such situations, it is helpful to try to relax. Here are some suggestions that may help (Benson, 1985):

• Find a quiet place. Do not insist on absolute silence; just find a spot where the noise is least disturbing.

• Adopt a comfortable position, relaxing your muscles (Figure 12.25). If you are not sure how to do so, start with the opposite: *Tense* all your muscles so you become fully aware of how they feel. Then relax them one by one, starting from your toes and working systematically toward your head.

• Reduce sources of stimulation, including your own thoughts. Focus your eyes on a simple, unexciting object. Or repeat something over and over—a sentence, a phrase, a prayer, or even a sound like "om"—whatever feels comfortable to you.

• Don't worry about anything, not even about relaxing. If worrisome thoughts keep popping into your head, dismiss them with an "Oh, well."

Some people call this practice meditation. People who spend a little time each day

FIGURE 12.25
Some people adopt special yoga or meditation techniques to reduce stress. Others find they can reduce stress without any formal procedure, just by finding a relaxing position, reducing their muscle tension, and taking a break from their most stressful concerns.

practicing this technique report that they feel less stress. Many of them improve their overall health (Benson, 1977, 1985).

Another step toward relaxation is to learn to interpret situations realistically. Some people fret forever about disasters that *might* happen or about something someone said that *might* be taken as an insult. Psychologists encourage people to reinterpret situations and events in less threatening ways.

EXERCISE

Exercise also can help to reduce stress. It may seem contradictory to say that both relaxation and exercise reduce stress, but exercise helps people relax. Exercise is a particularly helpful way to deal with nervousness about a future stressful event (Mobily, 1982). Suppose you are tense about something you have to do tomorrow. Your sympathetic nervous system becomes highly aroused in preparation for that event, yet there is nothing you can do about it. Under those conditions, the best approach may be to work off some of your excess energy through exercise and relax afterward.

Exercise can be a way of working off excess energy, especially when you are waiting for something to happen. Exercise also helps by improving overall condition; people in poor physical condition sometimes show excessive arousal to mild stressful events.

Regular exercise also prepares people for the unexpected. People in good physical condition react less strongly than other people do to stressful events (Crews & Landers, 1987). An event that would elevate the heart rate enormously in other people elevates it only moderately in a person who has been exercising regularly.

INOCULATION

Any stressful experience is less disturbing if you know what to expect, but it is hard to know what to expect if you have not been through the experience before. Sometimes a good solution is to provide people with a small-scale preview of a stressful experience

Practice at self-defense serves as a kind of inoculation against fear. The thought of being attacked is less frightening to one who has some idea of how to handle the situation.

they may have to face later. In other words, we can inoculate or immunize someone against certain kinds of stressful experience.

One way to inoculate people against stressful events is to have them practice ways of dealing with such events beforehand (Janis, 1983; Meichenbaum, 1985; Meichenbaum & Cameron, 1983). For example, the army has soldiers practice combat skills under realistic conditions, sometimes under actual gunfire. Another way is through role playing. A police trainee might pretend to intervene while two people act like a husband and wife engaged in a violent quarrel. If you are nervous about going to your landlord with a complaint, you might get a friend to play the part of the landlord and then practice what you plan to say.

Inoculation has proved successful with young people suffering from "dating anxiety." Some young people are so nervous about saying or doing the wrong thing that they avoid all opportunities to go out on a date. By means of role playing, in which they practice dating behaviors with assigned partners, they can be helped to feel less apprehensive (Jaremko, 1983).

CONCEPT CHECK

6. *Suppose you are nervous about giving a speech before a group of 200 strangers. How could you inoculate yourself to reduce the stress? (Check your answer on page 549.)*

SOCIAL SUPPORT

"Have you ever had a secret too shameful to tell? Have you stopped yourself from disclosing a personal experience because you thought others would think less of you? . . . Have you ever lied to yourself by claiming that a major upheaval in your life didn't affect you or, perhaps, didn't occur? If so you may be hurting yourself. Not because you have had a troubling experience but because you can't express it."
JAMES W. PENNEBAKER (1990)

A great many people have had a severely painful experience at one time or another. Perhaps you were beaten or sexually molested; perhaps you were responsible for someone else's injury; perhaps you attempted suicide; perhaps someone humiliated you in public. Whatever your experience, you may decide it was too painful even to think about, much less talk about. And therefore the pain builds up within.

People who have had painful experiences report that they feel much better after taking an opportunity to talk about them to someone—almost anyone (Pennebaker, 1990). A sympathetic friend or relative may provide not only a shoulder to cry on but also help in getting through the day. Some people who worry about their friends' or relatives' reactions will open up about their most private experiences to a near-stranger, especially someone they meet on a plane or out of town. (They do not worry about making a bad impression on someone they do not expect to meet again.)

In many cases, people gain the greatest support by talking with people who have lived through similar crises. Alcoholics Anonymous, for example, is composed of recovering alcoholics who try to help one another. Another example are the nurses in the intensive care units of hospitals who undergo constant, often severe stress (Hay & Oken, 1977). The unspoken (but rigidly obeyed) rule is never to refuse help to either a patient or a fellow nurse. They are surrounded by the sight, sound, and smell of patients who are suffering and dying. When a patient dies, it is often the nurse, not the doctor, who has to inform the relatives. At the end of the day, the nurses cannot simply go home and resume life as usual. They have to unwind, and they often do so by sharing their experiences with other nurses.

People find many ways to distract themselves from a stressful experience, especially while they are waiting to do something.

DISTRACTION

People who are trying to cope with stress caused by mild but persistent pain often resort to some sort of distraction. Distraction is not always helpful with prolonged pain, but it does help to reduce people's responses to temporary pains (Cioffi, 1991). For example, many people find they can reduce dental or postsurgical pain by playing video games or by watching comedies on television. The Lamaze method teaches women to cope with the pain of childbirth by concentrating on breathing exercises.

How effective a distraction is depends partly on whether or not a person believes that it will help. In one experiment, college students were asked to hold their fingers in ice water until the sensation became too painful to endure (Melzack, Weisz, & Sprague, 1963). Some of them listened to music of their own choice and were told that listening to music would lessen the pain. Others also listened to music but were given no suggestion that it would ease the pain. Still others heard nothing but were told that a special "ultrasonic sound" was being transmitted that would lessen the pain. The group that heard music and expected it to lessen the pain tolerated the pain better than the other two groups did. Evidently, neither the music nor the suggestion of reduced pain is as effective as both are together.

Distraction also helps us to cope with stress that is not painful. People who are concentrating on a difficult task find it helpful to take a break once in a while. They may go to a movie, read something entertaining, play a round of golf, or just daydream. Furthermore, trying to find the humor in a stressful situation often provides an effective distraction.

SOMETHING TO THINK ABOUT

Many experiments report that a placebo by itself serves as an effective painkiller for certain patients. Why might that be?

BELIEFS AS COPING STRATEGIES

- In the long run, I shall be more successful than most other people are.
- Sure I have my strengths and weaknesses, but my strengths are in areas that are important; my weaknesses are in areas that don't really matter.
- When I fail, it is because I didn't try hard enough or because I got some bad breaks. It is not because of any lack of ability.

Even when people suffer a hardship, such as a political defeat, they cope by looking at the bright side: We ran a good campaign; we carried forth an important message; maybe we'll win next time.

- No matter how bad (or good) things are, they are going to get better.

- Right now I'm sad that my wife (husband) left me, but in the long run I'll be better off without her (him).

- I lost my job, but in many ways it was a crummy job. The more I think about it, the happier I am that I lost it. I can get a better one.

For a given person at a given time, any of these statements may be correct or incorrect. Remember the "personal fable" of adolescence from Chapter 10? Most normal, happy people nurture various versions of that fable throughout life. They emphasize their strengths, downplay their weaknesses, and distort bad news to make things seem less bad, maybe even good (Taylor & Brown, 1988). To some extent these beliefs may help people to deal with the difficult and stressful times of life.

When a situation is undeniably bad, people may still find ways to deny it. Medics serving in the Vietnam War knew they were risking their lives every time they boarded a helicopter to go to the aid of wounded soldiers. Because they had no way to predict or control the enemy's actions, we might expect that they would have experienced extreme stress. In general, however, measurements of the activity of their autonomic nervous sys-

tem showed low levels of arousal on both flight and nonflight days (Bourne, 1971). Why? They had managed to convince themselves of their own invulnerability. They even told exaggerated stories about their close brushes with death as evidence to prove that they led a charmed life.

One study of 78 women who had surgery for the removal of breast cancer found that they coped with their stress and anxiety in three ways (Taylor, 1983):

First, they searched for some meaning in the experience. Many of them said they had become better people and had developed a new attitude toward life.

Second, they tried to regain a feeling of mastery over their lives. They wanted to believe that they knew why they had developed cancer and that they knew how to avoid a recurrence.

Third, they all sought to boost their self-esteem by comparing themselves with someone else who was worse off: "I'm glad I had only one breast removed instead of both, like some other women." "Sure, I had both breasts removed, but at least I was 70 years old at the time. It would have been worse if it happened when I was young." "It was terrible to have both breasts removed at age 25, but I was already married, and my husband has been sympathetic and supportive."

In short, people tell themselves, "I'm in control; my life is getting better; at least, things are better than they might have been." Is it good for mental health to remain unrealistically optimistic? On that question, psychologists disagree (Colvin & Block, 1994; Taylor & Brown, 1994). Certainly, some people manage to maintain excellent mental health without any apparent illusions about themselves. Although researchers have not yet measured the limits of optimistic thinking, it seems likely that the best attitude might be *slightly* unrealistic optimism.

▌ IN CONCLUSION

We discuss various aspects of psychology in different chapters—cognition, motivation, emotion, and so forth. That seems a reasonable way to organize a psychology textbook, but our experiences do not divide up so neatly into separate parts. As you have seen in this chapter, our emotions are closely linked to our biology, our motivations, and our memory and cognitions. Any factor that changes one aspect of our experience—say, cognition—has ripple effects on emotions and motivations as well.

- *Distraction.* Distracting a person's attention from the source of stress helps to reduce the stress. (page 547)
- *Beliefs.* A belief in one's capacity to succeed may help to reduce stress even if the belief is not entirely accurate. (page 547)

SUMMARY

- *Interpreting stressful events.* How successfully we cope with a stressful event depends largely on how we interpret the event. (page 543)
- *Prediction and control.* The best way to deal with stress is to try to attack the problem itself. Events are generally less stressful when people think they can predict or control them. (page 543)
- *Relaxation and exercise.* One way of coping with stress is to find a quiet place, relax the muscles, and eliminate distracting stimuli. Exercise can be a helpful way of handling nervous energy and enabling later relaxation. (page 545)
- *Inoculation.* Someone who has experienced a mild sample of a stressful experience is less stressed than are other people by a later, more intense version of the same experience. (page 546)
- *Social support.* Support and encouragement from friends and family help to alleviate stress. Many people cope with problems by talking with other people who have dealt with similar problems, such as members of self-help groups. (page 546)

SUGGESTION FOR FURTHER READING

Pennebaker, J. W. (1990). *Opening up.* New York: William Morrow and Company. A description of the stress-relieving value of discussing your most painful experiences, either with other people or with yourself in writing.

TERM

inoculation protection against the harmful effects of stress by earlier exposure to a small amount of it (page 546)

ANSWERS TO CONCEPT CHECKS

5. Your roommate's radio would be more disruptive. You can turn your own radio on or off, switch stations, or reduce the volume. You have no such control over your roommate's radio (unless your roommate happens to be very cooperative). (page 544)

6. Practice giving your speech to a small group of friends. If possible, practice giving it in the room where you are to deliver it. (page 546)

13 PERSONALITY

Several thousand people have the task of assembling the world's largest jigsaw puzzle, which contains over a trillion pieces. Connie Conclusionjumper examines twenty pieces very closely, stares off into space and announces, "When the puzzle is fully assembled, it will be a picture of the Houston Astrodome!" Prudence Plodder says, "Well, I don't know what the whole puzzle will look like, but I think I've found two little pieces that fit together."

Which of the two is making the greater contribution to completing the puzzle? We could argue either way. Clearly the task will require an enormous number of little, unglamorous accomplishments like Prudence's. But if Connie is right, her flash of insight will be extremely valuable in assembling all the little pieces. Of course, if the puzzle turns out to be a picture of two sailboats on Lake Erie, then Connie will have made us waste time looking for connections that are not there.

Some psychologists have offered grand theories about the nature of personality. Others have investigated why people with a certain type of personality act the way they do in a specific situation. We need both contributions. We begin with the grand, overall theories of personality. Then we turn to investigations of more limited aspects of personality. Finally, we consider methods of measuring personality characteristics. The module on social learning (Chapter 6) already presented how we learn certain aspects of our personality.

THEORIES OF PERSONALITY

Is personality rooted in one or two dominant motivations, such as sexuality or the desire for superiority?

Is personality influenced by unconscious motivations and thoughts?

What is a "healthy" personality?

"Every individual is virtually an enemy of civilization. . . . Thus civilization has to be defended against the individual. . . . For the masses are lazy and unintelligent . . . and the individuals composing them support one another in giving free rein to their indiscipline."
SIGMUND FREUD (1927/1953)

"It has been my experience that persons have a basically positive direction. In my deepest contacts with individuals in therapy, even those whose troubles are most disturbing, whose behavior has been most antisocial, whose feelings seem most abnormal, I find this to be true."
CARL ROGERS (1961)

What makes us tick? What makes us the way we are? At our core, are we humans good, bad, or somewhere in between?

The 17th-century philosopher Thomas Hobbes argued that humans are by nature selfish. Life in a state of nature, he said, is "nasty, brutish, and short." If we are to protect ourselves from one another, we must be restrained by a watchful government.

The 18th-century political philosopher Jean-Jacques Rousseau disagreed. He maintained that humans are good by nature and that "civilized" governments are the problem, not the solution. Although he conceded that society could never return to "noble savagery," he believed that education and government should promote the freedom of the individual. Rational people acting freely, he maintained, would advance the welfare of all.

The debate between those two viewpoints survives in modern theories of personality (Figure 13.1). Some theorists, including Sigmund Freud, have held that people are born with sexual and destructive impulses that must be held in check if civilization is to survive. Others, including Carl Rogers, have held that people will achieve good and noble goals once they have been freed from unnecessary restraints.

Which point of view is correct? Or does the truth lie somewhere between these extreme viewpoints? The study of human personality is complicated, and we can easily be tempted to emphasize one aspect to the exclusion of others. In this chapter I shall discuss the highlights of some complex theories and approaches. For a deeper understanding, read the "Suggestions for Further Reading" listed at the end of this module.

PERSONALITY AND CONCEPTIONS OF ITS ORIGIN

The term *personality* comes from the Latin word *persona*, meaning "mask." In the plays of ancient Greece and Rome, actors wore masks to indicate whether they were happy,

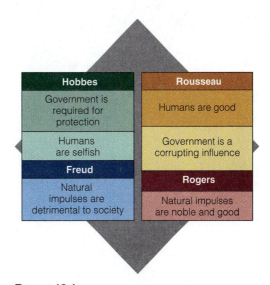

FIGURE 13.1
Philosophers Thomas Hobbes and Jean-Jacques Rousseau expressed opposite views on human nature. Psychologists Sigmund Freud and Carl Rogers also expressed opposite views. Freud, like Hobbes, stressed the more negative aspects of human nature; Rogers, the more positive or optimistic aspects.

FIGURE 13.2
According to the second-century Greek physician Galen, people's personalities depended on four humors. Clockwise from top left: sanguine, melancholic, phlegmatic, and choleric. Galen's theory was popular in Medieval Europe.

FIGURE 13.3
Sigmund Freud offered interpretations of dreams, slips of the tongue, psychological disorders, and other behaviors that people had previously considered "random" or "unexplainable." According to Freud, even apparently purposeless behaviors reveal the influence of unconscious thoughts and motivations. Freud's theories have had an immense influence on many people, not just on psychologists. For example, many literary commentators have offered psychoanalytic interpretations of novels and plays. Most psychological researchers, however, are skeptical of Freud's approach.

sad, or angry. Unlike a mask that one can put on or take off, however, the term *personality* implies something stable. **Personality consists of all the consistent ways in which the behavior of one person differs from that of others.**

The ancient Greeks believed that personality depended on which of four different "humors" (chemicals) predominated in a person's body (Figure 13.2). A predominance of yellow bile made people hot tempered. A predominance of black bile made people depressed. An excess of phlegm made people sluggish and apathetic. An excess of blood made people courageous, hopeful, and amorous. The ancient Greek theory persists in the English language in such terms as *phlegmatic* and *melancholic* (literally, "black-bile-ic").

Today, although we no longer believe in the four humors, we do believe that personality is influenced by other chemicals, such as hormones and neurotransmitters. It is further influenced by our experiences, including our observation and imitation of other people's behavior.

According to some historically influential theories of personality, differences in personality arise from the different ways in which people try to satisfy one central motive, such as the sex drive, the desire for superiority, or the drive to achieve one's full potential. We begin with Sigmund Freud, who concentrated on the sex drive and its ability to influence behavior indirectly, perhaps even unconsciously.

SIGMUND FREUD AND PSYCHOANALYSIS

Sigmund Freud's theory was the first of several psychodynamic theories. A **psychodynamic theory** relates personality to the interplay of conflicting forces within the individual, including some that the individual may not recognize consciously. Freud (1856–1939; Figure 13.3), an Austrian physician, developed theories on personality development that have had an enormous influence on psychologists and other students of human behavior. I shall caution you at the start, however, that Freud constructed his theories on evidence that most of us would regard as flimsy.

Freud would have liked to become a professor of cultural history or anthropology, and he wrote several books and articles about those topics in his later years. As a Jew in late 19th-century Austria, however, he knew he had little chance of becoming a university professor. The only professional careers open to Jews in his time and place were in law, business, and medicine.

Freud chose to study medicine, though he was never deeply committed to it. After receiving his medical degree, he worked in brain research and began to practice medicine only when he needed financial security. Even when he treated patients, he seemed more motivated by his theoretical interest in their psychological disorders than by a desire to relieve their distress.

Psychoanalysis and the Unconscious

Early in his career, Freud worked with the psychiatrist Josef Breuer, who had been treating a young woman with physical complaints that seemed to have no medical basis. As she talked with Breuer about her past, she recalled various traumatic, or emotionally damaging, experiences. Breuer proposed that recalling those experiences released pent-up emotional tensions. He called this release **catharsis,** a term Freud adopted in his own theory.

Freud began to apply Breuer's "talking cure" to his own emotionally disturbed patients. He referred to his method of explaining and dealing with personality as **psychoanalysis,** and to this day psychoanalysts remain loyal to that method and to Freud's theories (Figure 13.4).

Psychoanalysis is based on the assumption that each of us has an unconscious mind as well as a conscious mind (Figure 13.5). The **unconscious** has thoughts, memories, and emotions, although it often affects our behavior in an illogical fashion.

Psychoanalysis started out as a fairly simple theory: The unconscious contains memories of traumatic experiences, and the goal of psychoanalysts is to bring those memories to consciousness. That effort produces catharsis and relieves the patient of irrational and self-defeating impulses.

As Freud listened to his patients, however, he became convinced that the traumatic events they recalled were not sufficient to account for their abnormal behavior. Some

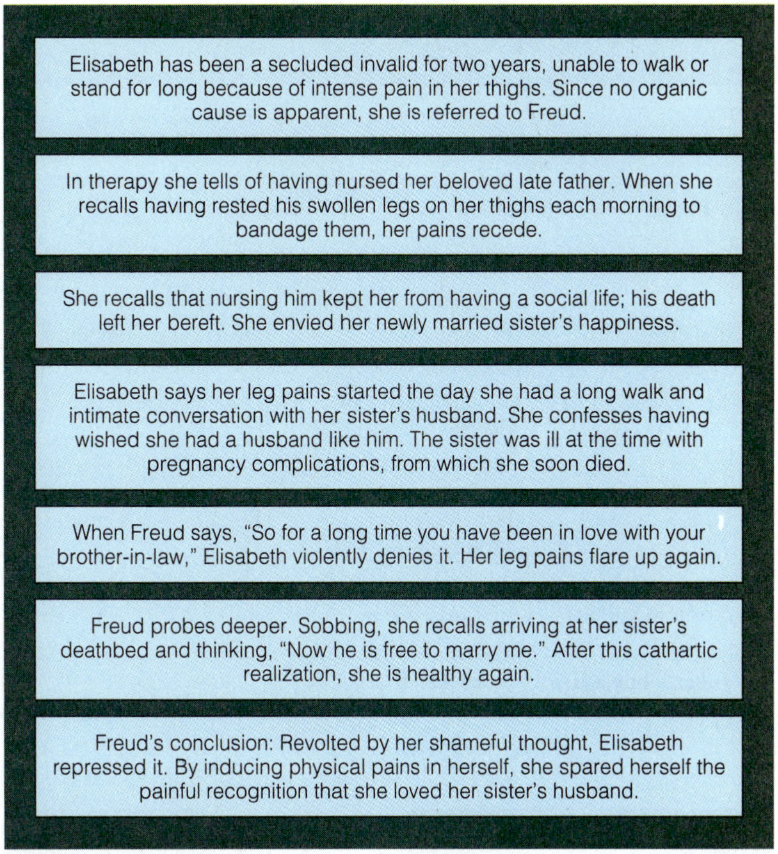

Elisabeth has been a secluded invalid for two years, unable to walk or stand for long because of intense pain in her thighs. Since no organic cause is apparent, she is referred to Freud.
In therapy she tells of having nursed her beloved late father. When she recalls having rested his swollen legs on her thighs each morning to bandage them, her pains recede.
She recalls that nursing him kept her from having a social life; his death left her bereft. She envied her newly married sister's happiness.
Elisabeth says her leg pains started the day she had a long walk and intimate conversation with her sister's husband. She confesses having wished she had a husband like him. The sister was ill at the time with pregnancy complications, from which she soon died.
When Freud says, "So for a long time you have been in love with your brother-in-law," Elisabeth violently denies it. Her leg pains flare up again.
Freud probes deeper. Sobbing, she recalls arriving at her sister's deathbed and thinking, "Now he is free to marry me." After this cathartic realization, she is healthy again.
Freud's conclusion: Revolted by her shameful thought, Elisabeth repressed it. By inducing physical pains in herself, she spared herself the painful recognition that she loved her sister's husband.

Figure 13.4
An example of Freud's psychoanalysis. (Based on Breuer & Freud, 1895/1957.)

Conscious mind
Acknowledged thoughts, memories, emotions
Psychoanalysis
Repressed thoughts, memories, emotions
Unconscious mind

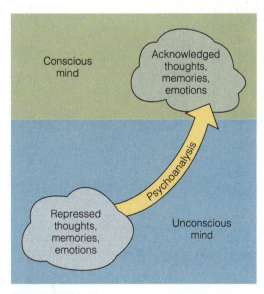

Figure 13.5
Freud believed that through psychoanalysis parts of the unconscious could be brought into the conscious mind, where a person could deal with them.

TABLE 13.1
Freud's Stages of Psychosexual Development

STAGE (APPROXIMATE AGES)	SEXUAL INTERESTS	EFFECT OF FIXATION AT THIS STAGE
Oral stage (birth to 1 year)	Sucking, swallowing, biting	Lasting concerns with dependence and independence; pleasure from eating, drinking, other oral activities
Anal stage (1 to 3 years)	Expelling feces, retaining feces	Orderliness, stinginess, stubbornness
Phallic stage (3 to 5 or 6 years)	Touching penis or clitoris Males: Oedipus complex Females: Electra complex	Difficulty feeling closeness Males: fear of castration Females: penis envy
Latency period (5 or 6 to puberty)	Sexual interests suppressed	—
Genital period (puberty onward)	Sexual contact with other people	

The beginning of psychosexual development is the oral stage, in which infants enjoy stimulation of their mouth—which for them means sucking, swallowing, and biting. They like putting things in their mouth and gnawing on them. According to Freud, if normal sexual development is blocked at this stage, the child will grow up continuing to get much pleasure from drinking and eating, as well as kissing and smoking. Perhaps this pipe smoker's mother weaned him too quickly—or let him nurse too long. And perhaps such an explanation is wrong. Like many of Freud's ideas, this one is difficult to test.

patients reacted strongly to past events that others took in stride. Why? He concluded that still earlier traumatic events, which were even harder to recall, predisposed certain patients to overreact. Those earlier events were, Freud said, in most cases sexual in nature.

STAGES OF PSYCHOSEXUAL DEVELOPMENT IN FREUD'S THEORY OF PERSONALITY

Freud believed that psychosexual interest and pleasure begin long before the individual achieves sexual maturity. He used the term **psychosexual pleasure** in a broad sense to include the good feelings arising from the stimulation of parts of the body. He maintained that the way we deal with psychosexual development influences nearly all aspects of our personality.

Freud proposed that young children have sexual tendencies that resemble those of more primitive mammals. Just as nonhuman mammals respond sexually to stimuli that do not excite most adult humans, children respond "sexually" to stimulation of the mouth, the anus, and other body zones. Freud collected no direct evidence for this view and in fact made no extensive observations of children. Rather, he reconstructed childhood experiences from the memories of his patients and other adults.

According to Freud (1905/1925), people have a psychosexual energy, which he called **libido** (lih-BEE-doh), from a Latin word meaning "desire." At different ages libido focuses on different parts of the body. Normally, it starts in the mouth and "flows" to other parts as the child grows older. Children go through five stages of **psychosexual development,** each with a characteristic sexual focus that leaves its mark on adult personality. If normal sexual development is blocked or frustrated at any stage, Freud said, a **fixation** occurs. Part of the libido becomes fixated at that stage; that is, it continues to be preoccupied with the pleasure area associated with that stage. Table 13.1 summarizes the stages.

The Oral Stage In the **oral stage,** from birth through the first year or so (Freud was vague about the age limits of all his stages), the infant derives intense psychosexual pleasure from stimulation of the mouth, particularly while sucking at the mother's breast. In the later part of the oral stage, the infant begins to bite as well as suck. A person fixated at this stage continues to receive great pleasure from eating, drinking, and smoking and may also have lasting concerns with dependence and independence.

The Anal Stage Around 1 to 3 years of age, children enter the **anal stage.** At this time they get psychosexual pleasure from their

Freud proposed that a "fixation" at an early stage of psychosexual development can alter the development of personality. For example, if toilet training is either too harsh or too lenient, someone may develop an "anal" personality, characterized by either extreme orderliness or extreme messiness. This hypothesis is difficult to evaluate scientifically, because it is not easily falsifiable. When we observe neat and orderly behavior, we can reinterpret that person's early toilet training as either too lenient or too harsh.

bowel movements. They may enjoy either the sensation of excreting feces or the sensation of holding them back. A person fixated at this stage goes through life "holding things back"—being orderly, stingy, and stubborn—or, less commonly, may go to the opposite extreme and become wasteful, messy, and destructive.

The Phallic Stage Beginning at about age 3, in the **phallic stage,** children begin to play with their genitals. They become more aware of what it means to be male or female. If parents teach children that touching their genitals is shameful, the children may become fixated at the phallic stage. According to Freud, boys with a phallic fixation are afraid of being castrated; girls with such a fixation develop "penis envy."

According to Freud, boys in the phallic stage experience an **Oedipus complex.** (Oedipus—EHD-ah-puhs—was a figure in an ancient Greek play by Sophocles. Oedipus unknowingly murdered his father and married his mother.) Freud claimed that a boy develops a sexual interest in his mother and competitive aggression toward his father. Eventually the boy learns to identify with his father and to shift his own sexual interests away from his mother. A boy who fails to resolve the Oedipus complex may forever feel anxiety and hostility toward other men.

Similarly, Freud asserted, young girls experience an **Electra complex,** named after a character in an ancient Greek play who persuades her brother to kill their mother, who had murdered their father. A girl with an Electra complex feels a romantic attraction toward her father and hostility toward her mother. Freud was vague about how girls resolve the Electra complex; he implied that few ever resolve it completely.

Freud's writings about boys' fear of castration, girls' penis envy, the Oedipus complex, and the Electra complex have long been controversial. Most developmental psychologists deny that children ordinarily show such tendencies.

The Latent Period From about age 5 or 6 until adolescence, Freud said, most children suppress their psychosexual interest. They enter a **latent period,** a time when they play mostly with peers of their own sex. Apparently a product of the way we rear children in Europe and North America, the latent period may not occur in certain unindustrialized societies.

The Genital Stage Beginning at puberty, young people take a strong sexual interest in other people. This is known as the **genital stage.** According to Freud, anyone who has fixated a great deal of libido at earlier stages has little libido left for the genital stage. But people who have successfully negotiated the earlier stages can now derive primary satisfaction from sexual intercourse.

Evaluation of Freud's Stages Was Freud right about these stages and about the consequences of fixation? His theory makes such vague predictions that it is almost impossible to test (Grunbaum, 1986; Popper, 1986). When it has been tested, the results have been unimpressive. For example, does strict toilet training lead to a combination of orderly, stingy, and stubborn behavior? According to most studies, it does not (Fisher & Greenberg, 1977). Do frustrations during the oral stage lead to later dependence problems and a craving for eating, drinking, and smoking? Maybe, although the studies to test this hypothesis have been weak (Fisher & Greenberg, 1977). Descriptively, it is true that infants get great pleasure from mouth stimulation and that older children and adults shift their attention to other body regions, especially the genitals. We have little evidence, however, to support the idea that fixation at a particular stage can direct later personality development.

FREUD'S DESCRIPTION OF THE STRUCTURE OF PERSONALITY

Personality, Freud claimed, consists of three aspects: the id, the ego, and the superego (Figure 13.6). (Actually, he used German words that mean *it, I,* and *over-I.* A transla-tor used Latin equivalents instead of English words.) The **id** consists of all our biological drives, such as sex and hunger. The id demands immediate gratification. The **ego** is the rational, decision-making aspect of the personality. The **superego** contains the memory of our parents' rules and prohibitions, such as, "Nice little boys and girls don't do that." Sometimes the id produces sexual or other motivations that the superego considers repugnant, evoking feelings of guilt. The ego may side with either the id or the superego; if it sides with the superego, it tries to avoid even thinking about the id's unacceptable impulses.

Most psychologists today find it difficult to imagine the mind in terms of three warring factions. They regard Freud's description as an occasionally useful metaphor at best.

CONCEPT CHECK

1. What kind of behavior would you expect of someone with a strong id and a weak superego? What behavior would you expect of someone with an unusually strong superego? (Check your answers on page 572.)

DEFENSE MECHANISMS AGAINST ANXIETY

According to Freud, an individual's personality is determined to a large degree by the way the unconscious mind deals with anxiety. To reduce the anxiety that certain thoughts and motivations cause, Freud said, we reject highly unpleasant thoughts from the conscious mind and force them into the unconscious.

According to Freud, the ego defends itself against conflicts and anxieties by relegating unpleasant thoughts and impulses to the unconscious. Among the **defense mechanisms** that the ego employs are repression, denial, rationalization, displacement, regression, projection, reaction formation, and sublimation (Figure 13.7). Ordinarily, we are not aware of our own repressions, rationalizations, and so forth. Defense mechanisms are normal ways of suppressing anxiety and are often adaptive, becoming a problem only if they prevent a person from dealing with reality.

Repression The defense mechanism of **repression** is motivated forgetting—the rejection of unacceptable thoughts, desires, and memories and their relegation to the uncon-

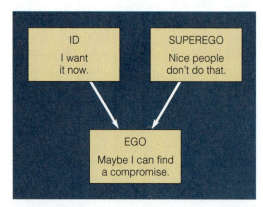

FIGURE 13.6

Freud described personality as a collection of three parts that are often in conflict with one another. The id *asks for immediate gratification of biological urges, such as the sex drive. The* superego *counters these impulses with lists of rules that we learned from our parents. The* ego, *torn between these two forces, makes the decision of what to do. According to Freud, we can understand certain people's behavior by assuming that their id is stronger than their superego or that their superego is stronger than their id.*

FIGURE 13.7
The ego—the rational I—has numerous ways of defending itself against anxiety, that apprehensive state named for the Latin word meaning "to strangle." These defense mechanisms try to ignore or avoid facing unpleasant reality, and they are part of an internal battle in that you fight against yourself.

scious. Repression is perhaps the most central concept in Freud's theory.

One example would be a woman seeing someone beating another person to death, and later not being able to remember what she saw. Another example: A man gives a speech and several members of the audience raise serious objections to what he says; later he forgets their objections.

Researchers have struggled to find unambiguous evidence to support the concept of repression. Investigators have exposed subjects to various unpleasant or threatening experiences, in the expectation that repression would interfere with their memories. However, in cases when subjects did have trouble remembering the events, a variety of alternative explanations appear to be possible

(Holmes, 1990). Outside the laboratory, repression is certainly not common in situations in which we might expect it. As discussed in Chapter 7, kidnapping victims, children who watched the death of their own parents, and others who endured similar miseries almost always remember the events intensely. Evidently, repression is not a robust or easily demonstrated phenomenon.

Denial The refusal to believe information that provokes anxiety is called **denial.** "This can't be happening" is a common first response most of us make to bad news. Whereas repression is the motivated forgetting of certain information, denial is an assertion that the information is incorrect.

For example, a doctor tells a woman that her child is mentally retarded. She refuses to accept this opinion and shops around for another doctor who will tell her the child is not retarded.

Rationalization When people attempt to prove that their actions are rational and justifiable and thus worthy of approval, they are using **rationalization.** For example, a student who wants to go to the movies instead of studying says, "More studying won't do me any good anyway." Someone who misses a deadline to apply for a job says, "I didn't really want that job anyway."

Displacement By diverting a behavior or a thought away from its natural target toward a less threatening target, **displacement** lets people engage in the behavior they prefer without experiencing severe anxiety.

For example, a man who is angry at his boss comes home and kicks his dog. He really wants to kick his boss, but that would cause him too much anxiety. Or a student who is angry at her professor screams at her roommate.

Regression A return to a more juvenile level of functioning, **regression** is an effort to avoid the anxiety of facing one's current role in life. By adopting a childish role, a person can escape responsibility and return to an earlier, perhaps more secure way of life. A person may also regress to an earlier stage of psychosexual development in response to emotionally trying circumstances.

For example, after a new sibling is born, a 5-year-old child may start wetting the bed again. Following a divorce or a business setback, a man may resort to daydreaming, getting drunk, or other immature behaviors.

Projection The attribution of one's own undesirable characteristics to other people is known as **projection.** When people project their own faults onto others, they generally do not deny that they themselves possess those faults (Holmes, 1978; Sherwood, 1981). However, by suggesting that the faults are widespread, they make them more acceptable and less anxiety provoking.

For example, someone says, "Everyone cheats on their income taxes," or "Every student cheats on a test now and then." What would you infer about that person's own behavior?

Reaction Formation In an effort to reduce anxiety and to keep undesirable characteristics repressed, people may use **reaction formation** to present themselves as the opposite of what they really are. In Shakespeare's play *Hamlet,* Gertrude says, "The lady protests too much, methinks." People who insist too vehemently that something is "absolutely" true often harbor secret doubts about whether it really is true.

For example, a man troubled by doubts about his religious faith may try to convert others to the faith. Someone with unacceptable aggressive tendencies may join a group dedicated to preventing violence against babies or animals. (Not everyone who proselytizes for a faith has deep doubts about it, of course, and not everyone who tries to pre-

Freud's own couch is now part of our history. What is the future of psychoanalysts' couches? Psychoanalytic interpretations range from reasonable to doubtful; in an individual case it is difficult or impossible to judge the accuracy of an analyst's interpretation.

vent violence is secretly a violent person. Different people can have different reasons for the same actions.)

Sublimation   The transformation of an unacceptable impulse into an acceptable, even an admirable, behavior is **sublimation**. According to Freud, sublimation enables a person to express the impulse without admitting its existence. For example, painting and sculpture may represent a sublimation of sexual impulses. Someone with unacceptable aggressive impulses may sublimate them by becoming a surgeon. Whether Freud is correct about sublimation is difficult to say; if the true motives of a painter are sexual, they are hidden well indeed. However, if Freud is correct, sublimation is the one defense mechanism that leads to socially constructive behavior.

CONCEPT CHECK

2. *Match the Freudian defense mechanisms in the top list with the situations in the list that follows.*

1. *Repression*	*5.* *Regression*
2. *Denial*	*6.* *Projection*
3. *Rationalization*	*7.* *Reaction formation*
4. *Displacement*	*8.* *Sublimation*

a. ___ A man who is angry with his neighbor goes hunting and kills a deer.
b. ___ Someone with a smoking habit insists that there is no convincing evidence that smoking impairs health.
c. ___ A woman with doubts about her religious faith tries to convert others to her religion.
d. ___ A man who beats his wife writes a book arguing that people have an instinctive need for aggressive behavior.
e. ___ A woman forgets a doctor's appointment for a test for cancer.
f. ___ Someone who has difficulty dealing with certain people resorts to pouting, crying, and throwing tantrums.
g. ___ A boss takes credit for a good idea suggested by an employee because "It's better for me to take the credit so that our department will look good and all the employees will benefit."
h. ___ Someone with an unacceptable impulse to shout obscenities becomes a writer of novels.

(Check your answers on page 572.)

MANIFESTATIONS OF THE UNCONSCIOUS IN EVERYDAY LIFE

Freud believed that the unconscious makes itself felt in nearly all aspects of ordinary life. Even an act that may be explained as "just a meaningless accident" reflects an unconscious motivation. For example, when one of Freud's patients "forgot" an appointment, Freud assumed the patient did not want to keep it. When a patient left something behind in Freud's office and had to come back to get it, Freud assumed that the patient enjoyed being with him and was unconsciously planting an excuse to return. Much of people's behavior and personality, Freud said, was based on unconscious motivations.

Freud also interpreted *slips of the tongue,* or what have come to be called "Freudian slips," as revelations of unconscious thoughts and motives. If you said "I leave you" when you intended to say "I love you," Freud would assume that your error revealed an unconscious rejection of your professed love.

Today, psychologists believe that most slips of the tongue and other such errors have multiple causes (Norman, 1981). Analyzing their causes is a difficult challenge, however.

WHAT'S THE EVIDENCE?

Freudian Slips

Freud claimed that what we say "by accident" reveals hidden motives. Many of Freud's claims are virtually impossible to test scientifically. This one can be tested, though not easily.

We could follow people around and record all their slips of the tongue, or we could ask them to record all their own slips. But we would still have to guess or infer the hidden motives of the people we were following. Also, the people who were recording their own slips would have to decide which slips to record. If they were familiar with Freud's theory, they might record only the errors that seemed to fit the theory and ignore those that did not.

A second method would be to induce a motive—hunger, for example—for the purposes of an experiment. Then we could ask the hungry subjects to read a certain passage, and we could count how many of their slips

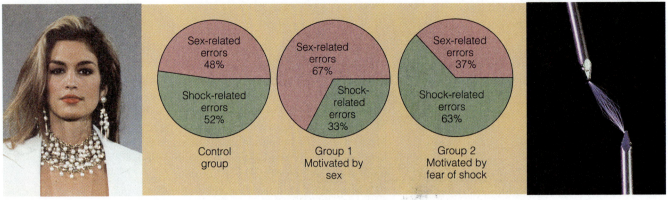

FIGURE 13.8

In the presence of an attractive woman, men made many sex-related slips of the tongue. When they were worried about shocks, they made shock-related slips of the tongue.

of the tongue had something to do with eating. We could repeat the experiment with people in whom we had induced a different motive, to see whether they made different slips.

However, most people make so few slips of the tongue that the experiment might go on for months without yielding significant results. To test Freud's theory, we need a procedure that increases the frequency of slips of the tongue. Michael Motley and Bernard Baars (1979) devised such a procedure.

Hypothesis When people are performing a difficult task on which they are likely to make slips of the tongue, the kinds of slips they make will depend on the kinds of motivations they are feeling at the moment.

Method The experimenters divided 90 male college students into three groups: a "sex" group, a "shock" group, and a control group. Those in the sex group were greeted by a very attractive female experimenter dressed in a sexy outfit and behaving in a seductive manner. Those in the shock group were met by a male experimenter who attached electrodes to their arms and told them the electrodes were connected to a "random shock generator" that might or might not give them one or more painful shocks at unpredictable times during the experiment. (No shocks were actually given.) Those in the control group were met by a male experimenter who attached no electrodes to them and made no mention of shocks. Thus one group should have a heightened sexual motivation, one group should have a strong fear of shock, and one group should be concerned with neither sex nor shock during the experiment.

The students watched a screen on which the experimenters flashed pairs of words or nonsense syllables, such as "HAT-RAM" and "RUF-GAM." Each pair was flashed for

1 second. A buzzer sounded 0.4 second after each pair appeared, telling the students to speak aloud the *previous* pair. So, for example, after seeing "RUF-GAM," they would have to say "HAT-RAM" (the previous pair), and remember "RUF-GAM" to say after the next pair. About 30% of the time, students made slips of the tongue. For example, they would say "HAT-RAM" as "RAT-HAM" and "RUF-GAM" as "GUF-RAM."

Some of the syllable pairs were designed to promote sex-related slips. For example, "GOXI-FURL" and "LOOD-GEGS" might be pronounced as "FOXY-GIRL" and "GOOD-LEGS." Other pairs were designed to promote shock-related slips. For example, "SHAD-BOCK" and "WOT-HIRE" might be pronounced as "BAD-SHOCK" and "HOT-WIRE." Still other pairs did not suggest any slips related to either sex or shock.

Results The men in the sex group made more than twice as many sex-related slips as shock-related slips. The opposite was true for the men in the shock group. Those in the control group made both types of errors about equally. Figure 13.8 illustrates the results.

Interpretation The results support Freud's claim that a strong motivation can increase the frequency of slips of the tongue related to that motivation. Slips of the tongue may indeed tell us something about a person's thoughts and desires.

But the results do not support Freud's contention that hidden motivations are the main cause of slips of the tongue. Slips were common in this experiment because the task was so difficult. Having to say one pair while preparing to say another produced conflict between the two pairs that a subject was trying to remember.

FREUD'S USE OF EVIDENCE AND HIS LEGACY

Freud has had an influence not only on psychology but also on art, literary criticism, and all the social sciences; his impact on the public viewpoint goes far beyond that of any other psychologist (Figure 13.9). But how good was his evidence? Unlike most of the psychologists we study, Freud conducted no experiments, surveys, or correlational studies. He simply spoke with patients and drew inferences from what they said and did. In a few cases above, I have remarked on the attempts of later psychologists to conduct scientific tests of Freud's ideas, and the usually unsuccessful outcomes of those studies. The other approach to evaluating his ideas is a careful biographical study of what Freud did and how he drew his conclusions. As more and more of Freud's letters and personal papers have become available, Freud biography has become a growth industry.

Much of the interest of biographers has focused on the first few years of Freud's development of psychoanalysis. In the 1890s, Freud proposed that the most common cause of psychological disorder was the experience of being sexually molested or abused in early childhood. A few years later he backed down from that position. According to Freud's own description of the events, he came to realize that his patients had misled him into believing they had been sexually abused in early childhood; in fact, he said, they had merely had childhood fantasies of sexual contact with their parents or other adults. The patients' early sexual fantasies were, nevertheless, very significant to them, and were the basis for their adult psychological problems.

To this day, scholars continue to debate why Freud changed his theory. According to one view (Masson, 1984), Freud was right the first time, and he simply lost the courage to defend his views about childhood sexual abuse. According to other scholars, however, Freud never had any good reason for such views in the first place. In his earliest writings (while he was emphasizing actual childhood sexual abuse) he made it clear that he was *inferring* his patients' sexual abuse from their symptoms, dreams, and so forth. The patients themselves vigorously denied that they remembered any such events.

A few years later, when Freud discarded his view about early sexual abuse, he claimed that his patients had *misled* him into believing they had been sexually abused. Scholars today point out that he was unjustified in

FIGURE 13.9
The fame of Sigmund Freud far exceeds that of any other psychologist. His picture has even been put on the Austrian 50-schilling bill.

saying his patients had misled him, when every statement about sexual abuse had come from Freud himself, not from the patients (Esterson, 1993; Powell & Boer, 1994; Schatzman, 1992).

Later, when Freud attributed his patients' psychological troubles to their childhood sexual fantasies, did his patients tell him about such fantasies? Again, the answer is negative. The existence of the fantasies was Freud's inference from the patients' symptoms, dreams, and speech; the patients themselves generally protested that they remembered nothing about the childhood sexual fantasies that Freud insisted they must have had. (Freud considered his patients' protests to be signs of emotional resistance, and therefore evidence that his interpretations were correct.)

What evidence did Freud have to support his interpretations? Apparently, his main evidence was simply the fact that he was able to construct a coherent story linking all of a patient's symptoms, dreams, and so forth to the sexual fantasies that Freud inferred must have occurred (Esterson, 1993). In short, Freud did not distinguish between his "results" and his "interpretations." When he inferred something about someone's Oedipus complex or repressions, he considered those interpretations to be observational results. Scientifically oriented psychologists today insist on different standards.

Given the weakness of Freud's evidence, should we simply disregard his theories? Some psychologists think so. Freud's initial evidence was weak, the research since then has done little to strengthen the case, and overall the Freudian approach is more myth than science. Other psychologists, however, continue to defend Freud's methods as a way to find meaning in otherwise haphazard and incoherent behaviors and thoughts (Nagel, 1994). Certainly Freud made a major contribution by focusing our attention on the hidden meanings beneath the surface of behavior. Even if we do not always agree with the particular interpretations that Freud gave, we can agree that behaviors do often have individual symbolic meanings.

NEO-FREUDIANS

Some psychologists, known as **neo-Freudians,** have remained faithful to parts of Freud's theory while modifying other parts. One of the most influential neo-Freudians was the German physician Karen Horney (HOR-nigh; 1885–1952; Figure 13.10), who believed that Freud had exaggerated the role of the sex drive in human behavior and had misunderstood the sexual motivations of women. She believed, for example, that the conflict between a child and his or her parents was a reaction to parental hostility and intimidation, not a manifestation of a sexual Oedipus complex or Electra complex. Horney contended that Freud had slighted the importance of cultural influences on personality and that he gave too little attention to helping his patients work out practical solutions to their problems. Still, Horney's views

were more a revision than a rejection of Freud's theories. Other theorists, including Carl Jung and Alfred Adler, broke more sharply with Freud. Although many psychologists call Jung and Adler neo-Freudians, the followers of Jung and Adler generally do not. Each offered a very different, very non-Freudian view of personality.

CARL G. JUNG AND THE COLLECTIVE UNCONSCIOUS

Carl G. Jung (YOONG; 1875–1961; Figure 13.11), a Swiss physician, was an early member of Freud's inner circle. Freud regarded Jung as a son, the "heir apparent" or "crown prince" of the psychoanalytic movement until their father-son relationship began to deteriorate (Alexander, 1982). At one point, Freud and Jung agreed to analyze each other's dreams. Freud described one of his dreams, but then refused to provide the personal associations that would enable Jung to interpret it, insisting that "I cannot risk my authority."

Jung was more forthcoming. He described a dream in which he explored the upper stories of a house, then explored its basement, and finally, discovering that the house

FIGURE 13.10

Karen Horney, a major neo-Freudian, revised some of Freud's theories and gave greater attention to cultural influences. She was a pioneer in the development of feminine psychology.

FIGURE 13.11

Carl G. Jung rejected Freud's concept of dreams hiding their meaning from the conscious mind: "To me dreams are a part of nature which harbors no intention to deceive but express something as best it can" (Jung, 1965).

a

c

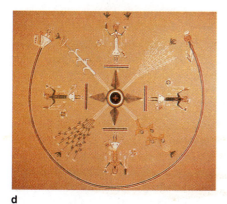

d

b

FIGURE 13.12

Carl Jung was fascinated with the similar images that show up in the artwork of different cultures. One recurring image is the mandala, which Jung believed to be a symbol of the self's striving for unity and wholeness. These mandalas are (a) a Hindu painting; (b) a mosaic from Beth Alpha Synagogue, Israel, from about 500 A.D.; (c) a Greek ceramic from about 550 B.C.; and (d) a Navajo sand painting, Southwestern United States.

had a subbasement, began to explore that. Jung thought the dream referred to his explorations of the mind. The top floor was the conscious; the basement was the unconscious; and the subbasement was a still deeper level of the unconscious, yet to be explored. Freud, however, insisted that the dream referred to Jung's personal experiences and frustrations (Hannah, 1976).

Jung's own theory of personality incorporated many of Freud's insights but put greater emphasis on people's search for a spiritual meaning in life and on the continuity of human experience, past and present. Jung believed that every person has a conscious mind plus a "personal unconscious"

(equivalent to Freud's "unconscious") and a collective unconscious. The personal unconscious represents a person's own experience. The **collective unconscious,** which is present at birth, represents the cumulative experience of preceding generations. Because all humans share a common ancestry, all have nearly the same collective unconscious. (Jung never explained how the collective unconscious might develop biologically.)

Jung drew his evidence for the collective unconscious from observations of various cultures. He pointed out that similar images emerge in the art of cultures throughout the world (Figure 13.12) and that similar themes emerge in religions, myths, and folklore.

Those images and themes also appear in dreams and in the hallucinations of people with severe psychological disorders. Jung inferred that these common themes and images derive from **archetypes,** the vague images that we all inherit as part of our collective unconscious.

Jung's impact on contemporary psychology is hard to judge. Some psychotherapists make extensive use of his ideas, and most are at least aware of them. Many of his ideas are vague and mystical, however, and difficult to deal with scientifically.

ALFRED ADLER AND INDIVIDUAL PSYCHOLOGY

Alfred Adler (1870–1937; Figure 13.13), an Austrian physician who, like Jung, had been one of Freud's early followers, broke with Freud because he believed that Freud was overemphasizing the sex drive and neglecting other, more important influences on personality. Their disagreement reached a peak in 1911, with Freud insisting that women experience "penis envy" and with Adler contending that women were more likely to envy men's status and power. The two were never reconciled.

Adler founded a rival school of thought, which he called **individual psychology.** To Adler this term did not mean "psychology of

the individual." Rather, it meant "indivisible psychology," a psychology of the person as a whole rather than a psychology of parts, such as id, ego, and superego. Adler agreed with Freud that childhood experiences have a crucial effect on personality, that many motives are outside conscious awareness, and that people can be helped to overcome their problems through a "talking cure." He put far more emphasis, however, on conscious, goal-directed behavior.

ADLER'S DESCRIPTION OF PERSONALITY

Several of Adler's early patients were acrobats who had had an arm or a leg damaged by a childhood illness or injury. Determined to overcome their disabilities, they had worked hard to develop the strength and coordination they needed to perform as acrobats. Perhaps, Adler surmised, people in general try to overcome their weaknesses and transform them into strengths (Adler, 1932/1964).

As infants, Adler pointed out, we are small, dependent creatures who strive to overcome our inferiority. People who do not succeed go through life with an **inferiority complex,** an exaggerated feeling of weakness, inadequacy, and helplessness. Even those who do manage to overcome their feelings of inferiority persist in their efforts to achieve.

According to Adler, everyone has a natural **striving for superiority,** a desire to seek personal excellence and fulfillment. Each person creates a **style of life,** or "master plan" for achieving a sense of superiority. That style of life may be directed toward success in business, sports, politics, or some other competitive activity. Or it may be directed toward "success" of a different sort: For example, someone who withdraws from life may gain a sense of accomplishment or superiority from being uncommonly self-sacrificing. Someone who constantly complains about real or imagined illnesses or disabilities may, by demanding help from friends and family, win a measure of control or superiority over them. Or someone may commit crimes in order to savor the attention they bring.

Adler recognized that people may not be aware of their own style of life and the assumptions behind it and may fail to realize that the real motive behind some word or action is to manipulate others. They may en-

FIGURE 13.13
Like Horney, Alfred Adler thought Freud overemphasized the sex drive. Adler was very interested in feelings of self-esteem. He was the first to talk about the possibility of a "healthy" personality, and not just a personality free from disorders. According to Adler, the key to a healthy personality was "social interest," a desire for the welfare of other people.

gage in self-defeating behavior because they have not admitted to themselves what their goals really are. Adler tried to determine people's real motives. For example, he would ask someone who complained of a backache, "How would your life be different if you could get rid of your backache?" Those who said they would become more active were presumably suffering from real ailments that they were trying to overcome. Those who said they could think of no way in which their life would change, or said only that they would get less sympathy from others, were presumably suffering from psychologically caused ailments or at least were exaggerating their discomfort.

Several of Alfred Adler's early patients were people who had overcome early injuries to become acrobats. He proposed that all of us have a natural striving to achieve superiority in some way.

CONCEPT CHECK

3. In Adler's theory, what is the relationship between striving for superiority and style of life? (Check your answer on page 572.)

ADLER'S VIEW OF PSYCHOLOGICAL DISORDERS

Any personality based on a selfish style of life is unhealthy, Adler (1928/1964) said. People's need for one another requires that they develop a **social interest,** a sense of solidarity and identification with other people. People with a strong social interest strive for superiority in a way that contributes to the welfare of the whole human race, not just to their own welfare. They want to cooperate with other people, not to compete. In equating mental health with a strong social interest, Adler saw mental health as a positive state, not just the absence of impairments.

In Adler's view, people with psychological disorders are not suffering from an "illness." Rather, they have set immature goals, are following a faulty style of life, and show little social interest. Their response to new opportunity is "Yes, but . . ." (Adler, 1932/1964). They are striving for superiority in ways that are useless to themselves and to others.

For example, one of Adler's patients was a man who lived in conflict with his wife because he was constantly trying to impress her and dominate her (Adler, 1927). In discussing his problems, the man revealed that he had been very slow to mature physically and had not reached puberty until he was 17 years old. Other teenagers had ignored him

and had treated him like a child. He was now a physically normal adult, but he was overcompensating for those years of feeling inferior by trying to seem bigger and more important than he really was.

Adler tried to get patients to understand their own style of life and to correct the faulty assumptions on which it rested. He urged them to strengthen their social interest and to strive for superiority in ways that would benefit both themselves and others.

ADLER'S LEGACY

Adler's influence on psychology exceeds his fame. His concept of the "inferiority complex" has become part of the common culture. He was the first to talk about mental health as a positive state rather than as merely the absence of impairments. Many later forms of therapy drew on Adler's innovations, especially his emphasis on the assumptions underlying a patient's behavior. Humanistic psychologists followed Adler in urging people to take responsibility for their own behavior and for modifying their style of life.

HUMANISTIC PSYCHOLOGY

Another general perspective on personality, **humanistic psychology,** deals with consciousness, values, and abstract beliefs, including the spiritual experiences and the beliefs that people live by and die for. According to humanistic psychologists, personality depends on what people believe and how they perceive the world. If you *believe* that a particular experience was highly meaningful, then it *was* highly meaningful. A psychologist can understand your behavior only by asking you for your own evaluations and interpretations of the events in your life.

(In theology, a *humanist* glorifies humans, generally denying or at least giving little attention to a supreme being. The term *humanistic psychologist* implies nothing about a person's religious beliefs.)

Humanistic psychology emerged in the 1950s and 1960s as a protest against both behaviorism and psychoanalysis, the dominant viewpoints in psychology at that time (Berlyne, 1981). Those two approaches, despite their many differences, are both rooted in *determinism* (the belief that every behavior has a cause) and in *reductionism* (the attempt to explain behavior in terms of its component elements). Humanistic psychologists turn away from these attempts to explain behavior in terms of its parts or causes. They claim that people make deliberate, conscious decisions about what to do with their lives. People may decide to devote themselves to a great cause, to sacrifice their own well-being, and to risk their lives. To the humanistic psychologist, it is pointless to try to ascribe such behavior to past rewards and punishments or to unconscious thought processes.

Humanistic psychologists seldom conduct research—at least not the kind of research that leads to reports of means and medians and other statistical data. In spite of the risks of relying on anecdotal evidence, they prefer to study unique individuals and unique experiences—the exceptions to the rule, not just the rule itself.

For example, humanistic psychologists study growth experiences—the moments that people identify as points of transition, when they may say, "Aha! Now I have become an adult," or "Now I have truly committed my life to this goal" (Frick, 1983). They also study **peak experiences,** moments in which a person feels truly fulfilled, content, and at peace. Some people report that they "feel at one with the universe" when they hear "thrilling" music, or take part in an emotional religious ceremony, or achieve some great accomplishment. Some mountain climbers who have scaled Mount Everest report what is literally a "peak" experience (Lester, 1983).

CARL ROGERS AND THE GOAL OF SELF-ACTUALIZATION

Carl Rogers, an American psychologist, studied theology before turning to psychology, and the influence of those early studies is apparent in his view of human nature. Rogers (Figure 13.14) became probably the most influential humanistic psychologist.

According to Rogers (1980), human nature is basically good. People have a natural drive toward **self-actualization,** which means the achievement of their full potential. Rogers holds that it is as natural for people to strive for excellence as it is for a plant to grow. The drive for self-actualization is the basic drive behind the development of personality. (To some extent, Rogers's concept of self-actualization is similar to Adler's concept of striving for superiority.)

Beginning at an early age, children evaluate themselves and their actions. They learn that what they do is sometimes good and sometimes bad. They develop a **self-concept,** an image of what they really are, and an **ideal self,** an image of what they would like to be.

FIGURE 13.14
Carl Rogers maintained that people naturally strive toward positive goals; they do not need special urging. He recommended that people relate to one another with "unconditional positive regard."

Rogers measured a person's self-concept and ideal self by handing the person a stack of cards containing statements such as "I am honest" and "I am suspicious of others." The person would then sort the statements into two piles: *true of me* and *not true of me.* Then Rogers would provide an identical stack of cards and ask the person to sort them into two piles: *true of my ideal self* and *not true of my ideal self.* In this manner he could determine whether someone's self-concept was similar to his or her ideal self. People who perceive a great discrepancy between the two generally experience distress. Humanistic psychologists try to help people overcome that distress, either by improving their self-concept or by changing their ideal self.

To promote human welfare, Rogers maintains, people should relate to one another with **unconditional positive regard,** a relationship that Thomas Harris (1967) has described with the phrase "I'm OK—you're OK." Unconditional positive regard is the complete, unqualified acceptance of another person as he or she is, much like the love of a parent for a child. If someone expresses anger, or even a desire to kill, the listener should accept that as an understandable feeling, even while discouraging the other person from acting on the impulse. This view resembles the Christian admonition to "hate the sin but love the sinner."

ABRAHAM MASLOW AND THE SELF-ACTUALIZED PERSONALITY

Abraham Maslow (Figure 13.15), another of the founders of humanistic psychology, proposed that people have a hierarchy of needs, an idea we considered in Chapter 11. The highest of those needs is *self-actualization,* the fulfillment of a person's potential. What kind of person achieves self-actualization, and what is the result of achieving it? Maslow (1962, 1971) sought to describe the self-actualized personality. He complained that psychologists concentrate on disordered personalities, reflecting the medical view that health is merely the absence of disease. They seem to assume that all personality is either "normal" (that is, bland) or undesirable. Maslow insisted, as Adler had, that personality may differ from the "normal" in positive, desirable ways.

To determine the characteristics of the self-actualized personality, Maslow made a list of people who in his opinion had achieved their full potential. His list included

FIGURE 13.15
Abraham Maslow, one of the founders of humanistic psychology, introduced the concept of a "self-actualized personality," a better-than-merely-normal personality, associated with high productivity and enjoyment of life.

people he knew personally as well as figures from history (Figure 13.16). He then sought to discover what they had in common.

According to Maslow (1962, 1971), people with a self-actualized personality show the following characteristics:

- An accurate perception of reality. They perceive the world as it is, not as they would like it to be. They are willing to accept uncertainty and ambiguity when necessary.
- Independence, creativity, and spontaneity. They follow their own impulses.
- Acceptance of themselves and others. They treat people with unconditional positive regard.
- A problem-centered outlook, rather than a self-centered outlook. They think about how best to solve a problem, not how to make themselves look good.
- Enjoyment of life. They are open to positive experiences, including those called "peak experiences."
- A good sense of humor.

Critics have attacked Maslow's description on the grounds that, because it is based on his own choice of subjects, it may simply reflect the characteristics he himself admired. In any case, Maslow set a precedent for other attempts to define a healthy personality as something more than a personality without disorder. Like Adler, he pointed to the possibility of a "healthier than normal" personality.

Figure 13.16

Harriet Tubman (left), one of the people Maslow identified as having a self-actualized personality, was one of the leaders of the Underground Railroad, a system for helping slaves to escape from the Southern states during the period before the Civil War. Maslow described the self-actualized personality by identifying a number of highly productive and admirable people, such as Tubman, and then determining what personality features they had in common.

Summary

• *Personality theories as views of human nature.* Personality consists of all the stable, consistent ways in which the behavior of one person differs from that of others. Theories of personality are closely related to conceptions of human nature. Some observers believe that human beings are basically hostile and need to be restrained (Hobbes, Freud). Others believe that human beings are basically good and are hampered by restraints (Rousseau, Rogers). (page 553)

• *Freud.* Sigmund Freud, the founder of psychoanalysis, proposed that human behavior is greatly influenced by unconscious thoughts and motives, that much of what we do and say has a hidden meaning. (page 554)

• *Freud's view of the unconscious.* According to Freud, unacceptable thoughts and impulses are relegated to the unconscious because they are threatening or anxiety provoking. Peo-

ple engage in repression and other defense mechanisms to exclude such thoughts and impulses from the conscious mind. (page 555)

• *Freud's psychosexual stages.* Freud believed that many unconscious thoughts and motives are sexual in nature. He proposed that people progress through stages or periods of psychosexual development—oral, anal, phallic, latent, and genital—and that frustration at any one stage can lead to a lasting fixation of libido at that stage. (page 556)

• *Slips of the tongue.* Unconscious thoughts influence many aspects of everyday life, including slips of the tongue, although other influences may be more important. (page 561)

• *Jung.* Carl Jung believed that all people share a "collective unconscious" that represents the entire experience of humanity. (page 564)

• *Adler.* Alfred Adler proposed that people's primary motivation is a striving for superiority. Each person adopts his or her own "style of life," or method of striving for superiority. (page 566)

• *Adler's view of a healthy personality.* According to Adler, the healthiest style of life is one that emphasizes "social interest"—that is, concern for the welfare of others. (page 567)

• *Humanistic psychology.* Humanistic psychologists emphasize conscious, deliberate decision-making; they oppose attempts to reduce behavior to its elements or to seek explanations in terms of unconscious influences. (page 568)

• *Rogers.* Carl Rogers focused attention on the discrepancies between a person's self-concept and his or her ideal self. He recommended that people relate to one another with unconditional positive regard. (page 568)

• *Maslow.* Abraham Maslow described a self-actualized personality, which he said was characteristic of people who achieve their full potential. (page 569)

Suggestions for Further Reading

Adler, A. (1954). *Understanding human nature.* Greenwich, CT: Fawcett. (Original work published 1927.) Adler's most general and most popular book.

Freud, S. (1924). *Introductory lectures on psychoanalysis.* New York: Boni & Liveright. Available in various paperback editions. This is Freud's attempt to describe the fundamentals of his theory to a general audience.

Maslow, A. H. (1962). *Toward a psychology of being.* Princeton, NJ: Van Nostrand. A good introduction to humanistic psychology.

Terms

personality all the stable, consistent ways in which the behavior of one person differs from that of others (page 554)

psychodynamic theory a theory that relates personality to the interplay of conflicting forces within the individual, including some that are unconscious (page 554)

catharsis the release of pent-up tension (page 555)

psychoanalysis Freud's approach to personality, based on the interplay of conscious and unconscious forces (page 555)

unconscious according to Freud, an aspect of the mind that influences behavior, although we are not directly aware of it (page 555)

psychosexual pleasure according to Freud, any enjoyment arising from stimulation of parts of the body (page 556)

libido in Freud's theory, a psychosexual energy (page 556)

psychosexual development in Freud's theory, progression through a series of five developmental stages, each with a characteristic psychosexual focus that leaves its mark on adult personality (page 556)

fixation in Freud's theory, a persisting preoccupation with an immature psychosexual interest as a result of frustration at that stage of psychosexual development (page 556)

oral stage Freud's first stage of psychosexual development, in which psychosexual pleasure is focused on the mouth (page 556)

anal stage Freud's second stage of psychosexual development, in which psychosexual pleasure is focused on the anus (page 556)

phallic stage Freud's third stage of psychosexual development, in which psychosexual interest is focused on the penis or clitoris (page 557)

Oedipus complex according to Freud, a young boy's sexual interest in his mother accompanied by competitive aggression toward his father (page 557)

Electra complex according to Freud, a young girl's romantic attraction toward her father and hostility toward her mother (page 557)

latent period according to Freud, a period in which psychosexual interest is suppressed or dormant (page 557)

genital stage Freud's final stage of psychosexual development, in which sexual pleasure is focused on sexual intimacy with others (page 557)

id according to Freud, the aspect of personality that consists of all our biological drives and demands for immediate gratification (page 558)

ego according to Freud, the rational, decision-making aspect of personality (page 558)

superego according to Freud, the aspect of personality that consists of memories of rules put forth by one's parents (page 558)

defense mechanism a method employed by the ego to protect itself against anxiety caused by conflict between the id's demands and the superego's constraints (page 558)

repression motivated forgetting; the relegation of unacceptable impulses or memories to the unconscious (page 558)

denial the refusal to believe information that provokes anxiety (page 560)

rationalization attempting to prove that one's actions are rational and justifiable and thus worthy of approval (page 560)

displacement the diversion of a thought or an action away from its natural target toward a less threatening target (page 560)

regression the return to a more juvenile level of functioning as a means of reducing anxiety or in response to emotionally trying circumstances (page 560)

projection the attribution of one's own undesirable characteristics to other people (page 560)

reaction formation presenting oneself as the opposite of what one really is in an effort to reduce anxiety (page 560)

sublimation the transformation of an unacceptable impulse into an acceptable, even an admirable, behavior (page 561)

neo-Freudians personality theorists who have remained faithful to parts of Freud's theory while modifying other parts (page 564)

collective unconscious according to Jung, an inborn level of the unconscious that symbolizes the collective experience of the human species (page 565)

archetypes according to Jung, vague images contained in the collective unconscious (page 566)

individual psychology the psychology of the person as an indivisible whole, as formulated by Adler (page 566)

inferiority complex an exaggerated feeling of weakness, inadequacy, and helplessness (page 566)

striving for superiority according to Adler, a universal desire to seek personal excellence and fulfillment (page 566)

style of life according to Adler, a person's master plan for achieving a sense of superiority (page 566)

social interest a sense of solidarity and identification with other people (page 567)

humanistic psychology a branch of psychology that emphasizes the capacity of people to make conscious decisions about their own lives (page 568)

peak experience an experience that brings fulfillment, contentment, and peace (page 568)

self-actualization the achievement of one's full potential (page 568)

self-concept a person's image of what he or she really is (page 568)

ideal self a person's image of what he or she would like to be (page 568)

unconditional positive regard complete, unqualified acceptance of another person as he or she is (page 569)

ANSWERS TO CONCEPT CHECKS

1. Someone with a strong id and a weak superego would be expected to give in to a variety of sexual and other impulses that other people would inhibit. Someone with an unusually strong superego would be unusually inhibited and dominated by feelings of guilt. (page 558)

2. a. 4, displacement; b. 2, denial; c. 7, reaction formation; d. 6, projection; e. 1, repression; f. 5, regression; g. 3, rationalization; h. 8, sublimation. (page 561)

3. In Adler's theory, a person's style of life is his or her method of striving for superiority. (page 567)

PERSONALITY TRAITS

Is personality consistent over time and from one situation to another?

What are personality traits?

In many ways all rocks are the same. If you plan to drop a rock and you want to predict when it will hit the ground, you do not need to know what kind of rock it is. If you skip a rock across a lake, throw it against a window, or use it to crack open a coconut, you can pretty well predict what will happen.

For certain other purposes, however, you need to know something about the rock. If you want to predict what will happen if you run an electric current through it, you have to know what kind of rock it is. If you want to determine a fair sale price for the rock, you need to know whether it is a diamond or a piece of granite.

Similarly, people resemble one another in some ways and differ in others. Psychologists investigate individual differences in two ways, called the nomothetic and the idiographic approaches. The word *nomothetic* (NAHM-uh-THEHT-ick) comes from the Greek *nomothetes,* meaning "legislator"; the **nomothetic approach** seeks general laws about how some aspect of personality affects behavior, often based on statistical comparisons of large groups of people. For example, we might make the nomothetic statement that people with a more *Machiavellian* personality tend to be highly manipulative and that people with a less Machiavellian personality tend to cooperate with others. We could apply that statement fairly directly to anyone, simply by measuring that person's amount of "Machiavellianism."

In contrast, the word *idiographic* is based on the root *idio-,* meaning "individual." The **idiographic approach** concentrates on intensive studies of individuals (Pervin, 1990). For example, certain psychologists have studied how people's goals in life affect their moods and their reactions to various events. Because different people have different goals, the investigators draw carefully qualified conclusions about how people with one kind of goal behave and how people with some other kind of goal behave (Emmons, 1991). The idiographic approach may lead to a conclusion that applies to more than just one person, but it is not meant to generalize to the whole population.

PERSONALITY TRAITS AND STATES

Meteorologists distinguish between climate (the usual conditions) and weather (the current conditions). For example, the climate in Seattle, Washington, is moister and cooler than the climate in El Paso, Texas, but on a given day the weather could be hot in Seattle or cool in El Paso. Similarly,

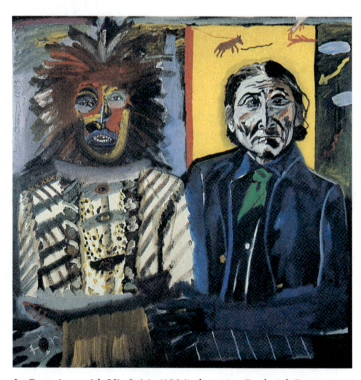

In Geronimo with His Spirit *(1984) the artist, Frederick Brown, implies that each of us has a "true self" that differs from the self we show the world. Personality includes underlying traits that remain stable over long periods of time as well as temporary states that can change from time to time, as easily as a person takes off one mask and puts on another.*

A temporary person-ality state *can be very different from the person's usual per-sonality trait. Singer Barbra Streisand is so shy and fearful in private life that she avoided public per-formances for years. Nevertheless, when on stage she can act very extraverted.*

psychologists differentiate between long-lasting personality conditions and tempo-rary fluctuations.

A consistent, long-lasting tendency in behavior, such as shyness, hostility, or talka-tiveness, is known as a **trait**. In contrast, a **state** is a temporary activation of a particu-lar behavior. People's behavior varies from time to time because they are in different states. For example, someone may have a trait of being highly talkative, yet enter a quiet state while in a library. The talkative trait is like a state of climate, which mani-fests itself in the long run, though not at every moment.

Note that both traits and states are de-scriptions of behavior, not explanations. To say that someone is talkative or quiet does not explain the person's behavior; it merely tells us what we are trying to explain.

CONCEPT CHECK

4. Two psychologists agree that a particular person is showing anxiety, but they argue about whether the anxiety is "trait anxiety" or "state anxiety." What do they mean by that distinction? How could they settle their argument? (Check your answers on page 581.)

THE SEARCH FOR BROAD PERSONALITY TRAITS

If we choose to describe people's personality in terms of traits, how many personality traits should we identify? One way to begin is

through an examination of our language. Presumably, if a particular personality trait is really important, any human language should have a word for it. A number of psy-chologists have pointed out that this assump-tion is just an assumption; still, it seems a rea-sonable one, considering how much attention people pay to other people's personalities.

Gordon Allport and H. S. Odbert (1936) plodded through an English dictionary and found almost 18,000 words that might be used to describe personality. Psychologists using this list deleted words that were merely evaluations (such as *pleasant* or *nasty*) and terms referring to temporary states (such as *confused*). In the remaining list they looked for clusters of synonyms, such as *affection-ate, warm,* and *loving,* and kept only one of the terms. When they found opposites, such as *honest* and *dishonest,* they also kept just one of the terms. (*Honesty* and *dishonesty* are different degrees of a single trait, not two separate traits.) After eliminating synonyms and antonyms, R. B. Cattell narrowed the list down to 35 traits.

THE "BIG FIVE" PERSONALITY TRAITS

Although some of the 35 personality traits that Cattell identified are not exactly syn-onyms or antonyms of one another, many of them overlapped enough to suggest that they were not independent traits. Furthermore, for practical purposes, psychologists would usually prefer to deal with a smaller number. Remember the principle of parsimony from Chapter 2: If we can explain most of person-ality with, say, 5 or 10 traits, we do not need to measure 35 or more traits.

To determine which traits correlate with one another and which ones do not, psychol-ogists use a method called *factor analysis.* For example, if measurements of *warmth, gregariousness,* and *assertiveness* correlate positively with one another, we can group them together into a single trait. But if *warmth* does not correlate highly with *self-discipline,* then they should be separate traits and not grouped together.

Using this approach, many researchers have found that they can describe most of the variation in human personality with what they call the **big five personality traits:** neuroticism, extraversion, agreeableness, conscientiousness, and openness to new ex-perience (McCrae & Costa, 1987). These five factors offer a powerful description of personality because each pertains to behavior in a wide variety of situations. The big five dimensions are described below (Costa, McCrae, & Dye, 1991). Note that the first two, neuroticism and extraversion, are the "biggest" of the "big five." Even psychologists who are skeptical of this model agree that neuroticism and extraversion are powerful traits that influence much of behavior (Block, 1995).

Neuroticism is a tendency to experience unpleasant emotions relatively easily. People high in neuroticism are relatively likely to experience anxiety, hostility, depression, self-consciousness, and impulsiveness. The opposite of neuroticism is emotional stability or self-control.

Extraversion is a tendency to seek new experiences and to enjoy the company of other people. Extraversion is associated with warmth, gregariousness, assertiveness, and excitement seeking. People high in extraversion enjoy meeting new people and tend to maintain a fairly stable, positive mood under most circumstances (Williams, 1990). The opposite of extraversion is introversion.

Agreeableness is a tendency to be compassionate toward others and not antagonistic. It implies a concern for the welfare of other people, closely related to Adler's concept of social interest. People high in agreeableness generally trust other people and expect other people to trust them.

Conscientiousness is a tendency to show self-discipline, to be dutiful, and to strive for achievement and competence. Research has shown that people high in conscientiousness tend to be better-than-average workers on almost any job (Barrick & Mount, 1991). They are likely to complete whatever task they say they will perform.

Openness to experience is the hardest of the big five to describe, and sometimes not an easy trait to demonstrate in certain populations. Roughly speaking, it is a tendency to enjoy new experiences, especially intellectual experiences, the arts, fantasies, and anything that exposes the person to new ideas.

Extraversion, one of the big five personality traits, includes a tendency to enjoy other people's company and a tendency to seek excitement.

which they call ambition *and* sociability— *changing the big five into the big six. How should psychologists determine whether or not to do so? (Check your answer on page 581.)*

PROS AND CONS OF THE BIG FIVE DESCRIPTION

To demonstrate that the "big five" traits provide a useful description for human personality, researchers must demonstrate that these five traits are nearly independent of one another and that they account for a major portion of the personality variation in many population samples, including both sexes, a wide range of ages, and a variety of cultures. For the most part, researchers have tested this hypothesis by repeating their original procedure on new samples of people. That is, they administer a questionnaire containing many personality descriptions (e.g., *friendly, competitive, shy,* and so forth) and ask people to rate themselves or other people on each description. Then the psychologists conduct a factor analysis to determine which descriptions correlate with one another.

SUPPORT FOR THE BIG FIVE DESCRIPTION

Many studies using this approach have concluded that the five-factor description is satisfactory for characterizing personality in

CONCEPT CHECK

5. *Some psychologists suggest that we should divide extraversion into two traits—*

both men and women, and that (in translation) the description also works in a variety of languages and cultures (Costa & McCrae, 1992). Certain differences do, however, occur among cultures. For example, the research sometimes finds that one or another of the personality traits, such as openness, does not show enough individual variation to be useful in some cultures (John, 1990). In some cultures, such as Botswana, the entire range of extraversion and neuroticism is shifted to lower values than one typically sees in Europe or America (Maqsud, 1992). Also, some studies have found five personality traits to be useful, but found a somewhat *different* five traits from the more established big five (Ormerod, McKenzie, & Woods, 1995). Psychologists have to make a judgment about whether these discrepancies are a serious problem, but most have concluded that the five-factor model works "well enough" across cultures.

How consistent is personality, as described by the five traits, across age? We can expect to find a few trends in personality change as people grow older. Generally, between ages 20 and 30, most people decline in the "thrill-seeking" aspect of extraversion (McCrae & Costa, 1994). Over the entire course of adulthood, most people show a slight decrease in neuroticism, extraversion, and openness; they show a slight increase in agreeableness and conscientiousness. As a rule, most people are impressively stable throughout adulthood (Costa & McCrae, 1994). In some cases, people make a deliberate effort to change some aspect of their personality, such as to overcome an addiction or to decrease their neuroticism. Change can occur and often does; still, such changes are in most cases slow and difficult (DiClemente, 1994). In short, the personality you have as a young adult is likely to mature as you grow older, but you are not likely to change drastically.

CRITICISMS OF THE BIG FIVE DESCRIPTION

In spite of the apparent success of the big five personality traits, a number of prominent psychologists caution against its whole-hearted acceptance.

Problem one: Nearly all of the data so far depend on written responses to questionnaires. Maybe what people say on questionnaires captures all the important dimensions of personality, and maybe it does not.

Problem two: The five-factor structure is theoretically unsatisfying. We have neither a psychological nor a biological explanation for why humans should have precisely five main personality traits instead of some other number, or why, if there are five, they should be these particular five (Block, 1995; Eysenck, 1992; Zuckerman, 1992).

Problem three: Choosing precisely five traits is arbitrary. Remember, R. B. Cattell initially identified 35 traits; factor analysis suggests that we can combine those 35 into 5 because various groups of the 35 traits correlate highly with one another. Still, they do not correlate perfectly. Some psychologists believe we could describe personality more adequately with 7 or 8 traits (Block, 1995; Cloninger, 1994), or even with Cattell's original 35. Still other psychologists, noting a positive correlation between extraversion and openness and a negative correlation between neuroticism and conscientiousness, believe we could get by with 3 factors instead of 5 (Eysenck, 1992).

Overall, how should we evaluate the five-factor description? The answer depends on our purposes. If we are interested in a good, practical way to describe a great deal of the variation in human personality while using only a small number of terms, the five-factor description works well. However, if we are interested in a complete theoretical understanding of personality, calling the five-factor description a fact of nature (as some have done) is an overstatement.

PERSONALITY VARIATION ACROSS SITUATIONS

When you are examining a photograph, ordinarily you simply hold the photo and look at its main features. For some purposes, however, you might get out a magnifying glass or a microscope to study some of the smaller details. Similarly, for some purposes we can describe human personality in terms of a few major traits, such as the big five; for other purposes, we need a more detailed analysis.

For example, although I consider myself conscientious, I admit I am much more conscientious on tasks I consider important than on tasks I consider just barely worth doing at all. You might consider yourself very honest because you would always return a lost wallet to its owner and because you would never cheat on your income taxes; nevertheless, you may find yourself telling each of your dating partners, "You are the only one I have ever loved." Indeed, because people's behavior varies so much from one situation to

According to critics of the big five personality description, any method that we choose for grouping data is arbitrary. For certain purposes we may find it convenient to separate people, or personality traits, into five groups. For other purposes, it might be more convenient to separate them into three, eight, or some other number of groups.

another, Walter Mischel (1973, 1981) formerly argued that we should abandon the whole idea of major personality traits.

Today, personality researchers, including Mischel, agree that people do have major personality traits. However, the fact remains that people's behavior varies across situations. For example, you and I may be equally conscientious, but we may be highly conscientious about different matters. We may also be equal on a scale of politeness–impoliteness, and yet you and I may be

polite or impolite in different ways or in different situations. Therefore, psychologists who want to understand the details of personality have to move beyond a measurement of major traits and examine each person's particular version of those traits. Without such a detailed focus, each of us may seem to be inconsistent: You are conscientious on some tasks, not on others; you are friendly in some situations, not in others. A detailed examination reveals considerably more consistency, however: You are almost always conscientious on the same kinds of tasks and almost always friendly in the same situations (Mischel & Shoda, 1995). Your personality consists of an assembly of learned behaviors. (Recall the discussion of social learning in Chapter 6.)

THE ORIGINS OF PERSONALITY

So far, this module has dealt only with a description of personality. Eventually we come to the more difficult question of why people differ in their personality. That is, what makes some people more extraverted, neurotic, agreeable, conscientious, or open than other people are?

The two major categories of influences are heredity and environment. To determine their possible influences, researchers have relied mostly on two kinds of data. First, they measure the similarities between monozygotic (identical) twins and the similarities between dizygotic (fraternal) twins. As Figure 13.17 shows, five studies conducted in separate locations indicated much greater similarities in extraversion between monozygotic pairs than between dizygotic pairs (Loehlin, 1992). Second, researchers compare the personalities of parents, their biological children, and their adopted children. As Figure 13.18 shows, parents' levels of extraversion correlate moderately with those of their biological children and almost not at all with those of their adopted children. Similarly, biologically related brothers or sisters who grow up together resemble each other moderately; unrelated children adopted in the same family do not develop similar personalities (Loehlin, 1992). The results shown in Figures 13.17 and 13.18 pertain to extraversion; similar studies provide a largely similar pattern for neuroticism and other personality traits (Heath, Neale, Kessler, Eaves, & Kendler, 1992; Loehlin, 1992; Viken, Rose, Kaprio, & Koskenvuo, 1994).

Overall, these results indicate a moderate contribution of heredity to personality development. Exactly how it contributes, we do not know. One possibility is that genetic factors influence the level of arousal of the brain and the autonomic nervous system, and that arousal levels in turn alter social behavior. Preliminary evidence, however, does not suggest any simple relationship between arousal

levels and personality traits (Brocke & Battmann, 1992; Stenberg, Risberg, Warkentin, & Rosén, 1990).

Personality contributors other than genetics are harder to identify. The consistently low (sometimes zero or negative) correlations between the personalities of parents and their adopted children suggest that personality differences do not depend much on the family environment. Many researchers believe that much of the variation among people's personalities relates to the **unshared environment**, the aspects of environment that differ from one individual to another, even within a family. Unshared environment is, because of its idiosyncratic nature, very difficult to investigate.

SEX DIFFERENCES IN PERSONALITY

How much of your personality depends on whether you are male or female? As a rule, tests of the big five personality traits show neither large nor consistent differences. Both women and men can be either high or low on conscientiousness, extraversion, and so forth. Specialized tests measuring certain subcomponents of these traits do show some reasonably consistent differences, although still not large ones. For example, women tend to have somewhat more anxiety, to be more trusting, and to score higher on a trait called "tendermindedness." Men tend to be more assertive, at least according to certain measures of assertiveness (Feingold, 1994).

It is possible to regard masculinity and femininity themselves as personality traits. These traits are not the same as being biologically male or female. Not all males are equally masculine; not all females are equally feminine.

According to the usual or stereotypical meanings of the terms, *masculinity* includes ambitiousness, self-assertiveness, and an interest in sports. *Femininity* includes an enjoyment of children, an enjoyment of beautifying the house and garden, and a tendency to be sympathetic to and understanding of other people.

Is it healthy to accept these roles wholeheartedly? Not if they limit one's choices in life. A man who loves taking care of children and who hates sports may worry that he is not very masculine; a highly assertive

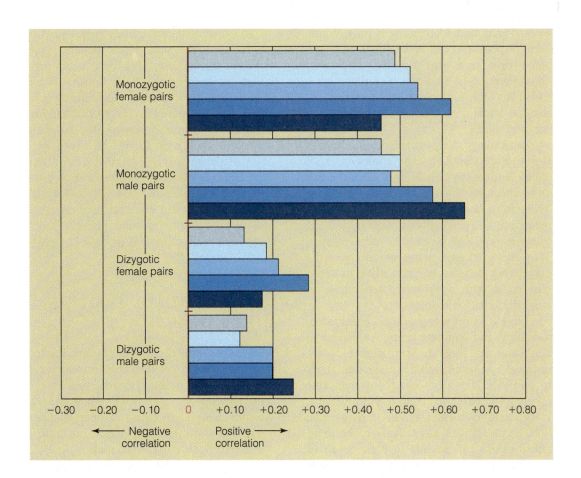

FIGURE 13.17
Five studies—in Britain, the United States, Sweden, Australia, and Finland—found larger correlations between the extraversion levels of monozygotic (MZ) twins than those of dizygotic (DZ) twins. (Based on data summarized by Loehlin, 1992.)

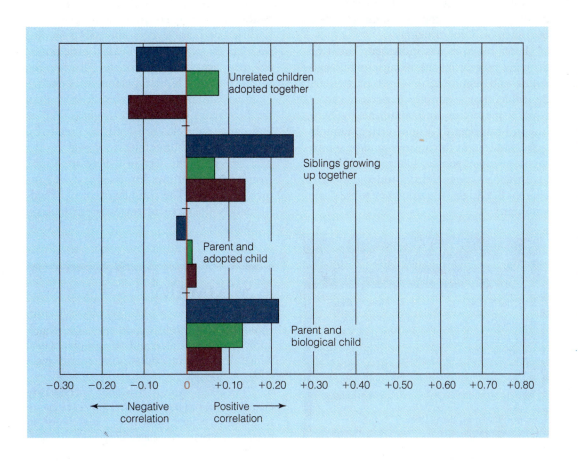

FIGURE 13.18
Three studies—in Britain, Minnesota, and Texas—measured extraversion in members of hundreds of families. Each found moderate positive correlations between parents and their biological children and between pairs of biologically related brothers and sisters. However, all found low or even negative correlations between parents and adopted children or between adopted children living in the same family. (Based on data summarized by Loehlin, 1992.)

woman may be told that she is unfeminine. Perhaps people would be healthier and happier if they felt free to combine masculinity and femininity in whatever way they like—to be, for example, ambitious, assertive, interested in children, *and* sympathetic to the needs of others.

Reasoning along these lines, Sandra Bem (1974) identified a psychological trait called **androgyny** (from the Greek roots *andr-* meaning "man" and *gyne-* meaning "woman"). According to Bem, androgynous people, as she originally conceptualized the trait, are equally masculine and feminine. They are not limited by one stereotype or the other; they can display masculine or feminine traits with equal ease, depending on what the situation requires.

Table 13.2 presents part of a checklist of masculine and feminine traits. According to Bem, you can measure your degree of androgyny by checking all the items that apply to yourself. If you check about the same number of masculine and feminine items, you are said to be androgynous. Such people, Bem predicted, are more likely to be mentally healthy and flexible in their behavior than are other people. Note that Bem made an important theoretical point: *Masculine* and *feminine* are not opposite poles of a single dimension; a person can be mostly one or the other, or both, or neither.

Later research has indicated that if androgyny merely means being equally masculine and feminine, it is not particularly desirable. For example, a person can be equally masculine and feminine by being low in both regards—unassertive, unambitious, indifferent to children, and unsympathetic to other people. Consequently, most investigators now define androgyny as a personality high in both masculinity and femininity.

Does androgyny confer any benefits greater than the sum of the benefits provided by masculinity and the benefits provided by femininity? Said another way, does being high in both masculinity and femininity give people some special kind of flexibility in their behavior due to their ability to switch from one to the other? Most of the research has failed to find any such special benefit, although many researchers continue to look for better evidence. To date, the evidence suggests that masculinity and femininity provide separate, independent benefits (Marsh & Byrne, 1991; Spence, 1984).

THE STATUS OF TRAIT RESEARCH

At the start of the discussion of traits, I noted that just as rocks are the same in some ways and different in others, personalities are the same in some ways and different in others. We find it useful to categorize personalities along a few dimensions, just as we find it useful to talk about types of rocks.

In some ways, however, the analogy between classifying rocks and classifying personalities breaks down. I do not refer simply to the fact that every individual personality is different from every other; in a similar sense, every piece of granite is a little different from every other piece, too. Rather, the problem is that human personalities change from one situation to another, far more than the properties of rocks do. Even as well as you know your closest friends and relatives, aren't you still sometimes surprised by the way one of them acts in a new situation? Aren't you sometimes surprised even at your own behavior? The complexity of personality makes this area of research particularly challenging.

TABLE 13.2
Sample Items from the Bem Sex-Role Inventory

MASCULINE ITEMS	FEMININE ITEMS
Ambitious	Affectionate
Assertive	Cheerful
Competitive	Compassionate
Makes decisions easily	Loves children
Self-reliant	Loyal
Willing to take risks	Sympathetic

Source: Based on Bem, 1974.

SUMMARY

• *Nomothetic and idiographic laws.* Psychologists seek both nomothetic laws, which apply to all people, and idiographic laws, which apply to individual differences. (page 573)

• *Traits and states.* Traits are personality characteristics that persist over time; states are temporary changes in behavior in response to particular situations. (page 573)

- *Five major traits.* Psychologists seek a short list of traits that describes as much of behavior as possible. Much can be explained by these five traits: neuroticism, extraversion, openness to new experience, agreeableness, and conscientiousness. (page 574)
- *Determinants of personality.* Studies of twins and adopted children indicate that heredity contributes to part of the observed differences in personality. Family environment evidently contributes rather little. Much of the variation in personality may be due to unshared environment, the special experiences that vary from one person to another even within a family. (page 578)
- *Sex differences.* On the average, men and women differ in small but fairly consistent ways in a few dimensions of personality. In addition, the personality traits of masculinity and femininity are somewhat independent of one another and distinguishable from being biologically male or female. Androgyny is a trait that combines the features of masculinity and femininity. (page 578)

SUGGESTION FOR FURTHER READING

Pervin, L. A. (1990). *Handbook of personality.* New York: Guilford Press. Contains summaries of contemporary theory and research on a wide variety of topics related to personality.

TERMS

nomothetic approach approach to the study of individual differences that seeks general laws about how some aspect of personality affects behavior, often based on statistical comparisons of large groups of people (page 573)

idiographic approach approach to the study of individual differences that concentrates on intensive studies of individuals (page 573)

trait a consistent, long-lasting tendency in behavior (page 574)

state a temporary activation of a particular behavior (page 574)

big five personality traits five traits that account for a great deal of human personality differences: neuroticism, extraversion, agreeableness, conscientiousness, and openness to new experience (page 574)

neuroticism tendency to experience unpleasant emotions relatively easily (page 575)

extraversion tendency to seek new experiences and to enjoy the company of other people (page 575)

agreeableness tendency to be compassionate toward others and not antagonistic (page 575)

conscientiousness tendency to show self-discipline, to be dutiful, and to strive for achievement and competence (page 575)

openness to experience tendency to enjoy new experiences, especially intellectual experiences, the arts, fantasies, and anything that exposes a person to new ideas (page 575)

unshared environment the aspects of environment that differ from one individual to another, even within a family (page 578)

androgyny tendency to be both masculine and feminine (page 580)

ANSWERS TO CONCEPT CHECKS

4. "Trait anxiety" is a tendency to experience anxiety in a wide variety of settings. "State anxiety" is anxiety evoked by a particular situation. Psychologists could observe whether this person's anxiety declines sharply when the situation changes. If it does, it is state anxiety. If not, it is trait anxiety. (page 574)

5. They should determine whether measures of ambition correlate strongly with measures of sociability. If they do, then ambition and sociability are two aspects of a single trait, extraversion. If they do not correlate strongly, then they are indeed separate personality traits. (page 575)

PERSONALITY ASSESSMENT

How can we measure personality?

How can we use measurements of personality?

A new P. T. Barnum Psychology Clinic has just opened at your local shopping mall and is offering a Grand Opening Special on personality tests. You have always wanted to know more about yourself, so you sign up. Here is Barnum's true-false test.

Questionnaire for Universal Assessment of Zealous Youth (QUAZY)

1. I have never met a cannibal I didn't like.   T   F

Most people tend to accept almost any personality assessment someone offers them, especially if it is stated in vague, general terms that each person can interpret to fit himself or herself. To determine the accuracy of a personality test, we need objective information, not just self-reports by satisfied customers.

2. Robbery is the only major felony I have ever committed.   T   F

3. I eat "funny mushrooms" less frequently than I used to.   T   F

4. I don't care what people say about my nose-picking habit.   T   F

5. Sex with vegetables no longer disgusts me.   T   F

6. This time I am quitting glue-sniffing for good.   T   F

7. I generally lie on questions like this one.   T   F

8. I spent much of my childhood sucking on telephone cords.   T   F

9. I find it impossible to sleep if I think my bed might be clean.   T   F

10. Naked bus drivers make me nervous.   T   F

11. Some of my friends don't know what a rotten person I am.   T   F

12. I usually find laxatives unsatisfying.   T   F

13. I spend my spare time playing strip solitaire.   T   F

You turn in your answers. A few minutes later a computer prints out your individual personality profile:

You have a need for other people to like and admire you, and yet you tend to be critical of yourself. While you have some personality weaknesses, you are generally able to compensate for them. You have considerable unused capacity that you have not turned to your advantage. Disciplined and self-controlled on the outside, you tend to be worrisome and insecure on the inside. At times, you have serious doubts as to whether you have made the right decision or done the right thing. You prefer a certain amount of change and variety and become dissatisfied when hemmed in by restrictions and limitations. You also pride yourself as an independent thinker and do not accept others' statements without satisfactory proof. But you have found it unwise to be too frank in revealing yourself to others. At times you are extraverted, affable, and sociable, while at other times you are introverted, wary, and reserved. Some of your aspirations tend to be rather unrealistic. (Forer, 1949, p. 120)

Do you agree with this assessment?

An experiment along these lines has been conducted a number of times with psychology classes (Forer, 1949; Marks & Kammann, 1980; Ulrich, Stachnik, & Stainton, 1963). Students started by filling out a questionnaire—one that looked fairly reasonable, not something as preposterous as the QUAZY. Several days later, each student received a sealed envelope with his or her name on it. Inside was a "personality profile," supposedly based on the student's answers to the questionnaire. The students were asked, "How accurately does this profile describe you?" About 90% rated it good or excellent. Some expressed amazement at its accuracy: "I didn't realize until now that psychology was an exact science." Of course, none of them realized that everyone had received exactly the same personality profile—the same one you just read.

The students accepted this personality profile partly because it vaguely and generally describes almost everyone and partly because people tend to accept almost *any* statement that an "expert" makes about them. Richard Kammann repeated the experiment but substituted a strange, unflattering personality profile that included statements like "Your boundless energy is a little wearisome to your friends" and "You seem to find it impossible to work out a satisfactory adjustment to your problems." More than 20% of the students rated this unlikely assortment of statements a "good to excellent" description of their own personality (Marks & Kammann, 1980).

The moral of the story is this: Psychological testing is tricky. If we want to know whether a particular test measures a particular person's personality, we cannot simply ask whether or not that person thinks it does. Even if a test is totally worthless— horoscopes, palm reading, or the QUAZY— many people will describe its results as a "highly accurate" description of themselves. To devise a psychological test that not only *appears* to work but also actually *does* work, we need to go through some elaborate procedures to design the test carefully and to determine its reliability and validity.

STANDARDIZED PERSONALITY TESTS

Psychologists have devised a great variety of personality tests; they add new ones every year. A **standardized test** is one that is administered according to specified rules and whose scores are interpreted in a prescribed fashion. An important step in standardizing a test is to determine the distribution of scores for a large number of people. We need to know the mean score and the range of scores for people in general and the mean and the range for various special populations, such as severely depressed people. Given such information, we can determine whether a given individual's score on the test is within the normal range or whether it is more typical of people with some disorder.

Most of the tests published in popular magazines have never been standardized. A magazine may herald its article "Test Yourself: How Good Is Your Marriage?" or "Test Yourself: How Well Do You Control the Stress in Your Life?" After you have taken the test and compared your answers to the scoring key, the article may tell you that "if your score is greater than 80, you are doing very well . . . if it is below 20, you need to work on improving yourself!"—or some such nonsense. Unless the magazine states otherwise, you can safely assume that the author pulled the scoring norms out of thin air and never even bothered to make certain that the items were clear and unambiguous.

Most of the "personality tests" you see in popular magazines are prepared by writers who have no idea how to standardize a test; your "results" on the test are meaningless. When psychologists standardize a personality test, they check the mean and range of scores, as well as the reliability and the validity of the test.

Many of the best-known and most widely used standardized personality tests were devised with almost no theoretical basis. Their authors simply wanted to measure some of the ways in which one person differs from another. We shall discuss some examples of well-established personality tests, but these may not be the final word. New tests with a clearer theoretical basis are on the way, including some that concentrate on measuring the "big five" personality dimensions (Costa & McCrae, 1995).

OBJECTIVE TESTS OF PERSONALITY

Some of the most widely used personality tests are based on simple pencil-and-paper responses. We shall consider one of them—the MMPI—in some detail because it is the most widely used of all personality tests (Piotrowski & Keller, 1989). We shall then consider the 16-PF more briefly.

THE MINNESOTA MULTIPHASIC PERSONALITY INVENTORY (MMPI)

The **Minnesota Multiphasic Personality Inventory** (mercifully abbreviated **MMPI**) consists of a series of true-false questions. The original MMPI, developed in the 1940s and still in use, has 550 items; the second edition, **MMPI-2**, published in 1990, has 567. Typical items are "My mother never loved me" and "I think I would like the work of a pharmacist." (The items I give in this text are re-wordings of the actual items.)

The original MMPI was devised *empirically*—that is, by trial and error (Hathaway & McKinley, 1940). The authors developed hundreds of true-false questions that they thought might be useful in identifying personality dimensions. They put these questions to people known to be suffering from depression, paranoia, and other psychological disorders, and to a group of hospital visitors, who were assumed to be psychologically normal. The researchers selected those items that most of the people in a given clinical group answered differently from most of the normal people. Their assumption was that if you answer many questions the way depressed people usually answer, you are probably depressed too. The MMPI had 10 scales, for reporting a depression score, a paranoia score, a schizophrenia score, and others. Later, other researchers found that they could use MMPI items to measure other personality dimensions as well (Helmes & Reddon, 1993).

The result was a test that worked, and still works, moderately well in practice. For example, the higher a person's score on the depression scale, the more likely that person is depressed. Some of the items on the MMPI made sense theoretically; some did not. For example, some items on the depression scale asked about feelings of helplessness or worthlessness, which are an important part of depression. But two other items were "I attend church regularly" and "Occasionally I tease animals." If you answered *false* to either of those items, you would get a point on the depression scale! These items were included simply because in the original sample of people, depressed people were more likely than nondepressed people to answer *false* on these items. Perhaps there was some good (if nonobvious) reason for that tendency, or perhaps the tendency was just a coincidence. In either event, the items were included on the depression scale.

THE MMPI-2

The MMPI was standardized in the 1940s. As time passed, the meaning of certain items, or at least of certain answers to them, changed. For example, how would you respond to the following item?

I believe I am important.   T   F

In the 1940s, fewer than 10% of all people marked this item true. At the time, "important" meant about the same as "famous," and people who called themselves important were thought to have an inflated view of themselves. Today we are more likely to say that every person is important.

What about this item?

I like to play drop the handkerchief.   T   F

Drop the handkerchief, a game similar to tag, dropped out of popularity in the 1950s. Most people born since then have never even heard of the game, much less played it.

To bring the MMPI up to date, a group of psychologists rephrased some of the items, eliminated some, and added new ones to deal with drug abuse, suicidal ideas, Type A personality, and other issues that did not concern the psychologists of the 1940s (Butcher, Graham, Williams, & Ben-Porath, 1990). Then they tried out the new MMPI-2 on 2,600 people selected to resemble the current

TABLE 13.3
The Ten MMPI Clinical Scales

SCALE	TYPICAL ITEM
Hypochondria (Hs)	I have chest pains several times a week. (T)
Depression (D)	I am glad that I am alive. (F)
Hysteria (Hy)	My heart frequently pounds so hard I can hear it. (T)
Psychopathic deviation (Pd)	I get a fair deal from most people. (F)
Masculinity-femininity (Mf)	I like to arrange flowers. (T = female)
Paranoia (Pa)	There are evil people trying to influence my mind. (T)
Psychasthenia (obsessive-compulsive) (Pt)	I save nearly everything I buy, even after I have no use for it. (T)
Schizophrenia (Sc)	I see, hear, and smell things that no one else knows about. (T)
Hypomania (Ma)	When things are dull, I try to get some excitement started. (T)
Social introversion (Si)	I have the time of my life at parties. (F)

mix of age, sex, race, and education in the United States. In other words, the psychologists restandardized the test. (Any test has to be restandardized from time to time. You may recall from the discussion of IQ tests that certain items once considered difficult are now considered relatively easy.)

The MMPI-2 has 10 clinical scales, as shown in Table 13.3. The various scales have 32 to 78 items each, scattered throughout the test, rather than clustered. Most people get at least a few points on each scale; psychologists look for any score that is much higher than average as a sign of possible difficulties. Figure 13.19 shows how MMPI-2 scores are plotted.

The MMPI-2 is only a minor revision of the original MMPI. Both tests are reasonably useful in measuring personality, but also subject to the criticism of being inefficient (Helmes & Reddon, 1993). That is, the test does not provide as much precision and accuracy as one might expect, considering the time and effort that the test requires.

THE GENERALIZABILITY OF THE MMPI

Your personality is such an integral part of what you are; is it really possible for one test to measure personality for all kinds of people? In particular, is the MMPI (or MMPI-2) a fair measure of personality for people of different ethnic and cultural backgrounds?

This is a difficult question to answer. The personality differences that occur within a given ethnic or cultural group are enormous compared to the very small differences that occur on the average between groups

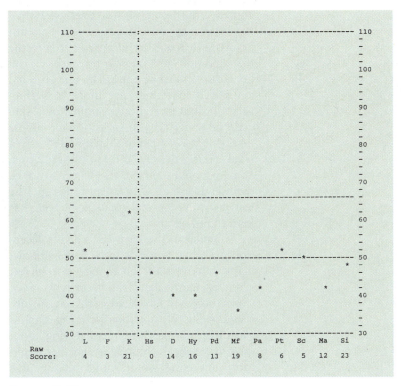

FIGURE 13.19
For the MMPI-2's 10 clinical scales, a score is plotted to profile an individual, as shown here. This is the profile of a middle-aged man with no psychological problems. A person with a disorder such as hypochondria or paranoia would have scores in the range of 65 or higher on the hypochondria or paranoia scales. (Source: Minnesota Multiphasic Personality Inventory-2, © by the Regents of the University of Minnesota. Data courtesy of R. J. Huber.)

(Greene, 1987b; Zuckerman, 1990). With regard to the small differences that do emerge between groups, we do not know whether they reflect real differences in personality or differences in interpreting what certain questions mean. Consequently, psychologists use the same norms for all races, although they are slightly more cautious about interpreting the scores of racial minorities, especially for those people who are most impoverished and least educated (Gynther, 1989).

DETECTION OF DECEPTION ON THE MMPI AND ELSEWHERE

Suppose you were taking the MMPI or some other personality test and you wanted to make yourself look mentally healthier than you really are. Could you lie on the test? Yes. Could anyone catch you in your lies? Again, yes.

The designers of both the MMPI and the MMPI-2 included in their test certain items designed to identify people who are consistently lying (Woychyshyn, McElheran, & Romney, 1992). For example, consider the items "I like every person I have ever met" and "Occasionally I get angry at someone." If you answer true to the first question and false to the second, you are either a saint or a liar. The test authors, convinced that there are more liars than saints, would give you two points on a special "lie scale." If you get too many points on the lie scale, a psychologist will refuse to trust your answers on the other items. Some people lie on the test to try to make themselves look *bad,* strangely enough. The test has some special items to detect that kind of faking also.

A similar method is used to detect deception on other types of tests. For example, many employers ask job applicants to fill out a questionnaire that asks them how much experience they have had with certain job-related skills. What is to prevent eager applicants from exaggerating or even lying about their experience? To find out whether applicants are lying, some employers include

among the authentic items a few bogus items referring to nonexistent tasks, as shown in Table 13.4.

According to the results of one study, almost half of all job applicants claimed experience at one or more nonexistent tasks (Anderson, Warner, & Spencer, 1984). Moreover, applicants who claimed a great deal of experience at nonexistent tasks also overstated their ability on real tasks. An employer can use answers on bogus items as a correction factor. The more skill an applicant claims to have on a nonexistent task, the more the employer discounts that applicant's claims of skill on real tasks.

SOMETHING TO THINK ABOUT

Could you use this strategy in other situations? Suppose a political candidate promises to increase aid to college students. You are skeptical. How could you use the candidate's statements on other issues to help you decide whether or not to believe this promise?

USES OF THE MMPI

The MMPI is useful to researchers who want to measure personality traits to see how they correlate with other traits or to test a theory of personality development. It is also useful to clinical psychologists who want to learn something about a client before beginning therapy or who want an independent measure of how much a client's personality has changed during the course of therapy (McReynolds, 1985).

How informative are the results to the client who actually takes the test? In some cases, they point out some problem to which the person had paid little attention. In other

TABLE 13.4 Part of an Employment Application, Designed to Determine Whether Applicants Are Lying About Their Skills			
How much experience have you had at:	None	A Little	Much
Matrixing solvency files?	___	___	___
Typing from audio-fortran reports?	___	___	___
Determining myopic weights for periodic tables?	___	___	___
Resolving disputes by isometric analysis?	___	___	___
Stocking solubility product constants?	___	___	___
Planning basic entropy programs?	___	___	___
Operating a matriculation machine?	___	___	___

cases, however, the results do little more than restate the obvious. For example, suppose you gave the following answers on the MMPI or MMPI-2:

I doubt that I will ever be successful.	True
I am glad that I am alive.	False
I have thoughts about suicide.	True
I am helpless to control the important events in my life.	True

A psychologist analyzes your answer sheet and tells you, "Your results show indications of depression." In a sense, this may seem so self-evident that you begin to question the whole point of taking the test. But even in a case like this, the results can be useful—not just for telling you that you are depressed (which you already knew), but for measuring *how* depressed you are at this moment (a basis for comparison of future results).

THE 16-PF TEST

The **16-PF Test** is another widely used standardized personality test. The term "PF" stands for personality factors. The test measures 16 factors, or traits, of personality. Un-like the MMPI, which was intended primarily to identify abnormal personalities, the 16-PF Test was devised to assess various aspects of normal personality. Raymond Cattell (1965) used factor analysis to identify the traits that contribute most significantly to personality. As we saw earlier in this chapter, other psychologists using factor analysis identified 5 major traits; Cattell found 16. He then devised a test to measure each of those traits. Because of the large number of factors, the results of his test apply to a rather wide range of behaviors (Krug, 1978).

When someone takes the 16-PF Test, the results are printed out as a **personality profile,** as Figure 13.20 shows. By examining such a profile, an experienced psychologist can determine the person's dominant personality traits.

Although the 16-PF Test was originally designed to assess normal personality, it does enable clinicians to identify various abnormalities, such as schizophrenia, depression, and alcoholism. Each disorder is associated with a characteristic personality profile (Figure 13.21). As with any test, it should be used cautiously, especially with people from different cultural backgrounds. Psycholo-

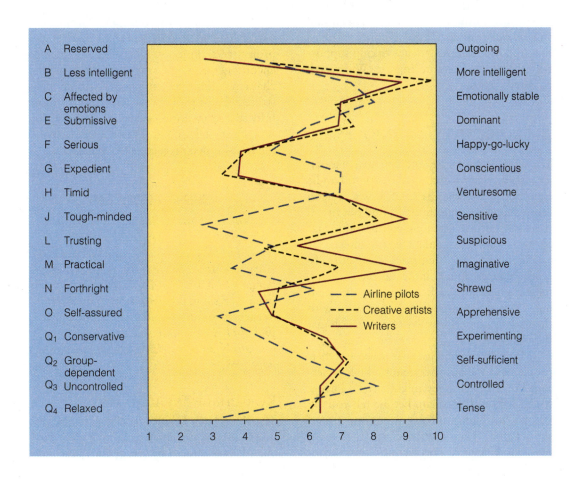

FIGURE 13.20
Personality profiles on the 16-PF test for airline pilots, creative artists, and writers. A personality profile shows whether people are high or low on a given trait. In this sample, writers were the most imaginative group. (Adapted from Cattell, 1988.)

FIGURE 13.21

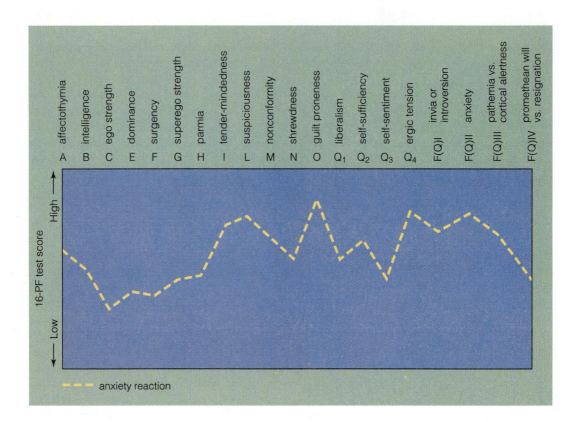

This personality profile, based on the 16-PF test, shows that this person is high in guilt, low in "ego strength." Cattell made up his own words for familiar concepts so that he could provide a precise definition that would not be confused with the everyday and vague meaning of a term such as depression. For example, surgency means something similar to cheerfulness and sociability. Parmia resembles adventurousness or boldness. (From Cattell, 1965).

gists have translated this test into other languages, but often something gets lost in translation. One study found that Mexican Americans taking the 16-PF in Spanish had substantially different personality profiles than did Mexican Americans taking supposedly the "same" test in English (Whitworth & Perry, 1990).

PROJECTIVE TECHNIQUES

The MMPI, the 16-PF, and similar personality tests are easy to score and easy to handle statistically, but they restrict how a person can respond to a question. To find out more, psychologists ask open-ended questions that permit an unlimited range of responses.

Simply to say, "Tell me about yourself" rarely evokes much information. In fact, most people find such invitations threatening. They may not be fully honest even with themselves, much less with a psychologist they have just met.

Many people find it easier to discuss their problems in the abstract than in the first person. For instance, they might say, "I have a friend with this problem. Let me tell you my friend's problem and ask what my friend should do." They then describe their own problem. They are "projecting" their prob-

lem onto someone else, in Freud's sense of the word—attributing their own characteristics to someone else.

Rather than discouraging projection, psychologists often make use of it. They use projective techniques, which are designed to encourage people to project their personality characteristics onto ambiguous stimuli. This strategy helps people reveal themselves more fully than they normally would to a stranger, or even to themselves. Let's consider two of the best-known projective techniques.

CONCEPT CHECK

6. Which of the following is a projective technique? (a) A psychologist gives a child a set of puppets with instructions to act out a story about a family. (b) A psychologist hands you a stack of cards, each containing one word such as tolerant, with instructions to sort them into two piles—a stack of cards that apply to you and a stack of cards that do not apply to you. (Check your answer on page 593.)

RORSCHACH INKBLOT TEST

The **Rorschach Inkblot Test** is probably the most famous projective technique of personality. It was created by Hermann Rorschach, a Swiss psychiatrist, who was interested in art and the occult. He read a book of poems by Justinus Kerner, a mystic writer, who had made a series of random inkblots and had then written a poem about each one. Kerner believed that anything that happens at random reveals the influence of occult, supernatural forces.

Rorschach made his own inkblots but put them to a different use. He was familiar with a word-association test then in use in which a person was given a word and was asked to say the first word that came to mind. Combining this approach with his inkblots, Rorschach showed people an inkblot and then asked them to say what came to mind (Pichot, 1984).

After testing a series of inkblots on his patients, Rorschach was impressed that their interpretations of the blots differed from his own. In a book published in 1921 (English translation 1942) he presented the 10 inkblots that still constitute the Rorschach Inkblot Technique. (Originally he had worked with a larger number, but the publisher insisted on cutting the number to 10 to save printing costs.) As other psychiatrists and psychologists began using these blots, they gradually developed the Rorschach into the projective technique we know today.

Administering the Rorschach The Rorschach Inkblot Technique consists of 10 cards similar to the one in Figure 13.22. Five are black and white; five are in color. A psychologist administering this procedure hands you a card and asks, "What might this be?" The instructions are intentionally vague. The assumption is that everything you do in an ill-defined situation will reveal something significant about your personality to the psy-

chologist—and the more poorly defined the situation, the better. The psychologist may keep a record of almost everything you do, including what you say you see, where and how you hold the cards, the length of any pauses between your responses, and so forth.

Sometimes people's answers reveal much, either immediately or in response to a psychologist's probes. Here is an example (Aronow, Reznikoff, & Moreland, 1995):

> (Card 5). **Client:** Some kind of insect; it's not pretty enough to be a butterfly.
>
> **Psychologist:** Any association to that?
>
> **Client:** It's an ugly black butterfly, no colors.
>
> **Psychologist:** What does that make you think of in your own life?
>
> **Client:** You probably want me to say 'myself.' Well, that's probably how I thought of myself when I was younger— I never thought of myself as attractive— my sister was the attractive one. I was the ugly duckling—I did get more attractive as I got older.

CONCEPT CHECK

7. Why would it be impossible to receive a copy of the Rorschach Inkblot Test by mail, fill it out, and mail it back to a psychologist to evaluate your answers? (Check your answer on page 593.)

Evaluation of the Rorschach Granted that people's answers on the Rorschach often contain a wealth of personal information, the key issue is whether or not psychologists can accurately interpret that information. In the 1950s and 1960s, certain psychologists made wild and unsupportable claims, even calling the Rorschach "an X ray of the mind." Those claims provoked equally enthusiastic criticisms. Part of the trouble is that the Rorschach provides unstructured answers that must be interpreted by a psychologist who, in many cases, has a preconceived notion about the client's problems.

For example, one depressed man replied as follows to one blot: "It looks like a bat that has been squashed on the pavement under the heel of a giant's boot" (Dawes, 1994, p. 149). This response illustrates both the reasons why many psychologists value the Rorschach so highly and the reasons why

FIGURE 13.22
In the Rorschach Inkblot Test, people look at a pattern similar to this one and tell what it looks like to them. The underlying theory is that in an ambiguous situation, anything someone does and says will reveal the individual's personality.

many other psychologists are so skeptical. On the one hand, as psychologist Robyn Dawes initially reacted, the response seems to provide a clear expression that the client felt overwhelmed and crushed by powers beyond his control—a perfect example of depression. On the other hand, as Dawes reacted after further contemplation, the Rorschach response itself had not really provided any unambiguous new information. The therapist had already *known* that the client was depressed, and he interpreted the response to match his expectations. If some client with a history of violence had made the same response, the therapist would have focused on the aggressive nature of the giant's foot stomp. If the client was prone to hallucinations or to paranoia, the psychologist would have made still other interpretations. That is, Rorschach interpretations depend on the psychologist's expectations at least as much as they do on what the client actually says. (Recall the need for double-blind procedures, as discussed in Chapter 2.)

A person's responses to the Rorschach can be used in two ways, as a projective technique or as an objectively scored test. The more traditional method of using it as a projective technique focuses on the content, such as themes of violence or themes of depression. Used in that manner, it faces the problem just described: The interpretations are mostly inferences based on the therapist's expectations. Nevertheless, defenders of the technique reply that they use it only as a way of starting a conversation and getting clients to talk more freely about topics they might be reluctant to discuss (Aronow, Reznikoff, & Moreland, 1995). Used in that way, the

technique is beyond criticism, but its limitations are clear: It is merely a conversation starter.

When the Rorschach is used as an objectively scored test, a psychologist counts particular kinds of responses and compares the results to the norms for the population. The use of standards developed by James Exner (1986) has greatly improved the ability of different psychologists to agree on their interpretation of a person's responses to the Rorschach. Thus, the reliability of the test is now far more respectable than it once was. Recall from Chapter 9, however, the difference between reliability and validity. Although measurements of Rorschach responses are now reasonably reliable (repeatable), the validity remains more doubtful. Statistically, psychologists can say that people with one kind of personality are more likely to show a certain pattern of responses and people with some other personality are more likely to show a different pattern (e.g., Weiner & Exner, 1991). However, the validity is not high enough for a psychologist to use Rorschach responses to diagnose anyone's personality with confidence. Even when the results suggest that someone probably has a psychological problem, they do not indicate with any certainty what the problem is (Vincent & Harman, 1991). Consequently, many psychologists have deep ethical qualms when they see their colleagues use Rorschach results to recommend that someone be committed to a mental hospital, or recommend for or against a parole decision for a prisoner (Dawes, 1994).

THE THEMATIC APPERCEPTION TEST

The **Thematic Apperception Test** (TAT) consists of 20 pictures like the one shown in Figure 13.23. It was devised by Christiana Morgan and Henry Murray as a means of measuring people's needs; it was revised and published by Murray (1943). Different sets of pictures are used for women, men, boys, and girls. The subject is asked to make up a story for each picture, describing what is happening, what events led up to the scene, and what will happen in the future. The pictures are all somewhat ambiguous but, except for the 20th card (which is blank!), they provide a better-defined stimulus than does the Rorschach.

People who take the TAT are expected to identify with the people shown in the pictures. That is why men are given pictures

FIGURE 13.23
In the Thematic Apperception Test, people look at a picture such as this one and tell a story about what is going on. Most people include material that relates to current concerns in their lives. (From Murray, 1971.)

showing mostly men, and women are given pictures showing mostly women. People usually tell stories that relate to recent events and concerns in their own lives, possibly including concerns they would be reluctant to talk about openly.

For example, one young man told the following story about a picture of a man clinging to a rope:

This man is escaping. Several months ago he was beat up and shanghaied and taken aboard ship. Since then, he has been mistreated and unhappy and has been looking for a way to escape. Now the ship is anchored near a tropical island and he is climbing down a rope to the water. He will get away successfully and swim to shore. When he gets there, he will be met by a group of beautiful native women with whom he will live the rest of his life in luxury and never tell anyone what happened. Sometimes he will feel that he should go back to his old life; but he will never do it. (Kimble & Garmezy, 1968, pp. 582–583)

This young man had entered divinity school, mainly to please his parents, but was quite unhappy there. He was wrestling with a secret desire to "escape" to a new life with greater worldly pleasures. In his story, he described someone doing what he really wanted to do but could not openly admit.

The TAT is often used in a clinical setting to get clients to speak freely about their problems. It is also used for research purposes. For instance, an investigator might measure someone's "need for achievement" by counting all the stories he or she tells about achievement. The same might be done for aggression, passivity, control of outside events, or dominance. The investigator could use the findings to study the forces that strengthen or weaken various needs and why certain groups of people express different needs.

For most purposes, the reliability of the TAT is rather low, generally about .3 (Kraiger, Hakel, & Cornelius, 1984). That is, someone who takes the test on two occasions is likely to give different answers, leading to different interpretations. One explanation is that the test measures current concerns, which change over time (Lundy, 1985). Generally, TAT results correspond better to what a person *has done recently* than to what he or she *will do in the future* (Anastasi, 1988). For that reason, it might be better to say that

the TAT measures "current concerns" rather than "needs."

USES AND MISUSES OF PERSONALITY TESTS

Before any drug company can market a new drug in the United States, the Food and Drug Administration (FDA) requires that it be carefully tested. If the FDA finds it safe and effective, it approves the drug for certain purposes, with a warning label that lists precautions, such as an advisory that pregnant women should not take it. After it is approved, however, the FDA cannot prevent a physician from prescribing it for some unapproved purpose and it cannot keep it out of the hands of people who should not be taking it.

Personality tests are a little like drugs: They ought to be used with great caution, and only for the purposes for which they have demonstrable usefulness. They are, at a minimum, helpful to psychologists as an interviewing technique, to help "break the ice" and get a good conversation started. Tests can also be useful as an aid in personality assessment by a clinical psychologist. Note that I said "as an aid," *not* "as a sufficient method of personality assessment." For example, suppose someone has an MMPI personality profile that resembles the profile typical for schizophrenia. Identifying schizophrenia or any other unusual condition is a signal-detection problem, as we discussed in Chapter 4—a problem of reporting a stimulus when it is present without reporting it when it is absent. Suppose (realistically) that people without schizophrenia outnumber people with schizophrenia by 100 to 1. Suppose further that a particular personality profile on the MMPI-2 is characteristic of 95% of people with schizophrenia and only 5% of other people. As Figure 13.24 shows, 5% of the normal population is a *larger* group than 95% of the schizophrenic population. Thus, if we labeled as "schizophrenic" everyone with a high score, we would be wrong more often than right. (Recall the representativeness heuristic and the issue of base-rate information, discussed in Chapter 8: Someone who seems "representative" of people in some rare category may not necessarily belong to that category.) Therefore, a conscientious psychologist will look for other evidence beyond the test score before drawing any conclusion. (The same,

Figure 13.24

Even the best personality tests make mistakes. A test to detect an unusual condition will often identify normal people as having the condition. Here, we assume that a certain profile occurs in 95% of people with schizophrenia and 5% of other people. If we relied entirely on this test, we would correctly identify 95 schizophrenic people, but we would also identify 495 normal people as having schizophrenia.

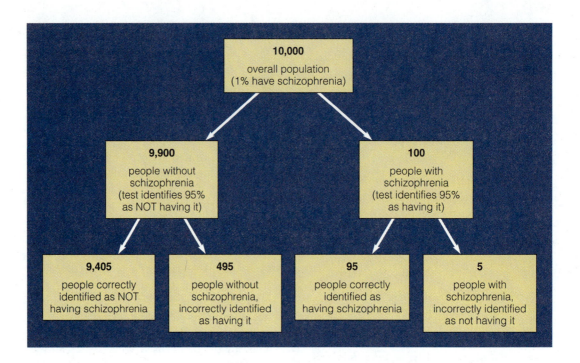

of course, should be said of any test. Scores on an IQ test or the SAT can be used as one of several factors in selecting students for a program; one should not make decisions based on a test score alone.)

Some employers use personality tests to screen job applicants, selecting only those who have the "right" personality. For example, some companies want to hire only people with an "aggressive" personality for sales jobs. Others want to eliminate anyone who shows signs of any psychological abnormality. As a rule, personality tests have a rather low predictive validity for this purpose; in many cases they have no demonstrated validity at all. For example, a personality test that claims to measure an "aggressive" personality may not measure the kind of aggressiveness that presumably helps in a sales job. For ethical, legal, and practical reasons, employers should use personality tests *only* when they have clear evidence that the results help them select the best job applicants more accurately than they could select without the tests.

Summary

• *People's tendency to accept personality test results.* Because most people are inclined to accept almost any interpretation of their personality based on a personality test, tests must be carefully scrutinized to ensure that they are measuring what they claim to measure. (page 582)

• *Standardized personality tests.* A standardized test is one that is administered according to explicit rules and whose results are interpreted in a prescribed fashion. Standards are based on the scores of people who have already taken the test. (page 583)

• *The MMPI.* The MMPI, a widely used personality test, consists of a series of true-false questions selected in an effort to distinguish among various personality types. The MMPI-2 is a modernization of the version developed in the 1940s. (page 584)

• *Detection of lying.* The MMPI and certain other tests guard against lying by including items on which nearly all honest people will give the same answer. Any other answer is probably a lie. An unusual number of "lying" answers will invalidate the results. (page 586)

• *The 16-PF Test.* The 16-PF Test, another standardized personality test, measures 16 personality traits. Although it was designed primarily to measure normal personality, its results do distinguish between normal and abnormal personalities. (page 587)

• *Projective techniques.* A projective technique—such as the Rorschach Inkblot Test or the Thematic Apperception Test—lets people describe their concerns indirectly while talking about "the person in the picture" or about some other ambiguous stimulus. The results from projective techniques are difficult to interpret and have unimpressive validity for making decisions about any individual. (page 588)

• *Uses and misuses of personality tests.* Personality tests can be an aid to assessing personality, but their results should be interpreted cautiously in conjunction with other evidence. They should be used for selection only when evidence clearly indicates that the results are valid for this purpose. (page 591)

SUGGESTION FOR FURTHER READING

Anastasi, A. (1988). *Psychological testing* (6th ed.). New York: Macmillan. A good textbook on both personality testing and IQ testing.

TERMS

standardized test a test that is administered according to specified rules and whose scores are interpreted in a prescribed fashion (page 583)

Minnesota Multiphasic Personality Inventory (MMPI) a standardized personality test consisting of true-false items, intended to measure various clinical conditions (page 584)

MMPI-2 the modernized edition of the MMPI (page 584)

16-PF Test a standardized personality test that measures 16 personality traits (page 587)

personality profile a graph that shows an individual's scores on scales measuring a number of personality traits (page 587)

Rorschach Inkblot Test a projective personality technique in which people are shown 10 inkblots and asked what each might be (page 588)

Thematic Apperception Test (TAT) a projective personality technique in which a person is asked to tell a story about each of 20 pictures (page 590)

ANSWERS TO CONCEPT CHECKS

6. (a) The puppet activity could be a projective technique, because the child is likely to project his or her own family concerns onto the puppets, using them to enact various problems. (page 588)

7. The Rorschach Inkblot Test must be administered in person by a psychologist who observes how you hold the cards, whether you rotate them, and anything else you do. The psychologist may also ask you to explain where you see something or why it looks the way you say it does. (page 589)

14 ABNORMAL BEHAVIOR

Over the past 4 months, George has struck and injured several dozen people, most of whom he hardly knew. Two of them had to be sent to the hospital. George expresses no guilt, no regrets. He says he would attack every one of them again if he got the chance. What should society do with George?

1. Send him to jail?
2. Commit him to a mental hospital?
3. Give him an award for being the best defensive lineman in the league?

Before you can answer, you must know the context of George's behavior. Behavior that seems normal at a party might seem bizarre at a business meeting. Behavior that earns millions for a rock singer might earn a trip to the mental hospital for a college professor. Behavior that is perfectly routine in one culture might be considered criminal in another.

Even when we recognize the context of someone's behavior, we may wonder whether it is "normal." Suppose your rich Aunt Tillie starts to pass out $5 bills to strangers on the street corner and vows that she will keep on doing so until she has exhausted her entire fortune. Is she mentally ill? Should the court commit her to a mental hospital and turn her fortune over to you as her trustee?

A man claims to be Jesus Christ and asks permission to appear before the United Nations to announce God's message to the world. A psychiatrist is sure that he can relieve this man of his disordered thinking by giving him antipsychotic drugs, but the man refuses to take them and insists that his thinking is perfectly normal. Should we force him to take the drugs, just ignore him, or put his address on the agenda of the United Nations?

Normal or abnormal? The distinction depends on the context of behavior and is often uncertain.

An Overview of Abnormal Behavior

Why do some people behave abnormally?
What are the most common kinds of abnormal behavior?

Students in medical school often contract what is known as "medical students' disease." Imagine that you are just beginning your training in medicine. One of your textbooks describes "Cryptic Ruminating Umbilicus Disorder":

"The symptoms are very minor until the condition becomes hopeless. The first symptom is a pale tongue." (You go to the mirror. You can't remember what your tongue is supposed to look like, but it *does* look a little pale.) "Later a hard spot forms in the neck." (You feel your neck. "Wait! I never felt *this* before! I think it's something hard!") "Just before the arms and legs fall off, there is shortness of breath, increased heart rate, and sweating." (Already distressed, you *do* have shortness of breath, your heart *is* racing, and you *are* sweating profusely.)

Sooner or later, most medical students decide they have some dreaded illness. The problem is imaginary; they merely confuse the description of some disease with their own normal condition. When my brother was in medical school, he diagnosed himself as having a rare, fatal illness, checked himself into a hospital, and wrote a will. (Today he is a successful physician.)

"Medical students' disease" is even more common among students of psychological disorders. As you read this chapter and the next, you may decide that you are suffering from some such disorder: "That sounds exactly like me! I must have Deteriorating Raving Odd Omnivorous Lycanthropy!"

Well, maybe you do and maybe you don't. Psychological disorders are just exaggerations of tendencies that nearly all of us have. The difference between "normal" and "psychologically disordered" is a matter of degree.

Concepts of Normal and Abnormal Behavior

How should we define abnormal behavior? If we try to be completely objective, we might define *abnormal* in a statistical manner as any behavior that differs very much from the average. By that definition, anyone who is unusually happy or unusually successful is "abnormal," and a condition such as severe depression would become "normal" if its prevalence in the population reached 51%. Ordinarily, when we say *abnormal,* we mean *troubled,* not just *different* (Wakefield, 1992).

The American Psychiatric Association (1994) has defined abnormal behavior as behavior that leads to distress (pain), disability (impaired functioning), or an increased risk of death, pain, or loss of freedom. We can question that definition as well. For example, when Martin Luther King, Jr., fought for the rights of African Americans, he engaged in

To determine whether a behavior is normal or abnormal, heroic or deeply disturbed, we have to know its social and cultural context. Here, Iranian worshippers flog themselves to reenact the suffering of an early Shi'ite martyr. In this context, self-flogging is a normal part of a religious ritual. In some other context, it might be a sign of psychological distress.

behaviors that entailed the risk of death, pain, and loss of freedom. But we regard his acts as heroic, not abnormal.

Another way to define abnormal would be to let people decide for themselves whether or not they are troubled. For example, someone with a good job and a loving family might say, "Everyone thinks I'm doing fine, but inside I feel miserable." According to a definition that focuses on distress, anyone who thinks he or she has a psychological problem *does* have a problem.

Fair enough, but what do we do about certain people who insist that they do *not* have a problem? Suppose someone babbles incoherently, urinates and defecates in the street, insults strangers, begs for dollar bills and then sets fire to them, while claiming to be doing all this in obedience to messages from the planet Chlorox? Suppose also that this person reports feeling no distress, does not wish to change, and refuses all offers of help. I would call this person abnormal or psychologically disordered, and I assume you would, too. If so, then what we mean by *abnormal* does not require a feeling of distress. We are, I think inevitably, making a value judgment. We mean that the "abnormal" condition is either undesirable to the affected people themselves, or unacceptable to the rest of us.

You will note, of course, that we are treading on dangerous ground. If we allow ourselves or our society to label people who are content with themselves as "abnormal," we run the risk of making some dreadful mistakes. For example, the government of the Soviet Union committed many of its political opponents to mental hospitals. In the United States, some psychologists and psychiatrists used to apply the label "self-defeating personality disorder" to battered women, suggesting that those women's psychological disorders brought about their abuse (Caplan, 1995). Loosely applying psychiatric labels can seriously damage people's lives. However, the message, I believe, is not that we should never identify anyone as abnormal, but that we should be extremely cautious about doing so.

SOMETHING TO THINK ABOUT

How would *you* define abnormal behavior?

ABNORMAL BEHAVIOR AS A CULTURALLY DETERMINED PHENOMENON

Each time and place has interpreted abnormal behavior according to its own worldview. People in the Middle Ages, for example, regarded bizarre behavior as a sign that the disturbed person was possessed by a demon. To exorcise the demon, priests resorted to prescribed religious rituals (Figure 14.1). In various parts of the world today, some cultures still talk about demon possession, some regard abnormal behaviors as biological disorders, and some have other interpretations.

We are accustomed to the idea that our culture tells us how to behave normally. To some extent a culture also tells people how to behave *abnormally*. For example, in one

FIGURE 14.1
Peculiar behavior was once explained as demon possession. Here, St. Zenobius exorcises devils (fleeing from the mouths of the possessed). At the time of this late 15th-century work, attributed to Botticelli, the priest Savonarola was exorcising the city with public burnings of luxury goods.

culture in Sudan, women have low status and very limited rights; if a woman's husband mistreats her, she has almost no defense. However, people in this society believe that sometimes a woman can be "possessed by a demon." During a demon possession, she loses control and starts screaming all sorts of "crazy" things that she "could not possibly believe," including insults against her own husband. The husband cannot scold or punish his wife for acting this way because, after all, it is not really she, but only the demon who is saying these things. The standard way to remove the woman's demon is to provide her with luxurious food, new clothing, an opportunity to spend more time with other women instead of with her husband, and more or less anything else she demands until the demon departs. Guess what: Demon possession occurs very frequently in this culture (Constantinides, 1977).

More examples: *Brain fag syndrome* is a psychiatric condition of headache, eye fatigue, and inability to concentrate—a common complaint among West African students just before exams. You might try explaining to your own professor that you cannot take the test tomorrow because you have brain fag syndrome, but unless you live in West Africa, I doubt your explanation will do you much good. You probably have heard the expression "to run amok." *Running amok* is a type of abnormal behavior recognized in parts of Southeast Asia, in which someone (usually a young man) runs around engaging in furious, almost indiscriminate, violent behavior (Berry, Poortinga, Segal, & Dasen, 1992). Such behavior is considered an understandable reaction to psychological stress, not a criminal offense.

Does running amok remind you of anything common in North America or Europe? How about the "celebrations" that occur after a sports team wins a major championship? (See Figure 14.2.) Like running amok, we regard such wild displays as temporary, excusable responses to overwhelming emotion.

Although we consider the fans' destructive celebrations to be "normal," their behavior illustrates an important point about conditions that we call "abnormal": Some people who are behaving "abnormally" are responding to suggestions, or they are imitating patterns of behavior they have observed in other supposedly abnormal individuals. For example, in a condition known as **disso-**

FIGURE 14.2

Following a victory in a major sports event, the home-town fans often celebrate with a property-destroying rampage. Under other circumstances, such acts would be considered criminal or insane; under these circumstances, our society excuses them as normal and expected.

ciative identity disorder or **multiple personality disorder,** a person alternates among two or more distinct personalities, each with its own behavioral patterns, memories, and even name, almost as if each personality were really a different person. Such conditions were at one time considered to be extraordinarily uncommon. Then, beginning in the 1950s, a few such cases received much publicity, such as the case of Chris Costner White Sizemore, featured in the book and the movie *The Three Faces of Eve,* written by her psychiatrists (Thigpen & Cleckley, 1957). Sizemore ("Eve") eventually told her own story, which was much different from her psychiatrists' version (Sizemore & Pittillo, 1977; Sizemore & Huber, 1988). (See Figure 14.3.) Then a few other people with dissociative identity disorder also received extensive publicity; by the early 1990s, some psychotherapists reported finding many such cases. If they are right, our society is experiencing an epidemic of dissociative identity disorder. Has the prevalence of this condition really increased that much? Have therapists become more acute at detecting something that has always been common? Or is the apparent prevalence increasing through power of suggestion, just as young men in Southeast Asia learn how to run amok and college basketball fans learn how to destroy

FIGURE 14.3

Chris Sizemore, the real "Eve" of The Three Faces of Eve, *exhibited a total of 22 personalities, including her final, permanent identity. A person who periodically changes personality and identity is said to have* dissociative identity disorder. *Each of those personalities by itself seems reasonably normal. Films, television, and other media often mistakenly refer to this condition as "schizophrenia." People with schizophrenia have only one personality; that personality, however, is abnormal in serious ways.*

property when their team wins a championship? In some cases, eager therapists may have unintentionally induced dissociative identity disorder by hypnotizing clients and asking whether they have another personality (Spanos, 1994). As you will recall from Chapter 5, people under hypnosis are often highly suggestible. In summary, just as we learn from our culture how we are supposed to act, we also learn—from our culture and even from our therapists—some of our options for abnormal behavior.

COMPETING VIEWS OF ABNORMAL BEHAVIOR

Among therapists and researchers today, *one influential point of view is that many psychological disorders are the result of biological disorders,* including genetics, brain damage, chemical imbalances in the brain, hormonal abnormalities, poor nutrition, inadequate sleep, various diseases, and overuse of certain drugs, including over-the-counter medications. *A second point of view is that some psychological disorders are the result of disordered thinking caused by early experiences.* That is essentially the Freudian point of view. Even many theorists who disagree

with Freud believe that traumatic experiences early in life may later distort people's thinking. *A third point of view is that some psychological disorders are learned reactions to a stressful or unsupportive environment* that the person is trying to cope with as well as possible.

For illustration, consider alcohol abuse. Someone may become an alcohol abuser because of a genetic tendency or other biological factors, the effects of early family life, or the stresses of current life. Naturally, these explanations are compatible with one another; a given individual may develop an alcohol problem for a combination of several reasons. Tracking down the causes of psychological disorders turns out to be quite a challenge.

THE CLASSIFICATION AND PREVALENCE OF PSYCHOLOGICAL DISORDERS

Any scientific study must be based on some accepted method for classifying information. In the study of abnormal behavior, we need to identify different types of disorders and we have to define them well enough to be sure that different therapists or researchers use each term in approximately the same way. For that reason, psychiatrists and psychologists have developed a reference book called *The Diagnostic and Statistical Man-*

DSM-IV is an aid to identifying and classifying various types of psychological disorders, much as a field guide helps observers identify the plants and animals they see. However, many people have mild disorders or disorders that do not neatly fit any of the DSM-IV categories.

ual of Mental Disorders (DSM), which is now in its fourth edition and therefore known as **DSM-IV** (American Psychiatric Association, 1994). DSM-IV lists the acceptable labels for all psychological disorders (alcohol intoxication, exhibitionism, pathological gambling, anorexia nervosa, sleepwalking disorder, stuttering, and hundreds of others), with a description of each and guidelines on how to distinguish it from similar disorders.

USES AND LIMITATIONS OF DSM-IV

DSM-IV serves a function a little like that of a nature field guide: A guide to butterflies, birds, or flowers enables a user to identify wildlife and to compare notes with others; if you use a field guide well, you can be sure that what you call a song sparrow is the same as what someone else calls a song sparrow. Psychologists and psychiatrists need something like DSM-IV to be sure that what one person calls schizophrenia is about the same as what another person calls schizophrenia.

The problem with this analogy between DSM-IV and a field guide is that birds come in distinct species, whereas psychological disorders form a continuum. For example, depression comes in different degrees, whereas a bird either is a song sparrow or is not. (Hybrids, which are crosses between two species, are rare in nature.) Depression can range from severe and long-lasting to mild and brief. Similarly, most of us have occasional bouts of fear, anxiety, hostility, or strange behaviors; if we are not classified as "abnormal" it is because our bouts of such behaviors are not quite frequent enough or not quite severe enough to cross the threshold from normal into abnormal.

Because psychological disorders are a matter of degree, statistics about their frequencies are arbitrary and potentially misleading. One survey of a random sample of about 20,000 people was conducted in three U.S. cities (Eaton et al., 1984; Regier et al., 1984). Trained interviewers tried to reach all the "usual residents" of each selected neighborhood, including those who lived at home and those who lived in institutions such as prisons, mental hospitals, and nursing homes. They found that about one-fifth of all adults were suffering from a psychological disorder of some sort (as defined by the American Psychiatric Association) and that close to one-third had suffered from such a disorder at some time during their life (My-

ers et al., 1984; Robins et al., 1984). A similar study conducted 10 years later reported higher frequencies of disorders, estimating that about 50% of all people endure some diagnosable psychological disorder at some point in their lives (Kessler et al., 1994). According to both surveys, the most common psychological disorders are phobia and related anxiety disorders, alcohol or drug abuse, and mood disorders (including depression), as shown in Figure 14.4. Although these surveys provide a useful gauge to the approximate frequencies of various disorders, the results necessarily reflect subjective judgments about how disabling someone's troubles must be before they constitute a psychological disorder. Some psychiatrists and psychologists, frankly, find some sort of disorder in a high percentage of the people they meet, and it may well be that all of us *are*, in fact, a bit disordered now and then. A small percentage of people have severe problems, a large percentage have mild problems, and the question of what percentage of people "have a problem" is fundamentally ambiguous.

Note in Figure 14.4 that depression and anxiety disorders are more common in

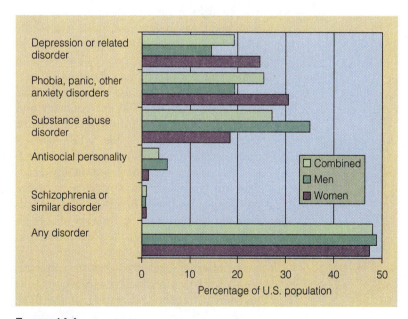

FIGURE 14.4
According to one extensive survey, about half of the population of the United States will suffer at least one psychological disorder at some time in life. (The figures for the individual conditions do not add up to the total percentage for "any disorder" because some people have more than one disorder.) However, the exact percentages depend on where one draws the dividing line between "normal" and "abnormal"; for each condition we can find many borderline cases. (Based on data of Kessler et al., 1994.)

women, whereas substance abuse and anti-social personality disorder are more common in men. The reasons for these differences are not clear. We shall consider the sex differences in depression later in this chapter.

CONCEPT CHECK

1. Which are the most common psychological disorders? (Check your answer on page 605.)

DSM-IV's AXES OF CLASSIFICATION

The clinicians and researchers who use DSM-IV classify each client along five separate *axes* (lists). A person may have more than one disorder on a given axis—for example, alcohol abuse and depression—or may have none at all. Axes I to III categorize specific disorders. Axis I lists disorders that have their onset at some time after infancy. These are the disorders that psychologists and psychiatrists encounter most frequently, the ones for which they can offer the greatest prospects for effective treatment. Table 14.1 lists some of the categories of disorder on Axis I.

Axis II lists disorders that generally persist throughout life, such as mental retardation and personality disorders (see Table 14.2). These conditions are almost part of the person himself or herself, rather than something the person has acquired. A **personality disorder** is a maladaptive, inflexible way of dealing with the environment and other people, such as antisocial behavior or an avoidance of other people. Whereas many other psychological disorders resemble medical disease to some extent, personality disorders are more like an integral part of the person, like being tall, or left-handed, or red-headed. People with personality disorders seldom complain about their condition and seldom seek treatment, except at the insistence of family, acquaintances, or an employer.

Axis III lists physical disorders, such as diabetes or alcoholic cirrhosis of the liver, that may affect a person's behavior. Ordinarily a psychotherapist does not treat a person for an Axis III disorder, but awareness of the Axis III disorder might affect interpretation or treatment of some disorder listed on Axis I or II.

Stress may intensify a psychological disorder and may affect the course of treatment. Axis IV indicates how much stress the person has had to endure, on a scale from 0 (almost no stress) to 6 (stress equivalent to being held hostage or to the death of one's child).

Some people with a psychological disorder are able to go on with their normal work and social activities; others are not. Axis V evaluates a person's overall level of functioning, on a scale from 1 (serious attempt at suicide or complete inability to take care of oneself) to 90 (happy, productive, with many interests).

THE IMPORTANCE OF DIFFERENTIAL DIAGNOSIS

The analogy between DSM-IV and a nature field guide, as previously discussed, works in some ways and not in others. Here is one final way in which it does work: Proper use of either guide alerts the user both to the expected features of each species *and* to the similar species from which we need to distinguish it. For example, if you see a bird and decide that it looks like a song sparrow, your field guide will also show you several other, somewhat similar kinds of sparrows. To be sure something is a song sparrow, you have to determine that what you see looks like a song sparrow and *not* like any of the other sparrows.

Similarly, in abnormal psychology, suppose someone says, "I feel unenergetic and pessimistic; I have trouble sleeping at nights; I don't have much appetite; and nothing brings me pleasure anymore." Given this information, a psychologist's first impulse might be to consider a diagnosis (label) of depression. However, the person's self-

Habitual, impulsive gambling is one kind of impulse control disorder.

TABLE 14.1
Some Major Categories of Psychological Disorders According to Axis I of DSM-IV

Disorders usually first evident in childhood or adolescence	*Examples:* *Attention-deficit hyperactivity disorder:* Impulsivity; hyperactivity; inability to pay attention to school or work *Tourette's disorder:* Repetitive movements, such as blinking an eyelid or twitching a hand; chanted sounds—in some cases, obscene words *Elimination disorders:* Bed-wetting; urinating or defecating in one's clothes *Stuttering:* Frequent repetition or prolongation of sounds, interfering with speech
Substance-related disorders	Alcohol abuse, cocaine abuse, opiate abuse, and abuse of other mind-altering substances
Schizophrenia	Deterioration of everyday functioning, along with either a lack of emotional response, or thought disorders, or hallucinations or delusions
Delusional (paranoid) disorder	Irrational beliefs, such as the belief that "everyone is talking about me behind my back" or that "I have discovered the secret that will solve all the world's problems if I can just get people to listen to me"
Mood disorders	Periods of depression serious enough to interfere with daily life, sometimes alternating with periods of mania, which is the opposite of depression
Anxiety disorders	Lingering anxiety at almost all times, unpredictable attacks of severe anxiety, or periods of anxiety that regularly occur when the person is confronted with a particular object or thought
Somatoform disorders	*Examples:* *Conversion disorder:* One or more physical ailments, such as blindness or paralysis, caused at least in part by psychological factors but not intentionally produced *Hypochondriasis:* Repetitive, exaggerated complaints of illness *Somatization disorder:* Recurrent complaints of pain and other ailments that are apparently not due to any physical disorder
Dissociative disorders	Loss of the memory of a person's own identity or the memory of past events, not caused by brain damage
Sexual disorders	*Examples:* *Pedophilia:* Sexual attraction to children *Exhibitionism:* Sexual pleasure from exposing oneself in public *Voyeurism:* Sexual arousal primarily from watching other people undressing or engaging in sexual intercourse *Fetishism:* Sexual arousal primarily from leather or other inanimate objects
Eating disorders	*Examples:* *Anorexia nervosa:* Refusal to eat, fear of being fat *Bulimia nervosa:* Binge eating alternating with weight loss
Sleep disorders	*Examples:* *Insomnia:* Frequent feeling of not being rested after a night's sleep *Sleep terror disorder:* Repeated periods of awakening suddenly in an experience of panic *Sleepwalking disorder:* Repeated episodes of leaving the bed, walking about, and not remembering the episode later
Impulse control disorders	A tendency to act on impulses that other people usually inhibit, such as the urge to gamble large amounts of money foolishly, the urge to steal something, or the urge to strike someone

Mental retardation	Intellectual functioning significantly below average; significant deficits in adaptive behavior
Personality disorders	*Examples:*
	Paranoid personality disorder: Suspiciousness; habitual interpretation of other people's acts as threatening
	Schizotypal personality disorder: Poor relationships with other people, odd thinking; neglect of normal grooming. This disorder is similar to schizophrenia but less extreme
	Antisocial personality disorder: Lack of affection for other people; tendency to manipulate other people without feeling guilty; high probability of getting into trouble with the law; low probability of keeping a job
	Borderline personality disorder: Lack of a stable self-image; trouble establishing lasting relationships with other people or making lasting decisions about values, career choice, even sexual orientation; repeated self-endangering behavior, such as drug abuse, reckless driving, casual sex, binge eating, shoplifting, and running up large debts
	Histrionic personality disorder: Excessive emotionality and attention-seeking; constant demand for praise
	Narcissistic personality disorder: Exaggerated opinion of one's own importance and a lack of regard for others (Narcissus was a figure in Greek mythology who fell in love with himself)
	Avoidant personality disorder: Avoidance of social contact; lack of friends
	Dependent personality disorder: Preference for letting other people make decisions; lack of initiative and self-confidence

Mental retardation and personality disorders are listed on Axis II because they are lifelong conditions and thus not easily changed.

description could also indicate some other problem, such as a malfunctioning thyroid gland, a stroke, the side effects of taking certain medications, withdrawal effects after quitting cocaine, or a grief reaction following the death of a loved one. The person could even be completely normal and just tired from a period of overwork. In short, even though the person's complaint may suggest depression, we do not have enough information yet to decide what the problem is.

Psychiatrists and clinical psychologists must learn to make a **differential diagnosis**—that is, a determination of what problem a person has, in contrast to all the other possible problems that might produce similar symptoms.

SUMMARY

• *Normal and abnormal behavior.* Although psychologists and psychiatrists try to be objective and scientific in identifying abnormal behavior, some judgments are necessarily difficult and dependent on value judgments. To avoid tyrannical subjugation of eccentric people, we should be very cautious about applying psychiatric labels to people who are not seeking help. (page 597)

• *Cultural influences on abnormal behavior.* Any culture provides not only examples of how to behave normally, but also how to behave abnormally. (page 598)

• *Multiple causes of abnormal behavior.* Abnormal behavior is the result of various combinations of biological factors, early experiences, and learned responses to a stressful or unsupportive environment. (page 600)

• *The Diagnostic and Statistical Manual.* Psychological disorders are classified in the *Diagnostic and Statistical Manual of Mental Disorders, Fourth Edition* (DSM-IV). This manual classifies disorders along five axes. Axis I and Axis II deal with psychological disorders; Axis III deals with physical ailments that may affect behavior; Axes IV and V provide means for evaluating a person's stress level and overall functioning. (page 600)

• *Axis I—disorders that last part of a person's life.* Axis I of DSM-IV lists disorders that usually begin after infancy and that have at least some likelihood of recovery. Three common disorders of this sort are anxiety disorders, substance abuse, and depression. (page 602)

• *Axis II—lifelong disorders.* Axis II of DSM-IV lists conditions that arise early and persist throughout a lifetime, such as mental retardation and personality disorders. (page 602)

• *Personality disorders.* Personality disorders are stable characteristics that impair a person's effectiveness or ability to get along with others. Examples of personality disorders are excessive dependence on others and excessive self-centeredness. (page 602)

• *Differential diagnosis.* Psychiatrists and clinical psychologists need to learn to consider all the possible diagnoses of a given condition, and to identify the correct one by eliminating all the other possibilities. (page 604)

SUGGESTION FOR FURTHER READING

American Psychiatric Association (1994). *Diagnostic and statistical manual of mental disorders* (4th ed.). Washington, DC. The standard guide to the classification and description of psychological disorders.

TERMS

dissociative identity disorder rare condition in which the personality separates into several identities. Also known as **multiple personality disorder** (page 599)

The Diagnostic and Statistical Manual of Mental Disorders, Fourth Edition (DSM-IV) book that lists the acceptable labels for all psychological disorders with a description of each and guidelines on how to distinguish it from similar disorders (page 600)

personality disorder a maladaptive, inflexible way of dealing with the environment and other people (page 602)

differential diagnosis a determination of what problem a person has, in contrast to all the other possible problems that might produce similar symptoms (page 604)

ANSWER TO CONCEPT CHECK

1. You are correct if you answered "anxiety disorders, substance-related disorders, and depression." You are also fully justified if you objected that "this is a meaningless question, because the answer depends on how many borderline cases are classified as disordered and how many are considered normal." (page 602)

ANXIETY AND AVOIDANCE DISORDERS

Why do some people take extreme measures to avoid something that is harmless or only slightly dangerous?

Why do some people develop strange habits and rituals?

You go to the beach, looking forward to an afternoon of swimming and surfing. Then someone tells you that a shark attacked two swimmers yesterday and has just been sighted close to shore. Do you venture into the water? What if the shark attack occurred a month ago and no shark has been seen in the area since then? Now would you go in? What if no shark has attacked anyone in this area, but someone saw a small shark there a few days ago? What if no shark has ever been seen within 50 miles of this particular beach, but recently you read a magazine story about shark attacks?

How much fear and caution is normal? Staying out of the water because you see a large shark is perfectly reasonable. Staying out of the water because of sharks you have read about is, by most people's standards, excessively cautious. If you refuse even to look at photographs of the ocean because they might *remind* you of sharks, you have a serious problem indeed.

It is normal to have a certain amount of fear and to avoid situations that might provoke fear. But excessive fear and caution are linked to some of the most common psychological disorders.

DISORDERS WITH APPARENTLY UNPROVOKED ANXIETY

Many psychological disorders are marked by a combination of fear, anxiety, and attempts to avoid anxiety. Anxiety, unlike fear, is generally not associated with a specific situation. We feel fear in the presence of a hungry tiger, but our fear passes as soon as we get away. But we cannot escape the anxiety we experience about dying or about our personal inadequacies. Some degree of anxiety is normal; it becomes a problem only when it interferes with our ability to cope with everyday life.

GENERALIZED ANXIETY DISORDER

People with **generalized anxiety disorder** are almost constantly plagued by exaggerated worries. They worry that "I might get sick," "My daughter might get sick," "I might lose my job," or "I might not be able to pay my bills." Although these people have no realistic reason for such worries—at least no more reason than anyone else—their worries persist and interfere with daily life. They grow tense, restless, irritable, and fatigued. About 5% of all people experience generalized anxiety disorder at some point in life, often in conjunction with depression, panic disorder, or other problems (Wittchen, Zhao, Kessler, & Eaton, 1994).

PANIC DISORDER

Panic disorder is an emotional disturbance found in about 1–2% of all American adults, women more than men; adults much more than children (McNally, 1990; Myers et al., 1984; Robins et al., 1984). People with this disorder have a fairly constant state of moderate anxiety and an overresponsive sympathetic nervous system; they respond to even mild stressors or mild exercise with a sudden increase in heart rate and blood adrenaline (Liebowitz et al., 1985; Nutt, 1989). This arousal sometimes provokes a full-fledged panic attack, accompanied by chest pains, difficulty in breathing, sweating, faintness, and shaking (see Figure 14.5). A panic attack generally lasts only a few minutes, although it may last an hour or more. During an attack, most people worry about fainting, dying, or going crazy (Argyle, 1988). People often interpret a panic attack as a heart attack or as a sign of an impending heart attack. After a few such attacks, those worries may grow more intense and may even trigger further panics.

Many people with panic disorder also have **social phobia,** a severe avoidance of other people and an especially strong fear of doing anything in public, where they might be embarrassed. Many also have **agorapho-**

bia—an excessive fear of open places or public places, from *agora*, the Greek word for "marketplace" (Reich, 1986). In addition, many of the relatives of people with panic disorder also have panic disorder, social phobia, or agoraphobia themselves (Goldstein et al., 1994; Kendler et al., 1995). Thus, panic disorder, social phobia, and agoraphobia seem to be different expressions of a single underlying predisposition.

Most psychologists believe that people with panic disorder develop their social phobia or agoraphobia because they are afraid of being incapacitated or embarrassed by a panic attack in a public place. In a sense, they are afraid of their own fear (McNally, 1990). To avoid the prospect of a public panic attack, they stay home as much as possible and almost never go out alone.

Panic disorder can become self-perpetuating (Figure 14.6). Many people deal with anxiety by taking a deep breath or two, to help calm themselves down. On the theory that "if a little is good, a whole lot will be better," they may continue breathing deeply, or hyperventilating. Hyperventilation expels carbon dioxide and therefore lowers the carbon dioxide level in the blood. If any event then increases the carbon dioxide level, this increased carbon dioxide raises the heart rate and causes trembling and other symptoms of a panic attack—the very thing the person was trying to avoid (Gorman et al., 1988; Woods et al., 1986). After a few such episodes, the likelihood of further attacks increases. One treatment for panic disorders is to teach the person to avoid hyperventilating (Wolpe & Rowan, 1988). Another is to teach the person to recognize sudden increases in heart rate and trembling as a sign of carbon dioxide fluctuations, and not as a sign of an impending heart attack.

When people discover that physical exertion sometimes triggers a panic attack, they may decide to avoid any sort of physical activity. As a result, they grow even more sensitive to the effects of physical activity; even slight exertion will raise the level of carbon dioxide in their blood. Consequently, some authorities recommend regular exercise as a way of decreasing panic disorder (Ledwidge, 1980).

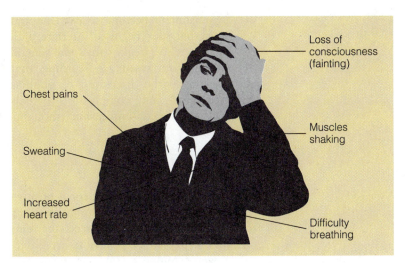

FIGURE 14.5
People subject to panic attacks experience moderate anxiety almost constantly, as well as occasional periods of intense anxiety. During a panic attack, the sympathetic nervous system intensely activates the heart and other organs. People are generally frightened by this experience; some believe they are having a heart attack.

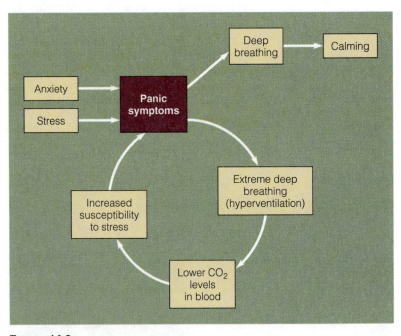

FIGURE 14.6
Deep breathing helps to calm a person, but extreme deep breathing increases the probability of another panic attack.

attacks and to adopt the attitude, *"If it happens, it happens."* Why would they make this recommendation? (Check your answer on page 617.)

DISORDERS WITH EXAGGERATED AVOIDANCE BEHAVIORS

People learn to avoid punishment, as we saw in Chapter 6. In some cases, their efforts to

CONCEPT CHECK

2. *Some psychologists advise people with panic attacks to stop worrying about their*

avoid punishment become so extreme and persistent that they begin to interfere with daily activities. We begin with some general observations on avoidance learning that are relevant to the discussion of phobias (extreme fears) and compulsions (rituals designed to avoid unpleasant thoughts or events).

AVOIDANCE LEARNING AND ITS PERSISTENCE

If you learn to do something for a positive reinforcement, you will extinguish your response soon after you stop receiving reinforcements. Avoidance behaviors are different, however. Suppose you learn to press a lever to avoid electric shocks. Soon you are responding steadily and receive no shocks. Now the experimenter disconnects the shock generator, without telling you. The extinction procedure has begun; you no longer need to press the lever. What will you do? You will continue pressing, of course. So far as you can tell, nothing has changed; the response still "works." *Avoidance behaviors are highly resistant to extinction*; once someone learns a response to avoid mishap, the response continues long after it ceases to be necessary.

Many people who watched the famous shower scene in the movie Psycho *became frightened of taking showers. Actress Janet Leigh, who portrayed the woman killed in that scene, was herself so terrified that she has only rarely taken a shower since then. That is, fears and phobias can be learned, either from one's own experiences or vicariously.*

You can see how this tendency would support superstitions: Suppose you believe that Friday the 13th is a dangerous day. You are very cautious every Friday the 13th, but occasionally some misfortune happens anyway. The misfortune confirms your belief that Friday the 13th is dangerous. The next Friday the 13th, nothing goes wrong. You conclude, "It helps to be careful on Friday the 13th. I was cautious all day long, and I avoided bad luck." *In other words, so long as you continue engaging in an avoidance behavior, you can never find out that you are doing something useless or unnecessary.*

CONCEPT CHECK

3. Suppose you are an experimenter, and you have trained someone to press a lever to avoid shocks. Now you disconnect the shock generator. Other than telling the person what you have done, what procedure could you use to facilitate extinction of the lever pressing? (Check your answer on page 617.)

PHOBIAS

Terror is the only thing that comes close to how I feel when I think of moths. Their willowy, see-through wings always seem filthy. I remember being stuck in a car with a huge moth, and my date, not knowing how terrified I was of moths, thought I was kidding when I told him I was afraid. It was terrible! I can feel it right now . . . the . . . feeling trapped and the moth with its ugly body flitting around so quickly, I couldn't anticipate where it would go next. Finally that creature hit me in the arm and I screamed—it felt dirty and sleazy and then it hit me in the face and I began to scream uncontrollably. I had the terrible feeling it was going to fly into my mouth while I was screaming, but I couldn't stop. (Duke & Nowicki, 1979, p. 244)

Phobias are extreme and persistent fears leading to avoidance behaviors, similar to a superstitious fear of Friday the 13th. Phobias are sometimes defined as "irrational fears," but that definition is inadequate. A fear of snakes or spiders is not irrational—some of them are dangerous. The intensity of someone's fear of snakes and spiders determines whether it is a normal fear or a phobia. Some people have such a strong fear of these creatures that they keep away from fields in which they might be lurking, stay away from unfamiliar buildings, avoid books that might have pictures of snakes or spiders, and don't talk to strangers who, after all, might like to *talk* about snakes or spiders.

⑰ A **phobia** is best defined as *a fear so extreme that it interferes with normal living*. Confronting the object of the phobia may lead to sweating, trembling, and rapid breathing and heart rate. In most cases, people with phobias are not so much afraid of the object itself but of their own reactions to it (Beck & Emery, 1985). They fear that they will have a heart attack or that they will embarrass themselves by trembling or fainting. In many ways, phobias are like panic disorder, except that phobias are aroused by a specific object or event, whereas panic attacks occur at less-predictable times.

Because most people with phobias are ⑱ well aware that their fears are exaggerated, it does no good to tell them not to be afraid. In fact, attempts to reduce phobias by providing information sometimes backfire. One city tried to combat the phobia of elevators by posting signs on elevators throughout the city: "There is no reason to be afraid of elevators. There is almost no chance at all that the cable will break or that you will suffocate." The signs actually *increased* the phobia of elevators.

The Prevalence of Phobias   How many people suffer from phobias? As with most other psychological disorders, phobias are exaggerations of normal behaviors. Depending on where we draw the line between phobias and normal fears, estimates of the prevalence of phobias range from 5% to 13% of the population (Myers et al., 1984). About twice as many women as men report phobias. Figure 14.7 shows the most frequently reported phobias. Figure 14.8 shows the prevalence of phobias by age. Note the early onset; phobias often begin in the teenage years (Burke, Burke, Regier, & Rae, 1990).

The Learning of Phobias   Although people seem to be born with a few fears, such as a fear of sudden loud noises, most fears are learned. Indeed, some phobias can be traced to a specific event, such as when one child got locked in a trunk and developed a phobia of closed places. Another person developed a phobia of water by diving into a lake and discovering a corpse (Kendler et al., 1995).

John B. Watson, one of the founders of behaviorism, was the first to demonstrate the

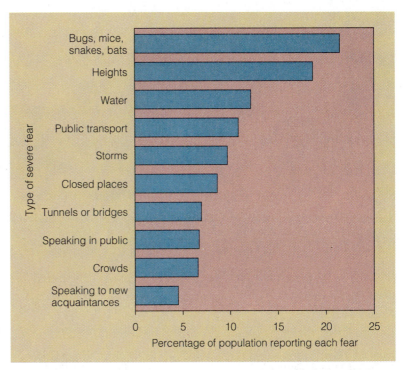

FIGURE 14.7
The most common phobias include snakes and other animals, heights, open places and crowds, and storms. Here, people reported their severe fears. Not all severe fears qualify as phobias, however.

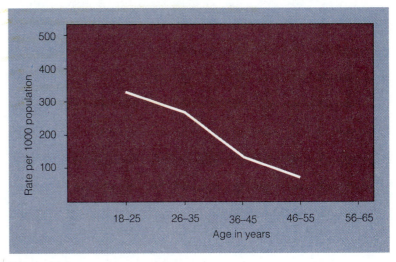

FIGURE 14.8
Most phobias are not lifelong conditions. Most young people with phobias lose them by middle age, either spontaneously or because of therapy.

possibility of learning a fear (Watson & Rayner, 1920). Today, we would consider it unethical to try to create a fear, especially in humans, but in 1920, researchers felt less restraint. Watson and Rosalie Rayner studied an 11-month-old child, "Albert B.," who ⑲ had previously shown no fear of white rats

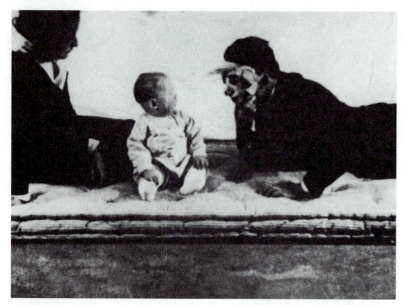

FIGURE 14.9
John B. Watson argued that most fears, including phobias, are learned. Watson first demonstrated that this child, Little Albert, showed little fear of small animals. Then Watson paired the presentation of a white rat with a loud, frightening noise. Little Albert became afraid of the white rat; he also began showing fear of other small animals, odd-looking masks, and other objects he had not previously feared. (Courtesy of Professor Benjamin Harris.)

or other animals (Figure 14.9). They set a white rat down in front of Albert, and then, just behind him, they struck a large steel bar with a hammer. The sudden sound made Albert whimper and cover his face. After seven repetitions, the mere sight of the rat would make Albert cry and crawl away. Watson and Rayner declared that they had created a strong fear and that phobias in general might develop along similar lines.

Although Watson and Rayner's study is open to serious methodological criticisms (Harris, 1979; Samelson, 1980), it led the way for later interpretations of phobias as learned responses. Watson and Rayner's explanation of phobias failed to answer some important questions: Why do people develop phobias toward objects that have never injured them? Why are some phobias much more common than others? And why are phobias so persistent?

CONCEPT CHECK

4. In classical-conditioning terms, what was the CS in Watson and Rayner's experiment? The UCS? The CR? The UCR? (Check your answers on page 617.)

Learning Fear by Observation

Contrary to Watson and Rayner's explanation, almost half of all people with phobias have never had a painful experience with the object they fear (Öst & Hugdahl, 1981). Are you afraid of snakes? Most people have at least a moderate fear of snakes, and a fair number have phobias about them. Have you ever been injured by a snake? Chances are, no. Why do so many people fear snakes when so few have ever been injured by one?

As noted in our consideration of social learning in Chapter 6, we learn many things by watching or listening to others. Perhaps we hear that someone has been injured by a snake, and we become afraid too.

That hypothesis is probably correct, but how can we demonstrate it? Susan Mineka and her colleagues demonstrated how monkeys learn fears by observing other monkeys (Mineka, 1987; Mineka, Davidson, Cook, & Keir, 1984). Her experiments show how animal studies can shed light on important human issues.

EXPERIMENT 1

Hypothesis Monkeys that have seen other monkeys show fear of a snake will develop such a fear themselves.

Method Monkeys that live in the wild generally develop a strong fear of snakes; however, monkeys reared in a laboratory show no fear of snakes. Mineka put a laboratory-reared monkey together with a wild-born monkey and let them both see a snake (Figure 14.10a). The lab monkey watched the wild monkey show signs of fear. Later she tested the lab monkey by itself to see whether it had acquired a fear of snakes.

Results When the lab monkey saw how frightened its partner was of the snake, it became frightened too (Figure 14.10b). It continued to be afraid of the snake when tested by itself even months later.

Interpretation The lab monkey may have learned a fear of snakes because it saw that its partner was afraid of snakes. But Mineka considered another possible, though less likely, interpretation: The lab-reared monkey may have become fearful simply because it observed the other monkey's fear. That is, maybe it did not matter *what* the wild-reared monkey was afraid of. To test this possibility, Mineka conducted a second experiment.

EXPERIMENT 2

Hypothesis   A monkey that sees another monkey show fear but does not know what the second monkey is afraid of will not develop the same fear itself.

Method   A monkey reared in a lab watched a monkey reared in the wild through a plate of glass. The wild monkey could look through another window, where it saw a snake. Thus, when the wild monkey shrieked and ran away from the snake, the lab monkey saw the wild monkey's fear but did not know what it was afraid of. Later the lab monkey was put close to a snake to see whether it would show fear.

Results   The lab monkey showed no fear of the snake.

Interpretation   To develop a fear of snakes, the observer monkey had to see that the other monkey was frightened of snakes, not just that it was frightened (Figure 14.10c).

Note that although the observer monkey had to see *what* the other monkey was afraid of, it did not have to see *why* it was afraid. Just seeing the other monkey's fear of the snake in Experiment 1 was enough. Humans not only observe other people's fears but also can tell one another what they are afraid of and why.

Why Some Phobias Are More Common Than Others   Imagine that you survey your friends. (You can survey them in fact, if you like, but in this case it's pretty easy to imagine what the results will be.) You ask them the following questions *in this order*:

- Are you afraid of snakes?
- Are you afraid of cars?
- Have you ever been bitten by a snake or seen someone else get bitten by a snake?
- Have you ever been injured in a car accident or seen someone else get injured in a car accident?

I think you know what results to expect: A fair number of people will admit being afraid of snakes, some of them extremely

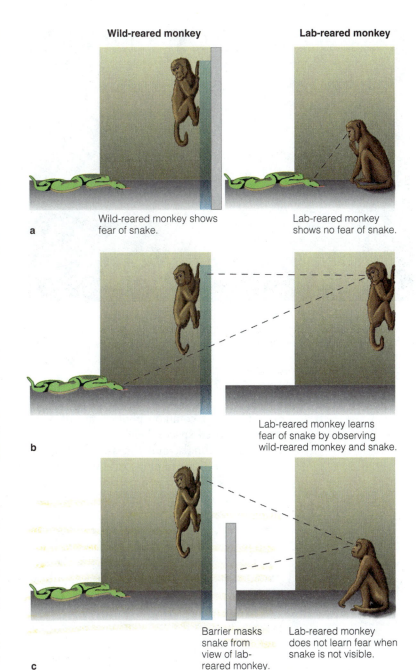

Wild-reared monkey **Lab-reared monkey**

a   Wild-reared monkey shows fear of snake.   Lab-reared monkey shows no fear of snake.

b   Lab-reared monkey learns fear of snake by observing wild-reared monkey and snake.

c   Barrier masks snake from view of lab-reared monkey.   Lab-reared monkey does not learn fear when snake is not visible.

FIGURE 14.10
A laboratory-reared monkey learns to fear snakes from the reaction of a monkey reared in the wild. But if the snake is not visible, the lab-reared monkey fails to learn fear.

afraid, even though very few have any first-hand experience with snakebites. Almost no one is afraid of cars, even though almost everyone has experienced or witnessed a car accident in which someone got injured. Why do people develop some fears more readily than others?

Phobias are most likely to develop for dangerous events that we can neither predict nor control. They also develop for events that give us occasional unpleasant experiences without any safe or pleasant experiences. Can you therefore explain why so many people have phobias of lightning and so few people have phobias of cars?

The most common phobias are of open spaces, closed spaces, heights, lightning and thunder, animals, and illness. In contrast, few people have phobias of cars, guns, or tools—even though injuries from cars, guns, and tools are quite common. One explanation for this tendency is that, as Martin Seligman (1971) put it, people may be inherently "prepared" to learn certain phobias. For millions of years people who quickly learned to avoid snakes, heights, and lightning probably have had a good chance to survive and to transmit their genes. We have not had enough time to evolve a tendency to fear cars and guns.

We have evidence to support this view from both monkey and human studies. Monkeys who watch a videotape of another monkey running away from a snake learn to fear snakes; monkeys who watch a monkey running away from a flower show no fear of flowers (Mineka, 1987). People who receive electric shocks paired with pictures of snakes quickly develop a strong and persistent response to snake pictures; people who receive shocks paired with pictures of houses show a much weaker response (Öhman, Eriksson, & Olofsson, 1975).

There may be other reasons why some phobias are more common than others. One is that we have many safe experiences with cars and tools to outweigh any bad experiences. We have few safe experiences with

snakes or spiders or with falling from high places. One study found that people who had extensive experiences with tarantula spiders lost their fears and sometimes even developed an interest in tarantulas as a hobby (Kleinknecht, 1982).

Another possible explanation is that people generally develop phobias for objects they cannot predict or control. Danger is more stressful when it takes us by surprise (Mineka, 1985; Mineka, Cook, & Miller, 1984). If you are afraid of spiders, for example, you have to be constantly on the alert for those tiny, unpredictable critters. Because you never know where they might be or when they might strike, you can never completely relax. Lightning is also unpredictable and uncontrollable. In contrast, you don't have to worry that electric outlets will take you by surprise. You have to be on the alert for cars when you are near a road, but not at other times.

The Persistence of Phobias Well-established phobias can last a lifetime. If you remember the discussion about avoidance learning, you can see why phobias are so difficult to extinguish: If you have learned to press a lever to avoid shock, you may not stop pressing long enough to find out that your response is no longer necessary. Similarly, if you stay away from snakes or heights or closed places because you have a phobia of them, you will never learn that your fear is exaggerated. In other words, you will not extinguish your fear.

Therapies for Phobias We shall consider general principles of psychotherapy in Chapter 15. Here, however, let us examine two therapies that were developed specifically for phobias—systematic desensitization and flooding.

As we have seen, phobias are persistent because people consistently avoid the object of the phobia. As long as people continue making their avoidance response, they cannot learn that the response is unnecessary; extinction does not take place. Therefore, the best way to extinguish a phobia is to expose a person to the object that arouses the fear. When nothing bad happens, the phobia fades.

The most common and most successful treatment for phobia is systematic desensitization, a method of reducing fear by gradually exposing people to the object of their fear (Wolpe, 1961). Someone with a phobia of snakes, for example, is first given training in methods of relaxation. Then the patient is asked to lie on a comfortable couch with relaxing music playing in the background and with the therapist nearby. The therapist asks the patient to imagine a small black-and-white photo of a snake. Next the patient is asked to imagine a full-color photo and then to imagine a real snake. After the patient has successfully dealt with all of those images, the same sequence is repeated with real photos and eventually with a real snake (Figure 14.11).

The process resembles Skinner's shaping procedure (Chapter 6): The patient is given time to master one step before going on to the next. The patient can say stop if the distress becomes too severe; the therapist then goes back several steps and repeats the sequence. Some people get through the whole procedure in a single 1-hour session; others need weekly sessions for 2 or 3 months. Systematic desensitization can easily be combined with social learning: The person with a phobia watches other people who display a fearless response to the object.

Some therapists use a high-tech approach (Rothbaum et al., 1995): The client is equipped with a helmet that displays a virtual-reality scene, as shown in Figure 14.12. Then, without even leaving the office, the therapist can expose the client to the object of his or her fears. For example, a client with a phobia of heights can go up a glass elevator in a hotel or walk across a narrow bridge over a chasm (Rothbaum et al., 1995). The virtual-reality technology gives the therapist excellent control of the situation, including even the option of turning off the display and removing the helmet, if the client becomes too fearful.

Flooding or **implosion** is a treatment in which the person is exposed to the object of the phobia suddenly rather than gradually (Hogan & Kirchner, 1967; Rachman, 1969) (Figure 14.13). (It is called "flooding" because the patient is "flooded" with fear.) If you had a phobia of rats, for example, you might be told to imagine that you were locked in a room full of rats crawling all over you and viciously attacking you. The image arouses your sympathetic nervous system enormously, and your heart rate and breathing rate soar to high levels (Lande, 1982).

The human sympathetic nervous system is not capable of maintaining extreme arousal for very long, however, and within a

FIGURE 14.11
One of the most effective therapies for a phobia is systematic desensitization, in which a therapist gradually exposes a client to the object of the phobia, first in imagination and later in reality. A similar procedure is exposure therapy; the therapist demonstrates a lack of fear of the object and encourages the client to do the same.

FIGURE 14.12
Some therapists provide a virtual-reality environment, so that a patient with a phobia of heights can experience heights under carefully controlled conditions.

FIGURE 14.13
Flooding is a procedure similar to systematic desensitization, except that in flooding the person is exposed suddenly, not gradually, to the object of fear. At first the person is terrified, but as the autonomic arousal decreases (as it inevitably does), the person realizes "I can handle this situation."

few minutes your heart rate and breathing rate begin to decline. A little later, you report that you feel more relaxed, even though the therapist continues to suggest gory images of what rats are doing to you. Once you have reached this point, the battle is half won. Remember, the main fear of people with phobias is that their own fear will be overwhelming or that it will lead to a heart attack; when they learn that they can withstand even the most frightening experience, they become less afraid of their own responses.

CONCEPT CHECKS

5. *In what way does systematic desensitization resemble extinction of a learned shock-avoidance response?*
6. *How is the flooding procedure related to the James-Lange theory of emotions, discussed in Chapter 12? (Check your answers on page 617.)*

OBSESSIVE-COMPULSIVE DISORDER

People with **obsessive-compulsive disorder** have two kinds of problems: An **obsession** is a repetitive, unwelcome stream of thought. For example, such people might find themselves constantly imagining gruesome scenes, worrying that they are about to kill someone, dwelling on doubts about their religion, or thinking "I hate my sister, I hate my sister." The harder they try to escape such thoughts, the more repetitive they become. A **compulsion** is a repetitive, almost irresistible action. Obsessions generally lead to compulsions, as an itching sensation leads to scratching.

The Persistence of Obsessions People with obsessive-compulsive disorder feel a combination of guilt and anxiety over certain thoughts or impulses. They feel persistent, frightening impulses—perhaps an impulse to engage in some sexual act they consider shameful, an impulse to hurt someone they love, or an impulse to commit suicide. They decide, "Oh, what a terrible thing to think. I don't want to think such a thing ever again." And so they resolve to shut the thought or impulse out of their consciousness.

However, the harder one tries to prevent a thought, the more intrusive it becomes. As a child, the Russian novelist Leo Tolstoy once organized a club with a most unusual qualification for membership: A prospective member had to stand alone in a corner *without thinking about a white bear* (Simmons, 1949). If you think that sounds easy, try it. You probably go months at a time without thinking about white bears, but when you try *not* to think about them, you can think of nothing else.

In one experiment, college students were asked to tape-record everything that came to mind during 5 minutes but to try *not* to think about white bears. If they did, they were to mention it and ring a bell. Subjects reported thinking about a bear a mean of more than six times during the 5 minutes (Wegner, Schneider, Carter, & White, 1987). Afterward, they reported that almost everything in the room reminded them of white bears. Evidently, attempts to suppress a thought are likely to backfire, even with an emotionally trivial thought such as "white bears." You can imagine what it must be like with severely upsetting thoughts.

One Type of Compulsion: Cleaning People with obsessive-compulsive disorder can have several kinds of compulsions. Some collect things. (One man collected newspapers under his bed until they raised the bed so high it almost touched the ceiling.) Others have odd habits, such as touching everything they see, trying to arrange objects in a completely symmetrical manner, or walking back and forth through a doorway nine times before leaving a building. I know of one obsessive-compulsive person who could not sleep at night until he had counted the corners of every object in the room to make sure that the total number of corners was evenly divisible by 16. If it was not, he would add objects to the room or remove objects from the room until it had an acceptable total of corners. (The Obsessive-Compulsive Foundation produces a button that says "Every Member Counts"!)

The most common compulsions are cleaning and checking. Obsessive-compulsive cleaning is similar to a phobia of dirt. Here is a description of a severe cleaning compulsion (Nagera, 1976):

"R.," a 12-year-old boy, had a long-standing habit of prolonged bathing and hand washing, dating from a film about germs he had seen in the second grade. At about age 12, he started to complain about "being dirty" and having "bad thoughts," but he would not elaborate. His hand washing and bathing became longer and more frequent. When he bathed, he carefully washed himself with soap and washcloth all over, including the inside of his mouth and the inside of each nostril. He even opened his eyes in the soapy water and carefully washed his eyeballs. The only part he did not wash was his penis, which he covered with a washcloth as soon as he entered the tub.

Coupled with his strange bathing habits, he developed some original superstitions. Whenever he did anything with one hand, he immediately did the same thing with the other hand. Whenever anyone mentioned a member of R.'s family, he would mention the corresponding member of the other person's family. He always walked to school by the same route, being careful never to step on any spot he had ever stepped on before. (After a while this became a serious strain on his memory.) At school, he would wipe the palm of his hand on his pants after any "good" thought; at home, he would wipe his hand on his pants after any "bad" thought.

R.'s problems were traced to a single event. Just before the onset of his exaggerated behaviors, R. and another boy had pulled down their pants and looked at each other. Afterward he felt guilty and full of anxiety that he might do the same thing again. The constant bathing was apparently an attempt to wash away his feelings of "dirtiness." The superstitious rituals were an attempt to impose rigid self-control. His underlying reasoning could be described as, "If I can keep myself under perfect control at all times, even following these rigid and pointless rules, I will never again lose control and do something shameful."

Another Type of Compulsion: Checking

An obsessive-compulsive checker "double-checks" everything. Before going to bed at night, he or she checks to make sure that all the doors and windows are locked and that all the water taps and gas outlets are turned off. But then the question arises, "Did I *really* check them all, or did I only imagine it?" So everything has to be checked again. And again. "After all, I may accidentally have unlocked one of the doors when I was checking it." Obsessive-compulsive checkers can never decide when to stop checking; they may go on for hours, and even then not be satisfied.

Obsessive-compulsive checkers have been known to check every door they pass to see whether anyone has been locked in, to check trash containers and bushes to see whether anyone has abandoned a baby, to call the police every day to ask whether they have committed a crime that they have forgotten, and to drive back and forth along a street to see whether they ran over anyone the last time through (Pollak, 1979; Rachman & Hodgson, 1980).

Why do checkers go on checking? According to some reports, they do not trust their memory of what they have done (Sher, Frost, Kushner, Crews, & Alexander, 1989). In one study, the experimenters asked several people—among them some obsessive-compulsive checkers—to read a list of words and to think their opposites. (For instance, when they saw "NORTH–S . . . ," they would think *south*.) Then the experimenters combined the two sets of words—the words on the list and their opposites—and asked the subjects to identify which words they had read and which ones they had only thought. The obsessive-compulsive checkers remembered about as accurately as the control group did, but their confidence in their answers was significantly lower. Compared to the control group, the checkers were less confident of their ability to distinguish between what had actually happened and what they had just imagined (Sher, Frost, & Otto, 1983).

Table 14.3 summarizes key differences between obsessive-compulsive cleaners and checkers. Table 14.4 lists some items from a questionnaire on obsessive-compulsive tendencies (Rachman & Hodgson, 1980). Try answering these questions yourself, or try guessing how an obsessive-compulsive person would answer them. The most common obsessive-compulsive answers are given on page 617. (The few items listed here are not sufficient to diagnose someone as obsessive-compulsive. So don't obsess about it if you agreed with all the obsessive-compulsive answers!)

Possible Predispositions or Causes About 2–3% of all people in the United States suffer from obsessive-compulsive disorder at some time during their lives (Karno, Golding, Sorenson, & Burnam, 1988). The disorder occurs most frequently among hardworking, perfectionistic people of average or above-average intelligence. It may develop either suddenly or gradually, usually beginning between the ages of 10 and 25. Nearly

TABLE 14.3
Obsessive-Compulsive Cleaners and Checkers

	CLEANERS	CHECKERS
Sex distribution	Mostly female	About equally male and female
Dominant emotion	Anxiety, similar to phobia	Guilt, shame
Speed of onset	Usually rapid	More often gradual
Life disruption	Dominates life	Usually does not disrupt job and family life
Ritual length	Less than 1 hour at a time	Some go on indefinitely
Feel better after rituals?	Yes	Usually not

Source: Rachman & Hodgson, 1980.

TABLE 14.4
Obsessive-Compulsive Tendencies

1. I avoid public telephones because of possible contamination. — T F
2. I frequently get nasty thoughts and have difficulty in getting rid of them. — T F
3. I usually have serious doubts about the simple everyday things I do. — T F
4. Neither of my parents was very strict during my childhood. — T F
5. I do not take a long time to dress in the morning. — T F
6. One of my major problems is that I pay too much attention to detail. — T F
7. I do not stick to a very strict routine when doing ordinary things. — T F
8. I do not usually count when doing a routine task. — T F
9. Even when I do something very carefully, I often feel that it is not quite right. — T F

Source: Rachman & Hodgson, 1980.
(Check typical answers on page 617.)

all people with obsessive-compulsive disorder have some insight into their own behavior and realize that their rituals are inappropriate. However, that realization does not stop the rituals.

Obsessive-compulsive disorder tends to run in families, suggesting a possible genetic basis. Many of the relatives who do not have obsessive-compulsive disorder have other anxiety disorders (Black, Noyes, Goldstein, & Blum, 1992).

Certain drugs have demonstrated substantial ability to suppress obsessions and compulsions, including Anafranil (generic name clomipramine). All such drugs inhibit the reuptake of the neurotransmitter serotonin after its release by presynaptic neurons; that is, the drugs prolong the effects of serotonin. The effectiveness of such drugs suggests that some disorder of the brain's serotonin synapses may be a cause or at least a predisposition to obsessive-compulsive disorder (Goodman et al., 1990; Leonard et al., 1989; Yaryura-Tobias, 1977). The details of this relationship are far from clear, and a whole new area of research is opening up.

▮ IN CLOSING

Phobias and obsessive-compulsive disorder illustrate some of the possible links between emotions and cognitions. At the risk of seriously oversimplifying, we could say that people with phobias experience emotional attacks because of their cognitions about some object, whereas people with obsessive-compulsive disorder experience repetitive cognitions for emotional reasons. In both conditions, most people are cognitively aware that their reactions are exaggerated, but mere awareness of the problem does not correct it. Dealing with such conditions requires attention to emotions, cognitions, and the links between them.

SUMMARY

• *Anxiety disorder and panic disorder.* People with generalized anxiety disorder or panic disorder experience extreme anxiety. Panic disorder is characterized by episodes of disabling anxiety, some of which may be triggered by hyperventilation. (page 606)

- *Persistence of avoidance behaviors.* Once an individual has learned a shock-avoidance response, the response may persist long after the possibility of shock has been removed. As with shock-avoidance responses, phobias and obsessive-compulsive disorder persist because people do not discover that their avoidance behaviors are unnecessary. (page 608)

- *Phobia.* A phobia is a fear so extreme that it interferes with normal living. Phobias are learned through observation as well as through experience. (page 608)

- *Common phobias.* People are more likely to develop phobias of certain objects than of others; for example, snake phobias are more common than car phobias. The objects of the most common phobias have menaced humans throughout evolutionary history. They pose dangers that are difficult to predict or control, and they are generally objects with which we have had few safe experiences. (page 609)

- *Systematic desensitization of phobias.* A common therapy for phobia is systematic desensitization, in which the patient is taught to relax and is then gradually exposed to the object of the phobia. Flooding is similar except that the person is exposed to the object suddenly. (page 612)

- *Obsessive-compulsive disorder.* People with obsessive-compulsive disorder try to avoid certain thoughts or impulses that cause anxiety or guilt. They also have repetitive behaviors. (page 614)

- *Types of obsessive-compulsive disorder.* Two common types of compulsion are cleaning and checking. Cleaners try to avoid any type of contamination. Checkers constantly double-check themselves and invent elaborate rituals. (page 614)

SUGGESTION FOR FURTHER READING

Beck, A.T., & Emery, G. (1985). *Anxiety disorders and phobias.* New York: Basic Books. Influential description of both the symptoms and the treatment of anxiety disorders.

TERMS

generalized anxiety disorder disorder in which people are constantly plagued by exaggerated worries (page 606)

panic disorder disorder characterized by a fairly constant state of moderate anxiety and occasional attacks of sudden increased heart rate, chest pains, difficulty in breathing, sweating, faintness, and shaking (page 606)

social phobia a severe avoidance of other people and an especially strong fear of doing anything in public (page 606)

agoraphobia excessive fear of open places or public places (page 606)

hyperventilation deep breathing (page 607)

phobia a fear so extreme that it interferes with normal living (page 609)

systematic desensitization method of reducing fear by gradually exposing people to the object of their fear (page 612)

flooding or **implosion** a therapy for phobia in which the person is suddenly exposed to the object of the phobia (page 613)

obsessive-compulsive disorder condition with repetitive thoughts and actions (page 614)

obsession a repetitive, unwelcome stream of thought (page 614)

compulsion a repetitive, almost irresistible action (page 614)

ANSWERS TO CONCEPT CHECKS

2. Worrying about anything—even panic attacks themselves—often prompts these people to hyperventilate, and hyperventilation can in turn lead to another panic attack. (page 607)
3. Temporarily prevent the person from pressing the lever. Only by ceasing to press does the person discover that pressing is not necessary. (page 608)
4. The CS was the white rat. The UCS was the loud noise. The CR and the UCR were a combination of crying and other reactions of fear. (page 610)
5. The method of extinguishing a learned shock-avoidance response is to prevent the response so that the individual learns that the failure to respond is not followed by shock. Similarly, in systematic desensitization the patient is prevented from fleeing the feared stimulus; he or she therefore learns that the danger is not as great as imagined. (page 614)
6. The flooding procedure is compatible with the James-Lange theory of emotions, which holds that emotions follow from perceptions of body arousal. In flooding, as arousal of the autonomic nervous system decreases, the person perceives, "I am calming down. I must not be as frightened of this situation as I thought I was." (page 614)

ANSWERS TO OTHER QUESTIONS IN THE TEXT

Typical answers for obsessive-compulsive people (page 616): 1. T 2. T 3. T 4. F 5. F 6. T 7. F 8. F 9. T

SUBSTANCE-RELATED DISORDERS

Why do people sometimes abuse alcohol and other drugs?

What can be done to help them quit?

How would you like to volunteer for a little experiment? I want to implant a device in your head to control your brain activity—something that will automatically lift your mood and bring you happiness. There are still a few kinks in it, but most of the people who have tried it say it makes them feel good at least some of the time, and some people say it makes them feel "very happy."

I should tell you about the possible risks: My device will endanger your health and will reduce your life expectancy by, oh, 10 years or so. Some people think it may cause permanent brain damage, but they have not proved that charge, so I don't think you should worry about it. Your behavior will change a good bit, though. You may have difficulty concentrating, for example. The device affects some people more than others. If you happen to be one of those it affects strongly, you will have difficulty completing your education, getting or keeping a job, and carrying on a satisfactory personal life. But if you are lucky, you may avoid all that. Anyway, you can quit the experiment any time you want to. You should know, though, that the longer the device remains in your brain, the harder it is to get it out.

I cannot pay you for taking part in the experiment. In fact, *you* will have to pay *me*. But I'll give you a bargain rate: only $5 for the first week and then a little more each week as time passes. One other thing: Technically speaking, this experiment is illegal. We probably won't get caught, but if we do, we could both go to jail.

What do you say? Is it a deal? I presume you will say no. I get very few volunteers. And yet if I change the term *brain device* to *drug* and change *experimenter* to *drug peddler,* it is amazing how many volunteers come forward.

For some people, using alcohol or drugs is apparently a harmless pleasure. For others, it is extremely destructive. In Chapter 5 we examined the effects of several drugs on behavior. Instead of reviewing all of those drugs again here, we shall focus on substance abuse, principally of alcohol and opiates—addictions that have been familiar to humans for centuries and which continue to be major problems today. Substance-related disorders are extremely widespread.

SUBSTANCE DEPENDENCE (ADDICTION)

Some people drink alcohol or experiment with other drugs only in moderation. Others continue until they jeopardize their health, their work or education, and the welfare of their family. Substance abusers do not all follow the same pattern; they may use the substance daily, only on weekends, or only during sporadic binges. Those who cannot quit a self-destructive habit are said to have a dependence on a substance or an addiction to

Addiction is in the user, not in the drug. Some people will continue using drugs even though they know the drugs endanger their health, limit their opportunities, and provide them with little pleasure.

it. It is difficult to draw broad generalizations about the behavior of people who have a substance dependence. Many people with a dependence ask themselves, "Am I an alcoholic?" or "Am I addicted?" and manage, for a time, to convince themselves that they are not, because they do not use the substance every day or because they are able to keep a job. The same is true, however, for many alcoholics and addicts. A person has a dependence or addiction if the substance is causing trouble in life and if the person has found himself or herself unable to quit.

Almost any substance can be addictive under certain circumstances. In one hospital ward where alcoholics were being treated, one of the patients moved his bed into the men's room (Cummings, 1979). At first the hospital staff ignored this curious behavior. Then, one by one, other patients moved their beds into the men's room. Eventually the staff realized what was going on. These men, deprived of alcohol, had discovered that they could get a "high" by drinking enormous amounts of water! By drinking about 7.5 gallons (30 liters) of water a day and urinating the same amount (which was why they moved into the men's room), they managed to alter the acid-to-base balance of their blood enough to produce something like drunkenness. They had become "water addicts." Is water addictive? *The addiction is not in the drug but in the user.*

Nevertheless, some substances are much more likely than others to be addictive. Apparently, either all or nearly all of the commonly addictive drugs stimulate types D_2 and D_3 dopamine synapses in the brain (Caine & Koob, 1993; Uhl, Blum, Noble, & Smith, 1993; Wise & Bozarth, 1987). Also, other things being equal, the more rapidly a substance enters the brain, the more likely it is to be addictive. Cigarettes are more addictive than cigars, for example, because smokers inhale cigarette smoke more deeply, allowing the nicotine to enter the bloodstream and reach the brain more quickly (Bennett, 1980). For the same reason, crack cocaine is more addictive than other forms of cocaine.

You have no doubt learned that cigarette smoking is based largely on nicotine addiction. "If that is so," you may have wondered, "why have so many smokers switched to low-tar, low-nicotine cigarette brands? Wouldn't those brands fail to satisfy a nicotine craving?" Yes, they would . . . *if they delivered low nicotine!* A low-tar, low-nicotine cigarette has the same kind of tobacco as other cigarettes, but a different filter. The special feature of the filter is a row of little air holes, as shown at the top of Figure 14.14. The idea is that air entering through the air holes will dilute the tobacco smoke coming through the barrel of the cigarette. People who smoke that way do indeed get low tar and nicotine. However, many smokers wrap their fingers around the air holes, either accidentally or intentionally. Some even wrap tape over the holes. Regardless of whether or not they cover the holes, people who switch to low-nicotine cigarettes generally inhale more deeply than they did when smoking regular cigarettes, and they smoke more cigarettes per day. As a result of all these changes in their smoking behavior, people smoking low-nicotine cigarettes inhale about as much tar and nicotine per day as do people smoking regular cigarettes (Benowitz, 1986; Kozlowski, Frecker, Khouw, & Pope, 1980).

SOMETHING TO THINK ABOUT

Are there any addictive behaviors that are beneficial? (If a behavior is beneficial, can we call it *addictive?*)

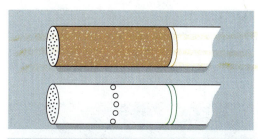

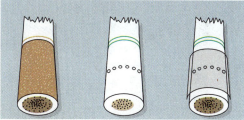

FIGURE 14.14

"Low-nicotine" cigarettes have a row of small holes in the filter; room air is supposed to enter through those holes and thereby dilute the tobacco smoke. If people smoke such cigarettes without covering the air holes, little tar and nicotine pass through the cigarette, as we see from the relatively clean filter tip. However, if people cover the holes with tape or (more commonly) with their fingers, they get about as much tar and nicotine as they would from any other filtered cigarette.

7. Methadone, an opiate drug, can be taken either as an injection (entering the blood rapidly) or as a pill (entering the blood slowly). Which route is more likely to lead to addiction? (Check your answer on page 626.)

PREDISPOSITION TO ADDICTION

Although only a minority of alcohol drinkers become alcoholics, many alcoholics become addicted before they reach age 25 (Cloninger, 1987). Some people try heroin once or twice and then quit; others inject themselves so frequently they eventually destroy every vein they can find (Dole, 1978). Why do some people become addicted while others do not?

Most of the research has dealt with alcoholism, the most common addiction, so we shall focus on predisposition to alcoholism. Might it be possible to determine in advance which people are most likely to develop into alcoholics? If we could identify those people early enough, we might be able to train them to drink in moderation or to abstain altogether.

GENETICS AND FAMILY BACKGROUND

There is convincing evidence that genetics plays some role in predisposition to alcoholism, although different studies give conflicting results about the size of that role (Cadoret, Troughton, & Woodworth, 1994). The close biological relatives of alcoholics are more likely to become alcoholics themselves than are the relatives of nonalcoholics (Gabrielli & Plomin, 1985). That holds true even when the children of alcoholics are adopted by people who are not alcoholics (Cloninger, Bohman, & Sigvardsson, 1981; Vaillant & Milofsky, 1982). However, people who have no alcoholic relatives should not consider themselves safe; even people with no family history of alcoholism sometimes develop an alcohol problem.

The incidence of alcoholism is greater than average among people who grew up in families marked by conflict between the parents, poor relationships between parents and children, and inadequate parental supervision of the children (Maddahian, Newcomb, & Bentler, 1988; Schulsinger, Knop, Goodwin, Teasdale, & Mikkelsen, 1986; Zucker & Gomberg, 1986). The culture in which children are raised also plays a role. For example, most Jewish families emphasize drinking in moderation, and relatively few Jews become alcoholics (Cahalan, 1978). That conclusion is more or less true of Italians as well. By contrast, the Irish tend to be more tolerant of heavy drinking, and alcoholism is more prevalent among people of Irish background (Vaillant & Milofsky, 1982).

Still, individuals differ. Not all children of alcoholic parents become alcoholics themselves, and not all children who grow up in a culture that tolerates heavy drinking become alcoholics. Again, how can we predict which people are most vulnerable to alcoholism?

Jewish and Italian cultures, which stress moderation, have a fair amount of alcohol use but relatively little alcohol abuse.

WHAT'S THE EVIDENCE?

Ways of Predicting Alcoholism

Perhaps a person's early behavior might offer some indicator of who is more likely or less likely to become an alcoholic. One way to find such a clue would be to record the presence or absence of various behaviors in hundreds of young people. Twenty years later we find out which of them have become alcoholics and determine which early behaviors would have predicted those outcomes. Such a study would take 20 years. Moreover, it might be difficult to find some of the subjects after that time, especially the alcoholics.

A more feasible approach would be to compare children of an alcoholic parent with children of parents who are not alcoholics. From previous studies, we know that more children of alcoholics will become alcoholics. Therefore, behaviors that are significantly more prevalent among the children of alcoholics may predict vulnerability to alcoholism.

In the first of the following studies, experimenters tested whether alcohol might be more rewarding to the sons of alcoholics than to the sons of nonalcoholics (Levenson, Oyama, & Meek, 1987). (The study focused on men because alcoholism is about twice as common in men as in women.)

EXPERIMENT 1

Hypothesis When people are put into a stressful situation, an opportunity to drink alcohol will reduce stress for almost everyone. It will have a greater effect on the adult sons of an alcoholic parent than on other men the same age.

Method The experiment was conducted on young men, half of them sons of an alcoholic father and half of them sons of nonalcoholic parents. The men were told that at a certain time they would receive an electric shock and at another time they would have to give a 3-minute speech on "What I like and dislike about my body." They watched a clock tick off the waiting time. Half of each group was given alcohol to drink at the start of the waiting period, and everyone who was offered alcohol drank it.

Results All of the men showed considerable stress, as measured by heart rate, restlessness, and self-reports of emotions. All of those who drank alcohol showed a lower heart rate and reported less anxiety. The easing of stress was more pronounced in those who had an alcoholic father (Figure 14.15).

Interpretation Men who are genetically vulnerable to alcoholism experience greater stress-reducing effects from alcohol than other men of the same age. Perhaps the degree to which alcohol relieves stress may provide a measure of vulnerability to alcoholism.

Two other experiments examined the possibility that young men who are vulnerable to alcoholism might have trouble estimating their own degree of intoxication (O'Malley & Maisto, 1985; Schuckit, 1985).

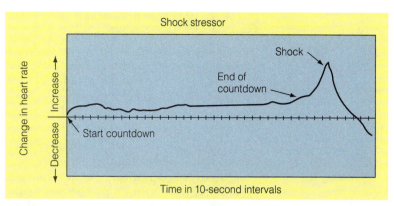

FIGURE 14.15
Changes in stress over time for a typical subject. The line goes up to indicate an increase in heart rate. Note that heart rate increased as soon as the countdown began and then remained stable. It rose toward the end of the countdown and again at the time of the shock or speech. Alcohol suppressed these signs of stress, especially for the sons of alcoholics. (From Levenson, Oyama, & Meek, 1987.)

Because these two experiments used practically the same method and reported the same pattern of results, I shall report them as one.

EXPERIMENT 2

Hypothesis Sons of an alcoholic father will underestimate how much they have been affected by the alcohol they have drunk.

Method Young men, some sons of alcoholic fathers and some sons of nonalcoholic parents, consumed drinks containing various amounts of vodka. None of them knew how much vodka was in the drinks. After consuming the drinks, they performed various motor and cognitive tasks. They also estimated how much vodka they had drunk and how intoxicated they were.

Results The sons of alcoholic fathers were just as much affected as the sons of nonalcoholics were in their motor and cognitive performance. However, they consistently underestimated how much vodka they had drunk and how intoxicated they were.

Interpretation Men who are not especially vulnerable to alcoholism are quick to recognize when they have started to become tipsy and generally stop drinking at that time. Men who are genetically more vulnerable to alcoholism are slower to recognize the signs of intoxication and continue drinking. Again, it may be possible to identify individuals who are particularly prone to alcoholism by testing their ability to monitor their own level of intoxication.

Every study has its strengths and its limitations, and you probably have noticed one of the major limitations of these studies on predisposition to alcohol abuse: They deal entirely with men. Starting with men is reasonable; after all, alcohol abuse is more common in men than in women. Still, someone needs to repeat these studies with women. The studies just discussed have other limitations, too; for example, they tested people's responses just once instead of repeatedly, and the studies were conducted in laboratory settings instead of normal drinking environments (Newlin & Thomson, 1990). As with most areas of research, investigators start with a fairly simple but limited design and then proceed with additional research to find out how broadly the conclusions apply.

TREATMENTS FOR ALCOHOLISM AND DRUG ADDICTION

At some point, someone with a drug or alcohol problem tries to quit. An estimated 10–20% do manage to quit on their own (Cohen et al., 1989), though not necessarily on the first try. A person may quit and relapse, quit and relapse many times before eventually succeeding. In many cases, however, people with a substance-abuse problem find that they cannot quit on their own. Eventually they "hit bottom"; they discover that they have damaged their health, their ability to hold a job, and their relationships with friends and family. At that point, they turn to others for help—either a mental-health professional or a self-help group such as Alcoholics Anonymous.

People who seek professional help improve their likelihood of long-term abstention, although there are no guarantees. Clinical psychologists spend an estimated one-fifth to one-fourth of their time with patients suffering from substance-abuse problems (Cummings, 1979). Addicts who check into a hospital for treatment can be supervised 24 hours a day to ensure full abstinence. **Detoxification refers to a supervised period to remove drugs from the body.** In the long run, however, most addicts respond just as well to outpatient treatment as they do to hospital treatment (Miller & Hester, 1986).

Therapists use many methods for helping people overcome substance-related disorders. In Chapter 15 we shall consider methods of therapy in general, as they apply to all types of disorders. Here we focus on methods that apply exclusively to substance abuse.

TREATING ALCOHOLISM

"If, when you honestly want to, you find you cannot quit entirely, or if when drinking, you have little control over the amount you take, you are probably alcoholic."
ANONYMOUS (1955)

"My mind is a dark place, and I should not be left alone there at night."
UNIDENTIFIED PARTICIPANT AT ALCOHOLICS ANONYMOUS MEETING

Alcoholism, the habitual overuse of alcohol, is the most common and most costly form of drug abuse in the United States and Europe. An estimated 25–40% of all hospital patients suffer from complications caused by alcohol abuse (Holden, 1987).

Alcoholics Anonymous The most widespread treatment for alcoholism in North America is **Alcoholics Anonymous (AA),** a self-help group of people who are trying to abstain from alcohol use and to help others do the same. In all large cities, and in many smaller cities and towns, AA meetings are held regularly in community halls, church basements, and other available spaces (Figure 14.16). The format for a meeting often includes study of the book *Alcoholics Anonymous* (Anonymous, 1955) and discussions of participants' individual problems; some meetings feature an invited speaker. The group has a strong spiritual focus, including a reliance on "a Power greater than ourselves," although AA has no affiliation with any particular religion. Although AA imposes no requirements on its members, it strongly encourages new members to attend 90 meetings during the first 90 days. (Those who miss one day can compensate by attending two or more meetings another day.) From then on, members attend as often as they like.

Millions of people worldwide have participated in the AA program. **One reason for its appeal is that all the members have gone through similar experiences.** If someone tries to make an excuse for drinking, saying, "You just don't understand how I feel," others can retort, "Oh, yes we do!" Fellow sufferers make very understanding listeners. A member who feels the urge to take a drink, or who has already had one, can call a fellow member day or night for support. There is no charge for attendance at meetings; members simply contribute what they can toward the cost of the meeting place. AA has inspired other "anonymous" self-help groups whose purpose is to help drug addicts, compulsive gamblers, compulsive eaters, and so forth.

Although AA members themselves have no doubt about the value of the program, research on its effectiveness has been scarce. One reason is that the organization is serious about its members' anonymity; it does not provide a list of members, and many of its meetings are closed to nonmembers.

About 50% of AA members abstain from alcohol altogether for at least 18 months after joining; others try to abstain but suffer occasional relapses (Emrick, 1987; Thurstin, Alfano, & Nerviano, 1987). Those results compare favorably to the results for alcoholics in other programs and for alcoholics who try to quit on their own. Still, because assignment to groups is not random, we cannot draw a firm conclusion. (Perhaps people who join AA are more highly motivated to quit than other alcoholics are.)

Antabuse In addition to or instead of attendance at AA meetings, many alcoholics seek medical treatment. Many years ago, investigators noticed that the workers in a certain rubber manufacturing plant drank very little alcohol. The investigators eventually linked this behavior to disulfiram, a chemical that was used in the manufacturing process. Ordinarily, the liver converts alcohol into a toxic substance, acetaldehyde (ASS-eh-TAL-de-HIDE), and then converts acetaldehyde into a harmless substance, acetic acid. Disulfiram, however, blocks the conversion of acetaldehyde to acetic acid. Whenever the workers drank alcohol, acetaldehyde accumulated in their body and they became ill. Over time, they learned to avoid all use of alcohol.

Disulfiram, under the trade name **Antabuse,** is now commonly used in the treatment of alcoholism (Peachey & Naranjo, 1983). Alcoholics who take a daily Antabuse pill become very sick whenever they have a drink. They develop a sensation of heat in the face, a headache, nausea, blurred vision, and anxiety. The threat of sickness is probably more effective than the sickness itself (Fuller & Roth, 1979). By taking a daily pill, a recovering alcoholic renews a decision not to drink. Those who actually do take a drink

FIGURE 14.16
Alcoholics Anonymous (AA) is the prototypical example of self-help groups. AA meetings are held throughout the United States and in many other countries throughout the world. Members share their experiences with one another and provide encouragement and help to members in need. A member who is fighting a craving for alcohol can call a fellow member for help at any time; each understands the problems that others are having. AA makes many recommendations, but its only requirement is that members try to overcome their alcohol problems.

in spite of the threat get quite ill, at which point they may decide not to drink again, or they may decide not to take the pill again!

CONCEPT CHECK

8. About 50% of Asians have a gene that makes them unable to convert acetaldehyde to acetic acid. Would such people be more likely or less likely than others to become alcoholics? (Check your answer on page 626.)

IS SUBSTANCE ABUSE A "DISEASE"?

You have no doubt heard people say that alcoholism is a disease or that drug abuse is a disease. It is hard to confirm or deny that statement, however, unless someone specifies exactly what the term *disease* means. (The medical profession gives the term no precise meaning, and the term has a wide variety of connotations.) When people call alcoholism or drug abuse a disease, they apparently mean that alcoholics and drug abusers should feel no guiltier about their condition than they would feel about having pneumonia.

Although the "disease" concept is far preferable to thinking of substance abuse as a sign of moral weakness, the concept has some implications that the data do not support.

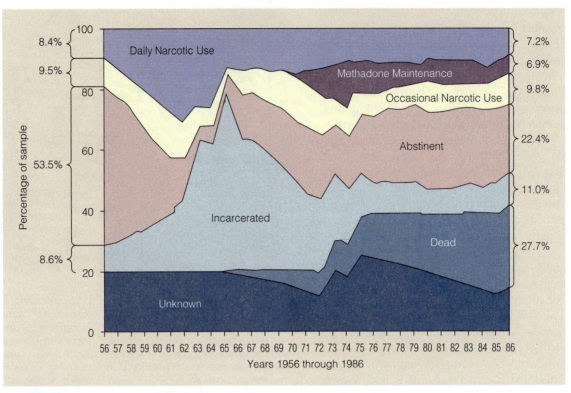

FIGURE 14.17
Researchers studied 581 young adult male narcotics addicts in 1962–1964. They asked these men about their previous drug use and located most of them again in later years to check on their progress. Over time, the results varied. Some died or went to prison; some continued using drugs as before; some decreased their use of drugs; and some abstained altogether. (From Hser, Anglin, & Powers, 1993.)

For example, the "disease" concept implies that alcoholism or drug abuse becomes inevitably worse over time. In fact, the long-term outcome for alcoholics and drug abusers varies enormously (Hser, Anglin, & Powers, 1993; Vaillant, 1983). As Figure 14.17 shows, some individuals deteriorate rapidly and severely, some reach a steady level of abuse, and still others show a gradual improvement in their condition over time.

Furthermore, to conceive of alcoholism strictly as a disease downplays the importance of environmental factors (Marlatt, 1978). Excessive drinking can sometimes be brought under control by altering the environment. For example, helping an alcoholic or drug user to get a job can improve the person's life and sometimes leads to decreased use of the substance (Platt, 1995).

The "Controlled Drinking" Controversy
Most physicians agree with Alcoholics Anonymous that the only hope for an alcoholic is total abstinence. Drinking in moderation, they insist, is out of the question.

A few psychologists, however, are not convinced that abstinence is the best advice for *all* alcoholics. Some alcoholics who try to abstain repeatedly fail; a few of these people do learn to reduce their drinking without eliminating it altogether. This is not to say that alcoholics can simply decide to drink in moderation; those who were capable of doing so would not have become alcoholics in the first place. Rather, the point is that a few people who fail to stick to an abstention program can learn (with difficulty) to drink a little less than they have been, to stay out of legal trouble, and in general to do themselves less damage. Psychologists have established a number of programs that try to teach alcoholics "controlled drinking," with at least occasional success. Generally, the more severe someone's alcohol problem, the less likely that person is to learn controlled drinking (Rosenberg, 1993). Beyond that generalization, psychologists have not yet found ways to predict which people might respond well to controlled drinking programs.

TREATING OPIATE ADDICTION

Before the year 1900, opiate drugs such as morphine and heroin were considered far less dangerous than alcohol (Siegel, 1987). In fact, many medical doctors used to urge their alcoholic patients to switch from alcohol to morphine. Then, around 1900, the use of opiates was made illegal in the United States, except by prescription for relief from pain. Since then, research on opiate use has been limited by the fact that only lawbreakers now use opiates.

Some users of heroin and other opiates try to break their habit by going "cold turkey"—abstaining altogether until the withdrawal symptoms subside, sometimes under medical supervision. Many people, however, experience a recurring urge to take the drug, even long after the withdrawal symptoms have subsided. For those who cannot quit, researchers have sought to find a nonaddictive substitute that would satisfy the craving for opiates without creating their harmful effects. Heroin was originally introduced as a substitute for morphine. Soon, however, physicians discovered that heroin is even more addictive and troublesome than morphine.

Today, the most common substitute for opiates is methadone (METH-uh-don). Methadone is chemically similar to both morphine and heroin and can itself be addictive. (Table 14.5 compares methadone and morphine.) When taken in pill form, however, methadone takes hours to enter and leave the bloodstream (Dole, 1980). (If morphine or heroin is taken as a pill, most of the drug is broken down in the digestive system and never reaches the brain.) Thus methadone does not produce the "rush" associated with intravenous injections of opiates; nor does it produce rapid withdrawal symptoms. Although methadone satisfies the craving for opiates without seriously disrupting the user's behavior, it does not eliminate the addiction itself. If the dosage is reduced, the craving returns.

Many addicts who stick to a methadone maintenance program are able to hold down a job and commit fewer crimes than they did when they were using heroin or morphine (Woody & O'Brien, 1986). Some of them, after discovering that they can no longer obtain a high from opiates, turn instead to the nonopiate drug cocaine (Kosten, Rounsaville, & Kleber, 1987). In other words, methadone maintenance programs

do not eliminate the addictive behaviors. At present, there is no reliable cure for opiate dependence.

TABLE 14.5 Comparison of Methadone with Morphine			
	MORPHINE	METHADONE BY INJECTION	METHADONE TAKEN ORALLY
Addictive?	Yes	Yes	Weakly
Onset	Rapid	Rapid	Slow
"Rush"?	Yes	Yes	No
Relieves craving?	Yes	Yes	Yes
Rapid withdrawal symptoms?	Yes	Yes	No

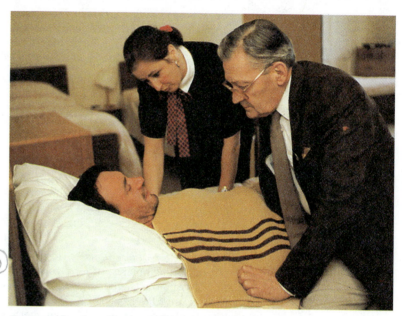

Going cold turkey: Heroin withdrawal resembles a severe bout of the flu, with aching limbs, intense chills, vomiting, and diarrhea; it lasts a week on average. Unfortunately, even after people have suffered through withdrawal, they are likely to experience periods of craving for the drug.

SUMMARY

• *Substance dependence.* People who find it difficult or impossible to stop using a substance are said to be dependent on it or addicted to it. (page 618)

• *Addictive substances.* Generally, the faster a substance enters the brain, the more likely it is to be addictive. Cigarette smokers inhale enough nicotine to satisfy an addiction, even if they smoke low-nicotine brands. (page 619)

- *Predisposition to alcoholism.* Some people may be predisposed to become alcoholics for genetic or other reasons. People at risk for alcoholism find that alcohol relieves their stress more than it does for other people. They also tend to underestimate how intoxicated they are. (page 620)

- *Alcoholics Anonymous.* The most common treatment for alcoholism in North America is provided by the self-help group called Alcoholics Anonymous. (page 622)

- *Antabuse.* Some alcoholics are treated with Antabuse, a prescription drug that makes them ill if they drink alcohol. (page 623)

- *The "disease" concept.* Whether or not substance abuse is a disease depends on how we define the term "disease." The long-term course varies among different alcoholics or drug abusers. Amount of substance use also depends on environmental factors, not just on a "disease" within the person. (page 623)

- *The "controlled drinking" controversy.* Whether alcoholics can be trained to drink in moderation is a controversial, unsettled question. A few alcoholics, especially those with a less severe problem, may learn to reduce their drinking and the harm it causes. However, for most alcoholics, controlled drinking is an unrealistic goal. (page 624)

- *Treatments for opiate abuse.* Some opiate users quit using opiates, suffer through the withdrawal symptoms, and manage to abstain from further use. Others substitute methadone under medical supervision. Although methadone has fewer destructive effects than morphine or heroin, it does not eliminate the underlying dependence. (page 625)

SUGGESTION FOR FURTHER READING

Marlatt, G. A., & Baer, J. S. (1988). Addictive behaviors: Etiology and treatment. *Annual Review of Psychology, 39,* 223–252. A review of the literature on who becomes an alcoholic or drug addict, why, and what can be done to help.

TERMS

dependence or **addiction** a self-destructive habit that someone cannot break (page 618)

detoxification supervised period to remove drugs from the body (page 622)

alcoholism habitual overuse of alcohol (page 622)

Alcoholics Anonymous (AA) a self-help group of people who are trying to abstain from alcohol use and to help others do the same (page 622)

Antabuse trade name for disulfiram, a drug used in the treatment of alcoholism (page 623)

methadone a drug commonly offered as a less dangerous substitute for opiates (page 625)

ANSWERS TO CONCEPT CHECKS

7. The injection route is more likely to lead to addiction. Other things being equal, the faster a drug reaches the brain, the more likely it is to become addictive. (page 620)

8. They are less likely than others to become alcoholics. This gene is considered the probable reason why relatively few Asians become alcoholics (Harada, Agarwal, Goedde, Tagaki, & Ishikawa, 1982; Reed, 1985). (page 623)

MOOD DISORDERS

Why do people become depressed?
What can be done to relieve depression?
How are depression and suicide related?

Even when things are going badly, most people remain optimistic that all will be well in the end. After the hurt and disappointment we feel when a relationship breaks up, we say, "Oh, well, at least I learned something from the experience." When we lose money, we say, "It could have been worse. I still have my health."

But sometimes we feel depressed. Nothing seems as much fun as it used to be, and the future seems ominous. For some people, the depression is severe and long-lasting. Why?

The appearance of depressed people mirrors their feelings of sadness and hopelessness, as this painting by Edvard Munch shows. Downcast eyes and sagging head and shoulders accompany slow movement. Suggestions to "smile" or "cheer up" fall on deaf ears.

DEPRESSION

When people say, "I'm depressed," they often mean "I am sad; life isn't going very well for me right now." In psychology, depression refers to a much more extreme condition. For example, Aaron Beck (1973) described one depressed woman who stood in front of an elevator for 15 minutes because she did not have enough desire to press the button. A serious depression lasts most of the day, day after day. The person experiences little interest, little pleasure, little reason for any productive activity. Even if life starts going well for the person, the depression persists.

Depressed people have trouble concentrating. Their appetite and sex interest decrease (Nofzinger et al., 1993). Their facial expression is typically sad. They feel worthless, fearful, guilty, and powerless to control what happens to them. Most of them consider suicide, and many attempt it. Depression is common at all ages, from adolescence through old age.

Nearly all depressed people experience sleep abnormalities (Carroll, 1980; Healy & Williams, 1988). (See Figure 14.18.) They enter REM sleep in less than 45 minutes after falling asleep (an unusually short time for most people). Most depressed people wake up too early and cannot get back to sleep. When morning comes, they feel poorly rested. In fact, early morning is usually the time when they feel most depressed. During most of the day they feel a little sleepy.

Depression, like any other psychological disorder, can vary in degree. For some people an episode of depression persists for months at a time and may recur periodically year after year. Bipolar disorder, also known as *manic-depressive disorder,* is a related condition in which a person alternates between periods of depression and periods of mania, which is the opposite extreme. We shall return to bipolar disorder later.

FIGURE 14.18

When most people go to sleep at their normal time of day, they progress slowly to stage 4 and then back through stages 3 and 2, reaching REM toward the end of their first 90-minute cycle. Depressed people, however, reach REM more rapidly, generally in less than 45 minutes. They also tend to awaken frequently during the night.

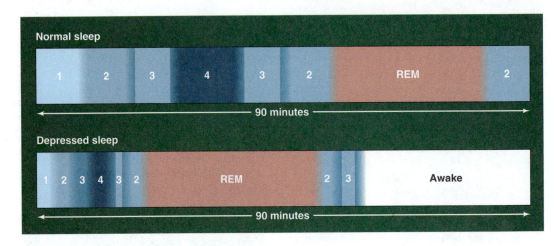

Many psychologists also distinguish between reactive and endogenous depressions. A **reactive depression** develops suddenly in reaction to a severe loss, such as the death of a spouse. An **endogenous depression** develops more gradually and cannot be traced to any single traumatic experience. Rather, it seems to result from internal, biological influences.

In practice, this distinction is difficult to draw. In most cases, one can identify both reactive and endogenous features that probably combined to produce depression. Moreover, classifying someone's depression as mostly reactive or mostly endogenous does not tell us whether the condition will respond better to drugs or to some form of psychotherapy (Gallagher-Thompson et al., 1992).

GENETIC PREDISPOSITION TO DEPRESSION

The fact that depression tends to run in families suggests that some people have a genetic predisposition to depression (see Figure 14.19). Depression is two to five times more common among the close relatives of a depressed person than it is in the population at large and is even more common among the relatives of people who developed depression before age 30 (Price, Kidd, & Weissman, 1987). Depressed people also have many relatives who, if not exactly depressed themselves, show sleep abnormalities similar to those of depression (Lauer, Schreiber, Holsboer, & Krieg, 1995), and many relatives who develop anxiety disorders or substance abuse (Kendler, Heath, Neale, Kessler, & Eaves, 1993; Kendler, Neale, Kessler, Heath, & Eaves, 1992). It is likely that certain families have genes that express themselves in different ways, leading to depression in some people and to other disorders in other people.

Adopted children who become depressed usually have more biological relatives than adopting relatives who are depressed (Wender et al., 1986). So far we do not have consistent evidence to indicate whether depression depends on one gene or several (Faraone, Kremen, & Tsuang, 1990). Chances are, a disposition to depression depends on different genes or gene combinations in different families.

THE SEX DIFFERENCE IN PREVALENCE OF DEPRESSION

From adolescence onward, at least in Europe and North America, women are about twice as likely as men to experience moderate to

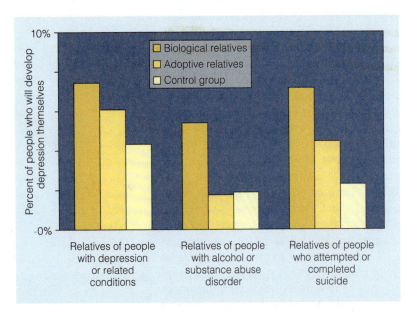

FIGURE 14.19

When compared with the incidence of depression in the general public, which is 5–10%, blood relatives of a depressed person are more likely to suffer depression themselves. (Based on data of Beardslee, Bemporad, Keller, & Klerman, 1983; Weissman, Kidd, & Prusoff, 1982.)

severe depression (Nolen-Hoeksema, 1990). We do not have enough good data to draw conclusions about sex ratios for depression in other cultures of the world. Why is depression more common in women than it is in men?

One possibility is that hormonal changes in women's menstrual cycles or as a result of pregnancy and childbirth trigger episodes of depression. For example, shortly after giving birth, a time of massive hormonal changes, some women enter a **postpartum depression.** Estimates of the frequency of postpartum depression vary widely, depending on whether one counts only the severe cases (about 1 per 1,000), the moderate cases (about 1 in 10), or the mild cases (about 3 in 10). However, most of the women who suffer moderate to severe postpartum depression have a history of other depressive episodes; the hormonal swing after giving birth is not so much a *cause* of depression as it is a trigger for an additional depressive episode (O'Hara, Schlechte, Lewis, & Wright, 1991).

The evidence does not make a convincing case that hormones account for the higher prevalence of depression in women than in men. Psychologists have considered a number of other hypotheses, such as that women are more likely than men to report their depression and seek help, that many depressed men get a diagnosis of alcoholism instead of depression, and that women become depressed in reaction to their lower status and power. Although each of these possibilities probably contributes to the sex difference in depression, the evidence does not strongly support any one of them as a fully adequate explanation (Nolen-Hoeksema, 1990). (For example, the fact that women have lower status and power than men does not explain why some women become depressed and other equally low-status women do not.)

Susan Nolen-Hoeksema (1990) has suggested another possibility: When men start to feel depressed, they generally try to distract themselves. They try not to think about whatever is making them depressed; they play basketball or watch a movie or do something else that they enjoy. Women are more likely to ruminate—to think about why they are depressed, to talk with others about their feelings, even to have a long cry. According to Nolen-Hoeksema (1991), ruminating about depression only makes it worse. The ruminative thoughts interfere with useful problem-solving and bias a per-

son toward a pessimistic appraisal of a situation. This explanation has the advantage of suggesting ways to help women (and men) avoid or minimize their depression. It does not, however, address the question of *why* women ruminate more and distract themselves less than men do.

EVENTS THAT PRECIPITATE DEPRESSION

As a rule, people become depressed when bad things happen to them. For example, most people are clearly depressed for at least the first two months after the death of a spouse (Thompson, Gallagher-Thompson, Futterman, Gilewski, & Peterson, 1991). Also, an unpleasant event in the life of either a mother or her child increases the likelihood of depressed feelings for both of them (Adrian & Hammen, 1993). However, the severity of an unpleasant event is a poor predictor of how depressed a person will become after it. Some people become depressed without any apparent stressful experience (Brown, Harris, & Hepworth, 1994), and some depressed people bring about their own stressful events (Hammen, 1991).

Illustrating the differences among people in their responses to a stressful event, one study took advantage of the fact that students in one California university had answered questionnaires about their mental health 2 weeks before a major earthquake hit in 1989. Psychologists asked the same students to fill out questionnaires 10 days and 7 weeks after the earthquake. The result was that students who were already somewhat depressed before the earthquake became very depressed afterward; students who were not depressed earlier suffered some distress but in most cases recovered rapidly (Nolen-Hoeksema & Morrow, 1991). In other words, a given event will produce depression in people who are highly vulnerable but probably not in other people.

So, what makes some people more vulnerable than others? One explanation is that severe losses early in life make people more vulnerable to depression later on. For example, adolescents who lose a parent through death or divorce are likely to react strongly to other losses later in life, even to routine events such as breaking up with a boyfriend or girlfriend (Roy, 1985).

People with poor social support also tend to be vulnerable to depression. As we saw in Chapter 12, social support helps people cope

Depression is most common among people who have little social support.

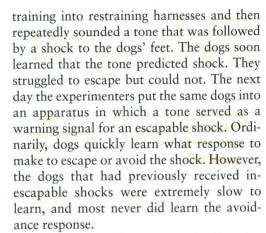

with stress. People with a happy marriage and close friends are less likely to become depressed or to remain depressed than are people who have no one to talk to about their troubles, or people who fail to make use of the social support that their friends offer (Rivera, Rose, Futterman, Lovett, & Gallagher-Thompson, 1991).

What matters in the onset of depression is not *what* events happen, but *how* people interpret them. For example, a trivial event such as not being invited to a party might contribute toward depression for someone who regarded the noninvitation as evidence of rejection by other people (Johnson & Roberts, 1995). To understand who becomes depressed and why, we have to understand how people think.

COGNITIVE ASPECTS OF DEPRESSION

Most people believe that every cloud has a silver lining. Show depressed people a silver lining and they wrap it in a cloud. Somehow they think differently from people who are not depressed. Do their thoughts lead to their depression?

THE LEARNED-HELPLESSNESS MODEL

According to one early influential theory, the learned-helplessness theory, people become depressed if their experiences teach them that they have no control over the major events in their lives. The learned-helplessness theory originated with some experiments with animals. While testing theories about avoidance learning in animals, Steven Maier, Martin Seligman, and Richard Solomon (1969) strapped some dogs with no previous

training into restraining harnesses and then repeatedly sounded a tone that was followed by a shock to the dogs' feet. The dogs soon learned that the tone predicted shock. They struggled to escape but could not. The next day the experimenters put the same dogs into an apparatus in which a tone served as a warning signal for an escapable shock. Ordinarily, dogs quickly learn what response to make to escape or avoid the shock. However, the dogs that had previously received inescapable shocks were extremely slow to learn, and most never did learn the avoidance response.

Why? Besides learning on the first day that the tone predicted shock, the dogs had also learned that the shock was inescapable. On the second day, when they started receiving shocks, they made no effort to escape. They had learned that they were helpless.

These "helpless" dogs resembled depressed people in several respects. The dogs were inactive and slow to learn. Even their posture and "facial expressions" suggested sadness. The experimenters proposed that the same process might operate in humans: People who, despite their best efforts, meet only with defeat and loss may come to feel "helpless" and fall into depression.

EXPLANATORY STYLES

The learned-helplessness hypothesis, though appealing, is no longer considered a viable explanation for depression, at least not in its original form. Experiments with humans failed to confirm that struggling with impossible tasks makes people feel depressed. It is not *failure* itself that makes people depressed, but *why people think they have failed*. For example, suppose you fail a French test. How bad you feel depends on why you think you failed:

• I failed because the test was so hard. This prof always makes the first test of the semester extra difficult just to scare us into studying harder.
• I failed because I'm the only one in the class who didn't take French in high school.
• I failed because I was sick and didn't get a chance to study.
• I failed because I'm stupid.

With any of the first three attributions for failure, you probably wouldn't feel very depressed. You would be attributing your failure to a temporary, specific, or correctable situation—a problem that has nothing to do with your abilities. But the fourth attribution applies to you at all times in all situations. If you make that attribution—and if your grades are important to you—you are likely to feel depressed about your low grade (Abramson, Seligman, & Teasdale, 1978; Peterson, Bettes, & Seligman, 1985). If you continue making similar attributions in many other situations, your depression may grow.

In a given situation, such as your low grade on a French test, you might have a good reason for one attribution or another. For example, perhaps you really are the only one in the class who did not take high-school French. Still, everyone has an explanatory style, a tendency to accept one kind of explanation for success or failure more often than others. For example, some people tend to use *internal* attributions, looking for a cause within themselves. ("I failed the French test because I did not study properly. I did well on the biology test because I spent many hours studying.") Other people tend to use *external* attributions, seeking causes outside themselves. ("I failed the French test because it was extremely hard. I did well on the biology test because it was easy.") People are not always consistent in how they explain their successes, but they tend to be very consistent, even over decades, in how they explain their failures. That is, people who generally blame themselves for their failures today will probably be doing the same thing 30 or 40 years from now (Burns & Seligman, 1989).

People who consistently take the blame for their own failures are said to have a *pessimistic* explanatory style, especially if their explanations for failure are stable and global. For example, "I failed the French test because I did not study hard" is an unstable explanation, because you can study harder next time. "I failed the test because I am poor at learning foreign languages" is a stable explanation, because it implies a permanent characteristic. "I failed the test because I am stupid" is not only stable but also global; it applies not only to foreign languages but to all kinds of learning.

Researchers can determine people's explanatory style by asking them to explain some of their successes and failures. They can also gauge the explanatory styles of famous people, even dead people, by reading their speeches and writings to find out what explanations they offered for successes and failures. Using this method, psychologists have found that pessimistic political leaders tend to be cautious, indecisive, and inactive. Leaders with an optimistic explanatory style (the opposite of a pessimistic style) tend to be bold, active, even risky (Satterfield & Seligman, 1994; Zullow, Oettingen, Peterson, & Seligman, 1988). (See Figure 14.20.) Athletes with a pessimistic style tend to give up after a defeat; for them, one defeat leads to another. Athletes with a more optimistic style keep on trying and even try harder after a defeat since, after all, they think the defeat was not their fault (Seligman, Nolen-Hoeksema, Thornton, & Thornton, 1990).

Although pessimism is hardly the same thing as depression, people with a pessimistic style are more likely than others to become depressed. Indeed, according to Aaron Beck (1973, 1987), depressed people consistently put unfavorable interpretations on the events of their lives. If someone walks by, the response is, "See, people ignore me. They don't like me." After any kind of loss or defeat, "I'm a loser. I'm hopeless." After any kind of win, "That was just luck. I had nothing to do with it." Depressed people exaggerate their failures, minimize their successes, and give themselves a very low evaluation. Given this explanatory style, almost any event seems like further grounds for feeling depressed. As we shall see in Chapter 15, effective psychotherapies for depression break people out

FIGURE 14.20
During the Gulf War of 1991, the speeches of U.S. President George Bush and Iraqi leader Saddam Hussein varied between optimistic and pessimistic styles. Both tended to make bold, risky decisions at about the same time they were making optimistic speeches; both were passive and cautious when they were making pessimistic speeches (Satterfield & Seligman, 1994).

of this cycle, helping them to stop seeing everything they do in a bad light.

CONCEPT CHECK

9. *Would depressed people be more or less likely than undepressed people to buy a lottery ticket? (Check your answers on page 636.)*

SEASONAL AFFECTIVE DISORDER

One variety of depression is known as **seasonal affective disorder, or depression with a seasonal pattern** (Figure 14.21). People with this disorder become seriously depressed once a year during a particular season. Although annual winter depressions have received the most publicity, annual summer depressions also occur (Faedda et al., 1993). Unlike most other depressed patients, people with seasonal affective disorder tend to sleep and eat excessively during their depressed periods (Jacobsen, Sack, Wehr, Rogers, & Rosenthal, 1987).

People with the winter variety of seasonal affective disorder respond to the amount of sunlight they see each day. Most

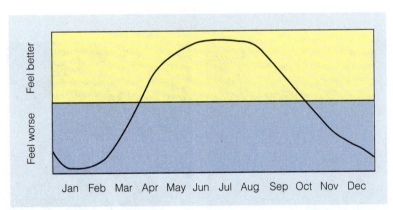

FIGURE 14.21
Most people have a slightly more pleasant mood during the summer (when the sun is out most of the day) than during the winter (when the day has fewer hours of sunlight). A small number of people—those with seasonal affective disorder—show an exaggerated tendency, feeling extremely good in the summer and seriously depressed in the winter. Seasonal affective disorder is more common in far-northern locations such as Alaska, where the summer days have many hours of sunlight and the winter days have few. It is unheard of in tropical locations such as Hawaii, where the amount of sunlight per day varies only slightly between summer and winter.

of us are more cheerful when the sun is shining than we are on cloudy days, but these people are unusually sensitive to the effects of sunlight. Seasonal affective disorder can be relieved by sitting for a few hours each day in front of a bright light after the sun sets or before it rises—artificially lengthening the day and resetting the body's biological clock (Wehr et al., 1986).

BIPOLAR DISORDER

People with bipolar disorder (also known as manic-depressive disorder) alternate between the extremes of mania and depression. In most respects, **mania** is the opposite of depression. When people with bipolar disorder are in the depressed phase, they are slow, inactive, and inhibited. When they are in the manic phase, they are constantly active and uninhibited. When depressed, they feel helpless, guilt ridden, and sad. When manic, they are either happy or angry. About 1% of all adults in the United States suffer from bipolar disorder at some time during their lives (Robins et al., 1984).

People in a manic phase have trouble inhibiting their impulses. Mental hospitals cannot install fire alarms in certain wards because manic patients pull the alarm repeatedly. They make costly errors of judgment, such as investing large sums of money in highly risky or poorly considered ventures. Even after their friends warn them of the risks, they plunge ahead.

The rambling speech of a manic person has been described as a "flight of ideas." The person starts talking about one topic, which suggests another, which suggests another. Here is a quote from a manic patient:

I like playing pool a lot, that's one of my releases, that I play pool a lot. Oh what else? Bartend, bartend on the side, it's kind of fun to, if you're a bartender you can, you can see how people reacted, amounts of alcohol and different guys around, different chicks around, and different situations, if it's snowing outside, if it's cold outside, the weather conditions, all types of different types of environments and types of different types of people you'll usually find in a bar. (Hoffman, Stopek, & Andreasen, 1986, p. 835)

Some people experience a mild degree of mania ("hypomania") almost always. They are productive, popular, extraverted, "life-of-the-party" types. Mania may become so serious, however, that it makes normal life impossible. The theatrical director Joshua Logan has described his own experiences with depression and mania. A few excerpts follow.

A SELF-REPORT: DEPRESSIVE PHASE

I had no faith in the work I was doing or the people I was working with. . . . It was a great burden to get up in the morning and I couldn't wait to go to bed at night, even though I started not sleeping well. . . . I thought I was well but feeling low because of a hidden personal discouragement of some sort—something I couldn't quite put my finger on. . . . I just forced myself to live through a dreary, hopeless existence that lasted for months on end. . . .

My depressions actually began around the age of thirty-two. I remember I was working on a play, and I was forcing myself to work. . . . I can remember that I sat in some sort of aggravated agony as it was read aloud for the first time by the cast. It sounded so awful that I didn't want to direct it. I didn't even want to see it. I remember feeling so depressed that I wished that I were dead without having to go through the shame and defeat of suicide. I couldn't sleep well at all, and sleep meant, for me, oblivion, and that's what I longed for and couldn't get. I didn't know what to do and I felt very, very lost. (Fieve, 1975, pp. 42–43)

A SELF-REPORT: MANIC PHASE

Here, Logan describes his manic experiences:

Finally, as time passed, the depression gradually wore off and turned into something else, which I didn't understand either. But it was a much pleasanter thing to go through, at least at first. Instead of hating everything, I started liking things— liking them too much, perhaps. . . . I put out a thousand ideas a minute: things to do, plays to write, plots to write stories about. . . .

I decided to get married on the spur of the moment. . . . I practically forced her to say yes. Suddenly we had a loveless marriage and that had to be broken up overnight. . . .

I can only remember that I worked constantly, day and night, never even seeming to need more than a few hours of sleep. I always had a new idea or another

conference. . . . It was an exhilarating time for me.

It finally went too far. In the end I went over the bounds of reality, or law and order, so to say. I don't mean that I committed any crimes, but I could easily have done so if anyone had crossed me. I flew into rages if contradicted. I began to be irritable with everyone. Should a man, friend or foe, object to anything I did or said, it was quite possible that I could poke him in the jaw. I was eventually persuaded by the doctors that I was desperately ill and should go into the hospital. But it was not, even then, convincing to me that I was ill.

There I was, on the sixth floor of a New York building that had special iron bars around it and an iron gate that had slid into place and locked me away from the rest of the world. . . . I looked about and saw that there was an open window. I leaped up on the sill and climbed out of the window on the ledge on the sixth floor and said, "Unless you open the door, I'm going to climb down the outside of this building." At the time, I remember feeling so powerful that I might actually be able to scale the building. . . . They immediately opened the steel door, and I climbed back in. That's where manic elation can take you. (Fieve, 1975, pp. 43–45)

BIPOLAR CYCLES

A manic period or a depressed period may last for months or for just a day. Figure 14.22 shows the mood ratings for a manic-

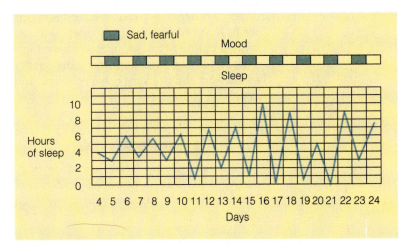

FIGURE 14.22
These records show one woman's 1-day manic periods alternating with 1-day depressed periods. Her days of cheerfulness alternated with days of fearfulness and sadness. (Based on Richter, 1938).

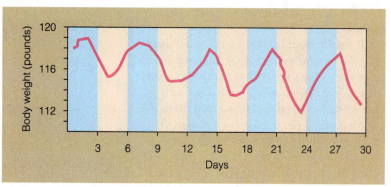

FIGURE 14.23
Records for a man who had 3-day manic periods (pink) alternating with 3-day depressed periods (blue). Note that he lost weight during manic times because of his high activity level. (Based on Crammer, 1959.)

depressive woman over 3 weeks (Richter, 1938). Note that she alternated day by day. She slept more on her cheerful days than on her sad days. Figure 14.23 shows the mood and body weight fluctuations for a manic-depressive man who had 3-day manic periods and 3-day depressed periods (Crammer, 1959). In many patients the depressed periods last longer than the manic periods.

A large number of artists, writers, and musical composers have suffered from depression or from bipolar disorder (Jamison, 1989). To test whether creative skills increase or decrease over various phases of the bipolar cycle, Robert Weisberg (1994) examined the works of the classical composer Robert Schumann, who is known to have had bipolar disorder. He found that Schumann produced more works during his manic phases than during his depressed phases. However, the compositions written during his depressed phases have been performed and recorded just as often as those written during his manic phases, on average. That is, judging from popularity, the quality of his work did not vary between manic and depressed phases.

CONCEPT CHECK

10. What are the similarities and differences between seasonal affective disorder and bipolar disorder? (Check your answer on page 636.)

■ SUICIDE

Many psychologically disturbed people attempt suicide, especially those who are depressed. Suicide is one of the most common

causes of death among young people. Figure 14.24 shows the estimated rates of suicide as a function of age (Boyd, 1983). Accurate records are hard to come by, because an unknown number of people disguise their suicides to look like accidents, either to reduce their family's anguish or to enable their survivors to collect life insurance.

Women make more suicide attempts than men, yet more men than women die by suicide (Cross & Hirschfeld, 1986). Most men who attempt suicide use guns or other violent means. Women are more likely to try poison, drugs, or other relatively slow, non-violent, uncertain methods (Rich, Ricketts, Fowler, & Young, 1988). Many women who injure themselves in suicide attempts are believed to be crying out for help and not really trying to kill themselves (Barnes, 1985). That is particularly true of young women. Unfortunately, some of them actually die, and others are disabled for life.

Suicide follows no dependable pattern. The fact that someone has talked about suicide—or has not talked about suicide—gives little indication of whether the person will actually attempt it. You may have heard people say that "someone who attempts suicide but survives will never actually commit suicide." That is simply untrue. In fact, one of the best predictors of future suicide attempts is a past suicide attempt (Beck, Steer, & Brown, 1993). Many people who attempt suicide give warning signals well in advance, but some do not. One study found that more than half of the people who made

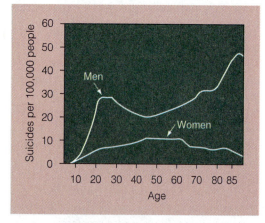

FIGURE 14.24
At every age, men are more likely than women to commit suicide, although a very large number of women (especially young women) make suicide attempts which they survive. For women, the probability of suicide is greatest in middle age. For men, it is high at about age 20, decreases during middle age, and rises again in old age. (From Boyd, 1983.)

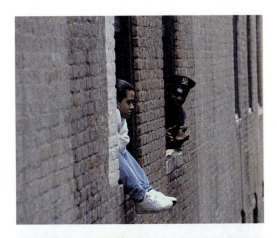

TABLE 14.6
People Most Likely to Attempt Suicide

- Depressed people, especially those with feelings of hopelessness (Beck, Steer, Beck, & Newman, 1993)
- People who have made previous suicide attempts (Beck, Steer, & Brown, 1993)
- People who have untreated psychological disorders (Brent et al., 1988), especially drug or alcohol abuse (Beck & Steer, 1989)
- People who have recently suffered the death of a spouse and men who have recently been divorced or separated, especially those who have little social support from friends and family (Blumenthal & Kupfer, 1986)
- People who during their childhood or adolescence lost a parent through death or divorce (Adam, 1986)
- People with guns in their home, particularly those with a history of violent attacks on others (Brent et al., 1988)
- People whose relatives have committed suicide (Blumental & Kupfer, 1986)
- People with low activity of the neurotransmitter serotonin in the brain (Mann, McBride, & Stanley, 1986)

a serious suicide attempt decided on suicide less than 24 hours before making the attempt (Peterson, Peterson, O'Shanick, & Swann, 1985).

However, certain factors are associated with an increased probability of attempting suicide. Anyone working with troubled people should be aware of these warning signals. Suicide attempts are most common among the types of people in Table 14.6.

If you suspect that someone you know is thinking about suicide, what should you do? Treat the person like a normal human being.

Don't assume that the person is so fragile that one wrong word will be disastrous. Don't be afraid to ask, "You have been looking depressed. Have you been thinking about suicide?" You may do the person a favor by showing that you are not frightened by the thought and that you are willing to talk about it.

Most people who threaten suicide are crying out for help; they are feeling pain, either mental or physical. You may not be able to guess what kind of pain someone is feeling. Be prepared to listen.

Urge the person to get professional help. Most large cities have a suicide prevention hotline listed in the white pages of the telephone directory.

SUMMARY

- *Symptoms of depression.* A depressed person takes little interest or pleasure in life, feels worthless, powerless, and guilty, and may consider suicide. Such a person has trouble sleeping, loses interest in sex and eating, and cannot concentrate. (page 627)

- *Predispositions.* Some people are predisposed to depression by genetic factors, by early experiences such as the loss of a parent, or by poor social support in adulthood. (page 628)

- *Sex differences.* Psychologists cannot convincingly explain why more women than men suffer depression. One hypothesis is that women are more likely to ruminate about their depression, and therefore aggravate and prolong it, whereas men are more likely to find some way of distracting themselves from their depression. (page 628)

- *Cognitive factors in depression.* People with a pessimistic explanatory style tend to blame themselves for their failures more than the facts actually warrant. Depressed people almost invariably have an extremely pessimistic explanatory style, seeing evidence of their own failures in almost everything that happens. (page 630)

- *Seasonal affective disorder.* Seasonal affective disorder is an uncommon condition in which people become depressed during the winter and somewhat manic during the summer. (page 632)

- *Bipolar disorder.* People with bipolar disorder alternate between periods of depression and periods of mania, in which they engage in constant, driven, uninhibited activity. (page 632)

- *Suicide.* Although it is difficult to know who will or will not attempt suicide, it is common among depressed people and people who show certain other warning signs. (page 634)

SUGGESTION FOR FURTHER READING

Beers, C. W. (1948). *A mind that found itself.* Garden City, NY: Doubleday. (Original work published 1908.) An autobiography of a man who recovered from a severe case of bipolar disorder.

TERMS

depression condition lasting most of the day, day after day, with a loss of interest or pleasure and a lack of productive activity (page 627)

bipolar disorder condition in which a person alternates between periods of depression and periods of mania (page 627)

reactive depression depression that develops suddenly in reaction to a severe loss (page 628)

endogenous depression depression that develops gradually, not traceable to any single traumatic experience (page 628)

postpartum depression period of depression some women experience shortly after giving birth (page 629)

learned-helplessness theory theory that some people become depressed because they have learned that they have no control over the major events in their lives (page 630)

explanatory style a tendency to accept one kind of explanation for success or failure more often than others (page 631)

seasonal affective disorder or **depression with a seasonal pattern** condition in which people become seriously depressed every winter, when the amount of sunlight per day is short (page 632)

mania condition in which people are constantly active, uninhibited, and either happy or angry (page 632)

ANSWERS TO CONCEPT CHECKS

9. Depressed people are less likely than others to buy a lottery ticket because they regard their chance of success as low on any task. (page 632)
10. Both seasonal affective disorder and bipolar disorder have repetitive cycles, sometimes with clocklike accuracy. However, people with bipolar disorder swing back and forth between two extremes, depression and mania, whereas most people with seasonal affective disorder alternate between depression and normal mood. (Some experience a slightly manic phase at the season opposite to the time of their depression.) (page 634)

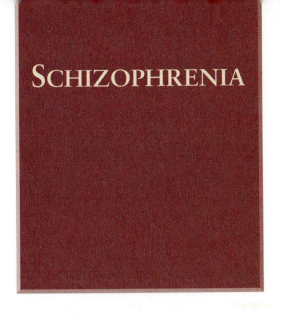

SCHIZOPHRENIA

What is schizophrenia?
What causes it?
What can be done about it?

How would you like to live in a world all your own? You can be the supreme ruler. No one will ever criticize you or tell you what to do. You can tell other people—and even inanimate things—what to do, and they will immediately obey. Every one of your fantasies becomes a reality.

Perhaps that world sounds like a heaven to you; I suspect it soon would be more like a hell. Most of us enjoy struggling to achieve our fantasies more than we would enjoy the immediate fulfillment of them.

Some people with schizophrenia live almost "in a world of their own," not always able to distinguish between fantasy and reality. They have trouble understanding what others say and trouble making themselves understood. Eventually they may retreat into a private existence, paying little attention to others.

THE SYMPTOMS OF SCHIZOPHRENIA

The widely misunderstood term *schizophrenia* is based on Greek roots meaning "split mind." However, the term does *not* refer to a split into two minds or personalities. Many people, including some who should know better, use the term *schizophrenia* when they mean *dissociative identity disorder* or *multiple personality*. As mentioned earlier in this chapter, people with dissociative identity disorder have several personalities, any one of which by itself might be considered normal.

In contrast, people suffering from schizophrenia have just one personality, but that personality is seriously disordered. The "split" in the schizophrenic "split mind" is a split between the intellectual and emotional aspects of the personality, as if the intellect and the emotions were no longer in contact with each other. (See Figure 14.25.) A person suffering from schizophrenia may seem happy or sad without cause or may fail to show emotions in a situation that normally evokes them. Such a person may even report bad news cheerfully or good news sadly.

To be diagnosed with schizophrenia, according to DSM-IV, a person must exhibit a deterioration of daily activities, including work, social relations, and self-care. He or she must *also* exhibit at least two of the following: hallucinations, delusions, incoherent speech, grossly disorganized behavior, certain thought disorders, or a loss of normal emotional responses and social behaviors. Exception: If someone has sufficiently severe hallucinations or delusions, no other symptoms are necessary. Finally, before assigning a diagnosis of schizophrenia, a psychologist or psychiatrist must rule out a number of other conditions that produce similar symptoms, including depression or bipolar illness, amphetamine or cocaine abuse, certain kinds of brain damage, the early stages of Huntington's disease, and so forth.

A little less than 1% of Americans are afflicted with schizophrenia at some point in life (Kessler et al., 1994). Some sources cite slightly higher or lower figures depending on how many borderline cases they include. Schizophrenia occurs in all countries and in

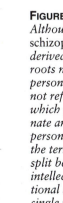

FIGURE 14.25
Although the term schizophrenia *is derived from Greek roots meaning "split personality," it does not refer to cases in which people alternate among different personalities. Rather, the term indicates a split between the intellectual and emotional aspects of a single personality.*

FIGURE 14.26
These portraits graphically illustrate their artist's progressive psychological deterioration. When well-known animal artist Louis Wain (1860–1939) began suffering delusions of persecution, his drawings showed a schizophrenic's disturbing perceptual distortions.

Schulsinger, Schulsinger, Mednick, & Teasdale, 1982).

SOMETHING TO THINK ABOUT
When we ask people to recall the childhood behavior of someone who later developed schizophrenia, what kinds of memory errors are likely, and why? (Recall the issues raised in Chapters 7 and 8.)

HALLUCINATIONS

Hallucinations are sensory experiences that do not correspond to anything in the outside world. Characteristically, people with schizophrenia hear voices and other sounds that no one else hears. Not all schizophrenic people hear voices, but most people who do are suffering from schizophrenia. The "voices" may speak only nonsense, or they may tell the person to carry out certain acts. Sometimes hallucinating people think the voices are real, sometimes they know the voices are coming from within their own head, and sometimes they are not sure (Junginger & Frame, 1985). Visual hallucinations are rare in schizophrenia, although a few have distorted or exaggerated visual experiences (Figure 14.26); visual hallucinations are more common after drug abuse.

DELUSIONS

Delusions are unfounded beliefs. Three of the more common types of delusions are persecution, grandeur, and reference: A **delusion of persecution** is a belief that one is being persecuted, that "people are out to get me." A **delusion of grandeur** is a belief that one is unusually important, perhaps a special messenger from God or a person of central importance to the future of the world. A **delusion of reference** is a tendency to interpret all sorts of messages as if they were meant for oneself. Someone with a delusion of reference may interpret a headline in the morning newspaper as a coded message or may take a television announcer's comments as personal insults.

DISORDERS OF EMOTION AND MOVEMENT

Many people with schizophrenia show little sign of emotion. Their faces seldom express emotion, and they speak without the inflections most people use for emphasis. When they do show emotions, the expressions are

all ethnic groups, although it is apparently rare in the tropics and especially prevalent in densely populated areas of cities. It is about as common among men as among women.

Schizophrenia is most frequently diagnosed in young adults in their teens or 20s. A first diagnosis is rare after age 30 and unheard of after age 45. The onset is sometimes sudden but is usually gradual. Most people with schizophrenia are described as having been "strange" children who had a short attention span, made few friends, often disrupted their classroom with "unusual" behaviors, and had mild thought disorders (Arboleda & Holzman, 1985; Parnas, inappropriate, such as laughing for no reason (Figure 14.27).

Some people with schizophrenia have a movement disorder called catatonia. **Catatonia** may take the form of either rigid inactivity or excessive activity; in either case, the person's movement pattern seems to be unrelated to events in the outside world.

THE THOUGHT DISORDER OF SCHIZOPHRENIA

One characteristic of schizophrenic thought is the use of *loose and idiosyncratic associations,* somewhat like the illogical leaps that occur in dreams. For example, one man used the words *Jesus, cigar,* and *sex* as synonyms. When he was asked to explain, he said they were all the same because Jesus has a halo around his head, a cigar has a band around it, and during sex people put their arms around each other.

Another characteristic of schizophrenic thought is *difficulty in using abstract concepts*. For instance, many people with schizophrenia have trouble sorting objects into categories. Many also give strictly literal responses when asked to interpret the meaning of proverbs. Here are some examples (Krueger, 1978, pp. 196–197):

Proverb: People who live in glass houses shouldn't throw stones.
Interpretation: "It would break the glass."
Proverb: All that glitters is not gold.
Interpretation: "It might be brass."
Proverb: A stitch in time saves nine.
Interpretation: "If you take one stitch for a small tear now, it will save nine later."

Because of this tendency to interpret everything literally, people with schizophrenic thought disorder often misunderstand simple statements. On being taken to the admitting office of a hospital, one person said, "Oh, is this where people go to admit their faults?"

Many schizophrenic people use vague, roundabout ways of saying something simple. For instance, one such person said, "I was born with a male sense" instead of "I'm a man." They often take many words to say nothing of importance, as in this excerpt from a letter one man wrote to his mother:

I am writing on paper. The pen which I am using is from a factory called "Perry & Co." This factory is in England. I assume this. Behind the name of Perry Co. the city

of London is inscribed; but not the city. The city of London is in England. I know this from my school-days. Then, I always liked geography. My last teacher in that subject was Professor August A. He was a man with black eyes. I also like black eyes. There are also blue and gray eyes and other sorts, too. I have heard it said that snakes have green eyes. All people have eyes. There are some, too, who are blind. These blind people are led about by a boy. It must be very terrible not to be able to see. There are people who can't see and, in addition, can't hear. I know some who hear too much. (Bleuler, 1911/1950, p. 17)

THE DISTINCTION BETWEEN POSITIVE AND NEGATIVE SYMPTOMS

Are all the various symptoms of schizophrenia independent, or do they form clusters? Many investigators distinguish between positive symptoms and negative symptoms of schizophrenia. (In this case, *positive* means *present*, and *negative* means *absent*; they do not mean *good* and *bad*.) **Positive symptoms** are behaviors that are notable because of their *presence* in schizophrenia—such as hallucinations, delusions, and thought disorder. **Negative symptoms** are behaviors that are notable by their *absence* in schizophrenia. For example, many people with schizophrenia show a lack of emotional expression, a lack of social interaction, a deficit of speech, a lack of pleasure, and a general inability to take care of themselves.

The research indicates that we should draw a further distinction, separating two groups of positive symptoms—"positive psychotic" symptoms (hallucinations and delusions) and "positive disorganized" symptoms (thought disorder, bizarre behavior, and inappropriate emotions). Hallucinations and delusions form a natural cluster; generally, people who have either hallucinations or delusions have the other as well. Similarly, the positive disorganized symptoms correlate with one another; people who have any one of them also tend to have the others (Andreasen, Arndt, Alliger, Miller, & Flaum, 1995). The negative symptoms form a third cluster.

Some patients have mostly positive symptoms; others have mostly negative symptoms. As a rule, both the positive psychotic and the positive disorganized symptoms fluctuate from time to time and respond favorably to treatments. Negative

FIGURE 14.27
A patient with disorganized schizophrenia may giggle for no apparent reason or engage in other bizarre behaviors.

symptoms tend to be more consistent over time and more difficult to treat (Arndt, Andreasen, Flaum, Miller, & Nopoulos, 1995). People with many negative symptoms have earlier onset and worse performance in school and on the job (Andreasen, Flaum, Swayze, Tyrrell, & Arndt, 1990).

■ TYPES OF SCHIZOPHRENIA

People with schizophrenia vary considerably in their symptoms; they also vary in their family histories, their results on brain scans, and their response to treatment. What we call "schizophrenia" may in fact include two or more separate conditions that produce overlapping symptoms, as it would be if medical doctors failed to distinguish among migraine headaches, tension headaches, and brain tumors (Heinrichs, 1993). Currently, psychologists distinguish among four types

FIGURE 14.28
A person suffering from catatonic schizophrenia may hold a bizarre posture for hours and alternate this rigid stupor with equally purposeless, excited activity. Such people may stubbornly resist attempts to change their behavior, but they need supervision to avoid hurting themselves or others. Catatonic schizophrenia is uncommon.

of schizophrenia, based on the behavioral symptoms. Although these distinctions are probably not the distinctions we shall eventually draw after we know more about the causes of schizophrenia (or the schizophrenias), the distinctions are useful for descriptive purposes.

Undifferentiated schizophrenia is characterized by the basic symptoms—deterioration of daily functioning along with some combination of hallucinations, delusions, inappropriate emotions, thought disorders, and so forth. However, none of these symptoms is unusually pronounced or bizarre.

Catatonic schizophrenia is characterized by the basic symptoms plus prominent movement disorders. The affected person may go through periods of extremely rapid, mostly repetitive activity alternating with periods of total inactivity. During the inactive periods he or she may hold a given posture without moving and may resist attempts to alter that posture (Figure 14.28). Catatonic schizophrenia is rare.

Disorganized schizophrenia is characterized by incoherent speech, extreme lack of social relationships, and "silly" or "odd" behavior. For example, one man gift wrapped one of his bowel movements and proudly presented it to his therapist. Here is a conversation with someone suffering from disorganized schizophrenia (Duke & Nowicki, 1979):

> **Interviewer:** How does it feel to have your problems?
>
> **Patient:** Who can tell me the name of my song? I don't know, but it won't be long. It won't be short, tall, none at all. My head hurts, my knees hurt—my nephew, his uncle, my aunt. My God, I'm happy . . . not a care in the world. My hair's been curled, the flag's unfurled. This is my country, land that I love, this is the country, land that I love.
>
> **Interviewer:** How do you feel?
>
> **Patient:** Happy! Don't you hear me? Why do you talk to me? (barks like a dog). (Duke & Nowicki, 1979, p. 162)

Paranoid schizophrenia is characterized by the basic symptoms plus strong or elaborate hallucinations and delusions, especially delusions of persecution and delusions of grandeur. Compared to other types of schizophrenia, paranoid schizophrenia generally has a later age of onset and a better prospect for recovery (Fenton & McGlashan, 1991). Most people with paranoid schizophrenia can manage their own lives reasonably well, except for their constant suspicion—for example, a suspicion that "I am surrounded by spies" or that "evil forces are trying to control my mind."

Paranoid schizophrenia tends not to run in the same families as other types of schizophrenia (Farmer, McGuffin, & Gottesman, 1987). In some ways, it resembles depression more than it resembles other types of schizophrenia (Zigler & Glick, 1988).

Many people fall on the borderline of two or more types of schizophrenia, perhaps switching back and forth between them. Switching is especially common between undifferentiated schizophrenia and one of the other types (Kendler, Gruenberg, & Tsuang, 1985).

CONCEPT CHECK

11. *Why are people more likely to switch between undifferentiated schizophrenia and one of the other types than, say, between disorganized schizophrenia and one of the other types? (Check your answer on page 645.)*

CAUSES OF SCHIZOPHRENIA

From all indications, schizophrenia has multiple causes. In most cases it probably begins with a biological predisposition, such as one based on genetics. However, the biological predisposition is not enough; not everyone with a biological predisposition to schizophrenia develops schizophrenia. Even people who do develop the condition vary in the type and severity of their symptoms. We shall examine what researchers currently understand about the causes of schizophrenia, but bear in mind that this understanding is tentative.

BRAIN DAMAGE

Unlike people suffering from other psychological disorders, people suffering from schizophrenia show minor but widespread brain damage (see Figure 14.29). The cerebral cortex is somewhat shrunken in one-fourth to one-third of all schizophrenic patients, and the cerebral ventricles (fluid-filled spaces in the brain) are enlarged on the average (Zipursky, Lim, Sullivan, Brown, & Pfefferbaum, 1992). Enlargement of the cerebral ventricles implies decreased space for neurons; thus it suggests mild brain damage. Most people with schizophrenia have cognitive and memory deficits similar to those of people with damage to the prefrontal cortex or the temporal cortex; these behavioral deficits do not depend on how long a person has had schizophrenia or on how long the person has been taking anti-schizophrenic drugs (Heaton et al., 1994; Saykin et al., 1994).

Furthermore, most people with schizophrenia show other brain abnormalities, such as decreased metabolic activity in the brain (Berman, Torrey, Daniel, & Weinberger, 1992), abnormal locations of certain

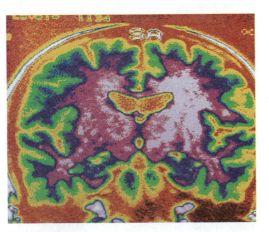
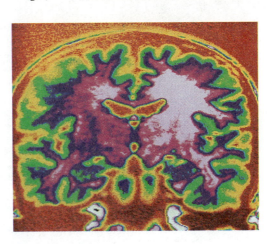

FIGURE 14.29
Many (though not all) people with schizophrenia show signs of mild loss of neurons in the brain. Here we see views of the brains of twins. The twin on the left has schizophrenia; the twin on the right does not. Note that the ventricles (near the center of each brain) are larger in the twin with schizophrenia. The ventricles are fluid-filled cavities; an enlargement of the ventricles implies a loss of brain tissue. (Photos courtesy of E. F. Torrey & M. F. Casanova/NIMH.)

neurons in the brain (Akbarian et al., 1993), and decreased activity at synapses that use the neurotransmitter GABA (Akbarian et al., 1995). Indications of brain abnormalities have been reported for patients in cultures as different as the United States and Nigeria (Ohaeri, Adeyinka, & Osuntokun, 1995).

Although the causes of the brain abnormalities are not certain, mounting evidence suggests that the abnormalities develop early in life, either before birth or early after birth. People with schizophrenia do not continue to lose neurons in adolescence or adulthood (Benes, 1995).

CONCEPT CHECK

12. *Following a stroke, a patient shows symptoms similar to schizophrenia. Where is the brain damage probably located? (Check your answer on page 645.)*

DOPAMINE IMBALANCE

Schizophrenia is commonly treated with drugs. All the effective drugs share one characteristic: They block dopamine synapses in the brain. In fact, the therapeutic effectiveness of these drugs is nearly proportional to their tendency to block those synapses (Seeman & Lee, 1975). Furthermore, large doses of amphetamine, cocaine, or other drugs that increase dopamine activity can induce a temporary state that closely resembles schizophrenia. These phenomena have led to the dopamine theory of schizophrenia, which holds that the underlying cause of schizophrenia is excessive stimulation of certain types of dopamine synapses. That stimulation may occur in part because other, competing synapses are being destroyed.

GENETICS

What causes the brain damage often associated with schizophrenia and the relative overactivity of dopamine synapses? Perhaps a particular gene produces chemicals that interfere with normal brain development, damage neurons, or alter the transmission at certain synapses. Substantial evidence supports this genetic predisposition for schizophrenia.

First, for adopted children who eventually develop schizophrenia, schizophrenia is more common among their biological relatives than it is among their adoptive relatives (Kety et al., 1994). Second, if one member of a pair of identical twins develops schizophrenia, there is almost a 50% chance that the other will develop it too (Gottesman, 1991). (See Figure 14.30.) That figure understates the role of genetics in schizophrenia, however, because a high percentage of the twins who do not develop schizophrenia will suffer from other serious psychological

FIGURE 14.30
The relatives of a schizophrenic person have an increased probability of developing schizophrenia themselves. Note that children of a schizophrenic mother have a 17% risk of schizophrenia even if adopted by a family with no schizophrenic members. (Based on data from Gottesman, 1991.)

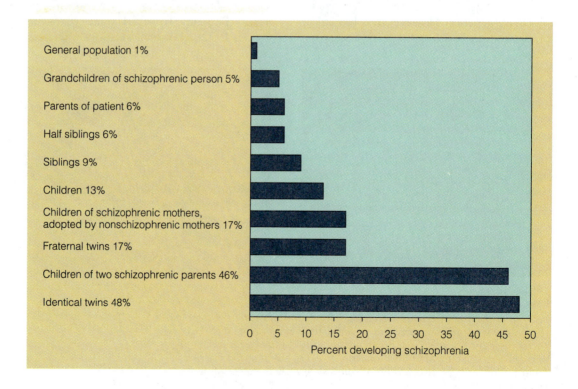

disturbances, including "borderline" schizophrenia (Farmer, McGuffin, & Gottesman, 1987; Kendler & Robinette, 1983). Furthermore, the schizophrenic twin and the non-schizophrenic twin run an equal risk of passing on schizophrenia to their children (Gottesman & Bertelson, 1989; Kringlen & Cramer, 1989). Apparently some gene or genes tend to increase the likelihood of schizophrenia. Even if a person with those genes does not actually develop schizophrenia, he or she still passes the genes to the next generation.

One focus of current research is to identify those people who have the genes for schizophrenia but do not show the symptoms. Identifying them could be useful for better understanding the genetics and for understanding how genetic influences combine with environmental influences. Psychologists have examined young people who are related to people with schizophrenia. Although these young people have not yet developed schizophrenia themselves, many of them will probably develop it later. Thus, any unusual behaviors they show are possible "markers" of vulnerability to schizophrenia—that is, these are behaviors found in people who more likely than others to develop schizophrenia.

Those markers include a number of symptoms of mild brain damage or abnormality (Cannon et al., 1994) and a failure to habituate normally to a repeated sound (Hollister, Mednick, Brennan, & Cannon, 1994). That is, many of these young people fail to filter out irrelevant information, responding to a repeated noise as much as they do to an unfamiliar noise.

Another possible "marker" is an impairment of **pursuit eye movements,** the movements necessary for keeping one's eyes focused on a moving object. About 80% of people with schizophrenia move their eyes in a series of rapid jerks instead of moving them smoothly (Holzman, 1985); they show this same impairment before they develop schizophrenia, during a schizophrenic episode, and after successful therapy (Holzman, 1988). The same impairment also occurs in many of their close relatives, but seldom in people who do not have a relative with schizophrenia (Blackwood, St. Clair, Muir, & Duffy, 1991; Clementz & Sweeney, 1990). Thus the impaired eye movement may help identify people who have the genes for schizophrenia.

EXPERIENCE

Assuming that genes predispose certain people to schizophrenia, what environmental factors determine whether or not those genes will be expressed as schizophrenia? Some years ago, psychologists suggested that mothers who gave a confusing mixture of "come here" and "go away" signals were likely to induce schizophrenia in their children. That theory has been discarded for several reasons.

One reason is that it does not fit the data on adoptions. The child of a schizophrenic parent who is adopted by normal parents has a high risk of developing schizophrenia, whereas other adopted children reared in the same family generally do not become schizophrenic. So it seems unlikely that confusing verbal signals from the mother are responsible for schizophrenia.

Another reason is that the suggested cause does not seem sufficient to produce the effect. Even abused and battered children seldom develop schizophrenia. It is hard to believe that confusing verbal signals would cause even greater damage.

Finally, the "bad mother" theory does not fit the course of the disorder over time. If the mother's behavior were the main cause of the problem, we would expect the child to improve when separated from her. In fact, schizophrenia usually develops in early adulthood—when most people become independent of their parents.

A more reasonable hypothesis is that the onset of schizophrenia may be *triggered* by stress. Note the word *triggered*. Although stress probably does not cause schizophrenia, it may aggravate the symptoms. The effect of stress is difficult to measure, however, because the term *stress* is imprecise and subjective; events that are stressful for one person may not be stressful for another.

Schizophrenia is slightly more common among people who are born in winter than in people born at other times. One possible explanation is that pregnant women who get feverish infections (which are most common in fall) may expose their fetuses to an extra risk during a critical stage of brain development. A fetus exposed to such a condition in fall would be born in winter.

Judith Rabkin (1980) reviewed studies in which schizophrenic people were asked to report any stressful events that had occurred during the months just before they developed schizophrenia. The frequency of stressful events turned out to be only slightly higher than normal. This finding could mean any of several things: The schizophrenic people may have forgotten the stressful events they experienced; stress may not be particularly significant in the onset of schizophrenia; the critically stressful events may have occurred more than a few months before the onset of the disorder; or people who are susceptible to schizophrenia may overrespond to very mild stress. We shall need further studies, preferably longitudinal studies, to decide among these possibilities.

INFECTIONS DURING EARLY DEVELOPMENT

A person born in the winter months is slightly more likely to develop schizophrenia than is a person born at any other time (Bradbury & Miller, 1985). No other psychological disorder has this characteristic. Moreover, investigators have clearly demonstrated this **season-of-birth effect** only in the northern climates, not near the equator. Evidently, something about the weather near the time of birth contributes to some people's vulnerability to schizophrenia.

One possible explanation relates to the fact that influenza and other epidemics are most common in the fall, especially in northern climates. Suppose a woman catches influenza or some similar disease in the fall. If she happens to be in the second trimester of pregnancy at the time, her illness may affect the fetus during a critical stage of brain development; she delivers that baby in the win-

ter. According to several studies, in years of a major influenza epidemic in the fall, the babies born 3 months later (in the winter) are at increased risk for schizophrenia, as diagnosed 20 or more years later (Kendell & Kemp, 1989; Mednick, Machon, & Huttunen, 1990; Torrey, Rawlings, & Waldman, 1988).

You might ask, if the brain damage occurs before or near the time of birth, why do the symptoms emerge so much later? One answer is that certain parts of the brain, especially the prefrontal cortex, go through a critical stage of development during the second trimester of pregnancy but do not become fully functional until adolescence. As the brain begins to rely more and more on those areas, the effects of the damage become more evident (Weinberger, 1987).

The causes of schizophrenia are still not understood; what is clear is that schizophrenia depends on a number of influences, not just a single cause. Genetics, stress, and prenatal exposure to illness are likely influences on schizophrenia, but exactly how these and other influences interact will be a topic of research for years to come.

SUMMARY

• *Symptoms of schizophrenia.* A person with schizophrenia is someone whose everyday functioning has deteriorated over a period of at least 6 months and who shows at least two of the following symptoms: hallucinations (mostly auditory), delusions, weak or inappropriate emotional expression, catatonic movements, and thought disorder. (page 637)

• *Onset.* Schizophrenia is usually first diagnosed in young adults. However, certain signs are evident in children, including mild thought disorder, lack of emotional contact with others, and impaired pursuit eye movements. (page 638)

• *Thought disorder of schizophrenia.* The thought disorder of schizophrenia is characterized by loose associations, impaired use of abstract concepts, and vague, wandering speech that conveys little information. (page 639)

• *Types of schizophrenia.* What we call *schizophrenia* may in fact consist of two or more separate conditions with overlapping symptoms. Psychologists distinguish four types of schizophrenia: undifferentiated, catatonic, disorganized, and paranoid. Some authorities believe paranoid schizophrenia resembles depression more than it does other types of schizophrenia. (page 640)

- *Brain damage.* Many people with schizophrenia show indications of mild brain damage. (page 641)
- *Role of dopamine.* Schizophrenia is relieved by various drugs that block dopamine synapses in the brain. For that reason, many people believe schizophrenia is due to overactivity at certain types of dopamine synapses, or to a relative overactivity of dopamine in comparison to other neurotransmitters. (page 642)
- *Combined forces of genetics and experience.* A predisposition to schizophrenia may be inherited. However, experience influences the timing and intensity of schizophrenic behavioral episodes. (page 642)
- *Season-of-birth effect.* Schizophrenia is more common in people born in the winter months, especially in cold climates. For that reason, some investigators believe that some cases of schizophrenia may be caused by a virus or bacterium contracted before or shortly after birth. (page 644)

SUGGESTION FOR FURTHER READING

Gottesman, I. I. (1991). *Schizophrenia genesis.* New York: W. H. Freeman. Review of research on the causes of schizophrenia.

TERMS

schizophrenia condition marked by deterioration of daily activities over a period of at least 6 months, plus either hallucinations, delusions, flat or inappropriate emotions, certain movement disorders, or thought disorders (page 637)

hallucination sensory experience that does not correspond to anything in the outside world (page 638)

delusion unfounded belief (page 638)

delusion of persecution belief that one is being persecuted (page 638)

delusion of grandeur belief that one is unusually important (page 638)

delusion of reference tendency to interpret all sorts of messages as if they were meant for oneself (page 638)

catatonia movement disorder, consisting of either rigid inactivity or excessive activity (page 639)

positive symptoms characteristics present in people with schizophrenia and absent in others—such as hallucinations, delusions, abnormal movements, and thought disorder (page 639)

negative symptoms behaviors that are present in other people—such as the ability to take care of themselves—but absent in schizophrenic people (page 639)

undifferentiated schizophrenia type of schizophrenia characterized by the basic symptoms but no unusual or especially prominent symptoms (page 640)

catatonic schizophrenia type of schizophrenia characterized by the basic symptoms plus prominent movement disorders (page 640)

disorganized schizophrenia type of schizophrenia characterized by incoherent speech, extreme lack of social relationships, and "silly" or "odd" behavior (page 640)

paranoid schizophrenia type of schizophrenia characterized by the basic symptoms plus strong or elaborate hallucinations and delusions (page 640)

dopamine theory of schizophrenia theory that the underlying cause of schizophrenia is excessive stimulation of certain types of dopamine synapses (page 642)

pursuit eye movements the movements necessary for keeping one's eyes focusing on a moving object (page 643)

season-of-birth effect tendency for people born in the winter months to be slightly more likely than other people are to develop schizophrenia (page 644)

ANSWERS TO CONCEPT CHECKS

11. With any disorder, symptoms are more severe at certain times than at others. Whenever any of the special symptoms of catatonic, disorganized, or paranoid schizophrenia become less severe, the person is left with undifferentiated schizophrenia. To shift between any two of the other types, a person would have to lose the symptoms of one type and gain the symptoms of the other type. (page 641)

12. The damage probably is located in the frontal or temporal lobes of the cerebral cortex, the areas that are generally damaged in people with schizophrenia. (page 642)

15

TREATMENT OF PSYCHOLOGICALLY TROUBLED PEOPLE

Vaclav Havel spent years as a political prisoner because of his criticisms of the Communist government of Czechoslovakia. Later, after he became president in the new, non-Communist government, he reflected on the tribulations his country was suffering:

People . . . are in a state of shock caused by freedom. It is similar to coming out of prison: When you are inside, you yearn for the moment when they will release you, but when it happens, you are suddenly helpless. You do not know what to do and even have a yen to go back, because at least you know what awaits you. You do not know what freedom will bring. ("A conversation with President Havel," 1992)

Some people are, in a sense, prisoners within themselves. Their freedom is limited by their own fears, thoughts, and habits. In a way they want to be released from all that, but in a way they also may resist freedom. They are not sure how to live without the limitations they have had for so long or how to accept full responsibility for their own decisions. Freedom, even psychological freedom, can be a bit intimidating.

Psychotherapists try to help people free themselves from their psychological shackles. We could compare the role of a psychotherapist to that of a physician, an educator, a member of the clergy, or a friend. Better yet, let's think of a psychotherapist as a kindly parole officer—someone who tries to help another person make the adjustment from a self-imposed prison into a world of new opportunities.

A psychotherapist assumes many roles, like those of friend, teacher, physician, even parole officer. A psychotherapist tries to help clients through their difficult times to reach a better, freer future. Here, a military psychologist gets acquainted with a Haitian girl in a refugee camp.

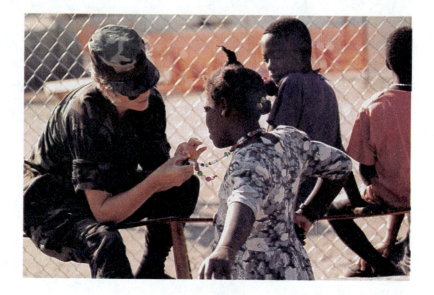

PSYCHOTHERAPY

What methods are used to help people overcome psychological disorders?

How effective are these methods?

Observation

If I don't drive around the park,
I'm pretty sure to make my mark.
If I'm in bed each night by ten,
I may get back my looks again.
If I abstain from fun and such,
I'll probably amount to much.
But I shall stay the way I am,
Because I do not give a damn.
DOROTHY PARKER (1944)

Psychotherapy is a treatment of psychological disorders, by methods that generally include a personal relationship between a trained therapist and a client. But psychotherapy does little good unless a client gives the proverbial damn.

Before the Second World War, almost all psychotherapists were psychiatrists, and most of them used Freudian methods. Since then, clinical psychologists, social workers, counseling psychologists, and others have begun to practice psychotherapy.

Both the number of therapists and the variety of methods they use have increased enormously (Garfield, 1981). Hundreds of identifiable forms of psychotherapy are available today. Psychotherapy is used for certain well-defined disorders, such as phobia, depression, and addiction, and for a wide variety of adjustment and coping problems that do not fall into any set category. In fact, close to half the people who consult a therapist are the "worried well" or the "nervous normals"—reasonably happy, successful people who would like to function even more successfully in some aspect of their life.

They consult a therapist not like a sick person seeing a physician but more like an athlete seeking advice from a coach.

In some types of psychotherapy, the therapist does most of the talking; in others, the therapist says little. Some emphasize past emotions; others emphasize current emotions; still others emphasize current behaviors and almost ignore emotions. Some therapists concentrate on helping clients understand the reasons behind their behaviors; others concentrate on changing the behaviors, and never mind where the behaviors came from in the first place. Some focus on the problems of the individual; some focus on problems of families or whole communities. In the following survey of common therapeutic methods, we shall see how therapists use different methods depending on what they consider the central problem of troubled people.

PSYCHOANALYSIS

A number of types of psychotherapy, known as **psychodynamic therapies,** attempt to unravel people's underlying drives and motivations. For example, both Sigmund Freud's procedure (looking for underlying sexual motives) and Alfred Adler's procedure (looking for underlying power and superiority motives) are considered psychodynamic. Here we shall focus on Freud's procedure.

Lawton Chiles dropped out of politics, received treatment for depression, and returned to become governor of Florida. The fact that someone has seen a therapist or is currently seeing a therapist does not imply a disabling or permanent problem.

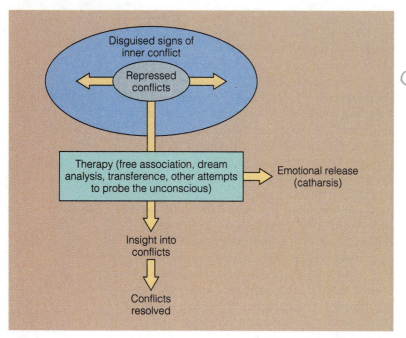

FIGURE 15.1
The goal of psychoanalysis is to resolve psychological problems by bringing to consciousness the unconscious thought processes that are responsible for the difficulty. Analysis literally *means "to loosen or break up, to look at the parts."*

Psychoanalysis, Freud's method of psychotherapy, was the first of the "talk" therapies. It is a method based on identifying unconscious thoughts and emotions and bringing them to consciousness, to help people understand why they do what they do and think what they think. Psychoanalysis is therefore described as an "insight-oriented therapy" in contrast to therapies that focus on changing thoughts and behaviors (Figure 15.1).

Freud believed that psychological problems were the result of unconscious thought processes and that the only way to control self-defeating behaviors was to make those processes conscious. Bringing them to consciousness, he thought, would produce **catharsis,** a release of pent-up emotions associated with unconscious thoughts and memories.

At first, Freud sought to gain access to his clients' unconscious through hypnosis. He soon abandoned that approach, however, and developed other methods of bringing unconscious material to consciousness: free association, dream analysis, and transference.

FREE ASSOCIATION

Free association is a method that Freud and his patients developed together. (Actually, a more accurate translation of the German expression would be "free intrusion.") In **free**

association, the client lies on a couch, starts thinking about a particular symptom or problem, and then reports everything that comes to mind—a word, a phrase, a visual image. The client is instructed not to omit anything, not to censor anything that might be embarrassing, and not to worry about trying to express everything in complete sentences.

The therapist listens for links and themes that might tie the patient's fragmentary remarks together. Freud believed that all behavior is determined, that nothing happens without a cause. (You will recall that behaviorists make the same assumption; see Chapter 6.) Even when the client jumps from one thought to another, the thoughts must be related in some way.

Here is a paraphrased excerpt from a free-association session:

A man begins by describing a conference he had with his boss the previous day. He did not like the boss's policy, but he was in no position to contradict the boss. He had had a dream. It was something about an ironing board, but that was all he remembered of the dream. He comments that his wife has been complaining about the way their maid irons. He thinks his wife is being unfair; he hopes she does not fire the maid. He complains that his boss did not give him credit for some work he did recently. He recalls a childhood episode: He jumped off a cupboard and bounced off his mother's behind while she was leaning over to do some ironing. She told his father, who gave him a spanking. His father never let him explain; he was always too strict. (Munroe, 1955, p. 39)

To a psychoanalyst, the links in this story suggest that the man is associating his wife with his mother. His wife was unfair to the maid about the ironing, just as his mother had been unfair to him. Moreover, his boss is like his father, never giving him a chance to explain his errors and never giving him credit for what he did well.

DREAM ANALYSIS

For thousands of years, people have been trying to divine the meaning of dreams. Some have said that dreams predict the future, others that they reveal the dreamer's personality.

Freud (1900/1955) agreed that dreams reveal something about personality, but he rejected the view that each detail has the same meaning for everyone. To understand a dream, he said, one must determine what associations each detail has for the dreamer. Each dream has a **manifest content**—the content that appears on the surface—and a **latent content**—the hidden content that is represented only symbolically in the actual experience. The only way a psychoanalyst can discover the latent content of a dream is to understand what each detail of the manifest content means to the dreamer.

To illustrate, Freud (1900/1955) interpreted one of his own dreams, in which he dreamed that one of his friends was his uncle. He worked out the following associations: Both this friend and another friend had been recommended for an appointment as professor at the university. Both had been turned down, probably because they were Jews. Freud himself had recently been recommended for the same appointment, but he feared he too would be turned down because he was Jewish. Freud's only uncle had once been convicted of illegal business dealings. Freud's father had said, however, that the uncle was not a bad man but just a simpleton.

What was the relationship between the two friends and the uncle? One of the friends was, in Freud's judgment, a bit simple-minded. The other had once been taken to court by a woman who accused him of sexual misconduct. Although these charges were dropped, some people might still feel that being accused was as bad as being convicted. By linking these two friends to his uncle, Freud interpreted the dream as meaning, "Maybe they didn't get rejected for the university appointment because they were Jews, but because one was a simpleton (like my uncle) and the other was regarded as a criminal (like my uncle). If so, I still have a chance to get the appointment."

To Freud, every dream represents a form of wish fulfillment. The wish may be disguised, but it is always there. For example, in his dream Freud was not wishing that his friend were his uncle. Rather, he was wishing that he would get the university appointment, and he was wishing that his friends had been rejected for some reason other than for being Jews.

Freud's theory seems to apply to many dreams. For example, people who have been deprived of food and water—and who, presumably, are wishing for food and water—have more frequent and more elaborate

According to Freud, the manifest content of a dream (that which appears) is a distorted representation of the latent content (its hidden meaning). To determine the latent content, one must determine what each element of the manifest content means to the individual.

dreams about eating and drinking than other people do (O'Nell, 1965). Note, however, Freud's leap of logic: Some dreams seem rather clearly to represent wish fulfillment, and certain others can, with a little effort, be interpreted as wish fulfillments; therefore, *all* dreams are wish fulfillments. Most psychologists today do not accept that conclusion.

You may hear people say that Freud thought all dreams had sexual symbolism. That is not true; Freud saw sexual symbolism in many dreams, but not in all. Curiously, however, in his writings, his examples of dreams with nonsexual symbolism are his own dreams, and his examples of dreams with sexual symbolism are invariably described as other people's dreams.

CONCEPT CHECK

1. A popular paperback purports to tell you what your dreams mean. It says that every element of a dream has a symbolic meaning, in many cases a sexual meaning. A ballpoint pen represents a penis, for example, and walking up a flight of stairs represents sexual arousal. Do you think Freud would agree or disagree with this book? (Check your answer on page 667.)

TRANSFERENCE

Some clients show exaggerated love or hatred for their therapist that seems inappropriate under the circumstances. Psychoanalysts call this reaction **transference,** by which they mean that clients are transferring onto the therapist what they actually feel toward their

PSYCHOTHERAPY

651

father or mother or some other important figure. Transference often provides a clue to the client's feelings about those people.

Psychoanalysts are fairly active in **interpretation** of what the client says—that is, they explain the underlying meaning—and may even argue with the client about interpretations. They may regard the client's **disagreement as resistance,** continued repression that interferes with the therapy. Resistance can take many forms; for example, a client who has begun to touch on some extremely anxiety-provoking topic may turn the conversation to something trivial or may simply "forget" to come to the next session.

Psychoanalysis today remains largely loyal to Freud's methods and theories, although many individual psychoanalysts put greater or lesser emphasis on particular issues (Karon & Widener, 1995). The goal is still to bring about a major reorganization of the personality, changing a person from the inside out, by helping people understand the hidden reasons behind their actions.

■ BEHAVIOR THERAPY

Behavior therapists assume that human behavior is learned and that it can be unlearned. They identify the behavior that needs to be changed, such as a phobia or an addiction or a nervous twitch, and then set about changing it through reinforcement, punishment, and other principles of learning. They may try to understand the causes of the behavior as a first step toward changing it, but unlike psychoanalysts, they are more interested in directly changing behaviors than in understanding their hidden meanings.

Behavior therapy begins with clear, well-defined behavioral goals, such as eliminating test anxiety or getting the client to quit smoking, and then attempts to achieve those goals through learning. Setting clear goals enables the therapist to judge whether or not the therapy is succeeding. If the client shows no improvement after a few sessions, the therapist tries a different procedure.

Systematic desensitization to treat phobias, which we examined in Chapter 14, is one example of behavior therapy. For other problems, behavior therapists use a variety of methods.

BEHAVIOR THERAPY FOR ANOREXIA NERVOSA

A behavior therapist treats anorexia nervosa (Chapter 11) by providing reinforcement for eating or for gaining weight. For example, one woman with severe anorexia nervosa was isolated from her family and placed in a small, barren hospital room (Bachrach, Erwin, & Mohr, 1965). She was told that she could not leave the room and could see no one except the nurse who came at mealtimes. She could obtain privileges—such as having a television or reading material, the right to leave the room, or the right to have visitors—only as a reward for gaining weight. This method may seem heartless, but life-threatening cases like this one demand drastic measures. The woman gradually gained weight and was released from the hospital when she reached 77 pounds (35 kilograms). After leaving, she lost some of the weight she had gained but not enough to endanger her life.

Behavior therapy can be combined with other therapeutic methods. In cases of anorexia nervosa, it is most effective when combined with family counseling designed to alter the family interactions that may have led to the problem (Russell, Szmukler, Dare, & Eisler, 1987).

BEHAVIOR THERAPY FOR BED-WETTING

Some children continue to wet the bed long after the usual age of toilet training. Most of them outgrow the problem, but occasionally it lingers on to age 5, 10, or even into the teens.

We now know that most bed-wetters have small bladders and thus have difficulty

Dr. Stephen Gullo uses a 5-pound model of fat to help motivate his weight-loss clients. Behavior therapists set specific goals, such as weight loss, and use conditioning and reinforcement techniques to help clients achieve those goals.

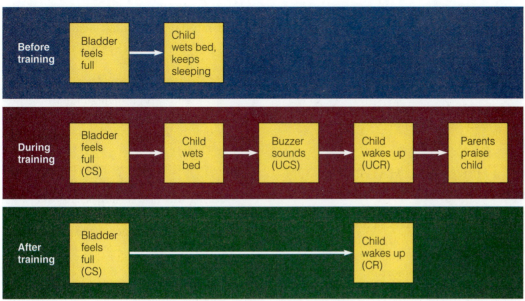

Before training	Bladder feels full	→ Child wets bed, keeps sleeping		

During training	Bladder feels full (CS)	→ Child wets bed	→ Buzzer sounds (UCS)	→ Child wakes up (UCR) → Parents praise child

After training	Bladder feels full (CS)	⟶ Child wakes up (CR)

FIGURE 15.2
A child can be trained not to wet the bed through use of classical-conditioning techniques. At first the sensation of a full bladder (the CS) produces no response, and the child wets the bed. This causes the buzzer to sound (the UCS), and the child wakes up (the UCR). By associating the sensation of a full bladder with a buzzer, the child soon begins waking up to the sensation of a full bladder alone, and will not wet the bed.

getting through the night without urinating. We also know that they are unusually deep sleepers who do not wake up when they wet the bed (Stegat, 1975).

The most effective procedure uses a simple device that makes use of classical conditioning. It trains the child to wake up at night and go to the bathroom without wetting the bed (Hansen, 1979). Here is how it works: Two thin pieces of metal foil separated by a piece of cloth are placed under the bottom sheet. The top piece of foil has holes in it, and wires connect the two pieces of foil to an alarm. If the child wets the bed, the moisture completes a circuit and triggers the alarm. In the early stages of conditioning, the alarm awakens both the child and the parents, and the child is taken to the bathroom to finish urinating.

The buzzer acts as an unconditioned stimulus (UCS) that evokes the unconditioned response (UCR) of waking up. In this instance, the body itself generates the conditioned stimulus (CS): the sensation produced by a full bladder (Figure 15.2). Whenever that sensation is present, it serves as a signal that a buzzer will soon sound. After a few pairings (or more), the sensation of a full bladder is enough to wake the child.

Actually the situation is a little more complicated, because the child is positively reinforced with praise for waking up to go to the toilet. Training with this device enables most, but not all, bed-wetting children to cease bed-wetting after 1–3 months of treatment (Bollard, 1982; Dische, Yule, Corbett, & Hand, 1983).

AVERSION THERAPY

Although behavior therapists rely mostly on positive reinforcement, they occasionally use punishments to try to teach clients an aversion (dislike) to some stimulus. For example, they might ask someone who is trying to quit smoking to smoke twice as many cigarettes as usual for a few days, to inhale rapidly (one puff every 6 seconds), or to smoke nonstop in a small, airtight room with overflowing ashtrays until there is little oxygen left to

Aversion therapy attempts to break a bad habit by associating it with something unpleasant. For example, someone trying to quit cigarettes might smoke in a small, poorly ventilated room until breathing becomes difficult. In other cases, a person might learn to associate cigarettes or some other undesirable habit with electric shocks or another kind of punisher.

breathe. The goal is to teach the client an aversion to smoking. At the end of this treatment, most people stop smoking at least temporarily, although they are likely to start again within a year (Poole, Sanson-Fisher, & German, 1981). Apparently, it is difficult to undo years of enjoyable smoking with a few unpleasant sessions.

THERAPIES THAT FOCUS ON THOUGHTS AND BELIEFS

Someone says to you, "Look how messy your room is! Don't you ever clean it?" How do you react? You might say, "Big deal. Maybe I'll clean it tomorrow." Or you might feel worried, angry, even depressed. If you get upset, it may not merely be because you were criticized, but because you want everyone to believe that you are scrupulously clean and tidy at all times. Some therapists focus on the thoughts and beliefs that underlie people's emotional reactions. Unlike psychoanalysts, these therapists are more concerned about what people are thinking right now than about early experiences that may have led to their thoughts.

RATIONAL-EMOTIVE THERAPY

Rational-emotive therapy is based on the assumption that people's emotions depend on their "internal sentences" such as "I can't be happy unless everyone thinks my room is clean" (Ellis & Harper, 1961). This therapy is called "rational-emotive" because it assumes that thoughts (rationality) lead to emotions.

Rational-emotive therapists (Ellis, 1987) hold that abnormal behavior often results from such irrational beliefs as these:

- I must perform certain tasks successfully.
- I must perform well at all times.
- I must have the approval of certain people at all times.
- Others must treat me fairly and with consideration.
- I must live under easy, gratifying conditions.

It is the word *must* that makes these beliefs irrational. Rational-emotive therapists try to identify people's irrational beliefs (which they may never have verbalized) and then contradict them. They urge clients to substitute other, more realistic "internal sentences." Rational-emotive therapists inter-

vene directly, instructing, persuading, and doing much of the talking. Here is an excerpt from a rational-emotive therapy session with a 25-year-old physicist:

Client: The whole trouble is that I am really a phony. I am living under false pretenses. And the longer it goes on, the more people praise me and make a fuss over my accomplishments, the worse I feel.

Therapist: What do you mean you are a phony? I thought that you told me, during our last session, that your work has been examined at another laboratory and that some of the people there think your ideas are of revolutionary importance.

Client: But I have wasted so much time. I could be doing very much better. . . . Remember that book I told you I was writing . . . it's been three weeks now since I've spent any time on it. And this is simple stuff that I should be able to do with my left hand while I am writing a technical paper with my right. I have heard Bob Oppenheimer reel off stuff extemporaneously to a bunch of newspaper reporters that is twice as good as what I am mightily laboring on in this damned book!

Therapist: Perhaps so. And perhaps you're not quite as good—yet—as Oppenheimer or a few other outstanding people in your field. But the real point, it seems to me, is that . . . here you are, at just twenty-five, with a Ph.D. in a most difficult field, with an excellent job, much good work in process, and what well may be a fine professional paper and a good popular book also in progress. And just because you're not another Oppenheimer or Einstein quite yet, you're savagely berating yourself.

Client: Well, shouldn't I be doing much better than I am?

Therapist: No, why the devil should you? As far as I can see, you are not doing badly at all. But your major difficulty—the main cause of your present unhappiness—is your utterly perfectionistic criteria for judging your performance. (Ellis & Harper, 1961, pp. 99–100)

2. *How does the idea behind rational-emotive therapy compare to the James-Lange*

theory of emotions, from Chapter 12? (Check your answer on page 667.)

COGNITIVE THERAPY

(16) **Cognitive therapy** seeks to improve people's psychological well-being by changing their cognitions—their thoughts and beliefs. Cognitive therapy is best known through the work of Aaron Beck with depressed patients (Beck, 1976; Hollon & Beck, 1979). According to Beck, depressed people are guided by certain thoughts or assumptions of which they are only dimly aware. He refers to the "negative cognitive triad of depression":

- I am deprived or defeated.
- The world is full of obstacles.
- The future is devoid of hope.

Based on these assumptions, which Beck calls "automatic thoughts," depressed people interpret ambiguous situations to their own disadvantage. When something goes wrong, they blame themselves: "I'm worthless and I can't do anything right." When an acquaintance walks past without smiling, they think, "He/she doesn't like me." They do not even look for alternative interpretations of the situation (Beck, 1991). Research has confirmed that depressed people are more likely than other people are to agree with such statements as "I'm a loser," or "Nothing ever works out right for me and it's all my fault," or "I never have a good time" (Hollon, Kendall, & Lumry, 1986).

The task of a cognitive therapist is to help people substitute more favorable beliefs. Unlike rational-emotive therapists, who in many cases simply tell their clients what to think, cognitive therapists try to get their clients to make discoveries for themselves. The therapist focuses on one of the client's beliefs such as "No one likes me." The therapist points out that this is a hypothesis, not an established fact, and invites the client to test the hypothesis as a scientist would: "What evidence do you have to support this hypothesis?"

"Well," a client may reply, "when I arrive at work in the morning, hardly anyone says hello."

"Is there any other way of looking at that evidence?"

"Hmm. . . . I suppose it's possible that the others are busy."

"Does anyone ever seem happy to see you?"

"Well, maybe. I'm not sure."

"Then let's find out. For the next week, keep a notebook with you and record every time that anyone smiles or seems happy to see you. The next time I see you we'll discuss what you find."

The therapist's goal is to get depressed clients to discover that their automatic thoughts are incorrect, that things are not so bad as they seem, and that the future is not hopeless. If one of the client's thoughts does turn out to be correct—for example, "My boyfriend is interested in someone else"—then the therapist asks, "Even if it's true, is that the end of the world?"

COGNITIVE-BEHAVIOR THERAPY

Many therapists combine important features of both behavior therapy and cognitive therapy to form **cognitive-behavior therapy**. Cognitive-behavior therapists set explicit goals for changing people's behavior, but in contrast to most behavior therapists, they put more emphasis on changing people's interpretation of their situations. For example, most of us get very upset if we see a clip on the news showing a fatal automobile accident; we would be much less upset if someone told us that the film was just a special-effects simulation (Meichenbaum, 1995). Similarly, cognitive-behavior therapists try to help clients distinguish between serious, real

Depressed people generally interpret ambiguous information to their own disadvantage. Cognitive therapists help them to reinterpret the situation. For example, people who do not talk to you may not realize you are lonely; you should not assume they are excluding you contemptuously.

problems and imagined or distorted problems. They help clients change their interpretations of past events, current concerns, and future possibilities. Cognitive-behavior therapy has become one of the most widespread forms of therapy in the United States.

HUMANISTIC THERAPY

As we saw in Chapter 13, humanistic psychologists believe that people can decide consciously and deliberately what kind of person to be and that people naturally strive to achieve their full potential. However, people sometimes learn to dislike themselves because others criticize and reject them. They become distressed by the incongruence (mismatch) between their self-concept and their ideal self. Humanistic therapists hold that once people are freed from the inhibiting influences of a rejecting society they can solve their own problems.

The best-known version of humanistic therapy is person-centered therapy, pioneered by Carl Rogers. It is also known as nondirective or client-centered therapy. The therapist listens to the client sympathetically, with total acceptance and *unconditional positive regard*, like the love of a parent for a child. Most of the time the therapist restates what the client has said in order to clarify it, conveying the message, "I'm trying to understand your experience from your point of view." The therapist strives to be genuine, empathic, and caring, rarely offering any interpretation or advice. Here is an example (shortened from Rogers, 1951, pp. 46–47):

> Client: I've never said this before to anyone. This is a terrible thing to say, but if I could just find some glorious cause that I could give my life for I would be happy. I guess maybe I haven't the guts—or the strength—to kill myself—and I just don't want to live.
>
> Counselor: At the present time things look so black to you that you can't see much point in living.
>
> Client: Yes. I wish people hated me, because then I could turn away from them and could blame them. But no, it is all in my hands. I either fight whatever it is that holds me in this terrible conflict, or retreat clear back to the security of my dream world where I could do things, have clever friends, be a pretty wonderful sort of person.

> Counselor: It's really a tough struggle, digging into this like you are, and at times the shelter of your dream world looks more attractive and comfortable.
>
> Client: My dream world or suicide.
>
> Counselor: Your dream world or something more permanent than dreams.
>
> Client: Yes. (A long pause. Complete change of voice.) So I don't see why I should waste your time. I'm not worth it. What do you think?
>
> Counselor: It's up to you, Gil. It isn't wasting my time. I'd be glad to see you, whenever you come, but it's how you feel about it. If you want to come twice a week, once a week, it's up to you.
>
> Client: You're not going to suggest that I come in oftener? You're not alarmed and think I ought to come in every day until I get out of this?
>
> Counselor: I believe you are able to make your own decision. I'll see you whenever you want to come.
>
> Client: I don't believe you are alarmed about . . . I see. I may be afraid of myself, but you aren't afraid for me.

The therapist provides an atmosphere in which the client can freely explore feelings of guilt, anxiety, and hostility. By accepting the client's feelings, the therapist conveys the message, "You can make your own decisions. Now that you are more aware of certain problems, you can deal with them constructively yourself."

CONCEPT CHECK

3. Answer the following questions with reference to psychoanalysis, cognitive therapy, humanistic therapy, and behavior therapy.
  a. In which type of therapy is the therapist least likely to offer interpretations of behavior and advice?
  b. Which type focuses more on changing what people do than on exploring what they think?
  c. Which two types try to change what people think? (Check your answers on page 667.)

FAMILY SYSTEMS THERAPY

In family systems therapy, the guiding assumption is that a troubled individual is probably part of a troubled family. In some

TABLE 15.1
Comparison of Five Major Types of Psychotherapy

TYPE OF PSYCHOTHERAPY	THEORY OF WHAT CAUSES PSYCHOLOGICAL DISORDERS	GOAL OF TREATMENT	THERAPEUTIC METHODS	ROLE OF THERAPIST
Psychoanalysis	Unconscious thoughts and motivations	To bring unconscious thoughts to consciousness; to achieve insight	Free association, dream analysis, and other methods of probing the unconscious mind	To interpret associations
Cognitive therapies	Irrational beliefs and unrealistic goals	To establish realistic goals, expectations, and interpretations of a situation	Dialogue with the therapist	To help client reexamine assumptions
Humanistic (person-centered) therapy	Reactions to a rejecting society; incongruence between self-concept and ideal self	To enable client to make personal decisions; to promote self-acceptance	Client-centered interviews	To focus the client's attention; to provide unconditional positive regard
Behavior therapy	Learned inappropriate, maladaptive behaviors	To change behaviors	Positive reinforcement and other learning techniques	To develop, direct, and evaluate the behavior therapy program
Family systems therapy	Distorted communication and confused roles within a family	To improve life of each individual by improving functioning of the family	Counseling sessions with whole family, or with individual talking about life in the family	To promote better family communication and understanding

cases, the person who first seeks treatment is the least disturbed member of the family; in any case, therapists are more effective if they can deal with a person's problems in the context of other family members. Marital counseling is a special kind of family system therapy, in which the therapist deals with a married couple.

Family systems therapy is not exactly an alternative to other forms of therapy; a family therapist may use psychoanalysis, behavior therapy, cognitive therapy, or any other technique. What distinguishes family therapists is that they prefer to talk with two or more members of a family together; even when they talk with just one member they focus on how that individual fits into the family. Their assumption is that many problems arise from poor communication or unreasonable demands within the family. Even when the psychological problem lies within a given individual (depression, alcoholism, or whatever), other family members have learned to treat the disordered person in certain ways; solving the problem requires changing the family environment as well as changing the individual's behavior (Clarkin

& Carpenter, 1995; Rohrbaugh, Shoham, Spungen, & Steinglass, 1995).

For example, one young man who had been caught stealing a car was taken to a psychologist. The psychologist, a family therapist, asked to talk with the parents as well. As it turned out, the father had been a heavy drinker until his boss pressured him to quit drinking and join Alcoholics Anonymous. Until that time, the mother had made most of the family decisions in close consultation with her son, who had become almost a substitute husband. When the father quit drinking, he began to assume more authority over the family, and his son came to resent him. The mother felt less needed and grew depressed.

Each member of the family had problems that they could not resolve separately. The therapist worked to help the father improve his relationship with both his son and his wife and to help all three find satisfying roles within the family (Foley, 1984).

Table 15.1 contrasts five major types of psychotherapy. Hundreds of additional types of therapy are available, including some that are quite different from the five I have

The novelist Leo Tolstoy observed, "All happy families resemble one another, but each unhappy family is unhappy in its own way." Family systems therapists find that most disturbed individuals are members of disturbed families.

described. About half of all U.S. psychotherapists, however, profess no strong allegiance to any single form of therapy. Instead, they practice **eclectic therapy,** meaning that they use a combination of methods and approaches. For example, an eclectic therapist might use behavior therapy with some clients, rational-emotive techniques with other clients, and occasionally borrow insights from psychoanalysis, person-centered therapy, and other therapies for use with all clients.

GENERAL TRENDS IN PSYCHOTHERAPY

The early practitioners of psychotherapy insisted on seeing each client one at a time, frequently, and long-term. Psychotherapy was, therefore, largely limited to people who could afford a rather expensive experience. Over the years, new methods have arisen for making psychotherapy less costly, less demanding, and in some cases more effective. We shall consider the possibilities of brief therapy, group therapy, and self-help groups; we shall also consider a strategy sometimes tried with clients who resist all efforts to help them.

BRIEF THERAPY

Psychotherapy can require a major commitment of time and money. An individual psychotherapy session generally lasts about 50

minutes; depending on the therapist and the nature of the client's problems, the sessions might be scheduled once a week or as often as every day. If the therapy begins with an open-ended plan to continue "as long as necessary," it can easily drag on for years. Indeed, many therapists, especially psychoanalysts, have assumed that frequent sessions over a long period of time are essential for a successful outcome, and regarded any client who quit after a few sessions as a dropout, a failure.

Eventually therapists realized that some of the apparent "failures" were really "premature successes" who did not need further treatment. In fact, about half of all the people who enter psychotherapy show significant improvement within 8 sessions, and three-fourths show improvement within 26 sessions (Howard, Kopta, Krause, & Orlinsky, 1986). (See Figure 15.3.)

As a result, many therapists began planning limits on the duration of therapy. At the start of **brief therapy,** or *time-limited therapy,* the therapist and client make an agreement about what they can expect from each other and how long the treatment will last—such as once a week for 2 months (Koss & Butcher, 1986). As the deadline approaches, both the therapist and the client are strongly motivated to bring the therapy to a successful conclusion. (How hard would you work on a term paper if you had no deadline to

Over the years, psychotherapists have altered their approach in many ways to meet their clients' needs, including brief therapy and group therapy. What will be the next trend? Here, two New York therapists offer therapy in a chauffeured van for the benefit of clients who would like to talk while on the way to work or on the way to the airport.

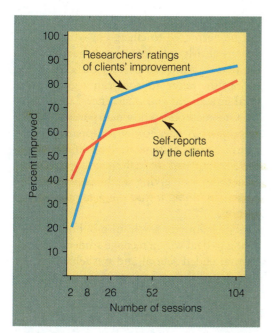

FIGURE 15.3
The relationship of the number of psychotherapy sessions and the percentage of clients improved. (From Howard et al., 1986.)

meet? How would a professor conduct class if your course were scheduled to continue "as long as necessary"? Without deadlines, few of us would apply ourselves as diligently as possible.)

Moreover, with a deadline agreed upon in advance, clients do not feel "deserted" or "rejected" when the therapy ends. They may return for an occasional extra session months later, but for a time they must get along without help. Any client who fails to make progress by the deadline should think about going to a different therapist. Many clients, probably most, prefer brief therapy to an indefinitely long commitment, and most clients with mild problems respond well to brief therapy.

Unfortunately, recent economic trends have created pressure for therapy to be extremely brief, sometimes too brief. A large percentage of people now receive health care through Health Maintenance Organizations (HMOs); they pay a fixed amount per month and then receive whatever medical care they need from the staff of the organization. Most HMOs offer brief therapy or "crisis intervention" as part of their services. In other words, anyone who belongs to such an HMO can get a few psychotherapy sessions (typically 3–20, depending on the HMO), without any extra payment. The advantage of this system is that many people who could

not afford psychotherapy otherwise can get some help during a time of distress (Hoyt & Austad, 1992). The disadvantage is that the HMO saves money by minimizing services. The organization provides only brief therapy, regardless of the severity of someone's problems. Any client who will need more than the allotted amount of treatment is either given a prescription for drugs instead of psychotherapy, or encouraged to see a therapist outside the HMO at the client's own expense (Karon, 1995).

Economically speaking, it is impossible to maximize the quality of care and at the same time minimize the cost. The goal of the HMOs, to provide good yet inexpensive therapy, is understandable; however, what some HMOs provide is simply too little. Working out a "cost-effective" solution will be a serious challenge.

GROUP THERAPY

The pioneers of psychotherapy dealt with their clients on a one-to-one basis. Individual psychotherapy has its advantages, most of all privacy. But for many purposes it is helpful to treat clients in groups. Group therapy is therapy that is administered to a group of people all at once. It first came into vogue as a method of providing help to people who could not afford to pay for a series of individual sessions. (Spreading the costs of a

Group therapy offers an opportunity for people to discuss their problems with others who have similar problems, under a therapist's supervision. Participants learn from one another's successes and failures; they also practice social skills.

session among 5–10 group members reduces the cost for each.) Eventually, therapists found that group therapy has other advantages as well. In particular, many clients seek help because of their failed relationships or because they have trouble dealing with other people. A group therapy session enables them to examine how they relate to others and to practice better social skills (Ballinger & Yalom, 1995).

SELF-HELP GROUPS

Self-help groups, such as Alcoholics Anonymous, operate much like group therapy sessions, except that they do not include a therapist. Everyone in the group both gives and receives help. People who have experienced a problem themselves can offer special insights to others with the same problem. They are particularly well prepared to deal with someone who says, "You just don't understand." They reply, "Oh, yes we do!" Self-help groups have another advantage: The members are available to help one another whenever someone needs help—often or seldom, without appointment, without charge.

Some self-help groups are composed of current or former mental patients. The members feel a need to talk to others who have gone through a similar experience, either in addition to or instead of treatment by a therapist. The Mental Patients' Association in Canada was organized by former patients who were frustrated and angry at the treatment they had received (or failed to receive), especially in mental hospitals (Chamberlin, 1978). Similar organizations in the United States and Europe enable former patients to share experiences with one another, provide support, and work together to defend the rights and welfare of mental patients.

PARADOXICAL INTERVENTION

Sometimes psychotherapists have to cope with patients who have no interest in helping themselves and who *like* being considered "mentally ill." Their behavior wins them attention and sympathy and gives them an excuse for not carrying out their obligations at home or at work (Fontana, Marcus, Noel, & Rakusin, 1972).

You are a psychotherapist trying to deal with someone who does not want to change. What do you do? You might decide that people should be free to choose how they will live. Or you might decide that people should *not* be permitted to engage in what you believe is clearly self-defeating behavior. Making that decision can be very difficult. If you choose the latter approach in a given situation, how might you intervene?

One method is known as **paradoxical intervention.** A paradox is an apparently self-contradictory statement. Paradoxical intervention consists of telling a person to do something but giving such an undesirable reason for doing it that the person will want to stop.

For example, a school psychologist was trying to deal with a teenage student who seldom attended school and misbehaved when he did attend. After a long series of other approaches had failed, the psychologist told him:

Psychologists sometimes find that children, somewhat younger than you, go through a phase in which they like to misbehave before they are able to become mature young men. This pattern is sort of like a last fling. . . . It seems that you have not passed through this childish phase yet. It is expected that you will be misbehaving and getting into trouble for a while longer than your mature friends until you grow up like them. . . . It seems it would be best for you if you didn't go to school until you grow through this childish stage; we don't want you to fight the urge to misbehave because you apparently aren't mature enough to control it.

After this conversation, the student's attendance and grades improved and his misbehavior declined (Kolko & Milan, 1983, p. 657).

Paradoxical intervention is used only as a last resort after more conventional forms of therapy have failed. Even then, it must be used with caution. Some people practice what they call "reverse psychology," which consists simply of telling someone to do the opposite of what they want the person to do; that practice can easily backfire (Haley, 1984). Paradoxical intervention is more than reverse psychology; it requires convincing the person that if he or she does the "recommended" action, it will be interpreted as a sign of childishness or some other undesirable characteristic. As with any other treatment, the therapist must constantly monitor the effects of the treatment.

EVALUATING THE EFFECTIVENESS OF PSYCHOTHERAPY

For the purpose of healing what ails your psyche, you can talk to someone who will be very curious about your childhood toilet training, someone who will compare your dreams to ancient myths and folktales, someone who will listen sympathetically without offering advice, or someone who will use learning principles to change your habits. You could also get a vigorous, almost painful, back rub or you could lie on the floor screaming to reenact the moment of birth. The list of possible therapies goes on, ranging from traditional, mainstream approaches to some odd and untested procedures. If you are spending just your own time and your own money, then the decision is entirely yours. However, in many cases a private or governmental health-insurance program pays for all or part of someone's treatment. Psychotherapy can sometimes become very expensive; some clients visit a therapist for as much as five or six sessions per week for months or even years, paying more than $100 per session. Before an agency starts paying for such a regimen, it wants to know whether the treatment will be sufficiently effective to justify the cost.

How can we measure the effectiveness of a treatment? You might imagine that someone could simply determine how much (if at all) people improve in their psychological well-being from the start to the end of treatment. That research method is inadequate, however. When would you guess people usually enter psychotherapy, when they are feeling better than usual or when they are feeling worse? Naturally, it is when they are feeling worse than usual, perhaps when they are feeling the worst they have ever felt. From that starting point, they have almost nowhere to go but up. That is, the apparent improvement in someone's condition might be due to natural fluctuations in psychological well-being, not to the effects of the therapy.

Hans Eysenck (1952) called attention to this issue by pointing out that about 65% of the people who never receive therapy for their psychological problems nevertheless improve in a year or two. Improvement without therapy is called **spontaneous remission.** To measure the effectiveness of psychotherapy, an investigator must compare the improvement of psychotherapy clients to the spontaneous remission rate.

WHAT'S THE EVIDENCE?

How Effective Is Psychotherapy?

In other chapters in this book, the "What's the Evidence?" section has highlighted a particular study. Here I want to describe a general research approach. Hundreds of research studies similar to this have been conducted, although each of them varies in its details (Kazdin, 1995).

Hypothesis Psychologically troubled people who receive psychotherapy will show greater improvements in their condition than similar people who do not receive therapy.

Method   For the results to be meaningful, participants must be assigned at random to the therapy and nontherapy groups. (Comparing people who sought therapy to those who did not seek it would be unfair, because the two groups might differ in the severity of their problems or their motivation for overcoming them.) In the best studies, people who contact a clinic about receiving therapy are all given a preliminary examination and are then randomly assigned to receive therapy at once or to go on a "waiting list" and begin therapy, say, six months later. At the end of six months, the investigators compare the amount of improvement by the therapy group and the amount of spontaneous remission by the waiting-list group.

How should the investigators measure the amount of improvement? Researchers cannot rely on the judgments of the therapists, who, after all, want to demonstrate the effectiveness of their procedures. For similar reasons they cannot ask the clients for an unbiased opinion on how much they have improved. Therefore, the researchers may ask a "blind" observer (see Chapter 2) to evaluate each client, without knowing who has received therapy and who has been on the waiting list. Or they may ask each person to take a standardized personality test, such as the MMPI. Unfortunately, the personality tests are far from perfect and a single evaluation by a blind observer uncovers only a limited amount of information. In short, this research method should be able to detect any major changes in clients' well-being, but it may overlook relatively subtle changes.

Many experiments on psychotherapy simply compare a group that received therapy to a control group that was on the waiting list. Other experiments, however, have compared groups receiving different kinds of therapy or different frequencies of therapy.

Results   Here we are not interested in the results of any single study. Most experiments have included only a modest number of people, such as 10 or 20 receiving therapy and a similar number on the waiting list. To draw a conclusion, we need to pool the results from a great many similar experiments. Psychologists use a method called **meta-analysis**, taking the results of many experiments, weighting each one in proportion to the number of participants, and determining the overall average effect. According to one meta-analysis that pooled the results of 475 experiments, the average person in therapy shows greater improvement than 80% of similarly troubled people who are not in therapy (Smith, Glass, & Miller, 1980). Figure 15.4 illustrates this effect.

Interpretation   One could easily complain that investigators have invested a great deal of effort for rather little payoff. After 475 experiments we can say that getting therapy is—usually—better than not getting therapy. This is a little like saying that if you are ill, medicine is better than no medicine, or that education is better than no education.

However, even if the conclusion seems unimpressive, it is a start. Next, of course, we want to know which kinds of therapy are best and for which disorders they are most effective. A more detailed examination of the meta-analysis data indicated that, as a rule, therapies using cognitive or cognitive-behavioral methods produced slightly larger benefits than other treatments, and that people suffering from depression or a simple phobia responded better to therapy than did people with vague, general complaints or all-pervasive problems (Singer, 1981; Smith et al., 1980). These results pave the way for additional, more detailed investigations.

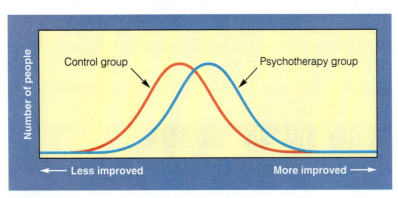

FIGURE 15.4

According to one review of 475 studies, the average person receiving psychotherapy shows more improvement than do 80% of similar, randomly assigned people not in therapy. Note that both groups show substantial variation; some untreated people progress better than some treated people. This comparison lumps together all kinds of therapy and all kinds of troubled people. (From Smith, Glass, & Miller, 1980.)

4. Although well-designed experiments on psychotherapy use a blind observer to rate clients' mental health, double-blind studies are virtually impossible. Why? (Check your answer on page 667.)

COMPARISONS OF DIFFERENT THERAPIES AND THERAPISTS

Although the meta-analysis indicated that cognitive and cognitive-behavioral therapies are the most effective, at least for treating certain kinds of disorders, the fact is that virtually every kind of therapy produces apparent benefits (Lipsey & Wilson, 1993; Stiles, Shapiro, & Elliott, 1986). That fact should surprise us, given that psychoanalysis, behavior therapy, person-centered therapy, and the others differ so sharply in their assumptions, methods, and goals. If all treatments succeed almost equally well, they must resemble one another more than we had thought.

If we compare results across therapists, we find the same remarkable similarity. Unquestionably, some individual therapists are vastly more successful than others are; however, differences based on the *credentials* of therapists are difficult to demonstrate. Of all the people suffering from psychological disorders—including alcohol abuse, phobias, anxieties, social adjustment problems, and so forth—some consult psychologists or psychiatrists, some talk with their physicians or clergy, some join a self-help group such as Alcoholics Anonymous, and some seek no help at all (Regier et al., 1993). (See Figure 15.5.) The research indicates that people who get help do better than those who get no help, but it does not indicate that psychologists and psychiatrists provide consistently better help than less specialized helpers do. Indeed, in some experiments, clients have been randomly assigned to talk with either an experienced therapist or a "caring" individual who had no formal training in psychology. Most clients gained about as much from consulting the inexperienced as the experienced therapists. In short, talking with someone about a psychological concern is generally helpful, but we have no evidence

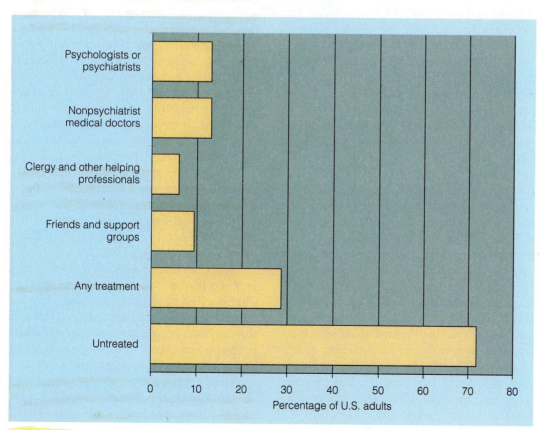

FIGURE 15.5

According to a survey of a random sample of U.S. adults, about 25–30% of all people get some sort of help for psychological problems within a given year. (Based on data of Regier et al., 1993.)

The research indicates that talking with an inexperienced but caring individual is about as helpful for most clients as talking with an experienced psychotherapist. The experienced therapist does offer certain advantages, however, including guaranteed privacy and a willingness to continue meeting and listening far longer than any friend would.

that the extensive experience or training of the therapist improves the results (Christensen & Jacobson, 1994; Dawes, 1994).

Is the conclusion, then, that if you are psychologically troubled, you may as well talk to your next-door neighbor instead of a psychotherapist? No. Not many of us have a friend or next-door neighbor with enough patience to listen to hours of personal ramblings. Furthermore, conversation with a professional psychotherapist has the significant advantage of being completely confidential; your therapist will keep secret anything you might say. You cannot be sure of that assumption after a conversation with a friend. Also, if you have symptoms that indicate a brain tumor or a hormonal imbalance or some other medical disorder, a well-trained psychotherapist should recognize that possibility and refer you to an appropriate medical specialist; an untrained person is less likely to note the medical warning signs. In short, although you can benefit by talking even to a completely inexperienced person, there are important advantages to seeing a professional psychotherapist.

Nevertheless, the research on psychotherapeutic effectiveness does suggest that we should be skeptical of therapists who make unrestrained claims that go beyond the

evidence. Some (repeat: *some*) therapists claim that their "years of clinical experience" enable them to determine whether or not someone was sane at the time of a crime, to predict which prisoners would be most dangerous if released on parole, to infer what was going on in someone's mind at the time of committing suicide, or to determine just by watching people whether or not they were sexually abused in childhood. Little or no evidence supports such claims (Dawes, 1994). In fact, according to Dawes (1994), a major reason why experienced therapists are *not* more effective than less experienced therapists is that too many experienced therapists become overconfident of their clinical intuition and rely on it instead of scientifically validated information and procedures. As in other matters, people do best when they recognize their own limitations.

SIMILARITIES AMONG PSYCHOTHERAPEUTIC METHODS

The fact that all forms of psychotherapy are almost equally effective implies that they all share some important features. For example, they all rely on the "therapeutic alliance"— a relationship between therapist and client that is characterized by acceptance, caring, respect, and attention. This relationship provides the social support that helps clients deal with their problems and acquire social skills that they can apply to other relationships. The research documents that clients who establish the strongest relationship with their therapists are the most likely to benefit from psychotherapy (Krupnick et al., 1994).

Moreover, in nearly all forms of therapy, clients talk about their beliefs and emotions, how they act, and why they act that way. They examine aspects of themselves that they ordinarily take for granted; in so doing, they gain self-understanding.

The mere fact of entering therapy, whatever the method, improves clients' morale. The therapist conveys the message "You are going to get better." Clients begin to think of themselves as people who can cope with their problems and overcome them. Just expecting improvement can lead to improvement.

Finally, every form of therapy requires clients to commit themselves to making some sort of change in their lifestyle (Klein, Zitrin, Woerner, & Ross, 1983). Simply by coming to the therapy session, they are reaffirming their commitment—to drink less, to feel less depressed, or to overcome a fear. They are also obliged to work on that change between sessions so that they can come to the next session and report, "I've been doing a little better lately." Improvement may depend at least as much on what clients do between sessions as on what happens in the sessions themselves.

Let us close this section with an illustration of how some therapists attempt to strengthen their clients' commitment to change (Haley, 1984). Suppose the problem is cigarette smoking. After discussing the habit with the client, the therapist casually mentions a "guaranteed cure" and then changes the subject. The client asks skeptically about the guaranteed cure, and the therapist says that it is not for everyone. "You probably wouldn't be interested."

"What do you mean I wouldn't be interested? What is it?"

"Well," replies the therapist, "part of the deal is that I can't tell you what the method is unless you agree to follow it."

"But how can I do that if I don't know what it is?"

"You're absolutely right. As I said, I don't think you would be interested."

Over the next few weeks the client keeps returning to the topic of the guaranteed cure, becoming more and more curious. Each time, the therapist refuses to describe it and tries to change the subject. Eventually the client says, "All right. Whatever this guaranteed cure thing is, I'll do it." The therapist encourages the client to discuss this decision with friends and return the next week. At that point the therapist finally reveals the plan:

"I want you to carry a little notebook with you and record every time you smoke a cigarette. When you come back next week I'll ask you to show it to me. For the first cigarette, you'll owe me a penny, in addition to my usual fee. For the second cigarette, you'll owe me two pennies. The next one will cost you four pennies, and so on. The price doubles for each cigarette."

The client leaves, disappointed by this unimpressive scheme but committed to follow it. The next week the client returns with $40.95, the charge for 12 cigarettes. "You dirty so-and-so! The first few cigarettes were cheap. But now they're getting expensive! I've smoked my last cigarette!"

The therapist pretends to be disappointed. "Nuts! There goes my trip to the Bahamas."

This treatment succeeds only because the client makes an irrevocable commitment to follow the therapist's plan. Once that commitment has been made, the battle is half won. Without such a commitment, success would be doubtful. Even with other therapies that do not make such an intentional ordeal of it, the client's commitment to change is essential.

ADVICE FOR POSSIBLE PSYCHOTHERAPY CLIENTS

At some point you or someone close to you may be interested in seeing a psychotherapist. If so, here is some advice to consider:

• Seeing a therapist does not mean that something is wrong with you. About half the people who consult a therapist have no diagnosable disorder; they merely want to talk with someone about a worry or concern.

• If you live in the United States, you can look in the white pages of your telephone directory under Mental Health Association. Call them and ask for a recommendation of a therapist. You can specify how much you are willing to pay, what kind of problem you have, and even what kind of theoretical orientation you prefer (or wish to avoid).

• If your religion is an important part of your outlook on life, you might prefer a therapist who shares your religion or at least sympathizes with your religious beliefs (Jones, 1994). You can check about this issue before making an appointment.

• Similarly, some clients prefer a therapist of their own ethnic background, sex, or sexual orientation because they believe such a person will understand them more easily (Allison, Crawford, Echemendia, Robinson, & Knepp, 1994). However, most therapists make a strong effort to be sensitive to people's diverse backgrounds. Ordinarily, the issue to consider is not whether the therapist will have trouble talking to someone of your background, but whether *you* will have trouble talking to someone of a different background.

• Be skeptical of any therapist who seems overconfident or arrogant. Clinical experience does not give anyone quick access to understanding your private thoughts.

• Even if your treatment is not labeled "brief therapy," expect some improvement within 6–8 weeks. If you do not seem to be making adequate progress, feel free to switch to a different therapist.

SUMMARY

- *Psychoanalysis.* Psychoanalysts try to uncover the unconscious reasons behind self-defeating behaviors. To bring the unconscious to consciousness, they rely on free association, dream analysis, and transference. (page 649)

- *Behavior therapy.* Behavior therapists set specific goals for changing a client's behavior and use a variety of learning techniques to help a client achieve those goals. (page 652)

- *Cognitive therapies.* Cognitive therapists try to get clients to give up their irrational beliefs and unrealistic goals and to replace defeatist thinking with more favorable views of themselves and the world. Many therapists combine features of behavior therapy and cognitive therapy, attempting to change people's behaviors by altering how they interpret the situation. (page 654)

- *Humanistic therapy.* Humanistic therapists, including person-centered therapists, assume that if people accept themselves as they are, they can solve their own problems. Person-centered therapists listen with unconditional positive regard but seldom offer interpretations or advice. (page 656)

- *Family systems therapy.* In many cases an individual's problem is part of an overall disorder of family communications and expectations. Family systems therapists try to work with all the members of a family. (page 656)

- *Eclectic therapy.* About half of all psychotherapists today call themselves "eclectic"— that is, they use a combination of methods, depending on the circumstances. (page 658)

- *Brief therapy.* Many therapists set a time limit for the treatment, usually ranging from 2 to 6 months. Brief therapy is about as successful as long-term therapy if the goals are limited. (page 658)

- *Group therapies and self-help groups.* Psychotherapy is sometimes provided to people in groups, often composed of people with similar problems. Self-help groups provide sessions similar to group therapy but without a therapist. (page 659)

- *Paradoxical intervention.* If other treatments fail because a client shows no desire to improve, a therapist sometimes "recommends" the undesirable behavior, while giving it an unpleasant meaning. (page 660)

- *Effectiveness of psychotherapy.* The average troubled person in therapy improves more than at least 80% of people not in therapy. The research has demonstrated small differences among types of therapy and no consistent differences based on the experience of the therapist. (page 661)

- *Similarities among therapies.* A wide variety of therapies share certain features: All rely on a caring relationship between therapist and client. All promote self-understanding. All improve clients' morale. And all require a commitment by clients to try to make changes in their lives. (page 664)

SUGGESTIONS FOR FURTHER READING

Bongar, B., & Beutler, L. E. (1995). *Comprehensive textbook of psychotherapy.* Oxford, England: Oxford University Press. Describes the theoretical assumptions and procedures of the most common forms of psychotherapy.

Dawes, R. M. (1994). *House of cards: Psychology and psychotherapy built on myth.* New York: Free Press. A harsh criticism of psychotherapists who rely on their intuitions and experience instead of scientific evidence.

Seligman, M. E. P. (1993). *What you can change . . . and what you can't.* New York: Fawcett Columbine. Description of both the possibilities and limitations of psychotherapy.

TERMS

psychotherapy treatment of psychological disorders by methods that generally include a personal relationship between a trained therapist and a client (page 649)

psychodynamic therapies treatments that attempt to unravel people's underlying drives and motivations (page 649)

psychoanalysis a method of psychotherapy founded by Sigmund Freud based on identifying unconscious thoughts and emotions and bringing them to consciousness (page 650)

catharsis release of pent-up emotions associated with unconscious thoughts and memories (page 650)

free association procedure in which a client lies on a couch, starts thinking about a particular symptom or problem, and then reports everything that comes to mind (page 650)

manifest content the content that appears on the surface of a dream (page 651)

latent content the hidden content of a dream that is represented only symbolically (page 651)

transference extension of a client's feelings toward a parent or other important figure onto the therapist (page 651)

interpretation a therapist's explanation of the underlying meaning of what a client says (page 652)

resistance according to psychoanalysts, continued repression that interferes with therapy (page 652)

behavior therapy treatment that begins with clear, well-defined behavioral goals, such as eliminating test anxiety, and then attempts to achieve those goals through learning (page 652)

rational-emotive therapy treatment based on the assumption that people's emotions depend on their "internal sentences" such as "I can't be happy unless everyone thinks my room is clean" (page 654)

cognitive therapy treatment that seeks to improve people's psychological well-being by changing their cognitions (page 655)

cognitive-behavior therapy treatment that combines important features of both behavior therapy and cognitive therapy, attempting to change people's behavior by changing their interpretation of their situations (page 655)

incongruence a mismatch between someone's self-concept and ideal self (page 656)

person-centered therapy (also known as nondirective or client-centered therapy) procedure in which a therapist listens to the client sympathetically, provides unconditional positive regard, and offers little interpretation or advice (page 656)

family systems therapy treatment provided for members of one family, generally meeting as a group (page 656)

eclectic therapy treatment that uses a combination of methods and approaches (page 658)

brief therapy (or time-limited therapy) treatment that begins with an agreement on what therapist and client can expect from each other and how long the treatment will last (page 658)

group therapy treatment administered to a group of people all at one time (page 659)

paradoxical intervention procedure in which a psychologist tells a person to do something but gives an undesirable reason for doing it in hopes that the person will want to stop (page 660)

spontaneous remission improvement of a psychological condition without therapy (page 661)

meta-analysis method of taking the results of many experiments, weighting each one in proportion to the number of participants, and determining the overall average effect (page 662)

ANSWERS TO CONCEPT CHECKS

1. Freud would disagree with the premise of this paperback. Freud believed that the symbolism of dream elements differed from one person to another. (page 651)

2. Rational-emotive therapy assumes that many thoughts lead to emotions. This assumption is the reverse of the James-Lange theory, which argues that emotion-related changes in the body give rise to thoughts. (page 654)

3. (a) humanistic therapy; (b) behavior therapy; (c) psychoanalysis and cognitive therapy. (page 656)

4. A double-blind design requires that neither the subjects nor the observers know which subjects received the experimental treatment and which ones were in the control group. It is not possible to prevent subjects from knowing whether or not they have received psychotherapy. (page 663)

MEDICAL THERAPIES

How do drugs and other medical interventions alleviate psychological disorders?

How effective are medical therapies?

Under what circumstances should they be used?

In his novel *The Idiot*, the Russian novelist Fyodor Dostoyevsky (1868/1969, pp. 245–246) described in the third person what he experienced just before each of his epileptic seizures: For a brief moment "it seemed his brain was on fire, and in an extraordinary surge all his vital forces would be intensified. The sense of life, the consciousness of self were multiplied tenfold in these moments. . . . His mind and heart were flooded with extraordinary light; all torment, all doubt, all anxieties were relieved at once, resolved in a kind of lofty calm, full of serene, harmonious joy and hope, full of understanding and knowledge of the ultimate cause of things."

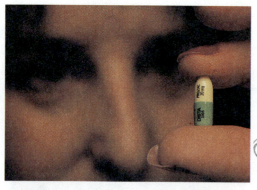

Psychiatric drugs have become a major industry. Drugs are available for the relief of anxiety, depression, schizophrenia, and other conditions. Two difficult issues arise: How effective are these drugs in comparison to other methods of treatment? And under what circumstances do the benefits outweigh the disadvantages?

Afterward Dostoyevsky debated with himself what to make of these moments of supreme bliss. Were they glimpses of the supreme beauty and harmony of the universe, moments when he could be at peace with his Creator? Or were all of these experiences just by-products of a diseased state of the brain?

This issue is not just a curiosity for scholars of Russian literature; it is central to medical therapies for psychological disorders. Said in other terms: Does happiness really "count" if it is induced by a physical change in the brain? In general, our society's answer to this question has been mixed. On the one hand, we do not want "normal" people to make themselves happier by taking drugs (or by trying to acquire the kind of epilepsy that Dostoyevsky had). We consider drug-induced happiness to be artificial, a poor substitute for the happiness people can find in real life. On the other hand, we *do* offer drugs to elevate the mood of depressed people, artificially bringing their mood up to "normal." If a depressed person, having recovered to normal mood, now wanted to increase the dosage to try for an even better mood, we probably would object (Nesse, 1991).

Medical therapies face philosophical issues of this type as well as practical and scientific issues. What are the effects of drugs and other medical treatments on people with psychological disorders? How do they work? And do they do more good than harm?

THE RATIONALE BEHIND MEDICAL THERAPIES

The various talk therapies we examined in the first module of this chapter all try to change people's thoughts and actions by providing new experiences. They rely on conversations between the client and the therapist or among members of a therapy group. The clients must be committed, or at least willing, to change certain aspects of their lives. Medical therapies differ from talk therapies in some important regards. They attempt to change brain functioning directly, rather than through experience. Once the physician and client have agreed to try a drug or some other medical treatment, there is no need for extensive or deep conversations. (To be sure, therapist and client might choose to have psychotherapy sessions in addition to the drugs, and they will at least meet periodically to evaluate the client's progress. Still, the drug's effects do not require talk sessions.) Moreover, clients do not need to make a commitment to changing their lives. They must agree to receive the treatment—or, if they are considered legally incompetent to decide, a legal guardian must agree—but no additional cooperation is necessary. The goal of medical therapies is to restore the brain to a normal physiological state, on the theory that normal physiology leads to normal behavior and experience.

Medical therapy for psychological disorders has a long and not altogether glorious history. For example, in the 1940s and 1950s a few physicians performed **prefrontal lobotomies** on thousands of patients, intentionally damaging parts of the prefrontal cortex in hopes of relieving schizophrenia and other disorders (Figure 15.6). The theoretical basis for this procedure was almost nonexistent and the surgical procedure was crude, even by the standards of the time (Valenstein, 1986). The surgeons who conducted the operations pronounced most of their patients improved and offered multiple excuses for why the others seemed unimproved or impaired. However, the patients suffered long-term losses of initiative and emotional expression, a decreased ability to concentrate, impaired social skills, and defects of memory and reasoning. After the advent of antidepressant and antischizophrenic drugs in the mid-1950s, people stopped performing lobotomies.

Another early medical therapy was insulin shock, a procedure in which people with schizophrenia were given an overdose of insulin to precipitate an epileptic-type convulsion, on the theory that people could not have epilepsy and schizophrenia at the same time. Insulin shock provided little if any benefit for people with schizophrenia and constituted an extremely unpleasant experience. Patients were exposed to heat, cold, water, and miscellaneous other treatments, generally on no theory other than the idea that "nothing else is working so we may as well give it a try." The medical therapies of today have to struggle to overcome the (deservedly) bad reputation established by the medical therapies of times past.

We shall discuss some of the current medical therapies for anxiety and avoidance disorders, depression, and schizophrenia. In Chapter 14, we already considered the use of

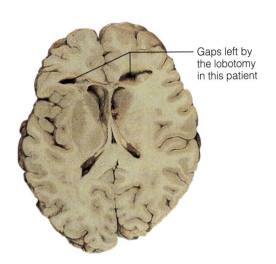

Gaps left by the lobotomy in this patient

Antabuse for alcohol abuse and methadone for opiate abuse.

DRUG THERAPIES FOR ANXIETY AND AVOIDANCE DISORDERS

Tranquilizers are among the most widely prescribed drugs in the United States (Robinson, 1987). The most common tranquilizers are the *benzodiazepines* (BEN-zo-die-AZ-uh-peens), including drugs with the trade names Valium, Librium, and Xanax. Benzodiazepines relieve anxiety, relax the muscles, induce sleep, and inhibit epileptic seizures. Sometimes they are prescribed for people with panic disorder, phobia, or other anxiety disorders; frequently they are also prescribed for people with no diagnosable disorder. For such people the drugs serve as a means of relieving an occasional episode of anxiety or as a sleeping pill. Benzodiazepines can be habit-forming, especially if used as sleeping pills.

Brain researchers now understand in reasonable detail how the benzodiazepines work. The neurotransmitter GABA stimulates receptors on a neuron's membrane, as shown in Figure 15.7. On its own, GABA attaches moderately easily to this receptor, opening a channel for chloride ions (Cl^-) to enter the neuron. Benzodiazepines alter the shape of the receptor complex to enable GABA molecules to attach more readily. Thus benzodiazepines indirectly facilitate transmission at these synapses (Macdonald, Weddle, & Gross, 1986). Facilitation of those synapses decreases anxiety and promotes sleep. Tranquilizers also reduce anxiety indirectly: People who have tranquilizers

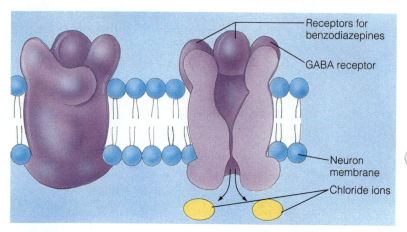

FIGURE 15.7

Benzodiazepine tranquilizers such as Valium and Librium attach to a site on the receptor complex for the neurotransmitter GABA. When they attach, they modify the shape of the receptor complex, making it easier for GABA to stimulate its receptor. Thus the benzodiazepines indirectly facilitate transmission at this synapse, enabling chloride molecules to enter the neuron. The effect on behavior is to relieve anxiety. (Based on Guidotti et al., 1986.)

available "as a crutch" are less worried about having an anxiety attack and are consequently less likely to have such an attack. Unfortunately, some people come to rely on tranquilizers for problems they could handle without drugs.

For people with obsessive-compulsive disorder, the drug clomipramine (Anafranil) and related drugs have demonstrated considerable effectiveness. Within 2 weeks on clomipramine, 50–60% of obsessive-compulsive patients experience noticeable relief from their symptoms (Clomipramine Collaborative Study Group, 1991). Clomipramine prolongs the effects of the neurotransmitter serotonin by preventing the presynaptic neuron from reabsorbing it. That is, after an axon releases serotonin from its terminal button, clomipramine causes the serotonin to remain longer than usual in the synapse, reexciting the postsynaptic neuron. The effectiveness of this drug suggests (but does not conclusively demonstrate) a biological basis for obsessive-compulsive disorder.

CONCEPT CHECK

5. Alcohol facilitates transmission at the GABA synapses. What effect should we expect if someone took both alcohol and a benzodiazepine tranquilizer? (Check your answer on page 676.)

BIOLOGICAL THERAPIES FOR DEPRESSION

Three types of drugs are used as antidepressants: tricyclics, monoamine oxidase inhibitors, and second-generation antidepressants. **Tricyclic drugs** (such as Tofranil) block the reabsorption of several neurotransmitters—dopamine, norepinephrine, and serotonin—after they are released by the terminal button (Figure 15.8). Thus tricyclics prolong the effect of these neurotransmitters on the receptors of the post-synaptic cell. **Monoamine** (MAHN-oh-ah-MEEN) **oxidase inhibitors** (**MAOIs**) (such as Nardil) block the metabolic breakdown of released dopamine, norepinephrine, and serotonin (Figure 15.8c). Thus MAOIs also prolong the ability of released neurotransmitters to stimulate the postsynaptic cell. MAOIs are not widely used, except for patients who suffer from a combination of severe anxiety and depression (Joyce & Paykel, 1989). **Second-generation antidepressants** (such as Prozac) are also called *serotonin reuptake blockers*. Like the tricyclic drugs, they act by blocking the reuptake of released neurotransmitters, but their effect is more narrowly limited to the neurotransmitter serotonin.

The effects of antidepressant drugs build up gradually. Some depressed people begin to experience relief within 1 week; most people have to take the drugs for 2 to 3 weeks before they notice any benefits. The relief from depression continues to increase over 6–8 weeks (Blaine, Prien, & Levine, 1983). What causes the gradual change in response?

The biochemical effects are complicated. While the drugs increase the amount of serotonin and other neurotransmitters that reach the synaptic receptors, the drugs also slowly decrease the sensitivity of those receptors (McNeal & Cimbolic, 1986; Sulser, Gillespie, Mishra, & Manier, 1984). Apparently, relief from depression requires both increased stimulation and decreased sensitivity.

These complex biochemical changes apparently relieve depression in part by improving the timing of the person's sleep patterns. Most depressed people have disorders of their 24-hour cycles. They are not as alert as other people during the day and not as sleepy at night. They wake up too early and cannot get back to sleep. Antidepressant drugs slowly restore their 24-hour cycles

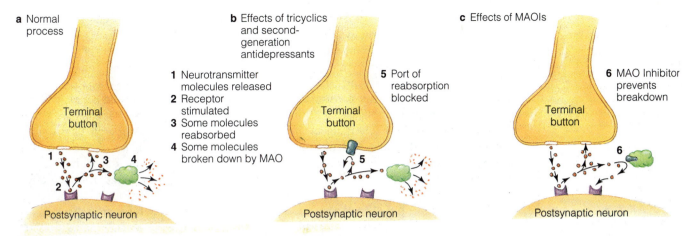

a Normal process

b Effects of tricyclics and second-generation antidepressants

c Effects of MAOIs

Terminal button

1 Neurotransmitter molecules released
2 Receptor stimulated
3 Some molecules reabsorbed
4 Some molecules broken down by MAO

5 Port of reabsorption blocked

6 MAO Inhibitor prevents breakdown

Terminal button

Terminal button

Postsynaptic neuron

Postsynaptic neuron

Postsynaptic neuron

FIGURE 15.8

Antidepressant drugs prolong the activity of the neurotransmitters dopamine, norepinephrine, and serotonin by two major routes. (a) Ordinarily, after the release of one of the neurotransmitters, some of the molecules are reabsorbed by the terminal button and other molecules are broken down by the enzyme MAO (monoamine oxidase). (b) Second-generation antidepressants prevent reabsorption of serotonin. The tricyclic drugs are less specific, preventing the reabsorption of dopamine, norepinephrine, or serotonin. (c) MAO inhibitors block the enzyme MAO. The result of any of these antidepressant drugs is to increase the stimulation of receptors on the postsynaptic neuron.

to normal at about the same rate at which they relieve depression (Healy & Williams, 1988).

CONCEPT CHECK

6. *The drug mianserin prolongs the release of dopamine, norepinephrine, and serotonin from the terminal button. Would mianserin increase or decrease the intensity of depression? (Check your answer on page 676.)*

ADVANTAGES AND DISADVANTAGES OF ANTIDEPRESSANT DRUGS

Antidepressant drugs alleviate depression for most adults, although they are seldom helpful with depressed children (Hazell, O'Connell, Heathcote, Robertson, & Henry, 1995). The drugs are convenient to use and are relatively inexpensive. Double-blind studies have consistently found that 50–70% of the adults who take tricyclic drugs experience an improvement in their mood, as compared to 20–30% of those who take placebos (Blaine, Prien, & Levine, 1983; Gerson, Plotkin, & Jarvik, 1988; Morris & Beck, 1974).

Overall, cognitive therapy is beneficial to a slightly higher percentage of depressed patients than drug therapy is, and its benefits are more likely to be long lasting (Robinson,

Berman, & Neimeyer, 1990). Cognitive therapy also has the advantage of producing no side effects. You might wonder why anyone would choose drug therapy. There are two reasons: First, drug therapy tends to work more quickly. (Remember, 2 months of psychotherapy is considered "brief psychotherapy." The drugs show benefits within 1–3 weeks.) Second, drug therapy is decidedly less expensive.

To a large extent, drug therapies are limited by the drugs' side effects. About one-third of the people who take tricyclic drugs experience dry mouth, dizziness, sweating, and constipation. A smaller number experience tremor, blurred vision, rapid heartbeat, impaired concentration, and other side effects (Blaine et al., 1983). In many cases, the side effects are severe enough to force people to stop taking the drugs or to reduce their dosage. The fact that many people cannot tolerate a large dosage is one major reason why only 50–70% of people gain significant benefits from the drugs.

The second-generation antidepressants, such as Prozac, became available in the 1980s. The advantage of these drugs is that they produce fewer side effects for most people; consequently most people can take them in larger dosages and experience greater relief from depression (Burrows, McIntyre, Judd, & Norman, 1988). In fact, because the side effects are generally so mild, some nondepressed people have taken Prozac—not in order to relieve depression (which they do not have), but in order to improve their personalities, to become more outgoing, or to feel "better than normal" (Kramer, 1993). In the controversies about this possibility, disputants have sometimes exaggerated both the likely benefits and the likely dangers of using Prozac for normal people. Still, most of us are unsettled by the idea of improving personality through drugs.

ELECTROCONVULSIVE THERAPY

Another well-known but controversial treatment for depression is electroconvulsive therapy, abbreviated ECT (Figure 15.9). In ECT, a brief electrical shock is administered across the patient's head to induce a convulsion similar to epilepsy. First used in the 1930s, ECT became popular in the 1940s and 1950s as a treatment for schizophrenia, depression, and many other disorders. It then fell out of favor, partly because antidepressant drugs and other therapeutic methods had become available and partly because ECT had been widely abused. Some patients were subjected to ECT hundreds of times without their consent. In many cases,

it was used as a threat to enforce patients' cooperation.

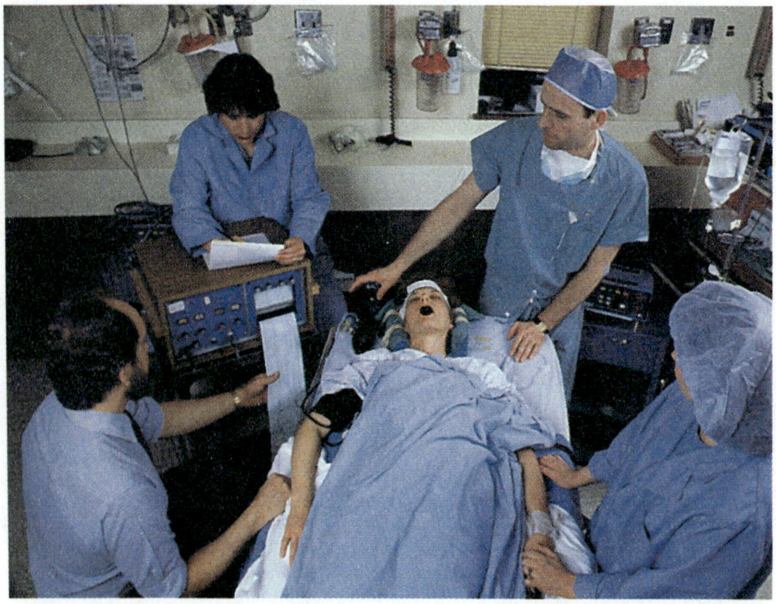

Beginning in the 1970s, ECT has made a comeback in modified form. Today it is used more selectively than it was in the past, mostly for severely depressed people who fail to respond to antidepressant drugs, whose thinking is seriously disordered, or who have strong suicidal tendencies (Scovern & Kilmann, 1980). For suicidal patients, this treatment has the advantage of taking effect rapidly, generally within a week. When a life is at stake, rapid relief is important.

ECT is now used only with patients who have given their informed consent, and its use is generally limited to six to eight applications on alternate days. The shock is less intense than it used to be, and the patient is given muscle relaxants and anesthetics to prevent injury and to reduce discomfort.

Exactly how ECT works is uncertain. Some have suggested that it relieves depression by causing people to forget certain depressing thoughts and memories. However, the data do not support that suggestion. Although ECT usually does impair memory, at least temporarily, there are ways to reduce the memory loss without lessening the antidepressant effect (Miller, Small, Milstein, Malloy, & Stout, 1981). Among the many effects of ECT on the brain, one may be of critical importance: By decreasing the sensitivity of synapses that inhibit certain neurons from releasing dopamine and norepinephrine, ECT increases the stimulation of dopamine and norepinephrine synapses (Chiodo & Antelman, 1980).

The use of ECT continues to be controversial. According to extensive reviews of the literature, ECT relieves depression for about 80% of the patients and generally produces fewer side effects than antidepressant drugs do (Fink, 1985; Janicak et al., 1985; Weiner, 1984). The brain shows no signs of damage, either immediately after the treatment or months later (Coffey et al., 1991). However, other researchers question those benefits and believe that the long-term side effects have been underestimated. Patients' rights groups, aware of how ECT has been abused at times, generally oppose its use. Furthermore, the procedure *seems* barbaric, and even its advocates frankly admit they do not know how it works. Because of the controversy and opposition, most psychiatrists hesitate to recommend it.

FIGURE 15.9
Electroconvulsive therapy today is administered only with the person's informed consent. It is given in conjunction with muscle relaxants and anesthetics to minimize discomfort.

LITHIUM THERAPY FOR BIPOLAR DISORDER

Many years ago, researcher J. F. Cade had the idea that uric acid might be effective in treating mania. To get the uric acid to dissolve in water, he mixed it with lithium salts. The resulting mixture proved effective, but eventually researchers discovered that the benefits depended on the lithium salts, not the uric acid.

Lithium salts were soon adopted in the Scandinavian countries, but they were slow to be accepted in the United States. One reason was that drug manufacturers had no interest in marketing lithium pills. (Lithium is a natural substance and cannot be patented.) A second reason was that lithium salts produce toxic side effects unless the dosage is carefully monitored. If the dosage is too low, it does no good. If it is slightly higher than the recommended level, it produces nausea and blurred vision.

Properly regulated dosages of lithium are the most effective known treatment for bipolar disorder (manic-depressive illness). Lithium reduces mania and protects the patient from relapsing into either mania or depression. It does not provide a permanent "cure," however; the person must continue to take lithium pills every day. When someone whose mood has become normal decides to quit taking the pills, mania or depression is likely to return within about 5 months (Suppes, Baldessarini, Faedda, & Tohen, 1991).

At this point, no one is certain how lithium relieves bipolar disorder. Many researchers believe its primary effects are on chemical pathways within neurons, not on transmission at a particular kind of synapse (Manji et al., 1991; Risby et al., 1991).

DRUG THERAPIES FOR SCHIZOPHRENIA

Before the discovery of effective drugs, the outlook for people with schizophrenia was bleak. Usually they underwent a gradual deterioration interrupted by periods of partial recovery. Many spent virtually their entire adult life in a mental hospital.

During the 1950s, researchers discovered the first effective antischizophrenic drug: chlorpromazine (klor-PRAHM-uh-ZEEN; trade name: Thorazine). Drugs that relieve schizophrenia are known as neuroleptic drugs. Chlorpromazine and other neuroleptic drugs, including haloperidol (HAHL-o-PAIR-ih-dol; trade name: Haldol), have enabled many schizophrenic people to escape lifelong confinement in a mental hospital. Although these drugs do not "cure" the disorder, a daily dosage does help to control it, much as daily insulin shots control diabetes. Since the 1950s, a majority of people with schizophrenia have improved enough to leave mental hospitals or to avoid ever entering one (Harding, Brooks, Ashikaga, Straus, and Breier, 1987).

All neuroleptic drugs block dopamine receptors in the brain, and their effectiveness in blocking those receptors is proportional to their effectiveness in relieving schizophrenia (Seeman, Lee, Chau-Wong, & Wong, 1976). One might assume, therefore, that schizophrenia is related to an excess of dopamine. However, the pattern is not that simple; extensive research has found no evidence that people with schizophrenia produce excessive amounts of dopamine or that they have excessive numbers of dopamine receptors (Jaskiw & Weinberger, 1992). A more likely hypothesis is that schizophrenia is related to the relative proportion between dopamine and other neurotransmitters, with dopamine appearing to dominate only because of a deficit of something else.

Neuroleptic drugs take effect gradually and produce a variable degree of recovery. Figure 15.10 shows one set of data concerning the rate of improvement with neuroleptics. As a rule, neuroleptic drugs produce their clearest effects if treatment begins shortly after a sudden onset of schizophrenia. The greater someone's deterioration before drug treatment begins, the slighter the recovery. Most of the recovery that will ever take place emerges gradually during the first month (Szymanski, Simon, & Gutterman, 1983). Beyond that point, the drugs merely maintain behavior but do not improve it. If an affected person stops taking the drugs, the symptoms are likely to return and to grow worse, though not in all cases (Figure 15.11). For a given patient, it is difficult to predict what will happen (Lieberman et al., 1987).

SIDE EFFECTS OF DRUG THERAPIES FOR SCHIZOPHRENIA

Neuroleptic drugs produce some very unwelcome side effects in certain people. The most serious is a movement disorder, tardive

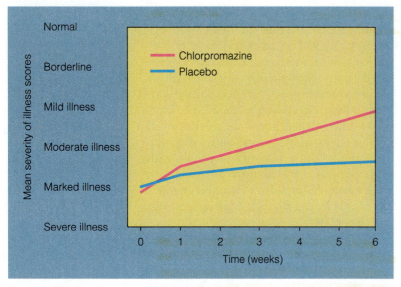

FIGURE 15.10
Antipsychotic drugs reduce psychotic symptoms gradually over several weeks. Placebo pills are noticeably less effective. (Data from Cole, Goldberg, & Davis, 1966; Davis, 1985.)

FIGURE 15.11
This graph indicates that during 2½ years following apparent recovery from schizophrenia, the percentage of schizophrenic patients who remained "improved" is higher in the group that received continuing drug treatment than in the placebo group. But it also shows that antipsychotic drugs do not always prevent relapse. (Based on Baldessarini, 1984.) Both the benefits and the side effects vary from one patient to another.

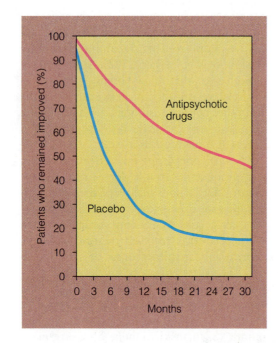

dict which patients will develop tardive dyskinesia and which ones will not.

Researchers have sought new drugs that could combat schizophrenia without causing tardive dyskinesia. On the theory that the symptoms of schizophrenia depend on one type of dopamine synapse and that tardive dyskinesia reflects changes at another type of dopamine synapse, researchers have experimented with drugs that specifically antagonize one or another type of dopamine receptor. Research has also focused on the relatively new drugs *clozapine* and *risperidone*, which relieve schizophrenia by combining moderate effects on dopamine synapses with additional effects on serotonin synapses. These new drugs have shown significant promise for relieving schizophrenia with a minimum risk of tardive dyskinesia; they also tend to relieve the *negative symptoms* of schizophrenia (such as social withdrawal) that other neuroleptic drugs fail to address (Carpenter, 1995; Meltzer, 1995).

CONCEPT CHECK

7. In Chapter 14, we considered the efforts that are made to diagnose schizophrenia as early as possible. Given what we know about neuroleptic drugs, why is early diagnosis so important? (Check your answer on page 676.)

DRUG THERAPY AND PSYCHOTHERAPY FOR SCHIZOPHRENIA

The degree of recovery produced by neuroleptic drugs varies, and drug therapy by itself is not a perfect solution. Some people with schizophrenia never have to enter a mental hospital, while others spend years in them and still others are in and out of hospitals throughout their life (Pokorny, 1978).

Although most psychologists and psychiatrists believe that psychotherapy by itself is not a very powerful treatment for schizophrenia, it can be a valuable adjunct to drug therapies. Highly stressful experiences sometimes aggravate schizophrenia and may cause a flare-up of problems that had been brought under control. If a patient faces constant criticism and hostility from relatives, the schizophrenic symptoms are likely to grow worse (Vaughn, Snyder, Jones, Freeman, & Falloon, 1984). Helping people with

dyskinesia (TAHRD-eev DIS-ki-NEE-zhuh), characterized by tremors and involuntary movements (Chouinard & Jones, 1980). Tardive dyskinesia is presumably related to activity at dopamine synapses, some of which control movement; however, the explanation for tardive dyskinesia is uncertain (Andersson et al., 1990). The condition is often permanent, although a patient who quits taking neuroleptic drugs at an early age has a good chance of recovery (Smith & Baldessarini, 1980). So far, physicians are unable to pre-

schizophrenia to cope with their environment can reduce the need for drugs. In some cases, family systems therapy improves the situation.

AN IMPORTANT QUESTION FOR FUTURE RESEARCH

Suppose we have a group of people seeking help for some disorder—for sake of illustration, let's say depression. The research tells us that various kinds of talk therapy would be effective for most depressed people. It also tells us that antidepressant drugs are helpful for most people. What it does not tell us is whether talk therapy and drug therapy are helpful to the *same* people. That is, are there some people who would respond better to talk therapy and others who would respond better to drug therapy? And within each category: Are there some people who would respond better to cognitive therapy and others who would respond better to, say, behavior therapy or psychoanalysis? Are there some who would respond better to one drug and others to a different drug? If so, how can we identify which treatment is best for a given individual?

Research has barely begun on these large and difficult questions. For example, according to one study of 239 depressed adults, those with better cognitive functioning responded best to cognitive psychotherapy, those with better social functioning responded best to a procedure called interpersonal psychotherapy, and those with severe depression that interfered heavily with their work performance responded best to antidepressant drugs (Sotsky et al., 1991). Another project, currently under way, is trying to identify which alcoholics are likely to respond well to Alcoholics Anonymous and which are more likely to respond to some other type of intervention. We shall need far more research in the future to begin to match people to the most appropriate treatment.

SUMMARY

* *Goal of medical therapies.* Medical therapies are designed to alter brain activity directly. (page 668)
* *Drugs for anxiety and avoidance disorders.* Tranquilizers are often used to control excessive anxiety. Clomipramine and related drugs have shown an ability to relieve the symptoms of obsessive-compulsive disorder. (page 669)
* *Effects of antidepressant drugs on the brain.* Tricyclic drugs and MAOIs are used to treat depression. Both types of drugs prolong stimulation of synaptic receptors by dopamine, norepinephrine, and serotonin. Second-generation antidepressants relieve depression by prolonging the action of serotonin only. For most people, second-generation antidepressants produce the mildest side effects. (page 670)
* *Effects of antidepressant drugs on behavior.* The effects of antidepressant drugs build up slowly over weeks. About 50–70% of depressed people benefit from taking these drugs, as compared to 20–30% of those who take placebos. (page 670)
* *Electroconvulsive therapy.* Electroconvulsive therapy has a long history of abuse; in modified form it has made a comeback and is now helpful to some depressed people who fail to respond to antidepressant drugs. (page 672)
* *Lithium treatment.* Lithium salts are the most effective treatment for bipolar disorder. (page 673)
* *Antischizophrenic drugs.* Certain drugs that block dopamine synapses often alleviate schizophrenia. Results are best if treatment begins before the person has suffered serious deterioration. (page 673)
* *Side effects of antischizophrenic drugs.* Drug treatment for schizophrenia sometimes produces a movement disorder called tardive dyskinesia. Atypical antipsychotic drugs have shown promise in relieving schizophrenia without inducing tardive dyskinesia. (page 673)

SUGGESTION FOR FUTHER READING

Heston, L. L. (1992). *Mending minds.* New York: W. H. Freeman. A nontechnical account of the use of drugs in psychiatry.

TERMS

prefrontal lobotomy surgical operation used in the 1940s and 1950s to interrupt communication between the prefrontal cortex and the rest of the brain (page 669)

tricyclic drugs drugs that block the reabsorption of the neurotransmitters dopamine, norepinephrine, and serotonin, after they are released by the terminal button, thus prolonging the effect of these neurotransmitters on the receptors of the postsynaptic cell (page 670)

monoamine oxidase inhibitors (MAOIs) drugs that block the metabolic breakdown of released dopamine, norepinephrine, and serotonin after their release from the terminal button, thus prolonging the effect of these neurotransmitters on the receptors of the postsynaptic cell (page 670)

second-generation antidepressants drugs that block the reuptake of the neurotransmitter serotonin by the terminal button (page 670)

electroconvulsive therapy (ECT) treatment in which a brief electrical shock is administered across the patient's head to induce a convulsion similar to epilepsy, sometimes used as a treatment for certain types of depression (page 672)

neuroleptic drugs drugs that relieve schizophrenia (page 673)

tardive dyskinesia a movement disorder characterized by tremors and involuntary movements (page 673)

ANSWERS TO CONCEPT CHECKS

5. The combined effect of alcohol and a benzodiazepine tranquilizer would decrease anxiety, relax the muscles, and induce sleep more effectively than either alcohol or a benzodiazepine could by itself. In fact, the combined effect can be so strong as to be dangerous, even fatal. People given prescriptions for benzodiazepine tranquilizers are warned not to take them in conjunction with alcohol. (page 670)

6. Mianserin should relieve depression and has in fact been used as an antidepressant. Although it acts by a different route from that of the tricyclics and MAOIs, it prolongs the stimulation of dopamine, norepinephrine, and serotonin receptors. (page 671)

7. Neuroleptics are more helpful to people in the early stages of schizophrenia than to those who have deteriorated severely. However, psychiatrists do not want to administer neuroleptics to people who do not need them because of the risk of tardive dyskinesia. Consequently, early and accurate diagnosis of schizophrenia is important. (page 674)

SOCIAL AND LEGAL ISSUES IN THE TREATMENT OF TROUBLED PEOPLE

What should society do about psychological disorders?

A group of nearsighted people, lost in the woods, were trying to find their way home. One of the few who wore glasses said, "I think I know the way. Follow me." The others burst into laughter. "That's ridiculous," said one. "How could anybody who needs glasses be our leader?"

In 1972 the Democratic party nominated Senator Thomas Eagleton for vice-president of the United States. Shortly after his nomination he revealed that he had once received psychiatric treatment for depression. He was subjected to merciless ridicule: "How could anybody who needed a psychiatrist be our leader?" In 1988 rumors circulated that the Democratic nominee for president, Michael Dukakis, had once received psychotherapy for depression. Although the rumors were apparently unfounded, they hurt Dukakis's standing in the polls.

A great many people suffer from a psychological disorder at some time during their life. Unfortunately, many people in our society consider it shameful to seek help for a psychological disorder. They struggle along on their own, like a nearsighted person who refuses to wear glasses, rather than admit they need help.

As a citizen and voter, you will have to deal with numerous issues relating to psychological disorders and therapies: Who, if anyone, should be confined to a mental hospital? Should mental patients have the right to refuse treatment? Under what circumstances, if any, should a criminal defendant be acquitted because of "insanity"? Can so-ciety as a whole take steps to prevent certain types of psychological disorders?

■ MENTAL HOSPITALS

About once every 8 seconds someone in the United States is admitted to a hospital or a nursing home because of a psychological problem (Kiesler, 1982b). Most of those people stay less than a month, but some stay years, even a lifetime. Hospitalization for psychological problems accounts for 25% of hospitalizations for all types of illness in the United States. Traditionally, we have told one another that we put people in these institutions "for their own sake." Sometimes that has been true, but often we have put people into mental hospitals for our own sake, because we found their behavior disturbing.

Until the 1950s, people with severe psychological disturbances were generally confined in large mental hospitals supported by their state or county. At the time most of those hospitals were built, severely disturbed mental patients had little hope of ever returning to society. Most of the hospitals were

Most large state mental hospitals were built long ago, when the goal of such institutions was to provide custodial care for patients who were likely to remain in the hospital for years, perhaps for life. Today, the goal of mental hospitals is to return people to society within a short time. Still, although the quality of such hospitals varies widely, many remain rather grim and uninviting.

located in remote country areas far from the patients' homes. (After all, the hospital staff expected to provide long-term custodial care, not to integrate the patients back into their own families and communities.) Frequently the hospitals resembled prisons (Okin, 1983). Patients had to depend on hospital attendants to cook the food, do the laundry, and make all the decisions. Little thought was given to helping patients learn the skills they would need if they were ever to leave. State hospitals claimed to provide psychiatric care, but most patients seldom saw a psychiatrist or psychologist. Moreover, state legislatures rarely furnished sufficient financial support to attract well-qualified, professional personnel. Some hospitals were better than others, but most of them were pretty grim places.

With the advent of antidepressant and anti-schizophrenic drugs in the 1950s, advances in psychotherapy, and changes in the

Community mental-health centers provide an alternative to state mental hospitals. A community mental-health center serves as a "halfway house"; people receive the amount of attention and supervision they need, but they are free to come and go and to live as normal a life as they can. Studies show that such alternatives to mental hospitals provide consistent advantages.

commitment laws, the number of long-term residents in mental hospitals began to decline, eventually reaching a level of about one-third what it was in 1950 (Pepper & Ryglewicz, 1982). The goal of mental hospitals is no longer to provide long-term custody, but instead to supply short-term care until a patient is ready to return home.

Unfortunately, however, many mental hospitals are still prisonlike institutions, ill suited to their new goals. Moreover, with the decline in mental-hospital populations, state legislatures have shown little interest in spending money on new, modern facilities.

DEINSTITUTIONALIZATION: THE CONCEPT AND THE REALITY

Given the unfortunate quality of many mental hospitals, many critics claim that people with mild to moderate problems are better off in community mental-health centers close to their own home. You might think of a community mental-health center as a "halfway house," not as restrictive as a mental hospital but not as unstructured as living at home. At a community mental-health center, each patient receives an appropriate amount of supervision and treatment, depending on his or her needs, but also enjoys some degree of independence, some freedom to come and go, and some contact with the "real world." Patients who have made sufficient progress may live at home and commute to the mental-health center during the day.

Several studies have compared these "alternative" forms of care with full-time confinement in mental hospitals. Every study has found that well-planned alternate care is as good as or better than care in mental hospitals in promoting psychological adjustment, in helping patients return to their school or job, and in restoring them to independent living (Braun et al., 1981; Kiesler, 1982a). Alternative care is also less expensive.

Such research prompted a movement toward **deinstitutionalization,** the removal of patients from mental hospitals. The idea is to give people the least restrictive care possible. Only those patients who cannot care for themselves or who are considered dangerous to society would be confined to mental hospitals. Others would be treated temporarily in a general hospital and then released (Kiesler, 1993). The rest would live in their own homes or in group homes and would receive care at community mental-health centers.

Unfortunately, many states got only half the message. They discharged great numbers of patients from their mental hospitals *without* planning adequate alternatives for care and housing (Pepper & Ryglewicz, 1982). By 1988, the population of mental hospitals declined to less than one-fourth of what it had been in 1955; however, a large number of people who would have been in mental hospitals are now in nursing homes; some are in prisons; others are homeless (Smith, Schwebel, Dunn, & McIver, 1993).

LEGAL ISSUES IN THE TREATMENT OF DISORDERED PEOPLE

In a democratic society, we treasure both freedom and security. Sometimes these values are in conflict. For example, the right of a psychologically disordered person to be free may conflict (or appear to conflict) with the right of other people to feel safe and secure. We shall consider several ways in which this conflict arises and the difficulties we have in resolving the conflict.

INVOLUNTARY COMMITMENT AND TREATMENT

A psychiatrist believes that Charles is severely schizophrenic. He cannot hold a job, he does not pay his bills or take care of his personal hygiene, and his neighbors consider him a nuisance. His family wants to commit him to a mental hospital, and the psychiatrist wants to give him drugs. But Charles refuses both courses, claiming that his family is "out to get him." Should he be permitted to refuse treatment?

We can argue this question either way. On the one hand, some seriously disordered people fail to recognize that there is anything wrong with them. On the other hand, some families have been known to commit aging or otherwise unwelcome relatives to mental hospitals just to get them out of the way. And some psychiatrists have given drugs and ECT treatments to people with only minor problems, doing them more harm than good. People often need treatment, but they equally need protection from inappropriate treatment.

Which people (if any) should be confined to a mental hospital against their will? In the

Deinstitutionalization is the process of releasing most mental patients from mental hospitals. Ideally, the released patients receive high-quality care in community mental-health centers or alternatives to the mental hospital. Unfortunately, in some cases mental hospitals have merely released patients without providing any alternative care. As a result, some former mental patients have no home, no job, and little prospect for a better life.

United States, laws vary from state to state. In some states, a court can commit patients to a mental hospital only if they are suffering from a mental disorder and are dangerous to themselves or others. The American Psychiatric Association has recommended that the laws be changed to allow commitment of any patient who "lacks capacity to make an informed decision concerning treatment" and who has a severe but treatable disorder (Bloom & Faulkner, 1987; Hoge, Sachs, Appelbaum, Greer, & Gordon, 1988). That is, they would rely on a judgment of the patient's competence rather than on whether the patient was dangerous. Regardless of how the law is stated, a judge has to make the final decision after a court hearing; the outcomes of such hearings vary haphazardly (Bloom & Faulkner, 1987).

Under a practice known as **preventive detention**, psychologically disturbed people who are considered dangerous to society can be involuntarily committed to a mental hospital to prevent them from committing crimes. This option raises some tricky

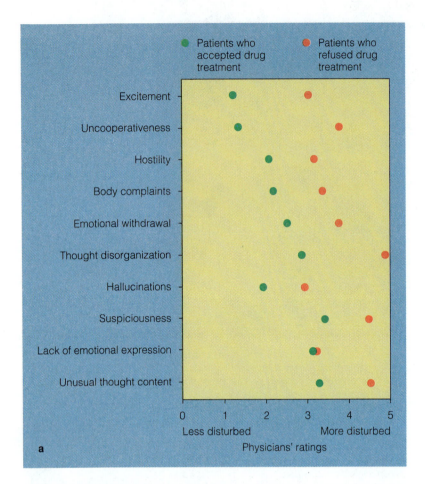

Excitement
Uncooperativeness
Hostility
Body complaints
Emotional withdrawal
Thought disorganization
Hallucinations
Suspiciousness
Lack of emotional expression
Unusual thought content

● Patients who accepted drug treatment
● Patients who refused drug treatment

0   1   2   3   4   5
Less disturbed   More disturbed
Physicians' ratings

a

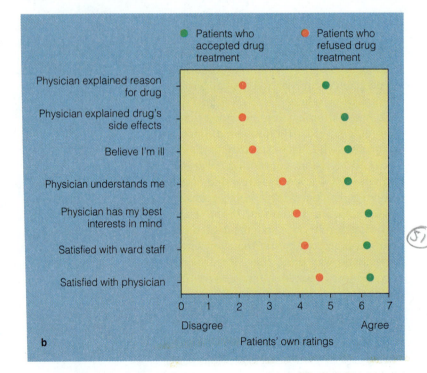

Physician explained reason for drug
Physician explained drug's side effects
Believe I'm ill
Physician understands me
Physician has my best interests in mind
Satisfied with ward staff
Satisfied with physician

● Patients who accepted drug treatment
● Patients who refused drug treatment

0   1   2   3   4   5   6   7
Disagree   Agree
Patients' own ratings

b

FIGURE 15.12
People with schizophrenia who refuse drug therapy impress their physicians as being seriously disturbed. The patients rate themselves as dissatisfied with their physicians and their treatments. (a) Physicians' ratings of their patients. High scores indicate greater disturbance. Those refusing treatment showed greater indications of disturbance on most scales. (b) Patients' self-ratings. The higher scores of patients who agreed to drug treatment indicate their higher satisfaction with how they have been treated. (Based on data from Marder et al., 1983.)

problems. Suppose a client tells a therapist, "Sometimes I feel like killing my boss." A few days later the client actually does kill the boss. Is the therapist legally to blame for failure to prevent this murder? Some courts have said that, indeed, the therapist has a duty to warn anyone whom a client has threatened to murder, or to impose preventive detention.

That ruling may sound reasonable, but imagine what happens in practice. You are the therapist; I am your client. I tell you that I felt like killing my neighbor yesterday because his barking dog kept me awake all night. You believe this was just an exaggerated way of saying that I was angry, not a serious threat of murder. But you're not completely certain of that; frankly, clinicians have great trouble determining whether a client is actually dangerous (Monahan, 1993). Given that you are not sure whether I am dangerous, you order me committed to a mental hospital—more to protect yourself against a lawsuit than to protect my neighbor with the barking dog. The result is that a number of psychotherapy clients who are not at all dangerous and who do not belong in mental hospitals may be committed to mental hospitals anyway.

Patients in a mental hospital have the right to refuse certain forms of treatment even if they have been involuntarily committed by a judge who decided that they needed those treatments (Appelbaum, 1988). What patients are likely to refuse treatment? According to their psychiatrists, many of them exhibit hostility, emotional withdrawal, and disorganized thinking (Marder et al., 1983). According to the patients themselves, they have good reason to be hostile and withdrawn; the hospital staff is trying to force them to submit to a treatment they consider unnecessary. Figure 15.12 compares patients with schizophrenia who refused drug treatment and patients who agreed to drug treatment. Understandably, decisions about enforced treatment can be very difficult.

SOMETHING TO THINK ABOUT

Thomas Szasz (1982) proposed that psychologically "normal" people write a "psychiatric will" specifying what treatments to give them, and what treatments to avoid, if they ever develop a severe psychological disorder. If you wrote such a will, what would you put in it? Or would you prefer to trust your judgment later, at the time of the disorder?

ARE MENTAL PATIENTS DANGEROUS?

Disputes about involuntary commitment often revolve around the question of whether someone is dangerous. Newspaper and television publicity about "mentally deranged" killers implies that many psychologically disordered people are dangerous. The impression of danger is compounded by selective reporting—we hear about the few mental patients who commit crimes and seldom about the many who do not. As a result, we perceive an *illusory correlation,* an apparent relationship between two unrelated or weakly related variables.

In times past, psychologists argued that former mental patients are no more dangerous than anyone else is. Further analysis of the evidence shows that their conclusion was overstated, because their evidence came from an era when only the best-recovered and least-dangerous mental patients ever got released from mental hospitals. Those very select patients were indeed not dangerous. However, today, when release from mental hospitals is a routine matter, we have to modify our conclusion.

For anyone, mental patient or not, the best predictor of violent or criminal behavior is the person's past history of violent or criminal behavior. As shown in Figure 15.13, mental patients with a past history of criminal arrests are likely to be arrested again; those with no previous arrests are likely to continue keeping a clean record (Cocozza, Melick, & Steadman, 1978). So the question is, how many mental patients fall into each category—those with a criminal past (and future), and those without? The results indi-

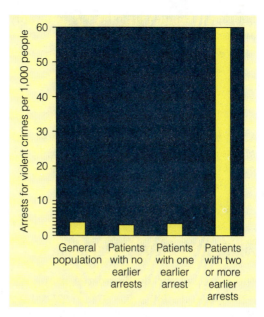

FIGURE 15.13
These arrest rates compare levels of violent crimes among the general population and mental patients. (After data reported by Cocozza, Melick, & Steadman, 1978.) Mental patients with a past history of criminal offenses are likely to continue to be dangerous; others are not.

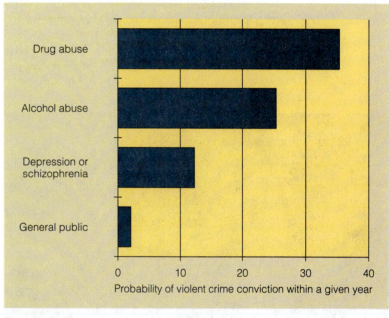

FIGURE 15.14
People diagnosed with certain psychological disorders are more likely than members of the general public to commit acts of violence within a given year. (Data from Monahan, 1992.)

cate that people with certain psychological disorders are more likely than the general public to commit violent acts; the probability is highest among people with alcohol or drug abuse (Monahan, 1992; see Figure 15.14). A few (very few) deeply disturbed mental patients commit extreme, senseless acts of violence, such as pushing a stranger in front of a subway train in a large city (Martell & Dietz, 1992). Such data do not justify a prejudice against people with psychological disorders,

SOCIAL AND LEGAL ISSUES IN THE TREATMENT OF TROUBLED PEOPLE

681

but they do caution us to be sure to identify and treat those mental patients who have a history of violence.

CONCEPT CHECK

8. *Why is it probably true that mental hospitals in some states contain more dangerous people than in other states? (Check your answer on page 685.)*

THE INSANITY DEFENSE

Most psychologically disordered people are not dangerous, but a few are. What should society do if such a person commits a felony?

Suppose in the midst of an epileptic seizure you flail your arms about and accidentally knock someone down the stairs, killing that person. Should you be convicted of murder? Of course not. Now, suppose that in the midst of severe hallucinations and

Courts have consistently ruled that the bizarreness of a crime does not by itself demonstrate insanity. In 1992, Jeffrey Dahmer was convicted of murdering and dismembering 15 men, cannibalizing some of them. The court ruled that he was sane; it granted that he was "abnormal" but maintained that he knew what he was doing.

delusions, you attack what you think is a giant insect, but in fact you are killing a person. In that case should you be convicted of murder?

British and American courts have traditionally ruled that you should not, because you are "not guilty by reason of insanity." Most people agree with that principle, at least for extreme cases. The problem is where to draw the line. Under what conditions should someone be judged legally insane? *Insanity* is a legal term, not a psychological or medical one, and its definition has gone through many changes over the years (Shapiro, 1985).

One point on which most authorities agree is that the crime itself, no matter how atrocious, does not demonstrate insanity. In Chapter 5 we considered the case of the "Hillside Strangler," who committed a long series of rapes and murders, but who was eventually ruled sane and sentenced to prison. The same decision was made for David Berkowitz, the "Son of Sam" murderer who killed a large number of women in the mid-1970s and claimed he was carrying out orders from "Sam," his neighbor's dog (Abrahamsen, 1985). In 1991, Jeffrey Dahmer was arrested after murdering and cannibalizing a number of men. The court found Dahmer sane also. In each of these cases, the crimes were ghastly and bizarre, but their bizarre nature did not demonstrate that the murderer was insane. In fact, each of the murderers knew what he was doing, knew it was wrong, and took steps to avoid getting caught. The juries therefore considered them sane.

In many other cases, a decision about sanity or insanity is very difficult; lawyers, physicians, and psychologists have long struggled to establish a clear and acceptable definition of *insanity*. One of the oldest, and perhaps the most famous definition, the **M'Naghten rule,** written in Britain in 1843, states:

To establish a defense on the ground of insanity, it must be clearly proved that, at the time of the committing of the act, the party accused was laboring under such a defect of reason, from disease of the mind, as not to know the nature and quality of the act he was doing; or if he did know it, that he did not know he was doing what was wrong. *(Shapiro, 1985)*

In other words, to be regarded as insane under the M'Naghten rule, people must be so disordered that they do not realize they are committing a criminal act. Many observers consider that rule to be somewhat narrow. They would like to broaden the definition of insanity to include "irresistible impulses"—acts similar to sneezing or hiccupping, which people could not inhibit for long, no matter how hard they tried. Under the **Durham rule,** established in 1954 in the case of a man named Durham, a U.S. court held that a defendant is not criminally responsible if the activity was "a product of mental disease or defect." That rule confused more than it clarified. Almost anything can be considered a mental disease or defect. And what does it mean to say that an act is a "product" of such a defect?

The **Model Penal Code**, written in the 1950s, attempted to clarify the definition of insanity:

A person is not responsible for criminal conduct if at the time of such conduct as a result of mental disease or defect he lacks substantial capacity either to appreciate the criminality (wrongfulness) of his conduct or to conform his conduct to the requirements of law. (Shapiro, 1985)

Again, the meaning is unclear. How does a jury decide whether a defendant lacked "substantial capacity" to appreciate wrongfulness or to conform behavior to the law? A jury hears such a case only in doubtful, borderline situations. If the defendant is clearly out of touch with reality, the police and district attorney ordinarily agree to bypass the trial and let the defendant enter a mental hospital. If the defendant has no serious signs of mental illness, the defense attorneys will not attempt an insanity defense, because they know that juries are reluctant to accept it. Necessarily, a jury that hears an insanity defense has a difficult judgment to make.

Under these difficult circumstances the jury will listen to the views of psychologists and psychiatrists who are called as "expert witnesses." However, given the vagueness of the law and the likely ambiguity of the situation, the expert witnesses often disagree with one another. Currently, the proper interpretation of the insanity defense is poorly defined. A jury that sympathizes with the defendant can use the insanity defense as a way of decreasing the penalty; a jury with less

sympathy can refuse to find the defendant insane. As a citizen, voter, and potential jury member, you should be alert for ways to bring more rationality to this portion of our legal system.

PREDICTING AND PREVENTING MENTAL ILLNESS

The traditional approach of psychologists and psychiatrists, beginning with Freud, has been to try to relieve psychological distress after it has developed. More recently, certain psychologists, especially community psychologists, began to pay more attention to prevention. **Community psychologists** focus on the needs of large groups rather than those of individuals. They distinguish between **primary prevention,** preventing a disorder from starting, and **secondary prevention,** identifying a disorder in its early stages and preventing it from becoming more serious.

Just as our society puts fluoride into drinking water to prevent tooth decay and immunizes people against contagious diseases, it can undertake measures to prevent certain types of psychological disorders (Albee, 1986; Goldston, 1986; Long, 1986;

Primary prevention of mental disorders relies largely on educating people about how they can avoid damaging their own mental health, that of their children, and that of their as yet unborn children.

Yoshikawa, 1994). For example, it can take the following actions:

- *Banning toxins.* The sale of lead-based paint has been banned because children who eat flakes of lead-based paint sustain brain damage. Other toxins in the air and water have yet to be controlled.

- *Educating pregnant women about prenatal care.* For example, women need to be informed that the use of alcohol or other drugs during pregnancy may cause brain damage to the fetus and that certain bacterial and viral infections during pregnancy may impair fetal brain development and increase the risk of psychological disorders.

- *Jobs.* Helping people who lose their jobs to find new work enables them to regain their self-esteem.

- *Child care.* Providing better day-care facilities would contribute to the psychological health of both parents and children.

- *Improved educational opportunities.* Programs that get young people more interested in their schoolwork have notable benefits in decreasing juvenile delinquency.

These techniques are aimed at primary prevention for the entire community. Secondary prevention techniques can be targeted at specific individuals who are just beginning to show symptoms of a particular disorder. For example, if we could identify people who are just in the preliminary stages of developing alcoholism or schizophrenia, psychologists might be able to intervene more effectively than they can if they wait until a later stage.

Although psychologists already know a certain amount about prevention, a great deal more remains to be discovered. Prevention turns out to be a difficult matter, requiring research and not just common sense.

SUMMARY

- *Mental hospitals.* Most mental hospitals were designed and built at a time when society expected mental patients to remain in them for a long time, even for a lifetime. Today, most patients stay a month or less. Large mental hospitals are not well designed to help restore people to society. (page 677)

- *Deinstitutionalization.* Community mental-health centers provide psychological care while permitting people some measure of free-dom. The care they provide is equal or superior to the care provided by large mental hospitals. However, many states have released patients from mental hospitals without supplying adequate community mental-health facilities. (page 678)

- *Involuntary commitment.* Laws on involuntary commitment to mental hospitals vary. In some states, people can be committed only if they are dangerous; in others, people can be committed if they are judged incompetent to decide about their own treatment. It is difficult to frame laws that ensure treatment for those who need it, while also protecting the rights of those who have good reasons for refusing it. (page 679)

- *Controversy concerning danger of mental patients.* Most mental patients are not dangerous; however, the risk of violent acts is somewhat higher among people with schizophrenia, depression, or substance abuse than it is for the general public. We need to distinguish between mental patients with a previous history of arrest and those with no such history. (page 681)

- *The insanity defense.* Some defendants accused of a crime are acquitted for reasons of insanity, which is a legal rather than a medical or psychological concept. The criteria for establishing insanity are vague and controversial. (page 682)

- *Prevention of psychological disorders.* Psychologists and psychiatrists are increasingly concerned about preventing psychological disorders. Many preventive measures require the cooperation of society as a whole. (page 683)

SUGGESTIONS FOR FURTHER READING

Ewing, C. P. (Ed.). (1985). *Psychology, psychiatry, and the law: A clinical and forensic handbook.* Sarasota, FL: Professional Resource Exchange. A review of procedures governing commitment to mental hospitals, the insanity defense, the right to refuse treatment, and other legal issues.

Sheehan, S. (1982). *Is there no place on earth for me?* Boston: Houghton Mifflin. The story of a young woman with schizophrenia and her life in and out of mental hospitals.

TERMS

deinstitutionalization removal of patients from mental hospitals (page 678)

preventive detention practice of involuntarily committing psychologically disturbed people to a mental hospital to prevent them from committing crimes (page 679)

M'Naghten rule rule that a defendant is not criminally responsible if, at the time of committing the act, the person was laboring under such a defect of reason, from disease of the mind, as not to know the nature and quality of the act he was doing; or if he did know it, that he did not know he was doing what was wrong (page 682)

Durham rule rule that a defendant is not criminally responsible if the activity was "a product of mental disease or defect" (page 683)

Model Penal Code rule that a person is not responsible for criminal conduct if at the time of such conduct as a result of mental disease or defect he lacks substantial capacity either to appreciate the criminality (wrongfulness) of his conduct or to conform his conduct to the requirements of law (page 683)

community psychologist psychologist who focuses on the needs of large groups rather than those of individuals (page 683)

primary prevention preventing a disorder from starting (page 683)

secondary prevention identifying a disorder in its early stages and preventing it from becoming more serious (page 683)

ANSWER TO CONCEPT CHECK

8. In some states, people can be involuntarily committed to mental hospitals only if they are dangerous. In other states, they can be committed if they are judged incompetent to make their own decisions. (page 682)

16

SOCIAL PSYCHOLOGY

In the *Communist Manifesto,* Karl Marx and Friedrich Engels wrote, "Mankind are more disposed to suffer, while evils are sufferable, than to right themselves by abolishing the forms to which they are accustomed. But when a long train of abuses and usurpations, pursuing invariably the same object, evinces a design to reduce them under absolute despotism, it is their right, it is their duty, to throw off such government." Vladimir Lenin later wrote, "A little rebellion, now and then, is a good thing."

Social psychologists find that influence depends not only on what someone says, but who says it and what the listeners think of that person.

Do you agree with those statements? Why or why not? Can you think of anything that would change your mind?

Oh, pardon. . . . That first statement was not from the *Communist Manifesto*—it was from the United States' Declaration of Independence. Sorry. And that second statement was a quote from Thomas Jefferson, not Lenin.

Do you agree more with these statements now that you know they were written by the founding fathers of the United States rather than by the founding fathers of communism?

What determines whether or not you will agree with someone who is trying to influence you? This question is one example of the issues of interest to **social psychologists**—the psychologists who study social behavior and how an individual influences other people and is influenced by other people.

Social psychology is a broad, diverse field that is difficult to define. I know I have just defined it as the study of social behavior and influence, but that term *social behavior* in turn gets defined very broadly, to include such matters as attitudes, persuasion, and certain aspects of self-understanding. A more useful characterization, if not exactly a definition, is that social psychology is a field that studies the everyday behaviors of more or less normal people, generally in their relationships with other people. In this chapter we shall consider several of the major fields of research and application in social psychology.

ATTITUDES AND CHANGING ATTITUDES

What are attitudes?

How do attitudes affect behavior?

What are the most effective means of persuading people to change their attitudes?

"**I**f you want to change people's behavior, first you have to change their attitudes." Do you agree?

Suppose you say yes. Now answer two more questions: (1) What is your attitude toward paying higher taxes? (2) If the government raises taxes, will you pay the higher taxes?

If you're like most people, you will say that (1) your attitude toward paying higher taxes is unfavorable, but that (2) if your taxes are raised, you will pay them. In other words, by changing the law, the government can change your behavior without changing your attitude.

So what effects do attitudes have on be-

havior? And what leads people to change their attitudes?

ATTITUDES, THEIR MEASUREMENT, AND THEIR INFLUENCE

An **attitude** is a like or dislike of something or somebody that influences our behavior toward that thing or person (Allport, 1935; Petty & Cacioppo, 1981). Your attitudes include an emotional component (the way you feel about something), a cognitive component (what you know or believe), and a behavioral component (what you are likely to do).

MEASUREMENT OF ATTITUDES

A common way of measuring attitudes is through the use of attitude scales, such as Likert scales, also known as summated rating scales (Dawes & Smith, 1985). On a Likert scale (named after psychologist Rensis Likert), a person checks a point along a line ranging from 1, meaning "strongly disagree," to 5 or 7, meaning "strongly agree," for each of several statements about a topic, as shown in Figure 16.1.

Checkmarks on an answer sheet are imperfect measurements of attitudes for several reasons. One problem is that different people have different styles of responding. For example, Japanese and Chinese people tend to put their checkmarks at or near the middle of the scale, whereas people in the United States tend to choose more extreme values (Chen, Lee, & Stevenson, 1995). Therefore a check-

Indicate your level of agreement with the items below, using the following scale:

	Strongly disagree		Neutral		Strongly agree
1. Labor unions are necessary to protect the rights of workers.	1	2	3	4	5
2. Labor union leaders have too much power.	1	2	3	4	5
3. If I worked for a company with a union, I would join the union.	1	2	3	4	5
4. I would never cross a picket line of striking workers.	1	2	3	4	5
5. Striking workers hurt their company and unfairly raise prices for the consumer.	1	2	3	4	5
6. Labor unions should not be permitted to engage in political activity.	1	2	3	4	5
7. America is a better place for today's workers because of the efforts by labor unions in the past.	1	2	3	4	5

Note: Items 2, 5, and 6 are scored the opposite of 1, 3, 4, and 7.

FIGURE 16.1
Likert scales—such as this one assessing attitudes toward labor unions—are commonly used in attitude research. Subjects rate the degree to which they agree or disagree with items that measure various aspects of some attitude.

Most people have a favorable attitude toward exercise, but only a few keep regular exercise habits. The attitudes that people express are not always closely related to behavior.

mark of "1" may not have quite the same meaning on an Asian answer sheet as it does on a North American answer sheet.

Another problem: People are not always aware of their own attitudes. Recall from Chapter 7 the difference between explicit and implicit memories: An implicit memory can affect behavior without the person's conscious awareness of the memory. Similarly, people can have implicit attitudes that affect their behavior without awareness (Greenwald & Banaji, 1995). For example, many people claim on answer sheets, and seem fully to believe, that they have no prejudices and that they treat all people equally. Nevertheless, they tend to give higher marks for essays they think men wrote than for essays they think women wrote, and they are more likely to evaluate an ambiguous act as "aggressive" if they saw an African American do it than if they saw a European American do it (Banaji & Greenwald, 1994). In tests of memory and cognition, they remember better and respond faster to stereotypical word combinations such as "black-lazy" than to counter-stereotypical combinations such as "black-brilliant" (Greenwald & Banaji, 1995). Generally, these same people are quite embarrassed to discover such signs of prejudice (Monteith, Devine, & Zuwerink, 1993). The point is, people sometimes have implicit, private attitudes that will not show up on answer sheets.

ATTITUDES AS PREDICTORS OF BEHAVIOR

It may seem obvious that attitudes influence behavior. If you have a positive attitude toward a certain brand of toothpaste, you probably will buy it. If you have a negative attitude toward your senator, you probably will vote for someone else.

Surprisingly, however, behavior often correlates rather weakly with attitudes (McGuire, 1985; Wicker, 1969). Why might

that be? One reason is that many variables other than attitudes also influence our behavior (Fishbein & Ajzen, 1975). For example, your favorable attitude toward new Porsches may not influence your buying behavior if you cannot afford an expensive car. Your favorable attitude toward getting good grades is no guarantee that you will devote yourself to your studies. Specific attitudes are better predictors than global ones; for example, your global attitude toward getting good grades may not predict much of anything, but your attitude toward studying your psychology textbook on Tuesday evening may be an excellent predictor.

The behavior of some people is more consistent with their attitudes than is the behavior of others. Some people are consistently inconsistent: Whenever they face an unfamiliar situation, the first thing they do is determine what is expected of them and what everyone else is doing. Such people, referred to as **high self-monitors** because they are constantly monitoring their own behavior to try to behave in the appropriate manner (Snyder, 1979), often behave in ways that do not match their attitudes.

ATTITUDE CHANGE AND PERSUASION

A great many people in this world will try to persuade you to change your attitudes and to do something that may or may not be in your best interests. They will ask you to give them your time, your money, your vote, your allegiance. Sometimes they will persuade you and sometimes they will not. The effectiveness of persuasion depends on *who* says *what, how,* and to *whom* (Hovland, Janis, & Kelley, 1953; Hovland, Lumsdaine, & Sheffield, 1949).

TWO ROUTES OF PERSUASION

Suppose you see a television advertisement in which your favorite actor or actress endorses some brand of cat food. The next time you go to the grocery store, will you buy that brand—presuming that you have a cat? You might; certainly many people would. Both advertisers and social psychologists have concluded that attractive or famous people tend to be more persuasive than unattractive, unknown people.

Now suppose that a little later you see your favorite actor or actress again, but this time endorsing a candidate for governor of your state. Now how do you react? Suddenly the celebrity has become much less persuasive. You probably think something like, "What makes him/her an expert on politics?"

Why didn't you ask the same question before? After all, great acting ability doesn't qualify someone as an expert on cat food any more than it does for politics. The difference is that your decision about cat food did not seem very important; you take the governor's race more seriously.

Richard Petty and John Cacioppo (1981, 1986) have proposed that certain kinds of persuasive influences weigh more heavily for some decisions than they do for others. When people take a decision seriously, they invest the necessary time and effort to evaluate carefully the evidence and logic behind each message. Petty and Cacioppo call this logical approach the **central route to persuasion**. In contrast, when people listen to a message on a topic of little importance to them, they may pay more attention to such superficial factors as the speaker's appearance and reputation or the sheer number of arguments presented, regardless of their quality. This superficial approach is the **peripheral route to persuasion**.

CONCEPT CHECK

1. You listen to someone who is trying to persuade you to change your major from astrology to psychology. Your future success may depend on making the right decision. You also listen to someone explain why a trip to the Bahamas is better than a trip to the Fiji Islands. You had no intention of going to either place. In which case will you pay more attention to the evidence and logic, following the central route to persuasion? (Check your answer on page 697.)

DELAYED INFLUENCE OF MESSAGES

In certain cases, a message may have no apparent influence on you at the time you hear it, but an important effect later. There are several reasons why a message can have a delayed effect; we shall consider two examples.

The Sleeper Effect Suppose you reject a message because of peripheral route influences. For example, you reject some new idea without giving it much thought, because you have a low opinion of the person who suggested it. If the idea is a good one, it may

Most political candidates will try both the central and peripheral routes to persuasion, depending on the situation. In debate and interviews, they try to impress with their knowledge and logic. In brief campaign appearances, they are more concerned with presenting an image, such as that of a "regular person just like you."

have a delayed effect. Weeks or months later, you may forget where you heard the idea and remember only the idea itself; at that time you evaluate it on its merits (Hovland & Weiss, 1951; Pratkanis, Greenwald, Leippe, & Baumgardner, 1988). Psychologists use the term **sleeper effect** to describe delayed persuasion by an initially rejected message (Figure 16.2).

FIGURE 16.2
The theory of plate tectonics and continental drift is one example of the sleeper effect. In 1912, Alfred Wegener proposed that until 225 million years ago, all of the earth's land was joined as a single supercontinent, Pangaea, from which our current continents divided and separated. At first, geologists dismissed and even ridiculed this theory. Four decades later, new evidence forced geologists to accept the idea of continental drift.

TABLE 16.1
The Political Platform of the U.S. Socialist Party, 1900

PROPOSAL	EVENTUAL FATE OF PROPOSAL
Women's right to vote	Established by 19th amendment to U.S. Constitution, ratified 1920
Old-age pensions	Included in the Social Security Act of 1935
Unemployment insurance	Included in the Social Security Act of 1935; also guaranteed by other state and federal legislation
Health and accident insurance	Included in part in the Social Security Act of 1935 and in the Medicare Act of 1965
Increased wages, including minimum wage	First minimum-wage law passed in 1938; periodically updated since then
Reduction of working hours	Maximum 40-hour work week (with exceptions) established by the Fair Labor Standards Act of 1938
Public ownership of electric, gas, and other utilities, and of the means of transportation and communication	Utilities not owned by government, but heavily regulated by federal and state governments since the 1930s
Initiative, referendum, and recall (mechanisms for private citizens to push for changes in legislation and for removal of elected officials)	Adopted by most state governments

Source: Foster, 1968, and Leuchtenburg, 1963.

ity to generate new ideas of its own (Nemeth, 1986). That is, by demonstrating the possibility of disagreement, the minority opens the way for other individuals to offer new suggestions different from the original views of both the majority and the minority.

One powerful example of minority influence is that of the Socialist Party of the United States, which ran candidates for elective offices from 1900 through the 1950s. The party made its best showing in 1912 when it received 6% of the vote in the presidential election. None of the Socialist candidates was ever elected senator or governor; only a few were elected to the House of Representatives (Shannon, 1955). Beginning in the 1930s the party's membership and support began to dwindle, until eventually the party stopped nominating candidates.

Was that because the Socialists had given up? No. *It was because they had already accomplished most of their original goals.* Most of the major points in the party's 1900 platform had been enacted into law (see Table 16.1). Of course, the Democrats and Republicans who voted for these changes always claimed the ideas were their own. Still, the Socialist party, though always a minority, had exerted an enormous influence on the majority.

Minority Influence Delayed influence also occurs if a minority group, especially one that is not widely respected, proposes a worthwhile idea: The majority may reject the idea at first but adopt it in some form later. By "minority group," I do not necessarily mean an ethnic minority; the minority may be a political minority or any other outnumbered group.

If a minority group keeps repeating a single, simple message and if its members seem to be united, eventually it has a good chance of influencing the majority's decision. The minority's united, uncompromising stance is important; it forces the majority to wonder, "Why won't these people conform? Maybe their idea is stronger than we thought." In many cases, majority members are slow to admit that the minority has swayed them; the minority's influence may increase over time (Wood, Lundgren, Ouellette, Busceme, & Blackstone, 1994). By expressing its views, a minority can also prompt the major-

2. At a meeting of your student government, you suggest a new method of testing and grading students. The other members immediately reject your plan. Should you become discouraged and give up? If not, what should you do? (Check your answer on page 697.)

WAYS OF PRESENTING PERSUASIVE MESSAGES

Most persuasive messages fall into one of two categories—do this to make something good happen, and do this to prevent something bad from happening. Either one can be effective, depending on the circumstances. Figure 16.3 shows a chain letter that has circulated widely throughout the world over several decades. It has been called a "mind virus" because of its ability to get people to duplicate and spread the letter (Goodenough & Dawkins, 1994). Many people who receive this letter cannot resist its command to make copies and send them to others, even if they regard it as a silly superstition. The letter claims to be offering "good luck" and "love," but it follows those promises with an implied threat: People who have failed to follow the instructions have been victims of terrible events. (They lost their job, lost a loved one, died, or had car problems!) The threat makes people feel nervous and uneasy if they decline to follow the instructions.

Sometimes fear messages are effective, as in the case of the St. Jude letter, but in other cases they are not. Appeals for money are often accompanied by implied threats, such as "If you don't send enough money to support our cause, then our political opponents will gain power and do terrible things." According to the research, messages that appeal to fear are effective only if they convince people that the danger is real (Leventhal, 1970). People tend to disbelieve an organization that exaggerates the threats or sends frequent "emergency" appeals.

Moreover, a fear message is effective only if people believe they can do something to prevent the threatened disaster. Frightening messages about AIDS have led many people to change their sex practices. Frightening messages about worldwide poverty or possible changes in the Earth's climate are less persuasive to most people, because they are less certain that they can do anything to make a difference.

AUDIENCE VARIABLES

Some people are more easily persuaded than others are, and a given individual may be more easily influenced at some times than at others. The ease of persuading someone depends on both person variables and situation variables.

Person Variables Would you guess that highly intelligent people are persuaded more easily, or less easily, than less intelligent people are? Actually, the answer depends on the message. Highly intelligent people are quicker to accept a new, complex scientific theory because they can understand the evidence better than less intelligent people can. Less intelligent people, on the other hand, are more likely to accept an illogical or poorly supported idea (Eagly & Warren, 1976).

Situation Variables Other things being equal, a persuasive message is more effective if the speaker can convey the message, "I am similar to you" or "My message is right for people like you." We like people who resem-

ble ourselves—in any way. In one striking illustration of this tendency, students were asked to read a very unflattering description of Grigori Rasputin, the "mad monk of Russia," and then rate Rasputin's personality on several scales such as pleasant to unpleasant, effective to ineffective, and strong to weak. All students read the same description except for Rasputin's birthdate: In some cases, the statement of Rasputin's birthdate had been changed to match the student's own birthdate. Students who thought Rasputin had the same birthdate as themselves liked him better than other students did. Nobody thought he was "pleasant," but many did rate him as "strong" and "effective" (Finch & Cialdini, 1989).

You can probably think of examples in which a speaker began by stressing his or her resemblance to the audience. "I remember when I was a student like you." "I grew up in

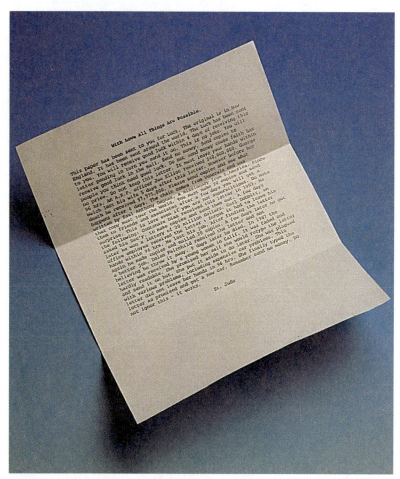

FIGURE 16.3
If you received a copy of this chain letter, would you copy it and send it to other people, as it requests? Why or why not?

a town similar to this one." "I believe in family values, and I'm sure you do too."

A persuasive message can become ineffective if people can generate arguments against it. For example, simply informing subjects a few minutes ahead of time that they are about to hear a persuasive speech on a certain topic weakens the effect of the talk on their attitudes (Petty & Cacioppo, 1977); this tendency is called the **forewarning effect**.

In the **inoculation effect**, people first hear a weak argument, then a stronger argument for the same conclusion. After they have rejected the first argument, they are likely to reject the second one also. In one experiment, subjects listened to speeches *against* brushing their teeth after every meal. Some of them heard just a strong argument (for example, "Brushing your teeth too frequently wears away tooth enamel, leading to serious disease"). Others heard first a weak argument, then 2 days later the strong argument. Still others first heard an argument *for* toothbrushing, then the strong argument against it. Only the subjects who heard the weak antibrushing argument before the

strong one resisted its influence; the other two groups found it highly persuasive (McGuire & Papageorgis, 1961). That is, people who have already rejected a weak argument are likely to reject a later, stronger argument for the same position. (If you want to convince someone, present some good evidence first; don't start with evidence they may see as faulty.)

CONCEPT CHECK

3. *If you want your children to preserve the beliefs and attitudes you try to teach them, should you give them only arguments that support those beliefs or should you also expose them to attacks on those beliefs? Why? (Check your answers on page 697.)*

COGNITIVE DISSONANCE

A few pages back, we considered whether people's behavior will change when their attitudes change. The theory of cognitive dissonance reverses the direction: It holds that when people's behavior changes, their attitudes will change (Festinger, 1957).

Cognitive dissonance is a state of unpleasant tension that people experience when they hold contradictory attitudes or when they behave in a way that is inconsistent with their attitudes. People try to reduce that tension in several ways: They can change their behavior to match their attitudes, change their attitudes to match their behavior, or adopt a new attitude that justifies their behavior under the circumstances (Wicklund & Brehm, 1976). (See Figure 16.4.) For example, Jane, a heavy smoker, believes that cigarette smoking is dangerous, and yet she smokes two packs a day. The inconsistency between her attitudes and her behavior creates dissonance, an unpleasant state of arousal. To reduce the dissonance, Jane can stop smoking, she can change her attitude—by deciding that cigarette smoking is not really dangerous after all—or she can adopt a new attitude, such as "smoking reduces my tension and keeps me from gaining weight." Although a person might adopt any of these three options, most of the research has focused on ways in which cognitive dissonance changes people's attitudes.

FIGURE 16.4
Cognitive dissonance is a state of tension that arises when people perceive that their attitudes do not match their behaviors. Theoretically, they could resolve this discrepancy by changing either their attitudes or their behavior, or by developing a new attitude or excuse to explain the discrepancy. Most of the research, however, has focused on ways in which cognitive dissonance leads to a change of attitudes.

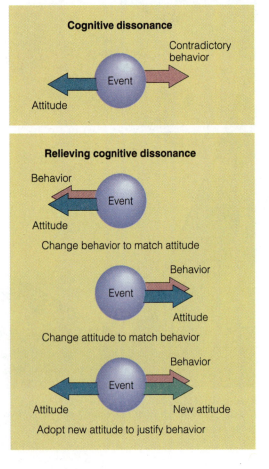

Cognitive dissonance

Contradictory behavior

Attitude

Event

Relieving cognitive dissonance

Behavior

Event

Attitude

Change behavior to match attitude

Behavior

Event

Attitude

Change attitude to match behavior

Behavior

Event

Attitude

New attitude

Adopt new attitude to justify behavior

EVIDENCE FAVORING COGNITIVE DISSONANCE THEORY

Leon Festinger and J. Merrill Carlsmith (1959) carried out a classic experiment demonstrating that cognitive dissonance can lead to attitude change. They created dissonance in college students by inducing them to lie to another student. Here's how the experiment worked: Seventy-one male undergraduates were invited to take part in an experiment on "motor behavior." Each subject was individually asked to perform a boring task—for example, rotating pegs on a board over and over again—for an hour. (The task was made as boring as possible, for reasons you will learn in a moment.) Afterward, the experimenter thanked each subject and explained that the study's actual purpose was to see whether the subjects' performance was affected by their attitudes toward the task. (This was not in fact the purpose.) The experimenter further explained that some subjects and not others were told that the experiment would be fun and interesting before starting.

As a matter of fact, the experimenter continued, right now the research assistant is supposed to inform the next subject, a young woman waiting in the next room, that the experiment will be fun and interesting. The experimenter excused himself to find the research assistant and then returned distraught a few minutes later. The assistant was nowhere to be found, he said. He turned to the subject and asked, "Would you be willing to tell the next subject that you thought this was an interesting, enjoyable experiment? If so, I will pay you."

Some students were offered $1; others were offered $20. Most of them, regardless of how much they were offered, agreed to tell the woman in the next room that the experiment was interesting. Presumably they experienced cognitive dissonance as they told this whopper of a lie. As they left, thinking the experiment was over, they were met by a representative of the psychology department who explained that the department wanted to find out what kinds of experiments were being conducted and whether they were educationally worthwhile. (The answers to these questions were the real point of the experiment.) Each subject was asked how enjoyable he considered the experiment and whether he would be willing to participate in a similar experiment later.

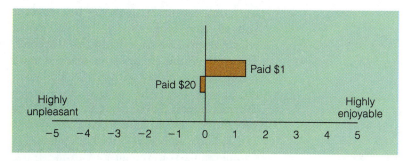

FIGURE 16.5

In a classic experiment demonstrating cognitive dissonance, subjects were paid $1 or $20 for telling another subject that they enjoyed an experiment (which actually was boring). Later they were asked for their real opinions. Those subjects who were paid the smaller amount said they enjoyed the study more. (Based on data from Festinger & Carlsmith, 1959.)

Which subjects do you think said they liked the experiment more, those who were paid $20 or those who were paid only $1? The students who received $20 said they thought the experiment was boring and that they wanted nothing to do with another such experiment. Those who received just $1 said they enjoyed the experiment and would be glad to participate again (Figure 16.5).

Why? According to the theory of cognitive dissonance, those who accepted $20 to tell a lie experienced little conflict. They knew they were lying, but they also knew why: for the $20. (In the 1950s, when this experiment took place, $20 was worth a great deal.) They had no reason to change their original opinion of the experiment—that they were bored to tears.

However, the students who had told a lie for only $1 felt a conflict between their true attitude toward the boring experiment and what they had said about it. The small payment did not provide them with a good reason for lying, so they experienced cognitive dissonance. Because it was too late to take back their lie, the only way they could reduce their dissonance was to change their attitude, to decide that the experiment really was interesting after all. ("I learned a lot of interesting things about myself, like . . . uh . . . how good I am at rotating pegs.")

In a second experiment (Aronson & Carlsmith, 1963), 4-year-old children (one at a time) were shown five toys: a tank, a steam shovel, plastic gears, a fire engine, and a set of dishes and pans. Each child was asked which toy looked like the best one, the second best, and so on. Then the experimenter said he would have to leave the room. He invited the child to play with the toys while he was gone, except, he insisted, "I don't want you to play with the _____," filling in whichever toy the child had ranked second. To some of the children he made a mild threat: "If you played with it, I would be annoyed." To others he made a more severe threat: "If you played with it, I would be very angry. I would have to take all my toys and go home and never come back again. . . . I would think you were just a baby."

The experimenter left for 10 minutes and watched each child through a one-way mirror. All the children dutifully avoided the forbidden toy. Then he returned and asked each child to tell him again which was the best toy, the second best, and so on.

All the children who had received the severe threat ranked the forbidden toy either first or second. They knew why they had avoided the toy, and they had no reason to change their mind about how much they wished they could play with it. However, almost half the children who had heard the mild threat lowered their evaluation of the forbidden toy. They had dissonant beliefs: "I really like that toy" and "I didn't play with it." Why hadn't they played with it? They didn't know. Was it because a man they had never met before said he would be "annoyed"—whatever *that* meant? That didn't sound like much of a reason. The only way they could relieve their dissonance was to convince themselves that they did not really like the toy very much.

CONCEPT CHECK

4. *Suppose your parents pay you to make a good grade in some course you consider boring. According to cognitive dissonance theory, are you more likely to develop a positive attitude toward your studies if your parents pay you $10 or $100? Would the theory of intrinsic and extrinsic motivation, discussed in Chapter 11, lead to the same prediction or a different one? (Check your answers on page 697.)*

SUMMARY

- *Attitudes.* An attitude is a like or dislike of something or somebody that influences our behavior toward that thing or person. (page 689)

- *Relationship between attitudes and behavior.* Attitudes are rather poor predictors of

behavior, especially a single behavior in a single situation, because many other factors influence behavior. (page 690)

- *Two routes to persuasion.* When people are considering an appeal on a topic of little importance, they are easily persuaded by the speaker's appearance and other superficial factors, regardless of the strength or weakness of the evidence. When people consider an appeal on a matter of importance to them, they pay more attention to the quality of the evidence and logic. (page 690)

- *Sleeper effect.* When people reject a message because of their low regard for the person who proposed it, they sometimes forget where they heard the idea and come to accept it later. (page 691)

- *Minority influence.* Although a minority may have little influence at first, it may, through persistent repetition of its message, eventually persuade the majority to adopt its position or to consider other alternatives. (page 692)

- *Influence of fear-inducing messages.* Whether or not messages that appeal to fear prove effective depends on whether people perceive the danger as real and on whether they think they can do anything about it. (page 692)

- *Forewarning and inoculation effects.* People evaluate the reasoning behind the persuasive messages they hear. If they have been warned that someone will try to persuade them of something, or if they have previously heard a weak version of the persuasive argument, they tend to resist the persuasive argument more strongly than they otherwise would have. (page 694)

- *Cognitive dissonance.* Cognitive dissonance is a state of unpleasant tension that arises from contradictory attitudes or from behavior that conflicts with a person's attitudes. When people behave in a way that does not match their attitudes, they reduce the inconsistency by changing either their behavior or their attitudes. (page 694)

SUGGESTION FOR FURTHER READING

Petty, R. E., & Cacioppo, J. T. (in press). *Attitudes and persuasion: Classic and contemporary approaches* (2nd ed.). Dubuque, IA: Times Mirror Higher Education. A complete yet readable review of research on attitudes and attitude change.

TERMS

social psychologists psychologists who study social behavior and how an individual influences others and is influenced by them (page 688)

attitude a like or dislike of something or somebody that influences our behavior toward that thing or person (page 689)

high self-monitor person who constantly monitors his or her own behavior in order to behave in what others consider the appropriate manner for each situation (page 690)

central route to persuasion method of persuasion based on careful evaluation of evidence and logic (page 691)

peripheral route to persuasion method of persuasion based on such superficial factors as the speaker's appearance and reputation or the sheer number of arguments presented, regardless of their quality (page 691)

sleeper effect delayed persuasion by an initially rejected message (page 691)

forewarning effect tendency of a brief preview of a message to decrease its persuasiveness (page 694)

inoculation effect tendency of a persuasive message to be weakened if people first hear a weak argument for the same conclusion (page 694)

cognitive dissonance a state of unpleasant tension that people experience when they hold contradictory attitudes or when they behave in a way that is inconsistent with their attitudes (page 694)

ANSWERS TO CONCEPT CHECKS

1. You will pay more attention to the evidence and logic, following the central route to persuasion, for the decision about your major. (page 691)

2. The fact that your idea was overwhelmingly rejected does not mean that you should give up. If you and a few allies continue to present this plan in a simple way, showing apparent agreement among yourselves, the majority may eventually endorse a plan similar to it—probably without giving you credit for suggesting the idea. (page 692)

3. You should expose them to weak attacks on their beliefs so that they will learn how to resist such attacks. Otherwise, they will be like children who grow up in a germ-free environment: They will develop no "immunity" and will be vulnerable when their beliefs are attacked. (page 694)

4. You will come to like your studies more if you are paid $10 than if you are paid $100. If you are paid only $10, you won't be able to tell yourself you are doing it only for the money. Instead, you will tell yourself that you must be really interested. The theory of intrinsic and extrinsic motivation leads to the same prediction: If you study hard in the absence of any strong external reason, you will perceive that you have internal reasons for studying. (page 696)

SOCIAL PERCEPTION AND COGNITION

How do we form impressions of other people?

How do we decide why someone behaves in a certain way?

Whenever you or I watch or hear something, we interpret the events in terms of our preconceptions. Of all the people who watched the O. J. Simpson murder trial, some concluded that he was innocent and some concluded that he was guilty—presumably revealing a difference in their expectations or beliefs. Shortly after a massacre of people in Lebanon in 1982, several audiences were polled concerning their reactions to the television news coverage. Pro-Israeli audiences were angry at the news programs'

anti-Israeli bias; pro-Arab audiences were angry at the *same* programs' anti-Arab bias (Vallone, Ross, & Lepper, 1985). Clearly, people's attitudes change the way they interpret information.

We inevitably form attitudes about other people and groups of people—good, bad, or indifferent. We decide whether or not we like people, whether or not we trust them. Once we have formed such attitudes, they can be very persistent, altering the way we perceive new information about those people. This module concerns *social perceptions*—our interpretations of the feelings, intentions, and personalities of other people.

▮ FIRST IMPRESSIONS

When you talk to someone you have never met before—say, the student sitting next to you in class—you begin to form an impression of how intelligent he or she is, how friendly, how energetic. Right or wrong, many people trust their first impressions. What information do we use in forming first impressions?

THE PRIMACY EFFECT

Our first impressions of others, correct or incorrect, are influential simply because they are first. Other things being equal, the first information we learn about someone influences us more than later information does (Belmore, 1987; Jones & Goethals, 1972). This tendency is known as the **primacy effect.**

Why are first impressions so influential? Partly, we simply pay more attention at first. Also, if our first impression of someone is unfavorable, we may not spend enough time with that person to form an alternative view. Moreover, our first impression can become a self-fulfilling prophecy. For example, suppose a psychologist hands you a telephone receiver and invites you to have a conversation with an attractive, appealing person of the opposite sex. Later, the psychologist hands you the same receiver and invites you to talk with a person described as much less attractive. You will act very differently toward these two people and probably elicit cheerful, sparkling conversation from the first and rather bland conversation from the second—even though the two people were in fact similar. (The psychologist chose at random which person would get which descrip-

If you were a new patient of Dr. Balamurali Ambati, the world's youngest doctor (at age 17), what would your first impression probably be? If you formed a first impression based only on his youthful appearance, you could be badly mistaken about his abilities. First impressions do not always linger, but sometimes they do.

tion; neither knew how the psychologist was describing them.) In short, your first impression of someone changes the way you act, and the way you act may influence the other person to live up to (or down to) your first impression (Snyder, Tanke, & Berscheid, 1977).

SOMETHING TO THINK ABOUT

In a criminal trial, the prosecution presents its evidence first. Might that give the jury an unfavorable first impression of the defendant and increase the probability of a conviction?

CONCEPT CHECK

5. Why do some professors avoid looking at students' names when they grade essay exams? Why is it more important for them to do so on the tests later in the semester than on the first test? (Check your answers on page 708.)

PHYSICAL CHARACTERISTICS

Many people hold strong (and often incorrect) beliefs that physical characteristics are related to psychological traits. As a rule, people regard their physically attractive acquaintances as highly sociable, dominant, sexually responsive, mentally healthy, intelligent, and socially skilled (Feingold, 1992a). One group of experimenters asked subjects to rate the personality and intelligence of students in a series of yearbook photographs (Dion, Berscheid, & Walster, 1972). The photographs had been selected to include equal numbers of attractive, average-looking, and less attractive students. The subjects rated the attractive students as more sensitive, kind, poised, and sociable than the others. They also predicted that the more attractive students would enjoy highly successful careers and happy marriages. Unattractive people, however, may be perceived as unpleasant, perhaps even threatening.

Physical characteristics have a great deal to do with how people are treated in various settings. Other things being equal, teachers expect better performance from attractive children than from unattractive children (Clifford & Walster, 1973). Attractive people are on average paid higher salaries than unattractive people are (Quinn, 1978). Juries often treat attractive defendants less harshly than unattractive defendants, unless the jury believes a defendant used his or her good looks to gain people's trust and then swindle them (Sigall & Ostrove, 1975; Stewart, 1980).

We also form impressions of others simply by watching them. For example, we judge people's emotions and personality traits by observing their facial expressions and their body movements (Lippa, 1983). You may infer that one woman is introverted because she makes small, tight gestures and that another is extraverted because she makes large, expansive gestures. You decide that one man is anxious and "uptight" because he twitches, fidgets, and trembles and that another is calm and composed because he makes smooth, controlled gestures.

Research suggests that when nonverbal information conflicts with verbal information, we are more likely to trust the nonverbal information, perhaps because nonverbal behavior is hard to modify voluntarily (Figure 16.6). That is, people lie with their words more often than they lie with their gestures (DePaulo, 1992). When a friend says, "I love you," but frowns, stands far away, and refuses to look at you, which do you believe—the verbal or the nonverbal statement?

FIGURE 16.6
People convey their feelings and attitudes both by what they say and by their body language—their posture, arm and leg positions, smile or frown, eye movements, and so forth. When someone's words conflict with the body language, we tend to trust the body language more. We know that people lie with their words more easily than they do with their posture.

■ SOCIAL COGNITION

Eventually we progress beyond first impressions. **Social cognition** is the process by which we combine and remember information about others and make inferences based on that information (Sherman, Judd, & Park, 1989).

ACCURATE AND INACCURATE JUDGMENTS

People's judgments of other people are often unreliable and inaccurate. As an extreme example, a mother and father may agree that their child is extraordinarily talented, even though the child's abilities are quite ordinary (Kenny, 1991). Less extreme examples occur widely; you may have an exaggerated favorable opinion of your friends and an unfairly low opinion of certain other people.

Why are social judgments so frequently inaccurate? The simple answer is that people frequently do not care whether their judgments are accurate. When you first met your college roommate, the two of you probably formed very favorable impressions of each other. You each *wanted* to form a favorable impression, and you were more willing to run the risk of overrating each other than to run the risk of prematurely ruining an important relationship (Friedrich, 1993). At the opposite extreme, a husband and wife who are on the verge of divorce seem more interested in supporting *unfavorable* views of each other than they are in accuracy (Fincham, Beach, & Baucom, 1987). For example, one may say that the other "only did the dishes to try to make me feel guilty for not doing them earlier." Nothing that either partner does seems to please the other one any more.

In many cases, we form a first impression and then stick to it, in spite of evidence to the contrary. We notice the behaviors that fit our expectations and reinterpret or ignore the behaviors that contradict our expectations (Jones, 1986). In other situations in which we are highly motivated to make accurate social judgments, we are capable of being much more careful (Hilton & Darley, 1991). For example, before deciding whether to start a business partnership with someone, you probably would spend a fair amount of time scrutinizing your prospective partner's character and honesty.

STEREOTYPES AND RACIAL PREJUDICE

A **stereotype** is a generalized, probably overgeneralized, belief or expectation about a group of people. A **prejudice** is a negative attitude about a group of people, such as a belief that some group is lazy or hostile. Do you have strong stereotypes or prejudices about members of any group? I presume you will say you do not. Now, what do you think about people who do have strong stereotypes and prejudices—members of the Ku Klux Klan or other white-supremacist groups, for example? I presume you will say that you think they are cruel, uncaring, unfair, probably ill-informed, probably stupid. Right? If so, consider that what you have just said about members of such groups is itself a very strong stereotype or prejudice.

My point is not that you are wrong to hold that prejudice—frankly, I share it. My point is that we almost invariably, almost inescapably form at least a few stereotypes about people, if not outright prejudices (Stangor & Lange, 1994; von Hippel, Sekaquaptewa, & Vargas, 1995). When I give a lecture to an undergraduate class, I explain some simple concepts and omit some complicated ideas; to a group of psychology professors, I would omit the simple concepts and discuss the more complicated ideas. My reason is my stereotype about undergraduates—that they have less background than professors do. Similarly, my stereotypes lead me to expect different behaviors from 6-month-old babies than from 20-year-olds. In effect, stereotypes "fill in the gaps" in our knowledge about someone until we have enough individual information to provide the details.

Some stereotypes are more or less correct, some are exaggerated, some are outright wrong, and some are untested hypotheses that might or might not be correct (Judd & Park, 1993). As already mentioned, peo-

Prejudices against people of different religions or ethnic groups can be very persistent. The war in Bosnia continues an ethnic battle that began centuries ago.

ple are not always motivated to form accurate judgments of other people. Sometimes they form stereotypes based on illusory correlations, because they remember unusual events more clearly than ordinary events. For example, if you are a European American and 90% of the people you ordinarily see in the course of a day are also European Americans, you probably will remember most clearly the behavior of the Latinos or African Americans that you have seen. If, in addition to *looking different* from the majority, a few members of a minority group *do* something unusual—such as being extra-polite, driving a car recklessly, or talking loudly in public—the combination is likely to make an especially strong impression (Hamilton & Gifford, 1976). Once such a stereotype forms, it can be quite persistent; anyone who does not fit the stereotype is dismissed as an "exception to the rule" (Rothbart & John, 1985).

European Americans' stereotypes and prejudices about African Americans have been of special concern to both social psychologists and the public at large. Early research by psychologists interpreted prejudices as Freudian-type defense mechanisms against anxiety; for example, people who were frustrated at their own lack of economic success might displace their anger from themselves or their circumstances onto helpless minority groups. Another approach in the early research was to look for personality traits that led some people to be inclined to hold powerless minority people in contempt (Duckitt, 1992).

Each of those approaches is probably valid to some extent; however, they do not fully explain current prejudicial attitudes. Since the Civil Rights Act of 1964, the civil rights movement, and the assassination of Martin Luther King, Jr., most European Americans have at least publicly embraced the principles of equal opportunity and equal rights. Schools and other institutions have been integrated; European Americans and African Americans have had far more contact with one another than they had in past eras. Psychologists therefore expected—naively, it now appears—that stereotypes and prejudices would fade away.

They have faded in some ways, but far from completely. Even those European Americans who say they have no prejudices and wish to have no prejudices often admit that under certain circumstances prejudices affect their behaviors. For example, in one study

European-American college students were asked for their reactions under various circumstances, such as "suppose an African-American person sits next to you on a bus," or "suppose an African-American family moves into the house next door to yours." In each case, the students were to describe how they believe they *would* respond and also how they *should* respond. Some students acknowledged discrepancies, saying they would react one way but should react a different way. They felt embarrassed, and even guilty, about their lingering prejudices (Devine, Monteith, Zuwerink, & Elliot, 1991).

An attitude commonly found among European Americans today is best described as **ambivalence** (literally, *both values*) toward African Americans. That is, they feel a mixture of favorable and unfavorable beliefs. They may hold a low opinion of many African Americans, and yet have great admiration for those individuals who have succeeded in overcoming barriers and disadvantages (Figure 16.7).

In one study college students, mostly European Americans, were assembled into teams to compete for prizes by answering "trivia" questions. Each team had a captain, who was selected by a rigged drawing. For

FIGURE 16.7
Many European Americans in the United States hold ambivalent attitudes toward African Americans; that is, they hold a mixture of strongly positive and strongly negative beliefs. They tend to admire and praise successful African Americans even more strongly than they admire and praise equally successful European Americans. However, they tend to be harsher toward unsuccessful or criminal African Americans than they are toward similar European Americans.

FIGURE 16.8
In the study by Hass, Katz, Rizzo, Bailey, and Eisenstadt (1991), European-American students evaluated the performances of their team captains (who were actually confederates of the experimenter). Successful African-American captains received higher ratings than successful European-American captains, but unsuccessful African-American captains received lower ratings than unsuccessful European-American captains. These results suggest that many European Americans have "ambivalent" feelings about African Americans—a mixture of favorable and unfavorable beliefs.

half the teams that captain was African-American; for the other half, European-American. All the captains were in fact confederates of the experimenter and were told exactly what to do. In some cases, the captains performed their tasks well and their teams won prizes; in other cases, the captains made one blunder after another and cost their team any chance of winning. Afterward, the members of each team were asked to evaluate their captain's performance. As Figure 16.8 shows, successful African-American captains got higher evaluations than successful European-American captains, but unsuccessful African-American captains got lower evaluations than unsuccessful European-American captains (Hass, Katz, Rizzo, Bailey, & Eisenstadt, 1991).

The apparent interpretation is that European-American students were showing their ambivalence toward African Americans: They praise successful individuals and scorn unsuccessful individuals. We must await further research to clarify the nature of such ambivalent attitudes. It would also be interesting to find out how African-American students would react to successful and unsuccessful European-American and African-American captains. As is often the case in research, one interesting study raises new questions that may inspire further studies.

OVERCOMING PREJUDICE

After prejudices and hostility have arisen between two groups, what can anyone do to break down those barriers? Simply getting to know each other better may help, but prejudices are sometimes rather stubborn. A more effective technique is to get the two groups to work toward a common goal.

Many years ago, psychologists demonstrated the power of this technique using two arbitrarily chosen groups, not different races (Sherif, 1966). At a summer camp at Robbers' Cave, Oklahoma, 11-to-12-year-old boys were divided into two groups in separate cabins. The groups competed for prizes in sports, treasure hunts, and other activities. With each competition the antagonism between the two groups grew more intense. The boys made threatening posters, shouted insults, and threw apples at one another's cabins. Clearly each group had developed prejudice and hostility toward the other.

Up to a point the "counselors" (the experimenters) allowed the hostility to take its course, neither encouraging it nor prohibiting it. Then they tried to reverse it by stopping the competitions and setting common goals. First they had the two groups work together to find and repair a leak in the water pipe that supplied the camp. Later they had the groups pool their treasuries to rent a movie that both groups wanted to see. Still later they had the boys pull together to get a truck out of a rut. Gradually hostility turned to friendship—except for a few holdouts who nursed their hatred to the bitter end! The point of the study is that competition leads to hostility; cooperation leads to friendship.

Working together toward a shared goal is an excellent way to overcome prejudice. When people associate their success with someone else's efforts, they naturally come to like that person and may generalize that attitude to similar others.

⬛ ATTRIBUTION

We often try to figure out why the people we observe behave as they do. Yesterday you won a million dollars in the state lottery. Today a classmate who had never seemed to notice you before asks you for a date. You wonder whether this sudden interest is the result of your charming personality or your new wealth. When we are not sure what is causing the behavior of someone we are observing, we *attribute* causes that seem appropriate. **Attribution** is the set of thought processes we use to assign causes to our own behavior and the behavior of others.

When someone behaves in an unusual way, we generally make an internal attribution. That is, we assume there is something unusual about this person; we do not assume that other people in the same situation would behave the same way. (If we knew more about the situation, we might be less confident of this attribution.)

INTERNAL CAUSES VERSUS EXTERNAL CAUSES

Fritz Heider, the founder of attribution theory, maintained that people often try to decide whether someone's behavior is the result of internal causes or external causes (Heider, 1958). Internal causes come from the person's stable characteristics, such as attitudes, personality traits, or abilities. External causes come from the situation, such as stimuli in the environment, the events of the day, and the rewards and penalties associated with certain acts. For example, your brother decides to walk to work every morning instead of driving. You could attribute his action to an internal cause ("He likes fresh air and exercise") or to an external cause ("He saves money" or "It allows him to walk past the house of that woman he's trying to meet").

We look for internal causes when someone does something unexpected, something that makes us say, "I wouldn't have done that." This tendency sometimes leads to misunderstanding between members of different cultures. Each person views the other's behavior as "something I would not have done" and therefore grounds for making an attribution about the other individual's personality. In fact, such behavior may be what the other person's culture dictates. For example, some cultures expect their members to cry loudly at funerals or to be emotionally demonstrative in other ways; other cultures expect their members to be more restrained in similar circumstances. People who are not familiar with other cultures may attribute a behavior to someone's personality and overlook the influence of the situation and the culturally determined response to it.

Harold Kelley (1967) proposed that we rely on three types of information in deciding whether to make an internal or an external attribution for someone's behavior:

- **Consensus information** (how a person's behavior compares with other people's behavior). If someone behaves the same way other people do in some situation, or the same way you imagine other people would, then you probably make an external attribution. If someone behaves in an unusual way, you look for an internal attribution, pertaining to something about that person instead of something about the situation.

- **Consistency information** (how the person's behavior varies from one time to the next). If someone seems almost always friendly, for example, you make an internal attribution ("this person is friendly"). If someone seems friendly at some times and less friendly at other times, you look for external attributions ("something just happened to cause this person's bad mood").

- **Distinctiveness** (how the person's behavior varies from one object or social partner to another). For example, if someone is friendly to most people, but unfriendly to one particular person, you make an external attribution for the unfriendly behavior. That is, you assume that person elicits unfriendly

behavior from an otherwise friendly person and that the behavior therefore does not reflect a personality trait.

CONCEPT CHECK

6. *Your friend Juanita returns from watching a movie and says it was excellent. The other people you heard commenting on this film disliked it. Will you be inclined to make an internal or an external attribution for Juanita's enjoyment of this movie? Why? (Distinctiveness, consensus, or consistency?) (Check your answers on page 708.)*

ERRORS AND BIASES

As the preceding experiment suggests, we often assume that people's behavior results from internal causes even when we know that some strong external cause may have been operating. Lee Ross (1977) calls this tendency to overemphasize internal explanations of other people's behavior the **fundamental attribution error.**

Moreover, people are more likely to attribute internal causes to other people's behavior than they are to their own behavior (Jones & Nisbett, 1972). This tendency is called the **actor-observer effect.** You are an "actor" when you try to explain the causes of your own behavior and an "observer" when you try to explain someone else's behavior.

The actor-observer effect has been demonstrated in a number of studies (Watson, 1982). In one of them, Richard Nisbett and his colleagues (1973) asked college students to rate themselves, their fathers, their best friends, and Walter Cronkite (a television news announcer at the time) on a number of personality traits. For each trait (such as "leniency"), the subjects had three choices: (1) the person possesses the trait, (2) the person possesses the opposite trait, and (3) the person's behavior "depends on the situation." Subjects checked "depends on the situation" most frequently when they were rating themselves, less frequently when they were rating their fathers and friends, and least often when they were rating Walter Cronkite. These results are consistent with the actor-observer effect; subjects made external attributions for their own behavior ("depends on the situation") and internal attributions for others' behavior ("they possess certain traits"). Figure 16.9 shows the results.

In another experiment (Jones & Harris, 1967), students were asked to read an essay another student had written, praising Fidel Castro, the Communist leader of Cuba. The investigators told some of the students that the writer had been assigned, almost forced, to take a pro-Castro position. The students were then asked to judge the writer's real attitude. Most students attributed at least a mildly pro-Castro attitude to the writer, even if they knew the author had been forced to write a pro-Castro essay. Figure 16.10 shows the results. That is, they attributed an internal cause to the writer's behavior, even though they knew about a strong external cause.

Why do we tend to explain our own behavior differently from that of others? There are several possibilities (Jones & Nisbett, 1972; Watson, 1982). First, because we observe our own behavior in many different situations, we realize how much it varies from one situation to another. (Recall Kelley's theory: You make external attributions when someone's behavior varies across time and across situations.)

Second, we tend to attribute unexpected, surprising behavior to internal causes. Our own behavior seldom surprises us, so we do not attribute it to internal causes.

A third reason is perceptual. We do not see ourselves as objects, because our eyes look outward and focus on our environment. We see other people, however, as objects in our visual field.

The perceptual explanation for the actor-observer effect has an interesting implication: If you could somehow become an object in your own visual field, then you might explain your own behavior in terms of internal traits, just as you tend to explain the behavior of others. In one innovative study, Michael Storms (1973) videotaped several subjects as they carried on a conversation. Before showing them the videotape, he asked them why they had said certain things and why they thought the others had said what they had. At first, most of the subjects attributed their own remarks to external causes ("I was responding to what the other person said") and attributed what the other people had said to internal causes ("He was showing off" or "She always says things like that"). Then Storms showed them the videotape and asked them the same questions. This time, many of them attributed their own behavior more to internal causes ("I

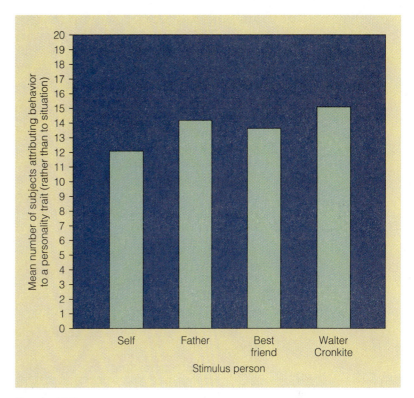

FIGURE 16.9
Subjects were asked whether certain people had certain traits, such as "leniency," or the opposite traits, such as "firmness," or whether "it depended on the situation." They attributed the most personality traits to news announcer Walter Cronkite (the person they knew least) and the fewest to themselves. That is, they were most likely to say their own behavior depended on the situation. (Based on data of Nisbett, Caputo, Legant, & Marecek, 1973.)

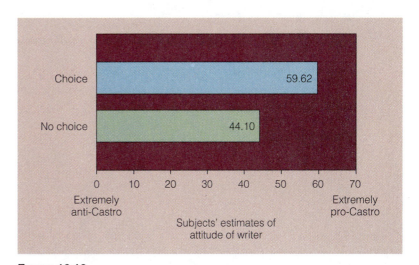

FIGURE 16.10
When subjects were told that a person chose to write a pro-Castro essay, they attributed pro-Castro attitudes to the writer. Even when they were told that the writer had been required to write the essay, they still attributed mildly pro-Castro attitudes to the writer. (Based on data from Jones & Harris, 1967.)

was being smart-alecky. . . . I was trying to act friendly"). That is, when people watched themselves, they reacted the way they did when watching other people—by making mostly internal attributions for behavior.

CONCEPT CHECK

7. *You go along with a crowd to see* Return of the Son of Sequel Strikes Back Again, Part 2. *Are you more likely to think that you really want to see the movie or that the others do? (Check your answer on page 708).*

SOMETHING TO THINK ABOUT

Try to explain these examples of behavior:

• Why did you choose to go to the college you are attending?

• Why did your roommate choose this college?

• Why are you reading this book right now?

• Why does your roommate study so much (or so little)?

Did you attribute internal causes or external causes for these behaviors? Did you rely more on external causes to explain other people's behavior or to explain your own?

People adopt a number of attributions to explain their defeats and failures. If you were a member of the basketball team of the Webb Institute of Naval Architecture, what attribution would you make after your team lost its 71st consecutive game?

USING ATTRIBUTIONS TO CONTROL PERCEPTIONS OF OURSELVES

Although we generally attribute our own behavior largely to external causes, we vary our attributions to try to present ourselves in a favorable light. For example, you may credit your intelligence for the good grades you get (an internal attribution) and blame unfair tests for your bad grades (an external attribution). Members of groups that are frequent victims of discrimination often blame their defeats on prejudice and discrimination—sometimes rightly, sometimes wrongly (Crocker & Major, 1989). Attributions that we adopt in an effort to maximize our credit for success and minimize our blame for failure are called **self-serving biases** (Miller & Ross, 1975; Van Der Pligt & Eiser, 1983).

We can also protect our image by adopting **self-handicapping strategies,** in which we create external causes as "decoy" excuses for our failures. Suppose you expect to do poorly on a final exam. You go to a party the night before and stay out until three in the morning. Now you can blame your low score on your lack of sleep and avoid having to admit that you might have done poorly anyway.

In an experiment on self-handicapping strategies, Steven Berglas and Edward Jones (1978) had college students work on problems; some students were given solvable problems and some were given unsolvable problems. Then the experimenters told all the students that they had done well. They wanted the students who had been given solvable problems to believe that they had performed skillfully and those who had been given unsolvable problems to believe that they had been lucky. (It had to be luck because the subjects knew they had not understood the problems!)

Next they told the subjects that the experiment's purpose was to investigate the effects of drugs on problem solving and that they were now going to pass out another set of problems. The subjects could choose between taking a drug that supposedly impaired problem solving and another drug that supposedly improved it. The subjects who had worked on unsolvable problems the first time were more likely than the others were to choose the drug that supposedly impaired performance. Because they did not expect to do well on the second set of problems anyway, they provided themselves with a convenient excuse.

In closing, we can see that attributions play an important role in social interactions. We are seldom fully aware of the reasons for our own behavior, much less someone else's. Consequently our attributions are based partly on our observations and partly on what we wish or imagine to be true. If someone you know passes by without saying hello, you might attribute that person's behavior to absent-mindedness, indifference to you, or outright hostility. If someone acts unusually friendly, you might attribute that response to your own personal charm, the other person's extraverted personality, or the other person's devious and manipulative personality. Whatever attributions you make are sure to influence your own social behaviors.

SUMMARY

* *First impressions.* We form first impressions of others on the basis of their appearance and their nonverbal behavior. (page 698)

* *Primacy effect.* Other things being equal, we pay more attention to the first information we learn about someone than to later information. (page 698)

* *Accuracy and inaccuracy.* People are frequently not motivated to judge other people accurately. They form opinions based largely on what they hope to be true, although they are capable of paying more attention to the evidence if accuracy of judgment becomes important to them. (page 700)

* *Stereotypes.* Stereotypes are generalized beliefs about groups of people. They are sometimes illusory correlations that arise from people's tendency to remember unusual actions clearly, especially unusual actions by members of minority groups. (page 700)

* *Racial prejudice.* European Americans in the United States sometimes show prejudice against African Americans even though they deny having any prejudice. One reason is that some European Americans have habits of prejudice that sometimes emerge, despite conscious efforts to overcome them. Another reason is that many European Americans have ambivalent attitudes toward African Americans, exaggerating both their praise for success and their criticism for mistakes. (page 701)

* *Attribution.* Attribution is the set of thought processes by which we assign causes to behavior. We attribute behavior either to internal causes or to external causes. According to Harold Kelley, we are likely to attribute behav-

ior to an internal cause if it is consistent over time, different from most other people's behavior, and directed toward a variety of other people or objects. (page 703)

* *Fundamental attribution error.* We are more likely to attribute the behavior of other people to internal causes than we are to attribute our own behavior to internal causes. (page 704)

* *Self-handicapping.* We sometimes try to protect our self-esteem by attributing our successes to skill and our failures to outside influences. (page 706)

SUGGESTION FOR FURTHER READING

M. P. Zanna & J. M. Olson (Eds.), *The psychology of prejudice: The Ontario symposium volume 7.* Hillsdale, NJ: Lawrence Erlbaum. Good collection of research on stereotypes and prejudices.

TERMS

primacy effect tendency to be influenced more by the first information learned about someone than by later information about the same person (page 698)

social cognition the process of combining and remembering information about others and making inferences based on that information (page 700)

stereotype an overgeneralization of either positive or negative attitudes toward a group of people (page 700)

prejudice negative attitude toward a group of people (page 700)

ambivalence a mixture of favorable and unfavorable beliefs about some person or group (page 701)

attribution the set of thought processes we use to assign causes to our own behavior and the behavior of others (page 703)

consensus information observations of how a person's behavior compares with that of others (page 704)

consistency information observations of how a person's behavior varies from one time to another (page 704)

distinctiveness observations of how a person's behavior varies from one object or social partner to another (page 704)

fundamental attribution error tendency to overemphasize internal explanations of other people's behavior (page 704)

actor-observer effect tendency to attribute internal causes more to other people's behavior than to one's own behavior (page 704)

self-serving biases attributions people adopt in an effort to maximize their credit for success and minimize their blame for failure (page 706)

self-handicapping strategies techniques for protecting self-esteem by creating external causes as decoy excuses for failures (page 706)

ANSWERS TO CONCEPT CHECKS

5. They want to avoid being biased by their first impressions of the students. That procedure is less important on the first test because they do not yet have a strong impression of the students. (page 699)

6. You probably will make an internal attribution for Juanita's enjoyment, attributing it to the fact that she is easy to please instead of attributing it to the quality of the movie. The reason is *consensus:* When one person's behavior differs from that of others, we make an internal attribution. (page 704)

7. You are likely to think that the others really want to go to the movie (an internal attribution) and that you are going because of the external situation (peer pressure). (page 706)

INTERPERSONAL ATTRACTION

How do people choose their friends?
How do people select their romantic partners?

William Proxmire, a former U.S. senator, used to give "Golden Fleece Awards" to those who, in his opinion, were most flagrant in wasting the taxpayers' money. He once bestowed an award on some psychologists who had received a federal grant to study how people fall in love. According to Proxmire, it was pointless to study love because people do not want to understand love. They prefer, he said, to let such matters remain a mystery, and therefore psychologists should stop doing research on love.

This module is about the information Senator Proxmire did not want you to know.

PEOPLE'S NEED FOR ONE ANOTHER

Think back to your first week at college. Did you feel lonely? Maybe not, if several of your closest friends went to the same college as you, or if you made some good friends rapidly. But many college students do feel lonely at the start. If you did, you may have spent hours on the telephone with friends and family back home, or you may have worked hard at establishing new friendships.

Clearly, people crave close, long-term relationships with other people. We have a "need to belong," a need to identify with a family or close group of friends, a need to be able to talk with someone about personal, confidential matters (Collins & Miller, 1994). Why do we need so much interaction with other people? Some psychologists have proposed that we learn this need from our early experiences with a nurturing parent. I shall not deny the importance of early nurturing experiences, but those experiences do not fully explain our strong social needs. If they did, we would find similar social needs in all other mammalian species. Bears, humans, porcupines, deer, and all the rest start life with a nurturing mother-infant relationship; nevertheless, some species develop a rich social life and some do not (Figure 16.11). Humans' need for social relationships might therefore be best regarded as a

FIGURE 16.11
Although all mammalian species start life with a nurturing mother-infant relationship, some species become highly social and some do not. Humans are among the highly social species. Evidently our social tendency is part of our basic nature.

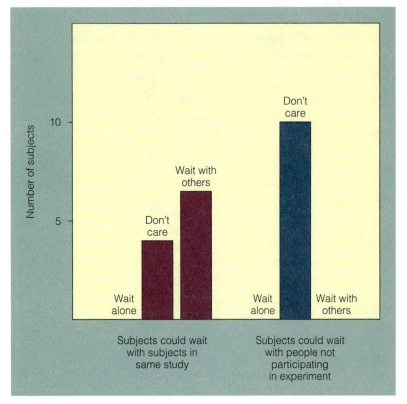

FIGURE 16.12

In Schachter's experiment, people who thought they were waiting for a procedure in which they would receive strong shocks preferred to wait with others who were about to undergo the same procedure. They had no particular desire to wait with people who were not participating in the same study. That is, miserable people like to be with other miserable people. In more general terms, we like to compare our reactions to those of other people who have had, or expect to have, similar experiences.

People who are facing an emotionally trying experience—such as firefighters, soldiers, or intensive-care nurses—prefer to be with others who have undergone or expect to undergo the same experience.

basic need, a part of our biological nature (Baumeister & Leary, 1995).

We treasure most highly our long-term relationships and we will make great efforts to try to maintain them. For example, when you finished high school you probably promised many of your friends that you would continue to see one another. If a close friend or relative leaves on a long trip, you

stay in touch with cards or phone calls. People who lose their closest friends or relatives through death, divorce, or other means often become depressed and even physically ill.

In addition to lasting relationships, we sometimes cultivate temporary friends for a limited purpose. For example, you might want to get together with some other students in a particular class to study for a test, or you might get together with a group for recreational sports.

Brief, casual affiliations can also be important to us for our own self-understanding. If you have just had some intense and trying emotional experience, you might want to be with other people who have had a similar experience, to compare your reactions to theirs and (you hope) demonstrate that you coped with the experience at least as well as they did (Kruglanski & Mayseless, 1990). People also like to associate with people who can set a good example. For example, cancer patients generally like to associate with other cancer patients, especially patients who are showing signs of recovery, who can provide an encouraging role model (Taylor & Lobel, 1989).

When people expect to face some difficult experience in the near future, they generally like to be with other people facing a similar predicament. The old saying goes, "Misery loves company." To test this saying, Stanley Schachter (1959) told subjects he was trying to measure the effects of electric shock on their heart rate and blood pressure. He told one group to expect substantial shocks; he told the other group to expect mild tickling or tingling sensations. Then he told subjects that they would have to wait about 10 minutes while the experimenter made some last-minute adjustments to the equipment. Some subjects were given a choice between waiting alone or waiting with other subjects in the same experiment. Other subjects were given a choice between waiting alone and waiting with students who just happened to be in the building (not subjects in the experiment). Subjects who expected only mild shocks had little preference; they were willing to wait anywhere or with anybody. But the subjects who expected strong shocks strongly preferred to wait with other subjects in the same experiment, as Figure 16.12 shows. In short, people in distress crave the company of people in similar distress. That is, misery loves *miserable* company. Short-term relationships like these can serve a variety of purposes, even if they do not develop into anything deeper or more lasting.

ESTABLISHING MORE LASTING RELATIONSHIPS

The world's population includes billions of people. During your lifetime you may personally see millions of them; you probably will get to know thousands of them by name at one time or another. But you will develop meaningful or lasting relationships with relatively few. How do you choose those people, or how do they choose you? Here we shall consider a few factors that are relevant to both friendships and dating relationships; in a later section we shall turn to issues that apply specifically to dating and marriage.

PROXIMITY

Proximity means closeness. (It comes from the same root as *approximate*.) We tend to choose as friends people who are in close proximity to us, who cross our path frequently. In one study, residents of a graduate housing project at the Massachusetts Institute of Technology were asked to list their three closest friends (Festinger, Schachter, & Back, 1950). The residents lived in two-story buildings with five apartments on each floor (Figure 16.13). On the average, they reported that about two-thirds of their closest friends lived in the same building, and of those about two-thirds lived on the same floor. People were most likely to make friends with their next-door neighbors.

At the start of a school year, Robert Hays (1985) asked college students to name two other students with whom they thought they might become friends. After 3 months, he found that more of the potential friends who lived close together had become friends than had those who lived farther apart.

Proximity influences romantic relationships as well. In an early study, James Bossard (1931) analyzed 5,000 marriage-license applications in Philadelphia and observed a clear relationship between proximity and marriage rates. More couples who lived one block apart got married than those who lived two blocks apart, and so forth. People tend to be more mobile today than they were when this study was conducted in 1931, but it is still true that the more often you cross paths with someone, the more likely you will develop a relationship with that person.

FAMILIARITY

Proximity increases the probability that two people will become friends or lovers partly by giving them more opportunities to meet and talk, and partly just by making them familiar with each other. Other things being equal, the more often we come in contact with another person—or with an inanimate object such as food or a painting—the more we tend to like that person or object (Saegert, Swap, & Zajonc, 1973; Zajonc, 1968). This tendency is known as the **mere-exposure effect**.

For romantic relationships, we can note an interesting exception to the mere-exposure effect: Extensive familiarity in early childhood can inhibit a later romantic interest. In Israel, many children are reared in kibbutzim, collective farms, from infancy to adolescence. However, young Israelis generally avoid dating people who grew up in the same kibbutz (Shepher, 1971). They regard one another almost like brother and sister.

THE SIMILARITY PRINCIPLE

Suppose you wrote a detailed description of yourself, including your age, ethnic background, physical attractiveness, political and religious beliefs, intelligence, academic interests, and attitudes toward sex and drugs. Next you get several of your closest friends to write detailed descriptions of themselves. Chances are, your friends' self-descriptions will match your own in most ways (Laumann, 1969). The tendency to associate with people similar to oneself is known, not surprisingly, as the **similarity principle**. Most people also date and eventually marry people

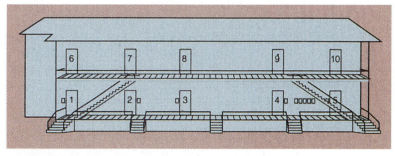

FIGURE 16.13
Students who lived in this graduate housing project generally chose friends who lived nearby. (From Festinger, Schachter, & Back, 1950.)

TABLE 16.2

The Pluses and Minuses of a Hypothetical Dating Relationship from the Standpoint of One Partner

	YOU	YOUR PARTNER	NET ADVANTAGE/ DISADVANTAGE TO YOU
Physical appearance	Average	Outstanding	Advantage
Prestige	Not well known	Popular	Advantage
Finances	Pay for most date expenses and occasional presents, provide nice car	Contributes very little	Disadvantage
Intelligence	Very high	Above average	Disadvantage
Annoying habits	Occasional swearing	Bad table manners	Uncertain
Loyalty	Dating no one else	Dates others often	Disadvantage
Attitudes	Conservative on most issues	Liberal on most issues	Disadvantage (to both people)

For the initial stage of attraction between a man and a woman, or even between two friends, physical appearance is highly important. In the long run, however, a couple must have some similar interests and values if their relationship is to thrive.

who closely resemble themselves in intelligence, attitudes, personality, and physical attractiveness (Plomin, DeFries, & Roberts, 1977). Couples who differ markedly in their education and interests may date for a while, but they are not likely to marry (Plomin, DeFries, & Roberts, 1977). Couples who differ in their extraversion or other personality traits may marry, but when they do they tend to have relatively troubled marriages (Russell & Wells, 1991).

Do you come to like people more when you find out that their beliefs and attitudes are similar to yours? That question turns out to be a little trickier than it sounds at first. If you are like most people, your "default setting" is to like every new person you meet until you see a reason to alter that judgment. If you think at all about a new acquaintance's beliefs and attitudes, you probably assume that he or she shares your own beliefs and attitudes, because most people do, don't they? After all, your opinions and actions are normal and correct, so of course most other people share them (Alicke & Largo, 1995). Therefore, finding a disagreement with someone may *lower* your liking of that person

more than finding agreement with a person *increases* your liking (Rosenbaum, 1986).

THE EQUITY PRINCIPLE

A business deal works best if each party entering into it believes that he or she is getting about as good a deal as the other party is. The same is true of friendships and romantic relationships. According to **exchange** or **equity theories,** social relationships are transactions in which partners exchange goods and services. In some cases, the businesslike nature of this exchange is fairly blatant. In the "Singles Ads" sections of some newspapers, those seeking a relationship describe what they have to offer ("35-year-old divorced male, 6′1″, business executive, athletic . . .") and what they want in return ("seeks warm, caring, attractive woman, age 27–33 . . ."). The ads resemble the "asked" and "bid" columns for the stock exchange (Kenrick & Trost, 1989). People do not run ads for nonromantic friendships, but the same principle applies: A good friendship has a balance of giving and taking.

As in business, a friendship or romantic relationship is most stable if both partners believe they are getting a fair deal. To illustrate, let's imagine that you compare the pluses and minuses of a relationship you have with someone you are dating, as shown in Table 16.2. (Ordinarily, of course, you would not tabulate these ratings in such a formal manner.) Note that the table shows that you consider yourself more desirable than your partner is in some regards, less desirable in other regards. You probably would note some additional pluses and minuses not listed in the table. Depending on which factors you think are most important, you might think you are getting a good deal or a poor one from this relationship. Simultaneously, your partner thinks about the pluses and minuses and also decides whether the exchange seems fair.

As you can begin to suspect by examining Table 16.2, it is difficult to develop a fair exchange in a relationship between people who are very different from each other. Here, one person is richer, more intelligent, and more loyal; the other is more attractive and more popular. Is one partner getting a better deal than the other is? Perhaps neither one is quite sure. Now imagine a relationship between two people who resemble each other. Both are equally attractive, equally popular, equally intelligent, and so forth. Therefore the exchange is fair; neither party is getting a better deal than the other is. In short, *the equity principle implies the similarity principle;* someone who seeks a fair, equitable relationship can achieve it most easily with a highly similar partner.

CONCEPT CHECK

8. *A person your own age from another country moves in next door to you. Neither of you speaks the other's language. Are you likely to become friends? What factors will tend to strengthen the likelihood of your becoming friends? What factors will tend to weaken it? (Check your answers on page 719.)*

SPECIAL CONCERNS IN SELECTING A MATE

Choosing a partner for a marriage (or a marriage-equivalent relationship) is different from choosing other kinds of friends, because of the extra dimension of raising children. Yes, I know, not everyone wants to get married, not all married couples plan to have children, and many unmarried people rear children. What I shall describe does not apply to everyone. Still, it applies to the large number of young people who might like to marry and have children, and it helps to explain a number of marriage customs and laws that have developed in similar forms in many cultures.

If you consider someone as a possible marriage partner, you have some special criteria. Not only do you want to find someone who will satisfy your own needs, but you

also want someone who will be a good parent to your children. That interest in your partner's parenting potential has some interesting and important consequences.

MEN'S PREFERENCES AND WOMEN'S PREFERENCES

Recall from Chapter 3 the *sociobiological approach,* the idea that our social behaviors are a product of evolutionary pressures. Sociobiologists analyze courtship and mating behaviors by noting how they contribute to reproduction (Buss, 1994; Kenrick, 1994).

For example, different species follow different reproductive strategies, ranging between two extremes: At one extreme, represented by most fish and insects, the strategy is to produce as many fertilized eggs as possible and then leave them to themselves. The large number of offspring compensates for the fact that each individual has only a tiny chance of survival. At the other extreme, represented by mammals and birds, the strategy is to produce a smaller number of offspring but give each one enough attention to ensure a reasonable chance for survival. (See Figure 16.14.)

However, males do not necessarily follow exactly the same strategy as females. A female mammal has little choice but to follow the few-offspring, extensive-care strategy. In humans, for example, a woman can have at most one delivery every nine months, and more realistically one every year or two during the twenty years or so when she is reproductively fertile. For her children to reach maturity, she needs to provide them with a great deal of her own attention and, if possible, get her mate to provide them with additional attention. Consequently, a woman

FIGURE 16.14
Two mating strategies: Produce large numbers of young, each of which has only a small chance for survival, or produce a small number and provide each with extensive care.

increases her chance of successful reproduction if she finds a mate who is fertile, healthy, and likely to provide substantial resources (psychological and physical) to help her rear the children. Once she finds such a mate, having any additional sex partners would not improve her success in rearing children, and might risk losing the support of her mate.

In contrast, a man could produce an enormous number of babies if he had enough fertile sex partners. You may recall from Chapter 11 that far more men than women report an interest in casual sex partners. The reason, say sociobiologists, lies in our evolutionary history: Occasionally, a man who has had sex with a casual partner has thereby spread his genes. Women with casual sex partners have gained no advantage and frequent disadvantages. Hence, evolution has equipped men and women with somewhat different behavioral tendencies.

However, although having sex with casual partners may occasionally spread a man's genes, it is generally a poor substitute for choosing a partner and raising a family together. (In many cultures, unmarried mothers have a very low probability of successfully rearing their children.) Most men in most cultures want to marry and help rear their children. Even so, a man has somewhat different concerns than a woman has in choosing a spouse, especially in regard to the age of a spouse. In every culture for which we have data, women report a preference for slightly older men (Kenrick, 1994), presumably because older men tend to have more wealth, more status, and more overall resources to provide. Women tend to be more concerned than men are about a potential mate's wealth, ambition, and intelligence—all good predictors of the resources a man could provide to children (Feingold, 1992).

Men in every culture prefer young women. Actually, young men—in their teens or early 20s—prefer women of approximately their own age. As men grow older, they start preferring women 5, 10, or 20 years younger than themselves. The reason, according to sociobiologists, is that women reach menopause and therefore stop being fertile at about age 40–50. Men have therefore evolved a tendency to find younger (probably fertile) women much more attractive than older women.

One more difference in the mating strategies of men and women: Barring some sort of

high-tech intervention, a woman can be sure that any baby she delivers is her own. For a man to be certain that a baby is his, he must believe that his mate has had sex with him alone. Consequently, although both men and women tend to be jealous and upset if their partner has sex with someone else, men tend to be more upset than women are. Most men report that they would be more distressed by a wife's having sex with another man than they would be if their wife became emotionally close to another man. Most women, however, say the reverse (Buss, Larsen, Westen, & Semmelroth, 1992). Cultures differ in how much they tolerate extramarital sexual affairs; for example, the Scandinavian cultures are relatively tolerant of such affairs but the Chinese condemn them harshly (Buss, 1994). In no culture, however, are affairs by wives considered more acceptable than those by husbands.

Table 16.3 summarizes sociobiological explanations of several differences between men and women.

CONCEPT CHECK

9. *Suppose astronauts discover humanlike beings on another planet, whose biology and culture resemble ours except that all men have exactly the same wealth, and women remain fertile all their lives instead of losing their fertility at menopause. What would you predict about the mate preferences of men and women on this planet? (Check your answer on page 719.)*

PHYSICAL ATTRACTIVENESS

What characteristics do you look for in a person you date and perhaps eventually marry? If you are like most college students, you say you want "a person who is intelligent, honest, easy to talk to, with a good sense of humor."

Now imagine a friend of yours says, "Hey, you're not doing anything this weekend, are you? How about going out on a blind date with my cousin who is visiting here for the weekend?"

"Well, I don't know," you reply. "Tell me about your cousin."

"My cousin is intelligent, honest, easy to talk to, and has a good sense of humor."

Do you go on the date? No. Why not? The reason is, your friend did not mention

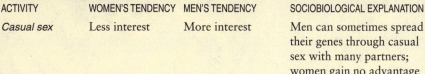

TABLE 16.3
Sociobiological Interpretations of Differences Between Men and Women in Their Choice of Mates

ACTIVITY	WOMEN'S TENDENCY	MEN'S TENDENCY	SOCIOBIOLOGICAL EXPLANATION
Casual sex	Less interest	More interest	Men can sometimes spread their genes through casual sex with many partners; women gain no advantage through multiple partners
Preferred age of spouse	Prefer older man	Prefer young woman	Older man more likely to have wealth and other resources; younger woman more likely to be fertile for many years
Sexual jealousy	Less upset by spouse's sexual affair	More upset by spouse's sexual affair	Sexual affair by wife decreases husband's confidence that her children are his

the cousin's appearance, so you infer that the cousin must be ugly. Were you being hypocritical when you said you wanted someone intelligent, honest, and easy to talk to? I think not. You did not mention appearance because you knew other people would take for granted your interest in good looks. (You also failed to mention that you prefer a date who speaks English; you don't mention preferences that you consider obvious.)

Social psychologists have found that when they ask college couples how much they like each other midway through a first date—yes, they actually did a study in which they polled couples in the middle of a date—the *only* factor that determined how much they liked each other was appearance (Walster, Aronson, Abrahams, & Rottman, 1966). Similarities of attitudes, personality, and intelligence counted for almost nothing. We should not find this result surprising; after all, midway through a first date, how much do two people know about each other, except for their appearance? Physical attraction is the first step in bringing a couple together. If the physical attraction is sufficient, the couple will spend enough time together to learn more about each other's intelligence, honesty, sense of humor, and other important personal qualities.

Why is physical appearance so important to us? Sociobiologists offer a simple explanation: Physical appearance is a good guide to a person's health, and health is extremely important in a mate (Kenrick,

1994). Never mind the possibility of your catching a contagious disease; an unhealthy mate has a decreased probability of successfully reproducing and of surviving long enough to rear any children to maturity. Also, if your potential mate is unhealthy for some genetic reason, then your children might inherit those same disadvantageous genes. Your preference for a healthy mate does not depend on your consciously understanding anything about reproduction or genetics. Throughout human evolution, the people most likely to pass on their genes by rearing healthy children have been those who found healthy mates. Therefore, you have been genetically programmed to prefer a mate who looks healthy.

"Is it true," you might ask, "that good-looking people are healthier than less attractive people?" Not always, of course; however, almost any condition that impairs people's health also makes their appearance less attractive, even if only by slowing down their gait or by decreasing their likelihood of smiling. By process of elimination, good-looking people have the highest probability of being healthy.

Furthermore, consider what "good looking" means. It is possible to take photographs of a large number of moderately similar people, all sitting in the same position and looking in the same direction, and get a computer to average their faces. Most people regard the resulting "averaged" face as highly attractive, more attractive than most

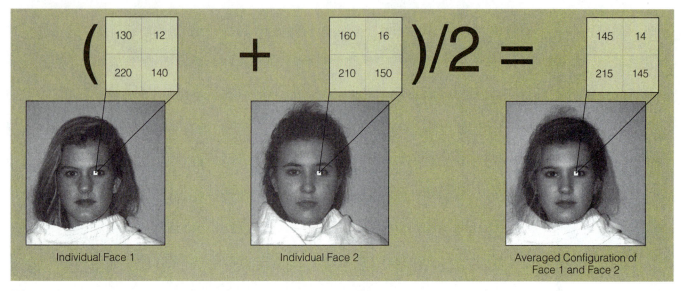

130	12
220	140

$+$

160	16
210	150

$)/2 =$

145	14
215	145

Individual Face 1   Individual Face 2   Averaged Configuration of
Face 1 and Face 2

FIGURE 16.15

A computer averaged a set of faces by measuring the gray value of each point on each picture and then producing a new picture with the average of the grays at each point. This set of photos illustrates the procedure for two original faces. The numbers are for illustrative purposes only. Especially after a large number of faces have been used, most people rate the resulting average face more attractive than most of the originals. (From Langlois, Roggman, & Musselman, 1994.)

of the original faces that composed the average (Langlois & Roggman, 1990; Langlois, Roggman, & Musselman, 1994). (See Figure 16.15.) In other words, a highly attractive face has about an average nose, about an average mouth, about average distance between the eyes, and so forth. If we note anything "unusual" about an attractive face, it is the face's unusual absence of irregularities—no crooked teeth, no skin blemishes, no major asymmetries or peculiarities. One can find a few exceptions to this "average = attractive" rule (Alley & Cunningham, 1991), but in general it holds pretty well.

Why is "normal" attractive? A normal, average face is probably a healthy face. The genes for a face similar to this one have successfully spread in the population, presumably for good reasons. Any face that departs much from the average may be a sign of either disease or genetic mutation. In other words, a face with regular, normal features is a probable indicator of good genes and good health.

ROMANTIC AND PASSIONATE LOVE

The term *love,* even in the sense of romantic love, means different things to different people, or even to the same person at different stages in life. We need to learn to distinguish several meanings.

DEFINING AND MEASURING LOVE

The poet Elizabeth Barrett Browning once asked, "How do I love thee? Let me count the ways." How do social psychologists count the ways of love?

In one of the first attempts to measure love, Zick Rubin (1970, 1973) developed scales of liking and loving. According to Rubin, liking includes a feeling of respect and admiration for someone. Two items from his liking scale are "In my opinion, _____ (fill in name) is an exceptionally mature person" and "_____ is one of the most likable people I know." Loving has to do with feelings of intimacy, absorption, and possessiveness. Sample items are "I feel that I can confide in _____ about virtually everything" and "It would be hard for me to get along without _____."

In one study, Rubin (1973) asked 182 college couples to rate their dating partners and their best friends on his liking and loving scales. Not surprisingly, the subjects rated both friends and romantic partners high on the liking scale, but they rated their romantic partners significantly higher on the loving scale. The scores on the two scales were positively correlated, though not perfectly. Apparently, you like almost all the people you love, but you may not love all the people you like. When Rubin asked the subjects how likely they were to marry their dating partner, they reported high probabilities only if they both liked and loved their partner.

Is love a single experience, or does it have multiple dimensions? Robert Sternberg (1986; Sternberg & Grajek, 1984) asked subjects questions about their experience of love and then analyzed the results to see whether the answers to each question correlated with the answers to others. He concluded that love has three main dimensions: *intimacy* (how well you can talk with and confide in your partner), *passion* (erotic attraction and the feeling of being in love), and *commitment* (an intention to continue in the relationship).

According to Sternberg, these three dimensions are somewhat independent. For example, a passionate relationship might be low in intimacy and commitment. And a marriage high in intimacy and commitment might be low in passion, more like a solid friendship. Most of us aspire to romantic relationships that are high on all counts: intimacy, passion, and commitment. Sternberg terms such ideal relationships "consummate loves."

Clyde and Susan Hendrick (1986) have identified three primary styles of love: *eros* (passionate, erotic love), *ludus* (uncommitted, game-playing love), and *storge* (STOR-gay; friendship love). (The strange-sounding labels are borrowed from Greek and Latin.) Hendrick and Hendrick also describe three secondary styles of love: *mania* (possessive and obsessive love), *pragma* (practical, list-of-benefits love), and *agape* (ah-GAH-pay; selfless, spiritual love). Table 16.4 shows some of the items used on a questionnaire to measure these six styles of love.

Hendrick and Hendrick (1986) also found that men tend to be more ludic (game playing and uncommitted), whereas women tend to be more storgic and pragmatic (inclined to see love as friendship or as a relationship based on practical considerations).

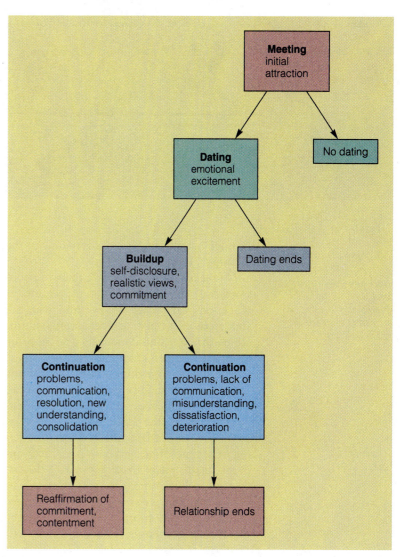

FIGURE 16.16
A romantic relationship begins with initial attraction. Of all the couples that experience initial attraction, a small percentage proceed to the dating stage; some of those advance to the buildup stage, and so forth. At each stage, the relationship can develop further or it can end.

Couples tend to share the same love style—that is, erotic partners choose erotic partners, and storgic partners choose storgic partners (Hendrick, Hendrick, & Adler, 1988). Relationships in which both partners share the same view of love tend to be more successful than relationships in which the partners have different views.

THE LIFE CYCLE OF ROMANTIC RELATIONSHIPS

Romantic relationships have a beginning, a middle, and sometimes an intentional end. George Levinger (1980, 1983) suggests that relationships go through five stages: initial attraction, buildup, continuation and consolidation, deterioration, and ending (Figure 16.16). Not all relationships, of course, go

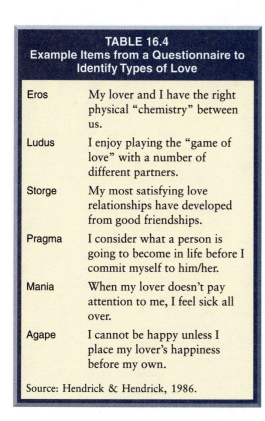

TABLE 16.4
Example Items from a Questionnaire to Identify Types of Love

Eros	My lover and I have the right physical "chemistry" between us.
Ludus	I enjoy playing the "game of love" with a number of different partners.
Storge	My most satisfying love relationships have developed from good friendships.
Pragma	I consider what a person is going to become in life before I commit myself to him/her.
Mania	When my lover doesn't pay attention to me, I feel sick all over.
Agape	I cannot be happy unless I place my lover's happiness before my own.

Source: Hendrick & Hendrick, 1986.

In a mature, lasting relationship, a couple can count on each other for care and affection through both the good times and the bad times. Here, two weary travelers wait for a train in Salzburg, Austria.

through all five stages. Here are some of the factors that affect each stage.

In the *initial attraction,* we form relationships with people we meet at school, at work, or near where we live and who are similar to us in age, socioeconomic status, ethnic background, and physical appearance. As couples enter the *buildup* stage, partners learn new things about each other, with women generally quicker than men to reveal their inner secrets (Dindia & Allen, 1992). Even at this point, however, the relationship may not be stable. In one study at the beginning of an academic year, 250 undergraduates each identified their "closest, deepest" relationship. Of these, almost half (47%) identified a romantic partner. Presumably those relationships were well into the buildup stage, if not beyond. But almost half of those "closest, deepest" relationships broke up by the end of the academic year (Berscheid, Snyder, & Omoto, 1989).

In the *continuation* stage, the relationship reaches a stable "middle age." By this time the partners have worked out a complex system of shared work and understandings. The excitement of constantly discovering new things about each other is over, and the partners may not arouse each other's emotions as intensely or as frequently as before (Berscheid, 1983). This does not mean that they no longer love each other. The emotion that persists in a mature relationship may become apparent only when the relationship is terminated by the death or departure of one of the partners.

As time passes, some relationships enter a stage of *deterioration.* Why? Exchange theories offer one explanation (Levinger, 1976): One of the partners has changed, for better or worse, and the exchange is no longer equally fair to both. According to one survey of 2,000 married people, the subjects who

felt they were not getting their fair share out of the relationship were more likely to engage in extramarital affairs, apparently to even the score (Walster, Traupman, & Walster, 1978). (Or was it the other way around? Did they first commit adultery and then justify their behavior by saying that their marriage was unrewarding?)

Some relationships finally arrive at an *ending.* One partner may decide to end the relationship before the other partner is even aware that a problem exists (Vaughan, 1986). It is rare that both partners decide to end a relationship at the same time. As a rule, college men are less sensitive to problems in their relationships than college women are, and men are less likely to foresee a breakup (Rubin, Peplau, & Hill, 1981). When the breakup comes, the men usually seem more upset than the women do (Bloom, White, & Asher, 1979). Perhaps women monitor relationships more carefully and prepare themselves for what lies ahead.

SUMMARY

- *People's need for one another.* People crave companionship of other people, especially others with whom they have felt emotionally close for a long time. This need can be regarded as part of human nature. (page 709)

- *Short-term affiliation.* People in distress or need gain strength from associating even briefly with other people, especially others who have undergone or who expect to undergo similar distressing experiences. (page 710)

- *Friendship.* People will generally choose friends and romantic partners who live near them, frequently come in contact with them, and resemble them in various ways. Relationships are most likely to survive and grow if each party believes that he or she is getting about as good a deal as the other person is. (page 711)

- *Marriage and similar attachments.* People have special considerations when choosing a possible marriage partner, because marriage implies a commitment to rearing children together. The behavior and interests of men are somewhat different from those of women, for reasons that make sense in a sociobiological framework. (page 713)

- *Physical attractiveness.* As a rule, attractive faces have normal, average features. An attractive face is, therefore, an indication that the person is probably normal and healthy. (page 714)

- *Liking and loving.* Although people generally like the people they love, loving and liking can be measured separately. (page 716)
- *Dimensions and types of love.* Love has several dimensions, including intimacy, passion, and commitment. Psychologists distinguish several types of love. (page 716)
- *Development of relationships.* Romantic relationships go through some or all of five stages: initial attraction, buildup, continuation and consolidation, deterioration, and ending. (page 717)

SUGGESTION FOR FURTHER READING

Buss, D. (1994). *The evolution of desire: Strategies of human mating.* New York: Basic Books. Discussion of evolutionary influences on men's and women's preferences in a mate.

TERMS

proximity (literally, closeness) tendency to choose as friends people with whom we come in frequent contact (page 711)

mere-exposure effect tendency to increase liking for everything and everyone that has become familiar (page 711)

similarity principle tendency to associate with people similar to oneself (page 711)

exchange or **equity theories** theories holding that social relationships are transactions in which partners exchange goods and services (page 712)

ANSWERS TO CONCEPT CHECKS

8. Proximity and familiarity will strengthen the likelihood of your becoming friends. The similarity principle will weaken it. Because of the difference in languages, you will have little chance, at least at first, to discover any similarities in interests or attitudes. In fact, proximity probably will not be a potent force because it serves largely as a means of enabling people to discover what they have in common. (page 713)

9. If all men are equally wealthy, women should have no reason to prefer older men and would presumably prefer men close to their own age. If women's fertility lasts as late in life as men's does, then the men on this planet should not have a strong preference for young women. (page 714)

INTERPERSONAL INFLUENCE

Under what circumstances do we conform to the behavior of others?

Under what circumstances do we behave as others tell us to?

Why do people act differently in groups from when they are alone?

In the spring of 1983, a strange epidemic swept through a Palestinian village in one of the territories occupied by Israel. The hospitals were flooded with people, mostly adolescents, complaining of headaches, dizzy spells, stomach pains, blurred vision, and difficulty breathing. The Palestinians accused the Israelis of poisoning the air or the water,

perhaps in an effort to sterilize the young Palestinian women. The Israelis replied with indignant denials.

Meanwhile, although physicians conducted extensive tests on all the patients, they could find nothing medically wrong. They studied the food, the air, the water, every possible source of poison or of contagious disease. They found no signs of anything that could cause any illness. Finally they concluded that all the symptoms were the result of anxiety, coupled with the power of suggestion (Paicheler, 1988). The Palestinians, understandably nervous about the political tensions in the region, *believed* they had been poisoned; this belief and the accompanying symptoms of illness spread from person to person just like a contagious disease.

We live in an ambiguous world. Often we do not understand what is happening or what we should do about it; when in doubt, we take our cues from what other people are doing or what they tell us to do. And that is fine—provided that the other people are better informed or wiser than we are.

CONFORMITY

Conformity means maintaining or changing one's behavior to match the behavior of others. The pressure to conform is sometimes overwhelming. Koversada, a small city on the coast of the Adriatic Sea, follows a custom of nudism, with a few exceptions such as dinners at formal restaurants. If a first-time visitor to the city tries walking around clothed, other people stop and stare, sometimes shaking their heads with disapproval. The clothed person feels awkward, out of place, and just as self-conscious as a naked person would be in a city of fully clothed people. Almost always, within 24 hours, a visitor to Koversada undresses to be like everyone else (Newman, 1988).

Conformity can also alter the way we perceive a situation, especially when our sensory experiences are ill defined. One example is an illusion known as the **autokinetic effect:** If you sit in a darkened room and stare at one small stationary point of light, the point eventually will seem to move. If someone says, "I see it moving in a zigzag manner" or "I see it moving slowly in a counterclockwise direction," you are likely to perceive it the

People tend to conform to the behavior of others, especially in ambiguous situations but sometimes even if they doubt the wisdom of the other people's behavior.

FIGURE 16.17
Choosing conformity: In Asch's conformity studies subjects were asked to match a line with one of three other lines on another card. They were surrounded by people who gave obviously wrong answers.

same way. You will perceive some movement on your own, but other people's suggestions can greatly alter the apparent speed and direction of the movement.

Early research suggested that people are most likely to conform their opinions in ambiguous situations that make it difficult for people to be sure of their own judgments (Sherif, 1935). For example, there is no absolute right or wrong on styles of clothing; and in matters such as politics, religion, or the movement of a single point of light in a darkened room, there may be a right answer, but we do not have enough information to be sure of that answer. Consequently, we rely to some extent on the opinions of others.

Would we also conform to the opinions or behaviors of others if we had adequate evidence to be sure that we are right and they are wrong? To answer that question, Solomon Asch (1951, 1956) carried out a now famous series of experiments.

Asch assembled groups of students and asked them to look at a vertical bar, as shown in the left half of Figure 16.17. This was defined as the model. He also showed them three other vertical bars (right half of Figure 16.17), and asked them which bar was the same length as the model. As you can see, the task is simple. Asch asked the students to give their answers aloud. He repeated the procedure with 18 sets of bars.

Only one student in each group was a real subject. All the others were confederates who had been instructed to give incorrect answers on 12 of the 18 trials. Asch arranged for the real subject to be the next-to-the-last person in the group to announce his answer so that he would hear most of the confederates' incorrect responses before giving his own (Figure 16.18). Would he go along with the crowd?

To Asch's surprise, 37 of the 50 subjects conformed to the majority at least once, and 14 of them conformed on more than half of the trials. When faced with a unanimous wrong answer by the other group members, the mean subject conformed on 4 of the 12 trials. Asch was disturbed by these results: "That we have found the tendency to conformity in our society so strong . . . is a matter of concern. It raises questions about our ways of education and about the values that guide our conduct" (Asch, 1955, p. 34).

Why did the subjects conform so readily? When they were interviewed after the experiment, some said they thought the rest of the group was correct or they guessed some optical illusion was influencing the appearance. Others said they knew their conforming answers were wrong, but went along with the group for fear of being ridiculed or thought "peculiar." Reactions of the nonconforming subjects were interesting too: Some were very nervous but felt duty bound to tell how the bars looked to them. A few seemed socially withdrawn, as if they paid no attention to anyone else. Still others were supremely self-confident, as if to say, "I'm right and everyone else is wrong. It happens all the time."

Asch (1951, 1955) found that one of the situational factors that influence conformity is the size of the opposing majority. In a series of studies, he varied the number of confederates who gave incorrect answers from 1 to 15. He found that the subjects conformed to a group of 3 or 4 as readily as

FIGURE 16.18
Three of the eight subjects in one of Asch's experiments on conformity. The one in the middle is the real subject; the others are the experimenter's confederates. (From Asch, 1951.) In this test of the power of group pressure to induce conformity, people had only to disagree with strangers for a short time. The correct answers were clear—yet most subjects felt a strong pressure to conform to what the majority said.

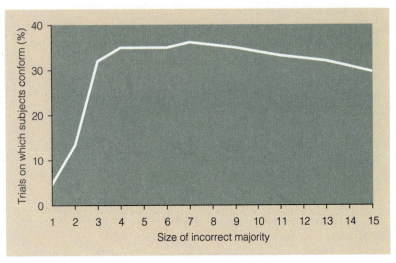

FIGURE 16.19
FIGURE 16.19
Asch (1955) found that conformity became more frequent as group size increased up to about three and then leveled off. But when subjects had an "ally," conformity decreased considerably.

they did to a larger group (Figure 16.19). However, the subjects conformed much less if they had an "ally." In some of his experiments, Asch instructed one of the confederates to give correct answers. In the presence of this nonconformist, the real subjects conformed only occasionally (Figure 16.20). Apparently, it is difficult to be a minority of one but not so difficult to be part of a minority of two.

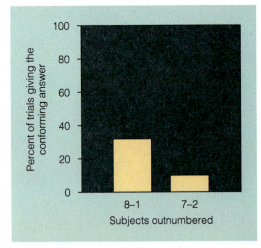

FIGURE 16.20
In Asch's experiments, subjects who were faced with a unanimous majority giving wrong answers conformed to the majority view on 32% of trials. Subjects who had one "ally" giving the correct answer were less likely to conform. Evidently it is difficult to be in a minority of one, but less difficult to be in a minority of two.

ACCEPTING OR DENYING RESPONSIBILITY TOWARD OTHERS

Sometimes other people encourage us to do something we would not have done on our own, as in the case of Asch's studies. Sometimes other people inhibit us from doing something we would have done on our own. We look around and see what others are doing—or *not* doing—and we say, "Okay, I'll do that too. I'll do my fair share—no more, no less." Why do people sometimes work together to help one another, and sometimes ignore the needs of others?

BYSTANDER HELPFULNESS OR APATHY

Suppose while you are waiting at a bus stop you see me trip and fall down, just 30 meters away from you. I am not screaming in agony but I am not getting up right away either, so you are not sure whether or not I need help. Do you think you probably would come over and offer your help? Or would you just stand there and ignore me? Before you answer, try imagining the situation two ways: First, you and I are the only people in sight. Second, there are a lot of other people nearby, none of whom is rushing to my aid. Does the presence of those other people make any difference to your response? (Note that it doesn't change *my* predicament. I am in the same amount of pain, regardless of whether one person or many people ignore me.)

Late one night in March, 1964, Kitty Genovese was stabbed to death near her apartment in Queens, New York. For 30 minutes, 38 of her neighbors listened to her screams. A few stood at their windows watching. None of them came to her aid or called the police. Why?

Bibb Latané and John Darley (1969) proposed that one reason the neighbors failed to help was **diffusion of responsibility**—the fact that we feel less responsibility for helping when other people are around than when we know that no one else can help. Latané and Darley suggest that no one helped Kitty Genovese because everyone knew that many other people *could* help her.

In an experiment designed to test this hypothesis, a young woman ushered either one student or two students into a room and asked them to wait a few minutes for the start of a market research study (Latané & Darley, 1968, 1969). She then went into the next room, closing the door behind her. There she played a tape recording that made it sound as if she had climbed onto a chair and had fallen off. For about 2 minutes she could be heard crying and moaning, "Oh . . . my foot . . . I can't move it. Oh . . . my ankle. . . ." Of the subjects who were waiting alone, 70% went next door and offered to help. Of the subjects who were waiting with someone else, only 13% offered to help.

Diffusion of responsibility is one possible explanation. Each person thinks, "It's not my responsibility to help any more than it is the other person's. And if we get blamed for not helping, it's as much that person's fault as it is mine." A second possible explanation is that the presence of another person changes the way we react to an ambiguous situation: "Does that woman need help or not? I'm not really sure. This other person isn't doing anything, so maybe she doesn't."

SOCIAL LOAFING

Sometimes your success and rewards depend entirely on your own efforts. For example, when you take a test in one of your college courses, you must work alone. (You can get into real trouble if you and a fellow student decide to "cooperate"!) In other cases, however, you work with other people as part of a team. For example, if you work for a company that gives workers a share of the profits, your rewards depend on both your own productivity and that of other workers. Do you work as hard when rewards depend on the group's productivity as when they depend on your efforts alone?

The answer is, probably not—at least under certain circumstances. In one experiment, students were told to scream and clap and try to make as loud a noise as possible, like cheerleaders at a sports event. Sometimes each student screamed and clapped alone; sometimes students acted in groups of 2 to 6; and sometimes they acted alone but *thought* that other people were screaming and clapping too. (They wore headphones so that they could not hear anyone else.) As a rule, a student who screamed and clapped alone made more noise than a student who was (or thought he or she was) part of a group (Latané, Williams, & Harkins, 1979). Social psychologists call this phenomenon **social loafing**—the tendency to "loaf" (or

In a tug-of-war or other task in which individuals pool their efforts, most people do not work as hard as they would when working alone. This is called "social loafing." However, if participants know that each individual's contribution will be measured separately, social loafing ceases and everyone puts out a full effort.

work less hard) when sharing the work with other people. Social loafing has been demonstrated for several other behaviors, not just for screaming. For example, suppose you were asked to "name all the uses you can think of for a brick" (such as *crack nuts, anchor a boat,* or *use as doorstop*) and write each one on a card. You probably would need a tall stack of cards if you were working by yourself, but you would fill out fewer cards if you were tossing them into a pile along with other people's suggestions, to be evaluated as a group (Harkins & Jackson, 1985).

At this point you may be thinking, "Wait a minute. When I'm playing on a basketball team, I try as hard as I can. I don't think I do any social loafing." And you are right; social loafing seldom occurs in team sports. (When it does, the fans boo.) The reason is that observers, including teammates, can easily see who is contributing and who is not. Even though the team wins or loses as a group, individual players also compete for recognition as individuals. People loaf in group projects if they expect no reward for an extra effort; they put out a full effort if they expect other people to notice their effort, or if they think they can contribute something that other group members cannot (Shepperd, 1993; Williams & Karau, 1991).

Social loafing is a robust phenomenon, easy to demonstrate in a variety of settings and in almost all populations of people. Generally, the effect is smaller when people consider the task a meaningful one or when they identify with and care about their group. (For example, we see little social loafing among members of a sports team or among soldiers in a war.) Other things being equal, men do more social loafing than women. (Perhaps women are more accustomed to working hard without getting credit.) Also, people in western cultures do more social loafing than do people in Asian cultures, which stress the value of helping one's group instead of just helping oneself (Karau & Williams, 1993).

In a way, many of the exceptions to social loafing are more surprising than the phenomenon itself. For example, during a national election, many people fail to vote, as we would expect based on social loafing. Nevertheless, most people do vote, and many people work for their candidate, contribute to their candidate, and make a surprisingly vigorous effort, considering how little chance one person has to influence the outcome of the election.

CONCEPT CHECKS

10. Given what we have learned about social loafing, why are most people unlikely to work hard to clean up the environment?
11. Suppose the head of a large library wants the library staff to pay more attention to getting all the books into their correct locations. Currently many of the books are misplaced and the staff seem to be "loafing" at rearranging them. What could be done to encourage greater efforts? (Check your answers on pages 728 and 729.)

VOLUNTEERISM

The preceding sections may have given an exaggerated impression. Perhaps you inferred that "no one ever takes responsibility for helping anyone else" and that "everyone is content to let someone else do the work." That conclusion is not correct, at least not for all the people all the time. When serious needs and problems arise in society, great numbers of volunteers respond with their time and money (Figure 16.21). For example, consider the problem of AIDS victims, some of whom find themselves shunned by strangers and virtually deserted by their family and friends. To meet this need, volunteer organizations have developed in many cities to provide "AIDS buddies," healthy people who offer comfort, assistance, and companionship to AIDS victims. Most of the people who volunteer to become AIDS buddies do not consider themselves to be at high risk for developing AIDS themselves; they do not have careers in psychology or medicine; they expect no reward or recognition for themselves. Apparently they volunteer simply as a way of expressing their values and their desire to help others (Omoto & Snyder, 1990). Volunteers also staff many other organizations devoted to health, education, environmental protection, and similar important causes. In short, some people—somehow—resist the pressures of bystander apathy and social loafing.

FIGURE 16.21
During an emergency, people abandon their usual tendencies toward bystander apathy and social loafing. Just after an earthquake in the San Francisco area, authorities ordered residents of one area to evacuate within 15 minutes. People who usually ignored one another immediately pitched in to help one another move their valuables.

GROUP DECISION MAKING

An organization that needs to make some decision will frequently set up a committee to look into the issues and make recommendations. We prefer a committee to an individual because the committee has more time, more total information, and fewer peculiarities and biases than any individual has. Nevertheless, a group is subject to the influences of conformity and social loafing, which sometimes interfere with its reaching the best possible decisions.

GROUP POLARIZATION

If a group is composed of people who nearly all lean in the same direction on a particular issue, the group as a whole will tend to move even further in that direction after they discuss that issue. Consequently, the group probably will vote for a more extreme decision than most of its members favored at the start (Lamm & Myers, 1978). This phenomenon is known as **group polarization.** Note that in this case *polarization* does not mean that the group breaks up into fragments who favor different positions. Rather, it means that the members of a group, after discussing the issues, move *together* toward one pole (extreme position) or the other. For example, a group of people who are opposed to abortion, or in favor of animal rights, or opposed to gun regulations will, after discussing the issue among themselves, generally become more extreme in their views than they had been at the start.

Group polarization occurs for at least two reasons: increased information and the pressure to conform (Isenberg, 1986). During the group discussion, the members become aware of new arguments and new information. If most of the members were leaning in one direction at the start, the group hears arguments mostly favoring that side of the issue (Burnstein & Vinokur, 1973, 1977). And as the members of the group become aware of the consensus during the discussion, they feel pressure to conform. The pressure to conform is strongest for people who see themselves as on the periphery, not fully accepted by the rest of the group (Noel, Wann, & Branscombe, 1995). They can increase their acceptance by the group if they emphasize how vigorously and extremely they support its views and goals.

GROUPTHINK

An extreme form of group polarization is known as **groupthink,** in which the members of a group suppress their doubts about a group's poorly thought-out decision (Janis, 1972, 1985). In some cases, dominant members of the group actually ask dissenters to

Many organizations try to resist the tendency toward groupthink—the tendency to stifle dissenting views and proceed to a possibly disastrous decision. During the Renaissance, European kings sometimes called on a "fool" (or court jester) to describe some proposal in a fresh and possibly amusing light. In a court composed largely of yes-men, the fool sometimes was the only person who could openly point out the folly of a proposed action without fear of reprisal. (From Roger von Oech's Creative Whack Pack; art by George Willett; © Roger von Oech 1992.)

be quiet; more often, dissenters silence themselves for fear of making a bad impression or disrupting the harmony of the group. One dramatic example of groupthink led to the Bay of Pigs fiasco of 1962. U.S. President John F. Kennedy and his advisers were considering a plan to support a small-scale invasion of Cuba at the Bay of Pigs. They assumed that a small group of Cuban exiles could overwhelm the Cuban army and trigger a spontaneous rebellion of the Cuban people against Fidel Castro and his government. Most of the advisers who doubted this assumption felt pressured to keep quiet; one who did express his doubts was told that he should loyally support the president, who had already made up his mind. Within a few hours after the invasion began, all the invaders were killed or captured. The decision makers themselves wondered how they could have made such a stupid decision.

Another example of groupthink was NASA's decision to launch the space shuttle

Challenger on a cold morning in 1986. The top decision makers let it be known that they had strong economic and public-relations reasons for launching the shuttle on schedule. Project engineers who knew the rocket booster was unsafe at low temperatures dutifully kept quiet and hoped for the best. Seventy-three seconds after the launch, the *Challenger* exploded because of an O-ring that was unable to function properly at low temperatures.

In both the Bay of Pigs incident and the *Challenger* disaster, group members who doubted the wisdom of the decision kept quiet and created an illusion of unanimous support. Originally, psychologists believed that groupthink occurs mostly in highly cohesive groups, such as fraternal or religious organizations, in which the members think it would be rude to criticize one another's views. Later research has found that almost all groups, not just cohesive ones, are capable of exerting pressure to conform (Aldag & Fuller, 1993).

Irving Janis (1985) suggests several techniques for reducing the likelihood of groupthink: Leaders should encourage dissent.

The group can be divided into subgroups to see whether, in independent discussions, they arrive at the same conclusions. Leaders should consult their advisers one by one in private. The group should seek the advice of outside experts, including those with dissenting opinions. Regardless of whether a leader takes such steps or not, members who entertain doubts about a decision should always remember the lessons of the Bay of Pigs and the *Challenger:* When much is at stake, it is better to risk angering one's leader than to go along with a possibly disastrous decision.

THE PSYCHOLOGY OF JURIES

Jury trials offer an important and rather unusual example of group decision making. Ordinarily the people who make important decisions for a company have been selected for their special competence, and they know that they will reap the rewards or suffer the consequences of their decisions. By contrast, a jury is composed of people with no special competence, who most likely do not know one another, and who need not even explain their decision, much less accept any personal consequences from it. Weighing all the conflicting evidence in a trial is a difficult task, and some jurors perform this task much more rationally than others do (Kuhn, Weinstock, & Flaton, 1994). The results of a jury trial depend, of course, largely on the evidence, but they also depend on the selection of jurors and the judge's instructions to the jury.

Jury Selection Before a trial begins, the judge, the prosecuting attorney, and the defense attorney interview prospective jurors in a process called *voir dire,* an Old French term meaning "to tell the truth." Prospective jurors are asked whether they have already formed an opinion based on accounts in the media, and whether for any other reason they would be unable to render a fair and impartial verdict. The judge excuses "for cause" anyone who could not render an impartial judgment. The two attorneys can ask the prospective jurors additional questions and make a certain number of *peremptory challenges,* rejecting prospective jurors without explanation. The permitted number of peremptory challenges may range from 2 or 3 in a routine case to 20 or more in a heavily publicized case. The attorneys use their

A jury trial begins with the *voir dire, a process of interviewing potential jurors and eliminating those who might be unable to reach a fair verdict based on the evidence.*

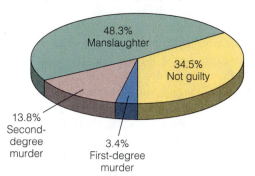

Death-qualified people

68% Manslaughter

17.3% Second-degree murder

1% First-degree murder

13.7% Not guilty

Death-scrupled people

48.3% Manslaughter

34.5% Not guilty

13.8% Second-degree murder

3.4% First-degree murder

FIGURE 16.22

Death-scrupled people are those who say they could never vote in favor of the death penalty; under current U.S. law, such people cannot serve on juries when the prosecution is seeking the death penalty. In a mock jury experiment, death-scrupled people were far more likely to vote "not guilty" than death-qualified people. This evidence suggests that excluding death-scrupled people tilts the jury toward conviction. (Based on data of Cowan, Thompson, & Ellsworth, 1984.)

peremptory challenges to eliminate jurors who seem to have a bias in favor of the other side. Presumably those who survive all the challenges by both sides constitute a fair, impartial jury.

Special problems arise in jury selection for death-penalty cases. Prior to 1968, any prospective juror who opposed the death penalty was excluded "for cause" from the jury of a murder trial. In the *Witherspoon* decision of that year, the Supreme Court ruled that opponents of the death penalty can be excluded for cause only if they are so opposed that they would vote against the death penalty in all cases, regardless of the evidence. People who are unconditionally opposed to the death penalty are referred to as *death-scrupled*. Those who are willing to consider the death penalty under certain circumstances are referred to as *death-qualified*—that is, they are qualified to serve on death-penalty cases.

Many social psychologists have challenged the wisdom of excluding death-scrupled people from juries. One objection is that more African Americans than European Americans are death-scrupled, as well as more women than men and more young people than older people (Fitzgerald & Ellsworth, 1984). Consequently, a young African-American defendant in a murder case often faces a jury composed mostly of older European-American men. A second objection is that death-qualified people tend to be more sympathetic to the prosecution,

while death-scrupled people tend to be more sympathetic to the defense (Fitzgerald & Ellsworth, 1984). A fair jury should include both kinds of people.

Several studies have compared the reactions of death-qualified and death-scrupled people to mock trials. In a particularly thorough study (Cowan, Thompson, & Ellsworth, 1984), adult (nonstudent) subjects watched a realistic 2½-hour videotape of a dramatized murder trial. They were then assigned to 12-person juries and asked to deliberate for an hour. Ten of the juries consisted entirely of death-qualified people; ten included 2 to 4 death-scrupled people. The videotape had been designed to present a borderline case. Evidently it succeeded, because no jury reached a verdict within the allotted hour. The juries that included death-scrupled people were more critical of the evidence presented by both the prosecution and the defense, and the death-scrupled people were more likely to vote for acquittal than the death-qualified people (Figure 16.22). Apparently, then, the exclusion of death-scrupled people makes juries less representative and decreases the defendant's chances of getting a fair trial in a murder trial.

Many attorneys as well as psychologists have argued for keeping death-scrupled people on juries, at least for the phase of the trial that considers guilt or innocence. So far, the courts and legislatures have asked for more research before they make any such decision.

The Judge's Instructions At various points during a trial, the judge may instruct the jury to ignore certain statements made by one of the attorneys or witnesses. According to the research, most jurors find that instruction difficult to follow (Sue, Smith, & Caldwell, 1973). Imagine yourself as a juror: You just heard someone say that the defendant failed a lie-detector test, but the judge says to ignore that statement, because the evidence is not admissible. How thoroughly could you ignore it?

At the end of a trial, the judge explains to the jury the relevant portions of the law as they apply to the case at hand. For example, the judge might explain that the prosecution has the "burden of proof"; if in doubt about the defendant's guilt, the jury should vote to acquit. In a death-penalty case, the judge explains to the jury what factors to weigh and how to weigh them in making a decision. Unfortunately, many judges give complicated and confusing instructions, apparently more concerned with *stating* the law than with making sure that the jurors *understand* the law (Diamond, 1993). Research has shown that alterations in the judge's instructions can greatly alter the jury's understanding and its probability of convicting or acquitting the defendant (Luginbuhl, 1992). Decision making by a jury is like other examples of group decision making: It can be strongly influenced by seemingly minor changes in procedures, instructions, or the makeup of the group.

SUMMARY

- *Conformity.* Many people conform to the majority view even when they are confident that the majority is wrong. An individual is as likely to conform to a group of three as to a larger group, but an individual who has an ally is less likely to conform to the majority. (page 720)

- *Diffusion of responsibility.* People in groups are less likely than an isolated individual to come to the aid of another because they experience a diffusion of responsibility. (page 722)

- *Social loafing.* People working together on a task tend to exert less effort than people who are working independently. However, they will work just as hard on the group task if they are evaluated on their individual performances or if they believe their contributions will make

a big difference to the group's success. (page 723)

- *Group polarization.* Groups of people who lean mostly in the same direction on a given issue often make decisions that are more extreme than the decisions most individuals would have made on their own. (page 725)

- *Groupthink.* Groupthink occurs when members of a cohesive group fail to express their opposition to a decision, for fear of making a bad impression or harming the cohesive spirit of the group. (page 725)

- *Psychology of juries.* Juries are groups of nonexperts who make important, even life-or-death, decisions. Social psychologists have investigated the influence of the judge's instructions and the selection of people to compose the jury. (page 726)

SUGGESTION FOR FURTHER READING

Cialdini, R. B. (1993). *Influence: Science and practice* (rev. ed.). New York: William Morrow & Co. One of the most enjoyable and entertaining psychology books ever written. Buy a copy and take it with you on vacation.

TERMS

conformity maintaining or changing one's behavior to match the behavior of others (page 720)

autokinetic effect the illusory perception that a point of light in a darkened room is in motion (page 720)

diffusion of responsibility tendency to feel less responsibility to help when other people are around than when we know that no one else can help (page 722)

social loafing tendency to "loaf" (or work less hard) when sharing the work with other people (page 723)

group polarization tendency for a group whose members lean in the same direction on a particular issue to become more extreme in its opinion after discussing the issue (page 725)

groupthink process in which the members of a group suppress their doubts about a group's poorly thought-out decision, for fear of making a bad impression or disrupting the harmony of the group (page 725)

ANSWERS TO CONCEPT CHECKS

10. For the task of protecting the environment, each person is part of a "group" with billions of other people. Social loafing is likely because many one-person contributions, such as picking up litter, would not earn individual credit or recognition. Also, each person thinks, "What good could one person do on such a gigantic problem?" When people believe their own contribution would not make a noticeable difference, they tend to engage in social loafing. (page 724)

11. One approach would be to make the contributions of each staff member more apparent (because social loafing is common when people do not see that their own efforts make much difference). For example, assign each person a different set of shelves and report data on which shelves have shown the greatest improvement in their orderliness. A similar approach can be used for other examples of loafing on the job. (page 724)

THE POWER OF THE SOCIAL SITUATION

Why do people sometimes engage in self-defeating behaviors?

How can we change the situation to minimize such behaviors?

Back in the 1960s, a number of world problems seemed to threaten the very future of civilization. The Vietnam War seemed to go on forever; the nations of the world seemed to be preparing for global nuclear war; racial injustice and discrimination were widespread in the United States; we were beginning to recognize how badly people were

People are often fond of citing ways in which technology has damaged human life: air and water pollution, the possibility of nuclear war, and so forth. But technology also enhances communication, education, and problem solving for people throughout the world. When people behave in self-defeating ways, we should look for ways to change the situation—through technology or other means—as an alternative to trying to change human nature.

damaging the environment. As a high-school and then college student at the time, I harbored grandiose dreams that I was going to save the world. I wasn't sure how—maybe through my great moral leadership (I told you I had "grandiose dreams"!), maybe through politics, maybe through psychological research. I hoped somehow to change human nature so that people would stop being so cruel and selfish.

Now here we are many years later, and I reflect on the people who really did improve the world in major and spectacular ways. Some of the people who come to mind made their impact through moral leadership or politics—Martin Luther King, Jr., Mother Teresa, Alexander Solzhenitsyn, Nelson Mandela, and others. But there have also been some people who improved the world through technology—a route that I never even contemplated during my youthful "save the world" fantasies. For example, the engineers who devised spy satellites made possible the international treaties banning tests of nuclear weapons. (Without the capacity to watch one another, competing countries would never have agreed to such treaties.) The engineers who developed computers, printers, and modems facilitated the spread of freedom of the press to every technologically advanced country. (Any country that lets people have computers lets them have printing presses.) These technological advances changed human *behavior* without changing human *nature*.

The general point here is that much of our behavior is controlled by the situation—sometimes the technological situation, sometimes the social situation. On occasion some person or social situation pressures us, or virtually compels us, to behave in cruel, uncooperative, even self-defeating ways. We need to recognize the power of these situations so that we can deal with them, change them, or avoid them altogether. Here we shall consider several situations that tend to elicit behavior that seems irrational, self-defeating, or uncivilized.

BEHAVIOR TRAPS

What would you think of someone who knowingly paid a great deal more for something than it was worth? Or someone who confessed to a crime even though the police admitted they did not have enough evidence for a conviction? Or someone who used up all of his or her resources at once instead of saving some for later? You probably would question that person's intelligence or sanity. And yet under certain circumstances you might find yourself acting the same way yourself. Sometimes we fall into a **behavior trap**—a situation that almost forces us into self-defeating behaviors. We call such situations "traps" because people wander into them without realizing the danger; once they see the danger, they cannot find their way out. We shall consider three examples—escalation of conflict, the prisoner's dilemma, and the commons dilemma.

ESCALATION OF CONFLICT

Sometimes a conflict or competition between two sides progressively escalates: After one side increases its effort and investment, the other side increases and surpasses the first sides's effort, prompting the first side to retaliate, and so forth. Eventually, both sides have invested far more than the original dispute was worth, but neither wants to quit and admit defeat.

For example, imagine you and I and a few other people are at an auction. The auctioneer explains that the next item up for bids is a dollar bill, which she will sell to the highest bidder, even if the highest bid is only a few cents. There is one catch, however; at the end, when someone finally buys the dollar bill, the second-highest bidder must pay his or her bid to the auctioneer also, receiving nothing in return. So, for example, if I bid 5 cents, you bid 10 cents, and the bidding stops there, you would buy the dollar bill for 10 cents and I would simply lose my 5 cents.

Suppose we both think this sounds like a good deal and we plunge right in. I bid 5 cents, you bid 10, I bid 15, and the bidding continues. Eventually you bid 90 cents and I bid 95. Now what do you do? If you let me have the dollar bill for 95 cents, you will lose 90 cents. So you bid a dollar, hoping at least to break even. What do I do? If I stop bidding, I lose 95 cents. But if I can buy the dollar for $1.05, I sustain a net loss of only 5 cents. So I bid $1.05. Then you bid $1.10, because you would rather lose 10 cents than lose a whole dollar. And so on. After a while we start to lose track of the economics and we start to get angry with each other. After all, as soon as one of us quits bidding, the other one "wins."

Psychologists have repeatedly set up such a situation to see what would happen. They have usually managed to sell their dollar bills for prices over $1, usually in the range of $3 to $5, and once for $25 (Brockner & Rubin, 1985). As soon as the bidding went over $1, bidders became increasingly distressed— sweating, trembling, sometimes even crying. Many of them offered excuses for themselves, such as "I'm sorry I behaved so irrationally, but I had a couple of beers before I came over here." (At the end of the experiment the psychologists always returned the money that the bidders paid them, although they had not promised to do so.)

The point of this study is not "here's a good scam you can use to work your way through college." The point is that once a person gets into a situation like this, it is hard to get out. And similar situations do arise in real life. The arms race between the United States and the Soviet Union was a classic example: From the end of World War II until 1991 (when the Soviet Union collapsed), the two countries devoted enormous sums of money to building weapons. Periodically critics asked, "Does it make sense to spend this much money on weapons?" And the reply was, "We have already spent an

After a government spends vast sums on a project—such as a space station or a superconducting supercollider—it is hard to stop the project, even if its completion will be extremely costly.

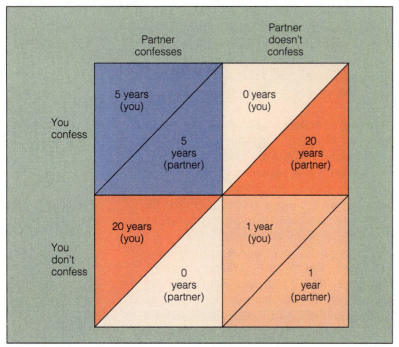

	Partner confesses	Partner doesn't confess
You confess	5 years (you) / 5 years (partner)	0 years (you) / 20 years (partner)
You don't confess	20 years (you) / 0 years (partner)	1 year (you) / 1 year (partner)

FIGURE 16.23
In the prisoner's dilemma, each person considering the choice alone finds it beneficial to confess. But when both people confess, they suffer worse consequences than if both had refused to confess.

enormous amount. Having spent so much already, we may as well spend a little more to be sure that we have more weapons than the other side."

Similar situations occur in everyday life (Staw & Ross, 1989). Someone who has lost money by gambling may continue gambling to avoid admitting that the original gambling was a mistake. Someone who has invested in a stock that lost money may hold onto the stock (and probably continue losing money) rather than sell it and accept the loss. A company that has invested millions in developing a new product may invest additional millions to finish the product, even though the product appears unpromising. Labor negotiations may persist fruitlessly because both sides need a "victory" to justify the strike they have already endured. Perhaps you can think of additional examples. Note that in each case, people behave in irrational ways because of a trapping situation.

COOPERATION AND COMPETITION IN THE PRISONER'S DILEMMA

In some situations you have a choice between two actions—one action that seems best for you and one that seems best for the whole group to which you belong. However,

if everyone in the group chooses the action that seems best for himself or herself, everyone will suffer. The problem is not simply human selfishness; the problem is inherent in the situation itself.

For example, consider the **prisoner's dilemma:** You and a friend are arrested and charged with armed robbery. The police take each of you into separate rooms and ask you to confess. If neither of you confesses, the police will not have enough evidence to convict you of armed robbery, but they can convict you of a lesser offense that carries a sentence of 1 year in prison. If either of you confesses and testifies against the other, the one who confesses will go free and the other will get 20 years in prison. If you both confess, you will each get 5 years in prison. And each of you knows that the other person has the same options. Figure 16.23 illustrates your choices.

If your friend does not confess, it is to your own advantage to confess—you go free instead of spending 1 year in prison. (Your friend will get 20 years in prison, but let's assume you are mostly interested in your own welfare.) If your friend does confess, it is still to your advantage to confess—you get only 5 years in prison instead of 20. So you confess. Your friend, reasoning the same way, also confesses, and you both get 5 years in prison. You both would have been better off if you had both kept quiet. The situation has fostered and almost compelled uncooperative, self-defeating behavior.

If you and your friend could have talked things over in advance, you would have agreed not to confess. Then when the police took you to separate rooms, you would each hope that the other would keep the bargain. And if your friend did keep the bargain, what should you do? Confess, of course! We're back where we started.

The two of you will behave cooperatively only if you can stay in constant communication with each other (Nemeth, 1972). If you and your friend can listen to everything the other one says, you both keep your pledge not to confess. You know that if one confesses, the other will retaliate immediately.

For experiments on the prisoner's dilemma, social psychologists have invented games in which each player chooses between two moves, one cooperative and the other competitive. The moves the players make determine their costs and rewards (Figure 16.24). To complicate matters (and make them more interesting), the game continues for many rounds. If one player chooses the competitive response on one trial, the other player can retaliate on the next. Players earn the most rewards if both choose the cooperative move. Frequently, however, one player chooses the competitive response, the other retaliates, both begin making only the competitive response, and both players lose rewards (Axelrod & Dion, 1988).

The prisoner's dilemma is analogous to many actual decisions that many of us face. For example, suppose you agree to buy my stamp collection for $300. I agree I will mail you the collection and you agree you will mail me the check. But then I wonder whether you are really sending me a check, so I decide to wait until I receive it before sending the stamps. You don't trust me to mail the stamps, so you decide to wait for the stamps before you send the check. As a result, we do not carry out the deal we both had accepted.

THE COMMONS DILEMMA

The commons dilemma is another case in which people hurt themselves as well as others by considering only their own short-term interests (Hardin, 1968). The **commons dilemma** takes its name from this parable: You are a shepherd in a small village with a piece of land—the commons—that everyone is free to share. Most of the time, your sheep graze on your own land, but when a few of them need a little extra grass, you are free to take them to the commons. There are 50 shepherds in the village, and the commons can support about 50 sheep a day. So if each shepherd takes an average of one sheep a day to the commons, everything works out fine. But suppose a few shepherds decide to take several sheep a day to the commons and save the grass on their own land. Not to be outdone, other shepherds do the same. Soon the commons is barren, useless to all.

The same holds true for any situation in which people overuse a resource that has a fixed rate of replenishment. If we cut down forests faster than trees can grow back and catch fish faster than they can reproduce, then sooner or later we exhaust our supplies of trees and fish (Figure 16.25).

Social psychologists have simulated the commons dilemma, like the prisoner's dilemma, in laboratory games. In one study,

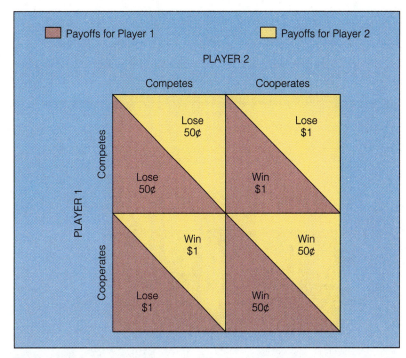

FIGURE 16.24
In this game based on the prisoner's dilemma, each player can choose the cooperative move or the competitive move. If both cooperate, each wins 50 cents; in other choices, one or both players lose money.

college students were asked to sit around a bowl that contained 10 nuts (Edney, 1979). They were told that they could take as many nuts as they wanted any time they chose. Every 10 seconds, the number of nuts remaining in the bowl would be doubled. The object of the game was to collect as many nuts as possible. Clearly, the rational strategy is to let the nuts double every 10 seconds for a while and then to "harvest" some to divide among the participants. But most of the groups never made it past the first 10 seconds. The subjects simply plunged in and grabbed as many nuts as they could, immediately exhausting the resources.

Fortunately, there are ways to avoid the tragedy of the commons. In some experiments (as in some real situations), people have resisted the temptation to gobble up resources for short-term profits by talking over the situation and agreeing on a sensible method for distributing the available resources (Messick et al., 1983; Samuelson, Messick, Rutte, & Wilke, 1984). By studying group behavior, social psychologists hope to find ways to help preserve our air, water, forests, petroleum, and the other resources of our worldwide commons.

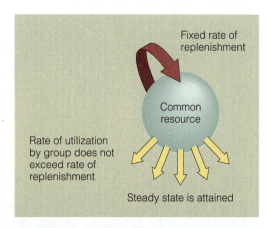

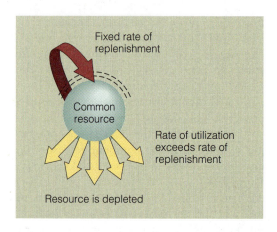

FIGURE 16.25
The commons dilemma: Unless the users agree to moderate their utilization of a common resource, it will soon be used up. For example, years of overfishing off the coast of Newfoundland so thoroughly depleted the fish population that the Canadian government had to ban commercial fishing.

STRATEGIES TO ELICIT COMPLIANCE

Compliance is the tendency to do what someone asks us to do. Sometimes people find ways to trap us into complying more than we would choose to do voluntarily. These are worth knowing about so that you can resist being tricked into doing something contrary to your best interests.

One technique is to make a modest request at first and then to follow it up with a larger second request. This is called the **foot-in-the-door technique.** When Jonathan Freedman and Scott Fraser (1966) asked suburban residents in Palo Alto, California, to put a small "Drive Safely" sign in their window, most of them agreed to do so. A couple of weeks later, other researchers asked the same residents to let them set up a large, unsightly "Drive Safely" billboard in their front yard for 10 days. They made the same request to a group of residents whom the first group of researchers had not approached. Of those who had already agreed to display the small sign, 76% agreed to let them set up the billboard. Only 17% of the

others agreed. Even agreeing to make as small a commitment as signing a petition to support a cause significantly increases the probability that people will later donate money to that cause (Schwarzwald, Bizman, & Raz, 1983).

In another approach, called the **door-in-the-face technique** (Cialdini et al., 1975), someone follows an outrageous initial request with a much more reasonable second one, implying an obligation that if you refused the first request you should at least compromise by agreeing to the second one. For example, I once received a telephone call from a college alumni association, asking me to show my loyalty by contributing $1000. When I apologetically declined, the caller asked whether I could contribute $500. And if not $500, how about $200? And so forth. I believe the original request for $1000 was not an honest statement of the expected contribution, but merely a manipulation to elicit my compliance with one of the lower requests.

Robert Cialdini and his colleagues (1975) demonstrated the power of the door-in-the-face technique with a clever experiment. They asked college students to agree to

Many stores use the "that's-not-all" technique, showing a high price that has been crossed off and replaced with a lower price. Have you ever wondered why the price is often at the bottom of the sales tag? Here's why: If the store owners want to raise the price, they can cut off the price at the bottom, write in a new (much higher) price, and then mark that one "down" to the new price. The price now in effect appears to be a bargain; the customer does not know that it is higher than last week's price.

spend 2 hours a week for 2 years working as counselors to juvenile delinquents. Not surprisingly, every student refused. Then the researchers asked, "If you won't do that, will you chaperone a group from the juvenile detention center for one trip to the zoo?" Half the subjects complied with this more modest request, as compared to only 17% of the subjects who had not first been asked to make the larger commitment.

Why did presenting the larger request first make the students more willing to comply with the smaller request? Apparently they felt that the researchers were conceding a great deal and that it was only fair to meet them halfway.

In the **that's-not-all technique,** someone makes an offer and then, before anyone has a chance to reply, improves the offer. The television announcer says, "Here's your chance to buy this amazing combination paper shredder and coffeemaker for only $39.95. But wait, there's more! We'll throw in a can of dog deodorant! And this handy windshield-wiper cleaner and a subscription to *Modern Lobotomist*! And if you act now, you can get this amazing offer, which usually costs $39.95, for only $19.95! Call this number!" People who hear the first offer and then the "improved" offer are more likely to comply than are people who begin with the "improved" offer (Burger, 1986).

CONCEPT CHECK

12. Identify each of the following as an example of the foot-in-the-door technique, the door-in-the-face technique, or the that's-not-all technique.

a. Your boss says, "We need to cut costs drastically around here. I'm afraid I'm going to have to cut your salary by 50%." You protest vigorously. Your boss replies, "Well, I suppose we could cut expenses some other way. Maybe I can give you just a 5% cut." "Thanks," you reply. "I can live with that."

b. A store marks its prices "25% off," then scratches that out and marks them "50% off!" Though the prices are now about the same as at competing stores, customers flock in to buy.

c. A friend asks you to help carry some supplies over to the elementary school for an afternoon tutoring program. When you get there, the principal says that one of the tutors is late and asks whether you could take her place until she arrives. You agree and spend the rest of the afternoon tutoring. The principal then talks you into coming back every week as a tutor. (Check your answers on page 739.)

WHAT'S THE EVIDENCE?

Obedience to Authority

Ordinarily, if someone you hardly know orders you to do something unpleasant, saying "You *have* to do this," you probably would refuse quite vehemently. Sometimes, however, you may get into a situation in which you feel obligated to obey unreasonable orders from someone who has no right to insist on your obedience. We might have thought that only people with a rigid, authority-worshipping personality would follow objectionable orders, but evidence has shown that some situations build up such powerful pressures that almost anyone obeys.

Research on this topic was inspired by reports of atrocities in the Nazi concentration camps during the Second World War. Those who had committed the atrocities defended themselves by saying they were only obeying orders. International courts rejected that defense, and outraged people throughout the world told themselves, "If I had been

FIGURE 16.26
In Milgram's experiment, a rigged drawing selected a confederate of the experimenter to be the "learner." Here, the learner is strapped to a device that is said to deliver shocks.

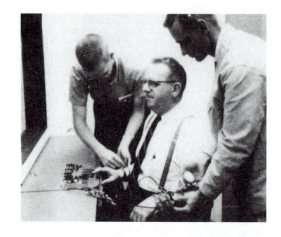

FIGURE 16.27
The "teacher" in Milgram's experiment flipped switches on this box, apparently delivering stronger and stronger shocks for each successive error the "learner" made. The situation was designed to appear realistic, although the device did not actually shock the learner.

there, I would have refused to follow such orders" and "It couldn't happen here."

What do you think? Could it happen here? Stanley Milgram (1974) set up an experiment to discover whether a carefully designed situation could trap people into obeying apparently dangerous orders. Milgram's experiment quickly became one of the most famous studies in psychology, with major ethical as well as scientific implications.

Hypothesis When an authority figure gives normal people instructions to do something that might hurt another person, at least some of them will obey, under carefully designed circumstances.

Method Two adult male subjects arrived at the experimental room—the real subject and a confederate of the experimenter pretending to be a subject. (They were not college students. The experimenters wanted results that would generalize to a broad population. They also wanted to minimize the risk that the subjects would guess the true purpose of the experiment.) The experimenter told the subjects that this was an experiment on learning and that one subject would be the "teacher" and the other the "learner." The teacher would read lists of words through a microphone to the learner, who would sit in a nearby room. The teacher would then test the

learner's memory for the words. Every time the learner made a mistake, the teacher was to deliver an electric shock as punishment.

The experiment was rigged so that the real subject was always the teacher and the confederate was always the learner. The teacher watched as the learner was strapped into the shock device, so he knew that the learner could not escape (Figure 16.26). In one version of the experiment, the learner was a middle-age man who said he had a heart condition. The learner never actually received any shocks, but the teacher was led to believe that he did.

The experiment began uneventfully. The teacher read the words and tested the learner's memory for them. The learner made many mistakes. The teacher sat at a shock generator that had levers to deliver shocks ranging from 15 volts up to 450 volts, in 15-volt increments (Figure 16.27). The experimenter instructed the teacher to deliver a shock every time the learner made a mistake, beginning with the 15-volt switch and raising the voltage by 15 volts for each successive mistake. As the voltage went up, the learner in the next room cried out in pain and even kicked the wall.

If a teacher asked who would take responsibility for any harm to the learner, the experimenter replied that he (the experimenter) would take responsibility, but he insisted that "while the shocks may be painful, they are not dangerous." When the shock reached 150 volts, the learner called out in pain and begged to be let out of the experiment, complaining that his heart was bothering him. Beginning at 270, he responded to shocks with agonized screams. At 300 volts he shouted that he would no longer answer any questions. After 330 volts he made no response at all. Still, the experimenter ordered the teacher to continue asking questions and delivering shocks. (Remember, the learner was not really being shocked. The screams of pain were played on a tape recorder.)

Results Of 40 subjects, 25 continued to deliver shocks all the way up to 450 volts. The people who did so were not sadists. They were normal adults, recruited from the community through newspaper ads. They were paid a few dollars for their services, and those who asked were told that they could keep the money even if they quit. (Not many asked.) People from all walks of life obeyed the experimenter's orders, including blue-collar workers, white-collar workers, and professionals. Most of them grew quite upset and agitated while they were supposedly delivering shocks to the screaming learner, but they kept right on.

Interpretation The obedience Milgram observed depended on certain factors that he put into the situation. One was that the experimenter agreed to take responsibility. (Remember the diffusion-of-responsibility principle.) Another factor was that the experimenter started with a small request, asking the subject to press the lever for a 15-volt shock, and then gradually progressed to stronger shocks. (Remember the foot-in-the-door principle; remember also Skinner's shaping principle.)

We can identify many other contributing factors, and we can imagine many ways to change the procedure that probably would change the results. Figure 16.28 and Figure 16.29 illustrate the results of a few variations

FIGURE 16.28
In one variation of his standard procedure, Milgram asked the teacher to hold the learner's hand on the shock electrode. This close contact with the learner decreased obedience to less than half of its usual level; still, some teachers continued following orders to deliver shocks. (From Milgram's 1965 film, Obedience.)

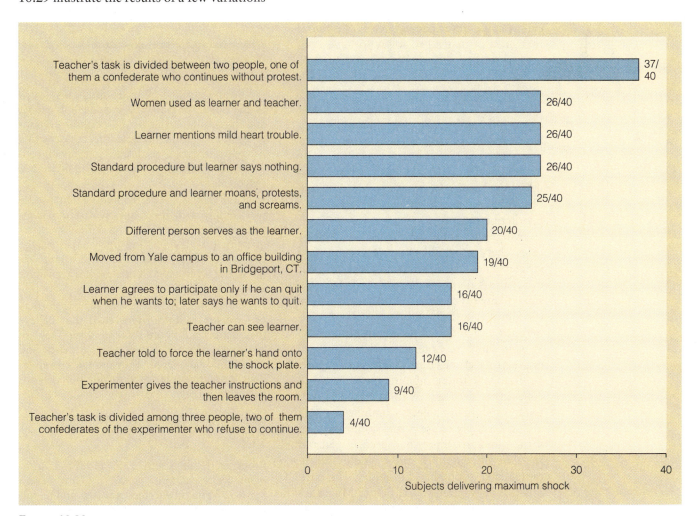

FIGURE 16.29
Milgram varied his procedure in many ways to find out what elements promoted or inhibited obedience. Division of responsibility increased obedience; an implication of personal responsibility decreased obedience. Under all conditions, some people obeyed and others did not.

in procedure that Milgram tried. For example, subjects were more obedient to an experimenter in the same room than to one who left. They were less obedient if they had to force the learner's hand back onto the shock plate. If additional "teachers" divided the task—the other "teachers" actually being confederates of the experimenter—a participant was very likely to obey if the others obeyed, unlikely if the others disobeyed.

Still, the remarkable conclusion remains that, under a variety of conditions, many normal people followed orders from an experimenter they just met, even though they thought they might hurt or even kill someone. Imagine how much stronger the pressure to obey orders from a government or military leader would be.

Ethical Issues   Milgram's experiment told us something about ourselves that we did not want to hear. No longer could we say, "Something like the Nazi concentration camps could never happen here." We found that most of us tend to follow orders, even quite offensive orders. We are indebted to Milgram's study for this important, if unwelcome, information.

However, although I am glad to know about Milgram's results, I doubt that I would have enjoyed being a subject in his experiment. Most of his subjects were emotionally drained by the experience and some were visibly upset to discover how readily they had obeyed orders to deliver dangerous shocks to another person.

Milgram's study prompted psychology researchers to establish much clearer and stricter rules about what an experimenter can ask a subject to do. Today, before the start of any psychological experiment—even the simplest and most innocuous—the experimenter is required to submit a plan to a Human Subjects Committee that must approve or reject the ethics of the experiment.

If anyone today submitted a proposal to conduct research similar to Milgram's study, the local Human Subjects Committee would almost certainly refuse permission. However, if the same procedures had been in place *at the time of Milgram's study,* would a committee have prohibited his study? The curious fact is, we aren't sure. Before Milgram's research, very few people expected his results to turn out the way they did. Milgram had asked a number of psychologists and psychiatrists to predict the results; nearly all replied that only a rare psychopathic weirdo would press levers to deliver severe shocks. A Human Subjects Committee that shared this expectation might have foreseen little ethical difficulty with Milgram's study. The unforeseen ethical problem underscores just how surprising Milgram's results were.

SOMETHING TO THINK ABOUT

Here is a version of the experiment that Milgram never tried: At the start of the experiment, we announce that the teacher and the learner will trade places halfway through the experiment so that the previous "learner" will start delivering shocks to the teacher. How do you think the teachers would behave then? What other changes in procedure can you imagine that might influence the degree of obedience?

SUMMARY

- *Behavior traps.*   Certain situations—such as the dollar auction, the prisoner's dilemma, and the commons dilemma—pressure even intelligent and rational people into self-defeating behavior. To avoid self-defeating behavior, people need to avoid or change such situations. (page 730)
- *Compliance.*   The likelihood that people will comply with the requests of others is increased when someone starts with a small request that is accepted and then makes a large request, or if someone starts with a large request that is refused and then makes a small request. (page 734)
- *Obedience.*   Many people obey the orders of a person in authority even if they believe their action will injure someone else. They are less likely to obey if they can see the person who would be injured. They are more likely to obey if other people are following orders without protest. (page 735)

SUGGESTIONS FOR FURTHER READING

Brockner, J., & Rubin, J. Z. (1985). *Entrapment in escalating conflicts.* New York: Springer-Verlag. Describes research on the dollar auction and similar behavior traps.

Milgram, S. (1975). *Obedience to authority.* New York: Harper & Row. Describes Milgram's classic experiments on obedience.

Terms

behavior trap situation that almost forces people into self-defeating behaviors (page 731)

prisoner's dilemma situation in which people have to choose between an act beneficial to themselves but harmful to others, and an act that is moderately beneficial to all (page 732)

commons dilemma situation in which people who share a common resource tend to overuse it and therefore make it unavailable in the long run (page 733)

foot-in-the-door technique method of eliciting compliance by first making a modest request and then following it with a larger request (page 734)

door-in-the-face technique method of eliciting compliance by first making an outrageous request and then replying to the refusal with a more reasonable request (page 734)

that's-not-all technique method of eliciting compliance in which someone makes an offer and then, before anyone has a chance to reply, improves the offer (page 735)

Answers to Concept Check

12. (a) Door-in-the-face technique; (b) that's-not-all technique; (c) foot-in-the-door technique. (page 735)

APPLIED PSYCHOLOGY

The term *applied psychology* refers to areas of psychology that are concerned primarily with solving practical problems. The term is analogous to "applied" areas in other disciplines. For example, chemists and physicists distinguish applied research, such as developing improved light bulbs, from pure or theoretical science, such as research into the structure of the atom. At least in psychology (and I suspect in chemistry and physics as well), the distinction between applied work and theoretical work is often cloudy. Good theories lead to practical applications, and new practical applications lead to new theories.

Virtually all areas of psychology have their practical applications. For example, research on memory suggests ways to improve study habits, research on decision making helps us understand gambling, and research on abnormal behavior leads to advances in clinical psychology. This final section of the book surveys three other fields of applied psychology that I have not previously emphasized: industrial-organizational psychology, ergonomics, and school psychology.

Applied psychologists work in many settings that you might not have thought of as psychology—such as selecting people for jobs, training them to do their jobs, and redesigning the machines to make them easier for people to use.

INDUSTRIAL-ORGANIZATIONAL PSYCHOLOGY

How do psychologists help employers select among job applicants?

Why are some people satisfied and other people dissatisfied with their jobs?

How do psychologists help employers design jobs to increase productivity and satisfaction?

Industrial-organizational psychology is the study of people at work. It deals with such issues as how to get the right person into the right job, how to train people for jobs, how best to determine salaries, and how to organize the workplace so that workers will be productive and satisfied. Industrial-organizational psychologists call upon their knowledge of social psychology, cognitive psychology, and standardized testing.

Let's begin with an example of a typical concern for industrial-organizational (I-O) psychologists (Campion & Thayer, 1989): A company that manufactures complex electronic equipment needed to publish reference and repair manuals for its products. The engineers who designed the devices could not devote the necessary time to write the manuals, and none of them were skilled writers, anyway. So the company hired a technical writer to prepare the manuals, but after one year the company gave her an unsatisfactory performance rating. The manuals she wrote contained too many technical errors; besides that, she was constantly complaining.

The writer countered that when she asked various engineers in the company to check her manuals or to explain technical details to her, they failed to provide the prompt help she needed. She found her job complicated and frustrating; her office was badly lit, noisy, and overheated; and her chair was uncomfortable. However, whenever she commented on these problems, she was told that she "complained too much."

In a situation like this, an industrial-organizational psychologist helps the company evaluate its possible solutions. First, the problem might be employee selection. Maybe the company hired the wrong person for this job. Maybe they should fire the current writer and hire someone who is an expert on electrical engineering, who is also an outstanding writer, and who *likes* a badly lit, noisy, overheated, uncomfortable office. However, if the company cannot find or afford such a person, it needs to improve the working conditions and provide the current employee with more training or more help with the technical aspects of the job.

SELECTION OF EMPLOYEES

If you have ever applied for a job, you are familiar with the hiring process from the standpoint of the job applicant. Now consider the process from the standpoint of the employer. As the personnel manager of a company, you can hire up to 12 new employees out of the 150 people who have applied. You want to hire the best people available; after all, if the people you hire do a poor job, they will get fired and so will you!

You also have to be careful about fairness in hiring. If some of the rejected applicants complain that you discriminated unfairly against them, you will have to defend

Industrial psychologists do research to determine the effectiveness of various ways of selecting employees for a job. For example, they find that most employers conduct interviews that are almost worthless for identifying good employees.

your hiring practices in court. U.S. laws prohibit employers from discriminating against women or racial minorities. The Americans with Disabilities Act of 1990 requires employers to make the workplace accessible to people with disabilities and prohibits discrimination against qualified people with disabilities.

So how should you proceed? If you have only as many applicants as you have jobs available, the decision is easy: You hire them all. Your decision is also easy if the job is so simple that virtually anyone can do it; you can then hire people at random. In most cases, however, an employer has more applicants than jobs, and some of the applicants are likely to be better workers than others. Industrial-organizational psychologists have devoted great research efforts to evaluating various methods of selecting employees.

INTERVIEWS

Go back to thinking of yourself as a job applicant. If you are being considered for a full-time job, the employer will probably ask you for an interview. The employer wants to talk with you, to learn more about you, indeed to look at you. Some employers put a great deal of confidence in the results of their interviews, using this first impression as a major factor in the hiring decision. Unfortunately, the research indicates that most interviews have poor validity for predicting the applicants' success on the job.

The common problems with interviews are that many interviewers ask irrelevant questions; they put different questions to different applicants; they take few notes; and they eventually make a subjective judgment based largely on how much they like the applicant (Schmitt, 1976; Thayer, 1983). In many cases interviewers favor the physically more attractive applicants and use other irrelevant criteria (Morrow, McElroy, Stamper, & Wilson, 1990).

In many regards, being interviewed is like taking a test. Can you imagine taking a test on which each student gets a different set of questions, many of which have nothing to do with the course? An interview becomes useful only if it is standardized, just as one might standardize a test: First the interviewer develops a set of questions clearly related to the job, such as "What experience do you have?" or "Would you be willing to do shift work?" The interviewer must ask all candidates the same questions and must "grade" the answers according to some unambiguous standard. Ideally each interviewee should be rated by a panel of people, not just by one person. Interviews conducted according to these principles have quite respectable reliabilities and validities, comparable to those of standardized cognitive tests (Campion, Pursell, & Brown, 1988).

COGNITIVE TESTS

How well people perform a job depends heavily on their job-related knowledge and skills. Some psychologists have proposed that the best way to select among job applicants is to measure their knowledge of information related to the job (Sternberg & Wagner, 1993). Other psychologists reply that a test of job knowledge makes sense only for experienced workers; with inexperienced job applicants, we should determine how fast they are likely to learn the job (Schmidt & Hunter, 1993).

One way to evaluate applicants is to test their cognitive abilities and perceptual-motor skills, using tests like the IQ tests we examined in Chapter 9. People who score high on tests of mental ability tend to learn almost any job quickly and perform it well. According to John Hunter and Frank Schmidt (1981, p. 1128), "Professionally developed cognitive ability tests are valid predictors of performance on the job . . . for all jobs . . . in all settings." That is probably an overstatement. (It could hardly be an understatement!) Still, for many jobs, cognitive tests are valid predictors; using test scores to select employees increases the company's productivity and saves money. It is also beneficial to employees, because those who are hired are more likely to succeed at their job.

One major impediment to using cognitive tests is that, on average, African-American and Latino applicants receive lower scores than do white applicants. In some cases that discrepancy poses no problem; depending on the job and the geographical location, an employer may attract an ample number of applications from well-qualified minority job seekers. In other cases, however, an employer who relies on cognitive tests hires relatively few minority candidates.

U.S. law makes some contradictory demands: Ordinarily, employers are obligated to hire their best-qualified applicants, and an employer is forbidden to use quotas in order to increase the hiring of ethnic minorities. However, if the result of hiring those best-qualified is to hire a disproportionately small number of minority applicants, then the courts may *require* an employer to use a quota system that was previously forbidden (Gottfredson, 1994). A number of employers have tried to solve this legal muddle by using separate norms for different groups. That is, they might compare a European American's test score only to those of other European Americans, and an African American's score to those of other African Americans. Then they might, for example, hire the top 20% of European-American applicants and the top 20% of African-American applicants. However, in response to public outcries, the government now considers this system to be just a quota in disguise (Sackett & Wilk, 1994). Currently, an employer who wishes to hire the best-qualified applicants and also to hire a culturally diverse workforce faces conflicting demands and no clear solution.

PERSONALITY TESTS

Some employers use personality tests, such as the MMPI, to help select employees. In some cases they are acting on someone's guess as to what kind of personality is best for a given job, and in some cases they are simply trying to eliminate applicants with potentially serious psychological disorders. The research indicates that scores on a personality test can be slightly, but only slightly, useful. You should not be surprised to learn that people who score high on conscientiousness tend to be good employees for almost any job; extraverted people tend to be good managers and salespeople, but show no advantage on other jobs (Barrick & Mount, 1991). People who score high on neuroticism show a slight disadvantage in their work performance (Tett, Jackson, & Rothstein, 1991). All of these trends are weak, however.

PHYSICAL STANDARDS

Suppose you apply for a job and are turned down with this explanation: "You're too short. We never hire anyone who is shorter than five-feet-ten."

Can employers do that? Employers who set physical standards for employees, such as a minimum height or a maximum weight, have been challenged in the courts. For example, women's groups have claimed that

Well-meaning employers are torn between two desires: On the one hand, they want to hire the applicants who will do the job best, and cognitive tests provide a reasonably valid predictor of job performance. On the other hand, the employers would like to hire a diverse workforce, and they have trouble doing so if they rely heavily on the results of cognitive tests.

a minimum-height standard discriminates against women.

The courts have ruled that employers can insist on certain physical standards if, and only if, they can demonstrate the importance of those physical standards for performance of the job. For example, police departments sometimes insist on a minimum height. They justify this requirement by saying that tall police officers can intimidate criminals. Imagine a thief who hears, "Drop your gun!" The thief turns and sees the police officer. If the police officer is tall, the thief drops the gun and goes quietly; if the police officer is short, the thief is likely to shoot.

So the police say, at any rate. Some courts have upheld the right of the police to set a minimum height; other courts have insisted the police abandon that requirement (Hogan & Quigley, 1986). The rule for physical standards is the same as the rule for cognitive tests: Any employer who sets such standards must demonstrate that they lead to the selection of better employees.

CONCEPT CHECK

1. To use cognitive tests, physical standards, or any other criteria for selecting employees, an employer must demonstrate that those criteria are valid. It is easier to validate criteria for jobs that have clear standards for success and failure (such as a sales job) than for jobs that are hard to evaluate (such as many desk jobs). Why? (Check your answer on page 752).

BIOGRAPHICAL DATA

I-O psychologists continue to search for other ways of predicting job performance. Using biographical data is valid for some jobs. For example, if an airline wants to identify which potential airplane pilots will complete their training program, one of the best predictors is this simple question: "As a child, did you ever make a model airplane that flew?" (Sackett & Wilk, 1994).

One type of biographical information most employers ask is, "How much previous experience have you had with this kind of job?" Some employers even specify in their job announcement some requirement, such as "Minimum 5 years experience." The research indicates that prior experience is, as you might expect, a benefit. However, beyond a certain point, additional experience is not additionally helpful. That is, a person with 2 or 3 years of experience has a definite advantage over someone with no experience, but someone with 12 years of experience has no dependable edge over someone with 8 years of experience (McDaniel, Schmidt, & Hunter, 1988).

An additional point about job experience that you might not guess: Previous experience is a better predictor of performance on relatively simple jobs than it is on the most complex jobs (McDaniel, Schmidt, & Hunter, 1988). Why? The answer is that the most complex jobs—rocket scientist, brain surgeon, and so forth—require complex kinds of knowledge and skill that not everyone can gain just through experience on the job.

SELF-SELECTION

One valuable, often overlooked way of finding the right person for a job is self-selection. In some cases an employer can narrow the applicant pool just by being honest about what the job requires (Parkinson, 1957). For example, consider this job announcement:

Wanted: Acrobat capable of crossing a slack wire 200 feet above raging furnace. Twice nightly, three times on Saturday. $250 per week. No health or accident insurance provided. Apply in person at Daredevil Circus.

In an extreme case such as this, only a thoroughly qualified person is likely to apply, and the employer does not need to screen a large number of applicants. With most jobs, of course, this appeal to self-selection is less effective.

WOMEN IN THE WORKPLACE

Times change. Before about the 1960s, relatively few women sought long-term careers; most expected to quit work when they got married or had their first child. Employers felt little pressure to hire women or to promote them on the same basis as men.

And then all that changed. As Figure A.1 shows, by the mid-1980s, most women, even mothers of preschoolers, had jobs outside the home (Matthews & Rodin, 1989). Even older women, who had grown up in an earlier era with much less support for women's careers, reentered the job market in many cases (Clausen & Gilens, 1990). For women as for men, work provides a source of income, an opportunity to meet people, and a sense of accomplishment.

Many employers have been slow to react to some special concerns of women at work, however. For example, mothers of preschool children may have trouble arranging consistently good day care for their children, and they are likely to miss work on days when their children are ill. I-O psychologists have surveyed working parents to find out what help their employers could provide. They find that in most cases it is still the mother who takes primary responsibility for the chil-

Women seldom reach the top levels of management, but those women who do—such as Ann Fudge, president of Maxwell House Coffee—are rated about as effective as men in similar positions.

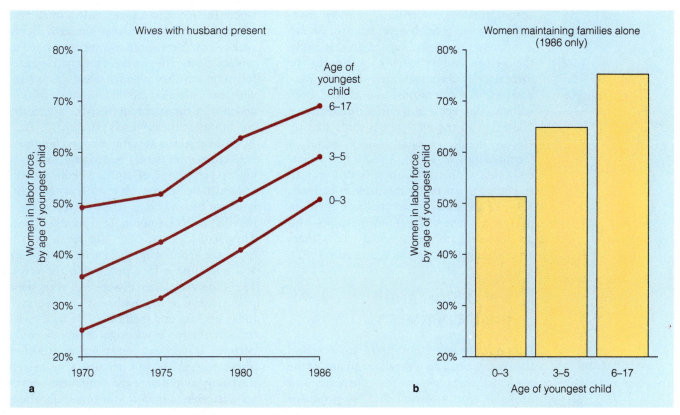

FIGURE A.1
(a) From 1970 to 1986, an increasing percentage of married women with children held jobs outside the home. During each year, women with older children were more likely to hold jobs than were women with younger children. (b) In 1986, most women who were caring for children without a husband held jobs outside the home. As with married women, these women were more likely to hold a job if their children were older. (Based on data from Matthews & Rodin, 1989.)

dren. Mothers report that they would like the opportunity to take days off from work to care for sick children and that they would like to have a day-care center at or near their workplace (Kossek, 1990). However, many day-care centers do not accept sick children, so on-site day-care does not necessarily alter women's rate of missing work (Goff, Mount, & Jamison, 1990).

In conjunction with the trend for more women to seek lasting careers, legislatures have changed the laws to prohibit employers from discriminating against women. However, in spite of legislation and employers' apparently good intentions, women still do not consistently advance as rapidly as men do in business. Companies hire women about as frequently as men for their lower-level management positions, but they tend to give men faster promotions and salary increases. Although women are frequently (and increasingly) promoted to the middle levels of management, it is still unusual for

women to reach the top levels. When women do reach high levels of leadership, they are generally rated as being about as effective as men at the same level. Women leaders get lower effectiveness ratings only in the military and similar settings with a preponderance of male subordinates and a tradition of giving and following orders (Eagly, Karau, & Makhijani, 1995).

Industrial psychologists have tried to understand why men continue to get most of the promotions, given that women who do get promoted seem highly successful. One hypothesis has been that many women put themselves at a disadvantage relative to men: They may interrupt their careers temporarily when they have a child, and because of family commitments, they may refuse a promotion that would require moving to a different city. Explanations such as these do not account for the whole story, however. In one study, industrial psychologists compared male and female managers in large U.S.

corporations, considering only those managers who had recently accepted a transfer to a different geographic region. In this study, the women had as much education as the men; none of them had interrupted their careers for family reasons; and all had been willing to accept a move to a different city. Nevertheless, the men in the study had received slightly greater salary increases (Stroh, Brett, & Reilly, 1992). The apparently inescapable conclusion is that women still face barriers to advancement in business. Some of those barriers come from their supervisors; others come from employees who are unwilling to let a woman boss them around (Eagly, Makhijani, & Klonsky, 1992).

JOB DESIGN AND JOB ENRICHMENT

If a professor failed most of the students and then complained about the low quality of the students, what would you suspect? You probably would suspect that the professor had set unreasonable grading standards, right? Similarly, if an employer reports that most new employees fail at some job, we should suspect that something is wrong with the job or with the employer's method of evaluating performance. For example, consider starting jobs in the life insurance business: Starting salaries are low, income depends heavily on commissions from sales, and new employees are expected to reach a high level of performance in a short time.

FIGURE A.2
I-O psychologists have conducted research to determine the best, safest, most efficient ways to perform even simple tasks. For example, the drawing on the left shows the right way to lift a brick, and the drawing on the right shows the wrong way, according to Gilbreth (1911).

Under these circumstances, only a small percentage of new employees succeed. Every year or two life insurance companies have to replace most of the workers they had so carefully chosen; they wonder what was wrong with their selection method. But the problem was not in the selection method, but in the conditions of the job itself (Thayer, 1977).

Industrial-organizational psychologists help companies design better jobs so that a higher percentage of workers will succeed. For example, in one job in a plywood plant, workers had to align strips of wood on a moving belt (Campion & Thayer, 1985). They had to bend over and reach out to move the strips while balancing on one leg and operating a foot pedal with the other. The supervisor was dissatisfied with their performance and grumbled that "workers today are lazy and inefficient." In fact, given the way the job was designed, no one could perform it without experiencing constant discomfort. After I-O psychologists helped the company redesign the equipment, workers were able to perform the task more effectively and with fewer complaints.

In other cases, the main fault of a job is its boredom. For many years, companies intentionally designed jobs, especially factory jobs, to be simple and repetitive so that even unskilled workers could complete their tasks without error. This strategy was based on the **scientific-management approach** to job design, also known as **Theory X**, which holds that employees are lazy, indifferent, and uncreative. According to that approach, employers should make the work as foolproof as possible and supervise the workers to make sure they are doing each task the right way (Figure A.2). The employer leaves nothing to chance, nothing to the worker's own initiative (McGregor, 1960).

This approach does have its strengths; clear and precise rules can be helpful to the worker as well as to the employer. For example, a wholesale bakery once called on psychologists to help reduce the rate of injury among employees. The psychologists identified several right and wrong ways to perform certain acts: Workers should not leave cardboard lying on the floor. At least one person must always be stationed at each end of the conveyor belt. Pans should not be stacked above the rear rail of the pan rack. The psychologists then helped the company set up a system for informing workers of their success in following these rules. Over time, the injury rate declined considerably (Komaki, Barwick, & Scott, 1978).

Jobs designed according to the scientific-management approach may be foolproof and safe, but in many cases they are also boring. An alternative to the scientific-management approach is the **human-relations approach** to job design, also known as **Theory Y,** which holds that employees like to take responsibility for their work, enjoy some variety in their job, and like to feel a sense of accomplishment. According to this approach, jobs should be made challenging and interesting (McGregor, 1960).

Proponents of the human-relations approach use **job enrichment,** a procedure of giving each employee responsibility for a task with clear meaning. For example, one way to arrange the work at a financial services corporation would be to have one employee keep one kind of records, another keep another kind of records, and so on. That is a scientific-management approach—foolproof but boring. Another way to arrange the work is for each employee to be in charge of the services for particular clients, keeping therefore a variety of different kinds of records and doing different things at different times. They are given a certain amount of flexibility in how and when they do various parts of the job. Information about how well they are doing their job comes to them directly, and not just to their supervisors. Employees whose jobs are "enriched" in this way report greater satisfaction because their job seems more meaningful than before, and they have a greater chance of catching any mistakes they make (Campion & McClelland, 1991). From the employer's standpoint, the enriched jobs are beneficial in most ways, although they pose two possible disadvantages: Training the workers takes longer than it would with a simpler job, and the workers performing enriched jobs expect to be paid more than before!

So, is the human-relations approach superior to the scientific-management approach? Not always (Campion & Thayer, 1985). Consider an analogy to education: Professor X tells students exactly what to read on which day, what facts to study for each test, and precisely what they need to do in order to get a good grade in the course. (This course is analogous to the scientific-management approach; it leaves nothing to the students' initiative.) Professor Y outlines some general issues to be discussed in the course, provides a long list of "suggested readings," lets the students control class discussion, and invites students to come up with their own ideas for projects instead of taking tests. (This course is analogous to the human-relations approach, though perhaps a little more extreme.) Which professor's class do you think you would like better?

My answer would be, "It depends." If I am extremely interested in the topic of the course and I have some ideas of my own that I would like to pursue, then I would prefer Professor Y's course, and I would consider Professor X's course tedious and insulting. But if I am just taking the course to satisfy a requirement and I do not have any ideas of my own, I probably would appreciate the precise structure of Professor X's class.

The same is true of jobs. Some workers, especially the younger and brighter ones, thrive on the challenge of an enriched job. Others, especially those who have been doing a simple job for many years, dislike the insecurity of having to learn new skills or to solve problems on their own (Arnold & House, 1980; Hackman & Lawler, 1971).

CONCEPT CHECK

2. "I want my employees to enjoy their work and to feel pride in their achievements." Does that statement reflect a belief in the human-relations approach or the scientific-management approach? (Check your answer on page 752.)

PAY AND WORK MOTIVATION

I-O psychologists like to quote this formula: "Performance is a function of ability times motivation." But what motivates people to work? "They work for money, of course," you reply. "Everyone knows that!" True, but "everyone" also knows that money is not the whole story. Given a choice among jobs, would you necessarily take the job with the highest pay? No. You also want a job with prestige, friendly coworkers, and an opportunity to accomplish something. (Recall the discussion of need for achievement in Chapter 11.) Some people prefer a desk job; some prefer an outdoors job; almost no one likes a physically exhausting job.

Still, pay is one factor in anyone's choice of jobs, and people will work harder if they think they can earn increased pay. Suppose you are the employer and you need to set the pay scale. You should set the salaries and wages high enough for you to hire and keep the workers you want. Beyond that, you might offer people higher salaries or performance bonuses, if you believe that such offers will motivate them to work harder or more effectively. Does increased pay lead to improved performance?

Yes, but only under certain circumstances, say industrial-organizational psychologists. When workers are paid by their unit of output (piecework) or when they can earn a bonus for high productivity, they generally increase their efforts. However, they complain about the constant pressure to work harder (Lawler, 1971). Also, if they have to achieve a very high performance goal in order to earn a pay bonus, they are likely to give up (Locke & Latham, 1991). That is, the goals are effective only if they are realistic goals.

Furthermore, workers who are paid on piecework often neglect other important chores that do not figure into their pay. For example, when salespeople are paid strictly on commission, they tend to compete for customers and to ignore such activities as checking stock and arranging displays (Vroom, 1964). A company that wants employees to attend to a variety of tasks may get better results if it pays them by the hour or by an annual salary.

Most of all, workers do not want to feel cheated. When employers grant bonuses to the best workers ("merit pay increases"), those who fail to receive a bonus may resent being overlooked, especially if they believe their employer evaluated their performance unfairly or inaccurately (Thayer, 1987). In many jobs, such as teaching in public schools, evaluating the contributions and merits of employees is extremely difficult.

According to J. Stacy Adams (1963), workers want to be paid as much as possible, but they also want to believe they are earning their pay. How would a worker react to being told that he or she was overpaid? Adams (1963) measured that effect with college students hired for temporary jobs as interviewers. Students in the control group were told their qualifications were exactly what the "employer" (the experimenter) was looking for. Those in the experimental group were told that they lacked the necessary experience for the job. The employer complained to each of the experimental subjects that the placement service had fouled up, called the placement service to find out what had gone wrong, got a busy signal, and finally said, "I guess I'll have to hire you anyway." He added that he would have to pay the same rate he was paying other, better-qualified employees.

Some employees in both the control group and the experimental group were paid by the hour. Others were paid a fixed amount for each interview they completed (piecework). Subjects who had been told they were unqualified worked harder than did subjects in the control group. They either produced a higher quantity of work, if they were paid by the hour, or a higher quality of work—fewer but longer interviews—if they were paid by the interview (see Figure A.3).

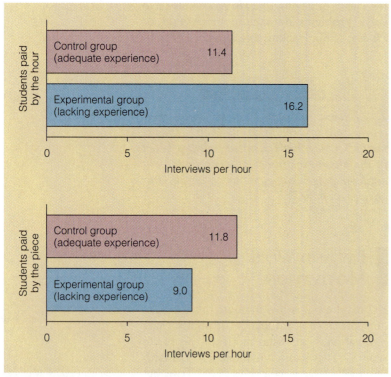

FIGURE A.3
Students who thought they were unqualified for a job as an interviewer (the experimental group) worked harder than those who believed they had adequate experience (the control group). If paid by the hour, people in the experimental group increased their quantity of work. If paid by the interview, they decreased their quantity and increased their quality.

In short, the workers who had been told they were unqualified tried to demonstrate either to themselves or to their employer (we cannot say which) that they were earning their pay.

Later researchers found that they could replicate these results only if they paid fairly high wages (Goodman & Friedman, 1971). If the wages were low, workers seemed to think, "That employer has a lot of nerve complaining about my qualifications while offering only the minimum wage!" This illustrates an important point about research: The results may depend on procedural details that were more important than investigators realized. One of the benefits of trying to replicate a study is that we find out which procedures are important for the outcome.

SOMETHING TO THINK ABOUT

We have considered the results for workers who believe they are overpaid. What would you expect workers to do if they believed they were underpaid?

JOB SATISFACTION

"A happy worker is a productive worker." Right? It sounds as if it should be. And yet most studies show that the correlation between job satisfaction and productivity is low, around .17 (Iaffaldano & Muchinsky, 1985).

If we think about it for a moment, we can understand why the correlation is so low. Could you imagine yourself being unhappy with a job and still highly productive? Sure: You do your job well, but you think you deserve a better job. Could you imagine yourself being unproductive on the job and nevertheless happy with it? Yes. It might be a great job; you know your own performance is just mediocre, but you love the job anyway.

Still, we cannot help but expect that satisfied workers should perform differently from dissatisfied workers in some consistent way. And they do: Satisfied workers are more likely than dissatisfied workers are to try to improve their skills, to help coworkers, to make constructive suggestions for improving the organization, and to spread goodwill about the organization (George & Brief,

What makes people enjoy their work? An archaeologist could probably find another job that paid better, and certainly a job that was less strenuous and a great deal less dusty. However, archaeology offers great prestige, interest, and a sense of accomplishment. People work because of a great many motivations.

1992). They also go beyond the call of duty. For example, both satisfied and dissatisfied workers usually show up for work on time under normal weather conditions, but right after a blizzard only the most satisfied workers make the effort to get to work (Smith, 1977).

INDUSTRIAL-ORGANIZATIONAL PSYCHOLOGY AND THE REST OF PSYCHOLOGY

As you have read this section, you may have found yourself wondering, "Is that really psychology? That sounds like business, or economics, or even law." Granted, industrial-organizational psychology overlaps heavily with these other fields. Psychology is a broad field; various parts of it overlap also with medicine, engineering, advertising, politics, and so forth.

However, it is also important to note the overlap between industrial-organizational psychology and other fields of psychology. I-O psychologists call upon the research in other areas of psychology, especially motivation, learning and memory, standardized testing, and social psychology. In turn, their findings contribute to new views in these other branches of psychology.

SUMMARY

• *The scope of industrial-organizational psychology.* Industrial and organizational psychologists study the behavior of people at work. They try to improve the productivity and satisfaction of workers by devising more effective methods of selection and training, pay incentives, and job design and job enrichment. (page 743)

• *Selection.* To choose among job applicants, employers use cognitive tests, interviews, biographical information, and physical standards. Each method has its advantages and disadvantages. If challenged in court, employers must be able to demonstrate that their methods are valid predictors of job performance. (page 743)

• *Job design.* Some employers try to provide simple, foolproof jobs. Others try to make the jobs interesting and challenging. Some workers perform better on simple jobs; others do best with interesting jobs. (page 748)

• *Work motivation.* People work for many reasons, including a sense of accomplishment, as well as for pay. Workers like to believe they are receiving fair pay for their work. Workers who believe they are being overpaid adjust either the quality or the quantity of their work to make it appear that they are earning their pay. (page 749)

• *Job satisfaction.* The correlation between satisfaction and productivity is low. However, satisfied workers are more likely than others are to perform citizenship tasks to help the organization. (page 751)

SUGGESTION FOR FURTHER READING

Muchinsky, P. (1993). *Psychology applied to work: An introduction to industrial and organizational psychology.* A thorough textbook surveying the major fields of industrial-organizational psychology.

TERMS

industrial-organizational psychology the study of people at work (page 743)

scientific-management approach or **Theory X** theory that employees are lazy, indifferent, and uncreative and that employers should therefore make the work as foolproof as possible and supervise the workers to make sure they are doing each task the right way (page 748)

human-relations approach or **Theory Y** theory that employees like to take responsibility for their work, like some variety in their job, and like to feel a sense of accomplishment (page 749)

job enrichment procedure of giving each employee responsibility for a task with clear meaning (page 749)

ANSWERS TO CONCEPT CHECKS

1. To determine the validity, the employer may compute the correlation between a test score (or height or any other criterion) and performance on the job. An employer who cannot accurately measure job performance cannot compute a meaningful correlation. (page 745)
2. The human-relations approach. (page 749)

ERGONOMICS, OR HUMAN FACTORS

What can psychologists contribute to the design of machines and their controls?

What kinds of displays are easiest for people to read and understand?

A few years ago, my son Sam, then about 16 years old, turned to me as he was rushing out the door with some friends. "Dad, could you go to my room and turn off the stereo for me?" he asked. I went to the stereo in his room and tried to find the "On-Off" switch. Failing that, I looked for something marked "Power." No such luck. I looked in vain for the manual. Finally, in desperation, I simply unplugged the stereo. (Eventually I learned that I could have turned it off by flipping one switch from "Tuner," which means radio, to "Tape," and then turning the tape player off.)

Learning to operate our increasingly complex machinery is one of the perennial struggles of modern life. Engineers design equipment so that it will work as effectively as possible from an engineering standpoint, but they do not always recognize the difficulties a nonengineer faces in learning to use the equipment.

Sometimes the resulting problems seem rather trivial, as when a father cannot figure out how to turn off his teenage son's stereo. But sometimes the problems are quite significant. Imagine an airplane pilot who wants to lower the landing wheels and instead raises the wing flaps. Or a worker in a nuclear power plant who does not notice a warning signal.

One specialized field of psychology attempts to facilitate the operation of machinery so that the average user can use it as efficiently and as safely as possible. This field is known as **ergonomics** or **human factors**. The term *ergonomics* is derived from Greek roots meaning "laws of work."

At some universities the ergonomics program is part of the psychology department; at others it is part of engineering; at still others it is administered jointly by both departments. Regardless of who administers the program, it necessarily combines features of both psychology and engineering, and generally computer science as well. Ergonomists test hypotheses about the perceptual, cognitive, and motor skills of people who use machines.

Ergonomics originated largely in military settings, where complex technologies sometimes required personnel to spot nearly invisible targets, to understand speech through deafening noise, to track objects in three dimensions while using two hands, and to make life-or-death decisions in a split second (Taylor, 1957). The military turned to psychologists to find out what skills their personnel could master and to redesign the tasks to fit those skills.

Ergonomists soon applied their experience to provide similar services for business and industry. They eventually discovered that careful design of machinery is important not just for complicated military and industrial gadgets but also for the everyday devices that all of us use. As Donald Norman (1988) pointed out, many intelligent and educated people find themselves unable to use all the features on a camera, a microwave oven, or a videocassette recorder; some have trouble setting the time on a digital watch. Sometimes they push doors that are supposed to be pulled or pull doors that are supposed to be pushed; they may even have trouble figuring out how to operate the shower in a hotel room. Ergonomists try to help design controls and displays so that people can quickly discern how to operate various devices. Let us consider several examples of ergonomics.

DESIGN OF MACHINERY

The combination of a person and a machine that the person operates is called a **person-machine system.** Proper operation of that system depends on a series of steps, as illustrated in Figure A.4. If the system fails, the fault could lie with the person, the machine, the communication between the two, or some outside factor such as heat or noise

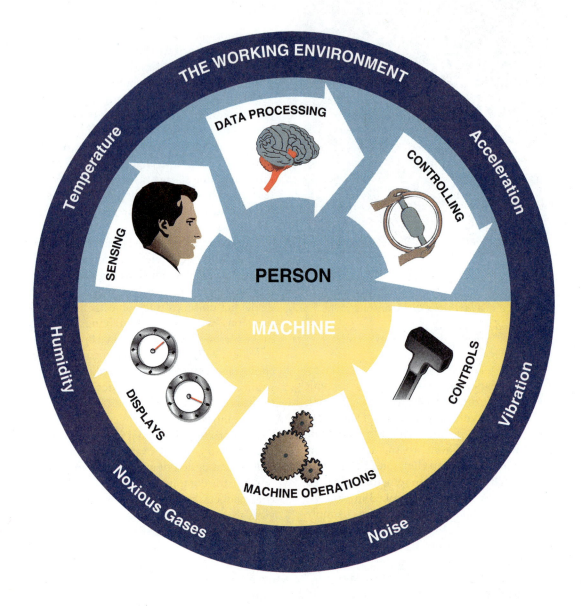

A person-machine system includes processes within the person, processes within the machine, and communication between the two. Various factors in the working environment, such as noise or heat, can interfere with the performance of either the person or the machine.

that interferes with the normal functioning of the person or the machine.

In designing machinery, ergonomists emphasize the **principle of compatibility:** People's built-in or learned expectations enable them to learn certain procedures more easily than others. For example, it is easier to learn that a burst of loud noise means danger than to learn that some melody means danger. For another example, we are accustomed to turning a knob clockwise to increase the volume on a radio or television; we expect to turn a knob clockwise on any new machine in order to increase almost anything. Similarly, we expect to turn a knob clockwise to move something to the right, counterclockwise to move something to the left (as we do when steering a car). Those examples may seem obvious, but in many cases ergonomists must do some trial-and-error research to find

the best way to set up the controls for some device.

CONCEPT CHECK

3. Which of the following are examples of the principle of compatibility?
a. A worker who is supposed to press a lever at any sign of danger responds faster to a visual danger signal than to an auditory danger signal.
b. People operate a home thermostat more easily if they have to push the control handle up to increase the temperature than if they have to push it down.
c. People can read a scale more easily if the numbers increase left to right (10-20-30-40-50) than if they increase right to left (50-40-30-20-10). (Check your answer on page 758.)

STANDARDIZATION OF CONTROLS

If you have long been in the habit of driving one model of car and now you try to drive a different model, you will make some mistakes at first. You reach for the turn signal and find that instead you have turned on your headlights or your windshield wipers. With a car, such mistakes generally are not too costly, and automobile manufacturers feel little pressure to standardize the controls of their cars.

With an airplane, however, the costs can be severe. Many years ago someone noted that most military plane crashes occurred when a pilot who was very experienced at flying one kind of plane suddenly had to fly another kind of plane. The pilot might then raise the wing when it was time to lower the landing gear, or make some other mistake because the controls were not in their familiar position. Flying a plane is especially complicated because of the large number of knobs and levers. Furthermore, the pilot often cannot afford to take the time to look at the knobs or levers.

To solve this problem, ergonomists worked out a standardized placement of knobs so that pilots would know where to find them even on unfamiliar aircraft (Bradley, 1959). The U.S. Air Force subsequently adopted a standard set of knobs for various controls, as shown in Figure A.5. Some shapes were chosen to make them easy to remember; for example, note that the knob that lowers the landing gear is shaped like a wheel. This system enables pilots to check whether they have the right knob just by feeling it.

READING INFORMATION DISPLAYS

In many jobs, people have to monitor a certain number of gauges to make sure their machinery is working properly. For example, a car has one gauge to tell you how much fuel is left in the tank, another to tell you whether the engine is overheating, probably another to tell you whether the car needs more oil. When you drive, you probably check each of those gauges periodically, or at least you check them at the start of each trip.

Now imagine the more complex task of monitoring the gauges in an airplane cockpit

FIGURE A.5

The U.S. Air Force adopted these standard shapes for the control knobs in its aircraft. Even if a pilot has never flown a particular aircraft before, he or she can count on being able to identify the knobs by their shape and feel. (From Sanders & McCormick, 1987.)

Supercharger   Mixture   Carburetor air   Landing flap   Landing gear

Fire extinguisher   Power (throttle)   rpm   Lift to reverse power

or other complex machinery. There may be dozens, even hundreds, of such gauges. Not only do you have to remember to check them all periodically, but you also have to remember what is a "good" reading on each gauge and what readings indicate possible danger.

Consider, for example, the set of gauges in the top row of Figure A.6. Each one represents the current measurement of a variable in some machine. If the machine is running properly, the first gauge should read about 70, the sec-

FIGURE A.6

Each gauge represents a measurement of a different variable in some machine, such as an airplane. The top row shows one way of presenting the information. The operator must check each gauge one at a time to find out whether the reading is within the safe range for that variable. The bottom row shows the information represented in a way that is easier to read. The safe range for each variable is rotated to the same visual position. At a glance the operator can detect any reading outside the safe zone.

ond should read about 40, the third should read about 30, and the fourth should read about 10. Note that you would have to check each gauge one at a time to find out whether all the readings were in the safe range.

Now examine the bottom row of Figure A.6. Here all the gauges have the same information as in the top row, but all the safe ranges appear in the same location—here, the 3 o'clock position on the dial. Now you can look at the row of dials and tell at a glance whether or not one of the readings is outside the safe zone. You do not have to check them one at a time—the odd reading stands out through preattentive processing (Chapter 4).

Now let's consider a more extreme example. Figure A.7 shows part of the control room of the Three Mile Island nuclear power plant as it looked prior to a nearly disastrous accident in 1979. The control room had an enormous number of knobs and gauges; a nuclear power plant is, after all, a complicated system. What you cannot see in the picture is that in certain cases the knob that controlled a variable was in one place and the gauge measuring that variable was in another place. An operator who noticed something wrong would have to run back and forth between the knob on one side of the room and the gauge on the other.

The redesigned control room was im-

FIGURE A.7
The Three Mile Island TMI-2 nuclear power plant had a complex and confusing control system, a small portion of which is shown here. Some of the important gauges were not easily visible to the operators, some of the gauges were poorly labeled, and many of the alarm signals had ambiguous meanings. The nuclear plant currently in operation at Three Mile Island has a much simpler and clearer operating system.

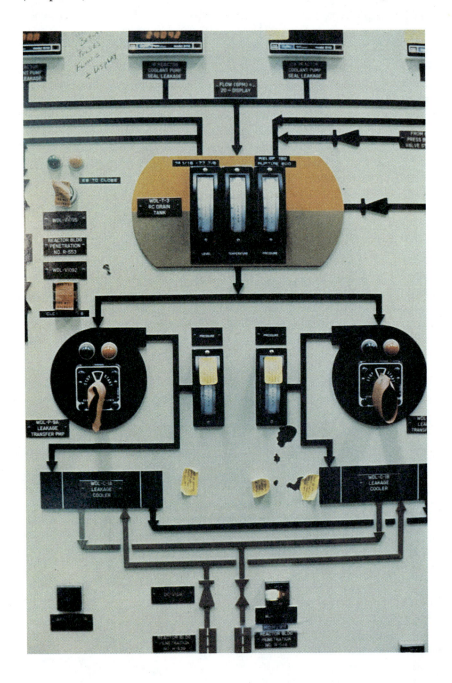

proved in many ways, grouping related gauges together in a logical sequence and placing the control knobs next to their associated gauges. From an engineering standpoint, the first room and the second room function about equally well, but from the human standpoint, the second room is far preferable.

READING DISPLAYS IN EVERYDAY LIFE

As a rule, most ergonomists work with large companies, helping them redesign machinery for the benefit of their workers. But in some cases ergonomists apply their skills for the benefit of people in everyday life.

For example, consider the problem of roadway signs. The government posts signs such as "Beware of falling rock," "Bridge slippery when wet," and "Drive slowly—school zone." In some parts of the United States and Canada, those signs might be posted in both English and Spanish or both English and French. But in parts of Europe, the signs would have to be posted in 20 or more languages. A more practical solution is to use a standard system of nonverbal signs, such as those shown in Figure A.8. Not only do these nonverbal signs break the language barrier, but they also have the advantage of being easy to read at a distance. Ergonomists conduct research to help design new signs that will be as easy as possible to understand and remember.

Ergonomists also help to evaluate warning signs. For example, suppose you take your younger cousin to a nearby lake. Do you let your cousin go into the lake, even though you see a "No swimming" sign? If so, you have ignored a warning sign. Research by ergonomists has demonstrated that people are more likely to heed a warning sign if the sign clearly explains the nature of the danger, the consequences of a mistake, and what one can do to avoid the risk (Wogalter et al., 1987). For example, you might assume the "No swimming" sign does not apply to your cousin because she is only going to wade a few feet into the water, not really swim. But imagine how you would react if the sign explained "No swimming—polluted water," "No swimming—quicksand," or "No swimming—poisonous snakes."

SOMETHING TO THINK ABOUT

Nuclear power plants store radioactive waste that will continue to be dangerous for tens of thousands of years. We cannot be confident that the English language or any other current language will still be in use for that long. What kind of warning sign could we attach to the nuclear waste to deter people of the future from endangering themselves?

SUMMARY

• *Ergonomics.* Ergonomists, or human-factors specialists, combine their knowledge of engineering and psychology to design machinery that is easy and safe for people to use. (page 753)

• *Principle of compatibility.* Ergonomists find that some ways of designing and arranging controls are easier than others are for people to learn, because people start with certain assumptions or expectations. (page 754)

SLIPPERY ROAD   PEDESTRIAN CROSSING   NO LEFT (RIGHT) TURN   DON'T BLOW YOUR HORN   MECHANICAL HELP   TELEPHONE

Danger signs   Instruction signs   Information signs

FIGURE A.8
Many countries throughout the world use these road signs; they communicate to drivers who speak a great variety of languages. Ergonomists do research to discover what signs are easiest to understand and remember.

- *Standardization of controls.* People make fewer mistakes if the controls are standardized so that someone who learns to operate one machine will also be able to operate other models. (page 755)

- *Design of displays.* Certain kinds of displays are especially easy to read because any abnormal, dangerous pattern stands out preattentively. (page 755)

- *Warning signs.* Warning signs are most effective if they include a brief explanation of the danger, the consequences of a mistake, and the way to avoid the danger. (page 757)

SUGGESTION FOR FURTHER READING

Norman, D. A. (1988). *The psychology of everyday life*. New York: Basic Books. A captivating discussion of everyday objects such as doors, cars, and telephones, and an explanation of what makes some of their designs good and other ones difficult to use.

TERMS

ergonomics or **human factors** field that attempts to facilitate the operation of machinery so that the average user can use it as efficiently and as safely as possible (page 753)

person-machine system the combination of a person and the machine which the person operates (page 753)

principle of compatibility principle that people will learn certain procedures more easily and more accurately than others because of people's built-in or learned expectations (page 754)

ANSWER TO CONCEPT CHECK

3. All three are examples of the principle of compatibility. (page 754)

SCHOOL PSYCHOLOGY

What sorts of special psychological conditions are common in school-age children?

What do school psychologists do about these conditions?

Imagine a group of 6- or 7-year-old children, either on a weekend or during summer vacation. How do you picture them spending their time? Talking, playing, running around, laughing, watching television perhaps. Left to their own choices, children find a mixture of active and inactive things to do. One of the things they will almost certainly *not* do is to sit silently for hours at a time, practicing their handwriting or arithmetic.

And yet, for five days a week during most of the year, we expect these same children to do exactly that: to sit silently except when called upon and to practice handwriting, addition, and other similarly unexciting tasks. At these times, any child who talks, laughs, or runs around may be labeled "abnormal"!

At one time or another, a great many children run into academic problems of one type or another. Some children simply have trouble sitting still or paying attention. Some get into trouble for misbehavior. Some have specialized problems with reading, spelling, arithmetic, or other academic skills. Some have distractions in their home life that prevent them from concentrating on their studies.

Other children have special gifts or talents; they master their schoolwork faster than other children and yearn for more. They may not get as much special attention as the slower children do; we tend to think that the brightest children have no problems or that they can take care of their own problems. But many of those children fall far short of achieving their great potential.

School psychologists are specialists who deal with the psychological condition of students, mostly in kindergarten through 12th grade. It is the task of school psychologists to try to identify a child's strengths and weaknesses and then plan a program to help the child build on the strengths or overcome the weaknesses. School psychologists also work with teachers and school administrators to plan strategies for coping with children who need special attention in the classroom.

WHAT SCHOOL PSYCHOLOGISTS DO

The role of school psychologists varies substantially, depending on the psychologists themselves, their education, and the school system for which they work. Broadly speaking, school psychologists identify educationally related needs of children, devise a plan to treat those needs, and then either implement the plan themselves or advise a child's teacher on how to implement it. As of 1992, an estimated 87,000 people were active as school psychologists worldwide (Oakland & Cunningham, 1992).

School psychology is not always taught in psychology departments. At some universities, the school psychology program is a branch of the Department of Education or of a special Department of Educational Psychology. In some countries it is possible to practice school psychology with only a bachelor's degree, but in the United States, the minimum is usually a master's degree. Job opportunities are much greater for people

For elementary-school children, to sit quietly by the hour, reading and writing, is biologically unnatural. Yet any child who does not comply is considered "abnormal"! School psychologists try to help both the students and the teachers.

with a doctorate degree. In the future, a doctorate may become necessary. The number of people employed as school psychologists has been growing sharply and is expected to continue growing. That is, job opportunities are good. Most school psychologists work for a school system; others work for consulting firms, mental health clinics, guidance centers, and other institutions.

Traditionally, one role of school psychologists has been to administer tests, including IQ tests, and interpret the results. IQ tests (see Chapter 9) are not easy to administer; for the results to be valid, the child must understand the instructions, the child must be able to work on the test with a minimum of distraction, and the school psychologist must know the limitations of the test. In a sense, the school psychologist uses the IQ scores the same way a detective uses a clue (Kaufman, Harrison, & Ittenbach, 1990). That is, the scores provide valuable information, but only in combination with other information. To take an obvious example, a school psychologist might take into account the fact that a child with a low IQ score had uncorrected visual or hearing deficits or that the child was a recent immigrant from a non-English-speaking country. It might be less obvious that a child was distracted by noises in the room or by emotional turmoil at home.

Over the years the task of school psychologists has broadened. One important event in the history of school psychology in the United States was the passage of a law, PL 94-142, in 1975 (French, 1990). **PL 94-142, the Education for All Handicapped Children Act,** specified that public schools must provide a "free and appropriate" education for all children, regardless of their deficits or limitations. It further stipulated that the federal government would provide extra funds in proportion to the number of children who need special education or other services. Those funds would contribute (at least to some extent) toward the additional cost of educating blind, deaf, or otherwise disabled students.

In order to implement this law, the state governments had to hire specialists, in many cases school psychologists, to test children and determine their special difficulties and needs. Those specialized difficulties include sensory impairments, learning disabilities, and serious emotional disturbances. Therefore, school psychologists have had to spend a great deal of time conducting a wide variety of tests and interviews to classify children's problems (Jackson, 1990).

Once a school psychologist has identified a child's problem, the next task is to devise a plan to deal with that problem. In some cases that plan may consist of simply advising the teacher to let a child with a mild hearing impairment sit closer to the front of the room or to permit certain children a little extra time when taking tests. In other cases the school psychologist may help the teacher find ways to cope with an impulsive, hard-to-discipline child or may help the teacher pace his or her lectures a little better to hold children's attention. In still other cases the school psychologist may set up counseling sessions with the child or the child's family to try to overcome emotional problems. In short, the school psychologist's role may range from educator to clinical psychologist. If the child has a severe problem, of course, the school psychologist refers the child to a medical doctor or other specialist.

EXAMPLES OF CONCERNS FOR SCHOOL PSYCHOLOGISTS

Imagine yourself as a school psychologist. On a given day you might have to deal with an enormous range of sensory, intellectual, and emotional concerns. Sometimes your day would be like solving a mystery: Here is a child whose school performance is disappointing; try to figure out the reason.

While the possible range of problems is enormous, some problems show up more frequently. Here is a quick survey of a few fairly typical conditions affecting school-age children.

SCHOOL PHOBIA

School phobia is a fairly uncommon condition, affecting about one child in a hundred, characterized by apprehension or even panic while in school, while preparing to go to school, or sometimes at the mere thought of school. Some children with this condition experience nausea, vomiting, dizziness, or headaches while in school, but at no other time. The term *school phobia* seems appropriate; the condition resembles other kinds of phobias.

Traditionally, most theorists have attributed school phobia to the child's anxiety at being separated from his or her parents, especially the mother. According to these theorists, children with a school phobia have an unhealthy family life with a mixture of extreme dependency and fear of desertion.

The evidence for that view is not convincing, however, at least not in most cases. A simpler, more parsimonious explanation is that the child really does fear school (Pilkington & Piersell, 1991). Most children with school phobias have encountered teachers who ridiculed them, children who bullied them, or other unpleasant or embarrassing school experiences.

The role of the school psychologist in such cases is to try to identify the basis of the fear and to develop a plan for dealing with it. The plan might consist simply of switching the child to a different class, or it might include efforts to teach the child more effective ways to deal with unpleasant classmates.

Research on school phobia indicates that it is usually the result of unpleasant experiences at school—being teased, bullied, or embarrassed.

ATTENTION-DEFICIT DISORDER

Suppose a teacher describes a boy in a first-grade class: "He is restless and unable to concentrate on schoolwork. He's easily distracted, impulsive, undeterred by threats of punishment, prone to temper tantrums, moody, and generally doing poorly in class." Would you regard this description as an indication that the boy has a serious problem and needs help? Or would you guess that he is a fairly typical 6-year-old?

The answer could be either, depending on degree. Many elementary-school children, especially boys, have occasional trouble sitting still and paying attention during class. A few have such persistent troubles that they do not make reasonable academic progress and perhaps do not even make many friends. If the child's restlessness and distractibility are severe, psychologists call the condition **attention-deficit disorder (ADD)**. At least two thirds of the children with ADD are boys. Because it is an exaggeration of tendencies common in young children, ADD is difficult to diagnose. Depending on where teachers and school psychologists draw the line separating "normal" from "troublesome," they might see attention-deficit disorder very rarely or in more than 10% of all children.

ADD is ordinarily first identified in children ages 5–7—in other words, within the first year or two after starting school. (The same behaviors at an earlier age would not be a problem, because no one expects a 4-year-old child to sit attentively in class.) Children with ADD have difficulties with many school activities, especially those that require planning a sequence of responses or focusing attention on a single task (Reardon & Naglieri, 1992). Some children outgrow ADD when they reach adolescence. Others have continuing problems of poor academic achievement, impulsive behavior, and sometimes delinquency (Thorley, 1984).

The most common treatment for attention-deficit disorder is the use of stimulant drugs, such as amphetamine or Ritalin. Such drugs are reasonably effective at reducing restlessness and improving attention for many children. However, ours is an over-medicated society. Sometimes it is tempting to seek a drug solution to a problem without checking other solutions first. So far, no one is certain how or why stimulant drugs are useful for children with ADD. Curiously, one study found that the drugs improve the attention span of normal children too, not just those with ADD (Zahn, Rapoport, & Thompson, 1980). School psychologists do not, of course, prescribe drugs themselves. In some cases they make recommendations to physicians; in other cases they advise teachers on behavioral means of controlling classroom behavior, either in addition to or instead of relying on drugs.

LEARNING DISABILITIES

You probably have heard the term *learning-disabled child*, and you may have assumed that it refers to some well-defined condition.

In fact, it is a very loose term applied to any child who performs normally in most regards but has trouble in one or more specific academic activities. Typically, such a child has normal vision and hearing, an IQ score within the normal range, and a history of adequate educational opportunities; nevertheless, the child reads poorly or cannot do arithmetic or fails in some other limited area. When observers have no ready explanation for the child's failure, we call the child's limitation a **learning disability.** In short, the term *learning disability* is, in many cases, little more than a name we give to our ignorance.

When school psychologists believe a particular child may be learning disabled, their task is to identify the nature of the child's disability as carefully as possible. They use a wide variety of tests, including academic tests and tests of neurological functioning (Gray & Dean, 1990). Once they understand a child's strengths and weaknesses, they can plan an academic program to take advantage of the strengths and to overcome or minimize the weaknesses.

GIFTED CHILDREN

Just as certain children find their schoolwork especially difficult, other children find it boringly easy. How should we handle especially talented or gifted children?

Some children are inattentive because they do not understand the material; others are inattentive because they understood long ago and have now become bored. School psychologists try to identify gifted children and recommend enriching activities to challenge their abilities.

One of the worst answers is simply to ask them to do more of the same thing they are already doing. For example, if a student finishes a page of long-division problems long before the rest of the class, the teacher might ask the student to complete another page of the same kind of problems. Or if a student completes a reading assignment in record time, the teacher might ask the student to read another assignment similar to the first, or worse yet, to reread the first assignment. Repetitive assignments such as these become demoralizing.

Most specialists in gifted education recommend challenging the child's creativity. In some schools, gifted children are placed in a special class with a special teacher, almost like the special classes for severely retarded children. In other schools, gifted children spend most of the day in regular classes but get "pulled out" for special enrichment classes at certain times (Vaughn, Feldhusen, & Asher, 1991). In still other schools, teachers provide these children with special challenges and opportunities without removing them from their regular classrooms. School psychologists have a hand in planning any of these approaches.

OTHER CONDITIONS

The conditions we have discussed are just the beginning of the list of concerns a school psychologist may face. Conduct disorder (misbehavior) and truancy are two fairly common problems that are quite difficult for most teachers to handle. Stuttering is a much less serious problem so far as teachers are concerned, although it can be embarrassing to the student. *Tourette's disorder* is a condition in which a child has repetitive tics and odd movements; some children with this condition periodically blurt out sounds and words. Schoolchildren may also have a great variety of medical conditions that impair their performance, such as epilepsy, paralysis, blindness, and deafness; they may be victims of sexual abuse or suffer other mistreatment.

As children grow older, school psychologists start to encounter anorexia nervosa, depression, schizophrenia, suicidal tendencies, and all sorts of other problems. School psychologists need at least to be able to identify the student's disorder and find the right specialist to treat it. In short, school psychologists need to be able to recognize an enormous variety of common and uncommon disorders and then recommend an appropriate strategy for each child.

"Mainstreaming" is placing children with disabilities in the same classes with other children, so far as possible. Under the supervision of a sympathetic teacher, mainstreaming can be a benefit to both the disabled child and the other children.

WHAT TO DO WITH DISABLED CHILDREN: THE MAINSTREAMING ISSUE

Finally, let us consider one major issue that affects school psychologists, as well as the rest of us: Should we put disabled children into special classrooms or into the same classrooms with other children?

Beginning in the 1970s, courts in the United States have insisted that each child has the legal right to an education in the "least restrictive environment" consistent with the child's abilities. That is, a child in a wheelchair, a child with dyslexia, or a child with some other disability should be educated in the same class with other children, if possible. Doing so is called **mainstreaming**. Sometimes a school works out a compromise, mainstreaming a child for part of the day but providing special education in another room at certain times.

Mainstreaming has some definite advantages: The disabled child avoids the stigma of being in a special class and gets a chance to deal with a wide range of other children— the kinds of people he or she will have to deal with on the job and in other aspects of life. The other children in the class gain the opportunity to learn respect for diversity, and they learn that a child who is disabled in one way may be highly capable in other ways.

Unfortunately, good ideas do not always work out well in practice. Teachers, after all, differ. Some do a marvelous job of including a disabled child in classroom activities; others are, frankly, less marvelous. When problems arise, school psychologists are sometimes called upon to help choose the best course of action.

SUMMARY

- *School psychologists.* School psychologists identify the problems that interfere with certain children's school performance. They then develop a plan to overcome those problems. (page 759)

- *Growth of school psychology.* The field of school psychology has been growing steadily, partly in response to the need for evaluation of children with disabilities. (page 760)

- *School phobia.* One of the problems that concern school psychologists is school phobia, a fearful and sometimes even panic-stricken avoidance of school. (page 760)

- *Attention-deficit disorder.* Another problem is attention-deficit disorder, a condition marked by restlessness, impulsiveness, and difficulty focusing attention. (page 761)

- *Learning disabilities.* Certain children have specialized academic difficulties, although their other skills are within the normal range. (page 761)

- *Gifted children.* Gifted children master their schoolwork quickly and find it boring. Such children thrive on opportunities to develop their creativity. However, many gifted children fear social rejection. (page 762)

- *Mainstreaming.* Schools try to educate disabled children in the least restrictive environment possible. Placing children with disabilities into the same classroom with other children has significant advantages, but can also pose some difficulties that school psychologists try to manage. (page 763)

Suggestion for Further Reading

Gutkin, T. B., & Reynolds, C. R. (Eds.). (1990). *The handbook of school psychology* (2nd ed.). New York: Wiley. A standard reference on all the tasks of school psychologists.

Terms

school psychologist specialist who deals with the psychological condition of students, mostly in kindergarten through 12th grade (page 759)

PL 94-142, the **Education for All Handicapped Children Act** U.S. law, passed in 1975, which specifies that public schools must provide a "free and appropriate" education for all children, regardless of their deficits or limitations (page 760)

school phobia a condition characterized by apprehension or even panic while in school, while preparing to go to school, or sometimes at the mere thought of school (page 760)

attention-deficit disorder (ADD) condition marked by severe restlessness and distractibility, particularly in a school setting (page 761)

learning disability condition in which a child fails in some limited academic area, although observers have no ready explanation for the child's failure (page 762)

mainstreaming educating impaired children in the same classrooms with other children (page 763)

EPILOGUE

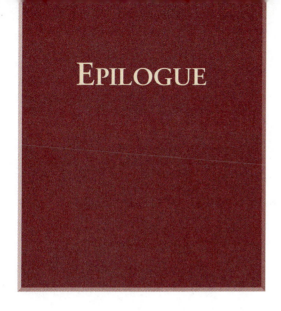

Here we are at the end of the book. As I have been writing and revising this book, I have imagined you sitting there reading it. I have generally imagined a student somewhat like I was when I was a college student, reading about psychology for the first time and often growing excited about something I had just read. I remember periodically telling my roommate, or my family, when I was home for a vacation, "Guess what I just learned in psychology! Isn't this interesting?" And I remember occasionally thinking, "Hmm. The book says such-and-so, but I'm not convinced. I wonder whether psychologists ever considered a different explanation. . . ." And I started thinking about possible research I might do if I ever became a psychologist.

I hope that you have had some of those same experiences yourself. I hope you have occasionally become excited about something you read, so that you thought about it and talked to other people about it. In fact, I hope you told your roommate so much about psychology that you started to become annoying. And I hope you have sometimes doubted some conclusion, imagining some research project you might like to conduct to improve and advance our knowledge.

Now, as I picture you reaching the end of the course, I'm not sure how you will react. You might be thinking, "Wow, I sure have learned a lot!" Or you might be thinking, "Is that *all*?" Maybe you are even reacting both ways: "I really have learned a lot. But it seems like there ought to be more. I still

don't understand what conscious experience is all about, and I don't understand why I react the way I do sometimes. And this book— *wonderful as it is*—hardly mentioned certain important topics. Like why do we laugh? How do we sense the passage of time? Why do people like to watch sports? How do people develop their political and religious convictions? Why do I feel like yawning whenever I see someone else yawn?"

If I didn't answer all your questions, there are two good reasons. One is that this is an introductory text; if you want to learn more, you should take additional courses or do some additional reading. The other reason is that psychologists do not know all the answers.

Perhaps some day you will become a psychological researcher yourself and add to the sum of our knowledge. If not, you can try to keep up to date on current developments in psychology by reading newspaper and magazine articles and an occasional book. One of the main goals of this book has been to prepare you to continue learning about psychology in that fashion. Try to read critically. If you pick up a book in the psychology section of your local bookstore, try to determine whether it is based on scientific evidence or just the author's own pronouncements. If you read an article in the newspaper, try to judge whether its conclusions follow from decent evidence. If it reports a survey, were the survey's questions unambiguous? If the article implies a cause-and-effect relationship, was the evidence based on experiments or only correlations? No matter what the evidence, can you think of a more reasonable, more parsimonious explanation than the one the author suggests?

Above all, remember that nearly all our conclusions are tentative. Psychological researchers seldom use the word *prove;* they have many ways of indicating moderate confidence. I once suggested to my editor, halfseriously, that we should include in the index to this book the entry "*maybe*—see pages 1–765." We did not include such an entry because our understanding of psychology is not really that bad—at least, not always. But be leery of anyone who seems a little too certain about some great new insight in psychology; the route from *maybe* to *definitely* is long and arduous.

To The Owner Of This Book

I hope that you have enjoyed *Introduction to Psychology,* Fourth Edition as much as
I enjoyed writing it. I would like to know as much about your experience
as you would care to offer. Only through your comments and those of others
can I learn how to make this a better text for future readers.

School _____ Your instructor's name _____

1. What did you like the most about *Introduction to Psychology,* Fourth Edition? _____

_____

_____

_____

2. Do you have any recommendations for ways to improve the next edition of this text? _____

_____

_____

_____

3. In the space below or in a separate letter, please write any other comments you have about the book. (For example, were
any chapters or concepts particularly difficult?) I'd be delighted to hear from you!

_____

_____

_____

_____

_____

_____

Optional:

Your name _____ Date _____

May Brooks/Cole quote you, either in promotion for *Introduction to Psychology* or in future publishing ventures?

Yes ☐   No ☐

Thanks!

Please photocopy this page and mail your comments to: James W. Kalat
c/o Brooks/Cole Publishing Company
511 Forest Lodge Road
Pacfic Grove, CA 93950

REFERENCES

Numbers in parentheses indicate the chapter in which a source is cited.

Abrahamsen, D. (1985). *Confessions of Son of Sam*. New York: Columbia University Press. (15)

Abramson, L. Y., Seligman, M. E. P., & Teasdale, J. D. (1978). Learned helplessness in humans: Critique and reformulation. *Journal of Abnormal Psychology, 87,* 49–74. (14)

"A conversation with President Havel." (1992, March). *World Press Review, 39*(3), 14–16. (15)

Adam, K. (1980). Sleep as a restorative process and a theory to explain why. In P. S. McConnell, G. J. Boer, H. J. Romijn, N. E. van de Poll, & M. A. Corner (Eds.), *Progress in brain research: Vol. 53, Adaptive capabilities of the nervous system* (pp. 289–305). Amsterdam: Elsevier/North Holland Biomedical. (5)

Adam, K. S. (1986). Early family influences on suicidal behavior. *Annals of the New York Academy of Sciences, 487,* 63–76. (14)

Adams, J. S. (1963). Wage inequities, productivity, and work quality. *Industrial Relations, 3,* 9–16. (A)

Adler, A. (1927). *Understanding human nature*. New York: Greenberg. (13)

Adler, A. (1928/1964). Brief comments on reason, intelligence, and feeble-mindedness. In H. L. Ansbacher & R. R. Ansbacher (Eds.), *Superiority and social interest* (pp. 41–49). New York: Viking. (Original work published 1928.) (13)

Adler, A. (1932/1964). The structure of neurosis. In H. L. Ansbacher & R. R. Ansbacher (Eds.), *Superiority and social interest* (pp. 83–95). New York: Viking. (Original work published 1932.) (13)

Adrian, C., & Hammen, C. (1993). Stress exposure and stress generation in children of depressed mothers. *Journal of Consulting and Clinical Psychology, 61,* 354–359. (14)

Akbarian, S., Viñuela, A., Kim, J. J., Potkin, S. G., Bunney, W. E., Jr., & Jones, E. G. (1993). Distorted distribution of nicotinamide-adenine dinucleotide phosphate-diaphorase neurons in temporal lobe of schizophrenics implies anomalous cortical development. *Archives of General Psychiatry, 50,* 178–187. (14)

Akbarian, S., Kim, J. J., Potkin, S. G., Hagman, J. O., Tafazzoli, A., Bunney, W. E. Jr., & Jones, E. G. (1995). Gene expression for glutamic acid decarboxylase is reduced without loss of neurons in prefrontal cortex of schizophrenics. *Archives of General Psychiatry, 52,* 258–266. (14)

Albee, G. W. (1986). Toward a just society: Lessons from observations on the primary prevention of psychopathology. *American Psychologist, 41,* 891–898. (15)

Aldag, R. J., & Fuller, S. R. (1993). Beyond fiasco: A reappraisal of the groupthink phenomenon and a new model of group decision processes. *Psychological Bulletin, 113,* 533–552. (16)

Aldrich, M. S. (1993). Narcolepsy. *Neurology, 42* (Suppl. 6), 34–43. (5)

Alexander, I. E. (1982). The Freud-Jung relationship—the other side of Oedipus and countertransference. *American Psychologist, 37,* 1009–1018. (13)

Alicke, M. D., & Largo, E. (1995). The role of the self in the false consensus effect. *Journal of Experimental Social Psychology, 31,* 28–47. (16)

Alley, T. R., & Cunningham, M. R. (1991). Averaged faces are attractive, but very attractive faces are not average. *Psychological Science, 2,* 123–125. (16)

Allison, K. W., Crawford, I., Echemendia, R., Robinson, L., & Knepp, D. (1994). Human diversity and professional competence. *American Psychologist, 49,* 792–796. (15)

Allport, G. W. (1935). Attitudes. In C. Murchison (Ed.), *A handbook of social psychology* (pp. 798–844). Worcester, MA: Clark University. (16)

Allport, G. W., & Odbert, H. S. (1936). Trait-names: A psycholexical study. *Psychological Monographs, 47* (Whole No. 211). (13)

Amato, P. R., & Keith, B. (1991). Parental divorce and the well-being of children: A meta-analysis. *Psychological Bulletin, 110,* 26–46. (10)

American Medical Association (1986). Council Report: Scientific status of refreshing recollection by the use of hypnosis. *International Journal of Clinical and Experimental Hypnosis, 34,* 1–12. (5)

American Psychiatric Association (1994). *Diagnostic and Statistical Manual of Mental Disorders* (4th ed.). Washington, D.C.: Author. (14)

American Psychological Association (1982). *Ethical principles in the conduct of research with human participants*. Washington, D.C.: Author. (2)

Anastasi, A. (1988). *Psychological testing* (6th ed.). New York: Macmillan. (9, 13)

Andersen, B. L. (1983). Primary orgasmic dysfunction: Diagnostic considerations and review of treatment. *Psychological Bulletin, 93,* 105–136. (11)

Andersen, B. L., Kiecolt-Glaser, J. K., & Glaser, R. (1994). A biobehavioral model of cancer stress and disease course. *American Psychologist, 49,* 389–404. (12)

Anderson, C. A. (1989). Temperature and aggression: Ubiquitous effects of heat on occurrence of human violence. *Psychological Bulletin, 106,* 74–96. (12)

Anderson, C. D., Warner, J. L., & Spencer, C. C. (1984). Inflation bias in self-assessment examinations: Implications for valid employee selection. *Journal of Applied Psychology, 69*, 574–580. (13)

Anderson, J. R. (1991). The adaptive nature of human categorization. *Psychological Review, 98*, 409–429. (8)

Andersson, U., Eckernäs, S.-Å., Hartvig, P., Ulin, J., Långström, B., & Hägström, J.-E. (1990). Striatal binding of ^{11}C-NMSP studied with positron emission tomography in patients with persistent tardive dyskinesia: No evidence for altered dopamine D_2 receptor binding. *Journal of Neural Transmission, 79*, 215–226. (15)

Andreasen, N. C., Arndt, S., Alliger, R., Miller, D., & Flaum, M. (1995). Symptoms of schizophrenia: Methods, meanings, and mechanisms. *Archives of General Psychiatry, 52*, 341–351. (14)

Andreasen, N. C., Flaum, M., Swayze, V. W., II, Tyrrell, G., & Arndt, S. (1990). Positive and negative symptoms in schizophrenia. *Archives of General Psychiatry, 47*, 615–621. (14)

Anisman, H., & Zacharko, R. M. (1983). Stress and neoplasia: Speculations and caveats. *Behavioral Medicine Update, 5*, 27–35. (12)

Anonymous (1955). *Alcoholics anonymous* (2nd ed.). New York: Alcoholics Anonymous World Services. (14)

Appelbaum, P. S. (1988). The new preventive detention: Psychiatry's problematic responsibility for the control of violence. *American Journal of Psychiatry, 145*, 779–785. (15)

Appley, M. H. (1991). Motivation, equilibration, and stress. In R. Dienstbier (Ed.), *Nebraska Symposium on Motivation 1990* (pp. 1–67). Lincoln, NE: University of Nebraska Press. (11)

Arboleda, C., & Holzman, P. S. (1985). Thought disorder in children at risk for psychosis. *Archives of General Psychiatry, 42*, 1004–1013. (14)

Argyle, N. (1988). The nature of cognitions in panic disorder. *Behaviour Research and Therapy, 26*, 261–264. (14)

Arkin, A. M., & Antrobus, J. S. (1978). The effects of external stimuli applied prior to and during sleep on sleep experience. In A. M. Arkin, J. S. Antrobus, & S. J. Ellman (Eds.), *The mind in sleep* (pp. 351–391). Hillsdale, NJ: Lawrence Erlbaum. (5)

Arndt, S., Andreasen, N. C., Flaum, M., Miller, D., & Nopoulos, P. (1995). A longitudinal study of symptom dimensions in schizophrenia. *Archives of General Psychiatry, 52*, 352–360. (14)

Arnett, J. (1990). Contraceptive use, sensation seeking, and adolescent egocentrism. *Journal of Youth and Adolescence, 19*, 171–180. (10)

Arnold, H. J., & House, R. J. (1980). Methodological and substantive extensions to the job characteristics model of motivation. *Organizational Behavior and Human Performance, 25*, 161–183. (A)

Aronow, E., Reznikoff, M., & Moreland, K. L. (1995). The Rorschach: Projective technique or psychometric test? *Journal of Personality Assessment, 64*, 213–228. (13)

Aronson, E., & Carlsmith, J. M. (1963). Effect of the severity of threat on the devaluation of forbidden behavior. *Journal of Abnormal and Social Psychology, 66*, 584–588. (16)

Arvey, R. D., and 51 others. (1994, December 13). Mainstream science on intelligence. *The Wall Street Journal*, A18. (9)

Asch, S. E. (1951). Effects of group pressure upon the modification and distortion of judgments. In H. Guetzkow (Ed.), *Groups, leadership, and men* (pp. 177–190). Pittsburgh, PA: Carnegie Press. (16)

Asch, S. E. (1955, November). Opinions and social pressure. *Scientific American, 193*(5), 31–35. (16)

Asch, S. E. (1956). Studies of independence and conformity: I. A minority of one against a unanimous majority. *Psychological Monographs, 70*(9, Whole No. 416). (16)

Ash, R. (1986, August). An anecdote submitted by Ron Ash. *The Industrial-Organizational Psychologist, 23*(4), 8. (6)

Atchley, R. C. (1980). *The social forces in later life* (3rd ed.). Belmont, CA: Wadsworth. (10)

Atkinson, J. W., & Birch, D. (1978). *Introduction to motivation* (2nd ed.). New York: D. Van Nostrand. (11)

Atkinson, R. C., & Shiffrin, R. M. (1968). Human memory: A proposed system and its control. In K. W. Spence & J. T. Spence (Eds.), *The psychology of learning and motivation* (Vol. 2, pp. 89–105). New York: Academic Press. (7)

Averill, J. R. (1983). Studies on anger and aggression: Implications for theories of emotion. *American Psychologist, 38*, 1145–1160. (12)

Axelrod, R., & Dion, D. (1988). The further evolution of cooperation. *Science, 242*, 1385–1390. (16)

Azrin, N. H., & Nunn, R. G. (1973). Habit-reversal: A method of eliminating nervous habits and tics. *Behaviour Research and Therapy, 11*, 619–628. (6)

Babcock, R. L., & Salthouse, T. A. (1990). Effects of increased processing demands on age differences in working memory. *Psychology & Aging, 5*, 421–428. (7)

Babich, F. R., Jacobson, A. L., Bubash, S., & Jacobson, A. (1965). Transfer of a response to naive rats by injection of ribonucleic acid extracted from trained rats. *Science, 149*, 656–657. (2)

Babkoff, H., Caspy, T., Mikulincer, M., & Sing, H. C. (1991). Monotonic and rhythmic influences: A challenge for sleep deprivation research. *Psychological Bulletin, 109*, 411–428. (5)

Bachevalier, J., & Mishkin, M. (1984). An early and a late developing system for learning and retention in infant monkeys. *Behavioral Neuroscience, 98*, 770–778. (7)

Bachrach, A. J., Erwin, W. J., & Mohr, J. P. (1965). The control of eating behavior in an anoretic by operant conditioning techniques. In L. P. Ullmann & L. Krasner (Eds.), *Case studies in behavior modification* (pp. 153–163). New York: Holt, Rinehart, & Winston. (11, 15)

Baddeley, A. D., & Hitch, G. J. (1974). Working memory. In G. H. Bower (Ed.), *Psychology of Learning and Motivation* (Vol. 8, pp. 47–89). New York: Academic Press. (8)

Baddeley, A. D., & Hitch, G. J. (1977). Recency re-examined. In S. Dornic (Ed.), *Attention and performance VI* (pp. 647–667). Hillsdale, NJ: Lawrence Erlbaum. (7)

Baddeley, A. D., & Hitch, G. J. (1994). Developments in the concept of working memory. *Neuropsychology, 8*, 485–493. (7)

Bahrick, H. (1984). Semantic memory content in permastore: 50 years of memory for Spanish learned in school. *Journal of Experimental Psychology: General, 113*, 1–29. (7)

Bahrick, H. P., Bahrick, L. E., Bahrick, A. S., & Bahrick, P. E. (1993). Maintenance of foreign language vocabulary and the spacing effect. *Psychological Science, 4*, 316–321. (7)

Bailey, J. M., & Pillard, R. C. (1991). A genetic study of male sexual orientation. *Archives of General Psychiatry, 48*, 1089–1096. (11)

Bailey, J. M., Pillard, R. C., Neale, M. C., & Agyei, Y. (1993). Heritable factors influence sexual orientation in women. *Archives of General Psychiatry, 50*, 217–223. (11)

Baird, J. C. (1982). The moon illusion: A reference theory. *Journal of Experimental Psychology: General, 111,* 304–315. (4)

Baker, G. H. B. (1987). Invited review: Psychological factors and immunity. *Journal of Psychosomatic Research, 31,* 1–10. (12)

Baker, T. B., & Tiffany, S. T. (1985). Morphine tolerance as habituation. *Psychological Bulletin, 92,* 78–108. (5)

Baker-Ward, L., Gordon, B. N., Ornstein, P. A., Larus, D. M., & Clubb, P. A. (1993). Young children's long-term retention of a pediatric examination. *Child Development, 64,* 1519–1533. (7)

Baldessarini, R. J. (1984). Antipsychotic drugs. In T. B. Karasu (Ed.), *The psychiatric therapies. I. The somatic therapies* (pp. 119–170). Washington, D.C.: American Psychiatric Press. (15)

Ballinger, B., & Yalom, I. (1995). Group therapy in practice. In B. Bongar & L. E. Beutler (Eds.), *Comprehensive textbook of psychotherapy: Theory and practice* (pp. 189–204). Oxford, England: Oxford University Press. (15)

Balloun, K. D., & Holmes, D. S. (1979). Effects of repeated examinations on the ability to detect guilt with a polygraphic examination: A laboratory experiment with a real crime. *Journal of Applied Psychology, 64,* 316–322. (12)

Banaji, M. R., & Greenwald, A. G. (1994). Implicit stereotyping and prejudice. In M. P. Zanna & J. M. Olson (Eds.), *The psychology of prejudice: The Ontario Symposium Volume 7* (pp. 55–76). Hillsdale, NJ: Lawrence Erlbaum. (16)

Bandura, A. (1977). *Social learning theory.* Englewood Cliffs, NJ: Prentice-Hall. (6)

Bandura, A. (1986). *Social foundations of thought and action.* Englewood Cliffs, NJ: Prentice-Hall. (6)

Bandura, A., Ross, D., & Ross, S. A. (1963). Imitation of film-mediated aggressive models. *Journal of Abnormal and Social Psychology, 66,* 3–11. (6)

Barber, T. X. (1979). Suggested ("hypnotic") behavior: The trance paradigm versus an alternative paradigm. In E. Fromm & R. E. Shor (Eds.), *Hypnosis: Developments in research and new perspectives* (2nd ed., pp. 217–271). New York: Aldine. (5)

Bard, P. (1934). On emotional expression after decortication with some remarks on certain theoretical views. *Psychological Review, 41,* 309–329. (12)

Barnes, R. (1985). Women and self-injury. *International Journal of Women's Studies, 8,* 465–474. (14)

Baron, J., & Norman, M. F. (1992). SATs, achievement tests, and high-school class rank as predictors of college performance. *Educational and Psychological Measurement, 52,* 1047–1055. (9)

Barrett, D. (1993). The "committee of sleep": A study of dream incubation for problem solving. *Dreaming, 3,* 115–122. (5)

Barrett, G. V., & Depinet, R. L. (1991). A reconsideration of testing for competence rather than intelligence. *American Psychologist, 46,* 1012–1024. (9)

Barrick, M. R., & Mount, M. K. (1991). The big five personality dimensions and job performance: A meta-analysis. *Personnel Psychology, 44,* 1–26. (13, A)

Bartlett, F. C. (1932). *Remembering.* Cambridge, England: Cambridge University Press. (7)

Bartoshuk, L. M. (1991). Taste, smell, and pleasure. In R. C. Bolles (Ed.), *The hedonics of taste* (pp. 5–28). Hillsdale, NJ: Lawrence Erlbaum. (4)

Bashore, T. R., & Rapp, P. E. (1993). Are there alternatives to traditional polygraph procedures? *Psychological Bulletin, 113,* 3–22. (12)

Bass, B. M., & Ryterband, E. C. (1979). *Organizational psychology* (2nd ed.). Boston: Allyn & Bacon. (10)

Bassok, M., & Holyoak, K. J. (1989). Interdomain transfer between isomorphic topics in algebra and physics. *Journal of Experimental Psychology: Learning, Memory, and Cognition, 15,* 153–166. (8)

Bateman, T. S., & Organ, D. W. (1983). Job satisfaction and the good soldier: The relationship between affect and employee "citizenship." *Academy of Management Journal, 26,* 587–595. (A)

Baum, A., Gatchel, R. J., & Schaeffer, M. A. (1983). Emotional, behavioral, and physiological effects of chronic stress at Three Mile Island. *Journal of Consulting and Clinical Psychology, 51,* 565–572. (12)

Baumeister, R. F., & Leary, M. R. (1995). The need to belong: Desire for interpersonal attachments as a fundamental human motivation. *Psychological Bulletin, 117,* 497–529. (16)

Baumrind, D. (1971). Current patterns of parental authority. *Developmental Psychology Monographs, 4*(1, part 2). (10)

Baylor, D. A., Lamb, T. D., & Yau, K.-W. (1979). Responses of retinal rods to single photons. *Journal of Physiology* (London), *288,* 613–634. (4)

Beach, F. A. (1950). The snark was a boojum. *American Psychologist, 5,* 115–124. (1)

Beardslee, W. R., Bemporad, J., Keller, M. B., & Klerman, G. L. (1983). Children of parents with major affective disorder: A review. *American Journal of Psychiatry, 140,* 825–832. (14)

Beck, A. T. (1973). *The diagnosis and management of depression.* Philadelphia: University of Pennsylvania Press. (14)

Beck, A. T. (1976). *Cognitive therapy and the emotional disorders.* New York: New American Library. (15)

Beck, A. T. (1987). Cognitive models of depression. *Journal of Cognitive Psychotherapy: An International Quarterly, 1,* 5–37. (14)

Beck, A. T. (1991). Cognitive therapy: A 30-year retrospective. *American Psychologist, 46,* 368–375. (15)

Beck, A. T., & Emery, G. (1985). *Anxiety disorders and phobias.* New York: Basic Books. (14)

Beck, A. T., & Steer, R. A. (1989). Clinical predictors of eventual suicide: A 5- to 10-year prospective study of suicide attempters. *Journal of Affective Disorders, 17,* 203–209. (14)

Beck, A. T., Steer, R. A., Beck, J. S., & Newman, C. F. (1993). Hopelessness, depression, suicidal ideation, and clinical diagnosis of depression. *Suicide and Life-Threatening Behavior, 23,* 139–145. (14)

Beck, A. T., Steer, R. A., & Brown, G. (1993). Dysfunctional attitudes and suicidal ideation in psychiatric outpatients. *Suicide and Life-Threatening Behavior, 23,* 11–20. (14)

Bellugi, U., Poizner, H., & Klima, E. S. (1983). Brain organization for language: Clues from sign aphasia. *Human Neurobiology, 2,* 155–170. (3)

Bellugi, U., Wang, P. P., & Jernigan, T. L. (1994). Williams syndrome: An unusual neuropsychological profile. In S. H. Broman & J. Grafman (Eds.), *Atypical cognitive deficits in developmental disorders* (pp. 23–56). Hillsdale, NJ: Lawrence Erlbaum. (2)

Belmore, S. M. (1987). Determinants of attention during impression formation. *Journal of Experimental Psychology: Learning, Memory, and Cognition, 13,* 480–489. (16)

Bem, D. J., & Honorton, C. (1994). Does psi exist? Replicable evidence for an anomalous process of information transfer. *Psychological Bulletin, 115,* 4–18. (2)

Bem, S. L. (1974). The measurement of psychological androgyny. *Journal of Consulting and Clinical Psychology, 42,* 155–162. (13)

Benes, F. M. (1995). Is there a neuroanatomic basis for schizophrenia? An old question revisited. *The Neuroscientist, 1,* 104–115. (14)

Bennett, W. (1980). The cigarette century. *Science 80, 1*(6), 36–43. (5, 14)

Benowitz, N. L. (1986). The human pharmacology of nicotine. *Research Advances in Alcohol and Drug Problems, 9,* 1–52. (14)

Benson, H. (1977). Systemic hypertension and the relaxation response. *New England Journal of Medicine, 296,* 1152–1156. (12)

Benson, H. (1985). Stress, health, and the relaxation response. In W. D. Gentry, H. Benson, & C. J. de Wolff (Eds.), *Behavioral medicine: Work, stress and health* (pp. 15–32). Dordrecht, Netherlands: Martinus Nijhoff. (12)

Berglas, S., & Jones, E. E. (1978). Drug choice as a self-handicapping strategy in response to noncontingent success. *Journal of Personality and Social Psychology, 36,* 405–417. (5, 16)

Berkow, R. (Ed.) (1987). *The Merck Manual* (15th ed.). Rahway, NJ: Merck Sharp & Dohme Research Laboratories. (11)

Berkowitz, L. (1983). Aversively stimulated aggression: Some parallels and differences in research with animals and humans. *American Psychologist, 38,* 1135–1144. (12)

Berkowitz, L. (1989). Frustration-aggression hypothesis: Examination and reformulation. *Psychological Bulletin, 106,* 59–73. (12)

Berlyne, D. E. (1981). Humanistic psychology as a protest movement. In J. R. Royce & L. P. Mos (Eds.), *Humanistic psychology: Concepts and criticisms* (pp. 261–293). New York: Plenum. (13)

Berman, K. F., Torrey, E. F., Daniel, D. G., & Weinberger, D. R. (1992). Regional cerebral blood flow in monozygotic twins discordant and concordant for schizophrenia. *Archives of General Psychiatry, 49,* 927–934. (14)

Berntson, G. G., Cacioppo, J. T., & Quigley, K. S. (1991). Autonomic determinism: The modes of autonomic control, the doctrine of autonomic space, and the laws of autonomic constraint. *Psychological Review, 98,* 459–487. (12)

Berntson, G. G., Cacioppo, J. T., & Quigley, K. S. (1993). Cardiac psychophysiology and autonomic space in humans: Empirical perspectives and conceptual implications. *Psychological Bulletin, 114,* 296–322. (12)

Berry, J. W., Poortinga, Y. H., Segal, H., & Dasen, P. R. (1992). *Cross-cultural psychology.* Cambridge, England: Cambridge University Press. (14)

Berscheid, E. (1983). Emotion. In H. H. Kelley, E. Berscheid, A. Christensen, J. H. Harvey, T. L. Huston, G. Levinger, E. McClintock, L. A. Peplau, & D. R. Peterson, *Close relationships* (pp. 110–168). New York: W. H. Freeman. (16)

Berscheid, E., Snyder, M., & Omoto, A. M. (1989). Issues in studying close relationships. In C. Hendrick (Ed.), *Close relationships* (pp. 63–91). Newbury Park, CA: Sage. (16)

Bilger, B. (1994, September/October). Keeping our words. *The Sciences, 34*(5), 18–20. (8)

Billy, J. O. G., Tanfer, K., Grady, W. R., & Klepinger, D. H. (1993, March/April). The sexual behavior of men in the United States. *Family Planning Perspectives, 25,* 52–60. (11)

Binet, A., & Simon, T. (1905). Méthodes nouvelles pour le diagnostic du niveau intellectual des anormaux [New methods for the measurement of the intellectual level of the abnormal]. *L'Année Psychologique, 11,* 191–244. (9)

Birnbaum, M. H., & Sotoodeh, Y. (1991). Measurement of stress: Scaling the magnitudes of life changes. *Psychological Science, 2,* 236–243. (12)

Bjorklund, D. F., & Green, B. L. (1992). The adaptive nature of cognitive immaturity. *American Psychologist, 47,* 46–54. (10)

Black, D. W., Noyes, R., Jr., Goldstein, R. B., & Blum, N. (1992). A family study of obsessive-compulsive disorder. *Archives of General Psychiatry, 49,* 362–368. (14)

Blackmore, S. (1994). Psi in psychology. *Skeptical Inquirer, 18,* 351–355. (2)

Blackwood, D. H. R., St. Clair, D. M., Muir, W. J., & Duffy, J. C. (1991). Auditory P300 and eye tracking dysfunction in schizophrenic pedigrees. *Archives of General Psychiatry, 48,* 899–909. (14)

Blaine, J. D., Prien, R. F., & Levine, J. (1983). The role of antidepressants in the treatment of affective disorders. *American Journal of Psychotherapy, 37,* 502–520. (15)

Blakemore, C., & Sutton, P. (1969). Size adaptation: A new aftereffect. *Science, 166,* 245–247. (4)

Bleuler, E. (1911/1950). *Dementia praecox, or the group of schizophrenias* (J. Zinkin, Trans.). New York: International Universities Press. (Original work published 1911.) (14)

Bliwise, D. L., Bliwise, N. G., Partinen, M., Pursley, A. M., & Dement, W. C. (1988). Sleep apnea and mortality in an aged cohort. *American Journal of Public Health, 78,* 544–547. (5)

Block, J. (1995). A contrarian view of the five-factor approach to personality description. *Psychological Bulletin, 117,* 187–215. (13)

Bloom, B. L., White, S. W., & Asher, S. J. (1979). Marital disruption as a stressful life event. In G. Levinger & O. C. Moles (Eds.), *Divorce and separation* (pp. 184–200). New York: Basic Books. (16)

Bloom, J. D., & Faulkner, L. R. (1987). Competency determinations in civil commitment. *American Journal of Psychiatry, 144,* 193–196. (15)

Blum, G. S., & Barbour, J. S. (1979). Selective inattention to anxiety-linked stimuli. *Journal of Experimental Psychology: General, 108,* 182–224. (4)

Blumenthal, S. J., & Kupfer, D. J. (1986). Generalizable treatment strategies for suicidal behavior. *Annals of the New York Academy of Sciences, 487,* 327–340. (14)

Bollard, J. (1982). A 2-year follow-up of bedwetters treated by dry-bed training and standard conditioning. *Behaviour Research and Therapy, 20,* 571–580. (15)

Bondi, M. W., Monsch, A. U., Galaski, D., Butters, N., Salmon, D. P., & Delis, D. C. (1994). Preclinical cognitive markers of dementia of the Alzheimer type. *Neuropsychology, 8,* 374–384. (7)

Booth, A., Shelley, G., Mazur, A., Tharp, G., & Kittok, R. (1989). Testosterone, and winning and losing in human competition. *Hormones and Behavior, 23,* 556–571. (2)

Booth-Kewley, S., & Friedman, H. S. (1987). Psychological predictors of heart disease: A quantitative review. *Psychological Bulletin, 101,* 343–362. (12)

Boring, E. G. (1930). A new ambiguous figure. *American Journal of Psychology, 42,* 444–445. (4)

Bornstein, R. F. (1989). Subliminal techniques as propaganda tools: Review and critique. *Journal of Mind and Behavior, 10,* 231–262. (4)

Bossard, J. H. S. (1931). Residential propinquity as a factor in marriage selection. *American Journal of Sociology, 38,* 219–224. (16)

Boswell, J. (1990). Sexual and ethical categories in premodern Europe. In D. P. McWhirter, S. A. Sanders, & J. M. Reinisch (Eds.), *Homosexuality/heterosexuality* (pp. 15–31). New York: Oxford University Press. (11)

Bouchard, T. J., Lykken, D. T., McGue, M., Segal, N. L., & Tellegen, A. (1990). Sources of psychological differences: The Minnesota study of twins reared apart. *Science, 250,* 223–228. (10)

Bouchard, T. J., Jr., & McGue, M. (1981). Familial studies of intelligence: A review. *Science, 212,* 1055–1059. (9)

Bourne, P. G. (1971). Altered adrenal function in two combat situations in Viet Nam. In B. E. Eleftheriou & J. P. Scott (Eds.), *The physiology of aggression and defeat* (pp. 265–290). New York: Plenum. (12)

Bouton, M. E. (1994). Context, ambiguity, and classical conditioning. *Current Directions in Psychological Science, 3,* 49–53. (6)

Bower, T. G. R., & Wishart, J. G. (1972). Effects of motor skill on object permanence. *Cognition, 1,* 165–172. (10)

Bowers, K. S., Regehr, G., Balthazard, C., & Parker, K. (1990). Intuition in the context of discovery. *Cognitive Psychology, 22,* 72–110. (8)

Bowlby, J. (1952). *Maternal care and mental health.* Geneva: World Health Organization. (10)

Boyd, J. H. (1983). The increasing rate of suicide by firearms. *New England Journal of Medicine, 308,* 872–874. (14)

Boynton, R. M. (1988). Color vision. *Annual Review of Psychology, 39,* 69–100. (4)

Bradbury, T. N., & Miller, G. A. (1985). Season of birth in schizophrenia: A review of evidence, methodology, and etiology. *Psychological Bulletin, 98,* 569–594. (14)

Bradley, J. V. (1959). *Tactual coding of cylindrical knobs.* (Technical Report No. 59–182). Dayton, OH: Wright Air Development Center. (A)

Brannon, L., & Feist, J. (1992). *Health psychology* (2nd ed.). Belmont, CA: Wadsworth. (12)

Bransford, J. D., & Johnson, M. K. (1972). Contextual prerequisites for understanding: Some investigations of comprehension and recall. *Journal of Verbal Learning and Verbal Behavior, 11,* 717–726. (7)

Bransford, J. D., & Stein, B. S. (1984). *The ideal problem solver.* New York: W. H. Freeman. (8)

Braun, P., Kochansky, G., Shapiro, R., Greenberg, S., Gudeman, J. E., Johnson, S., & Shore, M. F. (1981). Overview: Deinstitutionalization of psychiatric patients: A critical review of outcome studies. *American Journal of Psychiatry, 138,* 736–749. (15)

Bregman, A. S. (1981). Asking the "what for" question in auditory perception. In M. Kubovy & J. R. Pomerantz (Eds.), *Perceptual organization* (pp. 99–118). Hillsdale, NJ: Lawrence Erlbaum. (4)

Brent, D. A., Perper, J. A., Goldstein, C. E., Kolko, D. J., Allan, M. J., Allman, C. J., & Zelenak, J. P. (1988). Risk factors for adolescent suicide. *Archives of General Psychiatry, 45,* 581–588. (14)

Breuer, J., & Freud, S. (1957). *Studies on Hysteria* (J. Strachey, Trans. and Ed.). New York: Basic Books. (Original work published 1895.) (13)

Brocke, B., & Battmann, W. (1992). The arousal-activation theory of extraversion and neuroticism: A systematic analysis and principal conclusions. *Advances in Behaviour Research and Therapy, 14,* 211–246. (13)

Brockner, J., & Rubin, J. Z. (1985). *Entrapment in escalating conflicts.* New York: Springer-Verlag. (16)

Brooks-Gunn, J., & Furstenberg, F. F., Jr. (1989). Adolescent sexual behavior. *American Psychologist, 44,* 249–257. (10, 11)

Brophy, J. (1987). Socializing students' motivation to learn. *Advances in Motivation and Achievement, 5,* 181–210. (11)

Brower, K. J., & Anglin, M. D. (1987). Adolescent cocaine use: Epidemiology, risk factors, and prevention. *Journal of Drug Education, 17,* 163–180. (5)

Brown, G. W., Harris, T. O., & Hepworth, C. (1994). Life events and endogenous depression. *Archives of General Psychiatry, 51,* 525–534. (14)

Brown, R., & Kulik, J. (1977). Flashbulb memories. *Cognition, 5,* 73–99. (7)

Brown, R. J., & Donderi, D. C. (1986). Dream content and reported well-being among recurrent dreamers, past-recurrent dreamers, and nonrecurrent dreamers. *Journal of Personality and Social Psychology, 50,* 612–623. (5)

Brownell, K. D., & Rodin, J. (1994). The dieting maelstrom: Is it possible and advisable to lose weight? *American Psychologist, 49,* 781–791. (11)

Bruch, H. (1980). Preconditions for the development of anorexia nervosa. *American Journal of Psychoanalysis, 40,* 169–172. (11)

Bruck, M., Cavanagh, P., & Ceci, S. J. (1991). Fortysomething: Recognizing faces at one's 25th reunion. *Memory & Cognition, 19,* 221–228. (4)

Bruner, J. S., & Potter, M. C. (1964). Interference in visual recognition. *Science, 144,* 424–425. (8)

Buck, L., & Axel, R. (1991). A novel multigene family may encode odorant receptors: A molecular basis for odor recognition. *Cell, 65,* 175–187. (4)

Buck, R. (1994). Social and emotional functions in facial expression and communication: the readout hypothesis. *Biological Psychology, 38,* 95–115. (12)

Burger, J. M. (1986). Increasing compliance by improving the deal: The that's-not-all technique. *Journal of Personality and Social Psychology, 51,* 277–283. (8)

Burke, H. R. (1985). Raven's Progressive Matrices (1938): More on norms, reliability, and validity. *Journal of Clinical Psychology, 41,* 231–235. (9)

Burke, K. C., Burke, J. D., Jr., Regier, D. A., & Rae, D. S. (1990). Age at onset of selected mental disorders in five community populations. *Archives of General Psychiatry, 47,* 511–518. (14)

Burley, K. A. (1991). Family-work spillover in dual-career couples: A comparison of two time perspectives. *Psychological Reports, 68,* 471–480. (10)

Burns, M. O., & Seligman, M. E. P. (1989). Explanatory style across the life span: Evidence for stability over 52 years. *Journal of Personality and Social Psychology, 56,* 471–477. (14)

Burnstein, E., & Vinokur, A. (1973). Testing two classes of theories about group-induced shifts in individual choice. *Journal of Experimental Social Psychology, 9,* 123–137. (16)

Burnstein, E., & Vinokur, A. (1977). Persuasive arguments and social comparison as determinants of attitude polarization. *Journal of Experimental Social Psychology, 13,* 315–332. (16)

Burr, D. C., Morrone, M. C., & Ross, J. (1994). Selective suppression of the magnocellular visual pathway during saccadic eye movements. *Nature, 371,* 511–513. (8)

Burrows, G. D., McIntyre, I. M., Judd, F. K., & Norman, T. R. '(1988, August). Clinical effects of serotonin reuptake inhibitors in the treatment of depressive illness. *Journal of Clinical Psychiatry, 49* (Suppl. 8), 18–22. (15)

Bushman, B. J. (1993). Human aggression while under the influence of alcohol and other drugs: An integrative research review. *Current Directions in Psychological Science, 2,* 148–152. (12)

Bushman, B. J., & Cooper, H. M. (1990). Effects of alcohol on human aggression: An integrative research review. *Psychological Bulletin, 107,* 341–354. (12)

Buss, D. M. (1994). The strategies of human mating. *American Scientist, 82,* 238–249. (3, 16)

Buss, D. M., Larsen, R. J., Westen, D., & Semmelroth, J. (1992). Sex differences in jealousy: Evolution, physiology, and psychology. *Psychological Science, 3,* 251–255. (16)

Butcher, J. N., Graham, J. R., Williams, C. L., & Ben-Porath, Y. S. (1990). *Development and use of the MMPI-2 content scales.* Minneapolis: University of Minnesota Press. (13)

Cadoret, R., Troughton, E., & Woodworth, G. (1994). Evidence of heterogeneity of genetic effect in Iowa adoption studies. *Annals of the New York Academy of Sciences, 708,* 59–71. (14)

Cahalan, D. (1978). Subcultural differences in drinking behavior in U.S. national surveys and selected European studies. In P. E. Nathan, G. A. Marlatt, & T. Løberg (Eds.), *Alcoholism: New directions in behavioral research and treatment* (pp. 235–253). New York: Plenum. (14)

Cahill, L., Prins, B., Weber, M., & McGaugh, J. L. (1994). β-Adrenergic activation and memory for emotional events. *Nature, 371,* 702–704. (7)

Caine, S. B., & Koob, G. F. (1993). Modulation of cocaine self-administration in the rat through D-3 dopamine receptors. *Science, 260,* 1814–1816. (14)

Camara, W. J. (1988). Reagan signs ban on polygraph testing for job applicants. *The Industrial-Organizational Psychologist, 26,* 39–41. (12)

Camara, W. J., & Schneider, D. L. (1994). Integrity tests: Facts and unresolved issues. *American Psychologist, 49,* 112–119. (12)

Camel, J. E., Withers, G. S., & Greenough, W. T. (1986). Persistence of visual cortex dendritic alterations induced by postweaning exposure to a "superenriched" environment in rats. *Behavioral Neuroscience, 100,* 810–813. (3)

Cameron, P., Proctor, K., Coburn, W., & Forde, N. (1985). Sexual orientation and sexually transmitted disease. *Nebraska Medical Journal, 70,* 292–299. (11)

Campbell, S. S., & Tobler, I. (1984). Animal sleep: A review of sleep duration across phylogeny. *Neuroscience & Biobehavioral Reviews, 8,* 269–300. (5)

Campion, M. A., & McClelland, C. L. (1991). Interdisciplinary examination of the costs and benefits of enlarged jobs: A job design quasi-experiment. *Journal of Applied Psychology, 76,* 186–198. (A)

Campion, M. A., Pursell, E. D., & Brown, B. K. (1988). Structured interviewing: Raising the psychometric properties of the employment interview. *Personnel Psychology, 41,* 25–42. (A)

Campion, M. A., & Thayer, P. W. (1985). Development and field evaluation of an interdisciplinary measure of job design. *Journal of Applied Psychology, 70,* 29–43. (A)

Campion, M. A., & Thayer, P. W. (1989). How do you design a job? *Personnel Journal, 68,* 43–46. (A)

Campos, J. J., Bertenthal, B. I., & Kermoian, R. (1992). Early experience and emotional development. *Psychological Science, 3,* 61–64. (14)

Cannon, T. D., Zorilla, L. E., Shtasel, D., Gur, R. E., Gur, R. C., Marco, E. J., Moberg, P., & Price, R. A. (1994). Neuropsychological functioning in siblings discordant for schizophrenia and healthy volunteers. *Archives of General Psychiatry, 51,* 651–661. (14)

Cannon, W. B. (1927). The James-Lange theory of emotion. *American Journal of Psychology, 39,* 106–124. (12)

Cannon, W. B. (1929). Organization for physiological homeostasis. *Physiological Reviews, 9,* 399–431. (11)

Cantor, N., & Fleeson, W. (1994). Social intelligence and intelligent goal pursuit: A cognitive slice of motivation. In W. D. Spaulding (Ed.), *Integrative views of motivation, cognition, and emotion* (pp. 125–179). Lincoln, NE: University of Nebraska Press. (11)

Caplan, P. J. (1995). *They say you're crazy.* Reading, MA: Addison Wesley. (14)

Carey, S. (1978). The child as word learner. In M. Halle, J. Bresnan, & G. A. Miller (Eds.), *Linguistic theory and psychological reality* (pp. 264–293). Cambridge, MA: MIT Press. (10)

Carpenter, P. A., Just, M. A., & Shell, P. (1990). What one intelligence test measures: A theoretical account of the processing in the Raven Progressive Matrices test. *Psychological Review, 97,* 404–431. (9)

Carpenter, W. T. (1995). Serotonin-dopamine antagonists and treatment of negative symptoms. *Journal of Clinical Psychopharmacology, 15* (Suppl. 1), S30–S35. (15)

Carroll, B. J. (1980). Implications of biological research for the diagnosis of depression. In J. Mendlewicz (Ed.), *New advances in the diagnosis and treatment of depressive illness* (pp. 85–107). Amsterdam: Excerpta Medica. (14)

Carson, C. C., Huelskamp, R. M., & Woodall, T. D. (1993). Perspectives on education in America. *Journal of Educational Research, 86,* 259–310. (9)

Catania, J. A., Coates, T. J., Stall, R., Turner, H., Peterson, J., Hearst, N., Dolcini, M. M., Hudes, E., Gagnon, J., Wiley, J., & Groves, R. (1992). Prevalence of AIDS-related risk factors and condom use in the United States. *Science, 258,* 1101–1106. (11)

Cattell, R. B. (1965). *The scientific analysis of personality.* Chicago: Aldine. (13)

Cattell, R. B. (1987). *Intelligence: Its structure, growth and action.* Amsterdam: North-Holland. (9)

Cavell, T. A., & Woehr, D. J. (1994). Predicting introductory psychology test scores: An engaging and useful topic. *Teaching of Psychology, 21,* 108–110. (2)

Ceci, S. J., & Bruck, M. (1993). Suggestibility of the child witness: A historical review and synthesis. *Psychological Bulletin, 113,* 403–439. (7)

Ceci, S. J., Ross, D. F., & Toglia, M. P. (1987). Suggestibility of children's memory: Psycholegal implications. *Journal of Experimental Psychology: General, 116,* 38–49. (7)

Chamberlin, J. (1978). *On our own.* New York: Hawthorn. (15)

Chapanis, A. (1965). *Man-machine engineering.* Belmont, CA: Wadsworth. (A)

Charlton, S. G. (1983). Differential conditionability: Reinforcing grooming in golden hamsters. *Animal Learning & Behavior, 11,* 27–34. (6)

Cheetham, E. (1973). *The prophecies of Nostradamus.* New York: Putnam's. (2)

Chen, C., Lee, S., & Stevenson, H. W. (1995). Response style and cross-cultural comparisons of rating scales among East Asian and North American students. *Psychological Science, 6,* 170–175. (16)

Cherlin, A. J., Furstenberg, F. F., Jr., Chase-Lansdale, P. L., Kiernan, K. E., Robins, P. K., Morrison, D. R., & Teitler, J. O. (1991). Longitudinal studies of effects of divorce on children in Great Britain and the United States. *Science, 252,* 1386–1389. (10)

Chiodo, L. A., & Antelman, S. M. (1980). Electroconvulsive shock: Progressive dopamine autoreceptor subsensitivity independent of repeated treatment. *Science, 210,* 799–801. (15)

Chiueh, C. C. (1988). Dopamine in the extrapyramidal motor function. *Annals of the New York Academy of Sciences, 515,* 226–238. (3)

Chomsky, N. (1980). *Rules and representations.* New York: Columbia University Press. (8)

Chouinard, G., & Jones, B. D. (1980). Neuroleptic-induced supersensitivity psychosis: Clinical and pharmacological characteristics. *American Journal of Psychiatry, 137,* 16–21. (15)

Christensen, A., & Jacobson, N. S. (1994). Who (or what) can do psychotherapy: The status and challenge of nonprofessional therapies. *Psychological Science, 5,* 8–14. (15)

Cialdini, R. B. (1985). *Influence: Science and practice.* Glenview, IL: Scott, Foresman. (6)

Cialdini, R. B., Vincent, J. E., Lewis, S. K., Catalan, J., Wheeler, D., & Darby, B. L. (1975). Reciprocal concessions procedure for inducing compliance: The door-in-the-face technique. *Journal of Personality and Social Psychology, 31,* 206–215. (16)

Cioffi, D. (1991). Beyond attentional strategies: A cognitive-perceptual model of somatic interpretation. *Psychological Bulletin, 109,* 25–41. (12)

Cirignotta, F., Todesco, C. V., & Lugaresi, E. (1980). Temporal lobe epilepsy with ecstatic seizures (so-called Dostoevsky epilepsy). *Epilepsia, 21,* 705–710. (3)

Clark, H. H., & Chase, W. G. (1972). On the process of comparing sentences against pictures. *Cognitive Psychology, 3,* 472–517. (8)

Clarke, A. M., & Clarke, A. D. B. (1976). *Early experience: Myth and evidence.* New York: Free Press. (10)

Clarke-Stewart, K. A. (1989). Infant day care: Maligned or malignant? *American Psychologist, 44,* 266–273. (10)

Clarkin, J. F., & Carpenter, D. (1995). Family therapy in historical perspective. In B. Bongar & L. E. Beutler (Eds.), *Comprehensive textbook of psychotherapy: Theory and practice* (pp. 205–227). Oxford, England: Oxford University Press. (15)

Clausen, J. A., & Gilens, M. (1990). Personality and labor force participation across the life course: A longitudinal study of women's careers. *Sociological Forum, 5,* 595–618. (A)

Clementz, B. A., & Sweeney, J. A. (1990). Is eye movement dysfunction a biological marker for schizophrenia? A methodological review. *Psychological Review, 108,* 77–92. (14)

Clifford, M. M., & Walster, E. (1973). The effect of physical attractiveness on teacher expectation. *Sociology of Education, 46,* 248–258. (16)

Clifton, R., Siqueland, E. R., & Lipsitt, L. P. (1972). Conditioned head-turning in human newborns as a function of conditioned response requirements and states of wakefulness. *Journal of Experimental Child Psychology, 13,* 43–57. (10)

"Clinicopathologic conference" (1967). *Johns Hopkins Medical Journal, 120,* 186–199. (12)

Clohessy, A. B., Posner, M. I., Rothbart, M. K., & Veccra, S. P. (1991). The development of inhibition of return in early infancy. *Journal of Cognitive Neuroscience, 3,* 345–350. (10)

Clomipramine collaborative study group (1991). Clomipramine in the treatment of patients with obsessive-compulsive disorder. *Archives of General Psychiatry, 48,* 730–738. (15)

Cloninger, C. R. (1987). Neurogenetic adaptive mechanisms in alcoholism. *Science, 236,* 410–416. (14)

Cloninger, C. R. (1994). Temperament and personality. *Current Opinion in Neurobiology, 4,* 266–273. (13)

Cloninger, C. R., Bohman, M., & Sigvardsson, S. (1981). Inheritance of alcohol abuse: Cross-fostering analysis of adopted men. *Archives of General Psychiatry, 38,* 861–868. (3, 14)

Cocozza, J., Melick, M., & Steadman, H. (1978). Trends in violent crime among ex-mental patients. *Criminology, 16,* 317–334. (15)

Coffey, C. E., Weiner, R. D., Djang, W. T., Figiel, G. S., Soady, S. A. R., Patterson, L. J., Holt, P. D., Spritzer, C. E., & Wilkinson, W. E. (1991). Brain anatomic effects of electroconvulsive therapy. *Archives of General Psychiatry, 48,* 1013–1021. (15)

Cohen, J. D., Dunbar, K., & McClelland, J. L. (1990). On the control of automatic processes: A parallel distributed processing account of the Stroop effect. *Psychological Review, 97,* 332–361. (8)

Cohen, N. J., Eichenbaum, H., Deacedo, B. S., & Corkin, S. (1985). Different memory systems underlying acquisition of procedural and declarative knowledge. *Annals of the New York Academy of Sciences, 444,* 54–71. (7)

Cohen, N. J., & Squire, L. R. (1980). Preserved learning and retention of pattern-analyzing skill in amnesia: Dissociation of knowing how and knowing that. *Science, 210,* 207–211. (7)

Cohen, S., Lichtenstein, E., Prochaska, J. O., Rossi, J. S., Gritz, E. R., Carr, C. R., Orleans, C. T., Schoenbach, V. J., Biener, L., Abrams, D., DiClemente, C., Curry, S., Marlatt, G. A., Cummings, K. M., Emont, S. L., Giovino, G., & Ossip-Klein, D. (1989). Debunking myths about self-quitting: Evidence from 10 prospective studies of persons who attempt to quit smoking by themselves. *American Psychologist, 44,* 1355–1365. (14)

Cohen, S. L., & Cohen, R. (1985). The role of activity in spatial cognition. In R. Cohen (Ed.), *The development of spatial cognition* (pp. 199–223). Hillsdale, NJ: Lawrence Erlbaum. (8)

Coie, J. D., & Dodge, K. (1983). Continuities and change in children's social status: A five-year longitudinal study. *Merrill-Palmer Quarterly, 29,* 261–282. (10)

Coile, D. C., & Miller, N. (1984). How radical animal activists try to mislead humane people. *American Psychologist, 39,* 700–701. (2)

Cole, J. O., Goldberg, S. C., & Davis, J. M. (1966). Drugs in the treatment of psychosis. In P. Solomon (Ed.), *Psychiatric drugs* (pp. 153–180). New York: Grune & Stratton. (15)

Cole, N. S. (1981). Bias in testing. *American Psychologist, 36,* 1067–1077. (9)

Collins, A. M., & Loftus, E. F. (1975). A spreading-activation theory of semantic processing. *Psychological Review, 82,* 407–428. (8)

Collins, A. M., & Quillian, M. R. (1969). Retrieval time from semantic memory. *Journal of Verbal Learning and Verbal Behavior, 8,* 240–247. (8)

Collins, A. M., & Quillian, M. R. (1970). Does category size affect categorization time? *Journal of Verbal Learning and Verbal Behavior, 9,* 432–438. (8)

Collins, N. L., & Miller, L. C. (1994). Self-disclosure and liking: A meta-analytic review. *Psychological Bulletin, 116,* 457–475. (16)

Collins, W. A., & Gunnar, M. R. (1990). Social and personality development. *Annual Review of Psychology, 41,* 387–416. (10)

Colvin, C. R., & Block, J. (1994). Do positive illusions foster mental health? An examination of the Taylor and Brown formulation. *Psychological Bulletin, 116,* 3–20. (12)

Colwill, R. M. (1993). An associative analysis of instrumental learning. *Current Directions in Psychological Science, 2,* 111–116. (6)

Connine, C. M., Blasko, D. G., & Hall, M. (1991). Effects of subsequent sentence context in auditory word recognition: Temporal and linguistic constraints. *Journal of Memory and Language, 30,* 234–250. (8)

Comings, D. E., & Amromin, G. D. (1974). Autosomal dominant insensitivity to pain with hyperplastic myelinopathy and autosomal dominant indifference to pain. *Neurology, 24,* 838–848. (4)

Comstock, G., & Strasburger, V. C. (1990). Deceptive appearances: Television violence and aggressive behavior. Conference: Teens and television. *Journal of Adolescent Health Care, 11,* 31–44. (2)

Constantinides, P. (1977). Ill at ease and sick at heart: Symbolic behavior in a Sudanese healing cult. In I. Wilson (Ed.), *Symbols and sentiments* (pp. 61–84). New York: Academic Press. (14)

Corder, E. H., Saunders, A. M., Strittatter, W. J., Schmechel, D. E., Gaskell, P. C., Small, G. W., Roses, A. D., Haines, J. L., & Pericak-Vance, M. A. (1993). Gene dose of apolipoprotein E type 4 allele and the risk of Alzheimer's disease in late onset families. *Science, 261,* 921–923. (7)

Corkin, S. (1984). Lasting consequences of bilateral medial temporal lobectomy: Clinical course and experimental findings in H. M. *Seminars in Neurology, 4,* 249–259. (7)

Costa, P. T., Jr., & McCrae, R. R. (1992). Four ways five factors are basic. *Personality and Individual Differences, 13,* 653–665. (13)

Costa, P. T., Jr., & McCrae, R. R. (1994). Set like plaster? Evidence for the stability of adult personality. In T. F. Heatherton & J. L. Weinberger (Eds.), *Can personality change?* (pp. 21–40). Washington, D.C.: American Psychological Association. (13)

Costa, P. T., Jr., & McCrae, R. R. (1995). Domains and facets: Hierarchical personality assessment using the revised NEO Personality Inventory. *Journal of Personality Assessment, 64,* 21–50. (13)

Costa, P. T., Jr., McCrae, R. R., & Dye, D. A. (1991). Facet scales for agreeableness and conscientiousness: A revision of the NEO personality inventory. *Personality and Individual Differences, 12,* 887–898. (13)

Cowan, C. L., Thompson, W. C., & Ellsworth, P. C. (1984). The effects of death qualification on jurors' predisposition to convict and on the quality of deliberation. *Law and Human Behavior, 8,* 53–79. (16)

Craig, A. D., Bushnell, M. C., Zhang, E.-T., & Blomqvist, A. (1994). A thalamic nucleus specific for pain and temperature sensation. *Nature, 372,* 770–773. (4)

Craik, F. I. M., & Lockhart, R. S. (1972). Levels of processing: A framework for memory research. *Journal of Verbal Learning and Verbal Behavior, 11,* 671–684. (7)

Craik, F. I. M., & Watkins, M. J. (1973). The role of rehearsal in short-term memory. *Journal of Verbal Learning and Verbal Behavior, 12,* 599–607. (7)

Crammer, J. L. (1959). Water and sodium in two psychotics. *Lancet, i*(7083), 1122–1126. (14)

Crews, D. J., & Landers, D. M. (1987). A meta-analytic review of aerobic fitness and reactivity to psychosocial stressors. *Medicine & Science in Sports & Exercise, 19,* S114–S120. (12)

Crocker, J., & Major, B. (1989). Social stigma and self-esteem: The self-protective properties of stigma. *Psychological Review, 96,* 608–630. (16)

Cross, C. K., & Hirschfeld, R. M. A. (1986). Psychosocial factors and suicidal behavior. *Annals of the New York Academy of Sciences, 487,* 77–89. (14)

Crouter, A. C., Perry-Jenkins, M., Huston, T. L., & McHale, S. M. (1987). Processes underlying father involvement in dual-earner and single-earner families. *Developmental Psychology, 23,* 431–440. (10)

Cummings, J. L., & Victoroff, J. I. (1990). Noncognitive neuropsychiatric syndromes in Alzheimer's disease. *Neuropsychiatry, Neuropsychology, & Behavioral Neurology, 3,* 140–158. (3, 7)

Cummings, N. A. (1979). Turning bread into stones: Our modern antimiracle. *American Psychologist, 34,* 1119–1129. (11, 14)

Curry, S., Marlatt, A., & Gordon, J. R. (1987). Abstinence violation effect: Validation of an attributional construct with smoking cessation. *Journal of Consulting and Clinical Psychology, 55,* 145–149. (6)

Cutting, J. E. (1987). Rigidity in cinema seen from the front row, side aisle. *Journal of Experimental Psychology: Human Perception and Performance, 13,* 323–334. (4)

Czeisler, C. A., Johnson, M. P., Duffy, J. F., Brown, E. N., Ronda, J. M., & Kronauer, R. E. (1990). Exposure to bright light and darkness to treat physiologic maladaptation to night work. *New England Journal of Medicine, 322,* 1353–1359. (5)

Czeisler, C. A., Moore-Ede, M. C., & Coleman, R. M. (1982). Rotating shift work schedules that disrupt sleep are improved by applying circadian principles. *Science, 217,* 460–463. (5)

Dabbs, J. M., & Morris, R. (1990). Testosterone, social class, and antisocial behavior in a sample of 4,462 men. *Psychological Science, 1,* 209–211. (12)

Dackis, C. A., Pottash, A. L. C., Annitto, W., & Gold, M. S. (1982). Persistence of urinary marijuana levels after supervised abstinence. *American Journal of Psychiatry, 139,* 1196–1198. (5)

Dallenbach, K. M. (1951). A puzzle picture with a new principle of concealment. *American Journal of Psychology, 64,* 431–433. (4)

Damaser, E. C., Shor, R. E., & Orne, M. E. (1963). Physiological effects during hypnotically requested emotions. *Psychosomatic Medicine, 25,* 334–343. (5)

Damasio, A. R. (1994). *Descartes' error: Emotion, reason, and the human brain.* New York: G. P. Putnam's Sons. (12)

Damasio, H., Grabowski, T., Frank, R., Galaburda, A. M., & Damasio, A. R. (1994). The return of Phineas Gage: The skull of a famous patient yields clues about the brain. *Science, 264,* 1102–1105. (12)

Damron-Rodriguez, J. (1991). Commentary: Multicultural aspects of aging in the U.S.: Implications for health and human services. *Journal of Cross-cultural Gerontology, 6,* 135–143. (10)

Darley, J. M., & Shultz, T. R. (1990). Moral rules: Their content and acquisition. *Annual Review of Psychology, 41,* 525–556. (10)

Darling, N., & Steinberg, L. (1993). Parenting style as context: An integrative model. *Psychological Bulletin, 113,* 487–496. (10)

Darlington, R. B., Royce, J. M., Snipper, A. S., Murray, H. W., & Lazar, I. (1980). Preschool programs and later school competence of children from low-income families. *Science, 208,* 202–204. (9)

Darwin, C. (1859). *On the origin of species by means of natural selection.* London: Murray. (1)

Darwin, C. (1871). *The descent of man.* New York: D. Appleton. (6)

Darwin, C. (1872/1965). *The expression of emotions in man and animals.* Chicago: University of Chicago Press. (Original work published 1872.) (12)

Das, J. P. (1992). Beyond a unidimensional scale of merit. *Intelligence, 16,* 137–149. (9)

Davenas, E., Beauvais, F., Amara, J., Oberbaum, M., Robinzon, B., Miadonna, A., Tedeschi, A., Pomeranz, B., Fortner, P., Belon, P., Sainte-Laudy, J., Poitevin, B., & Benveniste, J. (1988). Human basophil degranulation triggered by very dilute antiserum against IgE. *Nature, 333,* 816–818. (2)

Davenport, D., & Foley, J. M. (1979). Fringe benefits of cataract surgery. *Science, 204,* 454–457. (4)

Davenport, W. H. (1977). Sex in cross-cultural perspective. In F. A. Beach (Ed.), *Human sexuality in four perspectives* (pp. 62–86). Baltimore: Johns Hopkins University Press. (11)

Davidson, R. S. (1966). Laboratory maintenance and learning of *Alligator mississippiensis. Psychological Reports, 19,* 595–601. (6)

Davis, J. M. (1985). Maintenance therapy and the natural course of schizophrenia. *Journal of Clinical Psychiatry, 46,* 18–21. (15)

Dawes, R. M. (1994). *House of cards: Psychology and psychotherapy built on myth.* New York: Free Press. (13, 15)

Dawes, R. M., & Smith, T. L. (1985). Attitude and opinion measurement. In G. Lindzey & E. Aronson (Eds.), *Handbook of social psychology* (Vol. 1, pp. 509–566). New York: Random House. (16)

Day, R. H. (1972). Visual spatial illusions: A general explanation. *Science, 175,* 1335–1340. (4)

Deacon, T. W. (1990). Problems of ontogeny and phylogeny in brain-size evolution. *International Journal of Primatology, 11,* 237–282. (8)

Deacon, T. W. (1992). Brain-language coevolution. In J. A. Hawkins & M. Gell-Mann (Eds.), *The evolution of human languages* (pp. 49–83). Reading, MA: Addison-Wesley. (8)

Deakin, J. M., & Allard, F. (1991). Skilled memory in expert figure skaters. *Memory & Cognition, 19,* 79–86. (8)

DeCasper, A. J., & Fifer, W. P. (1980). Of human bonding: Newborns prefer their mothers' voices. *Science, 208,* 1174–1177. (10)

Deci, E. L. (1971). Effects of externally mediated rewards on intrinsic motivation. *Journal of Personality and Social Psychology, 18,* 105–115. (11)

Deci, E. L., & Ryan, R. M. (1991). A motivational approach to self: Integration in personality. In R. A. Dienstbier (Ed.), *Perspectives on motivation* (pp. 237–288). Lincoln, NE: University of Nebraska Press. (11)

de Groot, A. D. (1966). Perception and memory versus thought: Some old ideas and recent findings. In B. Kleinmuntz (Ed.), *Problem solving* (pp. 19–50). New York: Wiley. (8)

DeLoache, J. S. (1989). The development of representation in young children. *Advances in Child Development and Behavior, 22,* 1–39. (10)

Delprato, D. J., & Midgley, B. D. (1992). Some fundamentals of B. F. Skinner's behaviorism. *American Psychologist, 47,* 1507–1520. (6)

DeLuise, M., Blackburn, G. L., & Flier, J. S. (1980). Reduced activity of the red-cell sodium-potassium pump in human obesity. *New England Journal of Medicine, 303,* 1017–1022. (11)

Dement, W. (1960). The effect of dream deprivation. *Science, 131,* 1705–1707. (5)

Dement, W. C. (1972). *Some must watch while some must sleep.* Stanford, CA: Stanford Alumni Association. (5)

Dement, W., & Kleitman, N. (1957a). Cyclic variations in EEG during sleep and their relation to eye movements, body motility, and dreaming. *Electroencephalography and Clinical Neurophysiology, 9,* 673–690. (5)

Dement, W., & Kleitman, N. (1957b). The relation of eye movements during sleep to dream activity: An objective method for the study of dreaming. *Journal of Experimental Psychology, 53,* 339–346. (5)

Dement, W., & Wolpert, E. A. (1958). The relation of eye movements, body motility, and external stimuli to dream content. *Journal of Experimental Psychology, 55,* 543–553. (5)

Dennett, D. C. (1991). *Consciousness explained.* Boston: Little, Brown. (1)

DePaulo, B. M. (1992). Nonverbal behavior and self-presentation. *Psychological Bulletin, 111,* 203–243. (16)

Deprés, J.-P., Pouliot, M.-C., Moorjani, S., Nadeau, A., Tremblay, A., Lupien, P. J., Thériault, G., & Bouchard, C. (1991). Loss of abdominal fat and metabolic response to exercise training in obese women. *American Journal of Physiology, 261,* E159–E167. (11)

Derogatis, L. (1986). Psychology in cancer medicine: A perspective and overview. *Journal of Consulting and Clinical Psychology, 54,* 632–638. (12)

Désir, D., VanCauter, E., Fang, V. S., Martino, E., Jadot, C., Spire, J.-P., Noël, P., Refetoff, S., Copinschi, G., & Golstein, J. (1981). Effects of jet lag on hormonal patterns. I. Procedure variations in total plasma proteins, and disruption of adrenocorticotropin-cortisol periodicity. *Journal of Clinical Endocrinology and Metabolism, 52,* 628–641. (5)

Detterman, D. K. (1979). Detterman's laws of individual differences research. In R. J. Sternberg & D. K. Detterman (Eds.), *Human intelligence* (pp. 165–175). Norwood, NJ: Ablex. (9)

Deutsch, J. A. (1983). Dietary control and the stomach. *Progress in Neurobiology, 20,* 313–332. (11)

Deutsch, J. A., Young, N. G., & Kalogeris, T. J. (1978). The stomach signals satiety. *Science, 201,* 165–167. (11)

DeValois, R. L. (1965). Behavioral and electrophysiological studies of primate vision. In W. D. Neff (Ed.), *Contributions to sensory physiology* (Vol. 1, pp. 137–178). New York: Academic. (4)

Devane, W. A., Hanuš, L., Breuer, A., Pertwee, R. G., Stevenson, L. A., Griffin, G., Gibson, D., Mandelbaum, A., Etinger, A., & Mechoulam, R. (1992). Isolation and structure of a brain constituent that binds to the cannabinoid receptor. *Science, 258,* 1946–1949. (3, 5)

Devine, P. G., Monteith, M. J., Zuwerink, J. R., & Elliot, A. J. (1991). Prejudice with and without compunction. *Journal of Personality and Social Psychology, 60,* 817–830. (16)

deWolff, C. J. (1985). Stress and strain in the work environment: Does it lead to illness? In W. D. Gentry, H. Benson, & C. J. deWolff (Eds.), *Behavioral medicine: Work, stress, and health* (pp. 33–43). Dordrecht, Netherlands: Martinus Nijhoff. (12)

Diamond, I. T. (1983). Parallel pathways in the auditory, visual, and somatic systems. In G. Macchi, A. Rustioni, & R. Spreafico (Eds.), *Somatosensory integration in the thalamus* (pp. 251–272). Amsterdam: Elsevier. (3)

Diamond, S. S. (1993). Instructing on death: Psychologists, juries, and judges. *American Psychologist, 48,* 423–434. (16)

DiClemente, C. C. (1994). If behaviors change, can personality be far behind? In T. F. Heatherton & J. L. Weinberger (Eds.), *Can personality change?* (pp. 175–198). Washington, D.C.: American Psychological Association. (13)

Diener, E. (1984). Subjective well-being. *Psychological Bulletin, 95,* 542–575. (12)

Dindia, K., & Allen, M. (1992). Sex differences in self-disclosure: A meta-analysis. *Psychological Bulletin, 112,* 106–124. (16)

Dion, K. E., Berscheid, E., & Walster, E. (1972). What is beautiful is good. *Journal of Personality and Social Psychology, 24,* 285–290. (16)

Dische, S., Yule, W., Corbett, J., & Hand, D. (1983). Childhood nocturnal enuresis: Factors associated with outcome of treatment with an enuresis alarm. *Developmental Medicine and Child Neurology, 25,* 67–80. (15)

Dixon, A., Ross, D., O'Malley, S. L. C., & Burke, T. (1994). Paternal investment inversely related to degree of extra-pair paternity in the reed bunting. *Nature, 371,* 698–700. (3)

Dixon, N. F. (1981). *Preconscious processing.* New York: Wiley. (4)

Dobrzecka, C., Szwejkowska, G., & Konorski, J. (1966). Qualitative versus directional cues in two forms of differentiation. *Science, 153,* 87–89. (6)

Dole, V. P. (1978). A clinician's view of addiction. In J. Fishman (Ed.), *The bases of addiction* (pp. 37–46). Berlin: Dahlem Konferenzen. (14)

Dole, V. P. (1980). Addictive behavior. *Scientific American, 243*(6), 138–154. (14)

Dollard, J., Miller, N. E., Doob, L. W., Mowrer, O. H., & Sears, R. R. (1939). *Frustration and aggression.* New Haven, CT: Yale University Press. (12)

Dorfman, D. (1994, September 6). Hilton may hold door open for takeover deal. *USA Today,* p. B-1. (8)

Dostoyevsky, F. (1960). *Notes from underground.* New York: E. P. Dutton & Co. (Original work published 1864.) (11)

Dostoyevsky, F. (1969). *The idiot.* New York: New American Library. (Original work published 1868.) (15)

Dowling, J. E. (1987). *The retina.* Cambridge, MA: Harvard University Press. (4)

Duckitt, J. (1992). Psychology and prejudice. *American Psychologist, 47,* 1182–1193. (16)

Duke, M., & Nowicki, S., Jr. (1979). *Abnormal psychology: Perspectives on being different.* Monterey, CA: Brooks/Cole. (14)

Duncan, J., Ward, R., & Shapiro, K. (1994). Direct measurement of attentional dwell time in human vision. *Nature, 369,* 313–315. (8)

Dwyman, J., & Bowers, K. (1983). The use of hypnosis to enhance recall. *Science, 222,* 184–185. (5)

Dykeman, B. (1989). A social-learning perspective of treating test-anxious students. *College Student Journal, 23,* 123–125. (6)

Eagly, A. H., & Crowley, M. (1986). Gender and helping behavior: A meta-analytic review of the social psychological literature. *Psychological Bulletin, 100,* 283–308. (10)

Eagly, A. H., Karau, S. J., & Makhijani, M. G. (1995). Gender and the effectiveness of leaders: A meta-analysis. *Psychological Bulletin, 117,* 125–145. (A)

Eagly, A. H., Makhijani, M. G., & Klonsky, B. G. (1992). Gender and the evaluation of leaders: A meta-analysis. *Psychological Bulletin, 111,* 3–22. (A)

Eagly, A. H., & Warren, R. (1976). Intelligence, comprehension, and opinion change. *Journal of Personality, 44,* 226–242. (16)

Earls, C. M. (1988). Aberrant sexual arousal in sexual offenders. *Annals of the New York Academy of Sciences, 528,* 41–48. (11)

Eaton, W. O., & Saudino, K. J. (1992). Prenatal activity level as a temperament dimension? Individual differences and developmental functions in fetal movement. *Infant Behavior & Development 15,* 57–70. (10)

Eaton, W. W., Holzer, C. E., von Korff, M., Anthony, J. C., Helzer, J. E., George, L., Burnam, A., Boyd, J. H., Kessler, L. G., & Locke, B. Z. (1984). The design of the epidemiologic catchment area surveys. *Archives of General Psychiatry, 41,* 942–948. (14)

Ebbinghaus, H. (1913). *Memory.* New York: Teachers College. (Original work published 1885.) (7)

Eccles, J. C. (1986). Chemical transmission and Dale's principle. In T. Hökfelt, K. Fuxe, & B. Pernow (Eds.), *Progress in brain research* (Vol. 68, pp. 3–13). Amsterdam: Elsevier. (3)

Edelman, B. (1981). Binge eating in normal weight and overweight individuals. *Psychological Reports, 49,* 739–746. (11)

Edney, J. H. (1979). The nuts game: A concise commons dilemma analog. *Environmental Psychology and Nonverbal Behavior, 3,* 252–254. (16)

Educational Testing Service (1994). *GRE 1994–95 guide.* Princeton, NJ: Author. (9)

Eibl-Eibesfeldt, I. (1973). *Der vorprogrammierte Mensch* [The preprogrammed human]. Vienna: Verlag Fritz Molden. (12)

Eibl-Eibesfeldt, I. (1974). *Love and hate.* New York: Schocken. (12)

Eikelboom, R., & Stewart, J. (1982). Conditioning of drug-induced physiological responses. *Psychological Review, 89,* 507–528. (6)

Eimas, P. D., Siqueland, E. R., Jusczyk, P., & Vigorito, J. (1971). Speech perception in infants. *Science, 171,* 303–306. (10)

Einstein, G. O., & Hunt, R. R. (1980). Levels of processing and organization: Additive effects of individual item and relational processing. *Journal of Experimental Psychology: Human Learning and Memory, 6,* 588–598. (7)

Ekman, P. (1992). Facial expressions of emotion: New findings, new questions. *Psychological Science, 3,* 34–38. (12)

Ekman, P. (1994). Strong evidence for universals in facial expressions: A reply to Russell's mistaken critique. *Psychological Science, 3,* 34–38. (12)

Ekman, P., & Davidson, R. J. (1993). Voluntary smiling changes regional brain activity. *Psychological Science, 4,* 342–345. (12)

Ekman, P., & Friesen, W. V. (1984). *Unmasking the face* (2nd ed.). Palo Alto, CA: Consulting Psychologists Press. (12)

Elaad, E. (1990). Detection of guilty knowledge in real life criminal investigations. *Journal of Applied Psychology, 75,* 521–529. (12)

Elkind, D. (1984). *All grown up and no place to go.* Reading, MA: Addison-Wesley. (10)

Ellis, A. (1987). The impossibility of achieving consistently good mental health. *American Psychologist, 42,* 364–375. (15)

Ellis, A., & Harper, R. A. (1961). *A guide to rational living.* Englewood Cliffs, NJ: Prentice-Hall. (15)

Ellsworth, P. C. (1994). William James and emotion: Is a century of fame worth a century of misunderstanding? *Psychological Review, 101,* 222–229. (12)

Emery, R. W. (1982). Interparental conflict and the children of discord and divorce. *Psychological Bulletin, 92,* 310–330. (10)

Emmons, R. A. (1991). Personal strivings, daily life events, and psychological and physical well-being. *Journal of Personality, 59,* 453–472. (13)

Emrick, C. D. (1987). Alcoholics Anonymous: Affiliation processes and effectiveness as treatment. *Alcoholism: Clinical & Experimental Research, 11,* 416–423. (14)

Enns, J. T., & Rensink, R. A. (1990). Sensitivity to three-dimensional orientation in visual search. *Psychological Science, 1,* 323–326. (4)

Erev, I., Wallsten, T. S., & Budescu, D. V. (1994). Simultaneous over- and underconfidence: The role of error in judgment processes. *Psychological Review, 101,* 519–527. (8)

Ericsson, K. A., & Charness, N. (1994). Expert performance: Its structure and acquisition. *American Psychologist, 49,* 725–747. (8)

Ericsson, K. A., Chase, W. G., & Falcon, S. (1980). Acquisition of a memory skill. *Science, 208,* 1181–1182. (7)

Ericsson, K. A., Krampe, R. T., & Tesch-Römer, C. (1993). The role of deliberate practice in the acquisition of expert performance. *Psychological Review, 100,* 363–406. (8)

Erikson, E. H. (1963). *Childhood and society* (2nd ed.). New York: Norton. (10)

Ernhart, C. B., Sokol, R. J., Martier, S., Moron, P., Nadler, D., Ager, J. W., & Wolf, A. (1987). Alcohol teratogenicity in the human: A detailed assessment of specificity, critical period, and threshold. *American Journal of Obstetrics and Gynecology, 156,* 33–39. (10)

Ernst, C., & Angst, J. (1983). *Birth order: Its influence on personality.* New York: Springer-Verlag. (10)

Eron, L. D. (1987). The development of aggressive behavior from the perspective of a developing behaviorism. *American Psychologist, 42,* 435–442. (12)

Esterson, A. (1993). *Seductive mirage.* Chicago: Open Court. (13)

Evans, D. A., Funkenstein, H. H., Albert, M. S., Scherr, P. A., Cook, N. R., Chown, M. J., Hebert, L. E., Hennekens, C. H., & Taylor, J. O. (1989). Prevalence of Alzheimer's disease in a community population of older persons. *Journal of the American Medical Association, 262,* 2551–2556. (7)

Exner, J. E., Jr. (1986). *The Rorschach: A comprehensive system* (2nd ed.). New York: Wiley. (13)

Eysenck, H. J. (1952). The effects of psychotherapy: An evaluation. *Journal of Consulting Psychology, 16,* 319–324. (15)

Eysenck, H. J. (1992). Four ways five factors are *not* basic. *Personality and Individual Differences, 13,* 667–673. (13)

Faedda, G. L., Tondo, L., Teicher, M. H., Baldessarini, R. J., Gelbard, H. A., & Floris, G. F. (1993). Seasonal mood disorders: patterns of seasonal recurrence in mania and depression. *Archives of General Psychiatry, 50,* 17–23. (14)

Falk, J. R., Halmi, K. A., & Tryon, W. W. (1985). Activity measures in anorexia nervosa. *Archives of General Psychiatry, 42,* 811–814. (11)

Fallon, A. E., & Rozin, P. (1985). Sex differences in perceptions of desirable body shape. *Journal of Abnormal Psychology, 94,* 102–105. (11)

Fantz, R. L. (1963). Pattern vision in newborn infants. *Science, 140,* 296–297. (10)

Farah, M. J. (1990). *Visual agnosia.* Cambridge, MA: MIT Press. (3)

Farah, M. J. (1992). Is an object an object an object? Cognitive and neuropsychological investigations of domain specificity in visual object recognition. *Current Directions in Psychological Science, 1,* 164–169. (3)

Faraone, S. V., Kremen, W. S., & Tsuang, M. T. (1990). Genetic transmission of major affective disorders: Quantitative models and linkage analyses. *Psychological Bulletin, 108,* 109–127. (14)

Farber, S. L. (1981). *Identical twins reared apart: A reanalysis.* New York: Basic Books. (9)

Farmer, A. E., McGuffin, P., & Gottesman, I. I. (1987). Twin concordance for DSM-III schizophrenia. *Archives of General Psychiatry, 44,* 634–641. (14)

Farmer, H. (1983). Career and homemaking plans for high school youth. *Journal of Counseling Psychology, 30,* 40–45. (11)

Farmer, H. S. (1987). Female motivation and achievement: Implications for interventions. *Advances in Motivation and Achievement, 5,* 51–97. (11)

Farmer, H., & Bohn, M. (1970). Home-career conflict reduction and the level of career interest in women. *Journal of Counseling Psychology, 17,* 228–232. (11)

Fausto-Sterling, A. (1985). *Myths of gender.* New York: Basic Books. (2, 8)

Fay, R. E., Turner, C. F., Klassen, A. D., & Gagnon, J. H. (1989). Prevalence and patterns of same-gender sexual contact among men. *Science, 243,* 338–348. (11)

Fawzy, F. I., Fawzy, N. W., Arndt, L. A., & Pasnau, R. O. (1995). Critical review of psychosocial interventions in cancer care. *Archives of General Psychiatry, 52,* 100–113. (12)

Feeney, D. M. (1987). Human rights and animal welfare. *American Psychologist, 42,* 593–599. (2)

Fehrenbach, P. A., & Thelen, M. H. (1982). Behavioral approaches to the treatment of aggressive disorders. *Behavior Modification, 6,* 465–497. (12)

Feingold, A. (1988). Cognitive gender differences are disappearing. *American Psychologist, 43,* 95–103. (9)

Feingold, A. (1992a). Good-looking people are not what we think. *Psychological Bulletin, 111,* 304–341. (16)

Feingold, A. (1992b). Gender differences in mate selection preferences: A test of the parental investment model. *Psychological Bulletin, 112,* 125–139. (16)

Feingold, A. (1994). Gender differences in personality: A meta-analysis. *Psychological Bulletin, 116,* 429–456. (13)

Fenton, W. S., & McGlashan, T. H. (1991). Natural history of schizophrenia subtypes. I. Longitudinal study of paranoid, hebephrenic, and undifferentiated schizophrenia. *Archives of General Psychiatry, 48*, 969–977. (14)

Fernald, D. (1984). *The Hans legacy: A story of science.* Hillsdale, NJ: Lawrence Erlbaum. (2)

Fernandez, E., & Turk, D. C. (1992). Sensory and affective components of pain: Separation and synthesis. *Psychological Bulletin, 112*, 205–217. (4)

Festinger, L. (1957). *A theory of cognitive dissonance.* Stanford, CA: Stanford University Press. (16)

Festinger, L., & Carlsmith, J. M. (1959). Cognitive consequences of forced compliance. *Journal of Abnormal and Social Psychology, 58*, 203–210. (16)

Festinger, L., Schachter, S., & Back, K. (1950). *Social pressures in informal groups: A study of human factors in housing.* New York: Harper. (16)

Fieve, R. R. (1975). *Moodswing.* New York: William Morrow. (14)

Finch, J. F., & Cialdini, R. B. (1989). Another indirect tactic of (self-)image management: Boosting. *Personality and Social Psychology Bulletin, 15*, 222–232. (16)

Fincham, F. D., Beach, S. R., & Baucom, D. H. (1987). Attribution processes in distressed and nondistressed couples: 4. Self-partner attribution differences. *Journal of Personality and Social Psychology, 52*, 739–748. (16)

Fine, M. A., & Schwebel, A. I. (1987). An emergent explanation of differing racial reactions to single parenthood. *Journal of Divorce, 11*, 1–15. (10)

Fink, M. (1985). Convulsive therapy: Fifty years of progress. *Convulsive Therapy, 1*, 204–216. (15)

Finkel, L. H., & Sajda, P. (1994). Constructing visual perception. *American Scientist, 82*, 224–237. (4)

Fischhoff, B. (1975). Hindsight ≠ foresight: The effect of outcome knowledge on judgment under uncertainty. *Journal of Experimental Psychology: Human Perception and Performance, 1*, 288–299. (7)

Fischhoff, B. (1992). Giving advice: Decision theory perspectives on sexual assault. *American Psychologist, 47*, 577–588. (11)

Fischhoff, B., & Beyth, R. (1975). "I knew it would happen"—Remembered probabilities of once-future things. *Organizational Behavior & Human Performance, 13*, 1–16. (7)

Fishbein, M., & Ajzen, I. (1975). *Belief, attitude, intention and behavior: An introduction to theory and research.* Reading, MA: Addison-Wesley. (16)

Fisher, S., & Greenberg, R. P. (1977). *The scientific credibility of Freud's theories and therapy.* New York: Basic Books. (13)

Fitzgerald, R., & Ellsworth, P. C. (1984). Due process vs. crime control: Death qualification and jury attitudes. *Law and Human Behavior, 8*, 31–51. (16)

Flatz, G. (1987). Genetics of lactose digestion in humans. *Advances in Human Genetics, 16*, 1–77. (3)

Flavell, J. (1986). The development of children's knowledge about the appearance-reality distinction. *American Psychologist, 41*, 418–425. (10)

Fletcher, R., & Voke, J. (1985). *Defective colour vision.* Bristol, England: Adam Hilger. (4)

Flynn, J. R. (1984). The mean IQ of Americans: Massive gains 1932 to 1978. *Psychological Bulletin, 95*, 29–51. (9)

Flynn, J. R. (1987). Massive IQ gains in 14 nations: What IQ tests really measure. *Psychological Bulletin, 101*, 171–191. (9)

Foley, V. D. (1984). Family therapy. In R. J. Corini (Ed.), *Current psychotherapies* (3rd ed, pp. 447–490). Itasca, IL: F. E. Peacock Publishers. (15)

Fontana, A. F., Marcus, J. L., Noel, B., & Rakusin, J. M. (1972). Prehospitalization coping styles of psychiatric patients: The goal-directedness of life events. *Journal of Nervous and Mental Disease, 155*, 311–321. (15)

Fordham, S. (1988). Racelessness as a factor in Black students' school success: Pragmatic strategy or pyrrhic victory. *Harvard Educational Review, 58*, 54–84. (10)

Forer, B. R. (1949). The fallacy of personal validation: A classroom demonstration of gullibility. *Journal of Abnormal and Social Psychology, 44*, 118–123. (13)

Forman, R. F., & McCauley, C. (1986). Validity of the positive control polygraph test using the field practice model. *Journal of Applied Psychology, 71*, 691–698. (12)

Forsberg, L. K., & Goldman, M. S. (1987). Experience-dependent recovery of cognitive deficits in alcoholics: Extended transfer of training. *Journal of Abnormal Psychology, 96*, 345–353. (5)

Foster, W. Z. (1968). *History of the Communist Party of the United States.* New York: Greenwood Press. (16)

Fox, B. H. (1983). Current theory of psychogenic effects on cancer incidence and prognosis. *Journal of Psychosocial Oncology, 1*, 17–31. (12)

Frankenhaeuser, M. (1980). Psychoneuroendocrine approaches to the study of stressful person-environment transactions. In H. Selye (Ed.), *Selye's guide to stress research* (pp. 46–70). New York: Van Nostrand Reinhold. (12)

Frankmann, S. P., & Green, B. G. (1988). Differential effects of cooling on the intensity of taste. *Annals of the New York Academy of Sciences, 510*, 300–303. (4)

Freed, C. R., Breeze, R. D., Rosenberg, N. L., Schneck, S. A., Kriek, E., Qi, J.-X., Lone, T., Zhang, Y.-B., Snyder, J. A., Wells, T. H., Ramig, L. O., Thompson, L., Mazziotta, J. C., Huang, S. C., Grafton, S. T., Brooks, D., Sawle, G., Schroter, G., & Ansari, A. A. (1992). Survival of implanted fetal dopamine cells and neurologic improvement 12 to 46 months after transplantation for Parkinson's disease. *New England Journal of Medicine, 327*, 1549–1555. (3)

Freedland, R. L., & Bertenthal, B. I. (1994). Developmental changes in interlimb coordination: Transition to hands-and-knees crawling. *Psychological Science, 5*, 26–32. (10)

Freedman, J. L., & Fraser, S. C. (1966). Compliance without pressure: The foot in the door technique. *Journal of Personality and Social Psychology, 4*, 195–202. (16)

French, A. R. (1988). The patterns of mammalian hibernation. *American Scientist, 76*, 568–575. (5)

French, J. L. (1990). History of school psychology. In T. B. Gutkin & C. R. Reynolds (Eds.), *The handbook of school psychology* (2nd ed., pp. 3–20). New York: Wiley. (A)

Freud, S. (1900/1955). *The interpretation of dreams* (J. Strachey, Trans.). New York: Basic Books. (Original work published 1900.) (15)

Freud, S. (1905/1925). *Three contributions to the theory of sex* (A. A. Brill, Trans.). New York: Nervous and Mental Disease Pub. Co. (Original work published 1905.) (13)

Freud, S. (1908/1963). "Civilized" sexual morality and modern nervousness. In P. Rieff (Ed.), *Freud: Sexuality and the psychology of love* (pp. 20–40). New York: Collier Books. (Original work published 1908.) (11)

Freud, S. (1927/1953). *The future of an illusion* (J. Strachey, Trans.). New York: Liveright. (Original work published 1927.) (13)

Frick, W. B. (1983). The symbolic growth experience. *Journal of Humanistic Psychology, 23,* 108–125. (13)

Friedman, M., & Rosenman, R. H. (1974). *Type-A behavior and your heart.* New York: Knopf. (12)

Friedman, M. A., & Brownell, K. D. (1995). Psychological correlates of obesity: Moving to the next research generation. *Psychological Bulletin, 117,* 3–20. (11)

Friedman, M. I., & Stricker, E. M. (1976). The physiological psychology of hunger: A physiological perspective. *Psychological Review, 83,* 409–431. (11)

Friedman, W. J. (1993). Memory for the time of past events. *Psychological Bulletin, 113,* 44–66. (7)

Friedrich, J. (1993). Primary error detection and minimization (PEDMIN) strategies in social cognition: A reinterpretation of confirmation bias phenomena. *Psychological Review, 100,* 298–319. (16)

Frijda, N. H. (1988). The laws of emotion. *American Psychologist, 45,* 349–358. (12)

Fuller, R. K., & Roth, H. P. (1979). Disulfiram for the treatment of alcoholism: An evaluation in 128 men. *Annals of Internal Medicine, 90,* 901–904. (14)

Gabrieli, J. D. E., Cohen, N. J., & Corkin, S. (1988). The impaired learning of semantic knowledge following bilateral medial temporal-lobe resection. *Brain and Cognition, 7,* 157–177. (7)

Gabrielli, W. F., Jr., & Plomin, R. (1985). Drinking behavior in the Colorado adoptee and twin sample. *Journal of Studies on Alcohol, 46,* 24–31. (14)

Gaito, J. (1976). Molecular psychobiology of memory: Its appearance, contributions, and decline. *Physiological Psychology, 4,* 476–484. (2)

Gallagher-Thompson, D., Futterman, A., Hanley-Peterson, P., Zeiss, A., Ironson, G., & Thompson, L. W. (1992). Endogenous depression in the elderly: Prevalence and agreement among measures. *Journal of Consulting and Clinical Psychology, 60,* 300–303. (14)

Gallup, G. G., Jr., & Suarez, S. D. (1980). On the use of animals in psychological research. *Psychological Record, 30,* 211–218. (2)

Gallup, G. G., Jr., & Suarez, S. D. (1985). Alternatives to the use of animals in psychological research. *American Psychologist, 40,* 1104–1111. (2)

Galton, F. (1978). *Hereditary genius.* New York: St. Martin's. (Original work published 1869.) (1, 9)

Garcia, J. (1990). Learning without memory. *Journal of Cognitive Neuroscience, 2,* 287–305. (6)

Garcia, J., Ervin, F. R., & Koelling, R. A. (1966). Learning with prolonged delay of reinforcement. *Psychonomic Science, 5,* 121–122. (6)

Garcia, J., & Koelling, R. A. (1966). *Psychonomic Science, 4,* 123–124. (6)

Garcia Coll, C. T. (1990). Developmental outcome of minority infants: A process-oriented look into our beginnings. *Child Development, 61,* 270–289. (10)

Gardner, H. (1985). *Frames of mind.* New York: Basic Books. (9)

Gardner, H. (1993). *Creating minds.* New York: Basic Books. (8)

Gardner, M. (1978). Mathematical games. *Scientific American, 239*(5), 22–32. (8)

Gardner, R. A., & Gardner, B. T. (1969). Teaching sign language to a chimpanzee. *Science, 165,* 664–672. (8)

Garfield, S. L. (1981). Psychotherapy: A 40-year appraisal. *American Psychologist, 36,* 174–183. (15)

Gastil, J. (1990). Generic pronouns and sexist language: The oxymoronic character of masculine generics. *Sex Roles, 23,* 629–642. (8)

Gawin, F. H. (1991). Cocaine addiction: Psychology and neurophysiology. *Science, 251,* 1580–1586. (5)

Gawin, F. H., & Kleber, H. D. (1986). Abstinence symptomatology and psychiatric diagnosis in cocaine abusers. *Archives of General Psychiatry, 43,* 107–113. (5)

Geiger, G., & Lettvin, J. Y. (1986). Enhancing the perception of form in peripheral vision. *Perception, 15,* 119–130.

Geiger, G., Lettvin, J. Y., & Zegarra-Moran, O. (1992). Task-determined strategies of visual process. *Cognitive Brain Research, 1,* 39–52. (8)

Gelb, S. A. (1986). Henry H. Goddard and the immigrants, 1910–1917: The studies and their social context. *Journal of the History of the Behavioral Sciences, 22,* 324–332. (9)

Gellhorn, E. (1970). The emotions and the ergotropic and trophotropic systems. *Psychologische Forschung, 34,* 48–94. (12)

Gelman, R. (1982). Accessing one-to-one correspondence: Still another paper about conservation. *British Journal of Psychology, 73,* 209–220. (10)

George, J. M., & Brief, A. P. (1992). Feeling good—doing good: A conceptual analysis of the mood at work–organizational spontaneity relationship. *Psychological Bulletin, 112,* 310–329. (A)

Gernsbacher, M. A. (1993). Less skilled readers have less efficient suppression mechanisms. *Psychological Science, 4,* 294–298. (8)

Gernsbacher, M. A., & Faust, M. E. (1991). The mechanism of suppression: A component of general comprehension skill. *Journal of Experimental Psychology: Learning, Memory, and Cognition, 17,* 245–262. (8)

Gerson, S. C., Plotkin, D. A., & Jarvik, L. F. (1988). Antidepressant drug studies, 1964 to 1986: Empirical evidence for aging patients. *Journal of Clinical Pharmacology, 8,* 311–322. (15)

Geschwind, N. (1970). The organization of language and the brain. *Science, 170,* 940–944. (3)

Gibson, J. J. (1968). What gives rise to the perception of movement? *Psychological Review, 75,* 335–346. (4)

Gick, M. L., & Holyoak, K. J. (1980). Analogical problem solving. *Cognitive Psychology, 12,* 306–355. (8)

Giebel, H. D. (1958). Visuelles Lernvermögen bei Einhufern [Visual learning capacity in hoofed animals]. *Zoologische Jahrbücher Abteilung für Allgemeine Zoologie, 67,* 487–520. (6)

Gilbreth, F. B. (1911). *Motion study.* London: Constable. (A)

Gilligan, C. (1977). In a different voice: Women's conceptions of self and morality. *Harvard Educational Review, 47,* 481–517. (10)

Gilligan, C. (1979). Woman's place in man's life cycle. *Harvard Educational Review, 49,* 431–446. (10)

Gilligan, C., & Attanucci, J. (1988). Two moral orientations: Gender differences and similarities. *Merrill-Palmer Quarterly, 34,* 223–237. (10)

Glass, D. C., Singer, J. E., & Pennebaker, J. W. (1977). Behavioral and physiological effects of uncontrollable environmental events. In D. Stokols (Ed.), *Perspectives on environment and behavior* (pp. 131–151). New York: Plenum. (12)

Goate, A., Chartier-Harlin, M. C., Mullan, M., Brown, J., Crawford, F., Fidani, L., Giuffra, L., Haynes, A., Irving, N., James, L., Mant, R., Newton, P., Rooke, K., Roques, P., Talbot, C., Pericak-Vance, M., Roses, A., Williamson,

R., Rossor, M., Owen, M., & Hardy, J. (1991). Segregation of a missense mutation in the amyloid precursor protein gene with familial Alzheimer's disease. *Nature, 349,* 704–706. (7)

Goff, S. J., Mount, M. K., & Jamison, R. L. (1990). Employer supported child care, work/family conflict, and absenteeism: A field study. *Personnel Psychology, 43,* 793–809. (A)

Gold, P. E. (1987). Sweet memories. *American Scientist, 75,* 151–155. (7)

Goldin-Meadow, S. (1985). Language development under atypical learning conditions: Replication and implications of a study of deaf children of hearing parents. In K. E. Nelson (Ed.), *Children's language* (Vol. 5, pp. 197–245). Hillsdale, NJ: Lawrence Erlbaum. (10)

Goldin-Meadow, S., Alibali, M. W., & Church, R. B. (1993). Transitions in concept acquisition: Using the hand to read the mind. *Psychological Review, 100,* 279–297. (10)

Goldman-Rakic, P. S. (1994). Specification of higher cortical functions. In S. H. Broman & J. Grafman (Eds.), *Atypical cognitive deficits in developmental disorders* (pp. 3–17). Hillsdale, NJ: Lawrence Erlbaum. (3)

Goldstein, E. B. (1989). *Sensation and perception* (3rd ed.). Belmont, CA: Wadsworth. (4)

Goldstein, M. D., Hopkins, J. R., & Strube, M. J. (1994). "The eye of the beholder": A classroom demonstration of observer bias. *Teaching of Psychology, 21,* 154–157. (2)

Goldstein, M. J. (1981). Family factors associated with schizophrenia and anorexia nervosa. *Journal of Youth and Adolescence, 10,* 385–405. (11)

Goldstein, R. B., Weissman, M. M., Adams, P. B., Horwath, E., Lish, J. D., Charney, D., Woods, S. W., Sobin, C., & Wickramaratne, P. J. (1994). Psychiatric disorders in relatives of probands with panic disorder and/or major depression. *Archives of General Psychiatry, 51,* 383–394. (14)

Goldston, S. E. (1986). Primary prevention. *American Psychologist, 41,* 453–460. (15)

Goodall, J. (1971). *In the shadow of man.* Boston: Houghton Mifflin. (2)

Goodenough, O. R., & Dawkins, R. (1994). The 'St Jude' mind virus. *Nature, 371,* 23–24. (16)

Goodman, G. S., Aman, C., & Hirschman, J. (1987). Child sexual and physical abuse: Children's testimony. In S. J. Ceci, M. P. Toglia, & D. F. Ross (Eds.), *Children's eyewitness testimony* (pp. 1–23). New York: Springer-Verlag. (7)

Goodman, P. S., & Friedman, A. (1971). An examination of Adams' theory of inequity. *Administration Science Quarterly, 16,* 271–288. (A)

Goodman, W. K., Price, L. H., Delgado, P. L., Palumbo, J., Krystal, J. H., Nagy, L. M., Rasmussen, S. A., Heninger, G. R., & Charney, D. S. (1990). Specificity of serotonin reuptake inhibitors in the treatment of obsessive-compulsive disorder. *Archives of General Psychiatry, 47,* 577–585. (14)

Goodman, P. S., & Friedman, A. (1971). An examination of Adams' theory of inequity. *Administration Science Quarterly, 16,* 271–288. (A)

Goodwin, C. J. (1991). Misportraying Pavlov's apparatus. *American Journal of Psychology, 104,* 135–141. (6)

Gorman, J. M., Fyer, M. R., Goetz, R., Askanazi, J., Liebowitz, M. R., Fyer, A. J., Kinney, J., & Klein, D. F. (1988). Ventilatory physiology of patients with panic disorder. *Archives of General Psychiatry, 45,* 31–39. (14)

Gorman, M. E. (1989). Error, falsification and scientific inference: An experimental investigation. *Quarterly Journal of Experimental Psychology, 41A,* 385–412. (8)

Gottesman, I. I. (1991). *Schizophrenia genesis.* New York: W. H. Freeman. (14)

Gottesman, I. I., & Bertelson, A. (1989). Confirming unexpressed genotypes for schizophrenia. *Archives of General Psychiatry, 46,* 867–872. (14)

Gottfredson, L. S. (1994). The science and politics of race-norming. *American Psychologist, 49,* 955–963. (A)

Graf, P., & Mandler, G. (1984). Activation makes words more accessible, but not necessarily more retrievable. *Journal of Verbal Learning and Verbal Behavior, 23,* 553–568. (7)

Gray, J. W., & Dean, R. S. (1990). Implications of neuropsychological research for school psychology. In T. B. Gutkin & C. R. Reynolds (Eds.), *The handbook of school psychology* (2nd ed., pp. 269–286). New York: Wiley. (A)

Green, D. J., & Gillette, R. (1982). Circadian rhythm of firing rate recorded from single cells in the rat suprachiasmatic brain slice. *Brain Research, 245,* 198–200. (5)

Green, D. M., & Swets, J. A. (1966). *Signal detection theory and psychophysics.* New York: Wiley. (4)

Greene, R. L. (1987a). Effects of maintenance rehearsal on human memory. *Psychological Bulletin, 102,* 403–413. (7)

Greene, R. L. (1987b). Ethnicity and MMPI performance: A review. *Journal of Consulting and Clinical Psychology, 55,* 497–512. (13)

Greeno, C. G., & Wing, R. R. (1994). Stress-induced eating. *Psychological Bulletin, 115,* 444–464. (11)

Greenough, W. T. (1975). Experiential modification of the developing brain. *American Scientist, 63,* 37–46. (3)

Greenwald, A. G., & Banaji, M. R. (1995). Implicit social cognition: Attitudes, self-esteem, and stereotypes. *Psychological Review, 102,* 4–27. (16)

Greenwald, A. G., Spangenberg, E. R., Pratkanis, A. R., & Eskanazi, J. (1991). Double-blind tests of subliminal self-help audiotapes. *Psychological Science, 2,* 119–122. (4)

Griffiths, M. D. (1990). The cognitive psychology of gambling. *Journal of Gambling Studies, 6,* 31–42. (8)

Gundlach, R. H. (1977). Sibship size, sibsex, and homosexuality among females. *Transnational Mental Health Research Newsletter, 19,* 1–7. (11)

Gusterson, H. (1992, May/June). Coming of age in a weapons lab. *The Sciences, 32,* 16–22. (10)

Gynther, M. D. (1989). MMPI comparisons of blacks and whites: A review and commentary. *Journal of Clinical Psychology, 45,* 878–883. (13)

Hackman, J. R., & Lawler, E. E. III (1971). Employee reactions to job characteristics. *Journal of Applied Psychology, 55,* 259–286. (A)

Hale, S., & Jansen, J. (1994). Global processing-time coefficients characterize individual and group differences in cognitive speed. *Psychological Science, 5,* 384–389. (9)

Haley, J. (1984). *Ordeal therapy.* San Francisco: Jossey-Bass. (15)

Hall, J. L., & Gold, P. E. (1990). Adrenalectomy-induced memory deficits: Role of plasma glucose levels. *Physiology & Behavior, 47,* 27–33. (7)

Hamilton, D. L., & Gifford, R. K. (1976). Illusory correlation in interpersonal perception: A cognitive basis of stereotypic judgments. *Journal of Experimental Social Psychology, 12,* 392–407. (16)

Hammen, C. (1991). Generation of stress in the course of unipolar depression. *Journal of Abnormal Psychology, 100,* 555–561. (14)

Hammond, W. R., & Yung, B. (1993). Minority student recruitment and retention practices among schools of professional psychology: A national survey and analysis. *Professional Psychology: Research and Practice, 24,* 3–12. (1)

Hannah, B. (1976). *Jung: His life and work.* New York: Putnam's. (13)

Hansen, G. D. (1979). Enuresis control through fading, escape, and avoidance training. *Journal of Applied Behavior Analysis, 12,* 303–307. (15)

Harada, S., Agarwal, D. P., Goedde, H. W., Tagaki, S., & Ishikawa, B. (1982). Possible protective role against alcoholism for aldehyde dehydrogenase isozyme deficiency in Japan. *Lancet, ii,* 827. (3)

Hardaway, R. A. (1990). Subliminally activated symbiotic fantasies: Facts and artifacts. *Psychological Bulletin, 107,* 177–195. (4)

Hardin, G. (1968). The tragedy of the commons. *Science, 162,* 1243–1248. (16)

Harkins, S. G., & Jackson, J. M. (1985). The role of evaluation in eliminating social loafing. *Journal of Personality and Social Psychology, 11,* 457–465. (16)

Harlow, H. F. (1958). The nature of love. *American Psychologist, 13,* 673–685. (10)

Harlow, H. F., & Harlow, M. K. (1965). The affectional systems. In A. M. Schrier, H. F. Harlow, & F. Stollnitz (Eds.), *Behavior of nonhuman primates* (Vol. 2, pp. 287–334). New York: Academic Press. (10)

Harlow, H. F., Harlow, M. K., & Meyer, D. R. (1950). Learning motivated by a manipulative drive. *Journal of Experimental Psychology, 40,* 228–234. (11)

Harlow, H. F., Harlow, M. K., & Suomi, S. J. (1971). From thought to therapy: Lessons from a primate laboratory. *American Scientist, 59,* 538–549. (10)

Harris, B. (1979). What ever happened to Little Albert? *American Psychologist, 34,* 151–160. (14)

Harris, G. C., & Aston-Jones, G. (1994). Involvement of D_2 receptors in the nucleus accumbens in the opiate withdrawal syndrome. *Nature, 371,* 155–157. (5)

Harris, R. J., Schoen, L. M., & Hensley, D. L. (1992). A cross-cultural study of story memory. *Journal of Cross-Cultural Psychology, 23,* 133–147. (7)

Harris, T. (1967). *I'm OK—You're OK.* New York: Avon. (13)

Harrison, A. O., Wilson, M. N., Pine, C. J., Chan, S. Q., & Buriel, R. (1990). Family ecologies of ethnic minority children. *Child Development, 61,* 347–362. (10)

Hass, R. G., Katz, I., Rizzo, N., Bailey, J., & Eisenstadt, D. (1991). Cross-racial appraisal as related to attitude ambivalence and cognitive complexity. *Journal of Personality and Social Psychology, 17,* 83–92. (16)

Hathaway, S. R., & McKinley, J. C. (1940). A multiphasic personality schedule (Minnesota): I. Construction of the schedule. *Journal of Psychology, 10,* 249–254. (13)

Hauri, P. (1982). *The sleep disorders.* Kalamazoo, MI: Upjohn. (5)

Hawkins, S. A., & Hastie, R. (1990). Biased judgments of past events after the outcomes are known. *Psychological Bulletin, 107,* 311–327. (7)

Hay, D., & Oken, D. (1977). The psychological stresses of intensive care unit nursing. In A. Monat & R. S. Lazarus (Eds.), *Stress and coping* (pp. 118–140). New York: Columbia University Press. (12)

Hays, R. B. (1985). A longitudinal study of friendship development. *Journal of Personality and Social Psychology, 48,* 909–924. (16)

Hazell, P., O'Connell, D., Heathcote, D., Robertson, J., & Henry, D. (1995). Efficacy of tricyclic drugs in treating child and adolescent depression: A meta-analysis. *British Medical Journal, 310,* 897–901. (15)

Healy, D., & Williams, J. M. G. (1988). Dysrhythmia, dysphoria, and depression: The interaction of learned helplessness and circadian dysrhythmia in the pathogenesis of depression. *Psychological Bulletin, 103,* 163–178. (14)

Heath, A. C., Neale, M. C., Kessler, R. C., Eaves, L. J., & Kendler, K. S. (1992). Evidence for genetic influences on personality from self-reports and informant ratings. *Journal of Personality and Social Psychology, 63,* 85–96. (13)

Heatherton, T. G., & Baumeister, R. F. (1991). Binge eating as escape from self-awareness. *Psychological Bulletin, 110,* 86–108. (11)

Heaton, R., Paulsen, J. S., McAdams, L. A., Kuck, J., Zissook, S., Braff, D., Harris, M. J., & Jeste, D. V. (1994). Neuropsychological deficits in schizophrenics. *Archives of General Psychiatry, 51,* 469–476. (14)

Heckhausen, H. (1984). Emergent achievement behavior: Some early developments. *Advances in Motivation and Achievement, 3,* 1–32. (11)

Heider, F. (1958). *The psychology of interpersonal relations.* New York: Wiley. (16)

Heilman, K. M. (1979). Neglect and related disorders. In K. M. Heilman & E. Valenstein (Eds.), *Clinical neuropsychology* (pp. 268–307). New York: Oxford University Press. (3)

Heinrichs, R. W. (1993). Schizophrenia and the brain. *American Psychologist, 48,* 221–233. (14)

Heit, E. (1993). Modeling the effects of expectations on recognition memory. *Psychological Science, 4,* 244–251. (7)

Held, R., & Hein, A. (1963). Movement-produced stimulation in the development of visually guided behavior. *Journal of Comparative and Physiological Psychology, 56,* 872–876. (10)

Heller, M. A. (1989). Picture and pattern perception in the sighted and the blind: The advantage of the late blind. *Perception, 18,* 379–389. (4)

Helmes, E., & Reddon, J. R. (1993). A perspective on developments in assessing psychopathology: A critical review of the MMPI and MMPI-2. *Psychological Bulletin, 113,* 453–471. (13)

Helzer, J. E., Robins, L. N., & McEnvoy, L. (1987). Posttraumatic stress disorder in the general population. *New England Journal of Medicine, 317,* 1630–1634. (12)

Hendrick, C., & Hendrick, S. (1986). A theory and method of love. *Journal of Personality and Social Psychology, 50,* 392–402. (16)

Hendrick, C., Hendrick, S., & Adler, N. L. (1988). Romantic relationships: Love, satisfaction, and staying together. *Journal of Personality and Social Psychology, 54,* 980–988. (16)

Henry, R. M. (1983). The cognitive versus psychodynamic debate about morality. *Human Development, 26,* 173–179. (10)

Hergenhahn, B. R. (1992). *An introduction to the history of psychology* (2nd ed.). Belmont, CA: Wadsworth. (1)

Herkenham, M., Lynn, A. B., deCosta, B. R., & Richfield, E. K. (1991). Neuronal localization of cannabinoid receptors in the basal ganglia of the rat. *Brain Research, 547,* 267–274. (5)

Herkenham, M., Lynn, A. B., Little, M. D., Johnson, M. R., Melvin, L. S., deCosta, B. R., & Rice, K. C. (1990). Cannabinoid receptor localization in brain. *Proceedings of the National Academy of Sciences, 87,* 1932–1936. (5)

Hernandez, L., Murzi, E., Schwartz, D. H., & Hoebel, B. G. (1992). Electrophysiological and neurochemical approach to a hierarchical feeding organization. In P. Bjorntorp & B. N. Brodoff (Eds.), *Obesity* (pp. 171–183). Philadelphia, PA: J. B. Lippincott. (11)

Herman, J., Roffwarg, H., & Tauber, E. S. (1968). Color and other perceptual qualities of REM and NREM sleep. *Psychophysiology, 5,* 223. (5)

Herrnstein, R. J., & Murray, C. (1994). *The Bell Curve.* New York: Free Press. (9)

Hershenson, M. (Ed.) (1989). *The moon illusion.* Hillsdale, NJ: Lawrence Erlbaum. (4)

Herzog, D. B., Norman, D. K., Gordon, C., & Pepose, M. (1984). Sexual conflict and eating disorders in 27 males. *American Journal of Psychiatry, 141,* 989–990. (11)

Hess, T. M., Donley, J., & Vandermaas, M. O. (1989). Aging-related changes in the processing and retention of script information. *Experimental Aging Research, 15,* 89–96. (7)

Hetherington, E. M. (1989). Coping with family transitions. Winners, losers, and survivors. *Child Development, 60,* 1–14. (10)

Hetherington, E. M., Cox, M., & Cox, R. (1982). Effects of divorce on parents and children. In M. E. Lamb (Ed.), *Nontraditional families* (pp. 233–288). Hillsdale, NJ: Lawrence Erlbaum. (10)

Hetherington, E. M., Stanley-Hagan, M., & Anderson, E. R. (1989). Marital transitions: A child's perspective. *American Psychologist, 44,* 303–312. (10)

Hilgard, E. R. (1971). Hypnotic phenomena: The struggle for scientific acceptance. *American Scientist, 59,* 567–577. (5)

Hilgard, E. R. (1973). A neodissociation interpretation of pain reduction in hypnosis. *Psychological Review, 80,* 396–411. (5)

Hilgard, E. R. (1979). Divided consciousness in hypnosis: The implications of the hidden observer. In E. Fromm & R. E. Shor (Eds.), *Hypnosis: Developments in research and new perspectives* (2nd ed., pp. 45–79). New York: Aldine. (5)

Hilton, J. L., & Darley, J. M. (1991). The effects of interaction goals on person perception. *Advances in Experimental Social Psychology, 24,* 235–267. (16)

Hines, M. (1982). Prenatal gonadal hormones and sex differences in human behavior. *Psychological Bulletin, 92,* 56–80. (11)

Hinton, G. (1979). Some demonstrations of the effects of structural descriptions in mental imagery. *Cognitive Science, 3,* 231–250. (8)

Hobson, J. A. (1988). *The dreaming brain.* New York: Basic Books. (5)

Hobson, J. A. (1992). Sleep and dreaming: Induction and mediation of REM sleep by cholinergic mechanisms. *Current Opinion in Neurobiology, 2,* 759–763. (5)

Hobson, J. A., & McCarley, R. W. (1977). The brain as a dream state generator: An activation-synthesis hypothesis of the dream process. *American Journal of Psychiatry, 134,* 1335–1348. (4)

Hobson, R. P. (1993). *Autism and the development of mind.* Hove, East Sussex, England: Lawrence Erlbaum Associates. (10)

Hoebel, B. G., & Hernandez, L. (1993). Basic neural mechanisms of feeding and weight regulation. In A. J. Stunkard & T. A. Wadden (Eds.), *Obesity: Theory and therapy* (2nd ed., pp. 43–62). New York: Raven Press. (11)

Hoffman, J. L. (1992). Supermelons? *Science, 255,* 665. (8)

Hoffman, L. W. (1989). Effects of maternal employment in the two-parent family. *American Psychologist, 44,* 283–292. (10)

Hoffman, R. E., Stopek, S., & Andreasen, N. C. (1986). A comparative study of manic vs. schizophrenic speech disorganization. *Archives of General Psychiatry, 43,* 831–838. (14)

Hogan, J., & Quigley, A. M. (1986). Physical standards for employment and the courts. *American Psychologist, 11,* 1193–1217. (A)

Hogan, R. A., & Kirchner, J. H. (1967). Preliminary report of the extinction of learned fears via short-term implosive therapy. *Journal of Abnormal Psychology, 72,* 106–109. (14)

Hoge, S. K., Sachs, G., Appelbaum, P. S., Greer, A., & Gordon, C. (1988). Limitations on psychiatrists' discretionary civil commitment authority by the Stone and dangerousness criteria. *Archives of General Psychiatry, 45,* 764–769. (15)

Hohmann, G. W. (1966). Some effects of spinal cord lesions on experienced emotional feelings. *Psychophysiology, 3,* 143–156. (12)

Holden, C. (1987). Is alcoholism treatment effective? *Science, 236,* 20–22. (14)

Hollister, J. M., Mednick, S. A., Brennan, P., & Cannon, T. D. (1994). Impaired autonomic nervous system habituation in those at genetic risk for schizophrenia. *Archives of General Psychiatry, 51,* 552–558. (14)

Hollister, L. E. (1986). Health aspects of cannabis. *Pharmacological Reviews, 38,* 1–20. (5)

Hollon, S. D., & Beck, A. T. (1979). Cognitive therapy of depression. In P. C. Kendall & S. D. Hollon (Eds.), *Cognitive-behavioral interventions* (pp. 153–203). New York: Academic Press. (15)

Hollon, S. D., Kendall, P. C., & Lumry, A. (1986). Specificity of depressogenic cognitions in clinical depression. *Journal of Abnormal Psychology, 95,* 52–59. (15)

Holmes, D. S. (1978). Projection as a defense mechanism. *Psychological Bulletin, 85,* 677–688. (13)

Holmes, D. S. (1990). The evidence for repression: An examination of sixty years of research. In J. Singer (Ed.), *Repression and dissociation* (pp. 85–102). Chicago: University of Chicago Press. (7, 13)

Holmes, T., & Rahe, R. (1967). The social readjustment rating scale. *Journal of Psychosomatic Research, 11,* 213–218. (12)

Holyoak, K. J., Koh, K., & Nisbett, R. E. (1989). A theory of conditioning: Inductive learning within rule-based default hierarchies. *Psychological Review, 96,* 315–340. (6)

Holzman, P. S. (1985). Eye movement dysfunctions and psychosis. *International Review of Neurobiology, 27,* 179–205. (14)

Holzman, P. S. (1988). A single dominant gene can account for eye tracking dysfunctions and schizophrenia in offspring of discordant twins. *Archives of General Psychiatry, 45,* 641–647. (14)

Honzik, M. P. (1974). The development of intelligence. In B. B. Wolman (Ed.), *Handbook of general psychology* (pp. 644–655). Englewood Cliffs, NJ: Prentice-Hall. (9)

Horn, J. L., & Donaldson, G. (1976). On the myth of intellectual decline in adulthood. *American Psychologist, 31,* 701–719. (9)

Horne, J. A. (1988). *Why we sleep*. Oxford, England: Oxford University Press. (5)

Horne, J. A., Brass, C. G., & Pettitt, A. N. (1980). Circadian performance differences between morning and evening 'types.' *Ergonomics, 23,* 29–36. (5)

Horne, J. A., & Minard, A. (1985). Sleep and sleepiness following a behaviorally "active" day. *Ergonomics, 28,* 567–575. (5)

Horner, M. S. (1972). Toward an understanding of achievement-related conflicts in women. *Journal of Social Issues, 28,* 157–175. (11)

Horvath, F. (1977). The effect of selected variables on interpretation of polygraph records. *Journal of Applied Psychology, 62,* 127–136. (12)

Hovland, C. I., Janis, I. L., & Kelley, H. H. (1953). *Communication and persuasion*. New Haven: Yale University Press. (16)

Hovland, C. I., Lumsdaine, A. A., & Sheffield, F. D. (1949). *Studies in social psychology in World War II: Vol. 3, Experiments on mass communications*. Princeton, NJ: Princeton University Press. (16)

Hovland, C. I., & Weiss, W. (1951). The influences of source credibility on communication effectiveness. *Public Opinion Quarterly, 15,* 635–650. (16)

Howard, K. I., Kopta, S. M., Krause, M. S., & Orlinsky, D. E. (1986). The dose-effect relationship in psychotherapy. *American Psychologist, 41,* 159–164. (15)

Howe, M. L., & Courage, M. L. (1993). On resolving the enigma of infantile amnesia. *Psychological Bulletin, 113,* 305–326. (7)

Hoyt, M. F., & Austad, C. S. (1992). Psychotherapy in a staff model health maintenance organization: Providing and assuring quality care in the future. *Psychotherapy, 29,* 119–129. (15)

Hser, Y.-I., Anglin, M. D., & Powers, K. (1993). A 24-year follow-up of California narcotics addicts. *Archives of General Psychiatry, 50,* 577–584. (14)

Hubel, D. H., & Wiesel, T. N. (1968). Receptive fields and functional architecture of monkey striate cortex. *Journal of Physiology* (London), *195,* 215–243. (4)

Hudson, W. (1960). Pictorial depth perception in sub-cultural groups in Africa. *Journal of Social Psychology, 52,* 183–208. (4)

Huff, D. (1954). *How to lie with statistics*. New York: Norton. (2)

Hughes, J. R., Higgins, S. T., Bickel, W. K., Hunt, W. K., Fenwick, J. W., Gulliver, S. B., & Mireault, G. C. (1991). Caffeine self-administration, withdrawal, and adverse effects among coffee drinkers. *Archives of General Psychiatry, 48,* 611–617. (5)

Hughes, J., Smith, T. W., Kosterlitz, H. W., Fothergill, L. A., Morgan, B. A., & Morris, H. R. (1975). Identification of two related pentapeptides from the brain with potent opiate antagonist activity. *Nature, 258,* 577–579. (5)

Hull, C. L. (1932). The goal gradient hypothesis and maze learning. *Psychological Review, 39,* 25–43. (1)

Hull, C. L. (1943). *Principles of behavior: An introduction to behavior theory*. New York: D. Appleton. (1, 11)

Hunt, E., & Agnoli, F. (1991). The Whorfian hypothesis: A cognitive psychology perspective. *Psychological Review, 98,* 377–389. (8)

Hunter, J. E., & Schmidt, F. L. (1983). Quantifying the effects of psychological interventions on employee job performance and work-force productivity. *American Psychologist, 83,* 473–478. (A)

Huntington's Disease Collaborative Research Group (1993). A novel gene containing a trinucleotide repeat that is expanded and unstable on Huntington's disease chromosomes. *Cell, 72,* 971–983. (1, 3)

Hyde, J. S., Fennema, E., & Lamon, S. J. (1990). Gender differences in mathematics performance: A meta-analysis. *Psychological Bulletin, 107,* 139–155. (9)

Hyman, B. T., van Hoesen, G. W., Damasio, A. R., & Barnes, C. L. (1984). Alzheimer's disease: Cell-specific pathology isolates the hippocampal formation. *Science, 225,* 1168–1170. (7)

Hyman, R. (1994). Anomaly or artifact? Comments on Bem and Honorton. *Psychological Bulletin, 115,* 19–24. (2)

Iaffaldano, M. T., & Muchinsky, P. M. (1985). Job satisfaction and job performance. *Psychological Bulletin, 97,* 251–273. (A)

Iggo, A., & Andres, K. H. (1982). Morphology of cutaneous receptors. *Annual Review of Neuroscience, 5,* 1–31. (4)

Inhoff, A. W. (1989). Lexical access during eye fixations in sentence reading: Are word access codes used to integrate lexical information across interword fixations? *Journal of Memory and Language, 28,* 444–461. (8)

Inouye, S. T., & Kawamura, H. (1979). Persistence of circadian rhythmicity in a mammalian hypothalamic "island" containing the suprachiasmatic nucleus. *Proceedings of the National Academy of Sciences, U.S.A., 76,* 5962–5966. (5)

Isaacs, E. A., & Clark, H. H. (1987). References in conversation between experts and novices. *Journal of Experimental Psychology: General, 116,* 26–37. (1)

Isenberg, D. J. (1986). Group polarization: A critical review and meta-analysis. *Journal of Personality and Social Psychology, 50,* 1141–1151. (16)

Jackson, J. H. (1990). School psychology after the 1980s: Envisioning a possible future. In T. B. Gutkin & C. R. Reynolds (Eds.), *The handbook of school psychology* (2nd ed., pp. 40–50). New York: Wiley. (A)

Jacobs, B. L. (1987). How hallucinogenic drugs work. *American Scientist, 75,* 386–392. (3, 5)

Jacobs, K. M., Mark, G. P., & Scott, T. R. (1988). Taste responses in the nucleus tractus solitarius of sodium-deprived rats. *Journal of Physiology, 406,* 393–410. (11)

Jacobsen, F. M., Sack, D. A., Wehr, T. A., Rogers, S., & Rosenthal, N. E. (1987). Neuroendocrine 5-hydroxytryptophan in seasonal affective disorder. *Archives of General Psychiatry, 44,* 1086–1091. (14)

James, W. (1884). What is an emotion? *Mind, 9,* 188–205. (12)

James, W. (1890). *The principles of psychology*. New York: Henry Holt. (1)

James, W. (1899/1962). *Talks to teachers on psychology*. New York: Dover. (Original work published 1899.) (8)

Jamison, K. R. (1989). Mood disorders and patterns of creativity in British writers and artists. *Psychiatry: Interpersonal and Biological Processes, 52,* 125–134. (14)

Janicak, P. G., Davis, J. M., Gibbons, R. D., Ericksen, S., Chang, S., & Gallagher, P. (1985). Efficacy of ECT: A meta-analysis. *American Journal of Psychiatry, 142,* 297–302. (15)

Janis, I. L. (1972). *Victims of groupthink*. Boston: Houghton Mifflin. (16)

Janis, I. L. (1983). Stress inoculation in health care. In D. Meichenbaum & M. E. Jaremko (Eds.), *Stress reduction and prevention* (pp. 67–99). New York: Plenum. (12)

Janis, I. L. (1985). Sources of error in strategic decision making. In J. M. Pennings and associates (Eds.), *Organizational strategy and change* (pp. 157–197). San Francisco: Jossey-Bass. (16)

Janson, P., & Martin, J. K. (1982). Job satisfaction and age: A test of two views. *Social Forces, 60,* 1089–1102. (10)

Jaremko, M. E. (1983). Stress inoculation training for social anxiety, with emphasis on dating anxiety. In D. Meichenbaum & M. E. Jaremko (Eds.), *Stress reduction and prevention* (pp. 419–450). New York: Plenum. (12)

Jaskiw, G. E., & Weinberger, D. R. (1992) Dopamine and schizophrenia—a cortically corrective perspective. *Seminars in the Neurosciences, 4,* 179–188. (15)

Jensen, A. R. (1980). *Bias in mental testing.* New York: Free Press. (10)

Jensen, A. R. (1993). Why is reaction time correlated with psychometric *g? Current Directions in Psychological Science, 2,* 53–56. (9)

Jéquier, E. (1987). Energy utilization in human obesity. *Annals of the New York Academy of Sciences, 499,* 73–83. (11)

John, O. P. (1990). The "big five" factor taxonomy: Dimensions of personality in the natural language and in questionnaires. In L. A. Pervin (Ed.), *Handbook of personality* (pp. 66–100). New York: Guilford Press. (13)

Johnson, D. (1990). Animal rights and human lives. Time for scientists to right the balance. *Psychological Science, 1,* 213–214. (2)

Johnson, M. H., Posner, M. I., & Rothbart, M. K. (1991). Components of visual orienting in early infancy: Contingency learning, anticipatory looking, and disengaging. *Journal of Cognitive Neuroscience, 3,* 335–344. (10)

Johnson, M. K., Hashtroudi, S., & Lindsay, D. S. (1993). Source monitoring. *Psychological Bulletin, 114,* 3–28. (7)

Johnson, S. L., & Roberts, J. E. (1995). Life events and bipolar disorders: Implications from biological theories. *Psychological Bulletin, 117,* 434–449. (14)

Johnston, J. C., & McClelland, J. L. (1974). Perception of letters in words: Seek not and ye shall find. *Science, 184,* 1192–1194. (8)

Johnston, J. J. (1975). Sticking with first responses on multiple-choice exams: For better or for worse? *Teaching of Psychology, 2,* 178–179. (Preface)

Johnstone, H. (1994, August 8). Prince of memory says victory was on the cards. *The Times (London),* p. 2. (7)

Jones, E. E. (1986). Interpreting interpersonal behavior: The effects of expectancies. *Science, 234,* 41–46. (16)

Jones, E. E., & Goethals, G. R. (1972). Order effects in impression formation: Attribution context and the nature of the entity. In E. Jones, D. Kanouse, H. Kelley, R. Nisbett, S. Valins, & B. Wiener (Eds.), *Attribution: Perceiving the causes of behavior* (pp. 27–46). Morristown, NJ: General Learning Press. (16)

Jones, E. E., & Harris, V. A. (1967). The attribution of attitudes. *Journal of Experimental Social Psychology, 13,* 1–24. (16)

Jones, E. E., & Nisbett, R. E. (1972). The actor and the observer: Divergent perception of the causes of behavior. In E. Jones, D. Kanouse, H. Kelley, R. Nisbett, S. Valins, & B. Wiener (Eds.), *Attribution: Perceiving the causes of behavior* (pp. 79–94). Morristown, NJ: General Learning Press. (16)

Jones, R. A. (1987). Cigarettes, respiratory rate, and the relaxation paradox. *International Journal of the Addictions, 22,* 803–809. (5)

Jones, S. L. (1994). A constructive relationship for religion with the science and profession of psychology. *American Psychologist, 49,* 184–199. (15)

Jones, S. S., Collins, K., & Hong, H.-W. (1991). An audience effect on smile production in 10-month-old infants. *Psychological Science, 2,* 45–49. (12)

Jonides, J., Kahn, R., & Rozin, P. (1975). Imagery instructions improve memory in blind subjects. *Bulletin of the Psychonomic Society, 5,* 424–426. (8)

Jouvet, M., Michel, F., & Courjon, J. (1959). Sur un stade d'activité électrique cérébral rapide au cours du sommeil physiologique [On a state of rapid electrical cerebral activity during physiological sleep]. *Comptes Rendus des Séances de la Société de Biologie, 153,* 1024–1028. (5)

Joyce, P. R., & Paykel, E. S. (1989). Predictors of drug response in depression. *Archives of General Psychiatry, 46,* 89–99. (15)

Judd, C. M., & Park, B. (1993). Definition and assessment of accuracy in social stereotypes. *Psychological Review, 100,* 109–128. (16)

Jung, C. G. (1965). *Memories, dreams, reflections* (A. Jaffe, Ed.). New York: Random House. (13)

Jurkovic, G. J. (1980). The juvenile delinquent as a moral philosopher: A structural-developmental perspective. *Psychological Bulletin, 88,* 709–727. (10)

Jusczyk, P. W. (1985). The high-amplitude sucking technique as a methodological tool in speech perception research. In G. Gottlieb & N. A. Krasnegor (Eds.), *Measurement of audition and vision in the first year of postnatal life* (pp. 195–222). Norwood, NJ: Ablex. (10)

Just, M. A., & Carpenter, P. A. (1985). Cognitive coordinate systems: Accounts of mental rotation and individual differences in spatial ability. *Psychological Review, 92,* 137–172. (8)

Just, M. A., & Carpenter, P. A. (1987). *The psychology of reading and language comprehension.* Boston: Allyn & Bacon. (8)

Kagan, J. (1984). *The nature of the child.* New York: Basic Books. (10)

Kagan, J. (1989). Temperamental contributions to social behavior. *American Psychologist, 44,* 668–674. (10)

Kagan, J., Reznick, J. S., & Snidman, N. (1988). Biological bases of childhood shyness. *Science, 240,* 167–171. (10)

Kagan, J., & Snidman, N. (1991). Infant predictors of inhibited and uninhibited profiles. *Psychological Science, 2,* 40–44. (10)

Kahneman, D., Fredrickson, B. L., Schreiber, C. A., & Redelmeier, D. A. (1993). When more pain is preferred to less: Adding a better end. *Psychological Science, 5,* 401–405. (4)

Kahneman, D., Slovic, P., & Tversky, A. (Eds.) (1982). *Judgment under uncertainty: Heuristics and biases.* Cambridge, England: Cambridge University Press. (8)

Kahneman, D., & Tversky, A. (1973). On the psychology of prediction. *Psychological Review, 80,* 237–251. (8)

Kaiser, M. K., Jonides, J., & Alexander, J. (1986). Intuitive reasoning about abstract and familiar physics problems. *Memory & Cognition, 14,* 308–312. (8)

Kalat, J. W. (1983). Evolutionary thinking in the history of the comparative psychology of learning. *Neuroscience & Biobehavioral Reviews, 7,* 309–314. (1, 6)

Kalat, J. W. (1995). *Biological Psychology* (5th ed.). Pacific Grove, CA: Brooks/Cole. (3)

Kales, A., & Kales, J. D. (1984). *Evaluation and treatment of insomnia.* New York: Oxford. (5)

Kales, A., Scharf, M. B., & Kales, J. D. (1978). Rebound insomnia: A new clinical syndrome. *Science, 201,* 1039–1041. (5)

Kales, A., Soldatos, C. R., Bixler, E. O., & Kales, J. D. (1983). Early morning insomnia with rapidly eliminated benzodiazepines. *Science, 220,* 95–97. (5)

Kamin, L. J. (1969). Predictability, surprise, attention, and conditioning. In B. A. Campbell & R. M. Church (Eds.), *Punishment and aversive behavior* (pp. 279–296). New York: Appleton-Century-Crofts. (6)

Kamin, L. J. (1974). *The science and politics of IQ.* New York: Wiley. (9)

Kanizsa, G. (1979). *Organization in vision.* New York: Praeger. (4)

Kanner, A. D., Coyne, J. C., Schaefer, C., & Lazarus, R. S. (1981). Comparison of two modes of stress measurement: Daily hassles and uplifts versus major life events. *Journal of Behavioral Medicine, 4,* 1–39. (12)

Kaplan, E. H. (1988). Crisis? A brief critique of Masters, Johnson and Kolodny. *Journal of Sex Research, 25,* 317–322. (11)

Kaplan, H. R. (1988). Gambling among lottery winners: Before and after the big score. *Journal of Gambling Behavior, 4,* 171–182. (11)

Karau, S. J., & Williams, K. D. (1993). Social loafing: A meta-analytic review and theoretical integration. *Journal of Personality and Social Psychology, 65,* 681–706. (16)

Karni, A., Tanne, D., Rubenstein, B. S., Askenasy, J. J. M., & Sagi, D. (1994). Dependence on REM sleep of overnight improvement of a perceptual skill. *Science, 265,* 679–682. (5)

Karno, M., Golding, J. M., Sorenson, S. B., & Burnam, A. (1988). The epidemiology of obsessive-compulsive disorder in five U.S. communities. *Archives of General Psychiatry, 45,* 1094–1099. (14)

Karon, B. P. (1995). Provision of psychotherapy under managed health care: A growing crisis and national nightmare. *Professional Psychology: Research and Practice, 26,* 5–9. (15)

Karon, B. P., & Widener, A. J. (1995). Psychodynamic therapies in historical perspective: "Nothing human do I consider alien to me." In B. Bongar & L. E. Beutler (Eds.), *Comprehensive textbook of psychotherapy: Theory and practice* (pp. 24–47). Oxford, England: Oxford University Press. (15)

Karrer, T., & Bartoshuk, L. (1991). Capsaicin desensitization and recovery on the human tongue. *Physiology & Behavior, 49,* 757–764. (4)

Kassin, S. M., & Lepper, M. R. (1984). Oversufficient and insufficient justification effects: Cognitive and behavioral development. *Advances in Motivation and Achievement, 3,* 73–106. (11)

Katz, S., Lautenschlager, G. J., Blackburn, A. B., & Harris, F. H. (1990). Answering reading comprehension items without passages on the SAT. *Psychological Science, 1,* 122–127. (9)

Kaufman, A. S., Harrison, P. L., & Ittenbach, R. F. (1990). Intelligence testing in the schools. In T. B. Gutkin & C. R. Reynolds (Eds.), *The handbook of school psychology* (2nd ed., pp. 289–327). New York: Wiley. (A)

Kaufman, L., & Rock, I. (1989). The moon illusion thirty years later. In M. Hershenson (Ed.), *The moon illusion* (pp. 193–234). Hillsdale, NJ: Lawrence Erlbaum. (4)

Kaye, K. L., & Bower, T. G. R. (1994). Learning and intermodal transfer of information in newborns. *Psychological Science, 5,* 286–288. (3)

Kazdin, A. E. (1995). Methods of psychotherapy research. In B. Bongar & L. E. Beutler (Eds.), *Comprehensive textbook of psychotherapy: Theory and practice* (pp. 405–433). Oxford, England: Oxford University Press. (15)

Keane, T. M., Wolfe, J., & Taylor, K. L. (1987). Post-traumatic stress disorder: Evidence for diagnostic validity and methods of psychological assessment. *Journal of Clinical Psychology, 43,* 32–43. (12)

Kelley, H. H. (1967). Attribution theory in social psychology. In D. Levine (Ed.), *Nebraska symposium on motivation* (Vol. 15, pp. 192–238). Lincoln, NE: University of Nebraska Press. (16)

Kendell, R. W., & Kemp, I. W. (1989). Maternal influenza in the etiology of schizophrenia. *Archives of General Psychiatry, 46,* 878–882. (14)

Kendler, K. S., Gruenberg, A. M., & Tsuang, M. T. (1985). Subtype stability in schizophrenia. *American Journal of Psychiatry, 142,* 827–832. (14)

Kendler, K. S., Heath, A. C., Neale, M. C., Kessler, R. C., & Eaves, L. J. (1993). Alcoholism and major depression in women. *Archives of General Psychiatry, 50,* 690–698. (14)

Kendler, K. S., Neale, M. D., Kessler, R. C., Heath, A. C., & Eaves, L. J. (1992). Major depression and generalized anxiety disorder. *Archives of General Psychiatry, 49,* 716–722. (14)

Kendler, K. S., & Robinette, C. D. (1983). Schizophrenia in the National Academy of Sciences–National Research Council twin registry—A 16-year update. *American Journal of Psychiatry, 140,* 1551–1563. (14)

Kendler, K. S., Walters, E. E., Neale, M. C., Kessler, R. C., Heath, A. C., & Eaves, L. J. (1995). The structure of the genetic and environmental risk factors for six major psychiatric disorders in women. *Archives of General Psychiatry, 52,* 374–383. (14)

Kenny, D. A. (1991). A general model of consensus and accuracy in interpersonal perception. *Psychological Review, 98,* 155–163. (16)

Kenrick, D. T. (1994). Evolutionary social psychology: From sexual selection to social cognition. *Advances in Experimental Social Psychology, 26,* 75–121. (16)

Kenrick, D. T., & Trost, M. R. (1989). A reproductive exchange model of heterosexual relationships. In C. Hendick (Ed.), *Close relationships* (pp. 92–118). Newbury Park, CA: Sage. (16)

Keon, T. L., & McDonald, B. (1982). Job satisfaction and life satisfaction: An empirical evaluation of their interrelationship. *Human Relations, 35,* 167–180. (10)

Keppel, G., & Underwood, B. J. (1962). Proactive inhibition in short-term retention of single items. *Journal of Verbal Learning and Verbal Behavior, 1,* 153–161. (7)

Kerns, L. L. (1986). Treatment of mental disorders in pregnancy: A review of psychotropic drug risks and benefits. *Journal of Nervous and Mental Disease, 174,* 652–659. (10)

Kerr, N. H. (1983). The role of vision in "visual imagery" experiments: Evidence from the congenitally blind. *Journal of Experimental Psychology: General, 112,* 265–277. (8)

Kessler, R. C., McGonagle, K. A., Zhao, S., Nelson, C. B., Hughes, E., Eshleman, S., Wittchen, H.-U., & Kendler, K. S. (1994). Lifetime and 12-month prevalence of *DSM-III-R* psychiatric disorders in the United States. *Archives of General Psychiatry, 5,* 8–19. (14)

Kety, S. S., Wendler, P. H., Jacobsen, B., Ingraham, L. J., Jansson, L., Faber, B., & Kinney, D. K. (1994). Mental illness in the biological and adoptive relatives of schizophrenic adoptees. *Archives of General Psychiatry, 51,* 442–455. (14)

Khalid, R. (1991). Personality and academic achievement: A thematic apperception perspective. *British Journal of Projective Psychology, 36,* 25–34. (11)

Kiesler, C. A. (1982a). Mental health and alternative care. *American Psychologist, 37,* 349–360. (15)

Kiesler, C. A. (1982b). Public and professional myths about mental hospitalization. *American Psychologist, 37,* 1323–1339. (15)

Kiesler, C. A. (1993). Mental health policy and mental hospitalization. *Current Directions in Psychological Science, 2,* 93–95. (15)

Kihlstrom, J. F. (1979). Hypnosis and psychopathology: Retrospect and prospect. *Journal of Abnormal Psychology, 88,* 459–473. (5)

Kihlstrom, J. F., Barnhardt, T. M., & Tataryn, D. J. (1992). The psychological unconscious. *American Psychologist, 47,* 788–791. (8)

Kim, S. (1989). *Inversions.* San Francisco, CA: W. H. Freeman. (4)

Kimble, G. A. (1993). A modest proposal for a minor revolution in the language of psychology. *Psychological Science, 4,* 253–255. (6)

Kimble, G. A. (1961). *Hilgard and Marquis' Conditioning and Learning* (2nd ed.). New York: Appleton-Century-Crofts. (6)

Kimble, G. A., & Garmezy, N. (1968). *Principles of general psychology* (3rd ed.). New York: Ronald. (13)

Kinsey, A. C., Pomeroy, W. B., & Martin, C. E. (1948). *Sexual behavior in the human male.* Philadelphia: W. B. Saunders. (11)

Kinsey, A. C., Pomeroy, W. B., Martin, C. E., & Gebhard, P. H. (1953). *Sexual behavior in the human female.* Philadelphia: W. B. Saunders. (11)

Klayman, J., & Ha, Y.-W. (1987). Confirmation, disconfirmation, and information in hypothesis testing. *Psychological Review, 94,* 211–228. (8)

Klein, D. F., Zitrin, C. M., Woerner, M. G., & Ross, D. C. (1983). Treatment of phobias. II. Behavior therapy and supportive psychotherapy: Are there any specific ingredients? *Archives of General Psychiatry, 40,* 139–145. (15)

Kleinknecht, R. A. (1982). The origins and remission of fear in a group of tarantula enthusiasts. *Behaviour Research & Therapy, 20,* 437–443. (14)

Kleinmuntz, B., & Szucko, J. J. (1984). A field study of the fallibility of polygraphic lie detection. *Nature, 308,* 449–450. (12)

Kleitman, N. (1963). *Sleep and wakefulness* (revised and enlarged edition). Chicago: University of Chicago Press. (5)

Kline, M., Tschann, J. M., Johnston, J. R., & Wallerstein, J. S. (1989). Children's adjustment in joint and sole physical custody families. *Developmental Psychology, 25,* 430–438. (10)

Kohlberg, L. (1969). Stage and sequence: The cognitive-developmental approach to socialization. In D. A. Goslin (Ed.), *Handbook of socialization theory and research.* Chicago: Rand McNally (10)

Kohlberg, L., & Hersh, R. H. (1977). Moral development: A review of the theory. *Theory into Practice, 16,* 53–59. (10)

Kolko, D. J., & Milan, M. A. (1983). Reframing and paradoxical instruction to overcome "resistance" in the treatment of delinquent youths: A multiple baseline analysis. *Journal of Consulting and Clinical Psychology, 51,* 655–660. (15)

Komaki, J., Barwick, K. D., & Scott, L. R. (1978). A behavioral approach to occupational safety: Pinpointing and reinforcing safe performance in a food manufacturing plant. *Journal of Applied Psychology, 63,* 434–445. (A)

Kopp, C. B. (1990). Risks in infancy: Appraising the research. *Merrill-Palmer Quarterly, 36,* 117–139. (10)

Koppenaal, R. J. (1963). Time changes in the strengths of A-B, A-C lists: Spontaneous recovery? *Journal of Verbal Learning and Verbal Behavior, 2,* 310–319. (7)

Koriat, A., Ben-Zur, H., & Sheffer, D. (1988). Telling the same story twice: Output monitoring and age. *Journal of Memory and Language, 27,* 23–39. (7)

Koss, M. P., & Butcher, J. N. (1986). Research on brief psychotherapy. In S. L. Garfield & A. E. Bergin (Eds.), *Handbook of psychotherapy and behavior change* (pp. 627–670). New York: Wiley. (15)

Koss, M. P., & Dinero, T. E. (1988). Predictors of sexual aggression among a national sample of male college students. *Annals of the New York Academy of Sciences, 528,* 133–147. (11)

Koss, M. P., Gidycz, C. A., & Wisniewski, N. (1987). The scope of rape: Incidence and prevalence of sexual aggression and victimization in a national sample of higher education students. *Journal of Consulting and Clinical Psychology, 55,* 162–170. (11)

Kossek, E. E. (1990). Diversity in child care assistance needs: Employee problems, preferences, and work-related outcomes. *Personnel Psychology, 43,* 769–791. (A)

Kosten, T. R., Rounsaville, B. J., & Kleber, H. D. (1987). A 2.5-year follow-up of cocaine use among treated opioid addicts. *Archives of General Psychiatry, 44,* 281–284. (14)

Koyano, W. (1991). Japanese attitudes toward the elderly: A review of research findings. *Journal of Cross-cultural Gerontology, 4,* 335–345. (10)

Kozel, N. J., & Adams, E. H. (1986). Epidemiology of drug abuse: An overview. *Science, 234,* 970–974. (5)

Kozlowski, L. T., Frecker, R. C., Khouw, V., & Pope, M. A. (1980). The misuse of "less hazardous" cigarettes and its detection: Hole blocking of ventilated filters. *American Journal of Public Health, 70,* 1202–1203. (14)

Kraiger, K., Hakel, M. D., & Cornelius, E. T. III (1984). Exploring fantasies of TAT reliability. *Journal of Personality Assessment, 48,* 365–370. (13)

Kramer, P. D. (1993). *Listening to Prozac.* New York: Viking. (15)

Kraut, R. E., & Johnston, R. E. (1979). Social and emotional messages of smiling: An ethological approach. *Journal of Personality and Social Psychology, 37,* 1539–1553. (12)

Kreskin (1991). *Secrets of the amazing Kreskin.* Buffalo, NY: Prometheus. (2)

Kringlen, E., & Cramer, G. (1989). Offspring of monozygotic twins discordant for schizophrenia. *Archives of General Psychiatry, 46,* 873–877. (14)

Krueger, B., & Neff, J. (1995, January 29). As killer dies, 2 women find diverging paths to peace. *News & Observer* (Raleigh, NC), pp. 1A, 4A. (12)

Krueger, D. W. (1978). The differential diagnosis of proverb interpretation. In W. E. Fann, I. Karacan, A. D. Pokorny, & R. L. Williams (Eds.), *Phenomenology and treatment of schizophrenia* (pp. 193–201). New York: Spectrum. (14)

Krug, S. E. (1978). Reliability and scope in personality assessment: A comparison of the Cattell and Eysenck inventories. *Multivariate Experimental Clinical Research, 3,* 195–204. (13)

Kruglanski, A. W., & Mayseless, O. (1990). Classic and current social comparison research: Expanding the perspective. *Psychological Bulletin, 108,* 195–208. (16)

Krupnick, J. L., Elkin, I., Collins, J., Simmens, S., Sotsky, S. M., Pilkonis, P. A., & Watkins, J. T. (1994). Therapeutic alliance and clinical outcome in the NIMH Treatment of Depression Collaborative Research Program: Preliminary findings. *Psychotherapy, 31,* 28–35. (15)

Kryger, M. (Ed.) (1993). Amphetamines and narcolepsy. *Sleep, 16,* 199–206. (5)

Kübler-Ross, E. (1969). *On death and dying.* New York: Macmillan. (10)

Kübler-Ross, E. (1975). *Death: The final stage of growth.* Englewood Cliffs, NJ: Prentice-Hall. (10)

Kuhn, D., Weinstock, M., & Flaton, R. (1994). How well do jurors reason? Competence dimensions of individual variation in a juror reasoning task. *Psychological Science, 5,* 289–296. (16)

Kulik, J. A., Bangert-Drowns, R. L., & Kulik, C. C. (1984). Effectiveness of coaching for aptitude tests. *Psychological Bulletin, 95,* 179–188. (9)

Lackner, J. R. (1993). Orientation and movement in unusual force environments. *Psychological Science, 4,* 134–142. (4)

LaFromboise, T., Coleman, H. L. K., & Gerton, J. (1993). Psychological impact of biculturalism: Evidence and theory. *Psychological Bulletin, 114,* 395–412. (10)

Laing, D. G., Prescott, J., Bell, G. A., Gillmore, R., James, C., Best, D. J., Allen, S., Yoshida, M., & Yamazaki, K. (1993). A cross-cultural study of taste discrimination with Australians and Japanese. *Chemical Senses, 18,* 161–168. (4)

Laird, J. D. (1974). Self-attribution of emotion: The effects of expressive behavior on the quality of emotional experience. *Journal of Personality and Social Psychology, 29,* 475–486. (12)

Lakoff, G. (1987). *Women, fire, and dangerous things.* Chicago: University of Chicago Press. (8)

Lamb, M. E. (1982). Maternal employment and child development: A review. In M. E. Lamb (Ed.), *Nontraditional families* (pp. 45–69). Hillsdale, NJ: Lawrence Erlbaum. (10)

Lamb, M. E., Frodi, A. M., Hwang, C.-P., & Frodi, M. (1982). Varying degrees of paternal involvement in infant care: Attitudinal and behavioral correlates. In M. E. Lamb (Ed.), *Nontraditional families* (pp. 117–137). Hillsdale, NJ: Lawrence Erlbaum. (10)

Lambert, N. M. (1981). Psychological evidence in *Larry P. v. Wilson Riles*: An evaluation by a witness for the defense. *American Psychologist, 36,* 937–952. (9)

Lamm, H., & Myers, D. G. (1978). Group-induced polarization of attitudes and behavior. *Advances in Experimental Social Psychology, 11,* 145–195. (16)

Land, E. H., Hubel, D. H., Livingstone, M. S., Perry, S. H., & Burns, M. M. (1983). Colour-generating interactions across the corpus callosum. *Nature, 303,* 616–618. (4)

Land, E. H., & McCann, J. J. (1971). Lightness and retinex theory. *Journal of the Optical Society of America, 61,* 1–11. (4)

Lande, S. D. (1982). Physiological and subjective measures of anxiety during flooding. *Behaviour Research and Therapy, 20,* 81–88. (14)

Landrine, H., Klonoff, E. A., & Brown-Collins, A. (1992). Cultural diversity and methodology in feminist psychology. *Psychology of Women Quarterly, 16,* 145–163. (1)

Lang, P. J. (1994). The varieties of emotional experience: A meditation on James-Lange theory. *Psychological Review, 101,* 211–221. (12)

Langer, E. J. (1975). The illusion of control. *Journal of Personality and Social Psychology, 32,* 311–328. (8)

Langlois, J. H., & Roggman, L. A. (1990). Attractive faces are only average. *Psychological Science, 1,* 115–121. (16)

Langlois, J. H., Roggman, L. A., & Musselman, L. (1994). What is average and what is not average about average faces? *Psychological Science, 5,* 214–220. (16)

Langworthy, R. A., & Jennings, J. W. (1972). Oddball, abstract olfactory learning in laboratory rats. *Psychological Record, 22,* 487–490. (1)

Larrick, R. P., Morgan, J. N., & Nisbett, R. E. (1990). Teaching the use of cost-benefit reasoning in everyday life. *Psychological Science, 1,* 362–370. (8)

Lashley, K. S. (1929). *Brain mechanisms and intelligence.* Chicago: University of Chicago Press. (3)

Lashley, K. S. (1950). In search of the engram. *Symposia of the Society for Experimental Biology, 4,* 454–482. (3)

Lashley, K. S. (1951). The problem of serial order in behavior. In L. A. Jeffress (Ed.), *Cerebral mechanisms in behavior* (pp. 112–146). New York: Wiley. (8)

Latané, B., & Darley, J. M. (1968). Group inhibition of bystander intervention in emergencies. *Journal of Personality and Social Psychology, 10,* 215–221. (16)

Latané, B., & Darley, J. M. (1969). Bystander "apathy." *American Scientist, 57,* 244–268. (16)

Latané, B., Williams, K., & Harkins, S. (1979). Many hands make light the work: The causes and consequences of social loafing. *Journal of Personality and Social Psychology, 37,* 823–832. (16)

Lauer, C. J., Schreiber, W., Holsboer, F., & Krieg, J.-C. (1995). In quest of identifying vulnerability markers for psychiatric disorders by all-night polysomnography. *Archives of General Psychiatry, 52,* 145–153. (14)

Laumann, E. O. (1969). Friends of urban men: An assessment of accuracy in reporting their socio-economic attributes, mutual choice, and attitude development. *Sociometry, 32,* 54–69. (16)

Laumann, E. O., Gagnon, J. H., Michael, R. T., & Michaels, S. (1994). *The social organization of sexuality: Sexual practices in the United States.* Chicago, IL: University of Chicago Press. (11)

Lavine, R., Buchsbaum, M. S., & Poncy, M. (1976). Auditory analgesia: Somatosensory evoked response and subjective pain rating. *Psychophysiology, 13,* 140–148. (4, 12)

Lawler, E. E. III (1971). *Pay and organizational effectiveness.* New York: McGraw-Hill. (A)

Lazarus, R. S. (1977). Cognitive and coping processes in emotion. In A. Monat & R. S. Lazarus (Eds.), *Stress and coping* (pp. 145–158). New York: Columbia University Press. (12)

Lazarus, R. S., Averill, J. R., & Opton, E. M., Jr. (1970). Towards a cognitive theory of emotion. In M. B. Arnold (Ed.), *Feelings and emotions* (pp. 207–232). New York: Academic Press. (12)

Ledwidge, B. (1980). Run for your mind: Aerobic exercise as a means of alleviating anxiety and depression. *Canadian Journal of Behavioral Science, 12,* 126–140. (14)

Lee, M. K., Graham, S. N., & Gold, P. E. (1988). Memory enhancement with post-training intraventricular glucose injections in rats. *Behavioral Neuroscience, 102,* 591–595. (7)

Leehy, S. C., Moscowitz-Cook, A., Brill, S., & Held, R. (1975). Orientational anisotropy in infant vision. *Science, 190,* 900–902. (10)

Leibowitz, S. F., & Alexander, J. T. (1991). Analysis of neuropeptide Y-induced feeding: Dissociation of Y_1 and Y_2 receptor effects on natural meal patterns. *Peptides, 12,* 1251–1260. (11)

Leibowitz, S. F., Hammer, N. J., & Chang, K. (1981). Hypothalamic paraventricular nucleus lesions produce overeating and obesity in the rat. *Physiology & Behavior, 27,* 1031–1040. (11)

LeMagnen, J. (1981). The metabolic basis of dual periodicity of feeding in rats. *Behavioral and Brain Sciences, 4,* 561–607. (11)

Lenneberg, E. H. (1967). *Biological foundations of language.* New York: Wiley. (10)

Lenneberg, E. H. (1969). On explaining language. *Science, 164,* 635–643. (10)

Leonard, H. L., Swedo, S. E., Rapoport, J. L., Koby, E. V., Lenane, M. C., Cheslow, D. L., & Hamburger, S. D. (1989). Treatment of obsessive-compulsive disorder with clomipramine and desipramine in children and adolescents. *Archives of General Psychiatry, 46,* 1088–1092. (14)

Lester, J. T. (1983). Wrestling with the self on Mount Everest. *Journal of Humanistic Psychology, 23,* 31–41. (13)

Leuchtenburg, W. E. (1963). *Franklin D. Roosevelt and the New Deal 1932–1940.* New York: Harper & Row. (16)

LeVay, S. (1991). A difference in hypothalamic structure between heterosexual and homosexual men. *Science, 253,* 1034–1037. (11)

Levenson, R. W. (1992). Autonomic nervous system differences among emotions. *Psychological Science, 3,* 23–27. (12)

Levenson, R. W., Oyama, O. N., & Meek, P. S. (1987). Greater reinforcement from alcohol for those at risk: Parental risk, personality risk, and sex. *Journal of Abnormal Psychology, 96,* 242–253. (14)

Leventhal, H. (1970). Findings and theory in the study of fear communication. In L. Berkowitz (Ed.), *Advances in Experimental Social Psychology* (Vol. 5, pp. 119–186). New York: Academic Press. (16)

Levin, M. (1994). Comment on the Minnesota transracial adoption study. *Intelligence, 19,* 13–20. (9)

Levine, R. V. (1990). The pace of life. *American Scientist, 78,* 450–459. (12)

Levinger, G. (1976). A social psychological perspective on marital dissolution. *Journal of Social Issues, 32,* 21–47. (16)

Levinger, G. (1980). Toward the analysis of close relationships. *Journal of Experimental Social Psychology, 16,* 510–544. (16)

Levinger, G. (1983). Development and change. In H. H. Kelley, E. Berscheid, A. Christensen, J. H. Harvey, T. L. Huston, G. Levinger, E. McClintock, L. A. Peplau, & D. R. Peterson (Eds.), *Close relationships* (pp. 315–359). New York: W. H. Freeman. (16)

Levinson, D. J. (1977). The mid-life transition: A period in adult psychosocial development. *Psychiatry, 40,* 99–112. (10)

Levinson, D. J. (1978). *The seasons of a man's life.* New York: Ballantine. (10)

Lewis, D. O., Moy, E., Jackson, L. D., Aaronson, R., Restifo, N., Serra, S., & Simos, A. (1985). Biopsychosocial characteristics of children who later murder: A prospective study. *American Journal of Psychiatry, 142,* 1161–1167. (12)

Lewis, D. O., Shanok, S. S., Grant, M., & Ritvo, E. (1983). Homicidally aggressive young children: Neuropsychiatric and experiential correlates. *American Journal of Psychiatry, 140,* 148–153. (12)

Lewis, M. (1995). Self-conscious emotions. *American Scientist, 83,* 68–78. (12)

Lewis, M., Sullivan, M. W., Stanger, C., & Weiss, M. (1991). Self development and self-conscious emotions. In S. Chess & M. E. Hertzig (Eds.), *Annual Progress in Child Psychiatry and Child Development 1990* (pp. 34–51). New York: Brunner/Mazel. (10)

Lewis, M., Thomas, D. A., & Worobey, J. (1990). Developmental organization, stress, and illness. *Psychological Science, 1,* 316–318. (10)

Lichtenstein, S., Fischhoff, B., & Phillips, L. D. (1982). Calibration of probabilities: The state of the art to 1980. In D. Kahneman, P. Slovic, & A. Tversky (Eds.), *Judgment under uncertainty: Heuristics and biases* (pp. 306–334). Cambridge, England: Cambridge University Press. (8)

Lieberman, J. A., Kane, J. M., Sarantakos, S., Gadaleta, D., Woerner, M., Alvir, J., & Ramos-Lorenzi, J. (1987). Prediction of relapse in schizophrenia. *Archives of General Psychiatry, 44,* 597–603. (15)

Liebowitz, M. R., Gorman, J. M., Fyer, A. J., Levitt, M., Dillon, D., Levy, G., Appleby, I. L., Anderson, S., Palij, M., Davies, S. O., & Klein, D. F. (1985). Lactate provocation of panic attacks: II. Biochemical and physiological findings. *Archives of General Psychiatry, 42,* 709–719. (14)

Lilie, J. K., & Rosenberg, R. P. (1990). Behavioral treatment of insomnia. *Progress in Behavior Modification, 25,* 152–177. (5)

Lilienfeld, S. O. (1993). Do 'honesty' tests really measure honesty? *Skeptical Inquirer, 18,* 32–41. (12)

Lindberg, N. O., Coburn, C., & Stricker, E. M. (1984). Increased feeding by rats after subdiabetogenic streptozotocin treatment: A role for insulin in satiety. *Behavioral Neuroscience, 98,* 138–145. (11)

Lindsay, D. S., & Read, J. D. (1994). Psychotherapy and memories of childhood sexual abuse: A cognitive perspective. *Applied Cognitive Psychology, 8,* 281–338. (7)

Link, N. F., Sherer, S. E., & Byrne, P. N. (1977). Moral judgment and moral conduct in the psychopath. *Canadian Psychiatric Association Journal, 22,* 341–346. (10)

Linn, R., & Gilligan, C. (1990). One action, two moral orientations—The tension between justice and care voices in Israeli selective conscientious objectors. *New Ideas in Psychology, 8,* 189–203. (10)

Linton, M. (1982). Transformations of memory in everyday life. In U. Neisser (Ed.), *Memory observed* (pp. 77–91). San Francisco: W. H. Freeman. (7)

Lippa, R. (1983). Expressive behavior. In L. Wheeler & P. Shaver (Eds.), *Review of personality and social psychology* (Vol. 4, pp. 181–205). Beverly Hills, CA: Sage. (16)

Lipsey, M. W., & Wilson, D. B. (1993). The efficacy of psychological, educational, and behavioral treatment. *American Psychologist, 48,* 1181–1209. (15)

Lisak, D., & Roth, S. (1988). Motivational factors in nonincarcerated sexually aggressive men. *Journal of Personality and Social Psychology, 55,* 795–802. (11)

Llaneza-Ramos, M. L. (1991). Perceived gender and drive for success. *Philippine Journal of Psychology, 24,* 59–64. (11)

Locke, E. A., & Latham, G. P. (1991). The fallacies of common sense "truths": A reply to Lamal. *Psychological Science, 2,* 131–132. (11, A)

Locke, E. A., Shaw, K. N., Saari, L. M., & Latham, G. P. (1981). Goal setting and task performance: 1969–1980. *Psychological Bulletin, 90,* 125–152. (11)

Locke, J. L. (1994). Phases in the child's development of language. *American Scientist, 82,* 436–445. (10)

Loeb, J. (1973). *Forced movements, tropisms, and animal conduct.* New York: Dover. (Original work published 1918.) (6)

Loehlin, J. C. (1992). *Genes and environment in personality development.* Newbury Park, CA: Sage. (13)

Loehlin, J. C., Willerman, L., & Horn, J. M. (1988). Human behavior genetics. *Annual Review of Psychology, 39,* 101–133. (3)

Loehlin, J. C., Horn, J. M., & Willerman, L. (1989). Modeling IQ change: Evidence from the Texas adoption project. *Child Development, 60,* 993–1004. (9)

Loehlin, J. C., Horn, J. M., & Willerman, L. (1994). Differential inheritance of mental abilities in the Texas Adoption Project. *Intelligence, 19,* 325–336. (9)

Loewi, O. (1960). An autobiographic sketch. *Perspectives in Biology, 4,* 3–25. (3)

Loftus, E. F. (1975). Leading questions and the eyewitness report. *Cognitive Psychology, 7,* 560–572. (7)

Loftus, E. F. (1992). When a lie becomes memory's truth: Memory distortion after exposure to misinformation. *Current Directions in Psychological Science, 1,* 121–123. (7)

Loftus, E. F. (1993). The reality of repressed memories. *American Psychologist, 48,* 518–537. (7)

London, E. D., Cascella, N. G., Wong, D. F., Phillips, R. L., Dannals, R. F., Links, J. M., Herning, R., Grayson, R., Jaffe, J. H., & Wagner, H. N. (1990). Cocaine-induced reduction of utilization in human brain. *Archives of General Psychiatry, 47,* 567–574. (5)

Long, B. B. (1986). The prevention of mental-emotional disabilities. *American Psychologist, 41,* 825–829. (15)

Longstreth, L. E. (1981). Revisiting Skeels' final study: A critique. *Developmental Psychology, 17,* 620–625. (9)

Loomis, J. M., Klatzky, R. L., Golledge, R. G., Cicinelli, J. G., Pellegrino, J. W., & Fry, P. A. (1993). Nonvisual navigation by blind and sighted: Assessment of path integration ability. *Journal of Experimental Psychology: General, 122,* 73–91. (8)

Lorenz, K. (1950). The comparative method in studying innate behaviour patterns. *Symposia of the Society for Experimental Biology, 4,* 221–268. (11)

Lorenz, V. C. (1990). State lotteries and compulsive gambling. *Journal of Gambling Studies, 6,* 383–396. (8)

Lowe, M. R. (1993). The effects of dieting on eating behavior: A three-factor model. *Psychological Bulletin, 114,* 100–121. (11)

Lubinski, D., & Benbow, C. P. (1992). Gender differences in abilities and preferences among the gifted: Implications for the math-science pipeline. *Current Directions in Psychological Science, 1,* 61–66. (9)

Lubinski, D., & Thompson, T. (1993). Species and individual differences in communication based on private states. *Behavioral and Brain Sciences, 16,* 627–680. (6)

Luginbuhl, J. (1992). Comprehension of judges' instructions in the penalty phase of a capital trial: Focus on mitigating circumstances. *Law and Human Behavior, 16,* 203–218. (16)

Lundy, A. (1985). The reliability of the thematic apperception test. *Journal of Personality Assessment, 49,* 141–145. (13)

Lykken, D. T. (1979). The detection of deception. *Psychological Bulletin, 86,* 47–53. (12)

Lykken, D. T., McGue, M., Tellegen, A., & Bouchard, T. J. (1992). Emergenesis: Genetic traits that may not run in families. *American Psychologist, 47,* 1565–1577. (3)

Lyness, S. A. (1993). Predictors of differences between Type A and B individuals in heart rate and blood pressure reactivity. *Psychological Bulletin, 114,* 266–295. (12)

Lynn, S. J., Rhue, J. W., & Weekes, J. R. (1990). Hypnotic involuntariness: A social cognitive analysis. *Psychological Review, 97,* 169–184. (5)

Maccoby, E. E. (1990). Gender and relationships. *American Psychologist, 45,* 513–520. (10)

Maccoby, E. E., & Jacklin, C. N. (1974). *The psychology of sex differences.* Stanford, CA: Stanford University Press. (10)

MacDonald, M. C., Pearlmutter, N. J., & Seidenberg, M. S. (1994). Lexical nature of syntactic ambiguity resolution. *Psychological Review, 101,* 676–703. (8)

Macdonald, R. L., Weddle, M. G., & Gross, R. A. (1986). Benzodiazepine, beta-carboline, and barbiturate actions on GABA responses. *Advances in Biochemical Psychopharmacology, 41,* 67–78. (5, 15)

MacLeod, C. M. (1988). Forgotten but not gone: Savings for pictures and words in long-term memory. *Journal of Experimental Psychology: Learning, Memory, and Cognition, 14,* 195–212. (7)

Macphail, E. M. (1985). Vertebrate intelligence: The null hypothesis. *Philosophical Transactions of the Royal Society, B308,* 37–51. (1)

Maddahian, E., Newcomb, M. D., & Bentler, P. M. (1988). Risk factors for substance use: Ethnic differences among adolescents. *Journal of Substance Abuse, 1,* 11–23. (14)

Madsen, K. B. (1959). *Theories of motivation.* Copenhagen: Munksgaard. (11)

Maehr, M. L., & Kleiber, D. A. (1981). The graying of achievement motivation. *American Psychologist, 36,* 787–793. (11)

Maier, N. R. F., & Schneirla, T. C. (1964). *Principles of animal psychology* (enlarged edition). New York: Dover. (6)

Maier, S. F., Seligman, M. E. P., & Solomon, R. L. (1969). Pavlovian fear conditioning and learned helplessness: Effects on escape and avoidance behavior of (a) the CS-US contingency and (b) the independence of the US and voluntary responding. In B. A. Campbell and R. M. Church (Eds.), *Punishment and aversive behavior* (pp. 299–342). New York: Appleton-Century-Crofts. (14)

Maki, R. H. (1990). Memory for script actions: Effects of relevance and detail expectancy. *Memory & Cognition, 18,* 5–14. (7)

Maki, R. H., & Serra, M. (1992). The basis of test predictions for text material. *Journal of Experimental Psychology: Learning, Memory, and Cognition, 18,* 116–126. (7)

Malamuth, N. M., & Donnerstein, E. (1982). The effects of aggressive-pornographic mass media stimuli. In L. Berkowitz (Ed.), *Advances in experimental social psychology* (Vol. 15, pp. 103–136). New York: Academic Press. (11)

Malamuth, N. M., Sockloskie, R. J., Koss, M. P., & Tanaka, J. S. (1991). Characteristics of aggressors against women: Testing a model using a national sample of college students. *Journal of Consulting and Clinical Psychology, 59,* 670–681. (11)

Malinosky-Rummell, R., & Hansen, D. J. (1993). Long-term consequences of childhood physical abuse. *Psychological Bulletin, 114,* 68–79. (12)

Malmquist, C. P. (1986). Children who witness parental murder: Posttraumatic aspects. *Journal of the American Academy of Child Psychiatry, 25,* 320–325. (7)

Mandler, J. M. (1990). A new perspective on cognitive development in infancy. *American Scientist, 78,* 236–243. (10)

Manji, H. K., Hsiao, J. K., Risby, E. D., Oliver, J., Rudorfer, M. V., & Potter, W. Z. (1991). The mechanisms of action of lithium. I. Effects on serotoninergic and noradrenergic systems in normal subjects. *Archives of General Psychiatry, 48,* 505–512. (15)

Mann, J. J., McBride, P. A., & Stanley, M. (1986). Postmortem monoamine receptor and enzyme studies in suicide. *Annals of the New York Academy of Sciences, 487,* 114–121. (14)

Mansky, P. A. (1978). Opiates: Human psychopharmacology. In L. L. Iversen, S. D. Iversen, & S. H. Snyder (Eds.), *Handbook of psychopharmacology: Vol. 12, Drugs of abuse* (pp. 95–185). New York: Plenum. (5)

Manuck, S. B., Cohen, S., Rabin, B. S., Muldoon, M. F., & Bachen, E. A. (1991). Individual differences in cellular immune response to stress. *Psychological Science, 2,* 111–115. (12)

Maqsud, M. (1992). Psychoticism, extraversion, and neuroticism among Botswana adolescents. *Journal of Social Psychology, 132,* 275–276. (13)

Marcia, J. E. (1980). Identity in adolescence. In J. Adelson (Ed.), *Handbook of adolescent psychology* (pp. 159–187). New York: Wiley. (10)

Marder, S. R., Mebane, A., Chien, C., Winslade, W. J., Swann, E., & Van Putten, T. (1983). A comparison of patients who refuse and consent to neuroleptic treatment. *American Journal of Psychiatry, 140,* 470–472. (15)

Marek, G. R. (1975). *Toscanini.* London: Vision. (7)

Margolskee, R. F. (1993). The biochemistry and molecular biology of taste transduction. *Current Opinion in Neurobiology, 3,* 526–531. (4)

Mark, V. H., & Ervin, F. R. (1970). *Violence and the brain.* New York: Harper & Row. (3)

Markman, E. M. (1990). Constraints children place on word meanings. *Cognitive Science, 14,* 57–77. (10)

Markman, E. M., & Hutchinson, J. E. (1984). Children's sensitivity to constraints on word meaning: Taxonomic versus thematic relations. *Cognitive Psychology, 16,* 1–27. (10)

Marks, D., & Kammann, R. (1980). *The psychology of the psychic.* Buffalo, NY: Prometheus. (2, 13)

Marlatt, G. A. (1978). Craving for alcohol, loss of control, and relapse: A cognitive-behavioral analysis. In P. E. Nathan, G. A. Marlatt, & T. Løberg (Eds.), *Alcoholism: New directions in behavioral research and treatment* (pp. 271–314). New York: Plenum. (14)

Marriott, F. H. C. (1976). Abnormal colour vision. In H. Davson (Ed.), *The eye* (2nd ed., pp. 533–547). New York: Academic Press. (4)

Marsh, H. W., & Byrne, B. M. (1991). Differentiated additive androgyny model: Relations between masculinity, femininity, and multiple dimensions of self-concept. *Journal of Personality and Social Psychology, 61,* 811–828. (13)

Marshall, W. L. (1988). The use of sexually explicit stimuli by rapists, child molesters, and nonoffenders. *Journal of Sex Research, 25,* 267–288. (11)

Martin, L. (1986). "Eskimo words for snow": A case study in the genesis and decay of an anthropological example. *American Anthropologist, 88,* 418–423. (8)

Masling, J. M., Bornstein, R. F., Poynton, F. G., Reid, S., & Katkin, E. S. (1991). Perception without awareness and electrodermal responding: A strong test of subliminal psychodynamic activation effects. *Journal of Mind and Behavior, 12,* 33–48. (4)

Maslow, A. H. (1962). *Toward a psychology of being.* Princeton, NJ: Van Nostrand. (13)

Maslow, A. H. (1970). *Motivation and personality* (2nd ed.). New York: Harper & Row. (11)

Maslow, A. H. (1971). *The farther reaches of human nature.* New York: Viking. (13)

Martell, D. A., & Dietz, P. E. (1992). Mentally disordered offenders who push or attempt to push victims onto subway tracks in New York City. *Archives of General Psychiatry, 49,* 472–475. (15)

Masson, J. M. (1984). *The assault on truth.* New York: Farrar, Straus, and Giroux. (13)

Masters, W. H., & Johnson, V. E. (1966). *Human sexual response.* Boston: Little, Brown. (11)

Matarazzo, J. D., & Wiens, A. N. (1977). Black Intelligence Test of Cultural Homogeneity and Wechsler Adult Intelligence Scale scores of black and white police applicants. *Journal of Applied Psychology, 62,* 57–63. (9)

Matheny, A. P., Jr. (1989). Children's behavioral inhibition over age and across situations: Genetic similarity for a trait to change. *Journal of Personality, 57,* 215–235. (10)

Matsui, T., Okada, A., & Kakuyama, T. (1982). Influence of goal setting, performance, and feedback effectiveness. *Journal of Applied Psychology, 67,* 645–648. (11)

Matthews, K. A., & Rodin, J. (1989). Women's changing work roles. *American Psychologist, 44,* 1389–1393. (A)

Matsumoto, D. (1994). *People: Psychology from a cultural perspective.* Pacific Grove, CA: Brooks/Cole. (2)

May, C. P., Hasher, L., & Stoltzfus, E. R. (1993). Optimal time of day and the magnitude of age differences in memory. *Psychological Science, 4,* 326–330. (7)

McCall, V. W., Yates, B., Hendricks, S., Turner, K., & McNabb, B. (1989). Comparison between the Stanford-Binet: L-M and the Stanford-Binet: Fourth edition with a group of gifted children. *Contemporary Educational Psychology, 14,* 93–96. (9)

McCaul, K. D., & Malott, J. M. (1984). Distraction and coping with pain. *Psychological Bulletin, 95,* 516–533. (4, 12)

McClelland, D. C. (1993). Intelligence is not the best predictor of job performance. *Current Directions in Psychological Science, 2,* 5–6. (9)

McClelland, D. C., Atkinson, J. W., Clark, R. A., & Lowell, E. L. (1953). *The achievement motive.* New York: Appleton-Century-Crofts. (11)

McClelland, D. C., Koestner, R., & Weinberger, J. (1989). How do self-attributed and implicit motives differ? *Psychological Review, 96,* 690–702. (11)

McClelland, J. L. (1988). Connectionist models and psychological evidence. *Journal of Memory and Language, 27,* 107–123. (8)

McClelland, J. L., & Rumelhart, D. E. (1981). An interactive activation model of context effects in letter perception: Part 1. An account of basic findings. *Psychological Review, 88,* 375–407. (8)

McClintock, M. K. (1971). Menstrual synchrony and suppression. *Nature, 229,* 244–245. (4)

McConnell, J. V. (1990). Negative reinforcement and positive punishment. *Teaching of Psychology, 17,* 247–249. (6)

McConnell, J. W. (1989, Summer). Reinvention of subliminal perception. *Skeptical Inquirer, 13,* 427–429. (4)

McCormick, M. C. (1985). The contribution of low birth weight to infant mortality and childhood morbidity. *New England Journal of Medicine, 312,* 82–90. (10)

McCormick, M. E., & Wolf, J. S. (1993). Intervention programs for gifted girls. *Roeper Review, 16,* 85–88. (11)

McCornack, R. L. (1983). Bias in the validity of predicted college grades in four ethnic minority groups. *Educational & Psychological Measurement, 43,* 517–522. (9)

McCrae, R. R., & Costa, P. T., Jr. (1987). Validation of the five-factor model of personality across instruments and observers. *Journal of Personality and Social Psychology, 52,* 81–90. (13)

McCrae, R. R., & Costa, P. T., Jr. (1994). The stability of personality: Observations and evaluations. *Current Directions in Psychological Science, 3,* 173–175. (13)

McDaniel, M. A., Einstein, G. O., & Lollis, T. (1988). Qualitative and quantitative considerations in encoding difficulty effects. *Memory & Cognition, 16,* 8–14. (7)

McDaniel, M. A., Schmidt, F. L., & Hunter, J. E. (1988). Job experience correlates of job performance. *Journal of Applied Psychology 73,* 327–330. (A)

McDougall, W. (1932). *The energies of men.* New York: Charles Scribner's Sons. (11)

McGaugh, J. L. (1990). Significance and remembrance: The role of neuromodulatory systems. *Psychological Science, 1,* 15–25. (7)

McGlynn, S. M., & Kaszniak, A. W. (1991). When metacognition fails: Impaired awareness of deficit in Alzheimer's disease. *Journal of Cognitive Neuroscience, 3,* 182–189. (7)

McGregor, D. M. (1960). *The human side of enterprise.* New York: McGraw-Hill. (A)

McGuire, W. J. (1985). Attitudes and attitude change. In G. Lindzey & E. Aronson (Eds.), *Handbook of social psychology* (Vol. 2, pp. 233–346). New York: Random House. (16)

McGuire, W. J., & Papageorgis, D. (1961). The relative efficacy of various types of prior belief-defense in producing immunity against persuasion. *Journal of Abnormal and Social Psychology, 62,* 327–337. (16)

McMahon, C. E. (1975). The wind of the cannon ball: An informative anecdote from medical history. *Psychotherapy & Psychosomatics, 26,* 125–131. (12)

McMurtry, P. L., & Mershon, D. H. (1985). Auditory distance judgments in noise, with and without hearing protection. *Proceedings of the Human Factors Society* (Baltimore, MD), pp. 811–813. (4)

McNally, R. J. (1990). Psychological approaches to panic disorder: A review. *Psychological Bulletin, 108,* 403–419. (14)

McNeal, E. T., & Cimbolic, P. (1986). Antidepressants and biochemical theories of depression. *Psychological Bulletin, 99,* 361–374. (15)

McReynolds, P. (1985). Psychological assessment and clinical practice: Problems and prospects. *Advances in Personality Assessment, 4,* 1–30. (13)

Meddis, R., Pearson, A. J. D., & Langford, G. (1973). An extreme case of healthy insomnia. *EEG and Clinical Neurophysiology, 35,* 213–214. (5)

Medin, D. L., & Shoben, E. J. (1988). Context and structure in conceptual combination. *Cognitive Psychology, 20,* 158–190. (8)

Mednick, S. A., Machon, R. A., & Huttunen, M. O. (1990). An update on the Helsinki influenza project. *Archives of General Psychiatry, 47,* 292. (14)

Meichenbaum, D. (1985). *Stress inoculation training.* New York: Pergamon. (12)

Meichenbaum, D., & Cameron, R. (1983). Stress inoculation training. In D. Meichenbaum & M. E. Jaremko (Eds.), *Stress reduction and prevention* (pp. 115–154). New York: Plenum. (12)

Meichenbaum, D. H. (1995). Cognitive-behavioral therapy in historical perspective. In B. Bongar & L. E. Beutler (Eds.), *Comprehensive textbook of psychotherapy: Theory and practice* (pp. 140–158). Oxford, England: Oxford University Press. (15)

Meichenbaum, D. H., & Goodman, J. (1971). Training impulsive children to talk to themselves: A means of developing self-control. *Journal of Abnormal Psychology, 77,* 115–126. (6)

Mello, N. K., & Mendelson, J. H. (1978). Behavioral pharmacology of human alcohol, heroin and marihuana use. In J. Fishman (Ed.), *The bases of addiction* (pp. 133–158). Berlin: Dahlem Konferenzen. (5)

Meltzer, H. Y. (1995). The role of serotonin in schizophrenia and the place of serotonin-dopamine antagonist antipsychotics. *Journal of Clinical Psychopharmacology, 15,* (Suppl. 1), S2–S3. (15)

Meltzoff, A. N., & Moore, M. K. (1977). Imitation of facial and manual gestures by human neonates. *Science, 198,* 75–78. (10)

Melzack, R., & Wall, P. D. (1965). Pain mechanisms: A new theory. *Science, 150,* 971–979. (4)

Melzack, R., Weisz, A. Z., & Sprague, L. T. (1963). Stratagems for controlling pain: Contributions of auditory stimulation and suggestion. *Experimental Neurology, 8,* 239–247. (12)

Mendelson, W. G. (1990). Do studies of sedative/hypnotics suggest the nature of chronic insomnia? In J. Montplaisir & R. Godbout (Eds.), *Sleep and biological rhythms* (pp. 209–218). New York: Oxford University Press. (5)

Mershon, D. H., Desaulniers, D. H., Kiefer, S. A., Amerson, T. L., Jr., & Mills, J. T. (1981). Perceived loudness and visually determined auditory distance. *Perception, 10,* 531–543. (4)

Mershon, D. H., & King, L. E. (1975). Intensity and reverberation as factors in the auditory perception of egocentric distance. *Perception and Psychophysics, 18,* 409–415. (4)

Mesmer, F. A. (1980). *Mesmerism: A translation of the original medical and scientific writings of F. A. Mesmer.* Los Altos, CA: William Kaufmann. (5)

Mesquita, B., & Frijda, N. H. (1992). Cultural variations in emotions: A review. *Psychological Bulletin, 112,* 179–204. (12)

Messick, D. M., Wilke, H., Brewer, M. B., Krammer, R. M., Zemke, P. E., & Lui, L. (1983). Individual adaptations and structural change as solutions to social dilemmas. *Journal of Personality and Social Psychology, 44,* 294–309. (16)

Messick, S., & Jungeblut, A. (1981). Time and method in coaching for the SAT. *Psychological Bulletin, 89,* 191–216. (9)

Metcalfe, J., & Wiebe, D. (1987). Intuition in insight and noninsight problem solving. *Memory & Cognition, 15,* 238–246. (8)

Michael, C. R. (1978). Color vision mechanisms in monkey striate cortex: Dual-opponent cells with concentric receptive fields. *Journal of Neurophysiology, 41,* 572–588. (4)

Milgram, S. (1974). *Obedience to authority.* New York: Harper & Row. (16)

Miller, D. T., & Ross, M. (1975). Self-serving biases in the attribution of causality: Fact or fiction? *Psychological Bulletin, 82,* 213–225. (16)

Miller, G. A. (1956). The magical number seven, plus or minus two: Some limits on our capacity for processing information. *Psychological Review, 63,* 81–97. (7)

Miller, J. G., & Bersoff, D. M. (1992). Culture and moral judgment: How are conflicts between justice and interpersonal responsibilities resolved? *Journal of Personality and Social Psychology, 62,* 541–554. (10)

Miller, L. L., & Branconnier, R. J. (1983). Cannabis: Effects on memory and the cholinergic limbic system. *Psychological Bulletin, 93,* 441–456. (5)

Miller, M. J., Small, I. F., Milstein, V., Malloy, F., & Stout, J. R. (1981). Electrode placement and cognitive change with ECT: Male and female response. *American Journal of Psychiatry, 138,* 384–386. (15)

Miller, N. E. (1985). The value of behavioral research on animals. *American Psychologist, 40,* 423–440. (2)

Miller, R. J., Hennessy, R. T., & Leibowitz, H. W. (1973). The effect of hypnotic ablation of the background on the magnitude of the Ponzo perspective illusion. *International Journal of Clinical and Experimental Hypnosis, 21,* 180–191. (5)

Miller, W. R., & Hester, R. K. (1986). Inpatient alcohol treatment: Who benefits? *American Psychologist, 41,* 794–805. (14)

Milner, B. (1959). The memory defect in bilateral hippocampal lesions. *Psychiatric Research Reports, 11,* 43–52. (7)

Mineka, S. (1985). The frightful complexity of the origin of fears. In F. R. Brush & J. B. Overmier (Eds.), *Affect, conditioning, and cognition* (pp. 55–73). Hillsdale, NJ: Lawrence Erlbaum. (14)

Mineka, S. (1987). A primate model of phobic fears. In H. Eysenck & I. Martin (Eds.), *Theoretical foundations of behavior therapy* (pp. 81–111). New York: Plenum. (14)

Mineka, S., Cook, M., & Miller, S. (1984). Fear conditioned with escapable and inescapable shock: The effects of a feedback stimulus. *Journal of Experimental Psychology: Animal Behavior Processes, 10,* 307–323. (14)

Mineka, S., Davidson, M., Cook, M., & Keir, R. (1984). Observational conditioning of snake fear in rhesus monkeys. *Journal of Abnormal Psychology, 93,* 355–372. (14)

Mischel, W. (1973). Toward a cognitive social learning reconceptualization of personality. *Psychological Review, 80,* 252–283. (13)

Mischel, W. (1981). Current issues and challenges in personality. In L. T. Benjamin, Jr. (Ed.), *The G. Stanley Hall Lecture Series* (Vol. 1, pp. 81–99). Washington, D.C.: American Psychological Association. (13)

Mischel, W., & Shoda, Y. (1995). A cognitive-affective system theory of personality: Reconceptualizing situations, dispositions, dynamics, and invariance in personality structure. *Psychological Review, 102,* 246–268. (13)

Miyake, A., Just, M. A., & Carpenter, P. A. (1994). Working memory constraints on the resolution of lexical ambiguity: Maintaining multiple interpretations in neutral contexts. *Journal of Memory and Language, 33,* 175–202. (7)

Moar, I., & Bower, G. H. (1983). Inconsistency in spatial knowledge. *Memory & Cognition, 11,* 107–113. (8)

Mobily, K. (1982). Using physical therapy activity and recreation to cope with stress and anxiety: A review. *American Corrective Therapy Journal, 36,* 77–81. (12)

Moffitt, T. E. (1993). Adolescence-limited and life-course persistent antisocial behavior: A developmental taxonomy. *Psychological Review, 100,* 674–701. (10)

Monahan, J. (1984). The prediction of violent behavior: Toward a second generation of theory and policy. *American Journal of Psychiatry, 141,* 10–15. (12)

Monahan, J. (1992). Mental disorder and violent behavior. *American Psychologist, 47,* 511–521. (15)

Monahan, J. (1993). Limiting therapist exposure to *Tarasoff* liability: Guidelines for risk containment. *American Psychologist, 48,* 242–250. (15)

Money, J., & Ehrhardt, A. A. (1972). *Man and woman, boy and girl.* Baltimore, MD: Johns Hopkins University Press. (11)

Monteith, M. J., Devine, P. G., & Zuwerink, J. R. (1993). Self-directed versus other-directed affect as a consequence of prejudice-related discrepancies. *Journal of Personality and Social Psychology, 64,* 198–210. (16)

Mook, D. G. (1990). Satiety, specifications, and stop rules: Feeding as voluntary action. *Progress in Psychobiology and Physiological Psychology, 14,* 1–65. (11)

Moorcroft, W. (1993). *Sleep, dreaming, and sleep disorders: An introduction* (2nd ed.). Lanham, MD: University Press of America. (5)

Moore, B. C. J. (1989). *An introduction to the psychology of hearing* (3rd ed.). London: Academic Press. (4)

Moore-Ede, M. C., Czeisler, C. A., & Richardson, G. S. (1983). Circadian timekeeping in health and disease. *New England Journal of Medicine, 309,* 469–476. (5)

Morgan, B. L. G., & Winick, M. (1989). Malnutrition, central nervous system effects. In G. Adelman (Ed.), *Neuroscience year* (pp. 97–99). Boston: Birkhäuser. (10)

Morris, J. B., & Beck, A. T. (1974). The efficacy of antidepressant drugs. *Archives of General Psychiatry, 30,* 667–674. (15)

Morrow, P. C., McElroy, J. C., Stamper, B. G., & Wilson, M. A. (1990). The effects of physical attractiveness and other demographic characteristics on promotion decisions. *Journal of Management, 16,* 723–736. (A)

Morrow, R. S., & Morrow, S. (1974). The measurement of intelligence. In B. B. Wolman (Ed.), *Handbook of general psychology* (pp. 656–670). Englewood Cliffs, NJ: Prentice-Hall. (9)

Moscovitch, M. (1985). Memory from infancy to old age: Implications for theories of normal and pathological memory. *Annals of the New York Academy of Sciences, 444,* 78–96. (7)

Moscovitch, M. (1989). Confabulation and the frontal systems: Strategic versus associative retrieval in neuropsychological theories of memory. In H. L. Roediger III & F. I. M. Craik (Eds.), *Varieties of memory and consciousness: Essays in honour of Endel Tulving* (pp. 133–160). Hillsdale, NJ: Lawrence Erlbaum. (7)

Moscovitch, M. (1992). Memory and working-with-memory: A component process model based on modules and central systems. *Journal of Cognitive Neuroscience, 4,* 257–267. (7)

Moscovitch, M., & Behrmann, M. (1994). Coding of spatial information in the somatosensory system: Evidence from patients with neglect following parietal lobe damage. *Journal of Cognitive Neuroscience, 6,* 151–155. (3)

Moskowitz, B. A. (1978). The acquisition of language. *Scientific American, 239*(5), 92–108. (10)

Motley, M. T., & Baars, B. J. (1979). Effects of cognitive set upon laboratory induced verbal (Freudian) slips. *Journal of Speech and Hearing Research, 22,* 421–432. (13)

Moyer, K. E. (1974). Sex differences in aggression. In R. C. Friedman, R. M. Richart, & R. L. VandeWiele (Eds.),

Sex differences in behavior (pp. 335–372). New York: Wiley. (12)

Mumford, M. D., & Gustafson, S. B. (1988). Creativity syndrome: Integration, application, and innovation. *Psychological Bulletin, 103,* 27–43. (8)

Munro, J. F., Stewart, I. C., Seidelin, P. H., Mackenzie, H. S., & Dewhurst, N. G. (1987). Mechanical treatment for obesity. *Annals of the New York Academy of Sciences, 499,* 305–312. (11)

Munroe, R. (1955). *Schools of psychoanalytic thought.* New York: Dryden. (15)

Murphy, G. L., & Medin, D. L. (1985). The role of theories in conceptual coherence. *Psychological Review, 92,* 289–316. (1)

Murray, H. A. (1938). *Explorations in personality.* New York: Oxford University Press. (11)

Murray, H. A. (1943). *Thematic Apperception Test manual.* Cambridge, MA: Harvard University Press. (13)

Murrell, J., Farlow, M., Ghetti, B., & Benson, M. D. (1991). A mutation in the amyloid precursor protein associated with hereditary Alzheimer's disease. *Science, 254,* 97–99. (7)

Myers, J. K., Weissman, M. M., Tischler, G. L., Holzer, C. E., III, Leaf, P. J., Orvaschel, H., Anthony, J. C., Boyd, J. H., Burke, J. D., Jr., Kramer, M., & Stoltzman, R. (1984). Six-month prevalence of psychiatric disorders in three communities. *Archives of General Psychiatry, 41,* 959–967. (14)

Nagel, T. (1994, May 12). Freud's permanent revolution. *New York Review of Books,* pp. 34–38. (13)

Nagera, H. (1976). *Obsessional neuroses.* New York: Jason Aronson. (14)

Naglieri, J. A. (1984). Concurrent and predictive validity of the Kaufman Assessment Battery for children with a Navajo sample. *Journal of School Psychology, 22,* 373–380. (9)

Nash, M. (1987). What, if anything, is regressed about hypnotic age regression? A review of the empirical literature. *Psychological Bulletin, 102,* 42–52. (5)

Nash, M. R., Johnson, L. S., & Tipton, R. D. (1979). Hypnotic age regression and the occurrence of transitional object relationships. Journal of *Abnormal Psychology, 88,* 547–555. (5)

Nash, M. R., Lynn, S. J., Stanley, S., & Carlson, V. (1987). Subjectively complete hypnotic deafness and auditory priming. *International Journal of Clinical and Experimental Hypnosis, 35,* 32–40. (5)

National Institute of Mental Health (1982). *Television and behavior: Ten years of scientific progress and implications for the eighties.* Rockville, MD: Author. (2)

Nebes, R. D. (1974). Hemispheric specialization in commissurotomized man. *Psychological Bulletin, 81,* 1–14. (3)

Nee, L. E., Eldridge, R., Sunderland, T., Thomas, C. B., Katz, D., Thompson, K. E., Weingartner, H., Weiss, H., Julian, C., & Cohen, R. (1987). Dementia of the Alzheimer type: Clinical and family study of 22 twin pairs. *Neurology, 37,* 359–363. (7)

Neiss, R. (1988). Reconceptualizing arousal: Psychobiological stakes in motor performance. *Psychological Bulletin, 103,* 345–366. (12)

Nelson, K. (1981). Individual differences in language development: Implications for development and language. *Developmental Psychology, 17,* 170–187. (10)

Nelson, K. E., Baker, N. D., Denninger, M., Bonvillian, J. D., & Kaplan, B. J. (1985). Cookie versus Do-it-again: Imitative-referential and personal-social-syntactic-initiating language styles in young children. *Linguistics, 23,* 433–454. (10)

Nelson, T. O., McSpadden, M., Fromme, K., & Marlatt, G. A. (1986). Effects of alcohol intoxication on metamemory and on retrieval from long-term memory. *Journal of Experimental Psychology: General, 115,* 247–254. (5)

Nemeth, C. (1972). A critical analysis of research utilizing the prisoner's dilemma paradigm for the study of bargaining. In L. Berkowitz (Ed.), *Advances in Experimental Social Psychology* (Vol. 6, pp. 203–234). New York: Academic Press. (16)

Nemeth, C. J. (1986). Differential contributions of majority and minority influence. *Psychological Review, 93,* 23–32. (16)

Nesse, R. M. (1991, November/December). What good is feeling bad? *The Sciences, 31*(6), 30–37. (15)

Newlin, D. B., & Thomson, J. B. (1990). Alcohol challenge with sons of alcoholics: A critical review and analysis. *Psychological Bulletin, 108,* 383–402. (14)

Newman, B. (1988, September 9). Dressing for dinner remains an issue in the naked city. *The Wall Street Journal,* p. 1. (16)

Nickerson, R. S., & Adams, M. J. (1979). Long-term memory for a common object. *Cognitive Psychology, 11,* 287–307. (7)

Nietzel, M. T., & Bernstein, D. A. (1987). *Introduction to clinical psychology.* Englewood Cliffs, NJ: Prentice-Hall. (9)

Nigg, J. T., & Goldsmith, H. H. (1994). Genetics of personality disorders: Perspectives from personality and psychopathology research. *Psychological Bulletin, 115,* 346–380. (3)

Nisbett, R. E., Caputo, C., Legant, P., & Marecek, J. (1973). Behavior as seen by the actor and as seen by the observer. *Journal of Personality and Social Psychology, 27,* 154–164. (16)

Nisbett, R. E., Fong, G. T., Lehman, D. R., & Cheng, P. W. (1987). Teaching reasoning. *Science, 238,* 625–631. (8)

Noel, J. G., Wann, D. L., & Branscombe, N. R. (1995). Peripheral ingroup membership status and public negativity toward outgroups. *Journal of Personality and Social Psychology, 68,* 127–137. (16)

Nofzinger, E. A., Thase, M. E., Reynolds, C. F., III, Frank, E., Jennings, J. R., Garamoni, G. L., Fasiczka, A. L., & Kupfer, D. J. (1993). Sexual function in depressed men: Assessment by self-report, behavioral, and nocturnal penile tumescence measures before and after treatment with cognitive behavior therapy. *Archives of General Psychiatry, 50,* 24–30. (14)

Nolen-Hoeksema, S. (1990). *Sex differences in depression.* Stanford, CA: Stanford University Press. (14)

Nolen-Hoeksema, S. (1991). Responses to depression and their effects on the duration of depressive episodes. *Journal of Abnormal Psychology, 100,* 569–582. (14)

Nolen-Hoeksema, S., & Morrow, J. (1991). A prospective study of depression and posttraumatic stress symptoms after a natural disaster: The Loma Prieta earthquake. *Journal of Personality and Social Psychology, 61,* 115–121. (14)

Norman, D. A. (1981). Categorization of action slips. *Psychological Review, 88,* 1–15. (13)

Norman, D. A. (1988). *The psychology of everyday things.* New York: Basic Books. (A)

Novick, L. R. (1990). Representational transfer in problem solving. *Psychological Science, 1,* 128–132. (8)

Nutt, D. J. (1989). Altered central alpha₂-adrenoceptor sensitivity in panic disorder. *Archives of General Psychiatry, 46,* 165–169. (14)

Nygard, R. (1982). Achievement motives and individual differences in situational specificity of behavior. *Journal of Personality and Social Psychology, 43,* 319–327. (11)

Oakland, T. D., & Cunningham, J. L. (1992). A survey of school psychology in developed and developing countries. *School Psychology International, 1,* 99–129. (A)

O'Brien, M., & Nagle, K. J. (1987). Parents' speech to toddlers: The effect of play context. *Journal of Child Language, 14,* 269–279. (10)

Ohaeri, J. U., Adeyinka, A. O., & Osuntokun, B. O. (1995). Computed tomographic density changes in schizophrenic and manic Nigerian subjects. *Behavioural Neurology, 8,* 31–37. (14)

O'Hara, M. W., Schlechte, J. A., Lewis, D. A., & Wright, E. J. (1991). Prospective study of postpartum blues. *Archives of General Psychiatry, 48,* 801–806. (14)

Öhman, A., Eriksson, A., & Olofsson, C. (1975). One-trial learning and superior resistance to extinction of autonomic responses conditioned to potentially phobic objects. *Journal of Comparative and Physiological Psychology, 88,* 619–627. (14)

Okin, R. L. (1983). The future of state hospitals: Should there be one? *American Journal of Psychiatry, 140,* 577–581. (15)

O'Leary, A. (1990). Stress, emotion, and human immune function. *Psychological Bulletin, 108,* 363–382. (12)

Oliver, M. B., & Hyde, J. S. (1993). Gender differences in sexuality: A meta-analysis. *Psychological Bulletin, 114,* 29–51. (11)

O'Malley, S. S., & Maisto, S. A. (1985). Effects of family drinking history and expectancies on responses to alcohol in men. *Journal of Studies on Alcohol, 46,* 289–297. (14)

Omoto, A. M., & Snyder, M. (1990). Basic research in action: Volunteerism and society's response to AIDS. *Personality and Social Psychology Bulletin, 16,* 152–165. (16)

O'Nell, C. W. (1965). A cross-cultural study of hunger and thirst motivation manifested in dreams. *Human Development, 8,* 181–193. (15)

Ormerod, M. B., McKenzie, J., & Woods, A. (1995). Final report on research relating to the concept of five separate dimensions of personality—or six including intelligence. *Personality and Individual Differences, 18,* 451–461. (13)

Orne, M. T. (1951). The mechanisms of hypnotic age regression: An experimental study. *Journal of Abnormal and Social Psychology, 46,* 213–225. (5)

Orne, M. T. (1959). The nature of hypnosis: Artifact and essence. *Journal of Abnormal and Social Psychology, 58,* 277–299. (5)

Orne, M. T. (1969). Demand characteristics and the concept of quasi-controls. In R. Rosenthal & R. L. Rosnow (Eds.), *Artifact in behavioral research* (pp. 143–179). (2)

Orne, M. T. (1979). On the simulating subject as a quasi-control group in hypnosis research: What, why, and how. In E. Fromm & R. E. Shor (Eds.), *Hypnosis: Developments in research and new perspectives* (2nd ed., pp. 519–565). New York: Aldine. (5)

Orne, M. T., Dinges, D. F., & Orne, E. C. (1984). On the differential diagnosis of multiple personality in the forensic context. *International Journal of Clinical and Experimental Hypnosis, 32,* 118–169. (5)

Orne, M. T., & Evans, F. J. (1965). Social control in the psychological experiment: Antisocial behavior and hypnosis. *Journal of Personality and Social Psychology, 1,* 189–200. (5)

Orne, M. T., & Scheibe, K. E. (1964). The contribution of nondeprivation factors in the production of sensory deprivation effects: The psychology of the "panic button." *Journal of Abnormal and Social Psychology, 68,* 3–12. (2)

Orne, M. T., Whitehouse, W. G., Dinges, D. F., & Orne, E. C. (1988). Reconstructing memory through hypnosis: Forensic and clinical applications. In H. M. Pettinati (Ed.), *Hypnosis and memory* (pp. 21–63). New York: Guilford Press. (5)

Ortony, A., & Turner, T. J. (1990). What's basic about basic emotions? *Psychological Review, 97,* 315–331. (12)

Oscar-Berman, M. (1980). Neuropsychological consequences of long-term chronic alcoholism. *American Scientist, 68,* 410–419. (7)

Öst, L.-G., & Hugdahl, K. (1981). Acquisition of phobias and anxiety response patterns in clinical patients. *Behaviour Research and Therapy, 19,* 439–447. (14)

Padgham, C. A. (1975). Colours experienced in dreams. *British Journal of Psychology, 66,* 25–28. (5)

Paicheler, G. (1988). *The psychology of social influence.* Cambridge, England: Cambridge University Press. (16)

Paikoff, R. L., & Brooks-Gunn, J. (1991). Do parent-child relationships change during puberty? *Psychological Bulletin, 110,* 47–66. (10)

Papini, M. R., & Bitterman, M. E. (1990). The role of contingency in classical conditioning. *Psychological Review, 97,* 396–403. (6)

Parke, R. D., Berkowitz, L., Leyens, J. P., West, S. G., & Sebastian, R. J. (1977). Some effects of violent and nonviolent movies on the behavior of juvenile delinquents. In L. Berkowitz (Ed.), *Advances in experimental social psychology* (Vol. 10, pp. 135–172). New York: Academic Press. (2)

Parker, D. (1944). *The portable Dorothy Parker.* New York: Viking. (14, 15)

Parkinson, C. N. (1957). *Parkinson's law.* Boston: Houghton Mifflin. (A)

Parmeggiani, P. L. (1982). Regulation of physiological functions during sleep in mammals. *Experientia, 38,* 1405–1408. (5)

Parnas, J., Schulsinger, F., Schulsinger, H., Mednick, S. A., & Teasdale, T. W. (1982). Behavioral precursors of schizophrenia spectrum. *Archives of General Psychiatry, 39,* 658–664. (14)

Pashler, H. (1994). Dual-task interference in simple tasks: Data and theory. *Psychological Bulletin, 116,* 220–244. (8)

Pate, J. E., Pumariega, A. J., Hester, C., & Garner, D. M. (1992). Cross-cultural patterns in eating disorders: A review. *Journal of the American Academy of Child and Adolescent Psychiatry, 31,* 802–809. (11)

Pate, J. L., & Rumbaugh, D. M. (1983). The language-like behavior of Lana chimpanzee: Is it merely discrimination and paired-associate learning? *Animal Learning & Behavior, 11,* 134–138. (8)

Patrick, C. J., & Iacono, W. G. (1989). Psychopathy, threat, and polygraph test accuracy. *Journal of Applied Psychology, 74,* 347–355. (12)

Patterson, C. J. (1994). Lesbian and gay families. *Current Directions in Psychological Science, 3,* 62–64. (10)

Pavlov, I. P. (1927/1960). *Conditioned reflexes.* New York: Dover. (Original work published 1927.) (6)

Peachey, J. E., & Naranjo, C. A. (1983). The use of disulfiram and other alcohol-sensitizing drugs in the treatment of alcoholism. *Research Advances in Alcohol and Drug Problems, 7,* 397–431. (14)

Pearce, J. M. (1994). Similarity and discrimination: A selective review and a connectionist model. *Psychological Review, 101,* 587–607. (6)

Peck, C. P. (1986). A public mental health issue: Risk-taking behavior and compulsive gambling. *American Psychologist, 41,* 461–465. (8)

Pedersen, N. L., Plomin, R., & McClearn, G. E. (1994). Is there G beyond *g*? (Is there genetic influence on specific cognitive abilities independent of genetic influence on general cognitive ability?) *Intelligence, 18,* 133–143. (9)

Pennebaker, J. W. (1990). *Opening up.* New York: William Morrow. (12)

Pepper, B., & Ryglewicz, H. (1982). Testimony for the neglected: The mentally ill in the post-deinstitutionalized age. *American Journal of Orthopsychiatry, 52,* 388–392. (15)

Pericak-Vance, M. A., Bebout, J. L., Gaskell, P. C., Jr., Yamaoka, L. H., Hung, W.-Y., Alberts, M. J., Walker, A. P., Bartlett, R. J., Haynes, C. A., Welsh, K. A., Earl, N. L., Heyman, A., Clark, C. M., & Roses, A. D. (1991). Linkage studies in familial Alzheimer disease: Evidence for chromosome 19 linkage. *American Journal of Human Genetics, 48,* 1034–1050. (7)

Perry, D. G., & Bussey, K. (1979). The social learning theory of sex differences: Imitation is alive and well. *Journal of Personality and Social Psychology, 37,* 1699–1712. (6)

Pert, C. B., & Snyder, S. H. (1973). The opiate receptor: Demonstration in nervous tissue. *Science, 179,* 1011–1014. (5)

Pervin, L. A. (1983). The stasis and flow of behavior: Toward a theory of goals. In M. M. Page (Ed.), *Nebraska symposium on motivation 1982* (pp. 1–53). Lincoln, NE: University of Nebraska Press. (11)

Pervin, L. A. (1990). A brief history of modern personality theory. In L. A. Pervin (Ed.), *Handbook of personality* (pp. 3–18). New York: Guilford Press. (13)

Peterson, C. (1983). Clouds and silver linings: Depressive symptoms and causal attributions about ostensibly "good" and "bad" events. *Cognitive Therapy and Research, 7,* 575–578. (14)

Peterson, C., Bettes, B. A., & Seligman, M. E. P. (1985). Depressive symptoms and unprompted causal attributions: Content analysis. *Behaviour Research and Therapy, 23,* 379–382. (14)

Peterson, L. G., Peterson, M., O'Shanick, G. J., & Swann, A. (1985). Self-inflicted gunshot wounds: Lethality of method versus intent. *American Journal of Psychiatry, 142,* 228–231. (14)

Peterson, L. R., & Peterson, M. J. (1959). Short-term retention of individual verbal items. *Journal of Experimental Psychology, 58,* 193–198. (7)

Petty, R. E., & Cacioppo, J. T. (1977). Effects of forewarning of persuasive intent and involvement on cognitive responses and persuasion. *Personality and Social Psychology Bulletin, 5,* 173–176. (16)

Petty, R. E., & Cacioppo, J. T. (1981). *Attitudes and persuasion: Classic and contemporary approaches.* Dubuque, IA: Wm. C. Brown. (16)

Petty, R. E., & Cacioppo, J. T. (1986). *Communication and persuasion: Central and peripheral routes to attitude change.* New York: Springer-Verlag. (16)

Pezdek, K. (1994). The illusion of illusory memory. *Applied Cognitive Psychology, 8,* 339–350. (7)

Pfungst, O. (1911). *Clever Hans.* New York: Holt. (2)

Phalet, K., & Claeys, W. (1993). A comparative study of Turkish and Belgian youth. *Journal of Cross-cultural Psychology, 24,* 319–343. (11)

Phelps, M. E., & Mazziotta, J. C. (1985). Positron emission tomography: Human brain function and biochemistry. *Science, 228,* 799–809. (1)

Phillips, R. G., & LeDoux, J. E. (1992). Differential contribution of amygdala and hippocampus to cued and contextual fear conditioning. *Behavioral Neuroscience, 106,* 274–285. (12)

Phillips, R. T., & Alcebo, A. M. (1986). The effects of divorce on black children and adolescents. *American Journal of Social Psychology, 6,* 69–73. (10)

Piaget, J. (1937/1954). *The construction of reality in the child* (M. Cook, Trans.). New York: Basic Books. (Original work published 1937.) (10)

Pichot, P. (1984). Centenary of the birth of Hermann Rorschach. *Journal of Personality Assessment, 48,* 591–596. (13)

Pilkington, C. L., & Piersel, W. C. (1991). School phobia: A critical analysis of the separation anxiety theory and an alternative conceptualization. *Psychology in the Schools, 28,* 290–303. (A)

Piotrowski, C., & Keller, J. W. (1989). Psychological testing in outpatient mental health facilities: A national study. *Professional Psychology: Research and Practice, 20,* 423–425. (13)

Pitman, R. K., Orr, S. P., Forgue, D. F., deJong, J. B., & Claiborn, N. M. (1987). Psychophysiologic assessment of posttraumatic stress disorder imagery in Vietnam combat veterans. *Archives of General Psychiatry, 44,* 970–975. (12)

Pitman, R. K., van der Kolk, B. A., Orr, S. P., & Greenberg, M. S. (1990). Naloxone-reversible analgesic response to combat-related stimuli in posttraumatic stress disorder. *Archives of General Psychiatry, 47,* 541–544. (12)

Platt, J. J. (1995). Vocational rehabilitation of drug abusers. *Psychological Bulletin, 117,* 416–433. (14)

Plomin, R., Corley, R., DeFries, J. C., & Fulker, D. W. (1990). Individual differences in television viewing in early childhood: Nature as well as nurture. *Psychological Science, 1,* 371–377. (3)

Plomin, R., & DeFries, J. C. (1980). Genetics and intelligence: Recent data. *Intelligence, 4,* 15–24. (9)

Plomin, R., DeFries, J. C., & Roberts, M. K. (1977). Assortative mating by unwed biological parents of adopted children. *Science, 196,* 449–450. (10)

Plutchik, R., & Ax, A. F. (1967). A critique of "determinants of emotional state" by Schachter and Singer (1962). *Psychophysiology, 4,* 79–82. (12)

Pokorny, A. D. (1978). The course and prognosis of schizophrenia. In W. E. Fann, I. Karacan, A. D. Pokorny, & R. L. Williams (Eds.), *Phenomenology and treatment of schizophrenia* (pp. 21–37). New York: Spectrum. (15)

Polivy, J., & Herman, C. P. (1985). Dieting and binging: A causal analysis. *American Psychologist, 40,* 193–201. (11)

Polivy, J., & Herman, C. P. (1987). Diagnosis and treatment of normal eating. *Journal of Consulting and Clinical Psychology, 55,* 635–644. (11)

Pollak, J. M. (1979). Obsessive-compulsive personality: A review. *Psychological Bulletin, 86*, 225–241. (14)

Pollatsek, A., & Rayner, K. (1989). Reading. In M. I. Posner, (Ed.), *Foundations of Cognitive Psychology* (pp. 401–436). Cambridge, MA: MIT Press. (8)

Polster, M. R. (1993). Drug-induced amnesia: Implications for cognitive neuropsychological investigations of memory. *Psychological Bulletin, 114*, 477–493. (7)

Polya, G. (1957). *How to solve it.* Garden City, NY: Doubleday Anchor. (8)

Pomeroy, W. B. (1972). *Dr. Kinsey and the Institute for Sex Research.* New York: Harper & Row. (11)

Poole, A. D., Sanson-Fisher, R. W., & German, G. A. (1981). The rapid-smoking technique: Therapeutic effectiveness. *Behaviour Research and Therapy, 19*, 389–397. (15)

Poole, D. A., & White, L. T. (1995). Tell me again and again: Stability and change in the repeated testimonies of children and adults. In M. S. Zaragoza, J. R. Graham, G. C. N. Hall, R. Hirschman, & Y. S. Ben-Porath (Eds.), *Memory and testimony in the child witness* (pp. 24–43). Thousand Oaks, CA: Sage Publications (7)

Popper, K. (1986). Predicting overt behavior versus predicting hidden states. *Behavioral and Brain Sciences, 9*, 254–255. (13)

Poulos, C. X., & Cappell, H. (1991). Homeostatic theory of drug tolerance: A general model of physiological adaptation. *Psychological Review, 98*, 390–408. (6)

Poulos, C. X., Wilkinson, D. A., & Cappell, H. (1981). Homeostatic regulation and Pavlovian conditioning in tolerance to amphetamine-induced anorexia. *Journal of Comparative and Physiological Psychology, 95*, 735–746. (6)

Povinelli, D. J., & deBlois, S. (1992). Young children's (*Homo sapiens*) understanding of knowledge formation in themselves and others. *Journal of Comparative Psychology, 106*, 228–238. (10)

Powell, R. A., & Boer, D. P. (1994). Did Freud mislead patients to confabulate memories of abuse? *Psychological Reports, 74*, 1283–1298. (13)

Powers, S., Barkan, J. H., & Jones, P. B. (1986). Reliability of the Standard Progressive Matrices Test for Hispanic and Anglo-American children. *Perceptual & Motor Skills, 62*, 348–350. (9)

Powlishta, K. K., & Maccoby, E. E. (1990). Resource utilization in mixed-sex dyads: The influence of adult presence and task type. *Sex Roles, 23*, 223–240. (10)

Pratkanis, A. R., Greenwald, A. G., Leippe, M. R., & Baumgardner, M. H. (1988). In search of reliable persuasion effects: III. The sleeper effect is dead. Long live the sleeper effect. *Journal of Personality and Social Psychology, 54*, 203–218. (16)

Premack, D. (1965). Reinforcement theory. In D. Levine (Ed.), *Nebraska symposium on motivation* (pp. 123–188). Lincoln, NE: University of Nebraska Press. (6)

Prentky, R. A., Knight, R. A., & Rosenberg, R. (1988). Validation analyses on a taxonomic system for rapists: Disconfirmation and reconceptualization. *Annals of the New York Academy of Sciences, 528*, 21–40. (11)

Price, R. A., Kidd, K. K., & Weissman, M. M. (1987). Early onset (under age 30 years) and panic disorder as markers for etiologic homogeneity in major depression. *Archives of General Psychiatry, 44*, 434–440. (14)

Prohaska, V. (1994). "I know I'll get an A": Confident overestimation of final course grades. *Teaching of Psychology, 21*, 141–143. (8)

Pullum, G. K. (1991). *The Great Eskimo vocabulary hoax.* Chicago: University of Chicago Press. (8)

Purves, D., & Hadley, R. D. (1985). Changes in the dendritic branching of adult mammalian neurons revealed by repeated imaging *in situ. Nature, 315*, 404–406. (3)

Qin, Y., & Simon, H. A. (1990). Laboratory replication of scientific discovery processes. *Cognitive Science, 14*, 281–312. (8)

Quadrel, M. J., Fischhoff, B., & Davis, W. (1993). Adolescent (in)vulnerability. *American Psychologist, 48*, 102–116. (10)

Quinn, R. P. (1978). Physical deviance and occupational mistreatment: The short, the fat, and the ugly. Master's thesis, University of Michigan Survey Research Center, University of Michigan, Ann Arbor. (16)

Rabkin, J. G. (1980). Stressful life events and schizophrenia: A review of the research literature. *Psychological Bulletin, 87*, 408–425. (14)

Rachlin, H. (1990). Why do people gamble and keep gambling despite heavy losses? *Psychological Science, 1*, 294–297. (8)

Rachlin, H., Siegel, E., & Cross, D. (1994). Lotteries and the time horizon. *Psychological Science, 5*, 390–393. (8)

Rachman, S. (1969). Treatment by prolonged exposure to high intensity stimulation. *Behaviour Research and Therapy, 7*, 295–302. (14)

Rachman, S. J., & Hodgson, R. J. (1980). *Obsessions and compulsions.* Englewood Cliffs, NJ: Prentice-Hall. (14)

Radin, N. (1982). Primary caregiving and role-sharing fathers. In M. E. Lamb (Ed.), *Nontraditional families* (pp. 173–204). Hillsdale, NJ: Lawrence Erlbaum. (10)

Raine, A., Venables, P. H., & Williams, M. (1990). Relationships between central and autonomic measures of arousal at age 15 years and criminality at age 24 years. *Archives of General Psychiatry, 47*, 1003–1007. (12)

Ramachandran, V. S. (1992). Filling in the gaps in perception: Part I. *Current Directions in Psychological Science, 1*, 199–205. (4)

Ramachandran, V. S., & Cobb, S. (1995). Visual attention modulates metacontrast masking. *Nature, 373*, 66–68. (4)

Ravussin, E., Lillioja, S., Knowler, W. C., Christin, L., Freymona, D., Abbott, W. G. H., Boyce, V., Howard, B. V., & Bogardus, C. (1988). Reduced rate of energy expenditure as a risk factor for body-weight gain. *New England Journal of Medicine, 318*, 467–472. (11)

Reardon, S. M., & Naglieri, J. A. (1992). PASS cognitive processing characteristics of normal and ADHD males. *Journal of School Psychology, 30*, 151–163. (A)

Rechtschaffen, A., Gilliland, M. A., Bergmann, B. M., & Winter, J. B. (1983). Physiological correlates of prolonged sleep deprivation in rats. *Science, 221*, 182–184. (5)

Redican, W. K. (1982). An evolutionary perspective on human facial displays. In P. Ekman (Ed.), *Emotion in the human face* (pp. 212–280). Cambridge, England: Cambridge University Press. (12)

Reed, T. E. (1985). Ethnic differences in alcohol use, abuse, and sensitivity: A review with genetic interpretation. *Social Biology, 32*, 195–209. (3)

Reeves, A. G., & Plum, F. (1969). Hyperphagia, rage, and dementia accompanying a ventromedial hypothalamic neoplasm. *Archives of Neurology, 20*, 616–624. (11)

Regan, T. (1986). The rights of humans and other animals. *Acta Physiologica Scandinavica, 128* (Suppl. 554), 33–40. (2)

Regier, D. A., Myers, J. K., Kramer, M., Robins, L. N., Blazer, D. G., Hough, R. L., Eaton, W. W., & Locke, B. Z. (1984). The NIMH epidemiologic catchment area program. *Archives of General Psychiatry, 41,* 934–941. (14)

Regier, D. A., Narrow, W. E., Rae, D. S., Manderscheid, R. W., Locke, B. Z., & Goodwin, F. K. (1993). The de facto U.S. mental and addictive disorders service system. *Archives of General Psychiatry, 50,* 85–94. (15)

Reich, J. (1986). The epidemiology of anxiety. *Journal of Nervous and Mental Disease, 174,* 129–136. (14)

Reicher, G. M. (1969). Perceptual recognition as a function of meaningfulness of stimulus material. *Journal of Experimental Psychology, 81,* 275–280. (8)

Reissland, N. (1988). Neonatal imitation in the first hour of life: Observations in rural Nepal. *Developmental Psychology, 24,* 464–469. (10)

Rescorla, R. A. (1968). Probability of shock in the presence and absence of CS in fear conditioning. *Journal of Comparative and Physiological Psychology, 66,* 1–5. (6)

Rescorla, R. (1985). Associationism in animal learning. In L.-G. Nilsson & T. Archer (Eds.), *Perspectives on learning and memory* (pp. 39–61). Hillsdale, NJ: Lawrence Erlbaum. (6)

Rescorla, R. A. (1988). Pavlovian conditioning: It's not what you think it is. *American Psychologist, 43,* 151–160. (6)

Ressler, K. J., Sullivan, S. L., & Buck, L. B. (1994). A molecular dissection of spatial patterning in the olfactory system. *Current Opinion in Neurobiology, 4,* 588–596. (4)

Rest, J. R. (1983). Morality. In P. H. Mussen (Ed.), *Handbook of child psychology* (4th ed., Vol. 3, pp. 556–629). New York: Wiley. (10)

Restle, F. (1970). Moon illusion explained on the basis of relative size. *Science, 167,* 1092–1096. (4)

Riccio, D. C. (1994). Memory: When less is more. *American Psychologist, 49,* 917–926. (7)

Rich, C. L., Ricketts, J. E., Fowler, R. C., & Young, D. (1988). Some differences between men and women who commit suicide. *American Journal of Psychiatry, 145,* 718–722. (14)

Richter, C. P. (1938). Two-day cycles of alternating good and bad behavior in psychotic patients. *Archives of Neurology and Psychiatry, 39,* 587–598. (14)

Richwald, G. A., Morisky, D. E., Kyle, G. R., Kristal, A. R., Gerber, M. M., & Friedland, J. M. (1988). Sexual activities in bathhouses in Los Angeles county: Implications for AIDS prevention education. *Journal of Sex Research, 25,* 169–180. (11)

Rips, L. J., Shoben, E. J., & Smith, E. E. (1973). Semantic distance and the verification of semantic relations. *Journal of Verbal Learning and Verbal Behavior, 12,* 1–20. (8)

Risby, E. D., Hsiao, J. K., Manji, H. K., Bitran, J., Moses, F., Zhou, D. F., & Potter, W. Z. (1991). The mechanisms of action of lithium: II. Effects on adenylate cyclase activity and beta-adrenergic receptor binding in normal subjects. *Archives of General Psychiatry, 48,* 513–524. (15)

Ristau, C. A. (1991). *Cognitive ethology.* Hillsdale, NJ: Lawrence Erlbaum. (5)

Ritz, M. C., Lamb, R. J., Goldberg, S. R., & Kuhar, M. J. (1987). Cocaine receptors on dopamine transporters are related to self-administration of cocaine. *Science, 237,* 1219–1223. (5)

Rivera, P. A., Rose, J. M., Futterman, A., Lovett, S. B., & Gallagher-Thompson, D. (1991). Dimensions of perceived social support in clinically depressed and nonde-

pressed female caregivers. *Psychology and Aging, 6,* 232–237. (14)

Rivers, P. C. (1994). *Alcohol and human behavior.* Englewood Cliffs, NJ: Prentice-Hall. (5)

Roberts, S. B., Savage, J., Coward, W. A., Chew, B., & Lucas, A. (1988). Energy expenditure and intake in infants born to lean and overweight mothers. *New England Journal of Medicine, 318,* 461–466. (11)

Roberts, T.-A. (1991). Gender and the influence of evaluations on self-assessments in achievement settings. *Psychological Bulletin, 109,* 297–308. (11)

Robins, L. N., Helzer, J. E., Weissman, M. M., Orvaschel, H., Gruenberg, E., Burke, J. D., Jr., & Regier, D. A. (1984). Lifetime prevalence of specific psychiatric disorders in three sites. *Archives of General Psychiatry, 41,* 949–958. (14)

Robinson, B. (1987, Feb. 16). Major classes of drugs continue on comeback trail. *Drug Topics, 131*(4), 67. (15)

Robinson, L. A., Berman, J. S., & Neimeyer, R. A. (1990). Psychotherapy for the treatment of depression: A comprehensive review of controlled outcome research. *Psychological Bulletin, 108,* 30–49. (15)

Rock, I., & Kaufman, L. (1962). The moon illusion, II. *Science, 136,* 1023–1031. (4)

Rodin, J. (1986). Aging and health: Effects of the sense of control. *Science, 233,* 1271–1276. (10)

Roese, N. J., & Jamieson, D. W. (1993). Twenty years of bogus pipeline research: A critical review and meta-analysis. *Psychological Bulletin, 114,* 363–375. (12)

Roffwarg, H. P., Muzio, J. N., & Dement, W. C. (1966). Ontogenetic development of human sleep-dream cycle. *Science, 152,* 604–609. (5)

Rogers, C. (1951). *Client-centered therapy.* Boston: Houghton Mifflin. (15)

Rogers, C. (1961). *On becoming a person.* Boston: Houghton Mifflin. (13)

Rogers, C. (1980). *A way of being.* Boston: Houghton Mifflin. (13)

Rogers, T. B. (1995). *The psychological testing enterprise: An introduction.* Pacific Grove, CA: Brooks/Cole. (9)

Rohrbaugh, M., Shoham, V., Spungen, C., & Steinglass, P. (1995). Family systems therapy in practice: A systemic couples therapy for problem drinking. In B. Bongar & L. E. Beutler (Eds.), *Comprehensive textbook of psychotherapy: Theory and practice* (pp. 228–253). Oxford, England: Oxford University Press. (15)

Rollman, G. B. (1991). Pain responsiveness. In M. Heller & W. Schiff (Eds.), *The psychology of touch* (pp. 91–118). Hillsdale, NJ: Lawrence Erlbaum. (4)

Rosch, E. (1978). Principles of categorization. In E. Rosch & B. B. Lloyd (Eds.), *Cognition and categorization* (pp. 27–48). Hillsdale, NJ: Lawrence Erlbaum. (8)

Rosch, E., & Mervis, C. B. (1975). Family resemblances: Studies in the internal structure of categories. *Cognitive Psychology, 7,* 573–605. (8)

Rose, J. E., Brugge, J. F., Anderson, D. J., & Hind, J. E. (1967). Phase-locked response to low-frequency tones in single auditory nerve fibers of the squirrel monkey. *Journal of Neurophysiology, 30,* 769–793. (4)

Roseman, I. J., Dhawan, N., Rettek, S. I., Naidu, R. K., & Thapa, K. (1995). Cultural differences and cross-cultural similarities in appraisals and emotional responses. *Journal of Cross-cultural Psychology, 26,* 23–48. (12)

Rosenbaum, M. E. (1986). The repulsion hypothesis: on the nondevelopment of relationships. *Journal of Personality and Social Psychology, 51,* 1156–1166. (16)

Rosenberg, H. (1993). Prediction of controlled drinking by alcoholics and problem drinkers. *Psychological Bulletin, 113,* 129–139. (14)

Ross, L. (1977). The intuitive psychologist and his shortcomings: Distortions in the attribution process. In L. Berkowitz (Ed.), *Advances in experimental social psychology* (Vol. 10, pp. 173–220). New York: Academic Press. (16)

Rothbart, M., & John, O. P. (1985). Social categorization and behavioral episodes: A cognitive analysis of the effects of intergroup contact. *Journal of Social Issues, 41,* 81–104. (16)

Rothbaum, B. O., Hodges, L. F., Kooper, R., Opdyke, D., Williford, J. S., & North, M. (1995). Effectiveness of computer-generated (virtual reality) graded exposure in the treatment of acrophobia. *American Journal of Psychiatry, 152,* 626–628. (14)

Rotton, J., & Kelly, I. W. (1985). Much ado about the full moon: A meta-analysis of lunar-lunacy research. *Psychological Bulletin, 97,* 286–306. (2)

Rovee-Collier, C. (1984). The ontogeny of learning and memory in human infancy. In R. Kail & N. E. Spear (Eds.), *Comparative perspectives on the development of memory* (pp. 103–134). Hillsdale, NJ: Lawrence Erlbaum. (10)

Rowe, D. C., Vazsonyi, A. T., & Flannery, D. J. (1994). No more than skin deep: Ethnic and racial similarity in developmental process. *Psychological Review, 101,* 396–413. (9)

Rowe, J. W., & Kahn, R. L. (1987). Human aging: Usual and successful. *Science, 237,* 143–149. (10)

Rowland, C. V., Jr. (Ed.) (1970). *Anorexia and obesity.* Boston: Little, Brown. (11)

Roy, A. (1985). Early parental separation and adult depression. *Archives of General Psychiatry, 42,* 987–991. (14)

Rozin, P. (1968). Specific aversions and neophobia as a consequence of vitamin deficiency and/or poisoning in half-wild and domestic rats. *Journal of Comparative and Physiological Psychology, 66,* 82–88. (11)

Rozin, P., & Fallon, A. E. (1987). A perspective on disgust. *Psychological Review, 94,* 23–41. (11)

Rozin, P., Fallon, A., & Augustoni-Ziskind, M. L. (1986). The child's conception of food: The development of categories of acceptable and rejected substances. *Journal of Nutrition Education, 18,* 75–81. (11)

Rozin, P., & Kalat, J. W. (1971). Specific hungers and poison avoidance as adaptive specializations of learning. *Psychological Review, 78,* 459–486. (11)

Rozin, P., Markwith, M., & Ross, B. (1990). The sympathetic magical law of similarity, nominal realism and neglect of negatives in response to negative labels. *Psychological Science, 1,* 383–384. (8)

Rozin, P., Millman, L., & Nemeroff, C. (1986). Operation of the laws of sympathetic magic in disgust and other domains. *Journal of Personality and Social Psychology, 50,* 703–712. (11)

Rozin, P., & Pelchat, M. L. (1988). Memories of mammaries: Adaptations to weaning from milk. *Progress in Psychobiology and Physiological Psychology, 13,* 1–29. (3)

Rubenstein, J. L. (1985). The effects of maternal employment on young children. *Applied Developmental Psychology, 2,* 99–128. (10)

Rubenstein, R., & Newman, R. (1954). The living out of "future" experiences under hypnosis. *Science, 119,* 472–473. (5)

Rubin, Z. (1970). Measurement of romantic love. *Journal of Personality and Social Psychology, 16,* 265–273. (16)

Rubin, Z. (1973). *Liking and loving: An invitation to social psychology.* New York: Holt, Rinehart, & Winston. (16)

Rubin, Z. (1974). Lovers and other strangers: The development of intimacy in encounters and relationships. *American Scientist, 62,* 182–190. (10)

Rubin, Z., Hill, C. T., Peplau, L. A., & Dunkel-Schetter, C. (1980). Self-disclosure in dating couples: Sex roles and the ethic of openness. *Journal of Marriage and the Family, 42,* 305–317. (10)

Rubin, Z., Peplau, L. A., & Hill, C. T. (1981). Loving and leaving: Sex differences in romantic attachments. *Sex Roles, 7,* 821–835. (16)

Ruch, J. (1984). *Psychology: The personal science.* Belmont, CA: Wadsworth. (3)

Ruderman, A. J. (1986). Dietary restraint: A theoretical and empirical review. *Psychological Review, 99,* 247–262. (11)

Ruderman, A. J., & Christensen, H. C. (1983). Restraint theory and its applicability to overweight individuals. *Journal of Abnormal Psychology, 92,* 210–215. (11)

Rudmin, F. W. (1994). Cross-cultural psycholinguistic field research. *Journal of Cross-cultural Psychology, 25,* 114–132. (8)

Rudy, J. W., & Sutherland, R. J. (1992). Configural and elemental associations and the memory coherence problem. *Journal of Cognitive Neuroscience, 4,* 208–216. (7)

Rumelhart, D. E., & McClelland, J. L. (1982). An interactive activation model of context effects in letter perception: Part 2, The contextual enhancement effect and some tests and extensions of the model. *Psychological Review, 89,* 60–94. (8)

Rumelhart, D. E., McClelland, J. L., & the PDP Research Group (1986). *Parallel distributed processing.* Cambridge, MA: MIT Press. (8)

Rusak, B. (1977). The role of the suprachiasmatic nuclei in the generation of circadian rhythms in the golden hamster, *Mesocricetus auratus. Journal of Comparative Physiology A, 118,* 145–164. (5)

Rushton, J. P. (1994). The equalitarian dogma revisited. *Intelligence, 19,* 263–280. (9)

Russell, C., & Megaard, I. (Eds.) (1988). *The general social survey, 1972–1986.* New York: Springer-Verlag. (12)

Russell, G. F. M., Szmukler, G. I., Dare, C., & Eisler, I. (1987). An evaluation of family therapy in anorexia nervosa and bulimia nervosa. *Archives of General Psychiatry, 44,* 1047–1056. (15)

Russell, J. A. (1994). Is there universal recognition of emotion from facial expression? A review of the cross-cultural studies. *Psychological Bulletin, 115,* 102–141. (12)

Russell, R. J. H., & Wells, P. A. (1991). Personality similarity and quality of marriage. *Personality and Individual Differences, 12,* 407–412. (16)

Saarinen, T. F. (1973). The use of projective techniques in geographic research. In W. H. Ittelson (Ed.), *Environment and cognition* (pp. 29–52). New York: Seminar Press. (8)

Sabo, K. T., & Kirtley, D. D. (1982). Objects and activities in the dreams of the blind. *International Journal of Rehabilitation Research, 5,* 241–242. (5)

Sachs, J. S. (1967). Recognition memory for syntactic and semantic aspects of connected discourse. *Perception and Psychophysics, 2,* 437–442. (8)

Sackett, P. R., & Wilk, S. L. (1994). Within-group norming and other forms of score adjustment in preemployment testing. *American Psychologist, 49,* 929–954. (A)

Sadger, J. (1941). Preliminary study of the psychic life of the fetus and the primary germ. *Psychoanalytic Review, 28,* 327–358. (2)

Saegert, S., Swap, W., & Zajonc, R. B. (1973). Exposure, context, and interpersonal attraction. *Journal of Personality and Social Psychology, 25,* 234–242. (16)

Salthouse, T. A., Mitchell, D. R., Skovronek, E., & Babcock, R. L. (1989). Effects of adult age and working memory on reasoning and spatial abilities. *Journal of Experimental Psychology: Learning, Memory, and Cognition, 15,* 507–516. (7)

Salzarulo, P., & Chevalier, A. (1983). Sleep problems in children and their relationship with early disturbances of the waking-sleeping rhythms. *Sleep, 6,* 47–51. (5)

Samelson, F. (1980). J. B. Watson's Little Albert, Cyril Burt's twins, and the need for a critical science. *American Scientist, 35,* 619–625. (14)

Samuelson, C. D., Messick, D. M., Rutte, C. G., & Wilke, H. (1984). Individual and structural solutions to resource dilemmas in two cultures. *Journal of Personality and Social Psychology, 47,* 94–104. (16)

Sanders, M. S., & McCormick, E. J. (1987). *Human factors in engineering and design* (6th ed.). New York: McGraw-Hill (A)

Santrock, J. W., Warshak, R. A., & Elliott, G. L. (1982). Social development and parent-child interaction in father-custody and stepmother families. In M. E. Lamb (Ed.), *Nontraditional families* (pp. 289–314). Hillsdale, NJ: Lawrence Erlbaum. (10)

Sappington, A. A. (1990). Recent psychological approaches to the free will versus determinism issue. *Psychological Bulletin, 108,* 19–29. (1)

Satterfield, J. M., & Seligman, M. E. P. (1994). Military aggression and risk predicted by explanatory style. *Psychological Science, 5,* 77–82. (14)

Sattler, J. M., & Gwynne, J. (1982). White examiners generally do not impede the intelligence test performance of Black children: to debunk a myth. *Journal of Consulting and Clinical Psychology, 50,* 196–208. (9)

Savage-Rumbaugh, E. S. (1990). Language acquisition in a nonhuman species: Implications for the innateness debate. *Developmental Psychology, 23,* 599–620. (8)

Savage-Rumbaugh, E. S., Murphy, J., Sevcik, R. A., Brakke, K. E., Williams, S. L., & Rumbaugh, D. M. (1993). Language comprehension in ape and child. *Monographs of the Society for Research in Child Development, 58,* serial no. 233. (14)

Savage-Rumbaugh, E. S., Sevcik, R. A., Brakke, K. E., & Rumbaugh, D. M. (1992). Symbols: Their communicative use, communication, and combination by bonobos (*Pan paniscus*). In L. P. Lipsitt & C. Rovee-Collier (Eds.), *Advances in infancy research* (Vol. 7, pp. 221–278). Norwood, NJ: Ablex. (8)

Saykin, A. J., Shtasel, D. L., Gur, R. E., Kester, D. B., Mozley, L. H., Stafiniak, P., & Gur, R. C. (1994). Neuropsychological deficits in neuroleptic naive patients with first-episode schizophrenia. *Archives of General Psychiatry, 51,* 124–131. (14)

Scarborough, E., & Furomoto, L. (1987). *Untold lives: The first generation of American women psychologists.* New York: Columbia University Press. (1)

Scarr, S. (1968). Environmental bias in twin studies. *Eugenics Quarterly, 15,* 34–40. (9)

Scarr, S., & Carter-Saltzman, L. (1979). Twin method: Defense of a critical assumption. *Behavior Genetics, 9,* 527–542. (9)

Scarr, S., Pakstis, A. J., Katz, S. H., & Barker, W. B. (1977). The absence of a relationship between degree of white ancestry and intellectual skills within a black population. *Human Genetics, 39,* 69–86. (9)

Scarr, S., Phillips, D., & McCartney, K. (1989). Working mothers and their families. *American Psychologist, 44,* 1402–1409. (10)

Scarr, S., Phillips, D., & McCartney, K. (1990). Facts, fantasies and the future of child care in the United States. *Psychological Science, 1,* 26–35. (10)

Scarr, S., & Weinberg, R. A. (1976). IQ test performance of black children adopted by white families. *American Psychologist, 31,* 726–739. (9)

Schacter, D. L. (1983). Amnesia observed: Remembering and forgetting in a natural environment. *Journal of Abnormal Psychology, 92,* 236–242. (7)

Schacter, D. L. (1985). Priming of old and new knowledge in amnesic patients and normal subjects. *Annals of the New York Academy of Sciences, 444,* 41–53. (7)

Schacter, D. L. (1986a). Amnesia and crime: How much do we really know? *American Psychologist, 41,* 286–295. (7)

Schacter, D. L. (1986b). Feeling-of-knowing ratings distinguish between genuine and simulated forgetting. *Journal of Experimental Psychology: Learning, Memory, and Cognition, 12,* 30–41. (7)

Schacter, D. L. (1987). Implicit memory: History and current status. *Journal of Experimental Psychology: Learning, Memory, and Cognition, 13,* 501–518. (7)

Schacter, D. L., Cooper, L. A., Delaney, S. M., Peterson, M. A., & Tharan, M. (1991). Implicit memory for possible and impossible objects: Constraints on the construction of structural descriptions. *Journal of Experimental Psychology: Learning, Memory, and Cognition, 17,* 3–19. (7)

Schachter, S. (1959). *The psychology of affiliation.* Stanford, CA: Stanford University Press. (16)

Schachter, S. (1982). Recidivism and self-cure of smoking and obesity. *American Psychologist, 37,* 436–444. (11)

Schachter, S., Christenfeld, N., Ravina, B., & Bilous, F. (1991). Speech disfluency and the structure of knowledge. *Journal of Personality and Social Psychology, 60,* 362–367. (8)

Schachter, S., Rauscher, F., Christenfeld, N., & Crone, K. T. (1994). The vocabularies of academia. *Psychological Science, 5,* 37–41. (8)

Schachter, S., & Singer, J. (1962). Cognitive, social, and physiological determinants of emotional state. *Psychological Review, 69,* 379–399. (12)

Schaie, K. W. (1994). The course of adult intellectual development. *American Psychologist, 49,* 304–313. (10)

Schank, R., & Birnbaum, L. (1994). Enhancing intelligence. In J. Khalfa (Ed.), *What is intelligence?* (pp. 72–106). Cambridge, England: Cambridge University Press. (9)

Schatzman, M. (1992, March 21). Freud: Who seduced whom? *New Scientist,* pp. 34–37. (13)

Scheibel, A. B. (1984). A dendritic correlate of human speech. In N. Geschwind & A. M. Galaburda (Eds.), *Cerebral dominance* (pp. 43–52). Cambridge, MA: Harvard University Press. (4)

Schellenberg, G. D., Bird, T. D., Wijsman, E. M., Orr, H. T., Anderson, L., Nemens, E., White, J. A., Bonnycastle, L., Weber, J. L., Alonso, M. E., Potter, H., Heston, L. L., & Martin, G. M. (1992). Genetic linkage evidence for a familial Alzheimer's disease locus on chromosome 14. *Science, 258,* 668–671. (7)

Schiffman, S. S. (1983). Taste and smell in disease. *New England Journal of Medicine, 308,* 1275–1279, 1337–1343. (4)

Schiffman, S. S., & Erickson, R. P. (1971). A psychophysical model for gustatory quality. *Physiology & Behavior, 7,* 617–633. (4)

Schlaug, G., Jäncke, L., Huang, Y., & Steinmetz, H. (1995). In vivo evidence of structural brain asymmetry in musicians. *Science, 267,* 699–701. (4)

Schlesier-Stropp, B. (1984). Bulimia: A review of the literature. *Psychological Review, 95,* 247–257. (11)

Schlossberg, N. K. (1984). Exploring the adult years. *The G. Stanley Hall Lecture Series, 4,* 101–154. (10)

Schmidt, F. L., & Hunter, J. E. (1993). Tacit knowledge, practical intelligence, general mental ability, and job knowledge. *Current Directions in Psychological Science, 2,* 8–9. (9, A)

Schmidt, R. A., & Bjork, R. A. (1992). New conceptualizations of practice: Common principles in three paradigms suggest new concepts for training. *Psychological Science, 3,* 207–217. (7)

Schmitt, A. P., & Dorans, N. J. (1990). Differential item functioning for minority examinees on the SAT. *Journal of Educational Measurement, 27,* 67–81. (9)

Schmitt, N. (1976). Social and situational determinants of interview decisions: Implications for the employment interview. *Personnel Psychology, 29,* 79–101. (A)

Schoenfeld, A. H. (1985). *Mathematical problem solving.* Orlando, FL: Academic Press. (8)

Schooler, C. (1972). Birth order effects: Not here, not now! *Psychological Bulletin, 78,* 161–175. (10)

Schuckit, M. A. (1985). Ethanol-induced changes in body sway in men at high alcoholism risk. *Archives of General Psychiatry, 42,* 375–379. (14)

Schulsinger, F., Knop, J., Goodwin, D. W., Teasdale, T. W., & Mikkelsen, U. (1986). A prospective study of young men at high risk for alcoholism. *Archives of General Psychiatry, 43,* 755–760. (14)

Schwartz, F. N. (1989, January-February). Management women and the new facts of life. *Harvard Business Review,* 65–76. (11)

Schwartz, G. E. (1987). Personality and health: An integrative health science approach. *The G. Stanley Hall Lecture Series, 7,* 125–157. (12)

Schwarzwald, J., Bizman, A., & Raz, M. (1983). The foot-in-the-door paradigm: Effects of second request size on donation probability and donor generosity. *Personality and Social Psychology Bulletin, 9,* 443–450. (16)

Scovern, A. W., & Kilmann, P. R. (1980). Status of electroconvulsive therapy: Review of the outcome literature. *Psychological Bulletin, 87,* 260–303. (15)

Scribner, S. (1974). Developmental aspects of categorized recall in a west African society. *Cognitive Psychology, 6,* 475–494. (4)

Scripture, E. W. (1907). *Thinking, feeling, doing* (2nd ed.). New York: G. P. Putnam's Sons. (1)

Seeman, P., & Lee, T. (1975). Antipsychotic drugs: Direct correlation between clinical potency and presynaptic action on dopamine neurons. *Science, 188,* 1217–1219. (14)

Seeman, P., Lee, T., Chau-Wong, M., & Wong, K. (1976). Antipsychotic drug doses and neuroleptic/dopamine receptors. *Nature, 261,* 717–719. (15)

Segal, K. R., & Pi-Sunyer, F. X. (1989). Exercise and obesity. *Medical Clinics of North America, 73,* 217–236. (11)

Segal, N. (1993). Twin, sibling, and adoption methods: Tests of evolutionary hypotheses. *American Psychologist, 48,* 943–956. (3)

Segall, M. H., Campbell, D. T., & Herskovits, M. J. (1966). *The influence of culture on visual perception.* Indianapolis, IN: Bobbs-Merrill. (4)

Sekuler, A. B., Palmer, S. E., & Flynn, C. (1994). Local and global processes in visual completion. *Psychological Science, 5,* 260–267. (4)

Seligman, M. E. P. (1970). On the generality of the laws of learning. *Psychological Review, 77,* 406–418. (6)

Seligman, M. E. P. (1971). Phobias and preparedness. *Behavior Therapy, 2,* 307–320. (14)

Seligman, M. E. P., Nolen-Hoeksema, S., Thornton, N., & Thornton, K. M. (1990). Explanatory style as a mechanism of disappointing athletic performance. *Psychological Science, 1,* 143–146. (14)

Selye, H. (1979). Stress, cancer, and the mind. In J. Taché, H. Selye, & S. B. Day (Eds.), *Cancer, stress, and death* (pp. 11–27). New York: Plenum. (12)

Sereno, S. C., Pacht, J. M., & Rayner, K. (1992). The effect of meaning frequency on processing lexically ambiguous words: Evidence from eye fixations. *Psychological Science, 3,* 296–300. (8)

Shafir, E. B., Smith, E. E., & Osheron, D. N. (1990). Typicality and reasoning fallacies. *Memory & Cognition, 18,* 229–239. (7)

Shallice, T., & Warrington, E. K. (1970). Independent functioning of verbal memory stores: A neuropsychological study. *Quarterly Journal of Experimental Psychology, 22,* 261–273. (7)

Shannon, D. A. (1955). *The Socialist Party of America.* New York: Macmillan. (16)

Shapiro, D. L. (1985). Insanity and the assessment of criminal responsibility. In C. P. Ewing (Ed.), *Psychology, psychiatry, and the law: A clinical and forensic handbook* (pp. 67–94). Sarasota, FL: Professional Resource Exchange. (15)

Shavit, Y., Terman, G. W., Martin, F. C., Lewis, J. W., Liebeskind, J. C., & Gale, R. P. (1985). Stress, opioid peptides, the immune system, and cancer. *Journal of Immunology, 135,* 834S–837S. (12)

Sheaffer, R. (1992). Psychic vibrations. *Skeptical Inquirer, 17,* 26–29. (2)

Sheaffer, R. (1993). Psychic vibrations. *Skeptical Inquirer, 17,* 138–140. (2)

Shepard, R. N., & Metzler, J. N. (1971). Mental rotation of three-dimensional objects. *Science, 171,* 701–703. (8)

Shepher, J. (1971). Mate selection among second-generation kibbutz adolescents and adults: Incest avoidance and negative imprinting. *Archives of Sexual Behavior, 1,* 293–307. (10)

Shepperd, J. A. (1993). Productivity loss in performance groups: A motivation analysis. *Psychological Bulletin, 113,* 67–81. (16)

Sher, K. J., Frost, R. O., Kushner, M., Crews, T. M., & Alexander, J. E. (1989). Memory deficits in compulsive checkers: Replication and extension in a clinical sample. *Behaviour Research and Therapy, 27,* 65–69. (14)

Sher, K. J., Frost, R. O., & Otto, R. (1983). Cognitive deficits in compulsive checkers: An exploratory study. *Behaviour Research and Therapy, 21,* 357–363. (14)

Sherif, M. (1935). A study of some social factors in perception. *Archives of Psychology, 27,* 1–60. (16)

Sherif, M. (1966). *In common predicament.* Boston: Houghton Mifflin. (16)

Sherman, S. J., Judd, C. M., & Park, B. (1989). Social cognition. In M. R. Rosenzweig & L. W. Porter (Eds.), *Annual Review of Psychology* (Vol. 40, pp. 281–326). Palo Alto, CA: Annual Reviews. (16)

Sherrod, D. R., Hage, J. N., Halpern, P. L., & Moore, B. S. (1977). Effects of personal causation and perceived control on responses to an aversive environment: The more control, the better. *Journal of Experimental Social Psychology, 13*, 14–27. (12)

Sherwood, G. G. (1981). Self-serving biases in person perception: A reexamination of projection as a mechanism of defense. *Psychological Bulletin, 90*, 445–459. (13)

Shimamura, A. P., Janowsky, J. S., & Squire, L. R. (1990). Memory for the temporal order of events in patients with frontal lobe lesions and amnesic patients. *Neuropsychologia, 28*, 803–813. (7)

Shimamura, A. P., Salmon, D. P., Squire, L. R., & Butters, N. (1987). Memory dysfunction and word priming in dementia and amnesia. *Behavioral Neuroscience, 101*, 347–351. (7)

Shogren, E. (1993, June 2). Survey finds 4 in 5 suffer sex harassment at school. *The Los Angeles Times*, A10. (2)

Shweder, R. A., & Haidt, J. (1993). The future of moral psychology: Truth, intuition, and the pluralist way. *Psychological Science, 4*, 360–365. (10)

Siegel, S. (1977). Morphine tolerance as an associative process. *Journal of Experimental Psychology: Animal Behavior Processes, 3*, 1–13. (6)

Siegel, S. (1983). Classical conditioning, drug tolerance, and drug dependence. *Research Advances in Alcohol and Drug Problems, 7*, 207–246. (6)

Siegel, S. (1987). Alcohol and opiate dependence: Reevaluation of the Victorian perspective. *Research Advances in Alcohol and Drug Problems, 9*, 279–314. (14)

Siegelman, M. (1974). Parental background of male homosexuals and heterosexuals. *Archives of Sexual Behavior, 3*, 3–18. (11)

Siegler, R. S. (1994). Cognitive variability: A key to understanding cognitive development. *Current Directions in Psychological Science, 3*, 1–5. (10)

Siegler, R. S., & Richards, D. D. (1982). The development of intelligence. In R. J. Sternberg (Ed.), *Handbook of human intelligence* (pp. 897–971). Cambridge, England: Cambridge University Press. (9)

Sigall, H., & Ostrove, N. (1975). Beautiful but dangerous: Effects of offender attractiveness and nature of the crime on juridic judgment. *Journal of Personality and Social Psychology, 31*, 410–414. (16)

Simmons, E. J. (1949). *Leo Tolstoy*. London: John Lehmann. (14)

Simons, R. L., Whitbeck, L. B., Conger, R. D., & Wu, C.-I. (1991). Intergenerational transmission of harsh parenting. *Developmental Psychology, 27*, 159–171. (6)

Singer, J. L. (1981). Clinical intervention: New developments in methods and evaluation. *The G. Stanley Hall Lecture Series, 1*, 101–128. (15)

Siqueland, E. R., & Lipsitt, L. P. (1966). Conditioned head-turning in human newborns. *Journal of Experimental Child Psychology, 3*, 356–376. (10)

Sizemore, C. C., & Huber, R. J. (1988). The twenty-two faces of Eve. *Individual Psychology, 44*, 53–62. (14)

Sizemore, C. C., & Pittillo, E. S. (1977). *I'm Eve*. Garden City, NY: Doubleday. (14)

Sjostrom, K. P., & Marks, A. (1994). Pretest and posttest confidence ratings in test performance by low-, medium-, and high-scoring students. *Teaching of Psychology, 21*, 12–16. (7)

Skeels, H. M. (1966). Adult status of children with contrasting early life experiences. *Monographs of the Society for Research in Child Development, 31*, 1–65. (9)

Skinner, B. F. (1938). *The behavior of organisms*. New York: D. Appleton-Century. (6)

Skinner, B. F. (1956). A case history in scientific method. *American Psychologist, 11*, 221–233. (6)

Skinner, B. F. (1960). Pigeons in a pelican. *American Psychologist, 15*, 28–37. (6)

Skinner, B. F. (1990). Can psychology be a science of mind? *American Psychologist, 45*, 1206–1210. (6)

Slobin, D. I. (1979). *Psycholinguistics* (2nd ed.). Glenview, IL: Scott, Foresman. (8)

Smith, C., & Wong, P. T. P. (1991). Paradoxical sleep increases predict successful learning in a complex operant task. *Behavioral Neuroscience, 105*, 282–288. (5)

Smith, D. E., & Cogswell, C. (1994). A cross-cultural perspective on adolescent girls' body perception. *Perceptual and Motor Skills, 78*, 744–746. (11)

Smith, E. E., Osherson, D. N., Rips, L. J., & Keane, M. (1988). Combining prototypes: A selective modification model. *Cognitive Science, 12*, 485–527. (8)

Smith, E. E., Shoben, E. J., & Rips, L. J. (1974). Structure and process in semantic memory: A featural model for semantic decisions. *Psychological Review, 81*, 214–241. (8)

Smith, F. J. (1977). Work attitudes as predictors of attendance on a specific day. *Journal of Applied Psychology, 62*, 16–19. (A)

Smith, G. B., Schwebel, A. I., Dunn, R. L., & McIver, S. D. (1993). The role of psychologists in the treatment, management, and prevention of chronic mental illness. *American Psychologist, 48*, 966–971. (15)

Smith, G. P., & Gibbs, J. (1987). The effect of gut peptides on hunger, satiety, and food intake in humans. *Annals of the New York Academy of Sciences, 499*, 132–136. (11)

Smith, J. M., & Baldessarini, R. J. (1980). Changes in prevalence, severity, and recovery in tardive dyskinesia with age. *Archives of General Psychiatry, 37*, 1368–1373. (15)

Smith, L. T. (1975). The interanimal transfer phenomenon: A review. *Psychological Bulletin, 81*, 1078–1095. (2)

Smith, M. L. (1988). Recall of spatial location by the amnesic patient H. M. *Brain and Cognition, 7*, 178–183. (7)

Smith, M. L., Glass, G. V., & Miller, T. I. (1980). *The benefits of psychotherapy*. Baltimore, MD: Johns Hopkins University Press. (15)

Smith, M. W. (1974). Alfred Binet's remarkable questions: A cross-national and cross-temporal analysis of the cultural biases built into the Stanford-Binet intelligence scale and other Binet tests. *Genetic Psychology Monographs, 89*, 307–334. (9)

Smith, S. S., O'Hara, B. F., Persico, A. M., Gorelick, D. A., Newlin, D. B., Vlahav, D., Solomon, L., Pickens, R., & Uhl, G. R. (1992). Genetic vulnerability to drug abuse: The D$_2$ dopamine receptor Taq1B1 restriction fragment length polymorphism appears more frequently in polysubstance abusers. *Archives of General Psychiatry, 49*, 723–727. (1)

Snodgrass, J. G., & Hirshman, E. (1991). Theoretical explorations of the Bruner-Potter (1964) interference effect. *Journal of Memory and Language, 30*, 273–293. (8)

Snyder, M. (1979). Self-monitoring process. *Advances in Experimental Social Psychology, 12*, 85–128. (16)

Snyder, M., Tanke, E. D., & Bersheid, E. (1977). Social perception and interpersonal behavior: On the self-fulfilling nature of social stereotypes. *Journal of Personality and Social Psychology, 35,* 656–666. (16)

Snyder, S. (1991). Movies and juvenile delinquency: An overview. *Adolescence, 26,* 121–132. (6)

Snyder, S. H. (1984). Drug and neurotransmitter receptors in the brain. *Science, 224,* 22–31. (3)

Solomon, R. L. (1980). The opponent-process theory of acquired motivation. *American Psychologist, 35,* 691–712. (12)

Solomon, R. L., & Corbit, J. D. (1974). An opponent-process theory of motivation: I. Temporal dynamics of affect. *Psychological Review, 81,* 119–145. (5, 12)

Solomon, Z., Mikulincer, M., & Flum, H. (1988). Negative life events, coping responses, and combat-related psychopathology: A prospective study. *Journal of Abnormal Psychology, 97,* 302–307. (12)

Sotsky, S. M., Glass, D. R., Shea, T., Pilkonis, P. A., Collins, J. F., Elkin, I., Watkins, J. T., Imber, S. D., Leber, W. R., Moyer, J., & Oliveri, M. E. (1991). Patient predictors of response to psychotherapy and pharmacotherapy: Findings in the NIMH Treatment of Depression Collaborative Research Program. *American Journal of Psychiatry, 148,* 997–1008. (15)

Sowell, T. (1994). *Race and culture.* New York: Basic Books. (6)

Spangler, W. D. (1992). Validity of questionnaire and TAT measures of need for achievement: Two meta-analyses. *Psychological Bulletin, 112,* 140–154. (11)

Spanos, N. P. (1987–88). Past-life hypnotic regression: A critical view. *Skeptical Inquirer, 12,* 174–180. (5)

Spanos, N. P. (1994). Multiple identity enactments and multiple personality disorder: A sociocognitive perspective. *Psychological Bulletin, 116,* 143–165. (14)

Spearman, C. (1904). "General intelligence," objectively determined and measured. *American Journal of Psychology, 15,* 201–293. (9)

Spence, J. T. (1984). Masculinity, femininity, and gender-related traits: A conceptual analysis and critique of current research. *Progress in Experimental Personality Research, 13,* 1–97. (13)

Spencer, D. D., Robbins, R. J., Naftolin, F., Marek, K. L., Vollmer, T., Leranth, C., Roth, R. H., Price, L. H., Gjedde, A., Bunnery, B. S., Sass, K. J., Elsworth, J. D., Kier, E. L., Makuch, R., Hoffer, P. B., & Redmond, D. E., Jr. (1992). Unilateral transplantation of human fetal mesencephalic tissue into the caudate nucleus of patients with Parkinson's disease. *New England Journal of Medicine, 327,* 1541–1548. (3)

Sperling, G. (1960). The information available in brief visual presentations. *Psychological Monographs, 74*(11, Whole No. 498). (7)

Sperry, R. W. (1967). Split-brain approach to learning problems. In G. C. Quarton, T. Melnechuk, & F. O. Schmitt (Eds.), *The neurosciences: A study program* (pp. 714–722). New York: Rockefeller University Press. (3)

Spiegel, D., Frischholz, E. J., Fleiss, J. L., & Spiegel, H. (1993). Predictors of smoking abstinence following a single-session restructuring intervention with self-hypnosis. *American Journal of Psychiatry, 150,* 1090–1097. (5)

Spira, A., et al. (1993). *Les comportements sexuels en France.* Paris: La documentation Française. (11)

Spitz, R. A. (1945). Hospitalism: An inquiry into the genesis of psychiatric conditions in early childhood. *Psychoanalytic Study of the Child, 1,* 53–74. (10)

Spitz, R. A. (1946). Hospitalism: A follow-up report. *Psychoanalytic Study of the Child, 2,* 113–117. (10)

Spring, B., Chiodo, J., & Bowen, D. J. (1987). Carbohydrates, tryptophan, and behavior: A methodological review. *Psychological Bulletin, 102,* 234–256. (3)

Squire, L. R., Amaral, D. G., & Press, G. A. (1990). Magnetic resonance imaging of the hippocampal formation and mammillary nuclei distinguish medial temporal lobe and diencephalic amnesia. *Journal of Neuroscience, 10,* 3106–3117. (7)

Squire, L. R., Haist, F., & Shimamura, A. P. (1989). The neurology of memory: Quantitative assessment of retrograde amnesia in two groups of amnesic patients. *Journal of Neuroscience, 9,* 828–839. (7)

Stangor, C., & Lange, J. E. (1994). Mental representations of social groups: Advances in understanding stereotypes and stereotyping. *Advances in Experimental Social Psychology, 26,* 357–416. (16)

Stapp, J., Tucker, A. M., & VandenBos, G. R. (1985). Census of psychological personnel: 1983. *American Psychologist, 40,* 1317–1351. (1)

Starr, C., & Taggart, R. (1992). *Biology: The unity and diversity of life* (6th ed.). Belmont, CA: Wadsworth. (3)

Staw, B. M., & Ross, J. (1989). Understanding behavior in escalation situations. *Science, 246,* 216–220. (16)

Stegat, H. (1975). Die Verhaltenstherapie der Enuresis und Enkopresis [Behavior therapy for enuresis and encopresis]. *Zeitschrift für Kinder- und Jugendpsychiatrie, 3,* 149–173. (15)

Stein, M., Miller, A. H., & Trestman, R. L. (1991). Depression, the immune system, and health and illness. *Archives of General Psychiatry, 48,* 171–177. (12)

Stenberg, G., Risberg, J., Warkentin, S., & Rosén, I. (1990). Regional patterns of cortical blood flow distinguish extraverts from introverts. *Personality and Individual Differences, 11,* 663–673. (13)

Sternberg, R. J. (1985). *Beyond IQ.* Cambridge, England: Cambridge University Press. (9)

Sternberg, R. (1986). A triangular theory of love. *Psychological Review, 93,* 119–135. (16)

Sternberg, R. J. (1991). Death, taxes, and bad intelligence tests. *Intelligence, 15,* 257–269. (9)

Sternberg, R. J., & Grajek, S. (1984). The nature of love. *Journal of Personality and Social Psychology, 47,* 312–329. (16)

Sternberg, R. J., & Wagner, R. K. (1993). The g-ocentric view of intelligence and job performance is wrong. *Current Directions in Psychological Science, 2,* 1–4. (A)

Sternberg, S. (1967). Two operations in character recognition: Some evidence from reaction-time measurements. *Perception and Psychophysics, 2,* 45–53. (8)

Stevens, A., & Coupe, P. (1978). Distortions in judged spatial relations. *Cognitive Psychology, 10,* 422–437. (8)

Stewart, I. (1987). Are mathematicians logical? *Nature, 325,* 386–387. (9)

Stewart, J. E. (1980). Defendant's attractiveness as a factor in the outcome of criminal trials: An observational study. *Journal of Applied Social Psychology, 10,* 348–361. (16)

Stewart, V. M. (1973). Tests of the "carpentered world" hypothesis by race and environment in America and Zambia. *International Journal of Psychology, 8,* 83–94. (4)

Stiles, W. B., Shapiro, D. A., & Elliott, R. (1986). "Are all psychotherapies equivalent?" *American Psychologist, 41,* 165–180. (15)

Stipek, D. J. (1984). Young children's performance expectations: Logical analysis or wishful thinking? *Advances in Motivation and Achievement, 3,* 33–56. (11)

Stolerman, I. P. (1991). Behavioural pharmacology of nicotine: Multiple mechanisms. *British Journal of Addiction, 86,* 533–536. (5)

Storms, M. D. (1973). Videotape and the attribution process: Reversing actors' and observers' points of view. *Journal of Personality and Social Psychology, 27,* 165–175. (16)

Strack, F., Martin, L. L., & Stepper, S. (1988). Inhibiting and facilitating conditions of the human smile: A nonobtrusive test of the facial feedback hypothesis. *Journal of Personality and Social Psychology, 54,* 768–777. (12)

Streather, A., & Hinson, R. E. (1985). Neurochemical and behavioral factors in the development of tolerance to anorectics. *Behavioral Neuroscience, 99,* 842–852. (5)

Streissguth, A. P., Barr, H. M., & Martin, D. C. (1983). Maternal alcohol use and neonatal habituation assessed with the Brazelton scale. *Child Development, 54,* 1109–1118. (10)

Streissguth, A. P., Sampson, P. D., & Barr, H. M. (1989). Neurobehavioral dose-response effects of prenatal alcohol exposure in humans from infancy to adulthood. *Annals of the New York Academy of Sciences, 562,* 145–158. (10)

Striegel-Moore, R. H., Silberstein, L. R., & Rodin, J. (1986). Toward an understanding of risk factors for bulimia. *American Psychologist, 41,* 246–263. (11)

Stroebe, M., Gergen, M. M., Gergen, K. J., & Stroebe, W. (1992). Broken hearts or broken bonds: Love and death in historical perspective. *American Psychologist, 47,* 1205–1212. (10)

Stroh, L. K., Brett, J. M., & Reilly, A. H. (1992). All the right stuff: A comparison of female and male managers' career progression. *Journal of Applied Psychology, 77,* 251–260. (A)

Stunkard, A. J., Sørensen, T. I. A., Hanis, C., Teasdale, T. W., Chakraborty, R., Shull, W. J., & Schulinger, F. (1986). An adoption study of human obesity. *New England Journal of Medicine, 314,* 193–198. (11)

Stuss, D. T., Alexander, M. P., Palumbo, C. L., Buckle, L., Sayer, L., & Pogue, J. (1994). Organizational strategies of patients with unilateral or bilateral frontal lobe injury in word list learning tasks. *Neuropsychology, 8,* 355–373. (7)

Sudzak, P. D., Glowa, J. R., Crawley, J. N., Schwartz, R. D., Skolnick, P., & Paul, S. M. (1986). A selective imidazobenzodiazepine antagonist of ethanol in the rat. *Science, 234,* 1243–1247. (5)

Sue, S., Smith, R. E., & Caldwell, C. (1973). Effects of inadmissible evidence on the decisions of simulated jurors: A moral dilemma. *Journal of Applied Social Psychology, 3,* 345–353. (16)

Sulser, F., Gillespie, D. D., Mishra, R., & Manier, D. H. (1984). Desensitization by antidepressants of central norepinephrine receptor systems coupled to adenylate cyclase. *Annals of the New York Academy of Sciences, 430,* 91–101. (14)

Suppes, T., Baldessarini, R. J., Faedda, G. L., & Tohen, M. (1991). Risk of recurrence following discontinuation of lithium treatment in bipolar disorder. *Archives of General Psychiatry, 48,* 1082–1088. (15)

Svanum, S., & Bringle, R. G. (1982). Race, social class, and predictive bias: An evaluation using the WISC, WRAT, and teacher ratings. *Intelligence, 6,* 275–286. (9)

Swash, M. (1972). Released involuntary laughter after temporal lobe infarction. *Journal of Neurology, Neurosurgery, and Psychiatry, 35,* 108–113. (3)

Szasz, T. S. (1982). The psychiatric will. *American Psychologist, 37,* 762–770. (15)

Szymanski, H. V., Simon, J. C., & Gutterman, N. (1983). Recovery from schizophrenic psychosis. *American Journal of Psychiatry, 140,* 335–338. (15)

Takeuchi, A. H., & Hulse, S. H. (1993). Absolute pitch. *Psychological Bulletin, 113,* 345–361. (4)

Tannen, D. (1990). *You just don't understand.* New York: William Morrow. (10)

Tassinary, L. G., & Cacioppo, J. T. (1992). Unobservable facial actions and emotion. *Psychological Science, 3,* 28–33. (12)

Taylor, F. V. (1957). Psychology and the design of machines. *American Psychologist, 12,* 249–258. (A)

Taylor, S. E. (1983). Adjustment to threatening events: A theory of cognitive adaptation. *American Psychologist, 38,* 1161–1173. (12)

Taylor, S. E., & Brown, J. D. (1988). Illusion and well-being: A social psychological perspective on mental health. *Psychological Bulletin, 103,* 193–210. (12)

Taylor, S. E., & Brown, J. D. (1994). Positive illusions and well-being revisited: Separating fact from fiction. *Psychological Bulletin, 116,* 21–27. (12)

Taylor, S. E., & Lobel, M. (1989). Social comparison activity under threat: Downward evaluation and upward contacts. *Psychological Review, 96,* 569–575. (16)

Teasdale, T. W., & Owen, D. R. (1984). Heredity and familial environment in intelligence and educational level: A sibling study. *Nature, 309,* 620–622. (9)

Tennen, H., & Affleck, G. (1990). Blaming others for threatening events. *Psychological Bulletin, 108,* 209–232. (12)

Terman, G. W., & Liebeskind, J. C. (1986). Relation of stress-induced analgesia to stimulation-produced analgesia. *Annals of the New York Academy of Sciences, 467,* 300–308. (4)

Terman, G. W., Shavitt, Y., Lewis, J. W., Cannon, J. T., & Liebeskind, J. C. (1984). Intrinsic mechanisms of pain inhibition: Activation by stress. *Science, 226,* 1270–1277. (4)

Terr, L. (1988). What happens to early memories of trauma? A study of twenty children under age five at the time of documented traumatic events. *Journal of the American Academy of Child and Adolescent Psychiatry, 27,* 96–104. (7)

Terrace, H. S., Petitto, L. A., Sanders, R. J., & Bever, T. G. (1979). Can an ape create a sentence? *Science, 206,* 891–902. (8)

Tesser, A. (1993). The importance of heritability in psychological research: The case of attitudes. *Psychological Review, 100,* 129–142. (3)

Tetlock, P. E. (1994). Good judgment in world politics: Who gets what right, when and why? Address at the Sixth Annual Convention of the American Psychological Society, July 2, 1994. (8)

Tetrud, J. W., & Langston, J. W. (1989). The effect of deprenyl (Selegiline) on the natural history of Parkinson's disease. *Science, 245,* 519–522. (3)

Tett, R. P., Jackson, D. N., & Rothstein, M. (1991). Personality measures as predictors of job performance: A meta-analytic review. *Personnel Psychology, 44,* 703–742. (A)

Thayer, F. C. (1987). Performance appraisal and merit pay systems: The disasters multiply. *Review of Public Personnel Administration, 7,* 36–53. (A)

Thayer, P. W. (1977). "Somethings old, somethings new." *Personnel Psychology, 30,* 513–524. (A)

Thayer, P. W. (1983). Industrial/organizational psychology: Science and application. *G. Stanley Hall Lecture Series, 3,* 5–30. (A)

Thieman, T. J. (1984). A classroom demonstration of encoding specificity. *Teaching of Psychology, 11,* 101–102. (7)

Thigpen, C., & Cleckley, H. (1957). *The three faces of Eve.* New York: McGraw-Hill. (14)

Thomas, A., & Chess, S. (1980). *The dynamics of psychological development.* New York: Brunner/Mazel. (10)

Thomas, A., Chess, S., & Birch, H. G. (1968). *Temperament and behavior disorders in children.* New York: New York University Press. (10)

Thompson, C. R., & Church, R. M. (1980). An explanation of the language of a chimpanzee. *Science, 208,* 313–314. (8)

Thompson, L. A., Detterman, D. K., & Plomin, R. (1991). Associations between cognitive abilities and scholastic achievement: Genetic overlap but environmental differences. *Psychological Science, 2,* 158–165. (9)

Thompson, L. W., Gallagher-Thompson, D., Futterman, A., Gilewski, M. J., & Peterson, J. (1991). The effects of late-life spousal bereavement over a 30-month interval. *Psychology and Aging, 6,* 434–441. (14)

Thompson, S. C. (1981). Will it hurt less if I can control it? A complex answer to a simple question. *Psychological Bulletin, 90,* 89–101. (12)

Thorley, G. (1984). Review of follow-up and follow-back studies of childhood hyperactivity. *Psychological Bulletin, 96,* 116–132. (A)

Thorndike, E. L. (1911/1970). *Animal intelligence.* Darien, CT: Hafner. (Original work published 1911.) (6)

Thurstin, A. H., Alfano, A. M., & Nerviano, V. J. (1987). The efficacy of AA attendance for aftercare of inpatient alcoholics: Some follow-up data. *International Journal of the Addictions, 22,* 1083–1090. (14)

Thyer, B. A., & Geller, E. S. (1990). Behavior analysis in the promotion of safety belt use: A review. *Progress in Behavior Modification, 26,* 150–172. (6)

Tiffany, S. T., & Baker, T. B. (1981). Morphine tolerance in rats: Congruence with a Pavlovian paradigm. *Journal of Comparative and Physiological Psychology, 95,* 747–762. (6)

Timberlake, W., & Farmer-Dougan, V. A. (1991). Reinforcement in applied settings: Figuring out ahead of time what will work. *Psychological Bulletin, 110,* 379–391. (6)

Tinbergen, N. (1958). *Curious naturalists.* New York: Basic Books. (3)

Titchener, E. B. (1910). *A textbook of psychology.* New York: Macmillan. (1)

Tolman, E. C. (1932). *Purposive behavior in animals and men.* New York: Century. (6)

Tolman, E. C., & Honzik, C. H. (1930). Introduction and removal of reward, and maze performance in rats. *University of California Publications in Psychology, 4,* 257–275. (6)

Tolstedt, B. E., & Stokes, J. P. (1984). Self-disclosure, intimacy, and the depenetration process. *Journal of Personality and Social Psychology, 46,* 84–90. (10)

Tolstoy, L. (1865, 1875/1978). *Tolstoy's letters,* Vol. I: 1828–1879. New York: Charles Scribner's Sons. (Original works written 1828–1879.) (10)

Tolstoy, L. (1983). *Confession.* New York: Norton. (Original work written 1882 but blocked from publication by the Russian censor.) (12)

Tomac, A., Lindqvist, E., Lin, L.-F. H., Ögren, S. O., Young, D., Hoffer, B. J., & Olson, L. (1995). Protection and repair of the nigrostriatal dopaminergic system by GDNF *in vivo. Nature, 373,* 335–339. (3)

Tombaugh, C. W. (1980). *Out of the darkness, the planet Pluto.* Harrisburg, PA: Stackpole. (4)

Torrance, E. P. (1980). Growing up creatively gifted: A 22-year longitudinal study. *Creative Child and Adult Quarterly, 5,* 148–159. (8)

Torrance, E. P. (1981). Empirical validation of criterion-referenced indicators of creative ability through a longitudinal study. *Creative Child and Adult Quarterly, 6,* 136–140. (8)

Torrance, E. P. (1982). "Sounds and images" productions of elementary school pupils as predictors of the creative achievements of young adults. *Creative Child and Adult Quarterly, 7,* 8–14. (8)

Torrey, E. F., Rawlings, R., & Waldman, I. N. (1988). Schizophrenic births and viral diseases in two states. *Schizophrenia Research, 1,* 73–77. (14)

Townsend, J. T. (1990). Serial vs. parallel processing: Sometimes they look like Tweedledum and Tweedledee but they can (and should) be distinguished. *Psychological Science, 1,* 46–54. (8)

Treisman, A., & Souther, J. (1985). Search asymmetry: A diagnostic for preattentive processing of separable features. *Journal of Experimental Psychology: General, 114,* 285–310. (4)

Trivers, R. L. (1972). Parental investment and sexual selection. In B. Campbell (Ed.), *Sexual selection and the descent of man, 1871–1971* (pp. 136–179). Chicago: Aldine. (3)

Tronick, E. Z., Morelli, G. A., & Ivey, P. K. (1992). The Efe forager infant and toddler's pattern of social relationships: Multiple and simultaneous. *Developmental Psychology, 28,* 568–577. (10)

Tschann, J. M., Johnston, J. R., Kline, M., & Wallerstein, J. S. (1990). Conflict, loss, change and parent-child relationships: Predicting children's adjustment during divorce. *Journal of Divorce, 13,* 1–22. (10)

Tulving, E. (1989). Remembering and knowing the past. *American Scientist, 77,* 361–367. (7)

Tulving, E., & Thomson, D. M. (1973). Encoding specificity and retrieval processes in episodic memory. *Psychological Review, 80,* 352–373. (7)

Turkheimer, E. (1991). Individual and group differences in adoption studies of IQ. *Psychological Bulletin, 110,* 392–405. (9)

Tversky, A., & Kahneman, D. (1981). The framing of decisions and the psychology of choice. *Science, 211,* 453–458. (8)

Tversky, A., & Kahneman, D. (1983). Extensional versus intuitive reasoning: The conjunctional fallacy in probability judgment. *Psychological Review, 90,* 293–315. (8)

Tversky, B. (1981). Distortions in memory for maps. *Cognitive Psychology, 13,* 407–433. (8)

U.S. Department of Labor. (1989, April). *Employment and Earnings* (Vol. 36, No. 4). Washington, D.C.: U.S. Government Printing Office. (10)

Udolf, R. (1981). *Handbook of hypnosis for professionals.* New York: Van Nostrand Reinhold. (5)

Uhl, G., Blum, K., Noble, E., & Smith, S. (1993). Substance abuse vulnerability and D_2 receptor genes. *Trends in Neurosciences, 16,* 83–88. (5, 14)

Ulrich, R. E., Stachnik, T. J., & Stainton, N. R. (1963). Student acceptance of generalized personality interpretations. *Psychological Reports, 13,* 831–834. (13)

Ulrich, R. S. (1984). View through a window may influence recovery from surgery. *Science, 224,* 420–421. (4)

Underwood, G. (1994). Subliminal perception on TV. *Nature, 370,* 103. (4)

Underwood, N. R., & McConkie, G. W. (1985). Perceptual span for letter distinctions during reading. *Reading Research Quarterly, 20,* 153–162. (8)

Vaillant, G. E. (1983). *The natural history of alcoholism.* Cambridge, MA: Harvard University Press. (14)

Vaillant, G. E., & Milofsky, E. S. (1982). The etiology of alcoholism: A prospective viewpoint. *American Psychologist, 37,* 494–503. (1, 3, 14)

Valenstein, E. S. (1986). *Great and desperate cures.* New York: Basic Books. (3)

Vallone, R. P., Ross, L., & Lepper, M. R. (1985). The hostile media phenomenon: Biased perception and perceptions of media bias in coverage of the "Beirut Massacre." *Journal of Personality and Social Psychology, 49,* 577–585. (16)

van der Meer, A. L. H., van der Weel, F. R., & Lee, D. N. (1995). The functional significance of arm movements in neonates. *Science, 267,* 693–695. (10)

Van Der Pligt, J., & Eiser, J. R. (1983). Actors' and observers' attributions, self-serving bias, and positivity. *European Journal of Social Psychology, 13,* 95–104. (16)

van Dyke, C., & Byck, R. (1982). Cocaine. *Scientific American, 246*(3), 128–141. (3)

Van Hoesen, G. W. (1993). The modern concept of association cortex. *Current Opinion in Neurobiology, 3,* 150–154. (3)

Van Hoesen, G. W., Hyman, B. T., & Damasio, A. R. (1991). Entorhinal cortex pathology in Alzheimer's disease. *Hippocampus, 1,* 1–8. (3)

Vaughan, D. (1986). *Uncoupling.* New York: Vintage Books. (16)

Vaughn, C. E., Snyder, K. S., Jones, S., Freeman, W. B., & Falloon, I. R. H. (1984). Family factors in schizophrenia relapse. *Archives of General Psychiatry, 41,* 1169–1177. (15)

Vaughn, V. L., Feldhusen, J. F., & Asher, J. W. (1991). Meta-analyses and review of research on pull-out programs in gifted education. *Gifted Child Quarterly, 35,* 92–98. (A)

Vernon, M. (1967). Relationship of language to the thinking process. *Archives of General Psychiatry, 16,* 325–333. (9)

Viken, R. J., Rose, R. J., Kaprio, J., & Koskenvuo, M. (1994). A developmental genetic analysis of adult personality: Extraversion and neuroticism from 18 to 59 years of age. *Journal of Personality and Social Psychology, 66,* 722–730. (13)

Vincent, K. R., & Harman, M. J. (1991). The Exner Rorschach: An analysis of its clinical validity. *Journal of Clinical Psychology, 47,* 596–599. (13)

Vokey, J. R., & Read, J. D. (1985). Subliminal messages: Between the devil and the media. *American Psychologist, 40,* 1231–1239. (4)

von Baeyer, C. (1988, September/October). How Fermi would have fixed it. *The Sciences, 28*(5), 2–4. (8)

von Hippel, W., Sekaquaptewa, D., & Vargas, P. (1995). On the role of encoding processes in stereotype maintenance. *Advances in Experimental Social Psychology, 27,* 177–254. (16)

von Restorff, H. (1933). Analyse von Vorgängen im Spurenfeld. I. Über die Wirkung von Bereichsbildungen im Spurenfeld [Analysis of the events in memory. I. Concerning the effect of domain learning in the memory field]. *Psychologische Forschung, 18,* 299–342. (7)

Vroom, V. H. (1964). *Work and motivation.* New York: Wiley. (A)

Vygotsky, L. S. (1978). *Mind in society.* Cambridge, MA: Harvard University Press. (10)

Wadden, T. A., & Stunkard, A. J. (1987). Psychopathology and obesity. *Annals of the New York Academy of Sciences, 499,* 55–65. (11)

Wagenaar, W. A. (1986). My memory: A study of autobiographical memory over six years. *Cognitive Psychology, 18,* 225–252. (7)

Wahba, M. A., & Bridwell, L. G. (1976). Maslow reconsidered: A review of research on the need hierarchy theory. *Organizational Behavior & Human Performance, 15,* 212–240. (11)

Wakefield, J. C. (1992). Disorder as harmful dysfunction: A conceptual critique of DSM-III-R's definition of mental disorder. *Psychological Review, 99,* 232–247. (14)

Wald, G. (1968). Molecular basis of visual excitation. *Science, 162,* 230–239. (4)

Waldman, I. D., Weinberg, R. A., & Scarr, S. (1994). Racial-group differences in IQ in the Minnesota transracial adoption study: A reply to Levin and Lynn. *Intelligence, 19,* 29–44. (9)

Waller, N. G., Kojetin, B. A., Bouchard, T. J., Jr., Lykken, D. T., & Tellegen, A. (1990). Genetic and environmental influences on religious interests, attitudes, and values: A study of twins reared apart and together. *Psychological Science, 1,* 138–142. (3)

Waller, N. G., & Shaver, P. R. (1994). The importance of nongenetic influences on romantic love styles: A twin-family study. *Psychological Science, 5,* 268–274. (3)

Wallesch, C.-W., Henriksen, L., Kornhuber, H. H., & Paulson, O. B. (1985). Observations on regional cerebral blood flow in cortical and subcortical structures during language production in normal man. *Brain and Language, 25,* 224–233. (3)

Walster, E., Aronson, E., Abrahams, D., & Rottman, L. (1966). Importance of physical attractiveness in dating behavior. *Journal of Personality and Social Psychology, 4,* 508–516. (16)

Walster, E., Traupman, J., & Walster, G. W. (1978). Equity and extramarital sexuality. *Archives of Sexual Behavior, 7,* 127–142. (16)

Walters, G. C., & Grusec, J. E. (1977). *Punishment.* San Francisco: W. H. Freeman. (6)

Warren, R. M. (1970). Perceptual restoration of missing speech sounds. *Science, 167,* 392–393. (8)

Washburn, M. F. (1908). *The animal mind.* New York: Macmillan. (1)

Wason, P. C. (1960). On the failure to eliminate hypotheses in a conceptual task. *Quarterly Journal of Experimental Psychology, 12,* 129–140. (8)

Watson, D. (1982). The actor and the observer: How are their perceptions of causality divergent? *Psychological Bulletin, 92,* 682–700. (16)

Watson, J. B. (1913). Psychology as the behaviorist views it. *Psychological Review, 20,* 158–177. (1, 7)

Watson, J. B. (1919). *Psychology from the standpoint of a behaviorist.* Philadelphia: Lippincott. (1)

Watson, J. B. (1925). *Behaviorism.* New York: Norton. (1, 7)

Watson, J. B., & Rayner, R. (1920). Conditioned emotional reactions. *Journal of Experimental Psychology, 3,* 1–14. (14)

Weaver, C. N. (1980). Job satisfaction in the United States in the 1970s. *Journal of Applied Psychology, 65,* 364–367. (10)

Webb, W. B. (1979). Theories of sleep functions and some clinical implications. In R. Drucker-Colín, M. Shkurovich, & M. B. Sterman (Eds.), *The functions of sleep* (pp. 19–35). New York: Academic Press. (5)

Wechsler, D. (1949). *WISC manual.* New York: Psychological Corporation. (9)

Wegner, D. M., Schneider, D. J., Carter, S. R., III, & White, T. L. (1987). Paradoxical effects of thought suppression. *Journal of Personality and Social Psychology, 53,* 5–13. (14)

Wegner, D. M., Wenzlaff, R., Kerker, R. M., & Beattie, A. E. (1981). Incrimination through innuendo: Can media questions become public answers? *Journal of Personality and Social Psychology, 40,* 822–832. (8)

Wehr, T. A., Jacobsen, F. M., Sack, D. A., Arendt, J., Tamarkin, L., & Rosenthal, N. E. (1986). Phototherapy of seasonal affective disorder. *Archives of General Psychiatry, 43,* 870–875. (14)

Weil, A. T., Zinberg, N. E., & Nelson, J. M. (1968). Clinical and psychological effects of marihuana in man. *Science, 162,* 1234–1242. (5)

Weinberg, R. A. (1989). Intelligence and IQ: Landmark issues and great debates. *American Psychologist, 44,* 98–104. (9)

Weinberg, R. A., Scarr, S., & Waldman, I. D. (1992). The Minnesota transracial adoption study: A follow-up of IQ test performances at adolescence. *Intelligence, 16,* 117–135. (9)

Weinberger, D. R. (1987). Implications of normal brain development for the pathogenesis of schizophrenia. *Archives of General Psychiatry, 44,* 660–669. (14)

Weiner, I. B., & Exner, J. E., Jr. (1991). Rorschach changes in long-term and short-term psychotherapy. *Journal of Personality Assessment, 56,* 453–465. (13)

Weiner, J. (1994). *The beak of the finch.* New York: Knopf. (3)

Weiner, R. D. (1984). Does electroconvulsive therapy cause brain damage? *Behavioral and Brain Sciences, 7,* 1–53. (15)

Weingardt, K. R., Loftus, E. F., & Lindsay, D. S. (1995). Misinformation revisited: New evidence on the suggestibility of evidence. *Memory & Cognition, 23,* 72–82. (7)

Weinstock, C. (1984). Further evidence on psychobiological aspects of cancer. *International Journal of Psychosomatics, 31,* 20–22. (12)

Weisberg, R. W. (1994). Genius and madness: A quasi-experimental test of the hypothesis that manic-depression increases creativity. *Psychological Science, 5,* 361–367. (14)

Weissman, M. M., Leaf, P. J., & Bruce, M. L. (1987). Single parent women: A community study. *Social Psychiatry, 22,* 29–36. (10)

Weitzman, E. D. (1981). Sleep and its disorders. *Annual Review of Neuroscience, 4,* 381–417. (5)

Weitzman, R. A. (1982). The prediction of college achievement by the Scholastic Aptitude Test and the high school record. *Journal of Educational Measurement, 19,* 179–191. (9)

Wellings, K., Field, J., Johnson, A., & Wadsworth, J. (1994). *Sexual behavior in Britain: The national survey of sexual attitudes and lifestyles.* New York: Penguin. (11)

Wells, G. L. (1993). What do we know about eyewitness identification? *American Psychologist, 48,* 553–571. (7)

Wender, P. H., Kety, S. S., Rosenthal, D., Schulsinger, F., Ortmann, J., & Lunde, I. (1986). Psychiatric disorders in the biological and adoptive families of adopted individuals with affective disorders. *Archives of General Psychiatry, 43,* 923–929. (1, 14)

Wenger, J. R., Tiffany, T. M., Bombardier, C., Nicholls, K., & Woods, S. C. (1981). Ethanol tolerance in the rat is learned. *Science, 213,* 575–576. (5)

Werner, E. E. (1989). High-risk children in young adulthood: A longitudinal study from birth to 32 years. *American Journal of Orthopsychiatry, 59,* 72–81. (10)

Westlake, T. M., Howlett, A. C., Ali, S. F., Paule, M. G., Scallet, A. C., & Slikker, W., Jr. (1991). Chronic exposure to Δ⁹-tetrahydrocannabinol fails to irreversibly alter brain cannabinoid receptors. *Brain Research, 544,* 145–149. (5)

Wheeler, D. D. (1970). Processes in word recognition. *Cognitive Psychology, 1,* 59–85. (8)

Wheeler, M. A., & Roediger, H. L. III (1992). Disparate effects of repeated testing: Reconciling Ballard's [1913] and Bartlett's [1932] results. *Psychological Science, 3,* 240–245. (7)

White, P. A. (1990). Ideas about causation in philosophy and psychology. *Psychological Bulletin, 108,* 3–18. (1)

Whitworth, R. H., & Perry, S. M. (1990). Comparison of Anglo- and Mexican-Americans on the 16-PF administered in Spanish or English. *Journal of Clinical Psychology, 46,* 857–863. (13)

Whorf, B. L. (1941). The relation of habitual thought and behavior to language. In L. Spier, A. I. Hallowell, & S. S. Newman (Eds.), *Language, culture, and personality* (pp. 75–93). Menasha, WI: Sapir Memorial Publication Fund. (8)

Wickens, D. D. (1970). Encoding categories of words: An empirical approach to meaning. *Psychological Review, 77,* 1–15. (7)

Wicker, A. W. (1969). Attitudes vs. action: The relation of verbal and overt behavioral responses to attitude objects. *Journal of Social Issues, 25*(4), 47–78. (16)

Wicklund, R. A., & Brehm, J. W. (1976). *Perspectives on cognitive dissonance.* Hillsdale, NJ: Lawrence Erlbaum. (16)

Widom, C. S. (1989). Does violence beget violence? A critical examination of the literature. *Psychological Bulletin, 106,* 3–28. (12)

Wiggins, S., Whyte, P., Huggins, M., Adam, S., Theilman, J., Bloch, M., Sheps, S. B., Schechter, M. T., & Hayden, M. R., for the Canadian collaborative study of predictive testing (1992). The psychological consequences of predictive testing for Huntington's disease. *New England Journal of Medicine, 327,* 1401–1405. (3)

Wild, H. M., Butler, S. R., Carden, D., & Kulikowski, J. J. (1985). Primate cortical area V4 important for colour constancy but not wavelength discrimination. *Nature, 313,* 133–135. (4)

Wilkins, L., & Richter, C. P. (1940). A great craving for salt by a child with corticoadrenal insufficiency. *Journal of the American Medical Association, 114,* 866–868. (11)

Willerman, L., Schultz, R., Rutledge, J. N., & Bigler, E. D. (1991). *In vivo* brain size and intelligence. *Intelligence, 15,* 223–228. (9)

Williams, D. G. (1990). Effects of psychoticism, extraversion, and neuroticism in current mood: A statistical review of six studies. *Personality and Individual Differences, 11,* 615–630. (13)

Williams, K. D., & Karau, S. J. (1991). Social loafing and social compensation: The effects of expectations of co-worker performance. *Journal of Personality and Social Psychology, 61,* 570–581. (16)

Williams, R. B., Jr., Lane, J. D., Kuhn, C. M., Melosh, W., White, A. D., & Schanberg, S. M. (1982). Type A behavior and elevated physiological and neuroendocrine responses to cognitive tasks. *Science, 218,* 483–485. (12)

Williams, R. W., & Herrup, K. (1988). The control of neuron number. *Annual Review of Neuroscience, 11,* 423–453. (3)

Wilson, E. O. (1975). *Sociobiology: The new synthesis.* Cambridge, England: Belknap. (3)

Wilson, J. R., and the editors of *Life* (1964). *The mind.* New York: Time. (4, 9)

Wilson, R. S. (1987). Risk and resilience in early mental development. In S. Chess & A. Thomas (Eds.), *Annual Progress in Child Psychiatry & Child Development 1986* (pp. 69–85). New York: Brunner/Mazel. (10)

Wimmer, H., & Perner, J. (1983). Beliefs about beliefs: Representation and constraining function of wrong beliefs in young children's understanding of deception. *Cognition, 13,* 103–128. (10)

Winner, E. (1986, August). Where pelicans kiss seals. *Psychology Today,* 24–35. (10)

Wise, R. A., & Bozarth, M. A. (1987). A psychomotor stimulant theory of addiction. *Psychological Review, 94,* 469–492. (14)

Wiseman, R. (1995). The megalab truth test. *Nature, 373,* 391. (12)

Wittchen, H.-U., Zhao, S., Kessler, R. C., & Eaton, W. W. (1994). DSM-III-R generalized anxiety disorder in the National Comorbidity Survey. *Archives of General Psychiatry, 51,* 355–364. (14)

Wogalter, M. S., Godfrey, S. S., Fontenelle, G. A., Desaulniers, D. R., Rothstein, P. R., & Laughery, K. R. (1987). Effectiveness of warnings. *Human Factors, 29,* 599–612. (A)

Wogalter, M. S., Marwitz, D. D., & Leonard, D. C. (1992). Suggestiveness in photospread line-ups: Similarity induces distinctiveness. *Applied Cognitive Psychology, 6,* 443–453. (7)

Wolfgang, M. E., Figlio, R. M., & Selin, T. (1972). *Delinquency in a birth cohort.* Chicago: University of Chicago Press. (10)

Wolgin, D. L., & Salisbury, J. J. (1985). Amphetamine tolerance and body weight set point: A dose-response analysis. *Behavioral Neuroscience, 99,* 175–185. (5)

Wolman, B. B. (1989). *Dictionary of behavioral science* (2nd ed.). San Diego, CA: Academic Press. (9)

Wolpe, J. (1961). The systematic desensitization treatment of neuroses. *Journal of Nervous and Mental Disease, 132,* 189–203. (14)

Wolpe, J., & Rowan, V. C. (1988). Panic disorder: A product of classical conditioning. *Behaviour Research and Therapy, 26,* 441–450. (14)

Wood, W., Lundgren, S., Ouellette, J. A., Busceme, S., & Blackstone, T. (1994). Minority influence: A meta-analytic review of social influence processes. *Psychological Bulletin, 115,* 323–345. (16)

Woods, C. W., Charney, D. S., Loke, J., Goodman, W. K., Redmond, E. E., Jr., & Heninger, G. R. (1986). Carbon dioxide sensitivity in panic anxiety. *Archives of General Psychiatry, 43,* 900–909. (14)

Woods, S. C. (1991). The eating paradox: How we tolerate food. *Psychological Review, 98,* 488–505. (11)

Woodward, E. L. (1938). *The age of reform.* London: Oxford University Press. (7)

Woodworth, R. S. (1934). *Psychology* (3rd ed.). New York: Henry Holt. (1)

Woody, G. E., & O'Brien, C. P. (1986). Update on methadone maintenance. *Research Advances in Alcohol and Drug Problems, 9,* 261–277. (14)

Woychyshyn, C. A., McElheran, W. G., & Romney, D. M. (1992). MMPI validity measures: A comparative study of original with alternative indices. *Journal of Personality Assessment, 58,* 138–148. (13)

Wright, D. B. (1993). Recall of the Hillsborough disaster over time: systematic biases in 'flashbulb' memories. *Applied Cognitive Psychology, 7,* 129–138. (7)

Wundt, W. (1902). *Outlines of psychology* (C. H. Judd, Trans.). New York: Gustav Sechert. (Original work published 1896.) (1)

Wundt, W. (1961). Contributions to the theory of sensory perception. In T. Shipley (Ed.), *Classics in psychology* (pp. 51–78). New York: Philosophical Library. (Original work published 1862.) (1)

Wyatt, G. E. (1994). The sociocultural relevance of sex research. *American Psychologist, 49,* 748–754. (11)

Yamamoto, J., & Kubota, M. (1983). The Japanese-American family. In G. J. Powell (Ed.), *The psychosocial development of minority group children* (pp. 237–247). New York Brunner/Mazel. (10)

Yarsh, T. L., Farb, D. H., Leeman, S. E., & Jessell, T. M. (1979). Intrathecal capsaicin depletes substance P in the rat spinal cord and produces prolonged thermal analgesia. *Science, 206,* 481–483. (4)

Yaryura-Tobias, J. A. (1977). Obsessive-compulsive disorders: A serotonergic hypothesis. *Journal of Orthomolecular Psychiatry, 6,* 317–326. (14)

Yates, B. (1985). *Self-management.* Belmont, CA: Wadsworth. (6)

Yoshikawa, H. (1994). Prevention as cumulative protection: Effects of early family support and education on chronic delinquency and its risks. *Psychological Bulletin, 115,* 28–54. (15)

Young, P. T. (1936). *Motivation of behavior.* New York: Wiley. (11)

Young-Ok, K., & Stevens, J. H., Jr. (1987). The socialization of prosocial behavior in children. *Childhood Education, 63,* 200–206. (6)

Zahn, T. P., Rapoport, J. L., & Thompson, C. L. (1980). Autonomic and behavioral effects of dextroamphetamine and placebo in normal and hyperactive prepubertal boys. *Journal of Abnormal Child Psychology, 8,* 145–160. (A)

Zajonc, R. B. (1968). Attitudinal effects of mere exposure. *Journal of Personality and Social Psychology, 9,* Monograph Suppl. 2, part 2. (16)

Zaragoza, M. S., McCloskey, M., & Jamis, M. (1987). Misleading postevent information and recall of the original event: Further evidence against the memory impairment hypothesis. *Journal of Experimental Psychology: Learning, Memory, and Cognition, 13,* 36–44. (7)

Zeki, S. (1980). The representation of colours in the cerebral cortex. *Nature, 284,* 412–418. (3)

Zeki, S. (1983). Colour coding in the cerebral cortex: The responses of wavelength-selective and colour-coded cells in monkey visual cortex to changes in wavelength composition. *Neuroscience, 9,* 767–781. (3)

Zeki, S. (1993). *A vision of the brain.* Oxford, England: Blackwell Scientific Publications. (4)

Zepelin, H., & Rechtschaffen, A. (1974). Mammalian sleep, longevity, and energy metabolism. *Brain, Behavior, and Evolution, 10,* 425–470. (5)

Zhang, Y., Proenca, R., Maffei, M., Barone, M., Leopold, L., & Friedman, J. M. (1994). Positional cloning of the mouse *obese* gene and its human homologue. *Nature, 372,* 425–432. (11)

Zigler, E., & Glick, M. (1988). Is paranoid schizophrenia really camouflaged depression? *American Psychologist, 43,* 284–290. (14)

Zigler, E., & Hodapp, R. M. (1991). Behavioral functioning in individuals with mental retardation. *Annual Review of Psychology, 42,* 29–50. (9)

Zigler, E., Taussig, C., & Black, K. (1992). Early childhood intervention: A promising preventative for juvenile delinquency. *American Psychologist, 47,* 997–1006. (10)

Zihl, J., von Cramon, D., & Mai, N. (1983). Selective disturbance of movement vision after bilateral brain damage. *Brain, 106,* 313–340. (3, 4)

Zipursky, R. B., Lim, K. O., Sullivan, E. V., Brown, B. W., & Pfefferbaum, A. (1992). Widespread cerebral gray matter volume deficits in schizophrenia. *Archives of General Psychiatry, 49,* 195–205. (14)

Zucker, R. A., & Gomberg, E. S. L. (1986). Etiology of alcoholism reconsidered. *American Psychologist, 41,* 783–793. (14)

Zuckerman, M. (1990). Some dubious premises in research and theory on racial differences. *American Psychologist, 45,* 1297–1303. (13)

Zuckerman, M. (1992). What is a basic factor and which factors are basic? Turtles all the way down. *Personality and Individual Differences, 13,* 675–681. (13)

Zuckerman, M., & Wheeler, L. (1975). To dispel fantasies about the fantasy-based measure of fear of success. *Psychological Bulletin, 82,* 932–946. (11)

Zullow, H. M., Oettingen, G., Peterson, C., & Seligman, M. E. P. (1988). Pessimistic explanatory style in the historical record. *American Psychologist, 43,* 673–682. (14)

Zwislocki, J. J. (1981). Sound analysis in the ear: A history of discoveries. *American Scientist, 69,* 184–192. (4)

CREDITS

This page constitutes an extension of the copyright page. We have made every effort to trace the ownership of all copyrighted material and to secure permission from copyright holders. In the event of any question arising as to the use of any material, we will be pleased to make the necessary corrections in future printings. Thanks are due to the following authors, publishers, and agents for permission to use the material indicated.

Chapter 3: 88: Figure 3.15 from J. G. Brandon and R. G. Coss, *Brain Research, 252,* pp. 51–61, 1982. Used by permission of R. G. Coss. **89:** Figure 3.17 reprinted by permission from *Nature, 315,* pp. 404–406 and Dale Purves. Copyright © 1985 Macmillan Magazines Ltd. **108:** Figure 3.37 from *Clinical Neuropsychology,* Third Edition, by Kenneth M. Heilman and Edward Valenstein. Copyright © 1993 by Oxford University Press, Inc. Reprinted by permission. **111:** Figure 3.40 (a) and (b) from "Specializations of the Human Brain," by Norman Geschwind, 1979, *Scientific American.* Copyright © 1979 by Scientific American, Inc. All rights reserved. Reprinted by permission.

Chapter 4: 135: Figure 4.16 reproduced from *Ishihara's Test for Colour Blindness,* Kanehara & Co., Ltd., Tokyo, Japan. A test for color blindness cannot be conducted with this material. For accurate testing, the original plate should be used. Reprinted by permission. **135:** Figure 4.17 reproduced from *Ishihara's Test for Colour Blindness,* Kanehara & Co., Ltd., Tokyo, Japan. A test for color blindness cannot be conducted with this material. For accurate testing, the original plate should be used. Reprinted by permission. **144:** Figure 4.24 from "Picture and Pattern Perception in the Sighted and the Blind: The Advantage of the Late Blind," by M. A. Heller, *Perception, 18,* pp. 379–389, 1989. Reprinted by permission from Pion, London. **157:** Figure 4.33 from "Fortysomething: Recognizing Faces at One's 25th Reunion," by M. Bruck, P. Cavanagh, and S. J. Ceci,

Memory and Cognition, 19, pp. 221–228, 1991. Reprinted by permission of M. Bruck. **158:** Figure 4.34 (b) from *Inversions,* by S. Kim. Copyright © 1989 by Scott Kim. Used with permission of W. H. Freeman and Company. **160:** Figure 4.37 from *Organization in Vision: Essays on Gestalt Perception,* by Gaetano Kanizsa, pp. 7, 8, & 9. Copyright © 1979 by Gaetano Kanizsa. Reprinted with permission of Praeger Publishers, an imprint of Greenwood Publishing Group, Westport, CT. **162:** Figure 4.40 (b) from "A Puzzle Picture with a New Principle of Concealment" by K. M. Dallenbach, *American Journal of Psychology, 54,* pp. 431–433, 1951. Copyright © by The Board of Trustees of the University of Illinois. **162:** Figure 4.41 (c) from *Mind Sights,* by Roger N. Shepard. Copyright © 1990 by Roger N. Shepard. Used with permission of W. H. Freeman and Company.

Chapter 5: 187: Figure 5.6 graphs from "Monotonic and Rhythmic Influences: A Challenge for Sleep Deprivation Research," by H. Babkoff, T. Caspy, M. Mikulincer, and H. C. Sing, 1991, *Psychological Bulletin, 109,* pp. 411–428. Copyright © 1991 American Psychological Association. Reprinted with permission. **190:** Figure 5.9 EEG recordings provided by T. E. LeVere. **192:** Figure 5.11 graph reprinted with permission from "Ontogenetic Development of Human Sleep-Dream Cycle," by H. P. Roffwarg, J. N. Muzio, and W. C. Dement, 1966, Science, *152,* pp. 604–609. Copyright © 1966 American Association for the Advancement of Science.

Chapter 7: 268: Figure 7.5 from "Considerations of Some Problems of Comprehension," by J. D. Bransford and M. K. Johnson in *Visual Information Processing.* W. G. Chase (ed.), 1973. Copyright Academic Press. Used by permission. **274:** Figure 7.13 reprinted with permission from "Acquisition of a Memory Skill," by K. A. Ericsson, W. G. Chase, and S. Falcon, 1980, *Science, 208,* pp. 1181–1182. Copyright 1980 American Association for the Advancement of Science. Reprinted by permission of the AAAS and K. A. Ericsson. **284:** Figure 7.17 based on "Long-Term Memory for a Common Object," by R. S. Nickerson and M. J. Adams, 1979, *Cognitive Psychology, 11,* pp. 287–307. Used by permission. **284:** Figure 7.18 (left) from "Semantic Memory Content in Permastore: Fifty Years of Memory for Spanish Learned in School," by Harry P. Bahrick, 1984, *Journal of Experimental Psychology: General, 113,* pp. 1–29. Copyright 1984 by the American Psychological Association. Used by permission of the author.

Chapter 8: 314: Figure 8.3 from "A Spreading-Activation Theory of Semantic Processing," by A. M. Collins and E. F. Loftus, 1975, *Psychological Review, 82,* pp. 407–428. Copyright 1975 American Psychological Association. Reprinted by permission. **317:** Figure 8.5 reprinted with permission from "Direct Measurement of Attentional Dwell Time in Human Vision," by J. Duncan, R. Ward, and K. Shapiro, 1994, *Nature, 369,* pp. 313–315. Copyright 1994 Macmillan Magazines

Ltd. **318:** Figure 8.6 reprinted with permission from "Mental Rotation of Three-Dimensional Objects," by R. N. Shepard and J. N. Metzler, *Science, 171,* pp. 701–703. Copyright 1971 American Association for the Advancement of Science. **329:** Logo courtesy of Dolby Laboratories. **359:** Figure 8.37 from "Parallel Distributed Processing Explorations in the Microstructure of Cognition," Vol. 1: *Foundations,* by David E. Rumelhart et al., p. 8, Figure 2. (Series in Computational Models of Cognition and Perception.) Copyright 1986 by MIT Press. Used by permission of the publisher.

Chapter 9: 374: Figure 9.5 from the Wechsler Intelligence Scale for Children: Third Edition. Copyright © 1990 by The Psychological Corporation. Reproduced by permission. All rights reserved. **377:** Figure 9.9 SAT questions selected from the Scholastic Assessment Test, College Entrance Examination Board. Reprinted by permission of Educational Testing Service, the copyright owner of the test questions. Permission to reprint the material does not constitute review or endorsement by Educational Testing Service or the College Board of this publication as a whole or of any other questions or testing information it may contain. **387:** Figure 9.12 from "Perspectives on Education in America," by C. C. Carson, R. M. Huelskamp, and T. D. Woodall, 1993, *Journal of Educational Research, 86,* pp. 259–310, Heldref Publications. **389:** Figure 9.14 from Black Intelligence Test of Cultural Homogeneity. Copyright © 1972 by Robert L. Williams, Ph.D. Reprinted by permission. **391:** Figure 9.15 reprinted with permission from "Familial Studies of Intelligence: A Review," by T. Bouchard et al., *Science, 212,* pp. 1055–1059, 1981. Copyright 1981 by the American Association for the Advancement of Science.

Chapter 10: 401: Figure 10.1 courtesy of Robin Kalat. **406:** Figure 10.8 modified from "Movement Produced Stimulation in the Development of Visually Guided Behavior," by R. Held and A. Hein, *Journal of Comparative Physiological Psychology, 56,* pp. 872–873. Copyright 1963 by the American Psychological Association. Adapted by permission of R. Held. **437:** Figure 10.30 graph from *Delinquency in a Birth Cohort,* by M. E. Wolfgang, R. M. Figlio, and T. Selin. Copyright © 1972 University of Chicago Press. Reprinted by permission.

Chapter 11: 477: Figure 11.14 reprinted by permission of Gene DeFoliart from *The Food Insects Newsletter,* March 1990.

Chapter 12: 515: Figure 12.6 based on "An Opponent-Process Theory of Motivation: I. Temporal Dynamics of Affect," by R. L. Solomon and J. D. Corbit, *Psychological Review, 81,* pp. 119–145. Copyright 1974 by the American Psychological Association. Reprinted by permission. **536:** Table 12.2 from "The Social Readjustment Rating Scale," by T. H. Holmes and R. H. Rahe in *Journal of Psychosomatic Research, 11,* pp. 213–218. Copyright 1967 by Pergamon Press, Ltd. Reprinted by permission of Elsevier Science Ltd., Oxford, England. **538:** Table 12.3 from "Comparison of Two Modes of Stress Measurement: Daily Hassles and Uplifts Versus Major Life Events," by A. D. Kanner, J. C. Coyne, C. Schaefer, and R. S. Lazarus, *Journal of Behavioral Medicine, 4,* p. 14. Copyright 1981 by Plenum Publishing Corporation. Adapted by permission. **539:** Figure 12.23 (left) from *Type A Behavior and Your Heart,* by Meyer Friedman and Ray H. Rosenman. Copyright © 1974 by Meyer Friedman. Reprinted by permission of Alfred A. Knopf, Inc.

Chapter 13: 585: Figure 13.19 from the Minnesota Multiphasic Personality Inventory-2. Copyright © by the Regents of the University of Minnesota, 1942, 1943 (renewed 1970), 1989. This profile from 1989. All rights reserved. **587:** Figure 13.20 adapted from *Handbook for the Sixteen Personality Factors,* by Raymond B. Cattell. Copyright 1970, 1988 by the Institute for Personality and Ability Testing, Inc. All rights reserved. Reproduced by permission. **588:** Figure 13.21 from *The Scientific Analysis of Personality,* by Raymond B. Cattell, 1965, Penguin Library. Reprinted by permission of Raymond B. Cattell. **590:** Figure 13.23 reprinted by permission of the publishers from Henry A. Murray, *Thematic Apperception Test,* Cambridge, Mass.: Harvard University Press, Copyright © 1943 by the President and Fellows of Harvard College, © 1971 by Henry A. Murray.

Chapter 14: 616: Table 14.3 and 14.4 from *Obsessions and Compulsions,* by Stanley J. Rachman and Ray J. Hodgson. Copyright © 1980. Reprinted by permission of Prentice-Hall, Inc., Englewood Cliffs, NJ. **621:** Figure 14.15 adapted from Levenson et al., "Greater Reinforcement from Alcohol for Those at Risk: Parental Risk, Personality Risk, and Sex," *Journal of Abnormal Psychology, 96,* pp. 242–253, 1987. Used by permission of the author. **624:** Figure 14.17 from "A 24-Year Follow-Up of California Narcotics Addicts," by Y. I. Hser, M. D. Anglin, and K. Powers, 1993, *Archives of General Psychiatry, 50,* pp. 577–584. Copyright 1993 American Medical Association. Reprinted by permission. **633:** Excerpts from Joshua Logan in *Moodswing,* by Ronald R. Fieve. Copyright © 1975 by Ronald R. Fieve. Published by William R. Morrow & Co. **633:** Figure 14.22 adapted from "Two-day Cycles of Alternating Good and Bad Behavior in Psychotic Patients," by C. P. Richter in *Archives of Neurology and Psychology, 39,* pp. 587–598, 1938. Copyright 1938 by the American Medical Association. Reprinted by permission. **634:** Figure 14.23 based on "Water and Sodium in Two Psychotics," by J. L. Crammer in *Lancet, 1*(7083), pp. 1122–1126, 1959. Used by permission of Lancet Ltd. **634:** Figure 14.24 from "The Increasing Rate of Suicide by Firearms," by J. H. Boyd in *New England Journal of Medicine, 308,* pp. 872–874, 1983. Used by permission.

Chapter 15: 649: Quote from "Observation" by Dorothy Parker, copyright 1928, renewed © 1956 by Dorothy Parker from *The Portable Dorothy Parker,* by Dorothy Parker, introduction by Brendan Gill. Used by permission of Viking Penguin, a division of Penguin Books USA Inc. **659:** Figure 15.3 based on "The Dose-Effect Relationship in Psychotherapy," by Kenneth I. Howard et al., 1986, *American Psychologist, 41,* pp. 159–164. Used by permission of Kenneth I. Howard. **662:** Figure 15.4 adapted from *The Benefits of Psychotherapy,* by M. L. Smith, G. V. Glass, and T. I. Miller, The Johns Hopkins University Press, 1980. Reprinted by permission. **670:** Figure 15.7 based on "Studies on Endogenous Ligands (Endacoids) for the Benzodiazepine/Beta-Carboline Binding Sites," by A. Guidotti, P. Ferrero, M. Fujimoto, R. M. Santi, and E. Costa, 1986, *Advances in Biochemical Psychopharmacology, 41,* pp. 137–148. Reprinted by permission. **674:** Figure 15.10 based on data from "Drugs in the Treatment of Psychosis," by J. O. Cole et al. In P. Solomon (ed.), *Psychiatric Drugs.* Copyright 1966 Grune & Stratton. Used by permission.

Chapter 16: 711: Figure 16.13 reprinted from *Social Pressures in Informal Groups: A Study of Human*

Factors in Housing, by Leon Festinger, Stanley Schachter, and Kurt Back, with the permission of the publishers, Stanford University Press. © 1950 by Leon Festinger, Stanley Schachter, and Kurt Back. **716:** Items from Zick Rubin's Liking and Loving Scales reprinted by permission of the author. **722:** Figure 16.19 adapted from "Opinion and Social Pressure," by Solomon Asch. *Scientific American,* November 1955. Copyright © 1955 by Scientific American, Inc. All rights reserved.

PHOTO CREDITS

Chapter 1: Page 3: Photo by T. R. Production/Superstock Inc. **Page 5:** Top photo by Bill Wisser/Gamma Liaison. Top right photo by Penelope Breese/ Gamma Liaison. Right middle photo by D. Abolafia/Gamma Liaison. Right bottom photo by J. Chenet/Gamma Liaison. Bottom middle photo by Kashi/Gamma Liaison. Bottom left photo by Cynthia Johnson/Gamma Liaison. Left middle photo by John Barr/Gamma Liaison. **Page 6:** Photo by J. Alvarez/Superstock Inc. **Page 7:** Photo by Sepp Seitz/Woodfin Camp & Assoc. **Page 8:** Photo by Black & White/Superstock Inc. **Page 9:** Photo courtesy of Dr. Michael E. Phelps & Dr. John Mazziotta, UCLA School of Medicine. **Page 10:** Right photo by Sandro Tucci/Time Magazine. Left photo by J. Novak/Superstock Inc. **Page 13:** Photo by Etienne de Malglaive/Liaison International. **Page 14:** Photo by Michael Heron/ Woodfin Camp & Assoc. **Page 15:** Photo by Tom McCarthy/Photo Network. **Page 17:** Photo by Phillip Wallick/Photo Network. **Page 18:** Right photo by Stephen Saks/Photo Network. Left photo by Phyllis Picardi/Photo Network. **Page 21:** Photo © The Walt Disney Company. **Page 22:** Photo by Rivera Collection/Superstock Inc. **Page 23:** Photo by Glenn Riley. **Page 25:** Photo courtesy of Wellesley College Archives and Notman. **Page 27:** Photo by Dario Perla/International Stock.

Chapter 2: Page 31: Photo by Glenn Riley. **Page 32:** Photo courtesy Commonwealth of Virginia/Division of Tourism. **Page 34:** Photo by Edinger/ Liaison. **Page 36:** Photo by Glenn Riley. **Page 37:** After Pfungst, 1911, in Fernald, 1984. **Page 38:** Photo by Harry Langdon/Shooting Star. **Page 39:** Photo by Orion Pictures Corporation. **Page 40:** Photo courtesy CFB Productions, Inc. **Page 41:** Photo © 1994 Center for Inquiry. **Page 43:** Photo by Richard T.

Nowitz/Photo Researchers, Inc. **Page 45:** Photo by Sally and Richard Greenhill. **Page 48:** Photo by Breese/Gamma Liaison. **Page 51:** Photo by S.S./Shooting Star. **Page 52:** Photo by T. Rosenthal/Superstock Inc. **Page 57:** Right photo by Chad Ehlers/Photo Network. Left photo by Porter Gifford/Gamma Liaison. **Page 58:** Photo by David Spiegel, M.D., Stanford University School of Medicine. **Page 59:** Photo © David Madison 1995. **Page 63:** Photo by AGE Spain/Superstock Inc.

Chapter 3: Page 71: Photo by M. Carlisle/Superstock Inc. **Page 72:** Photo by ZEFA. **Page 74:** Photo by CNRI/Science Photo Library. **Page 75:** Photo by ZEFA/The Stock Market. **Page 82:** Left photo by Gordon Langsbury/Bruce Coleman. Right photo by Rod Planck. **Page 83:** Photo by Galen Rowell/Mountain Light. **Page 84:** Photo by Tom Smart/Gamma Liaison. **Page 88:** Photo © Manfred Kage/Peter Arnold. **Page 91:** Photo by Dennis Kunkel, University of Hawaii. **Page 96:** Photo by Jim Bourg/Gamma Liaison. **Page 102:** Photos by Mao/Gamma Liaison. **Page 105:** Top photos by Dr. Colin Chumbley/Science Photo Library. Bottom photo courtesy of Dana Copeland. **Page 112:** Top photo by Burt Glinn/Magnum Photos, Inc. Bottom three from Figure 1 from "Observations on regional cerebral blood flow in cortical and subcortical structures during language production in normal man," by C. W. Wallesch, L. Henrikson, H. H. Kornhuber, and O. B. Paulson in *Brain & Language,* 25:224–233, 1985. Used by permission of Academic Press and O. B. Paulson.

Chapter 4: Page 121: Photo by Glenn Riley. **Page 122:** Photo by Dominique Malaterre of TILT. **Page 124:** Photo by Sally and Richard Greenhill. **Page 125:** Photos by Glenn Riley. **Page 126:** Photo by E. R. Lewis, F. S. Werblin and Y. Y. Zeevi. **Page 127:** Photo by Chase Swift/Swift Photography. **Page 128:** Photo by Ed Lallo/Liaison International. **Page 133:** Photo by Klaus Benser /ZEFA. **Page 139:** Photo by Lea Zuzuki/San Francisco Chronicle. **Page 140:** Photo by Rene. **Page 143:** Photo © 1994 Jack Vartoogian. **Page 145:** Photo by Richard Shock/Gamma Liaison. **Page 147:** Photo by Omikron/Science Photo Library. **Page 150:** Photo by Louis Psimoyos/Contact Press Images/ Colorific! **Page 155:** Courtesy of Toyota Motor Sales, USA Inc. **Page 156:** Photo by American Association of Advertising Agencies. **Page 157:** Figure 5.4 in "Fortysomething: Recog-

nizing Faces at One's 25th Reunion," by M. Bruck, P. Cavanagh, and S. J. Ceci in *Memory & Cognition,* 19:221–228, 1991. **Page 161:** Photo courtesy of McDonnell Douglas. **Page 164:** Collage by David Hockney, "Celia, Los Angeles, April 10 1982." Composite Polaroid, 18×40 in., © David Hockney, 1982. **Page 162:** Photos courtesy of K. M. Dallenbach from the American Journal of Psychology. © 1942 by the Board of Trustees of the University of Illinois. Used with permission of the University of Illinois Press. **Page 165:** Right photo by AP/World Wide Photos. Left photo by Russ Gilbert/San Diego Union. **Page 166:** Photo by Bettmann. **Page 168:** Photo by Globus Bros/ZEFA/ The Stock Market. **Page 169:** Figure 4.49: Photo by Clyde Tombaugh, Lowell Observatory Photograph. **Page 169:** Figure 4.50: Photos by Lara Hartley. **Page 170:** Photo by John Boykin. **Page 171:** Photo by John Boykin. **Page 172:** Photo by Steve McGurry/Magnum Photos, Inc. **Page 173:** Photo © Andrew Brilliant. **Page 174:** Photo by S. Schwartzenberg. © The Exploratorium. All rights reserved. **Page 177:** Photos by Mark Antman/The Image Works. **Page 182:** Photo by Tom McCarthy/Photo Network.

Chapter 5: Page 181: Photo by Mia & Klaus/Superstock Inc. **Page 183:** Photo by Brian Payne/Black Star. **Page 186:** Photo by San Diego Historical Society. **Page 187:** Photo by Eugene Richards/ Magnum Photos. **Page 188:** Top right photo by ZEFA/The Stock Market. Top left photo by Bill Terry/Photo Network. Bottom right photo by Valery Itskovich/Photo Network. Bottom left photo by Karen Lawrence/Photo Network. **Page 189:** Photo by Richard Nowitz/Black Star. **Page 192:** Photo by Susan Ashukian. **Page 193:** Photo by Yagi Studio/Superstock Inc. **Page 194:** Photo by Penny Tweedie/Impact. **Page 195:** Photo by AP/Wide World Photos. **Page 197:** Photo by Michael Philip Manheim/Photo Network. **Page 199:** Photo by Mary Evans Picture Library. **Page 200:** Photo by John Ficara/Woodfin Camp & Assoc. **Page 201:** Figure 5.14: Photo by Bill Aron/ Photo Researchers, Inc. **Page 201:** Figure 5.15: Photo by UPI/Bettmann. **Page 202:** Photo by AP/Wide World Photos. **Page 203:** Clockwise starting top left: Photo by Telegraph Colour Library/FPG International. Photo by Nikolay Zurek/FPG International. Photo by Lawrance B. Aiuppy/FPG International. Photo by Telegraph Colour Library/FPG International. Photo

Black Star. **Page 411:** Photo by Stephen Rapley. **Page 412:** Photo by Ann Dowie. **Page 416:** Photo by Ann Dowie. **Page 419:** Photo by Elizabeth Crews/Elizabeth Crews Photography. **Page 420:** Top photo by Jacyln Hasko/Stock Boston. Middle photo by Elizabeth Crews/Elizabeth Crews Photography. Bottom photo by Elizabeth Crews/Elizabeth Crews Photography. **Page 421:** Photo by Sally and Richard Greenhill. **Page 422:** Figure 10.19: Photo by Stephen Rapley. **Page 422:** Photo © Lars Topelmann. **Page 423:** Photo by Pugliano/Gamma Liaison. **Page 426:** Photo by Rick Smolan. **Page 427:** Photo by Alan Carey/The Image Works. **Page 429:** Photo from the Stanford Daily. **Page 431:** Figure 10.24: Photo by Forest McMullin/Black Star. **Page 431:** Figure 10.25: Photo by Olive Pierce/Black Star. **Page 432:** Photo by L. Mangino/The Image Works. **Page 433:** Photo by Harlow Primate Laboratory, University of Wisconsin. **Page 434:** Photo by Harlow Primate Laboratory, University of Wisconsin. **Page 435:** Photo © Joel Simon. **Page 436:** Photo by Sally and Richard Greenhill. **Page 437:** Photo by Stephen Frisch/Stock Boston. **Page 438:** Photo by Patrick Ward/Stock Boston. **Page 439:** Photo by R. Lord/The Image Works. **Page 440:** Photo by Chris Maynard/Gamma Liaison. **Page 442:** Photo by Galen Rowell/Mountain Light Photography. **Page 443:** Photo by Bettmann. **Page 446:** Photo by Sally and Richard Greenhill. **Page 447:** Photo by Bob Daemmrich/Stock Boston. **Page 448:** Photo by Jaques Chenet/Woodfin Camp & Assoc. **Page 449:** Photo by Catherine Ursillo/Photo Researchers, Inc. **Page 450:** Photo by Rene. **Page 450:** Right photo by John Boykin. Left photo © Joel Simon. **Page 453:** Right photo by Sally and Richard Greenhill. Left photo by Don Klump/The Image Bank. **Page 454:** Top right photo by Richard Pasley/Stock Boston. Top left photo by Frank Siteman/Stock Boston. Middle right photo by Daemmrich/The Image Works. Middle left photo by Larry Kolvoord/The Image Works. Bottom right photo by Garry D. McMichael/Photo Researchers, Inc. Bottom left photo by M. Green/The Image Works.

Chapter 11: Page 455: Photo by Steve Liss/Gamma Liaison. **Page 459:** Photo by Glenn Riley. **Page 460:** Photo by AP/Wide World Photos. **Page 463:** Top photo by Benn Mitchell/The Image Bank. Bottom photo by George Butler/Visions Photo Inc. **Page 465:** Top photo by David Halpern/Photo Researchers, Inc. Second down photo by

Gail Meese/Gail Meese Photography. Third down photo by Tony Arruza/The Image Works. Bottom photo by Arnold Zahn/Black Star. **Page 470:** Photo by J. M. Giboux/Gamma Liaison. **Page 471:** Photo by Stephanie Maze/Woodfin Camp & Assoc. **Page 478:** Photo by John Sholtis/The Rockefeller University. **Page 475:** Photo by Sally and Richard Greenhill. **Page 476:** Photo by The Image Bank. **Page 477:** Top photo by Peter Menzel/Stock Boston. Bottom photo by Gail Meese/Gail Meese Photography. **Page 479:** Photo by ZEFA. **Page 482:** Top right photo by Erich Lessing/Art Resource. Top middle photo by Fernando Botero/© Public Art Fund. Left reproduction of Sandro Botticelli/Art Resource. Bottom right photo by Carl Purcell/Photo Researchers, Inc. Bottom middle photo by Bettmann Archive. **Page 483:** Photo by Tony Freeman/Photo Edit. **Page 485:** Photo © Jay Dickman. **Page 486:** Reproduced by permission of The Kinsey Institute for Research in Sex, Gender, and Reproduction, Inc. Photo by Dellenback. **Page 491:** Top right photo by D. P. A./The Image Works. Top left photo by Thierry Mayer/Photo Researchers, Inc. Top middle photo by Ted Wood/Black Star. Bottom right photo by Ilene Perlman/Stock Boston. Bottom photo courtesy of the San Francisco AIDS Foundation. **Page 494:** Photo by Gail Meese/Gail Meese Photography. **Page 498:** Photo © 1995 Comstock, Inc. **Page 500:** Photo by David Tullis/UPI/Bettmann. **Page 501:** Top photo by Michael Speaker. Bottom photo by Elizabeth Crews/Elizabeth Crews Photography. **Page 503:** Photo by Bettmann. **Page 504:** Photo by Elizabeth Crews/The Image Works. **Page 505:** Photo by Gary Caskey/Reuters/Bettmann. **Page 506:** Photo by Craig Schwartz Photography/AP/Wide World Photos, Inc.

Chapter 12: Page 509: Photo © David Madison 1987. **Page 510:** Photo by Bob Daemmrich/The Image Works. **Page 511:** Photo by Petar Kujundzic/Reuters/Bettmann. **Page 512:** Reprinted with permission from "The return of Phineas Gage: Clues about the brain from the skull of a famous patient," by H. Damasio, T. Grabowski, R. Frank, A.M. Galabu, and A. R. Damasio in *Science*, 264. © 1994 American Association for the Advancement of Science. **Page 514:** Top photo by Matthews and Prudy/Planet Earth Pictures. Bottom photo by Christopher Morris/Time/Black Star. **Page 516:** Photo © 1995 Alon Reiniger/Contact Press Images. **Page 519:** Photo by Ann Dowie. **Page**

523: Photo by Tony Latham/Tony Stone Images. **Page 524:** Left photo by Ron Kimball/Ron Kimball Photography. Figure 12.14: Photo by John Boykin. **Page 525:** Figure 12.15: Photo by I. Eibl-Eibesfeldt. **Page 525:** Figure 12.16: Photo by I. Eibl-Eibesfeldt. **Page 525:** Figure 12.17: Photos by I. Eibl-Eibesfeldt. **Page 526:** Photos from *Unmasking the Face* (2d ed.) by P. Ekman and W. Friesen, 1984. Used by permission of P. Ekman. **Page 528:** Photo by John Boykin. **Page 529:** Photo by Alex Brandon/AP/Wide World Photos. **Page 530:** Photo by Jeffrey Muir Hamilton/Stock Boston. **Page 533:** Photo by Timothy Shonnard/Tony Stone Images. **Page 534:** Photo by Mark Richards. **Page 535:** Photo by Frankee (Jim Lenoir). **Page 536:** Photo © Robin Jareau/Stockworks. **Page 537:** Left photo by Barbara Campbell/Liaison International. Right photo by Gale Zucker/Stock Boston. **Page 539:** Photo by Peter Southwick/Stock Boston. **Page 540:** Top photo by Dennis Budd Gray/Stock Boston. Bottom photo by Bill Horsman/Stock Boston. **Page 543:** Photo by John Gaps III/AP/Wide World Photos. **Page 544:** Photo by Chris Brown/Stock Boston. **Page 545:** Photo by Tabuteau/The Image Works. **Page 546:** Top photo by Rorke/The Image Works. Bottom photo by Cindy Charles/Gamma Liaison. **Page 547:** Photo by Phyllis Picardi/Photo Network. **Page 548:** Photo by Mark Terrill/AP/Wide World Photos.

Chapter 13: Page 551: Photo by Dunn/Monkmeyer. **Page 552:** Photo by Bonnie Schiffman. **Page 554:** Figure 13.2: Photo by The Granger Collection, New York. **Page 554:** Figure 13.3: Photo © Archiv/Photo Researchers, Inc. **Page 556:** Right photo by Kindra Clineff/The Picture Cube. Left photo by Carol Palmer/The Picture Cube. **Page 557:** Right photo by Kindra Clineff/The Picture Cube. Left photo by The Bettmann Archive. **Page 560:** Photo from the Freud Museum London. **Page 562:** Right photo by Adam Hart-Davis/Science Photo Library. Left photo by UPI/Bettmann. **Page 564:** Figure 13.10: Photo by The Bettmann Archive. **Page 564:** Figure 13.11: Photo by Culver Pictures. **Page 565:** a: Photo by The Granger Collection, New York. b–d: Photos from The Archive for Research in Archetypal Symbolism, San Francisco. **Page 566:** Figure 13.13: Photo by UPI/Bettmann Newsphotos. **Page 567:** Photo by Rob Schoenbaum/Black Star. **Page 568:** Photo by The Bettmann Archive. **Page 569:** Figure 13.15: Photo by The Bettmann Archive. **Page 570:** Photo by The Bettmann Archive. **Page 573:** Reproduction courtesy of Frederick Brown. **Page 574:** Photo by John Hillery/Black Star. **Page 575:** Photo by J. Sulley/The Image Works. **Page 577:** Photo by Bob Daemmrich/The Image Works. **Page 582:** Photo by Glenn Riley. **Page 593:** Photo by Glenn Riley. **Page 590:** Photo by Louis Fernandez/Black Star. **Page 590:** Figure 13.23: From Thematic Apperception Test by Henry A. Murray, Harvard University Press, Cambridge, MA. © 1943 by the President and Fellows of Harvard College, © 1971 by Henry A. Murray. Reprinted by permission of the publisher.

Chapter 14: Page 595: Photo by Matthys Collection/Superstock Inc. **Page 596:** Photo by John Boykin. **Page 597:** Photo by Muzammil Pasha/Reuters/Bettmann. **Page 598:** Reproduction of "Three Miracles of St. Zenobius" (detail) by Botticelli from Art Resource. **Page 599:** Photo by Ian Barrett/Reuters/Bettmann. **Page 600:** Top photo by David Longstreath/AP/Wide World Photos. Bottom photo by Glenn Riley. **Page 602:** Photo by Jonathon Pite/International Stock. **Page 604:** Photo by Eli Reed/Magnum Photos, Inc. **Page 608:** Right photo by Los Angeles Times Photo. Left photo by Alfred Hitchcock/The Bettmann Archive. **Page 610:** Photo courtesy of Professor Benjamin Harris. **Page 612:** Photo by Dede Gilman/Photo Network. **Page 613:** Figure 14.11: Photo by Andrew Sacks/Andrew Sacks Pictures. **Page 613:** Figure 14.12: Photo by AP/Wide World Photos. **Page 616:** a: Photo by Glenn Riley. b: Photo by Collins/Monkmeyer. Left photo by Glenn Riley. **Page 618:** Photo by Al Cook/Stock Boston. **Page 620:** Photo by Phyllis Picardi/Stock Boston. **Page 623:** Photo by Jim McHugh/Visages/Colorific! **Page 625:** Photo by Mike Goldwater–Network/Matrix. **Page 627:** Photo of Edvard Munch painting by Erich Lessing/Art Resource. **Page 630:** Reproduction of Edward Hopper by Art Resource. **Page 631:** Right photo by Frederic Neema/Reuters/Bettmann. Left

photo by Steve Ball/Black Star. **Page 635:** Photo by Goldberg/Monkmeyer. **Page 639:** Photo by Benyas Kaufman/Black Star. **Page 640:** Photo by Grunnitos/Monkmeyer. **Page 641:** Photos courtesy of E. F. Torrey and M. F. Casanova/NIMH. **Page 644:** Photo by Hiller/Monkmeyer.

Chapter 15: Page 647: Photo by E. Faure/Superstock Inc. **Page 648:** Photo by Cindy Karp/NYT Pictures. **Page 649:** Photo by Pete Cosgrove/UPI/Bettmann. **Page 651:** Photo by Henry T. Kaiser/Photo Network. **Page 652:** Photo by Norman Lono/NYT Pictures. **Page 653:** Photo by Mimi Forsyth/Monkmeyer. **Page 655:** Photo by Ron Chapple/FPG International. **Page 658:** Top photo by Rob Nelson/Black Star. Bottom photo by Jim Estrin/NYT Pictures. **Page 659:** Photo by Mike Goldwater–Network/Matrix. **Page 661:** Right photo by Ken Fisher/Tony Stone Images. Left photo by Zigy Kaluzny/Tony Stone Images. **Page 664:** Photo by Erich Hartmann/Magnum Photos, Inc. **Page 668:** Photo by Seth Resnick/Stock Boston. **Page 669:** Photo courtesy of Dana Copeland. **Page 672:** Photo by James D. Wilson/Woodfin Camp & Assoc. **Page 677:** Photo by Jack Spratt/Black Star. **Page 678:** Photo by Bob Daemmrich/Stock Boston. **Page 679:** Photo by PF Bentley/Black Star. **Page 682:** Photo by Lee Celano/Reuters/Bettmann. **Page 683:** Photo by Annie Griffiths Belt/Aurora.

Chapter 16: Page 687: Photo by W. Gontscharoff/Superstock Inc. **Page 688:** Photo by Jose Azel/Aurora. **Page 690:** Photo by Charles Gupton/Stock Boston. **Page 691:** Photo by AP/Wide World Photos. **Page 693:** Photo by Glenn Riley. **Page 698:** Photo by Peter Morgan/Bettmann Newsphotos. **Page 699:** Photo by Bob Daemmrich/Stock Boston. **Page 700:** Photo by Paul Lowe/Magnum Photos Inc. **Page 701:** Top photo by Loren Santow/Impact Visuals. Bottom photo by Meryl Levin/Impact Visuals. **Page 703:** Top photo by Barbara Filet/Tony Stone Images. Bottom photo © Joel Simon.

Page 706: Photo by Jose Lopez/NYT Pictures. **Page 709:** Right photo by Tom Walker/Stock Boston. Top left photo by Jim Harrison/Stock Boston. Bottom left photo by Joe Bensen/Stock Boston. **Page 710:** Photo by Reed Saxon/AP/Wide World Photos. **Page 712:** Photo by Taylor-Fabricius/Photo Network. **Page 713 (right):** Photo by P. Quittemelle/Stock Boston. **Page 713 (left):** Photo by Joe McDonald/Natural Selection. **Page 715 (left):** Photo by Tom McCarthy/Photo Network. **Page 715 (right):** Photo by Esbin-Anderson/Photo Network. **Page 716:** Figure 2 from "Averaging Faces," by Langlois, Roggman, & Musselman in *Psychological Science,* vol. 5, no. 4. **Page 718:** Photo by John Boykin. **Page 720:** Photo by Bob Daemmrich/Stock Boston. **Page 721:** Photo by William Vandivert. **Page 723:** Photo by John Boykin. **Page 724:** Photo by Chuck Nacke/Black Star. **Page 726:** Photo by Billy Barnes/Stock Boston. **Page 730:** Photo by Raghu Rai/Magnum Photos, Inc. **Page 731:** Photo courtesy of NASA. **Page 734:** Photo by Greig Cranna/Stock Boston. **Page 735:** Photo by Ann Dowie. **Page 736:** Figures 16.26 & 16.27: Photos © 1965 by Stanley Milgram. From the film *Obedience,* distributed by Pennsylvania State University Audio Visual Services. **Page 737:** Figure 16.28: Photo © 1965 by Stanley Milgram. From the film *Obedience,* distributed by Pennsylvania State University Audio Visual Services.

Applied Psychology: Page 742: Photo by Erich Hartmann/Magnum Photos, Inc. **Page 743:** Photo by Bob Daemmrich/Stock Boston. **Page 745:** Photo by Mark Ludak/Impact Visuals. **Page 746:** Photo by Chester Higgins, Jr./NYT Pictures. **Page 751:** Photo by Kevin Coomb/Reuter/Bettmann Newsphotos. **Page 756:** Photo courtesy GPU Nuclear Corporation. **Page 759:** Photo by Susan Meiselas/Magnum Photos, Inc. **Page 761:** Photo by Lawrence Migdale/Stock Boston. **Page 762:** Photo by Grantpix/Monkmeyer. **Page 763:** Photo by Frank Siteman/Stock Boston.

INDEXES

NAME INDEX

SUBJECT AND GLOSSARY INDEX

fear of failure preoccupation with avoiding failure, rather than taking risks in order to succeed, 502

fear of success, 505

feature detector neuron in the visual system of the brain that responds to particular lines or other features of a visual stimulus, 157–61
   Gestalt psychology and, 165

femininity, 578–80

fetal alcohol syndrome condition marked by decreased alertness and other signs of impaired development, caused by exposure to alcohol prior to birth, 382, 403

fetal tissue, Parkinson's disease and, 96

fetishism, 603

fetus an organism more developed than an embryo but not yet born (from about 8 weeks until birth in humans), 402–4

"fight or flight," 101, 513

figure and ground an object and its background, 161

first impression, 698–99

fish, lateral line system of, 138

fixation in Freud's theory, a persisting preoccupation with an immature psychosexual interest as a result of frustration at that stage of psychosexual development, 556, 557

fixed-interval schedule rule for delivering reinforcement for the first response the subject makes after a specified period of time has passed, 251

fixed-ratio schedule rule for delivering reinforcement only after the subject has made a certain number of responses, 250

"flight of ideas," 632

flooding therapy for phobia in which the person is suddenly exposed to the object of the phobia, 613

fluid intelligence basic power of reasoning and using information, including the ability to perceive relationships, deal with unfamiliar problems, and gain new types of knowledge, 367–68, 371

food, learned associations with, 476

Food and Drug Administration (FDA), 591

food intake, homeostatic regulating system for, 473

food selection, motives in, 474–76

foot-in-the-door technique method of eliciting compliance by first making a modest request and then following it with a larger request, 734

forebrain the most anterior (forward) part of the brain, including the cerebral cortex and other structures, 100, 104
   tetrahydrocannabinol receptors in, 212

forewarning effect tendency of a brief preview of a message to decrease its persuasiveness, 694

forgetting, 289–90

formal-operations stage, 411, 416–17

fovea central part of the retina that has a greater density of receptors, especially cones, than any other part of the retina, 126

fraternal twins, 78
   extraversion levels of, 579
   IQ scores and, 391
   personality traits and, 578
   sexual orientation and, 494–95
   temperament and, 447

free association procedure in which a client lies on a couch, starts thinking about a particular symptom or problem, and then reports everything that comes to mind, 650

freebase cocaine, 213

free will alleged ability of an individual to make decisions that are not controlled by genetics, past experience, or environment, 7, 223
   vs. determinism, 6–8

frequency, sound wave, 138

frequency principle identification of pitch by the frequency of action potentials in neurons along the basilar membrane of the cochlea, synchronized with the frequency of sound waves, 140

Freudian slip, 561–62

frontal lobe portion of each cerebral hemisphere, critical for precise control of movement,

preparation for movement, and certain aspects of memory, 108, 110–11

frontal-lobe amnesia, 291–92

frustration-aggression hypothesis theory that frustration leads to aggressive behavior, 528

functionalism attempt to understand how mental processes produce useful behaviors, 22–23

fundamental attribution error tendency to overemphasize internal explanations of other people's behavior, 704

g Spearman's "general" factor that all IQ tests and all parts of an IQ test are believed to have in common, 366

GABA. *See* gamma-amino-butyric acid

gambler's fallacy belief that if a particular random outcome has not occurred recently, its probability of occurrence will increase, 341

gambling, psychology of, 338–42

gamma-amino-butyric acid (GABA)
   barbiturates and, 211
   benzodiazepines and, 669–70
   functions of, 95

ganglion cell neuron in the eye that receives input from the visual receptors and sends impulses via the optic nerve to the brain, 128

ganzfeld procedure, 40–41

gate theory theory that pain messages have to pass through a gate in the spinal cord on their way to the brain, and that the brain and receptors in the skin can send messages to the spinal cord to open or close the gate, 145

gender
   IQ score and, 386
   moral development and, 426–27
   social development and, 450–55

gender role the role each person is expected to play because of being male or female, 452–55

gene segment of a chromosome that controls chemical reactions that ultimately direct the development of the organism, 73–76
   addictive behavior and, 15
   Alzheimer's disease and, 293
   behavior and, 79
   dominant, 74
   identifying and localizing, 77
   recessive, 74
   sex-limited, 76
   sex-linked, 75–76
   transmission from one generation to another, 74

general adaptation syndrome condition characterized by weakness, fatigue, loss of appetite, and a general lack of interest, 534

generalized anxiety disorder disorder in which people are constantly plagued by exaggerated worries, 606

generativity versus stagnation conflict between a productive life and an unproductive life, 433

genetic counseling, 77

genetics
   addiction and, 620
   depression and, 628
   human behavior and, 77–81
   obesity and, 477–78
   personality traits and, 578
   principles of, 73–77
   psychological disorders and, 600
   sexual orientation and, 494–95

genitals, development of, 493

genital stage Freud's final stage of psychosexual development, in which sexual pleasure is focused on sexual intimacy with others, 557–58

genome, 77

Gestalt psychology approach to psychology that seeks explanations of how we perceive overall patterns
   feature detectors and, 165
   hearing and, 164–65
   pattern recognition and, 161–64

gifted children, 762

glaucoma condition characterized by increased pressure within the eyeball, resulting in damage to the optic nerve and therefore a loss of vision, 125
   marijuana and, 212

glia cell of the nervous system that insulates neurons, removes waste materials (such as dead cells), and performs other supportive functions, 87

glucagon hormone which the pancreas releases to convert stored energy supplies into blood glucose, 471

glucose a sugar, the main source of nutrition for the brain; the most abundant sugar in the blood, 471
   blood, emotionally arousing events and, 281
   brain cells and, 97
   short-term regulation of hunger and, 471–72

glutamate, functions of, 95

glycine, functions of, 95

goals, need for achievement and, 502–3

gonorrhea, 489

good figure in Gestalt psychology, the tendency to perceive simple, symmetrical figures, 164

Graduate Record Examination (GRE), 384

grammar, transformational, 348

"graveyard shift," industrial accidents and, 185

gray matter, 105

GRE. *See* Graduate Record Examination

group decision making, 724–28

group polarization tendency for a group whose members lean in the same direction on a particular issue to become more extreme in its opinion after discussing the issue, 725

group sex, 487

group therapy treatment administered to a group of people all at one time, 659–60

groupthink process in which the members of a group suppress their doubts about a group's poorly thought-out decision, for fear of making a bad impression or disrupting the harmony of the group, 725–26

guilty-knowledge test test that uses the polygraph to measure whether a person has information that only someone guilty of a certain crime could know, 517–18

habits, bad, operant conditioning and, 253

habituate to decrease a person's response to a stimulus when it is presented repeatedly, 406

hair cell, 139

Haldol, 673

hallucination sensory experience not corresponding to reality, such as seeing or hearing something that is not present or failing to see or hear something that is present, 205, 638

hallucinogen drug that induces sensory distortions, 214
   effects of, 210
   synapses and, 97

haloperidol, 673

hammer, 139

handwashing, compulsive, 614–15

happiness, 511, 529–31
   facial expression and, 526

hassles, most frequent, 538

Health Maintenance Organizations (HMOs), 659

health psychology field of psychology that deals with the ways in which people's behavior can enhance health and prevent illness and how behavior contributes to recovery from illness, 533–41

hearing, 138–42. *See also* auditory system
   Gestalt principles in, 164–65
   of newborns, 406
   threshold of, 153–54

hearing aid, 140

heart disease, stress and, 539–40

heart rate, emotion and, 519

helpfulness, bystander, 722–23

helping behavior, sex differences in, 451

hemisphere left or right half of the brain; each hemisphere is responsible for sensation and motor control on the opposite side of the body, 104

heredity
   chemical basis of, 73
   environment and, 80–81
   ethnic differences and, 392–93, 395
   IQ scores and, 390–93

personality traits and, 578
temperament and, 447
heroin
abuse of, 211–12
addiction to, treating, 625
effects of, 210
endorphin synapses and, 97
tolerance to, 216, 231
herring gull, mating behavior of, 82–83
hertz unit of frequency representing one cycle per second, 140
heterosexuality, 488
heterozygous having different genes on a pair of chromosomes, 74
heterozygous chromosome, 75
heuristic strategy for simplifying a problem or for guiding an investigation, 326, 331–32
availability, 335–37
gambling and, 341
representative, 334–35, 336, 591
hibernation, 183
hierarchy of needs Maslow's categorization of human motivations, ranging from basic physiological needs at the bottom to the need for self-actualization at the top, 466–67
anorexia and, 482
high self-monitor person who constantly monitors his or her own behavior in order to behave in what others consider the appropriate manner for each situation, 690
hindbrain most posterior (hind) part of the brain, including the medulla, pons, and cerebellum, 100, 103–4
hindsight bias tendency to mold our recollections of the past to fit the way later events turned out, 300–2
hippocampus forebrain structure believed to be important for certain aspects of memory, 104
damage to, memory and, 290–91
tetrahydrocannabinol receptors in, 212
Hispanics
cognitive testing and, 744–45
IQ score and, 386
in psychology, 13
histrionic personality disorder, 604
HMOs. *See* Health Maintenance Organizations
homeopathic medicine, 36–37
homeostasis maintenance of an optimum level of biological conditions within an organism, 462–63
motivation and, 465
homosexuality, 488, 493
influences on, 494–95
prevalence of, 488, 490
homozygous having the same gene on both members of a pair of chromosomes, 74
homozygous chromosome, 75
hope, 221
hormone chemical released by a gland and conveyed by the blood to other parts of the body, where it alters activity, 101–2
abnormalities, psychological disorders and, 600
depression in women and, 629
male
aggressive behavior and, 76
prenatal development and, 102
hospitalization, 677–78
human behavior
determinist assumption for, 7
genetics of, 77–81
phases of moon and, 50–51
human experimentation, ethical concerns in, 58
human factors field that attempts to facilitate the operation of machinery so that the average user can use it as efficiently and as safely as possible, 753–57
human intelligence, measurement of, 24–25
humanist, 568
humanistic psychologist, 221, 568
humanistic psychology branch of psychology that emphasizes the capacity of people to make conscious decisions about their own lives, 568–69
humanistic therapy, 656
other therapy techniques compared, 657

human-relations approach theory that employees like to take responsibility for their work, like some variety in their job, and like to feel a sense of accomplishment, 749
human sociobiology, 83–84
Human Subjects Committee, 58, 738
"humors," 554
hunger, 44
brain mechanisms of, 474
long-term regulation of, 473–74
physiological mechanisms of, 470–74
satiety and, 472–73
Huntington's disease an inherited condition marked by gradual deterioration of voluntary movement control and other behavioral functions, usually beginning in middle age, 14–15, 58, 544–45
gene causing, 77
Huntington's Disease Collaborative Research Group, 15, 77
hyperactivity disorder, attention-deficit, 603
hyperventilation deep breathing, 607
hypnosis condition of increased suggestibility that occurs in the context of a special hypnotist-subject relationship, 199–200, 650
as altered state of consciousness, 206–8
distortion of perception under, 205–6
faked, 206–8
inducing, 200–1
repressed memory and, 306
suggestibility and, 600
uses and limitations of, 201–5
hypochondria scale, 585
hypochondriasis, 603
hypoglycemia, 472
hypomania, 632–33
hypomania scale, 585
hypothalamus, 104
anorexia nervosa and, 481
hunger and satiety and, 474
sexual orientation and, 495–96
hypothesis testable prediction of what will happen under certain conditions, 34
leading to predictions, 33
premature commitment to, 333–34
in problem solving, 325–27
hysteria scale, 585

id according to Freud, the aspect of personality that consists of all our biological drives and demands for immediate gratification, 558
ideal self a person's image of what he or she would like to be, 568–69
identical twins, 78–79
extraversion levels of, 579
IQ scores and, 391–92
personality traits and, 578
schizophrenia and, 642–43
sexual orientation and, 494–95
temperament and, 447
identity achievment deliberate choice of a role or identity, 438
identity crisis search for self-understanding, 437–38
identity disorder, dissociative, 599–600, 637
identity foreclosure acceptance of a role that a person's parents prescribe, 438
identity versus role confusion conflict between the sense of self and the confusion over one's identity, 432
idiographic, 573
idiographic approach approach to the study of individual differences that concentrates on intensive studies of individuals, 573
idiot savant, 368
illness, psychomatic, 538
stress and, 538–41
illusion
auditory, 175
moon, 176–77
Muller-Lyer, 175–76
optical, 172–77
Ponzo, 205
waterfall, 158, 168
illusory correlation an apparent relationship based

on casual observation of unrelated or poorly related events, 50–51, 450, 681
imagination, 221
imitating copying a behavior or custom, 256–58
immune system, stress and, 538
implicit memory memory that influences behavior without requiring conscious recognition that one is using a memory, 295
amnesia and, 294–95
implosion therapy for phobia in which the person is suddenly exposed to the object of the phobia, 613
impulse-control disorders, 603
INAH3 nucleus, sexual orientation and, 495–96
incentive an external stimulus that prompts an action to obtain the stimulus, 463
incentive theory, motivation and, 465
incongruence a mismatch between someone's self-concept and ideal self, 656
incus, 139
independent variable the variable the experimenter manipulates to see how it affects the dependent variable, 52
indeterminism, 7
individual psychology the psychology of the person as an indivisible whole, as formulated by Adler, 566–67
induced movement perception that an object is moving and that the background is stationary when in fact the object is stationary and the background is moving, 168
industrial accidents, "graveyard shift" and, 185
industrial-organizational psychology study of people at work, 743–51
industrial psychologist, 12
industry versus inferiority conflict between feelings of accomplishment and feelings of worthlessness, 432
infancy
forming attachments during, 433–35
sensorimotor stage in, 412
temperament in, 446–47
infant
language development in, 420
thoughts and knowledge of, difficulties of inferring, 408–9
infant amnesia relative lack of declarative memories from early in one's life, especially before age 3 1/2 years, 296–97
infection, prenatal, schizophrenia and, 644
inferential statistics statements about large groups based on inferences from small samples, 65–66
inferiority complex an exaggerated feeling of weakness, inadequacy, and helplessness, 566
influenza, schizophrenia and, 644
information displays, reading, 755–57
information-processing model, view that information is processed, coded, and stored in various ways in human memory as it is in a computer, 270–76
informed consent a subject's agreement to take part in an experiment after being informed about what will happen, 58
inhibitory synapse, 92–94
initiative versus guilt conflict between independent behavior and behavior inhibited by guilt, 432
inoculation protection against the harmful effects of stress by earlier exposure to a small amount of it, 546
inoculation effect tendency of a persuasive message to be weakened if people first hear a weak argument for the same conclusion, 694
insanity defense, 682–83
insightful problem solving, 328–29
insight-oriented therapy, 650
insight problems, 328–31
insomnia failure to get enough sleep at night in order to feel well rested the next day, 195, 603
instinct, 92
instinct theory, motivation and, 465
instrumental conditioning process of changing behavior by following a response with reinforcement, 240

peak experience an experience that brings fulfillment, contentment, and peace, 568
pedophilia, 603
peg method mnemonic device in which a person first memorizes a list of objects and then forms mental images linking those objects to a list of names to be memorized, 287
"penis envy," 557, 566
perception interpretation of sensory information, 122
 depth, 168–72
 distortions of, hypnosis and, 205–6
 extrasensory, 38–39, 41
 feature detectors and, 159–61
 of minimal stimuli, 153–57
 of movement, 167–68
 pattern recognition and, 157–66
 pitch, 140
 absolute, 141
 size and depth relationship in, 173–75
 social, 698
 subliminal, 155–57
peremptory challenge, 726–27
periodic limb movement disorder condition occurring during sleep, marked by unpleasant sensations in the legs and many repetitive leg movements strong enough to interrupt sleep, 197
peripheral nervous system nerves that convey messages from the sense organs to the central nervous system and from the central nervous system to the muscles and glands, 99, 100
peripheral route to persuasion method of persuasion based on such superficial factors as the speaker's appearance and reputation or the sheer number of arguments presented, regardless of their quality, 691
permissive parents parents who are warm and loving but not demanding, 435
perpetual motion machine, 37, 327
personality all the stable, consistent ways in which the behavior of one person differs from that of others, 554
 Adler's description of, 566–67
 assessment of, 582–92
 Freud's description of, 558
 genetics and, 79
 Machiavellian, 573
 origins of, 578
 self-actualized, 569
 sex differences in, 578–80
 theories of, 553–69
 type A, 539–40
 type B, 539
 variation across situations, 576–78
personality disorder maladaptive, inflexible way of dealing with the environment and other people, 602, 604
 multiple, 599, 637
personality profile graph that shows an individual's scores on scales measuring a number of personality traits, 587
personality researcher, 12
personality test, 582–92
 employee selection and, 745
 objective, 584–88
 projective techniques and, 588–91
 standardized, 583–84
 uses and misuses of, 591–92
personality trait, 573–80
 "big five," 574–76
person-centered therapy (also known as nondirective or client-centered therapy) procedure in which a therapist listens to the client sympathetically, provides unconditional positive regard, and offers little interpretation or advice, 656
 other therapy techniques compared, 657
person-machine system combination of a person and the machine which the person operates, 753–54
person variables, persuasion and, 693
persuasion, 690–94
 audience variables and, 693–94
 central route to, 691

delayed influence of messages and, 691–92
 operant conditioning and, 252–53
 peripheral route to, 691
 routes of, 690–91
 ways of presenting messages and, 692–93
pessimistic explanatory style, 631
peyote, 214
phallic stage Freud's third stage of psychosexual development, in which psychosexual interest is focused on the penis or clitoris, 557
phenylalanine, 80–81
phenylketonuria (PKU) inherited disorder in which a person lacks the chemical reactions that convert a nutrient called phenylalanine into other chemicals; unless the diet is carefully controlled, the affected person becomes mentally retarded, 80–81
phenylthiocarbamide (PTC), 74
pheromone an odorous chemical released by an animal that changes the way other members of its species respond to it socially, 149–50
phi effect the illusion of movement created when two or more stationary lights separated by a short distance flash on and off at regular intervals, 168
phlegmatic, 554
phobia fear so extreme that it interferes with normal living, 601, 608–14, 649. See also fear
 learning of, 609–10
 persistence of, 612
 prevalence of, 609
 school, 760–61
 social, 606–7
 therapies for, 612–14
phoneme a unit of sound, 354–55
phonological loop, 276–77
 recency effect and, 284
physical attractiveness, mate selection and, 714–16
physical characteristics, first impressions and, 699
physical dependence condition in which a habitual drug user is driven to seek the drug in order to escape or avoid the unpleasant withdrawal effects that occur during abstention from the drug, 215
physical standards, employee selection and, 745
physiological arousal, emotion and, 511–18
pitch perception closely related to the frequency of sound waves, 138
pitch perception, 140
 absolute, 141
PKU. See phenylketonuria
PL 94–142 U.S. law, passed in 1975, which specifies that public schools must provide a "free and appropriate" education for all children, regardless of their deficits or limitations, 760
placebo an inactive pill that has no known pharmacological effect on the subjects in an experiment, 46
place principle identification of pitch by which auditory neurons are most active, 140
plateau phase, sexual arousal and, 492
pleasure, psychosexual, 556
polarization, group, 725
polygraph machine that simultaneously measures heart rate, breathing rate, blood pressure, and galvanic skin response, 516
 lie detection and, 516–17
pons structure adjacent to the medulla that receives sensory input from the head and controls many muscles in the head, 104
 fear reactions and, 527
Ponzo illusion, 205
positive reinforcement strengthening a behavior through the presentation of a favorable event, 245–46
positive symptoms characteristics present in people with schizophrenia and absent in others—such as hallucinations, delusions, abnormal movements, and thought disorder, 639–40
positron-emission tomography, brain activity and, 8–9
posthypnotic suggestion suggestion made to hypnotized subjects that they will do or

experience something particular after coming out of hypnosis, 202
postpartum depression period of depression some women experience shortly after giving birth, 629
postsynaptic neuron neuron on the receiving end of a synapse, 91–92
posttraumatic stress disorder (PTSD) condition in which people who have endured extreme stress feel prolonged anxiety and depression, 534–35
potassium ion, action potential and, 89–90
pragma, 717
preattentive process perceptual activity that occurs automatically and simultaneously across a large portion of the visual field, 166
precognition, 38
predictability, coping with stress and, 544–45
predictive validity ability of a test's scores to predict real-world performance, 384
prefrontal cortex area in the anterior portion of the frontal lobes, critical for planning movements and for certain aspects of memory, 110–11
 emotion and, 512
 language production and, 345
prefrontal lobotomy surgical operation used in the 1940s and 1950s to interrupt communication between the prefrontal cortex and the rest of the brain, 111, 669
pregnancy
 stress and, 537
 teenage, 438–39
prejudice negative attitude toward a group of people, 700–2
 overcoming, 702–3
Premack principle principle that the opportunity to engage in a frequent behavior will reinforce a less frequent behavior, 248
premarital questionnaire, 440
premature ejaculation, 492
prenatal before birth, 402
prenatal care, preventing mental illness and, 684
prenatal development, 402–4
 schizophrenia and, 644
 sexual anatomy in, 493
preoperational stage according to Piaget, the second stage of intellectual development, in which children lack operations, 411, 412–16, 417
 concept of conservation and, 415–16
 egocentric thinking in, 413–15
"preparedness," 242
presbyopia farsightedness, the inability to focus on nearby objects, 124–25
presynaptic ending, 91–92
preventive detention practice of involuntarily committing psychologically disturbed people to a mental hospital to prevent them from committing crimes, 679–80
pride, 523
primacy effect tendency to be influenced more by the first information learned about someone than by later information about the same person, 283, 698–99
primary motivation motivation that serves biological needs, 465–66
primary motor cortex strip in the posterior (rear) part of the frontal cortex that controls fine movements, such as hand and finger movements, 108, 110, 111
primary prevention preventing a disorder from starting, 683
primary somatosensory cortex strip in the anterior (forward) part of the parietal lobe that receives most touch sensation and other information about the body, 108, 110, 111
primary visual cortex, 107
primates, facial expressions of, 523–24
priming, 294
principle of compatibility principle that people will learn certain procedures more easily and more accurately than others because of people's built-in or learned expectations, 754

relearn something learned in the past than something being learned for the first time, 269, 294

reliability repeatability of a test's scores, 383
   test-retest, 383

religion, genetics and, 79

Renaissance, 6

repair and restoration theory theory that the purpose of sleep is to enable the body to recover from the exertions of the day, 185–87

replicable result result that can be repeated (at least approximately) by any competent investigator who follows the same procedure as the original study, 34–35

representative heuristic tendency to assume that if an item is similar to members of a particular category, it is probably a member of that category itself, 334–35, 336, 591 gambling and, 341

representative sample a selection of the population chosen to match the entire population with regard to specific variables, 44–45

repression according to Freudian theory, the process of moving a memory, motivation, or emotion from the conscious mind to the unconscious mind; motivated forgetting, 305–7, 558–60

reproduction, 81

research. See psychological research

resistance according to psychoanalysis, continued repression that interferes with therapy; second stage of response to stress, a stage of prolonged but moderate arousal, 534, 652

resolution phase, sexual arousal and, 492

respiration, emotion and, 519

responsibility
   diffusion of, 722–23
   toward others, accepting or denying, 722–24

resting potential electrical polarization that ordinarily occurs across the membrane of an axon that is not undergoing an action potential, 89–90

restless leg syndrome, 197

reticular formation set of neurons in the medulla and pons that receive information from sensory systems and respond by sending arousal messages to many areas of the forebrain, 104

retina layer of visual receptors covering the back surface of the eyeball, 114, 124, 126

retinal disparity the difference in the apparent position of an object as seen by the left and right retinas, 168–69

retinex theory theory that color perception results from the cerebral cortex's comparison of various retinal patterns, 133–34

retirement, adjustment to, 442–43

retrieval cue information associated with remembered material, which can be useful in helping to recall that material, 272, 285
   forgetting and, 289–90

retroactive interference impairment a newer memory produces on an older one, 267, 289

retrograde amnesia loss of memory for events that occurred prior to brain damage or other trauma, 290–91
   Korsakoff's syndrome and, 292

"reverse psychology," 660

"reverse sexual revolution," 487

reversible figure stimulus that you can perceive in more than one way, 161–62

risperidone, 674

Ritalin, attention-deficit disorder and, 761

rock music, subliminal messages in, 156

rod type of visual receptor that is adapted for vision in dim light, 126
   characteristics of, 127
   dark adaptation and, 127–28
   sensitivity to light wavelengths, 131

role diffusion experimentation with various roles or identities, 438

role playing
   coping with stress and, 546
   hypnosis and, 203, 204

romantic love, 716–18

romantic relationship
   equity principle and, 712–13
   familiarity and, 711
   life cycle of, 717–18
   proximity and, 711
   similarity principle and, 711–12

Rorschach Inkblot Test projective personality technique in which people are shown 10 inkblots and asked what each might be, 588–90

running amok, 599

s a "specific" factor that is more important for performance on some scales of an intelligence test than it is on others, 366

saccade quick jump in the focus of the eyes from one point to another, 355

sadness, facial expression and, 526

salivation, classical conditioning of, 225–27

salt deficiency, 475

sample
   random, 45
   representative, 44–45

sampling, 44–45, 48

Sapir-Whorf hypothesis, 349

SAT. See Scholastic Assessment Test

satiety experience of being full, of feeling no more hunger, 472–73
   brain mechanisms of, 474

savant, 368

savings method method of testing memory by measuring how much faster someone can relearn something learned in the past than something being learned for the first time, 269, 294

Schachter and Singer's theory of emotions theory that emotions are our interpretation of autonomic arousal in light of all information we have about ourselves and the situation, 520–23

schedule of reinforcement rule for the delivery of reinforcement following various patterns of responding, 250
   gambling and, 340

schema an organized way of interacting with objects in the world; in memory, a series of expectations used to guide one's reconstruction of events, 299, 411

schizophrenia condition marked by deterioration of daily activities over a period of at least 6 months, plus either hallucinations, delusions, flat or inappropriate emotions, certain movement disorders, or thought disorders, 58, 77, 591, 601, 603, 637–44
   brain damage and, 641–42
   catatonic, 640
   causes of, 641–44
   disorganized, 640
   dopamine imbalance and, 642
   drug therapies for, 673–75
   experience and, 643–44
   genetics of, 642–43
   infections during early development and, 644
   insulin shock and, 669
   paranoid, 640–41
   prefrontal lobotomy and, 669
   psychotherapy for, 674–75
   symptoms of, 637–40
   thought disorder of, 639
   types of, 640–41
   undifferentiated, 640

schizophrenia scale, 585

schizotypal personality disorder, 604

Scholastic Assessment Test (SAT) test of students' likelihood of performing well in college, 64, 66, 377–78
   predictive validity of, 384
   reliability of, 383
   utility of, 385

school phobia condition characterized by apprehension or even panic while in school, while preparing to go to school, or sometimes at the mere thought of school, 760–61

school psychologist specialist who deals with the psychological condition of students, mostly in kindergarten through the 12th grade, 12, 759

concerns for, 760–63
disabled children and, 763
role of, 759–60

school psychology, 759–63

science
   experimentation in, 40–41
   gathering and evaluating evidence in, 33–34
   principle of parsimony in, 36–41
   replicability in, 34–35

scientific-management approach theory that employees are lazy, indifferent, and uncreative and that employers should therefore make the work as foolproof as possible and supervise the workers to make sure they are doing each task the right way, 748

Scientific Revolution, 6

scientific theory, criteria for evaluating, 35–36

SD. See standard deviation

SE. See standard error of the mean

seasonal affective disorder condition in which people become severely depressed every winter, when the amount of sunlight per day is short, 632

season-of-birth effect tendency for people born in the winter months to be slightly more likely than other people to develop schizophrenia, 644

secondary motivation motivation that serves no biological need directly but develops as a result of specific learning experiences, 465–66

secondary prevention identifying a disorder in its early stages and mpreventing it from becoming more serious, 683

secondary visual area, 107

second-generation antidepressant drug that blocks the reuptake of the neurotransmitter serotonin by the terminal button, 670

second law of thermodynamics, 37

selective attrition tendency for some kinds of people to be more likely than others to drop out of a study, 56, 429

selective breeding, 81

self-actualization the achievement of one's full potential, 467, 568–69

self-actualized personality, 569

self-concept a person's image of what he or she really is, 568–69

self-efficacy perception of one's own ability to perform a task successfully, 259
   social learning and, 258–59

self-esteem, gambling and, 341–42

self-fulfilling prophecy, 56

self-handicapping strategy technique for protecting self-esteem by creating external causes as decoy excuses for failures, 706

self-help group, 660

self-hypnosis, cigarette smoking and, 202

self-punishment, social learning and, 259–60

self-reinforcement, social learning and, 259–60

self-selection, employee selection and, 746

self-serving bias attributions people adopt in an effort to maximize their credit for success and minimize their blame for failure, 706

semantic memory memory for factual information, 277, 295

semicircular canal, 142–43

sensation conversion of energy from the environment into a pattern of response by the nervous system, 122
   early studies of, 23

senses
   chemical, 147–50
   cutaneous, 143–46
   nonvisual, 138–50
   vestibular, 142–43

sensorimotor period, 408

sensorimotor stage according to Piaget, the first stage of intellectual development, in which an infant's behavior is limited to making simple motor responses to sensory stimuli, 411, 412, 417 sensory adaptation tendency of a sensory threshold to fall after a period when the sensory receptors have not been stimulated and to rise after exposure to intense stimuli, 154

sensory deprivation temporary reduction of vision, hearing, touch, and other forms of sensory stimulation, 55–56

sensory information, interpretation of, 153–77

sensory neuron neuron that carries information about touch, pain, and other senses from the periphery of the body to the spinal cord, 100

sensory store very brief storage of sensory information, 271

sensory threshold minimum intensity at which a given individual can detect a sensory stimulus 50% of the time; a low threshold indicates ability to detect faint stimuli, 153–55

serial-order effect tendency to remember the first and last items on a list better than those in the middle, 283

serotonin neurotransmitter that plays an important role in sleep and mood changes
    antidepressant drugs and, 670, 671
    functions of, 95
    mood changes and, 97
    suicide and, 635

serotonin receptor, lysergic acid diethylamide and, 214

serotonin synapse, obsessive-compulsive disorder and, 616, 670

serotonin uptake blocker, 670

set point level of some variable (such as weight) that the body attempts to maintain, 473, 479

sex
    depression and, 628–29
    need for achievement and, 504–5
    personality traits and, 578–80
    preferences in mate selection and, 713–14

sex chromosome chromosome that determines whether an individual will develop as a female or as a male, 75–76

sex drive, 485

sex-limited gene gene that affects one sex only or affects one sex more strongly than the other, even though both sexes have the gene, 76

sex-linked gene gene situated on the X chromosome, 75–76

sex-role inventory, 580

sexual abuse
    childhood, psychological disorder and, 563
    repressed memory and, 306

sexual anatomy, influences on, 493–94

sexual arousal, 492–93

sexual behavior, acquired immune deficiency syndrome and, 489–91

sexual disorders, 603

sexual harassment, 49

sexual identity sex a person regards himself or herself as being, 493–96

sexuality, anorexia and, 481

sexually transmitted disease (STD), 489

sexual motivation, 485–98
    rape and, 496–98
    surveys in, 486–89

sexual orientation a person's preference for male or female sex partners, 488, 493–96
    brain anatomy and, 495–96
    influences on, 494–95

"sexual revolution," 487

sexual symbolism, dreams and, 651

shadow, depth perception and, 171

shape constancy, 167

shaping technique for establishing a new response by reinforcing successive approximations to it, 244, 613

"shell shock," 535

short-term memory temporary storage of a limited amount of information, 271–72
    characteristics of, 273–76

signal-detection theory study of people's tendencies to make correct judgments, misses, and false alarms, 154

sign language, 346

similarity in Gestalt psychology, the tendency to perceive objects that resemble each other as belonging to a group, 162, 163

similarity principle tendency to associate with people similar to ourself, 711–12

single-blind study study in which either the observer or the subjects are unaware of which subjects received which treatment, 45–46

situation variable, persuasion and, 693–94

16-PF Test standardized personality test that measures 16 personality traits, 587–88

size perception, depth perception and, 173–75

skeletal pertaining to the muscles that move, the limbs, trunk, and head, 240

Skinner box, 243

skin senses, 143–46

sleep
    abnormalities of, 195–97
    brain activity during, 190–91
    evolutionary theory of, 187–88
    inadequate, psychological disorders and, 600
    leg movements during, 196–97
    non-REM, 189
    paradoxical, 188–89
    REM, 189
        depression and, 627, 628
        functions of, 191–93
    repair and restoration theory of, 185–87
    shifting schedules and, 184–85
    stages of, 188–93
        dreaming and, 189–91

sleep apnea condition in which a person has trouble breathing while asleep, 196

sleep deprivation, 186–87
    REM, 191–92

sleep disorder, 603

sleeper effect delayed persuasion by an initially rejected message, 277, 691

sleep talking, 196

sleep terror disorder, 603

sleepwalking, 196, 603

slip of the tongue, 561

smell, sense of, 148–50

social behavior, 688

social cognition process of combining and remembering information about others and making inferences based on that information, 700–3

social development, 429–44
    in adolescence, 436–39
    in childhood, 436
    ethnic and cultural influences on, 455–56
    family and, 447–50
    gender and, 450–55
    in middle adulthood, 440–42
    in old age, 442–43
    temperament and, 446–47
    in young adulthood, 439–40

social interest sense of solidarity and identification with other people, 567

social introversion scale, 585

social learning, 256–60
    self-efficacy in, 258–59
    self-punishment in, 259–60
    self-reinforcement in, 259–60

social-learning approach view that people learn by observing and imitating the behavior of others and by imagining the consequences of their own behavior, 256–60

social-learning theory, gambling and, 341

social loafing tendency to "loaf" (or work less hard) when sharing the work with other people, 723–24

social perception, 698

social phobia severe avoidance of other people and an especially strong fear of doing anything in public, 606–7

social psychologist psychologist who studies social behavior and how an individual influences others and is influenced by them, 12, 17, 688

social psychology approach, 17

Social Readjustment Rating Scale, 535–36

social situation
    power of, 730–38
    sex differences in, 451–52

social support
    coping with stress and, 546–47
    depression and, 629–30

sociobiology field that tries to relate the social behaviors of a species to its biology, particularly to its evolutionary history, 83–84, 713
    human, 83–84
    sex preferences in mate selection and, 715

sodium ion, action potential and, 89–90

sodium-potassium pump, 89–90

somatic nervous system nerves that control the muscles, 99, 100

somatization disorder, 603

somatoform disorder, 603

somatosensory cortex, primary, 108, 110, 111

somatosensory system, 144

sound, localization of, 141–42

sound waves vibrations of the air or of some other medium, 138–40

source amnesia remembering content but forgetting the manner of learning that content, 277, 304

SPAR method systematic way to monitor and improve understanding of a text by surveying, processing meaningfully, asking questions, and reviewing, 283

species-specific behavior a particular behavior that is widespread in one animal species but not in others, 92

speed reading, 357

spinal cord part of the central nervous system that communicates with sensory neurons and motor neurons below the level of the head, 100–1
    between cerebral cortex and, 103–4

split-brain phenomenon, 113–16

spontaneous recovery the temporary return of an extinguished response after a delay, 229–30

spontaneous remission improvement of a psychological condition without therapy, 661

spreading activation process by which the activation of one concept activates or primes the other concepts that are linked to it in a network, 315

stage of concrete operations according to Piaget, the third stage of intellectual development, in which children can deal with the properties of concrete objects but cannot readily deal with hypothetical or abstract questions, 416

stage of formal operations according to Piaget, the fourth and final stage of intellectual development, in which people deal with abstract, hypothetical situations, which demand logical, deductive reasoning and systematic planning, 416–17

standard deviation (SD) a measurement of the amount of variation among scores in a normal distribution, 64
    calculating, 68

standard error of the mean (SE), calculating, 68

standardization process of establishing rules for administering a test and for interpreting its scores, 381

standardized test test that is administered according to specified rules and whose scores are interpreted in a prescribed fashion, 583–84

Stanford-Binet IQ test a test of intelligence, the first important IQ test in the English language, 372–73
    bias of, 388
    predictive validity of, 384
    reliability of, 383

stapes, 139

startle response, 527

state temporary activation of a particular behavior, 574

statistically significant result effect that has a low probability of having arisen by chance, 66

statistics
    calculations in, 68–69
    descriptive, 62–64
    inferential, 65–66
    misleading, 62

stereotype overgeneralization of either positive or negative attitudes toward other people, 700–2

stimulant
abuse of, 213–14
effects of, 210

stimulus energy in the environment that affects what we do, 123
attention and, 316–17
conditioned, 226–27, 653
discriminative, 241–42
minimal, perception of, 153–57
subliminal, 155
sympathetic response and, 514
unconditioned, 226–27, 653

stimulus generalization in operant conditioning, the tendency to make a similar response to a stimulus that resembles one that has been associated with reinforcement; the extension of a conditioned response from the training stimulus to similar stimuli, 230–31, 241

stimulus-response psychology attempt to explain behavior in terms of how each stimulus triggers a response, 222

stirrup, 139

storge, 717

story memory, reconstruction in, 299–300

"stream of consciousness," 182

stress according to Hans Selye, the nonspecific response of the body to any demand made upon it; according to Lazarus, a situation that someone regards as threatening and as possibly exceeding his or her resources, 533–38
cancer and, 540–41
coping with, 543–49
depression and, 629
heart disease and, 539–40
Lazarus's approach to, 537–38
measuring, 535–37
psychosomatic illness and, 538–41
Selye's concept of, 533–34

striving for superiority according to Adler, a universal desire to seek personal excellence and fulfillment, 566

stroboscopic movement an illusion of movement created by a rapid succession of stationary images, 168

Stroop effect difficulty of naming the colors in which words are written instead of reading the words themselves, 358–59

structuralism attempt to describe the structures that compose the mind, 21–22, 221

structuralist, 221

stuttering, 603, 762

style of life according to Adler, a person's master plan for achieving a sense of superiority, 566

sublimation the transformation of an unacceptable impulse into an acceptable, even an admirable, behavior, 561

subliminal perception ability of a stimulus to influence our behavior even when it is presented so faintly or briefly or along with such strong distractors that we do not perceive it consciously, 155–57

subliminal stimulus, 155

substance abuse, disease concept of, 623–24

substance dependence, 618–19

substance P neurotransmitter responsible for much of the transmission of pain information in the nervous system, 145–46

substance-related disorder, 603, 618–25

substantia nigra, 96

sucking, habituation of, 406–7

suggestibility
eyewitness testimony and, 304–5
hypnosis and, 600
memory and, 302–4

suggestion
false memory and, 306
posthypnotic, 202

suicide, 62, 634–35
people most likely to attempt, 635

superego according to Freud, the aspect of personality that consists of memories of rules put forth by one's parents, 558

suprachiasmatic nucleus, circadian rhythm and, 184

surprise, facial expression and, 526

survey study of the prevalence of certain beliefs, attitudes, or behaviors based on people's responses to specific questions, 48–49
biasing, 50

surveyor bias, 49

survivor's guilt, 535

sympathetic nervous system system composed of two chains of neuron clusters lying just to the left and right of the spinal cord; the neurons send messages to the internal organs to prepare them for a burst of vigorous activity, 99, 101, 512–14
emotionally arousing events and, 281
functions of, 102
lie detection and, 515–17

sympathetic response, stimulus and, 514

synapse specialized junction between one neuron and another at which one neuron releases a neurotransmitter, which either excites or inhibits the next neuron, 16, 91–94
excitatory, 93
inhibitory, 92–94
synaptic cleft, 91–92
synaptic vesicle, 91–92

syphilis, 489

systematic desensitization method of reducing fear by gradually exposing people to the object of their fear, 612–13, 652

Tablas, 214

tardive dyskinesia movement disorder characterized by tremors and involuntary movements, 673–74

taste sensory system that responds to chemicals on the tongue, 147–48
food selection based on, 475
taste aversion, conditioned, 235–36

taste bud site of the taste receptors, located in the folds on the surface of the tongue, 147

taste receptor, 147–48

TAT. See Thematic Apperception Test

teenage pregnancy, 438–39

teenager, "personal fable" of, 438–39

telepathy, 38

television violence, aggressive behavior and, 34, 44, 54

temperament people's tendency to be active or inactive, outgoing or reserved, 446–47

temporal contiguity nearness in time, 232

temporal lobe portion of each cerebral hemisphere, the main processing area for hearing, complex aspects of vision, and certain aspects of emotional behavior, 108, 110

terminal button bulge at the end of an axon from which the axon releases a chemical called a neurotransmitter, 91–92

termination insomnia tendency to awaken early and to be unable to get back to sleep, 195

testosterone hormone present in higher quantities in males than in females
aggressive behavior and, 528
prenatal development and, 102
sexual anatomy and, 493

test-retest reliability repeatability of a test's scores between a test and a retest, 383

tetrahydrocannabinol (THC), 212
effects of, 210

texture gradient, depth perception and, 171

thalamus, 104

that's-not-all technique method of eliciting compliance in which someone makes an offer and then, before anyone has a chance to reply, improves the offer, 735

THC. See tetrahydrocannabinol

Thematic Apperception Test (TAT) projective personality technique in which a person is asked to tell a story about each of 20 pictures, 501–2, 504, 590–91

theory comprehensive explanation of natural phenomena that leads to accurate predictions, 35–36
criteria for evaluating, 35–26

Theory X theory that employees are lazy, indifferent, and uncreative and that employers should therefore make the work as foolproof as possible and supervise the workers to make sure they are doing each task the right way, 748

Theory Y theory that employees like to take responsibility for their work, like some variety in their job, and like to feel a sense of accomplishment, 749

thermodyamics, second law of, 37

thinking
egocentric, in preoperational period, 413–15
in parallel, 315–16
in series, 315–16

Thorazine, 673

thought
development of, 410–19
in infants, difficulties of inferring, 408–9
language and, 348–52
therapies focusing on, 654–56

thought disorder, schizophrenia and, 639

time-limited therapy, 658

tobacco, fetus and, 403–4

toddler, language development in, 420–21

Tofranil, 670

toilet training, 652
personality development and, 558

tolerance weakened effect of a drug after repeated use, 214, 215

tongue, 147

Torrance Tests of Creative Thinking, 330–31

Tourette's disorder, 603, 762

Tower of Hanoi puzzle, 291

toxins, banning, preventing mental illness and, 684

trait consistent, long-lasting tendency in behavior, 574. See also personality traits

tranquilizer drug that helps people to relax, 669–70
abuse of, 211
effects of, 210
insomnia and, 195
synapses and, 91
violent behavior and, 528
withdrawal from, 215

transference extension of a client's feelings toward a parent or other important figure onto the therapist, 651–52

transformational grammar, 348

triarchic theory Sternberg's theory that deals with three aspects of intelligence: the cog-nitive processes that occur, the situations that require intelligence, and how intelligence relates to the external world, 369–70, 371

trichromatic theory theory that color vision depends on the relative rate of response by three types of cones, 129–31

tricyclic drug drug that blocks the reabsorption of the neurotransmitters dopamine, norepinephrine, and serotonin, after they are released by the terminal button, thus prolonging the effect of these neurotransmitters on the receptors of the postsynaptic cell, 670

"triple blind," 46

tritanopia, 135

truancy, 762

t-test, 68–69

"tunnel vision," 125

Turing Test, 311

twins, 78
extraversion levels of, 579
IQ scores and, 391–92
personality traits and, 578
schizophrenia and, 642–43
sexual orientation and, 494–95
temperament and, 447

type A personality personality characterized by constant competitiveness, impatience, anger, and hostility, 539–40

type B personality personality characterized by easygoingness, lack of hurry, and lack of hostility, 539

UCR. See unconditioned response
UCS. See unconditioned stimulus
ultraviolet light, contact lens and, 126

unconditional positive regard complete, unqualified acceptance of another person as he or she is, 569, 656

unconditioned reflex an automatic connection between a stimulus and a response, 226

unconditioned reinforcer an event that satisfies a biological need, 249, 466

unconditioned response (UCR) an automatic response to an unconditioned stimulus, 226–27, 653

unconditioned stimulus (UCS) stimulus that automatically elicits an unconditioned response, 226–27, 653

unconscious according to Freud, an aspect of the mind that influences behavior, although we are not directly aware of it, 555
  collective, 564–66
  manifestations in everyday life, 561
  psychoanalysis and, 555–56
  understanding, self-monitoring of, 283

undifferentiated schizophrenia type of schizophrenia characterized by the basic symptoms but no unusual or especially prominent symptoms, 640

unilateral neglect, 108–9

United States Socialist Party, 1900 political platform of, 692

unshared environment the aspects of environment that differ from one individual to another, even within a family, 578

uplifts, most frequent, 538

utility usefulness of a test for a practical purpose, 385

vaginal intercourse, 487
  acquired immune deficiency syndrome and, 489

validity determination of how well a test measures what it claims to measure, 383–84
  construct, 384
  content, 383–84
  predictive, 384

Valium, 211, 669
  effects of, 210

vandalism, adolescence and, 437

variable, 52

variable-interval schedule rule for delivering reinforcement after varying amounts of time, 251

variable-ratio schedule rule for delivering reinforcement after varying numbers of responses, 250–51

variation, measures of, 64

ventromedial hypothalamus area of the brain in which damage leads to weight gain via an increase in the frequency of meals, 474

vestibular sense specialized sense that detects the direction of tilt and amount of acceleration of the head and the position of the head with respect to gravity, 142–43

vestibule, 142

vicarious punishment punishment observed to have been experienced by someone else, 258
  gambling and, 341

vicarious reinforcement reinforcement observed to have been experienced by someone else, 258
  gambling and, 341

Vietnam veterans, posttraumatic stress disorder and, 535

violence, televised, aggressive behavior and, 34, 44, 54

violent behavior, prediction and control of, 528–29, 681

vireous humor, 124

virtual-reality technology, therapy for phobias and, 613

visceral pertaining to the internal organs, 240

visible light, 123–24

vision, 123–36
  color, 129–36
    opponent-process theory of, 131–33
    retinex theory of, 133–34
    trichromatic theory of, 129–31
  detection of light in, 123–29
  disorders of, 124–26
  of newborns, 404–5
  preattentive and attentive processes in, 165–66
  tunnel, 125

visual area, secondary, 107

visual capture effect tendency to localize a sound as coming from a prominent visual feature (such as a loudspeaker or a ventriloquist's dummy), 175

visual constancy tendency to perceive objects as being unchanging in shape, size, and color, despite variations in what actually reaches the retina, 167

visual cortex
  feature-detector neurons in, 158
  primary, 107

visual-motor coordination, development of, 405–6

visual pathway, 107, 128–29

visual receptor, 126

visual system, 115
  brain damage and, 107–8

visuospatial sketchpad, 276

vitamin B1 deficiency, alcoholism and, 97, 291

voir dire, 726

volley principle identification of pitch by the fact that groups of hair cells respond to each vibration by producing an action potential, 140

volume, conservation of, 415

volunteerism, 724

von Restorff effect tendency to remember the distinctive of unusual items on a list better than other items, 269

voyeurism, 603

wages, work motivation and, 749–51

WAIS-R. See Wechsler Adult Intelligence Scale—Revised

waterfall illusion phenomenon in which prolonged staring at a waterfall and then looking at nearby cliffs causes those cliffs to appear to flow upward, 158, 168

Wechsler Adult Intelligence Scale—Revised (WAIS-R) IQ test originally devised by David Wechsler, commonly used with adults, 373–74
  bias of, 388

Wechsler Intelligence Scale for Children (WISC), 375

Wechsler Intelligence Scale for Children—Third Edition (WISC-III) IQ test originally devised by David Wechsler, commonly used with children, 373–74
  predictive validity of, 384
  reliability of, 383

weight loss, 478
  appetite and, 478–80

white matter, 105

Whorf hypothesis hypothesis that our language determines the way we think, 349–51

will, 221

Williams syndrome, 46–47

WISC. See Wechsler Intelligence Scale for Children

WISC-III. See Wechsler Intelligence Scale for Children—Third Edition

wish fulfillment, dreams and, 651

withdrawal
  caffeine, 213
  drug, 214–15

withdrawal effects experiences that occur as a result of the removal of a drug from the brain, 214

women
  job discrimination and, 440, 504–5
  in psychology, 13–14, 25
  in workplace, 746–48

word-association test, 589

words
  hearing as a whole, 352–53
  understanding in context, 353

word-superiority effect greater ease of identifying a letter when it is part of a whole word than when it is presented by itself, 357–58

working memory system that processes and works with current information, including three components—a central executive, a phonological loop, and a visuospatial sketchpad, 276–77

work motivation, pay and, 749–51

workplace, women in, 746–48

World Memory Championship, 265, 287

Xanax, 211, 669
  effects of, 210

X chromosome sex chromosome of which females have two per cell and males have one, 74–76

xenon, 112

Y chromosome sex chromosome of which males have one per cell and females have none, 74–76

yellow-blue color blindness, 135

Young-Helmholtz theory theory that color vision depends on the relative rate of response by three types of cones, 129–30

Zofran, 95

zone of proximal development the distance between what a child can do on his or her own and what the child can do with the help of adults or other children, 419

Theme Index

effectiveness of psychotherapy, 661–664

"Eskimos have many words for snow," 350

"experts were born with special talent," 323–324

extrasensory perception, 38–41

eyewitness testimony, 304–305

"false memory" vs. "recovered memory," 305–307

Freud's theories, limitations of evidence, 558, 559–560, 563–564, 651

Freudian slips, 561–562

full moon and mental disturbances, 50–51

general overview, 4, 33–37

homeopathic medicine, 36–37

homosexual orientation, prevalence of, 488

hypnosis and altered perceptions, 205–206

hypnosis and memory, 202–203

"hypnosis won't make you do anything that you would otherwise refuse to do," 204–205

influence of language on thought, 349–350

job satisfaction and job performance, 751

learning and memory in newborns, 406–407

learning fears by observation, 610–612

left-brain people and right-brain people, 116

lie detection, 515–518

"low nicotine cigarettes," 619

marijuana and antisocial behavior, 212

marriage and mental health, 51

mental imagery, 317–319

misleading statistics, 63

misleading survey results, 48–49

"never awaken a sleepwalker," 196

obedience to authority, 735–738

object permanence in infants, 408–409

old age and decline of memory, 297

personality test results, 582–583

"playing Dungeons and Dragons leads to suicide," 62

prediction of violent behavior, 528–529, 590

programs to improve IQ of low-scoring infants, 385–386

psychological disorders, prevalence of, 601

Rorschach inkblots, 588–590

sensory deprivation and behavior, 55–56

sexual orientation, origins of, 492–496

speed reading, advantages of, 357

"stick with first impulse on a multiple-choice item," xxx

stress, measurements of, 537

subliminal perception, 155–157

suggestibility of memory, 302–304

televised violence and aggressive behavior, 54

temporal contiguity and learning, 235

"to change people's behavior, change their attitudes first," 689, 694–696

vulnerability to alcoholism, 620–622

"we use only 10% of our brain," 116–117

"women cannot become outstanding chess players," 323

Genetic influences

and alcohol abuse, 620

and Alzheimer's disease, 73, 297

and color blindness, 76

and depression, 628

and environmental influences, 80–81

general principles, 73–81

and Huntington's disease, 14–15, 77

and IQ scores, 390–392

and obesity, 477–478

and obsessive-compulsive disorder, 616

and personality, 578, 579

and phenylketonuria, 80–81

and religious devoutness, 79

and schizophrenia, 642–643

and sexual orientation, 494–495

and television watching, 79

Sex and gender influences

and anatomical development, 493–494

and attention deficit disorder, 761

and careers in psychology, 13, 25

and communication with opposite sex, 452

and depression, 628–629

and family and career, 439–440

and frequency of sexual activity, 489

and gender roles, 452–455

and IQ and SAT scores, 388, 389

and job opportunities, 746–748

and language connotations, 350–351

and mate selection criteria, 713–715

and miscellaneous behaviors, 450–451

and moral reasoning, 426–427

and motivation to lose weight, 478–483

and need for achievement, 504–505

and olfaction, 149–150

and panic disorder, 606

and personality, 578–580

and phobia, 609

and preferred sexual activities, 84, 487, 488

and psychological disorders, 601

and relationship to genetics, 75–76

and sexual arousal, 492–493

and social behavior, 451–452

and social loafing, 724

and suicide, 634

Try-it-yourself demonstrations

attentive and preattentive visual processes, 166

blind spot, 128–130

breaking bad habits, 259–260

capacity of short-term memory, 273

closure in perception, 164

color blindness, 135

color blindness in retinal periphery, 126

consolidation of long-term memory, 275–276

creative scientific problem solving, 329–330

dark adaptation, 127–128

dating relationships, 439

encoding specificity, 285–286

facial expressions and emotions, 526

facial recognition, 157

feature detectors in vision, 158–159

forgetting of short-term memory, 274–275

foveal priming of peripheral vision, 160

framing of questions, 337

generalizing a solution to a related problem, 327–328

Gestalt perception, 161–164

hindsight bias, 300–302

insight problems, 328–329

localization of taste stimuli, 147

memory of meaning vs. wording of a sentence, 348–349

mind reading, 39–40

object movement vs. self-induced movement, 167

obsessive-compulsive disorder, 616

overconfidence, 332

perception of spots of different sizes and colors, 130–131

phobias, prevalence of different types of, 611

premature commitment to a hypothesis, 333, 335, 337

problem solving, 324–325

reading during an eye fixation, 356

recall vs. cued recall, 269

representativeness heuristic, 335

sensory adaptation, 154

shallow processing, 281–282

Stroop effect, 358–359

suppression of vision during saccadic eye movements, 355

thought avoidance, 614

Type A personality, 539

vestibular sensation and eye movements, 142

visual constancy, 167